HOUGHTON
★ MIFFLIN ★
SOCIAL STUDIES
★★ PROGRAM ★★

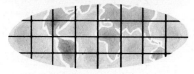

HISTORY

★ ★ ★

General Editor **HOWARD R. ANDERSON**
Map Editor **ROBERT M. CHAPIN, JR.**

A HISTORY OF THE
UNITED STATES

RICHARD C. WADE

HOWARD B. WILDER

LOUISE C. WADE

HOUGHTON MIFFLIN COMPANY · BOSTON

New York · Atlanta · Geneva, Ill. · Dallas · Palo Alto

ABOUT THE AUTHORS AND EDITORS

RICHARD C. WADE is Professor of American History at the University of Chicago. He has also taught at the University of Rochester and at Washington University in St. Louis. A distinguished urban historian, Professor Wade's published books include *Slavery in the Cities; The Urban Frontier;* and *The Negro in American Life,* a volume of readings of which he is the editor.

HOWARD B. WILDER served for many years as a teacher of history and as Head of the Social Studies Department at Melrose High School, Melrose, Massachusetts. Subsequently he became Principal of that school. He is also co-author of *This Is America's Story* and *The Making of Modern America.*

LOUISE C. WADE is Lecturer in History in the College of the University of Chicago. She has also taught at the University of Rochester and has served as a consultant to social studies curriculum committees. She is the author of *Graham Taylor, Pioneer for Social Justice.*

HOWARD R. ANDERSON, general editor, is past president of the National Council for the Social Studies. He was formerly Provost of the University of Rochester, Professor of Education at Cornell University, and Director of Social Studies in the public schools of Ithaca, New York. He is co-author of *The History of Our World.*

ROBERT M. CHAPIN, JR., map editor, is map-maker for *Time* and editor of the map programs in *The History of Our World* and *The Making of Modern America.* He has been a lecturer at Clark University, Worcester, Massachusetts, and a map consultant to the Department of Defense.

Consultants

For valuable suggestions in the preparation of the manuscript of *A History of the United States,* the authors, editors, and publisher are indebted to TREVOR COLBOURN, Professor of History, Indiana University; GILBERT C. FITE, Research Professor of History, University of Oklahoma; RAYFORD W. LOGAN, Professor of History, Howard University; JOHN L. SNELL, Professor of History and Dean of The Graduate School, Tulane University; and LEON H. CANFIELD, formerly of the College of the City of New York.

A History of the United States is a new book which, with the permission of Dr. Canfield, makes use of certain materials from *The Making of Modern America,* by Leon H. Canfield and Howard B. Wilder.

Contents

REFERENCE SECTION

LIST OF MAPS

LIST OF CHARTS

SPECIAL FEATURES

Listed below are only a few of the many special features appearing in this textbook. Closely integrated with the historical narrative are numerous additional factual and pictorial features which link the past to the present, re-create significant events in the nation's development, delineate forceful personalities or powerful movements, and present the controversy of the past in the words of those who shared in shaping the nation's future.

History and Historians

Henry Ford once expressed the opinion that "history is bunk." He could see little merit in a subject taught by "experts" who admitted they did not know all the facts about a given event and often disagreed on how to interpret the available evidence. Such fumbling, he felt, could never have produced the Model T!

Perhaps not. But the Model T is a rarity today, for the advances of automotive engineering and technology have long since displaced it. Our knowledge of history, like that of automotive engineering, is neither fixed nor unchanging, and each of us must learn to accept that idea. To be sure, history is based on facts — events taking place at a particular time and place. But the body of known facts is constantly growing. New information may come from an ancient manuscript, such as Yale University's Vinland map, or from excavations on the site of an old settlement, as when Viking remains recently were found in Newfoundland. New insights may be obtained from letters, diaries, and government documents. And each day and year history is being made. Historical research includes the discovery of new facts and the fitting of them into the body of knowledge already accumulated. In writing *A History of the United States* the authors have taken into account the great mass of new information made available by hundreds of scholars on a great variety of issues.

Equally important with new information are the conclusions drawn by scholars from the great body of facts related to a given problem. The same facts may be interpreted differently by different groups at different times. People in England and in the American colonies did not view the commercial regulations imposed by the mother country on the colonies in the same light. Nor did people in the North and in the South have the same view of events leading to the Civil War. In the past hundred years many historians have evaluated the causes leading to this tragic conflict. The relative importance attached to one cause or another has varied from one generation to the next and from one historian to another.

The continuing analysis and re-assessment of the past in the light of new information and new perspectives is the great contribution of historians. To the layman it may be upsetting to discover that some conclusion long accepted is being questioned as the result of new information or a shrewder analysis of the facts. But this problem of new interpretations is one which scientists constantly must face. Consider how man's view of the world has changed since Copernicus rejected the commonly accepted theory of the solar system. Or ponder the implications for mankind of Einstein's refusal to be bound by Newton's laws of physics. In writing *A History of the United States* the authors have tried not only to provide the most widely accepted interpretations of great events, but also to suggest various interpretations that deserve consideration and to make clear why these views merit attention.

The chief reason for writing *A History of the United States,* therefore, has not been to provide a body of information for students to memorize. It is rather to demonstrate how historians look at the past and to prepare each student to apply the lessons of history to his own experience. Living in a democracy, Americans must keep informed on many issues — local, national, international. They must be able to assess the conflicting views of scholars and crackpots, statesmen and demagogues. From the torrent of news and views poured out by the mass media of communication, Americans must learn to separate essentials from trivia. They must also develop the capacity to express informed views, the insights needed to choose able candidates for public office, and the courage to act in the light of their convictions.

History cannot give all the answers. But history provides information needed to understand the past and to think constructively about the future. More important, it provides a process which any intelligent person may follow in thinking about problems worth his while. In today's world it is vital for American citizens to be informed about issues and to know how to assess the worth of conflicting points of view.

Unit 1 | Europeans Establish an Independent Nation in the New World (1450-1783)

Americans pulling down a statue of King George III

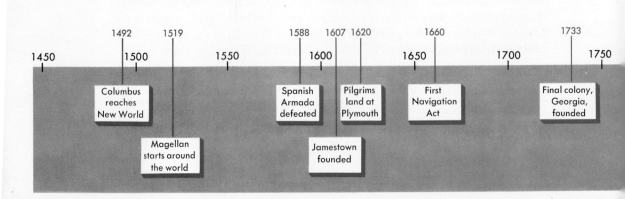

America's beginnings were closely related to developments in western Europe. During the 1400's new ideas were gaining acceptance, and trade and commerce were growing. European contacts with countries beyond the eastern Mediterranean aroused interest in plans for tapping their resources. As the century drew to a close, powerful monarchs, intent on accumulating wealth for their countries, sponsored voyages of exploration.

Three European powers — Spain, France, and England — pioneered in the settlement of the Americas. Spain, gambling on finding a western water route to the Orient, took the lead. The discovery of rich treasure in gold and silver enabled Spain to establish a powerful colonial empire based chiefly in the Caribbean islands, Mexico, and Peru. The French explored the St. Lawrence River Valley and the upper reaches of the Mississippi. Some French and Spanish families settled in the New World. For the most part, however, New Spain and New France were outposts of empire, encouraged because they promised to produce wealth for their mother countries.

The English settlements along the Atlantic seaboard were late in starting but in time outstripped the Spanish and French territories in population. One reason was the different pattern of settlement. English families came to America to build a new life for themselves and their children. Other reasons were the greater degree of self-government and the freedom from restrictions on religion and nationality that existed in the French and Spanish colonies. As a result, the English colonies not only surpassed New France and New Spain in population but established much healthier economies and sturdier governments.

The growing self-sufficiency of the English colonies led in time to rivalry with the mother country. Economic regulations which served the interests of England and threats to the freedom of colonial legislatures led to a period of growing tension during the 1760's and early 1770's. The American Revolution followed and resulted in England's recognition of the thirteen former colonies as "free and independent states."

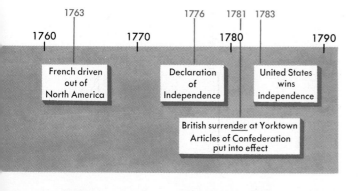

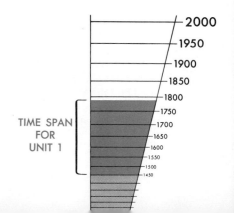

CHAPTER 1

Europeans Discover a New World

Indian drawing of Spanish conquest

. . . Here the people could endure no longer. They complained of the length of the voyage. But the Admiral cheered them up in the best way he could, giving them good hopes of the advantages they might gain from it. He added that, however much they might complain, he had to go to the Indies, and that he would go on until he found them, with the help of our Lord.

JOURNAL OF CHRISTOPHER COLUMBUS

1450–1700

These words, quoted from Columbus's journal, showed the explorer's determination to sail west until he came upon the fabulously rich lands of Asia. Columbus had departed from a Spanish harbor in August, 1492, with three small ships and about 90 men. Throughout the voyage the weather was good, but Columbus's crew became uneasy as they ventured farther and farther into uncharted waters. The sailors threatened to mutiny in early October, but, as his journal indicates, Columbus kept his firm resolve "to go to the Indies." A few days later the expedition sighted land. The Old World had made its historic contact with the New.

To understand why Europeans began to explore the New World at this time, we need to review the changes that had swept over Europe in the 1400's. Foremost among these developments were (1) the revival of trade and commerce, (2) the rise of national states controlled by powerful, wealthy rulers, and (3) the spread of new ideas which stimulated a growing curiosity about the world. These changes resulted in a period of great voyages of discovery in the late 1400's and early 1500's. In turn, these explorations led to the establishment of colonies in the Western Hemisphere by Spain, Portugal, France, Holland, and England. This chapter, therefore, will deal with the New World's roots in Europe.

1 *Changes in Europe Pave the Way for Discovery and Colonization*

Medieval society is divided into distinct classes. The thousand years between 400 and 1400 A.D. are generally called the Middle Ages (or the medieval period) in the history of western Europe. During these centuries European society included three major groups — the clergy, the nobles, and the peasants.

The primary responsibility of the clergy was the care of men's souls. In addition, the churchmen were the only teachers during the Middle Ages, and they also cared for the sick and disabled. The doctrines of the Catholic Church were generally accepted throughout western Europe, thus giving unity to medieval society.

The nobles were the landholders in the Middle Ages; and the peasants, most of them serfs, worked the land. The lord of each estate or manor supervised the work of his serfs, settled disputes among them, and protected them from enemy attack. The serfs who tilled the lord's land were bound to the soil. That is, if the manor passed from one noble to another, the serfs remained and served the new lord. Methods of farming were inefficient, and crop yields were low. Thus, the peasants made only a scanty living for themselves.

. . . .

CHAPTER FOCUS

1. Changes in Europe pave the way for discovery and colonization.
2. European explorers discover a New World.
3. Spain develops an empire in the Americas.
4. France establishes colonies in the New World.

Frequent warfare between brawling nobles was one of the curses of the Middle Ages. The lord of each manor was a law unto himself, and there were no national states as we know them today.

The Crusades create a demand for Eastern goods. During the later centuries of the Middle Ages, major changes were developing that would eventually disrupt the medieval way of life. First came the Crusades, beginning in 1096 and continuing into the 1200's. These military expeditions to the Holy Land in Asia Minor were inspired by the Popes and carried out by enthusiastic European nobles. The purpose of the Crusades was to win back the Holy Land from the Moslems, who were followers of the prophet Mohammed. The Moslems controlled not only Arabia and the lands along the eastern Mediterranean shore but northern Africa and much of Spain as well. Although the Crusades were at first successful, later expeditions to the Holy Land failed. Most people in Europe reluctantly accepted the fact that Jerusalem would remain under Moslem control.

Yet the Crusades had a tremendous influence on medieval Europe. The nobles who journeyed to the eastern Mediterranean came into contact with the startlingly different and more advanced Moslem civilization. Their own standard of living seemed crude by comparison. The Crusaders brought back samples of Eastern luxuries — spices, perfumes, brilliant dyes, jewels, ivory, glassware, silk, and tapestries. Although the Crusades failed to win the Holy Land, they whetted the appetite of Europeans for a variety of products from the East.

The revival of trade leads to the growth of cities. Throughout the early Middle Ages such Italian cities as Venice and Genoa had maintained trade with the Byzantine Empire.[1] Then, during the Crusades, Italian merchants had supplied the European armies in Asia Minor. Once the crusading fever had passed, these mer-

[1] The Byzantine Empire (map, page 4) was composed of the remnants of the eastern Roman Empire. Its capital was Constantinople, formerly called Byzantium.

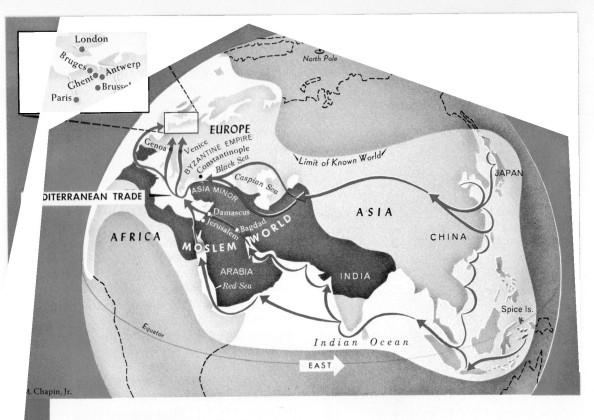

London
Bruges
Ghent · Antwerp
· Brussel~
Paris ·

North Pole

EUROPE
Genoa · Venice
BYZANTINE EMPIRE
Constantinople
Black Sea
~Limit of Known World~

Caspian Sea

MEDITERRANEAN TRADE

ASIA MINOR
· Damascus
Jerusalem · Bagdad

AFRICA
MOSLEM WORLD

ARABIA
~Red Sea

ASIA

CHINA

JAPAN

INDIA

Spice Is.

Equator

Indian Ocean

EAST

A. Chapin, Jr.

TRADE ROUTES BETWEEN EUROPE AND THE EAST

The trade routes between Europe and the East were avenues of traffic in ideas as well as products. Our system of Arabic numerals, for example, was brought by Arab merchants from India to Spain about 800 A.D. By the 1100's, the Mediterranean trade had introduced this number system to all Europe.

chants sought to meet the European demand for Eastern luxuries. Their agents scoured eastern Mediterranean ports in search of goods at bargain prices. These cargoes went directly to Italy and from there were shipped overland or carried by Venetian vessels to northern cities such as London, Antwerp, and Bruges (*broozh*).

Somehow the Eastern goods had to be paid for. As these imports flowed into Europe, gold and silver, never very plentiful, were drained away. Soon the Italian merchants began buying up products in western Europe that could be sold to traders from the East. This stimulated the production in western Europe of woolen fabrics, wines, metals, furs, and grain. The enterprising merchants who conducted this trade and many of the craftsmen or artisans who worked for them lived within medieval walled towns, or "burgs" (in French,

bourgs). Known as "burghers," or *bourgeoisie* (boor-zhwah-*zee'*), the merchants and artisans swelled the population of cities like Paris and London, Ghent, Bruges, Antwerp, and Cologne (see map above). Town life had never completely died out, even in the early Middle Ages, but now towns and cities grew larger and wealthier.

Townspeople become important. The rapid increase in the influence of the townspeople altered the balance of power among the other classes of society — the clergy, the nobles, and the peasants. The wealthy merchants in the growing cities were able to challenge the power and position of landholding nobles. And medieval towns provided a refuge for runaway serfs. If a serf lived for a year and a day in a free town, he became entitled to his freedom.

Before the Crusades, the great majority

4

of people in western Europe made their living from the land. By the end of the 1300's, the percentage of town and city dwellers had substantially increased. Because the prosperity of these townspeople depended upon trade, they were eager to preserve peace in order to increase the production of goods. For this reason they supported the efforts of kings to curb the warring nobles. Thus, the increase of East-West trade, the development of cities, and the growing importance of the townspeople all helped bring an end to the medieval way of life.

A rebirth of learning takes place in western Europe. Most people in Europe during the Middle Ages had little chance to get an education. Only a limited knowledge of Latin and Greek literature had been preserved by churchmen in the monasteries of western Europe. The Crusaders were surprised to find Moslem and Byzantine scholars thoroughly familiar with the civilizations of ancient Greece and Rome. Western interest in this classical culture was stimulated by the new trade ties with the Eastern lands and by the arrival of scholars from the Byzantine Empire. As a result, there was a rediscovery, or rebirth, of learning in western Europe, known as the *Renaissance* (ren-uh-*sahns'*).

Starting in wealthy Italian cities during the fourteenth century (1300's), the Renaissance spread over the rest of western Europe during the next two centuries. Universities, which had grown up during the late Middle Ages, had been concerned chiefly with the education of the clergy. Now they became crowded with young men eager to study the art and literature of the ancient Greeks and Romans. While Renaissance writers and artists still used religious subjects, they portrayed them in a more lifelike way. Also, they focused attention on the individual and the world they saw around them. Some Renaissance authors emphasized their independence by writing in the language of the people (French or Italian, for example) rather than in Latin, the language of the Church.

Renaissance scientists made great strides in their understanding of the nature of the universe. In the mid-sixteenth century the Polish astronomer Copernicus sought to prove that the sun, not the earth, was the center about which all the planets moved. Advances in the science of navigation allowed men to venture far out onto the oceans. Various instruments, such as the compass, astrolabe, and quadrant, enabled seamen to determine direction, measure latitude, and chart their course even when out of sight of land. Map makers acquired greater skill in indicating prevailing winds, currents, tides, channels, and harbors.

The printing press spreads knowledge. Undoubtedly the most important single advance in Renaissance Europe was the development of printing by a German named Johann Gutenberg in the mid-1400's. Before that time, books had been copied by hand, a process that was often inaccurate and always slow and expensive. By using movable metal type and a printing press, Gutenberg devised a quick, efficient, and cheap way of printing many copies of the same book. The value of this new process of printing was recognized immediately, and by 1500 there were more than a thousand printers in Europe. By increasing the number of books and reducing their cost, Gutenberg's printing process (1) stimulated the desire to read, (2) helped spread the new ideas of the Renaissance, and (3) aroused interest in distant lands.

Using an astrolabe to measure the altitude of the stars, navigators could determine their latitude at sea.

A Norwegian explorer, Helge Ingstad, has excavated remains of a thousand-year-old Norse settlement in Newfoundland. The excavated smithy shown here, with a stone anvil and remains of iron, is important evidence of the settlement's Norse origin, since neither Eskimos nor Indians in this area knew how to work iron.

Information about distant lands seeps into Europe. At the end of the fifteenth century most educated Europeans knew that the world was round, not flat. The ancient Greeks had first advanced this theory; and, though forgotten in the early Middle Ages, it had been revived in the twelfth century. The remarkable travels of the Venetian Marco Polo to the court of Kublai Khan, the Emperor of Cathay (China), seemed to confirm the theory. Polo had reached Cathay by crossing a vast land mass (Asia), at the end of which he found a large body of water. Presumably, it was thought, this was the same ocean that washed the shores of western Europe. When Marco Polo returned to Venice in 1295 after a 24-year absence, a book was published about his extraordinary journey. This volume stirred the imagination of Europeans and aroused their curiosity about Cathay and Cipangu (Japan), a country of "12,700 islands inhabited and uninhabited."

A few Europeans at this time may also have had some faint knowledge of distant lands to the *west* of their continent. In the ninth and tenth centuries Scandinavian seamen had explored and colonized Ireland, Iceland, and even Greenland. About the year 1000, a Viking named Leif Ericson had sailed west from Greenland, touched on the shores of North America, and win-tered in Newfoundland. Norse sagas told of Leif the Lucky's discovery of "Vinland," but these stories were little known outside of Iceland and the Scandinavian peninsula.

National states develop strong governments. While far-reaching changes were affecting ways of life and thought in Europe, political changes were also taking place. During the Middle Ages the unruly nobles had been able, for the most part, to disregard the authority of their kings. But after the Crusades some rulers in western Europe began to gain new strength. For funds they could now depend upon the prosperous townsmen, who realized that law and order would stimulate business. The assistance of the burghers enabled kings to hire soldiers to fight their battles and thus reduce the power of the nobles. By the late 1400's strong national states had emerged in Spain, Portugal, France, and England.

In Spain, for example, the marriage of Ferdinand of Aragon and Isabella of Castile made possible the union of the two most important Spanish states. They soon annexed more territory and in 1492 conquered the Moslem state in southern Spain. Meanwhile, Portugal had fought to protect its independence. King John II strengthened the royal power and established Portugal's lead in the voyages of discovery (page 8).

National rulers grew stronger in France and England too. French kings had begun to establish France's "natural boundaries" at the Pyrenees, the Alps, and the Atlantic. In England, following a bloody civil war, Parliament welcomed Henry Tudor to the throne as Henry VII in 1485. With the support of townsmen and independent farmers, this king and the Tudor monarchs who followed him brought order and prosperity to England. Neither Italy nor Germany achieved unification until much later, and hence they played no part as nations in the voyages of discovery or colonization.

Capital accumulates through increased trade. The revival of trade in the late Middle Ages paved the way for a vast expansion of commerce. Safer vessels and improved methods of navigation enabled merchants to ship large quantities of goods by way of the Atlantic Ocean and the North and Baltic Seas. As the volume of trade increased, so too did the wealth of commercial centers in Spain, Portugal, England, and France. The availability of surplus wealth, called *capital*, made it possible for countries to finance the costly voyages of discovery. None of the individual explorers had money enough of his own to embark on a long voyage. Instead, each was backed by funds from a royal treasury or from groups of bankers and merchants. The kings, merchants, and bankers who invested in voyages of discovery (and later in the establishment of colonies) expected to make money out of their ventures. As one historian has pointed out, "the voyages of discovery were calculated in the ledgers before they were charted in the logbooks."

National governments endorse mercantilism. The monarchs of the new national states adopted an economic policy known as *mercantilism*. According to this theory, wealth was measured by the amount of gold and silver that a country accumulated in its national treasury. Thus each nation tried to sell more goods abroad than it brought into the country. Only if the value of exports exceeded the value of imports could a country preserve and add to its gold and silver. It is easy to see, therefore, why mercantilism would encourage the founding of trading posts and colonies in distant parts of the world. These settlements could help make the mother country self-sufficient by providing raw materials and foodstuffs that she would otherwise have to import from other countries. In addition, the colonies would need finished goods and manufactures from the mother country. This exchange of manufactured goods for raw materials from the colonies would add to the surplus of gold and silver in the national treasury.

The European rulers were enthusiastic about the mercantile theory. So too were their economic allies, the merchants, for it meant government encouragement of trade and commerce. It also meant government support for explorations leading to the establishment of new trading posts in Africa, India, and the Far East. In time, mercantilism caused governments to support the founding of colonies in the New World. The mercantilists expected all these ventures to enrich the mother country. As the 1400's ended, then, the new national states in Europe had the economic desire, the financial resources, and the knowledge of navigation to explore, trade, and colonize beyond the fringes of the known world.

SPAIN BEFORE 1469

The marriage of Isabella of Castile and Ferdinand of Aragon in 1469 united the two largest Spanish kingdoms and thus laid the foundation for Spain's future greatness.

R. M. Chapin, Jr.

Religious changes divide Europe. One other change which influenced the exploration and colonization of the New World was the breakup of Catholic unity. By the end of the 1400's many European monarchs were critical of the Catholic Church because it refused to recognize national boundaries and collected revenues which the kings coveted for themselves. Merchants resented the Church's stand on the charging of interest by moneylenders. Other people complained about corruption in the Church and the poor education of some of the clergy.

Smoldering discontent came to a head in 1517 when a German churchman, Martin Luther, broke with the Catholic Church. He wrote a series of pamphlets which, thanks to the printing press, circulated widely. In time, Lutheran churches were founded in Germany, the Netherlands, and Scandinavia. Soon after Luther took his stand, John Calvin in Switzerland voiced a similar protest. Calvin's ideas spread to other countries, especially France and Scotland. Followers of Luther and Calvin, as well as others who broke away from the Catholic Church, were known as *Protestants.* In the latter half of the 1500's, the Catholic Church undertook widespread reforms. And a new religious order, the Jesuits, sought to win Protestants back to the Church. For a time, however, Catholics and Protestants fought religious wars in Germany, France, the Netherlands, and also in England.

The religious upheavals in Europe were closely connected with the exploration and settlement of the New World. Catholic missionaries, particularly Jesuit priests, accompanied Spanish, French, and Portuguese explorers and converted many Indians to Christianity. Protestants in quest of religious freedom were among the earliest settlers in the English colonies. The bitter religious controversies in Europe drove many people to the New World in search of a freedom denied them at home.

▶ CHECK-UP

1. Explain the roles of the clergy, the nobles, and the peasants in medieval society.

2. Why did the Crusades lead to increased trade? How did the revival of trade lead to the growth of cities? How did it affect the bourgeoisie? Why did the bourgeoisie tend to support the kings?

3. Why did western Europeans become interested in classical culture? What were the results of the Renaissance? Why was the development of printing important?

4. How was each of these related to interest in exploration: aids to navigation? knowledge of distant lands? rise of national states? accumulation of capital? mercantilism? religious changes?

• • • • • • • • • • • • • • • • • •

2 *European Explorers Discover a New World*

Portugal seeks a sea route to Asia. Portuguese mariners were the first Europeans to seek a water route to the East. Jealous of the wealth of Italian merchants who dealt in Eastern luxuries, the Portuguese resolved to find an alternate route to the riches of the East. Both their early interest and their final success were due in large part to a member of the royal family of Portugal, Prince Henry the Navigator. He established a famous maritime school at the southern tip of Portugal, where he gathered together the most talented geographers, map makers, and ship designers.

Portuguese sailors had already discovered the Azores and the Madeira Islands in the Atlantic (map, page 9). At the urging of Prince Henry, they began pushing farther and farther southward along the coast of Africa. The ship captains and their crews were reluctant to venture into unknown waters. Only the rich profits from the gold, ivory, and slaves which they could obtain in Africa encouraged them to continue southward. By the time of Prince Henry's death, Portuguese expeditions had reached Cape Sierra Leone and

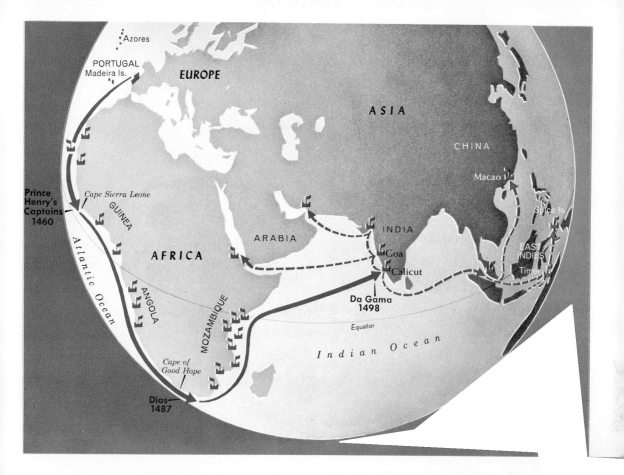

Azores

PORTUGAL
Madeira Is.

EUROPE

ASIA

CHINA

Macao

Prince
Henry's
Captains
1460

Cape Sierra Leone

GUINEA

Atlantic Ocean

ANGOLA

AFRICA

ARABIA

INDIA

Goa

Calicut

Spice Is.

EAST
INDIES

Timor

Da Gama
1498

MOZAMBIQUE

Equator

Indian Ocean

Cape of
Good Hope

Dias
1487

THE PORTUGUESE ROUTE TO THE EAST

Portugal's mariners spent nearly fifty years exploring a water route to the storied East. Note their progress southward along the west coast of Africa, around to the Cape of Good Hope, and finally to Calicut. Portuguese merchants established a fortified commercial empire (dashed lines and forts), which stretched from the Spice Islands to Angola.

charted the west African coast almost to the equator.

King John II of Portugal continued the work of Prince Henry. He also was eager to have Portuguese ships sail around Africa and tap the still richer markets of the East. During 1487 and 1488 Bartholomew Dias (*dee*'ahs) reached the southernmost tip of Africa. Dias called it the Cape of Storms, but the king changed the name to Cape of Good Hope. He believed that the way was now clear for Portuguese ships to sail around Africa to India.

Vasco da Gama reaches India by water. A decade later another Portuguese captain, Vasco da Gama (*vahs*'koh duh *gam*'uh), set out to follow Dias' route

around the Cape and continue on to India. In 1498, after a year's voyage, da Gama dropped anchor at Calicut on the western coast of India. Then, his ships loaded with spices and jewels purchased from the merchants of Calicut, he began the long trip back to Portugal. When he reached Lisbon in 1499, da Gama learned that his cargo was worth 60 times the entire cost of his two-year expedition. As word spread of da Gama's voyage, the Italian merchants realized that their long monopoly of the Eastern trade had come to an end.

The Portuguese moved at once to protect their trade route to India. They established forts on both the west and east coasts of Africa and also at the Cape of

9

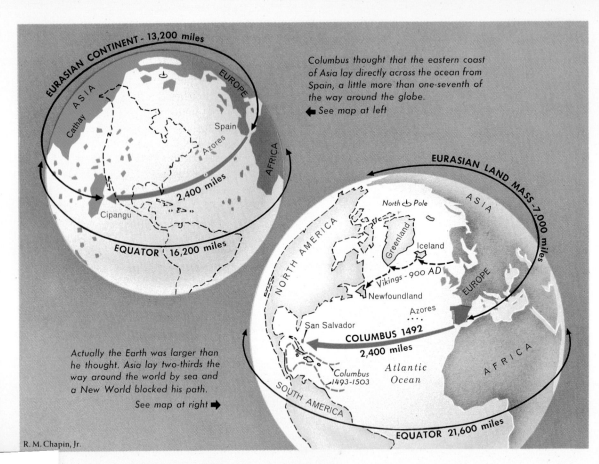

Columbus thought that the eastern coast of Asia lay directly across the ocean from Spain, a little more than one-seventh of the way around the globe.
◀ See map at left

Actually the Earth was larger than he thought. Asia lay two-thirds the way around the world by sea and a New World blocked his path.

See map at right ➡

R. M. Chapin, Jr.

COLUMBUS MISJUDGES THE DISTANCE TO ASIA

In 1492, Martin Behaim of Nuremberg constructed a terrestrial globe. Relying on accounts of travelers like Marco Polo and the guesses of the ancients, he devised an arrangement of land and water much like that imagined by Columbus (see upper left globe). Neither Behaim nor Columbus dreamed that a large land mass lay between western Europe and eastern Asia.

Good Hope. They fought off Moslem raiders in the Arabian Sea and won the right to establish trading posts in Calicut and Goa (*goh'uh*) in India. Portuguese mariners also discovered and traded with the Spice Islands (Moluccas) in the East Indies. Eventually they secured the island of Macao (*muh-kow'*) off the coast of China. In the long run, however, the Portuguese found it impossible to protect their vast trade empire. Portions of it fell to other colonial powers in the 1600's. But to the present time Portugal has held Angola, Mozambique, and Portuguese Guinea in Africa, Timor (*tee'mohr*) in the East Indies, and Macao in China. These are the last remnants of Portugal's once spectacular trade empire.

Columbus seeks Asia and finds a New World. The desire to share in the Eastern trade prompted Ferdinand and Isabella of Spain to invest in the search to find a *western* water route to Asia. Their agent was Christopher Columbus, a Genoese mariner who had sailed on many Mediterranean and African voyages and had made one trip to Iceland. He knew that the earth was round, but his estimate of the size of the earth and the extent of the Asian land mass was not very accurate. After reading Marco Polo's account, Columbus decided that Asia lay only a short distance west of the Azores. Had he known the truth, it is doubtful that he or any member of his crew would have risked a voyage into the unknown Atlantic. And it is almost certain that no monarch would have gambled on such a mad venture.

For eight years Columbus tried to interest someone in backing his scheme of sailing west to Asia. Finally, Ferdinand and Isabella agreed to finance the expedition. They commissioned him "Admiral of the Ocean Sea," provided three ships and a crew, and gave him a Latin letter of introduction to the Emperor of China. After more than two months at sea, Columbus and his men landed on San Salvador (also known as Watling Island) in the Bahamas on October 12, 1492. Later he sailed on to Hispaniola and Cuba, convinced that he had discovered islands off the coast of Asia.

Hailed as a hero upon his return to Spain, Columbus talked the Spanish rulers into financing three more voyages to the New World. He discovered more islands in the Caribbean, and on his last voyage (1502–1504) sailed along the shores of Central America. (On none of the four voyages did Columbus touch on territory now a part of the United States.) But he never found the wealth of the East Indies or had any use for his letter to the Emperor of China. Yet when Columbus died in 1506 — out of favor with the Spanish rulers — he still believed that he had discovered a western route to the East.

The world is divided between Spain and Portugal. News of Columbus's first voyage disturbed the Portuguese. They joined the Spaniards in an appeal to the Pope to settle their rival claims to the riches of Asia. In 1493 the Pope drew an imaginary north-south line 100 leagues (300 miles) west of the Cape Verde Islands (map, page 12). All non-Christian lands to the east of this line, including the route around Africa to India, would belong to Portugal. All non-Christian lands to the west of the papal Line of Demarcation (thus including the Western Hemisphere) would belong to Spain. But the Portuguese were still dissatisfied, so Spain consented in 1494 to a treaty which established the line 370 leagues (1110 miles) west of the Cape Verde Islands. This revised Line of Demarcation permitted Portugal to lay claim to what is now Brazil. At the time the line was finally settled, very little was known about the geography of the New World. Indeed, neither Spain nor Portugal suspected that a huge land mass lay between Europe and Asia. But both countries hoped that this division of the world would discourage other kings from sponsoring voyages of exploration.

England ignores the Line of Demarcation. King Henry VII of England was the first to defy the Line of Demarcation. He authorized a Genoese mariner named Giovanni Caboto "to seek out, discover and find whatsoever isles, countries, regions or provinces of the heathen and infidels, which before this time have been unknown to all Christians." On his first expedition in 1497, John Cabot (the English form of Caboto's name) probably reached Cape Breton Island and Newfoundland. But since he brought back no spices, gold, or jewels, Henry VII regarded the trip as a failure. Cabot made a second journey to North America in 1498. This time he explored as far south as the coast of what is now the United States, hoping to find a passageway through to Asia. But nothing came of this venture, and Henry VII refused to invest any more money in exploration. About the only thing the English had learned from Cabot's voyages was that the New World had a "barren shore," a "wooded coast," and "monstrous lumps of ice floating in the sea."

Spain and Portugal explore the New World. Meanwhile, Spanish and Portuguese mariners were exploring warmer, more promising regions. An Italian merchant-adventurer who sailed with a Spanish expedition was the first to conclude that South America was a separate land mass and not part of Asia. This man was Amerigo Vespucci (veh-*spyoo*'chih). In a series of letters which were widely circulated in Europe, he called the western land *Mundus Novus* (Latin for "New World"). The only way to reach Asia, he insisted, was to sail around the southern tip of the New World. A German map maker who read Vespucci's letters drew a map of the known world in 1507 and labeled the western land "America."

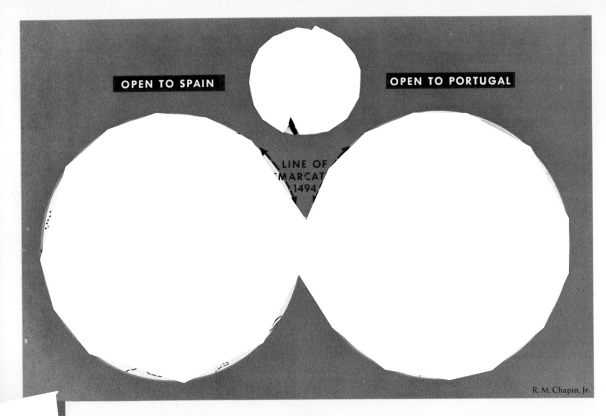

OPEN TO SPAIN   OPEN TO PORTUGAL

LINE OF
MARCAT
1494

R. M. Chapin, Jr.

THE WORLD DIVIDED

If Pope Alexander had been able in 1493 to see the world as he had divided it, the earth would have looked about like the globe at the top of the page. Although the Demarcation Line was revised for Portugal a year later by treaty (see hinged hemispheres), the Spanish retained claim to most of the Western Hemisphere. Where has Portuguese influence persisted to this day in the Americas?

At the same time that Vespucci was sailing for Spain, a Portuguese navigator named Pedro Cabral (kuh-*brahl'*), while trying to round Cape Verde in western Africa, touched the coast of Brazil. Cabral claimed this new territory for Portugal in 1500. Because it fell within the region granted to Portugal by the 1494 treaty, Brazil became a Portuguese colony.

Spanish explorers and adventurers continued to come to the Caribbean area. From the natives of the islands they heard about fabulously rich cities on the mainland. These stories spurred a Spaniard named Balboa to explore the narrow stretch of land separating the Atlantic and Pacific Oceans. Pushing through the jungles of Panama in search of these fabled cities in 1513, he came instead on the Pacific Ocean. Balboa's discovery was a bitter disappoint-

ment, for it meant that a New World did indeed stand in the way of a water route to Asia. Navigators redoubled their efforts to find a passageway to the Pacific either *through* the land or *around* it.

Magellan's crew sails around the world. Balboa's report led the Spanish government to hire Ferdinand Magellan, a Portuguese captain, to find a route around the New World. Departing in September, 1519, Magellan spent the winter along the coast of South America. His storm-tossed fleet then made its way through the treacherous Strait of Magellan and into the Pacific (see map above). A three-month voyage across that ocean, during which his men were desperately short of food and water, brought the expedition to the Ladrone Islands (now called the Marianas). Shortly afterwards Magellan was killed by natives in the Philippine Islands. The expedition pushed on, however, and in 1522 the one surviving ship, the *Victoria,* returned to her Spanish port.

Thus, in just 30 years (1492–1522), European mariners had stumbled on a new continent, explored its coasts and offshore islands, and charted a western water route to the East.

▶ CHECK-UP

1. Why was Portugal interested in explorations along Africa's west coast? How did these explorations lead to the discovery of a water route to India? Why was this discovery important?

2. Why did Columbus believe a westward route to Asia could be found? What were the results of his exploration? How did the Pope try to settle the rival claims to the riches of Asia?

3. How did it become clear that Columbus had discovered a New World? What was the significance of Magellan's voyage?

3 *Spain Develops an Empire in the Americas*

Columbus had been so certain that the Caribbean islands were part of the East Indies, that he had called the natives "Indians." Actually historians believe that the ancestors of these people were Asian nomads who crossed the Bering Strait some 25,000 to 40,000 years ago. From there they made their way through Alaska and eventually into the rest of North America and southward into Central and South America. Most of the Indians lived by hunting and fishing, but some tribes settled down and became skilled farmers.

Some Indian nations had advanced civilizations. In three areas of the New World the Indians had developed remark-

able civilizations. In the jungles of Guatemala and the Yucatan peninsula, the *Mayas* (*mah'*yuz) built imposing stone cities and applied intricate designs to pottery, wood, metal, and textiles. They developed a form of picture writing and even devised a calendar that was more accurate than the one used in Europe at that time. Farther north, on the Mexican plateau, the more warlike *Aztecs* built their capital city of Tenochtitlán (tay-nohch-tee-*tlahn'*), later Mexico City. The Aztecs, who had absorbed much of the civilization of the Mayas, ruled an empire of some five million Indians at the time of the Spanish conquests. In South America an even larger empire was efficiently administered by the *Incas* of Peru. A system of paved roads connected the distant parts of the Incan domain. The Incas excelled in agriculture and in working with copper, bronze, gold, and silver.

The most enduring contribution of the first inhabitants of the Western Hemisphere was their development of agriculture. The more highly civilized tribes built irrigation systems for watering their crops. By crossbreeding wild plants they produced Indian corn, or "maize." They also cultivated white and sweet potatoes, peanuts, pumpkins, squash, and tomatoes. And they knew how to extract and use quinine, vanilla, cacao (cocoa), and rubber. All of these products they eventually introduced to the European invaders.

The Spaniards conquer the Caribbean. The Spanish base in the Caribbean was the island of Hispaniola, to which Columbus brought colonists on his second voyage. There the Spanish conquerors, or *conquistadors,* carved out huge estates for themselves. They enslaved the natives, forcing them to work on sugar and cotton plantations. Under this system of forced labor, the Indians died in great numbers. So the Spaniards added to their labor force by purchasing Negro slaves transported from Africa by Portuguese slave-traders. Greed for gold drove the conquistadors into further exploration of the Caribbean. In 1508 Ponce de Leon (*pohn'* say day lay-*ohn'*) explored Puerto Rico. Within a few

SPANISH INFLUENCE IN THE UNITED STATES

Spanish rule long ago disappeared from North America, but much evidence survives of the influence of Spanish civilization in the American Southwest.

The Indians of the Southwest borrowed Spanish designs in fashioning beautiful silver jewelry. The squash blossom motif of this Navajo necklace traces back to a Spanish design.

The architecture of the Catholic missions is one of the richest legacies left by the Spanish who settled in the American Southwest. San Xavier Mission (above), built in the late 1700's, stands in the desert near Tucson, Arizona.

Spanish ranchers developed the Western saddle, many of which were decorated with fine leather work and embroidery (above). The Spanish also introduced horses to the New World. Many of these horses ran wild on the western plains and were captured by Indians. In the painting at left, George Catlin, an American artist, showed Comanche braves roping wild ponies.

R. M. Chapin, Jr.

SPANIARDS EXPLORE THE AMERICAS

The Spanish conquistadors found in the Americas three highly developed Indian civilizations (color). Hernando Cortés called Tenochtitlán, with its many waterways and movable bridges, "the Venice of the New World."

years the Spaniards also took Jamaica and Cuba. (See the map on this page for Spanish explorations in the New World.)

Cortés and Pizarro invade the mainland. One conquistador, young Hernando Cortés, led a band of some 600 Spaniards from Cuba to Mexico in 1519. When Cortés landed on the Mexican coast, the Indians hailed him as Quetzalcoatl (*kay'-tsal-kwaht' 'l*), a white god who tradition said would return some day. Cortés learned that the Indians resented Aztec control. Though his original intention had been to establish a trading post, he decided to take advantage of the confusion caused by his arrival. Spurred on by reports of fabulous riches farther inland, Cortés set out for the Mexican plateau to challenge the Aztec ruler. Eventually he engaged the Aztec warriors in battle. By 1521 Cortés had defeated the Aztecs and made himself master of their empire. The Spaniards seized enormous quantities of silver and gold in Mexico. When news of this

rich treasure got back to Spain, it touched off the first gold rush to the New World.

Some of these newcomers helped Francisco Pizarro plunder the Incan empire in South America. In 1531–1533 this Spanish conquistador sailed from Panama to Peru, scaled the Andes, and captured the Incan strongholds. Following Cortés' example in Mexico, Pizarro and his followers stripped the Incan towns of their riches and forced the natives to work for them.

The Spaniards penetrate into North America. Tales about the Seven Cities of Cíbola (*see'buh-luh*), rich with gold, and a spring whose waters restored youth and vigor drew Spanish explorers to areas of what is now the United States. Ponce de Leon, the governor of Puerto Rico, went in search of the fountain of youth. In 1513 he discovered Florida but not his magic spring. His attempts to found a colony in Florida were unsuccessful, but in 1565 the Spaniards did establish a base at St. Augustine. One Spanish expedition sailing from

15

Florida to Mexico in 1528 was caught in a hurricane. Its ships were wrecked in the Gulf of Mexico, and its members left to wander through Texas. Eight years later a few survivors, led by Cabeza de Vaca (kah-bay'sah day vah'kah), returned to Mexico with tales of the Seven Cities, which they had *not* seen, and wild "hunchback cows," which they *had* seen.

The lure of gold — not the first mention of American buffalo — inspired two more Spaniards to explore the North American mainland. Hernando de Soto, who had served under Pizarro in Peru, explored the area north of the Gulf of Mexico. He came upon the Mississippi River near the site of present-day Memphis in 1541, and when he died the following year, his men buried him in the river. Meanwhile, Coronado was leading an impressive force of Spaniards into territory that is now the southwestern United States. His men sighted the Grand Canyon in 1540, and they came across the

Pueblo Indians, whose large adobe dwellings (*pueblos*) amazed the Spaniards. Such discoveries, however, did not make up for their failure to find gold or silver. Although Spain laid claim to a large part of North America, the only Spanish settlements there were in Florida and in what is now the southwestern United States.

Spanish civilization is transplanted to New Spain. By the end of the sixteenth century there were some 200,000 Spanish settlers in Central and South America, Mexico, and the West Indies. They were governed by viceroys — representatives of the king who had vast powers over the conquistadors, settlers, missionaries, and Indians. Spain was proud not only of the extent of her New World empire but also of the transplanting of Spanish civilization to the wilderness. The Spanish cities in the New World were copied after those in the mother country, and they were justly proud of their cultural achievements. The first printing press in the New World was set up in Mexico City in the 1530's; and by 1551 Mexico City and Lima, Peru, each had a university.

In addition, Spain took pride in spreading Christianity to Indians in the New World. Catholic missionaries had accompanied the explorers and conquistadors and sometimes were explorers themselves. Missions, churches, and imposing cathedrals were built throughout the Spanish colonies. The clergy played an important role not only in spreading Spanish civilization but in trying to improve conditions among the Indians.

The power of Spain declines. The glittering wealth and prestige of Spain was beginning to tarnish by the end of the 1500's. For almost a hundred years gold and silver had poured into the Spanish treasury, making Spain the leading mercantile nation and the most powerful country in the world. Had Spanish rulers used this wealth to build up industries and to develop the navy, they might have been able to maintain Spanish power. Instead, they favored the army and neglected the navy, thus making it difficult for Spanish ships to protect the goose that laid the

---

England's Greatest "Sea Dog"

Of the English mariners who raided Spanish treasure ships in the late sixteenth century, the most famous was Sir Francis Drake. Not only did Drake enrich England's coffers with Spanish gold, but he also circumnavigated the globe in a voyage that contributed much to the understanding of world geography.

In 1577 Queen Elizabeth I equipped Drake with a fleet of five ships for a voyage of exploration. Drake followed Magellan's route until he passed through the Strait at South America's tip. Then he sailed north along the west coast of South America, plundering Chile and Peru. His other ships having abandoned the voyage, Drake continued sailing north and west in the *Golden Hind*. Along the way he sought vainly to find a northwest passage and a water route to the Atlantic Ocean which would take him back to England.

Drake landed in California near San Francisco Bay and claimed the region for England. (A brass plate on which the claim was inscribed was discovered in 1936.) The *Golden Hind* then sailed west across the Pacific, rounded Africa, and proceeded home to England, arriving in 1580. For his accomplishments, Drake was knighted by Queen Elizabeth.

golden eggs. Furthermore, Spain bought its manufactured goods from the merchants of the Low Countries (present-day Belgium and the Netherlands). These purchases drained off much Spanish gold. So, too, did wars in Europe. Corruption among government officials was still another reason for the decline of Spanish power.

Spain's envious neighbors took advantage of her difficulties. Dutch, English, and French vessels raided Spanish ships bringing gold and silver bullion and other precious cargoes from the New World. The English took the lead in harassing Spain. Fearless English "sea dogs" like John Hawkins and Francis Drake attacked Spanish treasure ships and even raided Spanish ports. In 1587 Drake boldly sailed into the harbor of the Spanish city of Cadiz and set fire to a royal fleet, thus "singeing the King of Spain's beard."

England defeats the Spanish Armada. In 1588 Philip II of Spain ordered his fleet, called the "Invincible Armada," to attack England. But the clumsy Spanish galleons suffered heavy losses while fighting in the English Channel. When the Spanish ships tried to return home by sailing around Scotland and Ireland, they were battered by heavy gales and many were wrecked on the rocky coasts.

Defeat of the Armada in 1588 marked a turning point in English and Spanish history. For Spain, it hastened the decline that had already set in. For England, the defeat of the Spanish fleet meant security from the threat of Spanish invasion. It also opened up opportunities for the English in the New World. Spanish power had rested not so much upon the Line of Demarcation as upon naval power in the Atlantic Ocean. An Englishman, Sir Walter Raleigh, put it this way: "[He] who rules the sea, rules the commerce of the world and to him that rules the commerce of the world belongs the treasure of the world and indeed the world itself."

▶ CHECK-UP

1. What advanced civilizations did the Spanish explorers find in the New World?

2. How did the Spaniards seek to profit from their conquests in the New World? Consider the Caribbean area, Mexico, and Peru. What did the Spaniards learn from the Indians?

3. What Spaniards explored vast areas in the southern part of what is now the United States? Why? What were the results? What efforts were made to transplant Spanish civilization to New Spain?

4. Why did Spain's power decline? What was the significance of the defeat of the Armada?

· · · · · · · · · · · · · · · · · · · ·

4 *France Establishes Colonies in the New World*

While Spain was building an empire in the New World, France showed only a mild interest in the Western Hemisphere. To be sure, French fishermen had heard about John Cabot's discovery of rich fishing banks off Newfoundland. Early in the 1500's they began making yearly trips to North America, curing their codfish on the mainland, and even trading with the Indians for furs.

France stakes out claims in the New World. France's first claim to territory in the New World rested upon the voyage of an Italian mariner, Giovanni da Verrazano (vehr-rah-*tsah'*noh). Commissioned by the French king in 1524 to find a passageway to the East, Verrazano explored the Atlantic coast from the Carolinas to Nova Scotia. He even entered what is now New York harbor and sailed up the Hudson River. (See the map on page 18 for French explorations in North America.)

Ten years later the French king sent Jacques Cartier (car-*tyay'*) to investigate the St. Lawrence River Valley in the hope that it might be a northwest passage to Asia. Cartier made three trips between 1534 and 1541. He explored the sites of

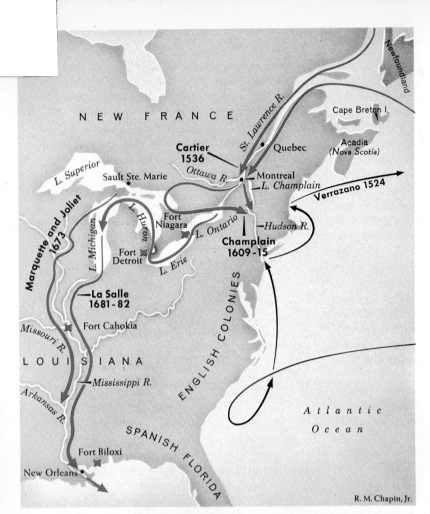

NEW FRANCE

Cartier 1536

St. Lawrence R.

Quebec

Cape Breton I.

Newfoundland

Acadia (Nova Scotia)

L. Superior

Sault Ste. Marie

Ottawa R.

Montreal
L. Champlain

Verrazano 1524

Marquette and Joliet 1673

L. Michigan

L. Huron

Fort Niagara

L. Ontario

Fort Detroit

L. Erie

Hudson R.

Champlain 1609-15

La Salle 1681-82

Fort Cahokia

Missouri R.

ENGLISH COLONIES

LOUISIANA

Mississippi R.

Arkansas R.

SPANISH FLORIDA

Atlantic Ocean

Fort Biloxi

New Orleans

R. M. Chapin, Jr.

THE FRENCH PENETRATE NORTH AMERICA

The French found no gold in northeastern North America. But in time they developed a rich fur trade with the interior. Their presence is reflected in the French names of many cities. Locate present-day Detroit and New Orleans on the map.

the future cities of Quebec and Montreal and reached the rapids of the St. Lawrence. His voyages failed to disclose a passageway through North America, but they did yield valuable geographical information. Cartier took this information back to France along with a cargo of iron pyrites, or fool's gold, and quartz crystals which he thought were diamonds.

During the remainder of the 1500's, French kings showed little interest in the far lands their explorers had claimed. They were much more concerned with religious and civil wars at home. Not until the early 1600's, when peace was restored, did French monarchs turn their attention to the planting of colonies in the New World.

France establishes colonies. The desire of French kings for colonies, like that of other European rulers at this time, reflected a belief in mercantilism. Trade was to

be carefully regulated so that exports would exceed imports. Thus, gold and silver would accumulate in the mother country's treasury. According to a French minister of finance, "only the abundance of money in a state . . . makes the difference in its greatness and power." Naturally, France expected whatever colonies she established in the New World to add to her "abundance of money."

The colonies planted by France in the Caribbean fulfilled this purpose. Plantations on the West Indian islands of Guadeloupe and Martinique yielded rich crops of sugar and tobacco. In North America, however, French colonies developed more slowly and were less profitable. French explorers still were more interested in finding a westward water passage to Asia than in planting settlements along the St. Lawrence River.

French explorers push into the interior of North America. One French explorer, Samuel de Champlain (sham-*plain'*), did understand the importance of the St. Lawrence Valley. For some thirty years, Champlain devoted himself to exploring the St. Lawrence and the surrounding land. He established the first permanent French settlement in North America at Quebec in 1608. The next year he discovered the inland lake which bears his name. Then he pushed farther into the interior, exploring the Ottawa River route to Lake Huron and the region around the Great Lakes. The journals which Champlain kept during his travels preserved much priceless information about the early history of New France.

In 1670 the governor-general of New France called a great meeting of Indian tribes at Sault Ste. Marie (*soo'saint'*muh-*ree'*), between Lakes Superior and Huron. In the name of the king of France he claimed all lands south and west of that point. Three years later, Louis Joliet and a Jesuit priest, Jacques Marquette, explored and claimed for France the headwaters of the Mississippi. They followed the river southward as far as the mouth of the Arkansas River. Not until 1682 did Robert Cavelier, Sieur de La Salle, travel the entire course of the Mississippi. At its mouth he claimed for France "possession of that river, of all the rivers that enter into it, and all the country watered by them." La Salle named this vast empire Louisiana in honor of his sovereign, Louis XIV.

Along the waterways of the interior of North America, the French built a series of forts. These military posts served as trading stations and missionary centers. The line of defense included Fort Niagara and Fort Detroit, Fort Cahokia near the junction of the Missouri and Mississippi Rivers, and Fort Biloxi near the Mississippi delta. The administrative headquarters of the southern portion of this territory was New Orleans, a city which the French laid out in 1718.

Farming is unprofitable in New France. Three fourths of the colonists of New France took up farming as an occupation, but few of them were successful. The growing season was short, and in some areas the soil was too rocky to raise anything except hardy grains. Many of the settlers were former soldiers who used inefficient, primitive methods of cultivation. The French government parceled out huge estates to French noblemen who tried to persuade farmers to work the land under conditions like those on a medieval manor. Few colonists had enough money to buy land, and renting a small farm was costly. Moreover, farmers had to sell their grain at prices set by the government. Thus, farming in New France was never very profitable. Unable to feed itself, the colony had to import food.

Fish and furs bring profits. Far more profitable than farming were fishing and fur trading. Most of the fishermen lived in Acadia (Nova Scotia) or Newfoundland or Cape Breton Island. They caught large quantities of cod, cured the fish themselves, and shipped it to Europe.

The fur trade attracted a colorful breed of men. Known as *coureurs de bois* (koo-rehr'duh-*bwah'*), or "forest runners," they usually depended on the Indians to trap the animals and prepare the pelts. In return for rich piles of furs, they traded trinkets, knives, hatchets, and later guns and liquor to the Indians. Shipped from Quebec and Montreal, these pelts brought high prices in Europe. Since it was important to maintain good relations with the Indians, the fur traders generally treated them well and often learned their languages. In New France, as in New Spain, few of the settlers were women, and many of the white men took Indian wives.

Profitable as the exports of fur and fish from New France were, they did not compare in value with the sugar, coffee, tobacco, and cotton produced in the French Caribbean colonies. This difference was reflected by the population growth of the two regions. The vast area of New France, stretching from the mouth of the St. Lawrence to the mouth of the Mississippi, had only about 15,000 white people in 1715. The tiny French colonies in the West Indies, on the other hand, had twice as many settlers.

New France attracts few settlers. The slow growth of New France was due in part to the inhospitable climate of the St. Lawrence River Valley and to the manorial system of landholding. But perhaps the main reason why New France grew so slowly was the lack of political and religious freedom.

The government of New France reflected the absolute monarchy of Louis XIV. The king appointed a royal governor with almost unlimited powers for the whole colony. Justice was handed down by royal magistrates under royal law, without jury trial. The government also closely supervised the economic life of New France, since the purpose of the colony was to provide raw materials to the mother country and buy her finished goods. Thus, exports of fur and fish went directly to France, and government regulations prevented the growth of any industry within New France.

Religious freedom was also lacking because the French government was determined to keep the colony Catholic. French Protestants, known as Huguenots (*hyoo'-guh-nots*), were hard-working and well-educated. Had they been allowed to emigrate to New France, they might have contributed much to the growth of the colony; but they were forbidden to leave France. Even when the government persecuted them, as it did in the late 1600's, they could only flee to some Protestant country in Europe or to the Dutch or English colonies in America.

The slow growth of New France becomes dramatically clear when compared to the progress of the English colonies, about which you will read in Chapter 2. The first permanent English settlement was founded only a year before Quebec. Yet in a little over 150 years the thirteen English colonies acquired a population of more than 1,500,000, while New France had only 60,000 people.

▶ CHECK-UP

1. Describe early French explorations in North America. What were the results? Why did France establish colonies in the early 1600's?

What routes were used by the French in exploring the interior of North America? What land did they claim?

2. Why did the French find fishing and the fur trade profitable? Why was farming unprofitable? Why was it that few settlers came to New France?

. . . .

Clinching the Main Ideas in Chapter 1

During the late Middle Ages, important changes occurred in Europe. By the end of the 1400's, townspeople in Europe had increased in numbers and wealth. To protect their new prosperity, they sided with the kings in checking the powers of the nobility. A growing number of peasants, free from the bondage of serfdom, owned or rented land or worked in the towns. Trade contacts with the East and the rediscovery of classical culture had awakened Europeans to new ideas and broadened their horizons.

The strong national states that developed in western Europe were ruled by ambitious monarchs. These rulers followed the mercantile theory; that is, they tried to export more goods than they imported and thus build up their treasuries. Eager to find new markets, they sponsored the spectacular voyages of discovery. Within some fifty years, Portuguese mariners found a water route around Africa to India and the Far East; Columbus, sailing westward to find Asia, accidentally discovered the New World; and Magellan's crew circumnavigated the globe.

Spain and Portugal, hoping to find gold and silver and precious stones, were the first countries to establish colonies in the New World. The French came next. The land they staked out in North America produced no precious metals or jewels, and not enough Frenchmen were attracted for thriving settlements to develop. The English, although they were the last of the Europeans to enter the scramble for New World colonies, were ultimately the most successful.

Chapter Review

Terms to Understand

1. sea power
2. Crusades
3. bourgeoisie
4. Renaissance
5. capital
6. viceroy
7. Calicut
8. 1492–1522
9. Spice Islands
10. Novus Mundus
11. Armada
12. northwest passage
13. mercantilism
14. Venice
15. Seven Cities of Cíbola
16. conquistadors

What Do You Think?

1. Why were the nations of western Europe ready to embark on great voyages of discovery in the late 1400's but not earlier?

2. Why were Portugal and Spain especially interested in finding new routes to the East?

3. Why did Spain derive so little lasting benefit from the riches of Mexico and Peru?

4. What did Raleigh mean when he said, "[He] who rules the sea, rules the commerce of the world and to him . . . belongs . . . the world itself"?

5. What were the basic ideas underlying mercantilism? How were these reflected in the colonial policies of Spain and France?

Using Your Knowledge of History

1. Give a report on why Venice became a middleman in the trade between the East and western Europe.

2. List the chief developments which paved the way for the voyages of discovery. In a parallel column, explain the significance of each.

3. Prepare a report on the civilizations of the Mayas, Aztecs, or Incas. Compare the cultural achievements of the Indians with those of Europeans at about the same period of time.

Extending Your Knowledge of History

For information on the discovery and exploration of the New World see J. B. Brebner, *The Explorers of North America, 1492–1806. Admiral of the Ocean Sea* is a fascinating biography of Columbus written by Samuel E. Morison. Exciting accounts of French explorers and explorations may be found in *The Parkman Reader.* Edited by Morison, this book contains selections from the writings of Francis Parkman. An article in the magazine *American Heritage* dealing with the Spanish explorers is "Conquest and the Cross" by Lewis Hanke (February, 1963).

CHAPTER 2

NOVA BRITANNIA.
OFFERING MOST
Excellent fruites by Planting in
VIRGINIA.

Exciting all such as be well affected
to further the same.

LONDON
Printed for SAMVEL MACHAM, and are to besold at
his Shop in Pauls Church-yard, at the
Signe of the Bul-head.
1609.

Advertisement for Virginia

English Colonies Dominate North America

1607–1763

Having undertaken, for the glory of God and advancement of the Christian faith, and the honor of our king and country, a voyage to plant the first colony in the northern parts of Virginia, [we] do by these presents, solemnly and mutually in the presence of God and one another, covenant and combine ourselves together into a civil body politic, for our better ordering and preservation, and furtherance of the ends aforesaid; and by virtue hereof do enact, constitute, and frame such just and equal laws, ordinances, acts, constitutions, and offices, from time to time, as shall be thought most meet and convenient for the general good of the colony. . . .

ADAPTED FROM THE MAYFLOWER COMPACT

The famous covenant quoted above was made by English men and women who had reached the difficult decision to forsake their homeland and try a new life in America. Thousands of their countrymen followed them during the 1600's. These people left England for a variety of reasons — religious persecution, political oppression, economic difficulties, and a thirst for adventure. By the time this exodus began to taper off in the next century, there were thirteen growing English colonies on the mainland of North America.

The patterns of living and types of government that developed in the English settlements varied. But in every one of the thirteen colonies there was more personal liberty, self-government, and religious toleration than existed in either New France or New Spain. This was an important reason for the rapid growth of the American colonies. And the greater population of the

22

thirteen colonies was an important factor in determining the outcome of the long conflict between England and France for control of North America. By 1763, scarcely a century and a half after the founding of the first permanent English settlement, England had won possession of the eastern half of the continent.

1 Conditions in England Encourage Colonization in America

England lagged behind Portugal, Spain, and France in exploring and colonizing the New World. More than a century elapsed between John Cabot's voyages to North America (page 11) and the first successful effort to establish an English colony. During the 1600's, however, the English more than made up for their late start. Their interest in colonization was closely tied to developments taking place within England itself.

England grows strong under the Tudors. Henry VII, who became king of England in 1485 (page 7), found himself ruler of a divided and poverty-stricken country. He and his successors subdued powerful nobles and built up the nation's wealth. The last of the Tudors, Queen Elizabeth I, ruled England from 1558 to 1603. The Queen and her advisers worked closely with Parliament and ruled the country well. During most of Elizabeth's long reign, her subjects were not much interested in planting colonies. "Good Queen Bess" was generally popular with her subjects, and very few Englishmen were dissatisfied with the government.

Most Englishmen belong to the Church of England. Nor did most Englishmen at this time have religious grievances serious enough to drive them to the New World. The Anglican Church, or Church of England, had been created by an act of Parliament in 1534. It was a *Protestant* church in the sense that it did not recognize the authority of the Pope. Instead, the Church of England accepted the English monarch as its "Supreme Head." In its beliefs and services, however, the Church of England was closer to the Catholic Church than to other Protestant churches. English Catholics opposed the Church of England, as did some Protestants, known as "dissenters." But the bulk of the English people were content with the Anglican Church.

England meets the Spanish threat. The great Spanish threat was another reason why Englishmen during most of Elizabeth's reign had little interest in colonization. The proud Philip II of Spain considered himself the foremost champion of Catholicism. He wanted to destroy the Church of England and drive Queen Elizabeth from her throne. In addition, Philip was angered by the raids of the Elizabethan sea dogs, which had seriously disrupted Spanish trade with the New World. But the Armada sent by Philip against England failed to even the score (page 17). Both before and after the great naval battle of 1588, English mariners found it more profitable to seize Spanish treasure ships or raid ports in New Spain than to start colonial ventures of their own.

Elizabeth encourages foreign trade. Although Queen Elizabeth showed little interest in establishing colonies during most of her reign, she did encourage the expansion of trade and commerce. The Queen chartered many joint-stock trading companies. Rich merchants, nobles, and Elizabeth herself bought shares in these

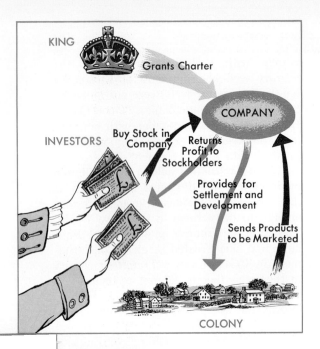

KING

Grants Charter

COMPANY

INVESTORS

Buy Stock in
Company

Returns
Profit to
Stockholders

Provides for
Settlement and
Development

Sends Products
to be Marketed

COLONY

ORGANIZATION OF A JOINT-STOCK COMPANY

The joint-stock company was a forerunner of the modern corporation. Note that stockholders supplied money for, and shared the profits of, overseas expansion.

companies. Their combined investments provided more money than any one person could supply; and all the stockholders shared the risks as well as the profits. The Muscovy Company developed a rich trade with Russia, while the Levant Company dealt with the Middle East. In 1600 the aged Queen chartered the East India Company, which became the most important of all the trading companies. Throughout the later 1500's, the English invested much of their surplus capital in such ventures.

The idea of colonies catches hold. The English geographer Richard Hakluyt (*hak*'loot) did more than any other individual to arouse his countrymen's interest in colonization. By explaining the advantages of New World colonies, he made the idea of *plantations* (meaning, in this connection, "new settlements") exciting and challenging. In *A Discourse Concerning Western Planting*, Hakluyt pointed out that English colonies on the North American mainland could prevent the "Spanish King from flowing over all the face . . . of Amer-

ica." Furthermore, English Protestants could look forward to converting the Indians to Christianity, thus leading them "from darkness to light . . . from the deep pit of hell to the highest heavens."

Hakluyt also argued that the New World could offer many Englishmen a better way of life. For several reasons, people were finding it hard to make a living in England. (1) Prices were high. Gold and silver from the New World had greatly increased the money supply in western Europe. This meant more money with which to buy a limited supply of goods — *inflation* we would call it today. The resulting higher prices made life hard for the common people. (2) Also, unemployment was widespread. As the market for wool increased, landlords fenced in large stretches of land for sheep-raising, and many farmers thus lost their livelihood.

As a result, England was "swarming," as Hakluyt said, with unemployed "able men." Many of these men landed in debtors' prison or were executed for small crimes. Hakluyt argued that it would be wiser to send the unemployed to American plantations. There they could be put to work mining gold and silver and raising crops needed by the mother country. They would also provide a market for manufactured goods from England. By the end of Elizabeth's reign many Englishmen had been won over to the idea of planting colonies in the New World. Within a short time, moreover, many of them found strong political and religious reasons for emigrating to America.

The Stuart rulers claim divine right. A new line of English rulers, the Stuarts, were responsible for the political and religious unrest. When Elizabeth, the last Tudor ruler, died in 1603, the crown of England went to James Stuart of Scotland. The arrogant James I came to London ready and all too willing to lecture his English subjects on the *divine right of kings.* According to this theory, the king was directly responsible to God and served as God's representative on earth. Therefore, it was the obligation of Parliament, the judges, and the English people to accept royal authority without question. Much to James's surprise, Parliament, the judges, and the English people did not agree with him. The King quarreled constantly with Parliament, and his son, Charles I, continued the battle.

Many Puritans are driven out of England. Just as the Stuarts wanted absolute political power in England, so too they wanted undisputed control over religious affairs. Both James I and Charles I tried to compel Catholics and Protestant dissenters to accept the doctrine and services of the Church of England. The Catholics were few in numbers and not well-organized. But the dissenters, who wanted to "purify" the Church of England of practices that seemed Catholic, caused a great deal of trouble. James met with the *Puritans,* as they were called. He listened to their proposals and decided that the troublemakers had to "conform themselves, or else I will harry them out of the land, or else do worse." His harsh laws and the severe penalties imposed on many dissenters drove them to Protestant countries in Europe or to the New World.

Charles I was even more harsh. He gave the Archbishop of Canterbury (the administrative head of the Church of England) a free hand during the 1630's to arrest Puritan preachers and sympathizers. Many of these unfortunate people were jailed, fined, whipped, or branded on the cheek with S.S., so that all good Anglicans could recognize them as "Sowers of Sedition." Such cruel treatment caused many Puritans to flee the country. Somewhere they hoped to establish a new and perfect society, a "city on a hill," as an example to England and the world. Crop failures, unemployment, and rising food prices prompted other Englishmen to accompany them.

Puritans and Parliament triumph. Meanwhile, Charles's quarrel with Parliament continued. In 1629 it reached such a point that the King dismissed Parliament and swore never to have it meet again. Eleven years later, however, Charles had become desperately short of money and had to call Parliament into session. But instead of granting the King the new taxes

that he wanted, its members insisted on discussing religious and political grievances. When the king tried to dismiss it, Parliament voted to raise an army and fight.

Two opposing groups began to muster forces for battle. One was composed of Englishmen who were loyal to the King, the divine-right theory of monarchy, and the Church of England. The other included those who believed that Parliament should be supreme over the King and who wanted to make Puritan changes in the Church of England. Civil war raged in England until the Puritans and Parliament gained the upper hand. In 1649, Charles I was executed. During the 1650's Parliament and the Puritans controlled England, and people who had supported the King were subjected to heavy taxes and punished in other ways. As a result, many of them fled to the New World.

Restoration of the Stuarts leads to the Glorious Revolution. After the death of Oliver Cromwell, the Puritan leader, neither the army nor Parliament could produce a strong leader. Thus, the way was open for the restoration of the Stuart kings in 1660.

Charles II (son of Charles I) got along fairly well with Parliament, though his religious policies annoyed both Protestant dissenters and Catholics. He was followed

---

TIMETABLE

SUCCESSION TO THE ENGLISH CROWN
(1485–1820)

House of Tudor	House of Stuart
1485 Henry VII	1660 Charles II
1509 Henry VIII	1685 James II
1547 Edward VI	1688 "Glorious Revolution"
1553 Mary	
1558 Elizabeth I	1689 William and Mary (1694)
	1702 Anne
House of Stuart	
1603 James I	**House of Hanover**
1625 Charles I	1714 George I
	1727 George II
Commonwealth	1760 George III
1649 **and Protectorate**	1820 George IV

by his brother, James II. James ignored Parliament, tampered with court decisions, levied heavy taxes, and showed open favoritism to fellow Catholics. In 1688, the Anglicans and dissenters in Parliament joined forces to drive James II out of England. This uprising was called the *Glorious Revolution.* At Parliament's invitation, William of Orange, the Protestant ruler of Holland, and his wife Mary (daughter of James II but also a Protestant) became king and queen of England.

Parliament was now able to turn its attention to settling problems that had bedeviled England for years. All factions agreed that Parliament was supreme. A Bill of Rights adopted in 1689 confirmed Parliament's right to levy taxes and promised regular sessions of Parliament. It also guaranteed the right of subjects to petition the king, to be tried by jury, and to be free from cruel and unusual punishment. Furthermore, in that same year, a Toleration Act granted freedom of religion to virtually all Protestant dissenters. Though Catholics were not included in this statute, they met with little interference after 1689.

English migration slows down. Thus, the main political and religious grievances that had driven Englishmen to the New World throughout the 1600's were removed. Englishmen had rejected the divine-right theory. They had secured a broad degree of religious toleration, though the Anglican Church remained the official church. Furthermore, economic conditions improved as unemployment declined, industry expanded, and foreign trade flourished. For all these reasons English emigration to the New World began to taper off in the early eighteenth century. By that time, however, England had a foothold on the North American continent that would have pleased Richard Hakluyt.

▶ CHECK-UP

1. In what ways did England gain strength under the Tudors? What were the causes of friction between Parliament and the Stuart kings?

2. Who were the Puritans? What were the results of the English civil war?

3. How did the various factors considered in the previous questions contribute to colonization in America? What economic reasons help to explain why English people migrated to America? Why did English migration begin to slow down by the end of the 1600's?

- -

2 *Virginia Is the First Successful English Colony*

The first English attempts to colonize the New World were sponsored during the 1580's by two adventurers — Sir Humphrey Gilbert and his half brother, Sir Walter Raleigh. But these early efforts at colonization were costly failures. Later English expeditions to the New World were financed by trading companies rather than by individuals.

James I charters two trading companies. Early in the reign of James I, the King was approached by a group of Raleigh's friends who wanted permission to start a settlement in America. At first the King was hesitant, but in 1606 he granted a charter authorizing them to settle the stretch of coast between present-day North Carolina and New England (map, page 28). The men who received this charter were divided into two trading companies. The London Company was to plant the "First Colony," and the Plymouth Company of Plymouth, England, was to start the "Second Colony." The directors of both trading companies hoped that the settlers in Virginia (a name given to the general region) would (1) establish trade relations with the Indians; (2) develop gold, silver, copper, and iron mines; and (3) perhaps even discover a northwest passage to Asia.

One provision of the charter proved to be of vital importance. It promised to the English colonists in Virginia certain rights

This sketch of a typical Indian village was drawn by John White, governor of an English settlement founded on Roanoke Island off the Carolina coast in the late 1500's. White embarked for England in August, 1587, for more supplies. When he returned to Roanoke Island three years later, the colony had vanished. The only clue to its fate was the word Croatoan *carved on a tree.*

and privileges which Spain and France had denied their New World colonists. The charter guaranteed to the settlers the right to "have and enjoy all Liberties, Franchises, and Immunities . . . as if they had been abiding and born within this our Realm of England or any other of our . . . Dominions." In other words, Englishmen were to take with them to the New World representative government, trial by jury, and the right to own personal property. At the time the charter was issued, this guarantee received little attention. But when the colonies quarreled with the mother country in the late 1700's, the Americans constantly referred to it.

Englishmen settle at Jamestown. Late in 1606 the London Company sent out 120 men in three small ships as their "first planters." The expedition reached Chesapeake Bay in April, 1607, and a month later selected a peninsula on the James River as the site of the settlement (map, page 35). It was an unfortunate choice, for Jamestown was located on low, swampy land, covered with trees, surrounded by Indians, and infested with malaria-carrying mosquitoes. Nonetheless, the colonists set to work building a fort, a storehouse, a church and frame houses.[1] A few crops were

[1] They did not build log cabins, which were unknown in America until Swedish settlers built them in Delaware in the late 1630's.

planted that first summer, but the settlers spent most of their time feverishly searching for gold and exploring the James River in hopes of finding a route to China. Many were killed by Indians; others perished of malaria or diseases contracted by drinking the brackish James River water. Within six months the population of Jamestown was cut in half.

John Smith takes control. Finally, Captain John Smith imposed an iron rule on Jamestown that probably saved it from disaster. He forced the colonists to build a blockhouse for protection against Indian attacks. He ordered the gold-seekers to clear the surrounding fields and plant corn. And from the Indians he obtained enough corn to see the starving colonists through the winter of 1608–1609. Meanwhile, the directors of the London Company wondered why Jamestown was not returning a profit. Worried by mounting financial losses, they called Smith back to London for consultation.

Smith had no sooner departed in the fall of 1609 than the colonists were plagued by crop failures, Indian attacks, disease, and their own quarrels. During this grim "starving time" they resorted to eating horses and dogs. When a British ship arrived in May, 1610, its commander decided the situation was hopeless. With the Jamestown survivors aboard ship, he set sail for England. But just as the ship reached the mouth of the James River, it was met by three vessels carrying 150 men and a huge store of supplies. This chance encounter saved the Jamestown colony.

Jamestown makes progress. Thereafter Jamestown slowly began to prosper. At first all the settlers had been forced to work for the London Company. Everything they produced went into the common storehouse, from which they could take only what they needed. Since those who worked hard were not rewarded for their efforts, the common-store system discouraged industry and ambition. But new charters in 1609 and 1612 gave the colonists title to more land and altered the system of landholding. Furthermore, the revised charters placed more power in the hands of a governor and an advisory council that was appointed by, and responsible to, the London Company.

The most important factor in Jamestown's rising fortunes, however, was the discovery of a profitable cash crop — tobacco. The native Virginia brand was "poor and weak, and of a biting taste." But

ENGLISH LAND GRANTS

Out of these original royal grants grew the thirteen English colonies. Study the map on page 120 for the later significance of the London Company's revised grant of 1609.

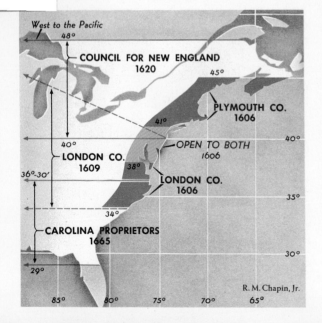

R. M. Chapin, Jr.

John Rolfe, husband of the Indian princess Pocahontas, learned how to grow and cure a milder strain. Immediately a market developed in England for Virginia tobacco. King James I tried to break the English of their "loathesome" habit of "drinking smoke." He even wrote a pamphlet in which he described tobacco smoking as "hateful to the nose, harmful to the brain, dangerous to the lungs." But he could not curb Englishmen's liking for Virginia tobacco. By 1617, Jamestown's yearly export of tobacco was worth about 20,000 pounds in English currency.

Slavery is introduced. The year 1619 saw two important developments in Jamestown. In August, a Dutch ship brought 20 Negroes to Jamestown; thus, the first Negroes came to Virginia. Until the mid-1600's comparatively few Negroes were imported, and most of these were servants rather than slaves. In 1661, however, the Virginia legislature recognized slavery as legal. Soon afterwards, the Negroes became an important source of labor in the colony, and the number sold by Dutch slave-traders sharply increased. One hundred years after the founding of Jamestown, Virginia had some 12,000 Negro slaves.

Representative government begins. Also in 1619 the London Company made important changes in the government of Jamestown. A "general assembly" was to be held yearly; and the governor, his council, and two representatives from each of the settlements around Jamestown were to attend. This assembly was empowered "to make and ordain whatsoever laws and orders" it thought "good and profitable." The governor and his councilors were appointed by the London Company, but the town representatives, or *burgesses*, were elected by the colonists. This assembly, known as the House of Burgesses, held its first session in July, 1619, in the little church at Jamestown. From this simple beginning grew the practice of representative government in the American colonies.

Virginia becomes a royal colony. Despite the introduction of tobacco farming, the Jamestown colony failed to produce the rich profits which the London Company expected. As a result, the Company directors fell to quarreling among themselves. In 1624, James I canceled the charter of Virginia and made the settlement a royal colony. The power to appoint the governor and councilors passed to the King. But James permitted the House of Burgesses to continue framing laws, although the governor could veto legislation that he considered unwise. Virginia's government became a model for later royal colonies.

Virginia continues to grow. Throughout the 1600's, the arrival of Negroes and white indentured servants swelled Virginia's population. Indentured servants were men and women too poor to pay their own way to the New World. They sold themselves into service to a ship captain or agent in return for their passage. Upon arrival in the colonies, they agreed to work for a certain period of years for a landowner or an artisan. At the end of this time they became free.

Another group of newcomers to Virginia were the supporters of Charles I who fled England after the triumph of Puritans and Parliament (page 25). Many of them became large landowners as they had been in England. Their tobacco plantations along the banks of the James, York, and Potomac Rivers were generally worked by indentured servants and slaves. By 1660 Virginia had a population of 30,000.

Settlers move inland. As the coastal area became occupied, later settlers had to take land above the *fall line* (map, page 55). This line marked the point on the rivers where waterfalls made navigation difficult. It was also a rough dividing line between the low-lying coastal area, known as the *tidewater,* and the upland plateau region, known as the *piedmont.* Above the fall line there were few plantations. Most of the Virginia piedmont was settled by small farmers who were Protestant dissenters. Each worked his own land, with the aid of a few indentured servants, and raised a variety of crops. By contrast, most of the tidewater region was divided among plantation owners who used slave labor to grow tobacco. Unlike the piedmont settlers, most of the tidewater planters belonged to the Anglican Church.

Virginia frontiersmen rebel. People of the piedmont and the tidewater regions disagreed on many points. The pioneers on the frontier wanted the colonial government to help them build roads and bridges, and they also wanted protection against Indian attacks. The piedmont settlers were also dissatisfied because their communities had not been granted the same number of representatives as the older settlements in the tidewater region. They thought they should have more adequate representation in the House of Burgesses. But the royal governor usually sympathized with the tidewater planters, who controlled the House of Burgesses, and little was done for the piedmont farmers. In 1676 this conflict came to a head when a frontier farmer named Nathaniel Bacon led a rebellion against the governor.

Bacon's men captured Jamestown, but when their leader died, the revolt collapsed. Governor Berkeley arrested many of the rebels and executed 23 of them. When Charles II heard of this harsh punishment, he exclaimed: "That old fool has killed more men in that naked country than I have done for the murder of my father." He replaced Berkeley with a more moderate governor, and Virginia's frontier settlers did get better protection against Indian raids. But the planters continued to control the colonial assembly.

▶ CHECK-UP

1. What trading companies were chartered by James I? How did the directors of these companies hope to profit from colonizing ventures? What promises were made to the colonists?

2. What problems plagued the Jamestown colonists? How were they met? What part did indentured servants and, later, slaves play in this settlement? How did representative government develop?

3. What were the differences between the tidewater and the piedmont? How did these differences lead to conflict?

• • • • • • • • • • • • • • • • • •

3 The New England Colonies Are Founded

Early ventures are not successful. While the Jamestown settlers were struggling for a toehold in the New World, the Plymouth Company attempted to establish a colony farther north. Settlers spent the winter of 1607–1608 near the mouth of the Kennebec River in what is now Maine. But they soon returned to England, and the Plymouth Company refused to finance another venture. Reorganized as the Council for New England in 1620, the company was granted the right to colonize and govern the territory between the fortieth and forty-eighth parallels (map, page 28). Struggling colonies were established by Sir Ferdinando Gorges in Maine and by John Mason in present-day New Hampshire. Far more successful were the settlements founded at Plymouth and Massachusetts Bay.

English Separatists decide to emigrate. The Plymouth colony was founded by English *Separatists*. These dissenters had no interest in purifying the Church of England; they wanted to break away from it entirely. A small band of Separatists had angered James I by actually withdrawing from the Church of England. Some were thrown into prison while "others had their houses beset and watched night and day," wrote William Bradford, a future governor of Plymouth colony. Most of these Separatists escaped to Holland, where they enjoyed religious freedom. But they found it hard to adjust to the language and customs of that country, and they were afraid that their children would grow up more Dutch than English. The older members of the congregation began to think seriously about emigrating to the New World.

The main obstacle was the cost, for these humble craftsmen and farmers could not afford to send the entire group to America. London businessmen advised them to form a joint-stock company. The Separatists bought as many shares in the company as they could, but most of the stock was purchased by investors who were also involved in the London Company. These stockholders agreed to (1) finance the voyage, (2) allow the Separatists to settle on land belonging to the London Company, and (3) guarantee them religious toleration in the Anglican colony of Virginia. In return, all profits from the settlement during the first seven years were to be divided among the shareholders. Thereafter property would be distributed among the individual settlers. In the end, 35 of the Separatists decided to take advantage of this offer and go to the New World.

Plymouth is founded. These Pilgrims or "saints" (as Bradford called them) were joined at Plymouth, England, by some 60 "strangers," that is, people who were not Separatists. In September, 1620, they all set sail in the *Mayflower;* and two months later they dropped anchor in what is now Provincetown harbor at the tip of Cape Cod. This land, the Pilgrims realized, was outside the boundaries granted to the London Company. But since so many of the passengers were ill, they decided to stay there for the winter and try to get a land grant from the Council for New England. When their scouts found a better location across Cape Cod Bay, the Pilgrims moved and in December they began building fortifications, a church, and homes at Plymouth (map, page 31). Half the *Mayflower* passengers died that first winter, but the Pilgrims remained hopeful.

From the Indians they learned how to plant Indian corn, how to make moccasins, and how to stalk wild turkeys. In the fall of 1621 an English ship brought supplies and new settlers; and, more important still, the Pilgrims gathered an abundant harvest. To celebrate their good fortune, they held a three-day feast of thanksgiving to which they invited the neighboring Indians.

The Pilgrims draw up the Mayflower Compact. Before the landing, the *Mayflower* passengers had elected John Carver, one of the Separatists from Holland, as their governor. They had agreed that laws

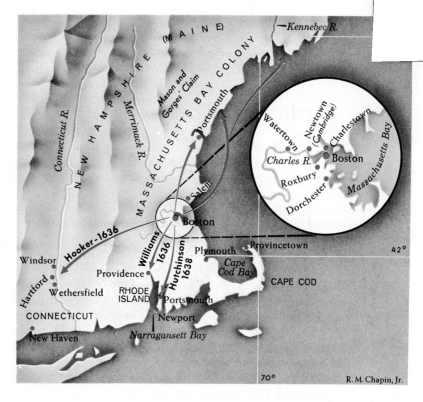

**EARLY SETTLEMENTS
IN NEW ENGLAND**

Boston was the center from which coastal New England was settled. For what reasons did groups leave Massachusetts and establish new towns?

approved by the majority of the settlers would be binding on saints and strangers alike. In this agreement, known as the *Mayflower Compact* (quoted on page 22), they promised to "covenant and combine ourselves together into a civil body politic, for our better ordering and preservation" and to frame "just and equal laws . . . for the general good of the colony." This famous document did not provide a detailed frame of government, but it set forth the idea that political authority must rest upon the will of the people.

Plymouth's growth is slow. Handicapped by lack of fertile soil, Plymouth grew slowly. The debts owed to the London merchants proved to be a disadvantage. Furthermore, the Pilgrims' strict religious views did not attract new settlers. Despite repeated requests, Plymouth never was able to secure a charter from the king. Finally in 1691 the settlement was joined to the Puritan colony founded nearby on Massachusetts Bay.

Puritans found the Massachusetts Bay Colony. Although James I's wrath had fallen on the Separatists, it was the larger body of Puritan dissenters who were persecuted during Charles I's reign. Some of these dissenters thought of seeking refuge in America. In 1628 a group of wealthy Puritans was given permission to settle within the territory belonging to the Council for New England. Under the name of the Massachusetts Bay Company, these Puritans secured a charter from the king. The charter resembled those given to other trading companies in that the colony would be administered by a governor and an elected assembly. But, unlike other charters, this one did not mention the location of the company's official headquarters. The members of the Massachusetts Bay Company took advantage of this loophole to emigrate to the colony themselves and take the charter with them. With full control in the hands of the settlers, Massachusetts was the first of the thirteen colonies to be founded as a self-governing colony.

In 1630 seventeen ships carried about a thousand Puritans to the shores of Massachusetts. Many others followed, and during the next decade they established a flourishing settlement of 20,000 people. Boston became the leading town in New England; but Charlestown, Roxbury, Dorchester, Newtown (later Cambridge), Watertown, and Salem also grew rapidly (map, page 31). Massachusetts Bay Colony included merchants, doctors, lawyers, teachers, and ministers, many of whom were college graduates. A recent historian has said of the colony: "Better organized than the expeditions that had led to the settlement of Jamestown and Plymouth, more richly endowed and more efficiently led, the Puritan experiment wore from the very outset an air of success."

Puritan town government is more democratic than colonial government. The government of the Massachusetts Bay Colony was not democratic. At first, Governor John Winthrop permitted only a very few of the settlers to vote. In 1634 he established an assembly of representatives from each town which met four times a year in Boston, but this General Court was closely controlled by the governor and his council. Only Puritan church members could vote for representatives and for the governor.

In spite of the undemocratic government of the colony as a whole, a democratic form of town government developed. Once a year all the citizens in each town gathered at the meeting house on the village green. There they discussed and voted on such local matters as defense, school policy, and selection of town officials. In these Puritan town meetings, authority rested with the assembled group.

Puritan ministers wield great influence. During its early years Massachusetts was greatly influenced by Puritan ministers. They set standards of behavior for all who came to the colony, whether they were Puritans or not. Since they wanted everyone to be able to read and interpret the Bible, the clergymen insisted on government support of education. The General Court ordered the towns to hire teachers and provide elementary schools. Moreover, it established Harvard College to prepare young men for the ministry. Disagreement with the Puritan leaders on religious matters was not tolerated, and many dissenters were banished from the colony. Some, like the Quakers (page 38), were whipped and mutilated and then threatened with death if they should return. Roger Williams and Thomas Hooker, founders of Rhode Island

and Connecticut, were religious refugees from the stern Puritan stronghold of Massachusetts.

Exiles from Massachusetts settle in Rhode Island. America's first great pioneer of religious liberty was Roger Williams. An English minister, he arrived in Boston in 1631. Williams opposed the election of government officials by church members only. He also believed that no official of church or state had the right to interfere with an individual's religious beliefs. "Persecution for cause of conscience is most evidently and lamentably contrary to the doctrine of Christ Jesus," said Williams. The Puritan ministers could not ignore this challenge to their authority, so in 1635 they got the General Court to expel Williams from Massachusetts. He spent the winter with friendly Indians and purchased from them a tract of land at the head of Narragansett Bay. There, in the spring of 1636, he and a few followers founded Providence Plantations in what is now Rhode Island.

Another exile from Massachusetts who fled to Rhode Island was Anne Hutchinson. Possessed of a "nimble wit . . . and a very voluble tongue," according to Governor Winthrop, Mrs. Hutchinson dared to challenge the authority of the Puritan clergy. Charged with being "deluded by the Devil," she was banished from the colony in 1638. With her husband and thirteen children and some of her supporters, she fled to Rhode Island and established a settlement at Portsmouth. Other religious rebels and outcasts from Massachusetts found a warm welcome in Rhode Island. The colony grew in spite of the scorn of strict Puritans, who referred to it as "Rogue's Island."

Rhode Island gets a charter. In 1644 Williams secured from Parliament a charter which united the settlements around Narragansett Bay. Some twenty years later Charles II granted Rhode Island a second charter, which clearly stated the principle of religious toleration. No person in the colony "shall be [in any way] molested, punished, disquieted, or called in question, for any differences of opinion in matters of religion." Protected by this guarantee, Quakers felt safe in Rhode Island and so too did non-Christians. One of the first Jewish communities in America was established at Newport. Rhode Island's second charter remained in effect (first as a charter and then as a state constitution) until 1842 — eloquent proof of Williams' forward-looking ideas.[2]

Pioneers settle the Connecticut valley. Thomas Hooker, a Puritan minister at Newtown (Cambridge), and the members of his congregation decided to seek a freer system of government and more fertile land. In the summer of 1636 they sold their homes and set out on foot for the Connecticut River valley. They settled at Hartford; and, before long, other settlers founded Wethersfield and Windsor nearby. Soon the three communities formed the self-governing colony of Connecticut. Though closely modeled after the Bay Colony, Connecticut's government did not require church membership in order to vote. In 1639, delegates from the three towns adopted a new plan of government called the *Fundamental Orders of Connecticut.*

New Hampshire and Maine attract settlers. Meanwhile, colonists were moving into the region north of Massachusetts. The settlements started in Maine and New Hampshire by Gorges and Mason (page 30) were little more than trading posts for several years. In time, pioneers from Massachusetts pushed northward into these areas, just as Hooker and his followers had moved into the Connecticut valley. The newcomers refused to recognize the authority of Gorges and Mason, and the Massachusetts General Court backed them up. In the 1640's, taking advantage of the Civil War in England (page 25), Massachusetts claimed control of both settlements. After years of bickering, New Hampshire broke away and secured its own royal charter from Charles II in 1679. But Maine remained part of Massachusetts until 1820.

The Indian threat leads to the New England Confederation. Most of the Eng-

lish colonists, unlike settlers in New France, looked on the Indians with scorn. Throughout the seventeenth century there was more or less constant warfare between English settlers and Indians over possession of the land. This prompted the New England colonists to consider measures for common defense. In 1643, representatives of Massachusetts Bay, Plymouth, and the Connecticut towns (Rhode Island was excluded) formed the *New England Confederation,* a "firm and perpetual league of friendship . . . for offense and defense." The Confederation put down a serious Indian uprising in 1675–1676, but this first attempt at colonial union was abandoned a few years later.

The Dominion of New England is short-lived. The next plan to unite the New England colonies was imposed by the British government in the 1680's. The New England colonies, New York, and the Jerseys (page 38) were united by royal order in the *Dominion of New England.* Their colonial assemblies were abolished. All power was now to rest with the royal governor, Sir Edmund Andros, who was re-

---

[2] Roger Williams, one of the few English colonists who treated the Indians like equals, was tolerant of their worship of the "Great Spirit."

The First Jews in America

The first man to set foot on American soil in 1492 may have been a Jew. His name was Luis de Torres, one of Columbus's sailors, who is mentioned in some accounts as the first man off the ship. In following decades, many Jews who were being persecuted in Europe came to the West Indies and South America.

The first Jews to settle in the original thirteen colonies arrived in New Amsterdam in 1654. These people were descendants of Spanish, Portuguese, and Dutch Jews who had been persecuted by the Spanish and exiled to Brazil. There the Jews made common cause with the Dutch, who in a series of wars with Spain and Portugal had gained a foothold in Brazil. When the Portuguese expelled the Dutch from Brazil, these Jews asked the Dutch for asylum in other parts of their empire. One haven was New Amsterdam.

In 1658 Jews from the Netherlands settled at Newport, Rhode Island. The Touro Synagogue, built at Newport in 1763, is the oldest synagogue in this country.

sponsible only to the king. Andros was a stiff-necked aristocrat with little sympathy for the Puritan colonists and no understanding at all of their pride in their colonial assemblies. His harsh rule and heavy taxes were deeply resented. The Bostonians were outraged when Governor Andros ordered them to open their Puritan meeting houses for the holding of Church of England services.

When news of the Glorious Revolution in England (page 26) reached the colonies, Andros was quickly overthrown and imprisoned. Connecticut and Rhode Island got back their former charters; but Massachusetts received a new charter in 1691, making it a royal colony. Massachusetts retained its General Court. The governor, however, was now to be appointed by the king. All adult males who owned a certain amount of property had the right to vote for members of the General Court; and religious toleration was assured to all Protestants. These provisions in the new charter slowly undermined the power of the Puritan clergy. Although Massachusetts had lost some of its political independence, it remained the largest, most prosperous, and most powerful of the New England colonies.

▶ CHECK-UP

1. What led the Pilgrims to embark for America? What is the significance of the Mayflower Compact? Why did the Puritans found Massachusetts Bay Colony? Why was it more prosperous than Plymouth?

2. In what sense was town government in Massachusetts more democratic than the government of the colony as a whole? How did Puritan clergy influence life in the colony?

3. Why did people from Massachusetts settle in Rhode Island and Connecticut? Why were the Rhode Island charters important? How did the Fundamental Orders of Connecticut differ from the Massachusetts plan of government?

4. What led to the establishment of the New England Confederation? Of the Dominion of New England? What happened to the Dominion?

. . . .

4 *Proprietors Establish Several Colonies*

Trading companies such as the London Company and the Plymouth Company gave the earliest colonies their start. Other colonies, however, were launched by *proprietors*. The English proprietors were usually favorites of the king or men to whom he was in debt. In either case the king granted a charter naming the person as proprietor or ruler of a particular tract of land in the New World.

Maryland becomes the first proprietary colony. Maryland, the first successful proprietary colony, was granted to Sir George Calvert, the first Lord Baltimore. A devout Catholic, he asked Charles I for a grant of land in America where he could establish a refuge for Englishmen of his faith. In 1632 the King named Lord Baltimore as the proprietor of territory extending from the south bank of the Potomac River north to the fortieth parallel (map, page 35). Baltimore died that same year but his son inherited the charter. He decided to name the colony "Mary's Land" after the King's Catholic wife, Queen Henrietta Maria.

In the spring of 1634, about 200 settlers, including many Catholics, landed at St. Mary's, near the mouth of the Potomac. They were followed by Protestants who settled near Annapolis farther north on Chesapeake Bay. From the Virginians, the Maryland settlers soon learned about tobacco, and in time the small farms gave way to large plantations devoted chiefly to the growing of this crop.

Maryland wins political and religious freedom. Maryland's charter had stated that all laws for the colony were to be made with the "advice, assent, and approbation of the freemen of the same province." The proprietor permitted the settlers to elect a representative assembly, but he refused to let the assembly do more

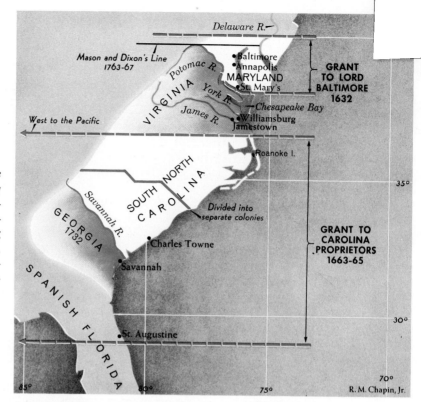

PROPRIETARY COLONIES
IN THE SOUTH

Although inland areas were barely explored and sparsely settled, the southern colonies had several prosperous coastal cities. Using the information on the map, roughly calculate the longitude and latitude of Savannah, Georgia.

than accept or reject laws which he proposed. Naturally, the colonists resented the fact that only the proprietor had the right to frame laws. Fearing an open revolt, Lord Baltimore finally gave way and permitted the Maryland assembly to propose as well as approve legislation.

The most important law was the Toleration Act passed in 1649. By that time, Protestant settlers in Maryland outnumbered Catholics, and the assembly passed this measure to guarantee freedom of worship to the Catholic minority. It granted religious freedom to those who professed belief in Jesus Christ. Thus, the Toleration Act protected Catholics, Anglicans, and most of the Protestant dissenters; but it was not as broad a guarantee of religious freedom as Roger Williams had secured in Rhode Island.

North and South Carolina are settled. Shortly after Charles II became king, a group of eight men approached him with a request to found a colony in the area between Virginia and Spanish Florida. They expected it to serve as a buffer state, protecting Virginia from Indian and Spanish attacks. They also hoped it would en-

rich the mother country by raising semitropical products. In 1663 Charles II granted the eight proprietors title to the land they wanted. Several years later, English settlers came to this region, called Carolina, and founded Charles Towne (later Charleston). Soon other Englishmen staked out plantations in the southern part of Carolina, while Virginia colonists claimed small farms in the northern part.

From the beginning, there were clear differences between the northern and southern portions of Carolina. The southern plantations grew rice and indigo and were worked by Negro slaves. The landowners lived like noblemen. Their social life centered around the gay port of Charles Towne. The northern part of Carolina was settled by Virginia frontiersmen, Quakers, and German farmers. They raised some tobacco but mostly corn and livestock, and they generally worked the land themselves. From its earliest days, political quarrels rocked the Carolina colony. Finally, the disgusted proprietors sold their rights to the king, and in 1729 North and South Carolina became separate royal colonies.

EUROPEAN INFLUENCE IN AMERICA

People from many lands have made America. The pictures below show just a few ways in which some of the earliest settlers in this country influenced American life.

The little Dutch settlement of New Amsterdam became New York City, shown here in the early 1700's. Though the English took over the town, its Dutch origin could still be seen in the narrow Dutch houses of stone and brick, with their sloping roofs.

Among the contributions of German settlers in Pennsylvania (called "Pennsylvania Dutch") were German cooking, the Conestoga wagon, and colorful designs like those on the candle box below.

Swedes settling in Delaware introduced the log cabin to America. Scotch-Irish pioneers borrowed the idea and built log cabins in their settlements along the frontier.

Lacy iron grillwork frames the balconies of many old buildings in New Orleans, the "Paris of America." Creole cooking, the famous Mardi Gras carnival, and the French names of many Louisiana families are other reminders of New Orleans' European background.

THE MIDDLE COLONIES

As in New England and the South, the original royal grants of land were subdivided and re-assigned many times. Parts of the Duke of York's grant were eventually administered by Penn and the New Jersey proprietors. Note that the earlier Swedish and Dutch settlements were appropriated by the English.

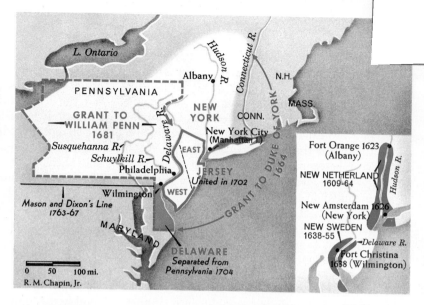

L. Ontario

PENNSYLVANIA

GRANT TO WILLIAM PENN 1681

Susquehanna R.
Schuylkill R.
Philadelphia

Wilmington

Mason and Dixon's Line 1763-67

MARYLAND

0   50   100 mi.

R. M. Chapin, Jr.

Hudson R.

Connecticut R.

Albany   N.H.

MASS.

NEW YORK   CONN.

New York City (Manhattan I.)

Delaware R.

EAST

JERSEY
United in 1702

WEST

GRANT TO DUKE OF YORK 1664

DELAWARE
Separated from Pennsylvania 1704

Fort Orange 1623 (Albany)

NEW NETHERLAND 1609-64

New Amsterdam 1626 (New York)

NEW SWEDEN 1638-55

Delaware R.

Fort Christina 1638 (Wilmington)

Hudson R.

The Dutch establish New Netherland. Although New York became an English proprietary colony in 1664, it began as a Dutch trading post. As early as 1609, the Dutch East India Company had hired an Englishman, Henry Hudson, to search the coast of North America for a westward passage. Hudson sailed his *Half Moon* up the Hudson River as far as present-day Albany. He told his employers about the fertile lands and friendly Indians in the valley, but he knew that the river was not a route to Asia. In 1621 the Dutch West India Company was chartered to colonize this region and develop trade. The Company's agents established a fur-trading post at Fort Orange (Albany), and staked out the settlement of New Amsterdam on Manhattan Island. The shrewd Dutch merchants completed a famous real estate deal by purchasing all of Manhattan Island from the Iroquois Indians for 24 dollars' worth of goods.

The population of New Netherland grew slowly. In part this was due to the strict regulations of the Dutch West India Company, which was far more interested in promoting the fur trade than in encouraging settlement. But the lagging rate of growth also resulted from the system of landholding. Under this system the Company gave a large tract of land to a *patroon,* who agreed to pay the costs of transporting 50 people to the colony to work his land. The patroon was in effect the lord of a large manor, and the people he brought to New Netherland had about the same rights as medieval serfs. Naturally this system attracted few settlers. It did, however, create a group of powerful families, such as the Van Rensselaers and the Schuylers, whose fortunes rested upon their extensive landholdings in the Hudson Valley.

New Netherland becomes New York. The Dutch settlements which grew up along the Hudson and in New Jersey and Delaware were in a hazardous position. They were tucked in between the more thickly settled New England colonies to the north and Virginia and Maryland to the south. The English looked upon the Dutch as intruders. They envied the Dutch their monopoly of the inland fur trade and their control of the splendid harbor of New Amsterdam. The Dutch realized this, but they were in no position to protect themselves. Their population was small, and their obstinate governor, Peter Stuyvesant, scared off possible settlers at the same time that he angered the burghers of New Amsterdam.

In 1664, Charles II of England declared that all the territory between the Connecticut and Delaware Rivers belonged to his brother James, the Duke of York. When an English fleet sailed into New Amsterdam and demanded that Governor Stuyvesant surrender, not one of the 8000 people in the town saw fit to support the unpopular governor. Although he swore and stomped his wooden leg, he could not prevent the Duke of York from taking control of New Netherland. Renamed New York, the colony became part of the Dominion of New England in the 1680's (page 33). But when that experiment collapsed, New York became a royal colony.

New Jersey and Delaware are founded. Included in the Duke of York's grant was the region of New Jersey, which had been settled by Dutch and Swedish pioneers. The new proprietor portioned out the land between the Hudson and Delaware Rivers to two of his friends. The province was soon divided into East Jersey and West Jersey. But early in the eighteenth century the rights to both Jerseys were surrendered to the king. New Jersey was then administered by the governor of New York until it became a separate royal colony in 1738.

Meanwhile, William Penn, proprietor of the neighboring colony of Pennsylvania, persuaded the Duke of York to give him control of the southern portion of the Delaware River. Though Swedish and Dutch settlers were already living there, Penn took possession and made the region part of Pennsylvania. The separate colony of Delaware was organized in 1704 but was controlled by the Penn family until the American colonies won independence.

Pennsylvania is founded as a refuge for Quakers. Pennsylvania, founded by William Penn, was the most successful of the proprietary colonies. Penn had infuriated his father, a wealthy admiral, by joining the Society of Friends. These people, also known as Quakers, believed that all men possessed an "inner light" which enabled them to hear God's commands without the aid of any clergymen. For their extreme views the Quakers were persecuted in England and in most of the American colonies. Penn himself spent time in prison for writing religious pamphlets.

When his father died, Penn inherited a claim of 16,000 pounds against Charles II. He persuaded the King to pay the debt by granting him land in the New World where he could establish a haven for Quakers. In 1681 Charles II gave Penn title to the land between Maryland and New York. The proprietor wanted to name the heavily forested region *Sylvania* (meaning "woods"), but the King added the prefix *Penn*. Unfortunately Charles II neglected to draw the boundaries clearly, and for many years Pennsylvania quarreled with New York and Maryland over conflicting land claims. The Pennsylvania-Maryland line was not settled until the surveyors Mason and Dixon drew the boundary in the 1760's.

Penn's charter showed that the day of great powers for the proprietor had passed. The English government wanted to tighten its control over the colonies, so it required that laws passed by the Pennsylvania assembly be approved by the king's council. Moreover, appeals from colonial courts were to go directly to the king. Yet, even within these restrictions, Penn devised a plan that gave his colony one of the most liberal forms of government anywhere in the New World. He guaranteed complete religious toleration for any person who worshiped the "one almighty and eternal God." He gave the vote to all men who either owned a small amount of land or paid taxes. And the legislature was to be elected by the colonists.

Pennsylvania grows and prospers. Penn and the first group of settlers arrived in the ship *Welcome* in 1682. After carefully studying the area, Penn picked out the site for Philadelphia on the Delaware River and had the first city plan drawn up. His relations with the Indians were excellent. Moreover, he made certain that settlers in Pennsylvania could either buy land cheaply or rent it for as little as a penny an acre. These advantages, as well as political liberty and religious toleration, attracted many immigrants to Pennsylvania. Penn stimulated interest in his "Holy Experiment" by circulating publicity about it in England, Ireland, and Wales, as well as in the Netherlands and Germany. Hundreds of oppressed people responded, many of them coming as indentured servants. By 1689 Pennsylvania had a population of 12,000; and Philadelphia, "the city of brotherly love," was on its way to becoming the largest colonial city.

Georgia is the last English colony. Pennsylvania was 50 years old before Georgia, the last of the English colonies, was planted on the American continent. Georgia was born as a charitable venture and as a bulwark against Spanish settlements to the south. Shocked by brutal conditions in British prisons, a wealthy Englishman named James Oglethorpe wanted to establish a refuge for poor but honest men who had been jailed for small debts. In 1732 Oglethorpe and a group of reformers secured title to the land between South Carolina and Spanish Florida. They decided to ban slavery in their colony, to prohibit the importation of rum and brandy, and to limit individual landholdings to 50 acres. The proprietors hoped that the settlers would produce silk and wine, thereby supplying goods which the mother country needed. It was also hoped that forts along Georgia's southern border would offer protection against Spanish and Indian raids.

The town of Savannah, at the mouth of the Savannah River, was established in 1733. English debtors were soon outnumbered by Welsh, Scotch, and German peasants seeking fertile land. Since none of these people showed any interest in silk or wine, the proprietors gave up that idea. Next they had to compromise on slavery and the sale of rum. Then the land policy was adjusted to permit large plantations in the Georgia lowlands. After two decades of feuding with the colonists, the well-intentioned proprietors surrendered their charter to the Crown. Georgia became a royal colony with a governor and council appointed by the king and an assembly chosen by the people.

English colonies in the far north and the Caribbean seem more important. The thirteen colonies on the mainland were the center of an arc of English territory in the New World. But, until the mid-1700's, the king and Parliament considered them far less important than the northern and southern outposts of this arc. In the north, the Hudson's Bay Company exploited the northern fur trade around the great inland body of water that had been discovered by Henry Hudson. The presence of Englishmen around Hudson Bay was menacing to New France, but the French colony did not have enough men to drive the English out.

England's Caribbean colonies constituted her southern outpost in the New World. Jamaica had been acquired in 1655, and there were prosperous English settlements on Barbados, Trinidad, St. Kitts, and other smaller islands, as well as on Bermuda farther north. From the English point of view, the Caribbean colonies and the Hudson Bay settlement were of greater value than the American colonies, for they produced the tropical products and furs that the mother country desired. From the point of view of the French government, however, all the English settlements in the New World were a threat to New France. By the 1750's the rivalry had become so keen that it erupted into a bitter struggle for control of North America.

▶ CHECK-UP

1. Why was Maryland established? How did the Maryland colonists achieve greater political rights and religious freedom? How was Carolina settled? What were the differences between the two parts of Carolina?

2. How did the Dutch establish New Amsterdam? Why did the English seize this colony? How were New Jersey, Delaware, and Georgia founded?

3. How did William Penn come to found a colony? Why did Pennsylvania prosper?

4. Why did England regard the Hudson Bay area and the Caribbean colonies as more valuable possessions than the thirteen colonies?

. . . .

5 *Britain Defeats France in the Struggle for North America*

Britain and France are rivals in the New World. Conflict in the New World between Great Britain and France was as

Map legend:

- English settlement
- English territory
- ✗ English fort
- French territory
- French settlement
- ✗ French fort
- Spanish territory
- ✝ Spanish mission

Map labels:

North Pole

Bering Strait · Alaska · Pacific Ocean

UNEXPLORED

Hudson Bay

Claimed by Russia, Spain and England

Newfoundland

St. Lawrence R. · Quebec · Montreal · Acadia (Nova Scotia)

NEW FRANCE

L. Superior · L. Michigan · L. Huron · L. Ontario · Detroit · L. Erie · Ohio R.

Mississippi R.

LOUISIANA

Atlantic Ocean

San Francisco De Asisi, 1776

Colorado R.

Santa Fe 1607

San Diego 1769

Guadelupe, 1659 (El Paso)

Rio Grande

San Antonio De Bejar 1718

NEW SPAIN

Monterrey

Natchez · Mobile · New Orleans

St. Augustine 1565

SPANISH FLORIDA

Bermuda

Gulf of Mexico

Bahama Is.

Mexico City · Vera Cruz

Cuba · Hispaniola · Puerto Rico · St. Kitts · Guadeloupe · Martinique · Barbados · Trinidad

Jamaica

WEST INDIES

Caribbean Sea

R. M. Chapin, Jr.

THE CONTEST FOR EMPIRE

On the eve of the French and Indian War, three nations held large claims in North America — the Spanish, with their many missions in the Southwest; the French, their forts and settlements connected by the Great Lakes and Mississippi River system; and the English, firmly settled along the Atlantic. Note that this seaboard area, though relatively small in size, was densely populated.

old as their earliest settlements. Both countries expected their colonies to produce, if not gold and silver, then at least a good quantity of furs, fish, naval stores, food, sugar, tobacco, and rice. Since the English and French colonies in the Caribbean were separate islands, competition there was less intense. But when both countries sought to control the fur trade in the interior of the continent and the rich fishing banks off the northern coasts, there was frequent trouble. Thus, when Jamestown was only six years old, it sent an expedition all the way to Acadia (Nova Scotia) to wipe out a handful of French settlers. Through most of the 1600's, however, neither the English colonies nor New France could spare enough men to wage an all-out attack. The French had more or less a free hand to explore the Mississippi River Valley, while the English planted colonies along the coast without opposition.

Rivalry leads to war. Toward the end of the seventeenth century, the picture changed. Relations between Britain and France grew worse after the overthrow of the Stuarts in the Glorious Revolution. England's new ruler, William of Orange, was a dogged foe of the French king, Louis XIV. The two countries were colonial rivals in North America and trade rivals in India. In addition, there was religious friction between Anglican England and Catholic France, and each country wanted to extend its control over the Netherlands.

For these various reasons, Britain and France launched a series of wars in 1689 that did not end until the defeat of Napoleon in 1815. These wars were fought in both Europe and America. (See table on this page.) The conflicts between England and France were of enormous importance for the American colonies. True, the fighting on this continent had only minor significance until the 1750's. But it gave the English colonists a chance to acquire political and military experience which later proved invaluable in their revolution against the mother country.

Each side has strengths and weaknesses. As the showdown between England and France approached, each of the contestants had certain advantages and disadvantages. (1) By 1750, English colonists outnumbered those in New France by more than twenty to one. In theory, the English colonies should have been able to produce large armies, but rivalry among the separate colonies made this impossible. Only when invasion threatened did the colonies muster an efficient fighting force.

(2) The English colonies had a more stable economy than did New France. In other words, a combination of agriculture, trading, and industry made the American colonies more self-sufficient than the French, who had to import much of their food and almost all of their supplies.

(3) Because the English controlled the seas, they could interfere with vital shipments to the French settlements along the St. Lawrence. But, in order to conquer that river valley, the English would have to capture the strategic French citadel at Quebec. As long as Quebec remained in

---

TIMETABLE

WARS INVOLVING ENGLAND AND FRANCE

In Europe	In America
1689–1697 War of the League of Augsburg	1689–1697 King William's War
1702–1713 War of Spanish Succession	1702–1713 Queen Anne's War
1740–1748 War of Austrian Succession	1744–1748 King George's War
1756–1763 Seven Years' War	1754–1763 French and Indian War
1778–1783 War of the American Revolution	1775–1783 War of the American Revolution
1792–1802 Wars of the French Revolution	1790–1800 Undeclared French War
1803–1815 Napoleonic Wars	1812–1814 War of 1812

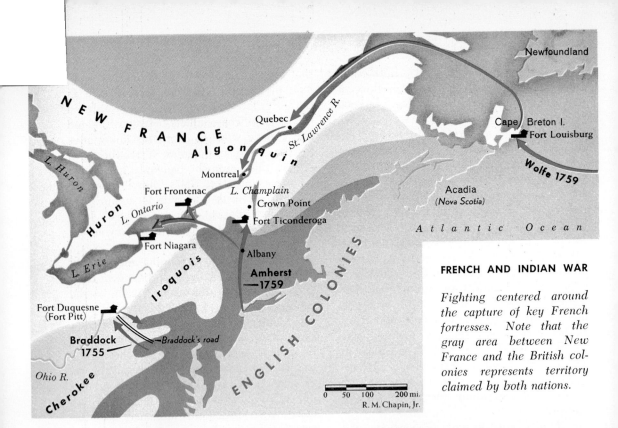

FRENCH AND INDIAN WAR

Fighting centered around the capture of key French fortresses. Note that the gray area between New France and the British colonies represents territory claimed by both nations.

R. M. Chapin, Jr.

French hands, New France was safe — despite British control of the seas.

(4) The government of New France was highly centralized, and there were no local assemblies to bother the royal governor with criticism. But the governor had to take orders from the French king and so was never able to act independently. This was an obvious disadvantage in a war that was fought so far away from France. The English colonies, on the other hand, were largely self-governing by 1750. This meant that it was difficult for the king or even the royal governors to control them. It was only when the colonists felt *their* interests to be at stake that they assumed greater responsibility for the war. They contributed substantially to winning control of both the region beyond the Appalachians and the fishing banks.

(5) Finally, the French had far better relations with the Indians than did the English. The Iroquois and the Cherokee were allied with the English, but all the other tribes sided with the French. In the long run, however, this did not prove too great a disadvantage to the English colonists. The rapidly increasing population of the English settlements provided more than enough man power to hold the Appalachian frontier.

The early wars bring no decision. During the first three wars fought by the English and French in North America, neither side made any great gains. The fighting that took place in America in these early wars had little lasting effect since the peace treaties were drawn up in Europe and tended to reflect European problems. To be sure, the English gained possession of Acadia and Newfoundland. Nevertheless, after half a century of conflict (1689–1748), neither the French nor the English had won supremacy on the North American continent.

The Albany Plan of Union is rejected. With the French danger growing more real every day, the British government decided to promote some type of colonial union. This would make it easier (1) to control colonial relations with the Indians and (2) to raise funds and military forces for colonial defense. In 1754 seven colonies sent delegates to a conference in Albany, which had been called by the British government. After discussing Indian affairs, the delegates turned their attention to a plan for uniting the colonies proposed by

Benjamin Franklin. His plan provided for a president-general appointed by the king and a council elected by the colonial assemblies. The council would handle Indian affairs, pass laws, and levy taxes for the common defense — all with the approval of the president-general and the Crown.

The Albany Congress accepted Franklin's proposal. Neither the British government nor the colonial assemblies, however, would give their consent. The king thought the Albany Plan gave too much power to the colonists, while the colonial assemblies thought it *took* too much power from them. "The Assemblies . . . thought there was too much *prerogative* [royal power] in it, and in England it was judged to have too much of the *democratic*," said Franklin.

War breaks out on the American frontier. Meanwhile, both England and France were watching each other's moves in the Ohio Valley. The French had strengthened their position by building a line of forts (map, page 40). Most menacing to the English was Fort Duquesne (doo-*kayn'*) at the forks of the Ohio (the site of present-day Pittsburgh). The English decided to let colonial speculators lay claim to large tracts of land in the hope that settlers would move into the interior. Ambitious Virginians promptly formed the Ohio Company and secured title to a 200,000-acre grant. Since the construction of Fort Duquesne threatened their plans for the Ohio Valley, the Virginians persuaded Governor Dinwiddie to protest to the French commander. For this delicate task, Dinwiddie picked George Washington, a 21-year-old surveyor and militia officer. In 1753, with a handful of men, Washington made his way through the wilderness to deliver the message. The French received him politely but refused to abandon Fort Duquesne.

Early the next year Governor Dinwiddie sent Washington back, this time in command of a small armed force. His orders were to drive the French away from the forks of the Ohio. But the enemy was strongly entrenched at Fort Duquesne, and after a brief skirmish Washington was forced to retreat. The French and Indian War actually started with this encounter in 1754. But its European counterpart, the Seven Years' War, did not begin until 1756.

The French take an early lead. For the first few years of the French and Indian War, the French had the upper hand. General Braddock and two crack British regiments set out to take Fort Duquesne in 1755. The English general put young Washington on his staff but unfortunately made little use of him. The British troops built a road (Braddock's Road) through the Pennsylvania wilderness; seven miles outside Fort Duquesne they were ambushed by the French and Indians. Braddock was mortally wounded, and the British were compelled to retreat.

Washington and the Virginia militia helped the survivors get out of the trap into which they had walked. But little could be done to stem the Indian raids against frontier settlements in Pennsylvania, Virginia, and Maryland. "These miserable English are in the extremity of distress," exulted a French captain in 1756, "and repent too late the unjust war they began against us." Moreover, the French were able to celebrate important victories in both India and Europe.

The tide turns for the British. The turning point came in 1757 when William Pitt joined the British cabinet. Pitt understood the strategic importance of North America in the global conflict. By paying his European allies to keep the French troops occupied in their theater of the war, Pitt was able to concentrate Britain's resources against New France. British naval power turned against Louisburg (on Cape Breton Island) and Quebec, while British troops took French forts in the interior.

Pitt inspired co-operation in the British government and in the colonies as well. For positions of responsibility in the army and navy, he picked able young men like Generals Jeffrey Amherst and red-headed General James Wolfe. Pitt also promised to give greater recognition to colonial officers. In return, the colonial assemblies agreed to increase the size of their militias.

The capture of Quebec assures Britain's triumph. Pitt's policies soon proved successful. In 1758 the French fortress of Louisburg fell to the British. In the interior George Washington had the satisfaction of helping British troops take Fort Duquesne, which was appropriately renamed Pittsburgh. The crowning victory, however, was the capture of Quebec in 1759. This task fell to Wolfe and Amherst, the former to approach by way of the St. Lawrence and the latter to lead an overland force. Amherst never got beyond the French forts at Ticonderoga and Crown Point (map, page 42), but Wolfe decided to gamble on a surprise attack. Having found an unguarded path up the steep cliffs that protected the French citadel, Wolfe led his men up the heights under cover of night. Early on the morning of September 13, his small army was ready for battle on the plains outside Quebec. The startled French commander, Montcalm, lacked the supplies to withstand a siege and so led his men out of the citadel to fight. In a brief but bloody battle, both Montcalm and Wolfe lost their lives. But

THE TREATY OF PARIS, 1763

The French and Indian War was only part of a global conflict, but for France it meant the loss of a huge empire in America. Compare with the map on page 40. What remained French in 1763?

English

Spanish

French

the British were victorious. With the fall of Quebec, Montreal was in a hopeless position and it surrendered in 1760. New France now belonged to Great Britain.

There were victories elsewhere for Pitt. In the Caribbean the French sugar islands of Martinique and Guadeloupe were seized. In India the French were completely routed. When Spain entered the war as an ally of France, Britain closed in on Cuba and the Philippines.

The Treaty of Paris is signed. The war was formally brought to a close by the Treaty of Paris in 1763. France surrendered to Great Britain its possessions east of the Mississippi with the exception of New Orleans. That city and French territory west of the Mississippi passed into the hands of Spain. Great Britain restored Cuba and the Philippines to Spain but received Florida in return. France was allowed to retain two tiny islands off the coast of Newfoundland for the use of French fishermen, but was forbidden to fortify them. Britain agreed to return Martinique and Guadeloupe to France.

Thus, the Treaty of Paris confirmed Britain's position as the dominant power in North America. From the Atlantic to the Mississippi and from Florida to Hudson Bay, English authority was unchallenged.

▶ CHECK-UP

1. Why were Britain and France rivals in the New World? Why did the rivalry become more bitter after 1689?

2. In the wars between France and Britain in America, what were the advantages and disadvantages of the French? Of the British? What was the purpose of the Albany Congress? Why did the Albany Plan please neither the colonial assemblies nor the British government?

3. Why were both the French and British interested in the Ohio Valley? How did each try to secure it? Why were the early years of the French and Indian War discouraging for the British? How did the situation change after 1757?

4. What territorial cessions were provided by the Treaty of Paris (1763)? What was the significance of Britain's victory?

Clinching the Main Ideas in Chapter 2

The quest for gold and silver had figured large in Cabot's voyage at the end of the fifteenth century and in the plans of Gilbert and Raleigh 90 years later. Yet the English did not plant permanent colonies in North America until the seventeenth century, and by then other than mercantile motives had become important. Religious, political, and economic unrest were the main reasons for the migration of Englishmen to the New World. In the 125 years between the establishment of Jamestown and the founding of the thirteenth colony, Georgia, the Atlantic coast became a patchwork of little towns, thriving ports, small farms, and broad plantations.

The thirteen English colonies differed in form of government, pattern of living, and the type of people they attracted. South Carolina, for example, was a royal colony, with a strong Anglican church, extensive plantations, slave labor, and aristocratic landowners. Rhode Island, on the other hand, was a charter colony, proud of its political independence, its religious toleration, and its free labor at work on the small farms and in the fishing villages. In comparison with the strict policies of French and Spanish colonization, English settlement in North America looked helter-skelter. Yet the thirteen colonies flourished.

The tiny settlements of the early 1600's had mushroomed to a total of 1,500,000 people just a century and a half later. These colonists were determined to hold their land against all comers. They fought off the Indians and, after 1689, French invaders too. By 1763 England had won control of the eastern half of North America. New France was eliminated, and New Spain had been greatly weakened.

Chapter Review

Terms to Understand

1. Anglican Church
2. Glorious Revolution
3. Mayflower Compact
4. New England Confederation
5. joint-stock company
6. divine right theory
7. common-store system
8. charter
9. burgesses
10. Separatists
11. piedmont
12. tidewater
13. patroons

What Do You Think?

1. Why did the idea of colonization catch hold in England during the early 1600's? Why did emigration slow down after 1688?

2. How was farming in the piedmont different from in the tidewater? Why?

3. Which colonies were most concerned about religious toleration? Explain why.

4. Why were the English eager to take over New Netherland?

5. Why was the mother country interested in establishing the Dominion of New England? What came of it? A plan of union also was discussed in 1754. Why? What came of it?

Using Your Knowledge of History

1. Had you lived in the 1600's, in which English colony would you have wanted to settle? Write a 300-word essay explaining the reasons for your choice.

2. Various factors (geographical, political, economic, religious) affected the settlement of New France and the English colonies. Make a chart in which you bring out similarities and differences for each of these factors.

3. List the rights and privileges which settlers in the English colonies came to enjoy. In parallel columns, point out the extent to which these rights and privileges were also enjoyed by colonists in New Spain and New France.

4. The French and Indian War was part of a great war fought in Europe, in India, and on the seas. Give an oral report to explain how this larger war came about.

Extending Your Knowledge of History

The English People on the Eve of Colonization, 1603–1630, by Wallace Notestein, provides vivid description of English life during that period. For information about the southern colonies, see two books by T. J. Wertenbaker: *The First Americans, 1607–1690* and *The Old South.* Samuel E. Morison deals sympathetically with the Puritans in *Builders of the Bay Colony,* while G. F. Willison describes Plymouth in *Saints and Strangers.*

CHAPTER 3

The Colonists Develop Distinctive Ways of Living

Early view of Princeton College

1607–1775

When John Pory came over from England, in 1619, to write his account of Virginia, he wrote: "Our cowkeeper here . . . on Sundays goes accoutered [dressed] all in fresh flaming silk; and a wife . . . of a collier of Croyden wears her rough beaver hat with a fair pearl hatband. . . ."

The New World did not care whether a man had been a knight or a cowkeeper before he came there. If he did well in the New World, his wife could dress in silk and nobody would think it odd. And that, too, has always been a part of the American dream — that a man should have a chance to do his best and rise in the world — that no man is better than another because his parents had money or titles or power.

ADAPTED FROM "AMERICA" BY STEPHEN VINCENT BENÉT

The growth of the thirteen English colonies would have been impossible without a constant flow of new settlers from Europe. Throughout the 1600's and 1700's colonial population increased at a rapid rate. Though the immigrants followed different patterns of living, all were striving to make a better life for themselves. One of the striking characteristics of colonial America was that so many of them succeeded in this goal.

A large majority of the colonists earned their livelihood by farming. For settlers in the Middle Colonies and the South, agriculture provided satisfactory returns. But in New England many settlers earned a living by fishing or in lumbering or the fur trade. Some farmers added to their income in those same ways. Despite the mother country's attempts to regulate colonial merchants, commerce was the most profitable occupation. It was not by accident that in

46

the 1700's colonial merchants began to replace the ministers as leaders of public opinion. The merchants and wealthy townspeople came to dominate colonial politics and also showed the greatest interest in education and the arts.

1 *The Colonial Population Increases Rapidly*

The American colonies grow at a startling rate. The population of the American[1] colonies increased from about 250,000 people in 1700 to approximately 2,500,000 in 1776. Since there was no official census until 1790, historians must rely upon contemporary estimates and records for colonial population statistics. Even allowing for some inaccuracy in these figures, a tenfold increase within 75 years represents a startling rate of growth.

Population increase was due in part to the high birth rate of the colonists. Families of ten or twelve children were common, and those of fifteen or twenty were not unusual. Patrick Henry was one of nineteen children; Benjamin Franklin was one of seventeen. Travelers in the American colonies frequently commented upon the large number of children who swarmed "like ants" or "like broods of ducks in a

---

[1] The term "American" was sometimes applied to English colonists in the early 1700's, but it did not come into common usage until the 1750's.

. . . .

CHAPTER FOCUS

1. The colonial population increases rapidly.

2. Living conditions vary among the colonists.

3. A prosperous economy is regulated by mercantile laws.

4. American trends develop in religion, learning, and the arts.

5. A colonial pattern of government emerges.

pond." One Englishman pointed out: "The good people are marrying one another as if they had not a day to live. I allege it to be a plot against the state, and the ladies (who are all politicians in America) are determined to raise young rebels to fight against old England."

Immigration also added to the population. After the early years, immigration from countries other than England became especially important. Prior to the 1690's, about 90 per cent of the colonists were of English stock. But in the 1700's English emigration tapered off, and many of the new arrivals came from Germany, northern Ireland, France, Switzerland, and Africa. By 1776 more than a third of the American population was of non-English origin.

German peasants make industrious settlers. The Germans formed one of the largest groups of immigrants in the eighteenth century. There were many reasons why German peasants left their homeland. At that time Germany was not yet a unified nation. Continual warfare among the princes of the many German states caused widespread destruction of the peasants' fields. Religious persecution of Protestant peasants by Catholic princes was another grievance. In addition, heavy taxation and the seizure of property by the warring factions convinced many Germans that their only hope was escape to the New World.

Many of these dissatisfied Germans heard of William Penn's "Holy Experiment" and his eagerness to secure new settlers. Ship captains spread word throughout the German states of their willingness to transport immigrants to America as indentured servants. As a result, thousands of Germans gathered in North Sea ports where they boarded vessels bound for Philadelphia.

Some German immigrants were able to pay their own way and to purchase rich farmland in America. They pushed up the valleys of the Delaware, the Schuylkill (*skool'*kil), and the Susquehanna Rivers (map, page 37). These German settlers clung to their old-country language and religion, methods of farming, and ways of cooking and dressing. Many travelers through the Middle Colonies commented on the neat, prosperous German farms with their distinctive stone barns. Already these people were called "Pennsylvania Dutch."[2] Though many of the Germans preferred Pennsylvania, others scattered throughout the colonies.

The Scotch-Irish settle on the frontier. Almost an equal number of Scotch-Irish came to America during these same years. The Scotch-Irish should not be confused with either the Scots or the Irish. They were originally Scots whom James I allowed to settle in northern Ireland on land taken from the Irish. In the early 1700's, Parliament forbade the Scotch-Irish to ship their dairy products, linens, and woolens to English markets. Faced with economic ruin, many of them decided to emigrate to the New World.

Finding that land along the coast was already occupied and relatively expensive, the Scotch-Irish moved to the unsettled frontiers of Pennsylvania, Maryland, Virginia, the Carolinas, and Georgia. Sometimes they settled in the wilderness without bothering to secure title to the land. As one of them explained, "it was against the laws of God and nature that so much land should be idle while so many Christians wanted it to labor on and to raise bread." Their steady westward drive has prompted historians to call the Scotch-Irish the "cutting edge of the colonial frontier."

French Huguenots flee to America. Some of the earliest, though not the most numerous, of the non-English immigrants were the French Protestants called Huguenots (page 20). Persecuted because of their religion, yet forbidden to settle in New France, the Huguenots fled from France to the Protestant countries of Europe. A few made their way to the American colonies. The Huguenots, many of whom were craftsmen or trained in a profession, quickly established themselves in colonial cities. The Reveres and Faneuils of Boston were of Huguenot background, as were the Manigaults of Charleston, South Carolina.

Involuntary immigrants swell the colonial population. Throughout the seventeenth century English officials persistently

[2] From the German word for "German," *Deutsch* (pronounced *doytch*).

dumped on American shores people who were considered undesirable. The first convicts were shipped to Virginia in 1617, and in the succeeding decades they were followed by prisoners of war, orphans, vagrants, and paupers. During the 1700's other European governments followed the British practice, and there was little that the colonists could do to stop it.

By far the largest number of unwilling immigrants, however, were African slaves. The British took over the slave trade from the Dutch in the eighteenth century, and with the aid of Yankee merchants, it became highly profitable. Ships carrying New England rum sailed for Africa, where they exchanged their liquid cargo for human cargo. Chained together, the Negroes were kept below decks in cramped, dark, unsanitary quarters. Poorly fed and given little or no exercise, many died before reaching the West Indies. When the survivors had adjusted to the change in food and climate, learned the meaning of English commands, and mastered the tasks to be performed on sugar and cotton plantations, they were shipped to the mainland and sold. (See map on page 59.)

The demand for slaves increases. The demand for slaves in the southern colonies grew rapidly. Plantation owners considered it wiser to invest in slaves than in indentured servants who would stay only a few years. Moreover, few indentured servants wanted to work with slaves on isolated plantations in Virginia, Georgia, or the Carolinas. Thus, the number of Negroes rose from about 25,000 in 1700 to nearly 400,000 at the outbreak of the Revolution. The vast majority of these slaves worked on tobacco, cotton, rice, and indigo plantations in the South. The expense of clothing, housing, and training slaves for jobs discouraged their widespread use in New England or the Middle Colonies. During the early 1700's, most northern colonists did not oppose slavery in principle, and some kept slaves as household servants. The only outspoken critics of slavery were the Quakers.

The nature of the colonial population changes. By the time the Revolution broke
(*Continued on page 53*)

LIFE IN THE COLONIES

By the mid-1700's the English colonies had been settled for a century or more. The colonists had not only conquered the wilderness but had begun to prosper. A distinctively American way of life had developed, as the pictures on pages 49–52 will show.

The restoration of Williamsburg, once the capital of colonial Virginia, has enabled present-day Americans to visit an eighteenth-century town. Above is the Duke of Gloucester Street in Williamsburg. Paul Revere's house (right), dating from 1760, is the oldest building in modern Boston. Visitors to this little house can see how townspeople lived in colonial New England.

Courtesy, Museum of Fine Arts, Boston, Abraham Shuman Fund

A prosperous Boston shipowner of the Revolutionary period, Isaac Winslow, had a portrait of his family (left) painted by Joseph Blackburn. Unlike Paul Revere, Winslow remained loyal to the Crown when the Revolution broke out and moved to Halifax, Nova Scotia.

Most of the colonists made their living by farming. In the picture above, the self-taught artist Edward Hicks painted a typical farm scene. Animals were a favorite subject of Hicks, who was also a coach and sign painter.

Early colonial women made most of their families' clothing. To twist flax or wool fibers into thread, they used spinning wheels (left).

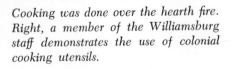

Cooking was done over the hearth fire. Right, a member of the Williamsburg staff demonstrates the use of colonial cooking utensils.

Left, Mystic Seaport, Connecticut, has been restored to look much as it did in late colonial times. Though most colonists farmed, many people in coastal towns, especially in the North, depended on the sea for their living. Fishing, whaling, shipbuilding, sailmaking, and ropemaking were active industries. Other colonial occupations included ironworking and glassblowing (below).

Above, left, a worker heats cast iron on a forge at the Saugus, Massachusetts, ironworks restoration. Some glass was made at Jamestown, as a present-day glassblower demonstrates (above, right), but the first successful glassworks was started in New Jersey in 1739. Before, glass had been rare in the colonies.

Since colonial people baked their own bread, every community had a mill where grain was ground into meal or flour. At left, a water wheel powers the gristmill at Old Sturbridge, Massachusetts, a present-day country town. Oxen were commonly used as draft animals in the colonies.

Earning a living was the colonists' first concern. But religion was also important, and interest in reading and the arts soon developed. Benjamin Franklin founded this library in Philadelphia (right).

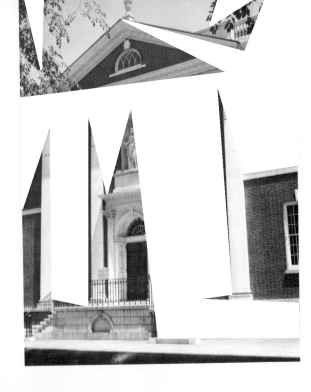

The evangelist George Whitefield (left) stirred up much religious enthusiasm during his tour of the colonies in the 1740's (page 61).

Prosperous colonists, appreciating the work of such artists as John Singleton Copley, often had their portraits painted. Below is Copley's portrait of Mrs. Ezekiel Goldthwait of Boston.

Courtesy, Museum of Fine Arts, Boston, Bequest of John T. Bowen in memory of Eliza M. Bowen

Courtesy, Museum of Fine Arts, Boston, Gift of James Longley

Colonists also admired the fine work of master craftsmen like Paul Revere. Revere made this silver tea set (above), which was presented to a Boston shipbuilder by his fellow citizens in honor of his completion of the frigate Boston.

52

out, then, the farmers and town dwellers of the American colonies were still primarily English in background. But sizable numbers of people from Ireland, Wales Scotland, France, Germany, Switzerland, Holland, and Sweden had joined them. "From this promiscuous breed," observed a French settler in 1782, "that race now called Americans have arisen." In his *Letters from an American Farmer*, Hector St. John de Crèvecoeur went on to say:

I could point out to you a family whose grandfather was an Englishman, whose wife was Dutch, whose son married a French woman, and whose present four sons now have four wives of different nations. . . . The Americans were once scattered all over Europe; here they are incorporated into one of the finest systems of population which has ever appeared. . . .

▶ CHECK-UP

1. Why did the population of the American colonies increase rapidly during the 1700's? From what countries did immigrants come to America? Why? Where did each of these groups generally settle?

2. What involuntary immigrants were brought to America?

· · · · · · · · · · · · · · · · · · · ·

2 *Living Conditions Vary Among the Colonists*

Class distinctions are not rigid. One of the striking characteristics of colonial life was the ease with which a person could better his position. Class differences existed in colonial America, but they were never as rigid as those in Europe. Gabriel Manigault, South Carolina planter, merchant, and slave trader, was the son of a penniless Huguenot craftsman. Benjamin Franklin's father was a poor Boston candlemaker.

On the frontier, class distinctions were less obvious than they were in colonial

towns and cities. As pioneers pushed westward up the rivers and streams, common hardships and dangers made social differences seem insignificant. In town society, one's "rank" was more important. Though social standing depended primarily on wealth, such factors as family background, education, length of residence, and political power all played a part. Clothes often showed whether a man or woman belonged to the "better sort," the "middling sort," or the "meaner sort." The farmer and his wife dressed in homemade garments, while the well-to-do merchant and his spouse wore silver-buckled shoes, starched ruffles, silks, satins, and powdered wigs. Social standing determined the assignment of church pews, and students were listed on college registers according to their families' rank.

Planters and merchants live comfortably. The "better sort" among the colonial population included the large landowners and the merchants in the port towns. The prosperous southern planter might own from 500 to 1000 or more acres of land and from 25 to 100 or more slaves. He often supervised the cultivation of his fields himself, for it was difficult to find competent overseers. The planter's house was usually a modest two-story structure, with kitchen, storehouses, dairy, and smokehouses as separate buildings. Few colonial plantation homes were as elaborate as George Washington's Mount Vernon or Thomas Jefferson's Monticello.

In the northern colonies, where agriculture was not so profitable, the merchants of Boston, New York, and Philadelphia dominated the social scene. Generally a merchant owned a wharf and warehouse and had a retail store nearby. As his profits piled up, he invested in additional ships, real estate, the fur trade, or the slave trade. The northern merchants were the bankers of the eighteenth century, lending money at interest rates as high as 10 per cent. These men often lived in handsome brick houses at the edge of town and took pride in their neatly cultivated gardens. They rode to and from their wharves in elegant carriages, and they dressed in the finest of imported clothes. Like the southern planters, the merchants imitated English aristocrats in their style of living. They would have been flattered to know that an English traveler in Boston in 1740 thought the "ladies and gentlemen dress and appear as gay . . . as courtiers in England on a coronation or birthday."

The middle classes form the bulk of the population. The "middling sort" of colonists included the professional people, the artisans, and the small farmers. They neither lived nor dressed as well as the planters and merchants, but they made a good living for themselves and their families. The professional group included lawyers, ministers, teachers, and doctors. Most of them lived in the cities in unpretentious houses with small gardens. Artisans and craftsmen were not as well-educated as the professional people, and their incomes generally were smaller. Their frame homes consisted of a shop on the first floor, with living quarters at the back or perhaps upstairs. The Paul Revere house in Boston (which may still be visited) is a good example of how the successful craftsmen lived. But silversmiths like Revere generally did better than shipwrights, millers, shoemakers, hatmakers, blacksmiths, weavers, candlemakers, or barrelmakers.

The small farmer of the mid-eighteenth century might own as much as 150 acres. He worked his land with the help of his family and perhaps a hired man or a slave or two. Farm homes were rough frame dwellings, sometimes little more than improved log cabins. The children had little schooling, and often the only reading material was the Bible and an almanac. Social gatherings for many of these farm families were limited to harvest parties, barn raisings, and religious meetings. The poorest farm people had to fashion their own homespun clothes and make their furniture and cooking utensils.

Indentured servants are near the bottom of the social scale. The lowest group on the social scale (except for slaves) consisted of indentured servants. These people, as we have seen, secured passage to the New World by selling their labor for a period of years. Many of them ran away before their term of service was up, and it was almost impossible to trace them. Those who did serve out their full term were usually rewarded with a small sum of money. With this, they could buy land or perhaps set themselves up as independent craftsmen. Many indentured servants and their descendants became respected members of their communities. At one time a third of the members of the Virginia House of Burgesses were former indentured servants.

Transportation and communication promote social change. The ease with which a colonist could improve his social position depended to some extent on transportation and communication. Many an ambitious man made a new start in a distant part of the colony or even in another colony altogether. Benjamin Franklin, for instance, left Boston for Philadelphia at the age of seventeen. He made a large part of this trip by boat, for there were few roads between Boston and Philadelphia in the 1720's. As time went on, however, roads did connect the major cities, and travelers who could afford it went by stagecoach. Boston, New York, and Philadelphia had regular, though infrequent, mail service in the early 1700's. When Benjamin Franklin became deputy postmaster general for the colonies in the 1750's, the number of deliveries was increased and postal service extended to the back country and the South. Such improvements in transportation and communication promoted social change and strengthened the ties among the thirteen colonies.

▶ CHECK-UP

1. What factors helped to determine the social standing of immigrants? How could a colonist move up the social ladder?

2. What groups of colonists were most prosperous? What groups were included in the middle class? What opportunity was there for indentured servants to get ahead? Compare standards of living of the different groups.

. . . .

3 *A Prosperous Economy Is Regulated by Mercantile Laws*

Because of their different climates and resources, New England, the Middle Colonies, and the South specialized in different occupations and the production of different crops. None of the thirteen colonies was economically self-sufficient. All of them relied on trade with the other colonies to market their surplus products and supply their needs. Even more important was trade with the mother country, which provided the colonies with most of the manufactured goods they needed. To regulate this trade, Parliament passed a number of laws. These laws were based on the mercantile theory — that the colonies existed for the benefit of the mother country — and so were known as mercantile laws.

Geography influences ways of making a living. Within most of the thirteen colonies, there were three distinct geographical areas — coastal plain, plateau, and mountains. The coastal plain in New England was only a narrow strip of land. To the south, however, this plain gradually broadened to the 200-mile stretch of low-lying fertile land known as the tidewater (page 29). Above the fall line lay the piedmont, a plateau that extended to the foothills of the mountains. To the west were the Appalachians, the mountainous spine of the colonies, including the Cumberland, Allegheny, and Adirondack Mountains.

Since the coastal plain and the plateau were suited to agriculture, most of the colonists lived in these regions and farmed the land. By the time of the Revolution, approximately 90 per cent of the colonists lived on farms, while the rest lived in villages, small towns, or cities. Most of the larger cities were ports located at the mouths of major rivers.[3]

[3] Philadelphia was the largest American city with a population of 40,000 in 1775. New York had 25,000 inhabitants and Boston, 16,000. Charleston was fourth in size with about 12,000.

New England develops a number of thriving occupations. In the New England colonies, the farmers raised corn, barley, oats, and vegetables and grazed livestock on the village commons. But the short growing season and the rocky land made it difficult for the farmers to supply much more than their own needs. A great deal of the food consumed in New England port towns came from the Middle Colonies. The moneymaking industries in colonial New England were fishing, shipbuilding, the rum and slave trade, iron manufacturing, and the fur trade.

Fishing. New England's most profitable industry was fishing. New England waters and the Grand Banks of Newfoundland teemed with cod, mackerel, bass, halibut, and sturgeon. The demand for fish in the

TIDEWATER AND PIEDMONT

The southern coastal plain (the tidewater) was ideal for plantation agriculture, while the piedmont was better suited to small farms. Note the differences in elevation of these two regions.

MAP STUDY

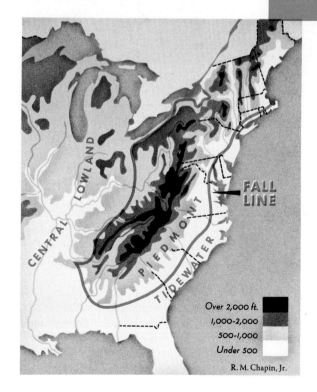

FALL LINE

CENTRAL LOWLAND

PIEDMONT

TIDEWATER

Over 2,000 ft.
1,000-2,000
500-1,000
Under 500

R. M. Chapin, Jr.

Catholic countries of Europe and in the Caribbean settlements provided a steady market. Thus, the fishing industry was vitally important to the northern colonies from an early date. Boston started exporting fish as early as 1633. Already Captain John Smith had declared: "Let not the meanness of the word Fish distaste you, for it will afford as good gold as the mines of Guiana . . . with less hazard and charge, and more certainty and facility." Soon every New England port had its fishing fleet operated by the men and boys of the surrounding countryside. The largest fish were hard to cure, so they were sold and consumed locally. The medium-sized fish were dried in the sun, packed, and exported to foreign markets. The smallest fish were chopped up, preserved in barrels of brine, and shipped to the West Indies as food for the slaves.

The most adventurous of the New England fishermen were the whalers. Throughout the 1600's they could harpoon whales within sight of the shore. As ship traffic on the Atlantic increased, however, the whales moved off and the fishermen had to pursue them into the Arctic Ocean and the south Atlantic. Even so, the daring whalers of Nantucket Island kept New England merchants well-supplied with sperm oil for lamps, whalebone and ivory for buttons, and ambergris for making perfume.

Shipbuilding. Shipbuilding was another important New England industry. The forests yielded an abundant supply of white pine, fir, and oak, as well as pitch pine for tar and turpentine. New England shipyards built most of the vessels used in the colonial trade. Also, because labor costs in the colonies were considerably lower than in England, many of the ships in the British navy were built in New England. In addition, the northern colonies supplied the British navy with naval stores — tar, pitch, rosin, turpentine, and rope.

Rum and slave trade. The distillation of rum was a profitable activity in New England. Rum, made from West Indian molasses, was a favorite colonial drink. Large quantities of rum were also shipped to Africa and traded for slaves. The same ships carried the Negroes to the West Indies and brought barrels of molasses back to New England on the last leg of the voyage. Many a New England merchant made his fortune in this way. Moreover, a sizable number of colonial workers were kept busy distilling the molasses into rum or building the special cargo ships used in this trade.

Iron. Still another New England industry was the manufacture of iron. There were ironworks at Lynn, Saugus, and Taunton, Massachusetts, as early as the 1640's. Though some of the bar iron was shipped to England, most of it was sold locally and made into anvils, pots and kettles, chains, anchors, nails, guns, and parts for wagons and sleighs.

Furs. New England also carried on a large fur trade, mostly in beaver skins. These were secured from the Indians in exchange for knives, cloth, and trinkets. Although English law prohibited the exchange of rum or guns for pelts, the colonists also traded these articles for furs from the Indians.

The Middle Colonies are the "bread basket" of North America. The land between the Hudson and Potomac Rivers was well-suited for general farming. Because the Middle Colonies shipped so much wheat to New England, the South, and the Caribbean, this region early became known as the "bread basket" of North America. These colonies also produced other cereal crops and large quantities of fruit and vegetables. One settler noted: "Peaches are of a fine flavor and in such amazing plenty that . . . hogs on a farm eat as many as they will, but yet the quantity that rot under the trees is astonishing. . . . Watermelons are in such plenty that there is not a farmer or even a cottager without a piece of ground planted with them." Rich pastures made the raising of cattle, sheep, and hogs profitable.

The woods of the Middle Colonies furnished timber for export, as well as a plentiful supply of beaver and otter pelts. The Dutch had early developed the fur trade in the Hudson River Valley, and the Scotch-Irish did most of the trapping on the Pennsylvania frontier. The lakes, rivers and coastal waters of the Middle Colonies also provided fish, clams, oysters, and lobsters, some of which were exported.

During the 1700's many small industries grew up around New York and Philadelphia. The countryside was dotted with flour mills, sawmills, iron forges, shipbuilding yards, and factories making glass, cloth, pottery, bricks, and potash. Of Germantown, Pennsylvania, a traveler wrote: "Most of the inhabitants are manufacturers, and make almost everything in such quantity and perfection, that in a short time this province will want very little from England."

Southern plantations produce tobacco, rice, and indigo. The South, like the Middle Colonies, was predominantly agricultural. There were distinct differences, however, in the kind of crops grown, the type of labor, and the size of landholdings. The tidewater of Virginia and North Carolina was devoted primarily to tobacco plantations. Slaves picked the tobacco leaves, cured them, bound them, and loaded the bales onto ships that carried the "noxious weed" to Britain. Rice and indigo were grown in the tidewater regions of South Carolina and Georgia. Rice was raised in swampy lowlands tilled by Negro slaves who worked in steamy heat and stood ankle-deep in mud for hours at a time. Indigo was grown on higher ground and could be tended by slaves when they were not needed in the rice fields. (The indigo plant yielded a bright blue dye that was highly prized by fashionable European ladies.)

During the later 1700's the amount of cotton grown in the South increased. So long as the seeds had to be removed by hand, however, cotton growing was not a very profitable way to use slaves.

The southern piedmont was an area of small farms. These were usually worked by the individual owner with the help of his sons and perhaps a slave or two. The piedmont farmers raised a variety of cereals, fruits, and vegetables and sold much of their produce to the plantations in the tidewater region. The fur trade was important along the Carolina and Georgia frontier, and many deerskins were shipped abroad from Charleston. The yellow pine forests of the southern colonies were valuable sources of lumber and naval stores.

Colonial industries develop. According to the mercantile theory (page 7), the colonies were expected to confine their trade to the mother country, sending her raw materials and buying finished goods in return. But in their early days the American colonies had little to export, and the English government did not pay much attention to colonial trade. As a result, the colonists were allowed to produce their own iron utensils, fashion beaver hats, make cloth from wool and flax, and manufacture hemp into rope. So long as colonial industry was limited, English officials did not complain.

As the colonies grew in number and size, however, they were tempted to do more manufacturing. The ironmasters of Massachusetts and Pennsylvania, for example, wanted to fashion all their bar iron into implements to be sold in the colonies. They did not want to export iron to England and then have to buy it back in finished goods at much higher prices. Similarly, textile producers considered it pointless to ship their raw wool to the mother country and then buy woolen cloth from English merchants.

The colonists also wanted to trade with non-British markets. New England rum distillers preferred a cheaper molasses from the French and Spanish Caribbean colonies to the more expensive British West Indian molasses. Yet, according to the mercantile theory, they could trade only with British colonies in the Caribbean. Southern planters were tempted to sell their tobacco, rice, and indigo in continental European markets. They did not like having to send them to the mother country, where British merchants collected a commission for selling them.

The Navigation Acts control colonial commerce. By the mid-seventeenth century the British government found it necessary to pass a series of laws regulating colonial trade and industry. The Naviga-

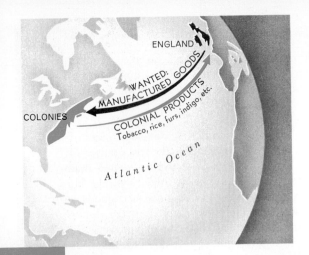
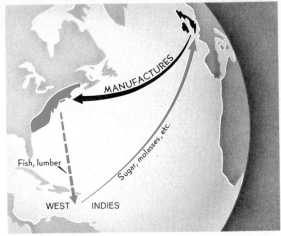

COLONIAL TRADE PATTERNS; THE "TRIANGULAR TRADE"

MAP
STUDY

The colonists discovered that direct trade with England led to an unfavorable balance of trade. As a result, they devised ways to exchange their native products for commodities which would improve their trade balance with the mother country.

tion Acts of 1660, 1663, and 1696 were the major pieces of legislation affecting trade.

(1) The Navigation Act of 1660 stated that any goods imported into, or exported from, any English possession had to be carried in ships built, owned, and manned by Englishmen or English colonists. This regulation was designed to head off the Dutch, French, and Spaniards, who might wish to share in the trade between England and the American colonies. The act also listed, or *enumerated,* certain articles produced in the colonies which had to be sent directly to England or sold in English colonies. These enumerated articles were sugar, tobacco, cotton, wool, and indigo, though the list was later extended to include rice, naval stores, furs, iron, and lumber. Non-enumerated products, such as fish, grain, and rum, could be sold directly by the colonists in any part of the world.

(2) The Navigation Act of 1663 was designed by Parliament to keep the colonies "in a firmer dependence" upon England and render them "yet more beneficial and advantageous." This law stated that all European cargoes headed for the colonies had to be sent to England first and reshipped from there in English vessels. In short, this act gave English merchants a monopoly over the colonial import trade, allowing them to collect commissions on all European goods that went to America.

(3) Among the New England merchants, who conducted much of the colonial carrying trade, there was considerable criticism and violation of the Navigation Acts. This, in turn, irritated the British merchants and they complained to Parliament. Finally, in 1696, Parliament passed still another Navigation Act "for preventing frauds and regulating abuses in the plantation trade." Under this act colonial governors had to take an oath that they would enforce the Navigation Acts. Customs collectors and inspectors could search ships, wharves, and warehouses and seize unlawful merchandise. Colonial laws that interfered with the Navigation Acts were set aside. Merchants accused of smuggling were tried in special courts without juries rather than before sympathetic colonial juries. During the early 1700's, efforts to enforce commercial regulations continued, and new restrictions were added. Whether or not they liked the Navigation Acts, the colonists had to obey them or run the risk of heavy penalties.

Mercantile laws regulate colonial industry. Steps were also taken to control colonial industries. The New England practice of buying French and Spanish molasses to make into rum angered English planters in the Caribbean. Parliament, therefore, passed the Molasses Act in 1733. This measure slapped a tax of sixpence a gallon on molasses imported to the Amer-

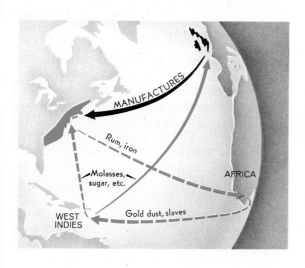
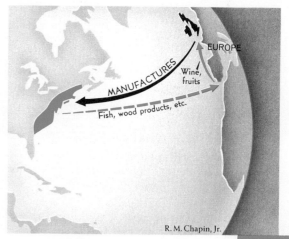

R. M. Chapin, Jr.

Analyze the trade patterns on each map, starting in each case from the American colonies. On the third map, why does the entire dashed-line triangle depend on the import of sugar and molasses from the West Indies?

ican colonies from the French and Spanish West Indies. The New England merchants were infuriated by this law. Some ignored it and smuggled molasses into unguarded harbors, but most of them grudgingly conducted their trade with the British West Indies.

English manufacturers obtained the same kind of protective legislation that Parliament gave to the Caribbean planters. The Woolens Act of 1699 stopped the shipment of woolen goods from one colony to another and prohibited the export of American woolen goods to European markets. The Hat Act of 1732 cut off the trade in beaver and felt hats and restricted the number of apprentices that a colonial hatmaker could hire. As a result, most of the New England beaver skins went to Britain to be made into fashionable fur hats. These hats were then shipped to the colonies and sold at prices which brought generous profits to the London hatters and British merchants. The Iron Act of 1750 forbade the manufacture of iron goods in the colonies but encouraged the production of pig and bar iron to be sent to England.

The colonists were angered by these laws which hampered one flourishing industry after another. One Bostonian voiced his disgust in this way: "A colonist cannot make a button, a horseshoe, nor a hobnail but some sooty iron monger or respectable button-maker of Britain shall bawl and squall that his honor's worship is . . . maltreated, injured, cheated and robbed by the rascally Americans."

Colonial currency is strictly regulated. According to the mercantile theory, as we have seen, wealth was measured by the amount of gold and silver that accumulated in the national treasury. England was eager, therefore, to make the American colonies pay cash for the goods they purchased. This drained English currency from America and meant that the colonies had little money in circulation. Debts were often settled by barter — that is, by the exchange of livestock, furs, and agricultural produce. Harvard College permitted one young man to pay his term bill with "an old cow worth 30 shillings Watertown rate, which died."

The colonists tried to remedy the lack of money by using Spanish, French, and Portuguese coins brought back from trade in the Caribbean. Many French guineas and Spanish dollars circulated in North America, though there were never enough to relieve the currency shortage. Massachusetts tried issuing silver shillings, the value of which depended on the colony's pine forests. But the British government soon prohibited these "pine tree shillings." Other colonists printed paper money with forests, farmland, or tobacco as security, but Par-

Pine tree shillings, about the size of a modern half dollar, circulated in Massachusetts for some thirty years.

liament passed laws forbidding the use of paper money in the colonies. From the mercantile point of view, these laws were necessary to protect the value of British currency. From the colonial point of view, however, the laws made the money shortage much worse.

Triangular trade patterns emerge. The laws limiting colonial trade and industry tested the wits of the colonists as well as their tempers. Since none of the colonies was self-sufficient, they had to trade in order to survive. Yet their freedom of trade was restricted by the Navigation Acts and the controls over colonial industry and currency. Consequently, the colonial merchants worked out patterns of trade whereby they marketed non-enumerated goods in non-English ports and picked up cargoes which could be exchanged in Britain for manufactured goods. They sold New England fish, for example, in Spain and Portugal; their ships then carried Mediterranean wine and fruit from these countries to England. Or grain and lumber from the Middle Colonies were exchanged in the West Indies for sugar and molasses that were taken to Britain. Since each of these routes involved at least one stop between the colonies and Britain, the trade came to be called the *triangular trade*.

Did mercantilism hurt or help the colonies? The effect of the mercantile legislation upon the American colonies has long been debated by historians. It is true that the colonies received many benefits from mercantilism. Their enumerated products had a steady market in the mother country. Some colonial industries, such as the production of indigo, bar iron, and naval stores, were encouraged by bonuses or

bounties from the British government. Parliament also prohibited the planting of tobacco in England or Ireland in order to give the American planters a larger market. In addition, the Navigation Acts stimulated shipbuilding and the transport trade in the colonies. Finally, the American colonies received military and naval protection and enjoyed trade advantages with other British possessions.

But after the end of the French and Indian War in 1763, some of the disadvantages of mercantilism became more obvious. The colonies were ready by that time to expand their manufacturing and increase their trade. The mercantile laws then seemed like a straitjacket that restricted the natural economic growth of the colonies. When Britain tried to tighten enforcement of the laws after 1763 and even passed new ones, the stage was set for an ugly quarrel between colonies and mother country.

▶ CHECK-UP

1. Describe the different geographical areas of the English colonies. What were the chief occupations in New England? In the Middle Colonies? In the South?

2. Why did Parliament pass the Navigation Acts? In what ways did these restrict colonial trade? Favor the colonies? How was this legislation regarded in the colonies?

3. How was colonial industry restricted? Why was there a shortage of currency in the colonies? How did the colonies try to cope with this problem? How did the colonies develop triangular trade patterns?

. . . .

4 *American Trends Develop in Religion, Learning, and the Arts*

As life in the New World became more secure, the colonists were able to take an interest in other things besides making a living. They found more time to read and write books, to publish newspapers, to establish schools, to encourage artists and musicians, and to start new churches. Under these circumstances, colonial culture — religion, education, science, literature, music, and art — flourished in the eighteenth century.

The clergy lose prestige. Clergymen, especially the Puritan ministers in Massachusetts, were very influential in the early years of the colonies (page 32). By the end of the 1600's, however, the clergy were no longer the undisputed leaders of colonial opinion. In part, this was due to the role of Puritan ministers in the witchcraft trials in Massachusetts in the 1690's. A wave of hysteria was touched off in Salem when several village girls accused certain townspeople of bewitching them. Within a few months a witch hunt was under way. Scores of men and women were accused of being the devil's agents, and nineteen were hanged before the frenzy died down. Increase Mather and his son Cotton Mather, both Puritan ministers, doubted the truth of the charges. But they and other clergymen did little to stop the trials or the hangings, and it was generally believed that the Puritan ministers approved. As a result, many colonists became critical of their religious leaders.

The arrival of non-English immigrants in the 1700's was another factor that undermined the privileged position of the Puritan (or Congregational) Church in New England and the Anglican Church (Church of England) in the South. Among the new settlers were Scotch-Irish Presbyterians, Quakers, French Huguenots, German and Scandinavian Lutherans, as well as Catholics and Jews. The mixture of religions led to greater tolerance in the colonies.

The Great Awakening occurs in the 1730's. A number of eloquent preachers tried in the 1730's to revive the earlier religious zeal of the colonists. Jonathan Edwards was one of the leaders in the *Great Awakening,* as this movement was called. A Congregational minister in Massachusetts, Edwards sought to dramatize for his parishioners the majesty of God's

mercy by contrasting it with the tortures of hell. He warned sinners and those who had fallen away from the church: "The God that holds you over the pit of hell, much as anyone holds a spider, or some loathsome insect over the fire, abhors you, and is dreadfully provoked; his wrath towards you burns like fire." More humane was George Whitefield, an English evangelist, who toured the colonies in the 1740's and helped establish the Methodist Church. The huge gatherings of the Great Awakening not only stirred religious fervor but also provided opportunities for isolated farm families and frontiersmen to mingle. In addition, the religious revival spurred the founding of a number of colleges to prepare ministers.

Educational opportunities are limited. Despite a growing interest in learning, many of the colonists could neither read

The most widely used schoolbook of the colonial period was the New England Primer. *This page from the primer helped children learn their ABC's.*

nor write. Moreover, it was difficult to get an education. There were no free, tax-supported public schools in any of the thirteen colonies. Massachusetts provided the best elementary schools, for the Puritan clergy had impressed upon local governments the need to educate children so they could outwit "that old deluder, Satan." A Massachusetts law of 1647 ordered towns of 50 householders to hire a schoolmaster and towns of 100 householders to set up a grammar school to prepare boys for college. But these requirements were not always carried out; half a century later they were being neglected in many towns. Furthermore, while these Massachusetts schools were *public* in the sense that they were open to all, they were *free* only to the children of very poor parents.

South of the Potomac, education lagged far behind the New England example. There was no strong religious motive to establish schools. Moreover, people were widely scattered on plantations and farms, thus making it difficult to bring teachers and students together. *Old-field schools,* on worn-out plantation lands, taught the basic elements of reading and writing to some white children, but most of the planters hired private tutors. In the southern cities the children of wealthy parents were taught in academies and *dame schools* held in private homes. Children of poorer parents attended charity schools or went without an education.

In the Middle Colonies instruction was left to religious groups. The schools run by the Quakers were usually the best.

Colleges are founded. Through most of the seventeenth century the only colonial college was Harvard, established in 1636. The sons of southern planters who wanted higher education generally traveled to universities in England. In 1693, however, the College of William and Mary was established in Virginia. Eight years later a third colonial college, Yale, was founded in New Haven, Connecticut.

The Great Awakening led to the founding of four more colleges — Rhode Island College (now Brown University) founded by Baptists; the College of New Jersey

(Princeton) founded by Presbyterians; Queen's College (Rutgers) founded by the Dutch Reformed churches; and Dartmouth, a Congregationalist school. At about the same time King's College (Columbia) was begun by Anglicans in New York City. The only colonial college that was not church-related was the Philadelphia Academy (later the University of Pennsylvania). Established by Benjamin Franklin and his friends in 1751, it was intended as a training school for political leaders rather than ministers.

Interest in science grows. Some colonists began to develop a strong interest in science. A number of them formed the American Philosophical Society. Its members included such men as the Quaker naturalist John Bartram and the astronomer David Rittenhouse of Philadelphia. Its most famous member, however, was Benjamin Franklin. Franklin knew a great deal about chemistry, horticulture, soil erosion and drainage, navigation, electricity, and optics. Like many later American scientists, Franklin was interested in the practical application of scientific knowledge. He devised more efficient chimneys and carriage wheels, invented the bifocal lens, designed an iron stove called the "Pennsylvania Fireplace," and introduced lightning rods and rocking chairs.

Judged by present-day standards, colonial medicine left much to be desired. Doctors placed great faith in "physicking" and bleeding their patients. Most doctors had no medical training, only a short apprenticeship with an older physician. In 1765, however, a medical school was established in Philadelphia, and it soon attracted a brilliant faculty. Franklin's friend Dr. Benjamin Rush taught there and studied the causes of yellow fever and mental illness. Churchmen like Cotton Mather and Jonathan Edwards were supporters of inoculation against smallpox, though comparatively few colonists accepted this medical advance. The unscientific practice of medicine accounts in part for the high death rate of the colonial period.

Almanacs and newspapers provide reading matter. Many colonists got their

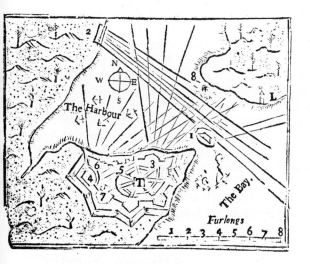

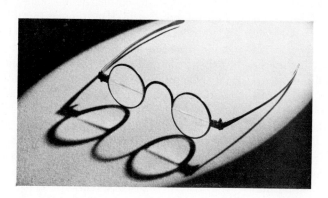

The inventive mind of Benjamin Franklin contributed to American life in many ways. His Pennsylvania Gazette *is believed to be the first American newspaper to print an illustration (top left) — a plan of Louisburg, the French fort on Cape Breton Island. Among Franklin's inventions were the Franklin stove (top right), which heated a room more efficiently than a fireplace, and bifocal glasses (above). Students will recognize the chair designed by Franklin (right) as a forerunner of the tablet-armed chairs used in classrooms today.*

medical information from yearly almanacs. These little books were popular reading matter during the eighteenth century. The almanacs offered weather predictions, calendars, recipes, poems, literary excerpts, jokes, and advice on many problems including physical ailments. The most popular was Franklin's *Poor Richard's Almanac*, which first appeared in 1732 and soon was selling 10,000 copies a year.

The first regular colonial newspaper was the *Boston News-Letter*, which appeared in 1704. It was a four-page sheet carrying stale European news and a few local business reports. By the time Ben Franklin took over the *Pennsylvania Gazette* in 1730, papers were printing more local news, some political reports, and also excerpts from English publications. But Franklin improved both the quantity and the quality of news in the *Pennsylvania Gazette* and eventually made it the most influential colonial newspaper. Franklin also started a magazine which bore the imposing title

The General Magazine and Historical Chronicle for all the British Plantations in America. Its content was entirely American: poems and essays from colonial newspapers and reviews of books and pamphlets published in the colonies.

Freedom of the press is defended. Colonial publishers had to take care that they did not offend British officials. If their articles were too critical, they might be arrested and fined or imprisoned, and their presses closed down. This happened to John Peter Zenger, a German printer and editor of the *New York Weekly Journal.* He was charged with libel for publishing articles which criticized the governor of New York. Zenger's colleagues hired an eminent Philadelphia lawyer, Andrew Hamilton, to defend him. For the British judges the only question was whether or not Zenger had printed the offending articles. For Hamilton the question was whether or not the articles were true. The jury accepted the lawyer's definition of libel and decided that since the articles were true, Zenger was not guilty of libel. This famous trial in 1735 paved the way for the establishment of two important principles — (1) freedom of the press in American journalism and (2) the right of the jury, not the judge, to decide whether printed matter is libelous.

The reading and writing of books increases. The growing prosperity and leisure of the colonists enabled more of them to read not only almanacs and newspapers but books and pamphlets as well. Most of the colonial writing in the seventeenth century had dealt with religion. Roger Williams, Thomas Hooker, Cotton and Increase Mather, and Jonathan Edwards all wrote pamphlets on religious matters. More widely read, however, was the poetry of Michael Wigglesworth, particularly his vivid description in *The Day of Doom.* The 1600's also produced some fine historians in John Smith, William Bradford, and John Winthrop.

Colonial writing of the next century reflected the rising standard of living. William Byrd II wrote a sprightly account of life and manners in Virginia and North Carolina. Judge Samuel Sewall of Boston kept a diary in which he recorded his financial transactions, his courtships, and his social engagements in great detail but gave only scant attention to religious affairs. (Neither Byrd's nor Sewall's diary was published until many years later.) A similar emphasis upon daily life rather than religious matters characterized Franklin's witty *Autobiography.*

Only a few of the colonists were able to collect libraries of their own. Even so, some of these private collections were surprisingly large for that time. William Brewster, one of the original Massachusetts Bay settlers, owned nearly 400 books at the time of his death. Two generations later, Cotton Mather and William Byrd II each built up libraries of more than 3500 volumes. Charleston was the first colonial city to establish a library supported by public funds. In Philadelphia, Franklin started the first subscription library,[4] and Boston, Newport, and New York quickly followed suit. By 1763 there were seventeen of these subscription libraries in the colonies.

The arts draw attention. The earliest settlers had no time for the fine arts. By the end of the 1600's, however, there were enough wealthy colonists to support silversmiths, cabinetmakers, and even architects. Of course many of the planters and merchants continued to import mahogany furniture, porcelain, glassware, and fabrics from England. But others took pride in colonial workmanship and bought from craftsmen like the silversmith Paul Revere. Peter Harrison of Newport was the colonies' finest architect. King's Chapel in Boston and Touro Synagogue in Newport are fitting memorials to his talent. Wealthy colonists were eager to sit for their portraits. As a result, painters like John Singleton Copley and Benjamin West not only became well-known for their oil portraits but made sizable sums of money as well.

Colonial musicians and dramatists had a harder time. The Puritans frowned on music and the theater and did little to en-

[4] A subscription library was open only to members, not to the general public.

courage these arts in New England. But New York, Philadelphia, and Charleston were more hospitable. There the upper classes attended concerts and performances of the best London plays. Even so, it was the late 1700's before there was enough interest in these arts to support American composers, dramatists, and performers.

Colonial towns influence the countryside. Most of the cultural life of the colonies was centered in the major towns. These cities also controlled colonial trade and influenced colonial politics. As the differences between urban and rural life increased, a rivalry developed between townspeople and the backcountry settlers. Farmers and frontiersmen were dependent on town markets to sell their produce and dependent on urban merchants for goods they needed. As the cities grew wealthier, the people of the countryside concluded that the merchants were living at their expense. A Connecticut farmer aired his resentment of the New York merchants when he expressed the hope that "the plumes of that domineering city may yet feather the nests of those whom they have long plucked." Though they were only a small percentage of the colonial population, city dwellers had a far greater influence on culture, economic development, and political power than the rural people.

Philadelphia is the most important city. Philadelphia was the leading American city in the eighteenth century. It had the largest population and had started the first colonial theater, the first subscription library, the first medical school, and the first art school. The stately brick mansions of the wealthy Quaker merchants were one of the sights of Philadelphia. When the very proper Bostonian John Adams paid his first visit to Penn's city, he noted in his diary that Puritan "morals . . . are much better, . . . our language is better, our taste is better, our persons are handsomer; our spirit is greater, our laws are wiser, our religion is superior, our education is better." Yet he soon found himself enjoying the lavish entertainment of Samuel Powel, one of Philadelphia's leading merchants. When Adams departed a few weeks later,

he bade farewell to "the happy, the peaceful, the elegant, the hospitable and polite city of Philadelphia." John Adams had discovered what another Bostonian, John Singleton Copley, had learned about Philadelphia; it was "a place of too much importance not to visit."

▶ CHECK-UP

1. What trends appeared during the 1700's in religion, education, science, literature, and the arts?

2. How did freedom of the press become an issue in New York? What was the significance of the Zenger case?

3. How did towns and cities play an important part in colonial life?

· ·

5 *A Colonial Pattern of Government Emerges*

Because the great majority of early settlers came from England, the political ideas and forms of government were English in origin. All of the English emigrants to the New World expected to take with them their fundamental rights as Englishmen. These included trial by jury, free speech, freedom from cruel and unusual punishment, and representative government. By and large, these rights became the basis for the thirteen colonial governments, and many years later were embodied in the United States Constitution.

Colonial governments vary. There were similarities as well as differences in the governments of the thirteen English colonies. Each colony had a governor, an advisory council, a representative assembly, and a system of courts. Yet even within this framework there was variation. By 1750, Connecticut and Rhode Island were the only colonies that elected their governors. The proprietary colonies — Maryland, Pennsylvania, and Delaware —

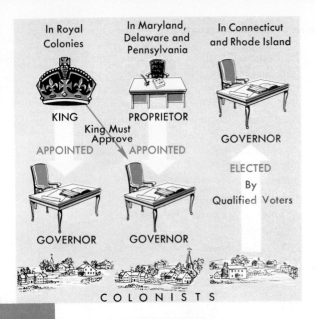

In Royal Colonies

In Maryland, Delaware and Pennsylvania

In Connecticut and Rhode Island

KING

PROPRIETOR

GOVERNOR

King Must Approve

APPOINTED

APPOINTED

ELECTED

By Qualified Voters

GOVERNOR

GOVERNOR

COLONISTS

THE COLONIAL GOVERNOR

The governor carried out the king's policy. Note that in most cases the colonists had no part in selecting him.

had governors appointed by the proprietors, who in turn bowed to the wishes of the king. The other eight colonies were royal colonies, with governors, judges, and advisory councils named by the king.

Colonial affairs are centralized in the Board of Trade. During the early years of settlement, as we have seen, Britain did not exercise strict control over her American colonies. Toward the end of the 1600's, however, the mercantile theory and the growing threat of war with France led Britain to tighten its colonial administration. The Navigation Act of 1696 (page 58) placed the administration of colonial policy in a Board of Trade and Plantations. The members of this Board were appointed by the king. They recommended candidates to be named royal governors, customs officials, and judges; and they sent instructions to the royal governors and supervised their administration. The Board also recommended legislation to Parliament. And it reviewed laws passed by the colonial assemblies, advising the king whether to accept or reject them. The Board of Trade got its information about colonial affairs from royal officials, colonial newspapers, and colonial agents stationed in London. Most skillful of these agents was Benjamin

Franklin, who for many years explained the problems of Pennsylvania to the Board of Trade and to Parliament.

The royal governors carry out the king's policy. Once the Board of Trade, Parliament, and the king decided on colonial policy, they informed the governors in America and held them responsible for enforcing it. The governors had the power to summon and dismiss colonial assemblies, approve or veto colonial legislation, grant pardons, and appoint officials. The veto and the power over appointments were the governors' most effective weapons against the colonial assemblies.

As time wore on, however, the governors found themselves in an uncomfortable position. If a governor vetoed legislation or quarreled with the assembly and then dismissed it, a new election had to be called. And a new election often resulted in an even more stubborn assembly. What was more important, the assemblies granted the funds out of which the governors' salaries were paid. In many instances, angry colonial assemblies flatly refused to pay the governors. One governor of North Carolina died in office with his salary eleven years overdue.

Some governors got along well with the assemblies and were liked by the colonists. But many of the governors were, to quote the New York Assembly, "entire strangers to the People they are sent to govern. . . . Their interest is entirely distinct." Franklin once charged that a number of the royal governors were "men of vicious characters and broken fortunes, sent by a minister to get them out of the way."

The councils act with the governors. Under the governor of a colony was a select group of 20 or 30 men who acted as his advisory council. The council also doubled as the upper house of the colonial legislature in some colonies; in other colonies it acted as a court of appeals. To be sure, the members of the council were colonists, not Englishmen. But, because they were drawn from among the governor's friends, they usually sided with him in case of conflict with the lower house.

Colonial assemblies are elected by the people. The colonial assemblies were the elective branch of colonial government. The earliest of these bodies was the Virginia House of Burgesses. Methods of electing representatives to the colonial assemblies varied. Generally the right to vote was limited to adult males who owned a certain amount of property and could meet certain religious qualifications. But the restrictions on suffrage varied from colony to colony. In the South a voter had to hold a given number of acres, but in northern colonies property was measured in terms of urban real estate, personal possessions, or annual income. If a man wanted to vote in Pennsylvania, he had to own 50 acres of partially cleared land or be worth 50 pounds, and he had to be a Christian. These restrictions on voting sound severe today; but in comparison with suffrage in England or elsewhere in Europe at that time, they were quite liberal. The surprising thing is that so few people took advantage of the opportunity to vote. Historians estimate that only about 25 per cent of the qualified voters cast their ballots in colonial elections.

Limited though the right to vote was, it nevertheless established the principle of representative government in the colonies. Furthermore, the practice of requiring a delegate to the colonial assembly to *live in the district he represented* was accepted early in the 1700's. This principle of "direct representation" differed from the English custom of "virtual representation," under which members of Parliament could represent districts in which they did not live.

Colonial assemblies increase their power. In general, during the 1700's, the colonial assemblies gained in power while the royal officials tended to lose power. The colonists maintained that only their assemblies should have the power to handle internal affairs. They felt that Parliament had no right to control their local affairs because the colonies had no representatives in that body. Thus, according to the colonists, all laws of Parliament levying taxes on the American colonists had first to be approved in the colonial assemblies. The colonial assemblies succeeded in gaining a large measure of control over taxation and the drafting of laws.

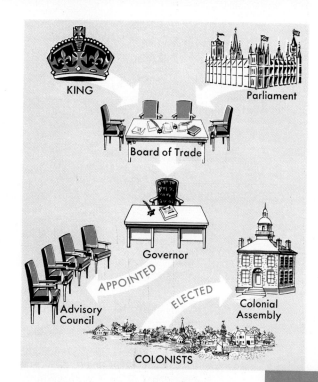

RELATIONS BETWEEN BRITAIN AND COLONIES

Note how the Board of Trade controlled the colonies, even though Americans had a voice in colonial government.

On the other hand, neither royal governors, nor king, nor Parliament considered that Parliament had surrendered its right to tax the colonies. As the British government saw it, the assemblies made their wishes known to the king and Parliament by passing laws. Each law was reviewed by the governor. If he approved, it was sent on to the Board of Trade and eventually might be accepted by Parliament. If the governor vetoed it, the colonial assembly would often pass a similar law and wait to see what the governor would do.

"Salutary neglect" aids the colonists. This difference in viewpoint between the colonies and the British government was of little practical importance before the 1750's. The economic value of the colonies was not yet fully realized. Moreover, their strategic or military importance did not dawn on the government until William Pitt became prime minister (page 43). To use the words of the English statesman Edmund Burke, the policy toward the colonies prior to the French and Indian War

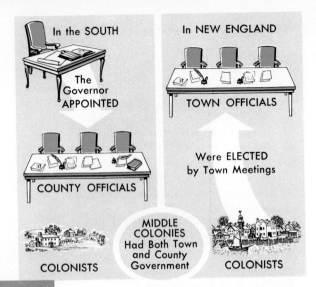

In the SOUTH

The Governor APPOINTED

COUNTY OFFICIALS

In NEW ENGLAND

TOWN OFFICIALS

Were ELECTED by Town Meetings

MIDDLE COLONIES Had Both Town and County Government

COLONISTS

COLONISTS

LOCAL GOVERNMENT IN THE COLONIES

Colonists maintained the English tradition of local self-government. Direct democracy was practiced in the town meeting. County governments existed in areas with scattered population.

was one of "salutary neglect." From the colonial point of view such neglect was a healthy thing. The lack of tight British supervision allowed the American colonists to evade mercantile laws and to gain the political experience which later proved so valuable.

Conflicts exist within each colony. It would be a mistake to conclude that the colonists were solidly united in their attitude toward British authority. Within each of the thirteen colonies there were differences that set one group of colonists against another.

(1) Speculators, for example, sought to buy up large tracts of land on the frontier and sell them at high prices to individual settlers. Frontiersmen bitterly resented this practice and tried to persuade the assemblies to prohibit it.

(2) Colonial currency was another subject of dispute. Debtors urged the assemblies to issue paper money or to mint coins, but the creditors sided with British authorities in trying to uphold the value of British currency.

(3) Religious quarrels arose in those colonies where all the people were taxed to support an established church, such as the Anglican Church in Virginia or the Con-

gregational Church in Massachusetts. Naturally those colonists who did not belong to an established church wanted the assembly to free them from such taxes.

(4) In all of the colonies backcountry settlers pleaded with the assemblies to provide better protection against Indians and more roads and bridges, but they seldom succeeded in obtaining these things.

(5) Finally, conflicts over representation in the assemblies caused an endless amount of trouble. The tidewater areas of the South and some towns and cities of the Middle and New England colonies had more representatives in the assemblies than did the rural population.

Internal quarrels over such matters caused riots and disorder in many of the colonies in the years before the American Revolution. British travelers in the colonies were not blind to these troubles. One predicted that if royal authority were removed and the colonists "left to themselves, there would soon be civil war from one end of the continent to the other." But after 1763 the British government altered its policy of "salutary neglect." By giving closer attention to colonial administration and by enforcing mercantile laws, Britain aroused anger and resentment in America. Playing upon these strong emotions, colonial leaders were able to unite the thirteen colonies behind their one common cause — preservation of their "fundamental rights as Englishmen." After the Revolutionary War, however, internal conflicts reappeared in the newly independent states.

▶ CHECK-UP

1. What was the role of the Board of Trade and Plantations? What sources of information were available to the Board? What was the role of Parliament in the administration of colonial affairs?

2. What were the respective roles of governor, council, and assembly in the colonies? What differences were there from one colony to another?

3. How had "salutary neglect" helped the colonists? What broad issues set one group of colonists against another? What common cause united the colonists?

Clinching the Main Ideas in Chapter 3

Expansion was the keynote of colonial life in the 1700's — expansion in the number of colonies, in amount of land claimed from the Indians, and, of course, in population. Most newcomers to the colonies, as well as the older settlers, were free to better themselves financially and socially. Social mobility — change in social status — became one of the striking characteristics of American colonial life. Eighteenth-century expansion had its tragic side, however, for it established the problem of slavery in America.

Most of the colonists earned their living by farming. Some supplemented this with fur trading and fishing. Still other Americans were engaged in trade and manufacturing. British regulations prevented manufacturers from expanding as they wished, but in spite of the mercantile laws they managed to prosper. The richer colonists had leisure time for cultural activities. Their support encouraged colonial craftsmen, architects, and painters.

It was these same people — merchants, planters, and professional men — who dominated colonial politics. They were leaders in the colonial assemblies, and they masterminded the struggles with the governors that resulted in greater power for the assemblies. By the end of the French and Indian War the merchants, lawyers, and planters were the recognized spokesmen for colonial public opinion. Since they felt most directly the effects of British administrative changes after 1763, it was natural that they should become leaders of the colonial opposition to the mother country.

Chapter Review

Terms to Understand

1. Board of Trade
2. established church
3. Great Awakening
4. class distinctions
5. grammar school
6. advisory council
7. naval stores
8. indentured servant
9. enumerated articles
10. triangular trade
11. representative government
12. Molasses Act of 1733
13. Woolens, Hat, and Iron Acts
14. Navigation Acts

What Do You Think?

1. "Europe, not England, is the parent country of America." Do you agree? Why?
2. Why was the triangular trade more profitable than direct trade between colony and mother country?
3. Why was there a scarcity of currency in the colonies? Why did the mother country forbid the colonies to issue paper money?
4. What interpretation of the word "representation" was used by Parliament? By the colonial assemblies? Why? What problems developed from this disagreement?
5. Why did class distinctions exist in the colonies? Why were class lines less rigid than in England?

Using Your Knowledge of History

1. Give an oral report on slavery in the New World. Tell where and why slavery was introduced, how slaves were obtained in Africa, and how the status of Negroes brought to the thirteen colonies changed from that of indentured servants to that of chattel slaves.
2. Prepare a chart bringing out the advantages and disadvantages to the thirteen colonies of the mercantile system.
3. Prepare a chart dealing with living conditions in New England, the Middle Colonies, and the South. Include such headings as occupations; imports and exports; education and recreation; literature and the arts.
4. Explain the role of each of the following in colonial government: governor, advisory council, representative assembly, and courts.

Extending Your Knowledge of History

Benjamin Franklin's entertaining *Autobiography* is available in several editions. The standard biography of Franklin is by Carl Van Doren. Esther Forbes has written *Paul Revere and the World He Lived In*, an excellent study of the artisan-patriot and eighteenth-century Boston. A comparable book about Philadelphia is Carl and Jessica Bridenbaugh's *Rebels and Gentlemen*.

CHAPTER 4

Liberty Tree

Britain's Colonial Policy Stirs Up Resistance

1763–1775

We cannot, I fear . . . , persuade them [the colonists] that they are not sprung from a nation in whose veins the blood of freedom circulates. . . . An Englishman is the unfittest person on earth to argue another Englishman into slavery.

EDMUND BURKE IN PARLIAMENT, MARCH 22, 1775

After the French and Indian War, Great Britain tried to establish firmer control over the thirteen colonies. The colonists, as we have already seen, were expected to supply raw materials to the mother country, buy finished goods from her, obey mercantile regulations, and pay enough taxes to cover the cost of defense and administration. During the war years British officials had blinked at some violations of the law rather than provoke a row with the Americans. After 1763, however, the British attitude hardened. This was reflected in stricter enforcement of mercantile legislation and in the passage by Parliament of higher taxes.

At the same time the colonial attitude toward the mother country was undergoing a change. Defeat of the French in North America made the colonists more secure. Security, in turn, bred self-confidence. Soon the colonists were not merely assuming but demanding the right to handle their own internal affairs, including taxation, in their assemblies. Parliament and King George III refused this demand.

It is true that before 1763, there had been some discord between the colonies and the mother country. But from 1763 until 1775 the colonists and the British government engaged in a dramatic war of nerves, punctuated from time to time by riots and disorder. Not until colonists and British troops clashed at Lexington and Concord, however, did actual fighting break out.

1 *The French and Indian War Causes Friction Between the Colonies and England*

Several disagreements between the American colonies and the mother country arose during the French and Indian War. Both wanted to check the power of the French and their Indian allies, but they disagreed over how to do this. British efforts to prevent the colonists from trading with the enemy were one source of trouble. Disagreement over the role of the colonial militia was another. British attempts to make the colonists help meet the costs of the war and of defense also irritated the Americans. And the war aggravated the currency shortage in the colonies. As we shall see, each of these problems caused friction, although they were largely forgotten in the celebration that marked the end of the war.

The colonists protest "writs of assistance." Although the colonies were permitted to trade non-enumerated goods (page 58) with France during peacetime, this trade became illegal when France and Britain were at war. Yet the colonists continued to do business with the French West Indies and New France even after Great Britain was officially drawn into the war in 1756. The colonists ignored repeated British warnings. The only concession they made was to conduct this illegal trade through neutral Spanish and Dutch ports. Consequently, when Pitt took office (page

. . . .

CHAPTER FOCUS

1. The French and Indian War causes friction between the colonies and England.
2. New British policies anger the colonists.
3. Colonial wounds are not healed.
4. Open resistance develops.

43), he authorized the colonial governors to do everything within their power to catch the smugglers. Also, Parliament approved the use of *writs of assistance,* or search warrants. These permitted customs collectors to search anywhere for smuggled goods. Armed with one of these writs, a customs official could break into private homes, search warehouses, and board ships to look for evidence that merchants were violating the trade laws.

When George III became king of England in 1760, Parliament had to re-issue the writs in his name. The merchants of Boston took this opportunity to lodge a protest. They hired James Otis, a young lawyer who was already a staunch foe of the royal governor of Massachusetts. Otis delivered a brilliant speech in which he charged that the writs violated the Englishman's right to be free of unreasonable search and seizure. "A man . . . is as secure in his house," said Otis, "as a prince in his castle." One colonist who heard the eloquent young lawyer thought that "Otis was a flame of fire! . . . American independence was then and there born." Actually independence had not yet been born, but Otis helped to stiffen the colonists' opposition to trade regulations.

Friction develops over the colonies' war effort. Another source of friction grew out of relations between the colonial militia and the British army. Except in case of war, each of the thirteen colonies was supposed to provide for its own defense. The colonial militia, in other words, was expected to defend the colonists against the Indians. But if war broke out with France, the British army and navy would help defend the American colonies. In actual practice, most of the money for arms, ammunition, and fortifications came from the British treasury. Moreover, the British provided most of the money for bribing the Indians to leave the colonists in peace.

Naturally, during time of war, the British expected colonial militiamen to fight with the British forces under the command of British officers. But after Braddock's defeat at the hands of the French and Indians (page 43), the colonists showed scant respect for the British army. At the same time, British officers felt contempt for the colonial militia. One commander described them as "a gathering from the scum of the worst people . . . who have wrought themselves up into a panic at the very name of Indians." Most of the colonial assemblies were reluctant to let their soldiers serve under British officers. The British General Amherst complained bitterly about "the sloth of the colonies in raising their troops and sending them to their rendezvous."

Financing the war is a problem. The British government had hoped that the Albany Congress of 1754 (page 42) would work out an agreement by which the colonies would share the cost of their defense. But this did not happen. As a result, when war broke out with France, the British government had to fall back on the unsatisfactory *requisition* system. This meant that Parliament asked, or requisitioned, the colonial assemblies to provide for their militia and contribute money or supplies for the British forces in America.

Most of the colonies refused these requests. Only Massachusetts, Connecticut, and New York came close to fulfilling their obligations. Other colonies claimed they were too poor to make any contribution. If their excuses were questioned, they pointed to the overdue salaries of their governors. Pennsylvania and Maryland, obviously too prosperous to plead poverty, dodged the requisitions on the grounds that their Quaker colonists opposed war. One British official complained that it was "the constant study of every province here to throw every expense on the Crown, and bear no part of the expense of this war themselves."

The currency shortage grows acute. The shortage of money in the American colonies was made worse by the war. Britain demanded that her troops be paid in cash but at the same time cut off the colonial trade which had brought in foreign coins. While all of the colonists felt the pinch, it was a dispute in Virginia that focused attention on the currency problem.

Patrick Henry attacks the crown. For a long time the Virginia House of Burgesses had paid Anglican clergymen in produce

— usually tobacco. When crop shortages caused the price of tobacco to rise, the clergy were in a position to make tidy profits. To prevent this, the House of Burgesses in 1758 passed a law providing that the clergy be paid in paper money, which had lost value, rather than in tobacco. But in 1759 Parliament set aside this act.

The clergy then sued for back pay, and one of these cases (known as the *Parson's Cause*) came to trial in 1763. Representing the Virginia taxpayers was a 27-year-old lawyer, Patrick Henry. Henry argued that the system of payment in produce was awkward. He criticized the Crown for setting aside the Virginia law and charged that this action was a denial of the rights of Englishmen. Henry also declared that George III, having "degenerated into a tyrant, . . . forfeits all rights to his subjects' obedience." The jury awarded the clergyman only one penny in damages, thus expressing its whole-hearted approval of Patrick Henry's fiery charges. The young lawyer's name became known throughout the colonies, and the next year he was elected to the House of Burgesses.

Victories cause rejoicing. The strains of war had made it clear that the colonies and mother country held sharply differing views on many questions. None of these differences was pushed to a showdown during the war years, however, for the British could not afford to provoke the colonists. For their part, the American colonists saw little reason to haggle about their rights, especially after the tide of war began to flow in Britain's favor. The capture of Fort Duquesne and Quebec, though achieved largely by British forces, caused great rejoicing in the colonies. When the peace terms of 1763 gave Britain control of French territory east of the Mississippi, there was still more celebrating. In the warm glow of victory, colonial grievances against the mother country were temporarily forgotten. Even James Otis went so far as to tell a Boston crowd that Britain and her colonies had identical interests. He warned: "What God in his providence has united, let no man dare attempt to pull asunder."

▶ CHECK-UP

1. How did the British government try to end colonial trade with the French after 1756? Why? What was the colonial reaction?

2. How did disagreements arise over the share of the colonies in fighting and paying for the war with France?

3. Why did the shortage of currency become more serious? What was the point at issue in the Parson's Cause?

4. How did victory over the French affect relations between the colonies and Britain?

· ·

2 *New British Policies Anger the Colonists*

Soon after the signing of the Treaty of Paris in 1763, the British authorities found that they had acquired a new set of problems. How, for example, were they to rule the French settlers in the St. Lawrence River Valley? What could be done to preserve the fur trade of the Ohio River Valley? How could the westward march of settlement be regulated? What policy should they follow toward the Indians in the region beyond the Appalachians? How could the colonies be made to obey the laws regulating trade? And how could the colonists be forced to pay at least part of the cost of colonial administration? Every one of these issues was important and had to be dealt with in the near future.

Yet the British government seemed incapable of planning an overall colonial policy. The leadership of the government changed frequently; problems were tackled by fits and starts; and decisions made by one ministry were later changed or repealed by another.

George III ascends the throne. British politics were further complicated after George III became king of England. The new monarch was opinionated and inexperienced in English politics. But he tried conscientiously to fulfill his obligations. George III soon found that Parliament was divided into many factions, each more interested in seeking personal advantages than in dealing with problems of state. These competing groups joined together to form shaky cabinets, which personal disputes were apt to topple at any time.

Toward the end of the 1760's, George III sought to build up the power of the monarchy by rewarding the "King's friends" in Parliament and by punishing his enemies. Any criticism of the monarchy and any suggestions for change or reform he took as a personal affront. As a result, those few members of Parliament who wanted to improve relations between Britain and the American colonies had almost no chance of getting their ideas across. After 1770, George III put his faith in Lord North, a politician as narrow-minded as the King himself. Together they set out to make the American colonies obey the King and Parliament.

The Proclamation of 1763 closes off the West. The first task facing the British government after the peace treaty of 1763 was to set up a policy for the newly acquired western lands. This problem had suddenly become important because of an Indian uprising called Pontiac's Conspiracy. When the war with France ended, British officials had cut off all bribes to their Indian allies. The Indians were also angry at English fur traders, who often cheated them. Meanwhile, French fur traders gave the Indians liquor and told them that French troops would soon return. A chieftain named Pontiac led the Indians in a sudden attack on British frontier posts, but the uprising was put down in 1764.

In the meantime, the British government had worked out a western land policy that it hoped would appease the Indians. The Proclamation of 1763 declared that the land west of the Alleghenies was "for the present" to be an Indian reserve. This territory was closed to settlers and speculators alike, and those who had already ventured into the region were to get out. Only the British Crown could purchase land west of the

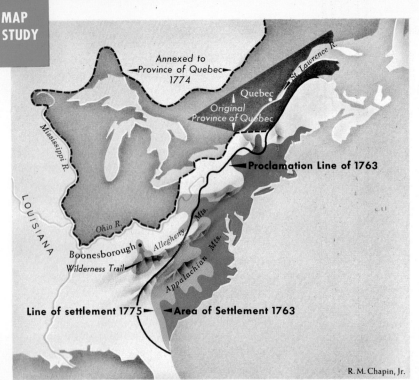

Annexed to
Province of Quebec
1774

St. Lawrence R.

Quebec

Original
Province of Quebec

Mississippi R.

Proclamation Line of 1763

LOUISIANA

Ohio R.

Alleghany Mts.

Boonesborough

Wilderness Trail

Appalachian Mts.

Line of settlement 1775 → ← Area of Settlement 1763

R. M. Chapin, Jr.

BRITISH ACTS CRAMP THE COLONIES

Both the Proclamation Line of 1763 and the Quebec Act stirred up resistance in the colonies. Compare the area of the original Province of Quebec with its extent under the Quebec Act. Note also that by 1775 settlers like Daniel Boone had pushed beyond the Proclamation Line.

mountains from the Indians, and no person could trade with the Indians unless licensed by the government.

The Proclamation of 1763 drew angry protests from the colonists. Some colonial assemblies charged that it violated their western land claims. These claims were based on their original charters, many of which had granted title to territory extending from sea to sea. (See the map on page 28.) Land speculators naturally opposed the Proclamation, for it practically put them out of business. But the real victims of the new policy were the individual settlers, many of whom had planned to head west as soon as the war with France ended. Some disregarded the Proclamation Line and crossed the mountains anyhow. Among them was Daniel Boone, who blazed the "Wilderness Road" into what is now Kentucky. By the late 1770's there was a thriving settlement at Boonesborough (see above map).

Grenville tackles the financial problem. Another problem that had to be faced was Britain's critical financial position. The British national debt had more than doubled during the war with France, and taxes had been greatly increased. George Grenville, prime minister from 1763 to 1765, realized that he could ask no further sacrifice from the people of England without risking serious trouble. Yet a yearly sum of 300,000 pounds was needed to pay for the costs of administering and defending the American colonies. It seemed only fair that the colonists pay half of this amount. Grenville believed that stricter enforcement of the mercantile laws plus a few new taxes would yield the 150,000 pounds per year needed from the Americans.

The British enforce trade regulations. Colonial customs receipts at the end of the war were enough to startle any minister of finance. Grenville found that it cost the British government 7600 pounds a year to collect 1900 pounds in revenue! One difficulty was that many customs officials were in league with smugglers. As the *Virginia Gazette* observed, the customs officials had learned that "the merchants' pay was more generous than the King's." So Grenville issued a series of orders to reform the colonial customs service. New writs of assistance were issued. British naval vessels were assigned to American waters to help catch smugglers. Dishonest officials were replaced by men who could not be bribed.

Finally, cases involving customs officials were moved from colonial courts to courts presided over by British judges and were tried without juries.

The colonial merchants led the outcry against these changes. They charged that colonial courts were being undermined and that writs of assistance violated a basic right of Englishmen. They protested, moreover, that British ships of war had no right to hover outside American ports and seize the cargoes of innocent shippers. British officials, ignoring these protests, were pleased to see the customs revenue increase from 1900 pounds in 1763 to 30,000 pounds four years later. Meanwhile, Grenville had pushed ahead with another measure to raise funds in the colonies.

The Sugar Act is passed. Grenville knew that there was widespread violation of the Molasses Act (page 58). It was believed, for instance, that four fifths of the molasses imported into Rhode Island was smuggled in from the non-British islands of the West Indies. Grenville therefore urged Parliament to pass the Sugar Act of 1764. By reducing the tax on foreign molasses from sixpence per gallon to three, Grenville hoped to discourage smuggling. He believed that the colonists would pay the new lower rates on non-British molasses without complaining. At the same time, the act raised the duties on sugar and certain other luxuries imported by the colonies. That Grenville was trying to raise money rather than to regulate trade was made clear by the preamble of the Sugar Act: "It is expedient that new provisions and regulations should be established for improving the revenue of this Kingdom." The money was to be used "for defraying the expenses of defending, protecting, and securing the British colonies and plantations in America."

Not only merchants and distillers but many other colonists in the North protested against the Sugar Act. They realized that any reduction in the rum-slave-molasses trade would deal an economic blow to the northern colonies. The Rhode Island Assembly sent an urgent petition to the Board of Trade, declaring that the colony could not exist without its foreign West Indian trade. But throughout the colonies there was further reason for concern — the fear that the Sugar Act threatened the power of their assemblies. If the government used the increased revenue to pay administrative expenses in the colonies, colonial assemblies might lose their control over the governors' salaries.

The Currency and Quartering Acts increase discontent. Grenville took two other unpopular steps. (1) He refused to let the colonists pay customs duties in colonial paper currency. The Currency Act of 1764 not only forbade the printing of paper money in the colonies but prohibited the use of paper money already in circulation for paying any obligations to the Crown. (2) Also, he devised a way to reduce the cost of maintaining troops in North America. Grenville believed that 10,000 British soldiers should be stationed in the colonies to protect them against Indian uprisings, to guard against any sneak attack by the French, and to maintain order. The Quartering Act of 1765 stated that where barracks were inadequate to house the British soldiers, public buildings, vacant houses, barns, and warehouses had to be provided for the use of the army at colonial expense. In addition, colonial assemblies were to furnish these troops with certain supplies — fuel, candles, vinegar, salt, bedding, cooking utensils, beer, cider, and rum.

The colonists lost no time in voicing their dislike of these new laws, especially the Quartering Act. Now that the French had been driven out of North America, the colonists saw no reason for a British army in America. Indeed, they looked upon Grenville's troops as an army of occupation. The Americans pointed out that there were few Indians in places like Charleston, Philadelphia, New York, and Boston, where the troops preferred to be stationed. The colonists especially resented the practice of congregating large numbers of troops in unruly colonies. These colonies correctly regarded the additional financial burden as a form of punishment.

The Stamp Act climaxes Grenville's program. To raise the remainder of the

150,000 pounds, Grenville suggested a direct tax in the form of "certain stamp duties." A stamp tax had been used in England for some time; and even before the French and Indian War, there had been talk of extending it to the colonies. To forestall criticism, Grenville gave the colonies a full year's notice of his plans. He even invited the colonial assemblies to propose alternative methods of raising the money if they objected to the stamp tax. When the assemblies came up with no new ideas, Grenville introduced the Stamp Act in Parliament. After a "languid debate," the measure was passed in 1765.

By the terms of this act, revenue stamps, costing from a halfpenny to ten pounds, were to be attached to newspapers, pamphlets, licenses, commercial and legal documents, deeds, playing cards, dice, advertisements, and almanacs. Violators of the law were to be tried in admiralty courts without a jury and punished by heavy fines. Grenville and his ministers expected the tax to be so evenly distributed that few people would resent it. To make the tax more acceptable to the colonists, only Americans were to be hired as stamp agents. Benjamin Franklin, in England at the time, opposed the act but assumed that the colonists would obey it. He even tried to obtain a stamp agent's commission for one of his friends in Pennsylvania.

The Stamp Act arouses opposition. Much to the surprise of Grenville — and Franklin — the Stamp Act aroused the fury of Americans. Publishers, lawyers, merchants, and financiers, who were hit the hardest, protested most loudly. But they rallied to their side anyone who purchased newspapers, almanacs, and playing cards. Colonial assemblies were quick to point out that the stamps were a form of *internal tax* (duty collected within the colonies), not a tax on imports for the purpose of regulating trade. Parliament, they grudgingly admitted, had the right to regulate their trade. But the assemblies insisted that only they could levy internal taxes. Patrick Henry introduced a set of resolutions in the Virginia House of Burgesses, one of which declared that the assembly had the "sole exclusive right and power to lay taxes and impositions upon the inhabitants of this colony."

During the summer of 1765 there were stamp riots in many colonial towns. Societies known as "Sons of Liberty" held parades of protest, forced stamp distributors to resign, and destroyed as many stamps as they could get hold of. Some British officials were tarred and feathered. In Boston, mobs ransacked the mansion of Chief Justice Thomas Hutchinson, destroying everything in the house and scattering in the street the manuscript of his *History of the Colony of Massachusetts Bay*. So far as Hutchinson was concerned, a rebellion had already begun. The "real authority of the government is at an end," he said; "some of the principal ringleaders in the late riots walk the streets with impunity; no officers dare attack them. No attorney-general prosecutes them, and no judges sit upon them." Most of the Sons of Liberty never were punished for their part in the Stamp Act riots.

The Stamp Act Congress voices colonial opposition. James Otis, by this time a member of the Massachusetts assembly, suggested a colonial conference to discuss the "common calamity of oppression." Delegates from nine colonies attended the Stamp Act Congress in New York in October, 1765. The more cautious members of this body drew up petitions to the King and to Parliament, in which they pledged allegiance to the Crown and promised obedience to acts of Parliament. But the bolder members supported a strongly worded Declaration of Rights and Grievances, in which they claimed for the colonists all the rights of Englishmen. They asserted that among those rights was freedom from taxation except "with their own consent, given personally or by their representatives." Since the colonists elected no representatives to Parliament, the Declaration demanded that control over internal taxation must rest with the colonial assemblies. Before adjourning, the congress approved a boycott, that is, a refusal to buy British goods, until Parliament repealed the obnoxious Stamp Act.

Historians have called the Stamp Act Congress "the opening move in the Revolution." It was important for a number of reasons. (1) As the first intercolonial assembly called by the colonists themselves, it helped to promote colonial unity. (2) The Declaration of Rights and Grievances presented the argument against taxation without representation. (3) This Declaration drew attention to the difference between British virtual representation and colonial direct representation (page 67). The delegates to the Stamp Act Congress, however, did not *ask* for direct representation in Parliament. They knew that, even if it were granted, they would be outvoted. They argued instead that the colonial assemblies should control internal taxation.

The Stamp Act is repealed. It was not the logic of the Declaration of Rights and Grievances that led to repeal of the Stamp Act but rather the economic effects of the boycott. The Sons of Liberty helped enforce the boycott by harassing people who bought British goods. Most of the colonial merchants supported the boycott. Though their business suffered, they knew they would gain in the long run if the system of tight Parliamentary control were broken. Trade with Britain fell off sharply, and English merchants were soon complaining to the Board of Trade. Finally the British government recommended repeal to Parliament. The Stamp Act was lifted in 1766.

The colonists ignore the Declaratory Act. Repeal of the Stamp Act did not mean that Parliament surrendered its authority to tax the colonies. Along with repeal went a new measure, the Declaratory Act. This act stated that Parliament had the right "to make laws and statutes of sufficient force and validity to bind the colonies and people of America . . . in all cases whatsoever." But the colonists were too busy celebrating repeal of the Stamp Act to protest against the Declaratory Act. A wave of loyalty swept through America, and statues were raised to George III. At this point the breach between Great Britain and the colonies might have been healed by wise statesmanship. Instead, however, the argument was renewed by the King's ministers.

▶ CHECK-UP

1. Why did the Proclamation of 1763 seem a wise policy to the British? Why did the colonists oppose it?

2. How did Grenville try to get the colonists to share the cost of defense and administration? Why did each of the following arouse great resentment: the Sugar Act, the Currency Act, the Quartering Act?

3. What was the Stamp Act? How did the colonies react to it? Why has the Stamp Act Congress been called "the opening move in the Revolution"? What led to repeal of the Stamp Act?

. . . .

3 Colonial Wounds Are Not Healed

The Townshend Acts renew the quarrel. In 1766 a new cabinet headed by William Pitt came to power in England. Pitt was sympathetic to the colonial grievances and might have been able to work out an understanding with the Americans. Unfortunately failing health forced him to withdraw from politics, and leadership of the cabinet then passed to Charles Townshend. Townshend did not share Pitt's desire to heal the colonial wounds. Rather, he wanted more revenue from the colonies so that he could lower taxes in England. Townshend realized that the Americans would protest any internal taxes he might suggest. He decided, therefore, to impose new duties on goods that the colonists had to import, for the Americans had not complained about these external taxes. The distinction between external and internal taxes struck him as "perfect nonsense," but he was willing to meet the colonists on their own terms.

The Townshend Acts, passed by Parliament in 1767, placed taxes on glass, lead, paint, paper, and tea imported into the colonies. Townshend also had Parliament

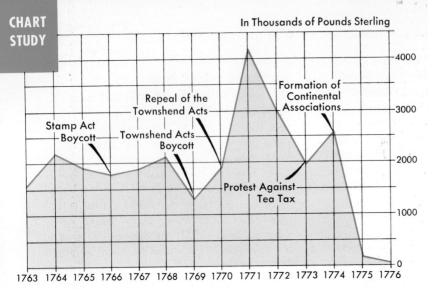

In Thousands of Pounds Sterling

Stamp Act
Boycott

Repeal of the
Townshend Acts

Townshend Acts
Boycott

Formation of
Continental
Associations

Protest Against
Tea Tax

—4000

—3000

—2000

—1000

—0

1763 1764 1765 1766 1767 1768 1769 1770 1771 1772 1773 1774 1775 1776

**RISE AND FALL OF BRITISH
IMPORTS**

*Fluctuations in the value of
imports from Britain reflect
American reaction to British
regulation. Note the decline
in imports following passage
of the Townshend Acts.*

suspend the New York Assembly for refusing to obey the Quartering Act. By disciplining one colony at a time, Townshend hoped to avoid Grenville's mistake of arousing all thirteen at once.

The colonies protest against the Townshend Acts. Colonial response to the Townshend Acts was immediate and emphatic. The colonists recognized that the suspension of the New York Assembly was a taste of what other assemblies could expect if they disobeyed acts of Parliament. Furthermore, the Americans were not impressed by the fact that the new taxes were external taxes. From their standpoint the taxes were unfair because the government had passed them to raise revenue, not to regulate trade. The money would be used to pay the salaries of royal officials and thus undermine the power of the colonial assemblies. Sam Adams of Boston summed up the colonial fears: "If our trade may be taxed, why not our lands? Why not the produce of our lands, and everything we possess or make use of? . . . If taxes are laid upon us in any shape without our having a legal representation where they are laid, are we not reduced from the character of free subjects to the miserable state of tributary slaves?" Another angry colonist, John Dickinson, wrote a series of essays entitled *Letters from a Farmer in Pennsylvania.* Dickinson argued that external taxes to regulate trade were legal; but external taxes designed to raise revenue, as in the Townshend Acts, were illegal because they had not been passed by the colonial assemblies.

Of course, not all the colonists followed the complicated argument about external versus internal taxes, and taxes to raise revenue versus taxes to regulate trade. Some Americans resorted to direct action. Once again there were riots in the major towns, tarring and feathering of British agents, and destruction of Crown property. When British customs officials tried to detain one of John Hancock's ships for payment of duty, angry Bostonians swarmed out to the wharf and drove the agents away "with clubs, stones, and brickbats."

Merchants and shopkeepers showed their displeasure with the Townshend Acts by renewing the boycott. They refused to handle goods subject to the Townshend duties, and many other British products as well. Much to the surprise of British officials, the colonists gave up drinking tea, let their frame houses go without paint, and cheerfully managed to do without other British goods. By the end of 1769, twelve of the thirteen colonies had joined a non-importation agreement. In that year alone, British trade with America declined by 700,000 pounds. While British merchants again sent urgent pleas to Parliament, further violence broke out in Boston.

Tension leads to the Boston Massacre. Following the protests over the Townshend Acts, additional British troops had been transferred to Boston. The people of that city naturally resented their presence and

78

chafed at the expense of quartering them. Furthermore, since the soldiers could work for pay in their spare time, they competed with Boston workers. There were frequent scuffles between townspeople and the "redcoats." Even the youngsters considered it good sport to pelt the soldiers with snowballs and rocks.

On March 5, 1770, these incidents reached a climax in the Boston Massacre. A large crowd gathered in front of the customs house to hurl insults and threats at the sentry on guard. When he called for reinforcements, Captain Thomas Preston and a small band of soldiers came to his aid. Thinking that the mob intended to break into the customs house, Preston ordered them to disperse. Instead they began clubbing the soldiers. In the confusion someone yelled "fire," and the soldiers did so. Five colonists lost their lives, including Crispus Attucks, a former slave.

Captain Preston immediately surrendered to the civilian authorities. When he and his soldiers were tried for manslaughter, they were defended by two Boston lawyers, John Adams and Josiah Quincy. Adams and Quincy had no sympathy for the British but felt that the soldiers should receive a fair trial. All were acquitted but two, who were given light punishment. Thereafter the tension growing out of the Boston Massacre died down.

Revision of the Townshend Acts brings a respite. For three years following the Boston Massacre, things were relatively quiet in the colonies. On the surface the quarrel seemed to be resolved. When Lord North became head of the British government in 1770, Parliament heeded his recommendation and repealed all of the Townshend taxes except the one on tea. The tea tax was left to remind the colonists that Parliament did have the right to levy external taxes. As George III remarked, "There must always be one tax to keep up the right, and as such I approve of the tea duty."

Interpreting partial repeal as a complete victory, the colonists resumed their tea-drinking habits and hastened to buy the latest British goods delivered to the shops.

Wrote one British official in Connecticut: "The people appear to be weary of their altercations with the mother country. A little discreet conduct on both sides would perfectly re-establish that warm affection and respect towards Great Britain for which this country was once remarkable."

The British attitude hardens. Beneath the surface, however, strong currents were sweeping Britain and America toward a showdown. In Great Britain there was renewed insistence that the mother country have absolute control over colonial government and trade. "The very word *colony*," argued one member of Parliament, "implies *dependency*." A member of the Board of Trade said: "The colonies are our subjects; as such they are bound by our laws." Many Englishmen feared that the colonies were growing so fast and becoming so prosperous that they would soon be able to "wrestle with us for pre-eminence." Also, there were urgent demands that the Americans be forced to pay a fair share of the tax burden.

Still other reasons explain the stiffer British attitude toward the colonies. Most Englishmen felt that Parliament should not share any of its powers with the colonial assemblies. Those "upstart" bodies had no right to challenge Parliament's authority to tax or to make laws for Englishmen in America. Colonists who had boycotted British goods or joined the Sons of Liberty were regarded as troublemakers. Most Englishmen looked upon Boston as the center of disobedience. They seldom referred to that city without adding adjectives like "mobbish," "unruly," or "saucy." In short, whatever sentiment had existed in Britain for seeking an understanding with the Americans evaporated in the early 1770's. The mother country seemed intent on forcing the colonies to obey all regulations of their trade and industry.

Some colonists desire a showdown with Great Britain. On the American side of the Atlantic, gains were made in the early 1770's by colonial leaders who favored a showdown with the mother country. These men were looked upon as radicals, since the majority of colonists at this time opposed

(*Continued on page 82*)

THE RISING TIDE OF RESISTANCE

Within ten years American resentment against the mother country's colonial policies rose to such heights that open rebellion finally broke out. This series of pictures shows how resistance developed in one part of the colonies — Boston and the neighboring towns.

 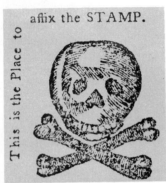

In 1765 Parliament levied a direct tax on the colonies. The Stamp Act required a seal or stamp (above left) to appear on newspapers, documents, and many other items. The colonists responded by printing a skull and bones (above right) wherever a stamp had to be affixed. Some Bostonians, the Sons of Liberty, took more drastic action, even tarring and feathering a few unfortunate stamp agents (right).

In 1768 the harried customs collectors in Boston requested additional troops from the mother country. As seen in the engraving by Paul Revere (below), a British fleet landed two regiments of soldiers in Boston. The stationing of these troops in the Massachusetts port further angered the townspeople, and many of them heckled the "redcoats."

In 1770 a clash between a Boston mob and the British soldiers resulted in the Boston Massacre. The Sons of Liberty circulated Paul Revere's engraving of the Massacre (right).

Three years later colonists disguised as "Mohawks" dumped tea into Boston Harbor (above) to protest the unfair advantage given the East India Company. Parliament passed the Coercive Acts to punish the "impudent" Bostonians. By 1775 the colonists were collecting arms for the day when they would have to resist actively. That day came in April, 1775, when Paul Revere (right, in a modern painting by Grant Wood) rode out from Boston to alert the countryside that British troops were marching to Concord to seize Patriot supplies. The outcome was open fighting between the Patriots and British troops at Lexington and Concord (below). The Revolutionary War had begun.

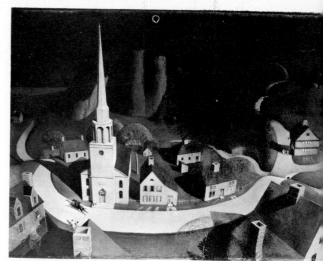

any drastic change in relations between Britain and America. A few years later, when the quarrel developed into a struggle for independence, the radicals won the name of *Patriots*. These people who favored stiff resistance to Britain, and who later urged complete separation, were drawn from all walks of colonial life. They included southern planters, New England merchants, artisans, small farmers, professional people, and urban laborers. The Patriots firmly believed that the time had come for a showdown with the mother country. John Adams, for example, wrote to Patrick Henry: "I expect no redress, but, on the contrary, increased resentment and double vengeance [from the British authorities]. We must fight."

Samuel Adams organizes the Committees of Correspondence. One of the most effective organizers of opposition to England was Samuel Adams of Boston. After graduating from Harvard, Adams studied law, and engaged in a number of unsuccessful business ventures. His real interest, however, was colonial politics. He bitterly opposed British authority and the colonial upper classes, both of whom he attacked while a member of the Massachusetts Assembly. Adams persuaded his friend Paul Revere to prepare an engraving of the Boston Massacre, so that other colonists could visualize the scene. He also sent hundreds of letters to colonial newspapers, thus keeping up the attack on British authority.

Adams' most brilliant stroke during these years was the organization of *Committees of Correspondence* for the exchange of ideas and plans of action. The first committee was established in Boston in 1772. Within a year a network of committees existed throughout the colonies. The members of these organizations, many of whom had been active Sons of Liberty, were ready to spread the alarm if the British committed any new "infringements and violations."

Dissatisfaction with British authority spreads. Sam Adams' influence was strongest in New England. There he could count on the aid of lawyers like his distant cousin John Adams, merchants like John Hancock, craftsmen like Paul Revere, and a host of other townsmen. These people could not have brought about the American Revolution by themselves. But in the early 1770's they were able to line up the aid of southern planters. As a result of exhausted tobacco lands and wasteful methods of marketing, many of the planters found themselves deeply in debt to British merchants. Their fields, houses, and slaves were heavily mortgaged. Virginia planters alone owed some two million pounds to British merchants. When southern assemblies passed bankruptcy laws allowing the planters to renounce their debts, Parliament declared the laws illegal. Many planters became convinced that the only way out of their financial difficulties was to break relations with Great Britain.

Many years later John Adams observed: "The Revolution was effected before the war commenced. The Revolution was in the minds and hearts of the people. . . . This radical change in the principles, opinions, sentiments, and affections of the people was the real American Revolution." Unyielding British ministers certainly had done their part to cause this "real American Revolution." But outspoken colonial leaders contributed to the conflict, for they used every opportunity to increase suspicion and hatred of British authority. By 1773, when the Committees of Correspondence had been established, they eagerly watched for the British government's next mistake. They did not have long to wait.

▶ CHECK-UP

1. What were the Townshend Acts? Why was this type of tax levied? Why were the colonists opposed to the Townshend Acts? How did the colonists show their opposition? What was the Boston Massacre?

2. Why did Parliament retain the tea tax when the other Townshend duties were repealed? How did the British colonial policy change?

3. Why were the Patriots considered radicals in the early 1770's? What steps did they take to strengthen opposition to Britain? Why did southern planters side with New England merchants in the dispute?

. . . .

4 *Open Resistance Develops*

The Tea Act angers the colonists. The huge British East India Company was almost bankrupt when Lord North came to power. Partly because of the colonial boycott of tea (page 78), a large surplus of that commodity had piled up in the Company's warehouses. Reduced sales and poor management resulted in serious financial loss. But the directors thought they could save the Company if Parliament would grant them a monopoly of the American tea trade. Lord North agreed, and in 1773 Parliament passed a Tea Act. It permitted the Company to export tea from its warehouses in England without paying the heavy export tax. This tea was to be carried to the colonies in Company ships and sold only by Company agents. Even though the Company had to pay the three-pence duty in the colonies (the only remaining Townshend tax), it still could undersell tea that was smuggled in from Holland.

Lord North thought that this measure would be accepted in the colonies, for it involved no new tax and it would provide cheaper tea. But the Tea Act was a mistake. It excluded colonial shippers from the transportation of tea, and it also deprived colonial merchants of one of their best-selling items. Patriot leaders promptly accused the British government of seeking to ruin colonial businessmen. This group also warned their fellow Americans not to let cheap tea blind them to Parliament's latest "act of aggression."

Boston Patriots hold a tea party. The people in Philadelphia and New York raised such a fuss about the arrival of the East India Company's tea ships that the captains refused to land the tea. "For the safety of your cargo, your vessels, and your person," the captains were advised to return to England. In Charleston, South Carolina, the merchants allowed the tea to be unloaded, but committees of planters and mechanics made sure that none of it was sold.[1]

In Boston the situation was complicated by Governor Thomas Hutchinson, whose attitude toward mob violence had been firmly fixed by the Stamp Act riots. He was determined to get even with the resistance leaders by allowing the tea ships to enter Boston harbor and unload. But the Patriots held mass meetings to protest the arrival of the tea ships and the payment of even "one farthing of duty." After such a meeting in December, 1773, the Bostonians donned blankets and Indian headdresses, marched to the wharves, boarded the ships, and dumped the tea chests into the water. The "Mohawks" were delighted with their well-planned "Boston Tea Party." In his diary John Adams described it as "the grandest event which has yet happened since the controversy with Britain opened."

Parliament responds with the Coercive Acts. Many colonists were shocked by this destruction of property. Both Benjamin Franklin and John Dickinson thought the East India Company should be repaid in full for "an act of violent injustice." George III, Lord North, and Parliament were furious. Since their authority had been challenged, they had to punish the offenders. Lord North devised a series of measures intended primarily to punish the colony of Massachusetts. These *Coercive Acts* were passed in 1774:

(1) The Boston Port Act closed the port of Boston until the owners of the tea had been repaid and until "the trade of Great Britain may safely be carried on there, and His Majesty's customs duly collected."

(2) The Massachusetts Government Act greatly limited the privileges of self-government in Massachusetts.

(3) An Administration of Justice Act permitted English officials in Massachusetts who were accused of serious offenses in connection with their duties to be tried in another colony or in England. This act was intended to assure the officials of a fair trial.

---

[1] Three years later this tea was auctioned off for the benefit of the Revolutionary Army.

(4) A new Quartering Act, which applied to all the colonies, placed on local authorities the responsibility of finding suitable quarters for troops.

In this dispute with Massachusetts, Lord North expected the other colonies to rally to Britain's side. But, while many Americans had disapproved of the Tea Party, Lord North miscalculated colonial response to the Coercive Acts.

The "Intolerable Acts" strengthen the Patriots. Sam Adams and the Committees of Correspondence swung into action. They dubbed the new laws the *Intolerable Acts* and pictured Massachusetts as a martyred colony, fighting to preserve the rights of all the colonies. The least the other colonists could do, argued the Massachusetts Patriots, was to come to the aid of the starving Bostonians. Soon after the Boston port was closed, supplies of food and clothing began pouring into the city, some of it from as far away as Philadelphia. Support for "our sister colony of Massachusetts Bay" was especially strong in Virginia. George Washington asked whether Americans should "sit supinely and see one province after another fall prey to despotism." Virginia's royal governor dissolved the House of Burgesses for endorsing this view. But the defiant burgesses met unofficially to conduct their affairs as usual.

The British chose this moment to pass another measure which still further aroused the colonists. The Quebec Act added to the province of Quebec the territory west of the Alleghenies and north of the Ohio River. The expanded province was to be ruled by the Crown. Preserving the traditions of New France, there would be no representative assembly, no jury trials, and of course no restrictions against Catholics. The Quebec Act pleased the French inhabitants of Quebec. (This helps to explain why, later on, Canada did not join the Americans in their fight for independence.) But the people of the thirteen colonies regarded the Quebec Act as another "intolerable" measure, believing its purpose was to deprive them of their western lands. They also felt that the act threatened their religious freedom. Naturally Patriot leaders played up these fears to unite the American colonists in opposition to the mother country.

The First Continental Congress assembles. During the spring of 1774 there was talk about holding another intercolonial congress. The Patriots liked the idea, for they remembered the successful outcome of the Stamp Act Congress. In June, 1774, Sam Adams persuaded the Massachusetts assembly to invite the other colonies to a Continental Congress to be held that fall in Philadelphia. According to the invitation, the delegates were

> to consult upon the present state of the colonies, and the miseries to which they are and must be reduced by the operation of certain acts of Parliament . . . and to deliberate and determine upon wise and proper measures to be by them recommended to all the colonies for the recovery and establishment of their just rights and liberties, civil and religious, and the restoration of union and harmony between Great Britain and the colonies, most ardently desired by all good men.

All the colonies except Georgia responded to this invitation. Their delegates were chosen in a variety of ways — some by the colonial assemblies, others by special conventions or by the Committees of Correspondence. Most of the 56 men who attended the First Continental Congress were merchants, lawyers, or large landowners. They represented every shade of opinion, from active Patriots, such as Sam Adams and Patrick Henry, to more conservative men, such as John Jay of New York and Joseph Galloway of Philadelphia. The "conservatives" were those Americans who hoped for a peaceable settlement of their differences with Great Britain.

There were many spirited debates in this Congress. But when the decisions were finally made, the delegates who favored a bold course of action had the necessary votes. This was due in no small part to Sam Adams' organizing ability. One delegate said of Adams, "He eats little, drinks little, sleeps little, thinks much, and is most decisive and indefatigable in the pursuit of his objects."

(*Continued on page 89*)

A NEW NATION TAKES SHAPE

The period of growing resistance against British rule and the revolution that followed form a memorable part of the American past. Americans have preserved many reminders of that past and of the people who helped to found the new nation.

Fort Ticonderoga on Lake Champlain (left) has been reconstructed to show what it was like in Revolutionary days.

The colorful drum at right once belonged to Ira Allen, brother of Ethan Allen. The Allen brothers were on the scene when the Green Mountain Boys captured Ticonderoga from the British in 1775. Paintings of scenes in American history also form a part of our heritage. Below, the Battle of Princeton (1777) was painted by the son of an American general, Hugh Mercer, who was fatally wounded there.

FOUNDERS OF THE NATION

Many portraits have survived of the men who helped found this nation. Among them are the portraits on these two pages, which represent the work of leading American painters of the colonial and federal periods. The bust of John Paul Jones was the work of a French sculptor.

George Washington at the Battle of Princeton, by Charles Willson Peale, from the Yale University Art Gallery, Maitland F. Griggs Collection.

John Paul Jones, bust by Jean Antoine Houdon, from the Addison Gallery of American Art, Phillips Academy, Andover, Massachusetts.

Thomas Jefferson, by Gilbert Stuart, from the Bowdoin College Museum of Art, Barney Burstein, Photographer, Boston, Massachusetts.

From left to right: Patrick Henry, by Thomas Sully, from the Colonial Williamsburg Collection. Alexander Hamilton, by John Trumbull, from the National Gallery of Art, Washington, D.C., Andrew Mellon Collection. James Madison, by George P. A. Healy, in the collection of The Corcoran Gallery of Art.

Samuel Adams, by John Singleton Copley, courtesy of the City of Boston, on deposit at the Museum of Fine Arts, Boston.

Benjamin Franklin, by Charles Willson Peale, from the Pennsylvania Academy of the Fine Arts.

John Adams, by Gilbert Stuart, from the National Gallery of Art, Washington, D.C., gift of Mrs. Robert Homans.

Of the many homes of the Presidents that have been preserved as memorials, Mount Vernon and Monticello are the best-known. The painting above shows the French general Lafayette visiting George Washington at Mount Vernon. Below are two rooms at Monticello, which Thomas Jefferson himself designed.

In the entrance hall at Monticello (above, left) is a seven-day clock invented by Jefferson. From the chair and worktable in his bedroom (above, right), Jefferson could look out at the surrounding gardens. Jefferson also designed buildings at the University of Virginia. The Rotunda (left) now houses administrative offices.

The Continental Congress takes action.
Proof of the strength of the Patriots came
when the Congress adopted a set of resolutions submitted by Suffolk County, Massachusetts. These Suffolk Resolves charged
that the Intolerable Acts had imposed a
"tyrannical" government upon Massachusetts. The people were urged to set up
their own government, prepare for war,
and break trade relations with the British
Empire. Then the Congress considered a
proposal for colonial union submitted by
Joseph Galloway and supported by all of
the conservatives and some of the moderates. This plan would have set up an
American legislature as a branch of the
British Parliament. When put to a vote,
six of the colonial delegations opposed the
Galloway Plan and five supported it. Thus,
the plan was defeated.

All factions of the Congress — Patriots,
moderates, and conservatives — joined
ranks in approving a Declaration of American Rights. This document accused Parliament of taxing the colonies unfairly and
burdening them with standing armies in
time of peace. Furthermore, Parliament
had dissolved their assemblies, disregarded
their petitions, and passed laws which were
"unjust and cruel." The Declaration then
flatly asserted that the colonists were "entitled to life, liberty, and property" and "to
a free and exclusive power of legislation in
their several provincial legislatures . . . in
all cases of taxation and internal polity
[political organization]."

Congress authorizes another boycott.
The final action of the First Continental
Congress was to call for another boycott
against Britain. This boycott, known as
the *Continental Association,* was a "non-
importation, non-consumption, and non-ex-
portation agreement." By these methods
the Patriots hoped to bring the British government to its knees. To enforce the boycott, committees were appointed in every
county, city, and town to watch for violations and to publish the names of offenders.
The actions of these vigilance committees
alarmed many colonists. Doubtless some
agreed with an Anglican clergyman, Samuel Seabury, who said, "If I must be enslaved, let it be by a king at least, and not
by a parcel of upstart lawless committee-
men."

**The British government refuses to
make concessions.** Despite occasional
grumbles, this latest boycott was very effective. British exports to the American
colonies declined in value from 2,500,000
pounds in 1774 to 250,000 pounds a year
later. Parliament was again flooded with
petitions from British merchants and manufacturers, all of them asking for concessions
to the colonies. In addition, two powerful
voices were raised in Parliament on America's behalf. Pitt left his sickbed to accuse
Lord North of following a "ruinous course."
"Every motive of justice and of policy, of
dignity and of prudence urges you to allay
the ferment in America." A few weeks
later Edmund Burke added a famous plea
for conciliation. But it was too late. The
vast majority of the members of Parliament
shared the determination of Lord North
and George III to put down rebellion in
the American colonies, no matter what the
cost. "Blows must decide whether they are
to be subject to this country or independent," said the King.

In a last-minute attempt to split the
united colonial front, Lord North offered
a Conciliatory Resolve in February, 1775.
It promised immunity from Parliamentary
taxation to any colony which raised enough
money to pay its share of the costs of defense and the salaries of royal officials.
Only a month later, however, Parliament
passed a Restraining Act which would
have severely limited New England's trade
with other parts of the Empire. This measure was soon extended to most of the other
colonies. Actually, news of the Conciliatory Resolve did not reach America until
after the King's soldiers and the colonists
had fought at Lexington and Concord.

**The opening shots of the Revolution
are fired.** The British commanding officer
in Boston, General Gage, had been named
military governor of Massachusetts. He
was instructed to arrest Sam Adams and
John Hancock for treason and to destroy
military supplies which the Patriots were
stockpiling in nearby Concord (map, page

91). Hearing of these new orders, Adams and Hancock slipped out to Lexington to avoid arrest. On Sunday, April 16, Paul Revere took a leisurely horseback ride to warn Adams and Hancock that the British were preparing to march. Two days later, the Boston Patriots learned that Gage was sending 700 British soldiers to Lexington and Concord. In the early hours of April 19, Paul Revere and William Dawes gal-

loped west to spread the alarm. They roused Adams and Hancock at Lexington and alerted the newly formed militia, called *minutemen*. But advance British units prevented Revere and Dawes from reaching Concord.

When the British soldiers marched into Lexington, they found a handful of minutemen assembled on the village green. Shots were exchanged and eight colonists were

CHART STUDY

BRITISH ACTION AND COLONIAL REACTION, 1765–1775

Britain's attempts to tighten its control over the colonies and the colonists' reaction to these attempts led to armed conflict between Britain and the Americans.

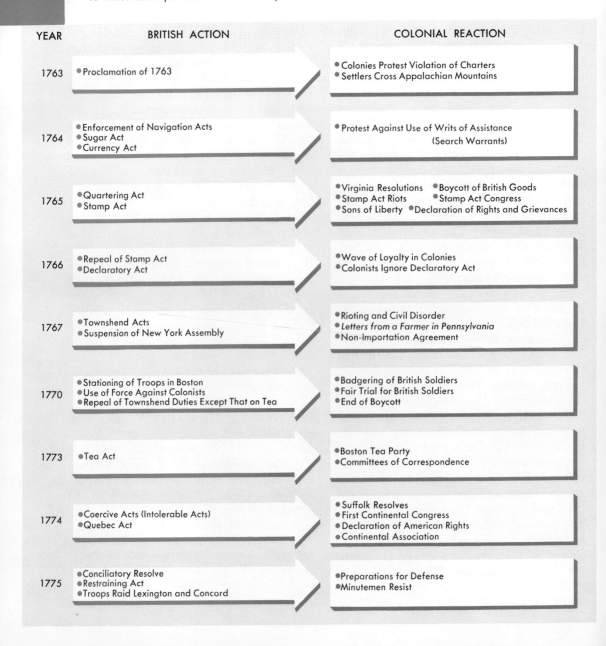

YEAR	BRITISH ACTION	COLONIAL REACTION
1763	• Proclamation of 1763	• Colonies Protest Violation of Charters • Settlers Cross Appalachian Mountains
1764	• Enforcement of Navigation Acts • Sugar Act • Currency Act	• Protest Against Use of Writs of Assistance (Search Warrants)
1765	• Quartering Act • Stamp Act	• Virginia Resolutions • Boycott of British Goods • Stamp Act Riots • Stamp Act Congress • Sons of Liberty • Declaration of Rights and Grievances
1766	• Repeal of Stamp Act • Declaratory Act	• Wave of Loyalty in Colonies • Colonists Ignore Declaratory Act
1767	• Townshend Acts • Suspension of New York Assembly	• Rioting and Civil Disorder • *Letters from a Farmer in Pennsylvania* • Non-Importation Agreement
1770	• Stationing of Troops in Boston • Use of Force Against Colonists • Repeal of Townshend Duties Except That on Tea	• Badgering of British Soldiers • Fair Trial for British Soldiers • End of Boycott
1773	• Tea Act	• Boston Tea Party • Committees of Correspondence
1774	• Coercive Acts (Intolerable Acts) • Quebec Act	• Suffolk Resolves • First Continental Congress • Declaration of American Rights • Continental Association
1775	• Conciliatory Resolve • Restraining Act • Troops Raid Lexington and Concord	• Preparations for Defense • Minutemen Resist

THE REVOLUTIONARY WAR BEGINS

The fighting at Lexington and Concord marked the beginning of the revolutionary conflict. The Battle of Bunker Hill was the first large-scale clash of arms. In the summer of 1775, Washington took command of the continental troops at Cambridge, Massachusetts.

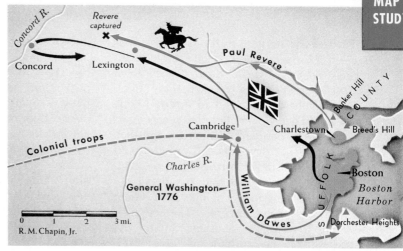

left dead or dying when the British pushed on to Concord. There they destroyed a small amount of ammunition which the Patriots had not yet removed. On the return march to Boston, the British suffered their heaviest losses. The colonists, like a swarm of angry hornets, stung the "redcoats" from behind trees and stone walls. A total of 273 British soldiers were killed or wounded. In contrast, there were only 93 colonial casualties.

The fighting at Lexington and Concord aroused colonists everywhere. To be sure, exaggerated versions of the encounter made the British troops sound like "butchers" and "massacrers of innocent people." But the fact that British troops had deliberately fired on American colonists was bound to have a strong impact on public opinion. The news of Lexington and Concord caused the members of the Second Continental Congress, who asse ıbled in Philadelphia in May, 1775, to raise a colonial army in order to fight back.

▶ CHECK-UP

1. Why did the colonists oppose the Tea Act? What was the result? What were the Coercive Acts? Why were they passed by Parliament? What was the response of the Patriots? How did the Quebec Act add fuel to the fire?

2. Why was the First Continental Congress held? How did conservatives and Patriots differ on steps to be taken? On what points did they agree? How was the Continental Association to be enforced? What were the results?

3. Why did the British and the Patriots come to blows at Lexington and Concord? What was the reaction of the members of the Second Continental Congress?

. . . .

Clinching the Main Ideas in Chapter 4

During the French and Indian War, friction developed between the colonies and the mother country. Regulation of trade was a major point of dispute, but shortage of currency and the control of colonial militia were other grievances. After 1763 still other problems widened the rift between the colonies and Great Britain.

Grenville's program, particularly his Sugar Act and Stamp Act, raised the question of whether Parliament or the colonial assemblies had the right to tax the colonies. In the Stamp Act Congress the Americans took the position that Parliament could levy only external taxes. Yet when Townshend tried external taxation, they decided that only *external taxes to regulate trade* were acceptable. The colonists found the boycott a potent weapon in fighting Parliament. It won repeal of the Stamp Act and revision of the Townshend taxes.

Destruction of the East India Company's tea, at a time when the Company was obeying an act of Parliament, posed a direct challenge to Lord North and George III. After the Boston Tea Party, the King, the prime minister, and Parliament were determined to bring the colonies to heel.

This was the purpose of the Coercive Acts, which the Americans labeled "intolerable." Those colonists who favored a showdown with the mother country used these measures and the Quebec Act to arouse public opinion. They dominated the proceedings of the First Continental Congress, and they made sure that the shots at Lexington and Concord were heard in the other colonies.

Some historians feel that the break between the American colonies and Great Britain was bound to come. The colonists, separated from the mother country by 3000 miles of ocean, had an empty continent at their back. "New soil," wrote the scholar Charles M. Andrews, "had produced new wants, new desires, new points of view, and the colonists were demanding the right to live their own lives in their own way." The British government was unable to adjust to these "new points of view," dominated as it was by statesmen whose chief concern was the regulation of the Empire in the interests of the mother country. The British ministers were no match for Sam Adams and his followers, who shrewdly used every British mistake to increase their own following. By 1775 the Patriots included merchants, planters, small farmers, and artisans who wanted a showdown with Britain. But they were not yet a majority of the colonial population.

Chapter Review

Terms to Understand

1. Parson's Cause
2. internal tax
3. Sons of Liberty
4. Coercive Acts
5. Stamp Act
6. boycott
7. Tea Act
8. Quebec Act
9. writs of assistance
10. Townshend Acts
11. First Continental Congress
12. Proclamation of 1763
13. Currency Act of 1764
14. Quartering Act of 1765
15. Committees of Correspondence

What Do You Think?

1. The English historian Green wrote: "With the triumph of Wolfe on the Heights of Abraham [outside Quebec] began the history of the United States." What did he mean?

2. In their discussion of Parliament's right to tax them, the colonists used such phrases as internal and external taxes, taxes to raise revenue and to regulate trade. Generally speaking, which type of tax was most acceptable to the colonists, and which was least acceptable? Why?

3. Which British policies would a New England merchant have found not to his liking? A Pennsylvania manufacturer? A frontiersman? A southern planter? A lawyer?

4. Grenville believed that 10,000 British troops should be stationed in the colonies to prevent French attacks and Indian uprisings and to maintain law and order. The colonists argued that Britain was burdening the colonies with the support of a standing army in time of peace. State the case for both positions.

Using Your Knowledge of History

1. List the reasons why the Proclamation of 1763 and the Quebec Act (1774) seemed to a British minister to be wise decisions. In a parallel column, explain why Americans rejected each of these "reasons."

2. Debate: *Resolved,* That after 1763 advantages to the colonies of being part of the British Empire outweighed disadvantages.

3. Write a brief account of the Boston Massacre, the Boston Tea Party, or the fighting at Lexington and Concord, as the event might have been described (a) in an American newspaper and (b) in an English newspaper.

4. List and evaluate the effectiveness of various methods and courses of action used by colonial leaders to mobilize public opinion against unpopular laws passed by Parliament.

Extending Your Knowledge of History

Read again Longfellow's "Paul Revere's Ride" and Emerson's "Concord Hymn" to see how these nineteenth-century poets dramatized the stirring events of 1775. In *The First American Revolution,* Clinton Rossiter traces the changing attitude of the colonists toward the mother country. Two readable biographies of Patriot leaders are John C. Miller's *Sam Adams* and Catherine D. Bowen's *John Adams and the American Revolution.*

CHAPTER 5

The United States Wins Its Independence

Battle of Yorktown

The battle, sir, is not to the strong alone; it is to the vigilant, the active, the brave. . . . If we were base enough to desire it, it is now too late to retire from the contest. There is no retreat but in submission and slavery! Our chains are forged. Their clanking may be heard upon the plains of Boston! The war is inevitable — and let it come! I repeat, sir, let it come!

PATRICK HENRY IN THE VIRGINIA CONVENTION, 1775

1775–1783

So spoke the eloquent Patrick Henry at the convention to choose Virginia delegates to a second Continental Congress. As the young lawyer prophesied, the Congress would do far more than strike back at the British for the clash at Lexington and Concord. Before it adjourned, it would conduct a long and bitter war for independence from Great Britain.

On the face of it, such a war seemed preposterous. The colonies were economically weak and politically inexperienced. Moreover, they did not even have a regular army until the Second Continental Congress authorized the raising of troops in 1775. Great Britain, on the other hand, was a leading world power.

Nevertheless, the American colonies eventually secured their freedom. Among the factors contributing to their victory were the persistence of Patriot colonists, the inspiring leadership of George Washington, the generous aid of the French, and a large dash of luck. How these forces combined to win the independence of the United States will be told in this chapter.

1 *The American Patriots Declare Their Independence*

The Second Continental Congress assembles. Before the First Continental Congress (page 89) adjourned in the fall of 1774, it had made plans for another assembly to be held the next spring if colonial grievances still had not been resolved. As we have seen, tension between the colonies and the mother country increased during that winter; and in April, redcoats and militiamen battled each other in Massachusetts. News of this fighting greeted the delegates who assembled in Philadelphia in May, 1775, for the Second Continental Congress.

The delegates were a distinguished group, many of them having served in the First Continental Congress. Three of them were destined to become Presidents of the United States (George Washington, John Adams, and Thomas Jefferson). A few delegates still hoped to patch up the differences with Britain, but the majority believed that only a show of armed strength by the Americans could win concessions. The Patriots felt that Britain would never come to terms with colonists who had resisted the mother country with force. They believed that complete independence was the only sensible objective. Nevertheless, the Patriots had to move cautiously. Although they were able to elect John Hancock president of the Congress, they did not always command a majority of the

CHAPTER FOCUS

votes. "Every important step," John Adams recalled, "was opposed, and carried by bare majorities."

Congress takes action. The first problem confronting Congress was what to do about the situation in Massachusetts. After halting the British advance at Concord, the minutemen had driven the redcoats back to Boston. Meanwhile, hundreds of volunteers swelled the ranks of the Massachusetts militia.

Congress decided to raise a Continental Army "for the defense of American liberty" and to incorporate the Massachusetts militiamen into this organization. At the suggestion of John Adams, George Washington was named commander-in-chief. Well-known for his role in the French and Indian War, a respected member of the Virginia House of Burgesses, and a staunch supporter of the colonial cause, Washington was an obvious choice. His selection was fortunate; for he had the wisdom, the patience, and the courage to persist in what often seemed like a hopeless struggle. Without Washington, it is doubtful that independence could have been achieved.

The vote in favor of Washington as commanding officer was unanimous, but Congress had a difficult time deciding on its policy toward Britain. In July, 1775, it adopted a "Declaration of the Causes and Necessity of Taking up Arms" to explain to King and Parliament why the colonists were fighting the British in Boston. But, they insisted near the end of this document, "we mean not to dissolve that union which has so long and so happily subsisted between us, and which we sincerely wish to see restored." The Congress also endorsed an Olive Branch Petition, written by the moderate John Dickinson. It begged George III to restrain his ministers and Parliament until an understanding could be worked out.

British policy grows harsher. During the summer and fall of 1775 most American colonists doubtless wished to preserve their ties with the British Empire. In the Second Continental Congress, too, those who wanted to reach a settlement controlled the

An old engraving of the Battle of Bunker Hill shows Charlestown in flames as British cannon bombard colonial forces on the peninsula.

BOSTON

CHARLES TOWN

majority of votes. Had the British government accepted the Olive Branch Petition, possibly discussions might have led to a compromise. But George III angrily rejected the petition as coming from an illegal assembly. He countered with a proclamation declaring the American colonies to be in a state of rebellion. He also approved an act of Parliament which prohibited all trade and other dealings with the colonies. Matters were made worse when the King sent 30,000 British troops plus foreign mercenaries (hired soldiers) to crush the rebellion. Many of the foreign troops were German soldiers called *Hessians*. Benjamin Franklin pointed out the irony in the British government's paying German soldiers to kill American colonists. Throughout the war, the presence of the Hessians stirred the colonists to greater resistance.

Colonial forces drive the British from Boston. Following the British retreat to Boston, colonial forces blockaded that city. Some of them occupied high ground in Charlestown (map, page 91), from which artillery could command the city. Unfortunately for the colonial cause, however, the Massachusetts militia lacked cannon.

On June 17, 1775, General Gage attacked the Americans on Breed's Hill in Charlestown, and after a bloody encounter (now known as the Battle of Bunker Hill) managed to dislodge them. Twice the colonial militia fought off the advancing British regulars. But the colonists ran short of am-

munition and had to withdraw as the third British assault was launched. Nevertheless, the Americans inflicted staggering losses on the British. General Gage reported to his superiors: "These people show a spirit and conduct against us they never showed against the French."

Two weeks after the Battle of Bunker Hill, Washington took command of the American army. After many discouraging months drilling the raw militiamen, he was able in March, 1776, to fortify Dorchester Heights overlooking Boston. For this purpose he used cannon which had been captured at Fort Ticonderoga and dragged overland to Massachusetts.[1] General William Howe, the new British commander, realized that the English position could not be defended. Howe and his troops evacuated Boston and sailed for Halifax, Nova Scotia, taking along a thousand gloomy British sympathizers.

Fighting breaks out elsewhere. After Patriot forces had captured Fort Ticonderoga and nearby Crown Point, the way to Canada was open. Realizing the value of Canada to the British as a base for attack, Washington urged Congress to take advantage of this opportunity. If Canada fell into American hands, Washington wrote, "success I think will most certainly crown our virtuous struggles." If it remained un-

---

[1] In May, 1775, Ethan Allen and the "Green Mountain Boys" had seized the British fort at Ticonderoga in northeastern New York.

der British control, "the contest at best will be doubtful, hazardous and bloody."

Late in 1775, Congress sent an expedition under General Richard Montgomery against Montreal and another under Colonel Benedict Arnold against Quebec. Montreal fell, but the combined forces failed to capture Quebec. In this fighting Arnold was wounded and Montgomery killed. Benedict Arnold and his men spent a miserable winter outside Quebec. When British reinforcements arrived in the spring, the sick and starving American troops had to withdraw to Ticonderoga. American hopes that the Canadians would join in the fight against the British were disappointed. The Canadians, satisfied with the Quebec Act (page 84), showed no desire to take part in the American rebellion.

There was better news from the South. During February, 1776, the Americans had won a sharp engagement against British sympathizers at Moore's Creek, North Carolina. A few months later, a force of 6000 militiamen successfully fought off a British naval attack on Charleston, South Carolina.

Thomas Paine speaks out for independence. Once the Patriots had taken up arms against the British, expressions of loyalty to the King and courteous petitions to Parliament seemed ridiculous. During the winter of 1775–1776 more and more Americans came to believe that severing all ties with Great Britain was the wisest course of action. A small pamphlet called *Common Sense* fanned enthusiasm for independence. Its author was Thomas Paine, an English tradesman who had been in America only a year. Paine modestly said, "I offer nothing more than simple facts, plain arguments, and common sense." Yet his pamphlet was so forceful and convincing that 120,000 copies were sold in three months.

Washington, Franklin, and other Patriots did their best to spread Paine's "flaming arguments." This was understandable, for the gist of Paine's message was "'tis time to part." He argued for independence on economic grounds: "As Europe is our market for trade, we ought to form no political connection with any part of it. 'Tis the true interest of America to steer clear of European contentions, which she can never do while, by her dependence on Britain, she is made the make-weight in the scale of British politics." Paine appealed to American pride: "There is something very absurd in supposing a Continent to be perpetually governed by an island." And he heaped sarcasm on George III: "Of more worth is one honest man to society, and in the sight of God, than all the crowned ruffians that ever lived." Some of Paine's charges about British tyranny were exaggerated, but this made his pamphlet all the more popular in the colonies. After the publication of *Common Sense*, public opinion veered sharply toward independence.

The colonies declare their independence. The final ties binding the American colonies to Great Britain snapped in the spring and summer of 1776. First, the Continental Congress opened American ports to the trade of all nations except Britain. In effect, this was a declaration of economic independence, for it severed commercial ties with Britain. In June, Richard Henry Lee, a delegate from Virginia, made the following proposal:

> That these United Colonies are, and of right ought to be, free and independent States, that they are absolved from all allegiance to the British Crown, and that all political connection between them and the State of Great Britain is, and ought to be, totally dissolved.

Shortly afterwards Congress appointed a committee of five — Thomas Jefferson, John Adams, Benjamin Franklin, Roger Sherman, and Robert R. Livingston — to prepare a document explaining the reasons "which impelled us to this mighty resolution." The committee asked Jefferson to prepare the first draft. Franklin and Adams made a few suggestions, and Congress approved further alterations in the document. On July 2, 1776, Congress endorsed Lee's resolution, and on July 4 it formally adopted Jefferson's Declaration of Independence. A few days later the text was read publicly in Philadelphia, and copies soon became available to all Americans. (See the next three pages.)

(*Text continued on page 100.*)

THE
DECLARATION OF INDEPENDENCE

In Congress, July 4, 1776
The Unanimous Declaration of the
Thirteen United States of America,

WHEN in the course of human events, it becomes necessary for one people to dissolve the political bands which have connected them with another, and to assume among the powers of the earth the separate and equal station to which the laws of nature and of nature's God entitle them, a decent respect to the opinions of mankind requires that they should declare the causes which impel them to the separation.[1]

We hold these truths to be self-evident, that all men are created equal, that they are endowed by their Creator with certain unalienable rights, that among these are life, liberty, and the pursuit of happiness. That to secure these rights, governments are instituted among men, deriving their just powers from the consent of the governed; that whenever any form of government becomes destructive of these ends, it is the right of the people to alter or to abolish it, and to institute new government, laying its foundation on such principles and organizing its powers in such form, as to them shall seem most likely to effect their safety and happiness. Prudence, indeed, will dictate that governments long established should not be changed for light and transient causes; and accordingly all experience hath shown, that mankind are more disposed to suffer, while evils are sufferable, than to right themselves by abolishing the forms to which they are accustomed. But when a long train of abuses and usurpations, pursuing invariably the same object, evinces a design to reduce them under absolute despotism, it is their right, it is their duty, to throw off such government, and to provide new guards for their future security. Such has been the patient sufferance of these colonies; and such is now the necessity which constrains them to alter their former systems of government. The history of the present King of Great Britain is a history of repeated injuries and usurpations, all having in direct object the establishment of an absolute tyranny over these states. To prove this, let facts be submitted to a candid world.

He has refused his assent to laws, the most wholesome and necessary for the public good.

He has forbidden his governors to pass laws of immediate and pressing importance, unless suspended in their operation till his assent should be obtained; and when so suspended, he has utterly neglected to attend to them.

He has refused to pass other laws for the accommodation of large districts of people, unless those people would relinquish the right of representation in the legislature, a right inestimable to them and formidable to tyrants only.

He has called together legislative bodies at places unusual, uncomfortable, and distant from the depository of their public records, for the sole purpose of fatiguing them into compliance with his measures.

He has dissolved representative houses repeatedly, for opposing with manly firmness his invasions on the rights of the people.

He has refused for a long time, after such dissolutions, to cause others to be elected; whereby the legislative powers, incapable of annihilations, have returned to the people at large for their exercise; the state remain-

---

[1] The Declaration has been modernized in spelling, capitalization, and punctuation.

ing in the meantime exposed to all the dangers of invasion from without and convulsions within.

He has endeavored to prevent the population of these states; for that purpose obstructing the laws for naturalization of foreigners, refusing to pass others to encourage their migrations hither, and raising the conditions of new appropriations of lands.

He has obstructed the administration of justice, by refusing his assent to laws for establishing judiciary powers.

He has made judges dependent on his will alone, for the tenure of their offices, and the amount and payment of their salaries.

He has erected a multitude of new offices, and sent hither swarms of officers to harass our people, and eat out their substance.

He has kept among us, in times of peace, standing armies without the consent of our legislatures.

He has affected to render the military independent of and superior to the civil power.

He has combined with others to subject us to a jurisdiction foreign to our constitution, and unacknowledged by our laws; giving his assent to their acts of pretended legislation:

For quartering large bodies of armed troops among us;

For protecting them, by a mock trial, from punishment for any murders which they should commit on the inhabitants of these states;

For cutting off our trade with all parts of the world;

For imposing taxes on us without our consent;

For depriving us, in many cases, of the benefits of trial by jury;

For transporting us beyond seas to be tried for pretended offences;

For abolishing the free system of English laws in a neighboring province, establishing therein an arbitrary government, and enlarging its boundaries so as to render it at once an example and fit instrument for introducing the same absolute rule into these colonies;

For taking away our charters, abolishing our most valuable laws, and altering fundamentally the forms of our governments;

For suspending our own legislatures, and declaring themselves invested with power to legislate for us in all cases whatsoever.

He has abdicated government here, by declaring us out of his protection and waging war against us.

He has plundered our seas, ravaged our coasts, burnt our towns, and destroyed the lives of our people.

He is at this time transporting large armies of foreign mercenaries to complete the works of death, desolation, and tyranny, already begun with circumstances of cruelty and perfidy scarcely paralleled in the most barbarous ages, and totally unworthy the head of a civilized nation.

He has constrained our fellow citizens taken captive on the high seas to bear arms against their country, to become the executioners of their friends and brethren, or to fall themselves by their hands.

He has excited domestic insurrections amongst us, and has endeavored to bring on the inhabitants of our frontiers, the merciless Indian savages, whose known rule of warfare is an undistinguished destruction of all ages, sexes, and conditions.

In every stage of these oppressions we have petitioned for redress in the most humble terms. Our repeated petitions have been answered only by repeated injury. A prince, whose character is thus marked by every act which may define a tyrant, is unfit to be the ruler of a free people.

Nor have we been wanting in attentions to our British brethren. We have warned them from time to time of attempts by their legislature to extend an unwarrantable jurisdiction over us. We have reminded them of the circumstances of our emigration and settlement here. We have appealed to their native justice and magnanimity, and we have conjured them by the ties of our common kindred to disavow these usurpations, which would inevitably interrupt our connections and correspondence. They too have been deaf to the voice of justice and of consanguinity. We must, therefore, acquiesce in the necessity which denounces our separation, and hold them, as we hold the rest of mankind, enemies in war, in peace friends.

We, therefore, the representatives of the United States of America, in General Congress, Assembled, appealing to the Supreme Judge of the world for the rectitude of our intentions, do, in the name, and by authority of the good people of these colonies, solemnly publish and declare, that these united colonies are, and of right ought to be, free and independent states; that they are absolved from all allegiance to the British Crown, and that all political connection between them and the State of Great Britain is and ought to be totally dissolved; and that as free and independent states, they have full power to levy war, conclude peace, contract alliances, establish commerce, and to do all other acts and things which independent states may of right do. And for the support of this declaration, with a firm reliance on the protection of divine Providence, we mutually pledge to each other our lives, our fortunes, and our sacred honor.

JOHN HANCOCK, *President*

NEW HAMPSHIRE
Josiah Bartlett
William Whipple
Matthew Thornton

MASSACHUSETTS BAY
Samuel Adams
John Adams
Robert Treat Paine
Elbridge Gerry

NEW YORK
William Floyd
Philip Livingston
Francis Lewis
Lewis Morris

NEW JERSEY
Richard Stockton
John Witherspoon

NEW JERSEY (cont'd.)
Francis Hopkinson
John Hart
Abraham Clark

PENNSYLVANIA
Robert Morris
Benjamin Rush
Benjamin Franklin
John Morton
George Clymer
James Smith
George Taylor
James Wilson
George Ross

DELAWARE
Caesar Rodney
George Read
Thomas M'Kean

MARYLAND
Samuel Chase
William Paca
Thomas Stone
Charles Carroll
of Carrollton

RHODE ISLAND
Stephen Hopkins
William Ellery

CONNECTICUT
Roger Sherman
Samuel Huntington
William Williams
Oliver Wolcott

VIRGINIA
George Wythe
Richard Henry Lee
Thomas Jefferson

VIRGINIA (cont'd.)
Benjamin Harrison
Thomas Nelson, Jr.
Francis Lightfoot Lee
Carter Braxton

NORTH CAROLINA
William Hooper
Joseph Hewes
John Penn

SOUTH CAROLINA
Edward Rutledge
Thomas Heyward, Jr.
Thomas Lynch, Jr.
Arthur Middleton

GEORGIA
Button Gwinnett
Lyman Hall
George Walton

The Declaration proclaims human liberty. The Declaration of Independence has proved to be a vital document in modern history. It argues the case for political liberty so forcefully that it has influenced not only American history but also the French Revolution, the movement for independence in Latin America, and the recent breakup of colonial empires in Asia and Africa. Oppressed people everywhere have rallied to Jefferson's call for freedom:

> We hold these truths to be self-evident, that all men are created equal, that they are endowed by their Creator with certain unalienable Rights, that among these are Life, Liberty, and the pursuit of Happiness.

When a government is "destructive" of these rights, stated the Declaration, the people are justified in seeking a new form of government.

After setting forth these general principles, the Declaration continued with specific charges against George III. The King was guilty of trying to establish "an absolute tyranny over these states," declared Jefferson; and to prove it, he listed all of the British government's "repeated injuries and usurpations." Many of these charges were exaggerated, but few Americans complained that Jefferson overstated the case against the King. The third and final section of the Declaration was a restatement of Richard Henry Lee's resolution that the colonies should be "free and independent States."

The Declaration forces the colonists to choose sides. The adoption of the Declaration of Independence marked a turning point in the quarrel between the mother country and the colonies. At the end of the French and Indian War, few — if any — of the English colonists wanted to break away from the British Empire. Yet, only thirteen years later, many of them cheered the Declaration of Independence. For the Patriots the adoption of the Declaration was a triumph. For many of the moderates and conservatives, it was something of a personal tragedy. They now had to decide whether to support King and Parliament or throw in their lot with the rebels.

▶ CHECK-UP

1. What steps were taken by the Second Continental Congress "for the defense of American liberty"? What evidence is there of sentiment favoring union with Britain? What British steps widened the breach between mother country and colonies?

2. How were the British driven from Boston? Why did Patriot forces invade Canada? What were the results?

3. On what grounds did Thomas Paine call for independence? By what steps did the colonies come to declare their independence?

4. What are the three parts of the Declaration of Independence? Why has this document been precious to all peoples seeking freedom? What problem did the Declaration pose for moderates and conservatives?

. . . .

2 *The Americans Fight Against Heavy Odds*

American allegiance is divided. Although the Declaration of Independence severed the ties between Great Britain and America, it did not unite all the colonists. Historians estimate that in 1776 roughly a third of the people were loyal to King and Parliament, a third were Patriots, and the rest were not committed to either side.

The Loyalists. Those Americans who opposed independence were known as Loyalists. The Patriots also scornfully called them *Tories*, a term applied in England to the political friends of George III and Lord North. Some of the Loyalists had been as fervent as any Patriot in demanding the rights of Englishmen. But they sincerely opposed separation from Britain as a solution to colonial problems. Loyalists were found in all groups in colonial society. Some were wealthy merchants and landowners who feared for their property if the Patriots won control in America. These people preferred the security of British rule, despite the inconvenience of British regulations, to the risk of popular rule by uneducated colonists. Many professional people — doctors, lawyers, and the Anglican clergy — wanted to preserve the ties with Great Britain. These Loyalists were prominent in the high society of Boston, Newport, New York, Philadelphia, Charleston, and Savannah. Throughout the colonies there also were scattered pockets of small farmers who sided with the British. Some of them simply wanted to take an opposite stand from Patriot leaders in their colonial assemblies; others felt a genuine loyalty to the British Crown.

After the adoption of the Declaration, some of the Loyalists left for Canada, the West Indies, or the British Isles. Others sought the protection of British troops in New York City and Philadelphia. Still others joined the British army and fought side by side with the King's soldiers. Although the remaining Loyalists went about their work and tried not to attract attention, some were deprived of their property or fined, jailed, or tarred and feathered. A few were even killed by angry mobs. "A Loyalist," said one Patriot, "is a thing whose head is in England, whose body is in America, and its neck ought to be stretched."

The Patriots. Another third of the colonial population in 1776 consisted of ardent Patriots. Many of them were craftsmen and mechanics in the towns and cities or small farmers in the backcountry. Tidewater planters, particularly those in Virginia, strongly supported independence, while in New England most of the merchants had joined the Patriots long before war broke out. So also had many lawyers who had risen to positions of leadership in the colonial assemblies. Throughout the colonies most of the non-Anglican clergy supported the Patriot cause. Just as the Patriots showed little sympathy for the Loyalists, so the latter group returned the compliment. One Loyalist charged that the Patriots were "an infernal, dark-designing group of men . . . obscure, pettifogging attorneys, bankrupt shopkeepers, outlawed smugglers . . . the refuse and dregs of mankind."

Uncommitted persons. The remaining third of the colonists were more or less neutral. Some had no interest in who won the struggle. Others were former moderates who saw some justice in each cause and thus found it hard to take sides. John Dickinson illustrates the difficult position in which many Americans found themselves. Dickinson had protested against the Townshend Acts in his famous *Letters from a Farmer in Pennsylvania.* But he opposed the use of force and therefore supported efforts to reach an understanding with the British. As a member of the First Continental Congress, he had drafted a petition to the King. In the Second Continental Congress he wrote the Olive Branch Petition which was sent to George III. The next year Dickinson argued against the Declaration of Independence. But having lost this fight, he resigned from Congress and enlisted in Washington's army.

Britain has advantages and disadvantages. The sharp divisions in American public opinion worked to Britain's advantage during the Revolutionary War. But the British faced a number of handicaps in their effort to suppress the American rebellion.

(1) They had to fight a war 3000 miles away from their base of supplies. Though Canada and the West Indies remained loyal, neither area could provide the supplies needed by the British army.

(2) The British government had at first thought that it would be a simple matter to stamp out the rebellion in Massachusetts. But when the war spread throughout the colonies, they realized they would have to wage war over a vast unfamiliar territory.

(3) Sea power gave the British a decided advantage, but many of the battles were fought far inland. And the American fighters could live off the land, even though the British held Philadelphia, New York, and other ports.

(4) Still another disadvantage for the British was the lack of enthusiasm for the war in England. Many members of Parliament criticized the use of Hessian troops, and some political opponents of the King's ministers pointed out that Americans were

fighting the cause of all Englishmen against tyranny. Moreover, there was concern lest Britain, by committing troops to fight in North America, would be vulnerable to attack by European enemies.

(5) Finally, frequent changes of British commanders in America contributed to a lack of consistent strategy.

For all these reasons, despite British victories in individual battles, the British were unable to inflict a blow decisive enough to drive Washington from the field.

The Patriots have some advantages. The Patriots had the advantage of fighting on their home ground. Knowing the lay of the land, they could assemble quickly for battle and, if defeated, retreat into the countryside to prepare to fight again. The Patriots generally avoided large-scale battles, preferring instead to attack British supply lines, pick off small units, and harass troop movements. One British official complained of the difficulty of "opposing an enemy that avoids facing you in the open field." Another Englishman exclaimed, "What an unfair method of carrying on a war!"

Probably the Patriots' greatest source of strength was George Washington. His firm belief in the justice of the Patriot cause enabled him to survive the strains of eight years of war. He worked to establish "order, regularity and discipline" in his unprofessional army; he won the respect of New Englanders, who at first were suspicious of a southern commander; he patiently pleaded with Congress for supplies; and he managed to control his officers, some of whom were jealous and spiteful. Modest about his own abilities, Washington desired only to win independence for the American colonies and then retire to his beloved Mount Vernon. It was typical of him that he insisted on serving without pay.

The Americans receive foreign aid. Assistance from foreign countries also greatly helped the Patriots. Congress had no sooner declared America's independence than it began seeking foreign aid. Excluded from trade with the British Empire, the Americans had to establish trade ties with other countries in order to secure arms and ammunition. The longstanding rivalry between France and Britain led Congress to hope for substantial aid from the French. Early in the war, Congress sent Benjamin Franklin and two other commissioners to Paris to seek aid and arrange a trade treaty. Later, John Jay was sent to Spain and John Adams to Holland. Still other agents were dispatched to Prussia, Austria, and Russia.

France, Spain, and Holland sent supplies to the Americans, thus giving invaluable assistance. At first this aid was secret, for none of the three countries wanted to risk war with Britain. After a decisive American victory at Saratoga (page 107), however, the Patriot cause looked more promising to European diplomats. In 1778, France was bold enough to sign a trade treaty and an alliance with the Americans. Later, both Spain and Holland were drawn into the war against Britain, though neither country actually allied itself with the United States.

In addition to assistance from foreign governments, many European officers crossed the Atlantic and volunteered their services to Congress. Though Washington did not find all of them easy to work with, the best of these foreign officers made valuable contributions to the American cause. Baron von Steuben, a Prussian officer, drilled the raw recruits of the Continental Army during the long winter at Valley Forge. Poland's Thaddeus Kosciusko (kos-ee-*us*'koh) instructed the Americans in military engineering. Another Pole, Count Pulaski (poo-*lah*'skih), gave his life at the siege of Savannah. The German Baron de Kalb also died during the war. Most valuable of all the foreign officers was the French Marquis de Lafayette, only 20 years old when he joined the Americans in 1777. He became a close personal friend and adviser of Washington.

The Patriot cause suffers from lack of unity. Despite these advantages — fighting on home ground, Washington's leadership, and generous foreign aid — lack of unity brought the Americans perilously close to defeat. Each of the thirteen states jealously guarded its powers and refused to surrender any of them to a central government. The Second Continental Congress had assumed responsibility for waging the war and governing in the name of the thirteen states. But Congress was poorly equipped for these large tasks. Fearful of a dictatorship, the delegates refused to give any real power to a president. Instead Congress set up committees to conduct foreign affairs, raise and spend money, and supervise the war effort. This proved to be an inefficient and cumbersome way of transacting business. American diplomats abroad, for example, were handicapped by confusing communications from Congress. And Washington had to spend much of his time begging congressional committees for soldiers, food, arms, and ammunition.

Raising money proves difficult. Congress tried to raise money in various ways, all without success. Since it had no power to levy or collect taxes, it asked each state to contribute a certain amount of money and supplies. But the response was disappointing. Of the 100 million dollars requested from the states, Congress received only four and a half million. Many farmers hid their horses or dismantled wagons rather than surrender them to Congress. And frequently they delivered spoiled vegetables and decayed meat to the Continental Army. Washington finally suggested to Congress that it cease all requisitions, for it was the "most uncertain, expensive, and injurious [method of raising money] that could be devised."

Congress also tried printing paper money. Immediately after the Battle of Bunker Hill it started issuing notes, called "Continentals," and eventually some 250 million dollars worth of paper money was authorized. In addition, the states were free to print money, and many did so. Altogether, Congress and the states turned out about 450 million dollars in certificates and notes. Since Congress had no gold or silver for which its notes could be exchanged, it asked the states to find "ways and means" to redeem them.

This reckless issue of paper money resulted in extreme inflation: prices rose and

Haym Salomon: Patriot and Financier

Many of those who work hardest for freedom do so because they know from experience what life is like without it. Such was the case with Haym Salomon (1740?–1785). A Jew of Portuguese descent, he was raised in Poland, a land that was partitioned to death by Europe's autocratic rulers. Salomon took part in an unsuccessful Polish struggle for freedom and migrated to New York in 1772. He quickly became a colonial sympathizer in the fight for American independence.

Salomon enjoyed success as a merchant and financier in America. With the money he made, he served the American cause in different ways. He joined the Sons of Liberty. He arranged for business loans to the struggling new government. He negotiated financial transactions between the French and American governments. Moreover, he gave generously from his own funds for supplies for the army.

On occasion, Haym Salomon's work as an agent took him behind the British lines in New York City, and he was twice arrested as a spy. In 1778, under sentence of death, he managed to escape. But Salomon's ordeals in prison had impaired his health. He died soon after the success of the cause he had worked for.

the value of paper money fell. By 1781 a pound of tea cost 90 dollars, a pair of shoes 100 dollars, and a barrel of flour 1575 dollars. Toward the end of the war, it was costing the government more to print paper bills than they were worth! No wonder the expression "not worth a Continental" came into common use.

Faced with financial chaos, Congress in 1781 appointed Robert Morris of Philadelphia as Superintendent of Finance. For the next few years he struggled with the problem and managed to improve matters. Loans from France, Spain, and Holland enabled him to meet government debts and to pay part of the back salaries due soldiers and officers.

Maintaining the army is a problem. Inflated currency and irregular paydays made it difficult for Washington to maintain an efficient fighting force. Enlistments were limited to one year, but not many Americans wanted to give a year's service

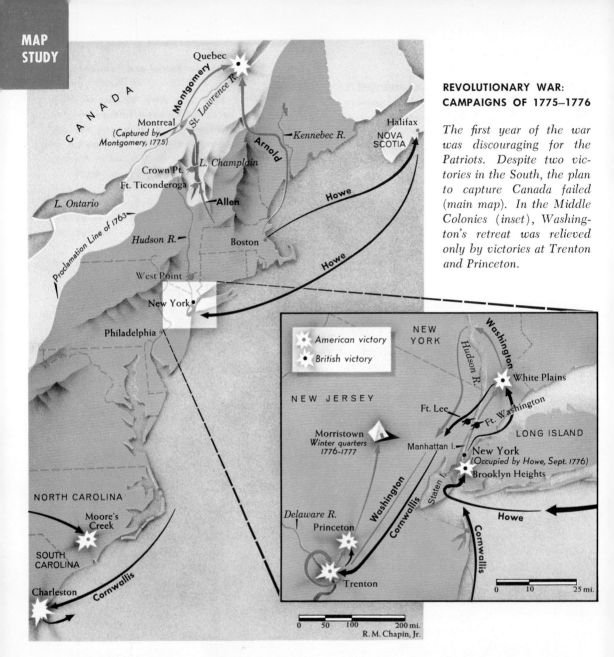

REVOLUTIONARY WAR: CAMPAIGNS OF 1775–1776

The first year of the war was discouraging for the Patriots. Despite two victories in the South, the plan to capture Canada failed (main map). In the Middle Colonies (inset), Washington's retreat was relieved only by victories at Trenton and Princeton.

R. M. Chapin, Jr.

when their chances of being paid were slim. Consequently, Washington had to rely on state militia to come to the aid of the regular army. These militiamen were willing to repel a British attack in their own state, but once the immediate danger passed, they wanted to return to their normal pursuits. These "part-time" soldiers, though essential to the American cause, made life difficult for Washington. He never knew how large his army would be from one month to the next.[2] The largest

army he ever had numbered about 20,000, including regulars and militiamen. During the winter months the army usually dwindled to three or four thousand. Fortunately, the British preferred to go into winter quarters in a port city. They never struck a decisive blow during the season when the Patriot forces were weakest.

Low salaries and irregular pay caused discontent among Washington's officers as well. At least one mutiny stemmed from these grievances, and it may have influenced Benedict Arnold's decision to spy for the British. Some officers actually plotted against Washington while he pleaded with

[2] All told, about 300,000 soldiers served at one time or another in the Revolutionary army. Approximately 5000 of them were Negroes.

Congress to provide food and clothes for his shivering troops. Realizing how uncertain the Patriot cause was, Thomas Paine issued the first of his *American Crisis* pamphlets in late 1776. With these words he sought to encourage the Americans:

These are the times that try men's souls. The summer soldier and the sunshine patriot will, in this crisis, shrink from the service of his country; but he that stands it *now* deserves the love and thanks of man and woman.

▶ CHECK-UP

1. What range of classes and views was reflected by the Loyalists? By the Patriots? By the uncommitted? What happened to the Loyalists?

2. What were the advantages and disadvantages of the British in the Revolutionary War? Of the Americans? In the case of the Americans, consider these factors: foreign aid, lack of unity, financial problems, and short-term army enlistments.

· · · · · · · · · · · · · · · · · · · ·

3 *Britain Strikes Blows But the Patriots Fight Back*

The British plan to take New York. When General William Howe and the British troops evacuated Boston in March, 1776 (page 95), they sailed to Halifax. There they devised a plan for crushing the American rebellion which called for an attack on New York City and capture of its valuable harbor. The British were confident of support from the large number of Loyalists in New York. They also believed that control of Long Island, Manhattan, and the Hudson River Valley would enable them to isolate New England from the rest of the colonies. For this purpose, General Howe gathered an army of 30,000 men, a quarter of them Hessians. Howe's army,

supported by a powerful British fleet commanded by his brother, Admiral Richard Howe, landed on Staten Island in the summer of 1776. But Washington had anticipated the British move. In April he had marched his troops from Boston to the western tip of Long Island. The Patriots entrenched themselves on Brooklyn Heights, hoping to protect Manhattan and beat back a British invasion of Long Island (map, page 104).

Washington abandons New York and New Jersey. The British plan to capture New York succeeded. In August the Howe brothers launched an attack on Brooklyn Heights and defeated Washington's forces. Under cover of fog the Americans managed to cross the river and take up a new position in northern Manhattan. But General Howe occupied New York City in September, and the Americans retreated northward. Washington's small army was defeated again at White Plains. The Patriots also lost valuable supplies when the British captured Fort Washington and Fort Lee on opposite sides of the Hudson River. Unable to cope with the large British army, Washington crossed the Hudson River and retreated southward across New Jersey.

Had General Howe acted more decisively, he might have wiped out the Continental Army. Instead he and his brother cherished the hope that the Americans would surrender. The British government had authorized the Howes to discuss peace terms, and they did carry on negotiations with Franklin, John Adams, and Edward Rutledge. Since the Americans insisted on complete independence, which the British refused to grant, the talks were broken off.

In the meantime, Washington in December, 1776, ferried his troops across the Delaware River into Pennsylvania. But the Patriot position remained perilous. Washington reported to Congress: "We have prevented them from crossing, but how long we shall be able to do it, God only knows, as they are still hovering about the river." The commander beseeched Congress to send him more troops, or "I think the game will be pretty well up." Instead of sending reinforcements to Washington, the members of Congress packed

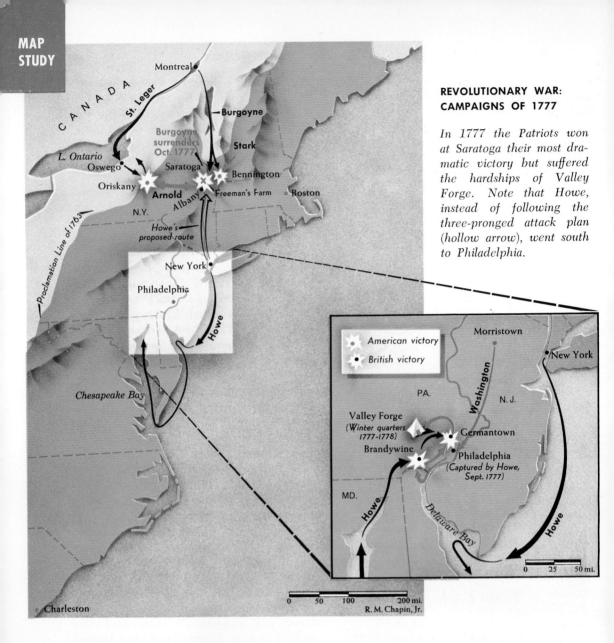

CANADA

Montreal

St. Leger

Burgoyne

Burgoyne surrenders Oct. 1777

Stark

L. Ontario

Oswego

Saratoga

Bennington

Oriskany

Arnold

Albany

Freeman's Farm

Boston

N.Y.

Howe's proposed route

Proclamation Line of 1763

New York

Philadelphia

Chesapeake Bay

Howe

Charleston

50   100   200 mi.

R. M. Chapin, Jr.

Morristown

★ American victory

● British victory

New York

PA.

Washington

N. J.

Valley Forge
(Winter quarters 1777-1778)

Germantown

Brandywine

Philadelphia
(Captured by Howe, Sept. 1777)

MD.

Howe

Delaware Bay

Howe

0   25   50 mi.

REVOLUTIONARY WAR: CAMPAIGNS OF 1777

In 1777 the Patriots won at Saratoga their most dramatic victory but suffered the hardships of Valley Forge. Note that Howe, instead of following the three-pronged attack plan (hollow arrow), went south to Philadelphia.

their belongings and fled from Philadelphia to Baltimore.

The Patriots strike back. As the year drew to a close, Washington still had received no reinforcements. Moreover, many of his soldiers were completing their term of enlistment and preparing to go home. On December 20 the commander informed Congress: "Ten days more will put an end to the existence of our army." But, with courage born of despair, Washington planned a surprise attack. On Christmas night, 1776, the Americans crossed the ice-clogged Delaware River and swept down on the Hessians quartered in Trenton, New

Jersey. Almost a thousand Hessians were captured, many still dazed from their celebration of Christmas. The only American casualties were four wounded men.

A week later, when the British thought they had the "old fox" hemmed in at Trenton, Washington again upset their calculations. Leaving his campfires burning to fool the British general, Lord Cornwallis, Washington marched around the main British force and attacked three regiments at Princeton. Unnerved by these actions of the American "country clowns," the British army withdrew to New York where it spent a comfortable winter. Washington's little army went into winter quarters at Morristown, New Jersey. Although the Americans had suffered heavy losses during the first year of the war, the sudden turn of fortune in the Trenton-Princeton campaign gave them renewed hope.

The British launch a three-pronged attack. The British in 1777 still hoped to conquer the American colonies by winning control of New York State and isolating New England. An elaborate plan called for three armies to meet near Albany (map, page 106): (1) General John Burgoyne was to lead 8000 British troops from Canada by way of Lake Champlain and the Hudson River. (2) Colonel Barry St. Leger (saint *lej'*er) was to bring an army of Loyalists and Indians from Fort Oswego on Lake Ontario eastward through the Mohawk Valley. (3) General Howe was to send part of the troops stationed in New York City to help Burgoyne.

This British plan was never carried out. It failed because Burgoyne and St. Leger encountered greater resistance than had been expected and because Howe failed to send reinforcements to Burgoyne. Instead of moving up the Hudson, Howe transported his troops by water to Chesapeake Bay and marched overland to capture the "rebel capital" of Philadelphia. Meanwhile, St. Leger's force met stiff resistance from backcountry Patriots and eventually retreated to Oswego. With Howe on his way to Philadelphia and St. Leger in retreat, Burgoyne was left to carry on alone.

Burgoyne surrenders at Saratoga. Unaware of his predicament, Burgoyne moved southward and quickly captured Ticonderoga in July, 1777. Thereafter he advanced more slowly. Americans sniped at his men and cut off supplies, and the countryside was much more rugged than he had expected. Furthermore, "Gentleman Johnny" traveled with heavy supplies of fancy clothing and choice wines, and this also slowed his advance. In August about 700 of Burgoyne's soldiers in search of supplies were captured near Bennington, Vermont, by John Stark and the Green Mountain Boys. About the same time, Burgoyne learned that he could expect no help from Howe and St. Leger. Nevertheless, he pushed on to the vicinity of Saratoga. In September, Burgoyne suffered heavy losses at the Battle of Freeman's Farm. As news of the fighting spread, hundreds of militiamen swelled the ranks of the American regulars. The outnumbered British fought and lost a second battle. Burgoyne then retreated to Saratoga and on October 17 surrendered his army of 5000 men to General Gates.

France comes to America's aid. The dramatic victory at Saratoga boosted the morale of the Patriots and won them an alliance with France. Since the beginning of the conflict, the French had secretly been sending arms and ammunition to America (page 102). News of the triumph at Saratoga convinced the French government that the Americans had a good chance of winning independence. Now France was willing to risk an open alliance.

Benjamin Franklin, representing the United States in Paris, made the most of the golden opportunity. In February, 1778, he had the pleasure of signing two treaties. One was a commercial treaty by which the United States and France granted full trade privileges to each other. The second was an alliance in which France promised to help the Americans win their freedom. In the event of war between France and Great Britain, neither France nor the United States would make peace without the consent of the other or "until the independence of the United States shall have been . . . assured by the treaty or treaties that shall terminate the war." When the British learned the terms of these two treaties, they declared war on France. But when Washington received word of the treaties, he declared that "no event was ever received with more heartfelt joy." The victory at Saratoga proved to be the turning point of the Revolutionary War, though at the time the Patriots were too hard-pressed elsewhere to realize it.

Howe takes Philadelphia. While Burgoyne was losing at Saratoga, General Howe was capturing Philadelphia. Because the British army traveled most of the way by sea, Washington had time to concentrate his forces to guard the approach to the city. But the outnumbered Americans were defeated at Brandywine Creek in September, 1777, and Howe occupied Philadelphia. Shortly afterward, when Washington tried to surprise a British detachment at Germantown, the Americans were again defeated. General Howe was then able to extend his control over the Delaware River and Delaware Bay.

When Franklin learned that Howe had taken Philadelphia, he remarked, "No, Philadelphia has captured Howe." There was a great deal of truth in this statement. Howe and the British officers settled down to enjoy a delightful winter of entertainment by Loyalist high society in Penn's beautiful city. Once again Howe had missed an opportunity to wipe out the battle-weary and discouraged Continental Army. Washington and the dwindling Patriot force went into winter quarters at Valley Forge, only 20 miles from Philadelphia.

Washington winters at Valley Forge. The winter of 1777–1778 was probably the darkest period of the war for the Patriots. Some officers and members of Congress became involved in a plot to replace Washington with General Gates. The plot failed, but Congress continued to ignore Washington's pleas for supplies. The troops at Valley Forge huddled in drafty cabins, hungry and cold. At one time, Washington wrote, "We had in camp not less than 2898 men unfit for duty by reason of their being barefoot and otherwise naked." A soldier described his plight in less elegant language: "Poor food — hard lodging — cold weather — fatigue — nasty cloaths — nasty cookery — vomit half my time. . . . Why are we sent here to starve and freeze?" Valley Forge lay in an area of fertile farmland where there was no scarcity of food. But the thrifty farmers preferred to sell food to the British for gold and silver coins rather than to the Continental Army for worthless paper money. The misery of that winter at Valley Forge was unrelieved until General Washington and his men learned about the signing of the French alliance.

CHECK-UP

1. Why did General Howe wish to take New York? Why was he tardy in following up victories? How did Washington strike back?

2. What was the British plan of attack in 1777? Why did it fail? What was the result? What treaties were signed by France and this country in 1778?

3. Why did Franklin think that Philadelphia had "captured" Howe? Why did the Patriots have to endure hardships during the winter of 1777–1778?

4 *Patriot Victories Assure American Independence*

The British make a new offer. The news of Saratoga had aroused a storm in Britain. Parliament criticized Lord North's government, blamed it for the Franco-American treaties, and demanded war with France. Alarmed at the prospect of fighting France as well as the Americans, Lord North made a final effort to end the American rebellion. He sent a peace commission to the colonies with an offer to revoke all laws passed since 1763 and to allow the Americans to tax themselves. But by this time the Continental Congress knew about the French treaties, and so it took a tough position in the discussions with Lord North's agents. Withdrawal of British troops and recognition of American independence were the only terms on which Congress would end the war. Lord North's offer was too little and too late to woo the Americans back into the British Empire.

The British move back to New York. In Philadelphia, General Howe, who had asked to be relieved of his command, was replaced by Sir Henry Clinton. In the spring of 1778, Clinton followed orders to evacuate Philadelphia and concentrate his

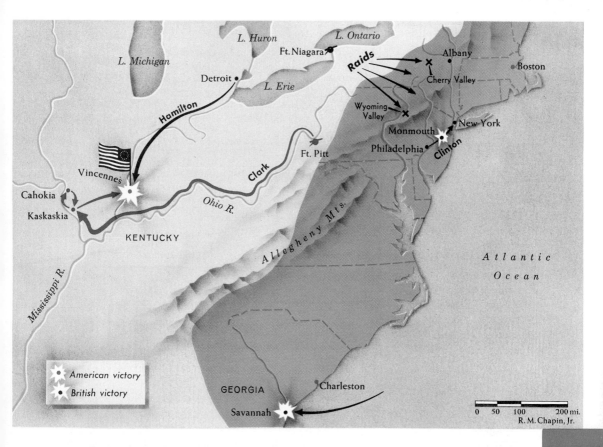

REVOLUTIONARY WAR: CAMPAIGNS OF 1778–1779

During these years, campaigns in the Northwest and in the South took on greater importance. By his victories in what are now Illinois and Indiana, George Rogers Clark won for the United States the Northwest Territory. The boundary of the colored area represents the Proclamation Line of 1763.

MAP STUDY

troops in New York. Washington tried without success to halt the British march across New Jersey. An American attack at Monmouth failed because General Charles Lee refused to obey Washington's orders. Clinton and the British forces settled down in New York, knowing that the Americans were not strong enough to dislodge them. For the next three years there was comparatively little fighting in the North. Elsewhere the initiative was taken by (1) American frontiersmen in the West, (2) American ships at sea, and (3) British troops in the South.

Americans win the Northwest. During the early years of the war there had been ruthless warfare on the frontier. Here the Americans were fighting not only British troops based at Detroit and Fort Niagara but also Indians and pro-British settlers.

Time and again forces of Indians and Loyalists raided the Wyoming Valley of Pennsylvania and the Cherry Valley of New York. American frontiersmen were eager to clear the region beyond the Allegheny Mountains of British troops. They hoped to put an end to raids on American outposts and open up the area which had been closed to settlement by the Proclamation Line of 1763. They also wanted to share in the fur trade reserved to the Canadians by the Quebec Act. But not until 1779 could Congress spare troops to march against the Iroquois Indians.

Early in 1778, Governor Patrick Henry of Virginia authorized George Rogers Clark, a Kentucky frontiersman, to lead a band of Americans into the country northwest of the Ohio River. Their goal was to capture the British posts at Kaskaskia,

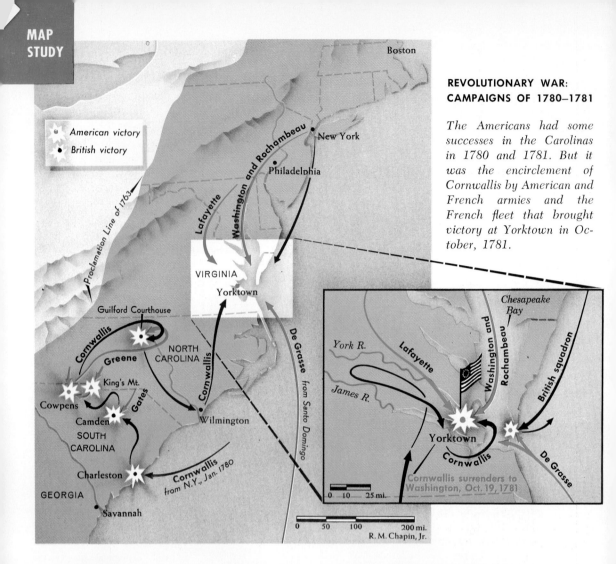

REVOLUTIONARY WAR: CAMPAIGNS OF 1780–1781

The Americans had some successes in the Carolinas in 1780 and 1781. But it was the encirclement of Cornwallis by American and French armies and the French fleet that brought victory at Yorktown in October, 1781.

American victory
British victory

Boston

New York

Philadelphia

Proclamation Line of 1763

Lafayette

Washington and Rochambeau

VIRGINIA
Yorktown

Guilford Courthouse

Cornwallis

Greene

NORTH
CAROLINA

Cornwallis

King's Mt.

Gates

Cowpens

Camden

SOUTH
CAROLINA

Wilmington

De Grasse from Santo Domingo

Charleston

Cornwallis
from N.Y., Jan. 1780

GEORGIA

Savannah

0   50   100   200 mi.
R. M. Chapin, Jr.

Chesapeake
Bay

York R.

Lafayette

Washington and Rochambeau

British squadron

James R.

Yorktown

Cornwallis

De Grasse

Cornwallis surrenders to
Washington, Oct. 19, 1781

0   10   25 mi.

Cahokia, and Vincennes (map, page 109). Clark and about 175 volunteers made their way to the Mississippi and seized Kaskaskia and Cahokia (in present-day Illinois). Then they doubled back and captured Vincennes (in present-day Indiana). When a British relief expedition from Detroit regained Vincennes, Clark and his men launched another attack early in 1779. In a march "too incredible for any person to believe," the Americans tramped 240 miles over flooded country to force the second surrender of Vincennes. The capture of Kaskaskia, Cahokia, and Vincennes was a factor in the British decision to give the Northwest to the Americans in the peace settlement of 1783.

War is waged on the sea. To carry on the war at sea, Congress authorized the purchase and construction of armed ves-

sels. These ships were too few and too small to threaten the powerful British fleet. But, by capturing merchant ships, they disrupted the enemy's supply lines. In this important work, they were aided by American *privateers* — privately owned armed ships that were licensed by the government to seize enemy vessels. At least 2000 privateers were commissioned either by Congress or by the states; three quarters of them were owned by New Englanders. One, the *Black Prince*, was reported to have "taken, ransomed, burnt, and destroyed" more than 30 British ships in less than three months. The privateers captured supplies and ammunition desperately needed by the Continental Army.

One of the ablest naval officers was John Paul Jones, a Scottish adventurer who volunteered his services to the Americans when war broke out. His skill and courage helped to establish the traditions of the young American navy. As captain of an old French ship renamed the *Bonhomme Richard* (buh-*nawm'* ree-*shahr'*), Jones won a spectacular encounter with a British frigate, the *Serapis* (seh-*ray'*pis), in September, 1779. To the delight of the Americans and the chagrin of the British, Jones raided English and Scottish coastal towns much as Drake had ravaged the Spanish coast two hundred years earlier (page 17).

The British win victories in the South. American naval victories were offset by losses in the South, where the British were aided by many Loyalists. (See map on page 110.) Late in 1778 the British occupied the important port of Savannah, Georgia, and in 1780 they took Charleston, South Carolina. At Charleston, a large number of American prisoners and valuable supplies fell to the British. General Gates, commanding the American forces in the South, suffered a crushing defeat at the hands of Lord Cornwallis near Camden, South Carolina, in August, 1780. By the end of that year the British controlled Georgia and South Carolina, though they met resistance from Patriot bands led by Francis Marion, Thomas Sumter, and Andrew Pickens.

British successes are checked. The Americans were more successful in checking the British advance into North Carolina. Frontiersmen routed a British army at King's Mountain in October, 1780, and General Nathanael Greene, who had replaced Gates, led the Americans to victory at Cowpens. At Guilford Courthouse, Lord Cornwallis won the battle but suffered such heavy losses that he had to abandon the attempt to conquer North Carolina. The British then retreated northward. Eventually they concentrated their forces near Yorktown, Virginia, on a peninsula jutting into Chesapeake Bay. Here the British army felt safe because supplies could be brought by sea and troops evacuated if necessary. Through most of 1781 and 1782 General Greene was busy mopping up small British units left behind in South Carolina. But it was not until December, 1782, that the Americans retook Charleston.

The American position remains in doubt. In spite of Greene's victories the outlook for the American cause seemed far from bright in the first half of 1781. British forces still held New York, and Cornwallis was entrenched in Virginia. Congress had increasing trouble raising money for Washington's army, enlistments were running

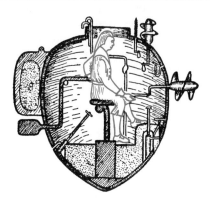

America's first submarine, the Turtle *(above), tried to sink British ships in New York Harbor in 1776. One man operated the* Turtle, *while today's atomic submarines have crews of over a hundred. Men of the submarine* Lafayette *(right) watch controls during a firing drill.*

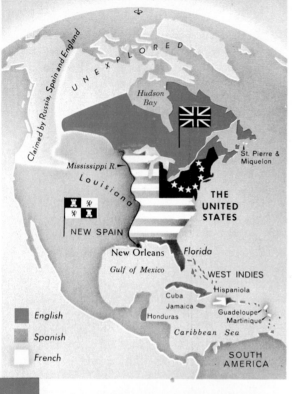

English

Spanish

French

THE NEW NATION IN 1783

For the second time in two decades (1763–1783), war had reshaped the map of North America. Compare this map with the one on page 44.

lower than before, and there had been several mutinies. "We are at the end of our tether," Washington confessed.

Meanwhile, the treason of Benedict Arnold was a humiliating blow to the Americans. Arnold, who had fought bravely at Quebec and Saratoga, was dissatisfied with his slow advance in rank and his inadequate salary. He began to sell military secrets to the British. In 1780 Arnold persuaded Washington to give him command of West Point, intending to surrender to the British this important Hudson River fortress. But Arnold's plot was discovered before he could carry it out. His British go-between, Major John André, was captured and hanged. Arnold himself escaped to the British and later fought against the Americans.

Despite setbacks, American prospects for victory were brightened by increasing help from France. Lafayette had returned to

France to plead with the French government for more aid. His efforts paid off handsomely. In 1780 Comte de Rochambeau (roh-shahn-*boh'*) and a force of 5000 soldiers arrived at Newport, Rhode Island, and the following year a powerful fleet under Admiral de Grasse put in at the French West Indies.

Cornwallis's surrender assures American victory. The Americans and the French now had the strength to attack the 7000-man British army at Yorktown. But Cornwallis saw no cause for alarm. He had chased off a small American force commanded by Lafayette, and had fortified the British position at Yorktown. Meanwhile, Washington had taken steps to make General Clinton think he was planning an attack on New York. Actually, however, Washington and Rochambeau hurried their forces to Chesapeake Bay for transportation to Yorktown. At the same time, de Grasse's fleet carrying 3000 more French troops sailed for Chesapeake Bay. The combined French and American army of 16,000 men then closed in on Cornwallis. Victory became certain when the French fleet beat off a British squadron bringing help to Cornwallis. The harassed British commander, blockaded by the French fleet and encircled by an army twice the size of his own, surrendered on October 19, 1781. The victory at Yorktown meant, for all practical purposes, that the war was over.

Britain seeks peace. When news of Cornwallis's surrender reached England, discontent with the war came to a head. Lord North resigned, and the new government was ready to yield to American demands for independence. But it took time to work out other details of the treaty, and for the British to negotiate with France, Spain, and Holland. The negotiations were conducted in Paris, with Benjamin Franklin, John Adams, and John Jay representing the Americans.

During the course of the talks, the Americans began to fear that France might try to set the Appalachian Mountains as the western boundary of the United States. This would have allowed France to give the territory between the Appalachians and the Mississippi to her ally, Spain. Spain

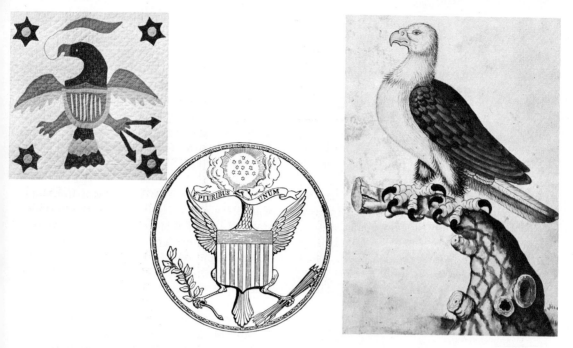

Congress in 1782 chose the bald eagle as the symbol to appear on the United States' official seal (middle). This handsome bird was a familiar sight in America at that time and also two hundred years earlier, when John White, governor of Roanoke colony, drew it in the 1580's (right). The new national symbol gained popularity, and craftsmen and artisans often used it as a decorative design. Note how the detail from a quilt of the 1800's (left) resembles the seal.

had entered the war on the understanding that France would help her seize Gibraltar from the British. Since the British still held Gibraltar in 1782, Jay and Adams suspected that France would try to compensate Spain with this American territory.

Contrary to the spirit of the Franco-American alliance in 1778, the Americans opened secret negotiations with the British. In November, 1782, the preliminary terms were signed, granting independence to the United States and establishing its western boundary at the Mississippi River. Naturally the French were irritated, but Franklin managed to smooth over "this little misunderstanding." He suggested that the French show their devotion to the United States by making another loan; and the nearly bankrupt French government did just that! Franklin, Jay, and Adams rendered their country valuable service by extracting a favorable treaty from the British and more money from the French.

The Treaty of Paris establishes American independence. The final terms were

set down in the Treaty of Paris, signed by the Americans and the British on September 3, 1783. "His Britannic Majesty" acknowledged the former American colonies "to be free, sovereign, and independent States." The boundaries of the new country were established at the Mississippi River in the West, Canada on the north, and the Florida frontier to the south[3] (map, page 112). Britain agreed to remove her troops from this area and to let Americans fish off the Grand Banks of Newfoundland. The Americans promised to place no legal obstacle in the way of British creditors who tried to collect prewar debts from American merchants and planters. It was also understood that Congress would "earnestly recommend" to the states the return of property taken from Loyalists. In addition, there was to be no further persecution of Loyalists. Finally, the Treaty of Paris stated that navigation of the Mississippi River should "forever remain free and open

[3] Parts of the northern and southern boundaries were disputed for some years afterward.

to the subjects of Great Britain, and the citizens of the United States."

The Americans gained the most under the terms of the peace. France had the satisfaction of helping to bring about Britain's loss of the thirteen colonies. But participation in the American Revolutionary War put the French government deeply in debt and also stirred up ideas of liberty and equality in French minds. That the French Revolution followed the American Revolution by only a few years was no coincidence. As for Spain, it failed to regain Gibraltar but received Florida, which had been ceded to Britain in 1763. And the spread of American revolutionary ideas into South America contributed to the eventual collapse of Spain's colonial empire.

▶ CHECK-UP

1. What was the British reaction to Saratoga? The American reaction to Lord North's peace terms? What happened when the British concentrated their forces in New York?

2. Why did George Rogers Clark invade the Northwest? What were the results? What successes did Americans have on the seas?

3. What successes did the British have in the South? How did the Patriots fight back? How was Cornwallis compelled to surrender? What was the outcome?

4. Why did the Americans open secret negotiations with the British? What were the provisions of the peace treaty?

. . . .

Clinching the Main Ideas in Chapter 5

The opening blows of the American Revolution were struck at Lexington and Concord when colonial minutemen clashed with British redcoats. This small encounter soon grew into a full-scale war for the independence of all the thirteen colonies. By 1776, British harshness and Patriot propaganda led many Americans to think it only "common sense" to break away from the British Empire. On July 4, 1776, Congress therefore adopted the Declaration of Independence.

The Revolutionary War was a fumbling war in many respects. Each of the thirteen states jealously guarded its sovereignty. In conducting the American war effort, the Second Continental Congress lacked any power to levy and collect taxes and had no machinery to carry out its decisions. Congress' most brilliant stroke was the appointment of George Washington as commander-in-chief of the Continental Army. An important factor in the war was the enlistment of French aid, which helped the Americans carry on until victory was achieved.

The British war effort also was confused. Each new commander introduced a different strategy. And no matter what plan was adopted, there was criticism of the war at home. The British people never gave their full support to this war against other Englishmen. As a result, Lord North's government grew steadily weaker. After the surrender at Yorktown, the British still had troops in South Carolina and New York. But fighting came to a halt because Britain no longer had the will to continue the war against her former colonies.

Franklin, Jay, and Adams protected American interests at the peace conference, and out of their bargaining came complete independence and a generous territorial settlement. How the Americans would use their freedom remained to be seen.

Chapter Review

Terms to Understand

1. Hessians
2. privateers
3. Loyalists
4. Patriots
5. Declaration of Independence
6. Olive Branch Petition
7. Valley Forge
8. *Common Sense*
9. Second Continental Congress
10. Treaty of Paris (1783)
11. French alliance
12. Yorktown

What Do You Think?

1. Why did the Second Continental Congress adopt the "Declaration of the Causes and Necessity of Taking up Arms" and endorse John Dickinson's "Olive Branch Petition"?

2. What were the advantages to Britain of retaining control of Canada throughout the Revolutionary War?

3. "As Europe is our market for trade, we ought to form no political connection with any part of it." Why did this argument advanced by Thomas Paine appeal to many Americans?

4. How would you assess credit and blame for the failure of British plans to isolate New England in 1777? For the surrender of Cornwallis at Yorktown in 1781?

5. In 1778 a British commission offered to revoke all laws passed since 1763 which affected the colonies and to permit the Americans to tax themselves. The Continental Congress rejected this. Why? Would these terms have been acceptable three years earlier? Why?

6. Why were George Rogers Clark's victories in the Northwest of vital importance to this country?

Using Your Knowledge of History

1. The Declaration of Independence makes a number of specific charges against George III. List five of these charges for which you can provide an example from the period before 1776.

2. Make a chart in which you list (a) ways of raising money and (b) ways of raising troops during the Revolutionary War. In a parallel column list how these things were done by this country during World War II. Then provide a brief paragraph in which you try to explain why some of the methods used in World War II were not used during the Revolution.

3. Debate: *Resolved,* French aid was the vital factor in assuring an American victory in the Revolutionary War.

4. Write an editorial about the Declaration of Independence from the point of view of a Patriot editing a colonial newspaper or a Tory editing an English newspaper.

Extending Your Knowledge of History

The American Heritage Book of the Revolution is a splendid pictorial survey of the war. Marcus Cunliffe, a British historian, has written a brief biography of Washington in *George Washington, Man and Monument.* Another Englishman, J. H. Plumb, has reassessed the role of George III in the article "Our Last King," in the magazine *American Heritage,* June, 1960. Much has been written about the Declaration, but one of the best books is probably Carl Becker's *The Declaration of Independence.*

Analyzing Unit One

1. A scholar of the Revolutionary War period has written that "there was a solid foundation of economic grievances" beneath the conflict between the mother country and the colonies. But "it was the invasion of Americans' political rights by Parliament after the Peace of Paris which precipitated the struggle." What were the causes of the economic discontent? Were they troublesome enough to have started a war between the mother country and the colonies? What political difficulties after 1763 reinforced earlier grievances? How did they provide just the right combination of forces to touch off the conflict?

2. One historian has claimed that our earliest politicians were "masters of the science and art of propaganda." Who were some of these colonial propagandists? How did they play upon grievances shared by many settlers in the English colonies?

3. What considerations and value judgments might have caused a Loyalist to conclude that the colonies should remain within the British Empire?

Unit 2

The New Nation Gains Respect at Home and Abroad (1781-1815)

Washington crossing the Hudson before his inauguration

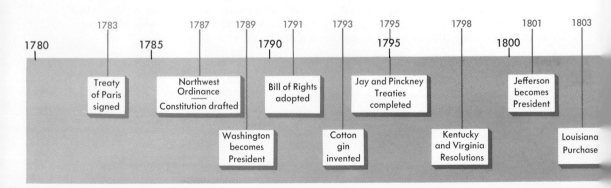

| 1780 | 1783 | 1785 | 1787 | 1789 | 1790 | 1791 | 1793 | 1795 / 1795 | 1798 | 1800 | 1801 | 1803 |

Treaty of Paris signed

Northwest Ordinance
Constitution drafted

Washington becomes President

Bill of Rights adopted

Cotton gin invented

Jay and Pinckney Treaties completed

Kentucky and Virginia Resolutions

Jefferson becomes President

Louisiana Purchase

Even before the struggle for American independence had been successfully concluded, members of the Second Continental Congress took steps to establish a central government for the thirteen states. The government established by the Articles of Confederation understandably bore little resemblance to the English model. Under the Articles, there was no chief executive who might act like a king, and there were no central courts which might overrule the decisions of state courts. Congress was denied the right to levy or collect taxes, lest it follow Parliament's practice of taxing unfairly.

By the mid-1780's it was clear that the Articles of Confederation left too much power in the hands of the states. Efforts to amend the Articles nevertheless ended in failure. Finally, a convention met in Philadelphia to devise a new government. The product of its deliberations was the Constitution. The new plan of government enlarged the government's legislative powers and provided for a chief executive and a system of national courts. But the most important achievement of the Constitutional Convention was the distribution of power between the states and the federal government. The "founding fathers" sought to establish an effective central government and at the same time to preserve the rights of the states.

To George Washington fell the task of translating the Constitution into a functioning government. His political associates, the Federalists, thought the federal government should be stronger than the states. Soon, however, an opposition group took shape that wanted to limit the powers of the federal government. After 1800 the Republicans controlled both Congress and the presidency. Delegates to the Constitutional Convention had feared that political parties would create conflict within the nation, but their appearance at an early date was a fortunate development; for they provided various groups with an opportunity to state their opinions and grievances.

Both Federalist and Republican administrations had to cope with violations of American rights on the seas. At the root of the problem was the nation's position as a neutral in the great wars between Britain and France. Both countries interfered with American trade, but the powerful British navy caused more trouble. Eventually the United States was drawn into war against the former mother country. The Americans gained little from the peace treaty which ended the War of 1812. But the very fact that the United States was willing to fight a "Second War of Independence" stimulated national pride.

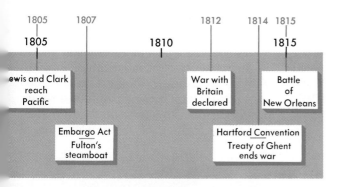

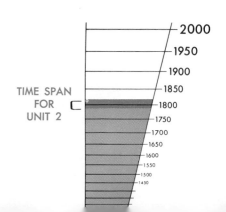

CHAPTER 6

The Constitution Establishes a Firm Union

Signing of the Constitution

1781–1789

Whilst the last members were signing it, Doctor Franklin, looking towards the president's chair, at the back of which a rising sun happened to be painted, observed to a few members near him, that painters had found it difficult to distinguish in their art a rising from a setting sun. "I have," said he, "often and often in the course of the session, and the vicissitudes of my hopes and fears as to its issue, looked at that behind the president without being able to tell whether it was rising or setting; but now at length I have the happiness to know that it is a rising and not a setting sun."

JAMES MADISON'S NOTES ON THE
SIGNING OF THE CONSTITUTION

The Revolution did more than sever American ties with Great Britain; it brought about changes within the new nation itself. New state governments were established. The state legislatures introduced social and economic changes which affected the American people, who by 1790 numbered about four million. But the chief problem in the years following the Treaty of Paris in 1783 was the creation of a central government.

During the Revolutionary War, the Americans had concentrated on winning independence; the problem of governing themselves had received little attention. To be sure, after considerable hesitation, the states adopted a plan of government known as the Articles of Confederation in 1781. But the weaknesses of the Confederation government soon became painfully obvious. Demands for a stronger central government led to the writing of the Constitution in

Philadelphia during the summer of 1787. Not all Americans shared the optimism reflected in Franklin's words quoted above, but the required number of states accepted the Constitution, and the new government was established.

This chapter is concerned with the events leading to the adoption of the Constitution and the factors which have enabled it, the oldest written constitution in the world, to stand the test of time.

1 *The Revolution Brings Important Changes*

State governments are established. The Declaration of Independence had made the thirteen colonies "free and independent States." It then became necessary to set up state governments for the former colonies. To define the powers of these new governments, Americans wanted written documents, like the colonial charters with which they were familiar. Rhode Island and Connecticut converted their colonial charters, with only slight alteration, into satisfactory state constitutions. But most of the states had to write entirely new documents. Many of the new constitutions included lists of personal rights guaranteed to each citizen. The famous English Bill of Rights of 1689 (page 26) served as a model for these "bills of rights."

The new state governments had many features in common. (1) Broad powers were given to the legislatures, most of which were made up of two houses. (2) All the state legislatures kept tight control over taxation. (3) Each state constitution provided for a governor. His powers, however, were strictly limited, for experience with royal governors had made the people cautious about allowing one man too much power. (4) The state constitutions listed the qualifications for holding office and for voting. To run for office, a man had to pay a certain amount of taxes or own a given amount of property. In general, the qualifications for holding office were higher than for voting. Vermont was the first state to give suffrage to all men over 21.

Church and state are separated. Many of the state constitutions provided for strict separation in affairs of church and state. This meant that a state government could not support an established church. In Virginia, for example, Thomas Jefferson and James Madison led the fight to sever all ties between the Anglican Church and the state. Adopted in 1786, their bill set an important precedent. To be sure, in Massachusetts the Congregational churches maintained an established position until the 1830's. But by the end of the Revolutionary period, most of the states had adopted the principle of separation of church and state. This principle was later affirmed in the First Amendment to the Constitution (page 150).

Land ownership is changed. Besides political changes, the Revolution opened up new economic opportunities, which Americans were quick to grasp. For one thing, land became more plentiful. The Proclamation Line of 1763 no longer held back the pioneers, and thousands of them pushed across the Appalachian Mountains in the 1780's. Also, the state governments had taken possession of land belonging to English proprietors or to the king. The new governments also seized Loyalist property. Much of this land was divided into small parcels and sold at reasonable prices to individual purchasers. Thus, the small farmer had an unusual opportunity to buy land in the settled areas of the new country. Furthermore, most of the state legislatures abolished the *quitrent*, the colonial land tax paid to the king or proprietor.

. . . .

CHAPTER FOCUS

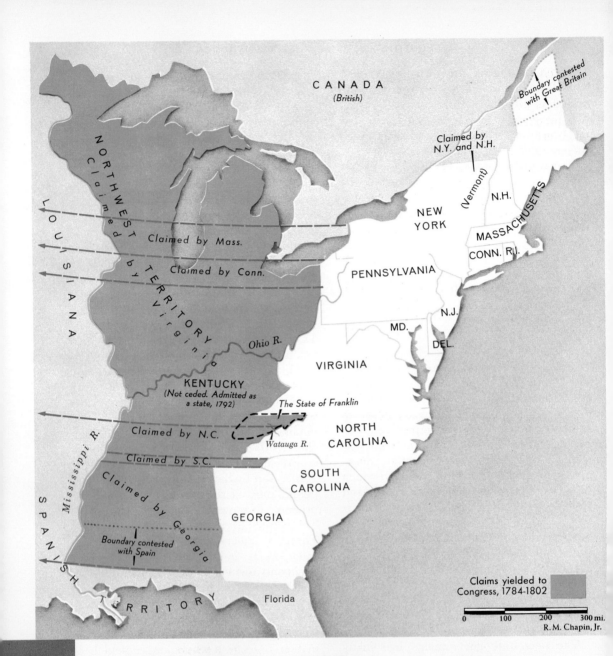

CANADA
(British)

Boundary contested
with Great Britain

Claimed by
N.Y. and N.H.

NORTHWEST

Claimed by Mass.

Claimed by Conn.

Claimed by Virginia

LOUISIANA

Ohio R.

KENTUCKY
(Not ceded. Admitted as
a state, 1792)

Claimed by N.C.

Watauga R.

The State of Franklin

Claimed by S.C.

Mississippi R.

Claimed by Georgia

SPANISH

Boundary contested
with Spain

TERRITORY

Florida

(Vermont)

N.H.

NEW
YORK

MASSACHUSETTS

CONN. R.I.

PENNSYLVANIA

N.J.

MD.

DEL.

VIRGINIA

NORTH
CAROLINA

SOUTH
CAROLINA

GEORGIA

Claims yielded to
Congress, 1784-1802

0   100   200   300 mi.

R. M. Chapin, Jr.

THE STATES RELINQUISH THEIR WESTERN CLAIMS

The original sea-to-sea grants in North America produced many conflicting state claims beyond the Appalachians. Note that Virginia's claim overlapped the claims of Massachusetts and Connecticut. Once the states had ceded their western claims, the way was paved for ratification of the Articles of Confederation. In the Northwest Territory, Congress provided a pattern by which territories might join the Union as equal states.

The states take steps against slavery. After independence had been declared, a number of Americans had spoken out against slavery and the slave trade. In his original draft of the Declaration of Independence, Jefferson had condemned the slave trade and blamed George III for it. The Second Continental Congress struck out this passage and in the following years took no steps against the traffic in slaves. But reformers hoped that the individual states would act to end the slave trade.

By 1786 all of the states except Georgia had banned the importing of slaves. Rhode Island had freed its slaves just before the Revolution started; Pennsylvania and Massachusetts abolished slavery during the course of the war. Other northern states provided for gradual emancipation of their slave population. In the South, where the number of Negroes was much larger, the problem of ending slavery was more difficult. Prominent Southerners such as Patrick Henry, Thomas Jefferson, and George Washington felt that slavery could not be reconciled with their belief in human rights. In his will, George Washington ordered all his slaves set free after his wife's death. Other planters took similar action, but none of the southern state legislatures proposed practical ways of ending slavery.

Education receives attention. Education was another matter of concern to the new state governments. Americans were aware of the importance of education for their young country, and some, including Thomas Jefferson, proposed the establishment of public school systems. These, however, did not appear until later. In 1789 Massachusetts confirmed its earlier colonial laws requiring local support of public schools (page 62), though enforcement of this measure was lax. In Massachusetts and elsewhere, private academies educated the sons of well-to-do families. Many of these academies were modeled after Andover (founded in 1778 in Massachusetts) and Exeter (1781, New Hampshire), both of which still exist. Most schools used Noah Webster's "blue-backed" speller, which first appeared in 1783. This speller and Webster's other textbooks became familiar to thousands of students in the late 1700's and in the next century as well. Together with Webster's dictionary, these books helped establish standards for American usage of the English language.

The number of colleges increased from nine at the outset of the Revolution to some 25 by 1800. Several had state support in addition to private grants and income from tuition. Though George Washington and others urged the establishment of a national university, this never came about.

The Articles of Confederation are proposed. As we have seen, the new state governments brought about some significant changes in American life after 1776. But the states had declared themselves to be "united," and therefore they had to set up a permanent central government. Shortly before the Second Continental Congress declared independence, it had appointed a committee to draw up a frame of government for the thirteen colonies. A document entitled *Articles of Confederation and Perpetual Union* was submitted to Congress in July, 1776. After more than a year, Congress approved the Articles and submitted them to the states for ratification. By early 1779, twelve states had ratified them, but the approval of all thirteen states was necessary for adoption of the Articles.

A dispute over western lands delays adoption of the Articles. Maryland was the state that held out against adoption of the Articles. The trouble stemmed from a dispute over ownership of land beyond the Alleghenies. Some of the colonial charters had granted title to lands stretching from "sea to sea"; moreover, in some instances the king had made overlapping grants of territory. The result was that seven states had western land claims. Virginia claimed the most land — all of present-day Kentucky, West Virginia, Ohio, Indiana, Illinois, Michigan, and Wisconsin (map, page 120). Maryland insisted that the states with western land claims surrender them to the central government. She argued that the land ought to be held for the benefit of the United States as a whole. Otherwise, landless states like Maryland would be dominated by giant states like Virginia.

Enough states agreed with Maryland's reasoning, or were jealous of the larger states, to pressure Virginia into surrendering its claims north of the Ohio River to Congress. The six other states with western land claims (New York, Massachusetts, Connecticut, North and South Carolina, and Georgia) followed Virginia's example.[1] Having won the argument, Maryland ratified

---

[1] The cession of western lands was not finally completed until 1802.

the Articles of Confederation in March, 1781.

The Articles set up a league of states. The Articles of Confederation created a "firm league of friendship" in which each state kept its sovereignty and independence. The central government consisted of a Congress which was to control foreign affairs, make war and peace, borrow money, regulate the value of coins, raise an army, and settle disputes between states.

The rights of the individual states were carefully safeguarded under the Articles of Confederation. Although each state had from two to seven delegates in Congress, a state delegation had only one vote. Hence, a large state could have no advantage over a small state. The states also retained all powers not specifically granted to the central government. Thus, the states kept the right to levy taxes, to issue paper money, and to control trade. These powers had been won in colonial times, and no state was yet willing to surrender them to a central authority. Congress could pass important laws only with the approval of nine of the states. Amendment of the Articles required the approval of all thirteen states.

The Articles also provided that a man would be a citizen of the state in which he resided as well as a citizen of the United States. Each state was to recognize the laws and court proceedings of every other state. Though many provisions of the Articles were altered by the Constitution that was later adopted, these two points were faithfully retained.

▶ CHECK-UP

1. What features did the new state constitutions have in common? What changes were made in the relationship of church and state? In landownership? What steps were taken against slavery? To further education?

2. What settlement was reached in the dispute over the ownership of western lands?

3. What powers were granted the central government under the Articles of Confederation? What powers were reserved to the states? How did the Articles strengthen the principle of national citizenship?

. . . .

2 The Weaknesses of the Confederation Become Apparent

The new government faces postwar problems. With the signing of the peace treaty in 1783, the new nation's troubles were by no means over. The new central government, based on the Articles of Confederation, had been in effect for two years. But a number of serious problems plagued the Confederation. Some of these resulted from defects in the Articles, particularly the limited powers granted to the central government. Others were brought on by a slump in trade, which led to hard times in the postwar years. Congress was effective neither in its direction of foreign affairs nor in its handling of problems at home. No wonder the Englishman Josiah Tucker confidently predicted:

As to the future grandeur of America and its being a rising empire under one head, whether republican or monarchical, it is one of the idlest and most visionary notions that ever was conceived even by writers of romance. . . . The Americans will have no center of union among them, and no common interest to pursue. . . . Their fate seems to be — *a disunited people*, till the end of time.

Even the American historian John Fiske, writing a century later, expressed the view that the Confederation had been a failure. He called the 1780's a "critical period" in American history.

More recently, historians have revised their opinion of the Articles of Confederation. They consider it remarkable that the thirteen proudly independent states consented to the establishment of *any* central government. Moreover, in view of the government's feeble powers, it was an accomplishment for the Confederation Congress to have provided as much direction as it did. Furthermore, the wise policy devel-

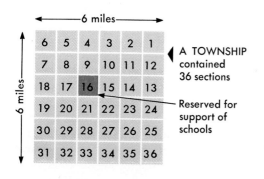

6 miles

A TOWNSHIP contained 36 sections

6	5	4	3	2	1
7	8	9	10	11	12
18	17	16	15	14	13
19	20	21	22	23	24
30	29	28	27	26	25
31	32	33	34	35	36

6 miles

Reserved for support of schools

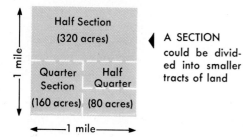

1 mile

Half Section (320 acres)

Quarter Section (160 acres)

Half Quarter (80 acres)

1 mile

A SECTION could be divided into smaller tracts of land

THE ORDINANCE OF 1785

Compare the checkerboard appearance of present-day midwestern farm land with the pattern set by the Ordinance of 1785.

oped by Congress concerning western lands was an important achievement.

Western settlers present their demands to Congress. Even before the Revolution was over, thousands of Americans had begun the long trek across the mountains. Some settled in the fertile valleys of Kentucky and Tennessee, and some went north of the Ohio River. Others bought land in Vermont. These pioneers wanted the government to help them fight the Indians who were allied with the British in Canada or with the Spaniards in Louisiana. They also wanted Congress to admit the newly settled areas to statehood. But Congress was slow to act. Because both New York and New Hampshire contested Vermont's land claims, Vermont had to remain an independent republic throughout the 1780's. Settlers along the Watauga River in what later became Tennessee formed the State of Franklin (map, page 120) and waited, unsuccessfully, for action by Congress. After making a western journey in 1784, George Washington reported to Congress that the loyalty of the West "hung by a hair." Washington urged Congress to consider the west-

ern demands: "Let us bind these people to us by a chain that can never be broken."

The Northwest Territory is organized. The Congress of the Confederation passed two laws that helped bind the West to the thirteen original states. These two measures dealt specifically with the Northwest Territory, the area bounded by the Ohio and Mississippi Rivers and the Great Lakes.

(1) The Land Ordinance of 1785 provided that the Northwest Territory be surveyed and divided into *townships* six miles square. Each township was subdivided into 36 *sections*, making each section one square mile or 640 acres. The land was to be sold at public auction for not less than one dollar per acre. Out of each township, one section was to be set aside for the support of public education. The plan established by the Land Ordinance resulted in a checkerboard pattern of land in the Northwest Territory and in other areas where it was later applied.

(2) In 1787 Congress passed the Northwest Ordinance, which provided a plan of government for the territory. In the first stage, Congress was to appoint a governor

and three judges to carry on the government. When the number of adult free males in the Northwest Territory reached 5000, the voters could elect a legislature to pass laws and they could send a nonvoting delegate to Congress. The territory was at some time to be divided into at least three, but not more than five, states. As soon as one of these divisions had a population of 60,000, it could petition Congress for admission to the union "on an equal footing with the original States in all respects whatever." The Northwest Ordinance forbade the introduction of slavery and guaranteed religious freedom. It required that schools should "forever be encouraged," and it guaranteed trial by jury, the sacredness of contracts, and freedom from cruel and unusual punishments.

These two important laws set the pattern for (1) the orderly sale of public land and (2) the organization of new territories that could eventually become states on terms of complete equality with the original thirteen. In fact, they have served as a basic model for territorial development ever since. Although Congress had no previous experience on which to draw except the English colonial pattern, these wise laws enabled the young nation to escape the problem of western "colonies." Forty years later, Daniel Webster suggested that no "one single law of any lawgiver, ancient or modern, . . . produced effects of more distinct, marked, and lasting character than the ordinance of '87."

Relations with Great Britain are unfriendly. Congress was less successful in its handling of foreign affairs. Great Britain was openly hostile to the new country. Franklin, writing from England in 1783, said: "We should, I think, be constantly upon our guard, and impress strongly upon our minds, that though it [Great Britain] has made peace with us, it is not in truth reconciled either to us, or to its loss of us." George III refused to dispatch a minister to the United States, though he did receive John Adams, the first American minister to Britain. Adams complained that he was coldly treated and often insulted by being asked whether he represented one state or thirteen.

In addition, Great Britain refused to evacuate its fur-trading posts within territory ceded to the United States by the Treaty of 1783. In defense of this violation, Britain charged that the Americans had failed to fulfill their promises about paying debts to British merchants and compensating Loyalists (page 113). It now seems clear, however, that the British held on to these posts in order to give Canadian fur traders time to strengthen their alliances with the Indians of the Northwest.

The new nation seeks trade. Americans wanted to resume trade with Britain after 1783. They soon found, however, that English merchants were determined to exclude them from commerce with overseas British possessions. Acts passed by Parliament banned American ships from the British West Indies and restricted the importation of American goods into England. Moreover, British merchants flooded the American market with their goods, thus hurting this country's manufacturers and shippers.

There was little that Americans could do to improve trade relations with Britain in the 1780's. But the new country did sign favorable trade treaties with France, Sweden, Prussia, and the Netherlands. Moreover, New England merchants succeeded in opening trade with China.

Foreign countries lack respect for the new nation. Spain was no friendlier than Great Britain during the 1780's. She wanted to make sure that the United States did not become a strong rival in America. So Spain ignored the provisions of the Treaty of Paris that fixed the southern boundary of the United States and guaranteed the free use of the Mississippi River (page 113). From their forts in Florida the Spanish encouraged the Indians to keep American settlers out of what is now Alabama and Mississippi. Spain also refused to let Americans use New Orleans as a port. This was a serious blow to western settlers, for it cut off the chief outlet for their produce.

Equally humiliating was the capture of American seamen by the Barbary pirates of North Africa (map, page 202). For years these pirates had terrorized the Mediter-

The Empress of China, *pictured on this Chinese fan, returned to New York in 1785 after a profitable trading voyage to Canton, China. The success of this pioneering venture prompted American merchants to develop more trade with the Far East.*

ranean and blackmailed even the strongest European countries. In the 1780's they tried the same tactics with the United States. But Congress was too poor either to pay sufficient ransom to satisfy the pirates or to wage war against them. The pirates captured many American merchant ships and imprisoned hundreds of American seamen.

Even the French government, which was officially allied to the United States, showed scant respect for the representatives of the weak Confederation. Jefferson, serving as American minister in Paris, sadly reported, "We are the lowest and most obscure of the whole diplomatic tribe."

Congress lacks authority at home. Not only did the new government command little respect abroad; it exercised little authority even at home. During 1782–1783 Congress requested eleven million dollars from the states. Having no way of compelling the states to pay their assessments, however, Congress received less than one and a half million dollars. As Robert Morris observed, asking the states to levy taxes for support of the Confederation was like "preaching to the dead." As Superintendent of Finance, Morris urged Congress to raise

funds by establishing duties on imports or levying taxes of one kind or another. But Congress lacked the power to take such steps, and the states blocked all attempts to amend the Articles. Finally Morris resigned in disgust. "To increase our debts, while the prospect of paying them diminishes," he commented, "does not consist with my ideas of integrity."

Congress' lack of control over the states led to other problems. The states printed paper money which quickly lost value. In Rhode Island the debtors, many of whom were farmers, won control of the legislature and passed a law requiring merchants to accept the worthless paper money. When the merchants refused to comply, farmers blockaded the towns and starved the businessmen into submission.

State tariff laws also caused trouble. Tariffs were intended to produce revenue for the states and protect local industry. Before long, however, neighboring states were using tariff measures to take revenge on each other. When New York taxed garden produce from New Jersey and Connecticut, both states struck back. Connecticut farmers boycotted New York markets, and

New Jersey slapped a heavy tax on a lighthouse which New Yorkers had built on the Jersey shore. Congress was powerless to stop such interstate warfare.

Another weakness in the government created by the Articles was the absence of national courts and of a strong executive branch. Each of the states had courts, but there was no national judiciary system. Congress could recommend a solution to a dispute between two states but had no way of enforcing its decisions. Nor could it enforce its own legislation; this was left up to the individual states. Congress established departments to handle foreign affairs, financial matters, and national defense; but these provided little leadership. Washington voiced the concern of many Americans when he described the Confederation as "a half-starved, limping government, always moving upon crutches and tottering at every step."

Shays' Rebellion reveals public discontent. Strife between creditors and debtors in Massachusetts aroused thé whole country to the dangers of weak central government. Property-owning creditors who controlled the Massachusetts government decided to pay off the state's war debt. To secure the necessary funds, a personal tax was levied on every resident of the state. Many of the farmers in western Massachusetts, who were already in debt and burdened by the rising cost of living, viewed this new tax as the last straw. Defeated in an effort to have paper money printed, as had been done in Rhode Island, the Massachusetts debtors tried to block the courts from holding sessions. The purpose was to prevent judges from ordering the seizure of property for nonpayment of debt. In central and western Massachusetts, farmers, mechanics, and laborers marched into the courthouses and released debtors from jail.

The climax came in the fall of 1786 when Daniel Shays, a Revolutionary veteran, took command of the discontented forces. Shays and his men, having closed several courts, tried to seize the arsenal at Springfield, Massachusetts. As recruits poured in, Shays' "army" swelled to almost 2000. But state militia finally put down the rebellion.

Shays was condemned to death but later was pardoned. Though law and order were reestablished in Massachusetts, thoughtful Americans were alarmed by the fact that Congress had been unable to take action to end the violence. John Jay wrote to Washington in 1786, "I am uneasy and apprehensive, more so than during the war."

Throughout the states, businessmen, merchants, property-owners, and middle-class people in general were beginning to recognize the need to strengthen the central government. Shays' Rebellion had the effect of uniting Americans in this opinion. By 1787 many of them agreed with Tom Paine that "thirteen staves and never a hoop will not make a barrel."

▶ CHECK-UP

1. What problems troubled the Confederation government? What is the present-day view of the Articles of Confederation?

2. What were the chief provisions of the Land Ordinance of 1785? Of the Northwest Ordinance? Why was this legislation important?

3. What issues after 1783 divided this country and Britain? Divided this country and Spain?

4. What problems arose because of Congress' lack of control over the states? What was Shays' Rebellion? Why was it important?

· · · · · · · · · · · · · · · · · · · ·

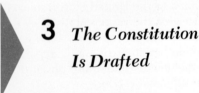

3 The Constitution Is Drafted

Preliminary meetings lead to united action. As early as 1780, Alexander Hamilton had warned: "The fundamental defect is a want of power in Congress. . . . The idea of an uncontrollable sovereignty in each state . . . will defeat the other powers given to Congress, and make our union feeble and precarious." This view was shared by Hamilton's friends in New York and by a group of prominent Virginians. It was a conference called by the latter group which eventually resulted in the Phila-

The Constitutional Convention met in Philadelphia's Independence Hall, so named because it had witnessed the signing of the Declaration of Independence. These two views show the historic building in the 1700's and two centuries later. The old tower was pulled down in 1781 and the present steeple erected in 1828.

delphia convention that drew up the Constitution.

Because Maryland and Virginia were quarreling over navigation rights on the Potomac River, George Washington brought the two sides together at Mount Vernon in 1785. At this meeting James Madison suggested a conference of all the states to discuss commercial problems. The supporters of a stronger central government hoped that such a gathering might result in amendments to the Articles of Confederation. But only five states sent delegates to the conference, which was held at Annapolis. Maryland, the host state, sent no representative at all. Alexander Hamilton then proposed still another conference, this one to meet in Philadelphia in May, 1787. Virginia endorsed the idea and chose Washington to head its delegation. Other states fell in line, and Congress gave its reluctant consent, providing that the meeting be held "for the sole and express purpose of revising the Articles of Confederation."

The Philadelphia Convention brings together famous Americans. The 55 delegates who at one time or another attended the Philadelphia meetings made up a notable group. Jefferson, who as American minister in Paris did not attend, called the delegates an "assembly of demigods." Two members of the Convention did have almost that standing with the American public: General Washington and the aging Benjamin Franklin. Among the other delegates were Robert Morris of Pennsylvania; James Madison and Edmund Randolph from Virginia; Alexander Hamilton from New York; John Dickinson now representing Delaware; and William Paterson of New Jersey. Absent, in addition to Jefferson, were John Adams and John Jay (both of whom were in Europe), as well as the leading defenders of states' rights, Sam Adams and Patrick Henry. The average age of the delegates was only 42 years. A majority of them were college graduates, and more than half were lawyers, although many of them had commercial interests as well. Most of the delegates had had experience in politics. Seven had been state governors, over half had served in Congress, and eight were signers of the Declaration of Independence.

The plan of government that these men were to write was given an "economic interpretation" by the historian Charles A. Beard in a book first published in 1913. Beard argued that since most of the delegates to the Constitutional Convention were men of property, they had an economic stake in establishing a powerful central government. And since most of them were creditors, they wanted a government strong enough to deal with domestic uprisings like Shays' Rebellion. It is true that most of the Founding Fathers were financially well-off. But this does not mean that they fashioned a new form of government to fit selfish needs. These men were representative of the best-educated and most politically experienced Americans of their time. They sincerely believed that a stronger central government was essential. Moreover, they felt sure that the Constitution would provide better government for farmers as well as merchants, for debtors as well as creditors. Time would prove that the interests of the delegates coincided with those of the nation. Historians today feel that Beard overstated his "economic interpretation" of how the Constitution came to be written. They are more apt to agree with James Madison:

> There never was an assembly of men, charged with a great and obvious trust, who were more pure in their motives, or more exclusively and anxiously devoted to the object committed to them than were the members of the Federal Convention of 1787.

The Convention holds secret sessions. The delegates began their deliberations on May 25, and their first action was to elect Washington chairman. Next they voted to conduct all their sessions in private and to allow no news releases or reports of their progress. Madison later explained why:

> [Throughout the debates] the minds of the members were changing, and much was to be gained by a yielding and accommodat-

ing spirit. Had the members committed themselves publicly at first, they would have afterwards supposed consistency required them to maintain their ground, whereas by secret discussion no man felt himself obliged to retain his opinions any longer than he was satisfied of their propriety and truth, and was open to the force of argument.

Our knowledge of what went on in the meetings comes chiefly from Madison's remarkable diary. In his own system of shorthand, he took down all that was said in debate and then worked until the early hours of each morning to transcribe his notes. Despite these labors Madison made some of the most useful contributions to the discussions. A student of past forms of government, Madison "always came forward the best informed man on any point in the debate," according to another delegate.

The delegates agree to draft a new document. The first major speech of the Convention was delivered by Edmund Randolph of Virginia. His outline of the type of government that the Virginia delegation wanted became known as the *Virginia Plan*. Early in his speech Randolph proposed "that a national government ought to be established consisting of a supreme legislative, judiciary, and executive." The Virginians themselves were aware that such a move would go beyond the Convention's authority to amend the Articles. But in the course of the discussions, Washington is supposed to have said:

> It is too probable that no plans we propose will be adopted. Perhaps another dreadful conflict is to be sustained. If to please the people, we offer what we ourselves disapprove, how can we afterwards defend our work? Let us raise a standard to which the wise and honest can repair. The event is in the hand of God.

Randolph's proposal to create a new government of three branches threw the Convention into excited discussion. But when the vote was taken on this resolution, the Convention agreed to establish a government consisting of three separate branches. Thus, they decided to create a new framework of government rather than just to amend the Articles. This decision may well be considered the most important vote during the entire Convention.

Large states clash with small states. The Virginia Plan called for a Congress of two houses in which the total number of delegates would be divided among the states according to the free population of each state. Congress would have the power to select the executive, and a system of national courts would be established.

It became clear that under the Virginia Plan, the more heavily populated states would control Congress. Naturally the small states were strongly opposed. Delegates from Connecticut, Maryland, Delaware, and New Jersey spoke out against the Virginia Plan. They eagerly awaited the arrival of New Hampshire delegates and wished that Rhode Island had not decided to boycott the Convention.

In mid-June, William Paterson of New Jersey presented an alternative plan based on the wishes of the small states. The *New Jersey Plan* called for a one-house legislature in which each state would cast only one vote, as in the Confederation Congress. But unlike the Articles of Confederation, the New Jersey Plan would allow Congress to regulate trade and to impose tariffs. It also would provide for an executive council and a federal judiciary, although the powers of both would be restricted by Congress.

The delegates reach a deadlock. For two weeks the delegates furiously debated the Virginia and New Jersey Plans. The heart of the quarrel was whether the central government would be given the power to control the states. Under the Virginia Plan, where representation in Congress was based on population, it would. Under the New Jersey Plan, where each state had equal power, it would not. Paterson angrily announced that he would "rather submit to a monarch, to a despot, than to . . . tyranny" by the large states. James Wilson of Pennsylvania shot back, "I never will confederate on his [Paterson's] principles."

The weather was hot and humid, and the tempers of the delegates were short. It was obvious to Washington that further debate

would not solve the problem, so on July 2 he called for a vote on the New Jersey Plan. The result was a tie: five states for; five opposed; Georgia delegates divided; New Hampshire still not there; and Rhode Island absent. "We were on the verge of dissolution," declared one delegate, "scarce held together by the strength of an hair."

The "Great Compromise" settles the controversy. At this crucial moment the Convention agreed to submit the problem to a compromise committee of one delegate from each of the eleven participating states. The Convention then adjourned for a few days "that time might be given to the committee, and to such as choose to attend the celebration of the anniversary of Independence." Washington and his Philadelphia host, Robert Morris, went trout fishing. Other delegates attended a Fourth of July benefit performance at the Opera House to raise funds for the ransom of Americans held by the Barbary pirates.

When the Convention reassembled, the compromise committee was ready to report. It suggested the creation of a two-house legislature composed of a House of Representatives and a Senate. To satisfy those who supported the Virginia Plan, members of the House were to be allotted to the states on the basis of population. The House members were to vote individually, not as part of a state delegation. To satisfy followers of the New Jersey Plan, the states would have equal representation in the Senate. Each state would elect two senators, who could vote individually. The legislative authority of the two bodies was to be equal except that the House would originate all bills for raising revenue. This "Great Compromise," as it came to be called, was accepted by the Convention on July 16.

The "three-fifths" compromise is approved. The compromise committee worked out a solution to another difficult problem. The southern states thought that slaves should be counted in deciding the number of representatives per state but should *not* be counted when direct taxes were to be levied.[2] Northerners protested, however,

---

[2] *Direct taxes* were to be levied upon the states on the basis of population (page 139).

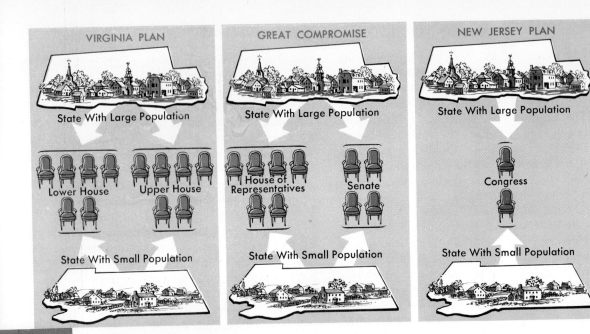

VIRGINIA PLAN — State With Large Population — Lower House — Upper House — State With Small Population

GREAT COMPROMISE — State With Large Population — House of Representatives — Senate — State With Small Population

NEW JERSEY PLAN — State With Large Population — Congress — State With Small Population

THE GREAT COMPROMISE

Compare the provisions of the Great Compromise with the proposals for apportioning representation in the Virginia and New Jersey Plans. Note that the Great Compromise included features of both plans.

that this would give Southerners an unfair advantage. The compromise committee suggested that five slaves be counted as three persons for purposes of representation as well as taxation. This solution was accepted by the delegates.

The executive and judicial branches are provided for. The delegates then turned to the question of the executive and judicial branches of the new government. Some delegates recommended that the executive branch be a committee rather than one individual. Some wanted the executive to serve for life, others for one year only. Some thought Congress should appoint the executive, others said the people should elect him. Finally, the delegates decided to entrust the executive powers to one man, to make his term of office four years, and to have him chosen by *electors*. These electors were to be selected by the states in whatever manner each of them chose. The electoral system (page 145) proved to be one of the clumsiest parts of the Constitution. It was designed to make the President independent of the legislative branch without putting his election directly into the hands of the people. The delegates believed that if the people were to elect the

President directly, they might vote only for local candidates because of lack of knowledge about leaders of other states.

Since both the New Jersey and Virginia Plans called for federal courts, the Convention had little trouble reaching an agreement about the judicial branch of government. Federal courts were provided for; the judges were to be appointed by the President. Most of the delegates probably assumed that the highest court, or Supreme Court, would decide if state or federal laws conflicted with the Constitution.

Final compromises are reached. During August the Convention ironed out disputes between slaveholding states and nonslaveholding states. Earlier, Madison had told the delegates that their real division of interest "did not lie between the large and small states; it lay between the northern and southern." The commercial North wanted a strong central government to control commerce, both interstate and foreign. The agricultural South, however, wanted to be able to buy and sell in the most favorable market anywhere in the world. The South feared that Congress, under northern influence, might set up tariff duties that would block the free flow of goods to and from the country. It also feared that Congress might interfere with the slave trade or sign commercial treaties that would be unfavorable to the South.

The delegates managed to find compromises that quieted these fears. Congress was given the power to regulate commerce among the states and with foreign nations. But specific limits on this power were adopted which made Southerners feel safer. (1) Congress could not prevent before 1808 the importation of slaves. It could, however, levy a tax of ten dollars on each imported slave. (2) Congress could not impose duties on exports. (3) A two-thirds vote was needed in the Senate to ratify a treaty. Thus the South (which at the time held about half the Senate votes) could probably defeat any treaty which might harm its interests. (4) Runaway or fugitive slaves were to be returned, even from free states, to their lawful masters.

The Convention adjourns. By September, 1787, the Convention had completed its outline for a new form of government. No delegate was satisfied with every part of the Constitution. Madison thought it "the best that could be obtained from the jarring interests of the states, and the miscellaneous opinions of politicians." But some disgruntled delegates had already walked out. Of the 55 men who had attended sessions, only 42 were present in mid-September. Of these delegates, only 39 were willing to sign the document. To get around this embarrassing situation, a phrase was inserted: "Done in Convention by the unanimous consent of *the States* present the 17th of September." During the signing of the document Franklin made his celebrated comment about the rising sun on the back of the presiding officer's chair (page 118).

▶ CHECK-UP

1. What illustrious Americans took part in the Constitutional Convention? What were their probable motives? Why were secret sessions held?

2. What was the importance of the decision to establish a government of three separate branches? Compare the Virginia and New Jersey Plans. What compromise was accepted by both large and small states?

3. What decisions were made concerning the executive branch? The judicial branch?

4. What issues divided northern and southern states? What compromises were reached?

· ·

4 *The Constitution Is Ratified*

The states consider ratification. The Philadelphia Convention provided that the Constitution be submitted to special state conventions. When nine states ratified it, the new government would go into effect for those states. By the fall of 1787 the Constitution had become the leading topic of discussion throughout the country. Those

---

Presidential Electors

American voters choose their President and Vice-President indirectly through the electoral college. The members of the electoral college, called "electors," are selected by the 50 states. The size of a state's electoral vote is determined by its representation in Congress.

Originally the members of the electoral college were supposed to use their own judgment in picking the best candidates for President and Vice-President. But with the advent of political parties, the role of the electors became less important. Now the party organizations in each state choose slates of electors. The electors are pledged to vote for their party's candidates if they receive a majority of the state's popular vote. Thus, practically speaking, the meeting of the electoral college a few weeks after election day is merely a formality.

Recently, however, some electors have exercised their constitutional right to vote for whom they please. In 1948 one of the Tennessee electors pledged to support Harry S. Truman bolted tradition and voted for Strom Thurmond of South Carolina. In the elections of 1960 and 1964, a number of southern electors refused to pledge support for any candidate and voted for their own choices.

who favored it called themselves *Federalists*. Opponents of the new federal union became known as *Antifederalists*. This group was in the unhappy position of fighting the Constitution while having to admit that the Articles had serious defects.

The lines between those who favored the Constitution and those who opposed it were not always clearly drawn. In fact, there is no simple explanation of why some people supported ratification of this document while others opposed it during 1787–1788. In general, the Federalists were willing to see the states surrender some of their powers to a stronger central government. The Federalists included many merchants, plantation owners, and professional people; yet some merchants and planters opposed the Constitution. The Antifederalists, on the other hand, did not want the states to lose any of their power. Sharing this viewpoint were small farmers and workingmen in the cities, as well as many debtors. Yet there was a strong pocket of Federalists in western Massachusetts, the center of Shays' Rebellion.

The battle for ratification was hard-fought. Had the Constitution been put to the test of a popular vote in the fall of 1787, it might have been defeated. Many Americans feared that if it were adopted, (1) the new government would destroy state sovereignty; (2) a standing army would violate the freedom of citizens; (3) taxes would be sharply increased; (4) agricultural interests would be sacrificed to commercial interests; and (5) individual liberties would be violated because the Constitution had no bill of rights. Yet within a few months the Federalists managed to dispel these fears. The Federalists made much of Washington's support of the Constitution and emphasized the General's willingness to serve as President if the document were ratified.

The Federalists' most convincing arguments appeared in a series of essays published in a New York newspaper. Signed "Publius," the 85 articles were actually written by Alexander Hamilton (who conceived the idea), James Madison, and John Jay. In clear, forceful language the authors outlined the weaknesses of the Articles and showed how the new government would remedy these defects. The essays were reprinted in many other newspapers and also published as a book entitled *The Federalist*. Hamilton, Madison, and Jay undoubtedly swayed many votes in the state ratifying conventions. To this day *The Federalist* remains one of the best interpretations of the Constitution and one of the most penetrating studies of government ever written.

Nine states ratify the Constitution. Four months after the signing of the Constitution, it had been ratified by Delaware, Pennsylvania, New Jersey, Georgia, and Connecticut. The first serious contest occurred in Massachusetts, where some of the rural delegates opposed the Constitution on the grounds that it would increase the power of the seaboard aristocrats. Only after John Hancock threw his wholehearted support to the Federalists did the scales tip in favor of ratification in Massachusetts. Next to fall in line were Maryland and South Carolina, early in 1788. After a heated struggle, New Hampshire became the ninth state to ratify. Thus, the Constitution was to go into effect for those nine states in June, 1788. But, without the participation of the key states of Virginia and New York, the success of the new plan of government would be in doubt.

Virginia and New York ratify. In Virginia the fight over ratification was fierce. James Madison, Governor Edmund Randolph, and John Marshall supported the Constitution, while Patrick Henry and George Mason fought against it. Referring to the members of the Constitutional Convention, Henry angrily asked, "Who authorized them to speak the language of *We the People*, instead of *We the States?*" James Madison patiently answered the Antifederalist criticism and promised to help secure a bill of rights once the new government was established. By the narrow vote of 89 to 79, Virginia finally approved the Constitution. Immediately Madison dispatched this news to New York, where the state ratifying convention was deadlocked.

Federalist strength in New York State centered in and about the city of New York and was led by Alexander Hamilton. The Antifederalists, led by Governor George Clinton, had at first been in the majority at the state convention. But, as the weeks of debate dragged on, and state after state ratified, some of the New York Antifederalists began to waver. Hamilton skillfully played on their fears of being excluded from the new government, and his *Federalist* essays influenced both the delegates and the public. Finally the news from Virginia helped him clinch the argument. By a narrow vote, the Federalists carried the state convention in July, 1788. New York thus became the eleventh state to ratify.

The new government is launched. It was now certain that the United States would try the new form of government. Preparations began for the election of a President, Vice-President, and members of Congress. In 1789, after the new government had actually taken over the reins of power, North Carolina voted to join the federal experiment. Not until 1790 did the Rhode Islanders take similar action.

In spite of the hard-fought contest over ratification, many Americans were hopeful about the future of the country under the Constitution. The poet Francis Hopkinson voiced their feeling in "The New Roof: A Song for Federal Mechanics":

Come muster, my lads, your mechanical tools,
Your saws and your axes, your hammers and rules;
Bring your mallets and planes, your level and line,
And plenty of pins of American pine:
For our roof we will raise, and our song still shall be,
Our government firm, and our citizens free.

▶ CHECK-UP

1. Who were the Federalists? The Antifederalists? In general, what fears were expressed by the latter? How were arguments against the Constitution met by the Federalists?

2. How was the Constitution to be ratified? Why was ratification by Virginia and New York of crucial importance? How was ratification secured in these states?

· · · · · · · · · · · · · · · · · · · ·

5 *The Constitution Meets the Test of Time*

The Founding Fathers draw upon past experience. Ever since 1787 the United States Constitution has served as a model for other written constitutions. The English Prime Minister William Gladstone once called it "the most wonderful work ever struck off at a given time by the brain and purpose of man." Yet the Constitution was not completely new, nor was it dashed off in a burst of inspiration. The Founding Fathers were too practical for that. All of them had experienced the restrictions of British colonial rule and the abuses of weak government under the Articles of Confederation. Most of them had studied enough history to know how different types of government had functioned in the past. In their debates they often referred to British politics and the powers of Parliament, and to the colonial assemblies, the state governments, and Congress under the Articles. The Founding Fathers made wise use of their knowledge of the past, but they also came up with ideas of their own to make the Constitution fit American needs.

The Convention sets up a federal system. One of the most difficult problems at Philadelphia concerned the distribution of power between the central government and the states. Under the Articles the central government had no real authority over the states and no power to deal directly with the people. The Philadelphia delegates agreed that the central government had to have more power but not so much that the states became merely administrative units. To solve this problem, they devised the *federal system*. This system provided a large measure of centralized control, yet preserved the benefits of state and local self-government. Under the federal plan, the states were to give up certain powers to the central government. In the exercise of these powers, the national government was to be supreme. In effect, it received those powers from the people and would be answerable to the people for the way in which they were carried out. The states, however, retained those powers not surrendered to the central government or forbidden by the Constitution.

State and federal authority is defined. In working out the federal system, the Convention delegates had carefully divided power between the federal government and the states. They listed, or enumerated, certain specific powers which the national government alone could exercise (page 142). Thus, the new Congress had many more powers than Congress under the Articles. Furthermore, its laws were binding upon every citizen. The states, however, kept control over voting qualifications, local governments, education, corporations, marriage and divorce, and the definition and punishment of ordinary crimes. Through their "police power" the states also supervised the health, safety, and welfare of their citizens. The skill with which the Founding Fathers distributed power between the federal government and the states is a major reason for the success of the Constitution.

The Convention sets up checks and balances. You have already read that the Constitution provided for separate legislative, executive, and judicial branches in the government. This system is called *separation of powers*. To make sure that no one branch got more than its share of power, the delegates to the Philadelphia Convention also added a system of *checks and balances*. The President, for example, can check Congress by vetoing legislation. In addition, the practice of *judicial review* has permitted the Supreme Court to check Congress by declaring laws unconstitutional. Congress, on the other hand, can check both the President and members of the Court through its power to impeach government officials for "treason, bribery, or other high crimes and misdemeanors."[3] Checks and balances were even set up within the legislative branch of government. Both houses of Congress, for example, have to approve a bill for it to become law.

[3] For explanation of impeachment, see page 139.

This complicated system of checks and balances has prevented the concentration of political power in any one branch of the government. Some critics have contended, however, that it leads to inefficiency and slows down the process of government.

The Constitution is flexible. At the time the Constitution was adopted, most Americans and Europeans thought of it as a detailed, specific, and fairly rigid plan of government. Yet time has proved it to be remarkably flexible. For example, the Constitution gives Congress the authority to "make all laws which shall be necessary and proper for carrying into execution the foregoing powers" (page 143). Through the years, Congress and the courts have interpreted this "necessary and proper" clause (also called the *elastic clause*) to fit the needs of the time. One of the earliest uses of this provision (as we shall find in Chapter 7) was the establishment by Congress of a national bank. The "general welfare" clause (page 142) is another source of flexibility in the Constitution, for Congress can decide what the general welfare requires. Another source of flexibility is the amendment process.

The Constitution can be amended. The members of the Constitutional Convention knew how difficult it had been to alter the Articles of Confederation. So they purposely provided four ways in which the Constitution could be amended (page 149). The Antifederalists especially appreciated this feature. Patrick Henry, for example, accepted ratification with these words: "I will be a peaceful citizen. My head, my hand, and my heart shall be at liberty to retrieve the loss of liberty, and remove the defects of that system, in a constitutional way."

The Bill of Rights is added. The very first amendments to the Constitution were intended to safeguard the rights of the individual. These ten Amendments, known as the *Bill of Rights,* were proposed by Congress in 1789 and went into effect in 1791 (pages 150–151). Among other things, the Bill of Rights guarantees to American citizens (1) freedom of religion, of speech, and of the press; (2) the right of peaceable assembly; (3) freedom from unauthorized

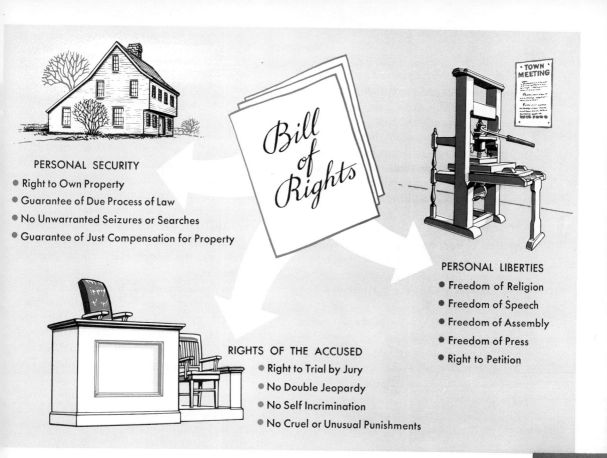

PERSONAL SECURITY
- Right to Own Property
- Guarantee of Due Process of Law
- No Unwarranted Seizures or Searches
- Guarantee of Just Compensation for Property

PERSONAL LIBERTIES
- Freedom of Religion
- Freedom of Speech
- Freedom of Assembly
- Freedom of Press
- Right to Petition

RIGHTS OF THE ACCUSED
- Right to Trial by Jury
- No Double Jeopardy
- No Self Incrimination
- No Cruel or Unusual Punishments

LIBERTIES GUARANTEED IN THE BILL OF RIGHTS

American civil liberties are guaranteed by the federal Bill of Rights and by the state constitutions. Note that the rights granted to individuals are safeguards against tyranny.

CHART STUDY

search; (4) fair and impartial trial by jury; (5) protection of life, liberty, and property; and (6) protection from cruel and unusual punishments. These guarantees of personal liberty were binding upon the national government, and similar bills of rights were already in most of the state constitutions. To satisfy those Americans who feared that the federal government would control the states, the Tenth Amendment asserts: "The powers not delegated to the United States by the Constitution, nor prohibited by it to the States, are reserved to the States respectively, or to the people."

Custom and usage have added to our form of government. There is still another way in which the government under the Constitution has adapted to changing conditions. Experience and custom have firmly established certain ways of doing things, as much as if they had been written into the Constitution. Our system of political parties, for instance, has greatly affected the operation of the government. The Founding Fathers did not foresee this development, nor would they have welcomed it. But political parties made their appearance in the 1790's and have been with us ever since. The committee system in Congress, the President's Cabinet, and the selection of presidential candidates by national conventions — these and other developments are outside the framework of the Constitution. Yet they have become vital parts of the governmental structure. So binding are these political customs that they are sometimes called the "unwritten constitution."

The Constitution has served the nation well. The changes that have been made in the original work of the constitutional delegates are remarkably few. The document they put together has remained the basis of the government of a great people for longer than any other single written document. It is indeed a tribute to the Fathers of the Constitution that the system of government they worked out has endured through the many startling changes which have taken place in this nation and in the world.

▶ CHECK-UP

1. What is a federal system of government? Why did the delegates favor this type of government? What is the system of checks and balances? Why was this included in the Constitution?

2. How did each of these make the Constitution more flexible: elastic clause, "general welfare" clause, provisions for amendment, the "unwritten constitution"?

3. Why was a Bill of Rights added to the Constitution?

. . . .

Clinching the Main Ideas in Chapter 6

The Declaration of Independence inaugurated a period of new political developments as well as social and economic changes. The new state governments guaranteed certain rights to the people. Increasing numbers of Americans were able to vote and hold office, and land became more easily available to small farmers.

It soon became clear that the most serious problem facing the states was weakness of the central government. The Articles of Confederation, adopted in 1781, provided for little more than a weak league of states. True, the Congress of the Confederation worked out a brilliant plan for incorporating new territory into the union. But in conducting foreign affairs and eliminating conflict at home, Congress was much less successful. Dissatisfaction with the Articles finally led to the Philadelphia Convention in 1787 and the adoption of a new plan of government.

What Madison called "the defects, the deformities, the diseases" of the Articles were remedied in the Constitution. The new system of government granted additional powers to the central authority without destroying the authority of the states. The federal government was divided into three departments, each of which had checks over the others. A Bill of Rights, adopted soon after the Constitution, provided for the protection of most individual liberties.

Those who favored the Constitution, known as Federalists, organized support for the new document and managed to bring about its ratification. By the summer of 1788, nine states had ratified the Constitution, and it thus became certain that the new government would be established. By 1790 all thirteen states had approved, and the new United States government was in operation.

Chapter Review

Terms to Understand

1. judicial review
2. Northwest Ordinance
3. checks and balances
4. custom and usage
5. Bill of Rights
6. Great Compromise
7. federal system
8. *The Federalist*
9. New Jersey Plan
10. Virginia Plan
11. separation of powers
12. elastic clause
13. quitrent
14. Shays' Rebellion
15. enumerated power
16. Articles of Confederation

What Do You Think?

1. How did the new state governments differ from the colonial governments?

2. How did the plan for dealing with "colonies" set forth in the Northwest Ordinance differ from Parliament's view of the relationship of colonies to the mother country?

3. Perhaps this country's greatest contribution to the theory of government is the federal principle, under which a strong central government could be established without destroying the already established state governments.

Explain, by referring to the Constitution, how this was accomplished.

4. In *Letters from a Farmer in Pennsylvania,* John Dickinson wrote: ". . . for who are a free people? Not those . . . whose government is reasonably . . . exercised, but those who live under a government so constitutionally . . . controlled, that proper provision is made against it being otherwise exercised." What did he mean? Did the Constitution provide this type of government? How?

5. Without the "Great Compromise," the Constitutional Convention might have ended in failure. Consider this compromise in terms of the "one man, one vote" principle implied in a recent Supreme Court decision.

Using Your Knowledge of History

1. List "weaknesses" in the Articles of Confederation and the provisions in the Constitution intended to remove these weaknesses.

2. Debate: *Resolved,* That conditions in 1787 made necessary the delegating to the central government of powers hitherto exercised by the states.

3. Patrick Henry accepted Virginia's ratification of the Constitution with these words: "My head, my hand, and my heart shall be at liberty to retrieve the loss of liberty, and remove the defects of that system, in a constitutional way." What "liberty" did Henry feel that Virginia had lost? How could such liberty be retrieved? Develop your views in a 250-word essay.

4. The United Kingdom has a system of government under which the prime minister is the head of the majority party in the House of Commons. The defeat of a major legislative proposal sponsored by him leads to an election, and no court has the right of judicial review. Give a report comparing this parliamentary system of government with ours. Bring out possible advantages and limitations of the parliamentary type of government.

Extending Your Knowledge of History

Contrast the gloomy views of the 1780's presented in *The Critical Period of American History, 1783–1789* by John Fiske, with the findings of recent research brought out in Merrill Jensen's *The New Nation: A History of the United States During the Confederation, 1781–1789.* An excellent account of the Constitutional Convention can be found in Carl Van Doren's *The Great Rehearsal.* Clinton Rossiter has edited *The Federalist Papers,* and their political impact is assessed by William F. Swindler in "The Letters of Publius," *American Heritage,* June, 1961.

The text of the Constitution of the United States, with explanatory notes, follows on pages 138–160.

THE CONSTITUTION OF
THE UNITED STATES
OF AMERICA

Pages 133–136 have described the basic principles which underlie the Constitution of the United States and make it the vital basis for the American government. Frequent references to it in this textbook indicate its influence upon the nation's history. It likewise provides the guidelines within which present-day laws are adopted and administered. It is not enough for Americans to read *about* the Constitution; they need to become familiar with the document itself.

The body of the Constitution is divided into seven Articles. Articles I, II, and III provide a blueprint for the organization and operation respectively of Congress, the President and other members of the Executive Department, and the federal courts. Article IV defines the relationships (1) between the states and (2) between the states and the federal government. Article V describes the methods of amending the Constitution, and Article VI covers certain general provisions. Ratification was dealt with in the seventh Article.

The vitality of the Constitution is revealed in the continuing process of amendment. Sometimes Amendments have been adopted in groups. Thus the first ten Amendments (the Bill of Rights) were ratified in 1791; while Amendments 13, 14, and 15 were added as a result of the Civil War. More recent Amendments, beginning with Amendment 16, have reflected changing conditions in the twentieth century.

The Constitution, modernized in capitalization and punctuation, is printed below in the wider column at the left. The actual words of the document are printed in regular type (like this: We the People). For easier reading, various headings and subheadings have been added in bolder type (like this: **Legislative Department, Congress in General,** and **Election and term of members**). Certain portions of the Constitution which are no longer in effect are printed in italic type (like this: *which shall be determined*).

Throughout the text you will find superior numbers (like this:[2]). These refer to the numbers in the narrower column at the right, where notes have been provided to help you understand the Constitution. Notice that the first note in each article begins a new series of numbers. The notes for the Amendments also begin a new series.

PREAMBLE

We the People of the United States,[1] in order to form a more perfect union, establish justice, insure domestic tranquillity, provide for the common defense, promote the general welfare, and secure the blessings of liberty to ourselves and our posterity, do ordain and establish this Constitution for the United States of America.[2]

ARTICLE I

Legislative Department

SECTION 1. **Congress in General**

All legislative powers herein granted shall be vested in a Congress of the United States, which shall consist of a Senate and House of Representatives.[1]

1. These opening words of the Constitution clearly indicated that the sovereign power (the power to establish a government or change it) belongs to the people.

2. The Preamble states the objectives of the Constitution.

1. Under the Great Compromise the Senate was to represent the states equally; in the House, membership was to be divided among the states according to population.

SECTION 2. The House of Representatives

a. Election and term of members. The House of Representatives shall be composed of members chosen every second year by the people of the several states,[2] and the electors[3] in each state shall have the qualifications requisite for electors of the most numerous branch of the state legislature.[4]

b. Qualification of members. No person shall be a representative who shall not have attained to the age of twenty-five years, and been seven years a citizen of the United States, and who shall not, when elected, be an inhabitant of that state in which he shall be chosen.

c. Apportionment of representatives and of direct taxes. Representatives and direct taxes shall be apportioned among the several states which may be included within this Union, according to their respective numbers,[5] *which shall be determined by adding to the whole number of free persons, including those bound to service for a term of years,[6] and excluding Indians not taxed,[7] three fifths of all other persons.*[8] The actual enumeration shall be made within three years after the first meeting of the Congress of the United States, and within every subsequent term of ten years, in such manner as they shall by law direct.[9] The number of representatives shall not exceed one for every thirty thousand, but each state shall have at least one representative; *and until such enumeration shall be made, the State of New Hampshire shall be entitled to choose three; Massachusetts, eight; Rhode Island and Providence Plantations, one; Connecticut, five; New York, six; New Jersey, four; Pennsylvania, eight; Delaware, one; Maryland, six; Virginia, ten; North Carolina, five; South Carolina, five; and Georgia, three.*

d. Filling vacancies. When vacancies happen in the representation from any state, the executive authority thereof shall issue writs of election to fill such vacancies.[10]

e. Officers; impeachment. The House of Representatives shall choose their Speaker and other officers; and shall have the sole power of impeachment.[11]

SECTION 3. The Senate

a. Number and election of members. The Senate of the United States shall be composed of two senators from each state, chosen *by the legislature thereof,*[12] for six years; and each senator shall have one vote.

b. Classification. Immediately after they shall be assembled in consequence of the first election, they shall be divided as equally as may be into three classes. *The seats of the senators of the first class shall be vacated at the expiration of the second year, of the second class at the expiration of the fourth year, and of the third class at the expiration of the sixth year,* so that one third may be chosen every second year;[13] *and if vacancies happen by resignation, or other-*

2. There is a new House every two years.

3. "Electors" in this context means voters.

4. This is the only voting qualification in the original Constitution. It meant, in effect, that the House would be a popularly elected body.

5. A direct tax is usually paid by the person on whom it is imposed; an indirect tax is usually shifted to the consumer by the person against whom it is levied. Amendment 16 now permits Congress to levy an income tax (a direct tax) without such apportionment.

6. This phrase refers to indentured servants.

7. Indians are now citizens.

8. "Persons" here means slaves.

9. A national census is taken every ten years. A law now provides that Congress shall reapportion membership of the House among the states after each census.

10. A special election is held in the state to fill a vacancy in the House.

11. Only the House has power to impeach a civil officer of the United States for "treason, bribery, or other high crimes and misdemeanors." See Article II, Section 4. The Senate tries cases of impeachment. See Article I, Section 3, clause "f."

12. Under Amendment 17 senators are now elected by voters who have the same qualifications as voters for members of the House. Thus, both houses are now popularly elected.

13. There is never a new Senate. The terms of only one third of its members expire in any election year.

wise, during the recess of the legislature of any state, the executive thereof may make temporary appointments until the next meeting of the legislature, which shall then fill such vacancies.[14]

c. **Qualifications of members.** No person shall be a senator who shall not have attained to the age of thirty years, and been nine years a citizen of the United States,[15] and who shall not, when elected, be an inhabitant of that state for which he shall be chosen.

d. **President of Senate.** The Vice-President of the United States shall be President of the Senate, but shall have no vote, unless they be equally divided.[16]

e. **Other officers.** The Senate shall choose their own officers, and also a President Pro Tempore,[17] in the absence of the Vice-President, or when he shall exercise the office of President of the United States.

f. **Trial by impeachment.** The Senate shall have the sole power to try all impeachments. When sitting for that purpose, they shall be on oath or affirmation. When the President of the United States is tried, the Chief Justice shall preside; and no person shall be convicted without the concurrence of two thirds of the members present.[18]

g. **Judgment in case of conviction.** Judgment in cases of impeachment shall not extend further than to removal from office, and disqualification to hold and enjoy any office of honor, trust, or profit under the United States; but the party convicted shall nevertheless be liable and subject to indictment, trial, judgment, and punishment, according to law.[19]

SECTION 4. **Election and Meetings of Congressmen**

a. **Method of holding elections.** The times, places, and manner of holding elections for senators and representatives shall be prescribed in each state by the legislature thereof; but the Congress may at any time by law make or alter such regulations, except as to the places of choosing senators.[20]

b. **Meeting of Congress.** The Congress shall assemble at least once in every year, *and such meeting shall be on the first Monday in December,* unless they shall by law appoint a different day.[21]

SECTION 5. **Rules of Procedure**

a. **Organization.** Each house shall be the judge of the elections, returns, and qualifications of its own members,[22] and a majority of each shall constitute a quorum to do business; but a smaller number may adjourn from day to day, and may be authorized to compel the attendance of absent members, in such manner, and under such penalties as each house may provide.

14. Amendment 17 provides for special elections to fill Senate vacancies, as in the case of the House. A state legislature, however, may give a governor power to make a temporary appointment until an election is held.

15. Age qualifications for a senator are higher than for a representative. Thus, the Senate includes older and more experienced men. This fact, as well as the longer term of senators and the continuous nature of the Senate, makes for a more stable legislative body.

16. This is the only duty assigned in the Constitution to the Vice-President. In recent years the Vice-President has been assigned many more responsibilities by the President.

17. "Pro tempore" means for the time being.

18. Impeachment is one case in which a two-thirds vote of those present is required.

19. If the Senate finds the officer guilty, it may remove him from office and disqualify him from holding another office under the United States. He may also be tried for the same offense in the courts.

20. Congressional elections are held on the Tuesday after the first Monday in November of the even-numbered years. Congress has also provided for a secret ballot.

21. Before 1933 the first regular session of a Congress began in December of the odd-numbered year and its last regular session began in December of the even-numbered year. See also Amendment 20.

22. Either house may refuse to seat a newly-elected member. Disputed elections may be settled in the House or Senate.

b. Rules of proceedings. Each house may determine the rules of its proceedings,[23] punish its members for disorderly behavior, and, with the concurrence of two thirds, expel a member.[24]

c. Journal. Each house shall keep a journal of its proceedings, and from time to time publish the same, excepting such parts as may in their judgment require secrecy;[25] and the yeas and nays of the members of either house on any question shall, at the desire of one fifth of those present, be entered on the journal.[26]

d. Adjournment. Neither house, during the session of Congress, shall, without the consent of the other, adjourn for more than three days, nor to any other place than that in which the two houses shall be sitting.

SECTION 6. **Compensation, Privileges, and Restrictions**

a. Pay and privileges of members. The senators and representatives shall receive a compensation for their services, to be ascertained by law, and paid out of the Treasury of the United States.[27] They shall in all cases, except treason, felony, and breach of the peace, be privileged from arrest during their attendance at the session of their respective houses, and in going to and returning from the same;[28] and for any speech or debate in either house, they shall not be questioned in any other place.

b. Holding other offices prohibited.[29] No senator or representative shall, during the time for which he was elected, be appointed to any civil office under the authority of the United States which shall have been created, or the emoluments[30] whereof shall have been increased during such time; and no person holding any office under the United States shall be a member of either house during his continuance in office.

SECTION 7. **Mode of Passing Laws**

a. Revenue bills. All bills for raising revenue shall originate in the House of Representatives;[31] but the Senate may propose or concur with amendments as on other bills.

b. How bills become laws. Every bill which shall have passed the House of Representatives and the Senate shall, before it become a law, be presented to the President of the United States;[32] if he approve he shall sign it, but if not he shall return it, with his objections, to that house in which it shall have originated, who shall enter the objections at large on their journal, and proceed to reconsider it. If after such reconsideration two thirds of that house shall agree to pass the bill, it shall be sent, together with the objections, to the other house, by which it shall likewise be reconsidered, and if approved by two thirds of that house, it shall become a law. But in all such cases the votes of both houses shall be determined by yeas and nays, and the names of the persons voting for and against the bill

23. Extensive rules of procedure have grown up covering the duties of officers and committees and the order and means of conducting business.

24. Expulsion from either house requires a two-thirds vote.

25. The Congressional Record is issued daily during sessions of Congress.

26. The vote of one fifth of those present is sufficient to cause the vote of each member to be recorded.

27. This provision served to strengthen the federal government. Unless the new government succeeded, members of Congress would receive no pay. The compensation of congressmen now stands at $30,000 annually, plus allowances for travel, clerk hire, stationery, and other uses. Congressmen also enjoy the franking privilege, or the right to send free any mail stamped with their names.

28. Legal action cannot be taken against congressmen for any statements made on the floor of Congress.

29. This section places certain limitations upon members of Congress.

30. This means salary or other compensation.

31. Tariff or income-tax measures are examples of revenue bills. By custom, bills appropriating money also originate in the House. Actually the Senate exerts about as much influence over revenue bills as does the House.

32. Before a bill is sent to the President, it must be passed in identical form by both houses. Differences are usually ironed out in a conference committee composed of members of both houses.

shall be entered on the journal of each house respectively. If any bill shall not be returned by the President within ten days (Sundays excepted) after it shall have been presented to him, the same shall be a law, in like manner as if he had signed it, unless the Congress by their adjournment prevent its return, in which case it shall not be a law.[33]

c. Approval or disapproval by the President. Every order, resolution, or vote to which the concurrence of the Senate and House of Representatives may be necessary (except on a question of adjournment) shall be presented to the President of the United States; and before the same shall take effect, shall be approved by him, or being disapproved by him, shall be repassed by two thirds of the Senate and House of Representatives, according to the rules and limitations prescribed in the case of a bill.[34]

SECTION 8. **Powers Granted to Congress**[35]

The Congress shall have power

a. To lay and collect taxes, duties, imposts, and excises;[36] to pay the debts and provide for the common defense and general welfare of the United States; but all duties, imposts, and excises shall be uniform throughout the United States;

b. To borrow money on the credit of the United States;[37]

c. To regulate commerce with foreign nations, and among the several states, and with the Indian tribes;[38]

d. To establish an uniform rule of naturalization, and uniform laws on the subject of bankruptcies throughout the United States;[39]

e. To coin money, regulate the value thereof, and of foreign coin, and fix the standard of weights and measures;

f. To provide for the punishment of counterfeiting the securities and current coin of the United States;

g. To establish post offices and post roads;

h. To promote the progress of science and useful arts, by securing for limited times to authors and inventors the exclusive right to their respective writings and discoveries;[40]

i. To constitute tribunals inferior to the Supreme Court;

j. To define and punish piracies and felonies committed on the high seas and offenses against the laws of nations;

k. To declare war,[41] grant letters of marque and reprisal,[42] and make rules concerning captures on land and water;

l. To raise and support armies,[43] but no appropriation of money to that use shall be for a longer term than two years;

m. To provide and maintain a navy;

33. If a President takes no action on a bill for ten days (Sundays excepted), it becomes a law without his signature provided Congress is still in session. If Congress has adjourned, the bill is dead. This is known as a "pocket veto."

34. A joint resolution, for example, must be passed and approved in the same manner as a bill.

35. Section 8 is one of the most important in the Constitution. A few other powers are granted to Congress, but the most important powers are listed here.

36. Congress under the Articles of Confederation had lacked the power to levy taxes. This power was of great importance in the growth of the national government.

37. Borrowing is generally by the issuance of government bonds or certificates of indebtedness.

38. This very important power was not exercised by Congress under the Confederation.

39. Bankruptcy legislation was largely left to the states until 1898.

40. This clause is the basis of our patent and copyright laws.

41. Congress alone has the power to declare war. But a situation may develop which gives Congress little choice.

42. This power to commission privateers to prey upon enemy commerce was used extensively in the War of 1812. The practice is no longer followed.

43. Congress has broad military powers.

n. To make rules for the government and regulation of land and naval forces;

o. To provide for calling forth the militia to execute the laws of the Union, suppress insurrections, and repel invasions;

p. To provide for organizing, arming, and disciplining the militia, and for governing such part of them as may be employed in the service of the United States, reserving to the states respectively the appointment of the officers, and the authority of training the militia according to the discipline prescribed by Congress;[44]

q. To exercise exclusive legislation in all cases whatsoever, over such district (not exceeding ten miles square) as may, by cession of particular states, and the acceptance of Congress, become the seat of the government of the United States,[45] and to exercise like authority over all places purchased by the consent of the legislature of the state in which the same shall be for the erection of forts, magazines, arsenals, dock-yards, and other needful buildings; — and

r. To make all laws which shall be necessary and proper for carrying into execution the foregoing powers, and all others powers vested by this Constitution in the government of the United States, or in any department or officer thereof.[46]

SECTION 9. **Powers Denied to the Federal Government**

a. *The migration or importation of such persons as any of the states now existing shall think proper to admit, shall not be prohibited by the Congress prior to the year one thousand eight hundred and eight,[47] but a tax or duty may be imposed on such importation, not exceeding ten dollars for each person.*

b. The privilege of the writ of habeas corpus shall not be suspended, unless when in cases of rebellion or invasion the public safety may require it.[48]

c. No bill of attainder[49] or ex post facto law[50] shall be passed.

d. No capitation or other direct tax shall be laid, unless in proportion to the census or enumeration herein before directed to be taken.[51]

e. No tax or duty shall be laid on articles exported from any state.

f. No preference shall be given by any regulation of commerce or revenue to the ports of one state over those of another;[52] nor shall vessels bound to, or from, one state be obliged to enter, clear, or pay duties in another.

g. No money shall be drawn from the treasury, but in consequence of appropriations made by law;[53] and a reg-

44. The federal government has greatly broadened its control over the militia.

45. This provision enables Congress to legislate for the District of Columbia.

46. This is the so-called "elastic clause." Whether it was to be interpreted strictly or broadly soon became a matter of bitter dispute between political parties. It is the basis for much legislation not authorized in any other provision. The taxing power and the commerce clause, in particular, have led to legislation that the authors of the Constitution did not foresee.

47. Congress could not stop the importation of slaves before 1808.

48. This writ prevents unreasonable imprisonment. A person arrested can demand to be charged with a specific crime or released. The Constitution does not say who may suspend the writ. Lincoln exercised this power, but the Supreme Court held that the action must be authorized by Congress.

49. This is a legislative measure which condemns a person without a trial in court.

50. This provision prevents legislation which would make an act a criminal offense after it was committed.

51. This provision eventually necessitated the enactment of Amendment 16 to permit the levying of an income tax.

52. The purpose of this clause was to insure equal treatment for all ports.

53. See note 31 on page 141.

ular statement and account of the receipts and expenditures of all public money shall be published from time to time.

h. No title of nobility shall be granted by the United States: and no person holding any office of profit or trust under them shall, without the consent of Congress, accept of any present, emolument, office, or title, of any kind whatever, from any king, prince, or foreign state.

Section 10. Powers Denied to the States[54]

a. No state shall enter into any treaty, alliance, or confederation; grant letters of marque and reprisal; coin money; emit bills of credit; make any thing but gold and silver coin a tender in payment of debts; pass any bill of attainder, ex post facto law, or law impairing the obligation of contracts; or grant any title of nobility.[55]

b. No state shall, without the consent of the Congress, lay any imposts or duties on imports or exports, except what may be absolutely necessary for executing its inspection laws; and the net produce of all duties and imposts, laid by any state on imports or exports, shall be for the use of the treasury of the United States; and all such laws shall be subject to the revision and control of the Congress.

c. No state shall, without the consent of Congress, lay any duty of tonnage; keep troops[56] or ships of war in time of peace; enter into any agreement or compact with another state, or with a foreign power; or engage in war, unless actually invaded, or in such imminent danger as will not admit of delay.[57]

54. For the powers reserved to the states, turn to Amendment 10.

55. Some of these powers are also denied to the national government; others may be exercised by the national government, but not by the states.

56. This does not prevent the state from having a militia. See Amendment 2.

57. Clauses "b" and "c" enumerate powers which may be exercised by a state only with the consent of Congress or in an emergency.

ARTICLE II

Executive Department

Section 1. President and Vice-President

a. Term of office. The executive power shall be vested in a President of the United States of America. He shall hold his office during the term of four years,[1] and, together with the Vice-President, chosen for the same term, be elected as follows:

b. Electors. Each state shall appoint, in such manner as the legislature thereof may direct, a number of electors, equal to the whole number of senators and representatives to which the state may be entitled in the Congress; but no senator or representative, or person holding an office of trust or profit under the United States, shall be appointed an elector.[2]

Former method of electing President and Vice-President.[3] *The electors shall meet in their respective states, and vote by ballot for two persons, of whom one at least shall not be an inhabitant of the same state with themselves. And they*

1. The four-year term without limitation as to re-election was a compromise among various plans.

2. Instead of placing the election of the Chief Executive directly in the hands of the voters, the Constitution provided for the selection of electors. The electors, in turn, would choose a President. Today electors usually are prominent party members whose votes are pledged to a given candidate.

3. This section has been changed by Amendment 12, adopted in 1804.

shall make a list of all the persons voted for, and of the number of votes for each; which list they shall sign and certify, and transmit sealed to the seat of government of the United States, directed to the President of the Senate. The President of the Senate shall, in the presence of the Senate and House of Representatives, open all the certificates, and the votes shall then be counted. The person having the greatest number of votes shall be the President, if such number be a majority of the whole number of electors appointed; and if there be more than one who have such majority, and have an equal number of votes, then the House of Representatives shall immediately choose by ballot one of them for President; and if no person have a majority, then from the five highest on the list the said house shall in like manner choose the President. But in choosing the President the votes shall be taken by States, the representation from each state having one vote; a quorum for this purpose shall consist of a member or members from two thirds of the states, and a majority of all the states shall be necessary to a choice. In every case, after the choice of the President, the person having the greatest number of votes of the electors shall be the Vice-President. But if there should remain two or more who have equal votes, the Senate shall choose from them by ballot the Vice-President.

c. **Time of elections.** The Congress may determine the time of choosing the electors and the day on which they shall give their votes; which day shall be the same throughout the United States.[4]

d. **Qualifications of the President.** No person except a natural-born citizen, *or a citizen of the United States, at the time of the adoption of this Constitution,* shall be eligible to the office of President;[5] neither shall any person be eligible to that office who shall not have attained the age of thirty-five years, and been fourteen years a resident within the United States.

e. **Vacancy.** In case of the removal of the President from office or of his death, resignation, or inability to discharge the powers and duties of the said office,[6] the same shall devolve on the Vice-President,[7] and the Congress may by law provide for the case of removal, death, resignation, or inability, both of the President and Vice-President, declaring what officer shall then act as President, and such officer shall act accordingly, until the disability be removed, or a President shall be elected.[8]

f. **The President's salary.** The President shall, at stated times, receive for his services a compensation, which shall neither be increased nor diminished during the period for which he shall have been elected, and he shall not receive within that period any other emolument from the United States, or any of them.[9]

4. The popular vote for electors takes place on the Tuesday after the first Monday of November in each "leap year." In mid-December the electors meet in their state capitals and cast their electoral votes.

5. Although the President today must be a natural-born citizen, the courts may interpret the clause to include a child born to American parents living outside this country.

6. The Constitution did not state who should determine this disability. One purpose of the Twenty-fifth Amendment is to clarify this point.

7. Tyler, the first Vice-President to succeed to the presidency because of the death of the incumbent, took the title as well as the powers and duties of that office and thus set a precedent.

8. In 1947 an act of Congress provided that the Speaker of the House and the President Pro Tem of the Senate should be next in line of succession, followed by the Cabinet officers in the order that their departments were established.

9. In 1949 Congress fixed this salary at $100,000 per year plus a tax-free expense account of $50,000.

g. Oath of office. Before he enter on the execution of his office, he shall take the following oath or affirmation: — "I do solemnly swear (or affirm) that I will faithfully execute the office of President of the United States, and will to the best of my ability, preserve, protect, and defend the Constitution of the United States."

SECTION 2.   Powers of the President[10]

a. Military powers; reprieves and pardons. The President shall be Commander-in-Chief of the Army and Navy of the United States, and of the militia of the several states, when called into the actual service of the United States;[11] he may require the opinion, in writing, of the principal officer in each of the executive departments, upon any subject relating to the duties of their respective offices,[12] and he shall have power to grant reprieves and pardons for offenses against the United States, except in cases of impeachment.

b. Treaties; appointments. He shall have power, by and with the advice and consent of the Senate, to make treaties, provided two thirds of the senators present concur;[13] and he shall nominate and, by and with the advice and consent of the Senate, shall appoint ambassadors, other public ministers and consuls, judges of the Supreme Court, and all other officers of the United States, whose appointments are not herein otherwise provided for, and which shall be established by law;[14] but the Congress may by law vest the appointment of such inferior officers as they think proper in the President alone, in the courts of law, or in the heads of departments.[15]

c. Filling vacancies. The President shall have power to fill up all vacancies that may happen during the recess of the Senate, by granting commissions which shall expire at the end of their next session.

SECTION 3.   Duties of the President

He shall from time to time give to the Congress information of the state of the Union,[16] and recommend to their consideration such measures as he shall judge necessary and expedient; he may, on extraordinary occasions, convene both houses, or either of them,[17] and in case of disagreement between them with respect to the time of adjournment he may adjourn them to such time as he shall think proper; he shall receive ambassadors and other public ministers;[18] he shall take care that the laws be faithfully executed,[19] and shall commission all the officers of the United States.

SECTION 4.   Impeachment

The President, Vice-President and all civil officers of the United States shall be removed from office on impeachment for, and conviction of, treason, bribery, or other high crimes and misdemeanors.

10. Sections 2 and 3 also are very important sections.

11. As Commander-in-Chief, the President exercises great power, especially in time of war.

12. No provision is made in the Constitution for the Cabinet or for Cabinet meetings. But the existence of executive departments is implied here, and the Cabinet developed during Washington's administration.

13. The President or his representatives draw up the treaty, which is then submitted to the Senate for ratification.

14. Ratification of treaties requires a two-thirds vote; ratification of appointments, a simple majority.

15. Congress, with the approval of the President, has given the Civil Service Commission responsibility for determining the fitness of job applicants, and for ranking them on civil service lists from which appointments are made.

16. Washington and Adams delivered their messages to Congress in person. Beginning with Jefferson and continuing up to Wilson, the Presidents sent written messages to Congress.

17. Special sessions are here provided for.

18. This clause gives the President the power to recognize or refuse to recognize a foreign government.

19. This clause is the basis of the President's executive power. Actually, the laws are carried out by the various departments and by special commissions and agencies.

ARTICLE III
Judicial Department

SECTION 1. **The Federal Courts**

The judicial power of the United States shall be vested in one Supreme Court, and in such inferior courts as the Congress may from time to time ordain and establish.[1] The judges, both of the Supreme and inferior courts, shall hold their offices during good behavior,[2] and shall, at stated times, receive for their services, a compensation, which shall not be diminished during their continuance in office.

SECTION 2. **Jurisdiction of the Federal Courts**

a. **Federal courts in general.** The judicial power shall extend to all cases, in law and equity, arising under this Constitution, the laws of the United States, and treaties made, or which shall be made, under their authority; — to all cases affecting ambassadors, other public ministers, and consuls; — to all cases of admiralty and maritime jurisdiction; — to controversies to which the United States shall be a party; — to controversies between two or more states; — *between a state and citizens of another state;* — between citizens of different states; — between citizens of the same state claiming lands under grants of different states, and between a state, or the citizens thereof, and foreign states, citizens or subjects.[3]

b. **Supreme Court.** In all cases affecting ambassadors, other public ministers, and consuls, and those in which a state shall be a party, the Supreme Court shall have original jurisdiction.[4] In all the other cases before mentioned, the Supreme Court shall have appellate jurisdiction, both as to law and fact, with such exceptions, and under such regulations as the Congress shall make.

c. **Rules respecting trials.** The trial of all crimes, except in cases of impeachment, shall be by jury;[5] and such trial shall be held in the state where the said crimes shall have been committed; but when not committed within any state, the trial shall be at such place or places as the Congress may by law have directed.

SECTION 3. **Treason**

a. **Definition of treason.** Treason against the United States shall consist only in levying war against them, or in adhering to their enemies, giving them aid and comfort.[6] No person shall be convicted of treason unless on the testimony of two witnesses to the same overt act, or on confession in open court.[7]

b. **Punishment of treason.** The Congress shall have power to declare the punishment of treason, but no attainder of treason shall work corruption of blood, or forfeiture except during the life of the person attainted.[8]

1. The organization of the Supreme Court and the establishment of lower courts was left to Congress. There are two main levels of inferior courts: district courts and courts of appeals.

2. Judges are appointed virtually for life.

3. In general two classes of cases come before the federal courts: (1) because of the nature of the case, for example, a case arising under the Constitution, federal laws, treaties, or affecting ships on the high seas or in United States waters; (2) because of the nature of the parties involved: the United States, a state, an ambassador, citizens of different states, etc. (See note 11, page 151.)

4. Most federal cases start in the United States district courts. Only the special cases here listed may be started in the Supreme Court. Much of the Supreme Court's work has to do with cases appealed from lower federal courts or from state courts (appellate jurisdiction).

5. Here a jury trial is provided only for criminal cases, but Amendments 5, 6, and 7 supplement this clause.

6. Note that the Constitution itself (and not Congress or the President) defines treason.

7. Convictions, therefore, are difficult.

8. The punishment of treason cannot be extended to a traitor's descendants.

ARTICLE IV

The States and the Federal Government

SECTION 1.   State Records

Full faith and credit shall be given in each state to the public acts, records, and judicial proceedings of every other state.[1] And the Congress may by general laws prescribe the manner in which such acts, records, and proceedings shall be proved, and the effect thereof.

SECTION 2.   Privileges and Immunities of Citizens

a. Privileges. The citizens of each state shall be entitled to all privileges and immunities of citizens in the several states.[2]

b. Extradition. A person charged in any state with treason, felony, or other crime, who shall flee from justice and be found in another state shall, on demand of the executive authority of the state from which he fled, be delivered up, to be removed to the state having jurisdiction of the crime.[3]

c. Fugitive workers. *No person held to service or labor in one state, under the laws thereof, escaping into another shall, in consequence of any law or regulation therein, be discharged from such service or labor, but shall be delivered upon claim of the party to whom such service or labor may be due.*[4]

SECTION 3.   New States and Territories

a. Admission of new states. New states may be admitted by the Congress into this Union; but no new state shall be formed or erected within the jurisdiction of any other state; nor any state be formed by the junction of two or more states, or parts of states, without the consent of the legislatures of the states concerned, as well as of the Congress.[5]

b. Power of Congress over territory and property. The Congress shall have power to dispose of and make all needful rules and regulations respecting the territory or other property belonging to the United States; and nothing in this Constitution shall be so construed as to prejudice any claims of the United States, or of any particular state.

SECTION 4.   Guarantees to the States

The United States shall guarantee to every state in this Union a republican form of government,[6] and shall protect each of them against invasion;[7] and on application of the legislature, or of the executive (when the legislature cannot be convened) against domestic violence.[8]

1. For example, a will legally drawn up in New Jersey would be approved in Connecticut courts even though it did not meet the requirements of Connecticut law. Some of the states are reluctant to accept divorce decrees granted in states where the laws are very lenient.

2. A citizen of Oregon going into California would be entitled to all the privileges of a citizen of California. See Amendment 14.

3. Usually the governor surrenders such a person. He may, however, exercise his judgment. There is no way to force him to surrender the accused.

4. This statement referred to the return of fugitive slaves. Amendment 13 made it invalid.

5. The power of admitting new states is here given Congress. No state may be deprived of any of its territory without its consent.

6. Congress may exercise this power by refusing to admit senators and representatives from a state. In an emergency the President could send federal troops to a state to preserve its republican form of government.

7. Invasion of a state, except from a neighboring state, would also mean invasion of the nation, and would call for action on the part of the national government.

8. In the case of domestic violence the federal government intervenes upon request. If national interests are threatened, the President may intervene even over the protests of the state.

ARTICLE V

Method of Amendment

The Congress, whenever two thirds of both houses shall deem it necessary, shall propose amendments to this Constitution, or, on the application of the legislatures of two thirds of the several states, shall call a convention for proposing amendments, which, in either case, shall be valid to all intents and purposes, as part of this Constitution, when ratified by the legislatures of three fourths of the several states, or by conventions in three fourths thereof,[1] as the one or the other mode of ratification may be proposed by the Congress; provided that *no amendments which may be made prior to the year one thousand eight hundred and eight shall in any manner affect the first and fourth clauses in the ninth section of the first article; and that* no state, without its consent, shall be deprived of its equal suffrage in the Senate.[2]

ARTICLE VI

General Provisions

a. Public debt. All debts contracted and engagements entered into, before the adoption of this Constitution, shall be as valid against the United States under this Constitution, as under the Confederation.

b. Supremacy of the Constitution. This Constitution, and the laws of the United States which shall be made in pursuance thereof; and all treaties made, or which shall be made, under the authority of the United States, shall be the supreme law of the land;[1] and the judges in every state shall be bound thereby, anything in the Constitution or laws of any state to the contrary notwithstanding.

c. Oath of office; no religious test. The senators and representatives before mentioned, and the members of the several state legislatures, and all executive and judicial officers, both of the United States and of the several states, shall be bound by oath or affirmation, to support this Constitution; but no religious test shall ever be required as a qualification to any office or public trust under the United States.[2]

ARTICLE VII

Ratification of the Constitution

The ratification of the conventions of nine states shall be sufficient for the establishment of this Constitution between the states so ratifying the same.[1]

1. The Constitution may be amended in four ways:

(1) An amendment may be proposed by two thirds of both houses of Congress and ratified by the legislatures of three fourths of the states, or (2) ratified by special conventions in three fourths of the states.

(3) An amendment may be proposed by a special convention, called upon application of two thirds of the state legislatures, and ratified by three fourths of the state legislatures, or (4) ratified by special conventions in three fourths of the states.

All amendments were added by (1) except Amendment 21, which was added by (2).

2. Note this further protection for the small states.

---

1. The supreme law of the land consists of: (a) the Constitution, (b) laws of Congress passed in accordance with the Constitution, and (c) treaties. The supreme law ranks above state and local laws that conflict with it. The Constitution does not say who shall determine whether a law passed by Congress is in accordance with the Constitution. Chief Justice John Marshall held that this power resided in the Supreme Court and that the federal courts had the right of judicial review.

2. Any religious qualification for federal office is ruled out.

---

1. This was a revolutionary provision, for delegates to the Constitutional Convention had been instructed to revise the Articles of Confederation, and unanimous consent of the states was required for such amendment.

AMENDMENTS TO THE CONSTITUTION

Amendment 1 (1791)[1]
Freedom of Religion, Speech, and the Press; Right of Assembly

Congress shall make no law respecting an establishment of religion, or prohibiting the free exercise thereof; or abridging the freedom of speech, or of the press; or the right of the people peaceably to assemble, and to petition the government for a redress of grievances.[2]

Amendment 2 (1791)
Right to Keep and Bear Arms

A well-regulated militia being necessary to the security of a free state, the right of the people to keep and bear arms shall not be infringed.[3]

Amendment 3 (1791)
Quartering of Troops

No soldier shall, in time of peace, be quartered in any house, without the consent of the owner, nor in time of war, but in a manner to be prescribed by law.[4]

Amendment 4 (1791)
Limiting the Right of Search

The right of the people to be secure in their persons, houses, papers, and effects, against unreasonable searches and seizures, shall not be violated, and no warrants shall issue but upon probable cause, supported by oath or affirmation, and particularly describing the place to be searched, and the persons or things to be seized.[5]

Amendment 5 (1791)
Guarantee of Trial by Jury; Private Property to be Respected

No person shall be held to answer for a capital, or otherwise infamous crime, unless on a presentment or indictment of a grand jury, except in cases arising in the land or naval forces, or in the militia, when in actual service in time of war or public danger; nor shall any person be subject for the same offense to be twice put in jeopardy of life or limb; nor shall be compelled in any criminal case to be a witness against himself, nor be deprived of life, liberty, or property, without due process of law; nor shall private property be taken for public use without just compensation.[6]

Amendment 6 (1791)
Rights of Accused Persons

In all criminal prosecutions, the accused shall enjoy the right to a speedy and public trial, by an impartial jury of the state and district wherein the crime shall have been

1. The first ten Amendments are known as the Bill of Rights. In general they protect the individual against the exercise of undue power by the federal government. The Supreme Court has extended some of the provisions of the Bill of Rights to the states.

2. Each individual is free to worship as he sees fit. He may speak, write, or print anything he wants to, except that he may not slander or libel others nor advocate violent overthrow of the government. Citizens may meet together for any lawful purpose provided they do not interfere with the rights of others. Finally, the people are free to petition the government to correct grievances or abuses.

3. In the late 1700's the militia was the country's chief defense. Hence its members had to own arms. Today most states regulate the sale and use of firearms.

4. This Amendment forbids the assignment of troops to private homes for food and shelter, except by law in wartime.

5. The government may not search a home, or arrest a person without good cause, and then only after the official who makes the search or arrest has obtained a legal warrant.

6. (a) Except for the armed forces in wartime, an individual may not be tried for crime except after indictment by a grand jury. (b) He may not be tried a second time for the same offense. (c) He is not obligated to testify against himself. The Supreme Court extended this provision to apply also in state court cases. (d) He may not have his "life, liberty, or property" taken from him except by regular legal

committed, which districts shall have been previously ascertained by law, and to be informed of the nature and cause of the accusation; to be confronted with the witnesses against him; to have compulsory process for obtaining witnesses in his favor; and to have the assistance of counsel for his defense.[7]

Amendment 7 (1791)
Rules of the Common Law

In suits at common law, where the value in controversy shall exceed twenty dollars, the right of trial by jury shall be preserved, and no fact tried by a jury shall be otherwise re-examined in any court of the United States than according to the rules of common law.[8]

Amendment 8 (1791)
Excessive Bail, Fines, and Punishment Prohibited

Excessive bail shall not be required, nor excessive fines imposed, nor cruel and unusual punishments inflicted.[9]

Amendment 9 (1791)
Rights Retained by the People

The enumeration in the Constitution of certain rights shall not be construed to deny or disparage others retained by the people.[10]

Amendment 10 (1791)
Powers Reserved to States and People

The powers not delegated to the United States by the Constitution, nor prohibited by it to the states, are reserved to the states respectively, or to the people.

Amendment 11 (1798)
Limiting the Powers of Federal Courts

The judicial power of the United States shall not be construed to extend to any suit in law or equity, commenced or prosecuted against one of the United States by citizens of another state, or by citizens or subjects of any foreign state.[11]

Amendment 12 (1804)
Election of President and Vice-President

The electors shall meet in their respective states and vote by ballot for President and Vice-President, one of whom, at least, shall not be an inhabitant of the same state with themselves; they shall name in their ballots the person voted for as President, and in distinct ballots the person voted for as Vice-President, and they shall make distinct lists of all persons voted for as President, and of all persons voted for as Vice-President, and of the number of votes for

proceedings. (e) His private property may not be taken by the government without fair payment.

7. If anyone is accused of a crime, (a) He is entitled to a prompt public trial before an impartial jury; (b) he must be clearly told what the charge against him is; (c) the witnesses against him must give their testimony in his presence; (d) the government must help him secure witnesses in his favor; and (e) he must be provided with a lawyer.

8. Except in minor cases, civil suits may be tried before a jury.

9. A person accused of a crime may in most cases be released from jail by posting a bond that he will not run away. This is called "being out on bail." Bail, fines, and punishments must be reasonable.

10. It was impossible to list in the Constitution all the rights of the people. This listing of certain rights does not imply that people do not have rights not listed.

11. This Amendment modifies Article III, Section 2, clause "a" to prevent a state from being sued by a citizen of another state or of a foreign country.

each, which lists they shall sign and certify, and transmit sealed to the seat of the government of the United States, directed to the President of the Senate; — the President of the Senate shall, in the presence of the Senate and House of Representatives, open all the certificates and the votes shall then be counted; — the person having the greatest number of votes for President shall be the President, if such number be a majority of the whole number of electors appointed; and if no person have such majority, then from the persons having the highest numbers not exceeding three on the list of those voted for as President, the House of Representatives shall choose immediately, by ballot, the President. But in choosing the President, the votes shall be taken by states, the representation from each state having one vote; a quorum for this purpose shall consist of a member or members from two thirds of the states, and a majority of all the states shall be necessary to a choice.[12] And if the House of Representatives shall not choose a President whenever the right of choice shall devolve upon them, *before the fourth day of March next following*, then the Vice-President shall act as President, as in the case of the death or other constitutional disability of the President. — The person having the greatest number of votes as Vice-President, shall be the Vice-President, if such number be a majority of the whole number of electors appointed, and if no person have a majority, then from the two highest numbers on the list, the Senate shall choose the Vice-President; a quorum for the purpose shall consist of two thirds of the whole number of senators, and a majority of the whole number shall be necessary to a choice.[13] But no person constitutionally ineligible to the office of President shall be eligible to that of Vice-President of the United States.

Amendment 13 (1865)[14]

Slavery Abolished

Section 1.   Abolition of Slavery

Neither slavery nor involuntary servitude, except as a punishment for crime whereof the party shall have been duly convicted, shall exist within the United States, or any place subject to their jurisdiction.

Section 2.   Enforcement

Congress shall have the power to enforce this article by appropriate legislation.

Amendment 14 (1868)

Civil Rights Guaranteed

Section 1.   Definition of Citizenship

All persons born or naturalized in the United States, and subject to the jurisdiction thereof, are citizens of the United States and of the state wherein they reside.[15] No state shall

12. Amendment 12 prevents another tied vote as in the election of 1800, and establishes the present procedure in the electoral college. Today the national conventions of the major parties nominate candidates for the presidency and vice-presidency. At the presidential elections in November, voters cast their ballots for electors who are usually pledged to vote for the candidates nominated by the conventions.

Then in December the President and the Vice-President are voted for separately by the electors in the state capitals. The lists of candidates, with the votes for each, are sent to the President of the Senate, who opens them in the presence of both houses.

If no candidate for President receives a majority, the election goes to the House, where the members vote by states for the three highest candidates. Each state casts one vote. A quorum consists of at least one member from two thirds of the states, and a majority of all the states is necessary for a choice.

13. If no candidate for Vice-President receives a majority, the Senate chooses a Vice-President from the two highest candidates. Again, a quorum consists of two thirds, and a majority of the whole number of senators is necessary.

14. Amendments 13, 14, and 15 resulted from the Civil War. In general, Amendment 13 freed the slaves, Amendment 14 was intended to guarantee civil rights to the freedmen, and Amendment 15 gave them the right to vote.

15. This is the only definition of citizenship in the Constitution.

make or enforce any law which shall abridge the privileges or immunities of citizens of the United States; nor shall any state deprive any person of life, liberty, or property, without due process of law; nor deny to any person within its jurisdiction the equal protection of the laws.[16]

Section 2. Apportionment of Representatives

Representatives shall be apportioned among the several states according to their respective numbers, counting the whole number of persons in each state, excluding Indians not taxed. But when the right to vote at any election for the choice of electors for President and Vice-President of the United States, representatives in Congress, the executive and judicial officers of a state, or the members of the legislature thereof, is denied to any of the male inhabitants of such state, being twenty-one years of age, and citizens of the United States, or in any way abridged, except for participation in rebellion, or other crime, the basis of representation therein shall be reduced in the proportion which the number of such male citizens shall bear to the whole number of male citizens twenty-one years of age in such state.[17]

Section 3. Disability Resulting from Insurrection

No person shall be a senator or representative in Congress, or elector of President and Vice-President, or hold any office, civil or military, under the United States, or under any state, who, having previously taken an oath, as a member of Congress, or as an officer of the United States, or as a member of any state legislature, or as an executive or judicial officer of any state, to support the Constitution of the United States, shall have engaged in insurrection or rebellion against the same, or given aid or comfort to the enemies thereof. But Congress may by vote of two thirds of each house, remove such disability.[18]

Section 4. Public Debt of the United States Valid; Confederate Debt Void

The validity of the public debt of the United States, authorized by law, including debts incurred for payment of pensions and bounties for services in suppressing insurrection or rebellion, shall not be questioned. But neither the United States nor any state shall assume or pay any debt or obligation incurred in aid of insurrection or rebellion against the United States, or any claim for the loss or eman-

16. Section I has become very important. It protects citizens against unjust actions on the part of state governments.

Many recent Supreme Court decisions related to segregation have been based in part on Amendment 14. Intended primarily as a protection for the freedmen, it has also become a protection to corporations. The Supreme Court has held a corporation to be a person within the meaning of this Amendment, and has declared unconstitutional many state laws which, it held, deprived a corporation of property without due process of law, or denied to a corporation the equal protection of the laws.

17. This section was intended to solve the political problem created by the freeing of the slaves. Each freedman would now count as one in apportioning representatives. Since this would increase the representation of the southern (Democratic) states, the Radical Republicans wanted to make sure that the Negroes, who were favorable to the Republican Party, were protected in the right to vote. Under this section, if 30 per cent of a state's adult male population were Negro, and if the Negroes were denied the right to vote, then the state would lose 30 per cent of its representatives in Congress. This provision has never been put into effect.

18. If any person who had held an office which required an oath to support the Constitution of the United States had violated that oath by taking up arms against the United States or by giving aid and comfort to the enemy, then he could not hold any office which would again

cipation of any slave; but all such debts, obligations, and claims shall be held illegal and void.[19]

Section 5.   Enforcement

The Congress shall have power to enforce by appropriate legislation the provisions of this article.[20]

Amendment 15 (1870)

Right of Suffrage

Section 1.   The Suffrage

The right of citizens of the United States to vote shall not be denied or abridged by the United States or by any state on account of race, color, or previous condition of servitude.[21]

Section 2.   Enforcement

The Congress shall have power to enforce this article by appropriate legislation.

Amendment 16 (1913)

Income Tax

The Congress shall have power to lay and collect taxes on incomes, from whatever source derived, without apportionment among the several states, and without regard to any census or enumeration.[22]

Amendment 17 (1913)

Direct Election of Senators

a. Election by the people. The Senate of the United States shall be composed of two senators from each state, elected by the people thereof, for six years; and each senator shall have one vote. The electors in each state shall have the qualifications requisite for electors of the most numerous branch of the state legislatures.[23]

b. Vacancies. When vacancies happen in the representation of any state in the Senate, the executive authority of such state shall issue writs of election to fill such vacancies: provided that the legislature of any state may empower the executive thereof to make temporary appointments until the people fill the vacancies by election as the legislature may direct.

c. Not retroactive. This amendment shall not be so construed as to affect the election or term of any senator chosen before it becomes valid as part of the Constitution.

Amendment 18 (1919)

National Prohibition[24]

Section 1.   Prohibition of Intoxicating Liquors

After one year from the ratification of this article the manufacture, sale, or transportation of intoxicating liquors

require such an oath. This limitation deprived the southern states of many leaders during Reconstruction.

19. Section 4 silenced any doubt about the validity of the national debt, but outlawed the Confederate debt. Confederate bonds were now worthless, and those who had lent money to the Confederacy were thereby punished. The former slave owners would receive no payment for their freed slaves.

20. Section 5 gave to Congress power to enforce the provisions of Amendment 14.

21. Amendment 15 limits the power of the states by denying them the right to exclude citizens from voting because of race, color, or previous condition of servitude.

22. The Supreme Court declared the income-tax law of 1894 unconstitutional on the ground that it was not apportioned among the states according to population. Amendment 16 grants to Congress power to levy a tax on incomes without reference to population.

23. Amendment 17 provides for direct election of United States senators. The qualifications needed to vote for senators shall be the same as for the lower branch of the state legislature.

24. Amendment 18 did not go into effect until one year after ratification. Wartime prohibition restrictions, however, caused the country to "go dry" sooner. Although Section 2 provided for concurrent power of enforcement, the Volstead Act was so strong that little power was left to the states. In *within, the importation thereof into, or the exportation thereof from the United States and all territory subject to the jurisdiction thereof for beverage purposes is hereby prohibited.*

Section 2.   Enforcement

The Congress and the several states shall have concurrent power to enforce this article by appropriate legislation.

Section 3.   Limited Time for Ratification

This article shall be inoperative unless it shall have been ratified as an amendment to the Constitution by the legislatures of the several states, as provided in the Constitution, within seven years from the date of the submission hereof to the states by the Congress.

Amendment 19 **(1920)**

Extending the Vote to Women

Section 1.   Woman Suffrage

The right of citizens of the United States to vote shall not be denied or abridged by the United States or by any state on account of sex.[25]

Section 2.   Enforcement

The Congress shall have power to enforce this article by appropriate legislation.

Amendment 20 **(1933)**

The "Lame Duck" Amendment

Section 1.   Terms of President, Vice-President, and Congress

The terms of the President and Vice-President shall end at noon on the 20th day of January, and the terms of senators and representatives at noon on the 3rd day of January, of the years in which such terms would have ended if this article had not been ratified; and the terms of their successors shall then begin.[26]

Section 2.   Sessions of Congress

The Congress shall assemble at least once in every year, and such meeting shall begin at noon on the 3d day of January, unless they shall by law appoint a different day.[27]

Section 3.   Presidential Succession

If, at the time fixed for the beginning of the term of the President, the President-elect shall have died, the Vice-President-elect shall become President. If a President shall not have been chosen before the time fixed for the beginning of his term, or if the President-elect shall have failed to qualify, then the Vice-President-elect shall act as President until a President shall have qualified; and the

Section 3 the idea of limiting the time for ratification by the state legislatures was first introduced. Amendment 18 was repealed by Amendment 21.

25. Amendment 19 further limited the power of the states to determine who may vote. In this case the right to vote may not be denied because of sex. In this Amendment and in others, Congress is given power to enforce the provisions by appropriate legislation.

26. Before 1933 many members of the "short session" of Congress meeting in December of even-numbered years had been defeated in the November elections. Congress as a whole, therefore, often stood for principles already rejected by the voters. Amendment 20 caused the terms of senators and representatives to end on January 3 instead of on March 4.

27. The regular session of the newly elected Congress begins on January 3, two months after the election, instead of thirteen months following it.

Congress may by law provide for the case wherein neither a President-elect nor a Vice-President-elect shall have qualified, declaring who shall then act as President, or the manner in which one who is to act shall be selected, and such person shall act accordingly until a President or a Vice-President shall have qualified.[28]

Section 4. Choice of President by the House

The Congress may by law provide for the case of the death of any of the persons from whom the House of Representatives may choose a President whenever the right of choice shall have devolved upon them, and for the case of the death of any of the persons from whom the Senate may choose a Vice-President whenever the right of choice shall have devolved upon them.[29]

Section 5. Date Effective

Sections 1 and 2 shall take effect on the fifteenth day of October following the ratification of this article.

Section 6. Limited Time for Ratification

This article shall be inoperative unless it shall have been ratified as an amendment to the Constitution by the legislatures of three fourths of the several states within seven years from the date of its submission.[30]

Amendment 21 (1933)
Repeal of Prohibition
Section 1. Repeal of Amendment 18

The eighteenth article of amendment to the Constitution of the United States is hereby repealed.[31]

Section 2. States Protected

The transportation or importation into any state, territory, or possession of the United States for delivery or use therein of intoxicating liquors, in violation of the laws thereof, is hereby prohibited.[32]

Section 3. Limited Time for Ratification

This article shall be inoperative unless it shall have been ratified as an amendment to the Constitution by conventions in the several states, as provided in the Constitution, within seven years from the date of the submission hereof to the states by the Congress.[33]

Amendment 22 (1951)
Presidential Term Limited
Section 1. Definition of Limitation

No person shall be elected to the office of the President more than twice, and no person who has held the office of President, or acted as President, for more than two years of

28. Section 3 makes provision for filling the office of President in case of death or failure to qualify before the time fixed for the beginning of his term.

29. In case the election is thrown into Congress because no candidate for either President or Vice-President receives a majority of the electoral votes, Congress may make provision for any situation arising from the death of any of the candidates.

30. As in the case of Amendment 18, a time limit was placed upon the state legislatures for the ratification of this Amendment.

31. In spite of widespread dissatisfaction with Amendment 18, it was generally believed that the difficulty of amending the Constitution would prevent its repeal. During the Great Depression, however, arguments in favor of Amendment 18 were no longer as strong as they had been. It was desirable to put men to work, to find uses for grain, and to gain sources of revenue.

32. Section 2 was designed to protect states which had laws prohibiting the use of liquor.

33. Section 3 was unique in that Congress made provision for the submission of this Amendment to conventions in the states. Ratification proceeded with unusual speed, and Amendment 21 was proclaimed a part of the Constitution before the end of 1933. The procedure followed in effect gave the people an opportunity to express their views on the question of a term to which some other person was elected President shall be elected to the office of the President more than once. But this article shall not apply to any person holding the office of President when this article was proposed by the Congress, and shall not prevent any person who may be holding the office of President, or acting as President, during the term within which this article becomes operative from holding the office of President, or acting as President during the remainder of such term.[34]

Section 2.   Limited Time for Ratification

This article shall be inoperative unless it shall have been ratified as an amendment to the Constitution by the legislatures of three fourths of the several states within seven years from the date of its submission to the states by the Congress.

Prohibition in voting for delegates to the state conventions.

34. The authors of the Constitution placed no limit on the number of terms a President might serve. Presidents Washington and Jefferson, however, decided against a third term. This practice became an unwritten custom observed by succeeding Presidents until 1940, when Franklin D. Roosevelt was elected for a third term. This Amendment did not apply to President Truman, who was then in office.

Amendment 23 (1961)
Presidential Voting in
the District of Columbia

Section 1.   Appointment of Electors

The District constituting the seat of government of the United States shall appoint in such manner as the Congress may direct:

A number of electors of President and Vice-President equal to the whole number of senators and representatives in Congress to which the District would be entitled if it were a state, but in no event more than the least populous state; they shall be in addition to those appointed by the states, but they shall be considered, for the purposes of the election of President and Vice-President, to be electors appointed by a state; and they shall meet in the District and perform such duties as provided by the twelfth article of amendment.[35]

35. Amendment 23 permits residents of Washington, D.C., to vote in presidential elections. Before this Amendment was adopted, they had not been able to vote for President because the Constitution provided that only states should choose presidential electors. The people of Washington still have no voice in their local government and are not represented in Congress.

Section 2.   Enforcement

The Congress shall have power to enforce this article by appropriate legislation.

Amendment 24 (1964)
Poll Tax Prohibited

Section 1.   Prohibition in National Elections

The right of citizens of the United States to vote in any primary or other election for President or Vice-President, for electors for President or Vice-President, or for senator or representative in Congress, shall not be denied or abridged by the United States or any state by reason of failure to pay any poll tax or other tax.[36]

36. Under Amendment 24 no citizen may be prevented from voting in a national election because he has not paid a poll tax or other tax. This Amendment does not, however, prevent making the payment of a poll tax a prerequisite to voting in state or local elections.

Section 2. Enforcement

The Congress shall have power to enforce this article by appropriate legislation.

Proposed Amendment 25

Presidential Disability[37]

Section 1. Accession of the Vice-President

In case of the removal of the President from office or of his death or resignation, the Vice-President shall become President.

Section 2. Replacing the Vice-President

Whenever there is a vacancy in the office of the Vice-President, the President shall nominate a Vice-President who shall take office upon confirmation by a majority vote of both Houses of Congress.

Section 3. The Vice-President as Acting President

Whenever the President transmits to the President pro tempore of the Senate and the Speaker of the House of Representatives his written declaration that he is unable to discharge the powers and duties of his office, and until he transmits to them a written declaration to the contrary, such powers and duties shall be discharged by the Vice-President as Acting President.[38]

Section 4. Resumption of power by the President

Whenever the Vice-President and a majority of either the principal officers of the executive departments or of such other body as Congress may by law provide, transmit to the President pro tempore of the Senate and the Speaker of the House of Representatives their written declaration that the President is unable to discharge the powers and duties of his office, the Vice-President shall immediately assume the powers and duties of the office as Acting President.[39]

Thereafter, when the President transmits to the President pro tempore of the Senate and the Speaker of the House of Representatives his written declaration that no inability exists, he shall resume the powers and duties of his office unless the Vice-President and a majority of either the principal officers of the executive department or of such other body as Congress may by law provide, transmit within four days to the President pro tempore of the Senate and the Speaker of the House of Representatives their written declaration that the President is unable to discharge the powers and duties of his office.[40] Thereupon Congress shall decide the issue, assembling within forty-eight hours for

37. This Amendment was approved by Congress in 1965 but had not yet received ratification by the end of that year.

38. The President himself can declare his incapacity and temporarily assign his function to the Vice-President.

39. If the President is incapacitated, but unable or unwilling so to inform Congress, the Vice-President and a majority of the Cabinet can take this action.

40. Note that the Vice-President and a majority of the

that purpose if not in session. If the Congress, within twenty-one days after receipt of the latter written declaration, or, if Congress is not in session, within twenty-one days after Congress is required to assemble, determines by two-thirds vote of both Houses that the President is unable to discharge the powers and duties of his office, the Vice-President shall continue to discharge the same as Acting President; otherwise, the President shall resume the powers and duties of his office.

Cabinet can override the President's decision that he is fit to resume his duties. Congress, however, must sustain this judgment.

Relating the Constitution to American History

Many issues and events in American history have been closely related to the provisions of the Constitution. Some of these issues have been touched on in preceding chapters; others will be described in later chapters as our country's history unfolds. On numerous occasions in the text there are page references to the Constitution itself. The following questions help to focus attention on the relation of the Constitution to these various aspects of American history.

Preamble and Article I

1. Why were forming "a more perfect union" and insuring "domestic tranquillity" given as reasons for establishing the Constitution?

2. Why did the Constitution provide that state legislatures should elect senators? Why was this method of election later changed?

3. Why did the Constitution provide that "bills for raising revenue shall originate in the House"?

4. What important powers that Congress had lacked under the Articles of Confederation were granted Congress by the Constitution? How has the last item in Section 8 affected the role of Congress?

5. Why was Congress forbidden to make an appropriation for the "support [of] armies . . . for a longer term than two years"?

6. What important powers does the Constitution assign to the national government but deny to the states? Can you suggest why?

Article II

1. Why did the Constitution provide that the President should be elected by electors appointed "in such manner as the [given state] legislature . . . may direct . . ."? What difference has the development of political parties brought about in the selection of electors?

2. What are the President's powers with reference to the armed forces and foreign affairs?

3. What provisions in Articles I and II provide "checks and balances" in the case of powers exercised by the legislative and executive departments?

Article III

1. Why did the members of the Constitutional Convention favor the establishment of a system of national courts?

2. Why might it seem desirable to give a national court jurisdiction in a controversy "between citizens of different states"?

3. Why does Article III specify trial by jury in criminal cases, "such trial . . . [to] be held in the state where the said crimes shall have been committed . . ."?

4. How does the Constitution define treason?

Article IV

1. What is the general intent of Sections 1 and 2? Why would these provisions be important in a new nation?

159

2. Relate the provisions of the Northwest Ordinance of 1787 to those in Section 3.

3. Why were the provisions in Section 4 included in the Constitution?

Articles V, VI, and VII

1. Contrast provisions for amending the Articles of Confederation and the Constitution. Why were the provisions, in each case, as they were?

2. Read the second paragraph in Article VI. What is the effect of this statement: ". . . and the judges in every state shall be bound thereby, anything in the Constitution or laws of any state to the contrary notwithstanding"?

3. Why did the members of the Constitutional Convention stipulate that the Constitution should be ratified by conventions held in the states? Why did they stipulate that it would go into effect if ratified by nine states?

Amendments

1. Why were the first ten Amendments added to the Constitution? What provisions in these Amendments are related to former grievances against the mother country?

2. What was the purpose of Amendment 9? Amendment 10? How was the power of the states affected by Amendment 11?

3. What was the primary purpose of Amendments 13, 14, and 15?

4. In what important respects were the rights of the states curtailed by Amendments 13, 14, 15, 18, 19, and 24? Why was each of these Amendments added to the Constitution?

5. Do you think that the changes with reference to the term of the President and the sessions of Congress are an improvement? Why?

6. What are the possible advantages and disadvantages of Amendment 22?

7. Why has Amendment 25 been proposed?

CHAPTER 7

Federalists Guide the New Ship of State

Inauguration of George Washington

The unity of government which constitutes you one people is . . . now dear to you. It is justly so, for it is a main pillar in the edifice of your real independence, the support of your tranquility at home, your peace abroad, of your safety, of your prosperity, of that very liberty which you so highly prize.

GEORGE WASHINGTON, FAREWELL ADDRESS, 1796

1789–1801

"Unity of government" was only a dream in 1789, when Washington first took office. Uncertainty clouded the future of the new government. The Confederation had left unpaid salaries and a number of debts, and the treasury was almost empty. At home the government had to develop policies which would win the confidence of its citizens. Abroad it had to win the respect of other nations. Obviously much depended on the wisdom and skill of the new nation's leaders. It was reassuring, therefore, to have the new government launched under the leadership of George Washington.

Thanks to such leaders as Washington, Hamilton, and John Adams, the Constitution was established on a firm foundation in the 1790's. Under their guidance, the government put into effect financial policies which encouraged prosperity at home and established the country's credit abroad. Despite turbulent changes in Europe and war between Britain and France, these leaders and their supporters maintained a policy of neutrality. Meanwhile, Thomas Jefferson and James Madison organized a loyal but active opposition party. Chapter Seven will examine the fortunes of the new republic during its first years.

1 *The New Government Gets Under Way*

In 1788 the Constitution went into effect for the eleven states which had ratified it. Within two years North Carolina and Rhode Island had joined the experiment. These thirteen states formed a country of roughly four million people, some 750,000 of them Negroes. One quarter of these Americans lived in New England, another quarter in the Middle States, and the remainder lived in the South. The vast majority of Americans lived on farms and plantations or in small towns. Only 3 per cent lived in cities of 10,000 or more.

The first elections are held. The old Congress of the Confederation had asked the states to hold elections for presidential electors, representatives, and senators. The first Congress under the new Constitution was scheduled to meet in New York on March 4, 1789. But the members were so slow in assembling that it was April before the new legislative body had a *quorum* (the number of members required to be present in order to do business). Congress' first act was to count the electoral ballots. By a unanimous vote Washington was elected President, and John Adams (second in the balloting) was named Vice-President. Not until late April, however, did Washington take the oath of office. This long delay disturbed some of the more ardent supporters of the Constitution. "The people will forget the new government before it is born!" cried a Boston Federalist.

Washington is inaugurated. Washington's journey from Virginia to New York

- -

CHAPTER FOCUS

1. The new government gets under way.
2. Hamilton presents a financial program.
3. Political parties are organized.
4. The new nation faces foreign problems.
5. Federalist power declines.

was a triumphal procession. Each of the towns through which the President-elect passed honored him with a celebration. He attended a public banquet in Philadelphia; Trenton erected a triumphal arch in his honor; and Princeton College gave him a reception. Thousands of New Yorkers lined the wharves as he crossed the Hudson River in a special barge rowed by harbor pilots in white uniforms.

On April 30, 1789, Washington took the oath of office on the balcony of Federal Hall. The crowds cheered, and then he stepped back inside to read his inaugural address to the members of Congress. Washington assumed his new responsibilities with genuine reluctance. Fifty-seven years old in 1789, he would have preferred the quiet life of Mount Vernon. "My movements to the chair of government," he wrote, "will be accompanied by feelings not unlike those of a culprit who is going to the place of his execution; so unwilling am I, in the evening of a life nearly consumed in public cares, to quit a peaceful abode for an ocean of difficulties."

Nevertheless, the nation's strongest guarantee of success was its new President. No other man commanded so much respect and trust. Few had worked as hard to win independence. His courage and determination were valuable assets in his new post. Washington did not have a brilliant or original mind, but he wisely surrounded himself with first-rate colleagues and often called upon them for advice. Jefferson said of him: "Perhaps the strongest feature in his character was prudence, never acting until every circumstance, every consideration, was maturely weighed." Once Washington made up his mind, nothing could turn him from the course he considered right and proper.

Knowing that his actions would set examples to be followed by his successors, the first President took care to establish good relations with the legislative and judicial branches of the government. Washington and his wife held many fashionable receptions and dinners for visiting dignitaries. The President, however, was never as concerned with pomp and ceremony as was the Vice-President. Adams suggested that the senators address the chief executive as "His Highness the President of the United States and Protector of their Liberties." Congress thought this sounded like monarchy and settled for plain "Mr. President," the form of address still used today.

Congress provides for executive departments. It was up to Washington and the first Congress to establish executive departments. While the Constitution mentioned such departments (page 146), it did not specify what they should be. In the summer of 1789 Congress created three departments — Foreign Affairs (later renamed State), Treasury, and War — each to be headed by a secretary. Congress also provided for a fourth executive position, Attorney General, to handle the legal business of the government.[1]

In filling these four positions, Washington looked for men who were qualified by education and experience, who had supported the Constitution, and who represented different sections of the country. A fellow Virginian, Thomas Jefferson, was the logical candidate for Secretary of State because of his diplomatic experience abroad. Alexander Hamilton, a New York lawyer and strong supporter of the Constitution, was appointed Secretary of the Treasury. Henry Knox of Massachusetts, an army officer who had served under Washington, became Secretary of War. The post of Attorney General went to Edmund Randolph, who had helped to secure ratification of the Constitution in Virginia.

The Constitution made no mention of a presidential Cabinet, but Washington established this custom. At first he called upon the department secretaries for written opinions on specific matters. Then he began bringing them together to discuss important problems. Early in Washington's second administration, these meetings began to be held regularly and became known as "Cabinet councils." In time the Cabinet became a permanent part of the government.

Congress establishes courts. To set up a federal court system, Congress passed the

[1] Congress also created the office of Postmaster General, but the Post Office did not become an executive department until 1872.

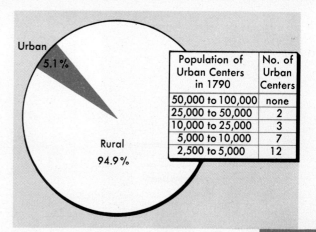

URBAN POPULATION IN 1790

The United States in 1790 was a nation of farms and small towns. Notice that only twelve urban centers had populations of more than 5000.

Population of Urban Centers in 1790	No. of Urban Centers
50,000 to 100,000	none
25,000 to 50,000	2
10,000 to 25,000	3
5,000 to 10,000	7
2,500 to 5,000	12

Urban 5.1%

Rural 94.9%

CHART STUDY

Judiciary Act of 1789. It provided for a Supreme Court made up of a Chief Justice and five associate justices.[2] In addition, there were to be three circuit courts and thirteen district courts. The act also provided for the appointment of United States attorneys to act as federal prosecutors and United States marshals to act as federal police.[3] All of the judges appointed under the Judiciary Act of 1789 had been strong supporters of the Constitution. John Jay, one of the authors of the *Federalist* essays, became the first Chief Justice.

The Judiciary Act of 1789 helped strengthen the central government. It permitted the Supreme Court to review state laws and state court decisions that involved the Constitution, treaties, or federal laws. Thus, the supremacy of federal courts over state courts was legally established. Furthermore, the marshals were directed to take a census of the country every decade beginning in 1790. The census information proved useful to Congress in making laws.

[2] The number of associate justices is now eight.
[3] The United States attorneys began their cases in the district courts, the lowest of the federal courts. Cases could be appealed to the circuit courts. Final appeal could then be made to the Supreme Court itself. In all the federal courts the justices wore robes like those used in English courts. But at Jefferson's request they omitted "the monstrous wigs" which British judges still wear.

(*Continued on page 165*)

George Washington

[1732–1799]

The son of a successful planter, George Washington was tutored at home and later served in the Virginia militia during the French and Indian War. After the capture of Fort Duquesne in 1758, he resigned his military post and was elected to the Virginia House of Burgesses. Had relations between the colonies and the mother country remained serene, Washington might well have lived the quiet life of a plantation owner. But he vigorously defended the American position in the quarrels with Britain and, as a result, was drawn into public life.

As early as 1770, Washington expressed readiness to use the sword as a "last resource" in defending American liberties. Though not a close associate of Sam Adams and Patrick Henry, he voted with them in the First Continental Congress. He was the only delegate who came to the Second Continental Congress in military uniform. When Congress asked Washington to become Commander-in-Chief of the Continental Army, he replied that he was not "equal to the command" but agreed to serve without pay for the duration of the conflict. Not until peace was signed did Washington return to Mount Vernon, "free from the bustle of a camp and the intrigues of a court."

Washington's plan to retire "from all public employments" was soon abandoned. He made an extended journey in 1784 to promote interest in western lands. He also corresponded with John Jay, Alexander Hamilton, and others who were actively trying to increase the powers of Congress by amending the Articles of Confederation. In 1787 Washington headed the Virginia delegation to the Philadelphia convention. He served as the convention's chairman and later helped Madison secure ratification of the Constitution in Virginia.

In the spring of 1789 he again left Mount Vernon, this time to reside in New York as President of the United States. His wisdom, courage, patience, and dignity contributed much to the success of the new government. But the rise of political parties baffled the first President, and abusive newspaper criticism during his second administration angered and hurt him. He was relieved to lay down the burdens of office in March, 1797, and return to his cherished Virginia plantation.

Recognized as a great man in his own lifetime, Washington's reputation soared to that of a demigod in the early nineteenth century. Recently a British historian offered this balanced judgment of the Father of our Country: "A good man, but not a saint; a competent soldier, not a great one; an honest administrator, not a statesman of genius; a prudent conserver, not a brilliant reformer. But in sum an exceptional figure."

The Bill of Rights is adopted. As we have seen (page 134), Congress soon provided for a Bill of Rights. During the months before the Constitution went into effect, many Federalists had come to agree with the Antifederalists that guarantees of individual rights should be added to the document. In 1789, therefore, Congress adopted the first ten amendments, and by the end of 1791 they had been ratified by the states. Prompt action in adding the Bill of Rights to the Constitution did much to allay the fears of Antifederalists.

▶ CHECK-UP

1. Why was Washington's election to the presidency important?

2. What executive departments were established? What men were appointed to head these departments? How did the Cabinet evolve?

3. What were the provisions of the Judiciary Act of 1789?

. . . .

2 *Hamilton Presents a Financial Program*

Financial problems are critical. The new government had inherited a large debt and an empty treasury from the Confederation. One of its first problems, therefore, was to secure revenue. In 1789 Congress passed a tariff act providing for the collection of low duties on imported goods. This revenue enabled the government to meet current expenses. But there remained the long-range problem of paying the national debt and thereby gaining the respect of foreign countries for the government.

Hamilton tackles the financial situation. Major credit for solving this problem belongs to the first Secretary of the Treasury, Alexander Hamilton. Still in his early thirties when he took office, Hamilton showed a remarkable grasp of financial affairs. Though never a wealthy man, he shared the viewpoint of successful merchants and large property owners. He was convinced that the central government would be strengthened by the establishment of sound financial policies. During his five and a half years as Secretary of the Treasury, Hamilton proposed a series of financial measures, most of which were adopted by Congress.

Hamilton calls for settlement of the public debt. Early in 1790, Hamilton sent to Congress a *Report on the Public Credit*. He recommended (1) that the foreign debt of 12 million dollars be paid in full; (2) that the domestic debt of 42 million dollars owed to the people of the United States be paid at full or face value; and (3) that the Revolutionary War debts owed by the states, amounting to 21 million dollars, be assumed and paid by the national government.

FEDERAL COURTS TODAY

The Constitution established a Supreme Court of the United States and directed Congress to create lesser courts as they became necessary. Note the use Congress has made of that power.

CHART STUDY

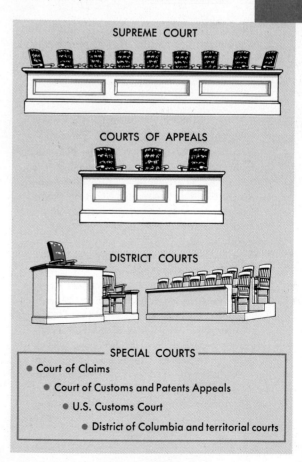

SUPREME COURT

COURTS OF APPEALS

DISTRICT COURTS

SPECIAL COURTS
- Court of Claims
- Court of Customs and Patents Appeals
- U.S. Customs Court
- District of Columbia and territorial courts

In support of these recommendations, Hamilton pointed out that the United States would not be truly independent until it repaid its financial obligations to such countries as the Netherlands and France. Furthermore, repaying the domestic debt was a matter of honor, for the government had promised to redeem its certificates of indebtedness. These certificates had been selling for far less than face value because of the Confederation's weak financial condition. The people holding them would have been glad, therefore, to accept less than full payment. But Hamilton insisted on redeeming the certificates at face value. As for the states' war debts, the Secretary said they should be taken over by the new government as "a measure of sound policy and substantial justice."

To meet these heavy financial obligations, Hamilton proposed that the federal government issue bonds to cover the entire public debt. In time the government would be able to pay its creditors and retire the bonds. Meanwhile, creditors would look to the central government, rather than to the states, for the money owed them. This would strengthen the federal government since creditors would have a personal stake in its success.

Taking the Census

Every ten years since 1790 the federal government has counted the population of the United States. Provision for a census was made in Article I of the Constitution. In 1790, some 200 workers counted 3,929,214 people. Of this number, 757,208 were Negroes, 697,681 of them slaves.

Over the decades, as the population has grown, the census-taking army has grown with it. In 1960 more than 150,000 enumerators were used to tabulate the nation's population of 179,323,175. The purposes of the census have also been broadened to describe the nature of the population as well as to determine its size. The Bureau of the Census tabulates Americans' ages, occupations, incomes, and other data. Such information is useful in charting the future growth and progress of the nation.

Congress adopts Hamilton's proposals on the public debt. There was little disagreement in Congress about paying the foreign debt. Full payment of the domestic debt, however, provoked some debate. People who held certificates of indebtedness naturally supported Hamilton's policy. Many of these people had acquired the certificates at far less than face value, and they stood to gain large sums if the proposal were adopted. Those who had no debt certificates or had sold them at a discount, on the other hand, opposed Hamilton's policy. Also taking this position were small landowners and wage-earners, who had no wish to be taxed to repay wealthy creditors. But Congress finally approved federal payment of the domestic debt at full value.

Hamilton's third proposal — assumption of the state debts by the federal government — aroused considerable turmoil. Some states (for example, Georgia) had not contracted large debts during the Revolution. Others (such as Virginia) had made sacrifices during the 1780's to repay their debts. These states thought it was unfair for the federal government to assume the debts of states which had failed to meet their financial obligations. Feeling ran high, and a test vote in the House of Representatives was won by Hamilton's opponents.

At this point Hamilton turned to Jefferson for help. Most southern congressmen opposed the assumption of state debts, but they were eager to have the national capital located on the Potomac River. Jefferson, Madison, and Hamilton reached an agreement. The two Virginians rounded up enough southern votes to pass Hamilton's assumption bill by a narrow margin. Then, with Hamilton's co-operation, they were able to win approval for establishing the capital on the Potomac after a ten-year period in Philadelphia. The exact site of the new Federal City was to be selected by Washington himself, and it was later named in his honor.

Hamilton recommends a national bank. Hamilton's second report to Congress urged the establishment of a national bank. He believed that such a bank would provide a safe place to keep government funds and

(Continued on page 168)

Alexander Hamilton

[1757–1804]

Born in the British West Indies, Alexander Hamilton was the son of a Scottish merchant and a French Huguenot mother. He was apprenticed to a shopkeeper at the age of eleven. But a few years later an article that he wrote, describing a hurricane, was noticed by a local businessman who decided to help the precocious youth get an education on the mainland. Thus, Alexander Hamilton entered King's College, now Columbia University, in 1773. He did well in his studies, but spent his spare time writing pamphlets attacking England.

In March, 1776, Hamilton joined the American Army and fought with Washington on Long Island the next summer. Washington made him a staff secretary with the rank of lieutenant-colonel and asked Hamilton to handle relations between the army and the Continental Congress. Soon the young officer was turning out reports on how to improve relations within the army and with Congress. After participating in the Battle of Yorktown, Hamilton resigned his commission and returned to New York City to study law.

He soon had a flourishing legal practice, yet devoted a good deal of attention to public affairs. One year in Congress convinced him that the Articles of Confederation needed drastic revision. Although he played a key role in bringing about the Philadelphia convention in 1787, Hamilton was too outspoken and impatient to exert much influence on the delegates. His *Federalist* essays, however, helped win public approval for the new government.

It was natural that Washington should think of his brilliant wartime aide when appointing government officials. As Secretary of the Treasury, Hamilton moved with his usual decisiveness. He kept Congress busy with one report after another. So many of his proposals were accepted that one Republican senator lamented, "Congress may go home. Mr. Hamilton is all-powerful, and fails in nothing he attempts."

After resigning from the Cabinet in 1795, Hamilton tried hard to retain power in the Federalist Party. He sought to influence the electoral vote in 1796 and again in 1800. He took issue with President John Adams on a number of occasions, and wrote an intemperate letter "concerning the public conduct and character of John Adams, Esq.," which helped defeat the Federalists in 1800. When Aaron Burr, Jefferson's first Vice-President, ran for governor of New York in 1804, Hamilton worked hard to defeat him. Soon afterwards, Burr challenged Hamilton to a duel. Though he did not believe in dueling, Hamilton accepted the challenge to prove his courage. On July 11, 1804, Hamilton was mortally wounded by Burr's first shot. His own gun was fired high, for he had no intention of shooting Burr.

would help the government sell its bonds. It also could issue a stable and uniform national currency, which would aid the country's business.

In 1791 Congress approved Hamilton's suggestion. It chartered a Bank of the United States for a period of 20 years with a capital stock of ten million dollars. The bank was to be under private management, but the Secretary of the Treasury could demand weekly statements of the bank's condition. The government was to purchase one fifth of the stock; the balance would be held by private individuals. The directors of the bank were authorized to establish branches in the states. The bank was given the right to issue bank notes (paper money). These notes could be used to pay taxes and debts to the government provided that the bank would redeem them on demand, in gold and silver coin.

Sharp differences develop over the bank bill. The bank bill brought cries of protest from Hamilton's opponents. Many Southerners predicted that the bank would help only the commercial North and not the agricultural South. A Georgia representative complained that Hamilton's scheme was "calculated to benefit . . . the mercantilist interests only; the farmers, the yeomanry, will derive no advantage from it." Madison attacked the bill on constitutional grounds, pointing out that the Founding Fathers had not authorized Congress to charter companies. Washington, troubled by the criticism of the bank bill, asked members of his Cabinet for their opinions.

Jefferson and Hamilton submitted reports which reflected two different interpretations of the Constitution. Jefferson argued for a *strict construction* of the Constitution. He challenged the bank bill on the grounds that it asked Congress to exercise powers which the Constitution had not "specifically enumerated." He believed, therefore, that it would be unconstitutional for Congress to charter a bank. Jefferson further warned that whenever Congress overstepped its powers, it would be taking "possession of a boundless field of power" to which no proper limits could be set. Hamilton, on the other hand, championed a *loose con-*

struction of the Constitution. He argued that the Constitution gave Congress the powers "necessary and proper" for carrying out its functions. Because a national bank would help Congress carry out such functions as borrowing money, making appropriations, and levying taxes, Hamilton argued that it would be constitutional.

The national bank is established. Washington studied the two papers carefully. He believed that the idea of a national bank was sound and accepted Hamilton's viewpoint that Congress had the "implied powers" to charter such an institution. In February, 1791, therefore, the President signed the controversial bank bill into law. But the furor over the national bank had sharpened the differences (1) between those who wanted to strengthen the central government and those who wanted to limit it; (2) between those who favored the economic interests of merchants and manufacturers and those who sided with the planters and farmers; (3) between those who agreed with Hamilton and those who agreed with Madison and Jefferson.

Congress passes another tariff act. Hamilton next turned his attention to raising money. The tariff of 1789 (page 165) was not producing enough revenue both to meet government expenses and to pay interest on the national debt. Hamilton proposed, therefore, that tariff rates be increased. In his *Report on Manufactures* (1791), he argued that higher duties would not only produce more revenue but also encourage manufacturing in the United States. More industry would reduce the need to import manufactured goods. In addition, increased manufacturing would promote the growth of cities, whose people would buy large amounts of food from American farmers. Finally, Hamilton pointed out that manufacturing plants would provide new jobs.

Congress was not enthusiastic about Hamilton's new proposal. Spokesmen for the farmers protested that they were already being taxed unfairly to help American manufacturing interests. And merchants who sold goods imported from foreign countries charged that higher duties would ruin their business. In the end, Congress approved another tariff act which raised some rates, gave added protection to certain manufacturers, and produced slightly more revenue for the Treasury. But it was not the high tariff measure that Hamilton had requested.

Congress levies a whiskey tax. Hamilton also proposed a tax on whiskey distilled within the United States. Not only would such a tax raise money, but it would also accustom people to the taxing power of the central government. Congress' approval of the whiskey tax came as a severe blow to western farmers. There was hardly a farmer in the western counties of Pennsylvania, Maryland, Virginia, and North Carolina who did not have a whiskey still. These farmers converted surplus corn and rye into whiskey because bad roads made the transportation of anything as bulky as grain expensive. In backwoods areas, where money was scarce, whiskey was actually used as currency. When the small farmers of the West heard about the whiskey tax, they protested that it would interfere with their way of making a living.

Farmers rebel against the whiskey tax. Hamilton knew how the frontier farmers felt, but he was determined to collect the whiskey tax and thereby strengthen the power of the central government. During 1794, Treasury agents were roughly handled in many frontier areas; the most serious disturbance broke out in western Pennsylvania. Hamilton insisted that open defiance of the government must be met with firmness. He persuaded Washington to mobilize 13,000 militiamen (a larger force than Washington had usually commanded during the Revolution!). As this army neared Pittsburgh, the opposition melted away. Leaders of the so-called Whiskey Rebellion were arrested, but only two were convicted and they were soon pardoned by the President. Hamilton had proved his point that federal taxes must be paid, but he had also made a great many enemies.

Hamilton recommends a national currency. The final part of Hamilton's financial program dealt with metal currency. Ever since colonial days there had been a shortage of coins, and much confusion resulted from the use of a variety of foreign coins. On Hamilton's recommendation, Congress passed the Mint Act of 1792 to deal with this problem. The act provided for the minting of gold, silver, and copper coins, based on the decimal system. There would be three gold coins: an eagle worth ten dollars, a half eagle, and a quarter eagle. Silver was to be coined into dollars, half dollars, quarters, dimes, and half dimes. Copper was to be used for cents and half cents. Since not enough gold and silver were available to mint an adequate supply of coins, however, foreign coins continued to be used.

The financial program promotes prosperity. Economic conditions had begun to improve even before Washington's inauguration. But there is no doubt that Hamilton's financial program did much to encourage prosperity. Paying the foreign debt strengthened the country's reputation abroad. Both government bonds and national bank stock soon sold at high prices. Trade between the states became brisk once state tariff barriers were eliminated. Also, foreign trade increased. Exports doubled between 1791 and 1794, and capital from foreign countries was eagerly invested in America. The infant republic, nearly bankrupt in the 1780's, was building an enviable financial reputation a decade later.

▶ CHECK-UP

1. What were Hamilton's recommendations with respect to the foreign debt, the domestic debt, and the war debts owed by the states? What were his reasons? Why was there more opposition to the last two proposals than to the first? How was passage of the assumption bill secured?

2. How did Hamilton justify the establishment of a national bank? What were to be its functions? On what grounds was the bank opposed? What were the results of this controversy?

3. Why did Hamilton propose a protective tariff? A tax on whiskey? What group or groups favored each? Opposed each? Why? What happened in each case?

3 *Political Parties Are Organized*

Hamilton's policies stir opposition. As Hamilton rounded out his program, the number of his enemies increased. Nearly every move he made — paying the national debt in full, taking over the state debts, starting the Bank of the United States, promoting tariffs, and levying taxes — stirred some group to opposition. Large landowners in the South and small farmers throughout the country were convinced that Hamilton's program brought them no benefits and, in fact, cost them money in increased taxes. The merchants, bankers, manufacturers, and land speculators, most of whom lived in the cities of the Northeast, gained most from the administration's financial policies. Thus, Hamilton's program tended to divide the South and West from the North and East, debtors from creditors, and merchants and manufacturers from farmers and planters.

These divisions contributed to the rise of political parties in the early 1790's. The Founding Fathers had not anticipated this development and, in fact, had hoped that political parties would not appear. Most of them had assumed that if groups were organized to influence government policy and legislation, tension and strife would result. President Washington often expressed his conviction that political parties were evil and should be avoided in America. Vice-President John Adams said in 1792, "There is nothing I dread so much as the division of the Republic into two parties, each under its leader." Yet political parties did arise in the 1790's, and their important role in the government soon became recognized as part of the unwritten constitution (page 135).

Jefferson and Madison organize the Republicans. Hamilton's opponents naturally rallied around Thomas Jefferson and James Madison. This group disliked Hamilton's financial policies and feared his plans to strengthen the central government. By strict interpretation of the Constitution, they hoped to preserve the powers of the individual states. In addition, the Jeffersonians felt that *all* citizens had the right to participate in the federal government.

To thwart Hamilton's plans, Jefferson and Madison organized a party, whose members took the name *Democratic-Republicans*, or simply *Republicans*. (This latter name should not be confused with the present-day Republican Party, which was not organized until the 1850's.) Jefferson and Madison corresponded regularly with political leaders who shared their views. To get their ideas before the public, they started a newspaper, the *National Gazette*, edited by the poet Philip Freneau. Madison contributed articles to the paper, outlining the position of "the Republican party, as it may be termed."

The Federalists support the administration. The people who approved of Hamilton's financial policies came together to form the Federalist Party. Most of them had fought as *Federalists* for ratification of the Constitution, and they adopted that name for their political organization. The strength of the Federalist Party centered largely in New England and the Middle States. The Federalists wanted to strengthen the central government and restrict the power of the states. Consequently they stood for loose interpretation of the Constitution. Many of the Federalists thought that political power should be entrusted to "gentlemen of principle and property," as Adams expressed it. Throughout the 1790's the Federalist organ was the *Gazette of the United States*, edited by John Fenno.

Jefferson and Hamilton become political opponents. The personal contrasts between Hamilton and Jefferson were as pronounced as their political differences. The Virginia planter was a tall, thoughtful man, who lived quietly and dressed simply. At the time he joined Washington's administration, he was 46 years old. Having traveled extensively in Europe, Jefferson was known on both sides of the Atlantic as a scientist, architect, musician, statesman, writer, and diplomat. Alexander Hamilton was in his mid-30's. A short, energetic man with a warm personality, he could charm even his opponents. While Jefferson came from a prominent family, his political sympathies lay with the rank and file of citizens. In contrast, Hamilton came from humble origins, yet he generally shared the interests of the well-to-do.

These two able members of Washington's Cabinet clashed constantly. Hamilton not only ran the Treasury Department but also gave directions to Congress and tried to influence Cabinet decisions on foreign policy. As Secretary of State, Jefferson usually opposed Hamilton in the Cabinet and worked closely with Madison to block Hamilton's measures in Congress. Despite the conflict between the two men, Washington persuaded them to remain at their posts during his first term of office. The President believed that the best way to resolve the quarrel was to keep both political leaders within the Cabinet.

The parties test their strength. The election of 1792 provided the first contest between the Federalists and the Republicans. President Washington, persuaded by his Cabinet to run again, was chosen unanimously by the electoral college. But there were two candidates for the vice-presidency — John Adams and Governor George Clinton of New York. The Federalists supported Adams, who won with 77 electoral votes. The Republicans backed Clinton and were encouraged by the fact that he won 50 electoral votes. Moreover, the Republicans gained a majority in the House of Representatives. Washington thus entered his second term with the prospect of more, rather than less, party conflict. Jefferson and Hamilton grew increasingly restive in the Cabinet. The former resigned at the end of 1793, and Hamilton left a year later. Both political leaders promptly began making plans for the election to be held in 1796. In the meantime, the Federalists and Republicans had begun arguing about a new issue — American policy toward foreign countries.

▶ CHECK-UP

1. What groups came to oppose Hamilton's policies? Why? How did this opposition lead to the organization of the Republican and Federalist Parties? Explain the major issues dividing these two parties.

2. Who were the leaders of the two parties? What was the significance of the outcome of the 1792 election?

• • • • • • • • • • • • • • • • • • • •

4 *The New Nation Faces Foreign Problems*

Americans at first sympathize with the French Revolution. In 1789, just a few months after Washington's first inauguration, the French Revolution began. Since it was a revolt of the French people against the absolute monarchy of Louis XVI and the privileged position of the nobility, Americans greeted the uprising enthusiastically. "In no part of the globe," wrote an American lawyer, "was this revolution hailed with more joy than in America." French costumes, mannerisms, and ideas were widely adopted, and Americans toasted each other with the French slogan "Liberty, Equality, and Fraternity." Bostonians changed the name of Royal Exchange Alley to Equality Lane; while in New York, Crown Street became Liberty Street. Americans celebrated each new victory in the French Revolution with songs, pageants, and "civil feasts." In the larger cities, democratic societies sprang up, modeled after French political clubs. Most of these societies favored the Republican Party. One of them, the Sons of Tammany in New York City, was closely allied with the Jeffersonians.

Federalists and Republicans disagree over France. As the French Revolution gathered force in the early 1790's, control passed from moderate leaders to extremists. Some Americans then began to have a change of heart. Many of Hamilton's followers distrusted the emphasis placed by French revolutionists on democracy and the rights of the common man. They also were alarmed by French attacks on religion and social position. Soon America heard that Lafayette had been forced to flee for his life, that the French king had been beheaded, and that France had been plunged into a Reign of Terror. Then even the more liberal Federalists lost sympathy with the revolutionists.

On the other hand, few Republicans criticized the French Revolution. Like Jefferson, they disapproved of the violence but hoped that it would soon give way to an orderly democratic government.

Washington proclaims American neutrality. Two developments finally forced the Washington administration to take a public stand on the French Revolution: (1) the outbreak of war between Great Britain and France, and (2) the arrival of a diplomatic representative from the French government.

By 1793 not only Britain but also Austria, Prussia, Spain, and Holland were at war with France. These countries were angered by the revolutionists' persecution of the French nobility and by their attempt to spread the doctrines of the French Revolution throughout Europe. In that same year the French republic decided to send a minister, "Citizen" Edmond Genêt (zhuh-*nay'*), to the United States. Technically this country was still allied with France, and the treaties of 1778 (page 102) obligated us to help France in case her West Indian possessions were attacked. Before 1793, President Washington had been able to stand aloof from fast-moving events in France. But when Britain, with its control of the seas, went to war with revolutionary France, and when it became known that Genêt was on his way, the President had to announce a policy.

As usual, Washington asked his Cabinet for opinions. And, as usual, Hamilton and Jefferson failed to agree. Hamilton argued that the treaties of 1778 had been signed by the French monarchy; and that once the monarchy was overthrown, the treaties no longer applied. He therefore urged a policy of neutrality. Jefferson, however, said the treaties bound the people of France and America. Hence they were still binding, even though both the French and the

Americans had changed their governments since 1778. Although he wished the United States to stay out of the European war, Jefferson felt that a declaration of neutrality would aid Great Britain.

After considering these two opinions, Washington arrived at a decision. On April 22, 1793, the President issued a proclamation which declared the United States to be neutral (though the word "neutrality" was not actually used). It informed France and Britain that the United States was "friendly and impartial," and it warned Americans to avoid hostile acts.

Genêt arouses resentment. The Neutrality Proclamation made little impression on Genêt, who had landed in South Carolina shortly before. Warmly welcomed by Republicans throughout the South, Genêt was in no hurry to present himself to the President. Before coming to Philadelphia, he organized expeditions of American volunteers to attack Spanish Florida and Louisiana, and he outfitted privateers to prey on British commerce.

When at last he called on President Washington, Genêt was coldly received. Even Jefferson was offended by the Frenchman's high-handed actions. Genêt, convinced that the American government did not reflect the feeling of the people, decided to appeal to them over the President's head. Angered by this brazen act, Washington asked France to recall Genêt. This was done, but because a new group had gained control of the French government, Genêt was afraid to return. He asked for, and was granted, permission to remain in the United States. Later he married a daughter of Governor George Clinton and lived in this country until his death.

Relations with Great Britain become strained. While the Republicans were sometimes embarrassed by the French government, the Federalists were not always pleased with Great Britain. Relations between the United States and Britain had been none too friendly in the 1780's. In disregard of the Treaty of 1783, the British had refused to remove their troops from the Northwest (page 124) or to pay for slaves carried off during the Revolution. More-

Detroit, shown here in 1794, was one of the western outposts that the British refused to give up after the Revolutionary War. Notice the stockade surrounding the settlement. Britain finally surrendered Detroit to the Americans in 1796.

over, the British steadfastly refused to let the United States trade with the British West Indies.

Another cause for resentment was British disregard for American rights on the high seas. After Britain and France went to war in 1793, the British fleet soon cut off France's trade with her colonies. The French government, therefore, opened its West Indian ports to commerce with neutral countries. American merchants were quick to engage in the profitable trade with the French West Indies. But they were dismayed when the British government ordered the seizure of all vessels trading with France or the French colonies. In enforcing this order, the British seized hundreds of American ships and cargoes. Many American seamen were *impressed*, or forced into British service, on the ground that they were Englishmen or deserters from the royal navy.

Federalists and Republicans fail to agree on policy toward Great Britain. Although these actions of the British distressed the Federalists, they still hoped that war with England could be avoided. They argued that the new country was not prepared for a long and costly struggle. The Federalists further pointed out that war would cut off imports, 90 per cent of which came from England. Duties on these imports provided a large part of the national government's revenue. Finally, Great Britain was fighting revolutionary France,

whose policies seemed wrong to the Federalists.

The Republicans were more critical of British interference with American shipping. Thomas Jefferson sent a strongly worded protest from the State Department, and the Republicans in Congress managed to push through an act suspending foreign trade for two months. Some even called for war.

Jay negotiates with Great Britain. President Washington was as anxious to keep peace with Great Britain as he had been to keep peace with France. He asked Chief Justice John Jay to go to England in 1794 to discuss American grievances. But Hamilton weakened the American position by confiding to the British minister in Philadelphia that under no circumstances would the United States fight Great Britain. Armed with this information, the British negotiators made few concessions. Thus, in the treaty that was signed, Jay had to settle for less than the United States expected.

In Jay's Treaty, Great Britain agreed to withdraw from the Northwest by June 1, 1796. Britain also agreed to submit for arbitration (settlement by a joint commission) certain disputed boundaries and the question of damages to American shippers. The British agreed to give the Americans some trade privileges in the British Empire, but far less than had been expected, especially in respect to the West Indies. On its part, the United States was to pay the pre-

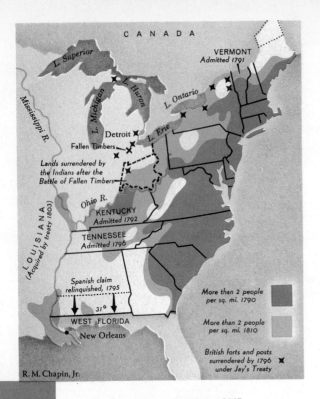

Map labels:
CANADA
VERMONT Admitted 1791
L. Superior
L. Huron
L. Michigan
L. Ontario
L. Erie
Mississippi R.
Detroit
Fallen Timbers
Lands surrendered by the Indians after the Battle of Fallen Timbers
Ohio R.
LOUISIANA (Acquired by treaty 1803)
KENTUCKY Admitted 1792
TENNESSEE Admitted 1796
Spanish claim relinquished, 1795
31°
WEST FLORIDA
New Orleans
More than 2 people per sq. mi. 1790
More than 2 people per sq. mi. 1810
British forts and posts surrendered by 1796 under Jay's Treaty

MAP STUDY

TREATIES OPEN WESTERN LAND TO SETTLEMENT

Jay's Treaty, Pinckney's Treaty, and also treaties with the Indians of the Northwest encouraged the settlement of western lands. Note the spread of population between 1790 and 1810.

Revolutionary debts due British creditors, and British vessels were to be admitted to American ports on favorable terms. Nothing was said about payment for captured slaves or about impressment of American seamen.

The Senate ratifies Jay's Treaty. When the terms of the treaty were announced, a storm of protest broke loose in the United States. Jay was accused of negotiating a Federalist "sellout" to Britain, and he was burned in effigy in many cities and towns. When Hamilton tried to defend the treaty in New York, his listeners hissed, booed, and threw stones. Even Washington was a target for criticism. Through the President's influence, however, the treaty was ratified by a bare two-thirds majority of the Senate in the summer of 1795. The terms were not what Americans wanted, but acceptance of Jay's Treaty preserved peace with Great Britain and secured American sovereignty in the Northwest. This treaty was also im-

portant for two other reasons: (1) it marked this country's first use of negotiation as a means of settling an international dispute; and (2) it prepared the way for settlement of the long dispute with Spain.

Pinckney concludes a treaty with Spain. The Spanish government was afraid that the United States, with her British troubles settled, might threaten the safety of Spanish Florida or Louisiana. Late in 1795, therefore, Thomas Pinckney was able to conclude a treaty with Spain. Pinckney's Treaty fixed the boundary between the United States and West Florida at the thirty-first parallel (map this page), and it guaranteed navigation rights on the Mississippi to American citizens. Spain also granted the use of New Orleans as a "port of deposit," where American goods could be transferred from river boats to ocean-going vessels without payment of regular duties. Westerners were pleased with this treaty. But they still hoped that New Orleans would eventually come under American control.

Americans move beyond the mountains. Before 1795, the urge to push west had been frustrated by hostile Indians and the presence of British and Spanish forces along the frontier. Congress had tried to improve Indian relations in 1790 by passing an act intended to curb greedy traders and land speculators. This act was difficult to enforce, however. As white settlers moved into the Northwest Territory, the Indians went on the warpath. They inflicted a crushing defeat on the frontier militia in 1791.

Three years later General Anthony Wayne won a decisive victory at the Battle of Fallen Timbers in what is now northwest Ohio. Indian chiefs then signed treaties which opened new frontier areas to white settlers. The withdrawal of British troops from fur-trading posts in the Northwest (Jay's Treaty) and the opening of the Mississippi to American navigation (Pinckney's Treaty) encouraged westward expansion. By the time Washington left office, Vermont, Kentucky, and Tennessee had been admitted to the Union.

Washington retires. As Washington's second term drew to a close, he looked forward to retirement at Mount Vernon.

Bitter personal attacks by political opponents and the constant quarrels of the Federalists and Republicans had saddened him. In 1796 his "Farewell Address" to American citizens was published in the newspapers. In this statement he warned of the evils of sectional jealousy and "the baneful effects of the spirit of party." He emphasized the need for continued neutrality and urged the country "to steer clear of permanent alliances with any portion of the foreign world." Washington's Farewell Address became one of this country's important public documents.

▶ CHECK-UP

1. How did Americans react to the French Revolution? Why did Federalists and Republicans come to disagree on policy toward France? What policy did Washington adopt?

2. Why had relations with Britain become increasingly unfriendly? How did the two American political parties differ on policy toward Britain? What good came from Jay's Treaty? What were its limitations?

3. What problems were solved by Pinckney's Treaty with Spain? Why did westward migration increase rapidly after 1795?

. . . .

5 Federalist Power Declines

The Federalists elect John Adams. As the election of 1796 drew near, rivalry between the Federalists and Republicans became more intense. The Federalists in Congress held a private conference, or *caucus*, and urged the election of John Adams for the presidency and Thomas Pinckney for the vice-presidency. A Republican caucus recommended Jefferson for President and Aaron Burr, a Republican leader in New York, for Vice-President.[4]

---

[4] In theory, the electors were to use their own judgment in voting for President and Vice-President. But the recommendations of the congressional caucuses obviously influenced their thinking.

Since Hamilton was not on good terms with Adams, he attempted to influence the electoral vote so that Pinckney would win. To that end, he appealed to southern Federalist electors to vote only for Pinckney, who came from South Carolina. But Adams' New England supporters, having learned of this trick, withheld electoral votes from Pinckney. The result was that Adams, a Federalist, was elected President by 71 electoral votes, while Jefferson, a Republican, became Vice-President with 68 votes. Pinckney came in third with 59. Adams never forgave Hamilton for the fact that he was "President by three votes."

John Adams is not popular. Descended from a Massachusetts Puritan family, John Adams had attended Harvard and then practiced law. He served in the Continental Congress and won distinction as a politician and diplomat before becoming Vice-President under Washington. No one questioned Adams' integrity, loyalty, sincerity, or intelligence, but he lacked the qualities which make for popularity. He was unbending, vain, tactless, and a poor judge of character. Nevertheless, "honest John" Adams was a courageous President. His main contribution was keeping the United States at peace during a time when the country could ill afford war.

The XYZ Affair leads to undeclared war. When Adams took office in 1797, the major countries of Europe were at war with France. Angry because the United States had signed Jay's Treaty, the French government had authorized its ships to seize American vessels carrying British goods. By the time Adams was inaugurated, about 300 American vessels had already been captured. Moreover, the government of France, now known as the Directory, had forced the American minister to flee the country. The more outspoken Federalists demanded that President Adams declare war against France.

Instead, Adams tried to reach an understanding with the Directory. He sent John Marshall and Elbridge Gerry to join the American minister, Charles C. Pinckney. Although the French government never recognized these envoys, certain persons claiming to speak for the Directory talked with the Americans. These French agents, later identified only as X, Y, and Z, made outrageous demands before they would agree even to discuss the seizure of American ships. When the French agents asked for a large sum of money for the "pocket of the Directory," Pinckney replied, "No, no; not a sixpence." The Americans finally put an end to this bargaining, and Marshall returned to America to inform Adams. Congress demanded to see the report, which was soon published as the "XYZ dispatches."

Americans were deeply aroused by the humiliating treatment of their envoys. "Millions for defense, but not one cent for tribute" became a popular slogan. Congress appropriated money to build up the American army and navy, and from 1798 to 1800 the United States and France waged an undeclared war at sea. While Americans captured scores of French vessels, they also suffered heavy losses.

France and the United States reach a settlement. Hamilton and his followers pressed Adams for war, but the President refused to yield. In fact, when Adams learned in 1799 that the French government would receive an American minister, he appointed a commission to re-open negotiations with France, even though he knew many Federalists would oppose this action. By the time the commissioners reached France, Napoleon Bonaparte had overthrown the Directory and made himself head of a new government. Napoleon proved easier to deal with than the Directory, and in 1800 the two countries signed an agreement to end the French-American treaties of 1778. In addition, France agreed to respect American rights on the high seas but refused to pay for the damage done to American shipping.

Though some Federalists had little liking for this agreement, President Adams never regretted the mission he sent to France. Toward the end of his life he said: "I desire no other inscription over my gravestone than: 'Here lies John Adams, who took upon himself the responsibility of peace with France in the year 1800.'"

Congress passes the Alien and Sedition Acts. Meanwhile, a new conflict had broken out between the Federalists and Republicans. The criticism of Adams' policies by Republican newspapers was beginning to hurt the Federalists. Moreover, the Republican Party was rapidly gaining new members, including many of the immigrants who came to this country in the 1790's. Alarmed by these developments, the Federalists decided to use the quarrel with France as an excuse for striking at the Republicans. Claiming a national emergency, they forced four controversial measures through Congress in 1798.

(1) The Naturalization Act required a foreigner to live fourteen years in the United States, rather than five years, before he could become a citizen and vote.

(2) The Alien Act permitted the President to deport aliens whom he judged "dangerous to the peace and safety of the United States."

(3) The Alien Enemies Act permitted the President to imprison or deport dangerous aliens in time of war.

(4) The Sedition Act authorized fines up to 5000 dollars and imprisonment for as long as five years for anyone who tried to hinder the operation of the government. This last measure was aimed specifically at Republican newspapers. It prescribed punishment for anyone who wrote or published "false, scandalous, and malicious" statements against the government, Congress, or the President, or statements which tended "to stir up sedition."

For the Federalists, the Alien and Sedition Acts were a costly mistake. Both Republicans and Federalists criticized the laws. Scores of people were kept from voting by the Naturalization Act. Though no one was ever prosecuted under the Alien Acts, thousands of foreign-born, citizens and aliens alike, deeply resented their enactment. The Sedition Act, on the other hand, was vigorously enforced. More than twenty Republican editors were arrested; and ten were convicted. Matthew Lyon, a Vermont congressman and editor, went to jail for saying that he saw in President Adams "every consideration of public welfare swallowed up in a continual grasp for power, an unbounded thirst for ridiculous pomp, foolish adulation, and selfish avarice."

Since the days of John Adams, government service has been a tradition in the Adams family of Massachusetts. President John Adams (see his picture on page 87) and his son John Quincy Adams (middle picture above) were born in neighboring salt-box houses just outside Boston (left). John Quincy Adams became the sixth President, and his son, Charles Francis Adams (right), served in the House of Representatives and as minister to Great Britain. Later generations of the Adams family continued the tradition of public service.

Kentucky and Virginia protest the Alien and Sedition Acts. The Republicans made good use of the Alien and Sedition Acts to denounce the Federalists. They attacked the laws as violations of the First Amendment, which guarantees freedom of speech and the press. Protests from Kentucky and Virginia carried the most weight. The Kentucky legislature adopted a set of resolutions drawn up in part by Thomas Jefferson. These resolutions held that the federal government had been formed by a *compact* (agreement) among the states, whereby each state relinquished certain definite powers to the central government. Since the states had not specifically granted Congress any power to pass the Alien and Sedition Acts, those acts were illegal. When Congress overstepped the powers granted to it by the Constitution, then the only "rightful remedy" was for the states to declare such acts "unauthoritative, void, and of no force" within their boundaries. Kentucky asked the other states to join in declaring the Alien and Sedition Acts null and void and in seeking their repeal at the next session of Congress. The Virginia legislature approved a similar set of resolutions drafted by James Madison.

None of the other state legislatures went this far in protesting against the Federalist measures. But the Virginia and Kentucky Resolutions had great impact. They raised the fundamental question of whether or not a state had the right to declare an act of Congress unlawful. This question of *states' rights* was to be raised many times in American history — especially by southern states in the decades before the Civil War. The immediate effect of the Kentucky and Virginia Resolutions was to provide ammunition for the Republicans in the election of 1800.

The Republicans win the election of 1800. By the end of the 1790's, many of the country's small farmers, skilled workers, and tradesmen had become members of the Republican Party. These Republicans, led by Jefferson and Madison, attacked the whole Federalist program: Hamilton's financial policy, loose interpretation of the Constitution, the growing centralization of government, increased taxes, failure to reduce the debt, and the money spent on the army and navy. The Alien and Sedition Acts, of course, became a special target of Republican orators.

The Federalists were embarrassed by quarrels within their party, the most serious of which was the rivalry between Hamilton and Adams. Then, too, Adams' efforts to keep peace with France were unpopular with many Federalist voters. George Washington's death in 1799 was still another handicap, for Washington had supported Federalist policies, and his loss was a blow to the party's prestige.

Jefferson was the Republican choice for President in the election of 1800, and the Republican caucus endorsed Aaron Burr as his running mate. The Federalist caucus, with little enthusiasm, backed John Adams for a second term and Charles Pinckney as Vice-President. Once again, Hamilton maneuvered to have the Federalist vice-presidential candidate elected President. This time his scheming made no difference; for when the electoral votes were counted, Adams had 65 and Pinckney 64, but Jefferson and Burr each had 73.

Thomas Jefferson becomes President. The tie vote meant that the House of Representatives had to choose between Jefferson and Burr for the presidency (page 145). The Federalists knew they could throw the choice to either Jefferson or Burr, or they could delay a decision indefinitely. Although the Republicans had obviously intended Jefferson to be President, many of the Federalist electors disliked him so much that they wanted to vote for Aaron Burr. At this crucial point Hamilton played the role of statesman. He knew from his experience in New York that Burr was a man without principles. Despite Hamilton's disagreement with Jefferson's views, he persuaded the Federalists to back his rival. On the thirty-sixth ballot, Jefferson was finally chosen. This confused election led to the adoption in 1804 of the Twelfth Amendment, which provided that the electors should cast separate ballots for President and Vice-President (pages 151–152).

The Federalists try to keep control of the courts. During the closing days of

Adams' administration, Congress passed a Judiciary Act establishing a number of new positions for judges. The Republicans naturally regarded this legislation as a trick of the Federalists to keep control of one branch of the federal government. It was rumored that Adams stayed up very late on his last day in office to sign the judges' commissions. Hence the new Federalist officeholders were called "midnight judges." Adams hoped that they would help to keep Federalist views alive. But, as you will read in later chapters, Adams' appointment, several weeks earlier, of John Marshall as Chief Justice of the Supreme Court was to have far greater influence in preserving Federalist principles.

▶ CHECK-UP

1. What was the French reaction to Jay's Treaty? What came of Adams' efforts to reach an understanding with the French government? What were the terms of the settlement reached in 1800?

2. What were the Alien and Sedition Acts? Why were these acts passed? What were the results of this legislation? What action was urged in the Kentucky and Virginia Resolutions?

3. What issues were raised in the election of 1800? How did Jefferson come to be elected President in 1800?

. . . .

Clinching the Main Ideas in Chapter 7

In the election of 1800 the Federalists lost control of the presidency and both houses of Congress. But during their twelve years in office, they had made significant contributions to the establishment of the Republic. In 1789 they had only a paper document — the Constitution — to guide them; by the time they left office, they had developed a workable government. The Federalists set the machinery of government in motion by creating the executive departments and establishing a system of federal courts. Under Hamilton's guidance the Federalists adopted economic policies that encouraged prosperity at home and won respect abroad. The Federalists recognized the importance of centering adequate power in the federal government; by their loose interpretation of the Constitution, they made this possible. Most important, the Federalists avoided war with both France and Great Britain, despite sharp criticism from opponents.

Thus, the Federalists served the new republic well. But they lacked what one historian has called "political common sense." By insisting on the importance of the well-to-do, they angered the majority of Americans who were small farmers and wage-earners. Federalist efforts to increase the power of the central government at times went too far, especially in the passage of the Alien and Sedition Acts. This extreme legislation frightened people who cherished state sovereignty and individual liberty as protected by the Bill of Rights. Jefferson and Madison worked skillfully to bring together in the Republican Party those Americans who were discontented with Federalist rule. In 1800 a decisive victory at the polls transferred the reins of government to Republican hands.

Chapter Review

Terms to Understand

1. XYZ Affair
2. implied powers
3. Cabinet
4. neutrality
5. caucus
6. impressment
7. states' rights
8. Jay's Treaty
9. Bank of the United States
10. loose interpretation
11. Pinckney's Treaty
12. Whiskey Rebellion
13. port of deposit
14. strict construction
15. Kentucky and Virginia Resolutions

What Do You Think?

1. One historian has expressed the view that "the downfall of the Federalists came because they had outlived their usefulness." Was it fortunate that the government came into the hands of the Federalists in 1789? Passed out of their hands in 1805? Why?

2. When western farmers balked at paying the tax on whiskey, the government mobilized 13,000 men to enforce the law. In what ways was this situation comparable (or not comparable) to the colonists' refusal to pay the Stamp Tax?

3. Jefferson and Madison believed that the Alien and Sedition Acts violated the Constitution. Why? In the Kentucky and Virginia Resolutions they argued that the states had the right to declare these acts null and void. Why? What fundamental question was raised by these resolutions?

4. Is an opposition party necessary in a democracy? Why? Was this the view of the men who wrote the Constitution? Why did political parties develop during Washington's years in office?

5. Was isolation a wise policy for this country in the 1790's? Why? Would it be today? Why?

Using Your Knowledge of History

1. Debate: *Resolved,* That the Sedition Act was a violation of the First Amendment.

2. Write an editorial that might have appeared in either a pro-Federalist or pro-Republican newspaper in the 1790's. Choose as your subject one of the following: the creation of the Bank of the United States; relations with France; the tariff; Jay's Treaty; or the Alien and Sedition Acts.

3. Prepare a chart comparing the views of Federalists and Republicans on specific issues grouped under such headings as federal-state relations, economic affairs, and foreign policy.

4. Write an essay dealing with the issue of free speech in an emergency — when criticism may destroy people's confidence in a democratic government and even lead to its overthrow.

Extending Your Knowledge of History

The party battles of the 1790's are vividly described by Claude G. Bowers in *Jefferson and Hamilton.* His sympathies clearly lie with Jefferson. For Federalist triumphs and troubles, see H. J. Ford's *Washington and His Colleagues* and the study by Stephen G. Kurtz, *The Presidency of John Adams.* There are good biographies of Hamilton (both entitled *Alexander Hamilton*) by Nathan Schachner and John C. Miller. Miller has also written *Crisis in Freedom* about the Alien and Sedition Acts.

CHAPTER 8

Capitol Building in 1801

Jefferson Takes the Helm

Still one thing more, fellow citizens — a wise and frugal government, which shall restrain men from injuring one another, shall leave them otherwise free to regulate their own pursuits of industry and improvement, and shall not take from the mouth of labor the bread it has earned. This is the sum of good government. . . .

THOMAS JEFFERSON, FIRST INAUGURAL ADDRESS, 1801

1801-1809

Thomas Jefferson was eager to heal the bitter party strife which characterized the election of 1800. In his inaugural address he not only described the "good government" which he promised to give his fellow Americans. He also reminded them: "We are all Republicans — we are all Federalists." By this, Jefferson meant that both parties agreed on the basic principles upon which the government had been founded. So successful was President Jefferson during his first administration that the country's voters returned him to office in 1804 with a thumping majority.

The Republicans had promised drastic changes in the Federalist system, yet once in power they proceeded with caution. Most of Hamilton's financial program was kept intact. Furthermore, Jefferson followed the lead of Washington and Adams in preserving American neutrality, though the methods he used to that end aroused much opposition. His boldest act, and one which certainly helped him win a second term, was the purchase of the vast Louisiana Territory in 1803. This chapter will examine the important developments which occurred while Jefferson was at the helm of government.

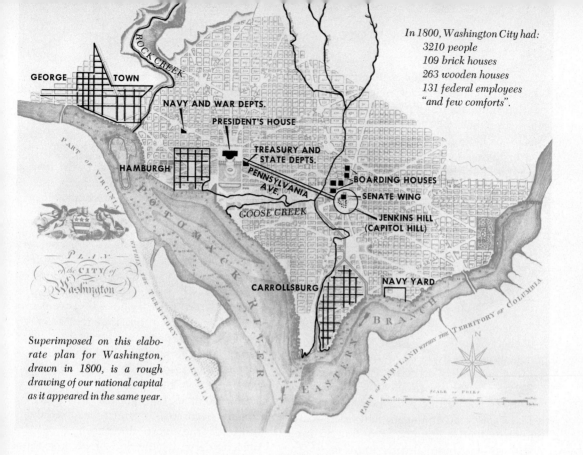

In 1800, Washington City had:
3210 people
109 brick houses
263 wooden houses
131 federal employees
"and few comforts".

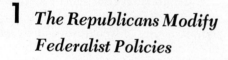

Superimposed on this elaborate plan for Washington, drawn in 1800, is a rough drawing of our national capital as it appeared in the same year.

1 The Republicans Modify Federalist Policies

The capital is moved to the Potomac. In 1800 the national government moved from Philadelphia to the new Federal City on the banks of the Potomac (page 166). Situated in a wilderness, Washington contained only a few shops and boarding houses scattered around the rising public buildings. It was a far cry from the atmosphere of Philadelphia, and those Federalists who still held office had a hard time

. . . .

CHAPTER FOCUS

1. The Republicans modify Federalist policies.

2. The Louisiana Purchase doubles United States territory.

3. Jefferson seeks to protect American rights.

adjusting to the new capital. One of them observed: "We want [lack] nothing here but houses, cellars, kitchens, well-informed men, amiable women, and other little trifles of this kind, to make our city perfect."

Jefferson, who took office in March, 1801, showed a keen interest in the growth of the city. He had suggested majestic Pennsylvania Avenue connecting the White House and the Capitol Building. He was on close terms with the Irish architect, James Hoban, who designed the White House, and the Englishman, Benjamin Latrobe, who helped plan the Capitol. Another of Jefferson's friends, Major Pierre Charles L'Enfant (lahn-*fahn'*), drew up an impressive plan for the city of Washington, with broad avenues radiating from the Capitol. When Jefferson began his term of office, however, few of these plans had been realized. Only one side of the Capitol was finished, and the White House was a barren mansion with few comforts for the new President. Pennsylvania Avenue was merely a clearing through the swamp, with a rough stone footpath for the daring pedestrian.

Jefferson introduces democratic customs. The simplicity of Jefferson's inauguration fitted the rough surroundings. With little ceremony the lanky Virginian walked from his lodgings to the unfinished Capitol. After taking the oath of office, he read his inaugural address to Congress in a voice so low that many had trouble hearing. Ill at ease as a public speaker, Jefferson soon gave up the practice of reading his messages to Congress. Instead, he sent them in writing, as did all his successors until the days of Woodrow Wilson (1913–1921).

Jefferson soon showed that he cared little for the social customs set by the Federalists. He received foreign diplomats in worn "yarn stockings, and slippers down at the heels." Members of the fastidious British delegation were shocked by the Republican President's "utter slovenliness and indifference to appearances." The British were in for further surprises. During the Federalist era, diplomats had been seated at presidential dinners according to rank, with the favored British minister at the head of the table. Jefferson abandoned this practice. At state dinners he substituted the "rule of pell-mell," letting his guests take any place they wanted at the table. Jefferson was a gracious host, however, combining the generous hospitality of a Virginia planter with the excellent food of a French gourmet. Because the President was a widower, the vivacious Dolley Madison, wife of James Madison, acted as official hostess at many state functions.

Jefferson appoints his Cabinet. Jefferson's closest advisers were his Secretary of State and Secretary of the Treasury, both of whom served eight years in his Cabinet. The Secretary of State was James Madison, a fellow Virginian and his friend of many years. In his fifties when he became a member of the Cabinet, Madison was unimpressive in appearance. But he was intelligent and well-read, and had won a reputation for his work in the Constitutional Convention and in Congress during the 1790's. Moreover, with Jefferson, Madison had played a leading role in the development of the Republican Party. Jefferson's Secretary of the Treasury was Albert Gallatin. A Swiss by birth, Gallatin had lived for many years in western Pennsylvania. He had defended the "whiskey rebels" and helped organize the Republican Party in that state. Gallatin had a thorough grasp of the principles of public finance, an area of government in which Jefferson was no expert. President Jefferson shrewdly named two Massachusetts men to other posts in the Cabinet. In this way, he hoped to win friends for his administration in the Federalist stronghold of New England.

Republicans become officeholders. There was great pressure on Jefferson to appoint Republicans to lesser government positions held by Federalists in 1801. Jefferson did not favor wholesale dismissals, but he recognized the importance of rewarding loyal party workers. The President stated the problem in this way: "How are vacancies to be obtained? Those by death are few; by resignation none." Jefferson appointed Republicans wherever vacancies occurred; and, in time, he did fire some of the more outspoken Federalist officeholders. By the end of his first term, he had appointed Republicans to about half the jobs at his disposal.

Congress reverses some Federalist policies. The Republicans used their majority in both houses of Congress to undo some of the work of the Federalists. Thus, when the Alien and Sedition Acts (page 176) expired, Congress refused to renew them. Jefferson freed the men imprisoned under the Sedition Act, and Congress appropriated funds to return the money they had paid in fines. Congress also restored the five-year residence requirement for naturalization.

The Republicans likewise reversed some of the Federalist financial policies. Congress repealed several taxes, including the one on whiskey. Steps were taken to save money and to reduce the public debt, which Jefferson and Gallatin believed should be paid off as quickly as possible. Government expenses were sharply cut, and the number of government officials employed at home and abroad was reduced. Furthermore, the Republicans in Congress cut the size of the army to 2500 men and reduced naval appropriations. These savings, plus the greatly increased income from the tariff, enabled the Republicans to make substantial pay-

(*Continued on page 184*)

Thomas Jefferson

[1743–1826]

Born and raised in the Virginia piedmont, Thomas Jefferson graduated from the College of William and Mary with an excellent education in the classics, an interest in science, and a curiosity about Virginia politics. He began practicing law in 1767, but a few years later took his bride to live on the sizable plantation he inherited.

Jefferson's political career began with his election to the House of Burgesses, where he worked closely with Patrick Henry and other representatives from the piedmont. As a Virginia delegate to the Second Continental Congress, Jefferson spoke infrequently but became well-known as a draftsman of committee reports — including the Declaration of Independence. Toward the end of 1776 the homesick Virginia planter left Philadelphia to return to his family at Monticello. Promptly elected to the Virginia legislature, he helped revise the land laws, rewrite the penal code, and bring about the separation of church and state.

In 1779 Jefferson succeeded Patrick Henry as Governor of Virginia. When the state militia was unable to stem a British invasion, the legislators fled Richmond and the governor himself narrowly escaped capture. When his term of office was over, Jefferson retired from public life to tend his neglected plantation and spend more time with his family, his books, and his studies. The death of his wife shattered these plans. To escape the grief at Monticello, Jefferson agreed to serve again in Congress.

During 1783 and 1784 Jefferson was an influential member of the committees which helped shape the country's western land policy. His report recommending a decimal system of coinage was later adopted by Alexander Hamilton. For the next few years Jefferson represented his country abroad. Although most of his time was spent in Paris, he traveled widely throughout Europe. He observed the political weaknesses of monarchies, studied city plans to get ideas for a future American capital, and conversed with scientists, architects, musicians, and writers. Returning to the United States in 1789, Jefferson was appointed Secretary of State. The next eighteen years of his life were marked by political conflict — the controversies with Hamilton; then as Republican Vice-President under a Federalist President; next as the organizer of the Republican Party and candidate for the presidency in 1800; and finally as President for two terms.

In the spring of 1809, Jefferson returned to his Virginia home. Yet even in retirement "the sage of Monticello" was often consulted by James Madison and James Monroe, his successors as President. In 1819 Jefferson persuaded the state legislature to charter the University of Virginia. He himself designed the school's main buildings and helped shape its curriculum and choose its faculty. During these last years, Jefferson corresponded with a former political antagonist, John Adams of Massachusetts. By strange coincidence, both Jefferson and Adams died on the fiftieth anniversary of the Declaration of Independence, July 4, 1826. In accordance with his wishes, the simple marker over his grave at Monticello reads: "Here was Buried Thomas Jefferson, Author of the Declaration of American Independence, of the Statute of Virginia for Religious Freedom, and Father of the University of Virginia."

ments on the national debt. By 1809 it had been pared from 83 million dollars to 57 million dollars.

The Republicans preserve the national bank. As we have seen, opposition to Hamilton's financial program had led to the formation of the Republican Party. The Bank of the United States was perhaps the most hotly debated part of this program. Yet, for good reason, the Republicans did not abolish the bank after they gained power. Jefferson still considered the bank to be in "deadly hostility" to "the principles and form of our Constitution." But both Jefferson and Gallatin realized that the bank was performing a vital economic service. Its destruction, they knew, would almost certainly threaten the country's prosperity. For this reason the Republicans retained the national bank, and Jefferson even authorized the opening of a branch office in New Orleans in 1803. Furthermore, since custom duties were a major source of government revenue, the Republicans kept the Federalist tariff in force. In a letter to a friend, Jefferson despaired of ever getting rid of Hamilton's financial system. "It mortifies me to be strengthening principles which I deem radically vicious." But, the President concluded, "what is practicable must often control what is pure theory."

The Republicans challenge Federalist control of the courts. Jefferson and other Republicans had regarded Adams' last-minute appointment of Federalist judges (page 178) as an "outrage on decency." The Republican Congress, therefore, repealed the Judiciary Act of 1801. This action prevented the new judges from taking office, but it did not change the situation in the established courts. The Republicans decided to impeach some judges and thus weaken the Federalist hold on the courts.

In 1804, House Republicans brought impeachment proceedings against a judge who had been insane for three years, and the Senate quickly upheld their charges. Then the Republicans went after Supreme Court Justice Samuel Chase, whose bias during the Sedition Act trials had been widely criticized. Jefferson desperately hoped that the impeachment charges against Chase would be upheld. But the two-thirds vote necessary to convict him could not be mustered in the Senate, and Chase returned triumphantly to the Supreme Court. After this setback, the Republicans gave up their attack on the judiciary.

The "Marbury v. Madison" decision strengthens the Supreme Court. The Republicans suffered still another defeat in the case of *Marbury v. Madison* (1803). William Marbury was an Adams appointee whose commission of office had not been delivered before the change of administrations. Marbury asked the Supreme Court to compel Secretary of State Madison to grant him his commission. He based his case on a section of the Judiciary Act of 1789 which authorized the Supreme Court to issue such instructions to the executive branch of the government.

Heading the Supreme Court was Chief Justice John Marshall, the Federalist appointed by John Adams just before he left office in 1801. Marshall and the other Federalist justices were in a tight spot. They believed that if they approved Marbury's request, Madison might ignore the Court's orders, thus weakening respect for the judiciary. If they rejected Marbury's request, it would be a victory for the Republicans. Marshall managed, however, to avoid both of these political pitfalls. In his decision he said that Marbury deserved his commission, but that the Court was powerless to make the Secretary of State deliver it. The Constitution had not authorized the Supreme Court to give directions to the executive branch of the government; therefore, Section 13 of the Judiciary Act of 1789 was unconstitutional.

Marshall's decision in *Marbury v. Madison* was a blow to the Republicans. It strengthened the federal judiciary by establishing the principle that the Supreme Court could declare acts of Congress unconstitutional. The Constitution had not specifically given this power of judicial review (page 134) to the Supreme Court; and the Republicans, of course, did not want the Court to have it. Jefferson complained that *Marbury v. Madison* set a dangerous precedent. It made of the Constitution "a mere thing of wax" which the justices "may twist and shape into any form they please." Yet the

Republicans could do nothing about the decision. *Marbury v. Madison* was the first of a number of important rulings handed down by John Marshall during his 35 years as Chief Justice.

▶ CHECK-UP

1. How did Jefferson's administration differ from preceding ones? What Federalist policies were reversed? Why did the Republicans make no greater changes?

2. How did Chief Justice Marshall assert the Supreme Court's right of judicial review in "Marbury v. Madison"?

• • • • • • • • • • • • • • • • • •

2 *The Louisiana Purchase Doubles United States Territory*

Jefferson takes an interest in the West. In his inaugural address Jefferson had expressed an interest in the "men of the western waters," those settlers who lived along the Ohio and Mississippi Rivers and their many tributaries. Jefferson had long favored those who tilled the soil, believing that the ideal nation would be one of small farmers. As President, he satisfied many of the requests of western settlers.

For one thing, the Westerners wanted an easing of the conditions under which government land could be purchased. In 1796 the Federalists had set the minimum price of public land at two dollars an acre and required a buyer to take at least 640 acres. Four years later the minimum purchase was reduced to 320 acres, with a down payment of 25 per cent of the price. This arrangement was still beyond the means of most farmers. Consequently, they had to buy smaller parcels of land at a far higher price per acre from land speculators. The Republicans came to their aid with a Land Act in 1804, which cut the minimum size of lots to 160 acres. Government land offices were opened west of the mountains and soon were doing a "land-office business" with appreciative settlers.

Jefferson and Secretary of the Treasury Gallatin pleased the Westerners in other ways as well. For example, the whiskey tax was repealed. Also, the Republican administration proposed the use of public funds to build roads, canals, and bridges in areas beyond the Appalachians. Nothing came of these projects until later. But it is easy to see why Jefferson was the favorite of voters in Kentucky, Tennessee, and the new state of Ohio (admitted in 1803).

France gains possession of the Louisiana territory. Soon after the Republicans came to power, the threat of foreign interference to the south and west became a serious problem. Since 1763, Spain had owned the vast territory, west of the Mississippi, known as Louisiana (map, page 188). The United States showed no great interest in this region at the time. But most Americans assumed, as did Jefferson, that the decaying Spanish empire would not hold on to Louisiana forever. Jefferson felt that as our population increased and began to need more land, we could "gain it [Louisiana] from them piece by piece." In the meantime, the Pinckney Treaty of 1795 guaranteed Americans free navigation of the Mississippi and the right to use New Orleans as a port of deposit.

During 1801, rumors began to circulate in New Orleans that Spain had secretly transferred Louisiana to France. The next year the American minister in Britain learned that Napoleon had indeed signed a secret treaty with Spain by which France regained Louisiana. Jefferson feared that France, unlike Spain, would actually occupy and settle Louisiana, making it the heart of a French empire in America. Napoleon clearly hoped to have Louisiana produce food for the French West Indies so that the islands would no longer be dependent on trade with the United States.

Jefferson is alarmed. In the spring of 1802, Jefferson sent a dispatch to the American minister in France, Robert R. Livingston. This document expressed American fears about French occupation of Louisiana, and Jefferson expected Liv-

ingston to make its contents known to
Napoleon. "There is on the globe," the
President wrote,

> one single spot, the possessor of which is our
> natural and habitual enemy. It is New Or-
> leans, through which the produce of three
> eighths of our territory must pass to market.
> . . . France, placing herself in that door,
> assumes to us the attitude of defiance. . . .
> The day that France takes possession of New
> Orleans, . . . we must marry ourselves to the
> British fleet and nation.

Jefferson's fears were increased later in
the year when the commander at New
Orleans suspended the right of deposit.
This action was a shattering blow to the
Westerners, for it threatened to stifle the
flow of American exports down the Mississippi and thence to Atlantic coastal ports
and overseas. Many Westerners demanded
a declaration of war against France and
Spain. The Federalists, who had long
wanted war with France, joined in the cry.

Jefferson tries to buy New Orleans.
Like Washington and Adams, Jefferson was
determined that "nothing but dire necessity should force us from the path of peace."
Jefferson had already instructed Livingston
to sound out Napoleon on the possibilities
of buying New Orleans and West Florida,
which Jefferson mistakenly assumed had
also been turned over to France. Early in
1803 he appointed James Monroe as a special envoy to assist Livingston in the negotiations. Congress appropriated two million dollars to pay for any unusual expenses
that might be incurred as a result of the
talks. Monroe left for Paris with instructions to offer up to ten million dollars for
the area around New Orleans plus West
Florida (map, page 174).

Napoleon sells all of Louisiana. Luck
was with the American commissioners.
Napoleon had suffered a series of reverses
that caused him to change his mind about
Louisiana. A slave revolt on the island of
Santo Domingo (Hispaniola) had met with
surprising success. A French army sent to
crush the uprising had failed to defeat the
slaves, and thousands of the soldiers had
died of yellow fever. The revolt threatened
to spread to other French possessions.
Moreover, an uneasy truce between France
and Britain seemed about to end. Napoleon knew that full-scale war in Europe
would require all his troops and more
money than he had in the treasury. Furthermore, he could not hope to protect both the
strife-ridden West Indies and Louisiana
from British naval attacks. So Napoleon
suddenly offered to sell the entire Louisiana territory to the United States.

The astonished Livingston had no instructions to buy this huge territory, but
he quickly accepted the French proposal.
When Monroe arrived, he also agreed to
the fantastic offer and the two Americans
drew up the final terms of the sale. In May,
1803, the treaty transferring Louisiana to
the United States was signed. The Americans agreed to pay fifteen million dollars.
Three quarters of this sum was to go directly to the French government; the rest
was to be used to satisfy American claims
for damages during the undeclared war
with France (page 176).

Monroe and Livingston were uncertain
about the exact boundaries of their "noble
bargain." The treaty merely described the
boundaries as those which Louisiana "now
has in the hands of Spain." Napoleon's ne-
gotiator admitted this description was vague

Haiti: The First Negro Republic

France's failure to put down an uprising on
Hispaniola in 1802 had far-reaching consequences. It enabled the United States to buy
Louisiana and resulted in the establishment of
the Negro republic of Haiti.

Haiti occupies the western third of Hispaniola. When the French Revolution broke out in
1789, slaves on Hispaniola demanded freedom. Attempts to suppress the slaves failed,
and they were freed by the French in 1793.

Haiti's great leader and hero was Toussaint
L'Ouverture, himself a slave until he was almost fifty. Toussaint governed Haiti ably until
Napoleon Bonaparte reversed French policy
and tried to reconquer all Hispaniola. Though
Toussaint was captured and sent to a French
prison to die, his countrymen fought on. In
1804 Haiti won its independence from France
and eventually became a republic.

but told the Americans, "I suppose you will make the most of it."

Reaction to the purchase is varied. The Louisiana Purchase delighted the "men of the western waters," and it pleased Republicans throughout the country. Jefferson summed up the advantages: "The territory acquired . . . has . . . doubled the area of the United States, and the new part is not inferior to the old in soil, climate, [and] productions. . . ." By "giving us the sole dominion of the Mississippi," said the President, "it excludes those bickerings with foreign powers which we know of a certainty would have put us at war with France immediately."

Yet Jefferson was embarrassed by certain aspects of the purchase. (1) For years he had criticized the Federalists for increasing the national debt; now he was adding fifteen million dollars at a single stroke. (2) He had attacked the Federalists for loose construction of the Constitution; but nowhere in that document was the federal government authorized to add land to the Union by purchase. (3) In his inaugural address Jefferson had claimed that this country possessed land enough "for our descendants to the hundredth and thousandth generation"; yet now he was doubling the amount of territory. The President was so troubled by these inconsistencies that he asked the Republicans in Congress to pass a constitutional amendment authorizing the federal government to purchase land. But few Republicans sympathized with Jefferson's doubts. Most of them urged immediate ratification of the treaty lest Napoleon change his mind.

The Federalists, for their part, objected strongly to the Louisiana Purchase. They charged that it was unconstitutional and unnecessary. The Federalists' political strength and their economic interests were centered in the commercial and manufacturing Northeast. Hence they were not concerned about the West, and they were suspicious of frontiersmen who voted overwhelmingly for the Republicans. Furthermore, the Federalists feared that cheap land in the West might drain people from the seaboard, thus ruining the prosperity of New England. An angry Bostonian charged that when the Mississippi was our western boundary, "we were confined within some limits. Now, by adding an unmeasured world beyond that river, we rush like a comet into infinite space."

The Louisiana Purchase is ratified. In spite of Federalist outcries, most Americans wanted the treaty ratified immediately. Jefferson's political associates advised him that there was no need, and no time, to seek an amendment to the Constitution. He finally relented, on the grounds that future Americans would excuse him for his method of acquiring Louisiana. In October, 1803, the Senate ratified the treaty, and the House appropriated the purchase money.

Two months later the United States took possession of Louisiana. Congress divided it into two territories: the Territory of Orleans, where most of the people lived, and the District of Louisiana[1] (map, page 188). The treaty had promised to the inhabitants full rights of citizenship, but this pledge was not fulfilled immediately. The Territory of Orleans was soon granted an assembly and a delegate to Congress, but its people did not become citizens until it was admitted as the state of Louisiana in 1812.

Spain and the United States argue over West Florida. Since the Louisiana Purchase treaty was vague about boundaries, it touched off a quarrel over ownership of West Florida (map, page 219). Napoleon said that France had not acquired West Florida from Spain and therefore could not have sold it to the United States. The Spanish government took the same position. But Jefferson was convinced that he had purchased West Florida too, and he was annoyed when the Spaniards refused to relinquish it. He hoped, however, that "in good time" Spain would agree to turn over the disputed territory. Jefferson's successor as President, James Madison, inherited this quarrel. When a revolt against Spanish rule broke out in West Florida, Madison took the opportunity to proclaim the region part of the United States (1810). Half the disputed area was added to the Territory of Orleans, and in 1813 the rest was attached to Mississippi Territory.

[1] The District was renamed the Louisiana Territory in 1805.

Map labels:
BRITISH TERRITORY
Lake of the Woods
OREGON
Lewis party return
49°
Boundary adjusted, 1818
(Portland) Columbia R
COUNTRY
Ft. Mandan (Bismarck)
Yellowstone R.
Clark party return
Mississippi R.
Pike, 1805-06
Snake R.
Rocky Mts.
Lewis and Clark, 1804-06
Missouri R.
TERRITORY OF LOUISIANA, 1805
Pacific Ocean
Platte R.
St. Louis
SPANISH TERRITORY
Pike's Peak
Pike, 1806
Boundary adjusted with Spain, 1819
Arkansas R.
Colorado R.
Red R.
New Orleans
Rio Grande
Pike, 1807
TERRITORY OF ORLEANS, 1804
LOUISIANA PURCHASE, 1803
0   100   300   500 mi.
R. M. Chapin, Jr.

MAP STUDY

AMERICA EXPANDS WESTWARD

Notice what vast distances Lewis, Clark, and Pike covered in exploring the Louisiana Purchase. After separating on the return trip, Lewis and Clark reunited near the junction of the Yellowstone and Missouri Rivers and went on to St. Louis.

Lewis and Clark reach the Pacific. Jefferson had long been curious about the region west of the Mississippi. Even before the Louisiana Purchase was completed, he had secured money from Congress for an expedition to the Pacific. To head this venture he chose his secretary, Meriwether Lewis, already an experienced explorer, and William Clark, a well-known Indian fighter and younger brother of George Rogers Clark. They were commissioned to explore the Missouri River and the farthest reaches of the Louisiana Territory and also to discover a route from the Missouri River to the Pacific.

In the spring of 1804, Lewis and Clark and a party of about 45 men started west from a point near St. Louis (map, this page). They followed the Missouri to the vicinity of what is now Bismarck, North Dakota, where they wintered among the Mandan Indians. With the aid of a French Canadian trapper and his Indian wife, Saca-jawea (*sak'*uh-juh-*wee'*uh), the expedition reached the headwaters of the Missouri. Then they pushed across the Continental (or "Great") Divide, which separates the Mississippi Valley from the Pacific watershed. In August, 1805, they came to a branch of the Columbia River and three months later reached the "roreing" ocean. After spending the second winter near the mouth of the Columbia, the group returned to St. Louis, arriving in September, 1806.

The daring Lewis and Clark expedition provided valuable information about the

Louisiana Territory. Their reports described strange wonders of nature, abundant resources, and opportunities for trade. Furthermore, their published journals yielded much information for mapmakers and future settlers. Thus the explorations of Lewis and Clark opened the way to the Far West. They also strengthened this country's claim to the Oregon Country.

Pike explores the Southwest. Lewis and Clark were not the only explorers of the new territory. In 1805 Zebulon Pike followed the Mississippi northward to find its headwaters. The next year Pike set out to explore the Southwest. Starting from St. Louis, Pike headed west to the Arkansas River. He followed this river until he reached the region near the Colorado peak which was later named in his honor. Turning south to find the source of the Red River, Pike and some of his men soon found themselves in Spanish territory. As they traveled the course of the Rio Grande — by mistake, Pike said — they were arrested by Spanish authorities for trespassing. When Pike was released, he returned by way of Texas to American territory. Although the Spaniards had taken his papers from him,

Pike remembered a great deal of what he had seen and brought back much useful information about the Southwest.

Jefferson is re-elected. Meanwhile, in the election of 1804, the Republican prospects for victory had been heightened by several factors. The country was prosperous, taxes had been cut, and in spite of the Louisiana Purchase, the national debt had been reduced. Although Republican changes had been less drastic than the Federalists had predicted, they were none the less real. The idea that the average citizen should have a share in the government was beginning to take hold. In an increasing number of states, presidential electors were chosen by popular vote. Thus, democratic practices were gaining headway. But the most brilliant stroke of Jefferson's first term had been the Louisiana Purchase.

For the election of 1804 the Republicans dropped Burr as Vice-President and named George Clinton in his place. The Federalists had trouble putting together a ticket, but their caucus finally decided to support Charles C. Pinckney for President. In the election, Jefferson swept the South, the West, and the Middle States. Much to the

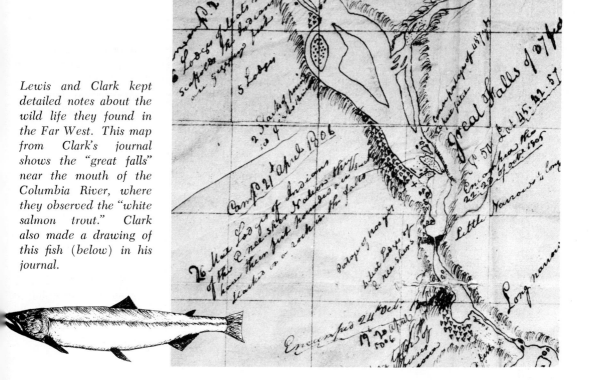

Lewis and Clark kept detailed notes about the wild life they found in the Far West. This map from Clark's journal shows the "great falls" near the mouth of the Columbia River, where they observed the "white salmon trout." Clark also made a drawing of this fish (below) in his journal.

embarrassment of the Federalists, he even carried most of New England.

Burr hatches a conspiracy. As Thomas Jefferson began his second term, one of the strangest episodes in American history unfolded. It centered about Aaron Burr, who in the summer before the election had mortally wounded Alexander Hamilton in a duel. For this and other reasons, Burr's political career was ruined.

During his last months as Vice-President, Burr began to plan a mysterious conspiracy involving the western lands. He corresponded with James Wilkinson, commander of the American troops in Louisiana, who was in the pay of Spain. Burr was also in close touch with the British minister to the United States, Anthony Merry. Historians still are not sure exactly what Burr was planning; there is little written evidence, and Burr himself told many conflicting stories. He may have been trying to carve a republic out of the Louisiana Territory, or to establish a buffer state between Louisiana and Mexico, or possibly to launch an attack on Spanish territory. At any rate, when Burr left office in 1805, he began a leisurely trip down the Ohio, stopping to confer with government officials, military commanders, and prominent Westerners. He stayed for a time with Harman Blennerhassett, an Irishman who had built a castle on an island in the Ohio River.

During 1806 Burr used Blennerhassett Island as his base to assemble an expedition of some 60 men and thirteen flatboats, equipped with arms and supplies. Toward the end of the year he and his followers departed, their exact destination still unknown. At this point Wilkinson thought twice about his involvement with Burr and wrote Jefferson about the former Vice-President's plans. Jefferson ordered Burr's arrest. Burr was soon captured and brought to Richmond, Virginia, to be tried for treason. Jefferson was eager to see Burr convicted, but Chief Justice Marshall, who presided at the trial, adhered strictly to the definition of treason found in the Constitution (page 147). Burr would not confess, and the government could not produce "two witnesses to the same overt act." The former Vice-President was therefore acquitted.

▶ CHECK-UP

1. In what ways did Jefferson show his interest in the West and Westerners? Why did he want to buy New Orleans and West Florida?

2. Why was Napoleon willing to sell the entire Louisiana territory? Why did the Louisiana Purchase embarrass Jefferson? On what grounds did the Federalists oppose it?

3. Why did the United States and Spain argue over West Florida? What was the outcome? What were the results of the Lewis and Clark expedition? Of Pike's explorations?

4. Why did Jefferson score an easy victory in 1804? What was the nature of Burr's plot?

· ·

3 Jefferson Seeks to Protect American Rights

During Jefferson's years in the White House, he faced a thorny problem in trying to protect American neutral rights on the seas. For one thing, pirates in the Mediterranean continued to plague American shipping. An even more serious situation, brought on by war between Britain and France, dominated Jefferson's second term.

The United States fights Mediterranean pirates. Ever since the 1780's, American shipping in the Mediterranean had suffered from attacks by the pirates of Tripoli, Tunis, Algiers, and Morocco (page 124). Washington and Adams had followed the example of European powers and the Confederation Congress in paying annual tribute to the Barbary states. Jefferson and Gallatin, while reluctant to spend money on a navy to fight the pirates, disliked paying tribute even more. Deciding on a show of force, Jefferson sent a small American squadron to the Mediterranean in 1801.

About the same time the Pasha of Tripoli declared war by chopping down the flag at the American consulate. For four years the American navy blockaded and bombarded Tripoli, finally forcing the Pasha to sign a favorable treaty in 1805. Soon afterwards agreements were reached with Morocco and Tunis. But Algiers did not come to terms with the United States until 1815.

Britain and France threaten American neutral rights on the seas. Meanwhile, the shaky truce between France and Britain (page 186) had given way to renewed warfare in 1803. By a series of masterly strokes, Napoleon managed to gain control of a large part of Europe. Great Britain, however, remained mistress of the sea. To cut off the trade of Napoleon and his allies, Great Britain issued *orders in council.* These orders said that if neutral ships went into the European ports controlled by Napoleon, they would not be considered neutral in British eyes.[2]

Napoleon, on the other hand, issued a number of decrees with the intention of stopping British exports to European ports. In the Berlin Decree (1806) he forbade all trade in British merchandise and closed French-controlled ports to ships coming from British ports. A year later, in the Milan Decree, he ordered the confiscation of all neutral ships that traded with the British Isles or let themselves be searched by British cruisers.

Since both Britain and France wanted to buy American foodstuffs, both encouraged American shippers to trade exclusively with them. But the Americans were caught in the bewildering crossfire of British orders and French decrees. Once again, American neutral rights were in danger.

Despite the British threat, American trade prospers. Although both warring powers tried to control American shipping after 1803, the British fleet was far more effective than the French. British men-of-war were stationed outside American harbors to keep watch on ships going in and out. Nevertheless, many American captains successfully ran the blockade. High prices for merchandise and rising freight rates

[2] The plight of American shippers was made worse by a British decision in the *Essex* case (1805). A British court held that an American vessel engaged in carrying enemy goods to an enemy port was subject to seizure even though it stopped en route in an American port. Scores of American vessels engaged in such broken voyages were captured by the British.

brought such fantastic profits that a merchant made money even if only a third of his ships succeeded in landing their cargo. This country's export trade in 1807 — despite the many ships seized — was the highest in its history until 1835.

The British navy seizes American sailors. The loss of American ships and cargoes to the British was less irritating than the loss of American seamen. *Impressment,* the forcing of men into service in the royal navy, had long been practiced in England. The food, discipline, pay, and living conditions were so bad on British warships that few men would volunteer for service on the "floating hells." Impressment was the British navy's way of recruiting English sailors. When Britain extended the practice to American sailors, there were angry protests in the United States.

The rapid growth of American commerce had made the situation worse. To get sailors for their merchant vessels, American shippers paid seamen high wages and gave them good food and fair treatment. Consequently, many British seamen deserted their ships when they reached American ports. They would secure naturalization papers (without waiting five years) and then sign aboard an American ship and claim protection of the American flag. The British government, holding to the principle "once an Englishman, always an Englishman," refused to recognize these deserters as Americans. Furthermore, the British even stopped American ships on the seas, searched them, and took off any seamen who had formerly served in the British navy or merchant marine. Mistakes were often made, accidentally or on purpose, and many native-born American sailors were carried off to serve on British vessels.

The "Chesapeake Affair" outrages Americans. Impressment almost led to war in June, 1807. An American frigate, the *Chesapeake,* left a Virginia port for the Mediterranean. About ten miles off the American coast, it was hailed and overtaken by a British warship, the *Leopard.* An officer of the *Leopard* boarded the *Chesapeake* on the pretext of delivering despatches but actually to search for British deserters. The American commander, Com-

A *cartoon of the early 1800's shows how American neutral rights (symbolized by President Jefferson) were threatened by Britain (George III, at left) and France (Napoleon, at right).*

modore Barron, told the British officer he had no deserters aboard and that he would not let his men "be mustered by any other but their own officers."

The British officer returned to his own ship. Then, without warning, the *Leopard* opened fire, killing three American sailors and wounding eighteen. Commodore Barron, having failed to prepare his ship for action, had no choice but to strike his colors. The British searched the ship and took away four men they said were deserters, three of whom were actually Americans. The unlucky *Chesapeake* was then left to limp back to port.

Americans were outraged by the "*Chesapeake* Affair," and many called for war. When the State Department protested to Britain, the British government agreed to pay damages and promised not to search American *warships*. But the British flatly refused to give up the practice of impressment, and they continued to stop and search American *merchant ships*. When Congress met in the fall of 1807, it voted funds to increase the size of the navy. Jefferson, however, wanted to avoid war if possible. The Republican majority in Congress agreed to give the President a chance to try "peaceable means of repressing injustice."

Jefferson tries an embargo on trade. The President decided to use an economic boycott to exert pressure on Great Britain. Jefferson's reasoning was that American ships could best avoid capture or attack by staying in their home ports. This policy would also interrupt the flow of American foodstuffs to both Britain and France. Jefferson thought that the two warring nations were so dependent on American trade that they would promise to respect our neutral rights in order to end the boycott.

The President had already signed a bill in 1806 to stop the import of many British manufactures into the United States. In December, 1807, he recommended, and Congress passed, an *Embargo Act*. By this measure no ships were permitted to leave United States ports for European ports, and no goods could be exported from this country. The embargo remained in effect for nearly fifteen months.

The embargo fails. Jefferson's Embargo Act failed to bring either France or Britain to terms. An unexpectedly large harvest in Britain in 1808 dulled the effect of the boycott there. And France, because of the British blockade, had not been able to carry on much trade with the United States anyway. The embargo did, however, have almost disastrous results in the United States.

As was to be expected, American exports fell alarmingly. Government income, most of which came from duties on imports, dropped to less than half its former level. Idle and rotting ships crowded every port along the Atlantic. Warehouses were soon bursting with products that could not be exported. A traveler observed of New York: "The streets near the water-side were almost deserted, the *grass had begun to grow* upon the wharfs." Shipbuilding came to a halt, and carpenters, sailmakers, and seamen were thrown out of work. Merchants went into bankruptcy. Farmers lost the European markets where they had sold their surplus produce. These financial losses were partly offset by an increase in manufacturing after 1807. But, in general, the American economy was badly hurt by the embargo.

The embargo arouses political opposition. The commercial Northeast suffered most and protested most against the Embargo Act. In the election of 1808, the Federalists won a majority of the seats in many state legislatures and elected several governors and members of Congress. Moreover, the Federalists encouraged smuggling across the Canadian frontier. When Jefferson signed a bill to insure strict enforcement of the embargo, the opposition became increasingly bitter.

Madison is elected President. For President in the election of 1808, the Federalists again backed Charles C. Pinckney. Jefferson urged the Republicans to support his Secretary of State, James Madison. But some Republicans who opposed the embargo preferred George Clinton of New York. When the electoral ballots were counted, Madison was the victor with 122 votes. Pinckney received 47 electoral votes, and Clinton, 6.

The retiring President did not want to saddle his successor with an unpopular policy. He knew that the embargo was playing into the hands of the Federalists and was having little effect on Britain or France. A few days before he left office in March, 1809, therefore, Jefferson signed a law repealing the Embargo Act.

▶ CHECK-UP

1. What steps did Jefferson take against the Barbary pirates?

2. What was Britain trying to achieve by its blockade of France? What was Napoleon's object in the Berlin and Milan Decrees? How did these measures affect the United States?

3. What is meant by "impressment"? Why did this British policy create problems for the United States?

4. What was the purpose of Jefferson's embargo? Why was it unsuccessful? What area and groups were most opposed to it?

. . . .

Clinching the Main Ideas in Chapter 8

In his later years, Jefferson was fond of saying that "the Revolution of 1800 was as real a revolution in the principles of our government as that of 1776 was in its form." Historians, however, have not agreed with Jefferson. Although the Republicans gained control of the executive and legislative branches in the 1800 election, they did not seek to bring about a revolution in the principles of government. Jefferson and Gallatin merely trimmed the edges of Hamilton's financial system; they decided not to disturb its keystone, the national bank. The Republicans could do little about Federalist control of the judiciary, and they had to accept Marshall's decisions, strengthening the hand of the central government. In foreign affairs, Jefferson stuck to his inaugural promise of no "entangling alliances." He showed favoritism to neither France nor Britain and managed to avoid war with both countries.

During his presidency, Jefferson's actions sometimes conflicted with the principles he had expounded in the 1790's. He increased expenditures for the navy, engaged in war with the Barbary pirates, and added territory to the Union even though the Constitution did not specifically authorize it. But Jefferson was wise enough to see that the country would gain by these measures. "What is practicable must often control what is pure theory," said the President.

Historians are agreed that Jefferson's decision to sign the Louisiana Treaty, in spite of his doubts about its constitutionality, was an act of statesmanship.

President Jefferson's hopes for "peaceful coercion" through the Embargo Act were not fulfilled. He found no formula for protecting American rights on the seas, but he did leave to his successor a country that was still neutral in the Napoleonic Wars.

Chapter Review

Terms to Understand

1. West Florida
2. blockade
3. Embargo Act
4. Burr conspiracy
5. Barbary states
6. judicial review
7. *Marbury v. Madison*
8. Louisiana Purchase
9. Chesapeake Affair
10. Lewis and Clark expedition
11. orders in council
12. Berlin and Milan Decrees

What Do You Think?

1. In 1802 Jefferson wrote: "The day that France takes possession of New Orleans . . . we must marry ourselves to the British fleet and nation." What did he mean? Recall that in Washington's administration Jefferson had been pro-French. Why was France more of a threat than Spain?

2. The Republicans, as an opposition party, had bitterly criticized Federalist policies. Yet, when the Republicans came to power, they made comparatively few changes. Why?

3. In urging the Senate to ratify the treaty providing for the purchase of Louisiana, Republicans found themselves advocating loose construction of the Constitution. The Federalists, who earlier had opposed strict construction, argued that the Purchase was unconstitutional. Why had the parties reversed their positions?

4. Beginning in 1806, what policies were advocated by Jefferson to compel Britain and France to respect American rights on the seas? How effective were these policies? Why? What groups in this country were hurt by them? Helped by them?

5. What similarities and differences do you see between Jefferson's embargo and the boycotts used by the colonists to wring concessions from Parliament?

Using Your Knowledge of History

1. Write brief answers to these questions regarding the Supreme Court's decision in *Marbury v. Madison:* (a) What did Marbury request? On what grounds? (b) What dilemma confronted Chief Justice Marshall? How did he solve it? (c) How did his "solution" help to establish the Supreme Court's right of judicial review?

2. Jefferson wanted to be remembered for founding the University of Virginia and for drafting the Declaration of Independence and the Virginia Statute of Religious Liberty. What conclusions do you draw from this expressed preference? Present your views about Jefferson in a brief editorial that might have been published in an American newspaper following Jefferson's death on July 4, 1826.

3. In a chart, show the restrictions on neutral shipping imposed by (a) the British orders in council and (b) Napoleon's Berlin and Milan Decrees. Then write a brief conclusion in which you (a) point out the difficulties these pronouncements created for neutral shipping and (b) the rights claimed as a neutral by the United States.

Extending Your Knowledge of History

Saul K. Padover has edited a collection of Jefferson's writings and has written a biography about the Virginian entitled *Jefferson*. Historians, like contemporaries of Jefferson and Burr, fail to agree on the latter's guilt. In *Aaron Burr*, Nathan Schachner acquits Burr of treason, whereas T. P. Abernethy finds him guilty in *The Burr Conspiracy*. On the exploration of the Louisiana Territory see *Lewis and Clark: Partners in Discovery*, by John Bakeless. Bernard De Voto's edition of *The Journals of Lewis and Clark* is lively reading.

CHAPTER 9

America Fights a Second War of Independence

Battle of Lake Erie

. . . The conduct of her [Britain's] government presents a series of acts hostile to the United States as an independent and neutral nation. British cruisers have been in the continued practice of violating the American flag on the great highway of nations, and of seizing and carrying off persons sailing under it. . . . our commerce has been plundered in every sea, the great staples of our country have been cut off from their legitimate markets, and a destructive blow aimed at our agricultural and maritime interests. . . .

JAMES MADISON, WAR MESSAGE TO CONGRESS, JUNE 1, 1812

1809–1815

For three tense years President James Madison tried to find a peaceful solution to the continuing problems of British interference with American trade and impressment of American seamen. When negotiation failed to change Britain's attitude, Madison tried Jefferson's policy of economic boycott. But Madison lacked sufficient diplomatic skill to achieve his goal. He was maneuvered into war by Napoleon's tactics, on the one hand, and the pressures of land-hungry southern and western Republicans in Congress, on the other.

In the conflict with Britain that followed, the United States neither gained nor lost any territory. In fact, the only satisfactory thing about the Treaty of Ghent was that it ended a war which neither Britain nor the United States wanted to continue. The war did, however, unleash a current of nationalist pride that strongly influenced the next generation of Americans. This chapter will discuss the events leading up to the war and the course of the fighting. We shall also see how Americans began to establish their economic and cultural independence.

1 Madison Continues the Struggle to Defend Neutral Rights

Madison follows in Jefferson's footsteps. Fifty-eight years old when he took the presidential oath, James Madison had behind him a distinguished career in government. He had been active in affairs of state since the 1780's, had played a leading role in the formation and adoption of the Constitution, and had served as Secretary of State. Yet, despite his ability, knowledge, and experience, Madison was not an outstanding President. Perhaps he had lived too long in Jefferson's shadow. At any rate, as President, Madison lacked the toughness and decisiveness that the times required.

In fairness it should be pointed out that Madison inherited a backlog of political quarrels which had built up under Jefferson. But he failed to resolve these disputes, and the Republican Party was thereby weakened. During his first term, the new President persuaded Gallatin to remain as Secretary of the Treasury, but the Pennsylvania financier resigned in 1814. James Monroe came to Madison's aid as Secretary of State in 1811, but he could not save the President from many errors in the conduct of the War of 1812. During most of his stay in the White House, Madison was not the master of his Cabinet, nor of the Republican Party, nor of Congress.

Madison continues economic coercion. Madison was committed to Jefferson's plan

. . . .

CHAPTER FOCUS

1. Madison continues the struggle to defend neutral rights.
2. The West and South want war with Great Britain.
3. The War of 1812 ends in a draw.
4. Americans strive for economic and cultural independence.

of putting economic pressure on Britain and France, a policy which he had helped devise. Though the Embargo Act was repealed just before Madison took office, Congress at the same time passed a Non-Intercourse Act. This act forbade trade with Great Britain and France and their colonies, but permitted trade with the rest of the world. The Non-Intercourse Act also stated that, if either France or Great Britain called off its restrictions on American shipping, the United States would renew trade with that country. In other words, Madison was still using an economic blockade against Britain and France. But the fact that American trade with other countries was now legal helped in some degree to revive the hard-hit seaports of New England and the Middle States.

In the hope of improving relations with Britain, Madison agreed to negotiations in 1809. Talks with the British minister in Washington, David Erskine, went well. Erskine assured the American government that the British orders in council would be lifted against American shipping if the economic boycott were ended. Without waiting for the approval of the British government, Madison considered the agreement binding. Hundreds of American ships consequently set sail for British ports. Then, suddenly, the British government rejected the agreement and recalled Erskine. The embarrassed American President restored non-intercourse against Great Britain, but he had no way of warning the American vessels that had already left port.

Congress tries the Macon Act. The Non-Intercourse Act was due to expire in March, 1810. To replace it, Congress passed the *Macon Act,* opening trade with all countries for one year. If either Britain or France withdrew its trade decrees — and the other failed to do so within three months — the Non-Intercourse Act would go back into effect against the offending country. Such bargaining did not add to American prestige, but the Macon Act did encourage American shipping. In the first year after the measure was passed, the value of American exports rose to more than 60 million dollars.

Napoleon takes advantage of the Macon Act. The person most displeased by the Macon Act was Napoleon, who up to this time had found America's commercial policy very satisfactory. The embargo had fitted in perfectly with his plans to stifle British trade, and the Non-Intercourse Act had served almost as well. But the Macon Act threatened France. It gave Britain a market in the United States which would help make up for loss of trade on the European continent. Furthermore, Britain's fleet continued to block American trade with France and French-held territory.

Nevertheless, the wily Napoleon saw in the Macon Act a chance to trap the United States into ending its trade with Britain. He might even be able to drag the Americans into war with the British. Napoleon announced through his foreign minister that France revoked the Berlin and Milan Decrees (page 191), "it being understood that, in consequence of this declaration, the English shall revoke their orders in council . . . ; or that the United States . . . shall cause their rights to be respected by the English." Then he added this touching postscript: "His Majesty loves the Americans. Their prosperity and their commerce are within the scope of his policy."

Napoleon springs a trap. President Madison accepted Napoleon's statement at face value. The President and his friends realized the risk involved in trusting Napoleon to fulfill his promise, but felt it was a worthwhile gamble. Madison's opponents, however, said that the President had fallen into a trap which "would catch us in an English war." Nevertheless, in November, 1810, Madison announced that non-intercourse would be resumed against Great Britain in three months unless the British repealed the orders in council. During these three months, evidence piled up that France was continuing the seizure of American ships. Despite this evidence, Congress in March, 1811, passed a law restoring non-intercourse against Britain. Thus, Napoleon achieved his goal of cutting off trade between the United States and Great Britain.

The economic boycott is felt in Britain. By the fall of 1811 the effects of the boycott were being felt in the British Isles. A shortage of food had been made worse by poor crops in the summer of that year. The ending of trade with America also reduced British exports and cut off raw materials needed by British factories. Petitions poured into Parliament asking for repeal of the orders in council so that trade could be resumed with America.

Unfortunately, the Madison administration knew little about these developments in England. After non-intercourse was restored, the American minister left his post in London, and Madison never sent a replacement. Thus the President had no way of knowing that a new British government had decided early in 1812 to yield to the demands of merchants and manufacturers. On June 16 the British government announced that the orders in council would be lifted, but this information reached Washington too late to have any effect. Meanwhile, as you will read in the next section, trouble on the American frontier had also been moving the United States to the brink of war with Great Britain.

PRIVATE INCOME FROM MANUFACTURING

Manufacturing grew steadily in the periods before and after the War of 1812. By 1859, factories were adding nearly half a billion dollars each year to the income of private citizens.

CHART STUDY

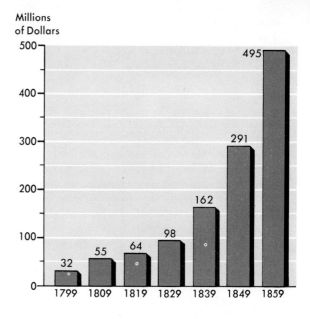

Millions of Dollars

Year	Amount
1799	32
1809	55
1819	64
1829	98
1839	162
1849	291
1859	495

▶ CHECK-UP

1. How did the Non-Intercourse Act differ from the Embargo? How did the Macon Act differ from the Non-Intercourse Act?

2. How did Napoleon take advantage of the Macon Act? What were the results?

• • • • • • • • • • • • • • • • • • • •

2 *The West and South Want War with Great Britain*

The population of the West expands. When Madison became President in 1809, almost a million people lived in the region west of the Alleghenies. These people had settled chiefly along the Ohio and Mississippi Rivers, for in those days navigable rivers were the main arteries of traffic. Most of the western settlers were farmers who sent their surplus produce by water to New Orleans and then to markets on the Atlantic seaboard and in Europe. Already a number of thriving cities had grown up in the West. Pittsburgh, at the head of the Ohio River, was an iron manufacturing center and a market where pioneers heading west bought supplies. Cincinnati was an important trading center farther down the Ohio. St. Louis, founded by the French in 1764, served as a headquarters for fur traders. The chief seaport of the West was New Orleans, its largest and most cosmopolitan city.

Westerners develop views of their own. By 1809 four new states had already been admitted to the Union — Vermont, Kentucky, Tennessee, and Ohio. The Territories of Illinois and Indiana were almost ready to seek admission, and the same was true of territories in the South that were to become the states of Alabama, Mississippi, and Louisiana. During Madison's administration these territories sent delegates to Congress. Though the territorial delegates could not vote, their views were shared by many Americans (1) in the newly admitted states and (2) in the western portions of some older states. Thus, representatives from the Georgia and Carolina piedmont, from western Pennsylvania and New York, and from the Maine districts of Massachusetts generally voted with congressmen from the four new states. During the early 1800's, the frontier point of view often contrasted sharply with the views of the southern planters and the manufacturers and merchants of the Northeast.

The South and West demand action against Britain. The loudest cries for action against Great Britain came not from the commercial Northeast, as might have been expected, but from the South and the frontier regions. New England merchants were making money, despite the seizure of American ships and the impressment of American seamen. They did not want to start a war which would ruin their trade. The South and the West had little interest in the profits and losses of New England merchants, though they did care about British seizure of American cargoes. European-bound ships carried produce from the West and South, and when cargoes were confiscated, the people of these regions suffered serious losses.

Where Is "the West"?

To Americans "the West" has always evoked images of pioneering adventure. But the geographical location of "the West" has changed through the years. Historically the term has meant the area beyond the frontier where civilization ended and wilderness began. Thus, the West was waiting for the first colonists. When Thomas Hooker and his flock left Massachusetts in 1636, for example, they "went west" and founded Hartford, Connecticut.

Before the Revolution the West lay mainly in the western areas of the thirteen colonies. After the war, settlers poured across the Appalachian Mountains. By 1812 the frontier had reached the Mississippi. Chapters 13 and 20 will describe how settlers filled in the West beyond that river. Today we use the terms Far West, Mountain West, and Midwest, but these refer to settled regions. The frontier West has virtually disappeared.

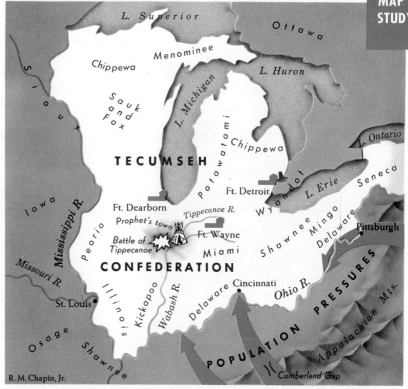

MAP STUDY

THE INDIAN LOSES THE OLD NORTHWEST

The tribes of the Tecumseh Confederation united to resist American expansionist pressures (see arrows). The Indian defeat at Tippecanoe shattered this union and enabled the American army to overcome the individual tribes.

R. M. Chapin, Jr.

But the settlers in the South and West had still other grievances against Britain and her ally, Spain. Frontiersmen believed that the British in Canada and the Spaniards in Florida were arming the Indians and encouraging them to attack American settlements. Spanish Florida had become a refuge for hostile Indians, pirates, and runaway slaves. When American settlers in West Florida rebelled against Spanish rule in 1810, Madison annexed the area to the United States (page 187). But this only whetted the southern appetite for the rest of Florida. At the same time angry Westerners demanded the conquest of Canada, so they could drive the British off the continent and end the alliance between redcoats and Indians.

The "War Hawks" control Congress. In the elections of 1810 many congressmen who had voted for the Macon Act were defeated. Voters in the West and frontier areas of the South elected a number of outspoken representatives who soon came to be called "War Hawks." Among these young men were John C. Calhoun of the South Carolina piedmont, whose grandmother had been scalped by Cherokee In-

dians; Felix Grundy of Tennessee, who had lost three brothers in Indian fighting; and Richard M. Johnson and Henry Clay of Kentucky.

The War Hawks, although a small minority in Congress, held the balance between northern and southern representatives and made the most of their position. They elected Henry Clay Speaker of the House of Representatives, and he in turn appointed War Hawks to the key committees. Clay allowed the War Hawks to deliver long, impassioned speeches. Johnson told the House: "I shall never die contented until I see her [Great Britain's] expulsion from North America, and her territories incorporated with the United States." And the Speaker added: "No man wants peace more than I, but I prefer the troubled ocean of war, demanded by the honor and independence of this country, . . . to the tranquil and putrescent pool of ignominious peace."

Indian trouble increases the tension. In 1811 the demands of the War Hawks took on new meaning as a result of growing unrest among the Indians of the Northwest. For many years these Indians had been unhappy about the steady advance

199

The Shawnee chief Tecumseh has been called "the most extraordinary Indian in history." Despite his brilliant leadership, Tecumseh failed to achieve his dream of a united Indian nation.

of white settlers. During Jefferson's administration federal agents had repeatedly called the Indians together to sign treaties giving tribal land to the United States government. The Indians' consent to these one-sided treaties was secured through small bribes and large contributions of whiskey. Such treaties led a remarkable Shawnee chief, Tecumseh, and his brother, called the Prophet, to organize Indian resistance. They formed an Indian Confederacy and persuaded the Indians to refuse both bribes and liquor. At the junction of Tippecanoe Creek and the Wabash River, in what is now Indiana (map, page 199), Tecumseh established his headquarters.

Wishing to strengthen his Indian union, Tecumseh went south in 1811 to arrange alliances with the Creeks and other tribes. William Henry Harrison, governor of the Indiana Territory, decided to take advantage of Tecumseh's absence to attack the Indian settlement. With a thousand-man force, Harrison marched north along the Wabash River until he came to Tippecanoe Creek. On a November day, the Indians

surprised the Americans in an attack just before dawn. The two sides suffered about equal losses in the Battle of Tippecanoe, but the better-armed Americans drove the Indians from their village and burnt it to the ground. Finding British arms and ammunition among the ruins, the Americans concluded that "British intrigue and British gold" were behind Tecumseh's confederacy. During the winter of 1811–1812 the western cry of "On to Canada!" was echoed by the War Hawks in Congress.

Congress declares war. Tension between the United States and Britain increased during the early months of 1812. Madison had no knowledge that the British government might revoke the orders in council, nor could he prove that the French decrees had been "absolutely and unconditionally" repealed. Meanwhile, the War Hawks stirred public opinion with reckless boasts. "The conquest of Canada is in your power," said Henry Clay. "The militia of Kentucky are alone competent to place Montreal and Upper Canada at your feet." As pressure for war mounted, Madison found it harder and harder to maintain a policy of peaceful negotiation. Finally, on June 1, 1812, the President asked Congress to declare war on Great Britain. Among the grievances he listed were (1) impressment of American seamen, (2) violation of American rights "and the peace of our coasts," (3) the British orders in council, and (4) the stirring up of the Indians on the frontier. No mention was made of the War Hawks' hunger for Canada and Florida.

Congress responded with a declaration of war. The voting in the House and Senate showed that the commercial Northeast stubbornly opposed the war. Support for the declaration came from the western arc stretching from Maine to Georgia. Such frontier states as Vermont, Kentucky, Tennessee, and Ohio were almost 100 per cent in favor of war with Britain.

Ironically, the United States went to war at the very time that Britain abandoned the policy which had plagued Jefferson and Madison (page 197). There is irony also in the fact that the frontier representatives in effect forced the war on commercial New England. One historian has said of the War of 1812 that it was "insisted upon by the South and the West in defense of the North which didn't want to be defended."

Madison is re-elected. Northern resentment against the declaration of war figured in the presidential election of 1812. The War Hawks, of course, supported Madison, as did most other Republicans from the South and West. But the northeastern Republicans, furious with Madison, backed De Witt Clinton of New York. The Federalists also gave their support to Clinton, who conducted a vigorous campaign against the war with Britain. The voting followed the same pattern as had the vote in Congress on declaring war. New England supported Clinton, the "peace candidate," as did large areas of the Middle States. The South and West voted solidly for Madison, giving him a majority of the electoral votes. The closest election since 1800, it demonstrated that public opinion was seriously divided on the war.

▶ CHECK-UP

1. Why were representatives from the West and South more bitterly opposed to British (and Spanish) policies than those from the Northeast? Who were the War Hawks?

2. What were the causes of Indian unrest in the Northwest?

3. Why did the United States declare war on Britain in 1812?

. . . .

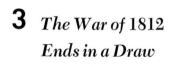

3 *The War of 1812 Ends in a Draw*

The United States is not prepared for war. The War Hawks anticipated a brief but glorious war with the British in Canada. Calhoun assured Congress that "in four weeks from the time that a declaration of war is heard on our frontier, the whole of

Upper and a part of Lower Canada will be in our possession." Yet the war was to last two and a half years, and the United States was to gain no new territory.

At the time Congress declared war, the American army consisted of fewer than 7000 men. Troops were poorly trained and were commanded by aged veterans who had seen little active service since the Revolution. Neither the President nor Congress had much success when they tried to increase the size of the army. Young men preferred to serve with their state militias. Some states even refused to let their militia be commanded by regular army officers.

The government bungled the financing of the war. Congress in 1811 had refused to recharter the national bank (page 168), and this resulted in financial distress during the war years. Because "Mr. Madison's War" was unpopular in some parts of the country, Congress was reluctant to increase tariff duties or levy taxes to help pay for the cost of the conflict. The government's attempts to sell bonds met with little success. Planters and farmers in the South and West lacked money to buy the bonds; and in the Northeast, the merchants, manufacturers, and bankers who did have money had no desire to purchase them. Thus, the sale of bonds brought in less than a third of the cost of the war. Considering Madison's political difficulties, the sad state of the army, and the haphazard financing of the war, it was fortunate for the United States that the British were kept busy in Europe trying to defeat Napoleon.

The invasion of Canada fails. The War Hawks' boast about taking Canada backfired. The American command unwisely chose to attack at widely scattered points (map, page 202) rather than to launch a single offensive. Although the British did not have a large force in Canada, they were able to hold off the invaders. In August, 1812, General William Hull, who had been ordered to invade Canada, surrendered Detroit to the British almost without firing a shot. Next, Fort Dearborn (on the present site of Chicago) fell to the Indians, who massacred the prisoners they took. The setbacks at De-

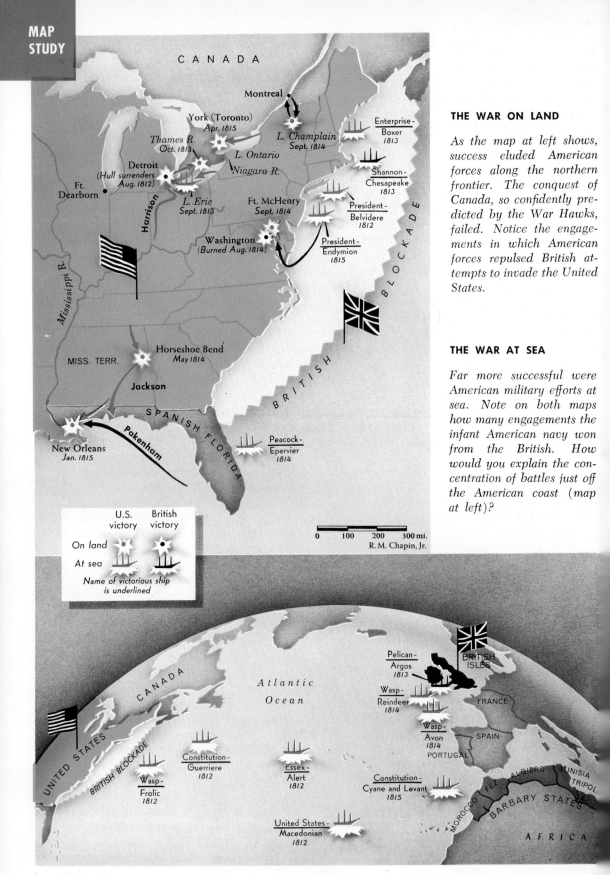

CANADA

Montreal

York (Toronto)
Apr. 1815

Thames R.
Oct. 1813

L. Champlain
Sept. 1814

Enterprise-
Boxer
1813

L. Ontario

Niagara R.

Detroit
*(Hull surrenders
Aug. 1812)*

Ft.
Dearborn

Harrison

Shannon-
Chesapeake
1813

L. Erie
Sept. 1813

Ft. McHenry
Sept. 1814

President-
Belvidere
1812

Mississippi R.

Washington
(Burned Aug. 1814)

President-
Endymion
1815

Horseshoe Bend
May 1814

MISS. TERR.

Jackson

SPANISH FLORIDA

Pakenham

Peacock-
Epervier
1814

New Orleans
Jan. 1815

BRITISH

BLOCKADE

THE WAR ON LAND

As the map at left shows, success eluded American forces along the northern frontier. The conquest of Canada, so confidently predicted by the War Hawks, failed. Notice the engagements in which American forces repulsed British attempts to invade the United States.

THE WAR AT SEA

Far more successful were American military efforts at sea. Note on both maps how many engagements the infant American navy won from the British. How would you explain the concentration of battles just off the American coast (map at left)?

U.S.
victory

British
victory

On land

At sea

*Name of victorious ship
is underlined*

0   100   200   300 mi.

R. M. Chapin, Jr.

Pelican-
Argos
1813

BRITISH
ISLES

CANADA

*Atlantic
Ocean*

Wasp-
Reindeer
1814

FRANCE

Wasp-
Avon
1814

SPAIN

PORTUGAL

UNITED STATES

BRITISH BLOCKADE

Constitution-
Guerriere
1812

Essex-
Alert
1812

Constitution-
Cyane and Levant
1815

Wasp-
Frolic
1812

ALGIERS

TUNISIA

TRIPOLI

MOROCCO

FEZ

BARBARY STATES

United States-
Macedonian
1812

AFRICA

troit and Fort Dearborn meant the loss of much of the Northwest. American forces tried twice more in 1812 to invade Canada, once by way of the Niagara River and once by way of Lake Champlain. Both efforts ended in humiliating defeat, chiefly because of inefficiency and jealousy among American officers and lack of disciplined troops.

The Northwest Territory is regained. During 1813 the Americans recovered the Northwest Territory, thanks to the energy and ability of young Captain Oliver Hazard Perry. He spent months building a fleet of ships on Lake Erie and training frontiersmen to handle them. In September, 1813, his ships met a British squadron at the western end of the lake and destroyed or captured every vessel. Perry reported to General William Henry Harrison: "We have met the enemy; and they are ours: two ships, two brigs, one schooner, and one sloop." Perry's victory gave the Americans control of Lake Erie and threatened the position of the British at Detroit, causing them to retreat into Canada. General Harrison pursued the British, and the two armies clashed at the Thames River. The Americans were the victors in that hard-fought battle. Tecumseh, now a British ally, was killed in the fighting. His death put an end to the Indian Confederacy.

Fighting in the North ends in a deadlock. Farther east a band of Americans captured York (Toronto), capital of Upper Canada, and set fire to the parliament buildings. But since the Americans did not control Lake Ontario, they had to retreat. In the summer of 1814 the Americans made a final attempt to invade Canada. Though ably led this time, they were stopped at the Battle of Lundy's Lane near the Niagara River. Meanwhile, the defeat of Napoleon in Europe made additional British troops available for the war in America. In the fall of 1814 a British force of about 11,000 men advanced southward along Lake Champlain. The British fleet on the lake, however, was defeated by Captain Thomas Macdonough, and the British troops were compelled to retreat. After more than two years of fighting, neither side had made any great gains along the northern frontier.

Americans score victories on the seas. American successes on the seas came as a surprise to the British. In size, the American navy was no match for the British fleet. In 1812, the United States had only 16 ocean-going warships compared to some 97 British war vessels in American waters. Hence, throughout most of the war, the British were able to blockade American ports and bottle up American ships. But when American frigates did escape from port, they scored some spectacular victories against British warships. Soon after General Hull surrendered Detroit to the British, his nephew, Captain Isaac Hull, revived American spirits with the first naval victory. Commanding the *Constitution* (later known as "Old Ironsides"), Captain Hull met the British frigate *Guerrière*, and his gunners soon turned it into a helpless hulk. Another American ship that fought brilliantly against the British was the *United States*, commanded by Stephen Decatur, whose naval career had started in the Barbary War.

American privateers also plagued the British. Large numbers of American privateers left home ports during the war to prey upon British commerce. They seized more than 1300 British vessels of various kinds. In time, however, the British all but drove American trade from the seas. As the British blockade tightened, exports fell to little more than one tenth of their prewar value.

The British attack Washington and Baltimore. Along the Atlantic coast, the British had little opposition. Using bases in Maine, they raided American seaports and fishing villages. In August, 1814, they landed a force that successfully attacked the city of Washington. President Madison, his Secretary of War, and the armed forces stationed in the city were caught by surprise. Five miles outside the city, some 6000 untrained militiamen were hastily assembled, but they broke before the British advance, leaving Washington at the mercy of the invaders. The city was in wild disorder as President Madison and his Cabinet snatched important papers and fled. Dolley Madison, who had been expecting dinner guests at the White House, paused long enough to rescue a Gilbert Stuart portrait of

George Washington. In retaliation for the burning of York (page 203), the British set fire to the Capitol, the White House, and other government buildings.

The British then shifted their attention to Baltimore; their troops marched overland while the fleet moved up Chesapeake Bay. An assault on Fort McHenry failed, however, and in October the British fleet and armed forces sailed away. A Washington attorney, Francis Scott Key, had watched the final bombardment of Fort McHenry from a boat in the harbor. When he saw the American flag still flying over the fort the next morning, he was inspired to write "The Star-Spangled Banner," which eventually became our national anthem.

Andrew Jackson defeats the British at New Orleans. The British launched their final attack of the war against New Orleans. This military operation gave the frontiersmen, who had done so much to start the war, a chance to make good on their boasts. The American forces were commanded by General Andrew Jackson. During the early years of the war Jackson had fought Creek Indians in the Mississippi Territory. At the Battle of Horseshoe Bend in 1814, he crushed the Indian forces and obtained from them a treaty which opened up the Southwest to settlement. Thus, he had already become a western hero when the Madison administration ordered him to New Orleans to defend that important city.

The Battle of New Orleans was fought between a British force of 8000 veterans of the Napoleonic Wars and a band of American militiamen, frontiersmen, pirates,[1] and sailors. Jackson ordered breastworks to be built and waited for the British to attack. The main assault opened on January 8, 1815. As the English troops advanced, Jackson's men poured a withering fire at them which, a British officer said, "mowed us down by whole sections." More than 2000 of the British troops were killed or

[1] Jean Lafitte was the leader of pirates who operated from islands off the Louisiana coast. Lafitte learned of the British plans to attack New Orleans, informed the Americans, and fought with Jackson. Because of this aid, Madison pardoned the pirates for their past crimes. But most of them followed Lafitte in returning to their outlaw life.

wounded; the entrenched Americans lost fewer than 25.

Though the Battle of New Orleans was a great victory for the Americans, it played no part in bringing the war to an end. In fact, with modern means of communication the battle would never have been fought, for British and American representatives had signed a peace treaty in Europe two weeks before. But the battle enabled Americans to feel that they had "won" the war. Moreover, it played an important part in Andrew Jackson's later career. The victory at New Orleans also silenced criticism in New England.

New England opposes the war. Throughout the War of 1812, Madison had been forced to contend not only with the British but also with the opposition of New England Federalists. As we have seen, these people objected to the war because it hurt their trade and because it was supported by Westerners who hoped to expand the country's frontiers. New Englanders displayed their opposition in many ways: (1) They refused to buy government bonds. (2) They refused to let their militia leave their home states. (3) They even traded openly with Canada, transporting goods across the border and shipping supplies under the protection of the British navy. (4) Moreover, the Federalists openly rejoiced at each of Britain's victories over Napoleon. When the British expeditionary force approached New Orleans, a prominent Federalist publicly wished it success.

The Hartford Convention meets. Federalist opposition to the war reached its climax when the Massachusetts legislature invited other New England states to meet in a convention. Its purpose was "to deliberate upon the dangers to which the eastern section of the Union is exposed by the course of the war." In December, 1814, Federalist delegates met in Hartford, Connecticut, for a three-week secret session. Their report sharply condemned the war but admitted that secession (withdrawal from the Union) could be justified only in case of extreme necessity. The right of a state to nullify (repeal) acts of Congress, however, was clearly set forth, in almost the

From a boat in Chesapeake Bay, Francis Scott Key (left) watched the "bombs bursting in air" as British ships bombarded Fort McHenry (above). Notice the flag over the fort. At far left is the actual flag that flew over Fort McHenry during the attack. This famous "star-spangled banner" is now displayed in the Smithsonian Institution.

same language as the Virginia Resolutions of 1798 (page 177):

> In cases of deliberate, dangerous, and palpable infractions of the Constitution, affecting the sovereignty of a State, . . . it is not only the right but the duty of such a State to interpose its authority. . . .

The Hartford Convention also proposed seven amendments to the Constitution. These were intended to strengthen Federalist New England and weaken the Republican South and West.

The Convention proves embarrassing to the Federalists. Three envoys were appointed to carry the recommendations of the Hartford Convention to President Madison. But when they arrived in Washington, the city had just learned of Jackson's victory at New Orleans and the signing of a peace treaty with Great Britain. This news touched off a wild celebration in the capital, and the Federalist envoys quietly slipped out of town. Little more was heard from New England on the subject of states' rights. And not much more was heard

from the Federalist Party, which came to be charged with treason by political opponents because of the ill-timed meeting at Hartford.

Though President Madison had been handicapped by Federalist opposition during the war, he had avoided the temptation to strike back at these outspoken critics. No sedition acts were passed to restrict the Federalists' right to find fault with the administration. Thus, freedom of speech and freedom of the press were not curtailed during the War of 1812.

The war ends. By 1814 both Great Britain and the United States badly wanted peace. Britain was staggering under a burden of debts and heavy taxes. There was danger, too, that war would start again in Europe, even though Napoleon had been defeated and exiled. As for the United States, its military plans had failed, its trade and income had been hard-hit, and New England was threatening nullification.

During the summer of 1814, five American commissioners began meeting with British representatives at Ghent (in Belgium). After many weeks of discussion, a treaty was

finally signed on Christmas Eve. The
Treaty of Ghent was unusual in that neither
side won or lost anything. It provided for
the return of "all territory, places, and possessions whatsoever taken by either party
from the other during the war." Nothing
was said about the impressment of American seamen or the violation of neutral rights
on the seas. These, however, were dead
issues, since Britain and France were no
longer at war. Other matters in dispute
were referred to arbitration commissions.
Commissioner John Quincy Adams said of
the document, "We have obtained nothing
but peace."

▶ CHECK-UP

1. In what ways was the United States unprepared for war? How and why did invasions
   of Canada fail? How did British efforts to
   invade this country from Canada fail?

2. What successes were achieved by the Americans and British, respectively, on the seas?
   How successful were the British in the Chesapeake region? What was the outcome of
   fighting at New Orleans?

3. How did New England Federalists show their
   opposition to the war? What was the Hartford Convention? Why was it a failure?
   What were the terms of the Treaty of Ghent?

. . . .

4 Americans Strive for Economic and Cultural Independence

**The war earns foreign respect for
America.** Since the outbreak of the wars
of the French Revolution in 1793, events
abroad had played a large part in shaping
the course of American politics. But ratification of the Treaty of Ghent in 1815
changed this pattern. Our political dependence upon Europe came to an abrupt end
in the so-called "Second War of Independence." The historian George Dangerfield
has weighed the effects of the war in these
words: "Once it had been won, or at any
rate not lost, the Americans realized that
they could no longer be considered a weak
sideline republic, clinging precariously to
the fringes of Christendom. Still less could
they be considered a mere tail to the European kite. They had gained a respectable
place in the family of nations."

The war stirs pride in America. One
important result of the war was the growth
of a national spirit. Prior to 1812 a man
thought of himself as, for instance, a Penn-
sylvanian or a New Englander. Even
Thomas Jefferson referred to Virginia as
"my country." The War of 1812 created in
the average American a new awareness of
the common bond he had with his fellow
Americans. This patriotism was stimulated
by the wartime naval victories and by
Jackson's triumph at New Orleans.

There was much evidence of this national
pride. "The Star-Spangled Banner" came
out of the War of 1812, and so too did
"Uncle Sam." The initials "U.S." (for
United States) appeared on boxes of army
supplies and were jokingly said to stand
for "Uncle Sam." This name was soon applied to the government, and soldiers were
called "Uncle Sam's" men.

Wartime letters often referred to the new
pride in the United States. Albert Gallatin,
for example, wrote in 1815: "The war has
renewed and reinstated the national feelings and character which the Revolution
had given, and which were daily lessened.
The people . . . are more Americans: they
feel and act more as a nation." And a
European traveler complained: "The national vanity of the United States surpasses
that of any other country. . . . It blazes
out everywhere, and on all occasions — in
their conversation, newspapers, pamphlets,
speeches, and books."

**Manufacturing gets a start in the
United States.** More than words were required, however, to win our economic independence from Great Britain. As long as
the United States was unable to manufacture the goods it needed, it would have to
import them from England. But during the
period between the winning of political independence and the end of the War of
1812, a number of developments helped lay

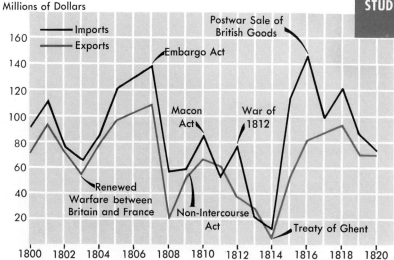

Millions of Dollars

IMPORTS AND EXPORTS, 1800–1820

Efforts to secure recognition of neutral rights affected the volume of American trade. Look at the sharp decline in imports after passage of the Embargo Act.

the basis for this country's economic independence.

During the late 1700's, a series of important inventions in England had revolutionized that country's manufacturing processes. At the time, this development, called the Industrial Revolution, had its greatest effect on the textile industry. Previously the spinning of thread and the weaving of cloth had been done at home on spinning wheels and hand looms. Now it was done in factories by power-driven machinery. The new machines could produce cloth much more rapidly than had been possible by hand methods. Wanting to preserve their headstart in the Industrial Revolution, British manufacturers jealously guarded the secrets of the new methods of production.

In 1790, however, American manufacturing took an important step forward when the first factory using textile machinery was constructed in this country. It was built under the direction of an Englishman, Samuel Slater. Forbidden by law to carry plans of spinning and weaving machines out of England, Slater had memorized the details of the machines before coming to this country. He wrote to Moses Brown, a wealthy Quaker farmer and merchant in Rhode Island, saying that he thought he could construct a cotton-spinning factory. Brown replied, "If thou canst do what thou sayest, I invite thee to come to Rhode Island." Slater accepted the offer and built a spinning factory beside a waterfall in

Pawtucket. A few other textile mills were started in the 1790's, but they found it difficult to compete with lower-priced British goods.

Manufacturing processes improve. Two developments foreshadowed the country's future use of mass production. One was the establishment in 1814 of the first manufacturing plant in which *all* processes of production were mechanized and carried on under one roof. This was a textile plant built in Waltham, Massachusetts, by Francis Lowell. A Boston merchant, Lowell had made a careful study of English textile machinery and returned to America to build the first power loom in this country. In his model Waltham factory every process of textile production, from raw cotton to finished cloth, was performed by machinery.

Equally important to the future of American manufacturing was Eli Whitney's development of the principle of *standardized* or *interchangeable parts*. After inventing the cotton gin in 1793 (page 227), Whitney had turned to the production of guns. In 1798, during the undeclared naval war with France, he signed a contract with the government for delivery of 10,000 guns within two years. A contract of this size was amazing because, like all manufactured goods in that period, guns had been produced one at a time. Each part was tailored to fit the particular musket under construction. Whitney, however, designed machines to produce large quantities of identical parts.

Eli Whitney manufactured muskets like the one above at this factory near New Haven, Connecticut. Using interchangeable parts in assembling the guns, Whitney laid the basis for modern mass production. Notice the row of houses provided by Whitney for his workers.

Eli Whitney Gun Factory, painting by William Giles Munson. Yale University Art Gallery, Mabel Brady Garvan Collection.

Using these "standardized" parts, his workmen could quickly assemble a musket. By this revolutionary process Whitney produced superior muskets at a lower price, in a shorter time, and in far greater quantity than had been possible before.

Manufacturing increases when trade with Europe is cut off. The Embargo and Non-Intercourse Acts naturally cut down the flow of British imports and so encouraged Americans to manufacture a variety of goods. Factories produced paper, liquor, guns, gunpowder, window glass, soap, leather goods, and earthenware. The production of iron goods and textiles expanded rapidly. By 1810, for instance, there were more than a hundred cotton mills in New England. When the outbreak of war in 1812 stopped almost all foreign trade, American wealth formerly tied up in shipping was invested in manufacturing.

Transportation methods improve. The growth of manufacturing and the westward trend of settlement were both stimulated by important developments in transportation during the early 1800's. So many improved roads were built that the period is often called the "turnpike era." The first such road was constructed between Phila-

delphia and Lancaster, Pennsylvania, in the 1790's (map, page 302). Tolls were collected at turnpike gates located at regular intervals along the road. In heavily traveled areas of the East, these toll roads made a profit; hence private companies were eager to build them. But for turnpikes to reach into the sparsely settled West, state or federal funds were needed. The bill admitting Ohio as a state provided that part of the money from the sale of land should be used for roads. A few years later President Jefferson and Secretary of the Treasury Gallatin proposed that a national road be built from the Potomac River to Ohio. Nothing came of this suggestion until 1811, when construction of the National Road began at Cumberland, Maryland. Its progress was slow during the war years. But the national government had taken a significant step in approving the use of federal funds for such a purpose.

Meanwhile, the steam engine was revolutionizing water transportation. The first experiments with steamboats took place before the War of 1812. In fact, as early as 1787 John Fitch had demonstrated to some of the delegates to the Constitutional Convention a vessel with paddles operated by steam. But perfecting the steamboat was the work of Robert Fulton and his financial backer, Robert R. Livingston. In 1807 their *Clermont,* a paddle-wheeler propelled by an English-built steam engine, traveled 150 miles up the Hudson River. Four years later the steamboat *New Orleans* introduced Westerners to this new mode of transportation. It steamed from Pittsburgh down the Ohio and Mississippi Rivers to New Orleans. In 1816 a river steamer made the first successful upstream voyage on the Mississippi. Within a few years steamboats were carrying the bulk of the Mississippi River cargo.

English influence remains strong in American culture. Changes in American cultural life after the Revolution were not as striking as they were in other fields. In 1783, Noah Webster had issued a call to his fellow citizens: "America must be as independent in literature as she is in politics, as famous for arts as she is for arms." Noah Webster did his best to promote cultural independence by publishing his schoolbooks and dictionary for the use of Americans (page 121). But the striving for cultural independence did not get far in the 1780's and 1790's. American thought and ideals were largely based on English standards, and this influence continued to be strong for at least another generation.

Nationalism affects the arts. In the early nineteenth century, however, it became fashionable for Americans to take a dim view of English culture. Englishmen naturally returned the compliment. The dispute reached a climax in 1820 when an English critic asked: "In the four quarters of the globe, who reads an American book? or goes to an American play? or looks at an American picture or statue?" True, Americans had not yet made a name for themselves in the arts. But it was clear that they were trying to establish a culture of their own.

American artists break away from English influence. English influence had been evident in the careers of American artists during the first years of the republic. Benjamin West (page 64) became Historical Painter to the King of England and ran an art school in London, where many American painters went to get their training. John Singleton Copley and John Trumbull, though never completely forsaking their American background, followed West to London. Eventually, however, American painters severed their ties with the English school. Gilbert Stuart, the best-known painter of this period, studied under West in London but returned to America in the early 1790's. Stuart painted a number of portraits of the first five American Presidents and also many important statesmen and men of wealth. Charles Willson Peale, founder of the Pennsylvania Academy of Fine Arts, gave encouragement to ambitious American artists. When the Capitol was rebuilt after the War of 1812, Congress commissioned John Trumbull to decorate the rotunda with historic American scenes. These included the signing of the Declaration, the surrenders of Burgoyne and Cornwallis, and Washington's resignation as commander-in-chief of the army.

The outstanding architect of this period was Charles Bulfinch, whose simple but elegant style gave an English look to many

GROWTH OF POPULATION, 1790–1820

The population of the United States in 1790 was slightly less than four million. The census of 1820 revealed that the number of Americans had more than doubled in 30 years.

CHART STUDY

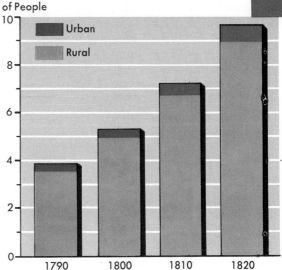

Millions of People

Urban
Rural

buildings in Boston. Thomas Jefferson turned to the classic styles of ancient Greece and Rome in designing the Virginia state capitol and buildings at the University of Virginia.

American writers become known. The American literary scene was not as barren as Englishmen liked to think. The poet Philip Freneau (page 170) had written verses praising political freedom during the Revolutionary years and later turned to themes of nature and American life. One of our first dramatists was Royall Tyler. His play *The Contrast*, produced in New York in 1787, emphasized the differences between a lazy, arrogant English aristocrat and an industrious, sincere American farmer. A group of Connecticut writers, known as the "Hartford Wits," turned out poems and essays that reflected the Federalist point of view. The western, Republican outlook was expressed by the novelist Hugh Henry Brackenridge, whose *Modern Chivalry* was published in installments between 1792 and 1815. Washington Irving finished his *History of New York by Diedrich Knickerbocker* in 1809. Ten years later the famous story of Rip Van Winkle and other Dutch legends of the Hudson River Valley appeared in Irving's *Sketch Book*.

A significant step in establishing our cultural independence of Britain was the appearance of American magazines and publishing houses. The *North American Review*, started in 1815, welcomed essays, poems, and stories by American authors. Moreover, the first American book publishing firm was established shortly after the end of the War of 1812. Its financial success led to the formation of other publishing companies. By the end of the 1820's about one quarter of the books sold in the United States were printed here.

Thus, American writers of the early 1800's began to make themselves heard. By midcentury, as we shall read later, a number of outstanding writers were to win a solid reputation for American literature.

▶ CHECK-UP

1. What was the effect of the War of 1812 on national spirit? On foreign opinion? On manufacturing? What was the significance

of the Waltham textile plant? Of Eli Whitney's development of interchangeable parts?

2. What improvements were made in transportation by land and water?

3. To what extent did American artists, architects, and writers of this period reflect English influence? What evidence was there of cultural independence?

• • • • • • • • • • • • • • • • • • •

Clinching the Main Ideas in Chapter 9

James Madison came to the presidency at a crucial moment. The struggle between Napoleon and Great Britain was reaching a climax, and neither side felt it could afford to respect the rights of neutrals. For three years Madison pursued the Jeffersonian policy of economic boycott. Though he did not know it, the policy worked well against Great Britain. Parliament voted to lift the orders in council at the very time that Congress was voting a declaration of war against Britain.

The demand for war came in large part from the planters, small farmers, and frontiersmen of the American South and West. Their motives were mixed. They wanted to punish Britain for interfering with American trade and impressing American seamen. But equally important was their desire to conquer Canada and Florida and to break British and Spanish ties with the Indians.

The War of 1812 brought none of the quick conquests which the War Hawks had predicted. American efforts to invade Canada were unsuccessful. But the American navy acquitted itelf well, both on the inland lakes and at sea. At New Orleans the British suffered a crushing defeat at the hands of Andrew Jackson, a colorful frontier general who became a national hero because of this victory. The war ended with the Treaty of Ghent, which restored the prewar boundaries but said nothing about the causes of the conflict.

From the standpoint of American morale, the War of 1812 was a "Second War of Independence." The United States, although ill-prepared for war, held its own against the British army and navy. Americans proved to themselves — and to the world — that they could fight a great power. Wartime victories and increasing economic in-dependence gave rise to a strong feeling of national pride, and spurred efforts to establish an American culture.

Chapter Review

Terms to Understand

1. Treaty of Ghent
2. standardized parts
3. National Road
4. Macon Act
5. War Hawks
6. nationalism
7. Industrial Revolution
8. Hartford Convention
9. Non-Intercourse Act
10. Battle of New Orleans
11. "Second War of Independence"

What Do You Think?

1. Madison "was maneuvered into war by Napoleon's tactics . . . and the pressures of land-hungry southern and western Republicans in Congress." Do you agree? How do you assess Madison's role?

2. During the early 1800's, representatives in Congress from the Georgia and Carolina piedmont, western Pennsylvania and New York, and the Maine districts of Massachusetts generally voted with representatives from the four new states of Vermont, Ohio, Kentucky, and Tennessee. This pattern of voting cut across such conventional sections as New England, middle states, the South, and the West. Why?

3. Why were the naval victories on Lake Erie and Lake Champlain of crucial importance to this country?

4. How do you explain New England's role in the War of 1812? Take into account developments before the declaration of war.

Using Your Knowledge of History

1. Give an oral report on one of these battles: Lake Erie, Lake Champlain, or New Orleans. Tell how the battle was won and also explain the importance of the victory.

2. In 1811, Congressman Richard M. Johnson of Kentucky said in the House: "I shall never die contented until I see her [Great Britain's] expulsion from North America, or her territories incorporated with the United States." Suggest the reaction to this statement of a Canadian newspaper editor and of the son of Loyalist parents who fled to Canada during the Revolutionary War.

3. Make a list of key inventions, developments, and improvements that revolutionized (a) American industry and (b) American transportation during the early 1800's. Explain briefly the importance of each.

Extending Your Knowledge of History

Glenn Tucker sheds light on frontier problems and troubles in *Tecumseh: Vision of Glory*. The same author has written a beautifully illustrated two-volume book on the War of 1812, *Poltroons and Patriots*. C. S. Forester deals with the naval phase of the war in *The Age of Fighting Sail*. Jeanette Mirsky and Allan Nevins let Eli Whitney tell the story of his important inventions in *The World of Eli Whitney*.

Analyzing Unit Two

1. James Madison once referred to "the defects, the deformities, the diseases" of the Articles of Confederation. What were these and how were they remedied in the Constitution?

2. One historian has said that the Federalist Party "contained more talent and virtue, with less political common sense, than any of its successors." What did the Federalists accomplish during the administrations of Washington and Adams? Why were they turned out of office by the voters in 1800?

3. In 1801, Thomas Jefferson wrote to a friend: "What is practicable must often control what is pure theory." To what extent did the administrations of Jefferson and Madison deviate from pure Republican theory of the 1790's? Why was this necessary?

Unit 3 | Democratic Changes and Territorial Expansion Alter the United States (1815-1850)

Wagon train in the Southwest

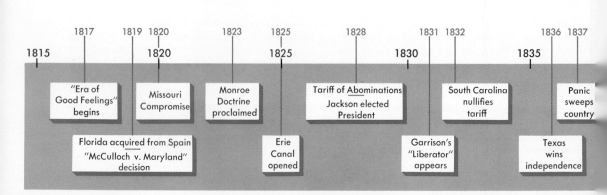

1815	1817	1819	1820	1823	1825	1828	1830	1831	1832	1835	1836	1837

"Era of Good Feelings" begins

Missouri Compromise

Monroe Doctrine proclaimed

Tariff of Abominations
Jackson elected President

South Carolina nullifies tariff

Panic sweeps country

Florida acquired from Spain
"McCulloch v. Maryland" decision

Erie Canal opened

Garrison's "Liberator" appears

Texas wins independence

A burst of nationalistic pride swept over the country after the War of 1812. The United States had held its own in a second war against the powerful British Empire, and this achievement strengthened the country's desire to chart an independent course. Congress was quick to protect American manufacturers against British competition. The Monroe Doctrine made clear our desire to avoid entanglements with Europe. Even artists and writers began to explore American themes.

At the same time, however, differences were developing among the various sections of the country. Most manufacturing and commerce were concentrated in New England. The South focused its energy on the spread of cotton plantations worked by slave labor. Most of the settlers who pushed westward into the Ohio River Valley and along the Mississippi were small farmers. People in these three sections seldom agreed on tariff policies, questions of money and banking, terms for the sale of government land, or slavery.

Many of these disagreements came to a head during the turbulent administration of President Andrew Jackson. There were noisy quarrels over government-financed internal improvements, the chartering of a second national bank, and the tariff. Underlying several public issues was the question of whether or not a state had to obey a federal law if it did not want to.

Other changes were taking place in the 1830's, many of them destined to have a greater impact on American life than the political controversies. Qualifications for voting and officeholding were altered to allow many more people to participate in elections and public life. Most of the northern and western states established tax-supported elementary schools. Magazines and newspapers increased in number and circulation, and efforts were made to reform the country's prisons and charitable institutions. In many respects, however, the most important reform movement of the Jacksonian Era was the spread of antislavery societies in the free states.

In the 1840's the opponents of slavery clashed head on with expansionists, who wanted to add more territory to the Union. The large territorial gains which resulted from the Mexican War again raised the question of slavery. Should slave labor be allowed to spread into the federal territories? Who had the authority to make this crucial decision? A compromise was hammered out in 1850 but it was merely a truce, not a final solution, to the ugly quarrel shaping up between the slave and free states.

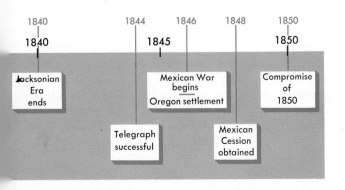

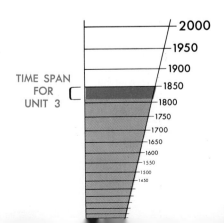

CHAPTER 10

Sectional Differences Check the Growth of Nationalism

Election Day at Independence Hall

1815–1828

[It is] gratifying . . . to witness the increased harmony of opinion which pervades our Union. Discord does not belong to our system. . . . The American people have encountered together great dangers and sustained severe trials with success. They constitute one great family with a common interest. . . . To promote this harmony in accord with the principles of our republican Government . . . , and to advance in all other respects the best interests of our Union, will be the object of my constant and zealous exertions.

JAMES MONROE, FIRST INAUGURAL ADDRESS, 1817

President Monroe, who succeeded James Madison in the White House, frequently referred in his speeches to the new national feeling that swept the country in the years after the War of 1812. In his inaugural address he called attention to the "increased harmony of opinion." In his first annual message to Congress, he rejoiced that "local jealousies are rapidly yielding to more generous, enlarged, and enlightened views of national policy."

Among the factors that encouraged the growth of nationalism were the far-reaching decisions of the Supreme Court under John Marshall. Surprisingly, many Republicans praised Marshall's decisions. Furthermore, as fear of the central government declined, the Republican Party took over a number of Federalist principles. Without much debate, Republicans in Congress passed a protective tariff, established a second national bank, and reached a diplomatic understanding with Britain. Indeed, the Republicans acted so much like Federalists that the two parties buried their differences during what was termed the "Era of Good Feelings."

Yet just beneath this placid surface ran strong currents of sectionalism. The special economic interests of the Northeast, the West, and the South led to political differences on the major issues of the day — the bank, the tariff, internal improvements, and slavery. During the 1820's these political differences helped to bring about the formation once again of two distinct political parties. This chapter will explain how the nationalist spirit of unity of 1815 gave way to sectional rivalry by 1828.

1 Nationalism Affects Politics and the Supreme Court

Party strife disappears. For almost a decade following the Treaty of Ghent, party politics in America were relatively calm. This was in sharp contrast to the heated battles of the 1790's and the bitter opposition of the Federalists during the War of 1812. Weakened by the Hartford Convention (page 204), the Federalist Party made a poor showing in the 1816 presidential election. James Monroe, Madison's Secretary of State, easily defeated the Federalist candidate, Rufus King. During his first term Monroe adopted enough Fed-

eralist principles to satisfy many former Federalist voters. Then, in the election of 1820, Monroe received every electoral vote except one. The President reflected national views and attitudes so accurately that the Federalist Party died out, and no new opposition party arose.

Monroe appointed extremely able men to his Cabinet, yet he remained the master of his administration. As Secretary of State, he named John Quincy Adams, a choice which gratified New England. For Secretary of War, Monroe wanted the rising young western politician Henry Clay. Clay, however, preferred to remain Speaker of the House, so the President appointed John C. Calhoun of South Carolina.

Shortly after his inauguration in March, 1817, Monroe announced plans for a tour of the country, something no other President had undertaken. He traveled through New England and as far west as Detroit. Wherever Monroe went, he was warmly received by the rank and file of Americans. Even Federalist newspapers outdid themselves in welcoming the President. The Boston *Columbian Centinel* described Monroe's cordial reception in an article entitled "Era of Good Feelings." The phrase quickly caught on in New England and soon was used throughout the country. Since then, the phrase "Era of Good Feelings" has been applied to the period of Monroe's presidency, though some historians believe it to be misleading in implying an absence of conflict.

British competition threatens American industry. The new sense of national unity helped solve some difficult economic problems. One of these was the need to protect from British competition the "infant industries" that had boomed during the War of 1812. American manufacturing had sharply increased after 1807, when trade with Britain was interrupted. Then, during the war years, American manufacturers found a ready market for their goods in their own country. At the same time British factories had turned out a surplus, and by 1815 their warehouses were bulging with goods.

When the war ended, British merchants were determined to regain their former trade with the United States. They flooded

American markets with manufactured goods deliberately priced below similar products made in this country. One member of Parliament declared that it was worthwhile for British merchants to take a loss on these goods "in order, by the glut, to stifle in the cradle those rising manufactures in the United States, which the war has forced into existence." These tactics drove many American manufacturers into bankruptcy. Of the 150 textile mills around Providence, Rhode Island, for instance, fewer than a dozen survived the deluge of English goods.

Manufacturers demand a protective tariff. Angry American manufacturers fought their British competitors in the only way possible. They asked Congress to enact a protective tariff. The demand was echoed by other groups whose national pride was hurt by British bullying. Even Thomas Jefferson, who had once urged that "our work-shops remain in Europe," admitted at the end of the war: "Manufactures are now as necessary to our independence as to our comfort. . . . We must now place the manufacturer by the side of the agriculturist."

Congress passes a new tariff act. Early in 1816, Congress passed a new tariff which raised the duties on many imported articles. Although the tariff rates were too low to give much help to the American "infant industries," they whetted the appetites of manufacturers for high protection.

The vote on the Tariff of 1816 was significant. The only organized groups to oppose it were northern merchants and shipowners, who profited from a brisk trade with Britain. Their spokesman was Representative Daniel Webster of Massachusetts, who voted against the tariff. There was some opposition among southern planters, who had no desire to pay higher prices just to help protect northern industry. Many Southerners, however, confidently expected that manufacturing would take hold in their region of the country. They had raw materials, water power, and man power. Consequently, many of them thought that the South soon would have textile factories that would benefit from tariff protection. Also,

Southerners were caught up in the wave of national feeling. John C. Calhoun of South Carolina argued for the Tariff of 1816 as a national necessity. "It is the duty of this country," he said, "as a means of defense, to encourage the domestic industry of the country." Calhoun added that the tariff would "form a new and most powerful cement."

Within a decade, however, the changing interests of Massachusetts and South Carolina would force Webster and Calhoun to revise their views on the tariff. By the late 1820's, manufacturers would outweigh the commercial interests in Massachusetts, and Webster would thus speak in favor of protective tariffs. Also by that time, the South, having abandoned its dreams of industrialization, would consistently oppose further tariff increases. Calhoun, like Webster, would shift with the changing tide. By the late 1820's the South Carolina leader would fervently oppose the tariff (page 233), though in 1816 he was one of its strongest advocates.

Congress charters a second national bank. The new feeling of nationalism also caused most Americans to support the President's suggestion of a second Bank of the United States. When the first bank's charter expired in 1811, Secretary of the Treasury Gallatin had unsuccessfully recommended renewal of the charter to Congress. The bank had no sooner closed its doors than the difficulty of maintaining a sound currency became apparent. In the absence of a national bank, state legislatures chartered a number of banks owned and operated by private individuals. Many of these state banks, especially in the West, issued large quantities of bank notes. These bank notes were circulated as paper money.[1] Unfortunately many of the state banks did not keep enough gold and silver on hand to redeem their notes. Thus the value of the paper money often declined. In the five years after 1811 the number of state banks

---

[1] The bank notes were not legal tender, and they were not issued by the state governments. Thus, technically, the states were not violating the Constitution, even though the state bank notes did interfere with Congress' exclusive power to regulate the currency.

almost tripled, and the amount of their bank notes more than doubled. The treasury of the United States suffered a loss because many of the bank notes accepted in payment of taxes were nearly worthless.

Congress could have remedied the situation by prohibiting the banks from issuing bank notes. Instead Congress decided to charter a second Bank of the United States in the hope that it could control the state banks. Madison signed the bank bill in April, 1816. Like its predecessor, the second bank had a 20-year charter, with the government owning one fifth of its stock and appointing a fifth of its directors. All government funds were deposited in the bank, and it could issue bank notes which would circulate as legal tender. In return for these privileges the bank was required to pay the government a "bonus" of one and a half million dollars.

The Supreme Court confirms the national bank. State banks now faced competition from the second national bank and the branches which it was authorized to establish. Moreover, the state banks resented attempts by the national bank to stabilize the currency and drive their bank notes out of circulation. At their request, a number of states passed laws taxing the branches of the national bank in an effort to destroy them. Matters came to a head when the cashier of the Baltimore branch of the national bank refused to pay a tax levied by the state of Maryland. A suit was brought in the state courts, which upheld the tax. The case was then appealed to the United States Supreme Court.

In this famous case, *McCulloch v. Maryland* (1819), Chief Justice John Marshall wrote one of the most important opinions in the history of American courts. He made it clear that Congress had only the powers given to it in the Constitution (Article 1, Section 8). He pointed out, however, that the very grant of power implied the right to use it in any necessary and proper way. What was more, no state could limit this right. Congress had decided that a national bank was "necessary and proper" in order to carry out its financial power of levying and collecting taxes and of borrowing

John Marshall, raised on the Virginia frontier, practiced law and served his country in several public offices before his appointment as Chief Justice of the United States.

money. "Let the end be legitimate," Marshall said, "let it be within the scope of the Constitution, and all means which are plainly adapted to that end, which are not prohibited, but consist [agree] with the letter and spirit of the Constitution, are constitutional." Furthermore, the states had no right to tax the national bank, for the taxation of federal agencies by the states "would defeat all the ends of government." The Supreme Court's decision in *McCulloch v. Maryland* upheld the constitutionality of the national bank and forbade the states to tax it.

Marshall's opinions strengthen the national government. Under Marshall's leadership, the Supreme Court handed down other decisions which protected the federal government against interference by the states. Several of these decisions, as in *McCulloch v. Maryland*, set aside state laws which conflicted with the Constitution. In the Dartmouth College case (1819), Marshall stated that the New Hampshire legislature could not change the old royal charter granted to Dartmouth College. The charter, he held, was a contract establishing obligations which the state was forbidden by the Constitution to alter. In another case (*Gibbons v. Ogden,* 1824), Marshall smashed a monopoly of the navigable waters of New York State — a monopoly granted by the New York legislature to Robert R. Livingston and Robert Fulton. He pointed out that navigation of the Hudson River involved interstate commerce, which, by the provisions of the Constitution, Congress alone was permitted to regulate.

John Marshall served as Chief Justice of the Supreme Court from 1801 to 1835. During this period Marshall personally wrote more than 500 decisions. In vigorous prose and clear logic, he translated his nationalistic views into law. To him the Supreme Court was more than a court. It was a platform from which he could proclaim to the nation those principles which gave life to the Constitution. In his decisions Marshall accomplished two important things. (1) By a broad interpretation of the Constitution, he strengthened the federal government at the expense of the states. (2) Through his energy and vigor, the Supreme Court gained an importance in the federal government which it retains to this day.

The Republican Party is "Federalized." The aging Thomas Jefferson was worried about the steady advance of Federalist principles in Marshall's court decisions. "The greatest object of my fear is the Federal Judiciary," he wrote. But few Republicans agreed with him. Most of them calmly accepted the Court decisions. Moreover, Republicans in Congress supported the national bank and protective tariff and voted funds to build the National Road (page 208) and maintain a strong army and navy. Approval of these measures was the "price" paid by the Republicans for the support of former Federalists during the Era of Good Feelings. By 1820 there was only one national political party, and Josiah Quincy quite rightly observed that it had "out-Federalized Federalism."

▶ CHECK-UP

1. Why was there less party strife in the decade after the War of 1812?

2. How did the British seek to regain their market for manufactures in America? What happened to the American "infant industries"? Why was the Tariff of 1816 opposed by Webster and favored by Calhoun? Why did these men reverse their stands by the late 1820's?

3. Why was a second Bank of the United States chartered in 1816? Why and how was it opposed by the state banks? How was the national bank strengthened by Marshall's decision in "McCulloch v. Maryland"?

4. What were the two broad goals achieved by the decisions written by Marshall? Explain and illustrate.

· ·

2 *American Foreign Policy Reflects National Pride*

Relations with other countries were well-conducted during Monroe's administration. As a result, Americans' pride in their nation continued to grow. Much of the credit for this situation belongs to John Quincy Adams.

American-British relations improve. During the first 25 years of the republic, relations with Great Britain had been stormy. After 1815, however, our affairs with Britain took a turn for the better.

(1) In that year John Quincy Adams, as Minister to Great Britain, signed an agreement with the British under which the United States regained its prewar trade privileges.

(2) In the Rush-Bagot Agreement (1817), the United States and Britain agreed to a policy of naval disarmament on the Great Lakes and Lake Champlain (except for a few gunboats needed for police purposes).[2]

---

[2] Later this agreement was extended to the entire Canadian-American boundary, thus making it the longest undefended border in the world.

(3) By another treaty, Great Britain in 1818 gave Americans permanent fishing privileges along certain parts of the Labrador and Newfoundland coasts. This Convention of 1818 also established the forty-ninth parallel as the northern boundary between the United States and Canada, from the Lake of the Woods west to the Rocky Mountains (map, page 188). The Oregon Country was to be "free and open" to the citizens of both the United States and Great Britain for ten years. At the end of this period, the arrangement was continued indefinitely, but it was understood that the agreement could be ended by either country on a year's notice.

Trouble arises with Spain. Relations with Spain were more troublesome. For many years Americans in Georgia and in the Mississippi Territory had complained about lawlessness in Spanish Florida. During the Napoleonic Wars, Spain withdrew so many troops from Florida that only Pensacola and St. Augustine had effective garrisons. The rest of the Florida peninsula was a refuge for runaway slaves, Indians, pirates, and smugglers.

Two British adventurers, Alexander Arbuthnot and Robert Ambrister, took advantage of this situation and openly encouraged the Creek and Seminole Indians to raid American territory. When these raids led to war between the Seminoles and the United States, the American government decided to force a showdown. Andrew Jackson was sent to the Florida border with orders to "adopt the necessary measures" to end the Indian threat. Jackson interpreted these instructions to mean that he could drive the Indians deep into Spanish territory. In 1818 he and his men swept across the Florida border and executed Ambrister and Arbuthnot. Jackson even captured Pensacola from the Spaniards and claimed the surrounding territory for the United States.

Jackson's hasty action put the Monroe administration in a difficult spot. Britain was outraged by the high-handed execution of two of her subjects, and Spain protested the invasion of her territory. President Monroe, hoping to buy Florida, did not

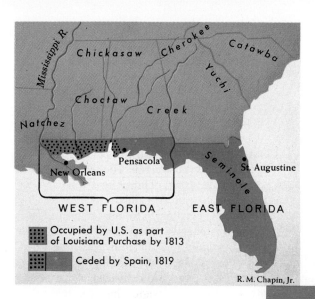

THE UNITED STATES ACQUIRES FLORIDA

Americans had claimed West Florida since the Louisiana Purchase, but not until 1819 did Spain cede both Floridas. Note that Alabama and Mississippi gained river outlets to the Gulf of Mexico.

want war with either country. He and every member of the Cabinet, with one exception, wanted to apologize to Spain and Britain for Jackson's raid. The one member who disagreed was Secretary of State John Quincy Adams. He proposed that Jackson's raid be used as a lever to force Spain to relinquish Florida. Adams finally brought Monroe and the Cabinet around to his point of view. Instead of an apology, a blunt note was delivered to the Spanish government. It demanded that Spain "either . . . place a force in Florida adequate . . . to the protection of her territory . . . or cede to the United States a province, of which she [Spain] retains nothing but the nominal possession."

Spain cedes Florida to the United States. Because the Spanish government was having trouble at home as well as in its Central and South American colonies, it was in no position to establish effective control over Florida. Therefore, by the Adams-Onís Treaty (1819), Spain ceded Florida to the United States. In return, the United States agreed to pay the claims that American citizens held against Spain to the amount of five million dollars.

By the same treaty the United States accepted a clearly defined southwestern boundary for the Louisiana Territory. This line, separating the United States from Spanish Mexico, proceeded in a steplike fashion from the Sabine River, alternately north and west to the forty-second parallel. It then followed that parallel to the Pacific (map, page 188). Thus, the United States gave up its claim to Texas as part of the Louisiana Territory. Adams regretted the necessity for this action, and many Southerners complained loudly. At this time, however, few Americans were living in Texas, and the Senate agreed with Adams that the other terms of the treaty were too favorable to turn down. The Senate promptly ratified the "transcontinental treaty." But Spain hesitated for two years, afraid that once the United States had Florida, it would aid the rebelling Spanish colonies in Latin America. Finally, in 1821, the Spanish government ratified the treaty, and Florida passed into American hands.

Spain loses her American colonies. One cause of Spain's weakness in the Florida affair grew out of troubles with her Central and South American colonies. For years the Spanish colonists had resented Spain's strict control over their government, commerce, and daily life. Feeling was bitter among the oppressed Indians; and the Creoles (people of Spanish or French blood born in the New World) were often at odds with Spanish administrators. Into this tense situation filtered ideas of freedom from the American and French Revolutions. A few bold leaders in the Spanish colonies started organizing for independence.

When Napoleon invaded Spain, the rebels took advantage of the situation. Starting in 1810, revolts flared up in many of the Spanish colonies. After the Napoleonic Wars, Spain re-established partial control over her American empire. But patriots like José de San Martín (sahn mar-*teen'*) in Argentina, Simón Bolívar (boh-*lee'*vahr) in Venezuela, and Bernardo O'Higgins in Chile continued the fight for independence.

The American government as well as many of its citizens sympathized with the uprisings in Latin America. Until the War of 1812 was over, however, the United States was too preoccupied with its own difficulties to aid the Spanish colonies in their revolt. Nor did Monroe, while he was trying to buy Florida from Spain, wish to take any action. In 1822, after the tottering Spanish government finally ratified the Adams-Onís Treaty, President Monroe officially recognized the independence of Mexico, Great Colombia, the Argentine confederation, Peru, and Chile.

Europe threatens the Americas. European monarchs feared the revolutionary ideas which had caused so much trouble in France and were shaking the Spanish empire. Near the end of the Napoleonic Wars, Russia, Prussia, Austria, and Great Britain formed an alliance (later joined by France). The purpose of this alliance was to resist all revolutionary movements. In the early 1820's, when rebellion broke out in Spain, the European powers (except for Great Britain) agreed that a French army should be sent into Spain to crush the uprising. This action restored the Spanish monarchy and led to rumors that the European powers might also try to recover Spain's American colonies.

In addition to the threat of European intervention in South America, Russia was seeking to increase its influence in North America. Russia already owned Alaska. Then, in 1821, the Czar extended Russian claims southward to the fifty-first parallel, well within the Oregon Country. Furthermore, Russia warned foreign ships not to approach within 100 miles of the Alaskan coast.

Britain proposes joint British-American action. Great Britain did not want to see Spain regain its American colonies. British trade with the former Spanish colonies had increased as their ties with the mother country were loosened. If Spanish authority were reimposed and if Spanish mercantile laws were again strictly enforced, British merchants would suffer. Moreover, the British government feared that France might gain territory in the Americas if she assisted Spain in putting down the revolts. Therefore, in 1823 George Canning, the British foreign secretary, suggested that the United

GREENLAND (Danish)

Claimed by Russia

BRITISH NORTH AMERICA

OREGON COUNTRY
(Joint British-U.S. occupation - 1818)

UNITED STATES

MEXICAN STATES (EMPIRE) 1822

Atlantic Ocean

Mexico City

Pacific Ocean

CUBA (Spanish)

REPUBLIC OF HAITI 1804

PUERTO RICO (Spanish)

BR. HONDURAS JAMAICA (British)

Caribbean Sea

INDEPENDENT CONFEDERATION OF CENTRAL AMERICA 1823

REPUBLIC OF GREAT COLOMBIA 1821
★ Bogotá

BRITISH GUIANA
SURINAM (DUTCH GUIANA)
FRENCH GUIANA

Equator

Amazon R.

EMPIRE OF BRAZIL 1822

PERU 1821
Lima ★

BOLIVIA 1825
La Paz ★
★ Sucre

Rio de Janeiro ★

PARAGUAY
★ Asuncion

CHILE 1818

UNITED PROVINCES OF RIO DE LA PLATA (ARGENTINA) 1816

★ Buenos Aires

Unoccupied

R. M. Chapin, Jr.

LATIN AMERICA TODAY

U.S.

MEXICO

CUBA
DOMINICAN REPUBLIC
HAITI
PUERTO RICO

BR. HONDURAS
HONDURAS
GUATEMALA
EL SALVADOR
NICARAGUA
COSTA RICA
PANAMA

Caracas
TRINIDAD-TOBAGO
BR. GUIANA
SURINAM
FR. GUIANA

VENEZUELA

COLOMBIA

Quito ★
ECUADOR

PERU ★

BRAZIL

Brasilia ★

Pacific Ocean

BOLIVIA

PARAGUAY

CHILE
Santiago ★

ARGENTINA

URUGUAY
Montevideo

■ Colonies

▨ Independent countries

THE WESTERN HEMISPHERE IN THE 1820'S

The large map shows the Western Hemisphere as it appeared when the Monroe Doctrine was proclaimed. Notice that several European nations held or claimed colonies in the Americas. The inset map shows Latin American republics and boundaries today.

MAP STUDY

221

The settlement of New Archangel (now Sitka) was the headquarters of Russian colonization in Alaska. The fort at right defended the settlement against Indians.

States and Britain jointly protest against any action European powers might take to restore the Latin American colonies to Spain.

Adams favors independent action. When Canning's proposal reached Washington, Monroe's Cabinet gave it immediate consideration. The President was inclined to accept. He consulted former Presidents Jefferson and Madison, both of whom favored a joint Anglo-American declaration. Secretary of State John Quincy Adams, however, opposed this plan. He thought the United States should act alone. His reasons were these: (1) He did not think the European nations would actually invade South America; and, if they did try, the powerful British navy would stop them anyway. (2) Canning had also proposed that the United States and Britain themselves promise not to annex any Spanish-American territory. But Adams thought it unwise to tie this country's hands, for there was always the possibility that Cuba or Texas might some day ask for annexation to the United States. (3) Russian expansion on the Pacific coast might make independent action by the United States necessary. If so, Adams did not want to have to consult Britain first.

In short, Adams argued, if the United States should act independently, the country still would be assured of British support. By rejecting Canning's proposal, the United States could avoid being a "cock-boat in the wake of the British man-of-war."

The Monroe Doctrine is proclaimed. Adams persuaded the President and the Cabinet to accept his point of view. Monroe announced the new policy in his annual message to Congress in December, 1823. In Monroe's own words, the important points were as follows:

(1) In the wars of the European powers in matters relating to themselves we have never taken any part, nor does it comport [agree] with our policy so to do. . . .

(2) With the existing colonies or dependencies of any European power we have not interfered and shall not interfere. . . .

(3) . . . The American continents, by the free and independent condition which they have assumed and maintain, are henceforth not to be considered as subjects for future colonization by any European powers. . . .

(4) . . . We should consider any attempt on their [the European powers'] part to extend their system to any portion of this hemisphere as dangerous to our peace and safety. . . .

The Monroe Doctrine has little immediate effect. Americans read the new policy with approval. Since it was in accord with their new nationalistic pride, they liked the bold warning which their President had issued. The European countries, however, considered the Monroe Doctrine to be of little importance. The British were annoyed because Canning's proposal for joint action had been rejected. Nevertheless, British and American interests in the Western Hemisphere were similar, and the Monroe Doctrine came at a time when the two countries were moving toward a long period of general understanding. France, Austria, Russia, and Prussia were unimpressed by Monroe's bold words. In fact, they considered the President's desire to guard the Western Hemisphere somewhat ridiculous in view of America's weak military position. But, knowing that the British navy would back up the Monroe Doctrine, they made no attempt to restore Spain's New World empire. Spain came to recognize the independence of her American colonies, and in 1824 Russia agreed to establish the southern boundary of Alaska at 54°40'. Consequently, the Doctrine was never really tested in this early period. Its real importance lay in the future, when it would become a cornerstone of American foreign policy.

▶ CHECK-UP

1. What important agreements improved American relations with Britain after 1815?

2. Why did the situation in Florida create problems? How did Andrew Jackson complicate the situation? How did John Quincy Adams turn Jackson's action to advantage? What were the terms of the Adams-Onís Treaty?

3. Why did Spain's American colonies begin to revolt? How were these revolts viewed by Spain, Britain, and the United States? What action was suggested by Canning? Why did Adams favor independent action?

4. What points were made in the Monroe Doctrine? How did the European powers view this statement of policy at the time? Why?

. . . .

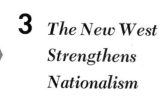

3 *The New West Strengthens Nationalism*

Pioneers move beyond the mountains. Still another development that strengthened national feeling in the United States was the rapid growth of the West. The War of

1812 was no sooner over than the westward movement of Americans increased to major proportions. By 1830, almost a third of the country's people lived beyond the Appalachian Mountains.

Americans went west for many reasons. The most powerful attraction was cheap, fertile land. Some land in the South was losing its fertility, and a growing population needed more land. Farmers in New England had long fought a discouraging battle with poor soil and a short growing season. Many of them now wanted to move on to more promising land. Hard times in the East after the war caused others to seek a new start in the West.

The removal of hostile Indians was important in encouraging westward migration. The power of the Indians had been broken by Tecumseh's death in 1813 and Jackson's decisive victory over the Creeks in 1814 (page 204). The British withdrawal to Canada and the expulsion of the Spaniards from Florida deprived the Indians of their European allies. With their power to resist American settlers shattered, many tribes were persuaded by government agents to move west of the Mississippi.

Turnpikes lead west. Better roads also stimulated the westward movement after 1815. A network of turnpikes began to appear (map, page 302). In the North, the Genesee and Catskill Turnpikes crossed New York State. From the Middle States, settlers took the Philadelphia-Lancaster pike and then followed the Forbes Road across the mountains to Pittsburgh, where they could continue by water on the Ohio River. The most heavily traveled route was the National Road between Cumberland, Maryland, and Wheeling on the Ohio River. Completed in 1818, this road was later extended to Vandalia, Illinois. Farther south, travelers took the Wilderness Road through Cumberland Gap.

Partly because of the direction of these roads, Americans tended to move west in parallel lines during the 1820's and '30's. New Englanders pushed into western New York, then along the Great Lakes, and eventually into Michigan and Wisconsin. Those from the Middle States and upper South who used the National Road generally settled in the southern parts of Ohio, Indiana, and Illinois and later in Missouri. Farmers from the Virginia and Carolina piedmont populated Kentucky and Tennessee. Planters from Virginia, the Carolinas, and Georgia established plantations in what are now the states of Alabama, Mississippi, and Louisiana.

Travel is difficult. The trip west was a hard one over rough roads with few accommodations along the way. Some families traveled on horseback or in large canvas-covered wagons — the *Conestoga* wagons. But many walked, carrying their few belongings or pushing wheelbarrows or carts. One Englishman said of the heavily traveled National Road:

> Old America seems to be breaking up and moving westward. We are seldom out of sight, as we travel on this grand track toward the Ohio, of family groups, behind and before us. . . . A cart and single horse frequently affords the means of transfer, sometimes a horse and a pack-saddle. Often the back of the poor pilgrim bears all his effects, and his wife follows, naked-footed, bending under the hopes of the family.

Once these people reached the Ohio River, they could travel on flatboats and "arks" and perhaps even the new steamboats.

Many travelers came down with frontier illnesses such as "fever and ague," a form of malaria. Another Englishman who observed these ailing pioneers wondered why they endured the "rugged road, the dirty hovels, the fire in the woods to sleep by, the pathless ways through the wilderness, the dangerous crossings of the rivers." The answer, of course, was the chance to buy cheap, fertile land and to make a new start in the West. As long as land was available, Americans pushed westward to claim it.

New states are admitted to the Union. So great was the westward surge of population that four new states were soon admitted to the Union: Indiana (1816), Mississippi (1817), Illinois (1818), and Alabama (1819). Already the population had spilled across the Mississippi. There was a wide belt of settlement along that river and even along the lower Missouri River. By 1818, the population of the Missouri Territory stood at 60,000, and territorial leaders were pushing for statehood.

Westerners demand better transportation. A large proportion of the people who settled in the West were farmers. They were soon raising more than they themselves could consume or sell to western towns. Thus, they had to seek other markets for their produce — plantations in the South, cities in the Northeast, or foreign countries. Until Europe recovered from the ravages of the Napoleonic Wars, it provided a large market for American farm products. But the logical market for western agricultural surplus was the industrial Northeast. The great problem was how to get the farm goods across the Appalachian Mountains to eastern markets and bring back manufactured goods to the West.

Western farmers soon found that it was too expensive to ship grain across the mountains. A bushel of western wheat before 1825 sold for 75 cents, but to send it overland from Pittsburgh to Philadelphia cost approximately twice that much. For this reason most western produce before 1825 was sent down the Mississippi and shipped by sea from New Orleans. Westerners used steamboats, flatboats, and other craft to transport their furs, hay, flour, grain, hemp, livestock, tobacco, whiskey, and lumber. Some farmers fed their grain to livestock, which was then driven across the mountains to market. But both western farmers and eastern merchants realized that some means of transportation cheaper than the turnpike and quicker than the long water route was needed. Until the railroad proved itself in the 1840's, the answer seemed to be canals.

The Erie Canal is a great success. Although a few short canals had been built earlier to get around falls or rapids in rivers, the canal era really started with the construction of the Erie Canal. In 1817 De Witt Clinton persuaded the New York State legislature to authorize the building of a canal between the Hudson River and Lake Erie. It would connect Albany and Buffalo, 363 miles apart, and would cost seven million dollars. At the time, the project

Americans in the early 1800's traveled by old means and new. Inns like the one at right served as stopping places for settlers heading westward. Horse power was also used in canal transportation (below). Meanwhile, inventors applied steam power to water travel. "Walk-in-the-Water" (below right) was the first steamer on the Great Lakes.

seemed so preposterous that opponents sarcastically called it "Clinton's Big Ditch." In spite of the ridicule, the canal was completed in 1825. Its success was instantaneous. Freight rates between Buffalo and Albany dropped from 100 dollars to 10 dollars a ton; travel time was cut from 20 days to 8. So heavy was the traffic on the Erie Canal that it paid for itself within nine years.

Among the most enthusiastic backers of the Erie Canal had been the merchants of New York City. They were amply rewarded for their foresight. The Canal enabled them to tap the rich upstate farmland and to reach into the Old Northwest for trade which would otherwise have gone to New Orleans. In the 1820's, New York City

pulled far ahead of its closest competitors — Philadelphia, Boston, and Baltimore. To be sure, it had a richer countryside to draw from and a better harbor. But the Hudson River and the Erie Canal had much to do with making New York the nation's largest city by 1830 and in greatly increasing its volume of trade.

The lesson of the Erie Canal was not lost on other cities and state legislatures. Baltimore announced plans for a Chesapeake and Ohio Canal, but it was never completed. Ohio strained its financial resources to build a canal linking Cleveland with the Ohio River. The canal boom lasted throughout the 1830's, producing some 3300 miles of canals, mostly in the North and West (map, page 302).

A plan for internal improvements fails.
Because both turnpikes and canals were expensive for the new western states to finance, Westerners looked to Congress for help. Politicians like Clay and Calhoun took up the cry for *internal improvements* to be paid for with national funds. Shortly after the War of 1812, President Madison had asked Congress to appropriate funds for building canals and roads. But he thought Congress should first pass an amendment to the Constitution to settle any question about the government's right to finance internal improvements.

Before Congress took any action, Calhoun proposed a bill to set aside for internal improvements the bonus of one and a half million dollars which the government received from the national bank (page 217). To this sum he suggested adding the annual dividends which the government received on its bank stock. Calhoun's Bonus Bill was strongly supported by the western states and also New York and Pennsylvania. The measure passed Congress in 1817 but was vetoed by Madison on his last day in office. Though the President sympathized with the purpose of the bill, he still wanted a constitutional amendment first.

Clay proposes the American System.
In 1824 Henry Clay presented a program that would combine internal improvements, a protective tariff, cheap land, and the national bank. He christened his program the *American System.* Clay tied up the western demand for internal improvements at national expense with the eastern desire for a protective tariff. Such a tariff would provide revenue for financing internal improvements and would also protect American manufacturers from European competition. This protection would make it possible to sell eastern manufactured goods in the growing markets of the West and South. In turn, these areas could give the workers of the North and East the foodstuffs and raw materials that they needed. In addition, Clay wanted the government to sell public land cheaply, and he believed the national bank was necessary to stabilize the country's economy. Thus, the American System would bind the different sections in an economic unit that would be almost self-sufficient in time of war or peace.

THE AMERICAN SCENE

AMERICAN WILDLIFE

as seen by JOHN JAMES AUDUBON

These beautifully detailed pictures of the little blue heron (left) and the now extinct passenger pigeon were just two of hundreds painted by Audubon. Born in Santo Domingo, Audubon came to this country in 1803 and spent the rest of his life capturing the color and beauty of American wildlife.

"I hope," Clay declared, "that it will yet be said, America is America's best customer."

Clay's American System had many enthusiastic backers, especially among Westerners. For the next two decades Clay campaigned tirelessly for his program, but it was never enacted into law. Most of the expense of internal improvements was left to the states or to private individuals.

Settlement of the West strengthens nationalism. As Americans moved across the mountains and established new homes in the West, their ties to their native states were weakened. Moreover, the new western states did not have the same roots in colonial history that the thirteen original states had. Western settlers, therefore, took greater pride in the nation as a whole than they did in their own states. And, as we have seen, the settlers looked to the federal government for land and for internal improvements. Thus the growing numbers of people beyond the mountains were a strong force for nationalism.

▶ CHECK-UP

1. Why did more settlers move westward after the War of 1812? What routes and means of travel were used? How did settlers in the West market their produce? Why did they demand improved transportation?

2. How did the Erie Canal benefit New York City? The West?

3. What was Madison's stand on federal support of internal improvements? What was Clay's American System? How was each section to benefit? Why did the westward movement strengthen nationalism?

. . . .

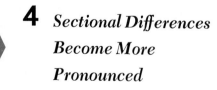

4 *Sectional Differences Become More Pronounced*

The sections develop conflicting interests. Up to this point, we have described the growth of national unity following the

War of 1812. Yet even during the Era of Good Feelings, a countercurrent of sectional rivalry existed. As the country rapidly expanded, each region — Northeast, South, and West — developed its own attitudes and viewpoints. These differences grew out of the special economic interests of each section and the efforts of politicians to get legislation from Congress that favored their own sections. From the 1820's to the 1860's, sectional rivalry was pitted against the spirit of nationalism in a continuing struggle.

(1) The *Northeast* in the 1820's was developing into a strong industrial center. As manufacturers became more influential than the trade and shipping interests, northeastern politicians tended increasingly to speak for the industrialists. To secure additional protection for American industry, manufacturers wanted higher tariffs. They favored the national bank because it kept the currency stable. And in general they favored internal improvements because increased East-West trade would benefit industry. But the northeastern manufacturers were only lukewarm about westward expansion. The West provided them with new markets for manufactured goods, but it also drew away their labor supply as ambitious workers migrated to the frontier. Moreover, as settlement of the West brought new states into the Union, New England's influence in Congress was reduced.

(2) The *South* developed a different point of view on tariffs and internal improvements. This was due in large part to the increasing importance of cotton in the South. Prior to the 1790's, cotton could be grown profitably only in the tidewater area. Although some species of cotton could be grown in the piedmont, the difficulty of removing seeds made it unprofitable. A cotton gin invented by Eli Whitney in 1793 remedied the problem. Whitney's machine quickly separated the seeds from the cotton fibers and thus made it possible for large crops of cotton to be processed rapidly. Cotton cultivation then spread through the piedmont region of the South, and later planters sought new lands along the Gulf coast and in the Southwest. In 1814 about 150,000 bales of cotton were produced, more than half of it in Georgia and South

Carolina. By 1825, however, production had jumped to 600,000 bales, and cotton cultivation had spread along the Gulf coast, up the Mississippi, and even into what is now Arkansas. The cotton crop was more valuable than all the other southern crops combined.

Because cotton cultivation was profitable, southern capital was expended on new land and slaves; little money was invested in manufacturing. Hence the South had to import its finished goods. Southerners preferred to buy manufactured goods from Britain, for that country bought most of the South's cotton. As a result, the South opposed protective tariffs, which would raise prices on imported articles. Southern planters favored western expansion because they needed new lands for cotton. But they insisted on the right to take slavery into the new territories. Finally, many Southerners opposed internal improvements. The navigable rivers of the South met their transportation needs, and they did not want the federal government to finance roads and canals that benefited only the North and West.

(3) The *West* had still a third point of view. It was a farming area in need of a market for surplus products. The Westerners therefore favored a government policy that made land available on easy terms and financed construction of roads and canals. The protective tariff was supported in western cities like Cincinnati, Louisville, and St. Louis, where there was some manufacturing. Most Westerners favored the second United States Bank during its early years. The bank made easy loans for the purchase of land, and it accepted notes from the state banks. An economic crisis in 1819, however, forced the national bank to change its policy. This in turn led Westerners to change their attitude about the bank.

A panic sweeps the country. The Panic of 1819 was due in part to the rapid expansion of American manufacturing during the War of 1812 and the distress caused by the postwar British competition (page 216). The rapid expansion of American farming was another factor. Surplus farm products

had been sold in Europe immediately after the war. But when European agriculture recovered, the demand for American goods declined and prices fell. Still another cause of the crisis was land speculation in the West. Thousands of settlers had purchased land on credit in the postwar years, and many of the land deals were financed by "wildcat banks." These state banks were eager to lend money, and so too was the national bank. But land speculation[3] had gotten out of hand by the latter part of 1818, and the directors of the national bank began to ask for repayment of their loans.

This tightening of credit and a sharp fall in farm prices touched off the Panic of 1819. Prices plummeted downward. In some places wheat fell from two dollars a bushel to 25 cents, and cotton dropped from 33 cents a pound to 10 cents. Factories closed their doors and thousands of people were thrown out of work. Western farmers who had taken land on credit could not repay their loans, and the banks foreclosed on their property.

During the depression that followed this panic, many "wildcat banks" were taken over by the United States Bank. So much land in the West and Southwest fell into the hands of the national bank that it was said: "The bank was saved and the people were ruined." Politicians assailed the bank as "the Monster" and blamed it for the country's troubles. Congress aided the Westerners with a new Land Act in 1820. It made possible the purchase of an 80-acre farm for only 100 dollars, but cash payment was required. Yet even after prosperity returned in 1824–1825, most Westerners continued to distrust the national bank and the eastern financiers who ran it.

Missouri's request for statehood leads to controversy. The Panic of 1819 had set the West against the East on economic issues. Another sectional conflict threatened when the territory of Missouri asked to be admitted to the Union. This development set the North against the South over the question of slavery. In 1818, when a bill to

---

[3] *Speculation* is buying with the hope of selling at a profit when prices rise.

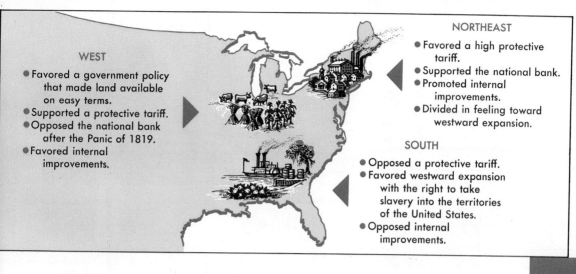

WEST
- Favored a government policy that made land available on easy terms.
- Supported a protective tariff.
- Opposed the national bank after the Panic of 1819.
- Favored internal improvements.

NORTHEAST
- Favored a high protective tariff.
- Supported the national bank.
- Promoted internal improvements.
- Divided in feeling toward westward expansion.

SOUTH
- Opposed a protective tariff.
- Favored westward expansion with the right to take slavery into the territories of the United States.
- Opposed internal improvements.

THE RISE OF SECTIONALISM

Sectional rivalry emerged as a countercurrent to the rising spirit of American nationalism. Note how special economic interests determined the opinions and attitudes of the people of the Northeast, the South, and the West.

CHART STUDY

make Missouri a state was introduced in the House of Representatives, James Tallmadge of New York offered the following amendment to the bill:

> That the further introduction of slavery or involuntary servitude be prohibited, except for the punishment of crimes . . . ; and that all children of slaves, born within the said state, after the admission thereof into the Union, shall be free but may be held to service until the age of twenty-five years.

The Tallmadge amendment narrowly passed the House but was defeated in the Senate. When Congress adjourned in March, 1819, the Missouri bill was still deadlocked.

Feeling over Missouri runs high. Whether Missouri should be admitted as a free or a slave state became a leading topic of discussion. Though there was some talk about slavery as a moral issue, the debate primarily concerned political and constitutional issues. With eleven free and eleven slave states, the North and the South had equal voting strength in the Senate. But a different situation existed in the House of Representatives, where each state's representation was based on population. In 1820 there were five million people in the free states, compared to the South's four and a half million, including the slaves. Thus, the House had more northern representa-

tives than southern and could pass measures like the Tallmadge amendment.

The right of Congress to legislate on slavery in the territories was also debated. Southerners insisted that Congress had no constitutional right to determine whether a new state would be slave or free. The North, on the other hand, held that the Constitution did give Congress the right to determine the status of slavery in new states. The Northerners claimed that Congress ought to approve the Tallmadge amendment and ban slavery in Missouri.

Northern legislatures and mass meetings adopted resolutions and signed petitions against the admission of Missouri as a slave state. Southern legislatures warned that Congress could not deprive Southerners of their property, meaning slaves, when they moved into the territories. One Georgian even predicted that passage of the Tallmadge amendment would break up the Union. The "momentous question" raised in the Missouri debate deeply disturbed Thomas Jefferson. It shattered the peace of the nation, he said, "like a fire bell in the night."

The Missouri Compromise is accepted. Fortunately, while the debate was going on, the northeastern counties of Massachusetts asked to be admitted to the Union as a separate state to be called Maine. Senator

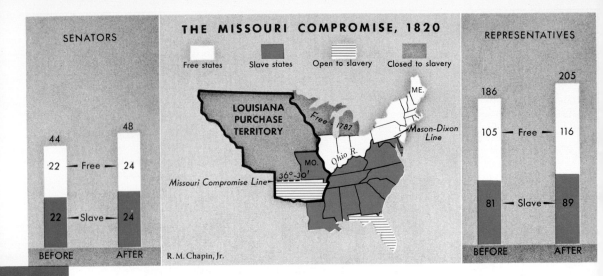

THE MISSOURI COMPROMISE, 1820

SENATORS

Free states
Slave states
Open to slavery
Closed to slavery

LOUISIANA PURCHASE TERRITORY

ME.
Free 1787
Mason-Dixon Line
Ohio R.
MO.
36°30'
Missouri Compromise Line

44
22 — Free — 22 — Slave
BEFORE

48
24 — Free — 24
AFTER

R. M. Chapin, Jr.

REPRESENTATIVES

186
105 — Free
81 — Slave
BEFORE

205
116
89 — Slave
AFTER

MAP STUDY

THE MISSOURI COMPROMISE

The first attempt by Congress to settle the issue of slavery in the territories maintained a balance in the number of free states and slave states. Since the two new states, Maine and Missouri, were each entitled to receive two seats in the Senate, representation of free states and of slave states remained equal in that body. How did the Compromise affect membership in the House?

J. B. Thomas of Illinois and Henry Clay saw an opportunity to break the Missouri deadlock. They proposed that Missouri be admitted as a slave state and Maine as a free state. In the rest of the Louisiana Purchase territory north of the parallel 36°30', slavery should be prohibited. Early in 1820 Congress accepted this compromise, and President Monroe signed it in March.

At the time, the arrangement satisfied the South because Missouri was to be a slave state. Also, it was generally believed that cotton could not be grown successfully north of 36°30'. The North accepted the compromise because it banned slavery from most of the Louisiana Purchase. Also, the Northerners felt the Compromise had established the right of Congress to determine the status of slavery in the territories. But time would show that the Missouri Compromise had not really solved the constitutional issue of slavery, and it had not even touched on the moral aspects of the question. To be sure, it had calmed the political waters for the time being. But John Quincy Adams warned that "the present question is a mere preamble — a title-page to a great, tragic volume."

The 1824 election is a sectional contest. Though all the candidates in 1824 still called themselves Republicans, it was clear that the one-party era had come to a close. The Republican caucus went through the motions of selecting a candidate — William H. Crawford of Georgia, Monroe's Secretary of the Treasury. Southern Republicans approved this choice, but other sections of the country were strongly opposed to Crawford. New England Republicans decided to back John Quincy Adams, Monroe's distinguished Secretary of State. The West produced two candidates. Henry Clay of Kentucky spoke out for the American System and nationalism. The Tennessee legislature nominated Andrew Jackson, hero of New Orleans and idol of the frontier.

When the electoral votes were counted, Jackson led with 99 votes from Pennsylvania, the Carolinas, and the West. Adams ran second with 84, mostly from New England and New York. Crawford, handicapped by a serious illness, came in third with 41, while Clay got only 37. Since no candidate had a majority of the electoral votes, the selection of a President rested with the House of Representatives.[4] Under

[4] There was no contest over the vice-presidency. John C. Calhoun had run on both the Jackson and Adams tickets, and he received a majority of the electoral votes for Vice-President.

the Twelfth Amendment, House members were to vote by states on the three highest candidates.

Adams is chosen to be President. Although out of the running for the presidency, Henry Clay as Speaker of the House could aid any one of the three candidates. Clay opposed Jackson because they were political rivals in the West and because he thought that Jackson lacked political experience. Though Clay and Adams were unlike in background and personality, they agreed on many of the issues of the day. Both favored a protective tariff, internal improvements, and the national bank. Clay may also have hoped that the New Englander would serve only one term and leave the way clear for Clay to run in 1828. At any rate, Clay gave his support to Adams. In February, 1825, the House elected John Quincy Adams President.

▶ CHECK-UP

1. Explain the rise of sectional views in the Northeast, South, and West with respect to protective tariffs, internal improvements, and western expansion.

2. What were the causes of the Panic of 1819? The results? Why did this panic cause Westerners to distrust the United States Bank?

3. Why did Missouri's request for statehood lead to controversy? What was the Tallmadge amendment? Why was it passed in the House but not in the Senate?

4. What were the terms of the Missouri Compromise? Why was the compromise approved in the North? In the South?

5. What men were presidential candidates in 1824? Why did Clay help Adams win?

· ·

5 *Bad Feeling Mars the Adams Administration*

A "corrupt bargain" is charged. Five days after Adams was chosen President, he announced the appointment of Henry Clay as Secretary of State. Immediately, Jackson's supporters charged the two men with making a "corrupt bargain." Historians doubt that Adams, the soul of honesty, promised a Cabinet post to get Clay's support in the House. But Clay's selection as Secretary of State — even before Adams himself had been inaugurated — seemed to many people to be proof of "the disgraceful traffic of Congressional votes for executive office." Jackson and his followers began calling Clay "the Judas of the West." They felt that because Jackson had received more electoral and popular votes than any other candidate, the House should have elected him. Many of them said Adams was "President by mistake."

These charges, which were to echo throughout Adams' administration, were a source of embarrassment to the cold, unbending President. While Adams was an extremely able man, he lacked the charm of Clay, the glamour of Jackson, and the political skill of Jefferson. He refused to use his control over government positions to reward his friends or punish his political enemies. When the next election came around, Adams found few people willing to work for him. By contrast, Jackson and his supporters had never stopped campaigning. The Tennessee legislature nominated Jackson again in 1825, and for the next three years he campaigned against Adams.

Adams' policies irritate Congress. Adams tried to ignore the sectional bitterness that had built up during his years as Secretary of State. He intended to be a strong, nationalistic President. Adams' first message to Congress was an extraordinary document. He called upon Congress to encourage farming and manufacturing; to construct roads and canals and improve the nation's harbors; and to build up the state militias and the army and navy. President Adams also asked Congress to promote the arts and sciences, establish a national university, standardize weights and measures, and build astronomical observatories, which he called "light-houses of the skies." Congress was amused but not impressed. It acted on few of these recommendations and even voted down an internal-improvements measure.

Average Rates on
Dutiable Imports

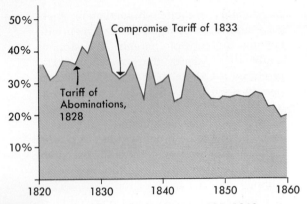

Compromise Tariff of 1833

Tariff of
Abominations,
1828

50%
40%
30%
20%
10%

1820   1830   1840   1850   1860

CHANGES IN THE TARIFF, 1821–1860

Tariff rates on dutiable imports reached a peak after the passage of the Tariff of Abominations and then began an uneven decline. Compare the average rate in 1830 with that of 1860.

Adams had been an outstanding Secretary of State; yet Congress rejected the foreign policy proposals he made as President. Both the United States and Great Britain were invited to a conference of South American republics at Panama. Adams was anxious to accept the invitation, for he saw a chance to increase American trade with South America. Congress, however, was slow to act. Southerners argued that the United States should not take part in a conference that included "men of color." Clay's enemies actually accused him of forging the invitation in the State Department. After three months of this kind of debate, Congress approved the appointment of two delegates. But one delegate died on the way to Panama, and the other failed to reach the conference before it adjourned.

A tariff dispute arises. More serious was the wrangling in Congress over the tariff. In spite of strong protests from southern planters and New England shippers, a new tariff act in 1824 gave more protection to manufacturers. Encouraged by this success, factory owners each year increased their demands for tariff protection. In 1827 congressmen from manufacturing states proposed a measure to raise rates on woolen goods as well as on iron, flax, hemp, cotton, and glass. It passed the House, but the vote in the Senate was a tie. Vice-President Cal-

houn cast the deciding vote against the measure. Thomas Cooper, president of South Carolina College, voiced the rising anger of Southerners:

> There is not a petty manufacturer in the Union, from the owner of a spinning factory to the maker of a hobnail . . . , who is not pressing forward to the plunder; and who may not be expected to worry Congress with petitions, memorials, and querulous statements for permission to put his hand into the planter's pocket.

The "Tariff of Abominations" pleases nobody. As the election of 1828 drew near, Jackson's backers looked around for some way to discredit Adams. The tariff issue seemed to offer a good opportunity. They proposed a tariff measure which would give a high degree of protection to manufacturers. This benefit would be offset, however, by the fact that the measure would also raise duties on raw materials, such as wool, which New England manufacturers needed to import. Jackson's supporters hoped that because the price for protection would be too high to pay, many northern votes would be cast against the bill. They further expected that these northern votes combined with solid southern opposition would defeat the tariff bill. The blame for this defeat could then be placed upon the New Englanders and their leader, Adams. John Randolph quite rightly charged that the bill was concerned with "manufactures of no sort, but the manufacturing of a President of the United States."

This elaborate scheme failed. Distasteful as the bill was to New Englanders, enough of their congressmen voted for the so-called "Tariff of Abominations" so that it passed in both houses. Adams signed the bill in May, 1828. Daniel Webster later explained: "Its enemies spiced it with whatsoever they thought would make it distasteful; its friends took it, drugged as it was."

The South protests the new tariff. The "Tariff of Abominations" provoked violent objections in the South. In Charleston, South Carolina, flags were flown at half-mast. Southerners talked openly about refusing to obey the tariff law and urged a boycott against products from the North.

The most impressive protest against the new tariff was written secretly by Vice-President Calhoun. In his unsigned *Exposition and Protest,* approved by a committee of the South Carolina legislature, Calhoun attacked the tariff as "unconstitutional, unequal, and oppressive." It was unconstitutional, he said, because it was not meant to raise revenue but to protect one field of industry at the expense of others. It was unequal and oppressive because the South, which purchased most of its manufactured articles from Europe, was the chief victim.

Calhoun went on to say that the remedy for such a situation lay in state action. He argued that the Union was a compact, or agreement, among sovereign states; and the states therefore had the right to judge whether this compact had been broken. If a state believed that an act of Congress was unconstitutional, a convention representing the people of that state should be assembled. If this convention found the federal government guilty of an unconstitutional act that would justify "the interposition of the state to protect its rights," the convention might declare the act "null and void within the limit of the state." The *Exposition and Protest* led to no action, however, until 1832 when South Carolina tried to declare new tariff proposals null and void (page 245).

New political parties take shape. During the unhappy Adams administration the Republicans made no pretense of being a united party. Some Republicans supported Adams and Clay, and the others followed Jackson. By 1828 this division had hardened into two distinct political parties. The Adams-Clay men called themselves *National Republicans,* because they favored a nationalistic program. Jackson's followers took the name *Democratic Republicans,* which soon became shortened to *Democrats.* In addition to his large personal following in the West, Jackson had the support of (1) Calhoun and Crawford in the South and (2) many of the wage earners and factory workers in the Northeast. The Jackson group talked states' rights in the South and promised greater opportunity for the ordinary citizen in the West and Northeast. In all sections of the country, Jackson supporters opposed Adams and Clay.

Jackson leads the Democrats to victory. Jackson and Adams tangled again in the presidential election of 1828. The Democrats, however, were much better organized than Adams' forces and had a long head start. As a result, Jackson won the contest, carrying Pennsylvania and all the states west of the Alleghenies and south of the Potomac. In the largest popular vote yet cast, he received nearly 650,000 as against about 500,000 for Adams. Calhoun was re-elected to the vice-presidency.

▶ CHECK-UP

1. Was Adams successful in reducing sectional bitterness? Why? How did Jackson supporters seek to use the tariff issue to discredit the President?

2. How did Calhoun support his contention that the Tariff of Abominations was "unconstitutional, unequal, and oppressive"? What remedy did he advocate?

3. What two political parties had evolved by 1828? How did Jackson enlist support in the Northeast and South as well as the West?

• •

Clinching the Main Ideas in Chapter 10

Nationalism in the postwar years took many forms and influenced many aspects of American life. National pride in wartime victories helped kill the Federalist Party and bring about a one-party "Era of Good Feelings." Pride in American development helped secure congressional approval of a protective tariff, a second national bank, and construction of the National Road. Nationalism underlay most of John Marshall's court decisions, and led to the issuing of the Monroe Doctrine. The rapid growth of the West also strengthened national pride.

Sectional rivalry, however, brought an end to the Era of Good Feelings. Conflict between the economic interests of the different regions of the country had much to do with the rising tide of sectionalism. Manufacturing interests in the Northeast demanded tariff protection; the West called for internal improvements; and the South opposed both, wanting to go its own way with slavery and cotton. Economic differences between northeastern financiers and western farmers came to the surface in the Panic of 1819. More important, the slavery issue set the North against the South. While the Missouri Compromise preserved the balance between slave and free states, it failed to resolve the basic differences between North and South.

In the presidential election of 1824, each of the sections tended to promote its own candidate. Though Jackson had the most votes, he lacked a majority; and John Quincy Adams was chosen President in the House of Representatives. His administration was plagued by the "corrupt bargain" charge and by quarrels with Congress that came to a head in 1828 with the Tariff of Abominations. That same year Adams was decisively beaten by Andrew Jackson, his rival for the presidency. Jackson, too, would find it necessary to cope with the forces of nationalism and sectionalism.

Chapter Review

Terms to Understand

1. Era of Good Feeling
2. *McCullough v. Maryland*
3. Dartmouth College case
4. Rush-Bagot Agreement
5. *Gibbons v. Ogden*
6. Monroe Doctrine
7. American System
8. Tallmadge amendment
9. internal improvements
10. Missouri Compromise
11. Tariff of Abominations
12. Panic of 1819
13. nationalism
14. sectionalism

What Do You Think?

1. What are the advantages and disadvantages of a compromise (for example, the Missouri Compromise) as the solution to a problem? Why are compromises necessary in a democracy?

2. Which groups were helped, and which were hurt, by the large issue of bank notes by state banks after 1811?

3. Was Adams wise in opposing joint British-American action to prevent European powers from thwarting independence movements in Spain's American colonies? Why?

4. Why was the Erie Canal the most successful of the many inland waterways constructed during the canal era?

5. Following the Panic of 1819, people in the West referred to the United States Bank as "the Monster." Why?

6. According to John Randolph, the 1828 tariff bill was concerned only with "the manufacturing of a President of the United States." What did he mean?

Using Your Knowledge of History

1. Define *nationalism* and *sectionalism*. List and briefly explain three policies or courses of action during the period 1800–1830 that reflect each of these ways of looking at things. A committee could work on this project.

2. Between 1800 and 1830 the economic interests of the Northeast, South, and West changed. Write two newspaper editorials, dated ten or fifteen years apart, dealing with a persistent issue such as the tariff. The policy advocated with respect to the given issue would be different in the two editorials.

3. During this period, a goal of American foreign policy was to reduce the influence of foreign powers in the Western Hemisphere. List and explain five important steps taken to further this goal.

4. Give a report entitled "Why Spain's American Colonies Revolted During the Early 1800's."

Extending Your Knowledge of History

Two of the best books on this period are *The Era of Good Feelings* and *The Awakening of American Nationalism* by the Englishman George Dangerfield. An interesting view of political developments as seen from the White House is recorded in *The Diary of John Quincy Adams*, edited by Allan Nevins. Dexter Perkins' *A History of the Monroe Doctrine* describes foreign policy during the 1820's. An interesting account of the westward movement after the War of 1812 can be found in Robert E. Riegel's *America Moves West*. A. F. Harlow writes about the canal craze in *Old Towpaths*.

CHAPTER 11

Andrew Jackson Dominates the Political Scene

Jackson's inaugural reception

Under our free institutions, I am sure the people in every part of the United States are too enlightened not to understand their own rights and interests, and to detect and defeat every effort to gain undue advantages over them.

ANDREW JACKSON'S FAREWELL ADDRESS, 1837

1828–1844

In the words quoted above, President Jackson summarized his faith in the good sense of the American people. During his eight years in the White House, Jackson was a colorful, vigorous, and controversial leader. While the Democrats idolized him, the National Republicans disliked him intensely. But Jackson's political strength rested on the solid support of the people. With the enthusiastic backing of the voters, Jacksonian politicians succeeded in carrying out a number of democratic reforms.

Throughout the Jacksonian Era — covering the administrations of Jackson and Martin Van Buren, his hand-picked successor — the forces of sectionalism and nationalism were in constant conflict. A native-born Southerner, Jackson sympathized with the states' rights argument, and he shared many of the sectional feelings of the West. Yet neither Jackson nor Van Buren, a New Yorker, endangered the welfare of the Union by yielding to extreme sectional demands. When South Carolinians tried to nullify a tariff act, Jackson asserted the federal government's power. And when he detected what he thought were special privileges for the second United States Bank, he refused to renew its charter. Sectionalism made some headway in the 1830's, but the course of national reform managed to hold it in check.

235

1 *Democracy Spreads During the Jacksonian Era*

Jacksonian democracy draws upon Jefferson's political philosophy. In the 1790's, Jefferson and his followers had promised the American people a share in the federal government. They had believed that more people should have the right to vote, and they respected the political wisdom of humble men, particularly the farmers. Yet, once in office, the Republicans had accomplished little in this direction. It remained for the followers of Andrew Jackson, who organized themselves as the Democratic Party in the late 1820's, to carry out the pledges of the Jeffersonians.

Coming from humble origins himself, Jackson believed in opening up new opportunities — educational, economic, and political — to the American people. He was not directly responsible for all of the sweeping changes made during the Jacksonian Era. Indeed one historian has said: "Jackson himself was a product, rather than the creator, of the new democratic spirit, for he rode into power on a tide of forces that had been gathering strength for more than a decade and which he had done little or nothing to bring into being." But Jackson was genuinely sympathetic with the effort to get rid of "special privilege" in American life. This democratic upsurge rested on the Jeffersonian belief in the worth of the individual. To this extent Jacksonian democracy was derived from Thomas Jefferson's political philosophy.

The suffrage is broadened. Perhaps the most important political change in the Jacksonian Era was the extension of the right to vote. The Constitution permitted each state to set its own voting restrictions. Every one of the thirteen original states had adopted property and religious qualifications for their voters, and all except New Jersey had limited the suffrage to men.[1] But the new western states that were admitted in the early 1800's generally permitted all free men to vote.

This trend worried many well-to-do Easterners, for it seemed to them, as Daniel Webster put it, "to be the part of political wisdom to found government on property." Yet Webster and his colleagues could do little to halt the demand for wider suffrage in the older states. During the next two decades so many states liberalized their voting requirements that by 1840 practically all free white men in the country could vote. Whereas only 350,000 persons had voted in the presidential election of 1824, more than a million went to the polls in 1828, and more than two million voted in 1840.

Other political changes are introduced. Other democratic political changes took place during these same years. For the first time men could run for office without having to meet property qualifications. More offices were made elective, and the power of the state legislatures to appoint judges and other local officials was restricted. In some states the governors, who had been given no veto power in the original state constitutions, were now entrusted with this weapon. There was even criticism of the electoral college. In one of his messages to Congress, Jackson suggested that the Constitution be amended to allow for direct popular election of the President and Vice-President. Nothing came of this bold suggestion. But the widening of the suffrage and the increasing responsibility of the

[1] New Jersey deprived women of the right to vote in 1807. Not until 1920 were American women permitted to vote in federal elections.

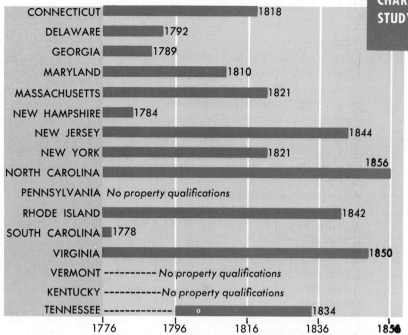

ABOLITION OF PROPERTY QUALIFICATIONS FOR VOTING

The date given in the chart indicates when the state abolished property qualifications for voting. (In some states, tax paying became an alternative.) After Tennessee, in 1796, no state entered the Union with property qualifications for voting.

State	Year
CONNECTICUT	1818
DELAWARE	1792
GEORGIA	1789
MARYLAND	1810
MASSACHUSETTS	1821
NEW HAMPSHIRE	1784
NEW JERSEY	1844
NEW YORK	1821
NORTH CAROLINA	1856
PENNSYLVANIA	No property qualifications
RHODE ISLAND	1842
SOUTH CAROLINA	1778
VIRGINIA	1850
VERMONT	No property qualifications
KENTUCKY	No property qualifications
TENNESSEE	1834

1776   1796   1816   1836   1856

voters were important political changes in the Jacksonian Era.

Political parties seek the support of the people. As more and more people took part in elections, the political parties showed increased interest in winning popular support. The newly organized Democratic Party took the lead. During the Adams administration, for example, the Democrats held community barbecues, parades, and frontier social gatherings. Moreover, they organized state and local branches of the Democratic Party and appointed political managers who were responsible for getting the voters to the polls. The Jackson men also circulated handbills and party newspapers to build up interest in campaigns. This new approach to the voters was so successful that in time the Democrats' opponents had to imitate them. Elections thus took on many features that are still familiar today.

The holding of party conventions to nominate candidates also reflected the rising democratic spirit. Presidential candidates had usually been selected by congressional caucuses (page 175). But in the 1830's the party nominating convention made its appearance. It was the brain child of an obscure third party, the Anti-Masons. The members of this party opposed secret societies and prided themselves on conducting open meetings. To stress their point of view, the Anti-Masons held a national convention in Baltimore in 1831 at which they selected a candidate for the presidency. They also adopted a platform, or set of principles in which they believed. Not to be outdone by this bid for popular support, the Democrats and the National Republicans also held conventions. Since then, the major parties have always held national nominating conventions and have usually adopted party platforms as well.

Workingmen seek to improve their position. The laborers and artisans in the eastern states were quick to use their newly won political power. They took a keen interest not only in the selection of a President but also in choosing congressmen and state and local officials. They banded together in Workingmen's Parties, the first of which was established in Philadelphia in 1828. These parties called for publicly supported schools, shorter hours, abolition of compulsory militia duty, and revision of the laws that imprisoned debtors. The Workingmen's Parties did succeed in electing some congressmen. They also influenced state legislatures to provide for tax-supported schools, revise the debtor laws, and reorganize the state militias. In addition, some laws were passed to improve working conditions in factories.

The political activity of the Workingmen's Parties alarmed some property owners. But it was not opposition from others so much as quarrels among themselves that stunted the growth of the Workingmen's Parties. They were further weakened when the Democratic Party began to weave the demands of the workingmen into its own platforms. This accounts for the fact that many laborers and artisans supported Jackson and Van Buren.

Jackson's inauguration is a democratic triumph. When he took the oath of office in March, 1829, Jackson was 61 years old and racked by a consumptive cough and painful headaches. But he was the hero of the common people, and his inauguration was the climax of their efforts at political reform throughout the 1820's. Hundreds of enthusiastic Democrats traveled to Washington to be on hand for the ceremonies. They cheered wildly after the President delivered his brief inaugural speech from the steps of the Capitol, though most of them could hear only a few words. Then they trailed him back to the White House for one of the most boisterous presidential receptions ever held. Men, women, and children jammed their way into the East Room, climbed upon the damask-covered chairs and sofas, and elbowed each other out of the way to catch a glimpse of their idol. Only after White House servants placed huge tubs of punch on the lawn did the unruly crowd leave the ruined parlors. "It was the People's Day, and the People's President," declared one happy Democrat.

Disgruntled opponents, however, observed that "the reign of King 'Mob' seemed triumphant." Daniel Webster noted: "People have come five hundred miles to see General Jackson, and they really seem to think that the country is rescued from some dreadful danger." He went on to point out that the new President's "friends have no common principle — they are held together by no common tie." To Webster it seemed extremely unlikely that the Democratic coalition — the groups which had joined together to put Andrew Jackson in the White House — would be able to keep him there for very long.

▶ CHECK-UP

1. What basic beliefs were reflected in Jacksonian democracy? What political changes gave the people greater control over their government? How did political parties seek to arouse greater interest and participation in politics?

2. What changes were sought by Workingmen's Parties? How successful were these parties? Explain.

2 Jackson Seeks to Unite His Followers

Sectional demands confront Jackson. Had the President been a less skillful politician, his winning coalition of 1828 might indeed have been smashed by his opponents in the election of 1832. Jackson headed a shaky political alliance of small farmers, southern planters, small businessmen, and artisans. There was "no common principle," as Webster noted, "no common tie" to hold these people together. The Democrats were united only by Jackson's personal appeal and their expectation that somehow the President would meet their demands.

In the West the small farmers and urban wage earners who voted for Jackson were bitter foes of the second national bank (page 216). They wanted a cheap and plentiful currency that would make it easier for them to pay their debts. But the Bank of the United States kept the currency on a sound basis, and this in turn forced state banks to keep their notes on a sound footing. Westerners, therefore, wanted Jackson to destroy the national bank. In addition, they hoped Jackson would provide internal improvements and cheap land.

The overwhelming concern of southern planters was the tariff. Angered by the Tariff of Abominations (page 232), they had managed to hold their tempers and vote for the Democratic ticket in 1828.

(Continued on page 240)

Andrew Jackson

[1767–1845]

Andrew Jackson's parents were Scotch-Irish immigrants who settled on the South Carolina frontier in the 1760's. Shortly before Andrew's birth, his father was killed by Indians. While still very young, the boy volunteered for service in the Revolutionary Army. His two brothers died in the war, and Andrew was imprisoned by the British. His mother managed to secure his release, but soon afterwards she died while nursing colonial soldiers in Charleston. Thus, Andrew Jackson found himself alone in the world at the age of fourteen.

Jackson tried farming on the frontier and school teaching before reading law in Charleston. Then in 1788 he packed his belongings and followed the Richmond Road west through the Cumberland Gap into Tennessee. There he settled in the village of Nashville, where he met Rachel Donelson Robards, a vivacious, pious woman who was separated from her husband. When word reached Nashville that Robards had divorced his wife, Rachel and Andrew Jackson were married. Two years later they learned that the divorce had only just been granted. The Jacksons promptly remarried, and no one at the time thought much of the legal confusion.

Andrew Jackson built a successful law practice in Tennessee and also took an interest in land speculation. In the 1790's he purchased land outside Nashville, where he ran a cotton plantation with slave labor, operated a small store, and eventually built a handsome house called "The Hermitage." Although most of Jackson's social and business relations were with the upper classes, his own experiences made him sympathetic to the needs of small farmers and wage earners. In the late 1790's, Jackson was plunged into debt when a Philadelphia merchant, from whom he had accepted notes for money owed to him, went bankrupt. Having worked his way out of that difficulty, he, like other western land speculators, was hurt by the Panic of 1819. As a result, Jackson was suspicious of paper money and hostile toward the national bank.

Jackson's Indian campaigns and his victory at New Orleans in the War of 1812 made him a national hero. But until the 1820's he had no great interest in politics. Then, his strong showing in the presidential election of 1824, and the "Corrupt Bargain" which he felt unfairly gave the prize to John Quincy Adams, helped whet Jackson's appetite. He worked hard for his sweeping victory in 1828. Yet his joy turned to sorrow a few weeks later, when his wife fell sick and died. Jackson was convinced that the cruel campaign rumors had caused Rachel's death.

Though not a learned man, Jackson was intelligent and shrewd, and had a knack for expressing his views in a way that ordinary persons could easily understand. As President, he himself prepared rough drafts of all major state papers, but he depended on advisers and Cabinet members to polish the language. Jackson was at the height of his popularity in the early years of his second administration. Even Harvard College, much to the chagrin of alumnus John Quincy Adams, gave Jackson an honorary degree in 1833. He spent his last years at the Hermitage, supervising the plantation, brooding over the problem of slavery, following the political fortunes of his protégé Van Buren, and paying daily visits to the grave of his wife.

After all, Calhoun was going to be Jackson's Vice-President, and many Southerners expected the new President to look to the experienced South Carolinian for advice. Moreover, Jackson himself had come from Carolina and owned a plantation in Tennessee. It was assumed, therefore, that he shared the planters' desire for a lower tariff and would act at once to repeal the Tariff of Abominations.

The urban vote for Jackson came largely from workingmen in the Northeast, where industry was by now firmly established. Small businessmen and some proprietors of state banks also voted for Jackson, because they wanted to see the Bank of the United States replaced by state banks. Many of Jackson's supporters in the Northeast hoped that he would follow the suggestions of the Workingmen's Parties for economic and social reforms.

The spoils system unites the Democrats. Jackson's supporters were divided on many crucial problems, but they all expected to share in government patronage. The rewarding of loyal party workers with government jobs was a familiar practice on both the national and state level. But since Jackson's followers had been kept out of government posts while John Quincy Adams was President, the pressure for jobs became tremendous after the election of 1828. Jackson sincerely believed that rotation in office — the appointment of new men to government jobs by the incoming President — was a healthy thing. In addition, being a man of deep loyalties, he wanted to satisfy as many of the job-seekers as possible. By turning out Adams' appointees, Jackson provided jobs for hard-working Democrats and also brought average citizens into the government as his campaign managers had promised. Other Presidents had said little concerning their patronage problems, but Jackson felt no reluctance about expressing his views. In a message to Congress the President said:

> The duties of all public officers are, or at least admit of being made, so plain and simple that men of intelligence may readily qualify themselves for their performance; and I can not but believe that more is lost by the long continuance of men in office than is generally to be gained by their experience. . . . In a country where offices are created solely for the benefit of the people, no one man has any more intrinsic right to official station than another.

Jackson was not a corrupt spoilsman. Like Jefferson, he removed only about one sixth of all the government officeholders. But since Jackson settled most of his patronage problems during the first year and a half of his administration, the changes seemed quite abrupt at the time. Democratic Party workers and newspaper editors who landed government jobs naturally applauded the President. But the Adams-Clay-Webster faction accused him of packing the federal offices with uncouth frontiersmen who could neither read nor write. During a Senate debate in 1832, a New Yorker defended the Democrats' patronage policy in these words:

> If they are defeated, they expect to retire from office. If they are successful, they claim, as a matter of right, the advantages of success. They see nothing wrong in the rule that to the *victor* belongs the spoils of the *enemy.*

Henceforth, the practice of rotation in office was known as the *spoils system.*

Cabinet appointments are another form of patronage. In addition to the spoils system, Jackson used Cabinet appointments to help hold the Democratic factions together. The choicest position, Secretary of State, went to Martin Van Buren, manager of the northern Jacksonians in the 1828 election. Calhoun, the southern manager, had been elected Vice-President, but Jackson also allowed him to name three Southerners to Cabinet posts. The remaining two positions went to Westerners, one of whom was Jackson's close friend, Senator John H. Eaton of Tennessee.

The Cabinet members tended to speak for the sections they represented, and they usually gave conflicting advice to the President. As a result, Jackson often sought the opinions of old political friends like Amos Kendall of Kentucky and William B. Lewis of Tennessee. These men held only minor government positions. But they were shrewd politicians who helped Jackson determine policy, interpret public opinion, and distribute government jobs. They met at the White House, often entering by the kitchen door to avoid publicity. They soon became known as the "kitchen cabinet."

Toward the end of Jackson's first term he reorganized his official Cabinet. This time he appointed members according to their political opinions, regardless of the section of the country from which they came. This idea of a Cabinet that agreed on policy was another new political development of the Jacksonian Era. It was a far cry from Washington's attempt to keep the feuding Jefferson and Hamilton in the same Cabinet.

Jackson's foreign policy pleases all the Democrats. His wise use of patronage helped Jackson hold the various factions of the party together. So too did his strongly nationalistic foreign policy. Ever since 1783, American ships had been either partially or completely excluded from the profitable British West Indian trade (page 124). Discovering that Britain would make concessions only if an American law discriminating against British trade was removed, Jackson obtained the necessary authority from Congress. He then made the offer to admit British ships sailing from the West Indies to the United States if West Indian ports were opened to American ships. Great Britain accepted this offer, but still denied to American ships the right to trade between the West Indies and Britain.

Jackson also worked out treaties with European countries to settle damage claims dating back to the Napoleonic Wars. One of these agreements was made with France in 1831. When the French failed to pay the first installment, Jackson angrily accused them of lack of good faith and threatened to take action. The French broke off diplomatic relations and demanded an apology. The President refused to apologize, but eventually he relented to the point of saying that "any intention to menace or insult the government of France" was "unfounded." Thereupon the quarrel was resolved, and soon French payments flowed with regularity into the American treasury.

▶ CHECK-UP

1. What three groups were included in the alliance which elected Jackson President? What changes were most desired by each?

2. What was the spoils system? How did it help to unite the Democrats? What principle was reflected in Jackson's appointments to his first Cabinet? In his reorganization of the Cabinet? What was the "kitchen cabinet"?

3. What negotiations did Jackson carry on with Britain and France? What was the outcome in each case?

. . . .

3 *Jackson Copes with the Demands of the West and the South*

Western Jacksonians want a liberal land policy. Soon after he took office, President Jackson received demands from both the West and the South. Jackson's western supporters, for example, were eager to secure changes in the government land policy. One of their spokesmen, Senator Thomas Hart Benton of Missouri, proposed a measure to aid "squatters" — settlers living on public land to which they had no legal title. His bill would allow actual settlers to make the first bid on land which they had cleared and were cultivating. Benton also asked for a gradual reduction in the price of land sold by the government.

New England manufacturers opposed these changes in land policy, for they feared that it would drain population from their region by encouraging workers to move west. In December, 1829, therefore, Senator Foot of Connecticut introduced a resolution to restrict temporarily the sale of public lands. Benton delivered a sharp reply. He was supported by Senator Robert Y. Hayne of South Carolina, who spoke for southern Jacksonians. Arguing that it was

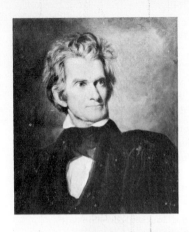

Three notable figures — Calhoun, Webster, and Clay — dominated Congress in the first half of the 1800's. South Carolina's John Calhoun (left) championed states' rights, while Daniel Webster (below) of New Hampshire defended the Union. Henry Clay (right) of Kentucky tried to satisfy sectionalist interests within the nationalist American System.

an abuse of federal power to cut off land sales, Hayne insisted that each state had the right to make its own decision. This was essentially the same position that Calhoun had taken in the South Carolina *Exposition and Protest* (page 233). Hayne concluded his speech by charging that eastern manufacturers were trying to rob the West of settlers just as they had robbed the South of its wealth through high tariffs.

Webster debates the nature of the Union. At this point Senator Daniel Webster of Massachusetts joined the debate. His concern was not with land policy but rather with the dangers of sectionalism. In January, 1830, he delivered his answer to the "South Carolina doctrine" of states' rights. Webster's eloquent rolling phrases and dra-

matic oratory thrilled the tightly packed Senate gallery. The federal government, asserted Webster, was not merely an instrument for carrying out the will of the states. "It is, sir, the people's constitution, the people's government; made for the people, made by the people, and answerable to the people." Within the limits of the powers granted in the Constitution, he said, the federal government must be the supreme authority. Otherwise, the Union would be no more than "a rope of sand." To Webster that would be a tragedy, for,

It is to that Union we owe our safety at home and our consideration and dignity abroad. It is to that Union that we are chiefly indebted for whatever makes us most proud of our country. . . . It has been to us all a copious fountain of national, social, and personal happiness. I have not allowed myself, sir, to look beyond the Union, to see what might lie hidden in the dark recess behind. I have not coolly weighed the chances of preserving liberty when the bonds that unite us together shall be broken asunder. I have not accustomed myself to hang over the precipice of disunion, to see whether, with my short sight, I can fathom the depth of the abyss below. . . . . While the Union lasts, we have high, exciting, gratifying prospects spread out before us, for us and our children. Beyond that, I seek not to penetrate the veil. God grant that in my day, at least, that curtain may not rise. God grant that, on my vision, never may be opened what lies behind.

Webster closed with the famous plea for "Liberty *and* Union, now and forever, one and inseparable."

Congress alters the land policy. This stirring defense of the federal union temporarily quieted the supporters of states' rights in the Senate, which then returned to its consideration of land policy. Congress eventually passed a measure permitting squatters to buy, for the actual cost of a survey, the lands they were living on and cultivating. Though the price of land was not reduced, Jackson indicated that he would favor such a step when government income no longer depended on land sales.

Jackson takes a stand on internal improvements. The western supporters of Jackson were also anxious to secure federal funds for internal-improvement projects. Uncertain as to Jackson's attitude toward such measures, they proposed construction of a road from Maysville to Lexington, Kentucky, at federal expense. The Westerners argued that it would serve a national purpose as a post road. Much to their dismay, Jackson vetoed the Maysville Road Bill. It was "a measure of a purely local character," he said, and therefore the road ought to be built with state funds. If Congress favored the use of federal funds for state internal improvements, Jackson declared, it should amend the Constitution to that effect.

Jackson's bold veto message cost him some support in the West, but he made up for the loss in several ways. During the rest of his term in office he approved a number of projects that involved two or more states. He also poured a large amount of government money into internal improvements in the federal territories. In fact, Jackson spent almost twice as much money on internal improvements as had President Adams, who had been a strong backer of Clay's American System. Furthermore, Jackson's Indian policy delighted the Westerners and helped them to forget the Maysville veto.

Jackson supports a harsh Indian policy. As a former Indian fighter, Jackson was sympathetic with the southern and western demand that the Indians be forced to move beyond the Mississippi River. The task of removing the Indians to the Louisiana Territory had been started by Jefferson but had proceeded slowly. By the 1830's white men were greedily eyeing the fertile land held by Indian tribes (map, page 199).

Several states decided to take matters into their own hands. Georgia, for example, laid claim to all the Cherokee lands within the state boundaries, even though the Indians held title to the land by federal treaties. The Cherokee had adopted the white man's way of life — cultivating their fields, operating schools, and even publishing a newspaper, the *Cherokee Phoenix*. Threatened with the loss of their lands, these Indians appealed to the United States Supreme Court. In the case of *Worcester v. Georgia* (1832), John Marshall ruled that Georgia had no jurisdiction in Cherokee territory. But the Chief Justice failed to reckon with Jackson. The President is supposed to have said, "John Marshall has made his decision; now let him enforce it." Of course, the Supreme Court had no power to enforce its ruling. When Jackson refused to use federal troops to protect the Cherokee tribes, the state militia hustled the Indians out of Georgia.

In 1834 Jackson persuaded Congress to establish an Indian Territory in what is now Oklahoma. He sent agents among the Indians to negotiate hundreds of "evacuation treaties" by which the tribes were paid to surrender their ancestral lands and move west. Many of them went peacefully, but in Florida it took a full-scale war to uproot the Seminole Indians. Despite its harshness, most Southerners and Westerners thoroughly approved of Jackson's Indian policy, since it opened to settlers thousands of square miles of fertile land.

Jackson is challenged on the issue of states' rights. The President's southern supporters liked his Indian policy and the Maysville veto, but they were less satisfied on the question of tariff rates. The Southerners waited impatiently to learn if the President would heed the warning about the tariff which had been given in the *Exposition and Protest.*

In the spring of 1830, while southern leaders were still stirred by the Webster-Hayne debate, they tried to commit Jackson to a states' rights policy. At a Democratic dinner marking the anniversary of Jefferson's birth, President Jackson was the guest of honor. After listening to lavish praise of Jefferson's defense of the states against the central government, Jackson was called on to deliver a toast. He rose to his full height of over six feet and, looking directly at John C. Calhoun, said: "Our Federal Union — it must be preserved!" Unmoved, Calhoun responded: "The Union — next to our liberty, the most dear!" After a pause, he added, "May we always remember that it can only be preserved by respecting the rights of the states and distributing equally the benefits and burdens of the Union."

Calhoun and Van Buren maneuver for position. Jackson's forthright defense of "our Federal Union" jolted the Southerners. Yet they waited throughout 1830 and 1831 to see whether Vice-President Calhoun or Secretary of State Van Buren would become Jackson's most influential adviser. The struggle between these two ambitious politicians was the talk of the capital. Van Buren called Jackson's attention to a letter revealing that Calhoun had wanted to punish Jackson for his raid into Florida during Monroe's administration (page 219). The President now interpreted this as a personal affront and referred darkly to the "insincerity" of his Vice-President.

Van Buren also used a controversy over the wife of a Cabinet officer to widen the breach between Jackson and Calhoun. Peggy O'Neale Timberlake, the attractive daughter of a Washington tavern keeper, had been admired by Senator John Eaton (page 240) before her husband died aboard a ship in the Mediterranean. Eaton wanted to marry the widow Timberlake but, knowing he would be included in Jackson's Cabinet, he consulted the President-elect. Jackson was convinced that the rumors about Peggy's past were as baseless as those which had hurt his own wife (page 239), and the marriage took place. Much to Jackson's surprise, however, Washington society refused to accept Mrs. Peggy Eaton. The leader of the social boycott was none other than Mrs. John C. Calhoun. Following her lead were the wives of the Cabinet officials appointed by Jackson on Calhoun's advice. Peggy's only public champion was the dapper widower Martin Van Buren.

The social tempest over Peggy Eaton perplexed and angered Jackson. When asked for advice, Van Buren suggested that both he and Secretary of War Eaton resign from the Cabinet. This would make it necessary for the three embarrassed Calhoun men to resign also. Jackson could then reorganize his official family, ridding himself of the undesirable Southerners. This is exactly what happened in the spring of 1831. Eaton was named governor of Florida Territory, and Van Buren was appointed minister to Great Britain. Van Buren's appointment required Senate approval, and since the vote was a tie, Calhoun (as presiding officer of the Senate) had the pleasure of blocking it. This petty action prompted Senator Thomas Hart Benton to remark that the Senate had "broken a minister and elected a Vice-President." He was quite right, for Van Buren had obviously become Jackson's closest adviser. Van Buren, not Calhoun, won the contest; and to him went the spoils — the vice-presidency in 1832 and the presidency four years later.

South Carolina tries to nullify tariff laws. After the Cabinet reorganization, Southerners realized they would get little support from either Jackson or Van Buren in their drive to reduce tariff rates. Then, in 1832 Congress passed a new tariff measure, which eliminated certain objectionable

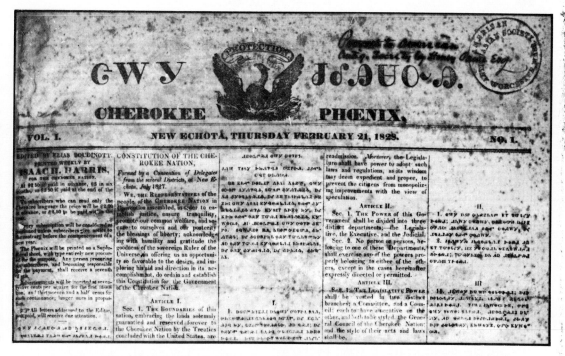

Articles in the Cherokee Phoenix *were printed in English and also in an alphabet invented specifically for the Cherokee language by an Indian named Sequoia. The first issue of the* Phoenix, *shown here, printed the text of the Cherokee Nation's constitution, which was closely modeled after that of the United States.*

features of the Tariff of Abominations. It did not, however, substantially lower rates. Calhoun began immediately to rally opposition in South Carolina. A special state convention adopted an ordinance *nullifying* the tariffs of 1828 and 1832 — that is, declaring them null and void. Federal and state officials were forbidden to collect customs duties in South Carolina after February 1, 1833. Moreover, secession from the Union was threatened if the federal government tried to use force "to reduce this State to obedience." Calhoun resigned the vice-presidency and was immediately elected to the Senate by South Carolina.

Jackson confidently met the challenge head-on. In a Nullification Proclamation, he made the following blunt statement:

I consider . . . the power to annul a law of the United States, assumed by one State, incompatible with the existence of the Union, contradicted expressly by the letter of the Constitution, unauthorized by its spirit, inconsistent with every principle on which it was founded, and destructive of the great object for which it was formed.

In addition, he asked Congress to pass a Force Bill, empowering him to use the army and navy against South Carolina if it resisted federal customs officials. Privately Jackson thundered against the "wicked demagogues" who were stirring up trouble in the South. He even threatened to "have the leaders arrested and arraigned for treason."

A compromise is reached. Meanwhile, forces on both sides were trying to find a face-saving compromise. South Carolina had expected other southern states to join in the fight for nullification, but none did. Consequently, the nullifiers were looking for a way out of an embarrassing dilemma. At the same time, the northern Jacksonians were fearful that the tariff dispute would split the party. And Jackson, despite all his bluster, was reluctant to send the army marching into South Carolina. When the President publicly recommended a downward revision in the tariff rates, Senator Henry Clay worked out a Compromise Tariff. Supported by the northern Jacksonians and by Senator Calhoun, the measure was approved by Congress. Rates remained about the same as they had been in the 1832 tariff. But the new measure enlarged the free list (goods that could come in duty-free) and provided for a gradual reduction of all rates in excess of 20 per cent.

On March 2, 1833, President Jackson signed both the Force Bill and the Compromise Tariff. Two weeks later the South Carolina convention repealed its Ordinance of Nullification and then proceeded to nullify the Force Bill. Both sides claimed victory. Jackson, it is true, had made South Carolina accept the tariff, but only after the rates had been lowered. South Carolina had backed down on its threat of secession, but it still claimed the *rights* of nullification and secession.

The compromise is not a permanent solution. The Compromise Tariff of 1833, like the Missouri Compromise of 1820, sidestepped the major issues at stake between the North and the South. Like the Webster-Hayne debate, it explored but did not solve the conflict about the nature of the Union. Some Americans held, as did Webster and Jackson, that the Union was "inseparable" and no state could withdraw from it. Other Americans, like Hayne and Calhoun, were convinced that any state (or group of states) could secede if it believed that its rights had been violated.

The Compromise Tariff did, however, enable the country to relax for a time from the tension aroused by these issues. It allowed Jackson to restore order within the Democratic Party. It also permitted the President to concentrate on his war against the Bank of the United States. Old Hickory was too shrewd to think that any permanent solution had been reached. He fully expected the "nullifiers in the South . . . to blow up a storm on the slave question next." But any new challenge to the Union, he quickly added, "*ought to be met.*"

▶ CHECK-UP

1. What changes in the government's land policy were sought by Westerners? Why were restrictions on the sale of public lands favored in the Northeast? What position was taken by Daniel Webster on sectionalism?

2. What was Jackson's policy concerning the spending of federal funds for internal improvements? Concerning the resettlement of Indians west of the Mississippi? What position did the Supreme Court take in the case of the Cherokees? Why was the Court decision ineffective?

3. What were the provisions of South Carolina's nullification ordinance? What was Jackson's reaction? How was this issue settled? What question remained unsettled?

∙ ∙

4 Jackson Kills the Bank of the United States

Jackson expresses his opinion of the bank. Unlike Jackson's stand against the threat of nullification, his fight against the Bank of the United States was not based on any feeling of nationalism. The President shared the West's hostility to the Bank and believed that it had caused the Panic of 1819 (page 228). Moreover, he felt that the bank enabled eastern businessmen to make money at the expense of southern planters and western farmers. Jackson also disliked the bank because its president, Nicholas Biddle, befriended Clay and Webster. Webster, in fact, was on the bank's payroll as a legal counselor.

During the 1828 campaign Jackson said nothing about the bank. But in 1829, he had an interview with Biddle, in the course of which he made his position clear: "I think it right to be perfectly frank with you — I do not dislike your bank any more than all banks. . . . I have read the opinion of John Marshall who I believe was a great and pure mind — and could not agree with him." (The Supreme Court, you will recall, had declared the bank to be constitutional in *McCulloch v. Maryland*. See page 217.) Jackson again questioned the constitutionality of the bank in a message to Congress. Meanwhile, his friend Senator Benton was accusing the bank of making "the rich richer and the poor poorer." Biddle's institution was "too great and powerful to be tolerated in a government of free and equal laws." The Democrats cheered the verbal brickbats hurled at the bank by Jackson and his advisers.

Clay and Biddle get Congress to recharter the bank. The charter of the bank was due to expire in 1836. But the bank's supporters decided to force the issue of recharter upon Jackson in the presidential election of 1832. This scheme was devised by Henry Clay, who hoped to be nominated by the National Republicans. Biddle, it seems, had grave doubts about challenging the former Indian fighter in the White House. But Clay and Webster put pressure on Biddle to seek recharter, and so in the summer of 1832 a bill to that effect was pushed through Congress. Clay was jubilant; he felt certain that he now had a popular issue on which to whip Jackson at the polls. "Should Jackson veto it, I shall veto him!" bragged the Kentucky senator.

Jackson vetoes the bank bill. As usual, Jackson met his foes head-on. To Van Buren he remarked that the bank "is trying to kill me, *but I will kill it.*" And kill it he did with a strongly worded veto message. Jackson insisted that the "authority of the Supreme Court must not . . . be permitted to control the Congress or the Executive when acting in their legislative capacities." He accused the bank of increasing sectional jealousy by arraying "section against section, interest against interest, and man against man, in a fearful commotion which threatens to shake the foundations of our Union." Though the logic of Jackson's veto message is open to dispute, it was warmly praised by those who detested the bank.

Jackson's stinging veto surprised friends of the bank. Webster called it "inflammable" and deplored its appeal to class prejudice. Clay, confident of his own election to the White House, agreed with Biddle that the President's veto had "all the fury of a chained panther, biting the bars of his cage." The National Republicans would have liked to override the veto but could not muster the necessary two-thirds majority in either house of Congress.

Jackson wins re-election. Rechartering of the bank, then, became the chief issue in the presidential campaign of 1832. The National Republicans staged their first nominating convention (page 237) and, as expected, chose Henry Clay. The Democratic convention naturally picked President Jackson to head its ticket. But the Democrats named Van Buren, not Calhoun, for the vice-presidency over the protests of disgruntled Southerners. To create a public impression of party unity, the Democrats adopted the rule that both the presidential and vice-presidential candidates must command the support of two thirds of the delegates in order to win the nomination.[2]

Strange as it may seem, both candidates in 1832 used Jackson's bank veto message as campaign literature. Clay had 300,000 copies distributed, believing that it would convince people to vote for the National Republicans. Jackson and the Democrats hammered away at the bank, repeating the criticisms that had been made in the veto message. With the lone exception of South Carolina (whose electoral votes were cast for a states' rights candidate), the Democrats rallied to Jackson's support. Henry Clay carried only six states, including his home state of Kentucky. The outcome of the 1832 election was a triumph for Jackson and the anti-Bank forces. They gleefully declared that at last "the Monster" had been "Biddled, Diddled, and Undone."

Government funds are placed in "pet banks." Jackson could have waited until the bank's charter expired in 1836 before removing government funds. But he was determined to destroy the bank as soon as possible. "I long for . . . repose on the Hermitage [his home in Tennessee]," he wrote in 1833. "But until I can strangle this hydra of corruption I will not shrink from my duty."

The President decided on a policy of gradual withdrawal of government funds from the bank. But first he had to make

[2] Not until 1936 was this "two-thirds rule" abandoned by the Democratic Party.

some Cabinet changes, for his Secretary of the Treasury was not willing to carry out his orders. Jackson promoted this man to the State Department and dismissed another Secretary before finally settling on Roger B. Taney (*tawn'ih*) of Maryland. After September, 1833, Secretary Taney deposited incoming government funds in carefully chosen state banks. At the same time he gradually withdrew government funds from the Bank of the United States and deposited them also in the selected state banks. Anti-Jacksonians promptly dubbed the lucky state banks the administration's "pet banks."

Inflation plagues the country. Jackson's fight against the bank brought financial troubles during the last years of his administration. Biddle was not one to accept defeat. During 1834 he called in bank loans and refused to make new ones. Then in 1835 he suddenly reversed his position and lent large sums of money on unusually generous terms. Moreover, the number of state banks more than doubled between 1829 and 1837, while their circulation of bank notes tripled. Both the "pet banks" and other state banks lent money on easy terms. Most of the paper money they issued declined in value; some of it was worthless from the very beginning. Biddle's action and the policies of state banks caused a sharp increase in the amount of money in circulation. This in turn led to a rise in prices, or *inflation*.

Distribution of surplus funds in the treasury was still another unsettling factor. By 1835 government revenue from the sale of western land and from tariff duties was sufficient to pay off the national debt. After that, money piled up in the treasury faster than the government could spend it. Clay proposed that the surplus be distributed among the states, hoping they would use it for internal-improvement projects. Jackson opposed the distribution scheme, but on the other hand he had no desire to cut off land sales in the West or tamper again with tariff rates. So he signed an act providing for the distribution of almost 28 million dollars among the states. While some states used the money for worthwhile construction or

for support of education, many squandered their share of the surplus.

Jackson tries to stem inflation. Worried by the mushrooming inflation, Jackson believed that the increase in paper money was chiefly responsible. To strike at what he felt to be the root of the problem, the President decided to reduce the amount of paper money in circulation and replace it with specie (coins of gold or silver), which had a stable value. In 1836 he issued the *Specie Circular*, which directed that in the future public lands were to be sold only for specie. Jackson's opponents accused him of high-handed methods in using an executive order, which needed no approval from Congress. They hoped to make this charge stick against "King Andrew's" associate, Martin Van Buren, in the coming election.

▶ CHECK-UP

1. Why was Jackson opposed to the Bank of the United States? Why did Clay and Biddle seek to have the Bank's charter renewed in 1832? How did Jackson's veto of the bank bill become a major issue in the election that year?

2. Why were government funds deposited in state banks after 1833? What factors contributed to inflation in the 1830's? What was the Specie Circular? Why did Jackson issue it?

5 *The Whigs Challenge Van Buren*

The Whigs organize. During Jackson's second term his political opponents began organizing a new party. They chose the name "Whig" because the British party of that name had opposed George III in the eighteenth century, just as they were opposing "King Andrew."

The new party included a variety of groups. (1) Almost all the former National

Republicans joined. (2) Many members were southern Whigs, mostly large planters and property owners. These people feared the effects of Jackson's policies on the profitable trade between southern cotton producers and New England textile manufacturers. (3) A third source of Whig strength included disillusioned third-party members. The Anti-Masons (page 237), for example, joined the Whigs in the mid-1830's. (4) So too did some of the antislavery advocates in the North, who soon earned the name "Conscience Whigs." (5) Finally, the new party picked up former Democrats who were angered by the nullification crisis, or the bank fight, or the struggle over internal improvements, or "King Andrew's" high-handed use of the veto power and executive orders.

In many respects the new Whig Party was a strange combination, but a few political principles served as rallying points. Most of the Whigs believed in Clay's American System (page 226). Like the National Republicans, they generally wanted internal improvements at federal expense, high tariffs, and a national bank. They put the preservation of the Union above any sectional interests, although they sometimes talked about states' rights out of deference to the southern wing of the party. To be sure, conflicts and contradictions existed within the Whig ranks. Thus, the Southerners were far less enthusiastic about high tariff rates than were the New England industrialists and less eager for internal improvements than were the western Whigs. And, of course, the Conscience Whigs held opposite views on the issue of slavery from the Southerners and many New England textile manufacturers. But on one point — opposition to President Jackson — the Whigs were firmly unified.

The Whigs run their "favorite sons." Clay and Webster, the principal leaders of the new party, managed the Whig campaign in 1836. Realizing that their party was too divided to hold a national convention, they decided to let popular Whig candidates run in each section of the country. They hoped these "favorite sons" would collect enough votes to prevent Van Buren

from winning a majority in the electoral college. In that case the election would be thrown into the House of Representatives, as had happened in 1824, and there the Whigs could select the next President.

The northeastern Whigs supported Daniel Webster, while southern Whigs rallied behind Senator Hugh L. White of Tennessee or Willie Mangum of North Carolina. In the Northwest the Whigs ran the aging William Henry Harrison, hero of the Battle of Tippecanoe (page 200). Afraid that Harrison might spoil the plan by speaking out on the issues, Whig managers gave these orders: "Let him say not one single word about his principles, or his creed — let him say nothing — promise nothing. . . . Let the use of pen and ink be wholly forbidden. . . ."

Van Buren wins the presidency. This elaborate "favorite sons" strategy failed. Everyone knew that Andrew Jackson wanted Vice-President Martin Van Buren to follow him in office, and this knowledge had won for Van Buren the unanimous nomination of the Democratic convention. In November, 1836, Jackson's loyal followers elected the Democratic candidate. Though Van Buren received only 25,000 more votes than the total Whig vote, he won a substantial majority in the electoral college.

The Panic of 1837 hits the country. Van Buren had no sooner entered the White House than he was caught up in the Panic of 1837. The trouble stemmed in part from the effects of Jackson's Specie Circular, which had abruptly ended western land speculation and started runs on banks. But the depression which followed as well as the panic itself were world-wide and probably would have afflicted the United States even if the Specie Circular had not been issued. British capitalists began calling in their American loans. This halted construction projects throughout the United States, forcing thousands of laborers out of their jobs. Factories closed down, swelling the ranks of the unemployed. Crop shortages added to the country's troubles. Many Americans suffered from starvation and exposure during the grim winter of 1837–1838. As the depression spread, many state banks had to close their doors.

Van Buren establishes the Independent Treasury. The Panic of 1837 forced the new President to spend most of his time wrestling with problems of finance and currency. Van Buren called a special session of Congress in September, 1837. Clay's distribution scheme (page 248) was repealed, for there was no longer a surplus in the treasury. Congress turned next to the problem of the country's banks. Since confidence in the "pet banks" had been shattered, Van Buren proposed a new plan for the handling of government funds. Under this plan, as money was paid in to the government, it would be stored (1) in the treasury at Washington, (2) in the vaults of the mint, or (3) in branch treasuries (subtreasuries) to be built in the principal cities.

First proposed in 1837, and known as the *Independent Treasury* system, this idea drew protests from the Whigs and also from some Democrats who preferred a third national bank. Nevertheless, Van Buren and the northern Democrats finally pushed the bill through Congress in 1840. For a brief time the government did keep its funds in subtreasuries, though the Independent Treasury was repealed by the Whigs in 1841. (It was re-established in 1846. See page 285.)

Relations with Great Britain are clouded. The Van Buren administration limped to an unimpressive close amid hard times at home and a threat of war with Great Britain. When an insurrection against the British broke out in Canada in 1837, many Americans crossed the border and volunteered their services to the rebels. In revenge, a small band of loyal Canadians crossed the treacherous Niagara River and seized an American ship, the *Caroline*, which had been used to supply the rebels. They cut it away from the dock, set it afire, and sent it over Niagara Falls. Van Buren's Secretary of State immediately demanded an explanation, but the British reply was unsatisfactory. This dispute smoldered until 1840, when a Canadian was heard to boast in a New York City tavern that he had killed an American during the *Caroline* attack. The man was promptly arrested on a murder charge by state officials. Failing to secure his release, the British foreign minister hinted at war and our State Department replied in the same tone. Not until after Van Buren had left office was the incident settled (page 253).

The Jacksonian Era ends. As Van Buren's administration came to an end, it was clear to most Americans that Jacksonian democracy had spent itself. Its major reforms accomplished, the Democratic Party split up into bickering factions. Calhoun and Van Buren were publicly airing their dislike for each other, and no one had arisen in the West to assume Old Hickory's mantle.

CHART STUDY

BUSINESS ACTIVITY, 1790–1860

The rise and fall of business activity results in periods of prosperity and depression. Note the ups and downs of the American economy in the period before the Civil War. Give particular attention to the Panic of 1837.

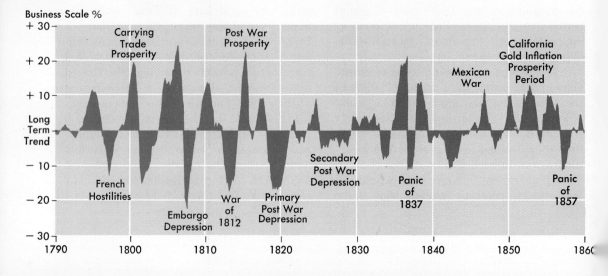

During the four years since Jackson's retirement, the country had been plunged into panic and depression and had quarreled with Great Britain. By 1840 the majority of Americans felt it was time to transfer power to the political opposition.

▶ CHECK-UP

1. Why did Jackson's political opponents choose the name "Whig"? What groups were included in this new party? On what points did the Whigs agree? Disagree? What was their strategy in the 1836 election?

2. What factors led to the Panic of 1837 and the depression that followed? What was the Independent Treasury system? Why was it established?

3. Why can it be said that the Jacksonian Era ended in 1840?

. . . .

6 The Whigs Win a Hollow Victory

An 1837 newspaper cartoon shows the effects of the Panic. A mother and child beg in the streets, while a crowd lines up in front of a failing bank.

The Whigs win the presidency. The Whigs had done their best to frustrate the Van Buren administration. They blamed the President for the Panic of 1837 and the depression that followed. They had delayed action on the Independent Treasury system. In the North the Whigs whispered that Van Buren was too friendly to the slave interests; in the South they claimed that he was sympathetic with those who sought to abolish slavery. In the East the Whigs charged that Van Buren was cruder than the roughest frontiersman; while in the West they circulated stories about the lavish "royal establishment" he was running in the White House. During Jackson's administration, shrewd political maneuvering had won for Van Buren the nickname "Little Magician." But the Little Magician had no magic that could cope with Whig lies or hard times. Though Van Buren's party reluctantly renominated him in 1840, the Democrats realized they were likely to lose.

Instead of nominating either Clay or Webster, the Whigs chose William Henry Harrison at their convention in 1840. Harrison had run surprisingly well in 1836, and the Whigs hoped that his military career would dazzle the voters. To hold the support of southern Whigs, the convention gave the vice-presidential nomination to John Tyler of Virginia. The Whig campaign featured songs, parades, and huge rallies. Whig orators contrasted the supposedly simple frontier habits of Harrison with the supposedly luxurious preferences of President Van Buren. A Democrat scornfully remarked of Harrison, "Give him *a barrel of hard cider*, and settle a pension of two thousand a year on him, and . . . he will sit the remainder of his days in his log cabin by the side of a sea-coal fire, and study moral philosophy." Immediately the jubilant Whigs turned this sarcasm to their advantage. "Old Tippecanoe" was per-

A Whig political rally featuring a log cabin and "a barrel of hard cider" was depicted on this "broadside" distributed by Harrison's supporters in 1840.

manently linked with hard cider and log cabins, which did him no harm in the eyes of many former admirers of Jackson. Though the popular vote again was close, Harrison and Tyler won an easy victory in the electoral college.

The Whig victory tarnishes. The first Whig administration soon ran into trouble. Both Clay and Webster had expected Harrison to be their puppet, but they had not agreed beforehand which of them would pull the strings. Clay preferred to remain in the Senate, where he could control legislation; Webster accepted the post of Secretary of State, where he could control the Cabinet. Meanwhile, President Harrison was besieged by Whig office-seekers. Having criticized the Democrats for using the spoils system, the Whigs found it embarrassing to fill government jobs under the same principle. Worn out by the pressure for patronage, discouraged by the rivalry between Clay and Webster, and weakened by old age, William Henry Harrison died a month after his inauguration. This was a major catastrophe for the Whig Party. Had Harrison lived, the Whigs might have been able to use him as a figurehead to hold the party together. But after Harrison's death, the western Whigs rallied around Clay, whereas the northeastern Whigs looked to

Webster. The southern Whigs took their orders from John Tyler, who became the country's tenth President.

Tyler quarrels with congressional Whigs. Tyler soon found himself at odds with Clay and the majority of Whigs in Congress. The President went along with Clay by approving repeal of the Independent Treasury and passage of a mild increase in tariff rates. But he vetoed as unconstitutional a bill for chartering a third national bank, which Clay had guided through Congress. Irritated but not yet discouraged, Clay pushed through another bank measure. To his amazement, Tyler vetoed that one too. Clay then called the Cabinet members together and persuaded every one of them, with the exception of Webster, to resign. This unprecedented action drew public attention to the Whig quarrels. Furthermore, Clay called the Whig congressmen into caucus and had them endorse a statement banning John Tyler from the Whig Party. The President was denounced as a traitor by northern Whigs and burned in effigy by the same crowds that had noisily campaigned for him only a year before.

The Webster-Ashburton Treaty is signed. Secretary of State Webster was the only Whig who sided with Tyler during this crisis, but he did so for reasons of his own. Webster refused to dance to any tune of Henry Clay's. Moreover, he was deep in negotiations with the British to settle both the *Caroline* feud (page 250) and a dispute over the boundary between Maine and Canada. The former dispute evaporated when the Canadian repudiated his claim of having killed an American and was acquitted of the murder charge.

The northeastern boundary dispute was more difficult to settle. It concerned some 12,000 square miles of territory in Maine and New Brunswick, where the boundary had been left uncertain by the Treaty of 1783. The inhabitants felt strongly about the issue, and on several occasions lumberjacks in the area had nearly come to blows. In 1842, Webster and a British diplomat, Lord Ashburton, worked out a compromise by which the United States received 7000 square miles of the disputed territory. The Webster-Ashburton Treaty also defined the boundary from Sault Ste. Marie to Lake of the Woods (map, page 289). Having won approval of the treaty, Webster resigned as Secretary of State in 1843.

Tyler looks to the South for support. Through the remainder of his presidency, President Tyler trod a lonely path. Both the northern and western factions of the Whig Party spurned him. Webster was out of the government, and Clay had already resigned his Senate seat to begin campaigning for the Whig nomination in 1844.

Tyler's closest allies were the southern Democrats, but many of them were lukewarm because of Tyler's public connection with the Whigs. During 1844, however, Tyler began courting the leader of the southern Democrats, John C. Calhoun. Though the South Carolinian held a seat in the Senate, he had not been active in national politics since the nullification controversy. Tyler gave Calhoun the opportunity to reassert his position of leadership in the party when he asked Calhoun to become Secretary of State. Calhoun accepted the appointment with the hope of building himself into a national figure. Actually, as we shall read later, Calhoun became known, not as a national leader, but as the foremost defender of southern rights.

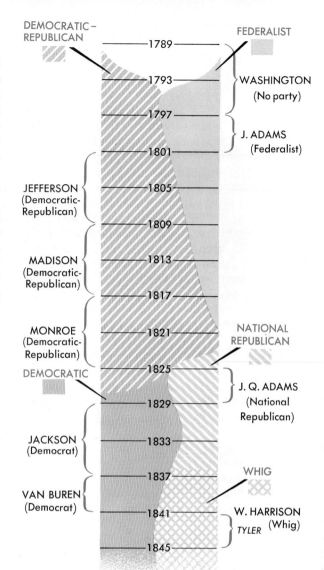

POLITICAL PARTIES, 1789–1845

This chart summarizes the development of political parties before 1845 and indicates party affiliations of the Presidents. Continuations of the chart appear in later chapters.

CHART STUDY

▶ CHECK-UP

1. Why did the Whigs nominate Harrison and Tyler in 1840? What was the result of the election? What factions arose in the victorious party? What was the outcome of Clay's quarrel with Tyler?

2. Why did Webster remain in Tyler's Cabinet? What were the provisions of the Webster-Ashburton Treaty? Why did Tyler look to the South for support?

Clinching the Main Ideas in Chapter 11

The Jacksonian Era saw the extension of the democratic process to include thousands of new voters, more elective offices, new party machinery, and new techniques of appealing to the people. It also marked the establishment of the spoils system in party politics. Jackson's vigorous use of executive power was a new development, as was his experiment with the idea of a Cabinet committed to support presidential policies.

The struggle between nationalism and sectionalism continued throughout the administrations of Jackson and Van Buren. Jackson unwaveringly defended the Union against the threat of nullification and secession. His fight to keep the Union "one and inseparable" in the 1830's undoubtedly strengthened the North's resolve a generation later to fight for preservation of the Union. Following the destruction of the Bank of the United States, however, infla-tion unsettled the nation's economy. As a result, Jackson's successor, Van Buren, was overwhelmed by the Panic of 1837 and the resulting depression.

The Democrats' inability to cope with the economic troubles of the late 1830's largely explains the Whigs' rise to power in 1840. But Whig harmony was destroyed by President William Henry Harrison's unexpected death. By the close of the Tyler administration in 1844, both the Whigs and the Democrats had changed their colors. The Democrats were leaning to the South and taking a much friendlier view of states' rights and strict construction than they had in Jackson's time. The Whigs were inclined toward the North. They were suspicious of the doctrine of states' rights and strongly attached to Webster's concept of an "inseparable" Union. Both parties, however, still drew votes from all sections of the country, and both were openly bidding for the support of the West.

Chapter Review

Terms to Understand

1. patronage
2. Panic of 1837
3. spoils system
4. "kitchen cabinet"
5. "pet banks"
6. Specie Circular
7. Webster-Ashburton Treaty
8. Nullification Proclamation
9. Jacksonian Era
10. *Worcester v. Georgia*
11. Independent Treasury

What Do You Think?

1. "Jackson himself was a product, rather than the creator, of the new democratic spirit. . . ." Do you agree? Explain.

2. Do you approve of Jackson's policy with respect to each of the following issues: the Bank, the Cherokee Indians, the Maysville Road, nullification? Explain your position on each.

3. Historians who call Jackson "King Andrew" also describe the rise of "Jacksonian democracy." How do you explain this seeming inconsistency?

4. Some contemporaries considered the extension of the suffrage to virtually all free whites as a revolutionary step. Why? Do you agree? Explain.

Using Your Knowledge of History

1. Debate: *Resolved,* That Jackson's veto of the bill to recharter the Bank of the United States was not in the public interest.

2. Write an editorial dealing with the Webster-Hayne debate from the point of view of either a New England newspaper or one published in South Carolina.

3. Make a classification of Jackson's policies in terms of whether each was generally approved or opposed in each of the sections (Northeast, South, and West). Explain why in each case.

Extending Your Knowledge of History

Arthur M. Schlesinger, Jr., provides a stimulating analysis of the Jacksonian Era in *The Age of Jackson.* A lively but less objective book, in which Jackson is always the hero, is *The Party Battles of the Jacksonian Period* by Claude G. Bowers. There are excellent interpretive essays on Calhoun and Jackson in Richard Hofstadter's *The American Political Tradition and the Men Who Made It.* Two books about Old Hickory by Marquis James are *Andrew Jackson, The Border Captain* and *Andrew Jackson, Portrait of a President.*

CHAPTER 12

The Jacksonian Era Witnesses Changes in American Life

A county election

In the history of the world the doctrine of Reform had never such scope as at the present hour. . . . We are to revise the whole of our social structure, the State, the school, religion, marriage, trade, science, and explore their foundations in our own nature.

RALPH WALDO EMERSON, "MAN THE REFORMER," 1841

1830–1850

So many changes appeared in American life during the Jacksonian Era that historians have called the period an "age of ferment." Industry was expanding, and new forms of transportation and communication hastened the spread of new ideas. Educational opportunities increased as free public-school systems were started in the northern and western states. A new reading public supported a growing number of newspapers and magazines and eagerly sought the word of outstanding authors and lecturers. New religions such as Mormonism appeared in the 1830's, and a few people experimented with settlements where property was held in common. The reforming urge found an outlet in the temperance movement, in seeking better care of the insane, the blind, and prisoners, and in the formation of peace societies. Far more controversial was the antislavery movement.

These wide-ranging reforms, Ralph Waldo Emerson noted, were the work of a "restless, prying, conscientious criticism." But the reform impulse was not a matter of politics; both Democrats and Whigs promoted it. Nor was it primarily religious, although a number of ministers were active reformers. Nor were the reforms of the Jacksonian Era equally distributed throughout the country. They were centered chiefly in the North and West. In this chapter we shall see what these changes were and how they affected life in the United States.

1 Industry Expands as Transportation and Communication Are Improved

American industry expands. American manufacturing, which had begun to grow during the period of Jefferson's embargo, survived British competition in the years following the War of 1812 (page 216). Then, with the aid of tariff protection after 1816, American industry developed rapidly. Textile manufacturing, with water power harnessed to run the machinery, was concentrated in New England. But a number of plants using steam power were built in the Philadelphia area in the 1830's. Technological improvements (new methods of production) were introduced in the manufacture of iron and metal tools. For example, cheaper and improved iron-tipped (and later steel) plows were produced. The value of manufactured goods rose from less than 200 million dollars in 1810 to over a billion dollars by mid-century.

Water transportation improves. The growth of industry depended to a considerable degree on improved transportation. In the 1830's the most efficient way to transport raw materials and finished goods, as well as agricultural products, was by water. We have already seen how New York City promoted the Erie Canal in the 1820's (page 225). The success of this project encouraged the construction of hundreds of miles of canals (map, page 302) with private and state funds and with money invested by European capitalists. The eastern seacoast towns were eager to get a share of the growing commerce with the West. Hence they sponsored a number of roads and canals. One of the most ambitious projects was the ten-million-dollar "Golden Link" between Philadelphia and Pittsburgh. Canal barges traveled west from Philadelphia to a portage railway, which carried the loaded boats over the crest of the mountains. An aqueduct high over the streets of Pittsburgh carried the barges into the "Western Waters" at the head of the Ohio River.

The number of steamboats on the Mississippi and Ohio Rivers increased sharply (page 209). They hauled grain, iron, and other products southward and brought back sugar, rice, and cotton. The steamboat reduced travel time between New Orleans and Pittsburgh from 100 days to 30 and cut the cost of transportation in half. A variety of flatboats and other vessels plied the same waters at a slower pace, carrying freight and western settlers.

As for ocean travel, the sailing ships called *packets* made regular Atlantic crossings. Built to withstand Atlantic gales, they made the trip in 18 to 20 days. Since regular sailings were scheduled from New York, that city captured a large portion of the transatlantic trade. There were a few steamships on the ocean, but as yet they provided no great challenge to the packets.

The first railroads are built. About the time that canal construction reached its peak, the steam railroad made its first appearance in this country. Cars propelled by gravity along an inclined railway track had been used in the early 1800's, but railway cars pulled by a steam engine were not developed until the late 1820's. Railroad construction was promoted primarily by the major cities. By 1830, Baltimore had built a fourteen-mile stretch of the Baltimore and Ohio Railroad. It was on this line that Peter Cooper's steam engine,

CHAPTER FOCUS

1. Industry expands as transportation and communication are improved.
2. An industrial society takes shape.
3. Educational opportunities are expanded.
4. American writers and artists achieve recognition.
5. Religious changes and reform movements reflect American society.
6. The antislavery movement divides the North and South.

The Tom Thumb, *one of this country's earliest steam locomotives, raced a horse-drawn coach on the Baltimore and Ohio Railroad in 1830 (above). Though the* Tom Thumb *led for awhile, its engine broke down and the horse won. Nevertheless, railroads soon showed their superiority over horse-drawn vehicles. Less than twenty years later, the much more advanced locomotive shown at right made transportation history when it pulled the first train out of Chicago in 1848.*

the *Tom Thumb,* made a trial run. A year later the Mohawk and Hudson Railroad joined Albany and Schenectady, New York. Soon Boston, eager to tap the trade of the Erie Canal, tied itself to the Hudson River by canal and rail. In the South, the merchants of Charleston financed the construction of 136 miles of track between their city and Hamburg, South Carolina. When completed, it was the longest railway in the world. By 1840 there were nearly 3000 miles of railroad track in the United States, most of it short lines connecting principal cities (map, page 303).

The early trains were hazardous. The wood-burning locomotives belched forth showers of sparks, menacing both passengers and countryside. An Englishwoman, Harriet Martineau, wrote of her travels in the United States during 1835:

One great inconvenience of the American railroads is that, from wood being used for fuel, there is an incessant shower of large sparks, destructive to dress and comfort, unless all the windows are shut, which is impossible in warm weather. Some serious accidents from fire have happened in this way; and during my last trip on the Columbia and Philadelphia railroad, a lady in the car had a shawl burned to destruction on her shoulders; and I found that my own gown had thirteen holes in it; and my veil, with which I saved my eyes, [had] more than could be counted.

There also were dangers of collisions and fatal accidents, for the early railroads had few safety devices. The rails, made of wooden beams covered with iron strips, often caused trouble when the strips came loose and wound around the wheels. Because the distance between the rails (called the *gauge*) varied on different railroads, the trains of one line could not run on the tracks of another.

Railroads threaten the canals and turnpikes. The canal and turnpike interests, recognizing the railroads as a threat, fought the newcomer with all the weapons at their command. In New York State, for example, canal promoters got a law passed prohibiting the railroads from carrying freight. Later, this law was amended to permit the railroads to haul freight during the winter months when canal operation was suspended. Elsewhere the railroads met opposition from those who had invested money in turnpikes, bridges, steamboats, and stagecoach companies. Many citizens thought it dangerous to travel at the giddy speed of fifteen miles an hour.

Yet the railroads had obvious advantages over other forms of transportation. Unlike canals they did not have to follow water-level routes, nor were they as much affected by floods, ice, and snow. They cost less to build than canals, and they provided faster travel than either canals or turnpikes. The uncomfortable open coaches were soon replaced with enclosed cars, which provided protection against cinders and dirt. The railroads quickly proved themselves profitable carriers of both passengers and freight, and adventurous investors poured money into railroad construction. Railroad promoters publicized their plans in newspapers and pamphlets and at public meetings. "It is almost impossible," noted one man in the 1830's, "to open a paper without finding an account of some railroad meeting. An epidemic on this subject seems nearly as prevalent throughout the country as the influenza."

The telegraph improves communication. Improvements in communication and transportation went hand in hand. As the railroad greatly speeded up travel, so the invention of the telegraph revolutionized communication. By 1837, Samuel F. B. Morse had perfected an electrical instrument by which combinations of dots and dashes could be transmitted over a metal wire. Morse was unable, however, to finance the construction of a telegraph line, nor could he find private investors who were interested. Finally he turned to friends in Washington, who persuaded Congress to appropriate 30,000 dollars for the construction of a line between Baltimore and Washington. In 1844, Morse set up his telegraph equipment in a room of the Supreme Court

in Washington. Then he tapped out a quotation from the Bible: "What hath God wrought!" and a friend in Baltimore received the message. The success of the telegraph was assured. Within a few years, New York was linked by telegraph with other eastern cities and even with Chicago.

New York City sets the pace. The brisk growth of New York City reflected the effect on American cities of the changes described in this section. New York took the lead in establishing telegraph connections with the rest of the country, just as it had pushed canal, turnpike, and railroad construction. By mid-century New York, with almost half a million inhabitants, was the country's most important city. New Yorkers had a plentiful supply of water piped from reservoirs; and gaslights lined the paved streets. Horse-drawn omnibuses handled the heavy traffic. Paid fire companies and uniformed policemen protected the city dwellers.

Other major cities introduced similar improvements at about the same time. But neither Philadelphia, Baltimore, Boston, Charleston, nor New Orleans could match the pace of New York. A traveler in New York in 1840 observed: "In the streets all is hurry and bustle; the very carts, instead of being drawn by horses at a walking pace, are often met at a gallop, and always at a brisk trot." He went on to note that the people "seem to enjoy this bustle, and add to it by their own rapid pace . . . as if under the apprehension of being too late." New York's enterprising populace set the pace for the emerging industrial society.

▶ CHECK-UP

1. How was water transportation improved during the 1830's? How was railroad construction promoted? Who were the opponents of the railroads?

2. What advantages did railroads have over canals and turnpikes? How did the telegraph revolutionize communication?

3. How had changes in transportation and communication affected a city such as New York by mid-century?

. . . .

2 *An Industrial Society Takes Shape*

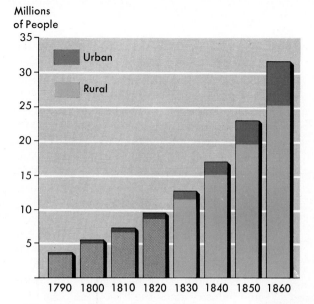

GROWTH OF POPULATION, 1830–1860

This chart shows the growth of population up to 1860, with emphasis on the years 1830–1860. Later charts on population will extend to the 1960's.

The growth of industry and improvements in transportation and communication had important effects on America's economic life. Among them were the development of a new kind of business organization and the forming of labor unions.

Businessmen form corporations. The earliest factories were small and had only a few pieces of machinery. Usually these factories were owned and run by one man, a family, or perhaps several partners. In the 1820's and 1830's, however, manufacturing establishments generally increased in size and in the amount of machinery they used. Because the establishment of these larger factories required much more money, some businessmen pooled their resources, or *capital*, in *corporations*. A corporation was permitted by law to sell shares of stock (certificates of ownership) to the general public and to use the money thus gained to carry on its business. With this capital a corporation could build larger factories and install more expensive machinery. It could buy greater amounts of raw materials and develop new markets for its manufactures. The profits could be used for further plant expansion or be paid as dividends to the stockholders according to the number of shares of stock owned by each. One of the earliest corporations was the Boston Manufacturing Company (1813), which owned textile plants in Massachusetts and New Hampshire as well as banks and insurance and real estate companies. Many of the corporations of this period were formed to develop means of transportation.

Immigration increases the population. Money and machines played an important part in the growth of American industry. But without an adequate supply of workers, the industrialists could never have carried out their plans. Fortunately plenty of good workers were available.

Many of the laborers who constructed the roads, canals, and railroads and who worked in the factories came from abroad. About 2,500,000 immigrants arrived during the 1830's and 1840's, whereas only 150,000 foreigners had come to this country in the 1820's. This sharp increase was due in part to expanding economic opportunities in the United States — (1) the opening up of western lands which could be purchased at a reasonable price and (2) the many jobs available in industry. Moreover, immigrants could get passage across the Atlantic for as little as 20 dollars. During the 1820's most of the immigrants had come from England, Northern Ireland, Wales, and Scotland. But in the next two decades increasingly large numbers of German and Irish immigrants arrived (page 305).

The proportion of Americans living in cities increases. Although many immigrants and native-born Americans moved west to take up farming, others settled in the cities, thus swelling the urban population. American cities were growing faster than the nation as a whole. In 1790 only one person in thirty had lived in a community with a population of 8000 or more; in 1820, one in twenty; and by 1840, one in twelve. Cincinnati was the fastest-growing city in the West. It was a trade center for the surrounding region and also a manufacturing and meat-packing center — hence its nickname "Porkopolis." In the Northwest the newer cities such as Chicago and Milwaukee were expanding rapidly. In the South the growing city of Mobile was able to snatch trade from Charleston and Savannah. New Orleans also was experiencing a period of phenomenal growth.

Urban growth in the Northeast was marked by a steady increase in the size of the older cities. A number of settlements between Albany and Buffalo became thriving communities because of increased trade and industry along the Erie Canal. And the growth of smaller towns centered around a particular factory or industry was spectacular. Northeastern cities not only attracted immigrants but also drew thousands of native-born Americans who left the land to work in the cities. New England farmers found it increasingly difficult to compete with the more fertile West. Some sold their land and moved west themselves. Those who stayed on their farms raised fruits, vegetables, and dairy products for nearby urban markets. Some farm families were so located that the men could care for the fields and livestock while the women and children took factory jobs.

Lowell is a "factory town." Lowell, Massachusetts, was a typical industrial town of the Jacksonian Era. Located on the falls of the Merrimack River, Lowell was a natural site for the many textile mills constructed there in the 1820's and 1830's. Mill owners recruited girls in their teens or early twenties from New England farm homes, offering them dormitory housing, close supervision, and attractive wages. The girls worked from sunup to sundown six days a week. Nevertheless, they found time to write and publish monthly magazines and to attend Sunday school and religious services. After the Panic of 1837 (page 249), however, wages were reduced and working conditions in Lowell worsened.

Other New England mills were poor rivals of those in Lowell. They paid less, enforced harsh work rules, and required women and children to work even longer hours. The unfortunate children who were employed in these mills at an early age were "brought up as ignorant as the Arabs of the desert."

Wage earners become dissatisfied. As factories grew larger, the worker had less and less personal contact with his "boss." In factories owned by corporations, the employer was a manager rather than an owner. These managers simply carried out the orders of the board elected by the corporation owners (stockholders). Both managers and owners were often more concerned with profits than with the welfare of the workers. Skilled workers, whose services were in great demand, could usually change jobs if they wished. But most factory workers had no way of securing better working conditions or higher wages. If they staged a protest meeting, as the Lowell girls did in the 1830's, they usually lost their jobs. If they tried to organize any opposition, they were not only fired but *black-listed*. This meant that their employer circulated their names to other employers so that no factory would hire them.

During the 1830's, workers grew increasingly uneasy. While inflation raised the cost of living, wages failed to keep pace. Indeed, many textile factories even cut wages because farm workers and newly arrived immigrants would work for lower pay.

The earliest labor organizations are short-lived. In the three years preceding the Panic of 1837, more than 150 labor organizations were formed in Boston, New York, Philadelphia, Baltimore, and other cities. Most of these small unions involved only one kind of worker. Women, moreover, had to form their own organizations. The first country-wide labor organization was the National Trades Union, established in 1834. This union favored a ten-hour day for all laborers, regulation of child labor in textile factories, and free, public education. By 1837 its membership had grown to more than 300,000 and it had conducted about 175 strikes.

The Panic of 1837 and the depression which followed undermined the National Trades Union and many other labor groups.

Yet these early efforts at unionization had made some important gains. Several state legislatures gave limited support to the ten-hour day, and President Van Buren ordered a ten-hour day for manual laborers employed by the federal government. More important was a decision handed down by the Massachusetts Supreme Court. In *Commonwealth v. Hunt* (1842), the court ruled that labor unions were legal organizations, not conspiracies as the courts had previously held. But the labor movement had little real success until after the Civil War.

▶ CHECK-UP

1. How did the growth of industry lead to the formation of corporations? What were the advantages of the corporation?

2. Why did immigration increase greatly during the 1830's and 1840's? Why did the urban population increase?

3. Why did working conditions begin to worsen in the late 1830's? How did employers try to keep workers from organizing?

4. What goals were sought by labor unions during the 1830's? What gains were made?

. . . .

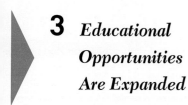

3 *Educational Opportunities Are Expanded*

From the earliest days of the republic, some Americans had urged the establishment of free, tax-supported schools extending from the elementary level to a national university. Nevertheless, in 1830 not a single state had tax-supported schools at which attendance was compulsory. During the Jacksonian Era, however, educational opportunities were broadened.

Demand for educational change grows strong. The demand for free, tax-supported schools was voiced by many groups. Reformers pointed out that since all free white men could vote, the nation must find a way of educating its citizens. Realizing that education was the key to a better life for their children, working people used their newly won votes and their influence in workingmen's parties and labor unions to demand free schools. A group of Philadelphia workingmen stated their case this way: "Our government is republican; our education should be equally so."

Nevertheless, many Americans opposed the drive for equal educational opportunity. Some complained that tax-supported schools would be too costly. A conservative newspaper said such schools would be a "compulsory application of the means [wealth] of the richer for the direct use of the poorer classes." Others argued that if farmers and laborers were educated, they would seek better jobs and thus upset the established order:

> The peasant must labor during those hours of the day which his wealthy neighbor can give to abstract culture of his mind; otherwise, the earth would not yield enough for the subsistence of all; the mechanic cannot abandon the operations of his trade for general studies; if he should, most of the conveniences of life . . . would be wanting.

Opposition also came from religious groups who had their own educational institutions and did not want to be taxed for public schools. Owners of other private schools thought they might lose many of their pupils if public schools were started.

Reformers promote free primary schools. Though the opponents of educational reform put up a stiff fight, they eventually lost. They had no leaders comparable to Horace Mann of Massachusetts or Henry Barnard of Connecticut, men who worked tirelessly to publicize the advantages of free elementary schools. As secretary of the Board of Education in Massachusetts, Horace Mann issued annual reports which were read by people throughout the country. By 1850 most states in the North and West had accepted the idea of tax-supported public schools. Approximately 80,000 elementary schools existed by that time, most of them in northern towns and cities.

Developments in education during the Jacksonian Era included new teacher training methods introduced by Horace Mann (right). At far right is the first public high school, founded in Massachusetts in 1821. By the late 1830's many schoolchildren were studying the McGuffey readers. The unhappy scene at right above appeared in one of these widely read books. Adults seeking knowledge enjoyed the new "penny dailies" sold on street corners (above).

Teacher training and textbooks are improved. Horace Mann and the other educational leaders realized that school buildings alone were not enough. They campaigned for better training of teachers, an enriched curriculum in the schools, and special instruction for retarded and delinquent children. Moreover, they wanted compulsory school attendance, employment of women as well as men in teaching positions, and the formation of teachers' organizations. In 1839, Mann established at Lexington, Massachusetts, the first state-supported school for training teachers. He also organized the first state teachers' association. Henry Barnard carried on similar work in Connecticut and Rhode Island.

The use of McGuffey's *Readers* was a step forward in American education. Noah Webster's spellers and grammars (page 121) continued to be widely used, but before the 1830's there were few good books for children to read. William Holmes McGuffey, a college professor, filled this gap. He prepared six readers for the elementary grades which offered poetry, patriotic stories, moral lessons, and a rich collection of interesting facts. Eventually adopted in 37 states, the McGuffey books introduced thousands of children to good reading.

Public high schools are started. Some Americans urged that high schools also be tax-supported. Boston, Massachusetts, led the way by establishing the first public high school in 1821. Six years later Massachusetts passed a law requiring every town with more than 500 families to provide a high school. New York City established a number of tax-supported "free academies." But progress was slow. By 1860 there were only 300 public high schools in the entire country, compared to more than 6000 private academies. Though most of the private schools taught boys only, a few schools for girls were opened. The most successful of these were Emma Willard's Female Seminary in Troy, New York, and Mary Lyon's Mount Holyoke Female Seminary (later Mount Holyoke College) in Massachusetts.

Higher education moves ahead. The new enthusiasm for education influenced American colleges. Thus, most of the new western states had a state college or university, though many of these institutions were inadequately financed and rated low in academic standards. Private colleges flourished in the Jacksonian Era, but many of them lasted only a few years. One educator remarked: "[They] rise up like mushrooms on our luxuriant soil. They are duly lauded and puffed for a day; and then they sink to be heard of no more."

College curriculums emphasized Latin, Greek, and mathematics, and to a lesser extent science, political economy, and moral philosophy. In many of these schools the teaching was uninspired and the libraries were pitifully small. An exception was Harvard College, which experimented with new methods of teaching history and the humanities. The founding of Oberlin College in Ohio (1833) attracted much attention as an experiment in higher education. Planned by New England reformers, Oberlin accepted women as well as men, and Negroes as well as whites.

Progress is made in science. A few colleges had on their faculties some of the outstanding scientists of the period. One was Benjamin Silliman, who for many years taught chemistry and natural science at Yale. He started the first American scientific periodical and wrote one of the earliest science textbooks. Another notable scientist was Joseph Henry, whose research in electromagnetism made possible Morse's telegraph. Henry taught at Princeton until 1846, when he was appointed director of the new Smithsonian Institution in Washington. The Institution was the gift of James Smithson, an English scientist who left a large bequest to the American government "for the increase and diffusion of knowledge among men."

During the Jacksonian Era, as throughout their history, Americans excelled in the practical application of scientific knowledge. Some machines, like textile machines and the steam engine, they borrowed from England; others, like the cotton gin and the telegraph, were invented by Americans. Many foreign travelers commented on the ability of Americans to put scientific knowledge to work in industry, transportation, and communication. One European expressed the opinion that the "social conditions and institutions of democracy" peculiarly fitted the Americans "to seek the immediate and useful practical results of the sciences."

Some medical advances are made. In medical science, better training of doctors helped to raise standards of practice. A number of medical schools were established during this period, and the American Medical Association was formed in 1847. In addition, states began to license doctors and dentists, though regulations were poorly enforced. Many Americans continued to "doctor" themselves with patent medicines, usually high in alcoholic content, which sold in enormous quantities.

American doctors made an outstanding contribution to medicine by developing anesthetics to prevent pain in surgical operations. In 1844, Dr. Horace Wells, of Hartford, Connecticut, demonstrated the value of nitrous oxide ("laughing gas") in pulling teeth without pain. Two years earlier, Dr. Crawford W. Long of Georgia had performed an operation in which he used ether to deaden pain, and in 1846 Dr. W. T. G. Morton successfully used ether in an operation at a Boston hospital.

Adult education flourishes. During the Jacksonian Era energetic adults who had not had a chance to obtain an education banded together to bring culture to their communities. Adult education took several forms. Workingmen started mechanics' institutes which offered night classes, sponsored lectures, and operated libraries and sometimes bookstores. A number of cities still have public halls or auditoriums that originated with the mechanics' institutes.

Mutual improvement societies sprang up in the North and West. These organizations, often called *lyceums,* held public lectures on art and science, followed by discussions. By 1850, more than 3000 lyceums were attended by Americans eager to hear such distinguished speakers as Ralph Waldo Emerson, Henry Barnard, and Horace Mann.

Newspaper circulation increases. As people acquired more education — whether in the schools or in the lyceums — the demand for newspapers, magazines, and books increased. The thirst for knowledge of an enlarged reading public in turn produced important changes in American newspapers. Before this time, newspaper circulation had been small and copies usually sold for six cents. In 1833, however, the New York *Sun* came out with a daily that was sold on the street corners for a penny. The *Sun's* example was soon followed by James Gordon Bennett, editor of the New York *Herald,* and Horace Greeley, who founded the New York *Tribune* in 1841. The editor-owners of these newspapers vied with each other to attract readers. Some played up sensational crime and scandal to increase circulation. But Greeley's *Tribune* gave serious coverage to the major developments of the day. Greeley also experimented with a weekly edition which sold by mail subscription throughout the North and West.

Certain inventions aided the progress of journalism. The telegraph drastically changed methods of gathering and transmitting news. Horace Greeley told Samuel Morse, "You are going to turn the newspaper office upside down with your invention." The Associated Press, a news-gathering agency formed in the 1840's, sold its dispatches to newspapers throughout the country. About the same time the Hoe cylinder press made possible the use of rotary printing machines. Still other improvements in printing and paper-making contributed to the rapid production of newspapers on a large scale. Soon every large city had at least one inexpensive daily. Among the most influential, in addition to the New York papers, were the Cleveland *Plain Dealer,* the Baltimore *Sun,* the Cincinnati *Gazette,* and the New Orleans *Picayune.*

Magazines encourage American authors. A growing number of magazines also served the larger reading public. Some of the magazines lasted only a few years. Others, such as educational and scientific journals, served special groups of readers. But some publications had a wide appeal and influenced public opinion. This was

---

Graham Crackers

Overeating has long been a problem of the American people. Meat, especially salt pork, was once consumed in enormous quantities because it was readily available and easy to preserve.

The Reverend Sylvester Graham of Connecticut (1794–1851) strongly opposed overeating. Graham had many likes and dislikes, some of them peculiar. He was a vegetarian and a fresh-air fiend and believed in exercising and bathing frequently. He crusaded against meat, alcohol, tobacco, coffee, featherbeds — and white bread. Graham argued that bread should be made of whole wheat flour instead of the refined flour used in white bread.

Many Americans became Graham followers, and at Graham boarding houses health seekers followed his principles religiously. As Graham's fame grew, whole wheat flour became known as Graham flour, and the crackers made from it were called Graham crackers. These crackers helped to pave the way for today's giant cereal industry.

especially true of *The Knickerbocker Maga-zine* and the *Southern Literary Messenger,* which, like the older *North American Review,* welcomed essays, stories, and poems by American authors.

The best-selling magazine of the mid-nineteenth century was *Godey's Lady's Book,* edited for many years by Sarah Josepha Hale. She was the author of "Mary Had a Little Lamb," a poem immortalized in the McGuffey *Readers.* In addition to illustrations of women's fashions, home furnishings, and architecture, Mrs. Hale published stories and poems by leading American authors. She also used the magazine to campaign for the education of women and for their employment as teachers, waitresses, and clerks.

▶ CHECK-UP

1. Why did demands for free, public education increase during the Jacksonian Era? What improvements were made in textbooks and teacher education? What progress was made in secondary and higher education?

2. What progress was made during this period in science? In medical practice? In adult education?

3. Why did the demand for newspapers, magazines, and books grow? What inventions made possible improved, low-cost newspapers?

* * * * * * * * * * * * * * * * * *

4 *American Writers and Artists Achieve Recognition*

Outstanding American authors appear. You will recall that British literary critics looked down on American authors in the early 1800's (Chapter 9). By the 1830's, however, American writers, and artists too, had begun to win fame on both sides of the Atlantic.

Irving. Washington Irving (page 210) was the first American author to achieve an international reputation. After living in England for a number of years, Irving returned to the United States and traveled in the West. The result was *A Tour on the Prairies* (1835), which introduced many Americans to the grandeur of their own country.

Cooper. Another author who won international fame with his descriptions of the American wilderness was James Fenimore Cooper. Both Americans and Englishmen eagerly read his *Leatherstocking Tales* (particularly *The Last of the Mohicans* and *The Pathfinder*). These novels made a folk hero of the frontiersman Natty Bumppo.

Bryant. William Cullen Bryant was a distinguished poet and editor. His poem "Thanatopsis," written before he was twenty, was at first rejected by the *North American Review* because its editor refused to believe that such a fine poem could be written by anyone "on this side of the Atlantic." Eventually an English edition of Bryant's poems firmly established his reputation on both sides of the Atlantic. By that time Bryant was part owner of the New York *Evening Post,* which he edited with great distinction for fifty years.

Poe. Edgar Allan Poe was a tragic man of talent. Forced by heavy debts to leave the University of Virginia, he spent some time in the army and then turned to writing. For the leading magazines of the day, especially the *Southern Literary Messenger,* he wrote brilliant articles, poems, and short stories. His eerie poetry, detective stories, and mystery tales won him fame, though never enough money. His physical and mental health declined after the death of his young wife, and in 1849 he was found dying in a Baltimore street.

Emerson. The most influential author of the period, in many ways a spokesman for the Jacksonian Era, was Ralph Waldo Emerson. Educated at Harvard and trained for the ministry, he resigned his pastorate in 1832. For the next three decades he devoted himself to lecturing and writing. Many of his lectures were published in a volume of essays; his poems were printed in the leading magazines and later published as a book. Emerson urged Ameri-

FRONTIER AMERICA

as seen by GEORGE CALEB BINGHAM

Western politicians like the speaker below appear in many of George Caleb Bingham's pictures. Bingham was born in Virginia but lived most of his life in Missouri. His realistic paintings and sketches depicted life in western settlements at a time when the Middle West was still America's frontier. At lower left is Bingham's sketch of a country fiddler.

Sketch from George Caleb Bingham: River Portraitist, *by John Francis McDermott, Courtesy Mercantile Library, St. Louis, Missouri. Copyright 1959 by the University of Oklahoma Press.*

cans to develop self-reliance, which he felt was important in a society that was rapidly becoming industrial and urban. In the next section you will read how his views influenced American religious thought.

American painters are inspired by American scenes. American artists of this period found much to inspire them in their native land. One group of landscape painters, known as the "Hudson River School," sought to capture on canvas the beauty of the Hudson Valley and the Catskill Mountains. The naturalist and artist John James Audubon spent a lifetime studying and drawing American birds and animals (page 226). His lifelike sketches of birds in their natural habitats were published in the 1830's. The Missouri artist George Caleb Bingham painted realistic

pictures of boatmen on the western rivers and politicians and voters in frontier cities.

Architects follow historic styles. While many Americans took greater interest in their own culture during the Jacksonian Era, architects continued to borrow from abroad. They were especially influenced by the classical buildings of ancient Greece. During those same years Americans were cheering Greek efforts to win independence from Turkish rule. As a result, hundreds of American towns received Greek names in the 1820's, and "Greek Revival" architecture became fashionable. Government buildings, banks, stores, and even some homes were built in the classic lines of ancient Greek temples. The architect Benjamin Latrobe used this style in designing the second Bank of the United States in

Philadelphia. He also preserved elements of the Greek style in rebuilding the national Capitol after the War of 1812.

By the 1840's the Gothic style began to influence American architects. New York City's Trinity Church and St. Patrick's Cathedral (begun in 1858) were Gothic buildings. So too was the Smithsonian Institution, which had the elaborate decoration favored by English architects of that period.

▶ CHECK-UP

1. Describe the work of the leading American authors of this period. What artists painted various aspects of the American scene?

2. What styles of architecture were representative of this period?

· ·

5 Religious Changes and Reform Movements Reflect American Society

Further evidence of "ferment" in the Jacksonian Era was a heightened interest in religion and the beginning of a number of crusades for human betterment.

The established churches undergo changes. The stern teachings of the Congregationalist and Presbyterian churches were softened in the early nineteenth century. Protestant doctrine was altered to fit the times; it allowed more room for a man

ements of classical architecture can be en in the Massachusetts meeting house ove, designed by Charles Bulfinch age 209). Benjamin Latrobe's design the second Bank of the United States p right) was a direct imitation of a eek temple. The Gothic style broke ay from classical rules to stress individual taste, as in Washington Irving's me "Sunnyside," seen here in a paint- by George Inness of the Hudson er School (right).

to win his own salvation by good works. Many people joined the Unitarians, who held that no individual's fate was predetermined. Unitarianism spread rapidly in the 1820's and soon rivaled the strength of Congregationalism in New England. Yet the writer Ralph Waldo Emerson and others as well felt that the Unitarian beliefs did not fit the religious needs of their generation. Like many men of his time, Emerson was a strong individualist. He believed that man should cultivate his own power of reason. Emerson also wanted man to develop to the fullest degree the small spark of divinity which he believed to be in everyone's soul. The surest route to an understanding of God, thought Emerson, was through an appreciation of Nature. Those who accepted Emerson's ideas called themselves *Transcendentalists*. They believed that men could "transcend" the need for organized churches and creeds, and establish their own relationship with the Creator and with the universe.

Religion on the frontier often took the form of *revivalism*. Enthusiastic throngs turned up at "camp meetings," where traveling preachers exhorted the people to give themselves to God. Some encouraged their listeners to show acceptance of the message by "the shakes" or other physical contortions. But such revivalists as Charles G. Finney asked Christians to seek salvation by performing charitable deeds. He and others like him were a strong force for turning Protestant religious enthusiasm toward social reform in the 1830's and '40's.

New religions are founded. Despite changes in the older religions, many dissatisfied people turned to new prophets. William Miller founded the Adventists in the 1840's, after causing considerable excitement with his prediction that the world was soon to end. The Mormon movement owed its origin to Joseph Smith, who claimed to have received divine records and revelations. These he published in the *Book of Mormon* and other writings, and established the Church of Jesus Christ of Latter-Day Saints (1830). Within a few years Smith gained thousands of converts in the United States and Great Britain.

The prophet and his followers lived for a time in Ohio and then in Missouri. But their tightly knit social organization roused the hostility of neighbors, and they were soon forced to seek refuge in an abandoned village in Illinois. By thrift and hard work the Mormons soon built a thriving settlement of 15,000 at Nauvoo. Still they aroused the bitterness of outsiders, however, especially after Smith sanctioned plural marriage for Mormon leaders. When an angry mob murdered Smith in 1844, Brigham Young, an extraordinarily able man, became the Mormon leader. Young directed the mass migration of the Mormons from Nauvoo to the basin of the Great Salt Lake in what was then Mexican territory. It was a tremendous undertaking, but the Mormons had the perseverance to push on. Under Young's guidance they turned their "promised land" into a prosperous co-operative community.

Catholics meet discrimination. The Mormons were not the only religious group to meet hostility. The rapid growth of the Catholic Church — from 600,000 members in 1830 to 3,500,000 in 1850 — alarmed many American Protestants. The increase was largely due to the arrival of Irish immigrants, almost all of them Catholic, and some German Catholic immigrants. Construction of new churches and parochial schools frightened a few Americans into taking direct action against the Catholics. Riots broke out in the larger cities. A convent in Charlestown, Massachusetts, was burned in 1834. And several writers published attacks on the Irish and the Catholics. At the same time, however, the new western states adopted constitutions which placed no political restrictions on Catholics, Jews, or agnostics. Furthermore, many of the older states removed religious tests for voting or holding public office.

Reformers seek changes in American society. Some Protestant churches in the 1830's and 1840's, as we have seen, placed increasing emphasis on "good works." Moreover, many Americans were disturbed by the social changes resulting from the growth of industry and of cities. As a result, the Jacksonian Era was marked by

The Mormons suffered extreme hardship on their westward migration. Even the women pulled hand carts through snowy mountain passes (above). Under Brigham Young's leadership, the Mormons settled in the valley of the Great Salt Lake in Utah. Their determination, industry, and irrigation of arid lands helped make Salt Lake City the prosperous community it is today (right).

the rise of reform movements that sought to relieve injustice and human suffering.

Ideal communities are founded. Some people went so far as to propose the establishment of new communities in which men and women could live more simply and happily. Emerson jokingly claimed that every man he met on the street had such a plan in his vest pocket. Some of these schemes were actually tried.

An English reformer, Robert Owen, came to America in the 1820's and established an "ideal" community in New Harmony, Indiana. But friction within the settlement and opposition from neighbors destroyed the harmony within a few years. Another experimental community was Brook Farm, which a group of Transcendentalists (page 268) started outside Boston in 1841. A number of writers lived at Brook Farm, trying to find a happy balance between intellectual and manual labor. But troubles developed among the community's members, and there was opposition from outside as well. Yet Brook Farm lasted longer than most of the ideal communities; it closed only after fire in 1846 destroyed the main building.

The temperance movement starts. Some reformers started a crusade against the use of intoxicating liquor. Drinking was indeed an evil during the Jacksonian Era. One man complained: "No keel of a vessel could be laid, no frame of a house or barn reared, in any of the Atlantic States; no log house be put together west of the mountains, without the presence of several gallons of New England Rum, Jamaica Spirits, or Western Whisky." The first effective organized movement against excessive drinking started in Boston in the 1820's, and the American Society for the Promotion of Temperance was soon formed. The *temperance* movement, calling for moderation in the use of liquor, won many converts. But there was also a growing feeling that total abstinence, or the *prohibition* of the use of liquor, was the best way to solve the problem.

Better care is given to criminals and the handicapped. Attitudes toward unfortunate members of society — such as the insane, the blind, orphans, and lawbreakers — underwent a great change during these years. Previously it had been the practice to imprison feebleminded and insane persons and treat them like animals. A strong-willed, courageous Unitarian, Dorothea Lynde Dix, made it her life work to aid these unfortunate people. After visiting the prison in Charlestown, Massachusetts, she petitioned the state legislature in 1843 to stop confining the insane "in cages, closets, cellars, stalls, pens! Chained, naked, beaten with rods, and lashed into obedience!" As a result of Dorothea Dix's untiring efforts, Massachusetts and many other states established public institutions for the insane. The number of private asylums also increased, and their facilities were improved.

Orphans and the blind also received attention. A Boston doctor, Samuel Gridley Howe, became interested in the problem of teaching blind children. In 1832 he established the model Perkins Institution for the Blind in Boston. A Philadelphia merchant and banker, Stephen Girard, left most of his immense fortune to the city of Philadelphia for the education of orphans. Not much public money was appropriated for the care of the blind or orphans, but private charity accomplished a great deal.

Prison reforms were also undertaken. Fewer crimes brought the death penalty, and laws which had imposed long prison terms for minor crimes were amended or repealed. Living conditions in prisons were somewhat improved, and prisoners were given work to do on the theory that they should be reformed as well as punished. Prisons were built in which each man had his own cell, thus separating habitual criminals from first offenders.

▶ CHECK-UP

1. What changes took place in religious thinking? What new religions were founded? Why did Catholics encounter discrimination?

2. What efforts were made to establish "ideal" communities? To further temperance?

3. What improvements were made in the treatment of the insane? Of prisoners?

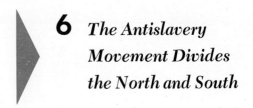

6 The Antislavery Movement Divides the North and South

Attitudes toward slavery change. Of all the reform movements, the crusade to abolish slavery was the most controversial. During the debate on the admission of Missouri (page 229), a few questions had been raised concerning slavery as a moral issue. But at the time neither the North nor the South was much concerned with that aspect of the problem. Some people living below the Mason and Dixon Line felt that slavery was wrong and would eventually have to go. Jefferson had often condemned the institution — "Nothing is more certainly written in the book of fate, than that these people are to be free" — but he offered no plan as to how it could be ended.

Colonization in Africa is suggested. The first organized effort to solve the slavery question was based on the idea of transporting American Negroes to Africa. In the first stages, free Negroes would establish a colony in Africa; later, slaves would be emancipated (freed) and sent across the Atlantic. The American Colonization Society, formed in 1817 with a nephew of George Washington as president, bought land in Africa in what is now Liberia and began sending free Negroes there as settlers. But the results were disappointing. The cost of transportation was higher than the society had expected, and Congress refused to help meet the expenses of the operation. Moreover, many of the Negroes died in Liberia; and a number of free Negroes and whites opposed the project. In its peak year the American Colonization Society sent only 800 emigrants to Liberia — compared to approximately 4500 Negroes born into slavery that year.

Emancipation is proposed. While American reformers were backing the colonization idea, British antislavery forces tried another approach. They argued for the emancipation of slaves in the British Empire with compensation, or payment, to slaveowners by Parliament; and in 1833 this objective was won. Encouraged by the British example, a few American reformers began to urge that slavery be ended in this country. But many Americans felt that paying slaveholders for their slaves would be too expensive. Moreover, the very fact that some people were demanding an immediate end to slavery caused Southerners to draw together in defense of what John Calhoun had called their "peculiar institution." Thus, the lines were formed for the long contest between North and South on the moral aspects of slavery.

Garrison demands abolition. A fiery New Englander named William Lloyd Garrison took the lead in demanding the immediate *abolition* of slavery in the United States. He believed that slavery was a "national sin" and should not be excused on the grounds of economic profit. The first issue of his newspaper, *The Liberator*, appeared on January 1, 1831. In it he hurled defiance at those who favored gradual emancipation or emancipation with payment to slaveholders. Garrison warned:

> I *will be* as harsh as truth, and as uncompromising as justice. On this subject I do not wish to think, or speak, or write, with moderation . . . I am in earnest — I will not equivocate — I will not excuse — I will not retreat a single inch — AND I WILL BE HEARD.

With the financial aid of two New York merchants, Garrison helped to establish the American Antislavery Society. He soon quarreled with the other members of the organization, however, and went his own way during the 1840's and '50's. He called on the northern states to secede from a Union which protected slavery; and he publicly burned the Constitution, charging that it compromised with "tyranny" and therefore was "an agreement with hell."

Garrison arouses Northerners. The approach Garrison took to the slavery question stirred up much opposition in the North. His bold language and his attack on the Constitution disturbed many Northerners. He made enemies among businessmen who were interested in the cotton textile industry and in protecting their trade with the South. Abolitionist meetings were broken up, speakers hissed and stoned, and printing presses and assembly halls torn down or burned. Garrison himself was mobbed in the streets of Boston in 1835 and barely escaped with his life. Less fortunate was the Illinois abolitionist Elijah Lovejoy, who was killed by an angry mob in 1837.

Garrison angers Southerners. In the South the abolitionists made even more violent enemies. White Southerners bitterly resented Garrison's attack on slaveholders as "greedy and relentless tyrants." Anger turned to alarm when the worst slave uprising the South had ever known took place in 1831. Led by Nat Turner, a Negro preacher, slaves in Virginia killed about 60 white people, most of them women and children. Southerners blamed Garrison and abolitionist propaganda for this violence.

The South quickly took steps to prevent further disturbances and to safeguard its institutions. State militias were reorganized. Laws were passed to stop the circulation of antislavery literature, and attempts were made to close the mails to such material. Georgia offered 5000 dollars for the arrest of Garrison, and other states dared abolitionists to come south and meet the punishment promised them.

Virginia rejects emancipation. Meanwhile, a movement had begun in Virginia to secure the state legislature's approval for the gradual freeing of slaves. Leading the opposition was Thomas Dew, soon to be named president of the College of William and Mary. He argued not only that slavery was an economic necessity in Virginia but that the institution of slavery was morally right. Emancipation, according to Thomas Dew, would ruin the Virginia planters, even if they were paid for their slaves. By a narrow majority, the Virginia legislature voted down the proposal for gradual emancipation. With this action died any hope that the South itself would put an end to slavery. White Southerners increasingly rallied to the defense of their "peculiar institution." Their determination to keep slavery was pitted against the determination of northern abolitionists to destroy it.

▶ CHECK-UP

1. How was "colonization" supposed to solve the slavery problem? What difficulties did this proposal encounter? Why was compensated emancipation not acceptable?

2. What was Garrison's solution? How did he justify it? How was his suggestion received in the North? In the South? Explain why in each case.

3. How did Thomas Dew justify slavery? What was the significance of the Virginia legislature's rejection of a proposal for gradual emancipation?

. . . .

Clinching the Main Ideas in Chapter 12

American society underwent many important changes during the 1830's and 1840's. Most of them tended to break down economic, intellectual, and social barriers. Hence historians have often referred to the period as an "age of ferment."

The industrial expansion of the Jacksonian Era was based on the introduction of new machines and new sources of power, as well as the spread of roads, canals, and railroads, which tied the nation together. Equally important was the rapid expansion of the laboring force. The first labor unions were short-lived, but workingmen used their votes to achieve a number of social reforms. Foremost among these was the establishment of tax-supported, free elementary schools.

The strong demand throughout the North and West for educational, cultural, and social reforms brought about other changes as well. Many new colleges appeared. Lyceums, penny newspapers, and magazines all catered to the demand for formal and informal education. The enlarged reading public in turn gave encouragement to American authors. The religious ferment of the 1830's and 1840's brought changes in established churches and produced new religions. Some Americans set out to reform the nation's drinking habits and its handling of prisoners, the insane, and the handicapped.

The most far-reaching reform, however, was the antislavery movement. Starting out as a leisurely debate, it became by the 1830's and '40's an uncompromising drive to abolish slavery in the United States. As a result, southern slave-owners rallied to the defense of their "peculiar institution." Though few Americans were ready to fight about slavery at this time, the scope of the coming controversy was clearly defined in the Jacksonian Era.

Chapter Review

Terms to Understand

1. lyceum
2. free academy
3. black-listed
4. camp meeting
5. packet ship
6. capital
7. corporation
8. abolition
9. Latter-Day Saints
10. Transcendentalist
11. *The Liberator*
12. temperance movement
13. patent medicine
14. Associated Press
15. Greek Revival

16. American Colonization Society

What Do You Think?

1. Had you been a New England farmer in the early 1800's, what factors would you have taken into account in deciding whether (a) to go West, (b) to get a job in a factory town, or (c) to stay where you were?

2. "By 1850 most states in the North and West had accepted the idea of tax-supported public schools." Why? Why was the idea not accepted in the South?

3. The development of the factory system was made possible by revolutionary changes in agriculture, communication, and transportation, as well as by the use of power to drive machines. Do you agree? Why?

4. With the increased building of railroads, interest in building canals declined. Why?

5. Garrison demanded the immediate abolition of slavery and scorned the idea of gradual emancipation or emancipation with payment to slaveholders. Why did he feel as he did? What can be said for the plans he rejected?

Using Your Knowledge of History

1. Study a physical map of the United States; then explain: (a) why New York was better located for trade with the West than Boston or Philadelphia; (b) why New Orleans became a more important port than Charleston; (c) why Chicago became a greater railroad center than Cincinnati.

2. Prepare a biographical report on one of the important reformers of this period. What did he advocate and why? What methods did he use? What was achieved?

3. Slogans are one way of calling attention to a needed reform. What slogans can members of the class suggest for the various reform movements discussed in this chapter?

4. Prepare a bulletin-board display of buildings in the Greek Revival and Gothic styles of architecture. What do you like (or not like) about each? What factors should be considered in deciding whether a particular style of architecture is "right" for a given building in a given place?

Extending Your Knowledge of History

An excellent summary of the sweeping changes during the Jacksonian Era is provided by Carl R. Fish in *The Rise of the Common Man.* Interesting accounts of the reform movements are found in *Young America, 1830–1840* by Robert E. Riegel, and in *The Fabulous Forties, 1840–1850* by Meade Minnigerode. A well-written study of the early stages of the antislavery movement is G. H. Barnes' *The Anti-Slavery Impulse, 1830–1844.* *Audubon's America* is a handsomely illustrated volume by Donald C. Peattie. Various issues of *American Heritage* contain excellent articles dealing with this period. Mrs. Hale is featured in "Mr. Godey's Lady" by Ralph Nading Hill (October, 1958); Washington Irving in "The Sunny Master of Sunnyside" by Curtis Dahl (December, 1961); the Mormon migration in "Best Prepared Pioneers in the West" by Ray A. Billington (October, 1956); southern plantation architecture in "The River Houses" by Clarence John Laughlin (June, 1956); the experiences of New England factory workers in "The Working Ladies of Lowell" by Bernard A. Weisberger (February, 1961); and Joseph Henry and the Smithsonian Institution in "Professor Henry and His Philosophical Toys" by Michael Blow (December, 1963).

CHAPTER 13

Wagon train camping

1820–1850

The United States Expands Westward to the Pacific

Land enough — land enough! Make way, I say, for the young American Buffalo — he has not yet got land enough; he wants more land as his cool shelter in summer — he wants more land for his beautiful pasture grounds. I tell you, we will give him Oregon for his summer shade, and the region of Texas as his winter pasture. Like all of his race, he wants salt, too. Well, he shall have the use of two oceans — the mighty Pacific and turbulent Atlantic shall be his. . . .

New Jersey Democratic State Convention, 1844

When the Treaty of Paris was signed in 1783, Americans thought they had more than enough land between the Atlantic coast and the Mississippi River. Yet 20 years later they added the vast Louisiana Territory to the Union and soon also acquired the Florida peninsula. Then, in the 1840's, Americans began to look westward for still more land.

In that decade an expansionist fever swept over the whole country. Northerners demanded that Oregon become American territory while Southerners insisted on the annexation of Texas. Both groups agreed that California should round out the coun-

try's "natural boundaries." So strong was this feeling that the issue of expansion dominated the presidential campaign of 1844. President Polk interpreted his election as a mandate, or demand from the voters, to expand westward and even to fight a war with Mexico if necessary to acquire more land. Expansion raised the question, however, of whether slavery should be permitted in newly acquired territory. The North and South nearly came to blows over this issue in 1850. Only the efforts of the compromiser, Henry Clay, and the champion of the Union, Daniel Webster, averted disaster.

1 *Americans Establish the Lone Star Republic*

Americans continue to move west.
Westward movement had been an ever-present factor in the nation's history — whether it was the early colonist venturing beyond the thin line of coastal settlements, or the later pioneer moving into the fertile lands of Louisiana. Whatever the period, American pioneers generally sought cheap land, greater opportunities, and a new start in life. New Englanders left small, rocky farms for the broad expanse of rich prairie soil. Southern planters abandoned fields worn out by cotton crops and moved west to stake out new plantations. In the Louisiana Territory and later in Oregon, California, and Texas, Americans found fertile land on which to grow wheat, corn, and cotton.

But expansion into these lands raised the disturbing question of slavery. Southern planters took slaves into the new territories, arguing that they were needed for cotton growing. Northerners increasingly felt that slavery was wrong and opposed its extension into new areas.

Expansion affects North-South relations. You will recall that in the Compromise of 1820 (page 230), Congress had drawn a line between slave and free territory in the Louisiana Purchase (except for Missouri) at 36°30′. During the 1830's and 1840's the free territory north of the Ohio River and the 36°30′ line filled rapidly with

. . . .

CHAPTER FOCUS

native-born Americans and immigrants. Michigan was admitted to the Union in 1837, and other non-slave territories were preparing for statehood.

Under these conditions, Southerners became worried about the balance of political power between slave and free states. They were also concerned over the scarcity of additional land for cotton growing. By the 1840's southern planters had occupied the most fertile parts of Georgia, Alabama, Mississippi, and Louisiana. So many of them had pushed over into Arkansas that it was admitted to the Union in 1836. The remainder of the Louisiana Territory south of 36°30′ (most of present-day Oklahoma) had been set aside for the Indians (page 243). To be sure, Florida was eligible for admission as a slave state. But Iowa and Wisconsin were about ready for statehood, and settlers were pushing into Minnesota. With the Senate equally divided between slave states and free states, admission of these three northern states would seriously upset the balance which had been the aim of the Compromise of 1820. As a result, Southerners showed a strong interest in nearby territory held by Mexico.

Texas attracts attention. From the planters' viewpoint the most attractive piece of Mexican territory was the province of Texas (map, page 277). This land included millions of acres of fertile land well-suited to the growing of southern crops. Over the protests of southern and western spokesmen, the United States had renounced its shadowy claim to Texas in the treaty with Spain in 1819 (page 220). Two years later Mexico won its independence from Spain, and Texas became a Mexican province. During the 1820's, the Mexican government was weak and unstable. Plagued by internal difficulties, it was never able to establish its authority over the outlying provinces. Only a few Spanish-speaking people lived in Texas, and only a thread of loyalty bound them to the central government at Mexico City.

Americans settle in Texas. Neither the Spanish nor the Mexican government objected to Americans' settling in Texas. Moses Austin, a Missouri mine-owner and banker who had been ruined by the Panic of 1819, received a large land grant from the Spanish governor of Texas in 1820. He died soon afterwards, but his son, Stephen F. Austin, managed to have the grant confirmed by the new Mexican government. Stephen Austin then started an American settlement in Texas. Soon other American promoters received similar grants of land.

In 1825 Mexico passed a colonization law which encouraged foreigners to settle in Texas and guaranteed their security. In return, it required foreigners to obey Mexican laws and observe the Catholic faith. But Mexican officials were not strict in enforcing this law. Consequently, hundreds of Americans poured into Texas seeking rich land, although they had no intention of living up to the Mexican restrictions. Before long, there were some 20,000 former American citizens and 2000 slaves living in Texas. Most of the Americans came from Alabama, Mississippi, Louisiana, and Tennessee.

The Mexican government soon realized that the ever-growing number of American settlers threatened its control of Texas. Mexican officials attempted to enforce a ban on slavery; they passed an immigration law forbidding any more Americans to enter Texas; and they sent troops to occupy the province. But the American settlers paid little attention to the laws on slavery and immigration, and new settlers continued to come to Texas.

Texas becomes independent. When a dictator, Santa Anna, took over the Mexican government, he decided that the Americans must obey Mexican laws. The Texans met this threat by issuing a declaration of independence. A struggle then developed between Mexican forces commanded by Santa Anna and Texans led by Sam Houston, former governor of Tennessee. On March 6, 1836, the Mexicans captured the Alamo, a fortified mission outside San Antonio. The American commander, William B. Travis, and his entire band of 187 men (including Davy Crockett and James Bowie) were killed. Three weeks later, at Goliad, 300 Texan soldiers who had surrendered were massacred by order of Santa Anna.

Suddenly the tide of battle turned. On April 21, Sam Houston surprised Santa Anna's army at San Jacinto (juh-*sin*'toh), defeated the Mexicans, and captured the dictator-general. To gain his release, Santa Anna signed an agreement promising that the Mexicans would retreat beyond the Rio Grande and that his government would recognize Texan independence. Although the Mexican Congress refused to accept this treaty, Mexico was too weak and disorganized to continue the war. For all practical purposes the Americans in Texas had won their independence at the Battle of San Jacinto.

Some Americans favor the annexation of Texas. The Texans promptly organized

Mexican forces stormed the walls of the Alamo. After a thirteen-day siege, the last of the 187 defenders was dead. "Remember the Alamo" became the battle cry of the Texans fighting for independence.

THE MEXICAN PROVINCE OF TEXAS: 1821-1836

THE LONE STAR REPUBLIC 1836-1845

THE STATE OF TEXAS TODAY

THE CHANGING SHAPE OF TEXAS

First explored by Spain, Texas was later part of French Louisiana and then became a Mexican province in 1821. In 1836, as the map shows, Texas became an independent republic with its capital at Austin. Note how the color treatment accents the changes in Texas' political status.

MAP STUDY

the "Lone Star Republic" with a constitution that made slavery legal. Sam Houston was elected the first president. Several courses of action were open to the new republic. (1) It could remain independent; (2) it could seek admission to the United States; (3) it could ally itself with Britain or France, both of whom wanted its trade. Because the great majority of Texans were Americans, they decided to seek admission to the United States.

Most southern Americans and many Westerners favored the annexation of Texas. Planters believed it would provide much-needed fertile soil for the further expansion of cotton growing. Southern politicians saw in Texas a golden opportunity to balance the growing strength of the free states. If four or five states were carved out of Texas, this would preserve a balance in the Senate. Western expansionists favored annexation since it would add desirable land to the growing nation.

Northerners oppose annexation. Many Northerners, however, argued against the annexation of Texas, and, as time went on, their number increased. Northern politicians opposed the addition of any slave territory, and they feared that Texas would be subdivided into a number of slave states.

Northern abolitionists attacked Texas annexation on the grounds that it would strengthen the institution of slavery. They charged that the struggle for Texan independence had been a slave-owners' conspiracy and that the same forces now wanted to drag the United States into a war with Mexico. Garrison wrote that Texas was full of "swindlers, gamblers, robbers, and rogues of every size and degree." These people, he charged, wanted "to extend and perpetuate the most frightful form of servitude the world has ever known."

The Texas question remains unsettled. President Andrew Jackson did not want to antagonize either the North or the South on the question of Texas annexation. He took no action, therefore, and did not even recognize the new republic until just before he left the White House in 1837. President Van Buren made it clear that he would follow Jackson's example and not press the matter of annexation. Thus rebuffed by the United States, Texas negotiated trade treaties with Britain and France. This worried the Southerners, for they had to compete with Texas cotton on the British market. They feared, moreover, that British abolitionists might get a foothold in Texas and seek to end slavery there.

AMERICANS SETTLE THE FAR WEST

*The Oregon and Santa Fe Trails were the primary over-
land routes by which settlers made the long trek to the
"Golden West." Note that the Mormons, while they had
a different starting point and destination, used the Oregon Trail to travel the plains and make the treacherous
Rocky Mountain crossing.*

Russian

54° 40'

OREGON COUNTRY

To Great
Britain, 1846

BRITISH

Vancouver I.

49°

Puget Sound

Astoria

Columbia R.

Willamette Valley

Ft. Walla Walla

Oregon City

Missouri R.

MINNESOTA TERRITORY

Mississippi R.

WIS.

OREGON
TERRITORY
1848

Rocky

MISSOURI TERRITORY

South Pass

42°

Ocean

California Trail

Sacramento R.

Salt Lake City

UTAH TERRITORY

Oregon Trail

Platte R.

Mormon route

IOWA

ILL. IND.

Nauvoo

New Harmony

Sacramento
San
Francisco

Gold discovered
1849

Mountains

Independence

Lawrence MISSOURI

California Cut-off

Colorado R.

Los Angeles

NEW MEXICO TERRITORY

Santa Fe

Santa Fe Trail

San Francisco

New York

MEXICO

NICARAGUA

Isthmus of
Panama

Gila R.

San Diego

Gila Trail

Rio Grande

TEXAS

Water
Routes

MEXICO

Pacific

California

~~ Main overland
route of forty-niners

⋈ Mountain Pass

⌐ Fort

0   100   300   500 mi.

R. M. Chapin, Jr.

Cape Horn

When John Tyler of Virginia became
President, Southerners redoubled their efforts to have Texas annexed. Tyler sympathized with them and asked John Calhoun, his Secretary of State, to prepare a
treaty with Texas. When the Secretary submitted the Texas treaty to the Senate in
1844, he urged its ratification on the
grounds that slavery was a "positive good."
Calhoun's argument offended antislavery
senators from the North and West, and they
made sure that the treaty failed to get the
necessary two-thirds vote. Thus, Texas annexation was certain to become an issue in
the presidential election of 1844.

▶ CHECK-UP

1. Why did Americans move westward? How
   did the westward movement affect North-
   South relations?

2. On what terms had Americans settled in
   Texas? Why did tension develop between
   them and the Mexican government? How
   did the Texans achieve independence?

3. What courses of action were open to the
   republic of Texas? How did each of the
   sections in this country feel about annexation of Texas? Why did Tyler and Calhoun
   fail to get Senate approval of annexation?

2 The United States Acquires Texas and Oregon

The United States and Britain claim Oregon. While Americans were settling in Texas, interest in far-off Oregon was also increasing. Spain and Russia had surrendered their rights to this desirable territory in 1821 and 1824 respectively (pages 220, 223). Oregon's boundaries thus were set at the forty-second parallel in the south and at 54°40′ in the north (map, page 278). Both Great Britain and the United States claimed the area, however, and each advanced strong arguments in its own behalf.

Americans pointed out that as early as the 1780's, Boston merchants were stopping along the Oregon coast to buy furs from the Indians. Captain Robert Gray discovered and named the Columbia River in 1792, and Lewis and Clark wintered on the Oregon coast. An enterprising fur trader, John Jacob Astor, established a trading post at Astoria near the mouth of the Columbia River in 1811.

British claims to Oregon were equally impressive. The British asserted that Francis Drake had anchored off Oregon in the sixteenth century. They also cited the fact that Captain James Cook in 1778 had mapped the northwest coast as far as Bering Strait. A few years later Captain George Vancouver had discovered and named Puget Sound and sailed around Vancouver Island. Moreover, Canadian fur traders drove Astor out of Oregon during the War of 1812. Thereafter the Hudson's Bay Company controlled the fur trade in the Pacific Northwest.

When American and British negotiators discussed boundary lines in 1818, they could come to no agreement on Oregon. They decided to leave the Oregon territory "free and open" to the citizens of both countries for ten years. Later, this friendly arrangement was renewed for an indefinite period.

Americans settle in Oregon. Public interest in Oregon was aroused in the early 1830's by a Boston schoolteacher, Hall Jackson Kelley, and a Cambridge merchant, Nathaniel Wyeth. Kelley and Wyeth, both ardent expansionists, proved that settlers could reach Oregon by an overland route. Wyeth's 1834 expedition to Oregon included a band of Methodist missionaries who settled in the fertile Willamette Valley. Their enthusiastic letters encouraged many American families to join them — not for the purpose of converting Indians but to farm. Soon afterward, the Presbyterians sent Marcus Whitman to establish a mission near Fort Walla Walla. Catholic missions were also started in Oregon.

Efforts to convert the Indians were not entirely successful. Whitman, his wife, and twelve others were massacred at their mission. But the missionaries did publicize Oregon. Their glowing descriptions of climate and soil were widely circulated in religious newspapers and magazines. As a result, many Americans traveled the 2000-mile Oregon Trail from Independence, Missouri, across the prairies, through the South Pass in the Rocky Mountains, to the Columbia River valley. The historian Francis Parkman described his experiences on this arduous journey in *The Oregon Trail* (1849). Other Americans went to Oregon by ship around Cape Horn.

In 1842 Webster and Ashburton (page 252), while settling other boundary problems, had no success in reaching agreement on the Oregon boundary. The next year the Americans in Oregon established a provisional government "until such time as the United States of America extend their jurisdiction over us." Canadian fur traders were alarmed at the influx of Americans south of the Columbia River, but, being outnumbered, they could do nothing about it.

Americans settle in New Mexico and California. Meanwhile, Americans had been settling in still other western regions. When Mexico won independence from Spain, the new government had let it be known that American traders would be welcome in New Mexico. As a result, American merchants developed trade with Santa Fe. Wagonloads of manufactured goods were hauled over the 800-mile Santa Fe Trail from Independence, Missouri (map, page 278). On the return trip the

Americans brought back gold, silver, furs, and mules. In pursuit of this profitable trade, some took up residence in Santa Fe.

Other Americans settled in California. When American ships stopped in California harbors to barter goods or buy supplies, some Yankee traders, whalers, and merchants stayed in this Mexican province. They were joined by sailors, artisans, fur traders, and adventurers. Descriptions of sunny California, its fertile valleys, and its magnificent harbors at San Diego and San Francisco soon filtered back to the United States. One of the most interesting accounts was Richard Henry Dana's *Two Years Before the Mast*. The lure of California led numerous bands of pioneers to undertake the long overland journey. Though the Americans were few in number, they hoped to free California from Mexican control and add it to the United States.

Expansion is viewed as America's "manifest destiny." Americans who wanted to expand the nation's boundaries justified this goal with an elaborate argument called *manifest destiny*. Apparently the phrase was first used by a newspaper editor who referred to "the fulfillment of our manifest destiny to overspread the continent allotted by Providence for the free development of our yearly multiplying millions."

Though the term "manifest destiny" was coined in the 1840's, the ideas implied in it were not new. The expansionists claimed that American occupation of Texas, California, and Oregon would be comparable to the addition of the Louisiana Territory and Florida. Just as the War Hawks had talked about stretching America's "natural boundaries" from the Gulf of Mexico to the "regions of the eternal frost," so the expansionists of the 1840's argued that the Atlantic and Pacific Oceans were our "natural boundaries." They believed that the supposedly "less energetic" people occupying neighboring lands would gladly surrender them to the hard-working Americans. Thus the New York *Herald* said about Mexico: "It is a part of our destiny to civilize that beautiful country and enable its inhabitants to appreciate some of the many advantages and blessings they enjoy."

Expansion becomes an election issue. "Manifest destiny" became an important issue in the 1844 presidential election. Henry Clay, who expected to get the Whig nomination, and Martin Van Buren, who hoped to be the Democratic candidate, tried to keep the expansion issue out of the campaign. They had agreed in private not to make an issue of Texas or Oregon, and each publicly stated that Texas annexation should be delayed. Neither man seemed to understand fully the deep interest of the voters in this question.

Clay did get the Whig nomination, and he dictated a platform which made no mention of Texas. But in the Democratic nominating convention, the expansionists of the South and West took control. They passed over Van Buren, who was too northern and had expressed opposition to slavery. They also passed over Calhoun, who was too southern and had strongly supported slavery. The Democrats settled on James K. Polk, once Speaker of the House of Repre-

---

The Donner Party

"Party" hardly describes what befell the Donner party, a group of pioneers from Illinois who set out for California in 1846. The expedition, organized by the Donner and Reed families, was slow in crossing the western prairies and desert. It arrived at the foothills of the Sierra Nevadas late in October, but snow was already falling. Unable to make their way through the deep snow of the mountain passes, the pioneers stopped at Truckee Lake, now Donner Lake, and built cabins for shelter.

Soon the members of the Donner party began to run out of food. They killed their cattle and preserved the meat in the snow until it was gone. When their bread ran out, the starving pioneers ate cattle hides. Finally, some resorted to cannibalism at the expense of those who had died.

Meanwhile, volunteers from the party had pushed over the mountains on snowshoes, starving and dying as they went. A few reached Sacramento to tell their horrible news to the settlers there. Then, rescue operations began. Of the 87 members of the Donner party, 47 were finally rescued.

(*Continued on page 285*)

AMERICANS MOVE WESTWARD

The Lewis and Clark expedition had whetted the interest of Americans in lands beyond the Mississippi. Exploration and settlement continued until by 1850 the nation extended to the Pacific.

Early adventurers became familiar with the customs of western Indian tribes. Right, the explorer Stephen Long participated in a parley with Pawnees near Council Bluffs, Iowa.

Much of our knowledge of Indian life and dress of the past comes from the work of the artist George Catlin. At left is Catlin's painting of a Blackfoot war chief and his family. Below, left, Sioux women scrape and stretch a buffalo skin.

Above, this shield of buffalo hide was used to foretell the future. If it fell face up when rolled on the ground, it promised success.

281

Mountain men like Jim Baker (right) were among the first to penetrate the plains and mountain regions. They were attracted by the rich fur trade and also acted as guides and scouts.

The trapper's life was lonely and sometimes dangerous but the fur trade brought good profits. Below, a frontiersman sets beaver traps in a mountain stream.

Pioneer missionaries like Marcus Whitman (below) stimulated interest in the fertile Oregon Country. Reports from the West led many Easterners to set out on the Oregon Trail.

Western forts like Laramie in Wyoming (above) served as trading posts and helped keep the Indians in check.

During the 1840's, two events — the Mexican War and the California gold rush — clinched American claims to the West and brought a horde of fortune seekers to the mining areas. The painting at left shows American troops passing through San Antonio on the long overland march to Mexico.

San Jacinto Museum of History Association

At right are pictured various methods used by the gold prospectors — digging, clearing rocks, panning dirt, and sifting out ore by a washing process.

The urge to get rich quick spread like an epidemic. Crews abandoned their ships in San Francisco harbor to seek their fortunes in the gold fields. Below, San Francisco is pictured in 1851.

Many American artists portrayed the "way westward," especially as the early trickle of pioneers swelled into a flood. Albert Bierstadt painted the above scene entitled "Nooning on the Platte." Rest periods helped maintain the strength of people and animals during the arduous overland journey. Right, another artist painted a steamboat called "Yellowstone" on the Missouri River. This form of transportation was limited to navigable rivers.

The two pictures above are sketches by J. Goldsborough Bruff, a forty-niner who kept an illustrated diary of his journey through the West. The sketch at left shows wagons being ferried on a raft across the Platte River. Right, travelers cook their meal over a fire of buffalo chips.

sentatives and a former governor of Tennessee. The Democratic candidate and the party platform came out in favor of annexing Texas and occupying all of Oregon.

The Democrats win with Polk. During the 1844 campaign the Democrats called for the extension of both slave and free territory. Their slogan was "The re-occupation of Oregon and the re-annexation of Texas." Thus, they managed to suggest that both of these areas had originally been American territory but had been bartered away by careless diplomats. The Whig candidate, Henry Clay, suddenly found himself in an uncomfortable spot. He tried late in the campaign to straddle the issue of annexation by stating that he would be glad to see Texas come into the Union on "just and fair terms." This angered the antislavery faction of the Whig Party and did not fully satisfy the proslavery southern Whigs.

A third party — the Liberty Party — also presented a candidate in the 1844 election. This party had been formed by abolitionists who, unlike Garrison, were interested in politics. Their presidential candidate, a former slave-owner named James G. Birney, campaigned against Texas annexation on the grounds that it would add more slave territory to the Union. Since Polk and, at the last minute, Clay, favored annexation, the Liberty Party won the support of many antislavery people. Nevertheless, it polled less than 3 per cent of the vote. The popular vote was closely split between Polk and Clay, but Polk had 170 electoral votes to Clay's 105. The Democrats also won control of both houses of Congress.

Polk is a forceful President. During the campaign the Whigs had ridiculed the Democratic candidate as a political unknown, a "dark horse." Though he was a friend of Andrew Jackson and had been active in politics for many years, Polk was not as well-known as Webster, Clay, or Calhoun. Nor did he have much popular appeal. But he was hard-working, diligent, and determined. Historians, who have learned a great deal from his diary, generally agree that Polk was the country's most effective President between Jackson and Lincoln.

When Polk took office, he noted in his diary that he wanted to lower the tariff, re-establish the Independent Treasury system (page 250), settle the Oregon dispute, and acquire California. The President actually succeeded in doing all of these things. In 1846 he signed a new tariff measure which sharply reduced rates. Southerners were jubilant, for it established the principle of a tariff for revenue only and not for the protection of American industry. In that same year Polk revived Van Buren's Independent Treasury, which continued to handle the government's finances until the 1860's.

Texas is annexed. Since Polk had campaigned on the issue of Texas annexation, he naturally hoped to get credit for adding Texas to the Union. But the outgoing President, John Tyler, stole a march on him. Tyler knew that it would be impossible to obtain a two-thirds vote in the Senate for a treaty of annexation. So he asked Congress for a *joint resolution*, which would require only a majority vote in both houses. Early in 1845, Congress passed a joint resolution annexing Texas, and Tyler had the pleasure of signing it three days before he left office. According to the terms of the resolution, Texas was to keep its public lands and pay its own debts. The people of Texas voted to accept these terms, and in December their state was admitted to the Union.[1]

The Oregon question is settled. Though President Polk missed the glory of annexing Texas, he still hoped to settle the Oregon issue and acquire California. "Fifty-four forty or fight!" became the slogan of those Americans who wanted all of Oregon. But Polk was sensible enough not to insist on a boundary of 54°40′. Relations with Mexico were strained in the spring of 1846, since that country resented the annexation of Texas and American interest in California. Because of this tense situation, Polk did not want to stir up trouble with Great Britain at the same time. The President let the British know, therefore, that he was

---

[1] In that same year Florida entered the Union as a slave state. But the balance between slave and free states was restored by the admission of Iowa in 1846 and Wisconsin in 1848.

willing to settle for a boundary at the forty-ninth parallel.

Fortunately, the British also were willing to compromise. They knew they could not match the growing number of Americans in Oregon. They further realized that the new settlements would eventually destroy the fur trade in the Columbia Valley. The British agreed, therefore, to divide Oregon at the forty-ninth parallel, provided they received Vancouver Island and retained navigation rights on the Columbia River. These terms were embodied in the Oregon Treaty ratified by the United States Senate in June, 1846. Thus Polk accomplished another of his objectives.

▶ CHECK-UP

1. What claims to Oregon did Great Britain and the United States each have? What efforts were made by each to settle in the region?

2. How had Americans come to settle in New Mexico and California? What did Americans mean by "manifest destiny"? How was such a policy justified?

3. How did expansion become an election issue in 1844? What was the outcome? How did Tyler bring about the annexation of Texas? How did Polk reach a settlement with respect to Oregon?

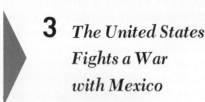

3 The United States Fights a War with Mexico

Relations with Mexico worsen. Let us now return to the quarrel between Mexico and the United States over Texas. Shortly after Congress passed the resolution annexing Texas, Mexico broke off diplomatic relations with the United States. Since the Mexican government had not yet recognized Texan independence, it considered this action of Congress insulting. In addition, Mexico insisted that the southern

boundary of Texas was the Nueces (noo-ay'sees) River, not the Rio Grande (map, page 287). President Polk ordered General Zachary Taylor and a small army force to station themselves at the Nueces River to protect Texas against invasion by Mexican troops. Then Polk sent a representative to Mexico to seek a settlement of the dispute.

Polk's special envoy, John Slidell, arrived in Mexico City with instructions to obtain Mexico's recognition of Texan independence and of the Rio Grande as Texas' southern boundary. In return, the United States would assume responsibility for two million dollars in unpaid American claims against Mexico. Slidell was also authorized to discuss the purchase of New Mexico and California and to offer Mexico as much as 40 million dollars for the two provinces. But the recently installed Mexican government was strongly anti-American and for political reasons dared not negotiate with Slidell. The disgusted Slidell wrote to President Polk that nothing could be done with the obstinate Mexicans "until they shall have been chastised."

Polk prepares for action. Annoyed by Mexico's refusal to talk with Slidell, Polk ordered General Taylor to cross the Nueces and take up a position on the north bank of the Rio Grande. Meanwhile, Polk sent secret orders to Commodore John D. Sloat of the United States Navy in the Pacific. Sloat was told to seize California if he learned definitely that Mexico had declared war against the United States. In addition, Polk's Secretary of State, James Buchanan, sent this message to the American consul in California:

Whilst the President will make no effort and use no influence to induce California to become one of the free and independent States of this Union, yet if the people should desire to unite their destiny with ours, they would be received as brethren, whenever this can be done without affording Mexico just cause for complaint.

The American consul, Thomas Larkin, took the hint. He immediately began to organize Americans in California in an effort to bring about separation from Mexico.

War with Mexico is declared. Early in May, 1846, Slidell returned to Washington and gave a discouraging report to the President. Polk then prepared a message to Congress asking for a declaration of war on the grounds that Mexico refused to receive Slidell and was behind in its payment of the claims of American citizens. Before he had a chance to deliver this message, news came that Mexicans had crossed the Rio Grande and attacked one of Taylor's patrols. Polk and General Taylor had considered the presence of American troops along the Rio Grande necessary for the protection of Texas. The Mexicans, however, regarded it as an act of aggression. They felt justified in attacking Taylor's patrol even though it was north of the Rio Grande.

When Polk learned of the attack, he promptly revised his message, and on May 11 it was delivered to Congress. Polk declared: "Mexico has passed the boundary of the United States . . . and shed American blood upon the American soil. . . . War exists, and, notwithstanding all our efforts to avoid it, exists by the act of Mexico herself." Two days later Congress declared war on Mexico.

The Mexican War is opposed by some Americans. Most Americans in the South and West were enthusiastic about the war. Of the 70,000 volunteers who enlisted, about 40,000 were Westerners and 20,000 were Southerners. Less than 8000 came from the Northeast, which was generally opposed to the Mexican War. The Massachusetts legislature called it a war of conquest. Abolitionists saw it as a slavery plot. James Russell Lowell spoke for them in the *Biglow Papers*. The expansionists, he charged, wanted "bigger pens to cram with slaves."

They jest want this Californy
So's to lug new slave-states in.

In the House of Representatives a young Illinois Whig, Abraham Lincoln, challenged President Polk to prove that the spot on which American blood was shed was actually American soil. But Whig opposition to the Mexican War was never as strong as Federalist opposition had been to the War of 1812 (page 204). For one thing, many

THE MEXICAN WAR

Although Americans considered all of the Lone Star Republic part of the Texas annexation, Mexico disputed the area shown. After her defeat, Mexico ceded not only Texas but the vast area cut off by the Kearny and Fremont "pincers."

MAP STUDY

southern Whigs favored the war. The two leading generals in the Mexican War were Whigs, and Whig politicians remembered what military reputations had done for Generals Jackson and Harrison. Finally, this war, unlike the War of 1812, went well for the Americans from the very beginning.

The United States wins the Mexican War. President Polk's plan was to occupy key areas of Mexico and force the enemy to accept American peace terms. Even before war was actually declared, General Taylor had driven the Mexicans out of the disputed area between the Nueces River and the Rio Grande. Then he crossed the Rio Grande and captured Monterrey, Mexico, in September, 1846. This gave the Americans control of northeastern Mexico. The newspapers hailed Zachary Taylor as a great hero and dwelt upon his popularity with the soldiers. They even speculated about "Old Rough and Ready" as a Whig presidential candidate for 1848.

Wary of Taylor's growing popularity, Polk entrusted the major campaign to another general, Winfield Scott. Scott, too, was a Whig, though less popular with the American public and his men, who called him "Old Fuss and Feathers." Polk ordered Scott to land at Veracruz, establish a base, and then move inland to Mexico City. Meanwhile, General Taylor was told to send part of his army to help Scott. The crafty Santa Anna seized this opportunity to launch an attack on Taylor's weakened forces at Buena Vista in February, 1847. Defeated by Taylor, however, Santa Anna turned back to defend Mexico City. Scott took Veracruz in March and then began his drive against Mexico City. The Americans captured the fortress of Chapultepec in August and the next month raised the American flag over the Mexican capital.

Polk's strategy in New Mexico and California was equally successful. In the summer of 1846, Colonel Stephen W. Kearny (*car*'nih) led a small army from Fort Leavenworth over the Santa Fe Trail and seized New Mexico without any opposition. Polk then ordered Kearny to direct operations in California. Actually Commodore Sloat had already taken Monterey, then the capital of California. Also commanding a small American force was the explorer-adventurer John C. Frémont, who had helped to establish a "California Republic" under the "Bear Flag." With some difficulty, Kearny brought the two forces under his command. By January, 1847, the conquest of California was complete.

Mexico accepts the peace terms. When Polk learned of the American victories in New Mexico and California as well as in Mexico, he sent a member of the State Department to confer with Santa Anna. When these negotiations collapsed, there was reckless talk in the United States about occupying all of Mexico. Indeed, Secretary of State Buchanan said, "Destiny beckons us to hold and civilize Mexico." In February, 1848, however, the Mexicans accepted a treaty embodying Polk's terms.

The treaty established the Rio Grande as the southern boundary of Texas. It provided for the cession to the United States of the provinces of New Mexico and California. This Mexican Cession included the present states of California, Nevada, and Utah and parts of New Mexico, Arizona, Colorado, and Wyoming (map, page 289). In return for this territory, the United States agreed to settle the claims of American citizens against Mexico and to pay the defeated government fifteen million dollars in cash.

The Gadsden Purchase rounds out America's southern boundary. Five years later the United States acquired still more land from Mexico. In this transaction the American government paid Mexico ten million dollars for a strip of land along the southern border of the Mexican Cession. This area was called the Gadsden Purchase after the American minister to Mexico, James Gadsden, who arranged the sale. Americans wanted this land because it provided the best railroad route between the Gulf states and the Pacific coast. With the Gadsden Purchase, expansionists were content for the time being. Though a few still talked about taking Cuba, the vast majority of Americans were satisfied that we had fulfilled "our manifest destiny to overspread the continent."

▶ CHECK-UP

1. Why did this country's annexation of Texas irritate Mexico? What steps were taken by Polk? What were the results? What reason was given for declaring war on Mexico?

2. How did the various sections feel about the war? What part was played in the war by each of the following: Taylor, Scott, Kearny, Frémont?

3. What were the peace terms ending the Mexican War? Why did the United States make the Gadsden Purchase?

• • • • • • • • • • • • • • • • • •

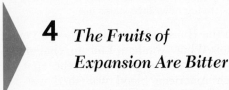

4 *The Fruits of Expansion Are Bitter*

The slavery issue is reopened. The annexation of Texas and the prospect of adding New Mexico and California to the

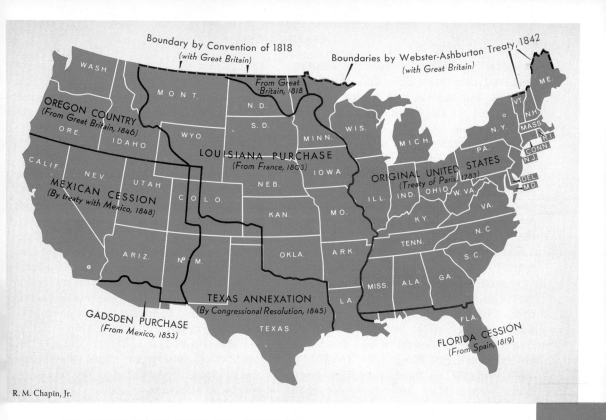

Boundary by Convention of 1818
(with Great Britain)

Boundaries by Webster-Ashburton Treaty, 1842
(with Great Britain)

WASH.

OREGON COUNTRY
(From Great Britain, 1846)

MONT.

From Great
Britain, 1818

N. D.

S. D.

MINN.

WIS.

ME.

VT.

N.H.

MASS.

N.Y.

R.I.

CONN.

N.J.

ORE.

WYO.

IDAHO

CALIF.

NEV.

UTAH

MEXICAN CESSION
(By treaty with Mexico, 1848)

LOUISIANA PURCHASE
(From France, 1803)

IOWA

NEB.

COLO.

MICH.

PA.

ORIGINAL UNITED STATES
(Treaty of Paris, 1783)

OHIO

ILL.

IND.

W. VA.

DEL.

MD.

ARIZ.

N. M.

KAN.

MO.

KY.

VA.

N. C.

TENN.

OKLA.

ARK.

S. C.

MISS.

ALA.

GA.

L A.

GADSDEN PURCHASE
(From Mexico, 1853)

TEXAS ANNEXATION
(By Congressional Resolution, 1845)

TEXAS

FLA.

FLORIDA CESSION
(From Spain, 1819)

R. M. Chapin, Jr.

THE UNITED STATES SPANS THE CONTINENT

With the Gadsden Purchase of 1853, the dreams of expansionists who had long supported the doctrine of manifest destiny were finally fulfilled. Use the map to trace the four-stage development of the United States' northern boundary.

MAP STUDY

Union revived the quarrel over slavery. Shortly after the Mexican War began, President Polk, hoping the war would be short, had asked Congress for money to purchase territory from Mexico. When an appropriation bill for this purpose was introduced into the House, a Democratic congressman from Pennsylvania, David Wilmot, attached an amendment to it. Known as the Wilmot Proviso, this amendment provided that "neither slavery nor involuntary servitude [should] exist in any part" of the territory acquired from Mexico.

President Polk did not feel strongly about the question of slavery in the territories, and he failed to see why the acquisition of Mexican land should disturb anyone. In his diary he noted that the Wilmot Proviso had occasioned an "exciting debate in the House." He called the amendment "mischievous and foolish" and added: "What connection slavery had with making peace with Mexico it is difficult to conceive."

Despite the President's opinion of it, the Wilmot Proviso caused spirited debate in Congress and throughout the country. Mass meetings, conventions, and state legislatures drew up petitions and passed resolutions, some endorsing the Proviso and others condemning it. In 1846 and again in 1847, the House of Representatives, dominated by the more populous free states, passed the Wilmot Proviso. Both times, however, it was defeated in the Senate by southern votes.

North and South disagree on the Wilmot Proviso. Most people in the northern states approved the Wilmot Proviso. The antislavery movement had grown rapidly in the North, and by the late 1840's the feeling was widespread that slavery was morally wrong. To be sure, not many Northerners were ready to abolish slavery where it legally existed south of the Mason and Dixon Line. But most of them felt that Congress should prevent the spread of slavery into any new territory. They were convinced,

289

moreover, that Congress had the constitutional authority to do this. To support their position, Northerners referred to this passage in Article IV, Section 3, of the Constitution: "The Congress shall have power to dispose of and make all needful rules and regulations respecting the territory or other property belonging to the United States" (page 148). They pointed out, furthermore, that Congress had used this power in establishing the 36°30' line of the Missouri Compromise.

Southerners, on the other hand, violently opposed Wilmot's amendment. Following the lead of John C. Calhoun, they supported the doctrine of noninterference. The territories belonged to all the states, they insisted, and Congress must supervise the territories for the benefit of all. The Southerners argued that the phrase "territory or other property" in the Constitution meant land. Hence, they said, Congress could regulate the sale of land but could not determine the status of slavery on that land. Furthermore, Southerners regarded slaves as a form of personal property and pointed to the Fifth Amendment, which guaranteed that no man could "be deprived of life, liberty, or property, without due process of law." According to this point of view, then, a citizen had the right to take his slaves into any territory, and it was the duty of the government to protect that right.

Compromises are proposed. Some Americans, especially in the Middle West, tried to work out a compromise on the problem of slavery in the territories. Two solutions were proposed:

(1) One compromise called for the extension of the Missouri Compromise line to the Pacific. In other words, the 36°30' line would become the dividing line between slave and free states from Missouri's western boundary to the west coast.

(2) The other solution was called *popular sovereignty* or *squatter sovereignty*. Under this plan the people who lived in each territory would decide for themselves whether slavery was to be permitted there. At first, every territory would be open to slave-owners. If the climate and soil attracted large numbers of slaveholders, then presumably the settlers would vote for the organization of a slave territory. In due time they would draw up a state constitution legalizing slavery. If, however, slaveholders were not in the majority, then the area would be organized as a free territory and eventually admitted as a free state.

Popular sovereignty does not solve the problem. Popular sovereignty was first suggested by Lewis Cass, a Democrat from Michigan, and was enthusiastically backed by an Illinois Democrat, Stephen A. Douglas. Most of its supporters did not feel strongly about slavery as a moral issue, and therefore were willing to let the settlers of a territory decide whether or not to permit slavery there. Supporters of popular sovereignty pointed out that this solution would take the issue of slavery out of Congress. But they were vague about one crucial point. They failed to say *when* the people of a territory should make the decision — at an early stage in territorial organization or not until the state constitution was adopted.

The politicians dodge the issue in 1848. The fierce debate over slavery in the territories still raged as the country prepared for the presidential election of 1848. Neither the Democrats nor the Whigs wanted to commit themselves. Hence both parties tried to ignore the dangerous question of slavery in the territories.

Within the Democratic Party there was a sharp division between antislavery and proslavery groups. In New York State, for example, the supporters of the Wilmot Proviso were called *Barnburners* because supposedly they were willing to "burn down" the Democratic "barn" to rid it of proslavery "rats." The regular Democrats were called *Hunkers* because they supposedly "hunkered" (hankered) for political office even at the sacrifice of principle. In other northern states the Democratic Party was similarly divided, while in the South the proslavery groups prevailed.

The proslavery delegates succeeded in controlling the Democratic convention. For President they nominated Lewis Cass of Michigan in the hope that his support of squatter sovereignty would take the voters' minds off congressional action on slavery in the territories. The Democratic platform said nothing about the status of slavery in the newly acquired Mexican Cession. Though Polk had not sought re-election, the Democrats claimed credit for winning the Mexican War under his leadership.

The Whigs were just as evasive. Their best-known figures were Daniel Webster and Henry Clay, but Webster was anti-slavery and Clay had lost in 1844. The Whig managers turned to the "Hero of Buena Vista," General Zachary Taylor. He was a Louisiana slave-owner, but as a new-comer to politics his views were unknown and he had not taken a public stand on slavery. In nominating Taylor, the Whigs were mindful of their smashing victory in 1840 with another military hero, General Harrison. The second spot on the Whig ticket went to a New Yorker, Millard Fillmore, who was mildly sympathetic to the Wilmot Proviso. To make certain that the campaign focused on Taylor's military career, the Whigs decided not to adopt a platform.

The Free Soil Party determines the outcome of the election. Widespread dissatisfaction with the Whigs and Democrats led to the formation of a third party in 1848 — the Free Soil Party. The Free Soilers made their stand on slavery very clear. Unlike the Liberty Party (page 285), which had favored abolition, this new third party merely opposed the extension of slavery into the territories. The Free Soil Party included a number of groups: (1) former members of the Liberty Party; (2) discontented antislavery Democrats; and (3) antislavery Whigs. With "Free Soil, Free Speech, Free Labor, and Free Men" as its slogan, the party's first convention nominated Martin Van Buren for the presidency.

The Free Soilers polled almost 300,000 votes in 1848. But since their strength was scattered throughout the North, Van Buren did not carry a single state. The Whigs won the presidency, though Taylor received only about 140,000 more popular votes than Cass. The Democrats kept control of both houses of Congress. But since the House of Representatives was closely divided between Whigs and Democrats, the dozen Free Soilers who were elected to Congress held the balance of power. Their influence in Congress, therefore, was much greater than their numbers would suggest.

▶ CHECK-UP

1. What was the Wilmot Proviso? What arguments were used by Northerners to support the view that Congress had the right to exclude slavery from the territories? By Southerners to deny Congress this right? What compromises were proposed?

2. Why did the question of slavery in the Mexican Cession create a problem for both parties? What did each do in the election of 1848? What was the position of the Free Soil Party?

• •

5 *The Compromise of 1850 Postpones a North-South Conflict*

When President Polk left office in March, 1849, a territorial government had been established in Oregon. But the bitter quarrel over slavery had prevented the territorial organization of either New Mexico or California. Under normal circumstances the new President and the deeply divided Congress might have had a breathing spell before tackling this problem. The discovery of gold in California, however, suddenly forced this issue upon Congress.

Gold is discovered in California. Early in 1848, gold was found in a millstream in the Sacramento valley.[2] The news spread

---

[2] The gold was discovered on the property of John Augustus Sutter, a Swiss who had built up a little "empire" in trading, trapping, and ranching. Though Sutter tried to keep the discovery a secret, the news quickly leaked out. Gold prospectors soon overran his property, with the result that Sutter's empire eventually crumbled into debt and ruin.

like wildfire along the Pacific coast, across the United States, and soon to all corners of the world. The remarkable "gold rush of '49" followed. Like bees to honey, the "forty-niners" swarmed into California, lured by visions of untold wealth. Farmers mortgaged their fields, clerks left their desks, ministers deserted their pulpits, and workmen dropped their tools to seek "that golden land." Those who could afford it made the perilous ocean trip around South America, others crossed the disease-ridden Isthmus of Panama. But most of the forty-niners traveled by covered wagon across the plains and mountains of the United States. Mexicans, South Americans, Europeans, and Chinese joined the Americans in staking out claims in California.

California requests admission to the Union. By the end of 1849 California had a population of over 100,000. The miners drank, fought, and gambled in a country that was practically without law and order. Informal police groups, called *vigilantes*, tried to enforce a rough kind of justice. But in the crowded cities of Sacramento and San Francisco, this was almost impossible. Prices skyrocketed, and everywhere in California conditions were chaotic.

Since Congress had taken no action to organize the Mexican Cession, President Taylor urged the people of California, New Mexico, and the Mormon state of Deseret (later named Utah) to draw up state constitutions. The Californians held a state convention at Monterey and drafted a constitution prohibiting slavery. A large popular majority ratified this constitution, and the Californians impatiently awaited congressional action. Meanwhile, New Mexico and the Mormon state also prepared for statehood.

Congressmen clash over slavery in California. When Congress assembled in December, 1849, southern members bitterly attacked President Taylor for allowing California to draw up a free state constitution. They repeated Calhoun's warning that the South was about to become a hopeless, permanent minority. Mississippi issued invitations for a southern convention. Many Southerners expressed the hope that this convention, to be held in Nashville, Tennes-

see, would recommend the secession of the slave states from the Union.

Northerners in Congress were just as angry and determined. They insisted that California be admitted as a free state immediately. Many of them also wanted to abolish slavery and the slave trade in the District of Columbia. Both northern and southern members of Congress came to the Capitol armed with revolvers and Bowie knives. According to the *Congressional Globe*, the sessions were marked by "threats, violent gesticulations, calls to order, and demands for adjournment. . . . The House was like a heaving billow. The clerk called to order, but there was none to heed him." Only after 63 ballots could the House choose a Speaker. President Taylor did nothing to relieve the tension and bitterness. In his message to Congress he naively recommended that they avoid "exciting topics of sectional character."

Clay offers a compromise. Fortunately Congress included two experienced legislators who well understood the gravity of the situation. Both Henry Clay and Daniel Webster were old men who had been disappointed in their hopes to become President. Both realized that extremists, whether northern or southern, would have to give ground if a national crisis were to be avoided. In January, 1850, Clay and Webster studied a draft of a speech which Clay intended to deliver in the Senate. Though Webster was a strong antislavery man, in this emergency he agreed to support Clay's proposals for compromise. With this assurance, Clay rose in the Senate to propose a series of measures. The most important were the following:

(1) That California be admitted as a free state.

(2) That territorial governments be established in New Mexico and Utah, without any restriction or condition on the subject of slavery.

(3) That the controversial boundary between Texas and New Mexico be determined by Congress and the Texan debt of ten million dollars be assumed by the federal government.

(4) That slave-trading, but not slavery, be prohibited in the District of Columbia.

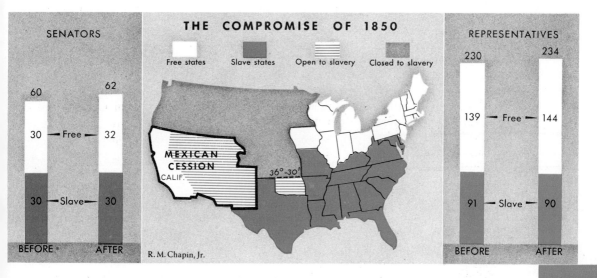

SENATORS

BEFORE	AFTER
60	62
30 — Free — 32	
30 — Slave — 30	

THE COMPROMISE OF 1850

Free states · Slave states · Open to slavery · Closed to slavery

MEXICAN CESSION
CALIF.
36°-30'

R. M. Chapin, Jr.

REPRESENTATIVES

BEFORE	AFTER
230	234
139 — Free — 144	
91 — Slave — 90	

MAP STUDY

THE COMPROMISE OF 1850

Like the Missouri Compromise 30 years earlier (map, page 230), the Compromise of 1850 offered only a temporary solution to the sectional dispute over the extension of slavery. Compare the representation in Congress of free states and slave states before and after the Compromise.

(5) That a more effective fugitive slave law be passed.

Congress debates the compromise. Clay defended his proposals in a powerful speech that stirred the packed Senate galleries. He warned the South that they would win none of their objectives by seceding from the Union. Instead they would risk "furious, bloody, implacable, exterminating" war and bring about the end of the Union. Clay declared that his resolutions "taken together, in combination," would provide "an amicable arrangement of all questions in controversy between the free and slave states."

The South's answer came a month later from Calhoun. Tired, ill, scarcely able to stand, Calhoun asked a colleague to read his speech. It was a document of despair. "The South asks for justice, simple justice, and less she ought not to take. She has no compromise to offer but the Constitution, and no concession or surrender to make." The ties that bound the states together, Calhoun had written, were slowly but surely breaking. Unity could be preserved only by assuring the South that it could remain in the Union with safety. The North, insisted Calhoun, must "cease the agitation of the slave question."

Three days later, Daniel Webster rose to defend Clay's proposals. Senators and visitors in the crowded chamber listened intently as the great orator delivered his "Seventh of March" speech.

I wish to speak today, not as a Massachusetts man, nor as a northern man, but as an American. . . . I have a part to act, not for my own security or safety, for I am looking out for no fragment upon which to float away from the wreck, if wreck there must be, but for the good of the whole, and the preservation of all; . . . I speak today for the preservation of the Union.

Warning that "peaceable secession" was impossible, Webster appealed to his colleagues to save the Union and the Constitution by enacting the compromise proposals into law. Webster's courageous support of the compromise undoubtedly helped save it. But his speech infuriated the abolitionists. They condemned him as a traitor to the antislavery cause, a second Benedict Arnold, a "fallen angel."

Free Soilers and antislavery Whigs and Democrats shared the abolitionists' disgust with Webster's Seventh of March oration. These people were cheered when William Henry Seward, a New York Whig, answered Webster. Senator Seward began his speech with this declaration:

> I am opposed to any such compromise, in any and all the forms in which it has been proposed, because . . . I think all legislative compromises radically wrong and essentially vicious.

Seward denied that the Constitution recognized slave property. It was contradictory, he said, for a "Christian nation" to protect the institution of slavery. "Britain, France, and Mexico have abolished slavery, and all other European States are preparing to abolish it as speedily as they can." Seward wound up his argument by appealing to a "higher law than the Constitution" — the moral law which was inalterably opposed to human bondage.

The Compromise of 1850 is adopted. The debate on Clay's proposals dragged on month after month. The burden of defending them passed from the elderly Clay and Webster to younger men, particularly Stephen A. Douglas of Illinois. Clay's proposals were submitted to a special committee, which recast them in the form of five separate bills. Several unforeseen events then made possible their passage in Congress.

Southern opposition to the Compromise of 1850 was blunted by the death of Calhoun late in March and by the position taken in the Nashville Convention (page 292). That gathering of Southerners, held in June, 1850, was controlled by moderates who refused to recommend secession. As a result, many southern congressmen dared to vote for the compromise bills. The measures faced major resistance, however, from President Taylor, who was opposed to the Compromise and threatened to veto the five bills. But shortly after delivering a Fourth of July speech, Taylor fell sick and died. The new President, Millard Fillmore, favored the Compromise and used all his influence to push it through Congress.

By September, 1850, the five measures embodying Clay's original proposals had been signed into law. Happy celebrations were held throughout the country. Webster wrote to a friend: "I can now sleep of nights. We have gone through the most important crisis that has occurred since the founding of this government, and whatever may prevail, hereafter the Union stands firm."

▶ CHECK-UP

1. Why did settlers rush to California after 1848? Why did California's request for admission as a free state lead to controversy? What compromise was proposed by Clay?

2. How was this compromise viewed by Calhoun? By Webster? By Seward? Why did the South come to accept the proposal?

. . . .

Clinching the Main Ideas in Chapter 13

America was in a hurry in the 1840's. Northerners, Southerners, and Westerners were on the move, and many feared that the unsettled parts of the Louisiana Purchase would not provide enough land. Settlers from the lower Mississippi Valley had moved into Texas and, after clashing with the Mexican government, had won their independence. Meanwhile, Americans had filtered into California's rich valleys, and hundreds of them had made the long trek to Oregon, still held jointly by the United States and Britain. The overwhelming majority of Americans in Texas, California, and Oregon, as well as many in the states, believed it was the country's "manifest destiny" to expand from sea to sea.

The Democratic candidate in 1844, James K. Polk, responded to this call. His promise to "re-annex" Texas and "re-occupy" Oregon won him the election. Congress annexed Texas in 1845, and the Oregon dispute was settled the next year. But Polk succeeded in acquiring New Mexico and California only after war with Mexico. The acquisition of this vast expanse of Mexican territory reopened the slavery question.

The bitter dispute over slavery in the territories threatened to disrupt the Union. But the Compromise of 1850 calmed the storm and postponed a conflict. Nevertheless, the growing differences between the free and slave states made it more and more difficult to find a mutually acceptable solution to the slavery problem.

Chapter Review

Terms to Understand

1. Rio Grande
2. manifest destiny
3. Oregon Trail
4. Gadsden Purchase
5. Wilmot Proviso
6. 54° 40′
7. 36° 30′
8. Nueces River
9. vigilantes
10. Liberty Party
11. Compromise of 1850
12. Santa Fe Trail
13. Free Soil Party
14. forty-ninth parallel
15. Lone Star Republic
16. Nashville Convention
17. joint resolution
18. Mexican Cession
19. popular sovereignty

What Do You Think?

1. Compare: (a) the Federalist position on the War of 1812 with the Whig position on the Mexican War; (b) the terms offered by Slidell with the actual peace settlement; (c) the acquisition of Texas with that of Oregon.

2. How would you have felt about this country's annexation of Texas had you been a Mexican? An American living in Texas? A southern planter? A northern abolitionist? A frontier farmer?

3. On what grounds did Southerners claim the right to take slaves into the territories? On what grounds did abolitionists claim that Congress had the right to exclude slavery from the territories?

4. What were the underlying causes of the Mexican War? The immediate causes? Do you think there would have been a conflict between this country and Mexico even if these "immediate causes" had not occurred? Why?

Using Your Knowledge of History

1. Six different flags have flown over Texas. Name them and give the years for each.

2. List the claims that the United States and Great Britain each had to the Oregon country.

3. Debate: *Resolved*, That the United States was justified in going to war with Mexico.

4. Explain how sectionalism held up the annexation of Texas for many years. What role did sectionalism play in the acquisition of (a) the Louisiana Territory, (b) Florida, and (c) Oregon?

Extending Your Knowledge of History

The drama of the westward movement is reflected in the books by Parkman and Dana cited in the text. Bernard De Voto has written two thrilling accounts of westward expansion, *Year of Decision, 1846* and *Across the Wide Missouri*. Other good accounts of western settlement are *The Far Western Frontier, 1830–1860*, by R. A. Billington, and Everett Dick's *Vanguards of the Frontier*. The California gold rush is described by S. E. White in *The Forty-Niners*. Allan Nevins has edited a valuable source in *Polk: The Diary of a President*. Walter Lord's *Time to Stand: The Story of the Alamo* is an exciting book. In *American Heritage* see "With Dana Before the Mast" by Samuel Shapiro (October, 1960); "The Storming of the Alamo" by Charles Ramsdell (February, 1961); "The Prairie Schooner Got Them There" by George R. Stewart (February, 1962); and "Carl Bodmer's Unspoiled West" by Marshall B. Davidson (April, 1963).

Analyzing Unit Three

1. In the period from 1820 to 1850, a number of political leaders tried hard to reach the White House — Henry Clay, John C. Calhoun, Daniel Webster, and Andrew Jackson. How do you account for the fact that Clay, Calhoun, and Webster failed, while Jackson succeeded?

2. In the 1840's, Ralph Waldo Emerson warned: "The United States will conquer Mexico, but it will be as the man who swallows the arsenic which brings him down in turn. Mexico will poison us." How did the Mexican Cession poison relations between the slave and free states? What effect did it have on political parties?

3. In the years after 1815 the country managed to avoid a showdown on the question of slavery and the nature of the Union by adopting a series of compromises — the Missouri Compromise, the Tariff of 1833 (which ended the crisis in South Carolina), and finally the Compromise of 1850. What issues were at the heart of this prolonged controversy? What did the compromises accomplish? What questions were side-stepped by the compromisers?

Unit 4

Sectional Differences End in Civil War (1850-1865)

Lincoln entering Richmond in April, 1865

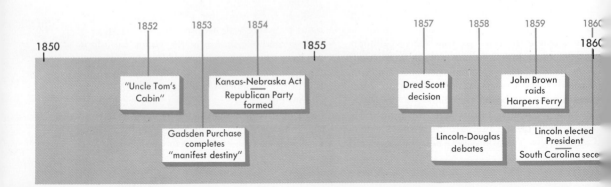

1850

1852 "Uncle Tom's Cabin"

1853 Gadsden Purchase completes "manifest destiny"

1854 Kansas-Nebraska Act
Republican Party formed

1855

1857 Dred Scott decision

1858 Lincoln-Douglas debates

1859 John Brown raids Harpers Ferry

1860 Lincoln elected President
South Carolina sece

The Compromise of 1850 provided a ten-year breathing spell. During this decade the North and the West drew closer together. Railroads carried food and raw materials from the Middle West to the East Coast and hauled manufactured goods in the opposite direction. The free states increased their manufactures and the output of their farms. The economic growth of both the North and the West was aided by the man power of European immigrants. Opposition to the spread of slavery in the territories provided still another bond between these two sections.

The South, on the other hand, increasingly drew in upon itself. Plantation owners, only a small proportion of the southern population, set the tone of public life. Southern capital was invested in land and slaves rather than in manufacturing. The entire region became convinced that cotton was, and always would be, "king." Those who dared to question the institution of slavery were silenced.

The 1850's were marked by violent quarrels between slave and free state representatives in Congress. Senator Stephen Douglas's bill concerning slavery in Kansas and Nebraska touched off violence between free soilers and proslavery settlers. The struggle in Kansas helped to establish a new political party — the Republicans. Opposed to the extension of slavery into the territories, the Republicans soon found supporters in all the free states.

As the 1850's wore on, bitterness between slave and free states heightened. One factor in the deepening split was the Dred Scott case, in which the Supreme Court ruled that the Constitution protected slave property everywhere in the Union. The Dred Scott decision figured in a series of debates between Abraham Lincoln, an Illinois Republican, and the Democratic Senator Douglas. Lincoln made such a favorable impression that the Republicans nominated him for the presidency in 1860.

Lincoln's election was the signal for South Carolina to secede from the Union. South Carolina was followed by other slave states, which then formed the Confederacy. The Confederate bombardment of a federal fort in Charleston Harbor marked the beginning of a long and tragic war. At first the Northerners fought to preserve the Union. But in 1863 the Emancipation Proclamation made the abolition of slavery an important objective of the war. Outnumbered in man power and resources, the Confederacy was unable to obtain substantial assistance from European countries. Only the skill of its generals enabled the Confederacy to hold out for four years. The surrender of Robert E. Lee to Ulysses S. Grant marked the fall of the Confederacy and established the fact that no state could secede from the Union.

CHAPTER 14

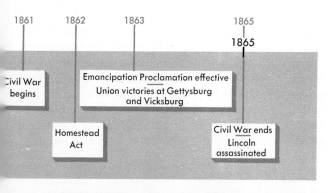

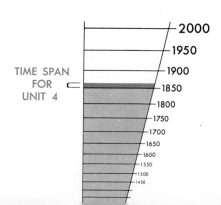

Early tool factory

The North and the West Draw Together

The fault of the Free States in the eyes of the South is not one that can be atoned for by any yielding of special points here and there. . . . Their crime is the census of 1860. Their increase in numbers, wealth, and power is a standing aggression. It would not be enough to please the Southern States that we should stop asking them to abolish slavery, — what they demand of us is nothing less than that we should abolish the spirit of the age.

JAMES RUSSELL LOWELL,
IN "THE ATLANTIC MONTHLY," 1861

1840–1860

By the mid-1800's there was a distinct difference in pace of life between the free states and the slave states. As James Russell Lowell pointed out in the above quotation, the census statistics told part of the story. Moreover, during the 1850's the people of the free states increased their industrial production and began to use machinery on their farms. A tidal wave of immigrants provided man power for building railroads and canals, working in the factories, and settling new farms in the Mississippi Valley and beyond. By 1860 the North and West far surpassed the South "in numbers, wealth, and power."

During the Jacksonian Era, Westerners and Southerners had agreed on many issues. In the 1840's, however, a re-alignment began to take place. The North and West drew closer together, and the South found itself increasingly isolated. During the 1850's the free states of the North and West were united by transportation routes, by economic ties, by social reforms, and by developments in the arts. Especially in the Northeast the 1840's and 1850's were marked by a period of remarkable literary activity. Even more important was the rapid spread of the antislavery movement throughout these sections of the country.

1 *The Economic Growth of the North and West Is Rapid*

Manufacturing continues to increase. The 1840's and '50's were characterized by rapid industrial growth, especially in the free states of the North and West. In these two decades the value of manufactured goods quadrupled, rising from about half a billion dollars in 1840 to almost two billion dollars by 1860. The number of people employed in factories almost doubled. Most manufacturing was still carried on in the North, though western industry was making rapid strides. In contrast to the amount of manufacturing in the rest of the country, the South in 1860 produced manufactured goods valued at only 155 million dollars.

New England's major industry was still textile production. Factories were enlarged, new ones built, and most of them converted from water to steam power. New looms made it possible to weave patterns in cloth, and new chemical dyes increased the range of colors.

In the Middle States the growing demand for iron in machines, steamboats, and construction, and scores of other uses led to an expansion of the iron industry. Foundries now used anthracite coal instead of wood or charcoal in the furnaces, and rolling mills replaced the old hand forges. Around 1850 a Kentucky ironmaster, William Kelly, devised a new process for mass-producing steel. But few Americans knew of Kelly's discovery until Henry Bessemer, an Eng-lishman, sought American patents on a similar process a few years later. Experimenting separately, Kelly and Bessemer had discovered that a blast of air directed at molten iron would remove its impurities. Despite the many advantages of steel over iron, the air-blast process was not widely used in the United States until later in the century.

New industries are started. American inventions gave rise to a number of new industries. In 1844 Charles Goodyear patented a method of *vulcanizing* rubber. His process of heating raw rubber with chemicals resulted in a product that would not crack in cold weather or melt under high temperatures. Goodyear's invention resulted in the development of a large rubber-goods industry. Another invention, Elias Howe's sewing machine, was not very satisfactory and few were sold. Isaac Singer made important improvements in the machine, however, and arranged for large-scale production. Mass advertising and the possibility of buying on credit resulted in the sale of more than 100,000 sewing machines by 1860.

Most of Singer's machines were bought by northern and western families, but many were also used in factories in the free states. Indeed, the use of industrial sewing machines revolutionized the production of clothing and shoes. By the beginning of the Civil War (1861), most of the shoes and boots sold in the free states were factory-sewn, and many of them had rubber soles and heels. Because they were mass-produced, they were lower in price than hand-stitched shoes. Most clothing sold in the North by 1860 was ready-made, machine-stitched, and relatively low-priced.

The West develops specialized industries. Manufacturing in the West naturally started later than in the northeastern states, and much of it was specialized. In many western communities the cutting and processing of lumber were important industries. There were, for example, factories for making barrel staves, railroad ties, shingles, and other wood products. Flour milling and the brewing of beer were also important. Chicago, St. Louis, and Cincinnati had many meat-packing plants and factories

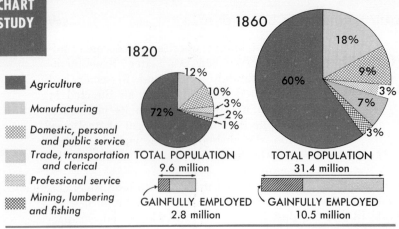

AMERICANS AT WORK, 1820 AND 1860

In 1820 nearly three fourths of all American workers earned their living in agriculture. Notice that employment in other fields increased by 1860. Manufacturing showed the greatest gain.

1820

1860

Agriculture

Manufacturing

Domestic, personal and public service

Trade, transportation and clerical

Professional service

Mining, lumbering and fishing

TOTAL POPULATION
9.6 million

TOTAL POPULATION
31.4 million

GAINFULLY EMPLOYED
2.8 million

GAINFULLY EMPLOYED
10.5 million

for tanning leather. Some meat packers used non-edible parts of hogs and cattle to make brushes, chemicals, glue, and fertilizer.

The use of farm machinery spreads. One of the West's most important industries in the 1840's and '50's was the manufacture of farm machinery. Western farmers had always wanted a steel plow light enough to be carried over the shoulder, yet strong enough to cut the tough prairie sod. John Deere, an Illinois blacksmith, produced the first steel plow in the 1830's. By the time the Civil War started, his factories were making 13,000 plows a year.

Wheat farmers began to use reapers and other types of machinery. Cyrus Hall McCormick had patented a steel-toothed reaper while he was living in Virginia in 1834. Although he demonstrated that his horse-drawn reaper could do the work of five men using scythes, his machine did not sell in the East. McCormick moved to Chicago and built a large factory which utilized Eli Whitney's principle of interchangeable parts (page 207). In addition, he sent agents throughout the West to sell reapers. Attractive advertising and credit plans increased sales. Although McCormick by 1860 was turning out 500 reapers a month, he could not meet the growing demand for his machine. Other manufacturers developed mechanical threshers and binders which enabled wheat farmers to keep pace with the reapers.

Machines enabled farmers in the West to provide food for industrial centers in the North and East and for large areas of the South as well.

More canals link the East and West. American farmers and manufacturers de-pended on railroads and water transportation for marketing their goods. The development of more east-west routes speeded up the exchange of farm products and manufactured goods. This exchange had two significant results: (1) It tended to bind the eastern and western sections of the country more closely together. (2) New canals and railroads began to drain traffic from the Mississippi River into the Great Lakes (maps, pages 302–303). Thus, the Miami and Erie Canal (1835) drew business away from Cincinnati. In 1848 the Illinois-Michigan Canal linked Chicago with the Illinois River. This canal diverted so much traffic to the Great Lakes that Chicago became a busy port even before it had railroad connections with the East.

Two other canals greatly strengthened the Great Lakes transport system. The Sault Ste. Marie Canal, linking Lakes Superior and Huron, enabled ships to carry iron ore from northern Michigan to mills in Cleveland and Chicago. At the other end of the Lakes, the Canadian-built Welland Canal by-passed Niagara Falls and enabled ships to go from Lake Erie into Lake Ontario.

While Milwaukee, Chicago, Detroit, Toledo, Cleveland, and Buffalo fattened on the Great Lakes-canal trade, cities farther south (such as St. Louis, Memphis, Louisville, and New Orleans) felt the effect of the reduced river traffic. Steamboat men on the Ohio and Mississippi Rivers tried to meet the competition of canals and railroads by cutting rates. In the 1850's, the river steamers vied with each other to attract passengers and freight, but it was a losing fight. By 1860 only 20 per cent of New

Orleans' trade came from western farms. A southern economist bitterly assailed the North for rolling back "the mighty tide of the Mississippi and its 10,000 tributary streams until their mouth, practically and commercially, is more at New York and Boston than at New Orleans."

Railroads cross the Appalachians. Railroads also played an important role in drawing the North and West together. As soon as the northeastern states recovered from the depression following the Panic of 1837 (page 249), they resumed railroad construction. Boston and Baltimore took the lead. By establishing rail connections with the Welland and Erie Canals, Boston captured a share of New York's trade with the West. By 1853 the Baltimore and Ohio Railroad completed the laying of tracks over the mountains to Wheeling, Virginia. At about the same time the Pennsylvania Railroad linked Philadelphia and Pittsburgh.

The gains scored by Boston, Baltimore, and Philadelphia finally stirred New York to action. For many years the success of the Erie Canal had stifled railroad construction in New York State. But in 1851 a line was completed between New York City and Albany. This line soon merged with a num-

(*Continued on page 304*)

Inventions of the mid-1800's eventually had enormous impact on the American economy. Singer's sewing machine (left) greatly changed clothes-making in both homes and factories. Goodyear's home experiments (right) led to vulcanization, thus enabling the rubber industry to develop. Agriculture was revolutionized by McCormick's reaper (below left); and the air-blast method of steel-making made possible the modern steel industry.

IMPROVED TRANSPORTATION

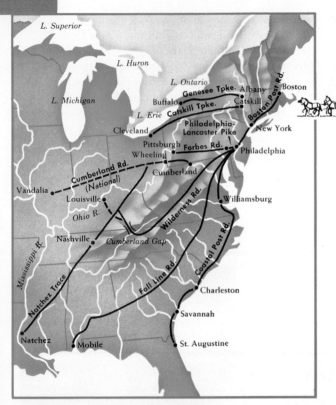

THE TURNPIKE ERA

In colonial times, overland transportation was slow and difficult. Even along the coast, there were few roads and these were poor. Settlers moving west seldom had roads to follow and so traveled along the winding river valleys. With the coming of the turnpike era, 1800–1840, road building boomed and land travel became more efficient. Improved roads, many of them financed by passenger tolls, served local travelers and pioneers alike. (Roads in dashed lines indicate later extensions.)

THE CANAL BOOM

The canal boom of the early 1800's also resulted in cheaper and more efficient transportation for goods and passengers. At first, private companies built canals to bypass rapids in streams. Later, since water transportation proved the best means of shipping products to eastern markets, western settlers urged their states to build canals connecting navigable rivers. By 1850, a system of canals linked the Atlantic coast with the Ohio and Mississippi valleys and these, in turn, with the Great Lakes.

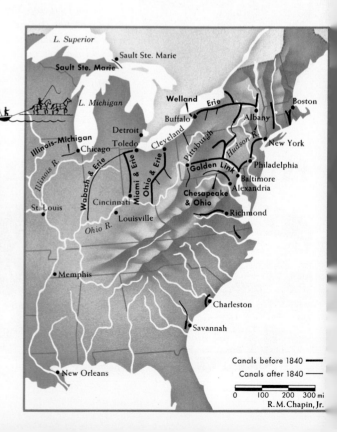

Canals before 1840 ▬▬

Canals after 1840 ▬▬

0   100   200   300 mi

R. M. Chapin, Jr.

SPEEDS THE NATION'S GROWTH

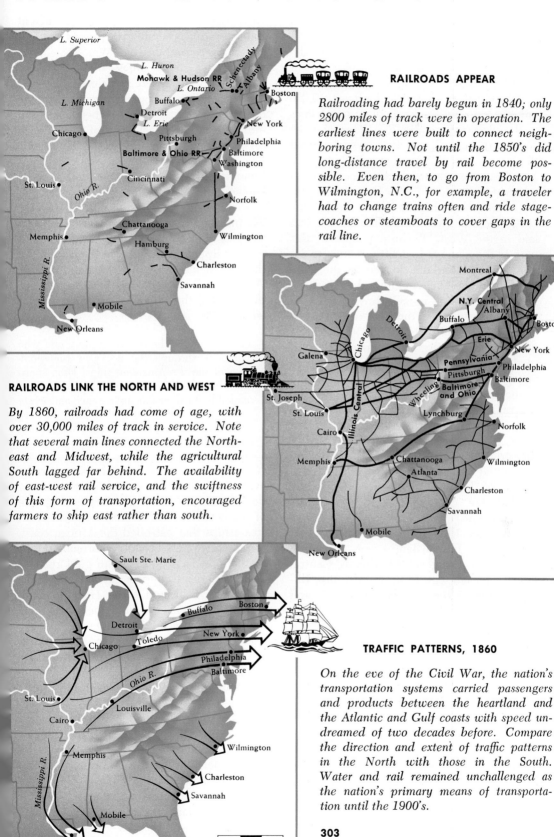

RAILROADS APPEAR

Railroading had barely begun in 1840; only 2800 miles of track were in operation. The earliest lines were built to connect neighboring towns. Not until the 1850's did long-distance travel by rail become possible. Even then, to go from Boston to Wilmington, N.C., for example, a traveler had to change trains often and ride stagecoaches or steamboats to cover gaps in the rail line.

RAILROADS LINK THE NORTH AND WEST

By 1860, railroads had come of age, with over 30,000 miles of track in service. Note that several main lines connected the Northeast and Midwest, while the agricultural South lagged far behind. The availability of east-west rail service, and the swiftness of this form of transportation, encouraged farmers to ship east rather than south.

TRAFFIC PATTERNS, 1860

On the eve of the Civil War, the nation's transportation systems carried passengers and products between the heartland and the Atlantic and Gulf coasts with speed undreamed of two decades before. Compare the direction and extent of traffic patterns in the North with those in the South. Water and rail remained unchallenged as the nation's primary means of transportation until the 1900's.

303

R. M. Chapin, Jr.

ber of small railroads between Albany and Buffalo to form the New York Central Railroad. Meanwhile, the Erie Railroad developed a route across the southern part of New York State.

By 1850 the country had almost 10,000 miles of railroad track. Four railroad lines — the Baltimore and Ohio, Pennsylvania, New York Central, and Erie — had crossed the mountains. Baltimore, Philadelphia, New York, and Boston had rail connections with western cities.

Railroads reach the West. During the 1850's most of the new railroad track was laid in the West. Because people in this part of the country had little money to invest, railroad builders looked to the state and federal governments for aid. The states helped by lending money, buying railroad stock, and guaranteeing the securities issued by the railroads. In 1850 Congress made its first land grant to encourage railroad construction. The land was given to states through which a line from Chicago to the Gulf of Mexico would pass. But the federal government retained alternate sections of land along this route, hoping that rising land values would offset the cost of the original land grant. This legislation committed the federal government to a policy of helping to finance this badly needed, but expensive, form of internal improvement.

It was the Illinois Central Railroad that received this federal land grant. Promoted by Stephen Douglas, the Illinois Central linked Chicago with Galena and Cairo, Illinois (both on the Mississippi River), and later with the Gulf port of Mobile. This was the first great north-south railroad built in the United States. Almost all other railroads built during the 1850's tied the West and the East together. Many lines crossed Michigan, Ohio, Indiana, and Illinois, and some pushed across the Mississippi River into Missouri and Iowa. The intersection of land and water routes made Chicago the rail center of the West. More than 10,000 miles of railroads were built in the West during the 1850's. Thus, the railroads, even more than the canals, drew traffic away from the Mississippi. And they pro-

vided the East and West with an efficient transportation system that proved a great advantage during the Civil War.

Clipper ships enjoy a brief glory. While railroads were reaching into the West, American clippers reigned supreme on the high seas. Noted for their long, slim hulls and tall masts, the first of these graceful ships had been built in the 1840's. Donald McKay of Boston was the most famous clipper designer, and his best-known ship was *Flying Cloud*. On her maiden voyage in 1851 this clipper traveled 374 miles in a single day, much faster than any packet or steamship of that time.

The clippers were used in the trade with the Orient and also in the Atlantic trade. Whenever they appeared in British ports, they excited the envy of shipowners, one of whom said:

> The reason will be evident to any one who will walk through the docks at Liverpool. He will see the American ships, long, sharp built, beautifully painted and rigged, and remarkable for their fine appearance and white canvas. He will see the English vessels, short, round, and dirty, resembling great black tubs.

Clippers also engaged in the slave trade, even though this had been outlawed by both the United States and Britain. Capable of outdistancing the British and American steamships that patrolled the African coast, the slave clippers brought enormous profits to their owners. During the gold rush of 1849, American clippers carried many fortune seekers around Cape Horn to California. *Flying Cloud* held the New York-San Francisco record of 89 days.

Clippers give way to steamships. Steamships soon lured most of the California traffic away from the clippers. Cornelius Vanderbilt and other steamship operators sent their vessels from New York to Panama or Nicaragua. Passengers and goods were transported across the Isthmus (via railroad after 1855) and then continued their voyage to California. The trip took a mere five weeks.

By 1860 the clippers had also lost some of their Atlantic trade to ocean-going steamers. In the 1850's, British ship-builders, with generous government assistance, introduced the screw propeller and iron hulls. The improved steamers crossed the Atlantic in less than two weeks and carried far more cargo than clippers or packets. Discouraged by this competition, many American investors transferred their capital from ocean shipping to railroads or manufacturing.

Foreign trade flourishes. The Panic of 1837 had dealt a crushing blow to the country's foreign trade. Between the mid-1840's and 1860, however, American trade steadily increased.[1] Imports were paid for by the export of southern cotton, western wheat and flour, and in the 1850's by California gold. Much of this trade was carried in American ships. Commerce with the Orient expanded sharply during these years as Americans secured new trading privileges in Chinese ports and in Siam. Most noteworthy, however, was Commodore Matthew C. Perry's success in opening up trade with Japan. In 1853 Perry sailed into Japanese waters, previously closed to most outsiders. This show of naval strength enabled him to arrange a commercial treaty with Japan which provided new markets for American merchants.

▶ CHECK-UP

1. What new industries contributed to the economic growth of the Northeast and West? What were the results of the development of more east-west routes for railroad and water transportation? Why did the importance of the Great Lakes system increase while the Mississippi declined in importance?

2. What major railroad systems had developed by the 1850's? How was the construction of a railroad connecting Chicago with the South subsidized?

3. Why were the clipper ships notable? Why did they soon give way to steamships? How did foreign trade fare during the 1850's?

. . . .

[1] The total value of imports and exports in 1843 was 125 million dollars. By 1860 the value of American foreign trade had climbed to 688 million dollars.

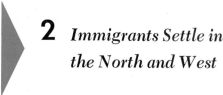

2 Immigrants Settle in the North and West

The tide of immigration swells. The number of people who came to American shores increased tremendously in the 1840's and '50's. By 1860 the United States had a white population of 27 million. Approximately 4 million of these people had come from other countries, and most of the foreign-born lived north of the Mason and Dixon Line.[2] The North and West, therefore, gained the benefits of the great tide of immigration. But these regions also had to deal with the social and economic problems of absorbing the newcomers.

Famine drives the Irish to America. The largest group of immigrants during these two decades was Irish. For some time Ireland had been troubled by potato rot, a plant disease which reached major proportions in 1845 when half the potato crop was lost. The disease and a drought caused even larger crop losses the following year. Ireland was so dependent on the potato for food that the crop failures meant starvation for many thousands of people. Those who had small savings or could barter their household goods for passage to America emigrated. Others secured money from friends or relatives already in the United States. Some made the crossing in the reeking holds of ships that had carried fish to European ports and took the desperate Irishmen to America as ballast on the return voyage. Many passengers died of malnutrition and disease on these transatlantic crossings. When Congress passed laws to improve conditions on immigrant ships, the shipowners evaded these restrictions by landing their human cargo at Quebec.

Most of the Irish immigrants in the 1840's and '50's settled in the cities of the Northeast. Some wished to be near relatives or friends already living in this area. Others took the first jobs they could find —

[2] The South had only 500,000 foreign-born in 1860.

as unskilled labor in factories, mines, and quarries, or on railroad or canal construction gangs. Though most of the Irish had been farmers in their homeland, they were generally too poor to buy land in this country. Hence the Irish colonies in Boston, New York, and Philadelphia expanded rapidly. Soon almost every industrial city of the Northeast had a sizable group of Irish who worked in textile plants, iron foundries, and small factories. Irish women and girls found employment as domestic servants, and some worked in the textile mills. By 1860 more than a million and a half Irish people had migrated to America.

German immigrants prefer the Middle West. The Germans accounted for another large proportion of the total immigration. More than a million Germans had come to America by 1860. Potato blight, poor harvests, and political unrest drove thousands of Germans from their homeland in the 1840's and early '50's. A number of well-educated Germans fled because they had taken part in an unsuccessful revolution in 1848. Many skilled craftsmen, put out of work by the introduction of machines, also sought a new life in the United States. These immigrants usually bought passage on merchant ships sailing from North Sea ports.

Once disembarked in America, the Germans tended to travel to the Middle West. Many bought farm land in Ohio, Indiana, Illinois, Iowa, and Wisconsin; smaller numbers settled in Missouri and Texas. They formed communities referred to as "New Germany's," and many of their towns had such Old World names as Berlin, Hanover, Dresden, Frankfort, Hamburg, and Westphalia. Western cities, especially St. Louis, Milwaukee, Cincinnati, and Chicago, also attracted the German newcomers. Craftsmen quickly found jobs in these industrial centers; and German writers, printers, doctors, lawyers, and teachers soon mastered English and found positions for themselves.

These German settlers left a definite mark on American life. Their love of music and their interest in physical fitness led to the formation of musical groups and athletic societies. German food, cigars, and beer spread well beyond the limits of the "New Germany's." So too did the German celebration of Christmas with decorated trees, carols, children's toys, and a Santa Claus who was far jollier than the Dutch Saint Nicholas. Perhaps the best-known German immigrant of this period was Carl Schurz, a political refugee who arrived in 1852 and practiced law in Wisconsin. He became active in American politics, served as an officer in the Union army during the Civil War, and was later elected to the Senate from Missouri.

Immigrants arrive from other lands. Ireland and Germany provided by far the largest number of newcomers at this time. But about half a million emigrants came from England, Scotland, and Wales during the 1840's and '50's. There were also Swiss and French immigrants and some French Canadians. In addition, a number of European Jews came to America in these decades. They generally settled in cities, where they worked as peddlers, merchants, clothing-manufacturers, teachers, and physicians. Some West Indian Jews of Spanish-Portuguese ancestry emigrated to southern cities. One of them, Judah P. Benjamin of New Orleans, was twice elected to the United States Senate.

About 70,000 Scandinavians also came to America before 1860. Bad harvests and economic depression had driven these people from Norway, Sweden, and Denmark. Some were drawn to the New World by glowing descriptions, such as this account by Fredrika Bremer, a Swedish writer:

> What a glorious new Scandinavia might not Minnesota become. Here would the Swede find his clear romantic lakes. . . . The climate, the situation, the character of the scenery agrees with our people better than any other of the American states.

The Scandinavians, like the Germans, preferred the Middle West. Large numbers of them settled on farms in northern Illinois, Iowa, Wisconsin, and Minnesota.

Opposition to immigration develops. Most Americans welcomed the tide of newcomers, but for various reasons some people felt hostile toward them. Religious prejudice was one reason for anti-immigrant feeling during the 1840's and '50's. Much of this kind of hostility was directed at the Irish, almost all of whom were Catholics. Unruly mobs burned Catholic churches and Irish homes in Philadelphia, and friction also appeared in Boston, New York, and Baltimore.

Economic conditions caused other Americans to find fault with the immigrants. In the Northeast the newcomers, eager to work even for low wages, displaced native-born American workers in many factories. The immigrants showed little interest in the labor movement, a fact which partly accounts for the weakness of early labor unions. Farther west, German and Scandinavian farmers competed with native-born Americans for choice parcels of land, and this, too, aroused jealousy.

Still further reasons account for the opposition to immigrants. The newcomers pouring into American cities crowded together in slums. In New York, for example, they took over the older Dutch housing on the lower East Side and in Greenwich Village. One-family homes were subdivided into tiny apartments, and boarders were packed into attics and cellars. Unscrupulous landlords filled the yards with wooden shanties to accommodate additional immigrants. Crime and disease festered in these crowded, dirty neighborhoods. Some European governments took advantage of America's "open-door" immigration policy by encouraging the departure of criminals, paupers, and the mentally ill. Many such newcomers ended up in American poor-houses and jails. Although some ports levied a small tax on all immigrants, there were no federal laws restricting immigration until after the Civil War.

Distrust of the immigrants developed for political reasons too. Political bosses in the cities controlled the immigrant votes, and the Irish or German bosses seldom saw eye-to-eye with native-born American politicians. As early as the 1820's the Irish had taken control of Tammany Hall (page 171), and by the 1850's they exerted a powerful influence in New York City politics. Moreover, some Americans were afraid that im-

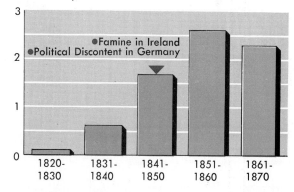

Millions of People

IMMIGRATION, 1820–1870

Immigration was an important reason for the increase in population from 1820 to 1870. Famine in Ireland and political unrest in Germany led many people to seek new opportunities in America.

CHART STUDY

migrants would not understand or support American democratic principles.

The immigrants themselves added to the increasing tension between groups. The Germans and Scandinavians, most of them Protestants, were critical of the Catholic Irish. And the Irish in turn looked down on the Negroes, with whom they sometimes competed for jobs and housing in northern cities.

An anti-immigrant political party is short-lived. Feeling against the newcomers was strong enough in the late 1840's to spawn an anti-immigrant, anti-Catholic organization in New York State. Called the "Supreme Order of the Star-Spangled Banner," it accepted as members only those who could prove that their parents and grandparents had been native-born and had never been Catholic. The organization soon spread to other states and took as its name the American Party. Determined to preserve "America for the Americans," the members promised to vote only for native-born candidates. When members were pressed for information about this new political party, they replied: "I know nothing." Soon they were called the Know-Nothing Party.

For a few years the Know-Nothings seemed to be gathering strength. In 1854 and 1855 they won control of Baltimore's city government. Their candidates became governors in several New England states, where opposition to the Irish was especially strong in factory towns. The Know-Nothings also scored political victories in California, where feeling ran high against the Chinese. Moreover, many Know-Nothing candidates won election to state legislatures and to Congress. After 1856, however, political attention focused on the quarrel over slavery, and Know-Nothing strength tapered off. By 1860 the party had disintegrated, though hostility to immigrants unfortunately had not disappeared.

Immigrants contribute to American life. The great tide of immigration in the 1840's and '50's, then, caused problems for the North and West. But the hard-working newcomers provided much of the man power that made possible the rapid industrial and agricultural growth of the free states. In time, the immigrants also enriched the cultural and intellectual life of the whole country.

▶ CHECK-UP

1. From what countries did large numbers of immigrants come to America during the 1840's and 1850's? Explain why in each case. Where did each tend to settle?

2. Why did opposition to immigration develop? What was the Know-Nothing Party?

. . . .

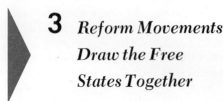

3 *Reform Movements Draw the Free States Together*

Many Jacksonian reforms continue. Many of the social changes that began in the Jacksonian Era (Chapter 12) were carried forward in the North and West during the 1840's and '50's. In addition to more public schools and state universities, the country's educational facilities were expanded by parochial schools and such Catholic colleges as Holy Cross (1843).

Dorothea Dix's campaign for better treatment of the insane made considerable headway in the 1850's. The lyceum movement continued to be popular. Newspaper circulation was increasing, and two new magazines, *Harper's New Monthly Magazine* and *The Atlantic Monthly,* appeared in the 1850's. Both soon had many readers.

Temperance laws are passed. Temperance leaders kept up their campaign against strong drink (page 269). Much publicity resulted from the activities of the Washingtonian Temperance Society, a group of former alcoholics who testified to the evils of liquor. One of the best-selling books of the 1850's was *Ten Nights in a Barroom and What I Saw There.* Thousands of people read this book or saw the play based on it.

The temperance leaders' greatest success, however, was the enactment of state laws prohibiting the sale of liquor except for medicinal purposes. The first such law was adopted in Maine in 1846; within a few years thirteen states, most of them in the North and West, had experimented with prohibition laws. But prohibition remained a subject of debate. Some protest came from immigrants who resented government interference with their drinking customs. Also, opponents of prohibition pointed out that temperance laws were difficult to enforce and that it was unwise to pass laws which would be violated.

Women secure new rights. During the Jacksonian Era, several academies and a few colleges, mostly in the North and West, had opened educational opportunities to women. Once educated, women asked for new rights and still other opportunities. A few remarkable women emerged as leaders of this campaign. In 1848, Lucretia Mott and Elizabeth Cady Stanton organized the first women's rights convention in Seneca Falls, New York. The delegates adopted a Declaration of Sentiments, modeled on the Declaration of Independence. This outspoken document criticized men for their tyranny over the opposite sex and demanded political, educational, and social equality for women. As a result of such efforts, several states granted new legal rights to women, for example, the right to control their own property after marriage. Many women found jobs in the teaching profession, largely because newly established training schools were open to both men and women.

For a short time, supporters of women's rights adopted a special costume. Instead of long skirts, they wore full, loose trousers and knee-length coats. This outfit was called the "bloomer" costume after Amelia Bloomer, who first described it in her crusading magazine. The public outcry against "Bloomerism" was so great, however, that the ladies soon gave it up.

These early feminists endured much ridicule and even hostility. Indeed, a long and unpopular campaign lay ahead for advocates of women's rights. Yet even in the 1850's they had the public support of such prominent men as the author Ralph Waldo Emerson, the newspaper editor Horace Greeley, and William Lloyd Garrison, the abolitionist.

The Negro meets obstacles in the North. A group of people who suffered even greater discrimination than women were the free Negroes living in the North and West. By 1860 only five states (Maine, Massachusetts, New Hampshire, Vermont, and Rhode Island) permitted Negroes to vote. Almost everywhere in the free states Negroes met discrimination in housing, jobs, schools, churches, and transportation. The legislatures of Ohio, Indiana, and Illinois actually prohibited Negroes from settling in those states. Ohio removed this ban in 1849; and a few years later Massachusetts forbade school segregation. But Negroes north of the Mason and Dixon line did not have rights or opportunities equal to those of white citizens. Moreover, whites who interested themselves in the Negro's plight devoted their efforts chiefly to the abolitionist cause.

The antislavery movement spreads. As you read in Chapter 12, few Northerners joined abolition societies in the 1830's. In fact, abolitionists of that period encountered much opposition in the North. But during the 1840's and '50's the antislavery movement grew rapidly. As spokesmen for the South became more unyielding in their defense of slavery, large numbers of north-

Elizabeth Blackwell received a medical degree in 1849, thus becoming the first licensed woman doctor in this country. In the 1850's, she and her sister opened a hospital for women in New York.

ern and western speakers, ministers, writers and organizers joined the cause of abolition. In the free states many people came to feel that slavery was morally wrong. They wanted Congress to ban slavery in federal territories and explore ways of ending it in the South.

The Gag Rule boomerangs. Abolitionist efforts seemed to thrive on opposition. This was demonstrated by the "Gag Rule" struggle in the House of Representatives. For several years the abolition societies had been sending antislavery petitions to Congress. Southern congressmen became so annoyed by these petitions that they sought to block consideration of them in the House of Representatives. In 1836 the House adopted a resolution which prevented discussion of any antislavery petition. Former President John Quincy Adams, serving as a congressman from Massachusetts, opposed this "Gag Rule." Though not an abolitionist,[3] he realized that the resolution violated the constitutional right of citizens to petition Congress. After eight years of

[3] Adams opposed slavery but, like many Americans, believed it would have to be eliminated gradually. Most abolitionists called for the immediate freeing of all slaves.

ABOLITIONIST LEADERS

The abolition movement attracted remarkable leaders, many of whom were clergymen and freed or escaped slaves. On these pages appear some of the outstanding abolitionists and scenes depicting their efforts.

One of the hardest working but least known abolitionists was Theodore Weld (right), who recruited many ministers, including Henry Ward Beecher, to the antislavery cause.

Theodore Weld

Beecher dramatized the plight of t *slaves by holding auctions in his chur* *(left). The money pledged by p* *rishioners went to buy the slaves th* *freedom.*

ceaseless effort, Adams managed to have the Gag Rule repealed.

The long struggle over the Gag Rule focused attention more sharply on the South's unwillingness to discuss the question of slavery. There was a growing awareness in the free states that the South seemed determined to retain its "peculiar institution." A few southern congressmen even wanted to establish new slave states in Latin America, to annex Cuba, and to reopen the slave trade with Africa. These views alarmed people in the free states and helped attract new members to the abolition societies. Thus, the South's unyielding position on the slavery question served only to increase antislavery sentiment throughout the North and West.

Abolition attracts able leaders. The antislavery movement in the 1840's and '50's enlisted the services of a remarkable group of speakers, organizers, and writers. Wendell Phillips, a wealthy Bostonian, closed his law office in the 1830's to devote himself to arousing antislavery sentiment in the North and West. Among the many ministers who aided the abolitionists, two of the best-known were William Ellery Channing, a Boston Unitarian, and Henry Ward Beecher, a New York Congregationalist. Beecher staged mock slave auctions in his church to demonstrate the evils of slavery.

The most skillful organizer was Theodore Weld, a man who preferred to work quietly behind the scenes. He advised the abolition societies, provided them with speakers, and guided the activities of converts to the antislavery movement. Weld helped make Oberlin College (page 263) a center of midwestern abolitionism. To answer the southern argument that the Christian scrip-

William Lloyd Garrison   Frederick Douglass

Garrison was one of the earliest and most determined of the abolitionists. After escaping from slavery to freedom, Douglass devoted his life to abolition and, after the Civil War, Negro rights.

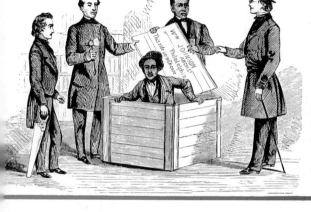

Sojourner Truth (above), a freed slave, campaigned for women's rights and aided in the underground railroad. One unusual slave escape was the shipment from Richmond to Philadelphia of Henry "Box" Brown (left) in a crate marked "This side up with care."

tures upheld slavery, Weld wrote *The Bible Against Slavery.*

The abolitionists also could count on the support of such writers as James Russell Lowell and John Greenleaf Whittier. The most widely read book of the 1850's was Harriet Beecher Stowe's *Uncle Tom's Cabin,* a vivid portrayal of the abuses of slave life.[4] Mrs. Stowe's abolitionist relatives had urged her to "write something that would make this whole nation feel what an accursed thing slavery is." Though she had just given birth to her seventh child, Mrs. Stowe promised to "write that thing," and the book was published in 1852. This novel and its stage version converted thousands of Northerners to the abolitionist cause, while angering many white Southerners who claimed that it gave an exag-

[4] Harriet Beecher Stowe and Henry Ward Beecher were sister and brother.

gerated picture of slavery. The importance of *Uncle Tom's Cabin* in molding northern opinion is suggested by President Lincoln's remark in 1863 when he first met Mrs. Stowe: "So you're the little woman who wrote the book that made this great war."

A number of leaders in the women's rights movement also became active in the antislavery cause. Among them were Elizabeth Cady Stanton and Lucretia Mott (page 308). The latter helped convert two South Carolina sisters, Sarah and Angelina Grimké, to the cause of abolition.

Many Negroes were also active abolitionists. Sojourner Truth, a freed slave, spoke at abolitionist meetings throughout the Midwest. Even more effective was Frederick Douglass, who fled from bondage in Baltimore, educated himself, and worked closely with the antislavery societies of New England. Douglass' autobiography sold well, and he was able to purchase his freedom and establish an abolitionist newspaper, the *North Star*.

The North helps fugitive slaves. As antislavery sentiment spread, free-state governments took steps to protect runaway slaves. A fugitive slave law passed in 1793 permitted a master or his agent to use force in returning a runaway slave from a free state to the South. Many Northerners felt, however, that once a slave reached free soil, he had earned his freedom and deserved to keep it. Moreover, cases of mistaken identity occasionally resulted in free Negroes being carried off to slavery. Hence many free states ignored the fugitive slave law. Several of these states passed "personal liberty" laws to protect free Negroes. When a fugitive slave from Virginia was captured in Boston in 1843, an angry mob rescued the Negro from his captors. Bostonians raised money to buy the man's freedom, and Whittier rejoiced, "No fetters in the Bay State — no slave upon our land!" The passage of an even stricter fugitive slave law as part of the Compromise of 1850 intensified northern efforts to help runaway slaves.

The abolitionists helped many slaves escape along the "underground railroad." Over this network of secret, zigzag routes, fugitive slaves were smuggled to places of safety in the North or to Canada. The Negroes hid by day and after dark were conducted from one hiding place to the next. Among the organizers of this escape route was Harriet Tubman, a fugitive slave herself. It has been estimated that by 1861 approximately 75,000 Negroes had traveled the underground railroad to freedom. Although this figure was a small percentage of the total slave population, the escape of these slaves heartened the abolitionists. On the other hand, the underground railroad angered and worried southern slave-owners, who vastly overestimated its success.

Opponents of slavery turn to politics. When the American Antislavery Society was formed in 1833 (page 271), its members had no intention of taking part in politics. They expected to reach their goal by organizing state and local societies, pub-

lishing antislavery newspapers, and working through the churches to expose slavery as a moral crime. In time, however, the abolitionists began to disagree on strategy. Garrison thought slavery could never be abolished under the Constitution, and he urged the North to withdraw from the Union. Most abolitionists, including Theodore Weld, preferred to co-operate whenever possible with the established political parties.

Since both the Whigs and Democrats ducked the slavery issue during the 1840's, a number of abolitionists turned to the Liberty Party (page 285). Then, in 1848 the Free Soil Party was organized (page 291). The Free Soilers in turn were absorbed by still another antislavery party, the Republican Party (page 341).

So well did the new Republican Party reflect the sentiments of voters in the North and West that the party won a majority of the free states in the election of 1856. Four years later the Republicans were strong enough to capture the North as well as the far western states of California and Oregon and thus to put Abraham Lincoln in the White House. Antislavery politics, therefore — and specifically the Republican Party — became another bond between the North and West.

▶ CHECK-UP

1. What progress was made in the 1840's and '50's by temperance leaders? What arguments were advanced against prohibition? What gains were made by women during this period? What kinds of discrimination did free Negroes encounter in the North and West?

2. What was the Gag Rule? How did it hurt the South?

3. Who were leaders in the abolition movement? What groups were especially involved? What methods were used by abolitionists to advance their cause?

4. What was done by free-state governments to help runaway slaves? Trace the evolution of antislavery political parties.

. . . .

4 Literature and the Arts Flourish at Mid-century

Literature, music, drama, and art provide a record of how people lived during a given period and indicate what things they thought were important. During the 1840's and '50's a burst of literary activity produced some of America's finest writing. This new interest in literature appeared chiefly in the North. The pace and challenge of life in the free states stimulated the authors of this period, and their novels, essays, and poems were acclaimed primarily by northern readers.

New England experiences a literary revival. Many of these authors lived in Boston or nearby Cambridge and Concord. This fact prompted one literary historian to refer to their activity as the "Flowering of New England." In addition to Ralph Waldo Emerson (page 265), this group included Longfellow, Hawthorne, Thoreau, Lowell, Whittier, and Holmes.

Longfellow. Henry Wadsworth Longfellow was probably the most widely praised poet of the mid-nineteenth century. Educated at Bowdoin College in Maine, he taught modern languages there before being appointed to the Harvard faculty. He spent his spare time in the study of his Cambridge home writing graceful, sentimental, optimistic poetry. Americans and many Europeans hailed each new volume — *Evangeline, Hiawatha, The Courtship of Miles Standish*, and many others. Though Longfellow once was America's favorite poet, most critics now consider him less important than other writers of this group.

Hawthorne. Nathaniel Hawthorne, a Bowdoin College classmate of Longfellow, was less cheerful about the fate of mankind. Hawthorne's stories were published in volumes entitled *Twice-Told Tales* and *Mosses from An Old Manse*. One of his novels, *The House of the Seven Gables*, is set in Salem, and another, *The Blithedale Romance*, reflects some of his experiences with the Transcendentalists (page 268). Hawthorne's best book, and one of America's finest novels, is *The Scarlet Letter* (1850), a study of the stern morality of Puritan New England.

Thoreau. A close friend and a neighbor of Emerson in Concord was Henry David Thoreau. A staunch individualist, Thoreau cared little for public acclaim. He lived simply and for a time like a hermit in a rough shack at Walden Pond. His intellectual life, however, was rich and full, and fortunately he kept a careful record of it in his notebooks. From this material he fashioned *A Week on the Concord and Merrimack Rivers* and his best book, *Walden, or, Life in the Woods* (1854). Thoreau opposed slavery and the Mexican War. Rather than pay taxes that would support the war, he went to jail. There he wrote the essay "Civil Disobedience" to justify his action. An eccentric and lonely man, Thoreau's death was little noted in 1862. But critics now consider him one of the most original of the New England writers.

Lowell, Holmes, and Whittier. Far better known at the time, though held in less regard today, were the poets James Russell Lowell, Oliver Wendell Holmes, and John Greenleaf Whittier. Lowell expressed his opposition to slavery and the Mexican War in *The Biglow Papers* (page 287). Later he turned to essays and editorial work on *The Atlantic Monthly* and *North American Review*. Oliver Wendell Holmes, a practicing physician in Boston, was highly respected for his scientific writings. He became much better known, however, for his volume of humorous essays, *The Autocrat of the Breakfast Table*, and for his poems "The Chambered Nautilus" and "Old Ironsides." More controversial were the antislavery tracts of the Quaker author John Greenleaf Whittier, who for three decades devoted most of his time to the abolitionist movement. Among his many poems was "Ichabod," a scathing attack on Daniel Webster for supporting the Compromise of 1850. "Snow-Bound," a description of New England country life, is one of his best-known poems.

A whaling scene from the same period as Melville's Moby Dick shows one peril of the whaler's life. In his novels Melville drew heavily on his own experiences as a sailor.

Melville and Whitman were New York writers. Two of the most significant writers of this period were Walt Whitman and Herman Melville, both of whom lived in New York. Though little noticed at the time, they are now considered among America's finest writers. Melville, who had little schooling, once wrote that "a whale-ship was my Yale College and my Harvard." In the 1840's he sailed on a whaler to the South Seas and lived for a time in Tahiti. Back in the United States, he wrote about his Pacific experiences in *Typee* and *Omoo*. His masterpiece, *Moby Dick* (1851), is an epic story of Captain Ahab's search for the great white whale, a symbolic quest which ends in death and destruction.

The other New Yorker who was little appreciated in his own day was Walt Whitman. He tried his hand at teaching, carpentry, printing, and journalism. His first volume of poems appeared in 1855, entitled *Leaves of Grass*. Whitman used new verse forms that bothered readers accustomed to the regular rhythm and rhyme of Longfellow's poetry. Moreover, Whitman wrote about such people as Indians and Negroes, sailors, carpenters, trappers, coachdrivers, and even tramps and criminals. Most poets, he believed, considered themselves "above the people." He wanted to be "of the people, partaking of the common idioms, manners, the earth, the rude visage of animals and trees, and what is vulgar."

For writing about these things, Whitman was denounced by one critic as a "New York rowdy." But Emerson understood Whitman's purpose, and in a letter to the poet he said he found in *Leaves of Grass* "incomparable things, said incomparably well."

Americans write history. American literature of this period was enriched by the work of several talented historians. In the 1830's George Bancroft began a twelve-volume *History of the United States,* which was a justification of American democracy. John L. Motley and William H. Prescott wrote romantic accounts of the Netherlands and the Spanish empire in the New World. One of the ablest American historians was Francis Parkman (page 279). Handicapped by poor health and failing eyesight, he nevertheless began in the 1850's a superb series of volumes on the dramatic struggle between Britain and France in the New World. The works of all these writers are still read, not only for their historical interest but also for their literary worth.

Interest in music increases. At midcentury not only did the American people read more books; they also displayed a growing interest in music. The immigration of trained German musicians invigorated American musical life. Many cities formed choral groups, string quartets, and orchestras. Regular opera seasons were started in New York, Boston, Philadelphia, Chicago,

San Francisco, and New Orleans, and several cities built imposing music halls. The most famous concert artist of the 1850's was the "Swedish nightingale," Jenny Lind.

Currier and Ives are the leading print-makers. Many features of American life were captured in the prints of Nathaniel Currier and James M. Ives. During the 1840's Currier established a reputation in New York as a lithographer.[5] Ives showed such ingenuity in coloring the prints that he became a partner in the 1850's. The company sold thousands of lithographs of steamboat wrecks, train accidents, and fires. Along with these disaster scenes, Currier and Ives turned out prints of rural landscapes, clipper ships, whaling vessels, Mississippi River steamers, locomotives, sports events, sleigh-riding and ice-skating in Central Park. The popular Currier and Ives prints gave color to the walls of countless American homes in the mid-1800's. Present-day historians are grateful to these print-makers for preserving so many scenes of nineteenth-century life.

Photography gets a start. The 1840's also saw the beginnings of photography in this country. The earliest photographs, called *daguerreotypes* (duh-*gair′*uh-types), were made by the Frenchman Louis Daguerre. This early form of picture-taking soon became popular in the United States. At first the subject's head had to be held firmly in place by an iron clamp to prevent him from moving during the long exposure. But shortly before the Civil War technical improvements enabled photographers to get a clear picture with only a brief exposure. Mathew B. Brady, realizing the possibilities of the camera, photographed the outstanding Americans of the period in his New York studio. After the outbreak of the Civil War, Brady brought his equipment to the battlefield and became the world's first war photographer (pages 362–363).

New forms of entertainment develop. Mid-century America saw the beginnings of the form of entertainment which later became the circus. In the 1840's Phineas T. Barnum, the great showman, established a

"museum" in New York City. Its offerings were varied — educational exhibits, stage performances, and freak shows. A brass band stationed outside drew attention to his "Wild West" show and to General Tom Thumb, only two feet and one inch tall. Barnum created a sensation when his "Grand Colossal Museum and Menagerie" toured the North and West in the 1850's. Not until 1871 did Barnum organize his famous circus, which he claimed to be "the greatest show on earth." Traveling by railroad, Barnum took his dwarfs, wax works, Swiss bell ringers, acrobats, and collection of animals to all parts of the country.

In the mid-1800's, huge audiences also attended the minstrel shows. White musicians blackened their faces and performed Negro songs and dances. These minstrels popularized such songs as "Dixie" and Stephen Collins Foster's "My Old Kentucky Home," "Old Black Joe," and "Oh! Susanna."

▶ CHECK-UP

1. Who were the chief New England authors of this period? For what type of writing is each known? Describe the work of Melville and Whitman.

2. What historians wrote during this period? What was the special interest of each?

3. Why are Currier and Ives prints important today? What progress was made in photography? What forms of entertainment were characteristic of this period?

. . . .

Clinching the Main Ideas in Chapter 14

The 1840's and '50's were crucial decades for the United States. During these years the North and West drew closer together, while the South found itself increasingly cut off from the interests of the rest of the country. Had the South been able to win the West to slavery, the story might well have been different. What happened instead was that economic, social, and political developments bound the North and the West closer together. This alliance enabled the free states to triumph in the conflict which was to split the North and South in the 1860's.

[5] A lithographer draws pictures on stones, inks the stones, and then transfers the pictures to paper.

The industrial growth of the North and West was made possible by ingenuity and inventiveness, wise use of resources and capital investments, and a labor force enlarged by immigration. At the same time the expansion of western farms and the use of agricultural machinery produced the necessary surpluses to feed the industrial workers. The exchange of farm and factory produce was dependent on roads, canals, river and lake transportation, and railroads.

The North and West exchanged ideas as well as food and manufactures. Thus, the people of these sections shared common cultural interests, though the literary accomplishments of the mid-1850's were chiefly centered in the Northeast. Citizens of the free states also responded in similar ways to the appeal of the abolitionists. At first only lukewarm about ending slavery, they became more concerned in the 1840's, and soon they were demanding that political parties take a strong stand against human bondage.

Chapter Review

Terms to Understand

1. rolling mill
2. vulcanizing
3. Middle West
4. clipper ship
5. Gag Rule
6. daguerreotype
7. federal land grant
8. Know-Nothing Party
9. underground railroad
10. Tammany Hall
11. *Uncle Tom's Cabin*
12. personal liberty law

What Do You Think?

1. A southern economist assailed the North for rolling back "the mighty tide of the Mississippi and its . . . tributary streams until their mouth . . . is more at New York and Boston than at New Orleans." What did he mean?

2. Why was the era of clipper ships so brief?

3. Why did anti-immigrant feeling run high during this period? Was there greater opposition than there had been 50 years earlier? Why?

4. By the 1850's, had Negroes achieved equal rights in the northern states? Explain.

5. What rights were women demanding in the '40's and '50's? Why did they encounter opposition? Have women achieved full equality today?

6. Thoreau was opposed to slavery and the Mexican War. Because of his views, he refused to pay taxes and so went to jail. Do you think his action was justified? Explain.

Using Your Knowledge of History

1. When they were alive, Longfellow was held in higher regard as a poet than was Whitman. Today they are usually ranked in the reverse order. Read selections from their works and report your conclusions to the class. Take into account their outlook on life, style of writing, subject matter, and verse forms used.

2. If you live in a community that had an early turnpike, canal, or railroad, see what you can learn about its history. Try to answer these questions in a report: (a) When did it reach your community? (b) How much was it used? (c) What was its effect on the community? (d) How significant is it today?

3. Prepare a report on the role of Negroes in the abolition movement.

4. Harriet Beecher Stowe's *Uncle Tom's Cabin* should be looked at in the light of a recent critique by J. C. Furnas, *Goodbye to Uncle Tom*. A committee might read both books and report its findings to the class.

Extending Your Knowledge of History

Interesting accounts of transportation can be found in *The Story of American Railroads* by S. H. Holbrook and in C. C. Cutler's *Greyhounds of the Sea: The Story of the American Clipper Ship*. On science, technology, and invention during these decades see *American Science and Invention: A Pictorial History*, edited by Mitchell Wilson. Russel Crouse's handsomely illustrated book *Mr. Currier and Mr. Ives: A Note on Their Lives and Times* is delightful. The standard book on the literary renaissance is *The Flowering of New England* by Van Wyck Brooks. For the antislavery movement, see Louis Filler's *The Crusade Against Slavery, 1830–1860*. *The Life and Times of Frederick Douglass* is an exciting autobiography. In *American Heritage*, see "The Know-Nothing Uproar" by Ray A. Billington (February, 1959) and "What Samuel Wrought" (about the telegraph) by Marshall B. Davidson (April, 1961).

AMERICA IN THE MID-1800's

By the mid-1800's America had changed considerably since colonial days. As the nation grew, changes occurred in economic activity, ways of living, and leisure-time interests. This picture essay highlights some of these new developments.

In the South, agriculture continued to be the chief occupation. Sugar and cotton were grown on plantations like the one above. Meanwhile, following the building of the first cotton mill in Pawtucket, Rhode Island (left), manufacturing spread rapidly in the North and to some cities in the West. The growing cities and towns hummed with activity. In the painting below, the artist exaggerated the frenzy that overtook people in New York on May 1, the city's traditional moving day.

As cities expanded, people required greater protection. By the 1850's a few cities were hiring uniformed policemen to replace the constables and lonely night watchmen (right) of former times. Fire companies (below, in a Currier print) raced to fires dragging their apparatus. Volunteer fire companies often vied with each other to be first on the scene.

Other services needed by growing cities included adequate water supplies. Below, a crowd gathered on Boston Common in 1848 to celebrate the inauguration of that city's water system.

Street vendors were a common sight —
(above) selling root beer; (right) bringing
milk from the country.

Though hard work was the
everyday lot of most Americans, some city dwellers felt
the need for physical exercise.
By the mid-1800's the larger
cities had well-equipped gym-
nasiums. The one pictured
at right provided athletic activities for Philadelphians.

With more leisure time, American city
and town dwellers enjoyed a variety
of activities. Lectures and dancing
were popular, lyceums flourished, and
theaters were more widely patronized
than in earlier days. Left, a painting
shows actors playing to a full house
in an elaborately ornamented theater
in New York.

319

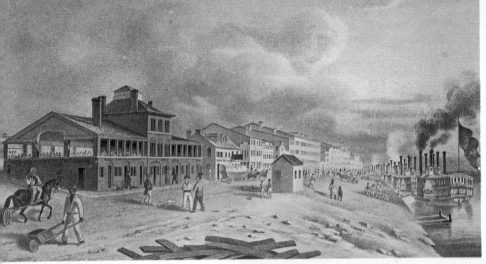

In the West, new towns were settled as old ones like St. Louis thrived. The painting above shows steamboats being loaded along the busy St. Louis river front.

Mail service helped to link the different parts of the country. In 1847 the United States issued its first postage stamps. At right, a painting shows the Pittsburgh Post Office as a busy meeting place in the mid-1800's.

During these years, larg numbers of American wom en eagerly read each issue o Godey's Lady's Book. Thi magazine offered stories an informative articles by lead ing writers, sheet music, an fashion plates (left). Aide by Godey's illustrations an by the sewing machin which was just coming int use, American women coul dress themselves in the late styles.

320

CHAPTER 15

The South Rallies Around Slavery

Steamboat on the Mississippi

Many in the South once believed that it [slavery] was a moral and political evil. That folly and delusion are gone. We see it now in its true light, and regard it as the most safe and stable basis for free institutions in the world.

JOHN C. CALHOUN, 1838

1830–1860

In the 1830's John C. Calhoun began his public defense of slavery, which he spoke of as the South's "peculiar institution." Many Southerners agreed with him that slavery was beneficial for both the Negroes and the whites. There were some, however, who still hoped that the South could find a substitute for slave labor. These people were aware of the growing opposition to slavery elsewhere in the world — in the free states, in Mexico, in Britain, and in France. They saw slavery abolished in the British West Indies and Mexico, and felt it was only a matter of time until the South would have to take the same step. By the mid-1800's, however, these Southerners had been silenced, and most white people in the South had rallied to the defense of slavery.

The rapid spread of cotton growing had made vast areas of the South dependent on slave labor. There was not enough manufacturing south of the Mason and Dixon Line to attract investors or to provide factory jobs for immigrants or native-born white workers. The way to get ahead in the South, therefore, was to acquire land and slaves and become a planter. Many southern whites who did not own slaves hoped to someday and therefore defended the institution of slavery. Throughout the 1850's many southern educators, clergymen, writers, and, above all, politicians staunchly defended the plantation system and slavery. Some of them, convinced that the South could survive as an independent slave republic, even began to talk about secession from the Union.

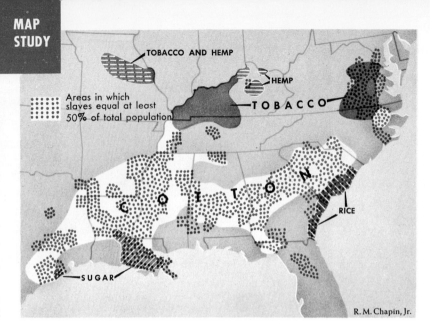

TOBACCO AND HEMP

HEMP

TOBACCO

Areas in which slaves equal at least 50% of total population

C O T T O N

RICE

SUGAR

R. M. Chapin, Jr.

COTTON IS KING

The economy of the prewar South was based on large-scale, cash-crop agriculture. Locate the major growing areas for five staple crops. Note the high concentration of slaves in the cotton-producing region.

1 *Cotton Becomes King*

Cotton cultivation spreads throughout the South. The South's major crops in the 1700's had been tobacco, rice, and indigo. Two developments in the 1790's, however, combined to make cotton the South's most important crop. These were (1) the invention of the cotton gin by Eli Whitney (page 227) and (2) the introduction of a new species of cotton which grew well in the uplands. As a result, cotton cultivation spread rapidly through the southeastern states, then along the Gulf coast, and finally into the lower Mississippi Valley and Texas.

By 1860 the Cotton Kingdom was a huge arc encompassing about three fifths of the South. The volume of the cotton crop had increased enormously. More than four times as much cotton was produced in 1860 as in 1830, and the value of the crop had increased proportionately. By 1860,

cotton constituted nearly two thirds of the total export trade of the United States.

Other crops are grown in the South. Tobacco, rice, and sugar cane, though outdistanced by cotton, were also important southern crops in the mid-nineteenth century. Like cotton, these crops were grown on plantations and cultivated by slave labor. Since tobacco had a relatively short growing season, it was raised chiefly in the more northern areas — Maryland, Virginia, and North Carolina, and across the mountains in Kentucky, Tennessee, and Missouri. Rice was cultivated in tidewater South Carolina and Georgia. Louisiana was the center of sugar-cane production. This crop, introduced in the 1790's, had caught on rapidly in the lower Mississippi Valley.

The upper South produced a variety of crops in addition to tobacco. Many farmers grew corn, wheat, rye, oats, peas, beans, and sweet potatoes, and raised hogs, sheep, and cattle. Hemp was important in Kentucky and Missouri.

Few advances are made in southern agriculture. Relatively little agricultural machinery was used in the South. Cyrus McCormick had spent years trying to interest Virginia farmers in his reaper before he moved to Chicago (page 300). But some southern farmers did take an interest in scientific agriculture. One was Edmund Ruffin of Virginia, who wrote extensively about the use of fertilizers, crop rotation,

CHAPTER FOCUS

1. Cotton becomes King.

2. Southern social classes are clearly defined.

3. Life in bondage is hard.

4. Southern whites defend slavery.

and soil drainage. Yet little of this information reached the small farmers of the South, who most needed to learn about improved methods of agriculture.

The South develops some manufacturing. The South's economic life, then, was based overwhelmingly on agriculture, and most of its surplus wealth or capital went into land and slaves. But some Southerners did invest in manufacturing. One South Carolinian, after visiting New England mills, urged that textile plants be established on the South's rivers and that poor white people be employed as factory workers. Though some southern mills were established in the mid-1850's, they faced fierce competition from New England factories and constantly required the investment of new capital.

A more successful industrial venture was the Tredegar Iron Works in Richmond, Virginia. Established in the late 1830's, this foundry was operated in part by skilled slave labor. By 1860 it was a leading producer of iron. Elsewhere in the South there were flour mills, sawmills, and other small plants. Most Southerners, however, showed little interest in manufacturing. They wanted no "greasy mechanics" or "filthy operatives," as one Georgia newspaper referred to factory workers. Although the South possessed some raw materials and a potential labor supply to support industry, in 1860 it was producing less than one tenth of the nation's manufactured goods.

The South builds some canals and railroads. The South was blessed with many navigable rivers flowing from the interior to the Atlantic or the Gulf of Mexico. Most of the large plantations bordered on rivers; their crops were sent to market on the James, Savannah, Alabama, and Tombigbee Rivers and, of course, the Mississippi. Southerners took great pride in their river transportation. They believed that the Mississippi and its many tributaries would always be the "great spinal cord" of the nation. They were not as eager, therefore, as the North and West to build surfaced roads, canals, or railroads.

Some canals were constructed in the South during the 1830's and '40's. The most ambitious one, Baltimore's Chesapeake and Ohio Canal (page 225), was never completed. Charleston, New Orleans, and other southern cities built short canals which linked the back-country to the major rivers and the leading ports.

Southern railroad construction was promoted chiefly by Baltimore and Charleston. As the Cotton Kingdom extended west, these cities had lost much of their coastal trade to Mobile and New Orleans. The older ports, therefore, tried to make up

The Tredegar Iron Works, in Richmond, Virginia, produced iron not only for the South but for markets throughout the country in the mid-1800's. During the Civil War, the Confederate government depended on the Tredegar Works for its cannon.

their losses by building railroads into the interior. Baltimore was most successful, for it established a railroad connection with the rich Ohio River Valley.

By 1860 railroad construction in the South had produced about one third of the country's total mileage of track. Two major trunk lines, the Baltimore and Ohio and the Illinois Central (page 304), linked southern cities with the North and the West. The rest of the South's railroads served mainly the cotton planters and the merchants who marketed their crops.

The South was economically dependent on the North. During the 1840's and '50's southern spokesmen expressed increasing irritation at the South's economic dependence on the North. The South provided cotton for the East and bought manufactured goods and much of its food from the free states. Moreover, northern merchants sold southern cotton to European markets. Northern packet ships would pick up the cotton in Mobile, New Orleans, and other southern ports and carry it to New York, Boston, or British ports, where the ships took on manufactured goods. (Some of these vessels also picked up Irish, English, and German immigrants at British or other European ports to take back to America.) The manufactured goods were then carried down the Atlantic coast to southern ports and sold at a profit. Northern merchants took anywhere from 2 to 10 per cent for their services in selling the cotton and in supplying southern planters with manufac-

tured goods. Southerners resented this loss of profits to the northern merchants.

Southern leaders held many conventions to find ways of reducing their economic dependence on the North. Usually these conferences ended with bitter words, such as these written by an Alabama journalist:

> At present, the North fattens and grows rich upon the South. We depend upon it for our entire supplies. We purchase all our luxuries and necessaries from the North. . . . The Northerners abuse and denounce slavery and slave-holders, yet our slaves are clothed with Northern manufactured goods, have Northern hats and shoes, work with Northern hoes, plows and other implements, are chastised with a Northern-made instrument, are working for Northern more than Southern profits. The slave-holder dresses in Northern goods, rides in a Northern saddle . . . sports his Northern carriage . . . drinks Northern liquors . . . spends his money at Northern watering places. . . . In Northern vessels his products are carried to market, his cotton is ginned with Northern gins, his sugar is crushed and preserved by Northern machinery; his rivers are navigated by Northern steamboats; . . . his Negroes are fed with Northern bacon, beef, flour, and corn; his land is cleared with a Northern axe, and a Yankee clock sits upon his mantelpiece.

The South places its confidence in King Cotton. Although the South recognized its economic dependence, it took no effective steps to change the situation. Instead of investing capital in merchant ships or in manufacturing, the South continued to pour its money into the expansion of the Cotton Kingdom. Southerners were reassured by the steady demand for raw cotton in the North and in Britain. Though the South had to import manufactured goods and food, textile manufacturers were dependent on the South for raw cotton to feed their machines. Southerners concluded that since the South produced two thirds of the world's cotton, they were in the driver's seat. It was in this spirit that a South Carolina senator boasted to northern colleagues in 1858: "You dare not make war on cotton — no power on earth dares make war upon it. Cotton is king."

What's in a Name?

A beautiful flowering plant is named after a South Carolina planter and diplomat who was also interested in scientific agriculture. While serving as the first United States minister to Mexico from 1825 to 1829, Joel Poinsett experimented with a plant that he later introduced in this country. Especially popular at Christmas because of its vivid red and green colors, the plant is called "poinsettia" in Poinsett's honor.

Trees often shaded the plantation houses of the prewar South. Notice the similarities and differences in the two plantation houses shown here. "Four Oaks," the dwelling at right, was the home of a large planter who lived near New Orleans. Small planters' residences, like the Georgia house at left, were less splendid.

▶ CHECK-UP

1. What were the chief crops in the South during the 1850's? In what region was each produced? Why was cotton important?

2. Why did the South lag behind the North in industrial development? In building canals and railroads? Why did Baltimore and Charleston promote railroad construction?

3. How was the South economically dependent on the North? Why did the South take no effective steps to change the situation?

. . . .

2 *Southern Social Classes Are Clearly Defined*

Social groupings are distinct in the South. The reforms of the Jacksonian Era had done much to break down class distinctions in the free states of the North and West. In the South, however, the lines were more clearly drawn between the planter and the small farmer, and between the small farmers and the "poor whites." But it was possible for white people to move from one class to another, especially on the frontier in Mississippi, Louisiana, Texas, and Arkansas. There, with hard work and good luck, a small farmer could save enough money to purchase more land and slaves and become a planter.

Thus southern society was not rigidly divided into classes of slave-owners, slaves, and "poor whites," though travel accounts and novels often give **that impression.** Many of the British and northern travelers in the South were so prejudiced against slaveholders that their accounts are unreliable. Present-day historians are further handicapped by the comparatively small number of documents from which to reconstruct southern life. Since both the small farmers and the "poor whites" were uneducated, they left few papers of any kind. The same was true of free Negroes and the slaves. Yet census figures, newspapers, magazines, court records, diaries, and letters enable historians to sketch the outlines of southern society in the 1850's.

The planters dominate southern society. The term "planter" was applied by the census takers to men who owned ten or more slaves and used them on cotton, tobacco, rice, or sugar plantations. A "large planter" owned a hundred or more slaves

Cades Cove, a community in the Great Smoky Mountains National Park, is maintained to show old ways of living. At left, men split logs to make rail fences.

Other skills of days gone by are carried on in southern mountain communities. The chairmaker above planes wood with a traditional tool called a draw knife. He uses no glue or nails but wets the wood, which then shrinks as it dries, making joints tight. The skill of sewing corn husk dolls (left) dates back to the days when families made toys for their children. The heads of the dolls are hickory nuts, with features drawn on.

and at least a thousand acres of land. "Small planters" had fewer than a hundred slaves and generally owned from several hundred to a thousand acres. In 1860 there were 140,000 large and small planters. They constituted only a small percentage of the southern white population. Yet the planters dominated southern society and controlled the economic and political life of the region. Northerners tended to think that most southern whites were slave-owning planters. In reality the planters were a small but very influential minority of the population.

The large planters lived in handsome plantation homes, tastefully furnished, with wide verandas and landscaped gardens.

They divided their time between the plantations and such cities as Charleston and New Orleans, where they attended social events and shopped for stylish clothes. Many of the wealthiest planters traveled in Europe. Children had private tutors and later attended academies. The boys usually went to southern colleges but in some cases to northern or British universities. Though the life of the large planter and his family was pleasant, it could be insecure. Floods, droughts, or insect plagues might destroy the planter's crops, and disease might thin the ranks of his slaves. Such losses would plunge him into debt, forcing him to sell some of his land, slaves, or perhaps the entire plantation.

The small planters lived in less spacious frame houses, sometimes unpainted and without landscaping. The planter's wife had to shoulder most of the household responsibilities. Many times she watched the youngest slave children in order to free their mothers for work in the fields. The small planter had to supervise the work of his slaves; unlike the large planter, he seldom could afford to hire an overseer. Moreover, he had little time to read or travel and not much money for his children's education. Like the large planter, however, he took great interest in politics.

The urban population was relatively small. There were thriving cities in the South — for example, New Orleans, Charleston, Richmond, Nashville, and Mobile. Even so, less than 10 per cent of the southern whites lived in communities of 2500 or more people. The population of these communities included such people as clergymen, teachers, doctors, and lawyers, as well as the merchants and tradesmen who did business with the planters. The urban upper classes and the planters had close ties. They mingled socially, and many of the lawyers and merchants invested in plantations. In fact, in 1860 half of Charleston's professional men were absentee plantation owners. Because of the ties between the planters and the professional classes and merchants, these urban groups strongly defended slavery and King Cotton.

Of course, artisans, mechanics, and laborers also lived in the cities and towns of the South. Their wages compared favorably with those paid in the North. Those immigrants who settled in the South usually found employment as artisans in the cities. Since the South had very few public schools, neither working people nor their children received much education. The white artisans and laborers of the South had to compete for jobs with free Negroes and with trained slaves who were hired out to work. In this bitter contest, the white workers often appealed to city councils or to state legislatures for protection of their jobs. Georgia in 1845, for example, prohibited Negroes, whether slave or free, from construction work on city buildings. Southern white workers had no direct stake in

slavery. But they feared Negro competition and so supported the slave system.

Small farmers form the bulk of the population. Approximately 75 per cent of the southern white population was made up of small farmers. They usually owned less than a hundred acres of land and worked it with the help of their children and perhaps a slave or two. Most of these people lived in the southern uplands and the foothills of the mountains. They raised wheat, corn, oats, sweet potatoes, and some tobacco, and kept a variety of livestock. Their surplus food was sold to the plantations.

The small farmers dwelt in sparsely furnished log houses. Their wives cooked over open fireplaces, using crude utensils. These families had practically no education, and many were illiterate. Their greatest enthusiasm was for revival meetings or other church gatherings. Their greatest hope was to be able to buy more land and slaves and move up into the ranks of the small planters. Some of these farmers found employment as overseers on large plantations. Since overseers' wages depended on the size of the cotton crop, and since they themselves did not own the slaves, these men often proved to be cruel taskmasters. The small farmers were ardent supporters of slavery. Frederick Law Olmsted, a Northerner whose observations about the South are reliable, said of these people: "They seem more than any other portion of the community to hate and despise the Negroes."

The "poor whites" live unhappy lives. The unfortunate people known as "poor whites" constituted about a sixth of the southern white population. Most of them lived in rough shacks perched in the highlands and mountainous regions and grew corn, vegetables, and sweet potatoes in the clearings. Many of them suffered from hookworm, malaria, and dietary deficiencies. Without jobs, medical care, or education, they lived a miserable existence. Abolitionists argued that the "poor whites" were victims of a society based on slavery. Southern leaders, however, denied that the condition of the "poor whites" had anything whatever to do with slavery. The English actress Fanny Kemble was one of the few travelers who ventured into the southern highlands to see these people. In her journal she observed that even the slaves scorned the poor whites.

Free Negroes are severely restricted. By 1860 the South had some 250,000 free Negroes, totaling about 6 per cent of its Negro population. Some had been freed by their masters; others had saved enough money to buy their freedom. These Negroes could be found in every slave state but were most numerous in the towns and cities of Virginia, Maryland, North Carolina, Kentucky, and Louisiana. Some of them were squatters on abandoned land, barely able to make a living. Others managed to buy land, and there were instances of free Negroes who owned slaves. Most of the free Negroes, however, were artisans and laborers in the cities. As we have seen, local laws often limited the jobs open to them. Because it was illegal to teach any Negro to read or write, few free Negroes in the South acquired an education. Many of them were "mistakenly" seized as runaway slaves. A few found their situation so trying that they voluntarily sold themselves to masters who promised kind treatment.

▶ CHECK-UP

1. Describe these social classes in the South: large planters, small planters, small farmers, "poor whites." What crops did each produce? What were the views of each on slavery?

2. What groups were included in the white urban population? What were their views on slavery?

3. About what percentage of the South's Negro population was free? Where did these Negroes live? What were their problems?

· ·

3 *Life in Bondage Is Hard*

Slaves have different status. Great differences existed within the ranks of the nearly four million slaves in the South in 1860. Their status depended on many factors — age, health, sex, type of employment, amount of training, and the size of the plantation or the kind of town where the slave lived. The character and disposition of his master and the slave's own personality were also factors. In general, slaves in the cities enjoyed better housing, a fuller and more varied diet, and a greater degree of independence than those on plantations.

The easiest situation for a plantation slave was service in the household, especially as the planter's valet or the wife's personal maid. Next in status came the slaves who worked as craftsmen on the plantation. Some of these slaves, if not needed by the planters, were hired out in the towns and allowed to live on their own. Most slaves were field hands who worked long hours under the direction of an overseer or a small planter. Those in the tobacco fields of the upper South generally fared better than the cotton hands. The cotton workers in turn were better off than the slaves who worked in the steaming rice swamps of Georgia or on the Louisiana sugar-cane plantations.

Laws regulate slavery. Hundreds of state and local laws regulated the institution of slavery. These slave codes denied the Negro the right to own property; he could not leave his master's land without permission; he could not gather with other slaves except for specific purposes, such as church services. Slaves could not be taught to read or write; they could not testify in court against a white person; they could not strike a white person even in self-defense. Slaves had to accept punishment inflicted by their masters; slave marriages were not recognized by law; and slave names had no legal standing. Since, as we have seen, few slave records remain, it is difficult to determine how strictly these laws were enforced. Historians have to weigh the conflicting claims of northern abolitionists and southern apologists, neither of whom painted completely accurate pictures of slave life.

The treatment of slaves varies. Some slaves were not badly treated by their masters. They lived with their own families in small cabins, had adequate though inexpensive clothing, and ate a nourishing though monotonous diet of corn meal, molasses, vegetables, and salt pork. Their masters gave them time off to hunt and fish, allowed them to hold their own social gatherings, and invited them to special affairs on the plantation. The slaves received some medical care, and a few (despite the laws) were taught to read by the planters' wives. Some slaves felt genuine affection for their masters; some masters returned this feeling and would never break up a slave family by selling any of its members.

On the other hand, many slaves were badly treated. These Negroes were crowded into rough shacks, were inadequately clothed in winter, and were poorly fed. They worked long hours and were cruelly punished for minor violations of strict plantation rules. Some masters showed little consideration for their slaves' family life and thought nothing of selling surplus slaves.

Such treatment naturally made unwilling workers of the slaves. They labored no harder than they had to. Moreover, many tried to escape from bondage by running away. Sometimes they struck back against cruel masters and on rare occasions organized rebellions against the system itself.

The internal slave trade continues. The slave trade was a cruel feature of slavery. Though Congress in 1808 had prohibited the importation of slaves, by the 1850's there was considerable smuggling of Negroes into the United States. Far greater in volume was the internal slave trade. As planters moved westward, they took some slaves with them. When the landowners had cleared their fields and laid out plantations, they needed many more slaves. These were purchased from areas which had a surplus of slaves, usually the states of the upper South. Washington, D. C., and New Orleans became centers of the domestic slave trade. After the Compromise of 1850 banned the sale of Negroes in the national capital (page 292), Richmond also became a leading market. Once the slaves had been auctioned off, many of them were transported by ocean packet or river boat to the plantations of their new masters. Others were chained together and marched overland to their destination.

Since the slave trade often broke up Negro families and sometimes even separated mothers from young children, it was bitterly criticized by Northerners. As early as the 1830's, abolitionist petitions sought to ban the slave trade not only in Washington but everywhere in the South. For eight years, however, the Gag Rule cut off discussion in the House of Representatives of the internal slave trade (page 309). When Clay offered his compromise proposals in 1850, he included a guarantee to southern planters that Congress would not interfere with the domestic slave trade. But this provision was not included in the laws finally passed by Congress.

Was slavery profitable? The question of whether or not slavery was economically profitable has long been debated. If slavery had proved uneconomical and the South had abandoned it for a system of free labor, the Civil War might have been avoided. Some historians argue that slavery in any event would have died out in time. They say the price of slaves was rising so fast in the 1850's that many planters could not afford to buy new slaves. Moreover, the slaves were a burden when they were too young, too old, or too ill to perform a full day's work. Some of these scholars conclude that if the South had been given more time, it eventually would have abandoned slavery. The angry demand of the abolitionists, however, antagonized the white Southerners into defending slavery. It finally took a war to decide the bitter controversy.

Most historians and economists give a different answer to the question of whether slavery was profitable. They say that slavery was an expanding, not a contracting, institution in the 1840's and '50's. The masters provided the Negroes with only the bare essentials of life, and in return they exacted a lifetime of unpaid labor. Few southern slaveholders condemned the system in the mid-1800's. Indeed after the early 1830's there was little serious thought in the South of finding a substitute for slavery. Even if Southerners doubted that slavery was profitable, they were determined to keep the South a "white man's country." To do this, they felt that the Negroes had to remain enslaved. In studying the origins of the Civil War, many historians place a great deal of emphasis on southern unwillingness to discuss alternatives to the slave system. The determination of southern whites to preserve their "peculiar institution" was, therefore, a major factor in the outbreak of the Civil War.

▶ CHECK-UP

1. How was the slave's life affected by the kind of work he did? By the character of his master or overseer?

2. What kinds of legal restrictions were there on slaves? Describe the slave's housing, food, medical care, and education?

3. How could slaves "protest" against slavery? Why was the domestic slave trade criticized by Northerners? What reasons are there to believe that slavery was profitable? Unprofitable? Why might the South have wished to retain an unprofitable slave system?

. . . .

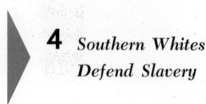

4 Southern Whites Defend Slavery

A leading historian of the prewar South has observed that between the deaths of Jefferson in 1826 and Calhoun in 1850, "a great change took place in the southern states. The liberal ideas of the eighteenth century were in large part discarded." Whereas the North and West experienced various reform movements, the South was little affected by the social ferment of the Jacksonian Era. Southern women showed less interest than their northern sisters in better opportunities for higher education or the opening of careers for women. There was only mild interest in the establishment of public schools, public libraries, penny newspapers, and lyceums.

White Southerners feel the need to defend slavery. Southern white people devoted much time and effort after the 1830's to a defense of slavery. They knew that

elsewhere in the world slavery was increasingly criticized. White Southerners met this challenge by ardently defending their "peculiar institution." Calhoun argued that Negro bondage was a "positive good," and a South Carolina governor called it "a national benefit" rather than "a national evil." A Virginia lawyer named George Fitzhugh announced in the early 1840's that "slavery, black or white, was right and necessary." He urged Southerners to take a "higher ground in defense of Slavery; justifying it as a normal and natural institution, instead of excusing and apologizing for it, as an exceptional one." Many southern educators, writers, ministers, and politicians proceeded to do this.

Southern educators defend slavery. Teachers in the private academies, colleges, and universities of the South were forced to toe the line on the question of slavery. Those who dared to speak or write against slavery usually lost their posts. By the 1850's few southern youths were sent to schools in the North. An irate Georgian offered one explanation: "I have never known a young man educated at Yale or Cambridge but what he returned to us a complete Yankee, and would lecture his parents in regard to the sin of holding human beings in Slavery."

Writers and publishers uphold slavery. After Garrison began publication of *The Liberator* in 1831, most southern states passed laws barring abolitionist literature from the mails (page 271). As time went on, these laws were rigidly enforced. Few northern papers or magazines printing articles on slavery were allowed to circulate in the South. Southern readers contented themselves with regional newspapers and magazines like *The Southern Literary Messenger, The Southern Review,* or *De Bow's Review.* These southern publications devoted an increasing amount of space to the defense of slavery.

Southern writers found that they had to turn out tracts defending slavery if they wanted the public to read their poems or novels. William Gilmore Simms, a South Carolina author, diligently wrote proslavery tracts but still was disappointed in the sale of his other works. In 1857 he complained

Cotton was king in the southern economy during the first half of the 1800's. This plantation scene on the Mississippi (top) shows slaves picking the ripe cotton, which was then loaded on wagons to be taken to the cotton gin (at left above, a model of Eli Whitney's invention). After the gins cleaned the seeds from the fibers, the cotton was packed into bales and hauled to a wharf for shipping to market. In the view of a New Orleans levee in 1855 (above right), cotton bales and sugar barrels are waiting to be loaded on a steamship.

that the South did not care "for literature or art. . . . You will write for & defend their institutions in vain. They will not pay the expense of printing your essays." At the same time, however, George Fitzhugh built a great reputation with proslavery books. He sought to prove that Negroes were racially inferior to whites, that slavery was beneficial for the Negroes, that free Negroes ought to be enslaved, and that free society

in the industrial North was a "failure." In the 1850's southern writers dashed off a score or more novels to counteract the effect of *Uncle Tom's Cabin*. These "anti-Tom" books painted a glowing picture of slavery, and most of them sold well.

Ministers justify slavery. Southern clergymen, reflecting the proslavery views of their parishioners, claimed that the Scriptures sanctioned slavery because of Biblical references to slaves and slave-owners. The defense of slavery on religious grounds was taken very seriously by most white Southerners. It played a large part in *The Pro-Slavery Argument* (1852), a collection of essays by prominent Southerners, including William Gilmore Simms.

At national gatherings of church people, northern and southern clergymen frequently clashed over slavery. In 1844 the Methodists voted to suspend a minister until he disposed of his slaves. As a result, angry southern Methodists formed their own regional organization. The following year, when the Baptists refused to engage a slaveholder as a missionary, Southerners formed a separate Baptist Convention. The Presbyterians managed to ward off a complete split until the late 1850's. In the pre-war decades, therefore, the South's Protestant churches became defenders of slavery.

Extremists speak for the South. Just as Southerners believed that the fiery abolitionist William Lloyd Garrison spoke for the entire North, so Northerners believed that southern extremists, or "fire eaters," reflected public opinion south of the Mason and Dixon Line. Among these were Edmund Ruffin (page 322), William Lowndes Yancey, and Robert Barnwell Rhett. In the 1840's Ruffin gave up publishing an agricultural journal to devote his full time to the defense of slavery. He traveled widely in the South, lecturing to vacationers at resorts, speaking at political rallies, and addressing agricultural conventions. He took pride in his homespun suits and never failed to tell listeners that he would not buy cloth manufactured in the North.

William Lowndes Yancey, an Alabama lawyer, spoke eloquently and tirelessly in defense of the plantation system. To increase the number and reduce the price of slaves, he advocated reopening the African slave trade. This action would have enabled small farmers as well as large planters to increase their slave holdings. Believing that the Constitution could not protect the South's way of life, Yancey urged secession from the Union and the creation of a separate Southern Republic. He influenced so many Southerners in the 1850's that he has been called "the orator of secession."

Robert Barnwell Rhett of South Carolina was an aristocratic planter and an active politician. As early as the 1830's he had called for amendments to the Constitution to protect the South. If that failed, he argued that the slave states should peacefully withdraw from the Union. Rhett believed that all tariff measures had been designed by Northerners to exploit southern planters. He served in the House of Representatives and for a brief time in the Senate. South Carolina's acceptance of the Compromise of 1850 so embittered Rhett that he resigned his Senate seat.

A Southerner attacks slavery. The "fire eaters" and other defenders of slavery monopolized southern pulpits, newspapers, magazines, and political platforms in the 1850's. There were southern whites who felt that slavery was morally wrong, and others who believed it to be unprofitable, but few expressed these opinions publicly. One southern farmer who did attack slavery on economic grounds was Hinton Rowan Helper of North Carolina. In 1857 he published a book entitled *The Impending Crisis of the South: How to Meet It.* Using the census figures of 1850, he argued that the South was far less productive than the North. He charged, moreover, that the region lagged behind the free states in cultural and intellectual development. Helper concluded that slavery was "the root of all the shame, poverty, ignorance, tyranny and imbecility of the South." *The Impending Crisis* delighted the abolitionists, and the Republicans used it as a campaign document in 1860. White Southerners angrily denounced Helper. His book joined the long list of antislavery publications rarely read in the South.

▶ CHECK-UP

1. How had southern opinion on slavery seemed to change by the 1830's?

2. What arguments were used by southern speakers, writers, and clergymen to justify slavery? For what reasons did Yancey and Rhett urge secession?

3. On what grounds did Hinton Helper criticize slavery?

Clinching the Main Ideas in Chapter 15

By 1860 many people in the free states felt that slavery was morally wrong and ought not be allowed to spread into the federal territories. Some of them were determined to end slavery in the South as well. Yet the white people of the slave states were just as determined to preserve their "peculiar institution." It mattered little to them that they were a minority within the United States or that most nations in western Europe and their immediate neighbor, Mexico, had abolished slavery.

Cotton had become the major crop of the South, and Southerners firmly believed that slave labor was necessary to maintain King Cotton. The life of the South was geared to the plantation economy — the trade, transportation, and politics of the region served the interests of the planter class. Moreover, professional people, artisans, small farmers, and even the "poor whites" shared the planters' view that the South must be kept a "white man's country." Jefferson Davis, a wealthy Mississippi planter and politician, declared in 1857 that "African slavery, as it exists in the United States, is a moral, a social, and a political blessing." A few southern extremists even urged secession from the Union in order to preserve white control and Negro bondage in the South.

Chapter Review

Terms to Understand

1. Cotton Kingdom
2. slave code
3. *The Impending Crisis*
4. small farmers
5. poor whites
6. small planters
7. large planters
8. domestic slave trade

What Do You Think?

1. "By 1860, cotton constituted two thirds of the total export trade of the United States . . . ," but the South "was producing less than one tenth of the nation's manufactured goods." What do these two statements tell you about the economy of the South and of the nation in 1860?

2. In what different ways was the South economically dependent on the North? Why?

3. Why has it been difficult for historians to reconstruct southern life in the 1850's?

4. Small and large planters combined made up only a small percentage of the South's white population. How then were they able to control the economic and political life of the region?

5. Why did white Southerners who questioned whether or not slavery was profitable nevertheless defend that institution?

Using Your Knowledge of History

1. In the 1850's, white artisans and laborers approved the slave system. A century later there was discrimination against Negroes in some labor unions and in the employment practices of some employers. Give your reactions in a brief essay.

2. (a) Economically what similarities were there between the South in colonial times and in the 1850's? (b) What differences? If two students report on (a) and (b), the whole class should help in formulating a conclusion.

3. Write a report contrasting the antislavery arguments used by abolitionists and those given by Hinton Helper in *The Impending Crisis*.

4. Before 1830 there had been a strong emancipation movement in the South. By 1860 there was none. List and explain the reasons for the South's "growing unanimity" on the issue of slavery.

Extending Your Knowledge of History

Clement Eaton has written an excellent survey of southern history, *The Growth of Southern Civilization, 1790–1860.* An authoritative book about slavery is Kenneth Stampp's *The Peculiar Institution.* F. L. Owsley has written social history in *Plain Folk of the Old South.* An accurate description of ways of life in the South is Frederick L. Olmsted's *Cotton Kingdom.* On urban slavery, consult *Slavery in the Cities* by Richard C. Wade. The southern defense of slavery is analyzed by W. S. Jenkins in *Pro-Slavery Thought in the Old South.*

CHAPTER 16

Antislavery meeting

1850–1861

The Slavery Issue Leads to Southern Secession

"A house divided against itself cannot stand." I believe this government cannot endure permanently half slave and half free. I do not expect the Union to be dissolved; I do not expect the house to fall; but I do expect it will cease to be divided. It will become all one thing, or all the other.

ABRAHAM LINCOLN, 1858

By 1858 many Americans, northern and southern, shared Lincoln's view that the Union could not endure "half slave and half free." Northerners were determined to keep slavery out of the territories, and many of them hoped to wipe it out where it legally existed. The slaveholders, on the other hand, were set on preserving their "peculiar institution." And they insisted on the right to take slaves into any federal territory.

Only eight years before, Congress had adopted the Compromise of 1850 to settle some of the grievances between the North and the South. Yet both sections soon found fault with this settlement, and throughout the 1850's tension between the slave and free states increased. In the territories this hostility led to clashes between free-soilers and slaveholders.

The breaking up of national political parties and the emergence of sectional parties increased the tension. The Whig Party disappeared soon after it was defeated in 1852. Within a few years the antislavery Republican Party took shape in the North and West. Meanwhile, proslavery forces increased their hold on the Democratic Party, and in 1860 it finally split into northern and southern factions. By that date Southerners were so fearful of the Republican Party that Abraham Lincoln's election to the presidency was the signal for seven slave states to secede from the Union.

1 *The North and South Reconsider the Compromise of 1850*

The Compromise benefits both North and South. The compromise measures of 1850 had averted an open break between the North and South (page 294), though neither side was entirely satisfied with the settlement. Each, however, had made some gains. The North welcomed the admission of California as a free state, especially since its addition shifted the balance between free and slave states in favor of the North. Moreover, most people believed that the rest of the Mexican Cession would remain free. The prohibition of the slave trade in the District of Columbia also pleased Northerners.

The South too could claim some victories in the Compromise of 1850. The strict Fugitive Slave Law obligated federal authorities to help return escaped slaves. And only the slave trade, not slavery itself, had been banned in the District of Columbia. Southerners also approved of the legislation permitting settlers to decide the status of slavery in Utah and New Mexico. This meant that the South had heard the last of the Wilmot Proviso, which would have banned slavery throughout the Mexican Cession (page 289).

The Compromise is an issue in the election of 1852. The presidential election of 1852 gave the voters an opportunity to voice their opinion of the Compromise. At the Democratic convention, the delegates

adopted a platform which praised the Compromise and opposed further agitation over slavery. But when it came to nominating a presidential candidate, the convention was deadlocked between two prominent supporters of popular sovereignty, Senator Stephen Douglas of Illinois and Lewis Cass of Michigan (page 290). Finally the delegates chose a little-known candidate from New Hampshire, Franklin Pierce.

Hopelessly divided between proslavery and antislavery Whigs, the convention of the Whig Party adopted a platform giving only lukewarm support to the compromise measures. For the presidential nomination it passed over President Fillmore and Daniel Webster, both of whom were closely associated with the Compromise. Instead, the convention chose General Winfield Scott, hoping that his military exploits in the Mexican War would attract the voters.

The Free Soil Party opposed the Compromise of 1850 because it made concessions to the South. Its candidate, John P. Hale, ran on a platform which criticized the Compromise and opposed the addition of any more slave states to the Union.

Pierce becomes President. The Democrats won handily in 1852. Pierce carried 27 states, Scott only 4. The Free Soilers polled only half as many votes as they had in 1848. It seemed clear, therefore, that the voters approved of the Compromise. Like the people, President-elect Pierce expected the Compromise to preserve the truce between the North and the South. But the new President, though well-meaning, was ineffective. He was dominated by Southerners in his Cabinet and by southern chairmen of the influential committees in Congress. The proslavery sympathies of the Pierce administration angered thousands of people in the North and West. Thus, although he predicted peace and prosperity in his inaugural address, President Pierce presided over a nation torn by sectional strife.

Northerners oppose the Fugitive Slave Act. The sense of relief which had swept the country after the adoption of the Compromise of 1850 soon vanished. Despite the fact that both the North and South had

A family of fugitive slaves rides north to escape their pursuers. If runaways could cross the Ohio River, their chances of finding help were good. But the Fugitive Slave Act meant that Negroes were not really safe until they reached Canada.

gained by the Compromise, people in both sections were greatly upset by certain (but not the same) parts of that settlement.

As we have seen, the Fugitive Slave Act enraged many Northerners (page 312). This law gave federal officials extraordinary powers to aid in the return of runaway slaves. When a slave-owner or his agent identified a Negro as a fugitive slave, the Negro would be taken before a federal judge. The suspect was denied trial by jury; and he could not summon witnesses or even testify in his own behalf. Heavy penalties were imposed on citizens who aided the runaways as well as on federal officials who failed to co-operate in capturing and returning fugitive slaves.

Abolitionists had raised loud cries against this measure from the moment Clay proposed it. When the law went into effect, thousands of Northerners who were not abolitionists joined in the protest. These people objected to the unconstitutional features of the measure, particularly the denial of trial by jury. Moreover, many Northerners were shocked by the arrest of Negroes who for years had lived peacefully in their communities.

Southerners object to the Compromise. Though most white Southerners had rejoiced when the Compromise of 1850 was adopted, they soon became disillusioned. For one thing, the Fugitive Slave Act provided much less protection than they had expected. One slave-owner found that it cost him 5000 dollars to recover a fugitive slave from Boston. Southerners also came to realize that the Utah and New Mexico Territories were too dry for plantation crops and therefore were not likely to become slave states. Moreover, the South was already outnumbered in the Senate and outvoted in the House by the more populous North and West.

Southerners look for a solution to their problem. In a gloomy mood, white Southerners cast about for ways to strengthen their section. One idea which received considerable support was to reopen the African slave trade. Another was the annexation of territory which might be carved into slave states. Southerners had already been eyeing northern Mexico, Central America, Cuba, and Santo Domingo. Still another proposal was that the federal government build a railroad linking Memphis or New Orleans with the West Coast, thus giving a boost to the economy of the South.

Desire for Cuba leads to the Ostend Manifesto. Both the Democratic Party and President Pierce proved sympathetic to southern proposals. Pierce felt that the annexation of Cuba would add glory to his administration. In 1853 he instructed the American minister in Spain to discuss the purchase of Cuba, but the Spanish government rejected the American offer. The next year three American ministers in Europe met at Ostend, Belgium, to clarify the American position on Cuba. They drew up a memorandum which became known as the Ostend Manifesto. This document declared that if Spain refused to sell Cuba, the United States would be justified in seizing the island by force. Though the Ostend Manifesto had been prepared for the State Department, it found its way into American newspapers. European governments were shocked by this aggressive document, and antislavery groups in the United States criticized the Pierce administration. The Secretary of State quickly denounced the Ostend Manifesto. Southern extremists then knew they would have to look elsewhere for ways of achieving their goals.

▶ CHECK-UP

1. What were the advantages of the Compromise of 1850 to the North? To the South? Were there any cases of an "advantage" proving to be less clear-cut than had been hoped? Explain.

2. Who were the candidates in the election of 1852? What was the outcome?

3. How did Southerners propose to strengthen their section? What was the Ostend Manifesto?

· · · · · · · · · · · · · · · · · ·

2 *The Kansas-Nebraska Act Has Far-reaching Consequences*

A transcontinental railroad route provokes a quarrel. After Oregon and California were added to the United States (Chapter 13), interest grew in the construction of a transcontinental railroad. A number of lines had crossed the Mississippi River by the early 1850's, and people were talking about a route to the West Coast. Both Northerners and Southerners agreed that a transcontinental railroad should be

built with federal aid in the form of land grants.

They did not agree on the route, however. Each of four proposals had enthusiastic supporters. A line could be built (1) from Chicago to St. Paul and west to the Oregon coast; (2) from Chicago through St. Louis to San Francisco; (3) from Memphis to Los Angeles; or (4) from New Orleans to San Diego (map, page 339). Northerners favored the routes westward from Chicago; Southerners preferred either the Memphis or New Orleans route.

Soon after he took office, President Pierce instructed his Secretary of War, Jefferson Davis, to survey the routes and make recommendations to Congress. When Secretary Davis, a Mississippian, submitted a report favoring the Memphis to Los Angeles route, angry Northerners vowed to block construction of such a railroad. They charged that the Pierce administration was bowing to the demands of Democratic slave-owners. In this tense situation a northern Democrat, Stephen Douglas of Illinois, proposed a compromise.

Douglas introduces the Kansas-Nebraska Bill. Douglas felt that the central

---

Filibusters

In their zeal to seize foreign territory for the extension of slavery, some southern adventurers invaded Mexico and Central American countries in the mid-1800's. The leaders of these private expeditions were called "filibusters," a term derived from a Dutch word meaning "pirate" or "plunderer." The most colorful filibuster was William Walker, who conquered Nicaragua, set up a government which received American recognition, and opened the country to slavery. After a year in power, however, Walker was forced to flee.

Another meaning of the word filibuster is better known today. Minority members of the United States Senate sometimes monopolize the floor with endless speeches in order to block legislative action. Such a delaying tactic is called a filibuster. The Senate is reluctant to ban filibustering because it would deprive the senators of their traditional right to unlimited debate.

route from St. Louis to San Francisco was the only one that both sections might accept. But first the vast region between the Missouri River and the Rockies would have to be organized into territories and opened to settlement. Once considered too dry for cultivation, this area was now recognized to be rich prairie farm land. Early in 1854, Douglas, as chairman of the Senate Committee on Territories, introduced a bill for this purpose.

Douglas had carefully planned this Kansas-Nebraska Bill to attract both northern and southern support in Congress. Since the region in question was north of 36°30′, it would be closed to slavery if the terms of the Missouri Compromise were applied (page 230). But Douglas's bill provided for two territories — Kansas south of the fortieth parallel and Nebraska north of that parallel. There were two important provisions in the final version of the bill. It stated (1) that the Missouri Compromise was "inoperative and void" and (2) that the people of the territories were "perfectly free to form and regulate their domestic institutions in their own way." In other words, squatter or popular sovereignty (page 290) would determine whether these territories were to be slave or free. Douglas and many others assumed that Nebraska would become free territory and Kansas would become slave territory. The bill, however, did not say *when* the decision on slavery should be made.

The Kansas-Nebraska Bill is passed. At the time Senator Douglas introduced his bill, he predicted that it would raise "a storm." The bill did indeed contain political dynamite. Antislavery congressmen called it a "gross violation of a sacred pledge," and most Northerners shared their alarm at the bill's rejection of the Missouri Compromise. Southern congressmen, determined to kill the 36°30′ line, worked hard to pass the Kansas-Nebraska measure. They argued that the Compromise of 1850 had already altered some features of the 1820 agreement and that squatter sovereignty was the only fair way to determine the question of slavery in the territories.

Fighting with skill and perseverance, Douglas managed to get his controversial bill through both houses of Congress. President Pierce, who favored the measure, signed it in May, 1854. Northern feeling was so strong against the Kansas-Nebraska Act, however, that Douglas said he could travel from Boston to Chicago by the light of the bonfires in which he was being burned in effigy.

The Kansas-Nebraska Act disrupts both parties. The vote in Congress on Douglas's bill revealed the serious split in both the Democratic Party and the Whig Party. The election of 1852 had dealt a fatal blow to

---

What Were Senator Douglas's Motives?

The motives of Stephen Douglas in sponsoring the Kansas-Nebraska Bill have been much debated. Some historians have pointed out that he owned western land which would rise in value if the transcontinental railroad were built from Chicago to St. Louis and then west. Also, opponents charged that he counted on the bill to win him southern Democratic support for the presidential nomination in 1856.

Undoubtedly Douglas did give careful thought to the political advantages and disadvantages of the measure. But many historians believe that Douglas was not acting for purely selfish reasons. He thought that a transcontinental railroad should be built and that the central route was the only one acceptable

to a majority of the members of Congress. Douglas was willing to repeal the Missouri Compromise because he honestly believed that popular sovereignty was the only way to decide the status of slavery in the territories. He did not sympathize with the passionate conviction of Southerners that slavery was morally right, nor did he share the equally passionate conviction of Northerners that slavery was morally wrong. For this reason he has sometimes been called "morally obtuse." But it is more accurate to say that Douglas wanted a railroad built and a new territory organized, and that he hoped in the process to strengthen the Democratic Party and perhaps to promote his own ambitions.

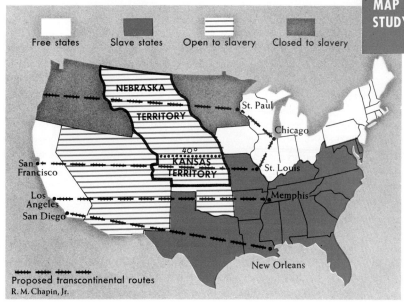

Free states   Slave states   Open to slavery   Closed to slavery

NEBRASKA TERRITORY

St. Paul

Chicago

San Francisco

40°

KANSAS TERRITORY

St. Louis

Los Angeles

San Diego

Memphis

New Orleans

Proposed transcontinental routes
R. M. Chapin, Jr.

KANSAS-NEBRASKA ACT

Using this map and the maps on pages 230 and 293, compare the areas opened and closed to slavery by the Missouri Compromise, the Compromise of 1850, and the Kansas-Nebraska Act.

the Whig Party. Moreover, Clay and Webster died shortly after that election. No other Whig leaders had the ability or stature to bridge the widening gap between the southern and northern wings of the party. As for the Democratic Party, the influence of Southerners in Pierce's administration irritated northern Democrats, many of whom were increasingly influenced by antislavery orators.

The vote on the Kansas-Nebraska Act emphasized these sectional differences. Almost all the southern Whigs and southern Democrats voted for the measure. Northern (or Conscience) Whigs voted solidly against it, and northern Democrats were divided. Some went along with Douglas and President Pierce and supported the bill; others opposed it. The northern antislavery Democrats drew up an *Appeal of the Independent Democrats in Congress.* In it they charged that Douglas's bill was "part and parcel of an atrocious plot to . . . convert it [Kansas and Nebraska] into a dreary region of despotism, inhabited by masters and slaves."

The Kansas-Nebraska Act increases sectional tension. Douglas had intended his bill to be a compromise measure, clearing the way for the construction of a transcontinental railroad. Instead, the new law shattered the truce between the North and South over slavery in the territories. Senator Charles Sumner of Massachusetts cor-

rectly gauged the effects of Douglas's legislation when he called it "at once the worst and best bill on which Congress ever acted." Sumner meant that it was the worst because it was a clear-cut victory for the "slave power." It was the best in that it "puts freedom and slavery face to face, and bids them grapple." Northern and southern congressmen were more clearly at odds after 1854 than ever before. In short, Douglas's fateful measure had renewed the quarrel over slavery in the territories. It also touched off an undeclared war in Kansas which has been called a "preliminary to the Civil War."

Free settlers and slaveholders struggle for Kansas. Nebraska's climate attracted only free-soil farmers. Control of Kansas, however, was bitterly contested between proslavery and antislavery factions. Settlers seeking good farm land came to Kansas from the Missouri and Ohio River Valleys. Their views on slavery were mixed. Only a small minority went into Kansas determined either to win it for slavery or to keep it free. But violent clashes between these small groups forced the rest of the settlers to take sides on the slavery question.

Both northern abolitionists and southern fire-eaters raised money and supplies to speed the settlement of Kansas. People from the free states moved into eastern and central Kansas, establishing the towns of Lawrence and Topeka. Proslavery settlers

The "sack of Lawrence" gave the nation a foretaste of the violence of the war to come. Proslavery Missourians (left) who had crossed into Kansas burned the free settlement of Lawrence. The Free State Hotel, in ruins after the attack (below right), was a special target because it was believed to have been built as a fort. To avenge Lawrence, John Brown (below left) led a murderous attack on proslavery settlers at Pottawatomie.

followed the Missouri River and founded the towns of Atchison, Leavenworth, and Lecompton. Few slave-owners as yet wanted to risk valuable property by moving their slaves into Kansas, but the proslavery men boldly declared in their paper, *The Squatter Sovereign,* that they were ready "to lynch and hang, tar and feather and drown, every white-livered abolitionist who dares to pollute our soil."

Kansas elections are indecisive. Serious trouble broke out in Kansas when the governor called for elections to set up a territorial legislature. From the beginning the free-soil farmers had outnumbered the proslavery settlers. But when the elections were held in 1855, thousands of armed proslavery Missourians moved into Kansas and voted illegally. More than 6000 ballots were cast, though only 1500 settlers were qualified to vote. As a result, the new legislature was overwhelmingly proslavery. Its first action was to pass laws legalizing and protecting slavery.

When the antislavery settlers realized that President Pierce supported the proslavery legislature, they resolved to establish their own government. They met in Topeka and drew up a constitution banning slavery. Then they elected their own legislature, chose a new governor, and petitioned Congress for admission as a free state. Pierce angrily denounced the free-state supporters as rebels and threatened to send troops into Kansas to uphold the proslavery governor and legislature.

Violence breaks out in "Bleeding Kansas." Encouraged by the President's support, the proslavery leaders decided to arrest the free-soil leaders. With the help of a federal marshal and armed Missourians (called "border ruffians" by their opponents), proslavery men marched on Lawrence in May, 1856. The town was pillaged and burned, and several men were killed. Soon afterwards, John Brown, a fanatical abolitionist, decided to avenge the "sack of Lawrence." He led an attack on a proslavery settlement at Pottawatomie Creek and brutally murdered five men. The territory became known as "Bleeding Kansas" during the months of guerrilla warfare that followed the "Pottawatomie Massacre." Two hundred lives were lost, and property damage was estimated at two million dollars. With the help of federal troops, the governor finally restored a semblance of order and broke up the meeting of the free-soil legislature at Topeka.

Sumner is attacked in the Senate. The struggle in Kansas echoed loudly in the halls of Congress. In May, 1856, Senator Sumner of Massachusetts delivered a long, abusive speech on the "Crime Against Kansas." He denounced the South and its attachment to slavery and slandered Senator Butler of South Carolina, who was absent. A few days later Preston Brooks, a member of the House of Representatives and Butler's nephew, entered the almost deserted Senate chamber where Sumner was working. With a heavy cane, Brooks beat Sumner about the head and shoulders until the senator lost consciousness. Sumner, for years an invalid after this attack, was hailed as a martyr in the North. Massachusetts enthusiastically re-elected him to the Senate, while Brooks' district in South Carolina re-elected him to the House. The violence in Congress, coupled with news of the "sack of Lawrence" and the "Pottawatomie Massacre," inflamed public opinion and had a direct bearing on the outcome of the election in 1856.

The Republican Party is established. The political effects of the Kansas-Nebraska Act were at once apparent in the North. While Douglas's bill was still being debated in Congress, northern opponents of the measure met to express their views. These gatherings included Conscience Whigs, antislavery Democrats, Free Soilers, and Know-Nothings. One group meeting in Ripon, Wisconsin, in February, 1854, had resolved that if Douglas's bill passed, they would "organize a new party on the sole basis of the non-extension of slavery."

Several months later a number of citizens met in Jackson, Michigan, and formally laid the foundation for a new party. They drew up a platform calling for (1) repeal of the Kansas-Nebraska Act, (2) repeal of the Fugitive Slave Act, (3) abolition of slavery in the District of Columbia, and (4) prohibition of slavery in the territories. The members of this group agreed to "co-operate and be known as *Republicans*." The new party rapidly gained strength in the free states. In the fall of 1854 many Republican candidates were elected to state offices in the North and West, and several won seats in the House of Representatives.

The Republicans narrowly lose the 1856 election. These victories gave the Republicans high hopes for the presidential race in 1856. At their first national convention, in Philadelphia, they chose John C. Frémont of California as their candidate. Frémont was well-known for his western expeditions and his part in the Mexican War (page 288). As a political newcomer, he had the further advantage of having expressed no opinions on the controversial questions of the 1850's. The delegates to the Republican convention came from many different political backgrounds — Whigs, Democrats, Free Soilers, Know-Nothings, and Prohibitionists — but all were from the North or West. They adopted a platform opposing the Kansas-Nebraska Act and the extension of slavery into the territories and demanding government aid for internal improvements. The Republican slogan in 1856 was "Free Soil, Free Speech, and Frémont."

The Democrats wanted a candidate who would be attractive to both the northern and southern wings of their party and who was not too closely connected with developments in Kansas. Although both Douglas and Pierce sought the nomination, the convention chose James Buchanan of Pennsylvania, minister to Great Britain during the Pierce administration. A third candidate in the 1856 election — former President Millard Fillmore — ran on the American Party (Know-Nothing) ticket.

Buchanan won the election easily with 174 electoral votes, compared to 144 for Frémont and 8 for Fillmore, though the popular vote was more evenly divided. The most significant fact about the 1856 election was the sectional division of the vote. Frémont carried New England and many other northern states, though not Indiana, Illinois, or Pennsylvania. Had Frémont captured Buchanan's state of Pennsylvania and either Indiana or Illinois, the Republicans would have won in 1856. This fact was not overlooked by Southerners. Even before the election they had talked about seceding from the Union if a "Black Republican" became President. After 1856 they redoubled their efforts to make sure no Republican would be elected in 1860.

Political Party Names

Party labels can be confusing. The Republican Party which emerged in the mid-1850's, for example, was not descended from the Republican Party which had developed under Jefferson's leadership over a half a century before. The Jeffersonian Republicans had become the Democratic Party of the Jacksonian Era, and Democrats today still regard Jefferson and Jackson as founders of their party. Present-day Republicans, on the other hand, trace their descent directly from the Republican Party which was born during the turbulent 1850's. Issues supported by the two major political parties have shifted through the years, but the party organizations have retained the traditional names.

▶ CHECK-UP

1. What were the terms of the Kansas-Nebraska Act? Why did Douglas introduce this measure? Why did it arouse resentment in the North? How did it disrupt both major political parties?

2. Why did free settlers and slaveholders become involved in a struggle for Kansas? What was the outcome in Kansas? In Congress?

3. What candidates were nominated by the Democrats and Republicans in 1856? What was the reaction in the South to the sectional division of the vote?

• • • • • • • • • • • • • • • • •

3 *Sectional Differences Are Sharpened*

James Buchanan, like Franklin Pierce, sincerely wanted to end the quarrel over slavery and restore harmony to the Union. But he was a weak and unimaginative President, who failed to understand the forces dividing the North and South. As a result, he too often became the victim rather than the master of events that occurred between 1857 and 1861.

The Dred Scott case stirs the nation. The first shock wave to sweep over the Buchanan administration resulted from the Supreme Court's decision in the Dred Scott case, handed down just two days after the President's inauguration. Dred Scott was a slave whose master had taken him from Missouri to Illinois, a free state, and then to a part of the Louisiana Territory declared free under the Missouri Compromise. Later he was returned to Missouri. Abolitionists persuaded Dred Scott to sue for liberation on the grounds that living in a free state and in free territory had given him the right to freedom. A lower court in Missouri decided in Scott's favor; but when the case was appealed to the state Supreme Court, this decision was set aside.

Dred Scott was then sold to a New Yorker. Scott's antislavery supporters decided to bring a test case before the federal courts. Claiming to be a citizen of Missouri, Scott brought suit for freedom against his owner (a citizen of another state) in a federal court. The court agreed to hear the case, and in so doing practically recognized Scott's claim that he was a citizen. But the jury voted against Scott. The case was then appealed to the Supreme Court of the United States. In due time, the Supreme Court held that the lower federal court had made an error in letting Dred Scott sue, since he was not a citizen of Missouri. According to Chief Justice Roger Taney, Negroes had not been considered citizens by the writers of the Constitution.

The Missouri Compromise is declared unconstitutional. If the Dred Scott decision had stopped there, the case probably would have caused less furor. But Chief Justice Taney went on to deliver an opinion on Dred Scott's claim to freedom. The Chief Justice declared that the Constitution distinctly recognized that slaves were property. He further stated that it pledged the federal government to protect owners in possession of their property in all the territories of the United States. Therefore, Congress had no power to regulate slavery in the territories, and the Missouri Compromise was unconstitutional. Only when a territory became a state of the Union could it decide for or against slavery. In short, the highest court in the land declared that slavery was legal in every part of the country where it was not forbidden by state law.

The Dred Scott decision increases tension. Southerners hailed the Dred Scott decision as their greatest victory in the slavery contest. The Supreme Court had upheld their right to take slaves into the territories. Moreover, it obligated the federal government to protect slavery, and it prohibited Congress from legislating against slavery in the territories. Southern jubilation contrasted sharply with the anger and dismay of Northerners. The Supreme Court decision dealt a serious blow to the new Republican Party, since it had been founded on the idea that Congress could ban slavery

in the territories. Senator William H. Seward of New York promptly denounced the Chief Justice's opinion as unconstitutional. Abraham Lincoln, a rising Republican politician in Illinois, said: "We know the Court that made it [the Dred Scott decision] has often overruled its own decisions, and we shall do what we can to have it overrule this."

The struggle for Kansas continues. News from Kansas further strained relations between the North and South. In June, 1857, a new governor ordered elections to be held for delegates to a convention that would draw up a new constitution for Kansas. Fearing that the election was rigged, the free-soil people refused to vote. Thus, the convention, held at Lecompton, was strongly proslavery and approved a constitution that protected slavery. In an election for members of the legislature, however, the free-soilers won by a narrow margin. This legislature then arranged to submit the Lecompton constitution to the voters. This time the proslavery people refused to vote, and the document was overwhelmingly rejected. A comparison of the two votes suggests that there were about 6000 proslavery and 10,000 free-soil voters in Kansas. Under popular sovereignty, Kansas would doubtless have approved a free-state constitution.

Throughout this struggle President Buchanan sided openly with the proslavery group. He requested Congress to admit Kansas as a slave state with the Lecompton constitution. In an effort at compromise, Congress requested the people of Kansas once again to vote on the Lecompton constitution. Again it was rejected by an overwhelming margin. Kansas thus won the right to become a free state. But it was not admitted to the Union until 1861, after southern representatives and senators had withdrawn from Congress.

Buchanan's clumsy effort to bring Kansas into the Union as a slave state had serious consequences. It caused an open break between the President and Senator Douglas, who had staked his political career on the principle of popular sovereignty. Buchanan's policy also angered northern Democrats and led to an open rupture in his own party. Moreover, it played into the hands of the Republicans, who could now say that squatter sovereignty was unworkable. Buchanan thought he was pleasing the Southerners, but they, too, were annoyed with him because in the end they lost Kansas.

The Panic of 1857 affects the free states. Meanwhile, the quarrel between the North and South extended even to economic affairs. In 1857 a financial crisis hit the country, and a depression followed. Like the Panic of 1837, this panic stemmed in part from land speculation and unsound banking practices (page 249). The shaky financing of railroad construction and the effects of a European economic crisis also contributed to the panic. The industrial Northeast was hardest hit, and during 1858 and 1859 thousands of factory workers lost their jobs. Farm prices in the free states also declined sharply. The South, on the other hand, experienced few ill effects from either the panic or the depression because the European demand for cotton remained steady.

Like most developments during the late 1850's the panic and depression heightened the tension between North and South. Southerners boasted that King Cotton and slavery had proved superior to an industrial system based on free labor. Some again argued that the slave trade should be reopened so that the "benefits" of the slave system could be spread more widely throughout the nation. Northerners, on their part, proposed a higher tariff and legislation to enable unemployed persons to acquire land in the West. But when Republicans in Congress introduced a new protective tariff bill, the Democrats added so many amendments that the final version of the Tariff Act of 1857 actually lowered rates. And while Congress passed a bill to reduce the price of land for settlers, southern Democrats persuaded President Buchanan to veto it. Republicans were furious, and northern Democrats concluded that Buchanan — though a Northerner — was in league with the slavery forces.

The Lincoln-Douglas debates attract attention. People throughout the country closely watched the congressional elections in 1858. Of special interest was the contest for the Senate seat in Illinois. Running for re-election was Senator Stephen Douglas, who had the enthusiastic support of the Democrats. The Republicans named a Springfield lawyer and former Whig congressman, Abraham Lincoln, to run against Douglas. Though not widely known outside the state, Lincoln was highly respected in Illinois as a skillful debater and political speaker. In his address to the Republican nominating convention, Lincoln made clear his position on slavery. "In my opinion," he said, "[the slavery quarrel] will not cease until a crisis shall have been reached and passed. . . . Either the opponents of slavery will arrest the further spread of it . . . or its advocates will push it forward till it shall become alike lawful in all the States, old as well as new, North as well as South." Douglas carefully studied Lincoln's speech and used it to attack the Republican candidate during the campaign.

When Lincoln invited Douglas to participate in a series of public debates, the Senator accepted. At first glance, the "Little Giant" (as Douglas was called) seemed to have the advantage. Handsome, self-confident, and nationally known, Douglas was at the peak of his career. Moreover, he was an eloquent orator and a shrewd judge of what voters were thinking. By contrast, Lincoln appeared awkward and ungainly. His thin, high-pitched voice compared unfavorably with Douglas's deep tones, and Lincoln never used the flowery oratory so popular in that era. Instead, he spoke to the heart of a question with logical reasoning that impressed his listeners. Not only the voters of Illinois but the whole country watched the battle of wits between "Honest Abe" and the "Little Giant."

Lincoln sharpens the slavery issue. The most important of the seven debates turned out to be the second one, held at Freeport, Illinois. Lincoln knew that Douglas's political strength lay in his support of popular sovereignty. Yet Douglas had also accepted the Dred Scott decision, which had declared slavery legal in all territories. Lincoln therefore asked his opponent whether the people of a territory could lawfully "ex-

The case of Dred Scott (*above*) widened the split between North and South over slavery in the territories. The Missouri Supreme Court, meeting in the St. Louis court house shown below, ruled that Scott's stay in free territory did not make him free. The U.S. Supreme Court upheld this decision.

The Dred Scott decision was sharply debated by Abraham Lincoln and Stephen Douglas (*standing behind Lincoln in the picture above*) during their contest for the Illinois Senate seat in 1858. In the following year, John Brown's raid at Harpers Ferry further inflamed the slavery issue. Brown was tried in Virginia (*below*) on charges of treason and conspiracy to incite a slave rebellion. Convicted and hanged, Brown by his violent action had helped to widen the gulf between North and South.

clude slavery . . . prior to the formation of a state constitution."

Douglas attempted to justify the stand he had taken, but it was like walking a tightrope. "The people have the lawful means to introduce it [slavery] or exclude it as they please," declared Douglas, "for the reason that slavery cannot exist a day or an hour anywhere, unless it is supported by local police regulations." By refusing to enact the necessary regulations, the people of a territory, according to Douglas, could in effect exclude slavery despite the decision of the Supreme Court. Lincoln had forced Douglas to choose between the Dred Scott decision and popular sovereignty. In his Freeport Doctrine, Douglas tried desperately to preserve the principle of popular sovereignty.

Douglas's reply satisfied voters in Illinois,

and he was elected to another six-year term in the Senate. But the Lincoln-Douglas debates damaged Douglas's reputation on the national scene. Many northern Democrats saw for the first time the essential conflict between popular sovereignty and the Dred Scott decision, and many of them felt dissatisfied with Douglas's hairsplitting Freeport Doctrine. Almost all of the southern Democrats were angry with Douglas, but for a different reason — he had chosen popular sovereignty over the Dred Scott decision in the Freeport debate.

Lincoln, although a loser in Illinois, emerged from the debates as a leading spokesman for the Republican Party. He had made a number of important points in the debates: (1) slavery was morally wrong; (2) it should not be permitted to spread into the territories, despite the Dred Scott decision; and (3) it should be contained within its existing limits where, Lincoln hoped, "it is in the course of ultimate extinction." This clear-cut position on the perplexing question of slavery made a deep impression on people in the North and West. They began talking about Abraham Lincoln as a possible presidential candidate for 1860.

John Brown's raid increases bitter feeling. The war of words was suddenly interrupted by an outburst of violence in October, 1859. The country was startled to hear that an armed force had seized the United States Arsenal at Harpers Ferry in Virginia. The man responsible for this act was John Brown, leader of the "Pottawatomie Massacre" in Kansas (page 341). Brown fervently believed that he had been chosen by God to destroy slavery. He planned to establish military outposts in the Virginia mountains, swoop down on the nearby plantations, and free the slaves. Ultimately he hoped to extend his operations throughout the South.

After months of planning, Brown decided to open his campaign at Harpers Ferry. With a band of some twenty followers, he seized the arsenal, captured several prisoners, and carried off slaves from a neighboring plantation. The local militia quickly surrounded the small band, and soon afterward Colonel Robert E. Lee arrived with a company of United States marines. Brown was taken prisoner, together with all of his followers who had not escaped or been killed. Brought to trial by state authorities in Virginia, Brown was judged guilty of murder, treason, and conspiracy, and was hanged in December, 1859.

This raid had serious consequences. Responsible northern leaders were shocked. Lincoln said: "Old John Brown has been executed for treason against a state. We cannot object, even though he agreed with us in thinking slavery wrong. That cannot excuse violence, bloodshed, and treason." Other Northerners, however, quickly turned John Brown into an abolitionist martyr. Thoreau described him as "an angel of light," and Emerson called him "the rarest of heroes, a pure idealist." Southern diehards claimed that the raid had been planned and financed by abolitionists. They feared that other attacks would follow and were certain that "Black Republicans" had masterminded the campaign. Senator Douglas, whose presidential ambitions had been heightened by his recent victory in Illinois, played upon the South's fears. He commented that "the Harpers Ferry crime was the natural, logical, inevitable result of the Republican Party."

▶ CHECK-UP

1. On what grounds did Dred Scott sue for freedom? What was the decision of the Supreme Court? What points were made by Chief Justice Taney in his opinion? How was this decision received in the South and North? Why?

2. Trace the steps whereby Kansas gained admission to the Union. What was Buchanan's position, and how did it increase tension? How did the Panic of 1857 affect the sectional conflict?

3. What was the Freeport Doctrine? How did it damage Douglas's standing in the Democratic Party? What were Lincoln's views on slavery?

4. How was John Brown's raid viewed in the South? In the North?

4 *The North and South Break Apart*

The year 1860 was a momentous one in American history. It opened with angry exchanges over the Harpers Ferry raid and John Brown's execution; it closed with the election of a Republican President and the secession of South Carolina.

The Democratic Party breaks in two. As the election of 1860 drew near, relations between northern and southern Democrats became increasingly strained. In April the party convention was held in Charleston, South Carolina. Senator Douglas clearly had more support for the presidential nomination than any other candidate. But southern diehards, bitterly opposed to squatter sovereignty, were determined to prevent his nomination.

Southern delegates who controlled the platform committee proposed that the party condemn popular sovereignty and uphold the Dred Scott decision. But the convention as a whole voted down this platform, for the majority of the delegates favored popular sovereignty. Unwilling to accept this outcome, the Alabama delegation walked out of the hall. Most of the delegates from seven other southern states followed. Since Douglas lacked the two-thirds vote needed for nomination, the convention adjourned without selecting a presidential candidate.

In June, Democratic delegates from the northern and border states gathered in Baltimore and nominated Douglas for President. The southern wing of the Democratic Party, at a separate convention in Baltimore, adopted a platform that affirmed the right of slaveholders to settle in the territories. The southern Democrats nominated John C. Breckinridge of Kentucky.

The Republicans nominate Lincoln. The open break in the Democratic Party was good news for the Republicans. In May thousands of excited delegates, onlookers, and newsmen poured into Chicago. The city had built a new hall for the convention. Called the Wigwam, this building could accommodate 10,000 people, but only the lucky ticket-holders got in. Outside, crowds milled around and cheered the parades that were staged for the ambitious candidates.

Inside the Wigwam the Republican platform committee drew up a carefully worded document. On the issue of slavery, it promised no extension into the territories. But it also promised not to interfere with the institution where it legally existed. Although this position disappointed the abolitionists, it satisfied many Northerners who opposed the spread of slavery but believed that Congress had no right to emancipate slaves in the South. The Republican platform also included important economic planks. It called for (1) a protective tariff, (2) free homesteads in the West, and (3) federal aid for a transcontinental railroad. These planks appealed to manufacturers and farmers in the North and West.

Several prominent Republicans wanted the presidential nomination, including Governor Salmon P. Chase of Ohio,[1] William H. Seward of New York, and Abraham Lincoln. But Chase was not well enough known, and Seward was *too* well-known. A speech in which Seward had predicted an "irrepressible conflict" between the North and the South was now held against him. Lincoln, on the other hand, had several advantages. He came from Douglas's own state of Illinois, had taken a clear-cut though moderate position on slavery in the 1858 debates, and was assured of widespread support in many areas of the North and West. Two immediate advantages, moreover, were the skillful political managers working for his nomination and the enthusiastic Lincoln supporters who packed the galleries of the Wigwam.

On the first ballot Seward led by more than 70 votes but lacked a majority. On the second ballot, many delegates shifted to Lincoln; and on the third he won the nom-

---

[1] Governor Chase had helped in the writing of the "Appeal of the Independent Democrats in Congress" (page 339).

POPULAR VOTE
(In thousands)

STATE	LINCOLN (Republican)	DOUGLAS (Democratic)	BRECKINRIDGE (Southern Democratic)	BELL (Constitutional Union)
DELAWARE	4	1	7	4
KENTUCKY	1	26	53	66
MARYLAND	2	6	42	42
MISSOURI	17	59	31	58
ARKANSAS	- - -	5	29	20
NORTH CAROLINA	- - -	3	49	45
TENNESSEE	- - -	11	64	69
VIRGINIA	2	16	74	74

ELECTION OF 1860 IN BORDER STATES

The popular vote in eight border states shows that the candidate receiving the electoral vote was not always the choice of a majority of the voters. Only 41 per cent of Delaware's popular vote was cast for Breckinridge.

ination. "There was a moment's silence," reported an eyewitness:

The nerves of the thousands, which through the hours of suspense had been subjected to terrible tension, relaxed, and as deep breaths of relief were taken, there was a noise in the Wigwam like the rush of a great wind, in the van of a storm — and in another breath, the storm was there. There were thousands cheering with the energy of insanity.

Another happy Lincoln fan said: "No language can describe it. A thousand steam whistles, ten acres of hotel gongs, a tribe of Comanches . . . might have mingled in the scene unnoticed."

The Constitutional Union Party is formed. A fourth party also offered a candidate in the 1860 election. The Constitutional Union Party, composed of remnants of the Whig and Know-Nothing organizations, took no stand on slavery. Its platform merely denounced "the creation and encouragement of geographical and sectional parties." This new party stood for "no political principle other than the Constitution of the country, the Union of the states, and the enforcement of the laws." At a convention in Baltimore, delegates of this party nominated John Bell of Tennessee for President.

Lincoln wins the election of 1860. During the campaign Lincoln followed the traditional practice of staying at home and letting his political managers do the electioneering. Douglas, however, broke this custom. He set off on a speaking tour to convince voters in the North and the South that popular sovereignty offered the only hope of preventing civil war over slavery. In the South, the campaign became a three-cornered struggle among Douglas, Breckinridge, and Bell. In the North and West, Lincoln had the edge over Douglas and a big lead over Bell.

When the ballots were counted, Lincoln had 40 per cent of the popular votes, Douglas 29, Breckinridge 18, and Bell 13. Lincoln, however, carried all the northern states (except part of New Jersey) as well as California and Oregon. He had 180 electoral votes, a clear majority. Breckinridge carried most of the South to win 72 electoral votes. Douglas carried only Missouri and part of New Jersey, while Bell won three border states.

Lincoln's victory alarms the South. Southerners found little comfort in the fact that Lincoln won less than half the popular vote. Nor did they attach much importance to the failure of the Republicans to win control of either the House or the Senate. The only thing that mattered to Southerners was that a "Black Republican" would soon occupy the White House. Said the Richmond *Examiner:* "With Lincoln comes something worse than slang, rowdyism, brutality . . . ; something worse than all the rag and tag of western grog-shops and Yankee factories. . . . With all those comes the daring and reckless leader of Abolitionists." The whole nation anxiously awaited the reaction of the slave states to Lincoln's election.

The southern states secede. The South Carolina legislature had remained in session

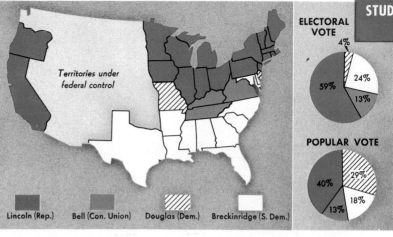

ELECTION OF 1860

The electoral results of 1860 clearly divided the nation along sectional lines. Note that the electoral percentages did not necessarily reflect the popular vote. (See chart on facing page for popular vote in the border states.)

ELECTORAL VOTE

4%
59%
24%
13%

POPULAR VOTE

40%
29%
18%
13%

Lincoln (Rep.)   Bell (Con. Union)   Douglas (Dem.)   Breckinridge (S. Dem.)

Territories under federal control

---

until the results of the election were known. Faced with the reality of a Republican victory, the legislators passed a bill calling for a convention to consider South Carolina's relation to the Union. This convention met in December, 1860. To the accompaniment of booming cannon, pealing bells, and general rejoicing in the streets of Charleston, the delegates unanimously passed an Ordinance of Secession. They declared that the Union "subsisting between South Carolina and other States . . . is hereby dissolved," and they formally repealed South Carolina's ratification of the Constitution. Commissioners were sent to Washington to arrange "for delivery of the forts . . . and other real estate" held by the United States government within the limits of South Carolina.

The other cotton states at once took up the question of secession. In Georgia, Alexander H. Stephens reminded delegates at a convention that the Republicans had as yet committed no acts of aggression. Lincoln, he pointed out, could do nothing unless "backed by power in Congress. . . . Why, then, I say, should we disrupt the ties of this Union, when his hands are tied — when he can do nothing against us?" In Mississippi, Jefferson Davis also cautioned delay; and in Texas, Governor Sam Houston used every means possible to prevent a secession convention. South Carolina's action, however, had brought matters to a head, and support for secession spread. By February 1, 1861, Mississippi, Florida, Alabama, Georgia, Louisiana, and Texas had followed South Carolina's example.

The southern Confederacy is formed. In that same month a convention of delegates from the seceded states met at Montgomery, Alabama, to organize a government for the South. They chose Jefferson Davis to be President. Davis had served as Secretary of War in Pierce's Cabinet and in the Senate. Alexander Stephens of Georgia was named Vice-President, despite his reluctance concerning secession. The two men took their oath of office in front of the courthouse in Montgomery.

The Montgomery convention also drew up a constitution for the Confederate States of America. Similar in many ways to the United States Constitution, this document accepted the doctrine of state sovereignty. Slavery was approved, and the Confederate Congress was denied the power to pass any law interfering with the right of property in slaves. The foreign slave trade was prohibited, however. It was recognized that any other policy on the slave trade would antagonize European governments, whose recognition the Confederacy hoped to win. The Confederate Congress was also denied the power to levy tariffs, although export duties could be established by a two-thirds vote in both houses. A simple method of amending the Constitution was approved. Nothing was said about the right of states to secede from the Confederacy.

By the time Lincoln was inaugurated on March 4, 1861, the Confederacy was raising funds and recruiting an army. It had sent commissioners to Washington to work out a treaty of recognition and to divide the common property of the states.

To be president of the Confederacy, the Montgomery convention chose Jefferson Davis, a Mississippian who had served in the United States Army and in Pierce's Cabinet. Davis's inauguration took place at the courthouse in Montgomery.

Why did the southern states secede? When the cotton states seceded, they acted on the theory that the Union was a compact, or agreement, among sovereign states. This compact, they argued, could be terminated by any of the states. But there were other reasons for their action.

(1) By 1860 the South was convinced that the political balance between slave and free states had been destroyed forever. California, Minnesota, and Oregon had joined the Union as free states in the 1850's, and no new slave states balanced them. Moreover, the population of the North and West was fast outstripping that of the slave states. The South endured this situation so long as it had the upper hand in the Democratic Party and the Democrats controlled the presidency, Congress, and the Supreme Court. This had been the situation during the Pierce and Buchanan administrations. But with the election of Lincoln, the handwriting was on the wall. A Republican had won the presidency, and the South believed it was only a matter of time until antislavery Northerners would also control both houses of Congress and the Supreme Court.

(2) The loss of political power, Southerners felt, would lead to loss of *economic* independence. The Republicans wanted high protective tariffs, internal improvements at federal expense, and free homesteads. Southern leaders feared that such measures would undermine the prosperity of the slave states. They were riding high with King Cotton, and they felt certain that textile manufacturers in the North and in Europe would continue to buy their major crop. Therefore, argued many Southerners, it was sensible to leave the Union before the Republicans brought about the economic ruin of the Cotton Kingdom.

(3) Still another reason why the southern states seceded from the Union — and many historians consider it the main reason — was to preserve slavery. Southerners believed that slave labor was essential to the production of cotton. Moreover, few Southerners

took seriously the Republican promise not to interfere with slavery in the states where it existed. They believed that the Republicans, once in power, would set out to end slavery everywhere in the United States. In the words of one North Carolinian, it was not Lincoln who alarmed the South but rather "the fundamental idea that underlies the whole movement of his nomination and . . . election. It is the declaration of unceasing war against slavery as an institution."

(4) Finally, the South held an unrealistic view of the future. Few Southerners believed that secession would lead to war. Indeed, it was a common saying that a lady's thimble could hold all the blood likely to be shed. Even abolitionists argued that the southern states should be allowed to secede in peace. Southerners expected, therefore, to leave the Union quietly and establish their own government. The way would then be open for possible expansion into Mexico, Central America, and the Caribbean. Some Southerners even looked forward to a time when the Confederacy would increase its manufactures, build a merchant marine, and produce its own food. In time the South might become self-sufficient, they thought.

Buchanan fails to take action. The four months between Lincoln's election and his inauguration proved a trying period for the country. Bewildered by what was happening, President Buchanan was incapable of providing guidance to Congress. In his annual message he said that the southern states had no right to secede but, on the other hand, Congress had no power to make them stay in the Union. Apparently Buchanan wanted only to keep the crisis within bounds until it became Lincoln's responsibility to deal with the situation.

In Springfield, Illinois, the President-elect waited out the awkward period before inauguration. He made no public assurances to Southerners that the Republican Party would protect slavery where it already existed. But he did correspond with men in the South who were loyal to the Union; and he also kept in close touch with developments in the border states, particularly Maryland and Missouri.

In the North and West there was serious disagreement on how to treat the seceding states. Many people could not believe that the South was serious about secession. Some abolitionists, on the other hand, felt that the southern states should be allowed to leave peacefully. Horace Greeley wrote in the New York *Tribune:* "We hope never to live in a republic where one section is pinned to the residue by bayonets." Other Northerners were opposed to a "hands-off" policy toward the Confederacy. They argued that the South had no right to secede and that the government should fight if necessary to preserve the Union.

Last-minute compromises fail. In this gloomy atmosphere, spokesmen for the border states tried to work out compromises. Senator Crittenden of Kentucky proposed several amendments to the Constitution, one of which would have re-established the 36°30′ line in the territories. But the Republicans were unyielding in their determination to keep slavery out of the territories. Their opposition helped kill the Crittenden proposals. Early in 1861 a peace convention, organized by the Virginia legislature, met in Washington. Twenty-one states took part in this convention, but its proposals received little consideration in Congress. It was clear that the time for compromise had passed. The country waited uneasily for Lincoln's inauguration and a statement of his policy.

▶ CHECK-UP

1. Who were the four presidential candidates in 1860? What was the position of each on slavery? Why did Lincoln win?

2. How did the southern states react to Lincoln's election? What efforts were made by leading Southerners to head off secession? How was the Confederacy formed? How did its constitution differ from that of the United States?

3. What was Buchanan's role in the secession crisis? What did Lincoln do prior to his inauguration? What conflicting views about secession were held in the North? What last-minute efforts at compromise were made?

. . . .

Clinching the Main Ideas in Chapter 16

In the brief span of ten years the United States moved from a widely accepted compromise on the issue of slavery to the verge of civil war. Many factors were responsible for this tragic development. The steady worsening of relations between the North and the South resulted in part from the continuing debate over slavery in the territories. The Compromise of 1850 had settled that question in the Mexican Cession, but the issue was raised again when the Kansas-Nebraska Act repealed the line of 36°30′. Northerners increasingly felt that Congress ought to pass laws excluding slavery from all the territories. Southerners argued that the federal government was obligated to protect slavery in all the territories and cited the Dred Scott decision to support their position.

Another factor in the tensions of the 1850's was the disappearance of national political parties. As long as there were Whig and Democratic voters in all areas of the country, political leaders made compromises to hold their parties together. But once the Whigs had disappeared, and the Republicans spoke for the North and West, and Southerners dominated the Democratic Party — then it proved impossible to fashion any more compromises between North and South.

Some historians have blamed the coming of the war on blundering statesmanship in the 1850's. Both Pierce and Buchanan were weak Presidents. It is also true that Douglas's Kansas-Nebraska Act helped to enlarge the area of conflict between North and South. Moreover, extremists on both sides aroused public opinion to the point where a separation between the slave and free states seemed acceptable to many people.

But at the heart of the controversy was slavery. Most white people in the South were determined to preserve the "peculiar institution." They felt that it was economically sound, that it was the only way to preserve the accepted social order, and that it was morally right. Slavery was the key factor in their way of life, and they were willing to sever ties with the Union in order to retain it. By the 1850's most Northerners had come to feel that human bondage was morally wrong. They were unwilling to let it spread to the territories, and many of them wanted to see slavery ended in the slave states. This was the basic cause of the impasse between the North and the South. The free states would make no concessions to southern demands that the federal government protect slavery. The slave states, fearing that a Republican administration would destroy their way of life, chose to leave the Union.

Chapter Review

Terms to Understand

1. Ostend Manifesto
2. "Bleeding Kansas"
3. John Brown's raid
4. Kansas-Nebraska Act
5. Dred Scott decision
6. Republican Party
7. Lecompton constitution
8. Lincoln-Douglas debates
9. Constitutional Union Party
10. Ordinance of Secession
11. Confederate States of America

What Do You Think?

1. Because the Compromise of 1850 averted an open break between the North and South, most Americans at the time welcomed this legislation. Within a few years, however, both Northerners and Southerners were finding fault with this Compromise. Why?

2. Douglas introduced the Kansas-Nebraska Bill as "a compromise measure, clearing the way for the construction of a transcontinental

railroad." Instead, it shattered the truce between the North and South over slavery in the territories. Northerners had accepted the principle of popular sovereignty in the Compromise of 1850. Why did they object to it in this case?

3. In 1858 Lincoln said: "Either opponents of slavery will arrest the further spread of it . . . or its advocates will push it forward till it shall become alike lawful in all the states. . . ." Were both of these alternatives equally possible? Why?

4. Seeking a last-minute compromise, Senator Crittenden of Kentucky proposed an amendment to re-establish the 36° 30′ line in the territories. A Senate committee of thirteen was constituted to consider this and other proposals. Six members of this committee were advocates of compromise. Robert Toombs of Georgia and Jefferson Davis of Mississippi, representing the lower South, were ready to accept the proposal if the majority of the Republican members would do so. But the five Republicans all voted against the plan. What conclusions can you draw?

5. The census of 1860 showed fewer than a hundred slaves in all the territories. Does this suggest that the South had profited from the Dred Scott decision? Does it seem likely that any more slave states would have sought admission to the Union? Why?

Using Your Knowledge of History

1. Prepare a five-column chart with these headings: Missouri Compromise, Wilmot Proviso, Compromise of 1850, Kansas-Nebraska Act, and Dred Scott decision. Provide the following information for each: (a) provisions for regulating slavery; (b) any other provisions; (c) the region affected; and (d) important consequences.

2. Prepare a four-column chart dealing with the election of 1860. For each party give this information: (a) candidate; (b) stand on slavery; (c) states carried; (d) electoral votes; and (e) percentage of popular vote.

3. Debate: *Resolved,* That the southern states were justified in seceding from the Union in 1860.

4. Write a brief essay explaining Douglas's Freeport Doctrine and why he held this view.

Extending Your Knowledge of History

A Decade of Sectional Controversy, by H. H. Simms, provides an interesting summary of the turbulent 1850's. On the role of the extremists see Arnold Whitridge's *No Compromise!* For the significance of events in Kansas, see two *American Heritage* articles: "The Needless Conflict" by Allan Nevins (August, 1956) and "Douglas, Deadlock, and Dissension" by Murat Halstead (June, 1960). Carl Sandburg's two-volume *Abraham Lincoln: The Prairie Years* is excellent. A condensed version is also available. Richard Hofstadter's interpretive essay on Lincoln in *The American Political Tradition* and the chapter on John Brown in *America in Crisis; Fourteen Crucial Episodes in American History,* edited by Daniel Aaron, are thought-provoking. Interesting biographical studies are *John Brown* by O. G. Villard, G. F. Milton's *The Eve of Conflict* about Stephen Douglas, and *The Liberator: William Lloyd Garrison* by John L. Thomas.

CHAPTER 17

North and South Fight a Bitter Civil War

We are not enemies, but friends. We must not be enemies. Though passion may have strained, it must not break, our bonds of affection. The mystic chords of memory, stretching from every battle-field and patriot grave to every living heart and hearthstone all over this broad land, will yet swell the chorus of the Union when again touched, as surely they will be, by the better angels of our nature.
ABRAHAM LINCOLN, FIRST INAUGURAL ADDRESS, 1861

Civil War cavalrymen

1861–1865

The responsibility for dealing with the deadlock between the North and the South became Abraham Lincoln's in March, 1861. His inaugural address included a moving plea to the Southerners to pause before the country was plunged into war. The new President urged caution and calm reflection "upon this whole subject." But in the South, as Alexander Stephens was to remark some years later, "the political atmosphere was charged to the bursting point, the storm had come." The bombardment of Fort Sumter in April marked the beginning of four terrible years of war.

The Civil War settled some of the ques-

tions about which the North and South had quarreled for years. It put an end to slavery and also to the idea that the states were sovereign and could secede from the Union at will. In this sense, the war marked the end of an era.

In other respects, the war marked the beginning of a new era. In its use of new weapons and tactics, as well as its concept of unconditional surrender, it was, in one historian's words, "the first of the world's really modern wars." Also, industry and mechanized farming expanded rapidly in the North and West during the war years. These developments contributed to important economic and social changes which are still going on. But the most important change which took place during the war and the following years concerned the relationship between Negroes and white people in the South. Lincoln's Emancipation Proclamation was the starting point for American Negroes in their slow advance from slavery to citizenship.

1 *The North and South Take Up Arms*

Lincoln is inaugurated. Abraham Lincoln's presidency began in an atmosphere charged with tension and emotion. Special precautions were taken to guard the President-elect during the train trip from Illinois to Washington and during the inaugural ceremonies. Thousands of people jammed the capital on March 4, 1861.

Lincoln's words were generous but firm. He promised not "to interfere with the institution of slavery in the States where it exists." He promised, moreover, to enforce the Fugitive Slave Act. It was a federal law, and he would enforce all such laws in all the states. For the same reason, he would collect the duties and taxes due the federal government, and he would "hold, occupy, and possess the property and places belonging to the Government." But in fulfilling these constitutional obligations, the new President added, "there needs to be no bloodshed or violence; and there shall

. . . .

CHAPTER FOCUS

1. The North and South take up arms.

2. The early years of the war bring no decision.

3. All-out war poses serious problems for both sides.

4. Victory for the North preserves the Union.

be none, unless it be forced upon the national authority."

In your hands, my dissatisfied fellow-countrymen, and not in mine, is the momentous issue of civil war. The government will not assail you. You can have no conflict without being yourselves the aggressors. You have no oath registered in heaven to destroy the government, while I shall have the most solemn one to "preserve, protect, and defend" it.

Lincoln appoints his Cabinet and other officials. While the country weighed the meaning of his eloquent words, Lincoln appointed his Cabinet, giving representation to as many factions as possible. Both of his rivals for the Republican nomination received Cabinet posts — William Seward became Secretary of State, and Salmon Chase, Secretary of the Treasury. In the early days of the administration Seward expected to exert great influence on the President, but Lincoln soon made clear that he would lead the government himself. Within a short time Seward was ready to admit that "the President is the best of us. . . . Executive ability and vigor are rare qualities, but he has them both." Lincoln's first Secretary of War, a Pennsylvania politician, was soon replaced by the capable Edwin Stanton, a northern Democrat who favored the preservation of the Union. To help hold the border states in the Union, Lincoln chose his Attorney General from Missouri and his Postmaster General from Maryland. A New Englander, Gideon Welles, became Secretary of the Navy. Fortunately for historians, Welles left a lively account of Cabinet meetings in his diary.

Lincoln was also careful about other government appointments. To represent the United States abroad, he recruited such distinguished men as Charles Francis Adams, son of John Quincy Adams, and the German-American Carl Schurz (page 306). Lesser government jobs went to Republicans whose claims to office were usually screened by the President himself. Lincoln intended to use his power of appointment to strengthen the young Republican Party.

Federal authority is tested at Fort Sumter. From the do-nothing Buchanan administration, Lincoln inherited a critical situation at Fort Sumter in Charleston Harbor. Except for Sumter and three others, all forts south of Virginia had already fallen into Confederate hands. Early in 1861 an unarmed government ship had tried to land men and supplies at Fort Sumter, but when South Carolina troops opened fire, the ship turned back. The day after the inauguration, Lincoln received an urgent request from Major Anderson, the commander at Fort Sumter, for reinforcements and supplies.

Fort Sumter thus became a test case of federal authority. If Lincoln let the fort fall to the Confederates, he would be accepting the fact of secession and indirectly recognizing the Confederate government. On the other hand, if he sent an armed ship to fight its way into Charleston Harbor, he would be accused of attacking the South. The President finally decided to send a relief ship carrying only food. On April 6 Lincoln dispatched a messenger to the governor of South Carolina, telling him of this

The people of Charleston climbed to the housetops to watch the bombardment of Fort Sumter in the harbor.

decision. The Confederate Secretary of State warned that firing upon Fort Sumter would "inaugurate a civil war greater than any the world has yet seen." Nevertheless, the Confederate cabinet instructed the commander at Charleston, General Beauregard, to demand Major Anderson's surrender.

The Confederates attack Fort Sumter. When Beauregard asked for the surrender of Fort Sumter, Anderson replied that he would not leave but that he would soon be starved out. General Beauregard regarded Anderson's answer as unsatisfactory, and early on the morning of April 12, Confederate guns opened fire on the fort. After 34 hours of bombardment, Major Anderson surrendered. He and his men were allowed to board the relief ship, which had helplessly watched the battle from the harbor.

The North rallies to Lincoln's support. The news from Fort Sumter put an end to talk in the North about the peaceful secession of the South. Men from all walks of life and from all parties rallied to the support of the Lincoln administration. Douglas spoke for the northern Democrats when he declared: "There are only two sides to the question. Every man must be for the United States or against it." On April 15 Lincoln issued a proclamation calling for 75,000 volunteers for three months of service. This request met with an enthusiastic response. Lincoln also proclaimed a blockade of the coast from South Carolina to Texas. The blockade was later extended to ports in North Carolina and Virginia.

The border states choose sides. When Lincoln called for volunteers, a crisis developed in the eight slave states which had not seceded. These states had to decide whether to join the Confederacy or remain loyal to the Union. Less than a week after the surrender of Fort Sumter, Virginia seceded, thus bringing the Confederacy to the very doors of Washington, D.C. This was a damaging blow to the administration, which had tried hard to hold Virginia in the Union. It also deprived the North of the services of Robert E. Lee, who might otherwise have commanded the Union forces. In Lee's mind, loyalty to his state outweighed his obligation to the Union.

(Continued on page 358)

Abraham Lincoln

[1809–1865]

Abraham Lincoln, the prairie statesman, is probably the best-loved figure in American history. His unique appeal springs from his frontier success story, from his role in the tragic Civil War, and from his great human qualities.

Born in a log cabin in the Kentucky wilderness, Lincoln soon moved with his family to southern Indiana and eventually to Illinois. Though his schooling was scanty, he showed a great interest in reading, even as a young boy. Lincoln's early ambition was to be a "steamboat man" on the Ohio River. But at the age of 21 he settled in the village of New Salem, Illinois, where he tended store, worked as a farm hand, served as village postmaster and deputy surveyor, and took part in the Black Hawk War. During the 1830's he served four terms as a Whig in the Illinois legislature. Soon after he was admitted to the state bar, and moved to Springfield where he established a successful law practice.

In Springfield, Lincoln met Mary Todd, a high-spirited Kentucky belle who was courted by many young men, including Stephen Douglas. Mary became Mrs. Lincoln in 1842. At times she found it hard to adjust to her husband's spells of melancholy and forgetfulness. Yet theirs was a successful marriage, and they took great joy in their sons — Robert, Edward, Willie, and Thomas. The childhood deaths of Edward and Willie were heavy blows.

During the Mexican War, Lincoln was a Whig congressman from Illinois. He challenged President Polk's explanation of the origin of the conflict. Because most of his Springfield constituents disagreed with him, Lincoln did not seek re-election in 1848. Although he did not join the public debate over the Compromise of 1850 or the Fugitive Slave Law, the Kansas-Nebraska Act roused him to action. Lincoln strongly opposed repeal of the Missouri Compromise and tried to reorganize the northern Whigs into a sectional party opposed to the extension of slavery in the territories. By 1856 he recognized the hopelessness of this effort and put his hopes for containing slavery in the new Republican Party.

Lincoln soon became the leading strategist of the Republican Party. He insisted that the new party should oppose the extension of slavery but not the existence of slavery in the South. Lincoln criticized "the monstrous injustice of slavery itself" but admitted that "if all earthly power were given me, I should not know what to do as to the existing institution." It was his opposition to the extension of slavery that won for Lincoln widespread support in the free states.

Lincoln grew and matured in the presidency as few other men have. Though constantly criticized, he never lost sight of the objectives of the war. Lincoln displayed no hatred toward the South, and never grew insensitive to the problems of other people. And he never exhausted his store of humorous anecdotes to illustrate human weaknesses, his own included.

The poet Edwin Markham wrote of this great American:

He held his place —
Held the long purpose like a growing tree —
Held on through blame and faltering not at praise.
And when he fell in whirlwind, he went down
As when a kingly cedar green with boughs
Goes down with a great shout upon the hills,
And leaves a lonesome place against the sky.

Arkansas, Tennessee, and North Carolina also seceded, despite the fact that in these states, as in Virginia, there was strong Union sentiment. Union feeling in north-western Virginia was so intense, in fact, that these counties split off from the mother state. They drew up a constitution, asked for admission as a separate state, and in 1863 came into the Union as West Virginia. The loyalty of this section of Virginia was of great strategic importance to the North, for through it passed the Baltimore and Ohio Railroad, Washington's major link with the West.

The other four border states — Dela-ware, Maryland, Kentucky, and Missouri — wavered. If the chief purpose of the war was to destroy slavery, they preferred to join the Confederacy. But if the war was to preserve the Union, then their sym-pathies lay with the North. Opposing loyal-ties often divided families in the border states, and in many tragic cases brother fought against brother. Lincoln was aware of the importance of Maryland, which vir-tually surrounded Washington and guarded Chesapeake Bay. He realized also that to control the Ohio and upper Mississippi Valleys, the Union needed Kentucky and Missouri. Thus, in Maryland, Kentucky, and Missouri, where sentiment was about evenly divided, Lincoln used federal troops to insure "neutrality." This policy provoked cries of dictatorship, but Lincoln felt that strong measures were necessary to keep these crucial states in the Union.

The North has greater resources but fewer able generals. As the states chose sides in the spring of 1861, the Union had distinct advantages in man power and re-sources. On the northern side were 23 states, with a population of more than 22 million. Army enrollments in the North exceeded those in the South by at least three to two; even so, the North had enough additional man power to fill factory jobs and farm the land. Furthermore, the north-ern states had nearly all of the iron, steel, textile, and munitions industries, as well as most of the banking capital of the country. Two thirds of the railroad mileage was in the North and West, and most of the mer-

chant marine and the navy remained under Union control.

As the war dragged on, these advantages in men and resources turned the tide for the Union. But in the early stages of the strug-gle, a lack of capable military leaders severely handicapped the North. Ever since the Mexican War, southern officers had dominated the army. Most northern gradu-ates of West Point stayed in the service for only a few years and then left to take up careers in business, railroading, engineering, or the professions. As a result, the Union was saddled with "dull and rusty" officers.

The South has military advantages but lacks essential resources. In contrast to the North, the South had a ready supply of ex-perienced officers. The Confederate Presi-dent, Jefferson Davis, was a West Point graduate, a veteran of the Mexican War, and a former Secretary of War. He could rely on Robert E. Lee, "Stonewall" Jackson, Joseph Johnston, and Albert Sidney Johnston — all intelligent, energetic, and ex-perienced military commanders. Moreover, the Confederate soldiers knew how to handle horses and firearms and adjusted more easily to outdoor living than did the rank and file of Union soldiers. The South also had a psychological advantage in fight-ing on its own soil. Southern soldiers were battling to defend their homes, while the North would have to invade the slave states in order to preserve the Union. Moreover, slavery was less of a disadvantage to the Confederacy than many people had pre-dicted. In the early years of the war, many of the Negroes continued to work in the fields, leaving the white men free to fight. (As the war went on, however, tens of thousands of Negroes left the plantations to follow the invading northern armies.)

These southern advantages weighed heavily in the early stages of the war. Later, however, they were more than offset by the South's inferior man power, natural re-sources, industry, and transportation. The eleven states of the Confederacy had a population of only nine million — of whom more than three million were slaves. Although the South possessed mineral re-sources, in general these had not been developed. Southern textile mills, iron and steel mills, and ammunition plants proved woefully inadequate to supply military needs. Also, the South found it increasingly difficult to keep railroad locomotives, cars, and tracks in repair. The Confederacy, therefore, was badly handicapped by shortages of food, clothing, weapons, and ammunition, and by breakdowns in transportation. The success of the northern blockade of southern ports aggravated these problems.

▶ CHECK-UP

1. What statements about slavery and secession were included in Lincoln's inaugural address? What considerations were reflected in his selection of a Cabinet? In his plan for bringing relief to Fort Sumter?

2. What was the effect in the North of the attack on Sumter? Why were the border states important? What factors influenced their decisions concerning secession?

3. What were the advantages of the North in the Civil War? Of the South? By the end of the war, which of these factors proved to be of crucial importance?

2 *The Early Years of the War Bring No Decision*

The strategy of the war unfolds. Neither the North nor the South expected the war to last long. Jefferson Davis hoped to establish the "natural frontier" of the Confederacy along the Mason and Dixon Line and the Ohio River, then up the Mississippi to the Missouri River, and northwestward to the Dakotas (map, this page). His plan was to win and hold the area south of this line and to establish trade relations with Britain and France.

The northern strategy was devised by the aged General Winfield Scott. He planned to cut off the Confederate states from overseas aid and thus compel them to surrender. To do this, the Union had to hold the border states, blockade Confederate Atlantic and Gulf ports, and win control of the Mississippi River from St. Louis to New Orleans. This done, Scott believed, the South would then have no alternative but to rejoin the Union.

THE NATION SPLITS

By 1861, the nation stood divided. Northern border states, still reluctant to abandon the Union, elected to fight with the North. Note that West Virginia, not admitted to the Union until 1863, was already separated from Virginia. In what resources did the North have a clear advantage?

MAP STUDY

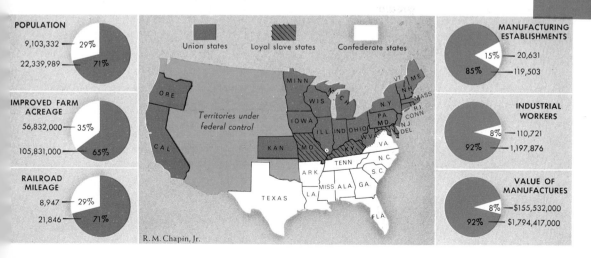

POPULATION
9,103,332 — 29%
22,339,989 — 71%

IMPROVED FARM ACREAGE
56,832,000 — 35%
105,831,000 — 65%

RAILROAD MILEAGE
8,947 — 29%
21,846 — 71%

Union states   Loyal slave states   Confederate states

Territories under federal control

MANUFACTURING ESTABLISHMENTS
15% — 20,631
85% — 119,503

INDUSTRIAL WORKERS
8% — 110,721
92% — 1,197,876

VALUE OF MANUFACTURES
8% — $155,532,000
92% — $1,794,417,000

R. M. Chapin, Jr.

THE CIVIL WAR, 1861–1862

On this and subsequent maps you will see how effectively the Union strategy of division and blockade worked. While individual battles were important, it was the relentless expansion of Union control (color) that made the southern defeat inevitable. Follow the Union's campaigns against Richmond during 1861–1862. While Union efforts to take Richmond failed, in the west and along the coast the North won significant victories.

Antietam
Sept. '62
MD.
Baltimore

Aug. '62
Bull Run
Washington

July '61
Manassas Junction
DEL.

Shenandoah Valley

Chesapeake Bay

Potomac R.

Fredericksburg
Dec. '62

Seven Days
June '62

James R.

York R.

Richmond

McClellan
McDowell, Pope, Burnside
Lee
Jackson

0   25   50 mi.

1861-62

UNION

Area of
control — Area
won

Movement — Battle
won

CONFEDERACY

Area of   control

Movement — Battle
won

MICH.

Chicago

New York

PA.

N.J.

Pittsburgh

Philadelphia

IND.

OHIO

ILL.

Cincinnati

W.VA.

Washington

Richmond

Ohio R.

Louisville

KY.

Cumberland Gap

Norfolk
Occ. May '62

MO.

Cairo

Ft. Donelson
Feb. '62

Ft. Henry
Feb. '62

Nashville

Aug. '61–
Mar. '62

N.C.

Memphis
Occ. June '62

TENN.

Tennessee R.

Chattanooga

Savannah R.

S.C.

Wilmington

Columbia

ARK.

Pittsburg Landing
(Shiloh) Apr. '62

Corinth

Mississippi R.

Atlanta

GA.

Charleston

Ft. Sumter
Surrendered
Apr. '61

MISS.

ALA.

Montgomery

Port Royal
Occ. Nov. '61

Vicksburg

Tombigbee R.

Alabama R.

Savannah

BLOCKADE

TEXAS

LA.

Port Hudson

Mobile

Pensacola
Occ. May '62

Jacksonville
Occ. Mar. '62
St. Augustine

Galveston

New Orleans
Occ. April '62

FLA.

UNION

0   50   100   200 mi.

R. M. Chapin, Jr.

Though Scott did not remain long in command of northern military operations, his successors adopted his overall strategy. The blockade proved effective, and the four northern border states remained in the Union. In both eastern and western areas of conflict, the Northern troops took the initiative from the beginning. In the East, the Union campaign centered on efforts to capture Richmond, Virginia, capital of the Confederacy.[1] In the West, Union fleets and armies sought to open the Mississippi River to northern commerce and drive a wedge between Confederate states east and west of that river.

Union forces lose at Manassas Junction. Because they believed that the war would be short, many Northerners urged Lincoln to move against the Confederate army and be done with it. In the columns of the New York *Tribune*, Horace Greeley kept agitating: "Forward to Richmond!" Moreover, many Union soldiers had signed up for only three months, and their term of enlistment would soon end. Despite their lack of training, General Irvin McDowell was ordered to lead them into battle. His target was Manassas Junction, a railway center about 35 miles south of Washington, D.C. (map, page 360). There, on July 21, near a stream called Bull Run, McDowell attacked a Confederate army commanded by General Beauregard.

At first, the Union troops made important gains. They were stopped, however, by General Thomas Jackson's "stonewall" defense and by the timely arrival of Confederate reinforcements under General Joseph Johnston. McDowell ordered his men to fall back, but the retreat soon turned into a disorderly flight. McDowell himself described the Union forces as "a confused mob, entirely demoralized." Over the dusty road to Washington streamed exhausted soldiers as well as congressmen, reporters, and even fashionably dressed ladies in carriages, who had come to witness the first northern victory.

Luckily for the North, the Confederate forces were too weary and disorganized to follow up their victory. Nevertheless, the

[1] The Confederate Congress voted to make Richmond the capital in May, 1861.

defeat at Bull Run shocked the overconfident North, and ended all talk of a 90-day war. Congress authorized the raising of an army of 500,000 three-year volunteers.

McClellan takes Union command in the East. Soon after the defeat at Bull Run, the President dismissed McDowell and appointed General George McClellan commander of the Army of the Potomac. McClellan was a graduate of West Point and had served in the Mexican War. A dapper, jovial man, he got along well with congressmen, was popular with soldiers, and showed great skill in organizing and training the army. In November, 1861, when the ailing General Scott retired, Lincoln made McClellan commander of all the Union armies. The new commander continued to drill his troops but seemed reluctant to engage the enemy. Although Congress and the newspapers again took up the chant "on to Richmond," the only report from McClellan's headquarters that winter was "all quiet on the Potomac." In the West, however, there was more action.

The war in the West begins. The Union's first move in the western campaign was to pierce the Confederate line of defense. This line ran from the Kentucky shore of the Mississippi River eastward into the central part of southern Kentucky (map, page 360). General Henry Halleck commanded the Union forces in the West, but credit for breaking through the Confederate line belongs to an officer who served under him, Ulysses S. Grant.

Grant's career before the war had been varied. A graduate of West Point and a veteran of the Mexican War, he had resigned from the army only to suffer reverses as a farmer and as a businessman. When the Civil War broke out, he was a clerk in his family's leather store in Illinois. Grant offered his services to the Union, and his reputation grew as he successfully carried out the tasks assigned him. Eventually he became commander of all the Union forces (page 375).

Grant opens the attack in Tennessee. Grant opened an offensive early in 1862. He moved first against Forts Henry and Donelson, which guarded the Tennessee and Cumberland Rivers and therefore were the keys to the interior of Tennessee. Grant was supported by Flag Officer Andrew Foote, who commanded a fleet of gunboats.

In early February, Fort Henry surrendered to Foote; ten days later, Fort Donelson also was captured. The Confederate forces in Fort Donelson had tried to break through the Union lines, only to be thrown back. When the commander asked for Grant's terms of surrender, the Union general made his famous reply: "No terms except unconditional and immediate surrender can be accepted." About 14,000 prisoners and 40 cannon were taken by

"Unconditional Surrender" Grant, as he came to be known.

Grant completes the conquest of western Tennessee. During the weeks that followed, Grant moved his forces southward along the Tennessee River. Meanwhile, Confederate forces were gathering at Corinth, Mississippi, a railroad junction near the Tennessee border. The Confederates, commanded by General Albert S. Johnston, made a surprise attack on the Union troops encamped near Pittsburg Landing, Tennessee. Johnston pushed back Grant's army on April 6, but the gallant Confederate commander was mortally wounded in this en-

THE AMERICAN SCENE

THE CIVIL WAR

as seen by MATHEW BRADY AND ALFRED WAUD

Brady's photographs (page 315) and Waud's sketches recorded scenes of the Civil War for people of their own time and for history. Below left is Brady's photograph of Waud, whose on-the-spot sketches (below, a Union charge) were reproduced as engravings in magazines. Opposite page: Brady took his cumbersome equipment to the camps of both Confederates (top left) and Union soldiers (bottom). He also photographed leading figures of the war — at top right, General Grant.

counter (Battle of Shiloh). The next day Union reinforcements gave Grant a decided edge in the heavy fighting. By the end of May the outnumbered Confederates had to abandon Corinth, and the Union conquest of western Tennessee was completed. The Confederate loss of Corinth meant that the railroad connection between Richmond and Memphis was cut, and another link lost in the railroad from the Ohio to the Gulf.

Union forces struggle for the Mississippi. While Grant had been moving south along the Tennessee River, a parallel advance was being made along the Mississippi River. Union troops and gunboats advanced to Memphis, Tennessee. After Memphis fell (June, 1862), the Union held the river as far south as Vicksburg, Mississippi.

Meanwhile, a naval expedition under Captain David G. Farragut paved the way for the capture of New Orleans. Two Confederate forts guarded the lower river, but the Union fleet, under Farragut, ran past their blazing guns and headed up the river to New Orleans. Lacking adequate defenses, the city became a scene of wild disorder. Bales of burning cotton along the waterfront and in ships cast adrift turned night into day. Crowds of panic-stricken people jammed the streets. The Confeder-

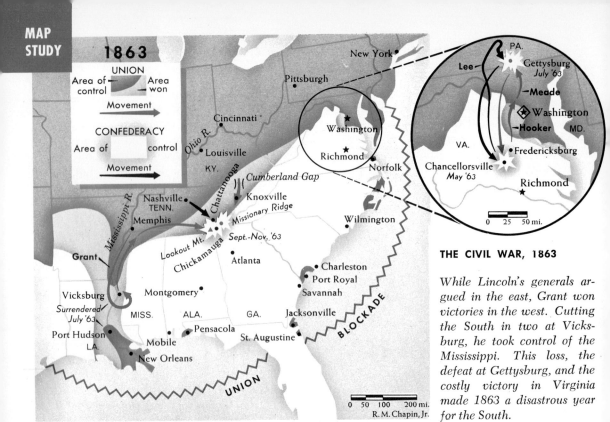

THE CIVIL WAR, 1863

While Lincoln's generals argued in the east, Grant won victories in the west. Cutting the South in two at Vicksburg, he took control of the Mississippi. This loss, the defeat at Gettysburg, and the costly victory in Virginia made 1863 a disastrous year for the South.

R. M. Chapin, Jr.

ate forces retreated, leaving New Orleans to be occupied by Union troops (May 1).

Thus, by the summer of 1862, the Mississippi was lost to the Confederacy except for the short stretch between Vicksburg and Port Hudson. But the Union objective had been to prevent the Confederate states west of the Mississippi from aiding the southern armies east of it. The Union could not achieve this goal until its troops had occupied all river ports, especially Vicksburg. Through this city the Confederacy obtained from the region west of the Mississippi food and also munitions shipped from Europe by way of Mexico and Texas.

The capture of Vicksburg reopens the Mississippi. General Grant was determined to take Vicksburg. Located on a high bluff, this city was a natural fortress. It could easily withstand an attack from the river, and the approach from the land side was almost as difficult. Grant launched his campaign late in 1862, but his army bogged down in the swamps north of Vicksburg. In Washington, the General's critics urged the President to dismiss Grant. But the President, mindful of McClellan's dallying tactics in the East, replied, "I can't spare this man: he fights."

In the spring of 1863 Grant made a daring move. Transporting his army to the west bank of the Mississippi River, he advanced thirty miles to the south. There with the help of gunboats which had steamed past the Confederate batteries at Vicksburg, Grant recrossed to the east bank. Living off the country, Grant defeated a Confederate army before it could reinforce Vicksburg. When in turn southern troops stationed in Vicksburg advanced against Grant, he drove them back. The Union army then settled down for a six-week siege, during which Union guns bombarded the city. Though desperately short of food, Vicksburg held out until July 4, 1863. Within a week, Port Hudson also surrendered, and on July 16 a cargo from St. Louis landed at New Orleans. Lincoln rejoiced that "the Father of Waters again goes unvexed to the sea." The Confederacy had lost control of one of its main arteries of transportation, and the Confederate states west of the Mississippi were for all practical purposes out of the war.

Union forces move slowly in the East. While Union forces in the West were achieving their goal, those in the East had little success. In February, 1862, after months of delay and inaction, Lincoln ordered McClellan to advance on Richmond. Instead of moving directly against the Confederate capital, McClellan transported his forces by sea to the peninsula between the York and James Rivers (map, page 360). With maddening caution, he approached the Confederate capital, always overestimating the size of the Confederate forces opposing him. By mid-May McClellan was only about five miles from Richmond, and the southern capital seemed doomed. But the Union general failed to strike.

Richmond is successfully defended. In late June, while McClellan waited for reinforcements, the situation changed dramatically. "Stonewall" Jackson's lightning thrusts in the Shenandoah Valley had compelled President Lincoln to hold back large forces to defend Washington. Now Jackson joined the Confederate forces under Robert E. Lee which were defending Richmond. The Confederates took the offensive, hammering away at McClellan in a series of engagements known as the Seven Days' Battles. McClellan drew back twenty miles to the James River, where his forces had the protection of the Union fleet. He then proposed to move south across the James and cut the railroads bringing supplies to Richmond. But this plan was rejected by Halleck, who had been appointed general-in-chief. Halleck ordered the Army of the Potomac to withdraw from the peninsula in order to reinforce the Union army based at Manassas.

The Peninsular Campaign was disappointing for the Union, even though Lee had lost more men than McClellan. Although McClellan had erred on the side of caution, major blame for the failure to capture Richmond must rest with Halleck for abandoning the campaign.

Pope is defeated at Bull Run. Most of McClellan's forces were now added to the command of General John Pope, a brash officer whom Halleck had brought with him from the West. Lee drew the overconfident Pope into the second Battle of Bull Run (August, 1862). The Union defeat was nearly as complete as McDowell's had been at Bull Run the year before. Thus, by the fall of 1862, Washington again faced the threat of invasion, and Lincoln again had to turn to McClellan. Restored to command, "Little Mac" wrote to his wife, "Again I have been called upon to save the country."

Lee's invasion is checked at Antietam. In September, 1862, Lee began an invasion of Maryland. His purpose was to cut Union railroad connections between East and West and then advance into Pennsylvania. Lee believed that Confederate sympathizers in Maryland would join his forces and that a southern victory in Union territory might influence foreign countries to support the Confederacy. McClellan followed Lee's army as it marched north, but even when he learned that Lee had split his forces, McClellan failed to attack. The two armies finally clashed at Antietam (an-tee'tum) Creek on September 17 in the bloodiest single day's fighting of the war. Neither side won the battle, but two days later the Confederates crossed back into Virginia.

McClellan made no effort to cut off the retreating enemy. Lincoln, bitterly disappointed, again dismissed McClellan, remarking, "I said I would remove him if he let Lee's army get away from him, and I must do so. He has got the 'slows.'"

Union forces suffer new defeats. The Battle of Antietam checked Lee's invasion of the North, but inferior military leadership continued to plague the Union. Lincoln had replaced McClellan with Ambrose Burnside, a handsome young general with impressive sidewhiskers. In December, 1862, Burnside attacked Lee at Fredericksburg, Virginia, but was badly defeated. The Union lost more than 10,000 men killed or wounded compared to Confederate losses of 5000. Within a few weeks, General Joseph Hooker replaced Burnside as commander of the Union army. Although Hooker restored morale, "Fighting Joe" proved no match for Lee and Jackson. The bloody battle at Chancellorsville, Virginia, in May, 1863, was perhaps Lee's greatest victory. But Confederate joy quickly turned to sorrow when it was learned that "Stonewall" Jackson had been mortally wounded by his own men when they mistook him for one of the enemy. Jackson's death was a terrible loss for the South.

Gettysburg marks the turning point. The long series of defeats had caused

The Civil War proved the advantages of armored warships. This fleet of Union ironclads, shielding its coal barges, successfully steamed past the bombardment from Confederate batteries at Vicksburg and aided in Grant's capture of that city.

morale to sag in the North. Knowing this, Lee again decided to invade Union territory. In June, 1863, crossing the Potomac with some 70,000 men, Lee advanced northward through Maryland into Pennsylvania (map, page 364). Panic swept the cities of Washington, Baltimore, and Philadelphia. The Union army, led by Hooker, moved along a parallel route but east of the Blue Ridge Mountains. On the eve of the most decisive battle of the war, Hooker, annoyed by Halleck's interference, resigned his command. President Lincoln replaced him with General George Meade. On July 1 the two armies clashed at Gettysburg.

The fighting raged for three days. On the third day, Lee made a desperate bid for victory. General George Pickett led 15,000 Confederate troops in a direct attack on the strong Union center. Crossing the open field, Pickett's men suffered terrible losses from the Union artillery. After hand-to-hand fighting at the top of Cemetery Ridge, what remained of the attacking force withdrew. Three fourths of Pickett's courageous men had been killed or wounded.

The next day Lee began the long retreat to the Potomac. Meade, who had lost nearly a third of his army, did not follow up his victory. "We had them within our grasp," mourned Lincoln; "we had only to stretch forth our hands and they were ours." "Still," he added later, "I am very grateful to Meade for the great service he did at Gettysburg."

The northern blockade of the South is effective. Meanwhile, during the first two years of the war, the Union navy co-operated with the army in the West and began its blockade of southern ports. Having only 24 steam-powered vessels in 1861, the Union government purchased propeller-driven steamers, side-wheelers, clipper ships, tugboats, and even ferryboats. By May, 1862, the Confederacy had lost all of its nearly 200 ports except Wilmington (North Carolina), Charleston (South Carolina), Savannah (Georgia), Mobile (Alabama), and Galveston (Texas). From these ports a few swift blockade runners carried southern produce to Bermuda and the West Indies, where it was exchanged for essential goods. Supplies for a time were brought in from Mexico. This source dried up, however, after the Union established control over the Mississippi and its ports.

The first ironclads appear. The need to break the blockade caused the Confederacy to experiment with ironclad ships. When the South seized the Norfolk, Virginia, navy yard in 1861, it captured a damaged 40-gun steam frigate called the *Merrimac*. The Confederates repaired this vessel, covered it with iron plate, and added a cast-iron ram to its prow. Rechristened the *Virginia*, this ironclad steamed out of Norfolk Harbor in March, 1862. Within a few hours it sank two Union warships.

The next day an even stranger vessel appeared off Norfolk to engage the *Merrimac*.

This was the *Monitor,* a Union ironclad. The deck of this "Yankee cheese-box on a raft" was nearly level with the water, and it was equipped with a revolving turret that carried two heavy guns. Since neither the *Monitor* nor the *Merrimac* seriously damaged the other, this first duel between ironclad men-of-war was a draw. It did, however, foreshadow the end of wooden warships. Although the *Merrimac* and some other ironclad rams menaced Union ships, the South lacked the resources to build and equip many such vessels. But the North steadily increased its naval might.

▶ CHECK-UP

1. What was the South's plan for winning the war? What was the North's plan? What success did the North have in advancing on Richmond in 1861?

2. How did Union land and naval forces co-operate in taking western Tennessee and opening up the Mississippi? How did Grant capture Vicksburg?

3. What was the outcome of the Peninsular Campaign? Why did Lee advance into Mary-land in the fall of 1862? Into Pennsylvania in 1863? What did Lincoln hope to achieve as these invasions were halted?

4. How was the North able to establish a block-ade of the South? How effective was it? What was the significance of the duel be-tween the "Monitor" and the "Merrimac"?

. . . .

3 *All-out War Poses Serious Problems for Both Sides*

While Union and Confederate forces faced each other in battle, the governments in Washington and Richmond struggled with pressing problems — recruiting sol-diers, financing the war, supplying the armed forces, and seeking the support of European powers. President Lincoln faced an additional dilemma in dealing with slavery in the border states and in territory captured from the Confederacy.

Both sides use a military draft. A critical problem for both governments was the recruitment of soldiers. In the early months, when enthusiasm ran high and most people thought the war would soon be over, volunteers enlisted faster than they could be armed and equipped. "After a time I had cut down my uniform so that I could see out of it and had conquered the drill sufficiently to see through it," wrote one Union private; "then the word came: on to Washington!" But by the end of 1861, enlistments fell off. Both governments then offered *bounties* (cash payments) to at-tract recruits. State and local governments added their own payments so that a volun-teer in the North might get as much as 1000 dollars in cash. The payment of bounties led to *bounty-jumping.* Some vol-unteers would desert after receiving a bounty in one town, enlist again in another place, and collect a second bounty.

Both sides also found it necessary to draft men for the armed forces. Before the end of 1862, the Confederacy issued a draft which made every able-bodied white male between the ages of 18 and 45 liable for service. The North, early in 1863, began to draft able-bodied male citizens from 20 to 45 years old. In both sections, however, high government officials, preachers, and teachers were exempt. Moreover, a drafted man could hire a substitute to take his place. In the North he could also get ex-emption from service by paying 300 dollars to the government.

Neither the Union nor the Confederacy developed a satisfactory system of com-pulsory service. Because northern draftees could buy their way out of service, some critics charged that the struggle was "a rich man's war and a poor man's fight." In several northern states, officials encoun-tered violent resistance to the draft law. In New York City four days of rioting fol-lowed the start of the draft in July, 1863. Nearly a thousand people were killed or wounded and much property was destroyed before troops could restore order.

War welfare work is developed. During the war great advances were made in caring for the soldiers. Noteworthy work was done by the United States Sanitary Commission, which foreshadowed the American Red Cross. This commission organized hospital units, sent men and women to nurse the wounded, and supplied the soldiers with clothing and comforts. Clara Barton was especially active in this work. In 1864 she became superintendent of nurses for the Union army, and after the war she directed the government's search for missing soldiers. The South had no organization like the Sanitary Commission, but state and county relief associations carried on the same type of work. Mrs. Jefferson Davis wrote that the women of the South "fed the hungry, cared for the orphans, deprived themselves of every wonted [customary] luxury to give it to the soldiers, and were amid their deprivations so cheerful as to animate even the men with hope."

Taxes and tariffs are levied in the North. To fight the war, both governments needed huge sums of money. The northern treasury was virtually empty when the war began. A few days before Lincoln's inauguration, Congress had enacted the Morrill Tariff, which raised rates well above the 1857 level. Secretary of the Treasury Chase recommended further increases. By 1864 tariff rates averaged 47 per cent, the highest in American history up to that time. This provided revenue for the government and also pleased northern manufacturers.

As the costs of the war mounted, Secretary Chase also proposed the adoption of internal taxes to add to government revenue. Eventually taxes were levied on all industries and many occupations as well as on the sale of liquor, tobacco, meat, carriages, yachts, and on hundreds of other items. Railroads, steamboats, and ferryboats had to pay taxes on their receipts. Moreover, the government for the first time imposed personal income taxes. Enforcement was lax, however, and the income tax was dropped after the Civil War.

The federal government sells war bonds. Since the money received from increased taxation fell far short of paying for the war, the federal government began to borrow money through the sale of bonds. To encourage the purchase of government bonds, a national banking system was established in 1863. By meeting certain financial requirements, a group of five or more persons could obtain a national bank charter. Such a bank had to invest at least one third of its capital in United States bonds. Upon deposit of these bonds with the Treasurer of the United States, the bank received national bank currency equal to 90 per cent of the market value of the bonds. This National Banking Act replaced the Independent Treasury System which had been in effect since 1846 (page 285). The new banks accomplished two things: (1) they created a market for government bonds and thus helped finance the northern war effort; and (2) they helped to provide a reliable national currency, which in time took the place of state bank notes.

Paper money is issued. The Union government adopted still another means of raising money. It issued paper money backed only by the government's promise to redeem it at some future date. These United States notes, called *greenbacks*, could be used to pay all debts, public or private, except customs duties and interest on the public debt. Because the value of the greenbacks depended on the government's ability to pay, they rose and fell with the fortunes of war. The greenbacks hit bottom in the gloomy summer of 1864, when they were worth only 39 cents on the dollar. Even when the war ended, a greenback was worth only about 67 cents.

As the purchasing power of the greenback declined, gold and silver became more valuable. When people began to hoard gold and silver and to pay bills in greenbacks, prices rose. Soon even small silver coins disappeared from circulation. The government met the need for fractional currency by issuing paper money for amounts as small as three cents. People called this paper currency *shinplasters*.

Industry booms in the North. The tremendous demand for military supplies caused northern industry to boom in the early 1860's. Manufacturers supplied clothing, shoes, arms, ammunition, cannon

Civilians as well as soldiers found their lives affected by the Civil War. Northern women, for example, took jobs filling cartridges (above).

Civilians in the South faced greater hardships than in the North. Lack of industry meant that damaged railroad tracks and cars (top) could not be repaired. Resulting shortages of goods led to soaring inflation, so that Confederate money (above) became valueless. But the soldiers of both sides suffered most. The Brady photo at left shows a Union hospital.

wagons, and many other goods for the army. At the same time industry continued to meet the needs of the northern civilian population. New factories were built; old ones expanded and installed more efficient machinery. Similarly, increased use of machinery enabled northern farmers to feed the Union forces as well as the civilian population. A tremendous expansion also took place in mining, the production of petroleum, and lumbering. The transportation facilities of the free states, especially railroads, handled a vast increase in freight.

This industrial growth brought large profits to many individuals in the North.

Government contracts, tariff protection, and "cheap" money stimulated the boom. Some businessmen took advantage of the government by selling inferior goods at high prices. So many uniforms of a poor-quality cloth called "shoddy" were sold to the government that the term came to be applied to any inferior goods.

Despite the industrial prosperity of the war years, many workers found themselves worse off than before the war, for prices rose faster than wages. Some workers organized unions and went on strike for higher pay. Others took advantage of the Homestead Act (1862), which permitted

THE GETTYSBURG ADDRESS

On November 19, 1863, President Lincoln spoke at the dedication of the Gettysburg battlefield as a national cemetery. In the midst of the troubles and bitterness of war, Lincoln expressed in a few unforgettable words the highest ideals of our democracy. Americans now treasure the Gettysburg Address as part of their national heritage.

FOURSCORE and seven years ago our fathers brought forth on this continent a new nation, conceived in liberty, and dedicated to the proposition that all men are created equal.

Now we are engaged in a great civil war, testing whether that nation, or any nation so conceived and so dedicated, can long endure. We are met on a great battlefield of that war. We have come to dedicate a portion of that field as a final resting place for those who here gave their lives that that nation might live. It is altogether fitting and proper that we should do this.

But, in a larger sense, we cannot dedicate — we cannot consecrate — we cannot hallow — this ground. The brave men, living and dead, who struggled here, have consecrated it far above our poor power to add or detract. The world will little note nor long remember what we say here, but it can never forget what they did here. It is for us, the living, rather, to be dedicated here to the unfinished work which they who fought here have thus far so nobly advanced. It is rather for us to be here dedicated to the great task remaining before us — that from these honored dead we take increased devotion to that cause for which they gave the last full measure of devotion; that we here highly resolve that these dead shall not have died in vain; that this nation, under God, shall have a new birth of freedom; and that government of the people, by the people, for the people, shall not perish from the earth.

---

them to claim 160 acres of free land in the West. Nevertheless, northern prosperity enabled almost every community to build new homes, churches, schools, hotels, and business establishments during the war years. Moreover, many city governments built parks, paved streets and sidewalks, and constructed water, gas, and sewage systems.

The South has trouble financing the war. Conditions in the South were very different. For one thing, the Confederacy had greater difficulty financing the war. In 1861 it seized federal property in the seceded states and renounced all southern debts to northern creditors. Such debts were to be paid to the Confederacy instead. But this income by no means covered the enormous expense of the war. Moreover, the Confederate government found it much more difficult than the Union to collect money through taxation. Although taxes were levied on personal property and on many commodities, few people had the cash to pay them. Both the Confederate government and the state governments issued bonds, but again few Southerners were able to buy them. The Confederacy also sought foreign loans. European governments hesitated to provide financial aid, however, when it seemed uncertain that the Confederacy would win the war.

The South, therefore, had to finance the war chiefly by issuing paper money backed only by the Confederate government's promise to redeem it. The Confederacy issued more than a billion dollars in paper money, and state and local governments also printed large amounts. This currency dropped in value as the fortunes of the Confederacy declined. As a result, prices skyrocketed until flour sold for 1000 dollars a barrel and a pair of shoes cost 200 dollars. Toward the end of the war, Confederate dollars were worthless.

The South suffers hard times. Thus, while the North and West experienced an economic boom during the war years, the South endured a steadily worsening economic crisis. Efforts were made to manufacture war materials and clothing, but the South's newly established factories lacked sufficient capital, machinery, and skilled workers. Abundant harvests provided the Confederacy with adequate food supplies during the first year of the war. In 1862, however, drought plagued many areas of the South, and during the rest of the war both soldiers and civilians were short of food.

A major cause of the South's economic troubles was the collapse of its transportation system. The northern blockade and the loss of the Mississippi River virtually paralyzed water transportation. Some key railroads fell into Union hands, while invading or retreating troops deliberately wrecked others. The South could neither buy nor manufacture replacements for engines, cars, or even tracks. Hence railroads were sometimes abandoned because it was impossible to maintain or repair them. The breakdown of southern rail transport hindered troop movements and the distribution of food. The South also suffered from profiteering, although there were fewer opportunities to make a dishonest dollar in the Confederacy than in the North.

Both North and South seek European support. From the outbreak of the war, both North and South realized the importance of gaining and holding the good will of European countries. The South hoped that its cotton and its free-trade policy would win diplomatic recognition — as well as loans and military supplies — for the Confederacy. The North hoped that its antislavery policy would appeal to Europeans and counted on its blockade of southern ports to cut off European trade with the Confederacy.

France and Britain at first favor the South. Early in the war the Confederacy attracted support both in Great Britain and France. Many members of the British upper classes thought that the North attached too great importance to equality and political democracy. Furthermore, British textile manufacturers would have welcomed an independent South able to supply raw cotton and to absorb manufactured goods. British shippers would have profited if the war were to undermine their chief competitors, the shippers of the New England and Middle Atlantic states. In addition, Englishmen who opposed slavery found it difficult to understand Lincoln's early statements that the war was being fought primarily to preserve the Union. Nevertheless, British reformers and humanitarians strongly supported the northern cause from the outset of the war. So also did labor leaders and workingmen, who favored the free labor system of the North over slavery.

The French upper classes, like the British aristocrats, tended to side with the Confederacy. French textile manufacturers, too, needed southern cotton. Moreover, the French ruler, Napoleon III, believed that a southern victory would weaken the Monroe Doctrine and provide an opportunity to extend French influence in the Americas. He would have recognized the Confederacy had he been able to persuade the British government to take this step.

Trouble brews between Britain and the North. Toward the end of 1861 a crisis developed which severely tested the diplomatic skill of Lincoln and Seward. Two Confederate commissioners to England and France — James Mason and John Slidell — were taken from the British steamer *Trent* by Captain Charles Wilkes, commander of a Union warship. Although this action clearly violated a principle for which the United States had fought in the War of 1812, Northerners hailed Wilkes as a hero. In Britain the reaction was quite different. Indignation reached such a pitch that the British began military and naval preparations and even sent 8000 troops to Canada. Fortunately for the Union cause, Lincoln realized the importance of disclaiming responsibility for Wilkes' action. He ordered the release of Mason and Slidell and thus averted the threat of war with Britain.

Nevertheless, friction between the North and Great Britain continued. For one thing, the Union blockade of the South was hurting the British. The blockade interfered with Britain's importation of southern cotton and the sale of British manufactures. Consequently, English merchants suffered losses, textile mills closed, and unemployment increased. The North, meanwhile, was angered because British shipyards were building commerce raiders for the Confederacy. These raiders, of which the *Alabama* was most famous, inflicted heavy losses on northern merchantmen. Matters came to a head in 1863 when the North learned that two powerful ironclad ships were being built in England for the Confederacy. Charles Francis Adams, the American minister to Britain, protested so sharply that the British government bought the ironclads to prevent their sale to the Confederacy.

The South loses European support. After 1863 the North's relations with Britain improved. The British textile industry increased its imports of cotton from other countries, thus lessening its need to trade with the Confederacy. Lincoln's Emancipation Proclamation, which became effective January 1, 1863 (page 373), convinced most Europeans that the North was fighting to abolish slavery as well as to restore the Union. Finally, Union victories made recognition of the Confederacy a bad risk. Except for Napoleon III's attempt to set up a puppet ruler in Mexico in defiance of the Monroe Doctrine (page 413), relations between the North and Europe became friendlier. The unwillingness of France and Great Britain to recognize the Confederacy sealed the fate of the slave states. Without aid from abroad, beset by economic troubles, and drained of its man power, the South was in a hopeless position.

Lincoln considers abolishing slavery. During the early years of the war, Lincoln and Congress repeatedly stated that the North's goal was not to conquer the South or interfere with its established institutions. Rather, the North was fighting to preserve the Union. Yet from the beginning of the conflict there were strong pressures on the Lincoln administration to abolish slavery. It was clear that the slaves contributed to the southern war effort. They tilled the fields, drove munition wagons, cooked in army camps, dug trenches, and built fortifications. It was also clear that the European governments would be less likely to aid the Confederacy if the Union announced its determination to end slavery. Pressure also came from the abolitionists, who kept pushing Lincoln to take action.

President Lincoln understood the problems which might arise if he took a firm stand in favor of emancipation. He could ill afford to antagonize the border states; nor could he afford to lose the support of those people in the North who were willing to fight to preserve the Union but not to free the Negro. Lincoln defined his position in these words:

> My paramount object in this struggle is to save the Union, and is not either to save or destroy slavery. . . . What I do about slavery and the colored race, I do because I believe it helps to save this Union; and what I forbear, I forbear because I do not believe it would help to save the Union.

In April, 1862, the Lincoln administration took its first steps toward emancipation. Congress voted to end slavery in the District of Columbia and pay the owners of the emancipated slaves. Two months later, an act of Congress abolished slavery forever in the territories of the United States. The President, meanwhile, had worked out a program of gradual emancipation with compensation for slave-owners in those border states which were willing to give up slavery. Much to his disappointment, Congress rejected the plan.

The Emancipation Proclamation is issued. Lincoln finally became convinced that he must use his authority as commander-in-chief to end slavery. It was, he said, "a military necessity, absolutely essential for the salvation of the nation, that we . . . free the slaves or be ourselves subdued." In July, 1862, he read to his Cabi-

Secretary of War Stanton said of the Negro troops who fought for the Union: "They have proved themselves among the bravest of the brave."

Courtesy of Chicago Historical Society

net a draft of a presidential proclamation. The members approved it, but Seward persuaded the President not to issue the statement until the North won a victory. The Battle of Antietam gave Lincoln his opportunity. On September 22, he announced that, at the beginning of the next year, he would declare "forever free" the slaves in any states or parts of states which were then in arms against the Union.

The presidential statement inspired both cheers and jeers. Probably most ·people in the North and in Europe approved. But some called it a publicity trick, and others criticized its failure to deal with slavery in the border states. In the congressional elections in November, 1862, the Democrats won more than thirty seats. Although this worried the Republican President, he was determined to carry out his plan. In a message to Congress, Lincoln said: "Without slavery the rebellion could never have existed; without slavery it could not continue."

On January 1, 1863, the Emancipation Proclamation went into effect. It defined the areas in rebellion against the government and declared that all slaves in those areas were legally free. It also welcomed into the Union forces all former slaves who wished to enlist. By the end of the war more than 186,000 Negroes had served in the Union army, many of them with officers' rank.

Steps are taken to abolish slavery. The Emancipation Proclamation provided no final solution to the problem of slavery. For one thing, it did not apply to the border states. And in the South, where the document was greeted with scorn, enforcement depended on whether the North defeated the Confederacy. Lincoln's proclamation paved the way, however, for more sweeping changes. Before the war ended, the border states of Missouri, Tennessee, and Maryland passed laws abolishing slavery. The Republicans, meanwhile, had proposed a Thirteenth Amendment to the Constitution which would abolish slavery everywhere in the United States and its territories. Congress approved the measure, and by December, 1865, enough states had ratified the amendment to make it a part of the Constitution (page 152).

▶ CHECK-UP

1. How did each side recruit soldiers? Why was the draft criticized?

2. How did the North finance the war? Explain the National Banking Act. Why did the purchasing power of the greenbacks decline? Why did industry and agriculture boom in the North during the war? How did the South try to finance the war? Why did the South suffer hard times?

3. Why did Britain and France tend to favor the South at first? What were causes of friction between Britain and the North? Why did the South lose European support after 1863?

4. What did Lincoln stress as the primary goal of the war? What antislavery steps were taken by Lincoln and Congress during 1862? What later steps were taken by the states and by Congress to abolish slavery?

· · · · · · · · · · · · · · · · · · ·

4 Victory for the North Preserves the Union

We return now to the closing military events of this tragic conflict. By the summer of 1863 (pages 359–366), Union forces had occupied western Tennessee and won control of the Mississippi River. In the East, they had failed to capture Richmond, the Confederate capital. But at Gettysburg the Union had checked Lee's invasion of the North in the most important battle of the war. On July 4, 1863, the North celebrated both the fall of Vicksburg and Lee's retreat from Gettysburg. Final victory, however, was still a long way off.

Fighting centers around Chattanooga. Following the surrender of Vicksburg, Grant began a drive into southeastern Tennessee to capture the important railroad junction of Chattanooga (map, page 364). In September, 1863, a Union army under General Rosecrans occupied Chattanooga without resistance. Thinking that the Confederate withdrawal was part of a general retreat into Georgia, Rosecrans set out in pursuit. But the Confederate leader, General Bragg, attacked the Union army at Chickamauga Creek. Rosecrans was saved from total defeat only by the stubborn stand of the Union left wing commanded by General George Thomas. Thomas came to be called the "Rock of Chickamauga."

As the Union armies fell back to Chattanooga, Bragg fortified two ridges, Lookout Mountain and Missionary Ridge, and cut most supply lines to Chattanooga. To avert a Union disaster, reinforcements were sent from the East, and General Grant assumed supreme command in the West. The army that had taken Vicksburg also soon appeared on the scene. Late in November, 1863, in a three-day battle Grant won a bril-

THE CIVIL WAR, 1864–1865

MAP STUDY

The final phases of the war were highlighted by Sherman's march to the sea and Lee's desperate efforts to prevent Grant from capturing Richmond. With the South again divided and Lee surrounded, a Union victory was assured.

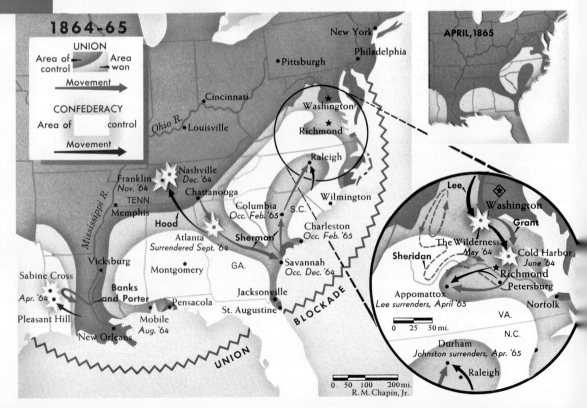

liant victory. The Confederates were driven from Lookout Mountain and Missionary Ridge.

Grant plans Union strategy. Even his former critics now recognized Grant's ability as a military commander, and in March, 1864, Lincoln named him commander of all the Union armies. General Grant went to Washington, met the President for the first time, and began planning Union strategy for crushing the Confederacy. Unlike his predecessors, Grant was patient, courteous, and considerate, not only to the President but also to subordinate officers. Most important, he could map out strategy and stick to his plan whatever the odds. Grant once described the "art of war" in these words: "Find out where your enemy is. Get him as soon as you can. Strike at him as hard as you can and keep moving on."

Under the plan Grant worked out, the Union armies in the West were to move southeastward into the very heart of the Confederacy. In the East, Union forces were to move against the Confederate capital. Meanwhile, the blockade would be tightened and an attempt would be made to capture Mobile, Alabama, one of the few ports still in Confederate hands.

Sherman takes Atlanta. Grant himself assumed direct command of the Union forces in the East, while William Tecumseh Sherman was put in charge of the western armies. With Chattanooga occupied by Union forces and the Confederates in retreat, the way was open for an invasion of Georgia. Sherman began the advance on Atlanta in May, 1864 (map, page 374). He was opposed by a smaller Confederate army under the able General Joseph Johnston, who had replaced Bragg.

By a series of flanking movements, Sherman forced Johnston to withdraw to the outskirts of Atlanta. At this critical moment, President Davis replaced Johnston with General John Hood. Hood directed two major attacks against the Union armies but was forced back into Atlanta. On September 2, the Confederates evacuated the city, and Sherman informed President Lincoln: "Atlanta is ours." The Union general seized or destroyed all Confederate supplies in the city.

Lincoln is re-elected. The news from Georgia helped Lincoln in the presidential campaign of 1864. Up to that time his re-election had by no means been certain. The regular Republicans and the War Democrats (northern Democrats who supported the Lincoln administration) held a joint convention in June, 1864. Calling themselves the Union Party, they nominated Lincoln for the presidency and Andrew Johnson, a War Democrat from Tennessee, for the vice-presidency. But many Republicans found fault with Lincoln's direction of the war and his cautious policy with respect to slavery. These "Radical" Republicans held a separate convention and nominated John C. Frémont. The regular Democrats named General McClellan as their standard-bearer. Though McClellan accepted the nomination, he rejected the Democratic platform, which called the war a failure and urged an immediate end to hostilities. The most extreme Democrats, those who openly sympathized with the Confederacy, became known as Copperheads.

If Frémont had succeeded in winning many Republican votes from Lincoln, McClellan might well have become President. Union victories, however, turned the tide for Lincoln. News that Farragut had captured Mobile and that Sherman had taken Atlanta forced Frémont out of the race and blunted the appeal of the Democrats. Lincoln won re-election by 212 votes to McClellan's 21. The voters gave the Union Republicans a majority in Congress and control of most of the state governments.

Sherman marches to the sea. In mid-November, after burning Atlanta, General Sherman and 60,000 Union troops began a march to the Atlantic coast. Their goal was Savannah, 300 miles to the southeast. Sweeping through an area some 60 miles wide, Sherman and his men took what they wanted in food and loot, then destroyed everything else. Harvested crops were carried off; livestock was slaughtered or led away. Railways were torn up, factories wrecked, warehouses and public buildings burned. Sherman's march destroyed communications between the Upper and Lower South and shattered Confederate morale. Savannah was besieged in December, and on Christmas, Lincoln received this message from Sherman: "I beg to present to you as a Christmas gift the city of Savannah, with one hundred and fifty heavy guns and plenty of ammunition, also about twenty-five thousand bales of cotton."

Sherman pushes northward. As the year 1865 opened, Sherman turned northward into the Carolinas to help Grant crush the Confederacy. Both Columbia, the capital of South Carolina, and Charleston fell into Union hands and suffered large-scale destruction. General Joseph Johnston and a poorly supplied Confederate army had been given the hopeless task of checking Sherman's advance. In April, 1865, Johnston finally surrendered to Sherman near Durham, North Carolina.

Grant launches the Wilderness campaign. At about the time that Sherman began his march through Georgia, Grant was leading the Army of the Potomac in an all-out drive to capture Richmond. The Union forces marched against the Confederate capital through a tangled, marshy woodland known as the Wilderness (map, page 374). Lee fought them every inch of the way, though his troops were hungry and short of supplies. But Grant was determined to "fight it out along this line," for he knew that the North had the resources and the man power to wear the Confederacy down. During the first months of the Wilderness campaign, Grant lost about 55,000 men. Such heavy losses were criticized in the North, but Lincoln never wavered in his support of "Unconditional Surrender" Grant.

Moving his army to the south bank of the James River, Grant advanced against Richmond by way of Petersburg. The Union lines were extended westward to cut Confederate railway connections with the West. Compelled to safeguard his only supply route, Lee had to abandon both Petersburg and the capital. Jefferson Davis and his government fled, and Lee's army tried to retreat to the southwest toward the mountains and a possible meeting with Johnston's forces. The Confederate situation was desperate; Lee's supplies were gone, and desertions and sickness further weakened the Confederate army. When Union cavalry and infantry blocked the escape route, Lee asked for surrender terms. "It is our duty to live," he said, "for what will become of the women and children of the South, if we are not here to support and protect them?"

Lee surrenders at Appomattox. On April 9, 1865, Lee and Grant met at a farmhouse in Appomattox Court House, a village about one hundred miles from Richmond. The short, stoop-shouldered Grant was still dressed in his mud-stained fatigue uniform; the handsome, white-haired Lee wore a new uniform, with a shining sword and bright red sash. In the parlor of the farmhouse they worked out the terms of surrender. Lincoln had already informed Grant that he was to give the Southerners "the most liberal and honorable terms." Accordingly, no Confederate officers or enlisted men were taken prisoner. Officers were allowed to keep their side arms, and all the Southerners who owned horses were permitted to keep them. In addition, Grant promised Lee food for his hungry army.

The war ends. And so, in the spring of 1865, the long, costly war to preserve the Union and free the slaves came to an end. More than 600,000 men had died, and as many more had either been crippled or lost their health. Large areas of the South had been devastated. Some four million Negroes now were free people, responsible — but inadequately prepared — for making their own way in the world.

President Lincoln understood the enormous problems now facing the country. During the winter of 1864–1865 he had worked out a humane policy for healing the wounds of war. In his Second Inaugural Address, Lincoln asked the nation to act "with malice toward none, with charity for all." To his Cabinet he expressed the hope that "there would be no persecution, no bloody work, after the war was over. . . . Enough lives have been sacrificed. We must extinguish our resentments if we expect harmony and union."

Lincoln is assassinated. It was unfortunate for the South as well as the North that Lincoln never had a chance to trans-

(Continued on page 378)

Robert E. Lee

[1807–1870]

The beloved Confederate commander was the son of "Light-Horse Harry" Lee, a cavalry officer in the Revolution. Young Robert Lee grew up in Alexandria, Virginia, and decided to follow in his father's footsteps. He entered West Point in 1825 and was graduated four years later near the head of his class and without a single demerit. During the next decade the young officer held a number of staff positions in and around Washington, D.C. His wife, a descendant of Martha Washington, made a gracious home for him and their seven children at "Arlington" on the banks of the Potomac River near the capital city. During the Mexican War, Lee fought bravely at the Battle of Buena Vista and served with distinction under General Winfield Scott in the advance from Veracruz to Mexico City. In the 1850's Lee was superintendent at West Point and the commander of a regiment in Texas. But his wife's failing health and financial problems led him to think about resigning from the army.

During the secession crisis, Lee argued that secession was revolution and would never happen in his day. Deeply shocked by South Carolina's decision to leave the Union, Lee sincerely hoped that his own state of Virginia would not take this action. But during the anxious months of waiting, he came to realize that, despite his love for the Union, it would be impossible for him to bear arms against the South. When Virginia joined the Confederacy in April, 1861, Lee resigned from the United States Army.

Robert E. Lee was the great hope of the Confederacy. Jefferson Davis fully trusted him, and his officers and soldiers revered him. Handsome, erect of carriage, courteous, and dignified, Lee embodied all the graces of a southern gentleman. Alexander H. Stephens described him as "the most manly and entire gentleman I ever saw." In the months after Appomatox, Lee was noted as being "rigid with self-respecting grief" over the defeat of the South. Even Union soldiers greatly respected the Confederate commander.

Instead of returning to "Arlington" at the end of the war, Lee chose a new career. He accepted the presidency of Washington College in Lexington, Virginia. There he gathered an enthusiastic faculty and student body, and proved that southern colleges once again could achieve academic excellence. Lee's conduct was exemplary in the difficult postwar years. He reaffirmed his loyalty to the United States government and refused to bear a grudge against Northerners. Repeatedly he counseled the people of the South to rebuild their economy as quickly as possible and to live in the future, not in the past. Lee died at Lexington, Virginia, and was buried there. The college was renamed Washington and Lee University in his honor.

late these principles into action. Soon after the surrender at Appomattox, he invited Grant to Washington. The general attended a Cabinet meeting with the President on the morning of April 14, and that evening Lincoln and his wife went to a play at Ford's Theater. During the performance a half-crazed actor named John Wilkes Booth crept into the presidential box. Thinking that he was avenging the South, Booth shot Lincoln in the back of the head, then jumped onto the stage, and escaped from the theater.[2] The unconscious President was carried to a house across the street, where shocked friends and associates soon gathered. Shortly after seven o'clock the next morning, the President breathed his last. Someone in the crowded room, probably Secretary Stanton, said, "Now he belongs to the ages."

▶ CHECK-UP

1. How did Sherman cut the Confederacy in two?

2. What candidates opposed Lincoln in 1864? What developments led to Lincoln's re-election?

3. How did Grant drive Lee out of Richmond and compel him to surrender?

4. Why was Lincoln's assassination a tragedy for both the North and the South?

. . . .

Clinching the Main Ideas in Chapter 17

Both the North and the South went to war believing that a brief conflict would determine whether states had the right to secede from the Union. Southern fire-eaters cheered when the first shot was fired against Fort Sumter. Northerners in a holiday mood went out to view the first

---

[2] The assassination of Lincoln was part of a plot to kill a number of Union leaders. That same night Seward was stabbed, and his son was injured trying to defend him. Grant, however, escaped attack. When cornered by federal agents late in April, Booth either shot himself or was shot. His accomplices were convicted on scanty evidence and hanged.

battle in northern Virginia. By the fall of 1861, however, both sides knew they were in for a long and bloody struggle.

As public opinion in the free states grew more hostile to slavery, Lincoln issued the Emancipation Proclamation and Congress approved the Thirteenth Amendment. In the end, therefore, the war was fought not only to preserve the Union but also to abolish slavery.

The North's main problem was finding a general competent to direct the Union war effort. Lincoln appointed and dismissed several commanders before he found Ulysses S. Grant and William T. Sherman. Northern man power, resources, and transportation had much to do with the outcome of the war. The farms and factories of the free states supplied the needs of the Union armies and the civilian population, and still produced surplus goods to sell abroad. In Abraham Lincoln the North had a leader of remarkable courage, forbearance, and understanding. Working patiently with temperamental generals and stubborn politicians, Lincoln achieved victory, saved the Union, and ended slavery.

The South was able to wage a long war because of the fighting qualities of the Confederate soldiers and the ability of such generals as Robert E. Lee, "Stonewall" Jackson, and Joseph Johnston. But the Confederate armies were undermanned and usually short of transport, artillery, munitions, and medical supplies. The collapse of southern agriculture and transportation during the later years of the war caused great hardship in many areas. The unwillingness of Britain and France to recognize the Confederacy was a crushing blow. These factors, plus the strangling effect of the northern blockade, doomed the South to defeat.

Of all the statesmen of the North and the South, Lincoln best understood the problems facing the country in April, 1865. His death was a tragic loss for all Americans. Robert E. Lee, when meeting with Grant at Appomattox, said that he "kept in mind President Lincoln's benignity, and surrendered as much to the latter's goodness as to Grant's artillery."

Chapter Review

Terms to Understand

1. commerce raiders
2. blockade runners
3. West Virginia
4. bounty-jumping
5. strategy
6. Vicksburg
7. Antietam
8. Peninsular Campaign
9. Atlanta
10. U.S. Sanitary Commission
11. *Monitor* and *Merrimac*
12. Emancipation Proclamation
13. Chancellorsville
14. Gettysburg
15. Appomattox

What Do You Think?

1. Considering the odds against the South in manpower and resources, why did the war last four years?

2. Why did some people in the North refer to the Civil War as "a rich man's war and a poor man's fight"?

3. Why did industry boom in the North during the war but not in the South?

4. Considering the costs of the Civil War, would it not have been better for Congress to pass a law providing for compensated emancipation of the slaves? Why was this not done?

Using Your Knowledge of History

1. Make a report on one of the outstanding military leaders or statesmen of the war. See *Statesmen of the Lost Cause: Jefferson Davis and His Cabinet*, by Burton J. Hendrick; or *Lincoln and His Generals* by T. Harry Williams.

2. Read Lincoln's great Second Inaugural Address. What can you learn from it? See also "The President Came Forward and the Sun Burst Through the Clouds" by Philip Van Doren Stern in *American Heritage* (February, 1958).

3. Study a map to see why Fort Henry and Fort Donelson were "keys to the interior of Tennessee." Write a brief essay to explain why control of this state was essential to the North's plans for victory.

4. Prepare a two-column chart to explain why certain groups in Britain favored the North while others favored the South.

Extending Your Knowledge of History

An excellent one-volume biography of Lincoln is Benjamin Thomas's *Abraham Lincoln*. Paul Angle has edited Lincoln's speeches and letters in *The Lincoln Reader*. A good study of the South during the war is Charles P. Roland's *Confederacy*. Two illustrated histories of the war are *The American Heritage Picture History of the Civil War* and *Divided We Fought*, edited by David Donald. Several good books about the Civil War have been written by Bruce Catton: *This Hallowed Ground, Stillness at Appomattox, America Goes to War,* and *Never Call Retreat*. Newspaper coverage of the Lincoln administration is the subject of Herbert Mitgang's entertaining book *Lincoln as They Saw Him*. Mary B. Chesnut left a spirited account of her wartime experiences in *A Diary from Dixie*. In *American Heritage* see "The Peaceable Ambassadors" (April, 1957) by Arnold Whitridge, "Prison Camps of the Civil War" (August, 1959), and "Grant at Shiloh" (February, 1960), the latter two both by Bruce Catton.

Analyzing Unit Four

1. Senator Charles Sumner charged that the squatter sovereignty provision of the Kansas-Nebraska Act "puts freedom and slavery face to face, and bids them grapple." Why did popular sovereignty fail to work in Kansas? Could it ever have provided a solution to the quarrel over slavery?

2. Senator William Henry Seward of New York predicted in 1858 that there would be "an irrepressible conflict" between the North and the South. Do you agree that civil war was irrepressible, or inevitable, by the late 1850's? Why?

3. Some historians feel that "bungling statesmanship" in the 1850's was a major cause of the war. Do you think that a more skillful politician than Buchanan could have fashioned another compromise in the late 1850's? Or negotiated a permanent solution to the quarrel over slavery? Give reasons.

Unit 5 | The Nation
Binds Up Its Wounds
(1865-1884)

Nomination of Grant at the Republican convention, 1868

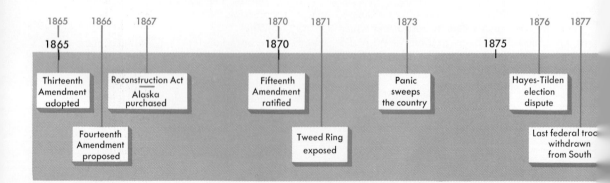

1865   1866   1867   1870   1871   1873   1875   1876   1877

1865   1870

Thirteenth Amendment adopted

Reconstruction Act
Alaska purchased

Fifteenth Amendment ratified

Panic sweeps the country

Hayes-Tilden election dispute

Fourteenth Amendment proposed

Tweed Ring exposed

Last federal troops withdrawn from South

The Civil War settled the questions of slavery and the right of secession from the Union. But no sooner had the conflict ended than all Americans, victors and vanquished, Negroes and whites, had to find solutions to other questions equally as complex.

The most pressing problems were agreement on the terms under which the Confederate states would be readmitted to the Union and the establishment of a new social order for freedmen and whites in the South. President Lincoln's tragic death complicated the situation, for no other political leader had his generous outlook or his political skill and prestige. Control of reconstruction passed into the hands of a closely knit faction of the Republican Party, the Radical Republicans.

The Radicals were determined to win immediate full suffrage for all freedmen and to make this a condition for representation of the former Confederate states in Congress. To achieve these objectives, the Radicals found it necessary to impose military rule on ten southern states. Some Radicals were genuinely concerned about making first-class citizens of the former slaves. Many others wanted Negroes to vote because their ballots would keep the Republican Party in power. When Republican leaders in the 1870's felt that they had enough votes in the North and West to win elections, their interest in southern Negroes slackened. Federal troops were withdrawn from the South, and the government made no effort to enforce voting or other civil rights for Negroes.

The reconstruction policies of the Radical Republicans angered many southern whites. As soon as federal troops were withdrawn, southern whites proceeded to establish the type of social order they thought best. It meant inferior jobs and loss of voting rights for most Negroes, and separation of the races in schools, trains, theaters, and eating places. Today it appears that one of the tragedies of reconstruction was the nation's failure to prepare the freedmen for the responsibilities of citizenship and to insure that they had the same opportunities for getting ahead as other citizens.

Ulysses S. Grant was President during the crucial period of reconstruction. Though Grant had been a highly effective general, he failed to comprehend the responsibilities of the presidency. Grant understood little about the problems of the South; nor was he aware of the political corruption which undermined state and local government during these years and which reached into his own administration.

CHAPTER 18

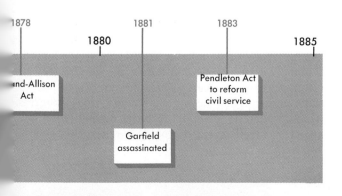

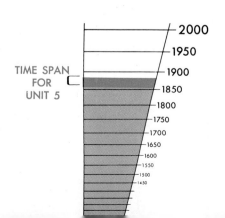

Richmond after the war

The Postwar South Experiences Change and Discord

The war being at an end, the Southern states having laid down their arms, and the questions at issue between them and the Northern states having been decided, I believe it to be the duty of everyone to unite in the restoration of the country and the re-establishment of peace and harmony.

ROBERT E. LEE, 1865

All Americans longed for the "re-establishment of peace and harmony" in the spring of 1865. But this hope was not realized until some time after Appomattox. President Lincoln's goal had been to restore the southern states to the Union on generous terms. His successor, Andrew Johnson, also tried to carry out a lenient policy in the *reconstruction,* or rebuilding, of the shattered South. But Johnson lacked the political strength and the personal prestige to win the co-operation of Congress. As a result, a group of Republican senators and representatives imposed a severe reconstruction program on the southern states.

During the reconstruction era, which lasted for about a decade, the country faced a series of difficult problems. In the North the armed forces had to be demobilized; and agriculture, industry, and the government itself had to adjust to peacetime conditions. But these problems were minor in comparison with those of the South. In the former Confederate states, cities and towns had been burned; factories, railroads, and bridges had been destroyed; and farm animals and harvested crops had been seized by northern armies. Because of the loss of property and the worthlessness of Confederate money and bonds, the South faced financial chaos. The southern states had to establish new governments, and Congress had to decide the terms upon which the seceded states could re-enter the Union.

The most pressing problem was the plight of the almost four million Negroes. Suddenly liberated, they desperately needed education and the means of making a living. In the prewar South, slavery had been not only a system of labor but also a social system. Now a new relationship between the races would replace slavery. One of the most bitterly contested issues during reconstruction was the question of whether northern Republicans or southern Democrats would determine the nature of this new relationship.

1 *Lincoln and Johnson Favor Lenient Reconstruction*

The South suffers heavy destruction. Since little fighting had taken place in the North, that area had not experienced much physical damage during the war. Large parts of the South, however, had suffered severe destruction. In the Shenandoah Valley of Virginia, one witness reported, there was "scarcely a fence worthy of the name from the Rapidan to Bull Run; and the fields . . . are now broad commons, with old landmarks obliterated, ditches filled up, quarters, cornhouses, and barns in ruins, while the lone and blackened chimneys of the once happy homestead stand like some old sentries on guard until the last." The same was true of the areas through which General Sherman had passed and also of

. . . .

CHAPTER FOCUS

1. Lincoln and Johnson favor lenient reconstruction.

2. Congress develops its own reconstruction program.

3. The South endures reconstruction.

4. A "New South" emerges.

large stretches in Arkansas, Tennessee, and northern Alabama.

Some southern cities had suffered extensive damage. Fire had destroyed Richmond. Most of the wharves in Mobile had been torn up, and explosions had ripped the heart of the city. A northern reporter who saw Columbia, South Carolina, at the end of the war wrote:

> It is now a wilderness of ruins. Its heart but a mass of blackened chimneys and crumbling walls. Two thirds of the buildings in the place were burned, including, without exception, everything in the business portion. Not a store, office, or shop escaped; and for a distance of three fourths of a mile on each of twelve streets there was not a building left.

Southern life is disrupted. Physical damage was not the only loss suffered by the South. The Thirteenth Amendment had wiped out a two-billion-dollar investment in slaves. Confederate money and bonds were worthless; most banks and insurance companies had closed their doors. So too had factories and mines. Storekeepers had little or nothing to sell, and food was scarce.

The federal government's policy of confiscation and taxation further hurt the South. All assets of the Confederate government were seized by Treasury Department agents, who were spurred on by the promise of a commission on the confiscated goods. Moreover, the federal government imposed taxes on the sale of private property, on shipping, and on cotton. This taxation and the seizure of property drained away money which the South desperately needed. Faced with economic ruin and the destruction of their way of life, many southern whites shared the views of the poet Henry Timrod, who wrote in 1867: "You ask me to tell my story for the last year. I can embody it all in a few words, *Beggary, starvation, death, bitter grief, utter want of hope.*"

The freedmen face staggering problems. Nevertheless, the southern whites were better able to cope with their problems than were the freedmen. The Negroes had suddenly been released from a life of bondage, a life in which they had received and carried out orders and in return had been provided with the bare necessities of life. Very few Negroes could read or write; and most had performed only manual labor. Yet the freedmen now had to find jobs, care for themselves, and fulfill the responsibilities of citizenship. Many Negroes exercised their freedom to move from place to place. Some drifted to the cities in the hope of finding better jobs and living conditions. Others traveled about searching for members of their families who had been sold to different masters. Some men deserted wives and children, who had no legal claims on them. A few freedmen joined bands of marauders, sometimes led by lawless whites.

Many freedmen become sharecroppers. Some of the freedmen stayed on plantations where they had been slaves, and worked for wages. But many of them hoped to acquire their own plots of land. They believed persistent rumors that the government would confiscate the land of former slaveowners and give every Negro "forty acres and a mule." When this failed to happen, many freedmen became *sharecroppers*. The sharecropping system developed because few southern landowners had the money to pay wages and few freedmen had the money to buy land. Consequently, large plantations were divided into small plots that were leased to freedmen and poor whites. The landowners furnished seed, tools, and domestic animals; the local storekeeper furnished household supplies on credit. When the sharecropper harvested his crop, he turned over part of it to the landowner and part to the storekeeper, and kept what was left for himself. Sharecropping spread rapidly throughout the South.

Southern states pass "black codes." The southern whites who controlled the state governments during 1865 and 1866 tried to regulate the freedmen's lives. They passed state laws, called *black codes,* that were based on northern vagrancy laws and on southern prewar regulations for slaves and free Negroes. Negroes were permitted to attend separate or *segregated* schools, to have their marriages sanctified, to give testimony in court, and to own property. But the black codes prevented them from holding office, serving on juries, voting, or owning arms. Some states barred Negroes from working as artisans or mechanics to keep them from competing with white labor. In the cotton states, where the Negroes were most numerous, the black codes called for the arrest of all able-bodied Negroes who had no jobs. If convicted of vagrancy, they were (1) fined and put to work on state chain gangs or (2) assigned to work for an employer who would pay the vagrant's fine and provide board but no wages.

Southern whites believed that the black codes were necessary to end confusion and to regulate relations between whites and freedmen. Harsh laws were essential, they argued, to put the Negroes to work and to "keep them in their place." Most Northerners, however, opposed the black codes. They considered the passage of these laws an attempt to make the Negroes slaves in everything but name.

Republicans differ on reconstruction policy. Meanwhile, the task of working out a reconstruction policy for the South fell to the Republicans who controlled the federal government. But the Republicans could not agree on a course of action.

The *Moderate Republicans* favored a generous policy toward the southern states. These Republicans believed that the South had learned its lesson. Since slavery, the root of the trouble, had been abolished, there was no further need to punish southern whites. Moreover, the Moderates took the position that the southern states had never really left the Union. They urged that a presidential pardon allow these states to resume their place in the federal Union.

The *Radical Republicans* took a different view, arguing that the Confederate states had actually left the Union and had been conquered by northern troops. These Republicans believed that Congress, not the President, should determine the conditions under which the southern states would be restored to the Union. While the Radical attitude toward southern whites was severe, toward the freedmen it was generous. The Radicals' concern for Negro rights stemmed in part from the genuine sympathy of those who had been abolitionists. But other Radicals were primarily interested in making Republican voters out of the southern Negroes. Without the votes of freedmen, the Republicans knew they might lose control of Congress once the southern states were readmitted.

Reconstruction politics, then, was a struggle between the Moderates and northern Democrats on one side and the Radicals on the other. During 1865 and 1866 the Moderate Republicans had the upper hand. But after the elections of 1866, the Radicals imposed their will on Congress, the Supreme Court, and the President, and, therefore, on the South. In the remainder of this section, we shall read about the reconstruction plans initiated by Lincoln and Johnson. The next section will take up the congressional program of reconstruction.

Lincoln develops a generous policy for restoring the Union. When large areas of Tennessee, Louisiana, and North Carolina fell into Union hands early in the war, Lincoln had appointed military governors in these states. Then the President worked out a plan for reconstructing southern states and permitting them to regain representation in Congress. In a presidential proclamation, Lincoln granted a full pardon to every southern citizen who would take an oath of allegiance to the Constitution. This did not apply, however, to high-ranking civil and military leaders. The proclamation also declared that when 10 per cent of the number of people who had voted in a state in 1860 had taken the oath to support the Union, they could organize a legal state government. Before the end of the war, Louisiana, Arkansas, and Tennessee had taken advantage of this generous "10 per cent plan" and had set up loyal governments.

The Radicals propose a stiffer plan. Lincoln's plan angered the Radicals. They thought he was being too easy on white Southerners and offered too little protection to the Negroes. Representative Thaddeus Stevens of Pennsylvania, formerly an abolitionist, spoke for the Radicals in the House. He declared that the actions of the South were "sufficient to justify the exercise of the extreme right of war — 'to execute, to imprison, to confiscate.'" Spurred on by such oratory, the Republicans in Congress proposed their own reconstruction plan in the Wade-Davis Bill. Congress passed this measure in July, 1864, during the closing hours of the congressional session.

The Wade-Davis Bill declared that Congress, not the President, should control reconstruction. It required a *majority*, not just 10 per cent, of the white male citizens in a seceded state to take the oath of al-

TIMETABLE

RECONSTRUCTION

1864–1865 Lincoln-Johnson reconstruction plans are aimed at pardoning South, not punishing it.

1864 Wade-Davis Bill, giving control of reconstruction to Congress, fails to gain Lincoln's approval.

1865 Thirteenth Amendment ends slavery.

1866 Civil Rights Act and Fourteenth Amendment (ratified in 1868) confer citizenship on Negroes.

1867 Reconstruction Act divides South into five districts occupied by federal troops. Southern state governments controlled by Radical Republicans.

1869 Congress adopts Fifteenth Amendment, intended to protect Negroes' right to vote. (Ratified in 1870.)

1870 Last of the southern states returns to Union.

1871 Ku Klux Act outlaws conspiracies against freedmen.

1872 Amnesty Act removes political restrictions from almost all Southerners.

1875 Civil Rights Act passed to protect Negroes' civil rights. (Never seriously enforced.)

1877 Last federal troops removed from South.

Representative Thaddeus Stevens (left) led the forces opposing President Andrew Johnson (right) in the fight over who should determine reconstruction policy.

legiance before a legal state government could be organized. Moreover, it declared that the new state constitutions must abolish slavery, refuse to pay old state debts, and prohibit former Confederate officers and political leaders from voting. Lincoln permitted the Wade-Davis Bill to die by refusing to sign it. This pocket veto[1] caused the Radicals to issue an angry declaration, in which they asserted the right of Congress to control reconstruction.

Lincoln's death weakens the Moderates. Shortly after Lincoln's re-election in 1864, the Radical Republicans renewed their campaign against the President's "10 per cent plan." They also pushed the Thirteenth Amendment through both houses of Congress. When ratified by the states, this measure would abolish slavery everywhere in the United States, including the border states. In addition, the Radicals blocked the seating in Congress of senators and representatives elected in Louisiana under the 10 per cent plan. Still, Lincoln had high hopes of completing reconstruction during the summer and fall of 1865, while Congress was adjourned. He expressed this optimistic view at his last Cabinet meeting on April 14, 1865.

Lincoln's assassination changed the

course of reconstruction. Had he lived, he might have been able to reorganize the southern states, rally Moderate Republican and Democratic support in Congress, and win over public opinion in the North. Thus, his generous plan might well have prevailed. Undoubtedly there would have been a bitter fight with the Radical Republicans, but Lincoln had the political skill and prestige to win such a battle. Lincoln's death actually strengthened the Radicals, for they claimed that the assassin was in league with southern conspirators. This conspiracy, they said, proved the need for a harsh policy in dealing with the unrepentant Confederates.

Andrew Johnson becomes President. The man who tried to carry out Lincoln's plan for reconstruction was honest, sincere, and courageous. Andrew Johnson had been born into a poor, nonslaveholding family in North Carolina. Lacking formal education, he started adult life as a tailor in eastern Tennessee. Johnson soon entered politics and served in the state legislature, as governor of Tennessee, and eventually in both houses of Congress. When Tennessee seceded, he denounced the action and remained in the Senate, the only southern senator to do so. Appointed by Lincoln as military governor of Tennessee, Johnson did an excellent job. This fact, plus his support of the Lincoln administration as a War Democrat, won him second spot on the Union ticket with Lincoln in 1864.

As President, however, Johnson had sev-

---

[1] A President can kill a bill which reaches his desk within ten days of the end of a congressional session by leaving it unsigned. This is called a *pocket veto.* See Article I, Section 7, of the Constitution (page 141).

eral handicaps. The fact that he was a Southerner and a Democrat made many Northerners suspicious of him during these years when emotions ran high. Moreover, Johnson could be obstinate and quick-tempered; indeed, he seemed to prefer to fight rather than negotiate with his political enemies. He lacked Lincoln's broad-minded approach to problems as well as the tact and understanding that were so badly needed in 1865.

Johnson tries to carry out Lincoln's program. When Andrew Johnson became President the Radical Republicans hailed him as an ally. They thought he would take their advice, and they also counted on the new President's well-known dislike of the southern planter class. Surely he would endorse the Radicals' proposals for dealing with the former Confederates. One of them said: "There will be no trouble now in running this government."

Johnson soon surprised the Radicals. First, he recognized state governments that had been formed under Lincoln's "10 per cent plan" in Louisiana, Tennessee, Arkansas, and Virginia. Second, he appointed military governors in the other southern states and pardoned all citizens except high Confederate officers, political leaders, and men who owned property valued at more than 20,000 dollars. Third, he held that the remaining southern states could re-enter the Union when they drafted constitutions which approved the Thirteenth Amendment and repudiated their war debts. Johnson's plan for reconstruction was similar to Lincoln's, though he did not specify the percentage of voters who had to take the oath of allegiance. Like Lincoln, he let each state decide who should vote on the new constitutions. Since this meant that Negroes would probably be denied the vote, the Radical Republicans were angered. But there was little they could do when Congress was not in session.

Throughout the summer and fall of 1865, Johnson pushed ahead with his plan for reconstruction. By December, all of the southern states except Texas had organized new governments and had been recognized by the President. Enough of them had ratified the Thirteenth Amendment (page 373)

to make it part of the Constitution. Moreover, the ten southern states had elected representatives and senators, and these men were ready to take their seats in Congress.

▶ CHECK-UP

1. What losses had the South suffered in the war? How did taxation and confiscation further hurt the South after the war? What problems confronted the freedmen? Why did many of them become sharecroppers?

2. What rights were denied to the Negroes under the black codes? What did southern whites hold to be the purpose of the codes?

3. What views on reconstruction were held by Moderate Republicans? By Radical Republicans? What was Lincoln's "10 per cent plan"? Contrast with the Wade-Davis Bill.

4. What were the major provisions in Johnson's plan for reconstruction?

• •

2 Congress Develops Its Own Reconstruction Program

The Radicals oppose Andrew Johnson's reconstruction program. When Congress assembled in December, 1865, it immediately took up the problem of southern reconstruction. The Radical Republicans angrily criticized Johnson's actions. They charged that he was overreaching himself in pardoning southern citizens. Now that the war was over, they argued, the President's broad emergency powers must be cut back and Congress must reassert itself. As the Wade-Davis Bill had made clear, the Radical Republicans believed that reconstruction was the business of Congress and not of the President.

Many Republicans were worried that their party would lose control of Congress. Before the war, five Negroes had been counted as three in determining the number of representatives for a state. Now that the

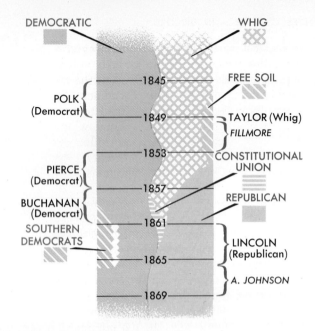

DEMOCRATIC   WHIG

POLK
(Democrat)

———1845——— FREE SOIL

———1849——— TAYLOR (Whig)
            FILLMORE

———1853——— CONSTITUTIONAL
            UNION

PIERCE
(Democrat)

———1857——— REPUBLICAN

BUCHANAN
(Democrat)

SOUTHERN
DEMOCRATS

———1861———

            LINCOLN
———1865——— (Republican)

            A. JOHNSON

———1869———

POLITICAL PARTIES, 1845–1869

CHART STUDY

The Republican Party, founded in 1854 to oppose the extension of slavery, rapidly replaced the Whig Party in national politics. (The next political chart is on page 526.)

freedmen would be counted equally with whites, the South would gain thirteen representatives. These would no doubt be Democrats if southern whites were allowed to control their state governments and exclude Negroes from the polls. The only way to prevent this, the Radicals reasoned, was to enforce the Negroes' right to vote and to make sure that they supported Republican candidates. "I am for Negro suffrage in every rebel state," said Thaddeus Stevens. And Senator Sumner of Massachusetts insisted, "If all whites vote, then must all blacks. . . . Without them the old enemy [the southern Democratic Party] will reappear, and in alliance with the Northern democracy, put us all in peril again."

It should be added that not only Radicals but also many Moderate Republicans were disturbed by what was happening in the reconstructed states. As we have seen, the new state governments had promptly passed black codes to control the freedmen. Moreover, the southern representatives elected to Congress included the Vice-President and several cabinet members of the Confederacy, a number of Confederate generals

and colonels, and more than 50 former members of the Confederate congress! For all these reasons, then, Congress voted against seating the southern representatives.

Congress protects the rights of Negroes. Congress next took steps to organize its own reconstruction program. It appointed a Joint Commission of Fifteen (six senators and nine representatives), which was largely dominated by Radicals. This committee was asked to study the problem of readmitting the southern states. Meanwhile, Congress pushed ahead with legislation to protect the freedmen.

First, it passed a bill to extend the life and powers of the Freedmen's Bureau. In March, 1865, Congress had set up this Bureau, for one year only, to provide food, clothing, and fuel to the freedmen. The Radicals now wanted the Bureau to (1) assign abandoned land to the freedmen, (2) establish hospitals and provide medical aid for the Negroes, (3) organize Negro schools, (4) encourage the freedmen to vote, and (5) help both Negroes and poor whites to find jobs. But President Johnson vetoed the bill on the grounds that some of its provisions were unconstitutional and that there was no need to expand the Bureau's activities. A few months later, however, Congress overrode the President's veto of another Freedmen's Bureau Bill.

Congress also passed a Civil Rights Act. This act declared that the Negroes were citizens of the United States and forbade the southern states to discriminate between Negro and white citizens. Johnson's veto of the bill not only infuriated the Radicals but disturbed many Moderate Republicans. The two groups lined up enough votes to override the President's veto in 1866.

Congress approves the Fourteenth Amendment. Radical Republican leaders realized that a later Congress could repeal the Civil Rights Act or that the Supreme Court might declare it unconstitutional. So the Joint Committee of Fifteen proposed that the act's basic principles be written into the Constitution. To that end, the Committee drafted an amendment which was passed by Congress in June, 1866, and sent to the states for ratification. The Fourteenth Amendment (page 153) had four main parts:

(1) Section One bestowed citizenship upon the Negroes and forbade any state to interfere with the civil and political rights of citizens.

(2) Section Two declared a penalty for any state which denied the right to vote to any adult male citizen except for "participation in rebellion, or other crime." Such a state was to have its representation in the House of Representatives reduced. This clause was intended to compel the southern states to allow freedmen to vote.

(3) Section Three dealt with Confederate leaders who were seeking state or national political office. It barred from public office anyone who had violated an oath to support the Constitution by engaging "in insurrection or rebellion" against the Union. Such a person was to be barred from office until pardoned by a two-thirds vote of Congress.

(4) Section Four forbade payment of the Confederate debt and the war debts of southern states. It also forbade the compensation of Southerners for the loss of their slaves.

President Johnson opposed the Fourteenth Amendment and urged the southern states to reject it. Ten of them did so by overwhelming majorities. Only Tennessee ratified the amendment, and Congress promptly readmitted this state to the Union (July, 1866).[2]

The Radicals gain strength in the elections of 1866. The congressional elections in 1866 gave the voters a chance to choose between Johnson's moderate plan for reconstruction and the more drastic proposals of the Radical Republicans. The President waded into the election campaign on behalf of Moderate Republican candidates. But his three-week "swing around the circle" of key cities proved disastrous. Hecklers interrupted his speeches, and the President angrily lashed back. Thaddeus Stevens called it "a very remarkable circus" with Andrew Johnson as the "chief clown." Johnson's efforts lost support for the Moderate candidates and damaged his own political stature.

[2] The Fourteenth Amendment became part of the Constitution in July, 1868.

The Radicals, by comparison, waged a clever campaign. They drew the voters' attention to the black codes and to the rejection of the Fourteenth Amendment by southern states. They also pointed to race riots in Memphis and New Orleans, where scores of Negroes had been killed or wounded, and to attacks on freedmen elsewhere in the South. These conditions, they said, showed the need for stronger action. To win the support of northern businessmen, the Radical Republicans promised to continue high protective tariffs and other government policies favorable to business.

When the ballots were counted, it was found that the Radicals had scored a victory. With a two-thirds majority in both houses of Congress, they could now push ahead with their reconstruction program in spite of presidential vetoes.

Congress passes the Reconstruction Act. Starting in March, 1867, the new Congress passed a series of reconstruction acts over Johnson's vetoes. These measures imposed the Radical program of reconstruction on the southern states. Senator Sumner had long held that the Confederate states had committed political "suicide" when they left the Union. Having been subdued by northern troops, he declared, these states had become "conquered territory" and should be treated as such. In the *North American Review,* James Russell Lowell expressed the Radical viewpoint: "We have the same right to impose terms and to demand guarantees . . . that the victor always has."

The basic Reconstruction Act did "impose terms" and "demand guarantees." It grouped the ten southern states that were still out of the Union into five military districts, each under a high-ranking army officer. These officers had the power to preserve order and to enforce martial law if necessary.

The Reconstruction Act also outlined the steps by which the states could be freed from military control. (1) Each state was to hold a convention of delegates chosen by all adult male citizens without regard to race or color (except those deprived of the vote for taking part in the war). (2) Each convention was required to adopt a state constitution that gave Negroes the right to vote. (3) This constitution was then to be approved by a majority of the voters in the state and also by Congress. (4) The legislature elected under the new state constitution must then ratify the Fourteenth Amendment. (5) When this Amendment became a part of the Constitution, any state that had taken these four steps would be allowed to return to its former position in the Union.

Through this Radical plan of reconstruction, the Negro would receive the right to vote, and enough whites would be deprived of suffrage to make it probable that the southern states would vote Republican.

Congress impeaches President Johnson. Meanwhile, the feud between President Andrew Johnson and the Radical Republicans was approaching a climax. When the President vetoed the Reconstruction Act, Congress promptly overrode the veto. At the same time the Radicals put through the Tenure of Office Act. This measure, also passed over his veto, was designed to trap the President. It provided that the President could not dismiss, without the consent of the Senate, any civil officer whose appointment had been approved by the Senate. Moreover, it specifically declared that any violation of this act would be a misdemeanor punishable by imprisonment.

Johnson decided to violate the Tenure of Office Act in order to test its constitutionality. He dismissed Secretary of War Stanton, who had been co-operating closely with the Radicals. Stanton refused to give up his office and for a time even barricaded himself in the War Department building. In February, 1868, the House impeached the President for "high crimes and misdemeanors."

Johnson's trial before the Senate was presided over by Chief Justice Salmon Chase. Thaddeus Stevens led the prosecution, which centered on charges that the President had violated the Tenure of Office Act. Republican senators were under great pressure to convict Andrew Johnson. Nevertheless, seven Republican senators courageously defied the Radical leaders and voted with the Democrats for acquittal. The vote, 35 to 19, was one less than the two thirds required for conviction.

Had the Radical Republicans been able to remove Johnson from office, the presiding officer of the Senate would have become President. Then the Radicals would have had control of the White House as well as Congress. In this event, the principle of separation of powers (page 134) would have been seriously impaired. But with the impeachment of Johnson, the Radicals had reached the peak of their power. Failure to

The Man Who Saved the Presidency

Because he voted "not guilty" at President Johnson's impeachment, Senator Edmund G. Ross of Kansas was called "the man who saved a President." Actually Ross did more: He helped save the office of chief executive from future domination by Congress.

Most Kansans were staunch Republicans and strongly opposed to President Johnson. Senator Ross, who had fought for the antislavery forces in Kansas and had served as a Union army major, felt the same way. Yet, in spite of terrific pressure from other senators and his constituents at home, Ross kept his vow to act as an impartial judge.

Six other Republican senators had already announced their intention of joining the Democrats in support of President Johnson. But on

the day of the verdict, the American people waited to hear from the one senator who had not yet declared himself. To impeach the President, the Republicans had to have one more vote — Senator Ross's.

Later Ross described his feelings as he stood before the packed Senate galleries: "I almost literally looked down into my open grave," he wrote, meaning that he could see the political ruin that lay ahead for him if he voted for acquittal. Nevertheless, Ross declared, "Not guilty," first in soft, wavering tones and then in a voice loud and clear. The years that followed were hard for Ross; but as hatreds cooled, people came to appreciate the wisdom of his decision. Kansas honored him, and so did the nation.

convict the President marked the beginning of their downfall.

The Southern states are readmitted. While the Radicals were plotting against Johnson, army officers were enforcing the Reconstruction Act in the five military districts of the South. Many civil officials in the Johnson state governments were removed. Delegates to constitutional conventions were elected, in many states chiefly by Negro voters. New state constitutions were drawn up under the provisions of the Reconstruction Act; and new legislatures, controlled by Radicals, ratified the Fourteenth Amendment. By the fall of 1868, seven of the ten southern states had been readmitted to the Union — in time for the freedmen to vote in the presidential election of that year. The military governors turned over the administration of these governments to the newly elected state officials, though some federal troops were stationed near at hand.

The election of 1868 shows the importance of Negro votes. The election of 1868 (page 403) dramatically illustrated the importance of the Negro vote in the South. The Republican candidate, General Grant, defeated a weak Democratic candidate. Though Grant won a one-sided victory in the electoral college, the popular vote was surprisingly close. Grant led his opponent by only 300,000 votes in a total of 5,700,000. Of the 700,000 Negroes who went to the polls in 1868, it is safe to assume that most voted for Grant. The Radicals were quick to note that without the freedmen's ballots, Grant would have received less than half the popular vote.

The Fifteenth Amendment is ratified. To protect still further the right of southern Negroes to vote, the Radicals proposed another amendment to the Constitution. The Fifteenth Amendment provided that suffrage should not be restricted because of "race, color, or previous condition of servitude." It became part of the Constitution in 1870. In that same year the three remaining southern states — Virginia, Mississippi, and Texas — were admitted to the Union after ratifying both the Fourteenth and Fifteenth Amendments. Most northern Republicans now assumed that reconstruction was completed and turned their attention to other matters.

▶ CHECK-UP

1. Why were the Radical Republicans opposed to Johnson's plan for reconstruction? What developments in the reconstructed states disturbed Republicans? What legislation did Congress pass to help Negroes?

2. Why did the Radical Republicans push for the adoption of the Fourteenth Amendment? What were its chief provisions? Why did the Radical Republicans gain strength in the 1866 election? What plan was provided for re-admitting a state to the Union?

3. On what grounds was President Johnson impeached? What was the result? How did the election of 1868 illustrate the importance of the Negro vote? Why was the Fifteenth Amendment proposed?

3 *The South Endures Reconstruction*

Southern whites resist reconstruction. For the South, reconstruction was far from finished when the last state was readmitted. The collapse of the Confederacy had completely disrupted the South's established way of life. At first, it had not been clear how southern whites would react to this staggering blow. When General Grant made a brief tour of the South in 1866, he reported, "I am satisfied that the mass of thinking men of the South accept the present situation of affairs in good faith."

There were warning signals, however, that many southern whites did not accept the "present situation in good faith." *De Bow's Review,* a leading southern journal, asked, "Is it possible that the North demands a miracle?" And Carl Schurz, who toured the South right after the war, told President Johnson that he found "among the southern people . . . a desire to preserve

This northern teacher taught freed slave children at the Penn School on an island off the South Carolina shore. This was one of the first schools built for freedmen in the South.

slavery in its original form as much and as long as possible." Despite the presence of federal troops, southern white people continued to resist many aspects of reconstruction. And eventually, after the soldiers left, they proceeded to readjust the relations between Negroes and whites in their states.

Many Northerners go south. After the war many Northerners moved to the South. Some whites volunteered to work in the hospitals set up by the Freedmen's Bureau. Others taught in Negro schools, providing a desperately needed service. Still others invested in new southern factories, mines, and railroads. But some of the northern whites were moved by the hope of personal profit rather than by the desire to help rebuild the former Confederate states.

Many Negroes who became leaders in the postwar South had formerly lived in the North. South Carolina's state treasurer, for example, was a Negro who had been educated in Glasgow and London and had served as a minister in New Haven, Connecticut. Most of the Negroes elected to Con-

gress from southern states during reconstruction had been educated in the North.

Republicans dominate the state governments. Because so many southern whites were barred from politics, power quickly fell into the hands of the freedmen and northern Republican agents. Northern politicians who went south after the war were called *carpetbaggers,* since presumably they carried everything they owned in a carpetbag (a kind of suitcase). While some of them were seeking power and advantage for themselves, many sincerely wanted to help the freedmen. The carpetbaggers were aided by *scalawags,* southern whites who co-operated with the Radical program of reconstruction. In general, southern whites scorned the scalawags as unprincipled self-seekers. Many scalawags, however, were people who had disapproved of slavery, had opposed secession, and had remained loyal (though silent) to the Union during the war. Together the carpetbaggers and scalawags directed the political activity of the freedmen, and all three groups held seats in the state legislatures. Only in South Carolina did Negroes ever outnumber whites in the legislature.

Reconstruction legislatures make changes. Since the reconstruction legislatures were something new in American politics, reporters from the North and from Europe covered their activities in great detail. One point often overlooked was the amount of worthwhile legislation adopted by these state governments. For example, the reconstruction legislatures appropriated money for public schools, something the South had neglected to do before the Civil War. These schools served both Negro and white children but were usually separate or segregated. The state governments also repaired roads, bridges, and public buildings that had been destroyed during the war. Many new hospitals and orphanages were built. Some states established relief programs for the poor. Moreover, the freedmen in the legislatures tried to equalize voting districts and to reform state criminal laws and judicial procedures. Many of these measures were patterned after northern state laws of the 1830's and '40's.

Some money is spent unwisely. The reform measures of the reconstruction legislatures were paralleled, however, by reckless spending and some corruption.[3] Extravagant sums were appropriated for statehouse furnishings, imported foods and luxury items for the legislators, and "traveling expenses." Railroad promoters received thousands of dollars, though many of the lines were never built. There was also theft of public funds; and some voters, legislators, and judges took bribes in return for votes or favors. Such unwise expenditures and the large sums needed to rebuild the South resulted in a sharp rise in state debts. South Carolina's public debt, for example, increased from 7 million dollars in 1865 to 29 million dollars in 1873. Tax rates on property rose sharply. Southern white landowners resented this trend; for they had to pay the taxes, while freedmen who owned no property escaped this burden.

Southern whites resort to violence. Many southern whites were likewise embittered by the extension of new rights and privileges to the Negroes. They knew that carpetbag rule depended on the votes of the freedmen. Hence some whites decided to

---

[3] Corruption and the extravagant use of public funds, it should be pointed out, were not restricted to the postwar South. During the same years northern and western state governments and scores of cities experienced corruption. Moreover, moral standards in the federal government reached a new low. This trend is discussed in Chapter 19.

disobey the new laws and frighten the Negroes in order to keep them away from the polls. Secret organizations such as the Ku Klux Klan, the Knights of the White Camellia, and the Society of the White Rose waged campaigns of terror.

The largest of these organizations was the Ku Klux Klan, organized soon after the war by restless young men in a small Tennessee town. News of their activities spread rapidly, and within a matter of months other chapters of the Klan were started. Officers were called dragons, hydras, titans, furies, and nighthawks, while the head of the Klan bore the title of Grand Wizard. Riding forth at night, dressed in white robes and hoods, the Klansmen struck terror in Negro homes. If the Negroes failed to heed the Klan's warning against political activity, they were whipped and their cabins were burned. The Klansmen and other white terrorists brutally attacked and even murdered many Negroes.

The Radical Republicans strike back. The spread of violence upset the Radical Republican program for the South and made a mockery of the Fourteenth and Fifteenth Amendments. In most cases, state governments failed to check the activities of these terrorist organizations. As a result, the federal government sent troops into southern states to supervise elections, and Congress passed additional laws.

(1) In 1870, Congress authorized the President to use force to put down "unlaw-

Hiram R. Revels of Mississippi (left) was the first Negro to sit in the United States Senate. The other men in this engraving were Negro representatives in Congress in 1872.

ful combinations." This same act declared that cases arising out of violations of the Fourteenth and Fifteenth Amendments were to be heard in federal rather than state courts.

(2) The Republicans also sponsored the Ku Klux Act (1871), which imposed stiff penalties on anyone who conspired against the freedmen.

(3) In addition, Congress approved another Civil Rights Act (1875), but only after deleting a provision that would have desegregated the public schools. This act guaranteed Negroes the right to serve on juries. It also provided that all persons, regardless of race, were entitled to "the full and equal enjoyment" of such public facilities as hotels, railroads, and places of amusement. But the Civil Rights Act of 1875 was never seriously enforced in the South.

White control is restored in the South. In spite of these measures, the Radicals were losing control of the southern state governments. The Klan and similar organizations had succeeded in frightening the Negroes away from the polls. Moreover, white employers threatened the freedmen with loss of their jobs if they dared support the Radicals. As the years went by, more and more southern whites regained the right to vote. Former Confederates were pardoned by Presidents Johnson and Grant, and young men reached voting age. Declining interest in the problems of reconstruction also accounted for the waning power of the Radical Republicans. Once the southern states were back in the Union, many Northerners did not care whether carpetbaggers and freedmen or former Confederates controlled state governments in the South. Now that the Negroes were free, most people in the North and West seemed to lose their concern for them.

This changing attitude was reflected in the Amnesty Act passed by Congress in 1872. This law removed the political limitations of the Fourteenth Amendment for all but a few hundred Southerners. In that same year the Freedmen's Bureau ceased to exist. Meanwhile, southern whites had regained control of the state governments in Virginia, Tennessee, North Carolina, and Georgia. Radical reconstruction govern-

ments survived in South Carolina, Florida, and Louisiana until 1877, but only because federal troops were stationed there. When the last troops were withdrawn in the spring of 1877, these three states joined the other southern states in giving white Democrats control of their governments. That fall President Rutherford Hayes, during a visit to Atlanta, told the Negroes that their "rights and interests would be safer" if southern whites were "let alone" by the federal government. As we shall see in the next section, President Hayes was greatly mistaken.

▶ CHECK-UP

1. Why did many Northerners move to the South after the war? Who were the carpetbaggers? The scalawags? What reforms were introduced by reconstruction legislatures? Why did state debts and taxes rise?

2. Why was the Ku Klux Klan organized? How did the federal government seek to put an end to violence? What were the provisions of the Civil Rights Act of 1875?

3. How were southern whites able to gain control of the state governments?

· · · · · · · · · · · · · · · · · · · ·

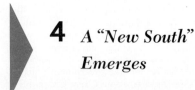

4 A "New South" Emerges

The South experiences further changes. Many southern whites felt that genuine reconstruction began with the withdrawal of federal troops and the establishment of white rule in the former Confederate states. Whether reconstruction began or ended in the mid-1870's, the South did undergo further economic, social, and political changes. These changes led Henry W. Grady, editor of the Atlanta *Constitution,* to refer in 1886 to "the New South." Ever since, historians have used this phrase to summarize the developments that took place in the South over the last 25 years of the century.

Plantations give way to small farms. You have read earlier in this chapter about the development of sharecropping on southern plantations. Slave-owning planters had been ruined by the war. After 1865 they had no laborers to work their fields, and they were fortunate if they could persuade sharecroppers to stay on their land. Gradually the prewar plantations were divided into smaller units of land. In Louisiana during the 1860's, for example, the number of farms rose from 17,000 to 28,000; over the same period the average size of Louisiana farms decreased from 536 acres to 247 acres. White men owned almost all of this land. Some of the landowners were businessmen who did not live on the land but held it as an investment.

White farmers as well as Negroes became sharecroppers. Since they were always in debt to the landowners and merchants, the sharecroppers found it impossible to buy their own land and thus break away from the system. Sharecropping also had the effect of continuing the reign of King Cotton. By the mid-1870's cotton production had climbed to the prewar level of about four million bales per year; by 1890 cotton production was up to eight million bales. This increase was a mixed blessing, however, since the price of cotton fell sharply — from fifteen cents a pound in the 1870's to five cents a pound in the 1890's. The harder the sharecroppers worked, the less their cotton was worth.

The South develops new industries. The Negro sharecroppers had few avenues of escape. But white tenant farmers could move to a city and take factory jobs, for by the late 1870's the New South was experiencing rapid industrial growth. Whatever southern capital was available went into new industry, and much northern capital was invested in southern railroads, lumbering, and iron and steel production. A former Confederate observed that many of the planters had been drawn to the cities: "The talent, the energy, the ambition, that formerly sought expression in the management of great estates and the control of hosts of slaves, now seeks a field of action in trade, [and] manufacturing enterprises."

Southern towns vied with each other to attract textile mills and other manufacturing plants. The number of textile mills increased sharply. Unlike the prewar plants, most were equipped with efficient machinery. Industrialists built modern iron and steel plants near Richmond, Chattanooga, and Birmingham. Throughout the South, lumber and flour mills, tanneries, and harness works were also established in the postwar years. In North Carolina the tobacco industry mushroomed. Largely as a result of the initiative of James B. Duke, North Carolina tobacco was sold widely throughout the country as chewing and smoking tobacco and as snuff. In the 1880's Duke secured a patent on the "ready-rolled" cigarette. As a result, he changed smoking habits, revolutionized the tobacco industry, and amassed a large fortune.

Industrialism stimulates the growth of cities. The development of new industries encouraged people to move to southern towns and cities. Around some of the new factories, particularly the textile plants, "mill towns" developed. The factory workers lived in company-owned houses and traded at company-owned stores. Since the mills paid wages in the form of rent and credit at the stores, these factory workers fared little better than rural sharecroppers.

The new textile mills and tobacco plants made cities out of many smaller towns. Meanwhile, the older cities like Nashville, New Orleans, Atlanta, and Savannah increased in size. The growth of the iron and steel industry led to the founding of a completely new city, Birmingham, Alabama, in the 1870's. Within twenty years, Birmingham had grown to 26,000 and already was calling itself the "Pittsburgh of the South." Nevertheless, despite this rapid industrial and urban growth, by 1900 only 18 per cent of the South's population lived in cities of 2500 people or more.

Negroes are barred from southern industry. Most of the factory jobs in the South were held by white people. The factory owners encouraged "poor whites" to come to the towns and cities, and they hired women and children as well as men. But almost no Negroes succeeded in finding factory jobs. The southern whites sought to keep Negro "hands" at work in the fields. Although many Negroes moved to the urban centers, they worked as servants or manual laborers.

In the postwar years, southern cities experienced the accelerated growth that had begun in northern cities at an earlier date. The development of Birmingham, Alabama, founded in 1871, was especially rapid.

By 1887, Birmingham had busy coke ovens (above) and soon became the iron and steel center of the "New South," a position which it still holds today. As in other cities, business and industry have begun to move into suburban areas. The industrial park pictured at right is just a few minutes' drive from the heart of Birmingham.

Negroes make advances in education. The strongest desire of many freedmen was to secure an education. Booker T. Washington, a Negro leader, said of this longing: "It was a whole race trying to go to school. Few were too young, and none too old, to make the attempt to learn. As fast as any kind of teachers could be secured, not only were day-schools filled, but night-schools as well."

The Freedmen's Bureau had established the first schools for Negroes. Aided by northern religious and charitable groups, it spent more than five million dollars on its educational program. State legislatures had appropriated state funds for Negro schools, but the sums were reduced after southern whites regained control of state and local governments. A few institutions of higher education for Negroes were started, thanks in large part to the contributions of wealthy Northerners. The most important of these were Atlanta and Fisk Universities and Hampton and Tuskegee Institutes.

Negroes' civil rights are restricted. Soon after federal troops were withdrawn from the South, Negroes began to lose the rights guaranteed them by the Fourteenth and Fifteenth Amendments and the Civil Rights Acts. At first the terrorism of the Ku Klux Klan kept them from voting. In time, white Southerners found other ways to hold down the Negro vote. Ballot boxes were stuffed with illegal votes, Negro communities were unfairly redistricted, and Negroes were not informed about the location of voting places. Moreover, discrimination was practiced against Negroes who traveled by railroad and who patronized hotels, restaurants, and theaters. The Supreme Court upheld this kind of discrimination with its decision in the Civil Rights Cases (1883). The Court ruled that the Fourteenth Amendment prevented *states* from discriminating against

Negroes. But, said the Court, the Amendment did not apply to private individuals or companies such as the railroad lines and owners of hotels, restaurants, and theaters. In effect, therefore, the Supreme Court rejected the Civil Rights Act of 1875.[4]

Southern state and local laws discriminate against Negroes. During the 1890's and the early 1900's, southern legislatures and city councils passed so-called "Jim Crow" laws,[5] making racial discrimination legal and compulsory. To keep Negroes from voting, the legislatures required voters to pay a poll tax or to prove that they could read and interpret passages from the state constitution. Poor, uneducated whites could get around these laws by means of the so-called *grandfather clause* in southern state constitutions. If a man could not meet the property and educational tests, he could still vote if he had been eligible to do so on January 1, 1867, or if he was the son or grandson of such a voter. (Negroes had not been eligible to vote at that time.) Some southern states passed *white primary* laws, which banned Negroes from voting in Democratic primary elections. These and other devices to keep Negroes from the polls violated the Fourteenth and Fifteenth Amendments. Nevertheless, Congress took no steps to reduce southern representation, as provided in the second section of the Fourteenth Amendment. The term "Solid South" came into use because in election after election white Southerners voted solidly Democratic, while Negroes were generally barred from voting.

Other "Jim Crow" state and local laws made segregation compulsory. Separate schools for Negroes and whites, already an accepted practice, became compulsory in the 1880's. Segregation spread to railroads, theaters, hospitals, cemeteries, parks, and beaches. City councils approved ordinances requiring segregated housing and even separate drinking fountains.

[4] It should be remembered that Negroes in the North also suffered from discrimination, especially in schools, housing, and employment. In fact, most of the cases that led to the 1883 decision had originated in the North.

[5] The term "Jim Crow" was applied to Negroes as early as the 1830's. Its origin is uncertain.

The Supreme Court approves "separate but equal" facilities. In time the Supreme Court had to rule on the constitutionality of "Jim Crow" laws. By far the most important case was *Plessy v. Ferguson* (1896). Eight of the nine justices upheld a Louisiana law requiring "separate but equal" accommodations for Negro and white passengers on the railroads. Laws requiring separation of the races, said the Court, "in places where they are liable to be brought into contact do not necessarily imply the inferiority of either race to the other." Justice John Marshall Harlan, however, dissented from the majority opinion. He wrote:

Our Constitution is color-blind, and neither knows nor tolerates classes among citizens. In respect of civil rights, all citizens are equal before the law. . . . The destinies of the two races in this country are indissolubly linked together, and the interests of both require that the common government of all shall not permit the seeds of race hate to be planted under the sanction of law.

Not until the middle of the twentieth century, as we shall see in later chapters, would Justice Harlan's view finally prevail. The Supreme Court then overturned the doctrine of "separate but equal," having earlier declared unconstitutional the grandfather clause (1915) and the white primary (1944). In the 1960's a constitutional amendment banned the poll tax in federal elections, and Congress passed new civil rights laws to protect Negro voting rights and guarantee Negroes equal access to public accommodations.

Booker T. Washington speaks for the Negroes. The leading spokesman for the Negroes in the New South was Booker T. Washington. Born a slave in Virginia in 1856, he acquired enough schooling to be admitted to Hampton Institute. In 1881 he founded Tuskegee Institute in Alabama. As principal of that school, he advocated vocational training for Negroes. Washington believed that the Negroes had to prove their economic worth to the New South before the whites would restore their social and political rights. He felt, therefore, that the schools should prepare Negroes to be

Booker T. Washington overcame heavy odds in his struggle for education. At a time when few opportunities were open to Negroes, he urged them to concentrate on education and learning a vocation.

good farmers, mechanics, and factory workers. Said Washington:

I would set no limits to the attainments of the Negro in arts, in letters or statesmanship, but I believe that the surest way to reach those ends is by laying the foundation in the little things of life that lie immediately about one's door. I plead for industrial education and development for the Negro not because I want to cramp him, but because I want to free him.

In 1895 Booker T. Washington delivered a speech at the Cotton States and International Exposition in Atlanta. It was the first time that a Negro had spoken to a large mixed audience in the South. Everyone waited to hear what he would say about the Negro's separate status. "In all things that are purely social," Washington said, "we can be as separate as the fingers, yet one as the hand in all things essential to mutual progress." Perhaps this was the only position a responsible Negro leader could take in 1895. But a few restless, well-educated Negroes resented Washington's "Atlanta Compromise." In the early 1900's

they would spearhead a movement to win not only equal economic opportunities for Negroes but equal social and political rights as well (page 580).

▶ CHECK-UP

1. What happened to cotton planting after the war? What industries were developed? Where were factory workers recruited?

2. How were the Negroes' civil rights restricted? How did the Supreme Court rule on Jim Crow laws in "Plessy v. Ferguson"?

3. What advances were made in Negro education? What type of education was stressed by Booker T. Washington?

. . . .

Clinching the Main Ideas in Chapter 18

Change and discord characterized the decade of reconstruction following the end of the Civil War. Southern farms, towns and cities, and railroads and bridges had to be rebuilt or repaired. Relations between the former Confederate states and the rest of the Union had to be clarified. And the position of the freedmen had to be defined. In 1865 it was uncertain whether southern whites would be allowed to establish the new order, or whether the Radical Republicans in Congress would impose their views on the South. Though some of the Radical Republicans were genuinely concerned with Negro rights, others were more concerned with building Republican strength in the South.

Lincoln and Johnson proposed moderate reconstruction plans which would have permitted most of the southern whites to participate in rebuilding their state and local governments. But the Radical Republicans considered this program too generous to the whites and unfair to the freedmen. They pushed through Congress their own brand of reconstruction. The Radical program provided for military control of the South and prevented the states from interfering with Negroes' civil rights. So long as federal troops were stationed in the South, Negroes and their white allies — carpetbaggers and scalawags — controlled the state legislatures. During these years they passed some unwise laws but also initiated many badly needed reforms in the state governments.

In the 1870's southern whites gradually regained political control. An Amnesty Act allowed former Confederates to vote again, the Ku Klux Klan and similar organizations frightened Negroes away from the polls, and the last federal troops were withdrawn in 1877. During the next two decades a "New South" emerged as manufacturing increased and cities grew rapidly. The new factories hired whites, however, and most of the Negroes remained sharecroppers on the land. State and local governments built a wall of restrictions around the Negroes during these years. It became extremely difficult for Negroes to vote, and they were segregated from whites in nearly all areas of life.

Chapter Review

Terms to Understand

1. Thirteenth Amendment
2. Fourteenth Amendment
3. Fifteenth Amendment
4. Radical Republicans
5. Moderate Republicans
6. Freedmen's Bureau
7. "10 per cent plan"
8. Wade-Davis Bill
9. grandfather clause
10. "Jim Crow" laws
11. white primary
12. carpetbagger
13. sharecropper
14. black codes
15. Amnesty Act
16. poll tax
17. reconstruction
18. scalawag
19. Tenure of Office Act
20. *Plessy v. Ferguson*
21. *Civil Rights Cases* (1883)
22. Ku Klux Klan
23. Civil Rights Act of 1866
24. Reconstruction Act of 1867

What Do You Think?

1. Why did sharecropping develop on many southern plantations after the Civil War?
2. What were the implications for white workers of the development of industry in the South? For Negroes? Why?
3. Why did the Radical Republicans gradually lose control of the southern state governments during the 1870's?
4. When the South produced four million bales of cotton in 1860, the slogan was "Cotton Is King." In 1890 eight million bales were produced. Was cotton still "King"? Why?
5. What was the significance of the Supreme Court's decisions in the *Civil Rights Cases* (1883) and *Plessy v. Ferguson* (1896)? On what grounds have these decisions been reversed in recent years?

Using Your Knowledge of History

1. In a two-column chart, compare the Lincoln-Johnson and the congressional plans of reconstruction.
2. Debate: *Resolved,* That the Radical Republicans went too far in identifying the interests of their party with the welfare of their country.
3. In 1895 Booker T. Washington made the so-called "Atlanta Compromise." What was it? Present (a) the reasons which you think moved him to suggest such a compromise at that time and (b) the grounds on which it could be criticized then and now.

Extending Your Knowledge of History

John Hope Franklin has written an authoritative volume entitled *Reconstruction After the Civil War.* Also useful is Kenneth Stampp's *The Era of Reconstruction.* An older book, *The Critical Year* by Howard K. Beale, concentrates on the events of 1866. Paul Buck describes the gradual reconciliation of North and South in *Road to Reunion, 1865–1900.* Booker T. Washington's autobiography, *Up From Slavery,* is interesting, and so too is C. Vann Woodward's study of segregation, *The Strange Career of Jim Crow.* Lee After the War by Marshall Fishwick is an interesting study of the southern leader's response to the postwar situation. Two good articles in *American Heritage* treat the angry political battles of reconstruction: "When Congress Tried to Rule" by Milton Lomask (December, 1959), and "Why They Impeached Andrew Johnson" by David Donald (December, 1956).

CHAPTER 19

Exhibit at Centennial Exposition

American Standards Change in the Gilded Age

No period so thoroughly ordinary had been known in American politics since Christopher Columbus first disturbed the balance of American society. . . . The moral law had expired. . . .

HENRY ADAMS, "THE EDUCATION OF HENRY ADAMS"

1868–1883

The changes and problems experienced by the South (Chapter 18) were not the only ones to develop in the years after the Civil War. Other changes and problems affected different sections of the country as well as the nation as a whole. In part, these changes and problems were related to the expansion of industry; in part, they resulted from a general lowering of moral standards. This condition is reflected in the chapter quotation from *The Education of Henry Adams*. The grandson of President John Quincy Adams, Henry Adams considered starting a career in public life. But he was so disillusioned by the lowered tone of

American society during the postwar years that he decided against a public career.

In national politics this decline in standards reached a climax during President Grant's administration (1869–1877). Grant proved to be a disappointing President. Unskilled in politics, he failed to establish his authority over the Republican Party. Moreover, he was victimized by unscrupulous businessmen and corrupt officeholders. As a result, Grant's eight years in the White House were marked by few achievements and tarnished by many scandals. His successors, Rutherford B. Hayes and Chester A. Arthur, tried to carry out reforms. But political spoilsmen, once in office, did not easily yield their power. Corruption also existed in city and state governments and among businessmen as well.

When Mark Twain wrote a novel about the postwar exploits of an ambitious businessman, he entitled it *The Gilded Age.* Historians have used the phrase ever since to describe American life in the 1870's and 1880's. On the positive side, this period was marked by vast industrial expansion and the development of farm land and mineral resources in the West. Though foreign affairs aroused little interest, there were several important developments. The United States purchased Alaska and showed new interest in islands in the Pacific. And, by calling for the removal of French troops from Mexico, our government reaffirmed the Monroe Doctrine.

1 *An Able General Makes a Disappointing President*

The country enters a period of economic expansion. In the years immediately after the Civil War, the North and the West experienced tremendous growth and expansion. By the 1870's even the South was beginning to share this growth. Many new railroads were built, and several lines extended to the Pacific coast. Iron and steel production increased in quantity and improved in quality. New industries, such as oil refining, gained national importance.

- -

CHAPTER FOCUS

1. An able general makes a disappointing President.

2. Grant serves a second term.

3. Hayes and Arthur undertake reforms.

4. Foreign affairs arouse little interest.

The industrial boom was accompanied by a rapid expansion of agriculture in the prairie states. Cattlemen fattened their herds on the grasslands farther west; while in the mountains, miners developed the country's rich mineral resources. War veterans provided much of the man power for this great expansion. In the 1870's and '80's, as in the prewar years, immigration brought additional workers to farms and factories. (These developments are more fully discussed in Chapters 20–22.)

This rapid economic expansion provided many opportunities to make money. Not all Americans, of course, were able to amass fortunes. Indeed, many farmers and laborers felt the pinch of hard times. But hundreds of Americans pioneering in new business ventures grew wealthy.

Corruption spreads. Unfortunately, the tide of prosperity was accompanied by dishonest practices and political corruption. Not a few stockbrokers and financiers cheated each other and small investors as well. Many businessmen used ruthless measures to drive competitors out of the field. A number of state legislatures voted large sums to build railroads that were never completed. And many public officials accepted bribes.

The Tweed Ring robs New York City. A notorious example of political corruption during the postwar years was the Tweed Ring in New York City. The leader of this band of thieving politicians was William M. ("Boss") Tweed, head of Tammany Hall, which controlled the city's Democratic organization. Tweed came to power by courting both the city's poor and its business leaders. He also had close connections with Republican politicians and shady financial promoters. In time, the Tweed Ring won control of the city council, installed a Tammany mayor, and even influenced the state government.

Tweed and his accomplices stole millions of dollars from New York City. Contractors agreed to pad their bills, at first only by 10 per cent but later by as much as 85 per cent. The "profits" went to the members of the Ring, with a generous cut for the contractor. In one transaction the city paid 179,000 dollars for forty chairs and three tables; in another, a plasterer drew 2,870,000 dollars for nine months' work. The taxpayers complained; the New York *Times* printed bitterly critical editorials; and Thomas Nast drew stinging cartoons for *Harper's Weekly*. But Boss Tweed merely replied, "What are you going to do about it?"

New Yorkers could do nothing about the Tweed Ring until 1871. Then, a member of the Ring who had fallen out with Tweed gave incriminating evidence to the *Times*. This information broke the Ring's power.

Some of the grafters fled, but others were prosecuted by a prominent attorney, Samuel J. Tilden, and sentenced to prison terms. Tilden won national acclaim when he convicted Tweed. Though other cities had "rings" and "bosses" during the Gilded Age, none was as infamous as the Tweed Ring.

Grant becomes President. Against the background of economic expansion, political corruption, and turmoil over reconstruction of the South, the American people elected General Grant President. They hoped that he, like General Washington, would be able to create order out of chaos. What they

THE AMERICAN SCENE

POLITICS IN THE GILDED AGE

as seen by THOMAS NAST

The Republican and Democratic Parties owe their traditional symbols — the elephant and the donkey — to cartoons by Thomas Nast (below). Nast not only advanced the art of political cartooning but, with drawings like the one at right, publicized the reformers' fight against corruption in government. In the cartoon at lower right, entitled "The Tammany Tiger Loose," Nast likened Tammany under the Tweed Ring to a brutal animal mauling the victimized republic while Boss Tweed and his henchmen enjoy the spectacle.

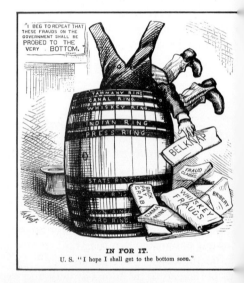

"I BEG TO REPEAT THAT THESE FRAUDS ON THE GOVERNMENT SHALL BE PROBED TO THE VERY BOTTOM."

IN FOR IT.
U. S. "I hope I shall get to the bottom soon."

failed to realize was that Grant, unlike Washington, had almost no political experience. Furthermore, Grant cared little about the Radical-Moderate quarrel over reconstruction. At first he had tended to side with Johnson, but later he broke with the President. The Radical Republicans then began courting Grant. Long before 1868, it was a foregone conclusion that the Republicans would nominate the General. At the Republican convention, Grant was chosen unanimously on the first ballot, and he accepted the nomination with a brief speech. One sentence seemed to sum up the public mood in 1868: "Let us have peace."

To run against the famous general, the Democrats chose Horatio Seymour, the wartime governor of New York. Seymour was not well-known to the voters, and he publicly disagreed with the Democratic promise to lower the tariff. Yet the Democrats did surprisingly well in the election. Though Seymour won only eight states, the popular vote was very close. As you read in Chapter 18, Grant's narrow margin in the popular vote prompted the Radical Republicans to pass the Fifteenth Amendment (page 391).

Grant is disappointing as President. In the White House, Ulysses S. Grant showed few of the qualities of leadership which had distinguished him on the field of battle. Though personally honest, he failed to keep a close check on government officials. Members of his Cabinet and even his own brother became involved in corrupt deals. Grant's strong sense of personal loyalty was a further disadvantage in the presidency, largely because he showed poor judgment in choosing his friends. Some of his army companions were appointed to positions of responsibility which they were incapable of filling. Grant's admiration for wealthy men caused him to fall into the clutches of Jay Gould and Jim Fisk, two notorious financial speculators. From other businessmen he accepted lavish gifts, including a completely furnished house in Philadelphia.

For political advice, Grant depended on ruthless, ambitious men, who were chiefly interested in furthering their own power. As a result, the spoilsmen of the Republican Party soon dominated him. Grant's Cabinet appointments likewise reflected his political shortcomings. As heads of most of the departments he named men of mediocre ability. The one exception was Hamilton Fish, Secretary of State. Fish demonstrated great skill in the conduct of foreign affairs (page 413), and he could have given the President sound advice on other problems. Unfortunately, Grant put his trust in the less competent members of his official family.

Civil service reform is considered. As the size of the government expanded and the number of employees increased, the appointment of inferior men to federal offices became a more serious problem. Even the most diligent department head could not check on the qualifications of all office seekers or resist the pressures of powerful politicians. Hence there were suggestions that the government adopt the British practice of selecting officials by competitive examinations. Senator Carl Schurz of Missouri introduced a bill to this effect, but it was killed by spoilsmen in Congress.

In 1871, however, Grant appointed a Civil Service Commission. This Commission recommended the establishment of competitive examinations, and at first President Grant seemed to agree. But in his second term the President deserted the civil service reformers and sided with those who regarded government jobs as rewards for political service. When Congress refused to appropriate funds for the Commission, Grant took no action. That was the end of civil service reform during the Grant administration.

Changes are made in taxes and tariffs. During Grant's first term Congress responded to widespread demands that wartime taxes be lifted. All internal taxes except those on liquor, tobacco, and a few other items were repealed. The income tax was also abandoned. But attempts to lower the wartime tariff rates ran into stubborn resistance from manufacturers. During most of his first term, Grant signed measures that raised tariff rates. Then, as the election of 1872 approached, some Republicans argued that a small cut would be politically wise. So Grant signed a bill reducing tariff rates. Three years later a new tariff act raised rates to their previous levels.

Grant's poor judgment leads to Black Friday. Grant's lack of insight into financial problems was revealed in the gold conspiracy of 1869. Jay Gould had devised a bold plan to buy most of the available gold in the country and then make a huge profit by forcing up the price of that metal. But he knew that the United States Treasury each month released several million dollars' worth of gold in exchange for government bonds. Unless the government sale of gold could be stopped, this scheme to corner the gold supply would fail.

Learning that the President might suspend the sale of gold to raise prices on farm commodities, Gould enlisted the help of Jim Fisk in his scheme. Both bought gold frantically. In order to persuade others to buy, Fisk implied that Grant was in on the scheme. In five days, the price of gold went up almost 17 per cent. Bankers and merchants, who needed gold to settle their international accounts, were desperate. They made frantic appeals to Grant, who seemed genuinely confused by the whole situation. Finally, Grant approved orders to sell government gold.

Meanwhile, Gould had been warned by the President's brother-in-law that the Secretary of the Treasury was going to start selling gold again. Gould, therefore, quietly began to sell out his holdings while Fisk was still feverishly buying. The crash came on September 24, 1869, a day remembered as "Black Friday." The price of gold dropped sharply, the stock market was badly shaken, and the country experienced a brief financial panic. Although a congressional investigating committee later held that Grant was not a party to the conspiracy, his social relations with Gould and Fisk shocked many people.

The Crédit Mobilier scandal involves high officials. Another scandal involved the construction of a transcontinental railroad. In 1862, Congress had approved land grants and loans to help two railroads undertake this gigantic task. The Union Pacific would build westward from Omaha, Nebraska, and the Central Pacific would build eastward from Sacramento, California (page 442). The chief stockholders of the Union Pacific formed a separate construction company called the *Crédit Mobilier* and voted this company profitable contracts.

The Crédit Mobilier was headed by Oakes Ames, a congressman from Massachusetts. His job was to distribute shares of stock among members of Congress where they would "do the most good" in securing legislative favors and preventing

---

Literature in the Gilded Age

The literature of the Gilded Age reflected the decline in standards that characterized American life during that period. Unlike the great literary output of the northern states in the years before the Civil War, the books of the 1870's and '80's were mostly mediocre.

Two exceptions were the works of Walt Whitman and Mark Twain (pages 314 and 432). In "Democratic Vistas" (1871), Whitman scored the "corruption, bribery, falsehood" that he saw in government and business. He charged that "society, in these States, is canker'd, crude, superstitious, and rotten." To Whitman the country's moral conscience seemed "either entirely lacking or seriously enfeebled." Mark Twain made similar charges in his novel "The Gilded Age" (1873), written with Charles

Dudley Warner. The leading character in this novel is Colonel Sellers, a businessman desperately eager to make a fortune by any means. In describing Colonel Sellers' experiences in Washington, Mark Twain expressed his scorn for the politicians of the 1870's.

But far more popular than either Whitman or Twain at this time were writers who followed the so-called "genteel tradition." These authors, who dealt with themes that were socially "proper" and often sentimental, avoided mention of any unpleasant reality. One of them referred to realistic writing as a "breath blown from the slums." Today the books of the genteel tradition are seldom read, but the works of Whitman and Mark Twain are classics of American literature.

interference with the Crédit Mobilier. Influential politicians were permitted to buy the stock at bargain prices. They were, of course, pleased with their bargain when the Crédit Mobilier paid annual dividends as high as 350 per cent. But in 1872 a stockholder who had quarreled with Ames turned over some damaging letters to the New York *Sun*. A congressional investigation then discovered that many prominent politicians, including Vice-President Colfax, were involved in the Crédit Mobilier. The committee recommended Ames' expulsion from Congress, but he denied that he had done anything wrong. His colleagues in the House merely passed a mild resolution of censure.

▶ CHECK-UP

1. How did the North and West prosper after the Civil War? What kinds of corruption accompanied this prosperity?

2. How did Boss Tweed build up a following in New York City? How did the Tweed Ring rob the people?

3. Why was Grant ineffective as President? What changes were made in taxation? In tariffs? What was Black Friday? The Crédit Mobilier scandal?

- - - - - - - - - - - - - - - - - - - -

2 *Grant Serves a Second Term*

As the election of 1872 approached, many people felt dissatisfied with Grant and his administration. In particular, a small band of Republicans, calling themselves Liberal Republicans, opposed Grant's re-election.

The Liberal Republicans oppose Grant. The Liberal Republicans held a convention in Cincinnati in May, 1872. The delegates who assembled there were a strange collection. Some were disgruntled politicians who had failed to get all the patronage they wanted from Washington. Others,

including a number of Democrats, were dissatisfied with reconstruction and thought the time had come to withdraw the troops from the South. Some delegates considered tariff reduction the critical issue; some were chiefly concerned with civil service reform. Still others were disturbed by the low level of Grant's appointments and the rumors of scandals. Opposition to Grant was the one thing on which all the Liberal Republicans agreed.

The strongest candidate to oppose Grant would have been Charles Francis Adams, former minister to Great Britain. Instead, the Liberal Republicans nominated Horace Greeley, the editor of the New York *Tribune*. Greeley was scarcely the best candidate to unite the opposition to President Grant. As an outspoken abolitionist, Radical Republican, and advocate of high tariffs, Greeley had acquired many enemies. The Liberal Republicans adopted a platform that condemned Grant, called for a less severe reconstruction policy in the South, and urged civil service reform.

Grant wins the 1872 election. When the regular Republicans renominated Grant, the Democrats faced a difficult decision. The only practical way to defeat Grant was to join with the Liberal Republicans. Yet Greeley had attacked the Democratic Party for years, and his views on the tariff clashed with those of most Democrats. It was with considerable reluctance, therefore, that the Democratic convention nominated Greeley and endorsed the Liberal Republican platform.

Greeley conducted a spirited campaign. He traveled widely and spoke frequently, doing his best to discuss the issues of the election. When the ballots were counted, however, Grant had an overwhelming majority of both the popular and the electoral vote. Greeley called himself the "worst beaten man who ever ran for high office."

The Panic of 1873 sweeps the country. President Grant had barely begun his second term when the country was plunged into a panic and depression. Signs of trouble had appeared as early as 1871, when more businesses than usual had failed. Devastating fires that swept Chicago that

AMERICANS AT LEISURE

as seen by WINSLOW HOMER

Though best-known for his ocean scenes, Winslow Homer sketched and painted many aspects of American life. During the Civil War, he had drawn battlefield scenes for a magazine. But in "The Fishing Party" (top) and "The Croquet Match" (left), Homer caught the carefree feeling of people enjoying a summer afternoon.

year and Boston in 1872 had used up close to 300 million dollars in insurance funds. Americans also had overinvested in railroads and factories. Another difficulty was that this country was dependent on European credit, and Europe had a depression from 1873 to 1878.

In September, 1873, the closing of the famous banking house of Jay Cooke and Company touched off the Panic of 1873. The New York Stock Exchange suspended trading for ten days "to save [Wall] Street from utter ruin." Soon factories stopped production, and farm mortgages were foreclosed. Thousands of industrial workers and farmers became destitute. Private charities and some city governments established soup lines to keep the unemployed and their families from starving.

The Panic of 1873 affected the outcome of the congressional elections of 1874. The Democrats, who blamed the Republicans for the country's economic ills, gained control of the House of Representatives for the first time since the Civil War. The Democrats likewise made gains in the Senate.

Greenbacks become a political issue. An important financial issue during Grant's second administration concerned the future of the greenbacks. Greenbacks, you will recall, were paper money issued by the Union government to raise funds during the Civil War (page 368). This paper money was not backed by gold or silver but depended for its value on the government's promise to redeem it. The value of greenbacks rose and fell, therefore, with the fortunes of war.

After the war, the government began gradually to *retire* the greenbacks; that is, they were taken out of circulation as they came into the Treasury. This policy aroused the opposition of debtors. Western farmers who had borrowed money to buy land and machinery, as well as wage earners and small businessmen who were in debt, wanted the government to keep the greenbacks in circulation. They argued that greenbacks expanded the volume of money in circulation and thus made it easier for them to repay their financial obligations.

Creditors, on the other hand, favored the retirement of the greenbacks. They believed that currency should be based on hard money, which did not rise and fall in value. Creditors were generally bankers, merchants, and large industrialists.

Greenbacks had become an issue in the election of 1868. During the campaign the Democrats had promised, if elected, to keep the greenbacks in circulation. The Democrats in general believed that the government should increase the supply of money fast enough to keep pace with or even outstrip the production of goods. Grant and the Republicans, however, opposed this viewpoint. After their victory in the election, the Republicans in Congress passed a measure which pledged the government to repay its bonds in "coin or its equivalent."

The government promises to redeem greenbacks in gold. As a result of the Panic of 1873 and the depression which followed, debtors asked Congress to issue more greenbacks. When the congressional elections in 1874 brought victory to the Democrats (page 406), the Republicans decided to act while they still controlled both houses of Congress. In 1875 they passed a Resumption Act, providing that after January 1, 1879, the government would exchange gold dollars for greenbacks. This act also required the treasury to build up a gold reserve for this purpose, and it set a limit on the number of greenbacks which could remain in circulation.

The Resumption Act represented a compromise between the views of creditors and those of debtors. Though the greenbacks stayed in circulation, their value was increased and kept constant by the gold reserve. But many of those who favored greenbacks and cheaper money were disappointed with the Resumption Act. They formed a Greenback Party and ran presidential candidates in 1876, 1880, and 1884. This party, however, never polled as much as 4 per cent of the popular vote.

More scandals are uncovered. Grant's second term, like his first, was troubled by instances of selfishness and corruption. In 1873 Congress passed a "Salary Grab Act," which increased congressional salaries by 50 per cent and, furthermore, made the raise effective for the preceding two years. The public raised such a storm of criticism that Congress repealed the measure the next year. A St. Louis newspaper exposed a "whiskey ring" which had defrauded the government of millions of dollars in taxes on liquor. One member of the ring, a revenue officer, had presented Grant with a team of horses and had given a valuable piece of jewelry to the President's private secretary. The secretary was tried but won acquittal, chiefly through Grant's intervention in the trial. In still another scandal, Grant's Secretary of War, William Belknap, was found to have accepted bribes from an employee in the Indian service. When Congress threatened to impeach Belknap, he resigned and thus escaped conviction.

Republicans divide into Stalwarts and Halfbreeds. These scandals tended to divide the Republican Party. The Liberal Republicans, who had rejected Grant as early as 1872, were joined by others alarmed at more recent evidence of widespread corruption. Moreover, persistent reports that Grant was considering a third term disturbed many Republicans.

As the election of 1876 approached, two factions within the Republican Party took shape. Those closest to Grant, and who hoped to secure a third term for the General, called themselves the *Stalwarts*. Their leader was Roscoe Conkling, Senator from New York. The Republicans who had parted company with Grant and his cronies were called *Halfbreeds*. Some were personal enemies of the Stalwarts, others were angry about the division of political jobs, and still others were concerned about honesty in government. The leader of the Halfbreeds was James G. Blaine, a Maine congressman. Determined to prevent Grant's renomination, Halfbreeds in the House of Representatives sponsored a resolution declaring that a third term would be "unwise, unpatriotic, and fraught with peril to our free institutions."

Hayes opposes Tilden in 1876. Taking the hint, Grant announced that after his term expired in March, 1877, he and his family would tour Europe. This left the Republicans free to select another candidate for the election of 1876. The Halfbreeds had enough strength to block the selection of Conkling or any other Stalwart. For their part, the Stalwarts produced damaging evidence of James G. Blaine's connections with a western railroad and thus prevented his nomination. Finally, the delegates agreed to name a compromise candidate, Rutherford B. Hayes, Governor of Ohio. Hayes was honest, had a good war record, and supported the Resumption Act and civil service reform. He had no ties with either the Stalwarts or Halfbreeds.

Encouraged by their gains in 1874, the Democrats were hopeful of victory when they gathered at their nominating convention. The delegates decided that their strongest candidate was Samuel J. Tilden of New York. Having broken the Tweed Ring, Tilden was carrying out reforms as governor of New York.

During the campaign, Democratic orators stressed the need for reform in government and called for improved relations between the North and South. Republican orators quoted their party platform, which called for civil service reform and continuation of the protective tariff. But most of their energy went into "waving the bloody shirt" — that is, accusing the Democrats of responsibility for the Civil War. The Republicans called the Democrats the "party of treason" while declaring themselves to be the "Grand Old Party" (GOP), which had saved the Union and promoted economic prosperity.

Election returns are disputed. On the morning after the election, it seemed certain that Tilden had won. The Republican campaign managers and most Republican newspapers conceded defeat. Tilden had a margin of 250,000 popular votes and had 184 undisputed electoral votes to 165 for Hayes. But the electoral returns from Florida, Louisiana, and South Carolina, as well as one vote from Oregon, were in dispute. To get a majority and thus win, Tilden needed only one of the 20 disputed electoral votes. Hayes, on the other hand, needed all of the electoral votes in question.

The dispute in Oregon was settled in favor of Hayes. In the three southern states, however, double sets of returns were forwarded to Washington. The carpetbag governments still in power in these states returned Republican electoral votes. But local Democrats, protesting that the elections had been unfair, sent Democratic electoral votes. The Democrats were especially angry about Louisiana, where Republican officials had thrown out enough so-called "fraudulent votes" to turn a Democratic majority of over 6000 into a Republican victory. Later research was to uncover "bare-faced skullduggery" on both sides, but many historians believe that Tilden probably should have had Florida's four electoral votes and Hayes the votes of the other states.

The election dispute is settled. Congress faced the problem of deciding which returns to accept. Although the Constitution provides for the opening and counting of the electoral votes before the combined houses of Congress, it fails to state exactly *who* should count the votes. For the next three months the Democratic House and the Republican Senate argued the point.

At last Congress broke the deadlock by creating an Electoral Commission to decide the dispute. The Commission included five representatives, five senators, and five Supreme Court justices. Of these, seven were Democrats, seven were Republicans, and one justice, David Davis of Illinois, was independent. But the election of Davis to the Senate upset the delicate balance of the

---

Waving the Bloody Shirt

In 1868 a Radical had displayed to Congress a nightshirt supposedly stained with the blood of an Ohio carpetbagger who had been beaten by Mississippi ruffians. Thereafter, whenever the Radicals asked for harsh legislation against the South, they were accused of "waving the bloody shirt." In the 1870's and '80's the Republicans "waved the bloody shirt" when they tried to revive wartime charges against the Democrats.

The year 1876 witnessed not only the disputed presidential election but also a great fair in Philadelphia to celebrate the nation's progress since the Declaration of Independence. Over eight million people visited this Centennial Exposition. Above is a view of the fair's Agricultural Building.

Electoral Commission. Another Supreme Court justice, a Republican, replaced Davis. The Commission divided along party lines and so, by a vote of eight to seven, gave all the disputed votes to Hayes.

To insure the Democrats' consent to this decision, the Republicans made certain promises. Hayes had already let it be known that he would withdraw the last of the federal troops from the South. In addition, he promised to put a Southerner in the Cabinet, to give Southerners more control over local patronage, and to grant subsidies for railroad construction in the South. In exchange for these promises, southern Democrats abandoned their protests and accepted the verdict of the Electoral Commission.

▶ CHECK-UP

1. What groups were included in the Liberal Republicans who opposed Grant's re-election? Who was their candidate? Why did the Democrats join with them?

2. What were the causes of the Panic of 1873? The results?

3. Why did greenbacks become an issue? What groups wanted them in circulation? Why? What solution was suggested in the Resumption Act?

4. Who were the Stalwarts? The Halfbreeds? Why did the Democrats expect to win the election of 1876? How did they lose it? What concessions were made to southern Democrats?

· · · · · · · · · · · · · · · · · · · ·

3 *Hayes and Arthur Undertake Reforms*

Hayes faces a difficult situation. In March, 1877, Congress declared Hayes the winner of the presidential contest by the narrow margin of 185 electoral votes to 184. But Hayes soon found that he was not to be judged on his own merits as President. Bitterly disappointed by Tilden's defeat, northern Democrats suspected Hayes of unduly influencing southern Democrats to accept the Electoral Commission's decision. The Democrats retained control of the House in 1876, and two years later they also won the Senate; thus Congress was hostile to the President. He even lacked the full support of his own party. The Stalwarts were disgruntled because they could not control Hayes. Conkling never missed an opportunity to refer to the President as "His Fraudulency" or "Rutherfraud" B. Hayes.

In spite of these obstacles, President Hayes went ahead with his program. He selected good men for his Cabinet. Carl Schurz became Secretary of the Interior, and a Halfbreed Senator from Ohio, John Sherman, was named Secretary of the Treasury. Most of the other members were former Liberal Republicans, and one was a

Southerner. Hayes promptly fulfilled his promise to withdraw federal troops from South Carolina and Louisiana. (They had already been pulled out of Florida.) Governments controlled by Democrats quickly replaced the reconstruction governments in those states.

Hayes tackles civil service reform. The President was in earnest about civil service reform. Early in his administration he proposed some general rules: (1) There would be no wholesale firing of competent officials; (2) job-seekers recommended by congressmen were to be investigated; (3) no relatives of the President's family were to be appointed; (4) no government officials could organize political parties or manage campaigns; (5) and no federal workers could be required to contribute to campaign funds. Despite this excellent start, few people shared the President's enthusiasm for civil service reform. Congress refused to pass the necessary laws to enforce the recommendations. Conkling and the Stalwarts laughed at Hayes' efforts and called them "snivel service reform."

Hayes did strike one damaging blow at the Stalwarts. He knew that Conkling's power rested on control of the New York Custom House, where the Stalwart leader had installed two of his supporters, Chester Arthur and Alonzo Cornell. They in turn gave Custom House jobs to political workers. Hayes instructed the Secretary of the Treasury to investigate the records of the New York Custom House. As a result, Arthur and Cornell were quickly removed from office.

"Soft-money" advocates become interested in silver. In currency matters, Hayes was a "hard-money" man. He had supported the Resumption Act in 1875, believing that it would hold the value of greenbacks steady. Actually, when that measure did go into effect in 1879, few people bothered to exchange their greenbacks for gold dollars. They knew that the value of the greenbacks was secured by the gold reserve in the Treasury. In fact, most of the "soft-money" people abandoned the greenback cause (except those who formed the Greenback Party). They turned their attention to silver and hoped that the government would inflate the currency (increase the amount of money in circulation) by minting silver dollars.

A great deal of silver had become available by the late 1870's. Since 1834, the government had been purchasing and coining both silver and gold at the ratio of 16 to 1. In other words, the government paid the same price for sixteen ounces of silver as it did for one ounce of gold. Because silver was actually worth slightly more on

---

Darwin on Evolution

One of the most important intellectual influences on American life in the years after the Civil War was the theory of evolution. Though the idea of gradual change in the natural world was not new, the proposition was clearly stated for the first time by Charles Darwin, an English scientist. In his book "On the Origin of Species" (1859), he argued that life on earth developed very slowly over millions of years. In this process, man was the most recent and highest form of life. Before the appearance of human life, the earth had been occupied by other species which managed to stay alive in a fiercely competitive world. The species which survived, said Darwin, were those best adapted to their environment — thus the phrase "survival of the fittest."

Darwin's theory of evolution had a tremendous impact on American thought. Some religious leaders argued that it was contrary to the Biblical story of the origins of the earth and the special creation of man by God. Yet in time many theologians accepted the theory of evolution and pointed out that it was God who started the remarkable process of selection in the first place.

Some social thinkers used the idea of "survival of the fittest" to explain the large fortunes amassed by industrialists in the late nineteenth century (page 459). Later on, however, many people felt that Darwin's theories of change should be used to support reform and social cooperation for the benefit of all mankind (page 482).

the open market, most of the American supply of that metal was sold to industrial users. In fact, the government purchased so little silver that a new coinage act in 1873 had made no mention of silver dollars. About the same time, however, rich deposits of silver were discovered in Colorado and Nevada. When the supply of silver increased, its price fell, and producers tried to sell the surplus metal to the government. Only then did they discover that the government was no longer coining silver dollars. Immediately they called the new coinage act the "Crime of '73."

Congress passes the Bland-Allison Act. Soft-money people, most of whom were in the West and South, demanded a change in the law. They found a spokesman in Richard P. Bland, a Democratic congressman from Missouri who had once been a Nevada miner. Bland, known as "Silver Dollar Dick," introduced a bill providing for the free or unlimited coinage of silver. But the hard-money men in Congress feared that this would lead to inflation by putting too much money in circulation. Led by Republican Senator William Allison of Iowa, they modified the bill to provide for *limited* coinage of silver.

The Bland-Allison Act (1878) required the treasury to buy, every month, two to four million dollars in silver bullion (the uncoined metal) at the market price. The bullion would be coined into dollars at the old ratio of 16 to 1. These dollars were to be accepted in payment of all debts. For convenience, silver certificates (paper dollars) would circulate in place of some of the "cartwheels," as the silver dollars were called. Because President Hayes considered the measure inflationary, he vetoed it; but Congress passed the law over his veto.

The Bland-Allison Act failed to live up to the expectations of the silver advocates and the debtors. Producers of silver were unhappy about the limit on government purchases. Debtors found that the new silver dollars were quickly absorbed by the rapidly expanding economy of the 1880's. Both groups, therefore, continued to demand *unlimited* coinage of silver.

The Republicans win in 1880. Hayes had announced in 1876 that he would serve only one term. As the election of 1880 drew near, he gave his support for the nomination to his Secretary of the Treasury, John Sherman, though most of the Halfbreeds preferred "Blaine of Maine." The Stalwarts, led by Roscoe Conkling, hoped to secure another term for Grant. The former President had returned from his tour of Europe and was obviously interested in the plans of the Stalwarts.

At the Republican convention, a deadlock developed in the balloting for Grant, Sherman, and Blaine. Then a stampede started for a "dark-horse" candidate — James A. Garfield, a congressman from Ohio and manager of the Sherman forces. On the thirty-sixth ballot, Blaine's delegates joined the Sherman delegates to nominate Garfield. As a concession to Conkling and the Stalwarts, the convention selected Chester Arthur for the vice-presidency.

The Democrats, weakened by the retirement of Tilden, chose as their presidential candidate General Winfield Scott Hancock of Pennsylvania. Hancock was not well-known, however, and failed to inspire the voters during the campaign. While the Democrats talked half-heartedly about civil service reform and tariff revision, the Republicans stood on their record of tariff protection and claimed credit for the return of prosperity. The Republicans also made much of Garfield's rise from modest beginnings. (He had once worked as a mule driver on the Ohio Canal.) In addition, Garfield and Arthur had the advantage of large campaign contributions from manufacturers who wanted high tariffs and from bankers who wanted sound money.

The popular vote in 1880 was closely divided. But Garfield carried the key states and won a decisive majority in the electoral college. The Republicans also gained control of Congress by a narrow margin.

Garfield clashes with the Stalwarts. During Garfield's brief administration, the bitter struggle between the Stalwarts and Halfbreeds continued. Garfield named Blaine as his Secretary of State and looked to him for advice. This angered Roscoe Conkling, who had carried New York State for the Republicans and thought he should be consulted on all appointments. The gap

Architecture during the late 1800's was advanced by such accomplishments as the Brooklyn Bridge, shown above before its completion in 1883, and the ten-story Home Insurance Building in Chicago (1884). This building, constructed with an iron and steel skeleton, is regarded as the first skyscraper.

between the President and the Stalwarts widened as many office seekers failed to win appointment.

In July, 1881, news flashed across the country that President Garfield had been attacked by an assassin. A disappointed, half-crazed office seeker named Charles Guiteau shot Garfield as he entered the Washington railroad depot. The assassin shouted: "I am a Stalwart and Arthur is President." Garfield lingered on, in constant pain, for two and a half months. When he died in September, Chester Arthur did become President.

Chester Arthur succeeds to the presidency. To the surprise of most observers, Arthur proved to be an able chief executive. Perhaps his sudden elevation to national leadership brought out untapped qualities. At any rate, he conducted the affairs of state ably and honestly. When irregularities were discovered in the Post Office Department, Arthur pressed charges against the guilty officials even though two of them were prominent Republican politicians. Moreover, he vetoed bills appro-

priating funds for unnecessary river and harbor improvements (known as "pork-barrel" legislation). His main achievement, however, came in civil service reform.

The Pendleton Act is passed. Shocked by Garfield's assassination, Americans for the first time gave serious attention to the recommendations of the civil service reformers. Under President Arthur's urging, Congress finally passed the Pendleton Act in 1883. This act forbade the assessment of federal officials for political contributions. It also authorized the President to appoint a Civil Service Commission, which would conduct competitive examinations for the classified service.[1] Appointments to such jobs and promotions within the federal service would be made from a list of eligible candidates who had taken the examinations.

The Pendleton Act at first applied only to some 15,000 workers in the customs districts and the post offices. This number amounted

[1] The *classified service* includes those jobs classified for appointment on merit.

to one seventh of the total government work force. But the act also gave the President authority to extend the number of jobs included in the civil service. Almost every chief executive since Arthur has done so until today civil-service regulations apply to nine tenths of all federal government employees.

▶ CHECK-UP

1. What groups made trouble for Hayes? What were his views on civil service reform?

2. Why did the coinage of silver become an issue in the '70's? What was the "Crime of '73"? What were the provisions of the Bland-Allison Act? Why did this measure fail to live up to the expectations of the soft-money interests?

3. How did Garfield gain the Republican nomination in 1880? How effective was Arthur as President? What were the provisions of the Pendleton Act?

. . . .

4 *Foreign Affairs Arouse Little Interest*

During the 1860's and '70's the American people were concerned about such internal problems as the war, reconstruction, economic expansion, the panic and depression, and the disputed election of 1876. Most people seemed to have little interest in foreign affairs. Nevertheless, in the years after 1865, the United States was involved in a number of international problems. Some of these had had their beginnings during the Civil War.

French plans in Mexico go awry. One of the more important issues during this period grew out of a violation by France of the Monroe Doctrine. Since its proclamation in 1823 (page 222), the Monroe Doctrine had seldom been challenged, largely because of the support given to its basic principles by Great Britain. But in 1861,

when the government of Mexico was in a state of confusion, Britain, France, and Spain sent vessels to Mexican ports to collect debts owed to them. Britain and Spain soon reached an agreement with Mexico and withdrew. But Napoleon III of France saw an opportunity to revive French colonial ambitions in the New World. He proceeded to establish an Austrian archduke, Maximilian, as his puppet ruler in Mexico. The United States, torn by war at this time, could do no more than protest to France against its military support of Maximilian.

When the Civil War ended, however, Secretary of State William H. Seward (who served throughout the Lincoln and Johnson administrations) took more vigorous action. An American army was sent to the Mexican border, and Seward requested Napoleon III to withdraw his troops from Mexico. Unwilling to risk war with the United States and worried about his relations with other European countries, Napoleon III decided to abandon his colonial venture. He recalled the French troops in 1867, leaving Maximilian to fend for himself. The Mexicans soon captured and executed the puppet ruler. Though Seward had not mentioned the Monroe Doctrine in the Maximilian affair, the American government had upheld its principles and thus strengthened the doctrine.

The "Alabama" claims are pressed. Another troublesome problem left over from the Civil War was a dispute with Great Britain over losses inflicted by Confederate commerce destroyers. These ships, including the *Alabama* (page 372), had been built in England and then allowed to "escape" into Confederate hands. At the end of the war, the United States demanded that Great Britain pay for the damage inflicted by these raiders. Some Americans even proposed that Britain surrender Canada to the United States.

President Grant and his Secretary of State, Hamilton Fish, inherited the unsettled problem of the *Alabama* claims. They had no sooner taken office than Charles Sumner, chairman of the Senate Committee on Foreign Relations, made matters worse with a sensational speech in

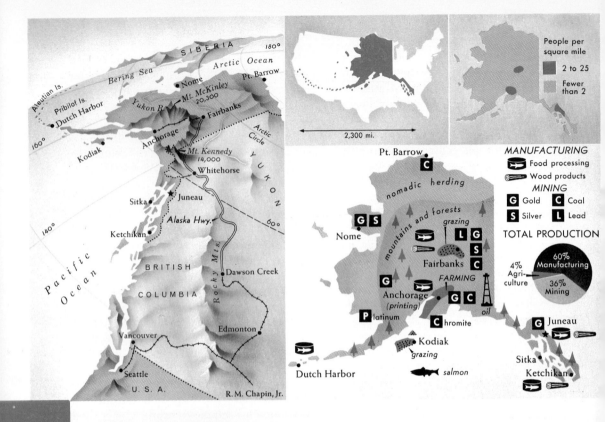

ALASKA: WHITE ELEPHANT TURNED GOLD

In 1867, Alaska seemed a barren wasteland. By contrast, modern Alaska is a land of enormous economic possibilities. Although vast in size, our last "frontier" state has as yet few people to develop its many resources. Note that agriculture accounts for a small percentage of total production. Look at the map on page 540 to compare Alaska's area and population with other outlying American territory.

the Senate. In addition to the direct damages, estimated at about fifteen million dollars, Sumner demanded two *billion* dollars in indirect damages. He based the claim for indirect damages on the theory that British aid to the Confederacy had prolonged the war. Since Sumner obviously hoped for the annexation of Canada in place of the two billion dollars, Secretary Fish was left in an embarrassing position. But Fish showed considerable skill in soft-pedaling Sumner's outrageous claim. At the same time he reminded the British that the United States could also build ships and release them to British enemies in future wars. Soon the British agreed to talk about the *Alabama* claims.

The Treaty of Washington is signed. In 1871 the two countries settled the dispute in the Treaty of Washington. By the terms of this treaty, Great Britain expressed regret for the escape of the Confederate raiders and agreed to submit the question of damages to arbitration. In 1872 an international court of arbitration awarded the United States fifteen and a half million dollars. The Treaty of Washington was an important step in establishing arbitration as a means for the peaceful settlement of international disputes. Moreover, it greatly improved American relations with both Great Britain and Canada.

Plans for expansion in the Caribbean fail. A new development during the post-Civil War years was the extension of United States influence into areas beyond the country's boundaries. Even after the expansionist era of the 1840's, some Americans hoped for the acquisition of still more territory. One such American was Secretary of State

Seward. He thought the United States should buy land in the Caribbean to be used as coaling stations for steamships and as naval bases for checking interference by European powers. But Congress rejected a treaty with the Dominican Republic that would have given the United States a base in that country. Meanwhile, Seward negotiated a treaty to purchase the Danish West Indies (now the Virgin Islands). The Senate also refused to ratify this treaty.

Seward purchases Alaska. In the Pacific, the policy of expansion was more successful. In 1867, Secretary of State Seward drew up a treaty with Russia for the purchase of Alaska at a cost of 7,200,000 dollars. Most Americans ridiculed this venture. Seward, they said, was buying "walrus-covered icebergs" in "a barren, worthless, God-forsaken region." Knowing that much of this opposition stemmed from ignorance, the Secretary of State waged an intensive campaign to inform Congress and the public about Alaska's rich resources. The facts impressed Senator Charles Sumner. With Sumner's help, the treaty was ratified, and the United States took possession of "Seward's Folly." For about two cents an acre, Americans had purchased some 600,000 square miles of territory rich in fish, furs, timber, coal, gold, and other resources.

The United States becomes interested in Pacific islands. In the same year that Alaska was purchased, the United States also took possession of the tiny Midway Islands, a thousand miles west of the Hawaiian Islands (map, page 540). Meanwhile, American traders and missionaries had become interested in Hawaii. Long before the Civil War, American clipper ships trading with China had stopped in Hawaii, and in time a number of Americans settled there. Many of them raised sugar cane and pineapples, which were marketed in the United States. In 1875, Secretary Hamilton Fish negotiated a trade agreement with Hawaii which permitted its sugar and other products to come into the United States duty-free. Twelve years later, a renewal of this treaty gave Pearl Harbor on the island of Oahu to the United States as a naval base. Secretary Fish and President

Grant also became interested in the Samoan Islands in the south Pacific. In the 1870's the United States leased a coaling station at Pago Pago (*pong'*oh *pong'*oh) on the island of Tutuila.

As yet, however, Americans showed little interest in expansion beyond the country's continental boundaries or in the scramble for colonies which most of the European powers had begun. Even the preliminary steps to extend American influence into the Pacific failed to arouse any degree of public enthusiasm.

▶ CHECK-UP

1. How did Napoleon III come to intervene in Mexican affairs? What happened when the United States asked him to withdraw French troops?

2. What were the "Alabama" claims? What extravagant claims were made for compensation? How was the dispute settled in the Treaty of Washington?

3. What efforts were made by Seward to expand into the Caribbean? With what results? How did this country acquire Alaska? Expand into the Pacific?

. . . .

Clinching the Main Ideas in Chapter 19

Grant's failure as President was a tragedy for the American people. A number of crucial issues faced the country during his administration — greenbacks, tariff policy, corruption in public life, and reconstruction. But Grant and the Stalwarts did little to solve these problems.

Nor were the Democrats or the reform-minded Republicans able to cope effectively with these issues. The Democrats were still handicapped by their record during the 1850's. Moreover, they offered a weak candidate for President in 1868 and again in 1872 when they joined with the Liberal Republicans to back Horace Greeley. In 1876 Samuel J. Tilden probably should have won the election, but the Electoral Commission awarded the disputed electoral votes to Rutherford Hayes. Both Hayes and

Chester Arthur were honest and able chief executives. During their administrations the power of the Stalwarts was broken, and Congress was sufficiently shocked by Garfield's assassination to approve civil service reforms.

Several important developments took place in foreign affairs during the Gilded Age. The Monroe Doctrine was strengthened when the United States protested French intervention in Mexico. Secretary of State Seward persuaded the Senate to approve the purchase of Alaska. And Hamilton Fish not only solved the crisis growing out of the *Alabama* claims but through the Treaty of Washington strengthened relations with Britain and Canada. For the most part, however, Americans during these years were not greatly interested in developments beyond their boundaries.

Chapter Review

Terms to Understand

1. Tweed Ring
2. Black Friday
3. "soft money"
4. Pendleton Act
5. Halfbreeds
6. Stalwarts
7. Panic of 1873
8. ratio of 16 to 1
9. Electoral Commission
10. silver certificate
11. Greenback Party
12. *Alabama* claims
13. Bland-Allison Act
14. Crédit Mobilier
15. Crime of '73
16. Resumption Act

What Do You Think?

1. Some critics of the American system of government hold that it does not raise the most able men to the presidency. What factors might they cite to support this criticism?

2. A government economic policy is likely to help one group more than another and may even seem to hurt some group. Can you give examples from this chapter?

3. What abuses were eliminated by civil service reforms? Does the merit system have any drawbacks?

4. President Hayes was handicapped because he lacked support both inside and outside of his own party. Why can this occur under the American system of government?

5. When "manifest destiny" was the cry, the will of a large segment of the population to expand seemed to outrun the willingness of the government to act. Yet when Secretary of State Seward sought to further expansion beyond this country's continental boundaries, the public showed little interest. How do you account for these reactions?

Using Your Knowledge of History

1. Senator Charles Sumner demanded two billion dollars in indirect damages from Britain, charging that British aid to the Confederacy had prolonged the Civil War. Write an editorial reaction to this claim such as might have appeared in a Canadian newspaper.

2. Imagine that you were the editor of a "reform" newspaper in 1882. Write an editorial demanding that Congress enact legislation reforming the civil service.

3. Report to the class on the French imperialist venture in Mexico during the 1860's. Bring out the situation in Europe as well as in America and what the French emperor hoped to achieve and why.

4. The Crédit Mobilier paid annual dividends as high as 350 per cent. Hold a class discussion in which you consider how such a payment was possible and what were the likely consequences. What would have been the annual return on 1000 dollars invested in this company's stock? What is considered a good return on a sound investment today?

Extending Your Knowledge of History

Matthew Josephson's *Politicos, 1865–1896*, provides a colorful account of political developments during this period. In *The Emergence of Modern America, 1865–1878*, Allan Nevins concentrates on economic and social developments. One of the best studies of Grant's administration is Nevins's *Hamilton Fish*. Mark Twain's *The Gilded Age* is a good introduction to this period. A recent effort to find a brighter side to the picture is *The Gilded Age: A Re-*

appraisal, edited by Wayne Morgan. Also see the article by Henry Darbee, "Mark Twain in Hartford: The Happy Years," in *American Heritage,* December, 1959. See also in *American Heritage* C. Vann Woodward's "The Low-est Ebb" (April, 1957) on the Grant administration; Louis W. Koenig's "The Election That Got Away" (October, 1960) on the dispute of 1876; and Robert L. Reynolds' "A Man of Conscience" (February, 1963) on Carl Schurz.

Analyzing Unit Five

1. What relationship between Negroes and whites was established in the southern states during 1865 and 1866? How was this relationship altered by the Radical Republicans after 1867? Why?

2. What was the reaction of southern whites to Radical reconstruction policy? How did they alter it after the federal troops were withdrawn? What was the Negro reaction, as expressed by Booker T. Washington, to the relationships which were established in the "New South"?

3. Had Lincoln lived, do you think he could have avoided the mistakes that were made during the reconstruction period? What do you think would have been a wise reconstruction policy? Why?

4. Henry Adams observed that "a great soldier might be a baby politician." Did President Grant's limitations as a political leader stem solely from the fact that he had been a soldier? What earlier military leader became a strong President? How do you account for the differences between these two men?

Unit 6 | Economic Change Transforms the Nation (1865-1900)

Grain elevators at New York railroad yards in the 1870's

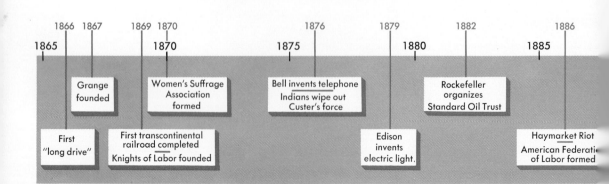

1865

1866 — Grange founded

1867

1869 — First transcontinental railroad completed / Knights of Labor founded

1870

1870 — Women's Suffrage Association formed

1875

1876 — Bell invents telephone / Indians wipe out Custer's force

1879 — Edison invents electric light.

1880

1882 — Rockefeller organizes Standard Oil Trust

1885

1886 — Haymarket Riot / American Federation of Labor formed

First "long drive"

One reason people lost interest in the reconstruction of the South and paid little attention to widespread political corruption was that there were so many other things to occupy their attention. The post-Civil War decades were marked by rapid industrial expansion and the settlement of the western plains. This mushrooming growth provided new opportunities for thousands of Americans and altered their lives in significant ways.

Slowed by the Civil War, the westward movement swelled to flood-tide proportions after 1865. Miners, ranchers, farmers, and townspeople arrived in such large numbers that nine western states were admitted to the Union between 1865 and 1900.

The country's industrial growth was even more spectacular. New industries, such as steel and oil, became "big business" almost overnight. Others — for example, flour-milling, meat-packing, lumber, textiles, and machine tools — increased in size and number, and their volume of production shot up dramatically. The booms in agriculture and industry were related, for farmers bought manufactured goods, particularly farm machinery, and sold their agricultural produce to food processors and ultimately to urban wage earners. Uniting the various segments of the economy were the railroads. By hauling raw materials and finished goods to all parts of the country, they played a vital role in the nation's economic expansion.

Most manufacturing and trade took place in cities. Urban growth during these decades, therefore, was as spectacular as the expansion of industry and agriculture. Opportunities to get ahead lured Americans from the countryside to expanding older cities and new towns. There they were joined by thousands of immigrants, who filled the ranks of unskilled labor. City governments were hard-pressed to cope with problems caused by the sudden growth. Inefficient city services and corrupt city officials were all too common.

In the cities wealthy people lived in luxury and the middle classes in relative comfort. But the poor people were crowded together in unsanitary and unsafe tenements. Low wages and inadequate housing constituted a heavy burden for most of the urban poor, many of them newcomers to this country. Yet, despite many problems, the United States made the transition to an industrial urban society more smoothly than did many other countries. The strains of adjustment did not destroy our basic framework of government. And during the early years of the twentieth century, remedies were found for many social injustices.

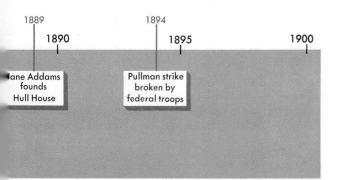

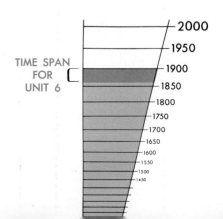

CHAPTER 20

Oklahoma land rush

Pioneers Settle the Last Frontier

We've broken land and cleared it, but we're tired of where we are.
They say that wild Nebraska is a better place by far.
There's gold in far Wyoming, there's black earth in Ioway,
So pack up the kids and blankets, for we're moving out today! . . .

STEPHEN VINCENT BENÉT, "WESTERN WAGONS"

1860–1890

It took the Pony Express ten days to carry the news of Lincoln's election from St. Joseph, Missouri, to Sacramento, California. The vast stretch of land over which the riders spurred their horses was still the Wild West of the frontier scouts and Plains Indians. Near Great Salt Lake in Utah, the Mormon settlement flourished; and Texas, California, and Oregon had become states. But elsewhere in the West there were only small bands of fur traders, miners, and soldiers.

Yet within the next 30 years the frontier was to vanish. By 1890 seventeen million people lived west of the Mississippi. The miners and cattlemen were followed by farmers expecting the western prairies and plains to be "a better place by far." Armed with modern rifles and protected by the United States Army, white people won control of the West from the Indians. Thousands of the country's original inhabitants died in battle or from disease as the white men completed the "taming" of the West.

Many of the farmers who staked out new homes in the West prospered. But others were bitterly disappointed. Drought, insect plagues, rising costs, falling prices for farm products, and the loneliness of the vast unsettled areas were among the problems that beset the pioneers. During the 1870's and 1880's western farmers formed new organi-

420

zations like the Grange and the Alliances, hoping to solve their problems by working together. The settling of the last frontier is a story of both achievement and heart-breaking disappointment.

1 Miners and Cattlemen Penetrate the West

Mining booms in the West. In 1859 most Americans were caught up in the heated quarrel over slavery and the coming presidential election. But Californians were more excited about new gold discoveries near Pike's Peak in the Colorado country. Thousands of "forty-niners" (page 292) left California for the new strike, and people from the Mississippi Valley and farther east soon joined them. Traveling in prairie schooners decorated with such signs as "Pike's Peak or bust!" these fortune hunters hoped to do as well as the forty-niners had in California. A few did strike it rich, but others found that the Colorado gold was buried too deep to reach. The unsuccessful miners coined a new motto — "Pike's Peak and busted!" — and drifted off to other parts of the West. The Colorado gold boom ended as quickly as it began. Then, in the years following the Civil War, mining companies invested in machinery that could reach the gold. Miners also discovered silver and lead in Colorado. Despite its mineral wealth, however, most of Colorado's settlers were ranchers and farmers.

Many of the miners who were "busted" in Colorado tried their luck in Nevada, at that time a part of Utah Territory. Gold

. . . .

CHAPTER FOCUS

1. Miners and cattlemen penetrate the West.

2. Indians give way to the advance of the farming frontier.

3. Farmers suffer hard times.

was discovered in 1859, and enormous quantities of silver were located in the fabulous Comstock Lode. During the next twenty years, the Comstock mines yielded more than 500 million dollars worth of gold and silver.

Lured on by the rich strikes in Colorado and Nevada, prospectors combed the slopes of the western mountains. They found gold and silver in what are now Idaho, Montana, Washington, and Wyoming. Far to the South, gold and silver were also discovered in the western part of New Mexico Territory. As a result, Arizona Territory was created. The last of the western gold rushes occurred in the Black Hills of Dakota Territory during the mid-1870's. In the Dakotas, however, as in the other western regions, the miners soon departed, leaving the land to be permanently settled by ranchers and farmers.

Life in the mining towns is rough. Each of the western strikes produced a mining town almost overnight. The most famous of these camp towns were Central City, Colorado; Virginia City, Nevada; Helena, Montana; Tombstone, Arizona; and Deadwood, South Dakota (map, page 425). Since no farms existed in these areas, food and other supplies had to be shipped in by wagon trains. Despite the high costs of construction, hotels, bars, stores, banks, and other buildings went up quickly. Some of the mining kings lived in elaborately furnished houses, attended by many servants. But most of the miners contented themselves with crude wooden shacks and frequent visits to the gaudy saloons that flourished in all the mining towns.

Perhaps the most colorful of the "roaring camps" was Virginia City, Nevada, perched on the side of a mountain above the Comstock Lode. Within a few months it had attracted a population of 20,000. When Mark Twain visited the mining frontier in the 1860's, he was fascinated by the turbulent life of Virginia City. In *Roughing It*, he described the town in these words:

Money was as plenty as dust; every individual considered himself wealthy, and a melancholy countenance was nowhere to be seen. There were military companies, fire

Miners worked on a wooden platform built deep within the mountain to dig out the riches of the Comstock Lode in Nevada (above).

Gold discoveries in South Dakota led to the founding of Deadwood (above), whose one street was lined mostly with saloons. Life in the mining towns was lawless and rowdy; but by 1900 Central City, Colorado, had an opera house, where famous singers performed (left).

The huge amounts of gold and silver taken from the mines attracted bandits. The Wells, Fargo express company had the dangerous job of shipping out the precious metals. Five armed guards rode on this wagon carrying 250,000 dollars in gold from Deadwood.

companies, brass-bands, banks, hotels, theaters, "hurdy-gurdy houses," wide-open gambling places, political pow-wows, civic processions, street-fights, murders, inquests, riots, a whiskeymill every fifteen steps, . . . a dozen breweries, and half a dozen jails and station-houses in full operation, and some talk of building a church. The "flush times" were in magnificent flower.

Vigilantes maintain order. The mining towns sprang up in areas of the West that had no organized state or local governments. In many areas there was not even a territorial government to help maintain law and order. As a result, violence was frequent. A resident of a Montana mining town reported that "not a day or night passed" without "fights, quarrels, wounds, or murders. The crack of the revolver was often heard above the merry notes of the violin." Yet, he noted, "underneath this exterior of recklessness, there was in the minds and hearts of the miners and businessmen of this society a strong and abiding sense of justice — and that saved the Territory."

In many of the mining camps private citizens formed vigilante groups (page 292) to maintain order and punish wrongdoers. During the winter of 1863–1864, Montana vigilantes caught and hanged 24 desperadoes who had committed robberies or murders. The miners in some areas organized local governments with elected officials. They regulated the size and type of claim a miner could stake out and required him to work it a certain number of days per week if he wanted to keep it. By the end of the Civil War, more than a thousand of these unofficial, self-governing mining districts existed in the Far West. Some of their rules were later embodied in the mining codes of the western states.

Transportation companies serve the mining camps. The growth of the mining towns brought much business to coach and freight companies. The first of the overland stagecoach lines was established in the late 1850's. With the help of a government subsidy, the Butterfield Overland Express carried mail and supplies between St. Louis and San Francisco. Following a winding route, the Butterfield stages required 24 days to make the trip each way. During 1860 the Pony Express carried mail from Missouri to California (map, page 425) in the remarkable time of 10 days. Starting at St. Joseph, Missouri, a rider carried the mail pouches to the next station 10 or 15 miles away, where he quickly changed horses. At intervals of about 75 miles a fresh rider took over. This was repeated many times before the mail reached San Francisco. But the Pony Express was destined to have a short life. The completion of a transcontinental telegraph put it out of business in 1861.

When the California miners spread into Colorado and Nevada, the Butterfield coaches and freight wagons were ready to serve them. Before long, however, another company — Wells, Fargo — had captured most of the business. In addition to stagecoaches for passengers and mail, Wells, Fargo maintained 6000 wagons and 75,000 oxen to carry supplies to the camp towns and minerals to the nearest railroad depot. Both freight wagons and stagecoaches were obvious targets for such western "bad men" as Jesse and Frank James and the three Dalton brothers. Other western characters won their reputations protecting law and order. Wild Bill Hickok was a stagecoach superintendent and a marshal before he was murdered in Deadwood.

Ranching originates in Texas. Another dramatic chapter in the opening of the West was written by the cattlemen. Long before Americans began filtering into Texas (page 275), the Mexicans had been raising cattle there. But few Mexican ranchers bothered to brand their cattle. When the Americans arrived in Texas, they assumed the herds were wild. They rounded up the wiry longhorn cattle, branded them, and thus acquired herds. In rounding up the cattle, the Texas ranchers used broncos, small muscular horses descended from Spanish stock.

Farther north on the grassy plains roamed cattle and horses that had broken away from the Mexican ranchers. Americans who ventured beyond the Mississippi as fur traders, explorers, or miners came across these herds and, like the Americans in Texas, set themselves up as ranchers. During the 1840's and '50's they butchered cattle to supply beef to people traveling west and also sold them horses. A few Texas ranchers began to drive their cattle to markets as far away as Illinois and California. But the difficulties of such a long trip made this practice uneconomical, and it was soon abandoned. By 1860 some five million longhorns crowded the Texas ranges. Though their hides could be marketed profitably, new transportation routes were needed before the beef could be sold to city dwellers in the North and East.

The "long drive" is organized. In the spring of 1866, Texas ranchers attempted

A herd of cattle on the long drive stretched across the rolling plain (above). Cowboys rode close beside to keep the cattle from straying. As western railroads were extended, and more cow towns grew up along the tracks, the long drives covered shorter distances. The artist Charles Russell, who himself worked for a time on a cattle ranch, showed in the painting at right how a cowboy lassoed an animal on the run.

the first of the organized "long drives." They set out to drive large herds of cattle to Sedalia, Missouri, where the Missouri Pacific railroad would ship them to market. In this first venture, heavy rains muddied the trails, unfamiliar woodlands confused the cattle, Indians harassed the cowboys, and Missouri farmers turned out with their shotguns to stop trespassing. Only a few of the cattle reached Sedalia, but they sold for 35 dollars a head compared to the 3 or 4 dollars they would have brought in Texas. The ranchers were determined to try again.

The cattle are marketed at cow towns. Fortunately, the cattlemen had the help of Joseph G. McCoy, who established a regular cattle market at Abilene, Kansas, on the Kansas Pacific Railroad. McCoy provided a hotel for the cattlemen and also built barns, stables, loading chutes, and pens. In 1868 some 75,000 head of cattle were brought to Abilene. Three years later the figure had increased almost tenfold. As settlers pushed farther west in Kansas and

the railroads extended their lines, new cow towns came into existence. One of these settlements, Dodge City, Kansas, became known as the "cowboys' capital." The cow towns, like the mining camps, were crowded with bars, saloons, and gambling houses. Here the cowboys could squander their earnings until they had to return to Texas for the spring roundup. They drank and fought as much as the miners.

The long drive was hard work. The cowboys' long drive to the cow towns was difficult and dangerous. It began with the spring roundup of the owner's cattle, the branding of new calves, and the selection of some 800 to 1000 head for market. Five or six cowboys conducted the cattle over the trail, allowing them to graze and stop at watering holes along the way. "It was tiresome grimy business for the attendant punchers," wrote one cowboy, for they "traveled ever in a cloud of dust, and heard little but the constant chorus from crackling of hoofs . . . the bellows, lows, and bleats of the trudging animals." At night the cowboys took turns riding around the herd to make sure that no rustlers stole the animals and that nothing frightened them into a stampede. During the lonely night patrols the cowboys often sang to quiet the cattle, setting new words to familiar tunes. These cowboy songs are now valued as authentic American folk music.

The long hours in the saddle, the dust and dirt, the heat and discomfort of the long drive have often been overlooked in romantic stories of the cowboy's life. So too have the dangers of the journey. In his lively *Log of a Cowboy*, Andy Adams described a critical experience on the trail:

Good cloudy weather would have saved us, but in its stead was a sultry morning without a breath of air, which bespoke another day of sizzling heat. We had not been on the trail over two hours before the heat became almost unbearable to man and beast. . . . Over three days had now elapsed without water for the cattle, and they became feverish and ungovernable. . . . They finally turned back over the trail, and the utmost efforts of every man in the outfit failed to check them. We threw our ropes in their faces, and when this failed, we resorted to shooting. . . . Six-shooters were discharged so close to the leaders' faces as to singe their hair, yet, under a noonday sun, they disregarded this and every other device

THE LAST FRONTIER, 1880

Miners and ranchers led the way to the filling in of the West. But the frontier disappeared so rapidly that mining towns and cattle trails soon were a matter of history.

MAP STUDY

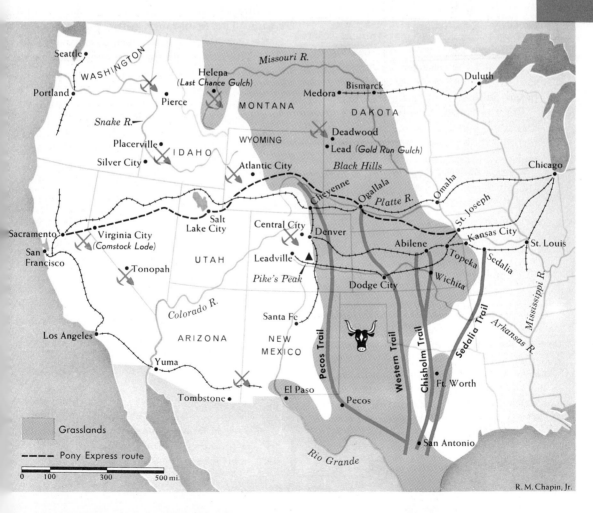

to turn them and passed wholly out of our control. In a number of instances wild steers deliberately walked against our horses, and then for the first time a fact dawned on us that chilled the marrow of our bones — *the herd was going blind.*

The bones of men and animals that lie bleaching along the trails abundantly testify that this was not the first instance in which the plain had baffled the determination of man. It was now evident that nothing short of water would stop the herd, and we rode aside to let them pass.

Cattle are fattened on the open range. The trails from Texas to the cow towns passed through the "open range." This term was applied to the government-owned grasslands of western Kansas and Nebraska, eastern Colorado, Wyoming, Montana, and the Dakotas. Huge herds of buffalo had lived on the wild grass of this region. But the building of railroads and the extension of the farming frontier had drastically reduced the buffalo herds by the 1870's. By this time also, most of the Plains Indians had been forced onto government reservations (page 428). With the passing of the buffalo and the Indians, the ranchers began to fatten their cattle on the open range before selling them to meat packers.

For a few years the open-range cattlemen flourished. Many newcomers sought their fortunes in the "cow country," and businessmen even formed cattle corporations as investments. Few of the ranchers purchased land from the government; they merely staked out informal claims to 30 or 40 square miles of open range and then

fought off all competitors. In time the ranchers, like the miners, developed their own vigilante groups, often called stock-growers' associations. These associations dealt with rustlers and regulated water rights. Since a water supply was essential, bitter struggles developed over "range rights" to the streams.

The cattle kingdom declines. For several reasons the open-range cattle industry declined rapidly after the mid-1880's. Sheepherders began grazing their flocks on the free grasslands, and the sheep ate the grass so close to the ground that the cattle could not graze after them. Moreover, farmers were buying land from the government and fencing off their acres with barbed wire. Then nature dealt a cruel blow to the cattlemen. The winters of 1885–1886 and 1886–1887 were unusually severe; thousands of cattle starved or were frozen to death. The intervening summer of 1886 was unusually hot and dry; the prairie grass withered away and watering places dried up. The open-range cattle industry never recovered from these two disastrous years.

Thereafter cattlemen purchased land and raised their herds on fenced-in ranches. This enabled them to concentrate on breeding, and in time they produced cattle far superior to the wiry longhorns. They also raised hay to feed the cattle in the winter. Many cowboys found employment on these combination ranch-farms. One of them reminisced in the late 1880's:

I remember when we sat around the fire the winter through and didn't do a lick of work for five or six months of the year, except to chop a little wood to build a fire to keep warm by. Now we go on the general roundup, then the calf roundup, then comes haying — something that the old-time cowboy never dreamed of — then the beef roundup and the fall calf roundup and gathering bulls and weak cows, and after all this a winter of feeding hay. I tell you times have changed.

▶ CHECK-UP

1. In what present-day states did mining booms develop? What new problem confronted forty-niners who tried to mine gold in Colorado? Describe life in the mining towns.

The Great American Desert

Early explorers of the Great Plains reported the area to be dry and practically treeless. As a result, the Plains became known as the Great American Desert and were left to the Indians, while the nation continued to fill out its borders in the Southwest and along the Pacific. In the mid-1800's, pioneers moving west onto the Plains discovered that this region was not a desert but afforded good opportunities for farming and ranching.

How did private citizens try to establish law and order? How were supplies brought in?

2. Describe the origins of ranching in Texas. What was the "long drive"? The "open range"? Why did the cattle industry boom and then decline after the mid-1880's?

· ·

2 Indians Give Way to the Advance of the Farming Frontier

For every forward step taken by the white man — miner, rancher, or farmer — the Indian had to step backward. Over a period of some 25 years after the Civil War, the western Indians fought a desperate but losing battle against the advance of the white man.

The western Indians oppose the white settlers. It has been estimated that about 300,000 Indians lived west of the Mississippi in the mid-1800's. This number included the Five Civilized Tribes — Cherokee, Choctaw, Chickasaw, Creek, and Seminole — which had been forcibly removed from the South in the 1830's and relocated in Indian Territory (now Oklahoma). Most of the western Indians belonged to the Plains tribes, who lived on the open range. These included the Sioux, Blackfeet, Crow, Pawnee, and Osage, and the fierce Apache and Comanche (map, page 428). The most formidable Indians in the mountains were the Nez Percé. In California the "Digger Indians," who lived off roots, tubers, and seed, were scorned by the Plains Indians and by the white man alike. All of these Indians naturally opposed the advance of the white settlers. Since most of them hunted wild animals for their food supply, they knew that settlement of the land would mean starvation for them. It was the Plains Indians who put up the stiffest fight against the white man.

The Plains Indians are dependent on the buffalo. The Plains tribes raised no

crops but for their food supply hunted wild animals — especially the buffalo. The Indians not only ate the buffalo meat but used the hides for clothing, moccasins, blankets, tepees, and shields. In earlier days the Indians had hunted the buffalo on foot. But after the 1500's they captured horses that had broken away from Spanish explorers (and later from Mexican ranchers) and became skillful riders. Entire tribes would follow the buffalo herds as they lumbered across the prairie.

The coming of the white men drastically affected the life of the Plains Indians. Most menacing of all the white men were the railroad builders, who had the buffalo shot to provide food for construction gangs. William F. Cody earned the nickname "Buffalo Bill" by killing more than 4000 buffalo in eighteen months for the Kansas Pacific Railroad. Thousands of the animals were shot to supply eastern markets with fashionable "buffalo robes." Other hunters killed the clumsy, weak-eyed animals just for sport, leaving the carcasses to rot on the plains. Some twelve million buffalo had roamed the plains in the 1850's. But so great was the slaughter that thirty years later only a few hundred remained. The Plains Indians had been stripped of their chief means of support.

The government moves the Indians to reservations. The government's Indian pol-

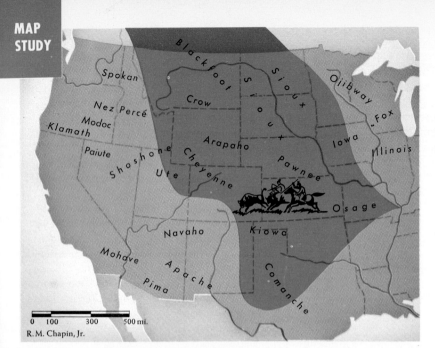

INDIANS OF THE WEST, 1800

With this map and those on pages 199 and 219, you can locate the lands of major Indian tribes before the coming of the white man. Note that the colored area represents the grasslands on which the buffalo ranged.

icies proved to be neither realistic nor humane. By the 1850's it had become clear that the Plains were not a "Great American Desert," as had once been thought. Someday the white man would want to claim that useful land from the Indians. The government, therefore, forced the Plains Indians to sign treaties which set off large areas called *reservations* for the Indians' use. Since the Indians were confined within the boundaries of the reservations, they had to abandon their old ways of hunting. The government agreed to supply the Indians on reservations with food and clothing, but by the 1870's corruption was widespread in every phase of the government's Indian policy. Spoiled meat and moth-eaten blankets were distributed to the Indians, and unscrupulous traders found ways to sell forbidden liquor to them. Moreover, the government violated its treaties with the Indians. The reservations were constantly reduced in size for the benefit of the miners, ranchers, or farmers who wanted the land.

Indian leaders were outraged by the treatment of their people, but appeals to Washington were useless. Many government officials agreed with the Westerners that the "only good Indian was a dead Indian." Time and again embittered Indians broke out of the reservations to raid settlements and ambush troops.

The Indians fight a losing battle. The Indians had few advantages in the bitter struggle with the white man. Their food supply steadily dwindled. Though some had rifles purchased from corrupt traders, most of their weapons were inferior to those of the United States Army. And, of course, the Indians could use neither the telegraph nor the railroads. But, in spite of these handicaps, the Indians forced the white men to fight a long and costly war.

The United States Army subdues the Indians. The Sioux tribes put up especially fierce resistance. Led by Little Crow, they went on the warpath during the Civil War. More than 700 white settlers lost their lives before the Indians were defeated and confined on a new reservation in the Dakota Territory. But the discovery of gold in the Black Hills brought a swarm of miners into this new reservation during the mid-1870's. When the Sioux began to gather under the leadership of Crazy Horse and Sitting Bull, the United States Army dispatched troops to round them up. Among the officers leading these troops was Colonel George A. Custer. In June, 1876, on the banks of the Little Big Horn River, Custer and over 200 cavalrymen were ambushed and slaughtered by the Sioux. The Indians were short of ammunition and food, however, and had to surrender in the fall.

Other tribes also waged a bitter fight.

INDIANS OF THE WEST, 1900

Despite numerous battles fought to retain their home-lands, Indians were con-fined to ever-shrinking res-ervations. Note that the Sauk from northern Wis-consin were settled in un-familiar land in Oklahoma. Tribes like the Navaho re-tained their land because the whites considered it useless.

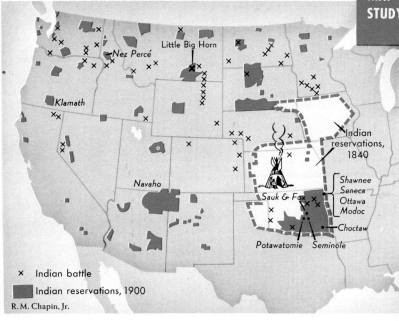

Little Big Horn
Nez Percé
Klamath
Navaho
Sauk & Fox
Indian reservations, 1840
Shawnee
Seneca
Ottawa
Modoc
Choctaw
Potawatomie   Seminole

× Indian battle

■ Indian reservations, 1900

R. M. Chapin, Jr.

The Nez Percé harassed miners in the Pacific Northwest until their leader, Chief Joseph, was captured, and hunger and disease weakened the tribe. The last organized Indian resistance was offered by the Apaches in New Mexico. When their leader, Geronimo, was captured in 1886, Indian warfare came to a close. These wars had reduced the Indian population west of the Mississippi by approximately one third.

The public attitude toward Indians changes. In the years after the Civil War, the government's Indian policy was occasionally criticized as expensive, corrupt, and cruel. Politicians paid no attention, however, so long as most of the voters favored a tough policy against the Indians. But in the early 1880's, after most of the Indians had been subdued, the public attitude began to change. This came about largely as a result of the book called *A Century of Dishonor* by Helen Hunt Jackson. This book recited the long record of government abuses and proposed that the Indians be given better opportunities. Mrs. Jackson's book became a best seller and strengthened those who sought to reform the government's Indian policy.

The government adopts a new policy. In 1887 Congress passed the Dawes Act, which established an entirely new Indian policy. The Dawes Act abolished most tribal organizations. It divided up the res-

ervations and offered a piece of land to any Indian who would cultivate it and give up allegiance to his tribe. After 25 years, the Indian would have a clear title to this land and would be granted full United States citizenship. Congress also appropriated money for Indian schools and soon made education compulsory for Indian children. (An act in 1924 granted full citizenship to all Indians.)

The Dawes Act could not be called a success. Most of the Indians remained loyal to their tribes and had no desire to become farmers. They lacked experience in agriculture, and the Indian schools provided inferior education. Moreover, the Indians' plots were too small and often unsuitable for farming. Some Indians fared better than others. After oil was discovered on the Osage lands in Oklahoma, some of these Indians became wealthy. But most of the others were barely able to make a living.

Settlers move onto the Plains. As the Indian threat diminished, a growing number of white families moved into the West. Actually the white man's invasion of the Great Plains[1] had begun during the Civil War. Some miners and prospectors had

---

[1] The Great Plains are generally considered to begin west of the ninety-eighth to hundredth meridian. This vast treeless region, stretching from Texas to Canada, usually receives less rain than the lands to the east.

White Bird, a Cheyenne Indian who fought in the Battle of the Little Big Horn at the age of fifteen, years later recreated his memory of "Custer's last stand" in a painting done on muslin (top left). Another survivor of the battle was Sitting Bull (left), a Sioux chief and medicine man, who continued to resist the Americans' invasion of Indian lands as long as possible. Many Indians today still live on reservations, but others, like the Navajo utility worker above, have jobs in industry.

settled down to farming in the 1860's. They were joined by Easterners seeking to escape the military draft and later by many veterans. An Easterner crossing the Plains on horseback in 1866 reported that he was hardly ever out of sight of ox or mule teams hauling wagons. But the greatest wave of settlers came in the 1870's and 1880's. Aside from the reduction of the Indian danger, two factors — the Homestead Act and the extension of the railroads — were especially important in this westward migration.

Congress provides for free homesteads. The Homestead Act became law in 1862 (page 369). Under this act, any American could become the owner of 160 acres of public land. All he had to do was live on it, cultivate it for five years, and pay a small fee to have his ownership recorded. The Homestead Act enabled many men to acquire farms and thus make a new start in the West. But it had its limitations. Much of the best land in the West had been given to railroads or bought by speculators; much of the free land available to homesteaders was too dry for cultivation. Moreover, many would-be farmers found they could not afford the cost of moving their families, buying equipment, fencing the land, and building even a crude house and barn. Nevertheless, there was a great rush for western land after the passage of the Homestead Act.

Railroads encourage settlement. Railroads, pushing steadily westward, helped to open up the Great Plains. The farmers and their families found it easier and safer to travel by railroad than by wagon. The railroads also carried the farmers' crops to market and brought back supplies from the East. Since the farmers who settled on the Plains provided business for the railroads, the railroad companies found it worthwhile to advertise the West. By describing — and no doubt exaggerating — the fertility of the prairie soil, they attracted Easterners and even European settlers. The railroads offered attractive rates to prospective farmers and also sold to settlers part of the land granted them by the government.[2]

Some pioneers live in sod houses. The earliest settlers on the Plains faced many hardships. Finding little timber, except along the creeks and rivers, they built their houses of prairie sod. The pioneer first plowed a strip of thick sod. With a spade he then cut the upturned sod into strips about three feet long. To make walls, he laid the sod strips in place and applied adobe mud (a mixture of earth, water, and grass or straw) to hold them together. Door frames and window frames were set in the walls. The roof was made of wood rafters covered with tar paper and a layer of sod on which grass and sometimes even sunflowers grew. The roof usually leaked in heavy rainstorms, but the sod house protected the pioneers against the bitter cold and scorching heat of the Great Plains. Furthermore, it was fireproof and could withstand severe windstorms.

Towns begin to appear on the Plains. It was not long, however, before the railroads brought building supplies to the Great Plains. Settlers then could build frame houses and barns. Small towns sprang up as stores, hotels, churches and schools soon surrounded the railroad depots. In 1882, an Iowa family that settled in Miller, South Dakota, built a two-story frame house, a lean-to, and a barn in less than a month. It took another two weeks to plaster the inside walls, build cupboards, and install

bookcases. When the newcomer's wife went shopping for groceries, she was amazed at how much "the town had improved . . . since I last rode out." There was such a shortage of labor that some families camped in tents until they could hire men to build houses.

Farmers use barbed wire and windmills. The Plains farmer was confronted by two problems which had not troubled farmers farther east. For one thing, he had to fence his land to keep out grazing cattle and also to mark off his holding in the vast, treeless plain. Because of lack of timber, wooden fences were out of the question. But in the 1870's barbed wire became available. Though the wire fencing sold for 20 dollars per hundred pounds, western farmers clamored for it. By 1890 mass production had reduced the price to 4 dollars per hundred pounds. Both farmers and ranchers by that time were fencing their acres with barbed wire.

The Plains farmers struggled with a second problem unique to their area — lack of rainfall. The soil was rich and the tough prairie grass retained enough moisture to survive. But when the farmers plowed the sod and tried to plant seed, much of the moisture escaped from the soil. Water lay from 50 to 200 feet below the surface. In many areas it was impossible to draw enough water by hand for the stock and for household use. To meet this problem, many farmers in the 1870's dug deep wells and built windmills. These steel windmills caught the strong prairie winds and pumped up from the wells the water needed by the homesteaders.

TIMETABLE

WESTERN STATES ADMITTED, 1861–1912

1861	Kansas	1889	Washington
1864	Nevada	1890	Idaho
1867	Nebraska	1890	Wyoming
1876	Colorado	1896	Utah
1889	North Dakota	1907	Oklahoma
1889	South Dakota	1912	New Mexico
1889	Montana	1912	Arizona

---

[2] See Chapter 21 for more about the growth of the western railroads (pages 442–443).

In 1895 Mark Twain was photographed on shipboard during a round-the-world lecture tour. Audiences flocked to hear the internationally famous writer.

New western states are admitted to the Union. The miners, ranchers, and particularly the farmers rapidly increased the population of the West. In 1860 less than five million people lived west of the Mississippi. Most of them were concentrated near that river or on the Pacific coast. By 1900, however, more than 20 million people lived in the trans-Mississippi West, and the Union had grown to include 45 states, 12 more than in 1860. (See the table on page 431, showing western states admitted from 1861 to 1912.)

Oklahoma Territory was settled in record time. On April 22, 1889, the unassigned lands in central Oklahoma were thrown open to homesteaders. At a given signal thousands of eager "boomers" raced across the border to stake out homesteads and buy town lots. By the end of the year, Oklahoma had a population of 60,000. Two territories developed — Oklahoma Territory in the central and western part and Indian Territory in the East. These two territories became the state of Oklahoma in 1907.

The frontier line disappears. In 1890 the Census Bureau issued a report stating that "the unsettled area" of the country "has been so broken into by isolated bodies of settlement that there can hardly be said to be a frontier line." Actually, vast areas of the West still remained unsettled. In the years after 1890 the government gave homesteaders four times as much land as before that date. Moreover, frontier living conditions continued to exist in many parts of the West. But the Census Bureau report called attention to the disappearance of a clear *line* separating populated areas from unsettled land.

In 1893 a young historian, Frederick Jackson Turner, told his colleagues: "Now, four centuries from the discovery of America . . . the frontier has gone, and with its going has closed the first period of American history." Turner and his students examined the effect on the American character of the availability of almost endless stretches of land. They concluded that the continuing opportunity to expand into the West had promoted democracy, nationalism, and individualism. Undoubtedly it did. But the settlement of the last frontier did not end the opportunity to develop new agricultural techniques. Nor did it interfere with the vast new challenges presented to the American people by the development of industry and the rise of cities.

Western life inspires writers. The taming of the West has been a favorite theme in American literature, movies, and television. Some of these portrayals are accurate; many are not. Fortunately we can learn the true nature of the West from some first-rate writers who took part in the westward movement.

Mark Twain was the best of these writers. Born Samuel Langhorne Clemens, he grew up in Hannibal, Missouri, on the banks of the Mississippi. In 1861 he considered joining the Confederate army but instead headed West. He tried his hand at prospecting in Nevada, worked for a time on a Virginia City newspaper, and mingled with colorful characters in San Francisco. It was in one of the mining camps that Mark Twain first heard the old tale of the "jumping frog," and in 1867 he brought out *The Celebrated Jumping Frog of Calaveras County and Other Sketches.* He soon followed it with an account of his western travels in *Roughing It.* Twain's experiences as a growing boy and young man in the Mississippi River Valley flavor his best-known books — *Life on the Mississippi, The Adventures of Tom Sawyer,* and *The Adventures of Huckleberry Finn.*

One of Twain's friends in San Francisco was a New Yorker named Bret Harte. Harte taught school in the gold mining towns and worked for several newspapers and journals in California. Among his first literary successes were the stories "The Luck of Roaring Camp" and "The Outcasts of Poker Flat." Harte's stories set the style for other local-color (regional) writers, but few equaled his ability to describe the life of the mining camps.

The physical grandeur of the Far West, particularly the mountains, was captured by the poet Joaquin Miller. His best volume of verse was *Songs of the Sierras.*

Hamlin Garland vividly portrayed the life of the farmer on the western Plains and prairies. His stories in *Main-Travelled Roads* described the hard physical labor, the loneliness, and the financial troubles of the prairie people. The pioneering experiences of Garland's own family provided the theme of *A Son of the Middle Border.* Ole Rölvaag, an immigrant from Norway, wrote a masterpiece about Norwegian farmers in the Dakotas — *Giants in the Earth.* Willa Cather, who grew up on the Nebraska frontier, used that area as the

THE AMERICAN SCENE

THE DISAPPEARING FRONTIER

as seen by FREDERIC REMINGTON

Remington served in the army during the wars against the Plains Indians, but he also lived for a time with friendly Indians. The colorful detail and realistic action of his paintings and sculptures captured western life of the late 1800's. In the statuette above, the cowboy's horse is shying away from a rattlesnake.

setting for two of her best novels — *O Pioneers!* and *My Antonia*.

Artists portray the West. Artists as well as writers were inspired by the trans-Mississippi West. Among the earliest was George Catlin. When living in Philadelphia in the 1830's, he saw his first Indians, members of a delegation that had visited the nation's capital. Catlin resolved that "the history and customs of such a people, preserved by . . . illustrations, are themes worthy of the lifetime of one man, and nothing short of the loss of my life shall prevent me from visiting their country and becoming their historian." Until his death in 1872, Catlin roamed the West, drawing and painting scenes of Indian life. He also collected many objects from the Indian villages. From time to time he displayed his impressive "Indian Gallery" in eastern cities and in Europe. Historians have found Catlin's detailed pictures an invaluable source of information about the western Indians.

Another artist who specialized in western themes was Frederic Remington. Remington left Yale in 1880 to travel in the West where he made hundreds of drawings of Indians, ranchers, and settlers. Many of these were sold to magazines, but others provided material for oil paintings which he turned out in his New York studio. Remington, like Catlin, realized the historic value of his western sketches. He said of his Indian drawings: "I knew the wild riders and the vacant land were about to vanish forever, and the more I considered the subject, the bigger the *forever* loomed." When Remington died in 1909, the West that he had sketched in his youth was already a thing of the past.

▶ CHECK-UP

1. Why was the buffalo important to the Plains Indians? Why did the government move the Indians to reservations? How was the government's treatment of the Indians criticized? What were the provisions of the Dawes Act?

2. How did the railroads and the Homestead Act contribute to the settlement of the West? What were the limitations of the Homestead Act? Why were barbed wire and windmills of crucial importance to the Plains farmers?

3. In what sense had the frontier disappeared by 1890? What writers and artists portrayed western life?

3 *Farmers Suffer Hard Times*

The future must have looked bright to many of the homesteaders who made the long trek westward in the years after the Civil War. Endless stretches of fertile land were theirs for the taking. More and better farm machinery, the spread of railroads, and improved methods of farming gave hope of prosperous times. But once settled on the land, farmers were beset with perplexing problems. In this section we shall examine some of the forces which helped and hindered the farmer.

Farm machinery increases. Back in the 1790's, when the republic was launched, about 90 per cent of the working people were farmers or worked on farms. A hundred years later, this figure had dropped to about 40 per cent. A much smaller percentage of the total work force was needed to raise food in 1890 because the productivity per worker had increased greatly. The increased use of farm machinery was chiefly responsible. Even before the Civil War, farmers had been using steel plows, reapers, mowers, and threshers (page 300). But after 1865 many new machines were introduced and old ones were improved.

James Oliver developed a steel plow suited for use on the tough sod of the Great Plains. Reapers also were improved by the addition of attachments which bound the grain in bundles. Other machines planted the seed at precise intervals and at the proper depth in the soil. A steam-powered threshing machine was introduced, and later the "combine," or complete harvester and thresher, came into use.

Between 1860 and 1900, the value of farm machinery tripled. During these same years, while the amount of farm land under cultivation doubled, the wheat harvest increased nearly four times, and corn production about three times. The use of machinery reduced the amount of human labor needed to turn out a bushel of wheat from three hours in 1830 to ten minutes in 1900.

Farmers specialize in certain crops. Once a farmer had invested in machinery for raising wheat or corn, he naturally wanted to continue growing that crop. Hence, more farmers began to specialize in the growing of a particular crop. The production of wheat moved westward, from Illinois and Indiana to the Dakotas, Minnesota, Nebraska, and Kansas. But the eastern variety of winter wheat could not survive the severe temperatures of the Plains. So the western farmers began to raise spring wheat and a sturdier breed of winter wheat. East of the Mississippi, farmers also specialized in the kinds of crops they grew. In the South, cotton and tobacco continued to be the leading crops. Farmers in Ohio, Indiana, and Illinois raised corn and also oats, rye, barley, and hay.

The government encourages new agricultural methods. The federal government promoted both the use of farm machinery and specialization in selected crops. The Department of Agriculture, established in 1862, collected statistics and published useful pamphlets for farmers. The Morrill Act, passed in 1862, provided for land grants to the states for establishing colleges of engineering and scientific agriculture. And in 1887 the Hatch Act authorized the creation of agricultural experiment stations. Over the years these experiment stations and the land-grant colleges have played an important part in educating American farmers and in developing new machines, new crops, and new techniques.

Farm prices drop but costs remain high. While farmers were moving onto the Plains, changes were taking place elsewhere in the world that reduced the demand for American agricultural exports. Vast new areas of farm land were being opened up in Argentina, Australia, and Canada. Improved methods of cultivation also increased production in many countries. As a result, the amount of food on the world market rose sharply and prices dropped. Since farmers

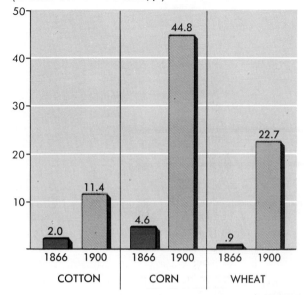

Millions of Acres
(in states west of the Mississippi)

CROP ACREAGE WEST OF THE MISSISSIPPI

The growth of farming west of the Mississippi can be measured in terms of land under cultivation. Compare the acreage used to produce cotton, corn, and wheat in 1866 and in 1900.

in the United States were producing more than Americans could consume, their surplus had to be sold on the world market. The American farmer thus became a victim of the falling prices of agricultural products in the 1870's and '80's.

The statistics are dramatic. A bushel of wheat brought about a dollar and a half in 1866, but only half a dollar in 1894. In this same year the price of cotton was only a sixth of what it had been in 1866. The price of corn dropped so low that some farmers found it cheaper to burn corn than to sell it and buy fuel.

While his income fell, the farmer's costs remained high. The cost of farm machinery and equipment took a major slice of his earnings. Neither the freight rates for shipping products to market, nor the cost of manufactured articles protected by high tariffs declined as much as the prices of farm products. Moreover, the hard-pressed farmers were charged high interest rates if they borrowed money or mortgaged their land. The spread of tenant farming from the South to other areas of the country re-

Sod houses sheltered pioneers on the Great Plains, where trees were scarce. The family shown at top right lived in western Kansas in the 1890's. An essential in Plains farming was the windmill, which pumped up water from great depths. The impact of agricultural machinery is visible in the modern wheat farming scene at right.

flected the farmers' financial troubles. By 1880 one fourth of all American farms were operated by tenants rather than by owners.

Drought and insects plague the farmers. High costs and falling prices were only part of the farmers' troubles. Many of them had moved onto the Plains in the 1870's and early 1880's when rainfall was unusually heavy. They refused to heed the cattlemen's warnings that the area was normally arid. Then came the scorching summer of 1886, followed by several more years of excessively hot, dry weather. A farmer in western Nebraska recalled the drought in these words:

> Corn did not sprout. On the hardland fringe the buffalo grass was . . . browned before the first of May. . . . The lake beds whitened and cracked in rhythmical patterns. . . . Rabbits grew thin and wild and coyotes emboldened. Covered wagons like gaunt-ribbed, gray animals moved eastward, the occupants often becoming public charges along the way.

Crops that survived the drought were often attacked by insects. Chinch bugs, corn borers, boll weevils, alfalfa weevils, and grasshoppers ruined many a farmer. Ole Rölvaag in *Giants in the Earth* describes the arrival of a "living, pulsating stream" of grasshoppers:

> . . . striking the backs of the helpless people like pebbles thrown by an unseen hand. . . . The whole place was a weltering turmoil of raging little demons; if one looked for a moment into the wind, one saw nothing but . . . a cloud made up of innumerable dark-brown clicking bodies. All the while the roaring sound continued. . . . They whizzed by in the air; they literally covered the ground; they lit on the heads of grain, on the stubble, on everything in sight . . . millions on millions of them.

When they had eaten every green shoot in the fields, the grasshoppers would disappear as suddenly as they had descended.

Farmers have other grievances. There was little the western farmers could do to overcome natural disasters or the expansion of farm production abroad. But they had other problems which they felt *could* be solved. Chief among them were (1) the high cost of transportation, (2) the shortage of money, (3) the indifference of political parties to farm problems, and (4) the loneliness of farm life.

(1) The blame for the high cost of transportation, according to the farmers, rested entirely with the railroads. The homesteaders charged that they had been lured to the Great Plains by favorable rates, only to find themselves at the mercy of the railroads. Farmers accused the railroad owners of hiking freight rates and charging exorbitant amounts for carrying crops to market. In the many areas that were served by only one line, the railroad could charge a high rate without fear of competition. Moreover, some railroads charged more to carry freight a short distance than to haul it hundreds of miles. The farmers thought the freight rates should be regulated.

(2) As prices continued to fall and costs remained high, the farmers found themselves short of money. Many of them went into debt by borrowing money at high interest rates or mortgaging their land. Few of them were able to pay off these obligations. Therefore, the farmers wanted to see more money put into circulation. At first they favored the greenbacks and hoped that the government would issue more paper money (page 406). But in the 1870's many farmers pinned their hopes on silver. The western cry for free and unlimited coinage of silver helped bring about passage of the Bland-Allison Act (page 411), which provided for limited coinage of silver. But since farm prices continued to fall, Westerners kept up their demand for *unlimited* coinage of silver. By the 1890's silver coinage was one of the major political issues in the country (page 517).

(3) Indifference on the part of Democratic and Republican politicians was another source of irritation to the farmers. Southern and western farmers wanted the same things from the government — regulation of the railroads, lower tariffs, and more money in circulation. Yet the politicians paid little attention to these requests.

National Democratic leaders assumed that they would get the southern white farmers' vote without passing any legislation to satisfy them. Likewise, Republican politicians took the western farmers' vote for granted because of the Homestead Act. Furthermore, in the West the state governments were often controlled by businessmen and lawyers. Not many farmers could afford to neglect their fields and hold public office. As a result, the farmers had little influence in state legislatures, and they found few supporters in Congress or in the courts.

(4) The loneliness of farm life was another problem. Western farms and ranches were often many miles apart. Without automobiles, radio, television, or telephones, the farm families felt isolated. They did not even have free mail service until 1896. Thus, there was little to relieve the hard physical work and the drabness of farm life. The author Hamlin Garland grew up on midwestern farms in the 1870's. But after visiting his parents in the Dakotas in the 1890's he wrote:

> The lack of color, of charm in the lives of the people anguished me. . . . All the gilding of farm life melted away. The hard and bitter realities came back upon me in a flood. Nature was as beautiful as ever . . . but no splendor of cloud, no grace of sunset could conceal the poverty of these people; on the contrary they brought out, with a more intolerable poignancy, the gracelessness of these homes, and the sordid quality of the mechanical daily routine of these lives.

Farmers join the Grange. The first organized effort to solve the farmers' troubles was directed by Oliver H. Kelley, a clerk in the Department of Agriculture. In 1867 he and six friends established the National Grange of the Patrons of Husbandry to provide farmers with social opportunities for discussing their problems. Kelley resigned his government job and devoted his energies to promoting the Grange. It was the Panic of 1873, however, that made the Grange an important national organization. The depression drove thousands of farmers into the Grange in hope of finding some way to improve their condition. By 1875 the Grange had 20,000 local branches with a membership of about 800,000. The movement found its greatest strength in the Middle West.

The Grange carried on a variety of activities. It held regular meetings where farm families gathered to discuss the leading issues of the day, exchange local news, and hear speakers. Hamlin Garland remembered that the Iowa Grange meetings were "important dates on our calendar. In winter 'oyster suppers' with debates, songs and essays, drew us all to the . . . school house and each spring, on the twelfth of June, the Grange Picnic was a grand turnout. It was almost as well attended as the circus."

The Grange also ran co-operative stores, grain elevators, packing plants, flour mills, and even banks and insurance companies. Farmers had long complained about *middlemen* — the businessmen who stood between the farmers and the consumers. Now they had a chance to by-pass the middlemen by dealing with Grange co-operative companies. Few of these ventures were financially successful, however. The farmers lacked business experience, and they faced strong opposition from established grain operators, packers, millers, and other businessmen. Most of the Grange "co-ops" failed after only a few years.

The Grangers go into politics. The Grangers had more success in politics. Grange leaders realized that unless they

could elect farm spokesmen to the state legislatures, they would never get state regulation of railroad rates. Hence the Grange encouraged political activity among its members. The Grange itself did not nominate candidates but gave its support to acceptable candidates of the various parties. In the early 1870's four midwestern states passed so-called "Granger laws," designed to regulate railroad and warehouse rates. The railroads refused to comply with these laws and appealed to the courts. Eventually the fight was carried to the United States Supreme Court.

The Supreme Court upholds Granger laws. A key decision handed down by the Supreme Court in regard to the Granger laws was *Munn v. Illinois.* This case dealt with an Illinois law that regulated warehouse rates for storing grain. In this case, as in the other Granger cases, businessmen argued that the state laws violated the Fourteenth Amendment by depriving them of property without due process of law. They argued that the word "person" as used in this Amendment could be interpreted to mean business corporation, and "property" could mean profits. But the Supreme Court upheld the Granger laws on the ground that the state had a right to regulate private property devoted to public use. In passing the Granger laws, declared the Supreme Court, the states were exercis-

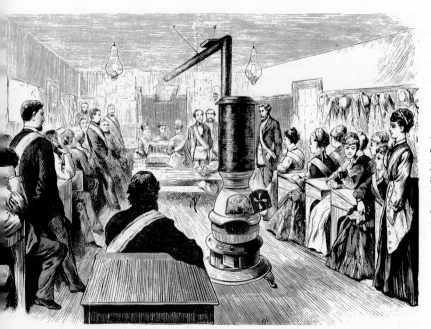

At grange meetings, like this one in an Illinois schoolhouse, farmers and their families met to discuss common problems. Through united effort, they hoped to reach solutions and put them into effect.

ing their police powers to protect the rights of citizens.[3]

Grange membership declines. These legal victories marked the high-water point of the Grange movement. When the Supreme Court upheld the Granger laws, many farmers assumed that they had won the battle. They felt that the Grange was no longer so necessary. Membership fell off, partly for this reason and partly because the Grange's unsuccessful business ventures had resulted in financial difficulties. Nevertheless, the Grange had performed a useful service. It provided social contacts for farm families and showed what farmers could accomplish through political action. They did not forget this lesson.

Other farm organizations appear. During the 1880's, as hard times continued in the Plains states and in the South, farmers formed organizations called Farmers' Alliances. The Alliances, like the Grange, held social gatherings, and tried running some co-operative stores known as "exchanges." Some of the Alliance members proposed a credit system called the *subtreasury* plan. They wanted the government to establish local warehouses where farmers could store nonperishable products until market prices were high enough to sell at a worthwhile profit. The farmers would be entitled to borrow from the government as much as 80 per cent of the current value of their stored goods.

From their beginning, the Alliances took an intense interest in politics. The platform of one Alliance declared that its purpose was "to unite the farmers of America for their protection against class legislation" and "to demand that the existing parties shall nominate farmers, or those who are in sympathy with them, for all offices within the gift of the people." As you will read in a later chapter, farmers' candidates showed surprising strength in the 1890 elections, chiefly because of campaigning by Alliance members (page 516). Both the Republican and Democratic Parties began to realize that the farm vote could be a major factor in elections.

[3] In the 1880's the Supreme Court reversed this decision and declared the Granger laws unconstitutional (page 496).

▶ CHECK-UP

1. How was farming affected by the increased use of machinery? How were farmers helped by the federal government? Why did farm prices decline even though the farmers' costs remained high?

2. How did nature plague farmers on the Great Plains? How did they feel about railroads, "cheap" money, the role of political parties? Explain why in each case.

3. What was the Grange? How did it help farmers? What was the significance of "Munn v. Illinois"? What types of farm aid did the Alliances propose?

• • • • • • • • • • • • • • • • • • • •

Clinching the Main Ideas in Chapter 20

After the Civil War, miners and cattlemen began to move into the vast stretch of land between California and the states along the Mississippi River. Rich strikes of gold and silver were discovered first in Colorado and then in other scattered locations throughout the mountainous West. Each discovery drew thousands of prospectors, and lively mining camps and towns sprang up overnight. After a few years, most of the miners drifted off to other sites or turned to farming or ranching.

From the mid-1860's to the mid-1880's, ranchers developed the western cattle industry on the open range. At first they drove full-grown steers from Texas to "cow towns" like Abilene, where the cattle were shipped by rail to meat-packing centers. Soon the ranchers were using the open range to graze young steers before selling them. But a series of harsh winters and unusually dry summers dealt a crippling blow to the industry. Moreover, sheepherders were moving to the open range, and farmers were fencing in the land with barbed wire. By the 1890's cattlemen had given up the "long drive" and were raising cattle on fenced-in ranches.

Farmers followed close on the heels of the miners and cattlemen. Encouraged by the Homestead Act and generous offers from the railroads, they moved onto the Great Plains in growing numbers. The Indians bitterly resisted this advance of the white man. But after years of bloody warfare, the army succeeded in subduing the Indians. The policy of confining the Indians on reservations was replaced by the Dawes Act, which promised land and citizenship to Indians who were willing to give up their tribal allegiance. Meanwhile, people had settled in so many parts of the West that the Census Bureau in 1890 reported the disappearance of the frontier line.

Despite the rich soil of the Great Plains, the western farmers faced many problems over which they had no control. In addition to such natural disasters as droughts and destructive insects, they had to cope with the problems of high railroad rates, rising costs for manufactured goods, and falling prices for farm products. Chiefly because of overproduction, both in this country and abroad, agricultural prices steadily declined. Unable to grasp the world-wide dimension of their problem, the farmers lashed out at railroads, bankers, middlemen, and politicians. To seek solutions, farmers banded together in such organizations as the Grange and the Alliances. In some midwestern states, farmer-influenced legislatures did pass regulatory laws which at first were upheld by the United States Supreme Court. Farm discontent continued, however, and by the 1890's the angry farmers were determined to take a more active role in politics.

Chapter Review

Terms to Understand

1. Comstock Lode
2. frontier line
3. open range
4. reservation
5. vigilantes
6. long drive
7. Homestead Act
8. Alliances
9. Pony Express
10. Hatch Act
11. cow towns
12. Grange
13. Oklahoma Territory

What Do You Think?

1. Explain the importance of the buffalo, barbed wire, and the windmill in the settlement of the West.

2. What can be said for and against vigilante justice on the mining frontier?

3. Why did interests of ranchers and farmers conflict? What adjustments were made?

4. Why do present-day Americans hold a different view of Indians than did settlers in the West after the Civil War?

5. The railroads helped to bring the long drive into existence and also to bring it to an end. Explain.

Using Your Knowledge of History

1. Emerson Hough said that the axe, the rifle, the boat, and the horse enabled the white man to conquer the West. Write a paragraph explaining how each contributed to this end.

2. Debate: *Resolved,* That the frontier was the most important factor in shaping the American character.

3. Read Chapters 3, 6, and 8 in Mark Twain's *Roughing It.* Report to the class on what you learn about "sharp" mining practices, frontier crime, and frontier justice.

4. Write two paragraphs contrasting the ways of living and the problems of farmers on the sod-house frontier, and on the Ohio Valley frontier some 80 years earlier.

Extending Your Knowledge of History

Two good books on the mining frontier are G. C. Quiett's *Pay Dirt* and William S. Greever's *The Bonanza West.* For information about the cattlemen's empire, see E. S. Osgood's *The Day of the Cattlemen;* Andy Adams's *The Log of a Cowboy;* and *The Negro Cowboys* by Philip Durham and Everett L. Jones. The fate of the Indians is discussed by William T. Hagan in *American Indians.* See also *The Hunting of the Buffalo* by E. D. Branch. F. A. Shannon in *The Farmer's Last Frontier* has portrayed the advance of the farmers onto the Plains. In *American Heritage* read "The Prairie Schooner Got Them There" by George R. Stewart (February, 1962); and "The Look of the Last Frontier" by Edgar M. Howell (June, 1961).

CHAPTER 21

American Industry Comes of Age

Transcontinental railroad completed

No other generation in American history witnessed changes as swift or as revolutionary as those which transformed the rural republic of Lincoln and Lee into the urban industrial empire of McKinley and Roosevelt.

"AMERICA: THE STORY OF A FREE PEOPLE,"
NEVINS AND COMMAGER

1860–1890

While some Americans were taming the West, others were pioneering in business and manufacturing. In so doing, they helped build the United States into the world's leading industrial nation. This amazing growth was made possible by skillful management, more effective use of natural resources, and the expansion of the country's labor supply. From a rural republic, the United States developed into a land of growing cities and rapidly expanding industry in the relatively short time span of one generation.

This dramatic change depended to a considerable degree on advances in transportation and communication. The construction of transcontinental railroads and the building of a network of telegraph and telephone lines revolutionized ways of living and of doing business. Such changes contributed to the growth of the oil and steel industries. Still in their infancy in the 1850's, both had become giants by 1900.

Industrial growth was directed by a shrewd group of businessmen, called "captains of industry," and it received encouragement from both state and federal governments. During the last decades of the century, leading businessmen and industrialists amassed enormous fortunes. How they spent their wealth in turn affected the country's social and cultural development.

In the following pages we shall consider the factors that brought about the rise of industry and also note some of its effects on our country.

1 *Transportation and Communication Improve*

The railroads played a vital role in the country's industrial and agricultural growth after 1865. They were the common element that influenced and stimulated all the tremendous economic activity that took place in the closing decades of the 1800's. They carried raw materials to the manufacturing plants and distributed the finished products to far-flung markets. Similarly, the railroads transported homesteaders to the West, brought them farm machinery and household goods, and hauled their crops to market. Without the railroads, rapid industrial growth would have been impossible.

Railroads prove their importance during the Civil War. You will recall that at the beginning of the Civil War the United States had about 30,000 miles of railroad track. Two thirds of this mileage was in the free states, most of it east of the Mississippi River. The railroads at this time carried about two thirds of the country's internal traffic. Yet it took the war to make clear the vital importance of the railroads. The Union used its east-west rail connections to transport food, arms and ammunition, and clothing to the troops, and some rail lines carried soldiers to the battlefield. At the same time, civilians continued to travel by railroad. During the war years nearly 5000 miles of new tracks were built in the North. The Confederacy, by contrast, found itself in a desperate situation when its railroads were captured or destroyed.

. . . .

CHAPTER FOCUS

1. Transportation and communication improve.
2. Steel and oil stimulate industrial growth.
3. Many factors aid industrial expansion.
4. Captains of industry leave their mark on American life.

Shortages of food and war supplies and the inability to move troops seriously hampered the South's war effort.

The transcontinental railroad is completed. By 1862 the importance of the railroads was so well-established that Congress voted to appropriate funds for a transcontinental line (page 404). The Central Pacific Railroad was to build eastward from Sacramento, and the Union Pacific would push westward from Omaha. The government promised generous aid to the two companies, giving them large grants of land as well as a free right of way through public land. For each mile of track laid, the railroad company received ten square miles of land, in alternate sections along the right of way. The government also offered to lend the railroads 16,000 or 32,000 or 48,000 dollars for each mile of road built. The amount depended on the nature of territory to be crossed — plains, foothills, or mountains.

The work progressed rapidly, despite such difficulties as transporting supplies, fighting Indians, and laying track through the Rocky Mountains. The Union Pacific's construction crews — chiefly war veterans and Irish immigrants — laid more than a thousand miles of track. The Central Pacific, employing Chinese laborers, built nearly 700 miles. On May 10, 1869, the two lines came together at Promontory Point near Ogden, Utah. A golden spike was driven into the final tie, and news of the event was flashed by telegraph to all parts of the country.

More transcontinental lines are built. Even before this first cross-country railroad was completed, the construction of other transcontinental lines had started. The Northern Pacific eventually extended from Minnesota across the northern plains to Oregon and Washington. The Southern Pacific ran from New Orleans across Texas and through the Gadsden Purchase to California. The Atchison, Topeka and Santa Fe also laid track in the Southwest; it stretched from Kansas through New Mexico and Arizona to the West Coast. (See the map on the next page for the routes of the western railroads.)

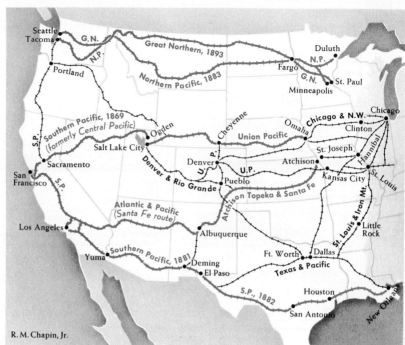

R. M. Chapin, Jr.

WESTERN RAILROADS, 1893

With the completion of the Great Northern Railroad, five transcontinental lines linked the Midwest and the Pacific. Note that in comparison with the railroads of 1880 (map, page 425), there were many more short, connecting lines by 1893. Why had the "long drives" from Texas to Kansas ended by the 1890's?

MAP STUDY

Each of the transcontinental lines had many feeders, or subsidiary routes. States and cities were eager to have as many rail connections as possible. Indeed, the railroad spelled the difference between growth and stagnation for many western communities. In order to encourage railroad construction and influence the location of routes, states and cities pledged enormous sums of money.

Railroads encourage settlement of the West. All of the transcontinental railroads helped promote the settlement of the West. The lines served the homesteaders and ranchers by shipping their products to eastern markets and bringing them manufactured goods in return. In some areas, as rapid settlement increased the railroads' volume of traffic, rates were reduced. Other railroads, however, continued to charge high rates regardless of growing profits.

The most satisfactory relations between settlers and a western railroad existed along the Great Northern route, running from Minnesota to Seattle, Washington. Credit

for the success of the Great Northern belongs to James J. Hill, one of the country's outstanding railroad builders. Hill insisted on high standards in the construction of roadbeds, track, and bridges. As a result, his railroad operated far more efficiently than many others.

Completed in 1893, the Great Northern was built too late to receive government land grants. Yet it did far more than the other western railroads to promote settlement along its right of way. Hill encouraged farmers in the East and in Europe to settle in the West, and he helped new communities build banks, schools, and churches. To create new markets for the settlers' produce, he arranged for steamship service between the Orient and the Pacific terminals of his railroad. Hill realized that the prosperity of the farms and ranches in Minnesota, the Dakotas, Montana, Idaho, Oregon, and Washington would create additional business for the Great Northern.

Railroads combine to form great systems. As new lines were built in the West,

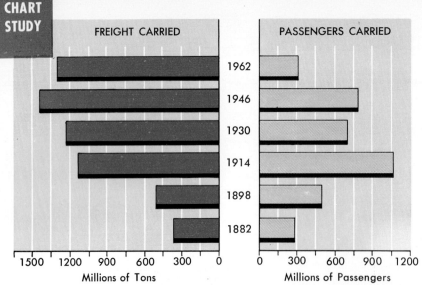

FREIGHT CARRIED | PASSENGERS CARRIED

1962
1946
1930
1914
1898
1882

1500 1200 900 600 300 0
Millions of Tons

0 300 600 900 1200
Millions of Passengers

VOLUME OF RAILROAD TRAFFIC, 1882–1962

Note the changing role of railroads. While passenger traffic has declined, the volume of freight carried has increased. The year 1946 reflects the extended use of railroads during and immediately following World War II.

the older railroads in the East were consolidated into a few large lines. Cornelius Vanderbilt masterminded a series of mergers which resulted in the giant New York Central System. With his profits from a steamship company, he bought several small New York railroads during the war years. Then, in 1869 he merged the New York Central (page 304) and the Hudson River Railroad, which provided service between New York and Buffalo. Vanderbilt continued to acquire connecting lines until he died in 1877. By then, the New York Central System reached into nineteen states and the Canadian province of Ontario. An able railroad manager, Vanderbilt double-tracked the Central's lines and, like Hill, insisted on well-constructed roadbeds, bridges, and embankments. Express trains, traveling over safe, smooth roadbeds, carried passengers from New York to Chicago in 24 hours.

Another large system that emerged during the late 1800's was the Pennsylvania Railroad. Having bought up smaller lines between Philadelphia and Pittsburgh (page 301), it extended its services to Chicago and St. Louis. By the end of the century the Pennsylvania Railroad also ran to Cleveland, Washington, D.C., and through New Jersey to the Hudson River. Free access to New York City was blocked by the New York Central, but the Pennsylvania Railroad tunneled under the Hudson River to reach the heart of the city.

Meanwhile, the Baltimore and Ohio reached northward to Philadelphia and westward to Chicago and St. Louis. In the South, the largest line was the Southern Railway System, linking Washington with New Orleans.

Rivalry develops for control of the railroads. The great profits brought by railroading in the late nineteenth century attracted financial adventurers. Probably the most unsavory were Daniel Drew and Jay Gould, who controlled the Erie Railroad. Since this line competed with the New York Central for freight between New York and Chicago, Cornelius Vanderbilt wanted to get control of the Erie. When Drew and Gould discovered that Vanderbilt was buying Erie stock, they issued thousands of shares of fraudulent stock. A struggle for control of the Erie followed. Finally, in 1868, with the railroad in serious financial trouble, Vanderbilt lost interest, and the "Erie war" was called off.

Another spectacular clash between railroad magnates took place in the 1890's. James J. Hill bought up the Northern Pacific (which competed with his Great Northern) and also purchased the Chicago, Burlington & Quincy in order to secure direct access to Chicago. This touched off a contest with Edward H. Harriman, another railroad magnate, who also wanted the Chicago, Burlington & Quincy. The struggle was resolved in 1901 when Hill and Harriman merged their railroad holdings to form the giant Northern Securities Company (page 558).

Some railroads engage in unfair practices. The railroad men carried on their struggles for control without much regard for the public interest. Thus, the managers of some railroads charged unfair rates or in other ways took advantage of the public.

(1) Some western lines overcharged farmers who had to use a particular carrier in sending crops to market (page 437).

(2) Many railroads showed favoritism in their rate schedules. Some shippers were charged lower rates than competitors using the same line. Similarly, certain cities and sections of the country received more favorable rates than others. In the 1870's it cost more to send freight directly from Rochester, New York, to St. Louis than to send it by way of New York City. Even over the same route the railroads often charged more for a "short haul" than for a "long haul."

(3) Another example of favoritism was the *rebate* or *kickback*, a practice whereby certain large shippers had part of their freight charges refunded by the railroad.

In addition to such unfair practices, some railroads failed to provide safe and efficient service. Certain railroads had been hastily and carelessly built. Too often, moreover, the tracks and roadbeds were inadequately maintained. It was said of the Erie Railroad that a passenger took his life in his hands when he boarded a train. All of these abuses angered the American public and finally led to government regulation of railroads in the late 1880's (page 496).

Technical improvements are made in railroading. In spite of the mismanagement of some lines, a number of improvements took place in railroading. Soon after the Civil War, coal-burning engines replaced the dangerous wood-burners of the 1850's. Also, the railroads adopted tracks of standard gauge or width, so that passenger and freight cars could be transferred from one company's lines to another's. George M. Pullman introduced the sleeping car in 1864. A few years later he brought out the first "restaurant cars," or diners. Greater safety was assured by the introduction of George Westinghouse's automatic air brake. Developed in 1869, the air brake permitted the engineer to apply the brakes on all cars at the same time. Other safety devices were the automatic block signal, which reduced the danger of collisions, and the safety coupler, which saved the lives of many trainmen.

The replacement of iron rails with steel rails was another improvement of far-reaching significance. The steel rails could safely support ten times as much weight, and they lasted twenty times as long. Consequently, larger, heavier locomotives could be used, more freight cars could be included in a single train, and each car could transport more weight. Steel was also used to build railroad bridges that could support the

Railroad travelers in the late 1800's could enjoy lavish meals in Pullman's dining cars.

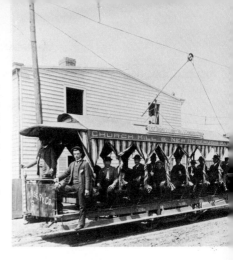

Electric trolley cars were first used in Richmond, Va., in the late 1880's (right). Managers of horse-drawn streetcar lines came from all over the country to inspect the new trolleys, which then appeared in other cities.

Other forms of city transportation in the late 1800's included San Francisco's cable cars. These colorful streetcars still carry San Franciscans up and down the city's steep hills (above). New York built an elevated railway line and experimented with steam-driven cars (right), but horse-drawn streetcars and carriages continued in use for a while.

heavier trains. In the country's largest cities, the railroading era produced some monumental stations. Earlier depots gave way to large train-sheds and elaborate waiting rooms. Designed by leading architects, some of these stations became landmarks in the nation's large cities. Notable examples were Grand Central Station and Pennsylvania Station in New York.

The rapid growth of railroads influences American life. In spite of two financial panics which temporarily slowed construction, the railroad network increased from 30,000 miles in 1860 to nearly 200,000 by 1900.[1] This was more railroad mileage

[1] American railroad mileage reached its peak, nearly 260,000 miles, in 1916. After that, competition from the Panama Canal and from trucks, automobiles, and airplanes gradually led to the abandonment of some unprofitable lines.

than in all Europe and amounted to nearly 40 per cent of the world total.

This great system of transportation played a vital role in the expanding American economy during the late 1800's. We have already seen how railroads promoted settlement of the West. The construction and maintenance of railroad lines also provided jobs for hundreds of thousands of workers. Moreover, the railroads were among the most important customers of many industries. Railroad development was closely connected with the growth of the steel industry, for example. The steel companies produced rails for the many new lines being built, while the railroads carried iron ore and coal to the steel mills and transported finished steel products to markets across the country.

The railroads also influenced the development of American cities during the postwar years. Railroads helped create the first modern suburbs by making it possible for city workers to live miles away from their place of employment. By the 1870's many major cities had suburbs whose residents depended on railroads. Typical of these new residential areas were the ring of suburbs around New York City, the "Main Line" communities west of Philadelphia, Hyde Park and Oak Park outside Chicago, and Palo Alto south of San Francisco.

Urban transportation is modernized. The growth of the cities, in turn, made new forms of urban transportation necessary. Horse-drawn carriages and streetcars were unable to handle the swelling city populations. New York experimented with steam-driven elevated railroads, while San Francisco developed cablecars. But the best solution to the problem of mass transportation proved to be electric-powered streetcars. Richmond, Virginia, was the first city to install trolley cars with overhead electric wires (1887). The electric streetcar was a great improvement over the dirty coal-burning trains and the elevated tracks that cut off light and air from the streets below.

During the 1890's most cities adopted the electric trolley as their major system of public transportation. Electricity also enabled Boston (1897) and New York (1904) to build subway lines.

Telegraph service is expanded. Methods of communication as well as transportation made rapid strides after the Civil War. Although the earliest telegraph lines were built in the 1840's (page 258), the country's first transcontinental telegraph line was not completed until 1861. It proved an immediate success. The rate for sending a message from Missouri to California soon dropped from a dollar a word to five dollars for a ten-word telegram. Rates were further reduced as new lines were constructed. Also, the invention of the duplex telegraph made it possible to send messages in both directions over the same wire at the same time. The multiplex telegraph, relaying many messages simultaneously, brought still lower costs and greater efficiency. Western Union became the leading telegraph company. By buying up competing companies, Western Union controlled the country's telegraph service by 1900.

Cyrus Field lays a transatlantic cable. Samuel Morse had no sooner invented the

The transoceanic cable and the telephone revolutionized communication. The old print at left shows the cable arriving in Newfoundland in 1866. Above, Alexander Graham Bell speaks over the telephone line that opened between New York and Chicago in 1892.

telegraph than some people began to consider the possibility of a cable between the United States and Europe. In the 1850's Cyrus Field made several attempts to lay such a cable across the Atlantic Ocean. Queen Victoria and President Buchanan sent messages to each other over a cable completed in 1858. This cable broke, however, and not until 1866 was Field able to re-establish transatlantic service. The cable reduced the time for sending messages from ten days by steamer to a matter of seconds. The new method of communication changed patterns of international trade and greatly speeded up the exchange of diplomatic messages between nations.

The telephone is introduced. The most revolutionary change in methods of communication was provided by the telephone. It was invented by a young teacher of the deaf, Alexander Graham Bell. He first displayed his "talking box" at the Philadelphia Exposition in 1876. It attracted little attention until the Emperor of Brazil, a visitor at the exposition, consented to listen to it. "It speaks! It speaks!" he is said to have exclaimed. From that moment Bell's instrument created a sensation.

Bell offered his invention to Western Union, only to have it rejected as an "electrical toy." The inventor soon found a financial backer, however, and the Bell Telephone Company was formed. By encouraging local communities to establish telephone service, the Bell system expanded rapidly, despite competition from other companies. The first commercial long-distance line, between Boston and Providence, Rhode Island, was opened in 1881. By 1900 nearly one and a half million telephones were in use in the United States. Since unified service was found to be more satisfactory, the giant American Telephone and Telegraph Company took over the Bell Company and gradually gained control of the most important telephone lines in the country.

▶ CHECK-UP

1. What contributions to the nation's economic development were made by railroads? How did the government encourage the building of the first transcontinental railroad? How did the Great Northern promote western settlement?

2. Why were small railroads merged to form large systems? What large systems were formed? Give examples of the unfair practices of some railroads.

3. What improvements took place in railroading? In urban transportation? In communication?

- - - - - - - - - - - - - - - - - - - -

2 *Steel and Oil Stimulate Industrial Growth*

The growth of modern manufacturing is best illustrated by the story of the expansion of the steel and oil industries, whose products play such an important part in modern American life.

Steel becomes a great industry. It was known before the Civil War that steel was much stronger than iron, but methods of producing steel were slow and expensive. William Kelly had perfected an air-blast method of making steel (page 299). But his discovery went unheralded until an Englishman, Henry Bessemer, applied for American patents on a similar process in 1857. During the Civil War a company in Michigan bought Kelly's patent, while another in Troy, New York, produced steel according to Bessemer's method. Shortly after the war the two companies merged their patent rights, and the process of making Bessemer steel spread rapidly. By 1876 a dozen Bessemer plants were in operation.

The open-hearth process of manufacturing steel was introduced from Europe during these same years. Using lower-grade ore and large quantities of scrap metal, it produced a steel of high quality that was well-suited for making locomotives. When the United States began building skyscrapers and producing automobiles and high-speed machinery, the demand for

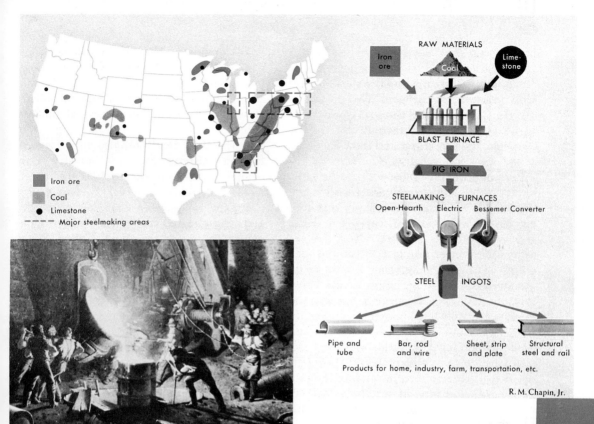

STEELMAKING

*Not all the deposits of raw materials shown on the map were known in the 1890's.
But the men who made steel followed the basic method outlined at right. With the
development of new equipment and techniques, steel has become a giant industry.*

open-hearth steel increased. By the early
1900's about one half of the steel produced
in this country came from open-hearth mills.
Total steel production rose from less than
600,000 tons in 1876 to more than ten million tons by 1900.

**New sources of raw materials are
discovered.** These improved processes of
manufacture made possible a great increase
in steel production. But it was also necessary to find larger supplies of iron, coal,
and limestone, all of which are needed in
the making of steel. The steel industry was
originally centered in western Pennsylvania
and the neighboring areas of Ohio, where
all the necessary raw materials were available. As the steel industry grew, however,
high-grade iron ore began to be mined in
northern Michigan and Minnesota. Oreboats on the Great Lakes brought enormous

quantities of ore to ports on the lower
Lakes, where it was loaded on railroad cars
for shipment to the Pittsburgh area. Pennsylvania remained the leading coal-mining
state, although rich veins were uncovered
in West Virginia, Ohio, and Illinois, as well
as other states. Largely because of the demands of the steel industry, coal production
rose from 25 million tons in 1865 to almost
270 million tons in 1900.

Steel centers develop. While Pittsburgh remained the leading steel city, important new steel centers grew up along
the Great Lakes. Using iron ore from Minnesota and coal from Ohio and Illinois,
blast furnaces were built along the Lake
Michigan shore of Illinois and Indiana.
Cleveland and Detroit also became steel
centers. Soon after iron ore and coal were
discovered near Birmingham, Alabama, that

city became the "Pittsburgh of the South" (page 395).

Andrew Carnegie builds a steel empire. Most powerful of the new steel producers was the Carnegie Steel Company near Pittsburgh. It was the creation of Andrew Carnegie, the shrewdest and most energetic of the steel industrialists.

Born in Scotland, Andrew Carnegie came to the United States and started work when he was only thirteen. His first job was bobbin boy in a cotton mill, earning a dollar and twenty cents a week. Next he became a messenger boy in a Pittsburgh telegraph office. After securing a position as private secretary to an officer of the Pennsylvania Railroad, Carnegie's energy and intelligence won him quick promotions. In time, he became superintendent of the railroad's important Pittsburgh division. Despite his success in railroading, Carnegie decided in 1865 to devote his time to ironmaking, an industry in which he had already invested most of his savings. Realizing the future possibilities of steel, he built the world's largest steel mill near Pittsburgh in the early 1870's.

Carnegie installed the new Bessemer furnaces and produced the kind of steel needed for railroad tracks. In fact, most of the steel rails sold in the 1880's came from his plant. Carnegie turned most of his own earnings and those of the company back into the business and thus was able to expand and modernize his steel plants. He also introduced new methods of accounting, offered bonuses to encourage executives and workers, and employed research scientists to find still better methods of producing steel.

Carnegie soon recognized the advantages to be gained from controlling the many branches of steel production. At first he demanded rebates from the railroads that carried his ore and finished products, but eventually he purchased his own railroads. In 1882 he bought out the country's largest coke producer.[2] Carnegie also bought up rights to ore fields and built a fleet of Great Lakes oreboats. The Carnegie Steel Company soon established a commanding lead in the industry. By 1900 it was making annual profits of nearly 40 million dollars, of which Carnegie's share was 25 million dollars.

The U. S. Steel Corporation is formed. Having mastered the steel industry, Carnegie decided to retire. In 1901 the investment and banking firm of J. P. Morgan and Company bought the Carnegie properties and consolidated them with other companies to create the giant United States Steel Corporation. With a capital investment valued at almost one and a half billion dollars, U. S. Steel produced over half of this country's iron and steel. The huge firm controlled every stage of the steelmaking process, from the mining of the ore to the distribution of the finished product.

Oil drilling begins. The oil industry got under way at about the same time as the steel industry. Before 1859, farmers had considered the seepage of oil a nuisance since it made streams impure and ruined their wells. Sometimes, however, this petroleum, known as "rock oil," was bottled and sold as a medicine.

In the early 1850's a young Dartmouth graduate, George H. Bissell, became interested in petroleum. He sent a sample of oil to a distinguished scientist, Benjamin Silliman of Yale University. Silliman reported that petroleum would make a good illuminant (source of light) and added that naphtha, paraffin, and lubricating oil could also be produced from it. Encouraged by this information, Bissell hired Edwin Drake to begin drilling for oil around Titusville, Pennsylvania. "Drake's Folly" occasioned jokes and laughter, but in 1859 Drake struck oil. Soon his well was yielding 20 barrels of oil a day.

Oil becomes big business. News of Drake's discovery brought hundreds of oil prospectors to western Pennsylvania. The Titusville area became thick with derricks, and the drilling of wells soon extended into West Virginia and Ohio. By the end of the Civil War over two million barrels of oil were being produced annually. For refining, the crude oil at first was transported

---

[2] Coke, made by baking coal, was essential in "firing" the blast furnaces.

Millions of Long Tons

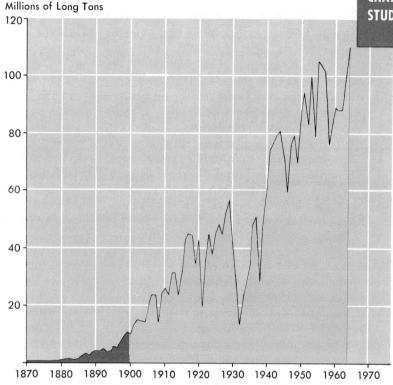

**GROWTH OF STEEL
PRODUCTION**

The increase in steel production from 1870 to 1900 is emphasized in this chart. Annual output was more than ten million long tons by the end of the century. Notice, however, the striking rise in production since 1900.

to Pittsburgh or Cleveland in river barges or in wooden tank cars hauled by teams of horses. But the barges leaked, and the tank cars often caught fire. Following the war, railroad tank cars built of iron carried most of the country's oil. After the turn of the century, underground pipe lines became the most common method of transporting oil. By then the industry was producing over 60 million barrels a year. Most of this oil was converted into kerosene to be used for lighting and heating. Before long, however, the mass production of automobiles (page 671) made gasoline a more important petroleum product.

John D. Rockefeller organizes the Standard Oil Company. John D. Rockefeller became master of the oil industry just as Carnegie controlled steel. Rockefeller developed into one of the most ambitious, relentless, and "sharp" industrialists of the late nineteenth century. Before he was 20, he had become a partner in a successful Cleveland produce firm. Having saved his profits, Rockefeller left the produce business after the war to form an oil refining company. He had already invested in a small oil refinery in Cleveland.

Though most refineries then were in Pittsburgh near the oil wells, Rockefeller recognized that Cleveland had better rail and water connections with national markets than Pittsburgh. Rockefeller also realized that pipe lines and the new tank cars would enable him to carry crude oil to his refinery. He modernized the Cleveland plant and soon built a second refinery with the newest improvements. In 1867 Rockefeller and several partners formed the Standard Oil Company of Ohio. Within five short years Rockefeller had a modern oil refining company with a capital investment valued at a million dollars.

Standard Oil builds a monopoly. Rockefeller and his associates now set out to win full control of the oil industry. Efficient operation enabled them to undersell competitors and still make money. Standard Oil soon acquired four fifths of the refineries in Cleveland alone.

Rockefeller delivered a heavy blow to his competitors by getting special privileges from the railroads. He persuaded a group of refiners in Pittsburgh and Philadelphia to join him in forming the South Improvement Company. This organization then made a secret agreement with the railroads, by which the railroads would sharply increase freight rates on oil for all refiners *except* the South Improvement Company. Furthermore, this company would receive rebates on the increased rates *paid by its competitors.* When news of this deal leaked out, the Pennsylvania legislature canceled the charter of the South Improvement Company. But Standard Oil was so powerful that it pressured the railroads into paying the rebates anyway.

Rockefeller found still other ways to dominate the oil industry. Rather than pay for the services of the independent pipe-line companies, Rockefeller built his own pipe lines. This move drove most of the independent pipe-line firms into bankruptcy. Standard also developed a nation-wide marketing system. An extensive network of sales offices sent Rockefeller regular reports about rival firms that were un-

derselling Standard products. These competitors were warned to withdraw from the race. If they refused, Rockefeller cut his prices until the opponent agreed to sell out. Standard could afford to take heavy losses in one area by raising its prices in another. Within fifteen years after he entered the industry, Rockefeller controlled 95 per cent of the country's oil refineries.

Though bitterly criticized in his time by competitors and others, Rockefeller made important contributions to the nation's economic growth. He found an oil industry composed of many small producers, few of which were efficiently organized. He left an industry of massive proportions, able to produce on a large scale and meet the ever-increasing demand for oil.

Other industries develop. New processes and business methods affected many other industries besides oil and steel. Dairy farmers were aided by new milking ma-

From a crude well drilled in Titusville, Pennsylvania, by Edwin Drake (in top hat in the picture at left above) has developed America's huge oil industry. Modern refining plants (above) work around the clock to convert crude oil into useful products. One of these products, gasoline, makes possible transportation by automobile and truck (left).

chines and cream separators. Gail Borden, founder of the Borden Milk Company, had worked out a process for producing condensed milk in the 1850's. After the Civil War, he built a plant in Texas and began large-scale production. New methods also revolutionized the flour milling industry. When the farmers on the plains began growing hard winter wheat in the 1870's, the millers had to develop new processes for grinding this grain. They found that steel rollers did a better job than the old millstones and produced a finer grade of flour. One of the biggest operators in the Minneapolis milling industry was Charles A. Pillsbury. Like Carnegie and Rockefeller, he was quick to utilize new improvements in his field.

Meat packing in the prewar days involved shipping hogs and cattle to Cincinnati or Chicago. There the animals were slaughtered and the meat salted down and packed in barrels for shipment to eastern markets. Sometimes animals were shipped all the way to the East Coast and butchered in local markets. The pattern of meat packing changed with the introduction of the refrigerator car. The cattlemen often did their own slaughtering and shipped the carcasses to Chicago in refrigerator cars. Some meat packing was done in Omaha and Kansas City, but the companies of Gustavus Swift and Philip Armour made Chicago the undisputed meat-packing center of the country. Their plants were equipped with conveyor belts and a wide variety of machines that cut, dressed, and packed the pork and beef. Moreover, the packers found uses for every possible by-product.

▶ CHECK-UP

1. What factors made possible the rapid growth of the steel industry after 1865? Where did steel centers develop? Why? What ideas enabled Carnegie to become a leader in steel production?

2. Why did oil become big business? What methods were used by Rockefeller and his associates to gain control of the oil industry?

3. What important changes were made in flour milling? In meat packing?

· · · · · · · · · · · · · · · · · ·

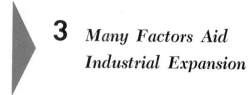

3 Many Factors Aid Industrial Expansion

Technology and invention spur industrial growth. What were the reasons for this country's remarkable industrial expansion in the late nineteenth century? One vital factor was the advance of *technology* — the practical application of science to industry. Advances in technology resulted in the invention or perfection of all sorts of machines, labor-saving devices, and scientific processes. The large-scale manufacture of steel, upon which the industrial age rests, would have been impossible without the new technology. Startling proof of the widespread interest in technology is found in the records of the United States Patent Office. From its establishment in 1790 up to 1860, the Patent Office granted only 36,000 patents. But in the next thirty years, it issued 440,000.

Electricity provides light and power. In the later 1800's, technology gave us a new and important form of power — electricity. In 1879 Thomas A. Edison had perfected an electric light bulb. Three years later he built a power station in New York City that provided electric current to 85 buildings. Edison's company soon merged with the General Electric Company. A major rival was the Westinghouse Electric Company, founded by George Westinghouse, inventor of the air brake (page 445). The Westinghouse Company developed generators and transformers for alternating current. This ultimately proved far more efficient than direct current, which Edison had originally used.

The use of electric power began to change the face of American cities. Office buildings and expensive homes installed electric lights. The electric arc lamp, developed in the 1870's, eventually replaced gas street lights. By making more efficient elevators possible, electric power prepared the way for the skyscraper. Electric trolley cars transformed urban transportation.

Despite the startling changes which electricity brought about in the late 1800's, however, its full impact was not felt until the twentieth century. Coal, rather than electricity, provided the power for railroads and fed the steam engines in the factories of the nineteenth century. In fact, coal was the country's major source of power from the Civil War to the First World War.

Resources are plentiful. An obvious factor contributing to the growth of industry was the country's abundant resources. During this period the steel industry found all the coal and iron ore it needed within the United States; likewise, the oil industry found vast resources of crude petroleum. The farmers of the Great Plains provided quantities of grain to keep the millers busy. Ranchers raised herds of cattle to supply the meat-packing firms. Forests yielded wood for furniture factories and paper mills. The railroads, of course, provided the necessary transportation, carrying farm products and raw materials to processing and manufacturing plants, and distributing the finished goods to markets all over the country.

Labor is available. The growing number of workers also contributed to the country's industrial expansion. The population of the United States more than doubled between 1860 and 1900, increasing from 31 million to 76 million. Part of this increase came from the arrival of some 14 million immigrants. Many of these new Americans took factory jobs in the cities where they disembarked or in other industrial centers. In addition, thousands of Americans left small farms in the eastern

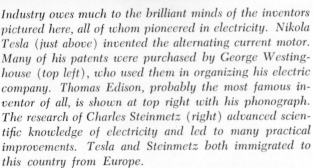

Industry owes much to the brilliant minds of the inventors pictured here, all of whom pioneered in electricity. Nikola Tesla (just above) invented the alternating current motor. Many of his patents were purchased by George Westinghouse (top left), who used them in organizing his electric company. Thomas Edison, probably the most famous inventor of all, is shown at top right with his phonograph. The research of Charles Steinmetz (right) advanced scientific knowledge of electricity and led to many practical improvements. Tesla and Steinmetz both immigrated to this country from Europe.

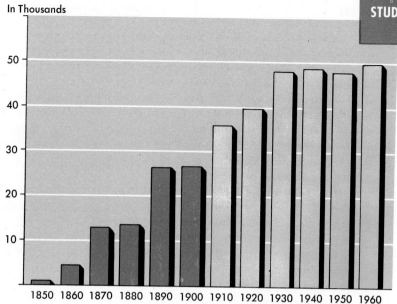

In Thousands

PATENTS GRANTED, 1850–1960

This chart features patents issued by the United States Patent Office from 1850 to 1900. The rapid increase in the number of inventions reflects advances in technology. A glance ahead to 1960 will show that the number of patents granted annually has nearly doubled since 1900.

1850 1860 1870 1880 1890 1900 1910 1920 1930 1940 1950 1960

---

and midwestern states to go to the cities. By 1900 more than 60 per cent of American workers had non-agricultural jobs.

Business develops new forms of organization. In the years following the Civil War, business leaders continued their search for more effective forms of business organization. Well before the war, many businesses had become *corporations* (page 259). A corporation received a charter from a state legislature, entitling it to conduct a certain kind of business. The corporation could raise capital by selling shares of stock (certificates of ownership). Stockholders received their share of the corporation's profits in the form of dividends, and they had the right to elect directors of the corporation. The corporation had definite advantages over a partnership or proprietorship. It could raise the large amounts of capital needed to build industrial plants and to buy machinery and raw materials. Moreover, the financial risks were divided among a large number of people, and the corporation was not affected by the death of individual stockholders.

During the 1870's many corporations formed *pools* in order to reduce competition. Pooling meant that corporations in the same line of business would agree to produce only a certain amount of goods and sell to only a certain part of the market.

For example, when the cordage manufacturers produced more rope and twine than the market could absorb, they formed a pool to control output and divide up the market. Some railroads formed pools, with the result that passengers and shippers had to pay higher rates. In the late 1880's the federal government prohibited railroad pools (page 496), but by that time the practice was already on the decline. Since a pool was a "gentlemen's agreement" and had no legal standing, its members often violated the agreement and tried to capture more than their share of the market.

Trusts prove more effective than pools. In the 1880's businessmen turned to still another kind of organization. The *trust* was a legal combination of corporations. Enough shares of stock in each of the associated companies were turned over to a single board of trustees to give it control over the combined organization. In return, the stockholders received trust certificates which entitled them to a share of the trust's profits. Management of the various corporations, however, rested in the hands of the trustees. The first trust was organized by John D. Rockefeller and his business associates. In 1882 the controlling shares of stock in a number of separate oil companies were turned over to a board of trustees, thus forming the Standard Oil trust.

Other businessmen soon saw the advantages of forming trusts. Competition among the associated companies was eliminated, and, unlike the pools, trusts were chartered by state legislatures. Standard Oil served as a model for many other trusts; the sugar, whiskey, and lead trusts were among the largest.

In time, the term "trust" came to mean any organization which held a monopoly, or near monopoly, in a certain industry.[3] The trusts conducted their business on a huge scale. They reduced costs by using specialized machinery, controlling their own raw materials and marketing, and processing many by-products for sale. But few trusts gave the consumers the benefit of their lower costs. Most of them increased prices once they had secured a monopoly, and the consumer had no choice but to pay the price or do without.

Businessmen form holding companies. When trusts were declared illegal (page 500), businessmen soon devised still another type of organization. *Holding companies,* like trusts and corporations, were chartered by state legislatures. A holding

[3] A *monopoly* is the exclusive, or almost exclusive, control of an industry.

company did not operate a business of its own but bought and held the controlling stock of other corporations. The board of directors of the holding company actually *owned* a controlling block of stock in each of the associated corporations rather than just holding shares of stock in trust. Like the trust, however, the holding company controlled the management of other corporations, set production schedules, and established marketing policies and prices. One of the earliest holding companies was the American Sugar Refining Company. In the 1890's the Standard Oil trust was dissolved, and a holding company, known as Standard Oil of New Jersey, was formed. This holding company bought the securities of the companies that had previously belonged to the trust. The largest of all holding companies was the giant United States Steel Corporation.

The federal government aids business expansion. In spite of the laws banning railroad pools and limiting the activities of the trusts, the national government was friendly to business during the late 1800's. The government felt little obligation to regulate the economic life of the country; instead it maintained a "hands off" or

CHART STUDY

FORMS OF BUSINESS COMBINATIONS

This chart shows three types of business combinations which contributed to the rise of "big" business in the United States after the Civil War. The diagrams illustrate simple forms of the pool, the trust, and the holding company.

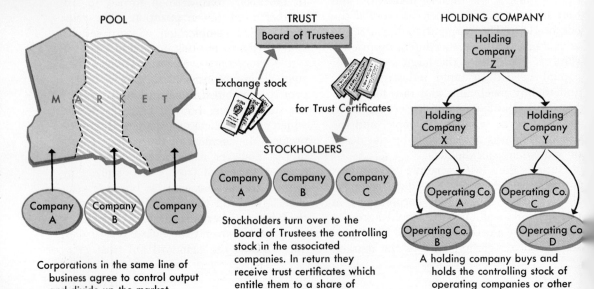

POOL

MARKET

Company A   Company B   Company C

Corporations in the same line of business agree to control output and divide up the market.

TRUST

Board of Trustees

Exchange stock for Trust Certificates

STOCKHOLDERS

Company A   Company B   Company C

Stockholders turn over to the Board of Trustees the controlling stock in the associated companies. In return they receive trust certificates which entitle them to a share of the trust's profits.

HOLDING COMPANY

Holding Company Z

Holding Company X   Holding Company Y

Operating Co. A   Operating Co. C

Operating Co. B   Operating Co. D

A holding company buys and holds the controlling stock of operating companies or other holding companies.

laissez-faire[4] attitude toward business, thus permitting the capitalist system to grow and expand freely. (Because of the small amount of government control, this system has also been called *private free enterprise*.) In fact, during the late nineteenth century the federal government not only refrained from regulation of business but encouraged industrial growth. Thus, the government substantially aided private business by (1) giving land grants and subsidies to railroads, (2) providing tariff protection against foreign competition to manufacturers, and (3) generally following financial policies favored by businessmen.

Captains of industry give direction to industrial expansion. The ingenuity and skill of certain leaders also promoted the nation's industrial growth. Shrewd businessmen like Carnegie and Rockefeller ran their companies efficiently, invested in the latest improvements and best machinery, cut costs wherever possible, and made the largest possible profits. These men guided the industrial expansion which resulted in an abundance of new products, created thousands of new jobs, and helped raise the country's standard of living. They have been called "industrial statesmen," "captains of industry," or "creators of wealth."

But there was another side to the picture. Some of these men were unscrupulous buccaneers like Daniel Drew and Jay Gould. Many of them exploited labor by paying the lowest possible wages. Most of the businessmen of the late 1800's believed in consolidation, not competition, and showed no mercy to small operators seeking a share of the market. John D. Rockefeller, Jr., compared the growth of a business like Standard Oil to the cultivation of an American Beauty Rose. It "can be produced in the splendor and fragrance which bring cheer to its beholder only by sacrificing the early buds which grow up around it. This is not an evil tendency in business. It is merely the working out of a law of nature. . . ." But businessmen who had been ruined by Standard Oil were not likely to agree. Some writers have charged that the "captains of

industry" could better be described as "economic spoilsmen" or "robber barons." In *The Age of the Moguls,* Stewart Holbrook strikes a balance:

> The best of them made deals, purchased immunity, and did other things which in 1860, or 1880, or even 1900, were considered no more than smart by their fellow Americans, but which today would give pause to the most conscientiously dishonest promoter. . . . I happen to believe that no matter how these men accumulated their fortunes, their total activities were of the greatest influence in bringing the United States to its present incomparable position in the world of business and industry.

America's industrial expansion is dramatic. Statistics highlight the story of America's industrial growth. On the eve of the Civil War, about one billion dollars was invested in manufacturing plants; by 1900 this type of investment had risen to almost ten billion dollars. During the same period, the value of the yearly output of manufactured goods zoomed from less than two billion dollars to some thirteen billion dollars. Industry before the war had still been centered in the Northeast. By the end of the century, however, other parts of the country had become industrialized. The Middle West had impressive iron and steel plants, oil refineries, meat-packing and flour-milling industries; the South had developed textile plants, tobacco companies, and a sizable iron and steel industry. In all sections the growth of industry had drawn people to the towns and cities. In 1860 one out of six people had lived in cities of 8000 or more; by 1900 one out of three lived in such cities. Still another measure of the country's industrial growth was the number of millionaires. The 1860 census listed only three, but by the end of the century almost 4000 Americans had achieved this position.

▶ CHECK-UP

1. How did the following contribute to the nation's industrial growth: electric power? natural resources? the expanding labor supply? Why was the corporation an effective form of business organization?

2. What was pooling? Why did trusts take the

---

[4] *Laissez faire* (pronounced *less′*ay *fair*) is a French expression meaning "leave alone."

place of pools? How did holding companies differ from trusts?

3. How did the federal government aid private business? How important were the captains of industry in the nation's economic development?

. . . .

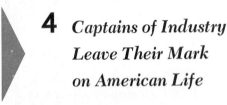

4 *Captains of Industry Leave Their Mark on American Life*

The industrialists defend their fortunes. The captains of industry felt no regrets about their methods of making money. A number of them had come from poor homes, had received little schooling, and had worked hard to reach the top. They felt entitled to the wealth they accumulated. John D. Rockefeller once said, "The good Lord gave me my money." Ministers in fashionable churches repeated this theme. In a famous lecture called "Acres of Diamonds," a Philadelphia clergyman told his listeners:

To secure wealth is an honorable ambition, and is one great test of a person's usefulness to others. . . . Money is power. Every good man and woman ought to strive for power, to do good with it when obtained. Tens of thousands of men and women get rich honestly. But they are often accused by an envious, lazy crowd of unsuccessful persons of being dishonest and oppressive. I say, get rich, get rich! But get money honestly, or it will be a withering curse.

Another justification of the industrial fortunes was based on the theory of *evolution* put forward in 1859 by the English scientist Charles Darwin (page 410). He suggested that those members of a group survived that were best adapted to their environment. Businessmen of the late 1800's applied the idea of the "survival of the fittest" to economic competition. This application of Darwin's theory came to be called *Social Darwinism*. Andrew Carnegie suggested that fierce competition was hard for the individual who lost, but was "best for the race, because it insures the survival of the fittest in every department."

The millionaires spend their money. Those industrialists who "survived" and made great fortunes had a zest for their work. Philip Armour once said: "I do not love the money. What I do love is the getting of it. . . . What other interest can you suggest to me? I do not read. I do not take any part in politics. What can I do?" While many of the businessmen concentrated on accumulating money, some of them were also eager to show the fruits of their success. In 1869 the historian Francis

During the 1880's polo became a popular sport among the young men of families who could afford to keep stables of polo ponies.

The public libraries built by Andrew Carnegie made book collections available to the people of many small towns across America. This painting shows the library at Fairfield, Iowa, not long after its construction.

Parkman had noted that "fine houses, fine clothes and sumptuous fare" were regarded by the Civil War profiteers as the "sum and substance of progress and civilization." The same was true of many of the men who made their fortunes later in the century.

The industrialists build imposing homes. One way for a captain of industry to show his wealth was by building an expensive house. Some of these houses were elaborate Gothic structures (page 267) with towers, gables, and ornate carving. A few captains of industry preferred medieval stone castles with drawbridges and moats. Those with better taste built distinctive houses designed by the architect H. H. Richardson.

By the 1880's New York captains of industry were setting a new trend with the houses they built along upper Fifth Avenue. These were modeled on French and Italian Renaissance town houses and country villas. The best of them were designed by the architect Richard Morris Hunt, who had studied in Paris and traveled widely in Europe. Few of the captains of industry were content with only a town house. They also built lavish houses at fashionable resorts like Newport, Rhode Island. The Vanderbilts hired Hunt to redesign "The Breakers" at Newport as an Italian villa.

The captains of industry who lived in these splendid houses also spent large sums to establish their place in "society." Their wives and daughters bought expensive clothes and jewels and entertained at elaborate dinners. Both town houses and summer homes had ballrooms large enough for a hundred or more dancers. Many families owned race horses and polo ponies or magnificent yachts.

Carnegie advocates a wiser use of money. Unlike many other wealthy men, Andrew Carnegie lived quietly and took little interest in fashionable society. In a magazine article, Carnegie declared that rich men should "set an example of modest, unostentatious living, shunning display or extravagance." They should consider "all surplus revenues" which came to them "simply as trust funds" to be administered for the benefit of the community. Wealthy men, said Carnegie, were blessed with the opportunity to make grants of money "from which the masses of their fellows will derive lasting advantages."

Carnegie practiced what he preached. He offered to build a library for any community willing to stock and maintain it. Ultimately some 2800 Carnegie Free Libraries were built in the United States and elsewhere. The steel master also gave many

PORTRAITS OF THE LATE 1800'S

by JOHN SINGER SARGENT

Many notable figures of the late 1800's had their portraits "done" by John Singer Sargent. At left is Sargent's portrait of Joseph Pulitzer, the Hungarian-born publisher of the New York *World*. Mr. and Mrs. Isaac Newton Phelps Stokes, the couple at right, were members of a prominent family in New York society.

millions to the Carnegie Foundation for the Advancement of Teaching, the Carnegie Institute of Technology in Pittsburgh, and other institutions of higher learning.

Businessmen patronize the arts. Few captains of industry were interested in the art, literature, and music of their own times. But many of them collected art objects and rare manuscripts of past centuries. Some of these collections eventually became the core of public museums and libraries. It has been estimated that J. P. Morgan (page 450) spent more than 60 million dollars on art and manuscripts. His rare books and manuscripts were housed in a beautiful library in New York which eventually was opened to the public. Morgan's art collection was given to the city's Metropolitan Museum of Art, of which he was president for many years.

Other captains of industry followed Morgan's example. The Henry Clay Frick Gallery and Guggenheim Museum in New York, the Mellon and Corcoran Galleries in Washington, and the Gardner Museum in Boston were all endowed by the wealthy families whose names they bear. The railroad fortune of Collis P. Huntington was given by a nephew to the famous Huntington Library in California. The captains of industry and their wives were also responsible for the construction of New York City's Metropolitan Opera House. Andrew Carnegie financed New York's famous Carnegie Hall, where concerts and recitals were given. Other industrialists contributed generously to the musical life of Boston, Philadelphia, Chicago, St. Louis, and other cities.

Captains of industry endow schools. Wealthy businessmen also aided the country's colleges and universities. Ezra Cornell, who made a fortune from the telegraph, founded Cornell University. Rail road money endowed Vanderbilt and Stanford Universities. John D. Rockefeller gave millions to the University of Chicago. Johns Hopkins University was endowed by a wealthy Baltimore banker and railroad man, while the tobacco fortune of James B. Duke eventually provided a trust fund for Duke University.

Artists and writers depict high society. Another mark of success was to have one's portrait painted by a well-known artist. The painter most favored by wealthy families was John Singer Sargent. Sargent's portraits of socially prominent Bostonians and New Yorkers made the viewer, according to one critic, "conscious of being in good company."

Among the American novelists who dealt with aspects of high society were William Dean Howells, Edith Wharton, and Henry James. Howells had published several books in the "genteel tradition" (page 404) before he wrote *The Rise of Silas Lapham,* a realistic study of a businessman's attempt to climb the social ladder. The success of Howells' novel encouraged other writers to focus their efforts on the realistic treatment of commonplace themes.

The novelist Edith Wharton was by birth and marriage a member of high society. Her intimate knowledge of life in New York, Boston, and Newport provided accurate background for such novels as *The House of Mirth* and *The Age of Innocence.*

Though born in New York, Henry James spent much of his life in England and on the continent. Many of his novels deal with the reactions of wealthy Americans traveling abroad and their influence on European society. Among his best novels are *Daisy Miller* and *The Portrait of a Lady.*

Horatio Alger points the "road to success." An author who influenced thousands of young readers, despite his lack of literary distinction, was Horatio Alger, Jr. Trained as a minister, Alger turned to the writing of boys' books and soon won a national reputation. Alger's 135 stories were all variations on one theme — the rise from "rags to riches" of the boy who worked hard, obeyed his parents, and was clean, courteous, and cheerful. The titles of these

stories reflect their optimism and happy endings — *Frank and Fearless, Onward and Upward, Luck and Pluck.* Alger died in 1899, but his books continued to be best sellers for many years.

▶ CHECK-UP

1. How did the industrialists justify their methods? In what ways did some millionaires show their wealth? Contrast with the views of Carnegie. How did captains of industry further the arts and education?

2. What artists and writers found their subjects in high society? What was the theme of Alger's books for boys?

• • • • • • • • • • • • • • • • • • • •

Clinching the Main Ideas in Chapter 21

In a few short decades the agricultural republic of the 1850's became an industrial, urban nation. Among the factors responsible for this transformation were the country's abundant natural resources, its genius for invention and business organization, a rapidly growing labor supply, new sources of power, and improved transportation and communication. Moreover, the federal government aided the industrial expansion in a number of ways. It granted land to the railroads, kept tariffs high, imposed few regulations on businessmen, and levied no income taxes.

As a result of all these factors, manufacturing increased tremendously in scope and volume between 1865 and 1900. New industries like steel and oil boomed, while the railroads crisscrossed the land, carrying raw materials to industrial plants and distributing finished goods to national markets. Many businessmen accumulated huge fortunes. Some spent their wealth to secure a place in high society. But others made lasting contributions to the nation's cultural life by endowing museums, libraries, and colleges.

Mass production of food and consumer goods meant a gradual rise in the standard of living for many Americans. But most of the industrial profits went to businessmen and stockholders. The immigrants and native-born Americans who provided the man power for industrial growth had little share in the nation's expanding wealth. Chapter 22 will describe the late 1800's from the viewpoint of the industrial workers and their families.

Chapter Review

Terms to Understand

1. pool
2. trust
3. rebate
4. rock oil
5. monopoly
6. holding company
7. "Erie war"
8. pipe lines
9. technology
10. corporation
11. U.S. Steel
12. *laissez faire*
13. "rags to riches"
14. short and long haul
15. transatlantic cable
16. private free enterprise
17. captains of industry
18. open-hearth steel
19. capitalist system
20. Northern Securities Company

What Do You Think?

1. After the Civil War, why did railroads sometimes charge more for a short haul than for a long haul?

2. Explain the theory of Social Darwinism. What was its origin? How was it justified?

3. Great industrialists and businessmen of the late 1800's have been called both "captains of industry" and "robber barons." Why? Which term do you think is more appropriate?

4. Why did both Pittsburgh, Pennsylvania, and Gary, Indiana, become important steel centers?

5. How did Andrew Carnegie seek to control the various branches of the steel industry? Why?

Using Your Knowledge of History

1. Debate: *Resolved,* That the use of electricity for light and power was the most im-

portant technological development in this country during the half century after 1865.

2. List the ten discoveries or inventions prior to 1915 which in your judgment did most to further this country's economic growth. Explain why you think so in each case.

3. Write an editorial commenting on Andrew Carnegie's views on personal wealth.

4. The nation's railroad network increased from about 30,000 miles in 1860 to nearly 200,000 miles in 1900. List and explain what you think are the five most important ways in which the railroads during this period contributed to the growth of the nation's economy.

Extending Your Knowledge of History

An excellent single volume on the growth of American industry is *Age of Enterprise: A Social History of Industrial America* by T. C. Cochran and William Miller. Other useful books are Ida Tarbell's *The Nationalizing of Business, 1878–1898;* Roger Burlingame's *Engines of Democracy* (on inventions and technology); and Samuel P. Hays' *The Response to Industrialism, 1885–1914.* For accounts of the railroad empires, see *American Railroads* by John F. Stover and *The Story of Western Railroads* by Robert E. Riegel. Matthew Josephson is critical of the captains of industry in *The Robber Barons;* Stewart Holbrook provides a balanced account in *The Age of the Moguls.* Frederick L. Allen's *The Great Pierpont Morgan* is a biography of J. P. Morgan In *American Heritage* see "The Legend of Jim Hill" by Stewart H. Holbrook (June, 1958) and "Epitaph for the Steel Master" by Robert L. Heilbroner (August, 1960), on Andrew Carnegie.

CHAPTER 22

An Urban Industrial Society Faces New Problems

So at last I was going to America! The boundaries burst.
The arch of heaven soared. A million suns shone out for
every star. The winds rushed in from outer space, roaring
in my ears, "America! America!"

MARY ANTIN, "THE PROMISED LAND"

Immigrants arriving in New York

1865–1900

In the years after 1865 the expanding economy of the United States attracted millions of immigrants seeking a better life. To them, as to the thousands of immigrants who had come earlier, this country seemed a land of golden opportunity. During the 1870's and '80's people from Ireland, Britain, Scandinavia, France, and Germany continued to pour into the United States. Thereafter the majority of the newcomers came from southern and eastern Europe — Italy, Greece, the Balkan countries, Austria-Hungary, Poland, and Russia.

Some of these people settled on western farms, but most found unskilled jobs in the cities of the Northeast and Middle West. At the same time the growing towns and cities attracted many native-born Americans from the countryside. As urban population rose sharply, most cities found themselves ill-prepared to deal with such problems as overcrowded slums and inadequate sanitation and other needs.

During these same years, low pay and poor working conditions led many Americans to join labor unions. Hoping to improve the workingman's lot, the unions sought the right to bargain with employers. On several occasions, violent strikes revealed the bitterness which existed between workers and management. At the same time, some individuals and organizations were working to improve relations between employers and employees, to remedy overcrowded conditions in cities, and to help immigrants get a better start.

CHAPTER TWENTY-TWO

1 *The United States Continues to Attract Immigrants*

Immigration increases. As you read in Chapter 21, the population of the United States jumped from 31 million in 1860 to 76 million by 1900. This growth resulted partly from a high birth rate and partly from increasing immigration. About 14 million foreigners came to American shores during this period (see chart, page 470). Though the number appears large in comparison with the 5 million who came to America between 1820 and 1860, the proportion of immigrants to the total population remained about the same — approximately 13 per cent. In other words, the nation's birth rate kept pace with the swelling tide of newcomers.

Reasons for immigration are unchanged. The motives of the immigrants who came to this country after 1865 were much the same as those of people who had come earlier. To them, this country was the "promised land" where they hoped to live a better life and give their children greater opportunities. They learned about these possibilities from relatives or friends who had already settled in the United States. Sometimes one exciting letter from America would persuade an entire village of people to leave their European homeland. Prospective immigrants also obtained information from American railroad agents offering western land at attractive prices,

and from spokesmen for American industries that needed factory workers. Agents for steamship lines competing for business also promoted immigration.

Opportunities in the United States seemed all the more inviting because of conditions in Europe. Many European countries were overpopulated. Both in farming areas and in cities, times were hard and jobs were scarce. Political oppression and religious persecution also caused some people to leave Europe. Still other reasons for leaving were heavy taxes and compulsory military service.

Many immigrants come from northern and western Europe. For about 25 years after the Civil War the majority of immigrants continued to come from northern and western Europe. Economic conditions in Ireland, for example, were still hard, though not as bad as during the famine years of the 1840's. Consequently many Irishmen joined friends and relatives in the United States. So also did large numbers of Welsh, Scottish, and English people. About half of the British immigrants were skilled workers, a much larger proportion than in any other group. They generally received higher wages than other newcomers and were also quick to join labor unions.

Many of the German and Scandinavian immigrants of the postwar years were country folk. Some of them settled on farms in the West, but many took unskilled jobs in mines, factories, and meat-packing and flour-milling plants. These newcomers, along with the Irish postwar immigrants, filled the demand for unskilled manual labor. By the mid-1890's, however, many of the Irish, German, and Scandinavian immigrants had acquired skills and enough knowledge of American ways to find better jobs.

By this time, moreover, economic conditions in northern and western Europe had improved. Though people continued to come to the United States from Ireland, Great Britain, Scandinavia, and Germany, the rate of immigration from these countries declined toward the end of the century.

Immigration from southern and eastern Europe increases. During much of the

- -

CHAPTER FOCUS

1. The United States continues to attract immigrants.
2. Crowded cities have many problems.
3. Workingmen organize national unions.
4. Workers strike, and management fights back.
5. Reformers try to help the underprivileged.

 (Continued on page 469)

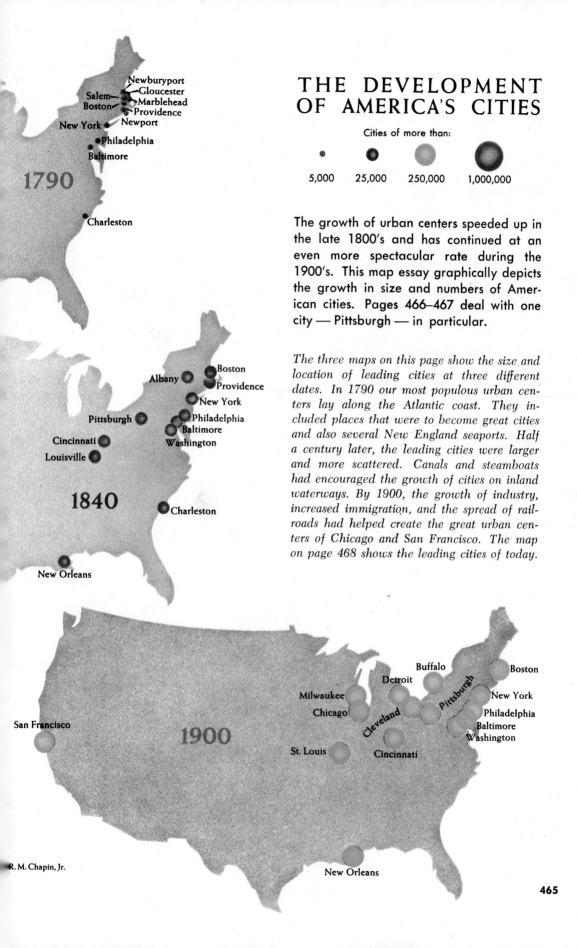

THE DEVELOPMENT OF AMERICA'S CITIES

Cities of more than:

| 5,000 | 25,000 | 250,000 | 1,000,000 |

The growth of urban centers speeded up in the late 1800's and has continued at an even more spectacular rate during the 1900's. This map essay graphically depicts the growth in size and numbers of American cities. Pages 466–467 deal with one city — Pittsburgh — in particular.

The three maps on this page show the size and location of leading cities at three different dates. In 1790 our most populous urban centers lay along the Atlantic coast. They included places that were to become great cities and also several New England seaports. Half a century later, the leading cities were larger and more scattered. Canals and steamboats had encouraged the growth of cities on inland waterways. By 1900, the growth of industry, increased immigration, and the spread of railroads had helped create the great urban centers of Chicago and San Francisco. The map on page 468 shows the leading cities of today.

1790

Newburyport
Gloucester
Salem
Marblehead
Boston
Providence
New York
Newport
Philadelphia
Baltimore

Charleston

1840

Albany
Boston
Providence
New York
Pittsburgh
Philadelphia
Baltimore
Cincinnati
Washington
Louisville
Charleston
New Orleans

1900

San Francisco
Buffalo
Boston
Detroit
Milwaukee
New York
Chicago
Cleveland
Pittsburgh
Philadelphia
Baltimore
Washington
St. Louis
Cincinnati
New Orleans

R. M. Chapin, Jr.

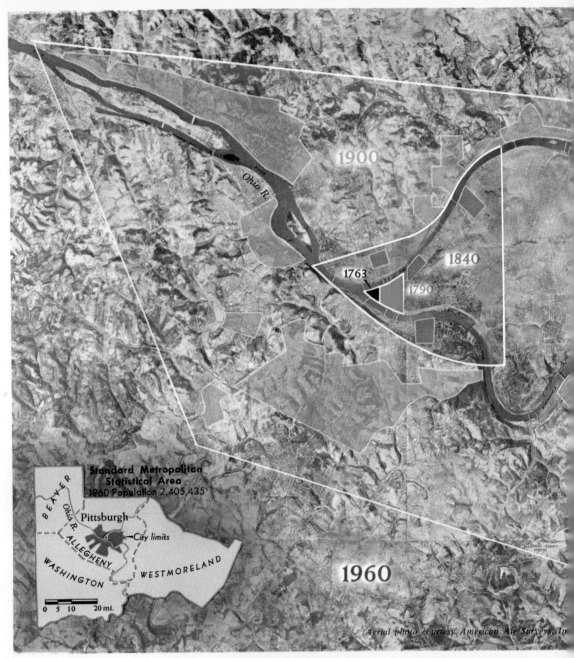

Standard Metropolitan
Statistical Area
1960 Population 2,405,435

BEAVER

Ohio R.

Pittsburgh

←City limits

ALLEGHENY

WASHINGTON

WESTMORELAND

0 5 10   20 mi.

1900

Ohio R.

1763

1790

1840

1960

Aerial photo courtesy American Air Surveys, In

The first-known sketch of Pittsburgh (below) showed the settlement in 1790. By the mid-1800's Pittsburgh had become a busy river port (right).

1960

1900

Allegheny R.

Monongahela R.

0 1 2 3 mi.

R. M. Chapin, Jr.

PITTSBURGH:
A Case Study in Urban Growth

Different colors on this aerial photograph of Pittsburgh illustrate the extension of population beyond what George Washington once called the "Land in the Fork" (black). This fork is formed by the junction of the Allegheny and Monongahela Rivers.

By 1790 (blue), the settlement's population stood at 376 inhabitants. Local merchants did a brisk business in land and supplies. Down the rivers flowed goods as well as settlers headed westward. By 1840, the triangle of settlement had expanded as residential and industrial towns (areas in dark red) grew up along the two branches of the Ohio. Iron and glass works were important industries in the city of 21,000 people. By 1900, Pittsburgh had become a sprawling steel center with a population of nearly 240,000. The dark green spots represent outlying industrial and residential areas.

Prosperity for Pittsburghers has always meant busy mills pouring out smoke. By 1946, air and water pollution and haphazard growth had become urgent problems. An urban renewal program began to clear the "Land in the Fork" of warehouses and parking lots, and smoke control restored the sparkling city landscape (below). Today, Pittsburgh is the core of a metropolitan area of over two million people.

Before industrial smoke was controlled, Pittsburgh was dark even at noontime (below).

467

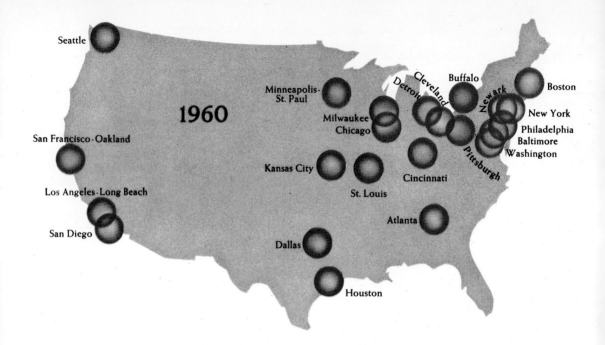

1960

Seattle

Minneapolis-
St. Paul

San Francisco-Oakland

Los Angeles-Long Beach

San Diego

Kansas City

Dallas

Houston

Milwaukee
Chicago

St. Louis

Cincinnati

Atlanta

Detroit

Cleveland

Buffalo

Newark

Boston

New York

Philadelphia
Baltimore
Washington

Pittsburgh

The map above shows the leading American cities in 1960. Because modern cities include suburban areas, the federal government has redefined urban centers as Standard Metropolitan Statistical Areas (SMSA). An SMSA is a large metropolitan area which acts as a single economic and social unit. The inset on the map of Pittsburgh (page 466) indicates the extent of that city's SMSA. Each of the cities above is an SMSA with over one million people in 1960.

Below are "growth profiles" of five American cities. As the key indicates, each column shows the growth between 1940 and 1960 of the core city (dark color), the suburban area (dashed line), and the metropolitan area as a whole (entire column). Percentage figures indicate the increase or decrease of the core city and of the metropolitan area. Note that each metropolitan area grew larger. But trends in core and suburban areas have not followed a uniform pattern.

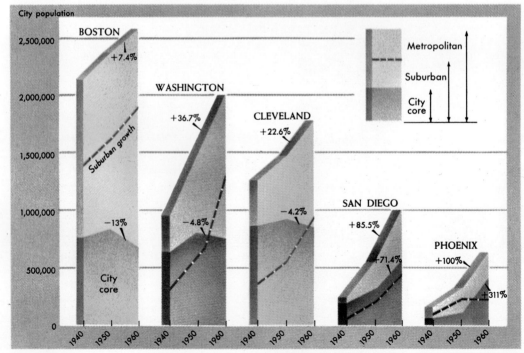

City population

2,500,000

BOSTON
+7.4%

2,000,000

WASHINGTON
+36.7%

CLEVELAND
+22.6%

1,500,000

Suburban growth

1,000,000

−13%

−4.8%

−4.2%

SAN DIEGO
+85.5%

+71.4%

PHOENIX
+100%

+311%

500,000

City
core

Metropolitan

Suburban

City
core

0

1940 1950 1960   1940 1950 1960   1940 1950 1960   1940 1950 1960   1940 1950 1960

R. M. Chapin, Jr

nineteenth century, emigration from Italy, Austria-Hungary, Russia, and Turkey had been prohibited by the governments of those countries. But in the 1870's laws were relaxed, enabling thousands of people to leave for the United States. People from Poland and the Balkan countries also joined the growing numbers who sought a better life across the ocean. Most of these immigrants were peasants, who had little chance of making a good living in their homelands. Many people left Russia to escape political and religious persecution. Anti-Jewish riots and harsh laws imposing restrictions on where they could live and what work they could do, caused large numbers of Jews to flee from Russia. Joining the Jewish refugees from Russia were Poles, Ukrainians, Lithuanians, and Finns.

During the 1870's immigration from southern and eastern Europe accounted for less than 5 per cent of the total number of newcomers to the United States. By the mid-1890's, however, half of the total number of immigrants came from these parts of Europe. And in the early 1900's the flow of people from southern and eastern Europe swelled to almost 75 per cent of the immigration tide.

The newer immigrants settle in cities. Few of these later immigrants took up farming in the United States. The best land in the West had already been claimed, and they lacked the money to travel west and buy land anyway. Most of them, therefore, settled in the urban centers of the Northeast, although a large number traveled by rail to Chicago. The new immigrants took jobs in factories, meat-packing plants, the garment industry, mines and lumber camps, and on construction projects. By 1910 foreign-born workers were filling more than half of the jobs in American industry. The willingness of workers from southern and eastern Europe to take the lower-paid, less-skilled positions enabled earlier immigrants to move into better jobs.

As in the earlier 1800's, few immigrants settled in the South. The southern states had fewer industrial jobs, and the competition of Negro labor tended to keep wages low. In the Northeast, Maine and Vermont also failed to attract immigrants. These states offered few factory jobs and little fertile land available for sale.

Some Americans favor restriction of immigration. The raising of the Statue of Liberty on an island in New York harbor came at an appropriate time — the mid-1880's. Great numbers of immigrants were responding to the invitation inscribed on the Statue's base:

> Give me your tired, your poor,
> Your huddled masses yearning to breathe free, . . .
> Send these, the homeless, tempest-tossed to me,
> I lift my lamp beside the golden door!

Yet, at this very time, some Americans were demanding that immigration be restricted. These people believed that more immigrants were being admitted than could be absorbed into American life. To some native-born Americans, the immigrants' religious practices, social customs, speech, and clothing seemed too foreign. They also accused the immigrants of being clannish and of refusing to learn English. This kind of criticism was especially directed at the immigrants from southern and eastern Europe, whose ways seemed much stranger than those of the earlier immigrants. Moreover, the immigrants were blamed for crowded conditions in the cities and for increases in crime, disease, and graft in city governments. Some Americans feared that the immigrants held dangerous political views. One businessman charged: "The [immigrant] leaders boldly proclaim that they come here not to enjoy the blessings of our liberty and to sustain our institutions but to destroy our government, cut our throats, and divide our property."

Labor union leaders likewise expressed some concern about immigration. They feared that the newcomers, by working for low wages, would cause union members to lose their jobs. They also suspected that employers would use immigrants to break strikes. In the 1890's some unions passed resolutions favoring the restriction of immigration. But foreign-born members of the unions opposed such resolutions.

Millions of People

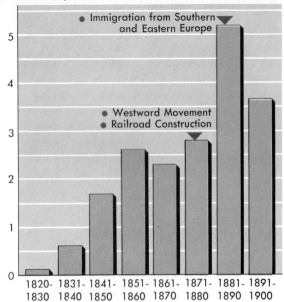

Immigration from Southern and Eastern Europe

Westward Movement
Railroad Construction

5

4

3

2

1

0

1820- 1831- 1841- 1851- 1861- 1871- 1881- 1891-
1830 1840 1850 1860 1870 1880 1890 1900

IMMIGRATION, 1871–1900

This chart shows immigration up to 1900 with emphasis on the years 1871–1900. Note the rapid increase in the number of immigrants. The chart on page 655 will trace the rise and fall of immigration up to the present.

As in the 1840's and '50's (page 307), religious prejudice was another reason for anti-immigrant feeling. Many Germans and Poles, and almost all of the Irish and Italian immigrants, were Catholic. Some people declared that Catholics would soon outnumber Protestants. It was even rumored that the Pope had plans to convert all Americans to Catholicism. Religious hostility was also aimed at the Jewish immigrants from eastern Europe. Though Jews had lived in this country from its earliest days, they did not arrive in large numbers until the late 1800's. Because their customs were unfamiliar to many native-born Americans, the Jews encountered much prejudice in the new country.

Chinese immigration is restricted. Along with the hostility toward immigrants in the East, there was growing concern about Chinese immigration to the West Coast states. During the 1860's Americans in the West had welcomed the arrival of Chinese "coolies" (workers) because of a

shortage of labor. A treaty with China in 1868 confirmed the right of the Chinese to come to the United States in unlimited numbers. Before long, however, American workers were finding that the coolies offered unwelcome competition. Demands for the restriction of Chinese immigration began to be heard. In 1882 Congress passed a bill that cut off all immigration from China for ten years. This restriction on Chinese immigration was extended in 1892 and then extended indefinitely in 1902. It marked a sharp reversal in this country's historic policy of admitting all newcomers without distinction as to place of birth.

Congress passes other restrictive measures. Meanwhile, eastern port cities were demanding a different kind of immigration law. These cities complained about the burden of supporting immigrants who were paupers, convicts, or insane. New York City threatened to close down its immigration depot unless Congress acted. This pressure caused Congress in 1882 to pass an act which excluded all such immigrants. The same law imposed a head tax of 50 cents (to be paid by the carrier) on every alien passenger, and required steamship companies to take back to their homelands any persons who were not admitted. In 1891 another law excluded persons suffering from contagious diseases.

Two other types of objections to unlimited immigration arose. First, labor groups objected to the practice of bringing immigrants into the United States under a contract to work for a specific employer. In 1885 Congress passed a law prohibiting contract labor. Second, many people thought immigrants should be required to pass literacy tests, proving that they could read and write. Such a bill passed Congress in 1896 but was vetoed by President Grover Cleveland. He insisted that it was better to

admit a hundred thousand immigrants who, though unable to read and write, seek among us a home and opportunity to work, than to admit one of those unruly agitators and enemies of governmental control who cannot only read and write, but delight in arousing by inflammatory speech the illiterate and peacefully inclined to discontent and tumult.

With the exception of the Chinese restriction measure, these early immigration laws were not aimed at newcomers from any particular country. Probably many Americans hoped that the laws would reduce the number of immigrants from southern and eastern Europe. But our European immigration policy remained basically unchanged until the 1920's (page 655).

▶ CHECK-UP

1. Why did immigration increase after the Civil War? Why did more immigrants come from eastern and southern Europe after about 1890? Why did these immigrants settle in cities?

2. Why did some Americans come to favor restriction of immigration? What restrictive measures were enacted?

. . . .

2 *Crowded Cities Have Many Problems*

Cities grow rapidly. As we have seen, the expansion of American industry in the years following the Civil War caused cities to grow rapidly. In or near the urban centers were found the steel mills, meat-packing and flour-milling plants, oil refineries, and machine-tool and clothing factories. Those cities grew most rapidly which provided the industries with adequate transportation facilities.

Immigrants arriving at an ever-increasing rate added to the city populations. At the same time, the job opportunities offered by expanding industry attracted large numbers of native-born people from the countryside. This was particularly true in the states east of the Mississippi River, where small farms could no longer compete with the mechanized farms of the Plains states. From 1870 to 1900 the number of Americans living in cities of 100,000 or more increased from four million to fourteen million.

During the same thirty years, three of the country's cities — New York, Chicago, and Philadelphia — acquired populations of more than a million people. Chicago enjoyed the most spectacular growth of any American city. Only a muddy trading post in the 1830's, it had become by 1860 an important rail center with a population of 100,000. Industrialization and further railroad expansion continued to boost the city's population. By 1900, Chicago had 1,700,000 inhabitants and was second only to New York City in size. New York and Brooklyn (they were consolidated in 1898) had over 3,000,000 people by the end of the century; Philadelphia had 1,300,000. Also startling was the growth of the iron and steel towns of Pittsburgh and Birmingham, and of Minneapolis as a flour-milling and lumber center. In the West, Denver, Seattle, San Francisco, and Los Angeles grew rapidly.

Many immigrants live in slums. Industrial expansion and the growth of urban populations changed the appearance of American cities. Small factories went up on vacant lots, while lofts and basements of existing buildings housed workrooms for cigar rollers, paper-box makers, and garment workers. People who had owned single-family homes in the core of the city moved to middle-class neighborhoods on the edges of the city or to the suburbs.[1] The homes they left were subdivided into small apartments for immigrants.

The need for city housing became so great that landlords began to build tenement (multiple-dwelling) buildings. In Philadelphia and Boston large numbers of two- and three-story frame tenements went up. Builders in New York preferred four- to six-story brick buildings with four apartments on each floor. In many instances the only running water and sanitary facilities were located outside the building at the back of the lot. In the 1890's the so-called "dumbbell tenement" began to appear in New York. Eight stories high, it packed 32 families into cramped quarters. A city

---

[1] For the growth of the middle-class suburbs see Chapter 23 (page 507).

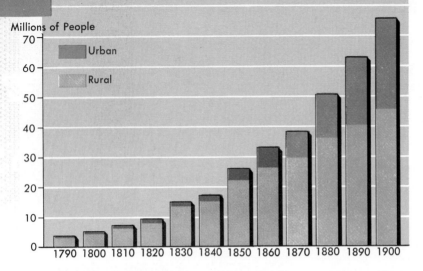

Millions of People

Urban

Rural

70
60
50
40
30
20
10
0

1790 1800 1810 1820 1830 1840 1850 1860 1870 1880 1890 1900

GROWTH OF POPULATION, 1870–1900

The population of the United States more than doubled between 1870 and 1900. An increasing proportion of Americans lived in urban areas.

block of these tenements could house some 1200 families. Slum areas where thousands of poor people huddled in squalid conditions sprang up in most large cities. Since Chicago could expand to the west, its tenements were never as high or as closely crowded together as those in New York. But ramshackle wooden structures and alley shacks blighted the entire western section of Chicago.

In 1890 Jacob Riis began to draw the nation's attention to the misery of the slums. This young Danish immigrant had become a newspaper reporter covering New York's immigrant neighborhoods. His articles in the New York *Sun* and his book *How the Other Half Lives* aroused the indignation of many Americans. Here is Riis' description of one New York slum building:

> The hall is dark and you might stumble over the children pitching pennies back there. Not that it would hurt them; kicks and cuffs are their daily diet. . . . All the fresh air that ever enters these stairs comes from the hall-door that is forever slamming and from the windows of dark bedrooms. . . . The sinks are in the hallway, that all the tenants may have access — and all be poisoned alike by their summer stenches. Hear the pump squeak? It is the lullaby of tenement house babes. In summer, when a thousand thirsty throats pant for a cooling drink in this block, it is worked in vain. But the saloon, whose open door you passed in the hall, is always there. The smell of it has followed you up.

Here is a door. Listen! That short, hacking cough, that tiny, helpless wail — what do they mean? They mean that the soiled bow of white you saw on the door downstairs will have another story to tell — oh! a sadly familiar story — before the day is at an end. The child is dying with measles. With half a chance it might have lived, but it had none.

City services are inadequate. City governments paid little attention to the spread of the slums in the 1880's and 1890's. Indeed, few services were provided for the poorer sections of any city. Although most of New York's streets were paved by 1880, streets in the slums were notoriously neglected. The west side of Chicago was a quagmire of mud and rubbish. There were few paved streets and almost no sidewalks in the slum districts. When the railroads built into Chicago, the city allowed tracks to be laid at street level. As a result, steam engines frequently crashed into horse-drawn vehicles.

City governments were little concerned with sanitation. Few slum areas had regular garbage collections, for example. In Chicago huge garbage containers on the street corners were seldom emptied and were infested by rats. Though Chicago drew its water supply from Lake Michigan, the city's refuse was dumped into the same body of water. Few cities had ordinances regulating the sale of food. Hence dealers

To document his reports, Jacob Riis photographed the people who lived and worked in the slums. The scene at right shows a New York street crowded with peddlers and buyers, horse cars, and children. Many immigrants of this period felt lucky to get a job in a "sweatshop," working long hours for low wages. The garment workers below must have been surprised that a newspaper reporter wanted to photograph them. Immigrant children often worked because their parents' wages were too meager to feed and clothe an entire family. But most of these children got more schooling than their parents had had. At lower right, students in an industrial school salute the flag.

were able to sell spoiled food and contaminated milk to the unwary public. As a result of such conditions, most large cities suffered frequent epidemics of typhoid fever and other diseases.

Hardly any parks or playgrounds brightened the urban slums. Children played on the streets, in the alleys, and in the dark hallways of the tenements. Though cities were beginning to install better street lighting in some areas, the slum neighborhoods were seldom adequately lighted at night. Jacob Riis pointed this out as one reason for the high crime rate in congested city areas. Riis discovered alleys in New York

inhabited by gangs of vicious thieves who frightened off even the police.

Municipal governments fail to cope with city problems. In general, city governments were unprepared to handle the problems that resulted from the rapid increase of population. Most American cities were governed by a mayor and a city council made up of aldermen elected from the various districts or wards. The mayor and council had a great deal of power. They determined how the city revenues would be spent; what buildings would be constructed; which streets repaired; and who would get the contracts for doing these jobs. In addition, the mayor and council hired many city workers, made appointments to boards and commissions, and sometimes named city court judges.

Before 1860, the responsibilities of city government were relatively light. Capable persons could serve on city councils while keeping their regular jobs. But in the later 1800's, the problems of governing the expanding cities became much more complex. Additional housing was desperately needed. Sanitary facilities — sewage disposal, water supply, and garbage collection — proved inadequate. Police and fire departments needed reorganization and expansion. Overwhelmed by the size of these problems, many capable men hesitated to seek office in city governments. Thus, the way was open for less scrupulous "bosses" to take over. The same sort of corruption that had plagued New York under Boss Tweed (page 401) took root in other cities. In the 1880's an English visitor, James Bryce, called city government "the one conspicuous failure in the United States."

City bosses court the immigrant vote. Many Americans laid the blame for bad city government on city bosses and immigrant voters. Newcomers to the crowded cities, particularly the immigrants, often found that the only "official" interested in their problems was the local political boss. He helped them find living quarters and jobs; and if they tangled with the law, he got them out of jail. During hard times he brought food to their families. In return, he expected the immigrants' votes.

But while the boss got most of his votes from the immigrants, he often received financial support from native-born Americans who wanted favors from the city council. The boss instructed his councilmen to grant contracts and other favors to men willing to finance the political machine. Thus, corruption was hardly a monopoly of the immigrants. Philadelphia remained "corrupt and contented" under native-born political bosses for nearly fifty years.

Some immigrants enter politics. Many political bosses of the late 1800's were themselves immigrants or the sons of immigrants. It is easy to understand why they were attracted to politics. Few of them had either the education or the money to build a career in business or the professions. But in politics they had an opportunity to advance. Out of the immigrant ranks came not only ward bosses but capable and honest politicians as well.

German and Irish immigrants were among the first newcomers to win public office. In many midwestern cities Germans held seats on the city councils, and some were elected mayors. German-born John Peter Altgeld was elected governor of Illinois in 1892. Boston had several Irish mayors, including John F. Fitzgerald, whose grandson, John F. Kennedy, became President in 1961. By the end of the century officeholders of German and Irish background were familiar figures in city, state, and even national politics. Not until the twentieth century, however, did immigrants from southern and eastern Europe have enough power to win political office.

▶ CHECK-UP

1. Why did cities grow rapidly after the Civil War? Why did slums develop? How were city services inadequate?

2. Why were city bosses interested in immigrants? Why did immigrants enter politics?

3 *Workingmen Organize National Unions*

Industrialization changes the worker's role. The rapid industrial growth of the late 1800's not only created thousands of new jobs but also made available many new goods and services. As a result of these changes, the American standard of living improved. Also, machines took over many backbreaking and dangerous operations formerly performed by workers. At the same time, however, industrialization had an unwelcome effect on the worker's role. Increasingly he became a mere cog in a huge industrial wheel. The value of a worker's skill, and the job security that it had given him, began to diminish. The skilled shoemaker, for example, found little satisfaction in operating a machine that punched eyelets in thousands of pairs of shoes every day. Moreover, a man who operated such a machine for ten years had little more skill than a newly hired worker.

Machinery, not labor, now became the most important factor in industrial planning. While machinery represented a large and permanent investment, labor could be hired and fired. Working people owned no land or machinery — they only had their labor to offer. In good times, employees worked ten or twelve hours a day, often for wages so low that they could not save for old age and hard times. When depressions came, they lost their jobs and suffered hardship. Supposedly industrial workers were free to bargain with employers for better wages, hours, and factory conditions. But actually they were at a great disadvantage. The manager of a large factory had no reason to listen to the complaints of an individual employee. As Theodore Roosevelt later expressed it, there was

a crass inequality in the bargaining relation between the employer and the individual employee standing alone. [For example] the

Jacob Riis (above), born in Denmark, became a police reporter in New York City. His accounts of slum conditions aroused Americans to the need for reform.

Labor in the late 1800's recognized Samuel Gompers (right) as its leader. Gompers arrived from England as a young boy and became an apprentice cigarmaker. He organized the AFL and served as its president for many years.

Three notable Americans of the late 1800's began life in this country as immigrants. German-born John Peter Altgeld (right) became the first Democratic governor of Illinois and won fame for his courageous stand on reform issues.

great coal-mining and coal-carrying companies, which employed their tens of thousands, could easily dispense with the services of any particular miner. The miner, on the other hand, could not dispense with the companies. He needed a job; his wife and children would starve if he did not get one.

Many workingmen believed there was only one way to solve their problem — they had to form unions strong enough to bargain with employers. Moreover, they argued, these unions should be nation-wide in scope, so that members could secure bargaining equality with large corporations.

The National Labor Union is unsuccessful. Following the Jacksonian period (page 260), few attempts had been made to organize workers on a national scale. But during the Civil War a shortage of skilled workers encouraged the efforts of union organizers. Within a few years, a number of crafts or trades had formed national organizations with a total of nearly 200,000 members. Among the most powerful of these were the printers, hatters, iron molders, machinists and blacksmiths, locomotive engineers, shoemakers, and cigarmakers.

In 1866, delegates from the national craft unions plus a number of local unions gathered in Baltimore to form the National Labor Union. This federation supported the movement for an eight-hour day. It also called for arbitration of labor disputes, currency reform, and co-operative factories run by craftsmen. At the peak of its popularity the National Labor Union represented some 600,000 workers. But during the hard times following the Panic of 1873, it fell apart. An unsuccessful attempt to nominate a presidential candidate had also weakened the union.

The Knights of Labor form one large union. Meanwhile, a movement to unite *all* working people in one big union had made progress. In 1869 the garment workers of Philadelphia, led by Uriah S. Stephens, founded the Noble Order of the Knights of Labor. At first this was a secret society, complete with ritual, oath, and handshake. Instead of organizing only skilled workers in separate trade unions, the Knights of Labor invited all workers to join its local lodges. To skilled and un-

skilled, male and female, white and Negro, citizen and alien (but not gamblers, liquor dealers, bankers, or lawyers) — the doors were open. The Knights' goal was to unite workers throughout the country into one huge union that could produce and distribute goods on a co-operative basis.

The Knights attracted few members, however, until Terence V. Powderly, a Pennsylvania machinist, was elected "Grand Master" in 1879. He toured the country urging the use of arbitration to settle labor disputes, prohibition of child labor, an eight-hour day, equal pay for women, and laws to protect workers' safety and health. In the mid-1880's the Knights made a big gain in membership after union men won a strike against the Missouri Pacific Railroad. Within a few months membership in the Knights of Labor soared from 100,000 to 700,000.

The popularity of the Knights of Labor declines. The Knights lost popularity just as quickly, however. One reason was the Haymarket Riot in Chicago. On May 4, 1886, a meeting was held in Haymarket Square to protest an attack by police on strikers. As the meeting was breaking up, the police appeared and ordered the men to disperse. Someone threw a bomb into the ranks of the police, and seven policemen and four civilians were killed. It was never learned who threw the bomb, but eight men believed to be anarchists were arrested.[2] Four of them were hanged, one took his own life, and the other three were imprisoned until Governor Altgeld of Illinois pardoned them in 1893.

Though the Knights of Labor had not organized the Haymarket Square meeting, the public believed that they were connected with the affair. Many skilled workers left the organization and rejoined their separate craft unions. Meanwhile, the Knights were also weakened by several unsuccessful strikes and by opposition to Powderly within the organization. By 1890 membership in the Knights of Labor had dwindled to 100,000 and continued to drop thereafter.

[2] *Anarchists* were opposed to all kinds of government and frequently advocated the use of violence to achieve their goals.

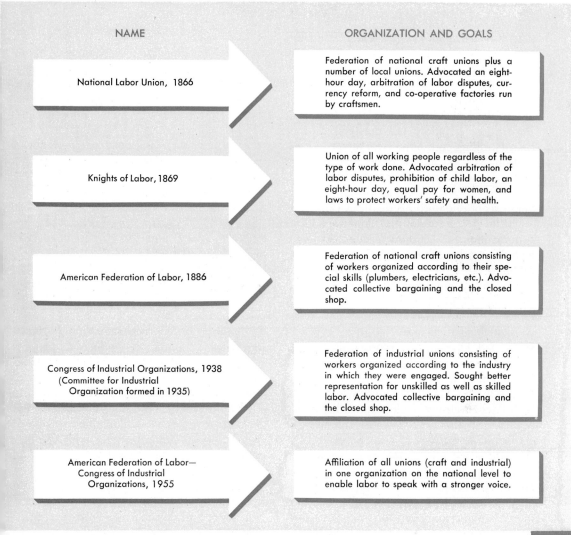

NAME	ORGANIZATION AND GOALS
National Labor Union, 1866	Federation of national craft unions plus a number of local unions. Advocated an eight-hour day, arbitration of labor disputes, currency reform, and co-operative factories run by craftsmen.
Knights of Labor, 1869	Union of all working people regardless of the type of work done. Advocated arbitration of labor disputes, prohibition of child labor, an eight-hour day, equal pay for women, and laws to protect workers' safety and health.
American Federation of Labor, 1886	Federation of national craft unions consisting of workers organized according to their special skills (plumbers, electricians, etc.). Advocated collective bargaining and the closed shop.
Congress of Industrial Organizations, 1938 (Committee for Industrial Organization formed in 1935)	Federation of industrial unions consisting of workers organized according to the industry in which they were engaged. Sought better representation for unskilled as well as skilled labor. Advocated collective bargaining and the closed shop.
American Federation of Labor—Congress of Industrial Organizations, 1955	Affiliation of all unions (craft and industrial) in one organization on the national level to enable labor to speak with a stronger voice.

DEVELOPMENT OF MAJOR NATIONAL LABOR UNIONS

Efforts to organize workers became national in scope after the Civil War. Note that the form of organization varied as unions attempted to strengthen the bargaining position of labor.

CHART STUDY

The American Federation of Labor is organized. The craft unions, meanwhile, were forming a federation destined to achieve much greater success than the old National Labor Union. The new organization was the work of Samuel Gompers, an English immigrant who had come to New York in 1863. Young Gompers found employment in the cigarmaking industry. In the cigar shop where he worked, it was the custom for the men to take turns reading out loud while the others rolled cigars. Gompers, who had been forced to leave school at an early age, was delighted with this practice. He also read widely on his own time, attended lectures, and studied employment practices and working conditions in New York City. During the 1870's he observed the effects of economic panic and depression on the labor movement and the failures of the National Labor Union's political efforts. He developed many ideas that he would later use in union organizing.

After becoming an officer in the cigarmakers' union, Gompers established new branches and raised union dues so that the organization would have emergency funds for hard times. He likewise worked out a plan for paying sickness, accident, and unemployment benefits to union members. By 1881 Gompers was able to persuade other craft unions to form a loose federation with the cigarmakers' union. This group of unions was reorganized as the American Federation of Labor (AFL) in 1886. Rather than enrolling individual workers, the Federation had as its members the national craft unions to which the workers belonged. Gompers served as AFL president every year except one until his death in 1924.

The AFL becomes the dominant labor organization. The new Federation collected regular dues from its member unions. With these funds, the AFL hired organizers to enlarge the membership and see that individual unions lived up to Federation standards. Gompers insisted that the AFL steer clear of party politics. While it supported Democratic or Republican candidates who favored labor, it opposed the formation of a labor party or the nomination of a labor candidate. Nor would Gompers have anything to do with radicals, anarchists, or anyone advocating changes in the capitalist system. Gompers wanted the AFL to work within the established economic system and to set realistic goals for itself. He thought it should be the Federation's purpose to engage in collective bargaining with employers on such issues as wages, hours, and working conditions. Moreover, he hoped to establish *closed shops*, in which employers would hire only men belonging to unions affiliated with the AFL. This would protect the jobs of union men and would strengthen the process of collective bargaining.

As these principles appealed to many craft unions, the membership of the Federation steadily grew. By 1900 it claimed the affiliation of unions with half a million members. The Knights of Labor still existed at the end of the century, and there were also some independent unions — the railroad brotherhoods, for example. The total of all organized workers was roughly 800,000, yet this was only a fraction of the total number of wage earners in the country. The majority of industrial laborers were unskilled and had no unions to represent them until the 1930's (page 698).

▶ CHECK-UP

1. How did industrialization affect workers? What was the National Labor Union? The Knights of Labor? How successful was each?

2. How was the AFL organized? Why was it comparatively successful?

. . . .

4 *Workers Strike, and Management Fights Back*

Labor and management hold opposing views. Behind the industrial disputes of the late 1800's were conflicting ideas as to the rights of labor. Workers in general felt that they had a right to their jobs and that employers should not abolish jobs, cut wages, or lengthen working hours without good reason. Union members thought that their leaders should be able to negotiate with employers regarding changes in wages, hours, or working conditions. To win and defend these rights, organized labor used the *strike* and the *boycott*. During a strike, the employees stayed away from their jobs in an attempt to force the employer to meet their demands. Workers also might boycott a struck factory by refusing to buy its products. Sometimes a boycott was carried a step further. Employees of companies that had dealings with a struck plant would refuse to handle that plant's products. This was called a *secondary boycott*.

The employer, on the other hand, believed that he should be allowed to operate the business as he saw fit. He felt that it was up to him to determine wages, hours, and working conditions. Many employers regarded union officers as "outside agitators" and refused to listen to them. If a worker was dissatisfied, the employer argued, let him find a job elsewhere. Employers had certain weapons they used in defending this "take-it-or-leave-it" attitude. They countered striking workers, for example, with *lockouts.* The employer would lock the workers out of the plant and refuse to resume operations until company terms were accepted. Another weapon was the *black list.* Names of union leaders would be circulated to other employers. This made it almost impossible for black-listed workers to find jobs. Employers also tried to defeat strikes by hiring non-union workers, or *strikebreakers.* And, of course, employers almost always had greater financial resources to carry them through an industrial conflict than did organized labor.

During the 1880's and 1890's, some 23,000 strikes took place in American industry, involving more than six and a half million workers. About a third of these strikes were successful: the workers won higher wages, shorter hours, or recognition of the right of unions to bargain. But the other strikes ended in compromise or failure.

Violence enters labor disputes. In their disputes both management and labor at times resorted to violence. Bloody fighting broke out in the Pennsylvania anthracite coal fields during the 1870's. The coal operators hired private investigators from the Pinkerton Detective Agency to break strikes and protect their property. Both sides were guilty of cruelty and bloodshed. Mine property was destroyed, and men who sympathized with the coal operators were beaten and even murdered. The violence was blamed on the "Molly Maguires," a secret group of disgruntled coal miners. The evidence gathered by a Pinkerton detective who worked his way into the Molly Maguires led to the arrest of 24 miners — all reputed to be "Mollies." Ten of them were hanged and the others imprisoned.

Federal troops break a railroad strike. Also in the 1870's a railroad strike paralyzed the lines east of the Mississippi and spread into the West. Railroad workers had become discontented with their long hours and poor working conditions. Moreover, they resented the blacklisting of men who dared to join such newly formed unions as the Order of Railway Conductors or the Brotherhood of Locomotive Firemen. Finally, they were angered by a series of wage cuts during the depression that followed the Panic of 1873.

Employees of the Baltimore and Ohio began to walk out in July, 1877. Within days the strike spread to other railroad lines. Train traffic in fourteen states virtually came to a standstill. Both state and federal troops were called out to protect railroad property and force the strikers back to work. When violence flared up in many cities, scores of people were killed or injured, and property valued at millions of dollars was destroyed. As a result, public opinion turned against the railroad workers. The defeated workers called off the strike and went back to their jobs at reduced wages.

Labor loses in the Homestead strike. The Haymarket riot of 1886 heightened public fear that radicals were running the labor movement. As we have seen, that outbreak helped to destroy the Knights of Labor, and labor felt its influence long afterward. Indeed, two major strikes in the 1890's failed partly because the public had little sympathy for the unions.

The first of these strikes occurred at the Carnegie Steel Company plant in Homestead, Pennsylvania. In 1892 the manager of the plant, Henry Clay Frick, announced a wage cut. Leaders of the union representing the Homestead workers protested. But before they could call a strike, Frick closed the plant, surrounded it with barbed wire, and hired deputy sheriffs to protect the property. Realizing that Frick intended to reopen the plant with strikebreakers, the workers forced the deputies to withdraw. Then Frick hired armed Pinkerton detectives. But the angry workers attacked the detectives, forcing them to surrender. A dozen lives were lost in this battle.

Frick then turned to the governor of Pennsylvania, who sent in the state militia. Order was soon restored, and the plant reopened with strikebreakers. A few days later an anarchist entered Frick's office and tried to assassinate him. Though the anarchist had nothing to do with the union or the strike, public opinion immediately turned against the union cause. Several months later a few of the steelworkers were taken back on company terms. But most of them lost their jobs, and their union lost more than half its membership.

Trouble breaks out in Pullman, Illinois. In 1893 another financial panic swept the country, and the depression which followed continued for several years. Most employers laid off workers and slashed wages; in return, many unions went on strike. This was the background of a hard-fought battle between the Pullman Palace Car Company and its employees.

George M. Pullman, head of the company, built sleeping and dining cars (page 445) and leased them to the railroads. Outside Chicago he had laid out a model company town named Pullman. The Pullman Company built and owned all the houses, stores, schools, and churches in this town.

In 1894, as the depression deepened, Pullman laid off one third of his employees and drastically reduced the wages of others. Yet rents and prices of food and clothing remained the same in the town of Pullman. In desperation the workers called a strike.

Eugene Debs and the American Railway Union came to their aid. Born in Indiana, Debs had worked his way up in the railroad craft unions. In 1893, he decided to form a union that all railroad workers — skilled or unskilled — could join. The American Railway Union soon had a membership of 150,000, including some of the Pullman Company workers. When the Pullman strike began, Debs proposed arbitration of

In 1860, women workers in a Lynn, Massachusetts, shoe factory went on strike. Dressed in their best clothes, they paraded through a snowstorm to publicize their cause (left). The Pullman railroad strike of 1893 was more violent. The federal government sent troops to ensure the movement of mail trains in and out of Chicago (below left). In the present-day scene below, representatives of labor and management meet with mediators to try to settle an industrial dispute.

the dispute, but the company rejected this offer. The union then refused to handle any Pullman cars attached to trains running into Chicago. The Pullman Company was aided by railroad owners who said they would fire employees who refused to handle Pullman cars. As a result, more workers joined the strike, and railroad transportation came to a standstill in the Midwest.

Government action breaks the Pullman strike. The railroad owners persuaded President Cleveland's Attorney General to secure an *injunction*[3] against the strikers. The injunction forbade the strikers to (1) interfere with the movement of United States mail through Chicago, (2) interfere with interstate commerce, or (3) damage railroad property. The railroad owners then attached mail cars as well as Pullman cars to trains coming into Chicago. By refusing to handle these trains, the strikers violated the injunction. The railroads then asked for federal troops to be sent in.

Over the protests of Governor Altgeld of Illinois, President Cleveland sent federal troops to Chicago. Angry union men and unruly hoodlums joined in the fighting that followed. Debs objected that the troops were not just protecting the mail and railroad property but were being used to break the strike. Because the American Railway Union was defying the injunction by continuing the strike, Debs and other union officials were arrested and sentenced to six months in jail. Debs appealed his case to the Supreme Court, but the Court upheld the decision on the grounds that the American Railway Union was engaged in a conspiracy to obstruct interstate commerce. Deprived of its leadership, the union abandoned the strike.

The Pullman strike failed for a number of reasons. (1) By granting an injunction and sending federal troops to enforce it, the government threw its weight on the side of the railroad owners. (2) Public opinion had at first been favorable to the Pullman workers. But when the strike spread to other railroads and violence broke out, many people concluded that the strike

[3] An injunction is a court order forbidding the performance of some particular act.

would lead to "anarchy." The American Railway Union was accused of looting and burning railroad property, though evidence suggests that hoodlums and perhaps even guards employed by the railroad companies were responsible for much of the violence. (3) Still another reason for the collapse of the strike was the failure of the labor unions to stand together during the crisis. The railroad brotherhoods were suspicious of Debs' union because it had lured away many of their members. And the AFL refused to support Debs because his union was independent and included unskilled workers.

The advantage rests with management. Thus, at the end of the 1800's, labor seemed to be at a disadvantage in its struggle with management. Business was well-organized and growing bigger, while union men had made but little progress in their efforts to build up bargaining power. Labor was regarded as a commodity which the worker "sold" for his wages. Corporations, on the other hand, seemed to have legal rights which were given a higher priority in the courts than those of employees. The widespread acceptance of these views helps to explain why public opinion did not back labor during this period and why government generally favored management.

▶ CHECK-UP

1. How did unions and management differ on the rights of labor? What weapons were used by each?

2. What bloody conflicts developed between labor and management? How did the government help to break the Pullman strike?

. . . .

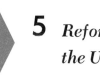

5 *Reformers Try to Help the Underprivileged*

The conditions described in this chapter troubled many Americans during the late 1800's. Thoughtful people were disturbed by the treatment of immigrants, the overcrowding and poor government of the cities, and the bitter struggle between labor and management.

Reformers organize. Some Americans formed organizations to seek solutions to these problems. The National Civic Federation, for example, sought to improve relations between employers and employees. Its president was a prominent businessman, Mark Hanna, and its vice-president was Samuel Gompers. Another organization, the National Municipal League, helped raise the standards of city government. The Immigrant's Protective League assisted newcomers in finding jobs and housing and gave them legal aid when needed. The National Conference of Charities and Corrections helped private charities to organize their work.

The need for reform is publicized. Newspapers and magazines of the late 1800's did much to acquaint the public with urban problems. Thus, Jacob Riis' writings revealed slum conditions; and Thomas Nast's cartoons in *Harper's Weekly* helped destroy Boss Tweed. Nast's powerful drawings (page 402) also attacked political corruption in state and federal government. *Harper's* and other magazines devoted articles to political corruption and industrial relations. The *Ladies Home Journal* campaigned for cleaner cities, more parks and playgrounds, and regulation of the sale of food and medicine.

Improvements are made in the cities. Widespread publicity, aroused citizens, and pressure from reform groups forced the cities to do something about their sloppy housekeeping. Streets were paved and kept cleaner, and sidewalks were added in many neighborhoods. Improved street lighting and larger, better-disciplined police forces helped to reduce crime. Moreover, cities began to build sewage plants and to provide safe water supplies. The cities also adopted ordinances to regulate the sale of food, milk, and medicine, though enforcement was often lax. Many towns and cities began to set aside land for parks.

By the end of the century most city governments were also attempting to regulate multiple dwellings. City regulations required landlords to install fire escapes, plumbing, and adequate lighting. The New York legislature banned the construction of "dumbbell" tenements and required all new apartment buildings to provide light, air, and open space for the tenants.

Churches show an interest in urban problems. By the 1890's many Protestant churches were beginning to take an interest in the problems of the cities. Some Protestant ministers were trained to apply Christian principles to all areas of life — including government, industrial relations, and social and economic problems. Preaching a message known as the *Social Gospel*, these ministers challenged the "survival of the fittest" theory that was used to justify selfish competition (page 458). They insisted that this principle should not be applied to human beings. Moreover, they argued, people should be helped to overcome handicaps imposed by outside forces — the immigrants' lack of knowledge of English, for example. By receiving such assistance, less fortunate people would become better able to adjust to life.

The "Social Gospel" ministers urged their parishioners to practice the principles of Christianity by helping underprivileged people. Churches in the heart of many cities began to offer a full schedule of clubs,

---

**Frederick Law Olmsted:
Builder of Public Parks**

During the Gilded Age the country's cities came to appreciate the importance of public parks, thanks in large part to the first "landscape architect," Frederick Law Olmsted. In the 1850's New York responded to the pleas of William Cullen Bryant for a city park. Olmsted's plans for Central Park won a contest in 1858, and for the next decade he supervised the park's development. Acres of swamp and pasture were transformed into lakes, woods, and meadows, with attractive paths for pedestrians and sunken roads for vehicles. Olmsted followed this achievement with the creation of many other city parks. He also landscaped the Capitol grounds in Washington, D. C.

Jane Addams combined administrative ability and a strong desire to help people in her successful work at Hull House (top right, in 1963). The photograph at right, taken not long before Miss Addams' death in 1935, shows her with children of the neighborhood.

classes, and playground activities. These churches, which were often supported by the wealthier suburban churches, did much to help the newcomers in the cities. Other religious groups also served city residents. The Young Men's and Young Women's Christian Associations provided social and physical activities for urban youth. The Salvation Army sought to help the poor of the city. Founded in England by "General" William Booth, its first American branch was established in 1880. The Army took religion to the tenements and distributed food and clothes to the needy.

Settlement houses aid the urban poor. Another institution established to combat the problems of city slums was the settlement house. The settlement house movement began at Toynbee Hall in the slums of east London. Jane Addams, a graduate of Rockford College in Illinois, visited Toynbee Hall in the 1880's and was deeply impressed by the work being done there. When she returned to Chicago, she pur-

chased a run-down mansion in an immigrant neighborhood and called it Hull House.

One of the first things Jane Addams did at Hull House was to start a kindergarten for the children of working mothers. But she and her associates soon discovered countless other ways to serve the community. They organized clubs and classes for all age groups and helped people find jobs and housing. They insisted on regular garbage collections in the area, and for a time, Jane Addams herself followed the garbage trucks to be sure the job was done properly. Over the years Hull House helped to secure parks and playgrounds for Chicago and to improve the schools. Its influence was also responsible for the passage of state laws to protect immigrants, ban child labor, and improve factory conditions.

Some reformers stress prohibition. Because many people believed that excessive drinking caused poverty, crime, and disease, the drive against intoxicating liquor gained new supporters in the late 1800's.

Some groups fought for the passage of state laws to prohibit the sale of liquor. They also formed a Prohibition Party and nominated presidential candidates from 1872 on. Much more influential in the battle against "demon rum" was the Woman's Christian Temperance Union (WCTU), founded in 1874. The leader of this organization was Frances E. Willard, a former teacher who stressed the importance of educating the public on the dangers of excessive drinking. Through speeches, pamphlets, and messages to school children, the WCTU reached a large number of people. The formation of the Anti-Saloon League in 1893 brought an energetic ally to the side of the WCTU. The prohibition forces redoubled their efforts, spurred on by the hope that America would soon be a "saloonless nation."

Women become more active in public life. In crusading for prohibition, establishing settlement houses, developing church social programs, and seeking public support for parks and playgrounds, women took an active part. In addition, the increased use of typewriters, telephones, and adding machines opened up a wide range of office jobs to women. Department and retail stores also employed far more women than in the pre-Civil War years. So too did industry; by 1900 one fifth of the country's industrial workers were women. Moreover, growing numbers of women were attending colleges and preparing for the professions of medicine, law, and the ministry.

Even before the Civil War, there had been some interest in woman suffrage. The movement gained new momentum, however, after the Fourteenth and Fifteenth Amendments guaranteed freedmen the right to vote. In 1869 the National Woman Suffrage Association was formed with Elizabeth Cady Stanton (page 308) as president.

THE AMERICAN SCENE

LIFE IN THE CITY

as seen by JOHN SLOAN

John Sloan captured the mood of the busy city in his pictures of New York life, as in the street scene below. Though he often chose to paint commonplace subjects, as in "Woman's Work" (left, below), his pictures showed the beauty that he found in everyday life and people. "Nature," said Sloan, "is what you see plus what you think about it."

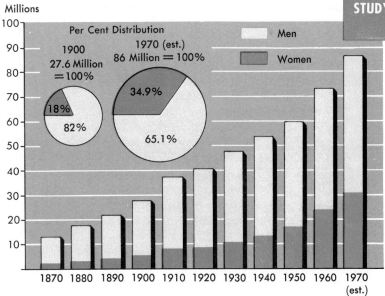

WOMEN AT WORK

Notice the rapid increase since 1870 in the number of women working outside the home. It is estimated that in 1970 more than a third of the people employed will be women.

Mrs. Stanton, Susan B. Anthony, and others worked relentlessly to carry their message to the public. In the cities they argued that women voters would insist on higher standards of municipal government. By the end of the century some states permitted women to vote in school board elections, but only four states — Wyoming, Colorado, Utah, and Idaho — had given women full suffrage rights.

Social theorists propose reforms. While some Americans directed their efforts toward specific reforms, a few pondered the basic causes of poverty. One of these thinkers was Henry George. He had long studied the gulf of misunderstanding that divided the people living in mansions on New York's Fifth Avenue from those who were crowded into the city's slums. In 1879 Henry George presented his ideas in a book called *Progress and Poverty.* According to George, those who owned land made money, while landless wage earners and renters were always poor. His solution to the problem of poverty was to levy only one tax — a tax on land. Another writer who held out the promise of a better life for all was Edward Bellamy. In a novel entitled *Looking Backward,* Bellamy described an idealistic co-operative society of the future. Both George and Bellamy attracted loyal, enthusiastic supporters.

Writers describe urban life. During this period American writers began to portray the problems of industrial, urban life. These writers owed much to the encouragement of William Dean Howells. As we read in Chapter 21, Howells defended "realism" in writing, by which he meant "the truthful treatment of commonplace material." Let the novel "portray men and women as they are; . . . let it speak the dialect, the language, that most Americans know — the language of unaffected people everywhere." Howells himself applied these lessons in *The Rise of Silas Lapham.* In another novel, *A Hazard of New Fortunes,* Howells described the men and women of Fifth Avenue and of the slums "as they were" and in their own language.

A talented young writer named Stephen Crane described the unhappy fate of a girl from the New York slums in his first novel, *Maggie: A Girl of the Streets.* The book shocked many readers, but Crane was not discouraged. In *The Red Badge of Courage* he wrote just as honestly about a young soldier's experience in the Civil War. In 1900, the year Crane died, another realist writer, Theodore Dreiser, published *Sister Carrie.* This novel was about a country girl who went to Chicago and fell upon evil ways but finally made a success of herself as an actress. Dreiser, like Crane, was criticized for writing so frankly about the problems of city life. Literary historians today, however, consider both Crane and Dreiser among the most important authors of their time. William Sydney Porter, writing under the name of O. Henry, described a wide variety of city people in his popular short stories. Some of his best stories were published in *The Voice of the City.*

Artists and photographers record the city's face. Several artists and photographers of the late 1800's shared the general interest in social problems. Technical advances enabled photographers to do more creative work with their cameras. Alfred Stieglitz, son of a German immigrant, was one of the first photographers to record the surging activity of New York's busy streets. In 1907 he took his most famous picture, "The Steerage," an unposed shot of immigrants. Lewis W. Hine also photographed immigrants as well as adults and children at work in factories and mines.

Some artists also chose to paint the life of the city streets. Robert Henri and a number of his students, including George Luks and John Sloan, spearheaded the realist movement. Because these artists avoided sentimentality and "prettiness" in their scenes of everyday life, their paintings seemed revolutionary at the time. The galleries and museums refused to show their work. One critic said they "deliberately and conscientiously paint the ugly wherever it occurs." After viewing their one and only show in 1908, another critic dismissed them as "the Ashcan School" of painting. Though unappreciated in the early twentieth century, these painters are highly regarded today for their introduction of realism into American art.

▶ CHECK-UP

1. How did reformers seek to help the underprivileged? How did the press help this movement? What improvements were made in the cities? What was the role of the churches? How did settlement houses help the poor?

2. Why was prohibition advocated by some reformers? What was the role of women in reform movements?

3. How did the problems of industrial-urban living influence certain authors? What artists and photographers depicted city life?

. . . .

Clinching the Main Ideas in Chapter 22

The fourteen million immigrants who came to America between 1860 and 1900 played an important role in the country's industrial expansion. Toward the end of this period, the number of immigrants from southern and eastern Europe increased. When some Americans voiced their opposition to the growing tide of immigration, Congress responded with a few restrictive laws. With the exception of the ban on Chinese immigration, however, the federal government took no drastic action during the nineteenth century to stop the flow of immigration.

One of the newcomers' greatest burdens was the miserable housing available to them in American cities. As more and more people poured into the cities, overcrowding became critical. By the end of the century some cities had made improvements, but slums continued to blight most of the urban areas.

Many of the immigrants became industrial workers. As industry grew large and companies became huge, impersonal corporations, workers sought to organize on a national scale in order to secure an equal bargaining position. After the Knights of Labor tried unsuccessfully to bring together skilled and unskilled workers in one organization, the American Federation of Labor became the major spokesman for organized labor. Composed of craft unions, its goal was to protect the jobs and improve the wages and working conditions of skilled laborers. Theoretically national unions and big business were free to bargain as equals. In fact, however, management was more powerful. At times government tilted the balance against labor by granting injunctions and by sending troops to help break strikes.

Industrial strife and disgraceful conditions in the cities troubled many Americans. Reformers publicized these problems and demanded better treatment for the immigrants and the poor. Social thinkers also proposed solutions for these problems, and writers and artists realistically portrayed life in the cities.

Chapter Review

Terms to Understand

1. "coolies"
2. slums
3. lofts
4. WCTU
5. AFL
6. anarchist
7. city "bosses"
8. closed shop
9. lockout
10. blacklist
11. injunction
12. Social Gospel
13. "dumbbell tenement"
14. Homestead strike
15. Pullman strike
16. Molly Maguires
17. Haymarket Riot
18. contract labor
19. Knights of Labor
20. National Labor Union
21. secondary boycott
22. strikebreaker
23. settlement house
24. "Ashcan School" of painting

What Do You Think?

1. What groups came to favor restrictions on immigration after about 1880? To oppose them? Explain why in each case.

2. Many blame bad city government on city "bosses." Why? Could it also be argued that bad municipal government made possible the rise of "bosses"? Explain.

3. Why have slums developed in our large cities?

4. In the late 1800's management regarded labor as "a commodity which the worker 'sold' for his wages." Explain the implications of this. What were the views of labor?

5. What values were stressed in the Social Gospel? Contrast them with the values implicit in Social Darwinism.

Using Your Knowledge of History

1. Prepare a two-column chart listing and explaining the weapons used (a) by labor in seeking higher wages and better working conditions and (b) by management in resisting such demands.

2. Debate: *Resolved,* That the United States government was justified in intervening in the Pullman strike.

3. Give an example of "realism" in writing. What is the opposite approach to realism? Give an example. On what grounds has each been praised? Condemned?

4. Prepare a chart contrasting (a) the organization, (b) the goals, and (c) the policies of the Knights of Labor and of the AFL.

Extending Your Knowledge of History

A brief but well-balanced study of immigration was written by Maldwyn Jones, *American Immigration.* See also Carl Wittke's interesting *We Who Built America* and Oscar Handlin's interpretation of the immigrant's experience, *The Uprooted.* An excellent study of urban problems during this period is A. M. Schlesinger's *The Rise of the City, 1878–1898.* For first-hand accounts of urban problems see Jane Addams's *Forty Years at Hull-House;* Mary Antin's *The Promised Land;* and Jacob Riis's *How the Other Half Lives. Labor in America* by F. R. Dulles should be supplemented with Samuel Yellen's account of the post-Civil War strikes, *American Labor Struggles.*

Analyzing Unit Six

1. Surveying the country's economic growth in the postwar decades, Henry Adams observed: "The generation between 1865 and 1895 was . . . mortgaged to the railways and no one knew it better than the generation itself." Explain how the railroads nourished the industrial and agricultural growth of the postwar period. What impact did the railroads have on the cities?

2. The people who settled the trans-Mississippi West had to contend with many problems which they had not anticipated. What

difficulties confronted the miners, the cattlemen, and the farmers? How did each of these groups adjust, or try to adjust, to its major problems?

3. American cities in the postwar decades came in for a good deal of criticism. Their governments were often corrupt and inefficient, and many cities were blighted by slums. What caused these troubles? How do you account for the fact that the cities continued to grow? That they became cultural centers as well as economic centers?

Unit 7 | Politics and Foreign Policy Reflect the Growth of Industry (1880-1900)

American steamship in a Chinese port around 1890

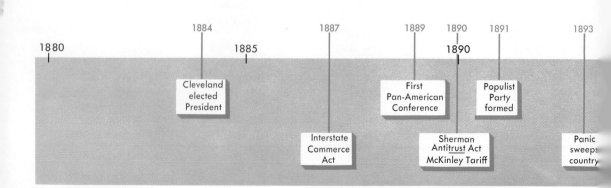

1880

1884
Cleveland
elected
President

1885

1887
Interstate
Commerce
Act

1889
First
Pan-American
Conference

1890
1890
Sherman
Antitrust Act
McKinley Tariff

1891
Populist
Party
formed

1893
Panic
sweeps
country

Before the Civil War, both Whigs and Democrats had tried to ignore the question of the extension of slavery into the western territories. Similarly, in the closing decades of the 1800's the Democrats and Republicans appeared unwilling to cope with problems arising out of the country's tremendous economic growth. In fact, both major parties were far more concerned with the possession of political power than in tackling such issues as tariff reform, inadequate wages and working conditions, or the decline in farm prices.

On more than one occasion, the consequences of ignoring important issues has been the formation of a new political party. Thus, failure of the Whigs and Democrats to take a stand on the extension of slavery in the 1850's had led to the rise of the Republican Party. Again, in the 1890's, a third party took a stand on many of the questions avoided by the Republicans and Democrats during post-Civil War years.

The Populist Party had its greatest strength in the western states, and its chief interest was improving the farmers' lot. In the election of 1896, the Populists called for a more vigorous federal government to protect the interests of farmers and workers, thus clashing with the Republican concept of a limited federal government sympathetic to businessmen. William Jennings Bryan, the eloquent candidate of both the Populists and the Democrats, was defeated. Nevertheless, many Populist ideas lived on long after the Populist Party had collapsed.

Meanwhile, during the 1880's and 1890's a debate over the role of the United States in foreign affairs had developed. Pressures arising from this country's widening economic interests, and from the position taken by ardent expansionists, led the United States to annex the Hawaiian Islands and to acquire other bases in the Pacific. When Cuba began a rebellion against Spanish rule, this country eventually plunged into the conflict to help the Cubans win independence. The treaty ending the Spanish-American War gave the United States possession of Puerto Rico and the Philippines and signaled the nation's increasing involvement in world affairs.

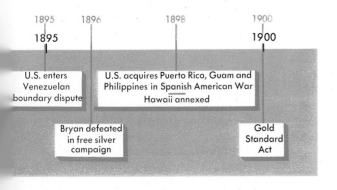

1895   1896   1898   1900

1895   1900

U.S. enters Venezuelan boundary dispute

U.S. acquires Puerto Rico, Guam and Philippines in Spanish American War
Hawaii annexed

Bryan defeated in free silver campaign

Gold Standard Act

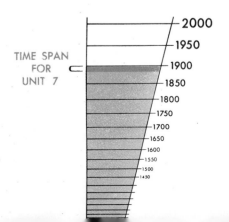

TIME SPAN FOR UNIT 7

2000
1950
1900
1850
1800
1750
1700
1650
1600
1550
1500
1450

CHAPTER 23

Bicycling in the '90's

Conservatives Control Both Parties

In a country so full of change and movement as America, new questions are always coming up and must be answered. . . . Neither [political] party has anything definite to say on these issues; neither party has any principles, any distinctive tenets. . . . Both have [certain] war cries, organizations, interests enlisted in their support. But those interests are in the main the interests of getting or keeping the patronage of the government.

James Bryce, "The American Commonwealth," 1888

1884–1895

As the chapter quotation points out, not many clear-cut differences separated the two major parties in American politics during the 1880's. Political contests revolved around personalities more often than they concerned principles. In fact, there seemed to be greater differences *within* each party on the major issues — tariff rates, currency reform, and regulation of railroads and trusts — than there were between the Democrats and the Republicans. The cement which held each of the parties together was the desire for office and political power. Both parties tended to be conservative. Despite the "change and movement" that Bryce spoke of, political leaders saw little need to re-examine the direction or goals of American life.

Though the two major parties lacked well-defined differences, they continued to wage hard-fought election campaigns. In this chapter we shall read how, in the election of 1884, the Democrats won the presidency for the first time since the 1850's. Four years later the Republicans narrowly regained the presidency. But in 1890 the Republicans lost many seats in Congress to the Democrats, chiefly because of discontent among farmers and wage earners.

Throughout the 1880's, however, most middle-class citizens seemed satisfied with the general trend of American life. As their standard of living rose, these people had little concern for such problems as low farm prices, slum conditions, labor agitation, or political quarrels.

1 *Both Parties Ignore the Need for Change*

The parties avoid the major issues. Neither the Republicans nor the Democrats in the 1880's showed much concern with the changing American scene. The mushroom growth of cities and the increasing numbers of people employed in industry were bringing about changes in ways of living. But the majority of Americans felt that any adjustment to these changes should be an individual matter and was not a proper concern of the government. They believed that elected officials should deal with political affairs only. Since voters felt this way, few members of Congress called for laws dealing with industrial disputes, farmers' problems, or the issues posed by the growth of big business. Nor did most of the Presidents who served between 1868 and 1900 seem deeply concerned with the problems resulting from economic and social changes. One historian has said of the 1880's that "politics were in dead center, not because there were no issues, but because the politicians refused to recognize and act on the issues."

The two parties are closely matched. During the 1880's the two major parties fiercely competed for office. But neither of the parties stood for any clear-cut principles. To be sure, the Republicans were more apt to respond to the pleas of the business community. They also relied on the votes of midwestern farmers, who remained loyal to the Republican Party because of the Homestead Act and government subsidies to western railroads. The

. . . .

CHAPTER FOCUS

1. Both parties ignore the need for change.
2. The Democrats gain control under Cleveland.
3. The Republicans return to power under Harrison.
4. Many Americans enjoy a better life.

Democrats, on the other hand, could always count on heavy majorities in the South and on a substantial vote from immigrants in the expanding cities.

Despite these differences in voter support, each of the two parties represented a wide variety of interests. Some Democrats and some Republicans favored high tariffs and "hard money" and opposed government regulation of railroads or trusts. Yet other members of both parties held opposite views. Thus, in most elections the parties avoided taking a forthright position on any of these issues. In 1879 a young scholar named Woodrow Wilson summed up the American political situation in these words: "No leaders, no principles; no principles, no parties."

Since there was little choice between the parties, Democratic and Republican strength was fairly evenly balanced. Between 1868 and 1900 the Republicans controlled the White House for 24 years and the Democrats for only 8. But these figures are somewhat misleading. In 1868 Grant's margin of victory in the popular vote was close, and in the 1876 election the Democrats had a majority of the popular, though not the electoral, votes. When the Democrats finally captured the White House in 1884, their candidate, Grover Cleveland, won because he carried New York State by a narrow margin. Moreover, from 1880 to 1900, congressional seats were fairly evenly divided between the two parties. But more than one President during the last 30 years of the century had to deal with a Congress in which the opposing party dominated one or both houses.

Favoritism mars party politics. In some ways, the national political parties were like the organizations built up by city bosses. National political leaders saw to it that their organizations were properly financed and did their utmost to line up the votes needed for victory. Just as the city boss granted favors to municipal contractors, so the national party bosses promised favors to those who made substantial contributions to campaign funds. For example, government subsidies to railroad builders or promises about tariff rates brought thousands of dollars into political

Thomas Nast satirized the railroads' influence in the Senate with this cartoon of a locomotive senator blowing off steam.

favors. Since Congress was seldom firmly controlled by either party, political bosses were often unable to carry out their campaign pledges. As a result, some businessmen decided to run for office themselves. Usually they preferred the Senate.[1] A senator had more prestige, his vote counted for more than a representative's, and he had a greater opportunity to influence legislation. By the 1890's, so many wealthy men held seats in the Senate that it was called the "millionaires' club." A Kansas journalist, William Allen White, had this to say about the powerful businessmen-senators:

A United States senator . . . represented something more than a state, more even than a region. He represented principalities and powers in business. One senator, for instance, represented the Union Pacific Railway System, another the New York Central, still another the insurance interests of New York and New Jersey. . . . Coal and iron owned a coterie [group] from the Middle and Eastern seaport states. Cotton had half a dozen senators. And so it went.

Reformers are ineffective. Some Americans protested against the corruption and short-sightedness of the major political parties. The Liberal Republicans had tried to block Grant's re-election in 1872 (page 405), but they fell apart shortly afterward. Nevertheless, voices continued to be raised against political corruption and in favor of the extension of civil service and municipal reform. But reform-minded citizens too often devoted themselves to a particular problem. They failed to work out a far-reaching program of reform that could become the basis of a political movement. Grange leaders, for example, concentrated their energies on farm problems and cared little about factory workers' low wages and even less about urban slums. The labor organizers, who might have joined forces with immigrants and farmers, were usually hostile to the newcomers and uninterested in agricultural problems. Consequently, the

campaign chests. Pensions were promised to win the votes of Civil War veterans. Moreover, party bosses could still offer government jobs to their supporters, although the Pendleton Act had begun to reduce the amount of patronage at their disposal (page 412). Sometimes during the heat of election campaigns, politicians used party funds to bribe voters.

The practice of buying political favors was so widespread by the 1890's that some wealthy persons made large contributions to *both* parties. One large corporation gave generously to the Democratic and Republican campaign funds in 1892 and defended its action as "the politics of business." During a congressional investigation of Jay Gould's political contributions, the railroad tycoon proudly announced: "I was a Republican in Republican districts, a Democrat in Democratic districts. But everywhere I was for Erie!"

Some businessmen run for office. By the 1890's many businessmen concluded that they paid too high a price for political

[1] At this time, United States senators were still elected by state legislatures. This meant that the majority party in a legislature virtually appointed a senator, often as a reward for financial support to the party.

reformers of the 1870's and '80's were generally ineffective in national politics. James G. Blaine dismissed them as "the worst possible upstarts, conceited, foolish, vain. They are noisy but not numerous . . . , ambitious but not wise, pretentious but not powerful."

▶ CHECK-UP

1. Why did political parties of the late 1800's avoid taking a firm stand on major issues? How did favoritism mar party politics?

2. Why did businessmen run for office? Why were reformers ineffective?

. . . .

2 The Democrats Gain Control Under Cleveland

We left off the country's political history in Chapter 19 with President Arthur's administration. As he completed his three years in the White House, the Democrats and Republicans waged one of the bitterest — and closest — presidential contests in American history.

The Republicans nominate Blaine. President Chester Arthur's creditable record in the White House would ordinarily have entitled him to nomination for another term. But his support of civil service reform had annoyed both factions of the Republican Party. His former Stalwart friends disowned him, and his Halfbreed opponents mistrusted him. Thus, when the Republican nominating convention met in 1884, President Arthur had little support. Instead, the delegates nominated James G. Blaine, the "man from Maine."

Some Republicans had opposed Blaine's nomination. Included in this group were such young men as Henry Cabot Lodge of Massachusetts and Theodore Roosevelt of New York. One Liberal Republican ac-

cused Blaine of having "wallowed in spoils like a rhinoceros in an African pool." Most of these men refused to support their party's candidate. Instead, they offered to help the Democrats if that party nominated an honest candidate. These Republicans were promptly nicknamed "Mugwumps" or "assistant Democrats." Lodge and Roosevelt, however, changed their minds about bolting the Republican Party. To avoid being shut out of party affairs, they broke with the Mugwumps and reluctantly accepted Blaine's nomination.

The Democrats pick Cleveland. The Mugwumps applauded the Democrats' choice of Grover Cleveland, Governor of New York, as their presidential candidate. Cleveland had been an honest, plodding lawyer in Buffalo, New York, when the Democratic bosses were looking for a respectable candidate for mayor in 1881. Cleveland had accepted the nomination and then surprised both politicians and voters in Buffalo by campaigning on the principle that "a public office is a public trust." "Public officials," he explained, "are the trustees of the people, and hold their places and exercise their powers for the benefit of the people."

Elected by a large majority, the new mayor had fought corrupt aldermen and won the support of the reformers. The resulting publicity helped him secure nomination and election as governor of New York in 1882. Grover Cleveland won more than one contest against Tammany Hall representatives in the state legislature, and this fact added to his reputation for honest, efficient government. Said one delegate to the Democratic convention of 1884, "We love him for the enemies he has made."

The campaign is bitter. Both parties offered similar platforms in 1884 — vague promises of tariff revision, extension of civil service, and regulation of the trusts. But the campaign had little to do with these issues. Instead it revolved around personal charges and counter-charges that made it the roughest campaign since Jackson and Adams fought each other in 1828. James G. Blaine was a man of charm and a brilliant speaker. But the Democrats were quick to

Throughout his presidency, Grover Cleveland held to his belief that "a public office is a public trust." Cleveland made some bitter political enemies but is ranked as one of the most capable Presidents of the late 1800's.

remind the voters of Blaine's irregular railroad deals.[2] They also charged that he was a Halfbreed spoilsman who would carry the quarrel between Halfbreeds and Stalwarts (page 407) all the way to the White House. Cleveland, in contrast to Blaine, was not an exciting speaker. When the Republicans could find no way to attack his political career, they investigated his private life. They publicized his hiring of a substitute in the Civil War, but ignored the fact that he had to support a widowed mother and his sisters.

Two events on the eve of the election may have influenced the outcome. When Blaine received a group of Protestant clergymen in New York, one of them called the Democrats the party of "rum, Romanism, and rebellion." Blaine failed to take issue with this slur against Catholics, and news-

---

[2] In 1876 it had been revealed that Blaine, as Speaker of the House, helped an Arkansas railroad secure a land grant and personally profited from the deal.

men rushed the story into print. That same day Blaine attended a lavish dinner party for Republican campaign contributors. Reporters wrote colorful accounts of Blaine's "feast" with the "money kings."

The Democratic victory is close. When the results were in, Cleveland had won by a narrow margin. Out of ten million votes Cleveland had only 29,000 more than Blaine; the electoral vote was 219 to 182. The Mugwumps had played an important role in the election. They had campaigned hard for Cleveland, and in New York State they were especially effective. Though Cleveland carried New York by only 1149 votes, that state's electoral votes were crucial in the outcome of the election. The Halfbreed-Stalwart quarrel within Republican ranks also helped Cleveland. Had Roscoe Conkling, the Stalwart leader, aided Blaine, the Republicans might have carried New York. Instead, Conkling refused to participate in the campaign, declaring that he did not engage in "criminal practice."

Cleveland defines his concept of the presidency. The new President set out to administer the federal government as honestly and efficiently as he had governed the city of Buffalo and the state of New York. He intended to appoint competent people to government jobs and then see that they executed the laws fairly. In Cleveland's opinion, the President could *suggest* legislation to Congress, and should veto acts that he considered unwise. But, according to Cleveland, it was not the President's duty to *lead* Congress. Rather, Cleveland considered himself the "umpire" of the federal government. It was the President's job to see that the rules were obeyed and that no individual or group was either deprived of their rights or granted special favors.

Cleveland's veto of a minor agricultural bill illustrates his view of the presidency. When western farmers were hard hit by drought in 1886, Congress passed a bill appropriating 10,000 dollars to help them buy seed for the next planting. To Cleveland, this measure looked like favoritism. In his veto message he said:

I do not believe that the power and duty of the General Government ought to be extended to the relief of individual suffering which is in no manner properly related to the public service or benefit. . . . The lesson should constantly be enforced that *though the people support the Government, the Government should not support the people.* . . . Federal aid in such cases encourages the expectation of paternal care on the part of the Government and weakens the sturdiness of our national character.

Cleveland hoped to bring capable men into government service. But he was subjected to great pressure by party workers and political bosses for government jobs. Strongly in favor of civil service, Cleveland extended the list of jobs covered by the Pendleton Act. But the "everlasting clatter for office" forced him to fill most of the unclassified positions with loyal Democrats. Ardent civil-service reformers, most of whom were Mugwumps, objected. When the President referred to his critics as "impracticable friends," Carl Schurz, speaking for the Mugwumps, replied: "Your attempt to please both reformers and spoilsmen has failed."

Cleveland vetoes a pension bill. The President's desire to avoid favoritism toward a special group of citizens influenced his handling of pensions for war veterans. Sometimes claimants who were rejected by the Pension Bureau requested their congressmen to secure the passage of private bills granting them relief. Most of the post-Civil War Presidents signed these private pension bills without close examination. Cleveland, however, carefully investigated each of the measures. He approved some 1500 of the private pension bills, more than Grant, Hayes, Garfield, and Arthur combined. But he also vetoed more than 200 of them. For example, he refused a pension for a widow whose husband had been shot, not in the war, but by a neighbor while hunting. Another widow was denied relief because her husband, after being captured by the Confederates, ended up fighting for the South.

The Grand Army of the Republic, a powerful veterans' organization, was angered by Cleveland's vetoes and accused him of displaying "rebel sympathies." In 1887 it influenced Congress to pass a Dependent Pension Bill. This measure would have given a pension to any veteran who had served three months and who was disabled, regardless of the date or cause of the disability. Cleveland vetoed this measure on the grounds that it would show favoritism to veterans.

Federal land is reclaimed. Cleveland was equally strict with individuals and corporations which had violated the terms of land grants. Certain railroads which had received land grants, and some cattlemen, mineowners, and lumber companies who claimed government land, had not lived up to the terms of their agreements. From these people Cleveland reclaimed more than 80 million acres of land and restored it to the national domain.

Federal administration is improved. Three of the laws passed during Cleveland's administration reflected his interest in governmental efficiency.

(1) The Presidential Succession Act (1886) provided that, if both President and Vice-President should die or be disabled, Cabinet members would succeed to the presidency in the order of the creation of their offices by Congress. This meant that the Secretary of State would succeed to the presidency after the Vice-President.[3]

(2) The Electoral Count Act (1887) was intended to prevent another disputed election like that of 1876. It provided that a state's electoral vote must be accepted unless rejected by both houses of Congress. If more than one set of returns were sent in, and if the two houses could not agree on which to approve, Congress must accept the set approved by the governor of the state.

(3) In 1887 Congress repealed the Tenure of Office Act (page 390), after a long struggle between President Cleveland and the Republican Senate. This action strengthened the independence of the executive branch of the federal government.

Railroad regulation is demanded. Meanwhile, mounting public protests finally convinced the Senate that it should investigate the railroads. It had become

---

[3] This act was replaced by another Presidential Succession Act in 1947. See page 785.

clear that some railroads were taking advantage of the farmers or of the public (pages 437, 445). During 1885 a committee headed by Senator Cullom of Illinois studied the activities of the railroads and early the next year submitted a report criticizing the unfair practices carried on by some of them. The Cullom Committee Report also recommended the appointment of a special committee of experts to iron out the differences between the railroads and the people who used their services.

Then, in October, 1886, the Supreme Court handed down a decision which made government action seem more necessary than ever. Ten years before, the Supreme Court had upheld the legality of the state Granger laws, which regulated railroad rates (page 438). But in a case called *Wabash, St. Louis and Pacific Railroad Company v. Illinois,* the Court reversed its earlier decision. It now held that the states had no right to regulate interstate commerce or to interfere with traffic moving across state lines. This power, declared the Court, had been conferred by the Constitution upon Congress. The Court even forbade a state to set rates on interstate railroad traffic within its own borders. The Granger laws, for all practical purposes, were meaningless, after the *Wabash* case was decided.

Farmers and shippers called for immediate action by the federal government. If the states could no longer regulate the railroads, then Congress, they argued, must do so under its power to control interstate commerce. Important spokesmen in both parties urged some kind of government regulation.

Congress passes the Interstate Commerce Act. The result was the Interstate Commerce Act, passed by Congress in 1887. This important law forbade (1) favoritism in rates among persons, places, or commodities; (2) rebates; (3) higher rates "for a shorter than for a longer distance over the same line, in the same direction"; (4) unreasonable or unjust rates; and (5) pooling arrangements. To enforce these restrictions, the act provided for the creation of an Interstate Commerce Commission (ICC).

The five members of this regulatory commission were to be appointed by the President with the consent of the Senate. None of them could be a railroad stockholder or employee, and no more than three members could belong to the same political party.

The Interstate Commerce Act set a precedent that has become increasingly important. It established the principle that the government could regulate private business engaged in interstate commerce. President Cleveland had some misgivings about signing the act into law because it ran counter to the government's traditional "hands-off" policy toward business. But the abuses of the railroads had become so glaring that the President and many Americans felt government action was necessary to protect the public welfare.

The Interstate Commerce Act proves difficult to enforce. It soon became clear, however, that regulation of the railroads would not be easy. The Interstate Commerce Commission could investigate a complaint against a railroad and then rule whether or not the new law was being violated. An accused railroad could then appeal the Commission's ruling to the federal courts. This proved to be a great advantage to the railroads because they could hire skillful lawyers and in many cases could count on judges being favorable to them.

Between 1887 and 1905, sixteen of the Commission's rulings were appealed to the Supreme Court by the railroads; in only one of these cases did the Court decide in favor of the Commission. Obviously the Interstate Commerce Commission was powerless to regulate the railroads. In fact, a corporation lawyer confidentially advised a railroad executive in 1892:

The Commission, as its functions have now been limited by the Courts, is, or can be made, of great use to the railroads. It satisfies the popular clamor for a government supervision of railroads, at the same time that such supervision is almost entirely nominal [in name only]. . . . The part of wisdom is not to destroy the Commission, but to utilize it.

Still, the Interstate Commerce Act had at least established the principle that railroads were subject to government regulation and had laid the basis for more effective legislation in later years.

Controversy arises over tariff rates. In addition to railroad regulation, many Americans at this time believed that new tariff legislation was necessary. High tariffs for the protection of American industry had been a part of the Republican Party's program since the Civil War. In the early 1880's, to be sure, President Arthur had decided that rates could be lowered without hurting American business. He appointed a tariff commission, which studied the problem and then recommended a 20 per cent reduction in rates. When the necessary legislation was introduced in Congress, however, lobbyists went to work and, in the end, many rates were actually raised. The so-called "Mongrel Tariff" was enacted into law in 1883, but few were satisfied with it.

Industrialists argued that still higher rates were necessary to protect them from competition with European industrial countries, particularly England. They pointed out that thousands of American jobs and the rising standard of living depended on the economic well-being of American industry. Farmers and many consumers, on the other hand, felt differently. They argued that excessively high tariff rates enabled manufacturers to monopolize the American market and then charge any price they pleased. The opponents of a high tariff also declared that it was at least partly responsible for a shortage of currency. Because of high tariff rates, the United States treasury was actually collecting about 100 million dollars a year more than it paid out. Lowering the tariff would reduce the treasury surplus, put more money into circulation, and result in lower prices for manufactured goods.

Cleveland calls for tariff reduction. When Cleveland entered the White House, he knew little about the details of the tariff issue. But he soon educated himself by poring over the recommendations of the tariff commission and studying the rate schedules. He realized that the treasury surplus resulted in large part from high tariff rates. He also believed that it would be unwise to spend the surplus on unjustified pensions for veterans or "pork barrel" projects which politicians wanted for their home districts. Cleveland concluded that most American industries would not be hurt by moderate tariff reductions while continued high tariff rates would impose an unfair burden on consumers.

By 1887 Cleveland had decided to recommend a moderate reduction in tariff rates. Cabinet members and other Democratic leaders warned him that the tariff was too touchy an issue to bring up before a presidential election. But with characteristic bluntness Cleveland replied: "What is the use of being elected or re-elected if you don't stand for something?" In a message to Congress the President said: "Our present tariff laws ought to be at once revised and amended." He referred to the treasury surplus as "a hoarding place for money needlessly withdrawn from trade and the people's use, thus crippling our

"The Grange Awakening the Sleepers" is the title of this cartoon showing farmers about to be run over by a train symbolizing railroad abuses. Though the Grange succeeded in arousing the farmers to action, the Supreme Court in the Wabash case ruled against the state Granger laws.

national energies." Cleveland made it clear that he did not favor *free trade,* or the removal of all tariff duties. He favored protection for American industry but warned businessmen not to demand "immense profits instead of moderately profitable returns." The President declared: "It is a condition, not a theory, that confronts us."

Cleveland's tariff recommendation fails. The Democratic majority in the House of Representatives responded to Cleveland's tariff message by passing a bill to lower rates. But Republicans in the Senate substituted a bill providing for high rates. With the two houses thus deadlocked on tariff legislation, the issue was left for the voters to decide at the polls in 1888.

▶ CHECK-UP

1. Why was Cleveland nominated in 1884? Why was Arthur not nominated? What was the result of the election?

2. What was Cleveland's conception of the presidency? Why did Cleveland veto some pension bills? How did he seek to improve the efficiency of the federal government?

3. On what grounds did the Supreme Court reverse its decision on the Granger laws? What were the provisions of the Interstate Commerce Act? How were these to be enforced? Why was enforcement difficult?

4. Why did farmers and industrialists disagree about tariff rates? Why did Cleveland recommend revision of the tariff? What was the outcome?

· ·

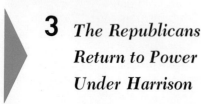

3 *The Republicans Return to Power Under Harrison*

The Republicans win the election of 1888. Many of the Democratic bosses were unhappy about Cleveland's forthright stand on the tariff. Nevertheless, the Democratic convention in 1888 renominated the Presi-

dent without the formality of a ballot. The Democratic platform endorsed moderate downward revision of tariff rates. The Republican convention nominated Benjamin Harrison, a corporation lawyer from Indiana and grandson of President William Henry Harrison. "Young Tippecanoe," as he was called, strongly supported a high tariff.

Claiming that the Democrats' tariff plans threatened American business, the Republican fund raisers secured large contributions from corporations. Republican speakers and campaign literature tried to convince the voters that Cleveland actually favored "free trade." Removing tariff barriers would force American factories to shut down, they charged, and thus cause American workingmen to lose their jobs.

In the face of Republican "free trade" charges, the Democrats found it hard to convince voters that moderate tariff reductions would benefit the country. The Tammany organization in New York was only lukewarm in its support of Cleveland, and the Grand Army of the Republic actively opposed him because of his pension bill veto. Few of the Mugwumps rallied to Cleveland's support in 1888. To add to the President's troubles, the British minister in Washington was tricked into writing a letter in support of Cleveland. The letter was published, and not only cost Cleveland many Irish votes in New York but also seemed to confirm Republican charges that British industrialists were backing efforts to lower American tariff rates.

When the ballots were counted, Cleveland had about 100,000 more votes than Harrison. But the Republicans had carried the pivotal states of New York and Indiana by narrow margins, and this was enough to give Harrison a majority of 65 electoral votes. The Republicans retained control of the Senate and also won a slim majority in the House of Representatives.

Harrison relies on party bosses. The new President lacked Grover Cleveland's rugged independence and courage. In fact, Harrison seemed content to follow the advice of such prominent Republicans as James Blaine, Senators Sherman of Ohio

Election night called out large crowds in 1888 as it does now. An early projection screen shows election returns to New Yorkers.

and Quay of Pennsylvania, and John Wanamaker, a Philadelphia department store millionaire. "When I came into power," President Harrison later admitted, "I found that the party managers had taken it all to themselves. I could not name my own Cabinet. They had sold out every place to pay the election expenses." Included in Harrison's Cabinet were Blaine as Secretary of State and Wanamaker as Postmaster General. The new President promptly fired all Democratic officeholders outside the classified list and gave their jobs to Republican Party workers.

The House adopts the Reed rules. Eager to push their legislative program through Congress, the Republicans ran into trouble from the Democrats in the House. The Democrats did not have enough votes to block passage of bills. Nevertheless, by refusing to answer the roll call, they could prevent the House from attaining a quorum; and without a quorum, no business could be transacted. The Republican Speaker of the House, Thomas B. Reed, put up with this maneuver for a while. But one day in 1890, when the roll call again failed to produce a quorum, Reed instructed the clerk to count all the silent Democrats as present. He then declared that a quorum existed. Such an action had no precedent in Congress, and the Democrats shouted angry

threats. But Speaker Reed restored order with this question: "The Chair is making a statement of fact that the gentleman . . . is present. Does he deny it?"

Soon afterward the House Republicans pushed through two new rules. One prohibited motions made simply to obstruct action. The other permitted the Speaker to count as present members who were actually in the House, even if they did not answer the roll call. These rules greatly increased the power of the Speaker, and the unhappy Democrats started calling Reed a "Czar." Nevertheless, when the Democrats regained control of the House, they retained the Reed rules.

Harrison signs a pension measure. The way was now clear for the Republicans to fulfill their campaign promises to the voters. Most insistent were the veterans. In 1890 Congress passed and Harrison signed the Dependent Pension Act, similar to the bill that Cleveland had vetoed (page 495). The new law increased the number of pensioners from about 700,000 to nearly 1,000,000. Payments to veterans and their widows jumped from about 90 million dollars in 1888 to nearly 160 million dollars by the end of Harrison's term of office.

Government regulation of the trusts is demanded. In the same year that the pension act was passed, Congress approved three laws of much greater importance. The most significant was a measure authorizing government regulation of businesses that engaged in interstate commerce.

As we have seen, government regulation of railroads had been attempted in the Interstate Commerce Act. By 1890 the pressure was mounting for the federal government also to take action against the "trusts," as large corporations were called (page 455). Corporations were chartered by state legislatures, but once the charters had been granted, the states had little or no power over them. Moreover, corporations chartered in any one state were then free to do business anywhere in the country. Since New Jersey and Delaware had charter laws especially favorable to corporations, many businesses were chartered in those two states, regardless of where their offices or plants were actually located.

The early efforts of state governments to restrict the industrial giants were even less successful than the Granger laws had been against the railroads. Corporations found protection in the Fourteenth Amendment, which provides that no state may deprive any *person* of life, liberty, or property *without due process of law*, nor deny to any *person* the *equal protection of the laws*. The words in italics caused endless arguments in the courts. At first, the Supreme Court held that the Fourteenth Amendment applied only to individuals and not to corporations. But in 1886 the Court reversed its position and declared that a corporation was a *person* within the meaning of the Amendment. The Court then set aside state regulatory laws on the grounds that they interfered with the liberty or property of corporations. This ruling of the Supreme Court made the states powerless to control big business.

Congress passes an antitrust act. In response to public demand, Congress turned its attention to certain large corporations, whose great power and ruthless methods had been revealed by investigations. President Harrison urged Congress to consider the question of "how far the restraint of those combinations of capital commonly called 'trusts' is a matter of Federal juris-

diction." Some congressmen argued that the trusts, unlike the railroads, were not engaged in carrying goods across state lines. Moreover, trusts had state charters and their plants were located within state boundaries. Therefore, these lawmakers concluded, Congress had no power to regulate them. But other congressmen interpreted their powers more broadly. Since the trusts produced goods that were sold in interstate commerce, they believed that Congress had the right to regulate such corporations.

Congress used its authority over interstate commerce to pass the Sherman Antitrust Act in 1890. (The act took its name from Senator John Sherman of Ohio.) The new law forbade (1) "every contract, combination in the form of trust or otherwise, or conspiracy, in restraint of trade or commerce among the several states, or with foreign nations" and (2) attempts to monopolize any part of such trade. The act authorized the Attorney General to prosecute illegal combinations, break them up into their separate parts, and subject the promoters to fines and jail sentences. Persons injured by illegal trusts were entitled to seek damages in federal courts.

The Sherman Antitrust Act proves ineffective. As in the case of the Interstate Commerce Act, the vague wording of the Sherman Antitrust Act was welcomed by corporation lawyers. A humorist said of the act, "What looks like a stone wall to a layman, is a triumphal arch to a corporation lawyer." Legal experts argued about the meaning of such phrases as "in the form of trust," "in restraint of trade," and the words "combination," "conspiracy," and "monopoly." President Harrison's Attorney General made no real effort to enforce the law, and those cases which did get into the courts were usually decided in favor of the trusts.

The Supreme Court's decision in the Knight Company case (1895) illustrates how the courts undercut the Sherman Act. The American Sugar Refining Company had purchased refineries in Philadelphia which, with its other holdings, gave it control of more than 95 per cent of the coun-

(*Continued on page 505*)

AMERICAN INDUSTRY MOVES FORWARD

New machines, techniques, and business methods accelerated the expansion of American industry in the late 1800's. In our own time, America's talents for invention and leadership continue to reshape business and industry.

Eli Whitney's use of standardized parts (page 207) had laid the basis for mass production. In the early 1900's, Henry Ford incorporated Whitney's idea in the assembly-line production of automobiles. Above, in 1914, workers at the Ford plant in Michigan assembled Model T's at the rate of one every 93 minutes. Today, though the manufacture of an automobile is vastly more complicated, the finished product still rolls off an assembly line (right).

Other businessmen and industrialists soon recognized the advantages of assembly-line methods of production. Assembly lines today are found in almost every kind of manufacturing, from heavy industry to food processing. At right, workers stationed along a moving assembly line package salmon in an Oregon canning plant.

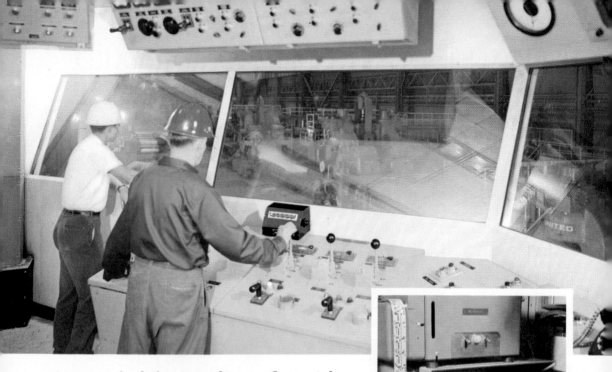

Automation has had as far-reaching an effect on industry as the assembly line. Above, a steelworker uses an electronic control board to direct processes formerly done by hand labor. Punched tape fed into a computer (right) controls the operation of a blast furnace.

Scientific research improves old products and devises new ones. Left, an oil industry scientist tests fuels for jet airplanes. The soil in the picture below has been treated with another petroleum product. Because it helps the soil retain heat and moisture, this product could help extend the growing season in cold climates.

The products of American industry have taken the drudgery out of everyday tasks. By 1923 electric kitchens had made cooking easier (above). Today even more appliances are available (right).

Household appliances like those pictured above have lightened the work of homemakers. Industry produces many other labor-saving devices. Snowplows, for example, swiftly clear the highways (right), thus making practical the operation of automobiles in snowy climates.

A high standard of living has meant increased leisure time for most Americans. As a result, the manufacture of sports and recreation equipment has become a thriving field in American industry. Sales of pleasure boats (right) have grown tremendously in recent years.

503

Today American industry is world-wide in scope. Not only are American products sold abroad but many companies have foreign branches. Right, a barge on the Rhine River carries American petroleum products past an ancient German castle.

The management of complex business organizations has become a highly skilled profession (above, left). To process the rapidly growing volume of business records, a new television filing system has been developed. Individual documents are recorded on magnetic video tape. Office workers can retrieve a particular item on a television screen at the touch of a button (above, right).

Other vital operations in industry are market research, advertising, and merchandising. Businessmen study what people need, want, or might like. Advertising informs the public how products can be used and enjoyed. Retail stores offer the products in convenient, attractive displays (left). Today the American consumer can choose from a greater variety of goods than ever before.

504

try's sugar refining business. The government accused the company of violating the Sherman Act and asked the Court to declare the purchase illegal. The Supreme Court refused, on the grounds that the mere purchase of sugar refineries "bore no direct relation to commerce between the states or with foreign nations."

Thus, during the 1890's large corporations had nothing to fear from the Sherman Antitrust Act. Although several small business associations were successfully prosecuted, no trust was broken up. One effect the act did have was to cause many businessmen to establish holding companies (page 456). And, oddly enough, the act was successfully applied against four unions. The Supreme Court ruled that the American Railway Union, for example, was an organization "in the form of a trust" and that its activities in the Pullman strike constituted a "conspiracy in restraint of trade" (page 481).

The Sherman Silver Purchase Act is passed. Senator Sherman's name was attached to another major law in 1890. Passage of the Sherman Silver Purchase Act was the result of pressure from debtors, western farmers, and silver mine owners. Ever since the 1870's the farmers, concerned about the falling prices on farm commodities, had urged the free and unlimited coinage of silver (page 411). This would increase the volume of money in circulation and make it easier for farmers to repay their financial obligations.

The Bland-Allison Act of 1878 had pumped some silver money into circulation, but during the 1880's the economy expanded so rapidly that the additional currency was quickly absorbed. Consequently the Farmers' Alliances (page 439) redoubled their demands for more silver dollars. Also, during 1889 and 1890 North and South Dakota, Wyoming, Montana, Idaho, and Washington were admitted to the Union. Although most of the congressmen from these states were Republicans, they strongly favored increased coinage of silver. Eastern Republicans, who generally opposed free silver, were willing to consider compromise legislation if the Westerners

would support a high-tariff measure. This understanding paved the way for passage of the Sherman Silver Purchase Act in July, 1890, and a new tariff law a few months later.

The Sherman Silver Purchase Act, like the Bland-Allison Act, provided for limited, not unlimited, coinage of silver. It authorized the government to buy up to 4,500,000 ounces of silver each month at the market price. This silver bullion was to be used as a base for issuing treasury certificates (paper money) redeemable in gold or silver. The Silver Purchase Act brought mixed reactions. The mine owners were happy because the new law enabled them to sell most of their monthly output of silver to the government. Farmers and debtors generally were dissatisfied because they felt the act did not put enough additional money into circulation. They still wanted unlimited coinage of silver. Supporters of the gold standard opposed the measure because it brought more silver-backed currency into circulation which had to be redeemed in gold on demand. This, they felt, might be a threat to the gold reserves in the national treasury.

The McKinley Tariff is passed. The third important piece of legislation passed

---

Mr. Dooley

Probably more than any other people on earth, Americans like to laugh at themselves. The humorous remark about the Sherman Antitrust Act on page 500 was made by Finley Peter Dunne (1867–1936), a Chicago newspaperman. Dunne was a humorist in the tradition of Mark Twain, Will Rogers, and other commentators on the events of their times. Finley Peter Dunne created "Mr. Dooley," an Irish-American saloonkeeper and philosopher. Mr. Dooley took a dim view of many aspects of American life, among them the trusts and big business. Dooley's biting wit was circulated in books and newspapers and was greatly appreciated by millions of chuckling readers.

in 1890 was a tariff bill. The Republicans had considered the outcome of the 1888 election an endorsement of their stand on protection. Thanks to their understanding with the congressmen from the new western states, they had the votes to pass a new tariff measure. William McKinley of Ohio, chairman of the House Ways and Means Committee, introduced a bill which would raise rates to the highest level yet in American history. The McKinley Tariff, which became law in October, 1890, contained three new features:

(1) In an effort to gain the good will of western farmers, the act placed import duties on certain agricultural products — wheat, corn, potatoes, eggs, bacon, and barley. Actually these products were imported only in very small quantities; but the Republicans hoped to convince the farmers that they would be aided, rather than hurt, by high tariffs.

(2) The act also included a *reciprocity* clause. This clause, in effect, said to foreign countries: "I'll treat you as you treat me." Certain commodities (raw sugar, molasses, tea, coffee, and hides) were placed on the "free list" — that is, they could be sent into the United States without tariff

"Will somebody show Uncle Sam how to see through the silver trouble?" was the question posed by this cartoon which appeared during the silver-gold controversy of the late 1800's.

duties. But the reciprocity provision gave the President authority to impose duties upon these commodities whenever the country exporting them to us placed "unjust and unreasonable" duties on their imports of American products.

(3) The third new feature of the McKinley Tariff was a *bounty* (or payment) to American sugar growers. Most of the sugar consumed in the United States was grown outside the country, and this commodity had been placed on the free list. To protect American sugar growers from foreign competition, the McKinley Tariff provided that they be paid a bounty of two cents a pound on all sugar grown within the country. This feature satisfied American sugar growers because of the bounty they received. It also satisfied the sugar *refiners*, who were able to get raw foreign sugar duty-free and therefore more cheaply.

The McKinley Tariff proves unpopular. The Republicans in Congress were content with their achievements. Besides passing several important laws, they had appropriated more than a billion dollars — in pensions, sugar bounties, bills to improve rivers and harbors, postal subsidies to steamship lines, and naval appropriations. When "Czar" Reed was told that expenditures had reached that total, he snapped, "This is a billion-dollar country."

Some Americans, however, were dissatisfied with the work of this Congress. Farmers and wage earners found little to be happy about in the new legislation. The Silver Purchase Act had not noticeably increased prices on farm products, and the antitrust law was powerless against monopolistic businesses. Moreover, when the new tariff went into effect, prices on manufactured goods rose sharply. While everyone had to pay more for heavily protected manufactured goods, agricultural imports were so small that the McKinley Tariff helped farmers hardly at all.

The Democrats gain in the 1890 elections. Secretary of State James G. Blaine had warned his fellow Republicans about the political dangers of a tariff that would "protect the Republican Party only into speedy retirement." The congressional elections in 1890 proved Blaine's fears to have

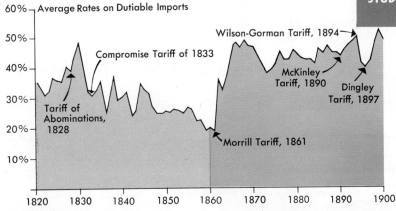

CHART STUDY

CHANGES IN THE TARIFF, 1861–1900

This chart shows changes in the tariff up to 1900 with emphasis on the years 1861–1900. Average rates remained high. A chart on page 677 shows changes in the tariff since 1900.

Average Rates on Dutiable Imports

Compromise Tariff of 1833

Wilson-Gorman Tariff, 1894

McKinley Tariff, 1890

Dingley Tariff, 1897

Tariff of Abominations, 1828

Morrill Tariff, 1861

been well-founded. The Democrats elected 235 members to the House of Representatives, while the Republicans won only 88 seats. Among those congressmen who went down to defeat was William McKinley, "the guardian angel of protection." The Republicans kept control of the Senate, however, and for the next two years were able to block legislation initiated by the Democratic House.

▶ CHECK-UP

1. Why did Harrison win the election in 1888? What new rules increased the power of the Speaker of the House of Representatives?

2. Why were the states unable to regulate trusts? What provision in the Fourteenth Amendment gave the trusts protection? Why was the Sherman Antitrust Act ineffective?

3. Why did Congress pass the Sherman Silver Purchase Act? What were its provisions? How was this act regarded by those who favored free silver? By those who opposed it?

4. Explain the new features of the McKinley Tariff Act. What groups were dissatisfied with the new tariff? Why?

• • • • • • • • • • • • • • •

▶ **4** *Many Americans Enjoy a Better Life*

Despite widespread dissatisfaction among farmers, laborers, and immigrants in the late 1800's, many Americans found themselves better off than ever before. The growing middle class included those Americans who never expected to have great wealth but who lived much more comfortably than the poor. The ranks of the middle class were expanding to include people of many different occupations — teachers, ministers, lawyers, doctors, office workers, shopkeepers, salesmen, and a growing number of skilled factory workers. Their incomes enabled them to enjoy more than the bare necessities of life, and they were generally content with the way things were going in the late 1800's. Middle-class standards of taste, comfort, and morality had become idealized as "the American way of life" and were imitated or envied by those who could not afford them.

The American standard of living rises. Many middle-class Americans lived in the expanding urban centers. As newcomers swarmed into the cities, the older, native-born inhabitants often moved outward to the city limits or beyond (page 471). This movement was made possible by the development of city transportation systems. First the horse-drawn streetcar, then the steam railroad, and finally electric trolleys enabled people to travel rapidly and conveniently within large urban areas. Quiet residential suburbs soon surrounded the industrial, commercial, and tenement districts of every large city. Many more Americans of the middle-income groups continued to live in smaller cities and towns. Enjoying home ownership, relatively steady jobs, and a rising standard of living, middle-class citizens sought no change in existing conditions and so generally held conservative views.

A rising standard of living enabled middle-class families of the late 1800's to furnish their parlors with fringed furniture, hangings, and an abundance of pictures, statuettes, and knick-knacks.

Vast quantities of inexpensive mass-produced articles helped raise the standard of living for middle-class people of the late 1800's. They bought ready-made clothes and shoes, mass-produced carpets and furniture, and an abundance of factory-made knickknacks for their homes. The parlors of middle-class homes were cluttered with sentimental pictures, bamboo stands, glass domes sheltering wax flowers, and horsehair upholstered loveseats. Running water, bathtubs, gas lamps, sewing machines, and pianos were within the financial reach of most of these people. Even the more prosperous farmers could afford some of these comforts.

Public school attendance increases. Better education has generally helped to raise standards of living, and middle-class Americans benefited from a number of new educational developments in the late 1800's. Perhaps most important was the increasing number of public schools. In 1880 about ten million children attended public schools. But before the end of the century the number had climbed to fifteen million, and more than 30 states had laws which made attendance compulsory. Even more remarkable was the growth of high schools. In 1880 some 110,000 students were enrolled in fewer than 800 high schools. Only 20 years later the country had 5500 high schools, attended by more than 500,000 students.

Colleges and universities offer greater opportunity. Some middle-class families during this period could afford to send their young people to private colleges, but many more enrolled in state-supported colleges and universities. A number of these state institutions had been established under the Morrill Act of 1862, which gave federal land grants to the states (page 435). Proceeds from the sale of this land were used to establish "land-grant colleges" providing instruction in agriculture and engineering. Co-education became the rule in these colleges, even though this policy at first met with opposition. Among the women's colleges founded during these years were Vassar, Wellesley, Smith, and Bryn Mawr.

Not only were colleges increasing in numbers and enrollment; they also were raising their standards. By the 1890's some colleges had begun to offer courses in modern history, the social sciences, and modern foreign languages. Science courses were expanded and laboratories built. Many institutions adopted the German practice of teaching small groups of advanced students in *seminars.* Harvard introduced the elective system, under which students were permitted a choice of courses instead of having to follow a required program. In 1876 Johns Hopkins University became the first institution chiefly concerned with graduate studies. There, and at Harvard and Yale, college graduates could carry on advanced studies and research without having to travel to European universities.

Public libraries make books available. The growing interest in reading among middle-class Americans brought about a substantial increase in the number of public libraries. By 1900 the United States had over 9000 free circulating libraries housing nearly 47 million books. The generosity of Andrew Carnegie, as we have seen, made possible the building of libraries in many small towns.

The Chautauqua movement provides education and entertainment. Another important educational force was the Chautauqua movement. This institution, founded at Lake Chautauqua, New York, in 1874, enabled people to combine the pleasures of summer camp life with reading, lectures, and discussions. Thousands of people came from every state to hear prominent educators, ministers, reformers, writers, and statesmen. Among the most popular sessions were talks and readings by such well-known humorists as Mark Twain, "Bill" Nye, and James Whitcomb Riley. Enthusiastic Chautauqua fans organized study groups in their home towns and pursued a program of reading and discussions through the winter months. Eventually the Chautauqua lecturers traveled on regular winter circuits. A vast number of books and pamphlets were supplied to Chautauqua reading clubs throughout the country. Middle-income Americans, eager for educational

opportunities denied them in their youth, especially appreciated the Chautauqua movement.

More Americans listen to music. Many Americans were developing an interest in music. By the end of the century most of the largest cities had their own symphony orchestras. An outstanding conductor was Theodore Thomas, who came to this country from Germany as a small boy. He organized his own symphony orchestra and toured the country, introducing many Americans to serious music. Such conductors as Leopold Damrosch and his son Walter Damrosch, both German-born, also brought symphonic music to thousands of Americans. In addition, many cities formed choral and operatic societies. While these groups often engaged European soloists, they drew heavily upon foreign-born Americans who had extensive musical training.

Some cities established conservatories to prepare musicians and music teachers, and colleges and universities introduced music courses. Walter Damrosch taught for many years at the New York Institute of Musical Art (later merged with the Juilliard School of Music). The first professor of music at Columbia University was the American composer Edward MacDowell. After studying in Germany, MacDowell returned to

A growing number of women's colleges offered broader education than the earlier "academies." Here a class at Wellesley College meets in a chemistry laboratory.

Americans of the late 1800's enjoyed a good band concert, especially if it was conducted by John Philip Sousa (above). Recorded music was a popular novelty. At right is one of the earliest phonographs, operated by a handcrank.

the United States and won acclaim as a concert pianist, teacher, and composer. Among his many piano and orchestral compositions were the *Woodland Sketches,* which included "To a Wild Rose" and "To a Water Lily."

Band concerts were very popular in the late 1800's. Many small towns had bandstands in their parks, where concerts were regularly held in good weather. The band music of John Philip Sousa, "the March King," was especially popular. A former Marine band conductor, Sousa formed his own band in the 1890's and toured both this country and Europe. Thomas A. Edison's phonograph, invented in the 1870's, opened new musical opportunities to thousands of Americans. Wax records of marches, waltzes, operatic arias, and popular songs sold in great numbers. Among the most enduring of the hit songs of the 1890's were "After the Ball," "A Bicycle Built for Two," and "Oh Promise Me."

Another important musical development in the 1890's was the growth of interest in ragtime and "the blues" — two ingredients that later were blended in jazz. During the 1870's and '80's, Negro musicians replaced whites in the minstrel shows and experimented freely with new rhythms and dance routines. As the popularity of the minstrel shows declined, the Negroes began to give regular performances in the cafés of New Orleans, Memphis, and St. Louis. The "blues" singers adapted Negro folk songs to strong rhythmic accompaniments, while performers like Scott Joplin wrote ragtime compositions for the piano. By the end of the decade the whole country was listening to ragtime tunes, and the younger generation had invented a wide variety of ragtime dance steps.

More people are interested in sports. Whether they lived in villages, small towns, or cities, increasing numbers of Americans had both the time and the money to enjoy a variety of sports. They watched games played by professionals and participated in sports themselves. The game of baseball had been played in a variety of forms since colonial days. By the 1840's, standardized rules and a diamond-shaped playing field had been adopted. During the Civil War, the game was learned by soldiers from all parts of the country and became increasingly popular.

In 1869, the first professional team, the Cincinnati Red Stockings, was organized, and seven years later the National League of Professional Baseball Clubs was founded. By 1900 the rules of the game were standardized, the professional teams had agreed upon a ball not too lively and not too "dead," and gloves and a catcher's mask had been introduced. Baseball had become the national pastime.

Meanwhile, the colleges had enthusiastically taken up the game of football, a modification of English rugby. Rivalry between football teams became so heated, especially in the East, that one college president in the '90's feared the degree of B.A. would soon stand for "Bachelor of Athletics." The annual Yale-Princeton football game on Thanksgiving Day in 1893 drew more than 50,000 spectators.

Smaller crowds of equally dedicated fans turned out to watch professional boxing matches. Boxers usually fought with bare fists, often for 40 or 50 rounds. In 1889 the famous John L. Sullivan fought 75 rounds with Jake Kilrain in what proved to be the last bare-knuckle championship fight. Sullivan won 20,000 dollars and a diamond belt, but three years later he lost to "Gentleman Jim" Corbett. By the 1890's professional boxers fought three-minute rounds and used padded gloves.

Swimming and boating were popular family sports during the late nineteenth century. Many resorts catered to families of moderate income, who enjoyed their rowboats and canoes as much as the captains of industry did their yachts. Roller-skating, ice-skating, lawn tennis, golf, archery, and croquet were other popular recreations. Bicycling became a favorite sport of Americans after its introduction in the 1870's. The earliest bicycles were awkward and even dangerous vehicles. An enormous front wheel was fitted with pedals, and the tires were solid. The rider sat above the front wheel, a position from which he was often pitched over the han-

dlebars. In the '80's, however, the "safety" bicycle introduced low wheels of equal size and pneumatic tires. Soon thousands of Americans owned bicycles, and young and old, male and female, enjoyed week-end rides to the country. Others bicycled to the new soda fountains where they could buy "pop" and other "soft" drinks, as well as chewing gum, another innovation of this period.

Americans enjoy theatrical entertainment. Among other amusements of the postwar decades were musical comedy and vaudeville, which grew in popularity as the minstrel shows began to wane. Many Americans also enjoyed melodramas, which often told the story of an innocent country girl lured to the wicked city and saved at the last minute from the clutches of an evil man. By the 1880's most American cities had theaters which presented serious drama as well. Large audiences applauded such famous stage personalities as Sir Henry Irving and Sarah Bernhardt from overseas and the American actor Edwin Booth. Traveling companies, headed by one or more stars, performed in Philadelphia, New York, and Boston and then toured the cities of the interior. One of the best of these road companies was headed by John Drew and Maurice Barrymore. The latter's three children, John, Lionel, and Ethel, were later to become famous stage and screen stars.

A world's fair celebrates American progress. The four-hundredth anniversary of Columbus' discovery of the New World came in 1892. To celebrate this event, the city of Chicago held a World's Columbian Exposition. The job of converting 600 acres of lakeside dunes into parks, lagoons, and fairgrounds proved so difficult that the exposition did not open until 1893. The fair's main buildings, called the "White City," were designed in the classical tradition, painted white, and illuminated by 5000 electric arc lights. One building that did not follow the classical theme of the fair was the Transportation Building; it was the work of a brilliant Chicago architect, Louis Sullivan.

The 28 million people who visited the fair in the summer of 1893 were deeply im-

In the 1890's bicycling was a favorite recreation of middle-class Americans. The bicycle as we know it had replaced the high-wheeled velocipede (top left). A more fashionable pastime was lawn tennis (above), brought to this country from England in 1874. Annual lawn tennis tournaments were soon being played at Newport, Rhode Island, the summer resort of eastern society. Princeton and Rutgers played the first college football game in 1869. By 1890, when this Harvard team was photographed (left), football was the leading college sport.

pressed by the evidence of their country's progress. The fair's great halls displayed the developments in industry, transportation, communication, and agriculture that had made the United States a leader among the nations of the world. A Palace of Fine Arts exhibited the works of outstanding American painters and sculptors. The achievements of the "weaker sex" were set forth in the Woman's Building. The fair's playground was the Midway, with sideshows, a Ferris Wheel and reproductions of foreign villages, cafés, and bazaars.

Hamlin Garland's reaction to the Chicago fair was typical. He wrote immediately to his aged parents in Dakota: "Sell the cook stove if necessary and come. You *must* see this fair." They came and, like thousands of other Americans, were moved "to tears of joy" by "the wonder and beauty of it all."

▶ CHECK-UP

1. What groups of people were included in the expanding middle class? How did the middle-class standard of living improve? How did educational opportunities increase? What was the Chautauqua movement?

2. What developments took place in music? Sports? The theater? What was the significance of the Columbian Exposition?

Visitors to the Columbian Exposition marveled at the splendors to be seen. Displays in buildings like Machinery Hall (right) and the Electricity Building heralded the wonders of the century to come.

Clinching the Main Ideas in Chapter 23

During the 1880's each of the two major political parties tended to be conservative. They were not much concerned with the rapid changes taking place in the country nor troubled by social problems of the times. As long as their candidates could win elections by ignoring controversial issues, they did so. Their primary aim was to win and hold public office.

Grover Cleveland was more independent and courageous than other Presidents between 1865 and 1900. But he was sometimes reluctant to use his power as President to provide leadership for Congress. As a result, his effort to lower the tariff was thwarted. Harrison not only raised the tariff but also yielded to demands for veterans' pensions and "pork-barrel" legislation financed out of the treasury surplus.

Growing awareness of unfair practices by railroads and large corporations led to the passage of two important pieces of legislation — the Interstate Commerce Act and the Sherman Antitrust Act. These two acts marked the beginning of government regulation of railroads and corporations. But neither measure was seriously enforced in the 1890's, and loopholes enabled corporation lawyers to win court cases.

Though some groups, notably farmers and industrial workers, were growing increasingly dissatisfied, the fact remains that many Americans were generally satisfied with conditions during the 1880's. More people were achieving middle-class standards, and large numbers of them were not directly affected by such problems as falling farm prices and growing labor unrest. To many people, the beautiful buildings and industrial marvels of the World's Columbian Exposition seemed to summarize the achievements of the American way of life.

Chapter Review

Terms to Understand

1. Mugwumps
2. ICC
3. Reed rules
4. bounty
5. reciprocity
6. private pension bill
7. Interstate Commerce Act
8. Sherman Antitrust Act
9. land-grant college
10. McKinley Tariff Act
11. Electoral Count Act (1887)
12. Sherman Silver Purchase Act
13. Columbian Exposition
14. Chautauqua

What Do You Think?

1. Concerning political parties during the 1880's and 1890's, the statement is made, "there often seemed to be greater differences *within* each party on the major issues . . . than there was between the Democrats and the Republicans." How was that possible? Is it true today?

2. Cleveland said: ". . . though the people support the government, the government should not support the people." What did he mean? Do you agree? Explain.

3. What groups favored higher tariff rates during the 1880's? Lower rates? Explain why in each case.

4. Why was modern transportation an important factor in making modern urban centers possible?

5. How did the Electoral Count Act make a repetition of the disputed election of 1876 impossible?

Using Your Knowledge of History

1. The leisure-time activities of a people are often considered important keys to their character. In a paper of 300 words see if you can point out some of the chief characteristics of Americans.

2. Some have said that American education has reduced the level of illiteracy but has not led to a significant rise in the reading of books. Hold a discussion to bring out the pro's and con's in regard to this viewpoint.

3. Write an editorial on the McKinley Tariff showing why it was not likely to help farmers.

4. Prepare a report on some aspect of the growth of the cities during this period, using information found in Arthur M. Schlesinger's *The Rise of the City*.

Extending Your Knowledge of History

A stimulating interpretation of this period can be found in Ray Ginger's *Age of Excess*. A sampling of *The American Commonwealth* by James Bryce will also give the flavor of the 1880's. Matthew Josephson's *The Politicos, 1865–1896* is useful for this period. So also is Allan Nevins's biography of a Democratic President, *Grover Cleveland: A Study in Courage*. For social changes in this period, see F. R. Dulles's *America Learns to Play*. *American Heritage* has several notable articles about this period: on the 1884 election, "The Dirtiest Election" by Marvin and Dorothy Rosenberg (August, 1962); on the Sherman Antitrust Act, "The Law to Make Free Enterprise Free" by Thurman Arnold (October, 1960); and on the Chicago Fair, "The Great White City" by Jessie H. Hirschl (October, 1960).

CHAPTER 24

The Country Chooses Between Gold and Silver

Bryan speaking

Having behind us the producing masses of this nation and the world, supported by the commercial interests, the laboring interests, and the toilers everywhere, we will answer their demand for a gold standard by saying to them: You shall not press down upon the brow of labor this crown of thorns, you shall not crucify mankind upon a cross of gold.

WILLIAM JENNINGS BRYAN, 1896

1890–1900

Though many Americans became more prosperous during the 1880's, others had good reason to be discouraged with their situation. In Unit Six we saw that the farmers, particularly in the West, faced serious problems in their struggle to make a living. We also noted the hardships suffered by immigrants in the cities and the difficulties confronting workingmen in their efforts to win bargaining rights with employers. In 1893 the condition of many Americans became even worse when a severe depression swept the country. Banks failed and savings were wiped out; factories closed their doors and unemployment soared; farm prices continued to fall.

The politics of the 1890's reflected the mounting discontent of many Americans. Leaders of dissatisfied groups in the West and South abandoned the two major political parties and formed the Populist Party, which became one of the strongest third parties in our history. The Populists campaigned for free silver and also proposed a number of political reforms. Political strife came to a climax in the bitterly contested election of 1896. The Democrats and Populists fought for Bryan and free silver, while the Republicans backed William McKinley and the gold standard. McKinley won, and during his administration the gold standard was legalized. The Populists had gone down to defeat, yet many of the measures they proposed eventually became law.

CHAPTER TWENTY-FOUR

1 *Political Unrest Leads to a New Political Party*

As the 1890's opened, both Democratic and Republican leaders continued to concentrate their efforts on winning and holding office. For the most part they ignored the complaints of discontented voters. Despite the serious problems that demanded attention, the politicians saw no threat to the established two-party system. But rising dissatisfaction among western farmers soon changed the situation.

Farmers register their discontent in 1890. By the end of the 1880's southern and western farmers faced staggering problems. Despite shrinking prices for their crops, the farmers had to pay high prices for farm machinery, high interest on mortgages, and high shipping rates to the railroads. Droughts and insect plagues added to their difficulties. During the 1880's the farmers had begun to voice their discontent through the Alliances (page 439), which had replaced the Grange. Then, in 1890 the leaders of the Alliances agreed to work together in the upcoming congressional elections. They tried to persuade the major parties to run candidates who were sympathetic to the farmers' problems. Whenever this failed, they promised support to independent candidates. The Alliances pressed for free silver, government ownership of the railroads, lower interest rates, and restrictions on the foreclosure of farm mortgages. They also urged adoption of the subtreasury plan, whereby the farmers

. . . .

CHAPTER FOCUS

1. Political unrest leads to a new political party.
2. Cleveland experiences his "luckless years."
3. Free silver loses in the election of 1896.
4. The Republicans consolidate their gains.

would receive credit from the government for storing grain in government warehouses (page 439).

The farmers were surprisingly successful in the elections of 1890 (page 506). They won control of twelve state legislatures, elected six governors, and sent two senators and some fifty congressmen to Washington. Most of these candidates ran on the Democratic ticket, though in some western states they ran as candidates of third parties. The Democrats also gained support because of widespread dissatisfaction with the McKinley Tariff and the Sherman Antitrust and Silver Purchase Acts.

A new third party is organized. Farm leaders were so encouraged by the outcome of the 1890 elections that they decided to push ahead with plans for a national political party. Representatives of the Alliances met in Cincinnati in 1891 to work out the details. A few spokesmen for the Knights of Labor also attended. Another convention, held in St. Louis early the following year, adopted the name "People's Party," though the new organization also became known as the Populist Party. The delegates adopted a statement of purpose which opened with these ringing words:

> We meet in the midst of a nation brought to the verge of moral, political, and material ruin. Corruption dominates the ballot-box, the legislatures, the Congress, and touches even the ermine of the bench [the courts]. The people are demoralized. . . . The newspapers are largely subsidized or muzzled, public opinion silenced, business prostrated, homes covered with mortgages, labor impoverished, and the land concentrating in the hands of capitalists. . . .

Before adjourning, the Populists decided to hold a presidential nominating convention that summer in Omaha.

The Republicans renominate Harrison. Disheartened by their losses in the 1890 elections, the Republicans doubted that President Harrison could win re-election in 1892. Yet the delegates at the Republican convention that year had little choice but to renominate their unpopular leader and to defend the legislation enacted during his administration. They readily endorsed a plank in their platform which promised to uphold "the American doctrine of protection." But the silver issue caused trouble. Delegates from the silver-mining states wanted to commit the party to free silver. A large number of eastern Republicans, however, opposed the Sherman Silver Purchase Act of 1890, even though their congressmen had voted for it in order to gain western support for a higher tariff (page 505). Now they were determined to block any more concessions to the silver Republicans. In the end, the convention adopted a compromise plank, which declared that the Republican party favored *bimetallism*, "the use of both gold and silver as standard money." Thus, the Republicans neither rejected the Sherman Silver Purchase Act nor committed the party to free silver.

The Democrats decide on Cleveland. By 1892 the Democratic Party also was badly split. Most southern and western Democrats, representing the agricultural wing of the party, favored tariff reduction and the free coinage of silver. Eastern Democrats generally wanted to keep the protective tariff and the gold standard. These Democrats, who included both industrialists and wage earners, believed that American prosperity depended on a high tariff and a currency backed by gold.

Grover Cleveland, who had practiced law in New York City during Harrison's administration, was still the outstanding figure in the Democratic Party. The former President viewed with misgivings the "uprising" of southern and western Democrats in 1890. Alarmed by the clamor for free silver, Cleveland issued a public statement declaring that "the greatest peril would be invited by the adoption of . . . the dangerous and reckless experiment of free, unlimited, and independent silver coinage."

The Democratic convention of 1892 was a tug of war between the two factions of the party. The silver delegates charged that Cleveland's nomination would surrender "the rights of the people to the financial kings of the country." But the eastern Democrats had enough votes to nominate the former President. The convention made two concessions, however, to the southern and western delegates. Its platform included a pledge to lower the tariff, and it nominated for Vice-President a champion of free silver from Illinois, Adlai E. Stevenson.[1] Although the Democratic platform called for the use of both gold and silver, Cleveland had already made clear his opposition to the free and unlimited coinage of silver.

The Populist Party proposes far-reaching reforms. In July the new third party held its convention in Omaha. The enthusiastic Populists adopted a platform which outlined their many grievances. The monetary planks in the Omaha Platform included: (1) the free and unlimited coinage of silver; (2) an increase in the nation's money to not less than 50 dollars per person in the country; (3) an income tax, graduated so that those with higher incomes paid proportionately higher taxes; and (4) adoption of the subtreasury scheme proposed by the Alliances.

The Populists also demanded a number of changes in the government. Their platform called for government ownership and operation of railroad, telegraph, and telephone systems; secret ballots in elections; a single term for Presidents and Vice-Presidents; and election of senators by popular vote rather than by state legislatures. The Knights of Labor delegates at the Populist convention added three other planks to the platform: adoption of an eight-hour day for government workers; prohibition of labor spies in industrial disputes; and restrictions on immigration.

When the convention voted its approval of the platform, pandemonium broke loose. According to one reporter, "fifteen thousand people yelled, shrieked, threw papers, hats, fans, and parasols, gathered up banners, mounted shoulders. . . . The two bands were swamped with noise." The Populists wound up their meeting with the nomination of James B. Weaver of Iowa as their presidential candidate. He was a former

[1] His grandson, also named Adlai E. Stevenson, was the Democratic presidential candidate in 1952 and 1956 and later served as American Ambassador to the United Nations.

officer in the Union army and had been active in agricultural reform movements. His running mate was a former Confederate general from Virginia.

The campaign of 1892 is spirited. The Democrats had little trouble raising money for their campaign chest in 1892. Industrialists who had fought Cleveland in 1888 because of his stand on the tariff now contributed generously to the Democratic Party. They felt that Harrison could not be re-elected and that it was important to put a conservative Democrat into the White House.

The Populists carried on an enthusiastic campaign in 1892. The party managers were grateful even for five-cent contributions from the debt-ridden farmers. Though they lacked the funds to circulate literature or buy billboard advertising, the Populists offered a number of colorful orators. In Kansas, the voters listened to "Sockless" Jerry Simpson, who got his nickname from criticizing his opponent's silk stockings in the 1890 campaign. Mary E. Lease, a Kansas pioneer, held forth against Wall Street bankers and told the farmers to "raise less corn and more hell." Minnesota produced Ignatius Donnelly, an effective political organizer and speaker. The eastern newspapers made fun of these "calamity howlers" and "political rainmakers" but failed to dampen the enthusiasm of the Populist crusaders.

Cleveland wins a second term. Despite the Populist efforts, the Democrats won a sweeping victory in 1892. Cleveland received a clear margin in the popular vote and won 277 electoral votes to 145 for Harrison. The Democrats also won control of both houses of Congress. For the first time since before the Civil War, the Democrats controlled not only the presidency but also Congress.

Nevertheless, the new third party had shown surprising strength. Weaver polled over a million votes and won 22 electoral votes. Moreover, the Populists elected ten congressmen and five senators. They were strongest in the Great Plains and silver-mining states. Southern Populists did not run as well as western candidates, but for the first time since reconstruction the political control of the southern Democrats had been threatened.

▶ CHECK-UP

1. What demands were made by the Alliances in the election of 1890? What was the outcome? Why were both major parties split by 1892? What did the platform adopted by each major party that year say about free silver and protection?

2. What reforms were demanded by the Populists? What was the outcome of the election of 1892? Evaluate the showing of the Populists in this election.

"Sockless Jerry" Simpson campaigns for the Populist cause at Harper, Kansas, in 1892. Once a Republican, Simpson served several terms in the House of Representatives as a Populist.

2 *Cleveland Experiences His "Luckless Years"*

The election of 1892 had returned the Democrats to power, apparently with fair prospects ahead. But, as it turned out, President Cleveland's second term was plagued by economic depression, congressional quarrels, and an ever-widening breach within the Democratic Party.

The Panic of 1893 hits the country. When Grover Cleveland returned to the White House in March, 1893, an economic depression had already swept over most of Europe. A few weeks after the inauguration the Panic of 1893 struck at this country's economic strength, and a severe depression followed. Within six months, 8000 businesses had failed, 156 railroads were bankrupt, and 400 banks had closed their doors. Prices of farm products, already low, fell still lower. One fifth of the country's factory workers lost their jobs. Visitors to the Columbian Exposition in Chicago contrasted the "White City" with the surrounding "Black City," where thousands of unemployed persons sought shelter in public lodging houses and stood in soup lines for food. This scene was repeated in every major industrial city and in many smaller towns as well. The depression that followed the Panic of 1893 lasted through 1896, and some of its effects continued even longer.

The causes of this depression were complex. They included (1) the decline in farm prices during the 1880's, (2) overexpansion of industry and railroads, (3) a loss of overseas markets because of the European depression, and (4) the recalling of capital invested in the United States by Europeans. Some Democrats blamed the Panic on the "billion-dollar Congress" (page 506) and the McKinley Tariff, both of which had cut into the treasury surplus. Many Republicans, on the other hand, charged that the Sherman Silver Purchase Act had destroyed faith in the country's currency and thus had caused the Panic.

Hoarding threatens the gold reserve. President Cleveland agreed with American businessmen that "congressional legislation touching the purchase and coinage of silver" was a primary cause of the financial crisis. The Sherman Silver Purchase Act had authorized the government to buy practically the entire output of American silver mines. Nevertheless, the price of silver had followed a downward trend. By 1893 the bullion in a silver dollar was worth only 60 cents, and after the panic of that year it fell to 49 cents. But the value of the dollar was not in question, for the treasury continued to redeem, on demand, all silver and paper money with gold. Banks were hoarding their gold and getting rid of their treasury certificates. People who had both silver and gold dollars were spending the silver and saving the gold. Moreover, the government had to settle its foreign obligations in gold, because gold was the international medium of exchange. Thus there was a steady flow of gold out of the treasury. Bankers and financiers feared that the government would soon run out of gold and that the much cheaper silver dollar would take the place of the gold dollar as the standard of monetary value. The effect would be a tremendous rise in prices. This, of course, was what the western and southern farmers wanted, but it would have meant disaster for many banks and businessmen.

The Sherman Silver Act is repealed. When the amount of gold in the government reserve fell below the minimum of 100 million dollars,[2] President Cleveland decided that repeal of the Sherman Silver Purchase Act was necessary. Calling Congress into special session, he asked for repeal of the law in order to make American currency "so safe . . . that those who have money will spend and invest it in business and enterprise instead of holding it." Spokesmen for the southern and western farmers, together with the western "silverites," put up a stiff fight. In the House, "Silver Dick" Bland (page 411) and William Jennings Bryan, a young congressman from Nebraska, pleaded with the lawmakers to ignore Cleveland's request. Nevertheless,

---

[2] This figure had been established by the Resumption Act of 1875 (page 407).

the repeal bill was enacted in the fall of 1893. The eastern press congratulated Cleveland for saving the "honor of the country." But Bryan warned the victors that they had not buried the demand for free silver. In time, he prophesied, the issue would "lay aside its grave clothes. . . . It will yet rise."

The gold reserve continues to shrink. Repeal of the Sherman Silver Act checked the flow of silver into the treasury. It failed, however, to stop the drain on gold, chiefly because the government continued to redeem silver certificates and treasury notes in gold. Twice during 1894 the treasury sold gold bonds to increase its gold reserve, but this step failed to check the outflow of gold. People who paid gold for the government bonds got the gold back merely by presenting greenbacks, silver dollars, or silver and treasury certificates for redemption in gold. By 1895 the reserve had fallen to 41 million dollars. Both bank-

A cartoon published during the gold crisis of 1896 shows President Grover Cleveland trying to raise the level of the gold reserve "thermometer."

ers and the government began to wonder how much longer the country could remain on the gold standard.

Cleveland preserves the gold standard. Feeling that it was vitally important to maintain the gold standard, President Cleveland agreed to a plan suggested by the financier J. P. Morgan. A group of Wall Street bankers, headed by Morgan, would pay 62 million dollars in gold for government bonds. The bankers further agreed (1) to secure half of this gold abroad and (2) *not* to withdraw gold from the treasury by redeeming government notes. Because the bankers made a large profit on this transaction, Cleveland was bitterly criticized by southern and western Democrats as being "the tool of Wall Street." But the President had stopped the drain on the gold reserve and had re-established confidence in the gold standard. In 1896, another series of bonds was quickly purchased by small investors, and the gold reserve rose to 128 million dollars.

The Wilson-Gorman Tariff is passed. In saving the gold standard, Cleveland had widened the split in the Democratic Party between urban-industrial and rural-agricultural groups. Cleveland's sincere effort to make good on the party's pledge to lower the tariff did little to heal this breach.

When Congress met in 1893, Representative William Wilson of West Virginia introduced a bill to lower tariff rates. This bill passed the House without much difficulty, but met resistance in the Senate. Lobbyists went to work on the senators to secure amendments that would protect special interests, among them sugar growers, wool producers, and iron and steel manufacturers. Under the direction of Senator Arthur Gorman of Maryland, a Democrat, more than 600 amendments were added to the bill. In its new form, the Wilson-Gorman bill was scarcely less protective than the McKinley Act. For example, bounties to American sugar producers were abandoned (page 506), but high rates were restored on sugar imported into the United States. When the Senate voted on the sugar rates, Representative Wilson declared: "The question is . . . whether this is a gov-

BUSINESS ACTIVITY, 1860–1900

Panics and depressions interrupted the nation's economic progress between 1860 and 1900. Compare the length and the depth of the depressions which followed the Panics of 1873 and 1893.

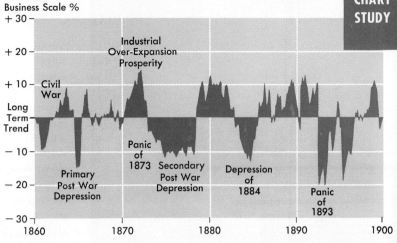

Business Scale %

Civil War — Long Term Trend — Industrial Over-Expansion Prosperity — Primary Post War Depression — Panic of 1873 — Secondary Post War Depression — Depression of 1884 — Panic of 1893

1860   1870   1880   1890   1900

---

ernment by the American people for the American people, or a government of the sugar trust for the benefit of the sugar trust."

The Populists in Congress voted against the amendments raising tariff rates but failed to defeat them. They did succeed in adding an amendment calling for a direct tax of 2 per cent on all incomes over 4000 dollars. Some congressmen attacked this tax as an outrageous "prejudice against the accumulation of wealth." Nevertheless, the legislators left the income-tax provision in the Wilson-Gorman bill.

President Cleveland found himself in a difficult position when the bill reached his desk. If he signed it, he would be approving a measure which he considered a piece of "party perfidy and dishonor." But if he vetoed it, the McKinley Tariff would remain in effect. Since there was little prospect of securing genuine tariff reduction, Cleveland let the bill become law in August, 1894, without his signature.

The Supreme Court rules against the income tax. The income-tax provision of the Wilson-Gorman Tariff was soon appealed to the Supreme Court. The opponents of the tax charged that it was a penalty being levied on about 85,000 people out of the total population of 68 million. But its supporters, including most of the people in the West and South, argued that it was a fair way of taxing the wealth of the country. In 1895 the Supreme Court decided by a five-to-four margin that the tax was unconstitutional. The Court ruled that an income tax was a direct tax; and according to the Constitution, Congress must

apportion direct taxes among the states on the basis of population (page 143). Thus, the Court reversed a decision handed down in 1881 which had upheld the constitutionality of the income-tax law passed during the Civil War.

The government does nothing about the depression. Even before this Court decision, the mood of the country was, as one historian put it, "growing dangerously sullen." The depression had thrown thousands of people out of work, and farm prices had fallen to desperately low levels. Bands of unemployed men roamed the country, and in the cities thousands of families lacked adequate food, clothing, and shelter. Most Americans believed that the government had no responsibility for the welfare of these unfortunate people. They assumed that prosperity would sooner or later return to both farm and factory, and meanwhile it was up to the individual to see his way through hard times. Many private organizations did what they could to relieve the suffering.

This line of reasoning had been followed during earlier panics and depressions and continued to be accepted in the 1890's. But the depression which followed the Panic of 1893 also produced some new ideas. In their Omaha Platform the Populists had expressed the belief that the government should bear some responsibility for the public welfare. Following up this idea, Jacob Coxey, an Ohio Populist, proposed in 1894 that the federal government issue 500 million dollars in paper money to finance a public-works program. Local communities

People cheered Coxey's army on its way to Washington, but when Coxey tried to speak in front of the Capitol, he was arrested, and the army went home.

would use their share of this money to pay unemployed men a dollar and a half per eight-hour day of manual labor. To dramatize this scheme, Coxey called for "armies" of unemployed men to march on Washington. A small band actually reached Washington but when Coxey set foot on the Capitol lawn, he was arrested for trespassing. Coxey's "army" soon broke up, and (until some 40 years later) nothing came of the proposal for a public-works program.

Cleveland's administration draws to a close. As the congressional elections of 1894 drew near, there was growing discontent with the Democratic administration. The depression continued to plague the country. Moreover, everything Cleveland did seemed to antagonize some group or section. The repeal of the Sherman Silver Purchase Act had angered people in the South and West. Though the Democrats controlled Congress, Cleveland could not carry out the pledge of tariff reform. And labor groups were outraged when the President sent troops to support a federal court injunction in the Pullman strike (page 481). The unpopularity of the Democratic ad-

ministration enabled both Populists and Republicans to make gains in 1894. The Populists polled a total of almost 1,500,000 votes, half again as many as in 1892. The Republicans regained control of both the House and the Senate. But many of the laws passed during the next two years were vetoed by President Cleveland, whom the Republicans nicknamed "His Obstinacy."

With the advantage of hindsight, most present-day historians regard Cleveland as the strongest President between Lincoln and Theodore Roosevelt. It is true that he was often stubborn and at times did not fully understand the problems that faced the country during the 1890's. But Cleveland was intelligent, honest, and courageous. His willingness to go to the voters on the issue of tariff revision cost him re-election in 1888. And his insistence on preserving the gold standard cost him control of his party in 1892.

▶ CHECK-UP

1. What were the causes of the Panic of 1893 and the depression that followed? Why was gold hoarded? What steps were taken by Cleveland to save the gold standard?

2. Why was Cleveland unable to make good on his pledge to lower tariff rates? What happened to the income tax provided for in the Wilson-Gorman bill? Why was the mood of the country "dangerously sullen"?

3. What were the two views about the government's responsibility for public welfare? Why did Republicans regain control of Congress in 1894?

• • • • • • • • • • • • • • • • • • • •

3 *Free Silver Loses in the Election of 1896*

The Republicans nominate McKinley. As the election of 1896 approached, the Republicans felt optimistic. They confidently noted the widespread criticism of Cleveland in the South and West. The

Atlanta *Constitution,* a Democratic paper, said: "Grover Cleveland will go out under a greater burden of popular contempt than has ever been excited by a public man since the formation of the government." Some Republicans boasted that their party could nominate a "rag baby" for the presidency and still win the election.

One Republican who had a definite candidate in mind was Marcus Alonzo Hanna of Ohio, a wealthy businessman who turned to Republican politics in the 1880's. "Mark" Hanna had taken a young congressman from Canton, Ohio, under his wing. William McKinley (page 506), Hanna believed, had the qualities needed for a successful political career. When McKinley was defeated for re-election to the House in 1890, Hanna persuaded him to run for the governorship of Ohio. Soon after McKinley won that office, Hanna began lining up delegates for the Republican convention of 1896. When the convention met in St. Louis, it nominated McKinley for President on the first ballot.

The Republican platform promised continued tariff protection, the issue with which McKinley was most closely associated in the public mind. Although delegates from the silver-mining states wanted recognition of silver coinage in the Republican platform, the vast majority of delegates were firmly committed to the gold standard. On this issue the Republican platform said:

> We are . . . opposed to the free coinage of silver, except by international agreement with the leading commercial nations of the earth, which agreement we pledge ourselves to promote, and until such agreement can be obtained, the existing gold standard must be maintained.

Since there was little chance of persuading European countries to change their monetary systems, the Republicans were actually pledging themselves to preserve the gold standard. Some of the silver delegates walked out of the convention, threatening to help the Democrats if that party nominated a free-silver candidate.

The Democrats choose Bryan. Several weeks later, when the Democrats gathered in Chicago, the silver delegates were clearly in control of the convention. The party platform condemned Cleveland's handling of the Pullman strike, called for downward revision of the tariff, and supported the income-tax provision which the Supreme Court had recently declared unconstitutional. As for the silver issue, the Democratic platform stated:

> We demand the free and unlimited coinage of both silver and gold at the present legal ratio of sixteen to one without waiting for the aid or consent of any other nation.

One of the delegates who spoke in favor of this platform was William Jennings Bryan. Trained as a lawyer in Illinois, Bryan had moved to Nebraska, where he was elected to the House of Representatives in 1890. Among Westerners he had won acclaim for his battle against the McKinley Tariff and against repeal of the Silver Purchase Act. When the Nebraska legislature failed to elect him senator in 1894, Bryan supported himself by writing for newspapers and lecturing on the Chautauqua circuit. By 1896 he was well-known to Democratic politicians of the South and West. Only 36 years old at the time, Bryan was an experienced orator with a powerful, melodious voice that carried throughout the convention hall. The delegates listened intently as Bryan defended the planks in the platform and assured the convention that the monetary issue was the most important of all. To the advocates of the gold standard, he said:

> You come to us and tell us that the great cities are in favor of the gold standard; we reply that the great cities rest upon our broad and fertile prairies. Burn down your cities and leave our farms, and your cities will spring up again as if by magic; but destroy our farms and the grass will grow in the streets of every city in the country.

Bryan closed his "Cross of Gold" speech with the eloquent warning quoted on the first page of this chapter. The delegates wildly cheered their new-found leader and nominated him for the presidency on the fifth ballot.

The Populists decide to support Bryan.
When the Populists gathered in St. Louis,
they faced a difficult choice. The Democrats had adopted their key issue — free
silver — and nominated a man whom the
Populists liked. But if the Populists merged
with the Democrats and supported Bryan,
they knew it would be difficult, if not impossible, to revive their party after the
election. Said one Populist leader, "If we
fuse [with the Democrats], we are sunk. If
we don't fuse, all the silver men will leave
us for the more powerful Democrats."

Some Populist delegates were strongly
opposed to fusion with the Democrats.
Southern Populists were reluctant to join
hands with certain conservative Democrats
whom they had been fighting for years.
Other Populists feared that the Democrats
were interested only in free silver and not
in the other planks of the Omaha Platform.
If the Populists dismantled their party in
1896, then their comprehensive program of
reforms would soon be forgotten.

The majority of the Populist delegates,
however, felt that the free-silver candidate
would have a fair chance of winning the
election if they joined with the Democrats.

James Weaver, the Populist candidate of
four years before, said, "I would nominate
him [Bryan] outright, and make him our
own, and then share justly and rightfully
in his election." The convention finally
heeded this advice. It nominated Bryan
for the presidency and Thomas Watson of
Georgia for the vice-presidency.

Bryan campaigns for free silver. Before 1896 a presidential candidate had
usually let his political manager do most of
the active campaigning. But William Jennings Bryan broke with tradition. Traveling more than 18,000 miles, he delivered
over 600 speeches in 29 states. Sometimes
he appeared before large rallies, but most
of his talks were made to small groups of
people in villages and towns.

Bryan geared his campaign to the free-
silver issue. He pictured the Republicans
as a party of Wall Street financiers and
other rich men who used their wealth to run
the government for their own advantage.
He implied that the free coinage of silver
would help workingmen by putting more
money into circulation and would bring
prosperity to all Americans. An effective
campaign document in the South and West

*This delegation of McKin-
ley supporters traveled from
Cook County, Illinois, to
shake hands with the Re-
publican candidate at his
home in Canton, Ohio.*

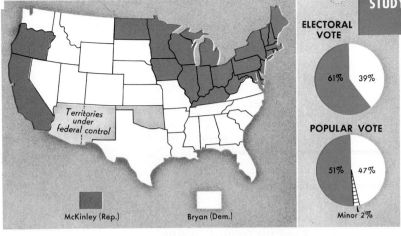

ELECTION OF 1896

The so-called "metal election" indicated a sharp rural-urban division. Note the states where McKinley and Bryan each was strongest. Two per cent of the vote was for candidates of minor parties.

Territories under federal control

ELECTORAL VOTE

61% 39%

POPULAR VOTE

51% 47%

McKinley (Rep.)   Bryan (Dem.)   Minor 2%

was a little book by William Harvey entitled *Coin's Financial School*. It consisted of lectures delivered by "Professor Coin" on the advantages of free silver. A best-seller in the mid-1890's, the book was widely quoted by Bryan's supporters.

Mark Hanna runs McKinley's campaign. Mark Hanna ran the Republican campaign along traditional lines. McKinley stayed at home in Canton, Ohio, where he received friendly delegations and delivered short statements from his front porch. Republican Party workers, however, were spurred on by Hanna to reach as many voters as possible. The Republicans had little trouble collecting over three million dollars for the campaign. The money was used for pamphlets, for billboards picturing McKinley as "the advance agent of prosperity," and for gold lapel pins to identify supporters of the gold standard. Toward the end of the campaign Hanna used more direct methods. He urged Republican businessmen to make their contracts and orders dependent on the election of McKinley. Thus, farmers were warned that if Bryan were elected, their mortgages would not be renewed. Workingmen were paid off before the election and told not to return to work if the Democrats won. The conservative press became almost hysterical about Bryan and the prospect of a Democratic-Populist administration. One journalist noted: "Probably no man in civil life has succeeded in inspiring so much terror, without taking life, as Bryan."

McKinley wins the election. In the final test of strength, McKinley received over seven million votes — 600,000 more than Bryan. McKinley's margin of victory was the largest of any President since Grant defeated Greeley in 1872. As the map on this page shows, McKinley's 271 electoral votes came from the New England and Middle Atlantic states plus a number of western and midwestern states. Bryan's 176 electoral votes came from the South, most of the Plains states, and the silver-mining West. By stressing free silver and the farmers' plight, and by saying little about urban and industrial problems, Bryan had lost the support of city voters. In fact, he managed to lose labor as well as business support in nearly all the urban areas outside the South. Furthermore, the depression had begun to lift in 1896. There had been a noticeable increase in farm prices even during the campaign. Some historians have suggested that if the election had been held in August instead of November, more midwestern states would have voted for Bryan and he might have won the presidency. In any case the Republicans now controlled the government. Mark Hanna wired McKinley in Canton, Ohio: "God's in his Heaven, all's right with the world!"

As for the Populists, their party was never again a serious factor in a presidential election. Nevertheless, many of the reforms which they had proposed· in the Omaha Platform (page 517) continued to gain support. In fact, as we shall see in later chapters, a number of them were eventually adopted.

▶ CHECK-UP

1. What was the stand of the Republican Party in 1896 on the tariff and the gold standard? What important planks were included in the Democratic platform? What dilemma confronted the Populists at their nominating convention?

2. Contrast the campaigns of Bryan and McKinley. Why did the latter win?

· · · · · · · · · · · · · · · · · · · ·

4 *The Republicans Consolidate Their Gains*

The outcome of the election was welcomed by industrialists, financiers, and conservatives who had feared Bryan and the Populists. The Republicans interpreted their victory as endorsement by the voters of the gold standard, the protective tariff, and a "hands-off" attitude toward business. During the McKinley administration, Congress followed these policies.

McKinley moves into the White House. The new President was a handsome man

POLITICAL PARTIES, 1869–1897

CHART STUDY

Voters sought solutions to social and economic problems through third parties. The Populists, strongest of the reform groups, declined in strength after 1896. (See the next political chart on page 669.)

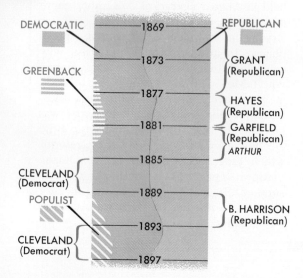

who dressed well, made friends easily, and was proud of his resemblance to Napoleon. The journalist William Allen White said McKinley "walked among men like a bronze statue . . . determinedly looking for his pedestal." After McKinley's inauguration, Mark Hanna continued to be an intimate adviser of the President. Though McKinley offered to appoint his campaign manager as Postmaster General, Hanna preferred the Senate. After winning election to that body in 1897, Hanna exerted great influence in the writing of laws and advised McKinley on appointments.

Congress raises tariff rates. Though the issue of gold versus silver had claimed most attention in the campaign, Congress first acted on the tariff. McKinley called Congress into special session and asked for a new tariff law. The result was the Dingley Tariff (1897), which established the highest average rate level up to that time in American history. The new bill also restored the reciprocity provision of the McKinley Tariff, a feature which had been omitted from the Wilson-Gorman Tariff of 1894. The President actually negotiated several treaties based on the reciprocity provision. But the Republican senators who favored high tariffs blocked approval of the treaties. They ignored the President's warning that "the period of exclusiveness is past. . . . Reciprocity treaties are in harmony with the spirit of the times; measures of retaliation are not."

The money supply increases. The Republicans delayed action on the monetary problem until 1900. For one thing, as we have seen, prosperity had begun to return — for both the farmer and the businessman. One reason for better times, strangely enough, was an increase in the amount of currency in circulation, the very thing that Bryan and the farmers had wanted. This was brought about, not by an increase in the amount of silver, but rather by an expansion in the supply of gold. The development of a cheap process of extracting gold from low-yield ores was one reason for the expansion of gold production. Even more significant were new gold discoveries in Alaska, South Africa, and Australia.

When gold was discovered on the Klondike River in the 1890's, thousands of prospectors — including women — swarmed to Canada's Yukon Territory.

American production of gold from the Klondike strike alone almost doubled in the decade after 1896. As the price of gold fell, the government purchased more gold and issued more money. The amount of money in circulation in the United States increased from 24 dollars per person in 1893 to 34 dollars by 1910.

The gold standard is formally established. The return of prosperity during the McKinley administration took the edge off political discontent among farmers and industrial workers. Undoubtedly this made it easier for the Republicans to pass legislation formally adopting the gold standard. The Gold Standard Act (or Currency Act) of 1900 made the gold dollar the standard unit of value in American currency. Though only four years had passed since the battle over free silver, this measure stirred up little controversy in Congress.

▶ CHECK-UP

1. What were the major provisions of the Dingley Tariff? Why was the reciprocity provision ineffective?

2. How did the increased amount of gold on the world market relieve this country's monetary problem? What was the Gold Standard Act? Why did this law arouse little controversy?

. . . .

Clinching the Main Ideas in Chapter 24

The decade of the 1890's was marked by controversy. On one side of the dispute were industrialists, financiers, and merchants; on the other were farmers and wage earners. The newly formed Populist Party tried to speak for many of those who were dissatisfied. In their Omaha Platform, the Populists called for sweeping reforms. They believed that the federal government should concern itself with the well-being of all citizens. Many other Americans, however, believed the government should preserve a "hands-off" policy in the nation's economic affairs. Those who had been successful under the existing system felt there was no reason for the government to interfere in the affairs of private citizens.

Politics in the 1890's reflected these opposing points of view. There was little difference between the policies advocated by Cleveland and Harrison in the election of 1892, but a vast gulf separated them both from the Populist candidate. During his second administration President Cleveland had the support of many Republicans in his fight to repeal the Silver Purchase Act and save the gold standard. But depression had swept the country after 1893, and Cleveland was unfairly blamed for the economic crisis. Southern and western Democrats, meanwhile, rallied behind the cause of free silver, which seemed to them the best way to put more money into circulation.

By 1896 the silver Democrats had won control of their party and nominated William Jennings Bryan for President. The Populists also supported Bryan in 1896, but the combined strength of the two parties failed to overcome the Republicans and gold Democrats who backed McKinley. The 1896 election was a victory for the gold standard and the protective tariff.

Chapter Review

Terms to Understand

1. Panic of 1893
2. Dingley Tariff
3. Coxey's "army"
4. free silver
5. *Coin's Financial School*
6. Gold Standard Act
7. Klondike strike
8. Populist Party

What Do You Think?

1. In 1894 many Americans called a two per cent tax on annual incomes over 4000 dollars an outrageous "prejudice against the accumulation of wealth." Why? What would be the attitude today?

2. In 1894 the bullion in a silver dollar was worth only 49 cents. Why was the value of the dollar not in question?

3. In 1894 Jacob Coxey proposed that Congress appropriate 500 million dollars for a public works program. The program would enable unemployed workers to earn a dollar and a half per day on approved projects. Why did this "radical" suggestion receive no serious consideration from Congress?

4. "Probably no man in civil life has succeeded in inspiring so much terror, without taking life, as Bryan [in 1896]." Why did many Americans fear Bryan?

5. Why was free silver not an issue after 1896?

Using Your Knowledge of History

1. Compare the platforms and campaign methods of the Republican and Democratic Parties in 1896.

2. Write an editorial for a Republican newspaper, giving that party's reaction to Bryan's statement ". . . you shall not crucify mankind upon a cross of gold."

3. List the important planks in the Omaha Platform of the Populist Party. Which of these have since been enacted into law?

4. Most Americans in the 1890's believed that "it was up to the individual to see his way through hard times." Discuss in class why this view was held and whether it is held today. What is your own view?

Extending Your Knowledge of History

Interesting first-hand accounts of the political turmoil in the 1890's can be found in James B. Weaver's *A Call to Action;* William Jennings Bryan's *The First Battle: A Story of the Campaign of 1896;* and *Memoirs of William Jennings Bryan.* A first-rate study of the political problem can be found in Paul W. Glad's *McKinley, Bryan, and the People.* For more information about the Populists, see *The Populist Revolt* by John D. Hicks and the early chapters of *The Age of Reform* by Richard Hofstadter. An interesting study of the winning candidate in 1896 is Margaret Leech's Pulitzer Prize winner, *In the Days of McKinley.* She also wrote "The Front Porch Campaign," an article in *American Heritage,* December, 1959. William Allen White takes a critical view of the Republicans in *Masks in a Pageant,* whereas Herbert Croly is favorable to McKinley's campaign manager in *Marcus Alonzo Hanna.* A good biography of Bryan is Paxton Hibben's *The Peerless Leader.*

CHAPTER 25

The United States Acquires Overseas Possessions

A new consciousness seems to have come upon us — the consciousness of strength — and with it a new appetite, the yearning to show our strength. . . . Ambition, interest, land hunger, pride, the mere joy of fighting, whatever it may be, we are animated by a new sensation.
WASHINGTON POST, 1898

Dewey at Manila

1887–1900

In Chapter 19 you read about the United States' relations with other countries during the years just after the Civil War. Most Americans at that time did not give much thought to foreign problems. The country was growing rapidly, and troublesome domestic problems occupied their attention. Foreign affairs seemed so remote from American life that the New York *Sun* declared: "The diplomatic service has outgrown its usefulness. . . . It is a costly humbug and sham. . . . Instead of making ambassadors, Congress should wipe out the whole service." Yet even during the 1870's and '80's there was some evidence that the United States' ties with Latin America were growing closer and that American interest in the Pacific was increasing.

Then, during the 1890's, Americans definitely began to "look outward." For one thing, they were influenced by the example of European powers which were acquiring colonies and extending their influence. Also, some Americans felt an obligation to carry their own standards of living to less civilized areas of the globe. More important, however, the country's industrial growth had awakened Americans to the advantages of world markets for manufactured goods and to the need for new sources of raw materials.

As a result of this change in attitude, the United States played a more active role in foreign affairs during the 1890's. We took a new interest in Latin American affairs, and we acquired possessions in the Pacific and the Caribbean. This new consciousness of world position came to a climax in the Spanish-American War.

CHAPTER TWENTY-FIVE

1 *The United States Takes Greater Interest in Its Neighbors*

In the late 1880's this country became increasingly aware of its role in the Western Hemisphere.

Blaine promotes interest in Latin America. Unlike many Americans in the 1870's and '80's, James G. Blaine was an ardent expansionist. He thought the United States should dominate the Caribbean and the Pacific, and he even believed that in time this country would annex Cuba, Puerto Rico, Hawaii, and Canada. Blaine twice served as Secretary of State. During his brief tenure in that office under Garfield in 1881, he tried to arouse interest in building a canal across Central America. At the time, few people shared his enthusiasm for such a waterway, and nothing came of his proposal.

Blaine arranges a Pan-American Conference. Blaine's program for improving relations between the United States and the countries of Latin America was more fruitful. He was disturbed by the fact that these countries bought most of their manufactured goods from Great Britain and Germany. Blaine wanted to secure the Latin American market for the United States' manufacturers. In 1881 the Secretary of State invited the Latin American governments to discuss the matter at a Pan-Amer-

ican Conference. But after Garfield's assassination, the meeting was canceled. Then, in 1889, the idea of a hemispheric conference was revived. As Secretary of State under President Harrison, Blaine presided over the first Pan-American Congress. Delegates from nineteen nations gathered in Washington for the meetings.

Blaine presented two proposals at this first Pan-American Conference. (1) He wanted to lower tariff barriers between the United States and Latin American countries; and (2) he wanted to establish the use of arbitration as a means of settling disputes. The Latin American delegates rejected both proposals. They had no desire to import American manufactured goods at higher prices than European goods, and most of their exports were already being shipped to the United States duty-free. While they were not opposed to the idea of arbitrating disputes, they feared that the United States would dominate any such proceedings.

The Pan American Union is formed. The delegates did agree to establish a Pan American Union. The purpose of this organization was to collect and distribute information about the customs, laws, and trade of the Latin American countries. Its permanent headquarters were established in Washington, and early in the 1900's Andrew Carnegie donated money to build the handsome Pan American Union building on Constitution Avenue. The Pan American Union has played a useful role in promoting better understanding and friendlier relations among the countries of this hemisphere.

Blaine offends Chile. Soon after the first Pan-American Conference ended, the United States became involved in a dispute with Chile. During a revolt against the Chilean government in 1891, the American minister in that country openly sided with its president. Moreover, the American government seized a Chilean rebel ship which had bought arms in San Diego, California. Chilean resentment against the United States flared up. When sailors from a United States warship went ashore in Valparaiso, Chile, they were attacked. In

---

CHAPTER FOCUS

1. The United States takes greater interest in its neighbors.

2. Interest in expansion leads to acquisition of Hawaii.

3. American interest in Cuba leads to war with Spain.

4. The United States wins the Spanish-American War.

James G. Blaine sought to establish more constructive ties between the United States and the Latin American nations. The Pan-American Conferences, first called by Blaine, have furthered this goal. An outgrowth of the inter-American movement is the Organization of American States (page 761), founded at the Bogotá Conference in 1948. Above right, the OAS Council meets at the Pan American Union.

the fighting that followed, two Americans were killed, and a number were wounded. Secretary Blaine demanded an apology and payment of an indemnity from Chile. At first the government established by the victorious rebels refused to meet Blaine's demands. But when President Harrison talked about war, Chile changed its position, apologized, and paid the indemnity. Blaine's handling of the affair, however, convinced many Latin Americans that they had been wise in rejecting his arbitration proposal at the Pan-American Conference.

Arbitration settles the Bering Sea controversy. Blaine's enthusiasm for arbitration was put to the test in a quarrel with Great Britain. The argument concerned the right of the United States to protect the seal herds on the Pribilof Islands in the Bering Sea (map, page 414). When the United States purchased Alaska from Russia, it had also received the Aleutian Islands and certain rights over the Bering Sea. The privilege of hunting seals in the

Bering Sea had been granted by the United States government to a private corporation. But by the 1880's many poachers, chiefly Canadians, were hunting the seals in the open waters of the Bering Sea. American revenue cutters began to seize Canadian vessels. Then, in 1890, Secretary Blaine protested to the British government.[1]

Blaine claimed that the Bering Sea was a "closed sea" under the protection of the United States; hence the Canadians had no right to hunt the seals. He contended, moreover, that their wholesale slaughter of seals threatened to wipe out the herd. Great Britain, on the other hand, denied that the United States had any special rights in the Bering Sea. Britain claimed there was no reason why Canadians should not hunt seals in waters outside the three-

[1] Canada had become a self-governing dominion within the British Empire in 1867, but Canadian foreign policy was controlled by the British government until after World War I.

mile limit — the usual extent of a nation's authority under international law. Finally the two countries agreed to submit the dispute to a court of arbitration. In 1893 the court decided against the United States, and Great Britain received half a million dollars in damages. New restrictions on the hunting of seals were drawn up, however, and these were eventually accepted by Great Britain, Russia, Japan, and the United States.

The Alaskan boundary is fixed. Settlement of the Bering Sea dispute was followed a few years later by an agreement on the Alaskan boundary. The United States had acquired Alaska within the limits established by a treaty between Russia and Great Britain in 1825. But the southeastern boundary was vaguely defined. The discovery of gold in the Klondike during the 1890's made the fixing of this boundary important, because entrance to the region was gained through the Alaskan panhandle (map, page 414). Canada claimed parts of this panhandle which would give it access to the sea. In 1903 the dispute was referred to a court of arbitration, and the boundary was eventually fixed in line with American claims.

A dispute between Venezuela and Great Britain involves the United States. Arbitration was used in still another dispute with Great Britain, but only after the United States and Britain had come close to war. Soon after the Chilean crisis died down, the United States found itself in the middle of a bitter quarrel between Venezuela and Great Britain. These two countries had long disagreed over the boundary line between Venezuela and British Guiana. When gold was discovered in this jungle area, Venezuela insisted that Great Britain was extending its territorial claims. But the British government refused to submit the dispute to arbitration. In 1887 Venezuela broke off diplomatic relations and appealed to the United States for help. Again Britain turned down an offer of arbitration.

In 1895 the situation took a new turn. Richard Olney, Secretary of State during Grover Cleveland's second term, sent a blunt note to the British Foreign Minister. Olney repeated the American offer to arbitrate the dispute and went on to say that Britain was violating the Monroe Doctrine. He suggested that the British relinquish Guiana altogether. "Three thousand miles of intervening ocean make any permanent political union between a European and an American state unnatural and inexpedient," Olney said. The controversy with Venezuela, he continued, was "one in which both its [the United States'] honor and its interests are involved and the continuance of which it cannot regard with indifference. . . . The United States is practically sovereign on this continent. . . ."

Cleveland threatens war over Venezuela. The British Foreign Minister did not reply to Olney for several months. Then he not only refused arbitration but also stated that in his opinion the Monroe Doctrine did not apply to this dispute and was not recognized in international law anyway. Indignant at this reply, President Cleveland stated that the Monroe Doctrine did apply to this disagreement and claimed a place for the doctrine in international law. Moreover, he sent a special message to Congress asking authority to appoint a commission to study the boundary line. Cleveland added that if Britain rejected the decision of the special commission, the United States would use "every means in its power" to protect Venezuelan territory, no matter what the consequences. Congress quickly approved the President's proposal, and spokesmen from both parties supported his position.

The President's implied threat of war jolted the British government. Since it was facing a serious uprising in South Africa and had no desire to fight the United States, Britain agreed to co-operate with the boundary commission. But before the commission's report was completed, Britain and Venezuela signed a treaty which turned their quarrel over to international arbitration. Although a final settlement in 1899 awarded most of the territory to Great Britain, Americans were satisfied because they had upheld their interpretation of the Monroe Doctrine. Moreover, they had demonstrated their readiness to fight a great power in support of the doctrine.

▶ CHECK-UP

1. How did Blaine arrange a Pan-American Conference? What proposals did he make? What was the outcome? How did the controversy with Chile affect relations with Latin America?

2. What was the issue in the Bering Sea controversy? What did this country claim? How was the dispute settled? How was the Alaska-Canada boundary dispute settled?

3. What was the issue in the dispute between Britain and Venezuela? What position was taken by Britain? By the United States? How was the dispute settled?

. . . .

2 *Interest in Expansion Leads to Acquisition of Hawaii*

During the pre-Civil War years the westward movement had rounded out the nation's continental boundaries. But the long contest over slavery and then the Civil War itself had dulled the American appetite for more territory. To be sure, Seward added Alaska and the Midway Islands, but schemes to annex the Dominican Republic and the Virgin Islands had ended in failure (page 415). By the mid-1880's, however, a number of factors rekindled American interest in acquiring more territory.

The United States searches for new markets. A major reason for the growing interest in new territory was the country's industrial and agricultural growth. Because of greater use of machinery, farmers produced more food and raw materials than Americans needed. Hence they hoped to sell their surpluses outside the United States. Industrialists were interested in securing access to new sources of raw materials and new markets. Foreign markets became especially important in the 1890's when the depression cut the purchasing power of American consumers. The value of American exports jumped from 400 million dollars in 1870 to nearly a billion and a half dollars by 1900.

Senator Albert J. Beveridge of Indiana was one who recognized the economic forces behind the search for new markets. In a speech in 1898, he explained:

American factories are making more than the American people can use; American soil is producing more than they can consume. Fate has written our policy for us; the trade of the world must and shall be ours. We will establish trading posts throughout the world as distributing points for American products. We will cover the ocean with our merchant marine. We will build a navy to the measure of our greatness. Great colonies governing themselves, flying our flag and trading with us, will grow about our posts of trade.

Additional motives inspire expansionists. Some Americans were interested in expansion for other than economic reasons. There were those who felt that expansion in the 1890's was a natural continuation of the drive to achieve "manifest destiny" half a century before. James G. Blaine, for example, assured Americans that Canada would "ultimately seek . . . admission to the union." Theodore Roosevelt asserted that the government should shape its policy "with the view to the ultimate removal of all European powers from the colonies they hold in the Western Hemisphere." Senator Henry Cabot Lodge of Massachusetts thought that "from the Rio Grande to the Arctic Ocean there should be but one flag and one country." Rising politicians like Roosevelt, Lodge, and Beveridge also pointed out that European countries were seizing territory and extending their influence in Africa, Asia, and the Pacific. They felt that the United States should join the race for colonies.

Additional support for expansion came from missionaries and from those who believed in "Anglo-Saxon" superiority. Missionaries hoped to carry Christianity to "heathen" peoples. Others believed that

Britain and the United States had an obligation to introduce their political institutions and their way of life into other parts of the world. A Congregational minister named Josiah Strong presented this idea in *Our Country: Its Possible Future and Its Present Crisis.* This popular book argued that "the Anglo-Saxon, as the great representative of these two ideas . . . civil liberty . . . and pure *spiritual* Christianity . . . is divinely commissioned to be, in a peculiar sense, his brother's keeper."

Expansionists favor a stronger navy and merchant marine. If the United States extended its interests beyond its continental boundaries, it would obviously need a larger merchant marine and navy. While serving as Secretary of State in 1881, James G. Blaine had found that the United States ranked twelfth among the nations of the world in naval power. Before leaving office, Blaine persuaded Congress to establish a Naval Advisory Board to work for larger appropriations. Under President Arthur, funds were voted to build four steel warships equipped with both steam power and sails. During succeeding administrations, Congress authorized the construction of battleships, cruisers, gunboats, and torpedo boats. By 1900 the United States had the third largest navy in the world, surpassed only by Great Britain and Germany. The merchant marine had also grown, as a result of government subsidies for carrying mail overseas and because of the increase in American exports.

The most influential supporter of the new naval policy was Alfred Thayer Mahan. A lecturer at the Naval War College in Newport, Rhode Island, Mahan wrote a number of articles and books, in which he argued that the powerful nations were those which controlled the sea lanes. Navies and merchant marines protected the life-lines to colonies and markets; the resulting commerce brought prosperity and power to the mother countries. Mahan urged the government to build up the navy and merchant marine and acquire colonies and naval stations in the Caribbean and Pacific. He also favored the construction of a canal across Central America. Mahan

warned that the United States must become a strong naval power if it wanted to survive in a world where "nation is arrayed against nation." "Whether they will or no," he predicted, "Americans must now begin to look outward."

The United States acquires territory in the Pacific. One of the first Pacific territories to attract American attention was Samoa. In the 1870's the United States acquired a coaling station on the Samoan island of Tutuila (page 415). Germany and Great Britain were also interested in Samoa, and the three countries had made an informal agreement to supervise the islands. But constant friction and commercial rivalry led the three countries to send armed vessels to the islands in 1889. A clash was threatening when a sudden hurricane destroyed most of the warships. This disaster relieved the tension, and the three powers agreed to establish a joint protectorate over the islands. Ten years later, Samoa was divided between the United States and Germany; the United States acquired Tutuila and some smaller islands. Great Britain was rewarded with the Gilbert and Solomon Islands, also in the Pacific.

By the end of the century the United States had acquired about fifty other Pacific islands, most of them small and many of them uninhabited. Some of these islands were used by the navy as coaling stations, and few Americans ever heard of them until World War II. But in the 1890's American involvement in Hawaii excited much attention.

American interest in Hawaii increases. In Chapter 19 we traced the story of Hawaiian-American relations as far as 1887, when the United States gained exclusive rights to Pearl Harbor as a naval base. By this time, white businessmen dominated the economy of Hawaii. They owned most of the sugar plantations while native-born Hawaiians and Chinese and Japanese laborers worked in the fields. A reciprocity treaty allowed Hawaiian sugar to enter the United States duty-free, and this sugar made up 99 per cent of Hawaii's exports.

The McKinley Tariff of 1890 dealt a heavy blow to the Hawaiian economy.

Liliuokalani (top left), who followed her brother as ruler of Hawaii, lost her throne when the American sugar planters established a republican government. Sugar (left) is still Hawaii's major export, with pineapples ranking second. But the islands' climate and beautiful beaches and scenery (above) have made tourism the biggest industry.

Since it allowed *all* foreign sugar, not just Hawaiian sugar, to be admitted duty-free to the United States, Hawaiian sugar lost its favored position. The Hawaiian sugar-planters urged immediate annexation to the United States, arguing that this was the only way to save the islands' sugar industry. Meanwhile, the Hawaiian people were rallying to the support of a new Queen, Liliuokalani (lee-*lee*'oo-oh-kah-*lah*'nee). Openly hostile to the white businessmen, she opposed annexation.

In 1893 "Queen Lil's" efforts to rid her government of American influence pro-voked the planters to revolt. The Americans were aided by the United States minister to Hawaii, John L. Stevens, who ordered marines to be landed at Honolulu. The queen was deposed, and the Americans formed a provisional government. Stevens wrote to the State Department: "The Hawaiian pear is now fully ripe, and this is the golden hour for the United States to pluck it."

Hawaii is annexed. The Harrison administration signed a treaty of annexation with the Hawaiian provisional government and sent it to the Senate. There it was

RELATIONS WITH OTHER COUNTRIES, 1880–1900

ISSUE	OUTCOME
Pan-American relations	Delegates to the first Pan-American Conference in 1889 set up a permanent agency for strengthening inter-American relations—forerunner of the Pan American Union.
Attack on American sailors in Chile, 1891	Chilean government apologized and paid an indemnity to the United States.
Protection of fur seal herds in the Bering Sea	In 1893 an international tribunal (France, Sweden, Italy) denied the American claim to a "closed sea." Regulations for the protection of the fur seal herds were agreed upon by the nations engaged in hunting in the Bering Sea.
Boundary dispute between Venezuela and British Guiana. (The United States viewed Great Britain's refusal to arbitrate as a violation of the Monroe Doctrine.)	A court of arbitration in 1899 awarded most of the disputed territory to British Guiana. The United States was satisfied because the American interpretation of the Monroe Doctrine was upheld.
Alaskan boundary dispute	Court of arbitration fixed the boundary in line with American claims in 1903.
Rivalry over Samoa	In 1899 Samoa was divided between the United States and Germany with the United States retaining Tutuila and some smaller islands.
Hawaiian-American relations	Hawaii was annexed to the United States in 1898.
Spanish-American relations	War with Spain (1898) ended in an American victory. Puerto Rico, Guam, and the Philippine Islands were ceded to the United States by the terms of the Treaty of Paris.
Cuban-American relations	Cuba gained its independence from Spain. The United States assumed the role of protector. Cuba remained under American military occupation until 1902.
Annexation of the Philippine Islands	The Philippine Islands were annexed to the United States in 1899.

delayed by the Democrats, who were suspicious of the part played by Americans in the Hawaiian "rebellion." When Cleveland began his second term in March, 1893, he withdrew the treaty from the Senate. A special investigating committee reported that the rebellion would have failed without Stevens' help and that the majority of the Hawaiian people opposed annexation. Though unable to restore Queen Liliuokalani to her throne, Cleveland did refuse to consider another treaty of annexation.

There the matter rested until President McKinley took office. He negotiated a new treaty to annex the Hawaiian Islands, but it too failed to get the necessary two-thirds vote in the Senate. In 1898, however, after the United States had gone to war with Spain, Hawaii's value as a naval base became clear. Both houses of Congress approved a joint resolution, by which Hawaii was annexed to the United States.[2]

▶ CHECK-UP

1. Why did interest in overseas markets and expansion increase during the 1880's and '90's? How did this attitude affect the navy? The merchant marine?

2. How did the United States acquire part of Samoa? Why did Americans in Hawaii favor annexation by this country in the 1880's and '90's? Why was annexation opposed? How and why was it finally brought about?

• • • • • • • • • • • • • • • • • •

3 American Interest in Cuba Leads to War with Spain

Americans show interest in Cuba. The war with Spain which helped to hasten the annexation of Hawaii grew out of American interest in Cuba. On several earlier occasions American attention had been drawn to this island. Before the Civil War, some Southerners had talked of annexing Cuba as a suitable area for the extension of slavery (page 336). Interest in Cuba was revived in 1868 when a rebellion broke out against the Spanish government. That revolt lasted for ten years and ended with the defeat of the rebels, though Spain promised some self-government and emancipation of the slaves. But toward the end of the century, the Cuban people tried again to win their independence. American

[2] A precedent for this action had been established in 1845 when Texas was annexed by joint resolution of Congress (page 285).

tariff legislation played a part in the outbreak of a revolt against Spain.

Revolt breaks out again in Cuba. By the late 1880's large amounts of American and European capital were being invested in Cuban sugar plantations. American interest in Cuba was heightened not only by these investments but also by the fact that most Cuban sugar was sold to the United States. Under the McKinley Tariff, this sugar could enter free of duty. As a result, production nearly doubled. But the Wilson-Gorman Tariff (page 520) restored a 40 per-cent duty on sugar imported into the United States. This was a damaging blow to the Cuban economy, coming as it did at the same time as the 1893 depression. Exports declined, the price of Cuban sugar fell, plantations were closed, and unemployment increased. Smoldering discontent with Spanish rule flared into open revolt in 1895.

The fighting in Cuba was savage. Determined to win this time, the rebels took to the hills to carry on guerrilla warfare. Their leader, Maximo Gomez, launched a campaign to destroy the sugar plantations and thus cut off the Spanish government's revenue. The rebels also hoped that the United States would intervene to protect American property in Cuba.

General Weyler, the Spanish commander, was unable to stop the rebel raids. Convinced that Cuban civilians were aiding the guerrilla fighters, Weyler imprisoned thousands of people — including old men, women, and children — in barbed-wire enclosures. Starvation and disease took a heavy toll in these camps; perhaps as many as 200,000 Cubans died.

Some Americans demand intervention. American expansionists favored immediate action by the United States in Cuba. Theodore Roosevelt declared that failure to aid the Cuban rebels would be an act of cowardice and an "unpardonable sin." Congress passed a resolution asking President Cleveland to extend recognition to the rebels. He ignored the suggestion and said he suspected there were "outrages upon both sides, if the truth were known." During 1897 President McKinley also pursued a cautious policy. When the Spanish government removed General Weyler, the President hoped that a settlement with the rebels might be worked out.

Newspapers arouse American public opinion. Americans were concerned about Cuba for several reasons — sympathy for the rebels, resentment against Spain's harsh policy, the nearness of the island to the United States, and the heavy losses suffered by American investors in Cuba. This concern was fanned into anger by propaganda printed in American newspapers.

The newspapers of the 1890's were different in many respects from those of pre-Civil War years. Independent editors like Horace Greeley had been replaced by editors whose chief interest was to sell more papers. Newspapers had come to give less coverage to politics and far more space to crime and scandal. Sensational news (and special features like society pages, cartoons, photographs, and comic strips) helped to boost newspaper circulation from 3 million copies in 1870 to over 24 million by 1900.

The brutalities of the Cuban rebellion provided the kind of material the newspaper publishers wanted to print, and they took full advantage of this opportunity. Among the more aggressive papers were Joseph Pulitzer's New York *World* and William Randolph Hearst's New York *Journal*. These rival newspapers carried shocking stories about the civilian camps in Cuba. In their frantic efforts to whip up public feeling, they accepted all the material offered by the rebels and by Cuban exiles. These accounts were frequently exaggerated and sometimes untrue, but they further aroused American public opinion against Spain.

The de Lôme letter angers Americans. Two diplomatic crises early in 1898 heightened the war fever. The first stemmed from the publication of a letter written by the Spanish minister to the United States, Dupuy de Lôme, to a friend in Havana. In this private correspondence, de Lôme referred to President McKinley as "weak and a bidder for the admiration of the crowd, besides being a would-be politician

who tries to leave a door open behind himself while keeping on good terms with the jingoes [war advocates] of his party." A rebel sympathizer stole this letter from the Havana post office, and the New York *Journal* published it. Democrats and even some Republicans had said far worse things about McKinley, but the *Journal* blew up the story until the letter seemed an insult to the nation. Although de Lôme promptly resigned and his government apologized for his "indiscretion," the incident damaged Spanish-American relations.

The "Maine" is sunk. Less than a week later, Americans were shocked by a great tragedy. Because of the disorders in Cuba, the United States battleship *Maine* had been sent to Havana to protect American lives and property. On the night of February 15, a terrific explosion sank the *Maine* with the loss of two officers and 258 of the crew. An American naval court of inquiry at once conducted an investigation. It reported to the President:

> In the opinion of the court the *Maine* was destroyed by the explosion of a submarine mine which caused the partial explosion of two or more of the forward magazines. The court has been unable to obtain evidence fixing the responsibility for the destruction of the *Maine* upon any person or persons.

The American public paid slight attention to the second of these quoted sentences. Nor did it accept the report of a Spanish board of inquiry which declared that the disaster had been caused by an explosion of the ship's ammunition. Moreover, few people considered the possibility that Cuban rebels might have blown up the vessel to draw the United States into war with Spain. Most Americans blamed the Spanish government for the disaster, and the newspapers also expressed this view. Both the *Journal* and the *World* accused Spain of foul play, and a new slogan — "Remember the *Maine*" — swept the country. Responding to the public mood, Congress appropriated 50 million dollars for military preparations.

Spain accepts American demands. Though the press and the expansionists

Headlines in the New York Journal *declared that the destruction of the* Maine *had been no accident. At right is the first photograph of the ruined ship, taken the day after the explosion.*

clamored for war, many Americans were reluctant to support this stand. Those who had little interest in expansion were opposed to intervention in Cuban affairs. Business leaders were afraid that war would disrupt trade and interfere with the country's recovery from the depression of the mid-1890's.

For a time McKinley resisted the clamor for war within his own party. He sincerely wanted to avoid war and to continue negotiations with the Spanish government. In March, 1898, the United States demanded that Spain arrange an immediate armistice in Cuba and abolish the concentration camps. By April 9, after strong pressure from the United States minister and from the Pope, Spain agreed to the armistice as well as to other American requests. The American minister cabled from Madrid: "I hope that nothing will now be done to humiliate Spain, as I am satisfied that the present Government is going . . . as fast and as far as it can."

The United States declares war on Spain. In spite of Spain's acceptance of

the American demands, Congress declared war. Responsibility for this development rests largely upon President McKinley. He feared that a peaceful solution would divide the Republicans, bring losses to them in the congressional elections that year, and give the Democrats a campaign issue in 1900. Hence, on April 11, two days after Spain met the American demands, the President delivered a war message to Congress. He asked for authority to stop the hostilities in Cuba, stating that intervention was necessary to protect American commerce and business and to end a conflict which was "a constant menace to our peace."

In reply to McKinley's message, Congress adopted a resolution granting the President's request and proclaiming the independence of Cuba. To this resolution was attached the so-called Teller Amendment, stating that it was not the intention of the United States to "exercise sovereignty, jurisdiction, or control over said island except for the pacification thereof." The United States promised that once

539

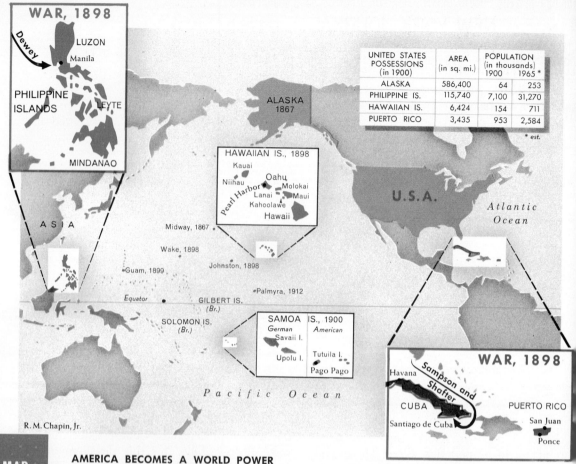

UNITED STATES POSSESSIONS (in 1900)	AREA (in sq. mi.)	POPULATION (in thousands) 1900	1965 *
ALASKA	586,400	64	253
PHILIPPINE IS.	115,740	7,100	31,270
HAWAIIAN IS.	6,424	154	711
PUERTO RICO	3,435	953	2,584

* est.

R. M. Chapin, Jr.

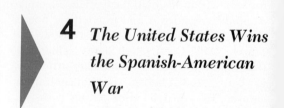

MAP STUDY

AMERICA BECOMES A WORLD POWER

By 1900 the United States had island possessions in the Pacific and Caribbean. As you read about the Spanish-American War, consult the inset maps. The chart at top right shows area and population of American possessions in 1900. Today Alaska and Hawaii are states, and the Philippines are an independent republic.

Cuban independence had been established, it would "leave the government and control of the island to its people." The Teller Amendment was a concession to those who were willing to fight a war to *free* Cuba but not to *annex* it.

▶ CHECK-UP

1. Why did American interest in Cuba increase? Why did some Americans come to favor intervention? What was the effect of the de Lôme letter? Of the sinking of the "Maine"?

2. What demands did the United States make on Spain? Why did McKinley deliver a war message to Congress even though Spain had accepted earlier terms? How did Congress respond? What was the Teller Amendment?

4 *The United States Wins the Spanish-American War*

Dewey wins a victory in Manila Bay. From the first it was evident that fighting at sea would play an important part in the Spanish-American War. The United States Navy was prepared for immediate action; its equipment was modern, and its officers and men were alert and well-trained. Even before war was declared, Theodore Roosevelt, Assistant Secretary of the Navy, had sent instructions to the commander of the Pacific squadron. He told Commodore George Dewey to keep the fleet "full of coal." When war was declared, Dewey was to leave Hong Kong for Manila and launch "offensive operations" in the Spanish-owned Philippine Islands.

On April 30, Dewey steamed into Manila Bay (map, page 540) and on the next day attacked the Spanish squadron in the harbor. In a short time the old Spanish ships were sunk or disabled, the shore batteries silenced, and nearly 400 Spanish seamen killed or wounded. The superior American ships suffered little damage, and only eight Americans were wounded. The newspapers played up this sudden victory and outdid themselves in praise of Commodore Dewey. The President thanked him for his "splendid achievement" and promoted him to rear admiral.

Manila is taken by the Americans. Dewey still faced the problem of occupying Manila, but for this task he needed an army. Pending its arrival, he declared a blockade of the city. It was the end of May before any reinforcements reached Dewey and another two months before he had enough men to take Manila. Aided by Filipinos in revolt against Spanish rule, the American troops captured the city of Manila on August 13, 1898. By that time, however, Spain had signed an armistice, and the war in Cuba had come to an end.

The army is unprepared for war. In a letter to Theodore Roosevelt, the American Ambassador to Great Britain, John Hay, called the Spanish-American conflict "a splendid little war." From the point of view of those who had favored American intervention, it may have been a "splendid" war. But from the point of view of the men who fought in it, the Spanish-American War was a tragedy of errors. Army officers who had fought Indians on the plains were at a loss to direct a campaign in Cuba. Supply officers ran out of repeating rifles and had to equip many soldiers with old-fashioned single-shot guns. Heavy woolen uniforms were issued to men fighting under a tropical sun. Sanitary facilities and medical supplies in many of the camps were inadequate, and much of the food

was unfit to eat. Though fewer than 400 Americans were killed in battle, over 5000 died from intestinal disorders, typhoid, malaria, and other diseases.

The American fleet blockades Santiago. When the war started, the United States Atlantic fleet established a blockade of Cuba. Rear Admiral Sampson cruised off the coast of Cuba, hoping to intercept a Spanish squadron which had left the Cape Verde Islands soon after the declaration of war. Three weeks passed without word of the Spanish ships commanded by Admiral Cervera (sair-*vay'* rah). The New York *Journal* and *World* hinted at surprise raids along the Atlantic coast, thereby creating panic in many coastal towns and cities. In spite of the watchfulness of the American fleet, the Spanish squadron managed to slip into the harbor of Santiago on the southeastern coast of Cuba (map, page 540). The embarrassed American commander then took up a position outside the harbor and waited for a military force to join in the attack on Santiago.

Land forces attack Santiago. Meanwhile, an American expeditionary force had been assembling in Tampa, Florida. Joining the regular army regiments was a volunteer unit known as the Rough Riders, commanded by Colonel Leonard Wood and Theodore Roosevelt, who had resigned as Assistant Secretary of the Navy. Shortages of arms, ammunition, food, clothing, and medical supplies soon became evident. In the midst of great confusion, some 17,000 men under General Shafter finally embarked for Cuba. By the end of June, this force was ready to attack Santiago.

Although the Spanish forces defending Santiago numbered fewer than 2000, they put up stiff resistance. After some hard fighting, during which Roosevelt's Rough Riders led an attack on San Juan Hill, the Americans won control of hills northeast of Santiago. Despite the fact that the Americans greatly outnumbered the Spaniards, there was talk of drawing back from the outskirts of Santiago. The Americans were short of supplies and were suffering from disease. Even Roosevelt admitted, "We are within measurable distance of a terrible military disaster."

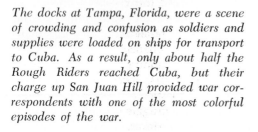

The docks at Tampa, Florida, were a scene of crowding and confusion as soldiers and supplies were loaded on ships for transport to Cuba. As a result, only about half the Rough Riders reached Cuba, but their charge up San Juan Hill provided war correspondents with one of the most colorful episodes of the war.

Spain admits defeat. Fortunately for the Americans, the Spanish forces were even more discouraged. Convinced that they could not hold Santiago, the Spaniards decided that Admiral Cervera must try to escape. But when the Spanish fleet steamed out of the harbor on July 3, American vessels closed in. One after another, the Spanish ships were crippled by gunfire and sunk or driven ashore. Two weeks later the Spanish garrison in Santiago surrendered to the Americans. After the fall of Santiago, a second American force invaded Puerto Rico, also a Spanish possession at this time. The Americans encountered little resistance and received a warm welcome from the Puerto Ricans.

Unable to continue the struggle, the Spanish government asked for peace terms. An armistice was signed on August 12, the day before Manila fell. Under the terms of the armistice, Spain was to (1) withdraw its forces from Cuba immediately; (2) sur-render all authority over Cuba; (3) cede Puerto Rico and Guam (an island in the Pacific) to the United States; and (4) allow American troops to occupy Manila "pending the conclusion of a treaty of peace which shall determine the control, disposition, and government of the Philippines."

The Peace of Paris is signed. American and Spanish commissioners met at Paris in October, 1898, to draw up the final treaty of peace. Disagreement soon arose over the Philippine Islands. Because Manila had not been occupied until the day after the armistice was signed, Spain argued that the Philippines should be restored to her. At the beginning of the war few people in the United States would have favored annexation of these distant islands. In fact, most Americans knew little about them. Even President McKinley later confessed: "When we received the cable from Admiral Dewey telling of the taking of the Philippines, I looked up their

THE UNITED STATES ACQUIRES OVERSEAS POSSESSIONS

location on the globe. I could not have told where those darned islands were within 2000 miles." Soon, however, the country was discussing the advantages of annexing the Philippines. Mark Hanna called the islands "a strategic point" that would give the United States a "foothold" in the markets of the Orient. Many missionaries favored annexation, and so too did people who feared that Germany might try to annex the islands if the United States did not. President McKinley reached the conclusion that public opinion favored our taking over the Philippines.

Spain had no alternative but to accept this decision. The negotiators did agree, however, that the United States should pay 20 million dollars for the Philippine Islands. On December 10, 1898, the Peace of Paris was signed. It guaranteed a free Cuba and ceded Puerto Rico, Guam, and the Philippines to the United States.

Annexation of the Philippines becomes a major issue. For the next two months the treaty was hotly debated in the United States Senate. The main controversy concerned the annexation of the Philippines. An Anti-Imperialist League, formed in 1898, had rallied public opinion against annexation of these islands. Such men as former Presidents Cleveland and Harrison, Andrew Carnegie, William Dean Howells, and Mark Twain opposed ratification of the treaty.

The anti-imperialists used a number of arguments. (1) For one thing, they said, governing the Filipinos and Puerto Ricans as colonists would violate the principles set forth in the Declaration of Independence and the Constitution. (2) A Filipino uprising against the United States showed that these people did not want to be ruled by Americans. (3) Moreover, annexation of the Philippines would increase military expenditures and might lead to entanglement in the Far East. (4) It was inconsistent to pass the Teller Amendment, disclaiming any intention of annexing Cuba, and then to annex the Philippine Islands, Puerto Rico, and Guam.

The treaty is ratified. Supporters of the treaty used familiar arguments — the need for naval bases and markets and the obligation to "uplift and civilize and Christianize" the Filipinos. But they were unable to muster a two-thirds vote in the Senate. At this point William Jennings Bryan came to their aid. Though he had supported the war to free Cuba, Bryan opposed the annexation of the Philippines. But he thought the matter should be settled by the voters in the election of 1900. The best way to present the issue, said Bryan, was to ratify the treaty and then let the people decide whether to keep the Philippine Islands or to free them. This argument led some Democratic senators to vote for the treaty. On February 6, 1899, the Senate ratified the Peace of Paris by a vote of 57 to 27.

McKinley is re-elected. In 1900, then, the voters had a chance to pass judgment on McKinley's handling of both foreign and domestic affairs. The Republican convention enthusiastically renominated the President, but a struggle developed for second place on the ticket. A majority of the delegates favored the colorful Theodore Roosevelt, who had been elected governor of New York after returning from Cuba. Though some bosses, including Mark Hanna, opposed Roosevelt because he was too independent, the Rough Rider won the vice-presidential nomination. Afterward, Hanna said to McKinley, "We have done the best we could. Now it is up to you to live!" The Democratic convention nominated Bryan and Adlai E. Stevenson, the free-silver Democrat who had been Vice-President during Cleveland's second term.

During the campaign the Democrats raised the issues of imperialism, free silver, and the tariff. But the return of prosperity had dulled the voters' interest in tariff rates and free silver. So Bryan concentrated on the evils of annexing the Philippines and urged immediate independence for the islands. The Republicans claimed credit for the return of prosperity, declaring that the McKinley administration had brought a "full dinner pail" to every worker. McKinley and Roosevelt defended Republican foreign policy and the terms of the treaty with Spain. They promised to put down

the insurrection in the Philippines and appealed to patriotic pride with the slogan
"Don't haul down the flag."

In the end, McKinley defeated Bryan by
a larger margin than in 1896. Only the
Solid South and the silver-mining states
supported the Democratic candidate. Apparently most Americans favored the
Republican administration and its handling
of domestic affairs as well as annexation of
the Philippines.

▶ CHECK-UP

1. Why was Dewey able to win a decisive
   naval victory at Manila Bay but unable to
   take Manila until several months later?
   What evidence is there that the army was
   unprepared to invade Cuba? What events
   led to the surrender of Santiago?

2. What were the terms of the armistice ending
   the Spanish-American War? How did the
   annexation of the Philippines come to be
   included in the peace treaty?

3. What arguments were advanced by those
   who favored annexation of the Philippines
   and ratification of the peace treaty? By
   those who were opposed? What did the
   election of 1900 seem to indicate with respect to the attitude of most Americans toward the war and the peace?

. . . .

Clinching the Main Ideas in Chapter 25

Within a few short years the United
States assumed a new role as a world
power with overseas responsibilities. The
change had begun quietly in the 1870'
with the Hawaiian and Samoan treaties and
had gathered speed in the 1880's. Secretary
of State Blaine's interest in closer ties with
Latin America was the prelude to American
intervention in the Venezuela boundary
dispute. In this affair, the United State
demonstrated its intention of applying the
Monroe Doctrine in the affairs of the Western Hemisphere, even at the risk of wa
with Great Britain. The Venezuelan con
troversy as well as disputes involving the
Bering Sea and the Alaskan boundary
helped to establish the use of arbitration in
international affairs.

The change in foreign policy had become
more apparent by the time the United
States annexed Hawaii and declared wa
against Spain. American expansionists were
arguing that the country needed Caribbean
and Pacific possessions to provide naval
bases as well as new markets and new
sources of raw materials. Furthermore, as
prosperity returned in the late 1890's
Americans were ready to "look outward."

The cry to "free Cuba" appealed to some
Americans because of their sympathy for
the oppressed Cubans and to others because of their economic interests in the
island's sugar production. As a result of
the brief war with Spain, the country found
itself the custodian of the remnants of the
Spanish colonial empire. Puerto Rico
Guam, and the Philippines became American possessions. In the election of 1900 the
voters seemingly endorsed the country's
new foreign policy by giving McKinley a
decisive majority over Bryan.

Chapter Review

Terms to Understand

1. "closed sea"
2. naval power
3. jingoes
4. Rough Riders
5. Klondike
6. de Lôme letter
7. Peace of Paris
   (1898)
8. Teller
   Amendment
9. three-mile limit
10. Pan American
    Union
11. coaling station
12. Anti-Imperialist
    League

What Do You Think?

1. Contrast the original purpose of the Monroe Doctrine with the purpose for which it was
applied in the Venezuelan boundary dispute.

2. What different motives caused many
Americans in the late 1800's to favor colonial
expansion? To oppose it?

3. Why was Spain unable to offer more effective resistance to United States naval and

land forces in the West Indies and in the Philippines?

4. What were the chief characteristics of the colonial empire envisioned by Senator Beveridge in 1898 (see quotation on page 533)?

5. In 1880 this country ranked twelfth among the world's naval powers; twenty years later it ranked third. Why?

Using Your Knowledge of History

1. Draft a statement such as might have been issued by Queen Liliuokalani to her people in 1893 when American planters encouraged a revolt that caused her to be deposed.

2. Debate: *Resolved,* That the United States was not justified in going to war with Spain.

3. Plan an informal debate to examine the soundness of the four arguments (page 543) advanced by anti-imperialists in opposing annexation of the Philippines.

4. Write a letter such as might have been written by an American soldier who sailed from Florida to Cuba to take part in the siege of Santiago. Take into account factors mentioned in this chapter.

Extending Your Knowledge of History

Books written by Alfred Mahan and Josiah Strong are worth sampling to get the attitude of the expansionists. Another interesting first-hand account is Theodore Roosevelt's *The Rough Riders.* An excellent study of the forces that brought about the Spanish-American War is Julius Pratt's *Expansionists of 1898.* For the war itself see Frank Freidel's lively volume *The Splendid Little War.* See also "Manifest Destiny and the Philippines" in *America in Crisis,* edited by Daniel Aaron. Appropriate articles in *American Heritage* are "The Needless War with Spain" by William E. Leuchtenburg (February, 1957); "The Enemies of Empire" by Harold A. Larrabee (June, 1960); "How We Got Guantanamo" by Robert D. Heinl (February, 1962); and "The Great White Fleet" by Frank Uhlig, Jr. (February, 1964).

Analyzing Unit Seven

1. One historian has written: "There is no drearier chapter in American political history than . . . the period from the end of reconstruction to the Populist revolt of the 1890's." What were politicians concerned with during these years? What issues were they purposely avoiding? Why?

2. The election of 1896, focusing on the issue of free silver versus the gold standard, was "both deeper and less dangerous than contemporaries realized." In what sense was the fight over silver less important than many people thought at the time? In what sense

did the election represent a more fundamental clash between the interests of farmers and those of the business community?

3. It is the judgment of one historian that the "American people were not led into [the Spanish-American] war; they got the war they wanted." How did the activities of the expansionists prepare Americans for this type of war? What groups finally persuaded the McKinley administration to declare war on Spain? What were their motives? Why were the anti-expansionists unable to prevent the annexation of the Philippine Islands?

Unit 8 | Americans Crusade at Home and Abroad (1900-1918)

College women demanding the vote in the early 1900's

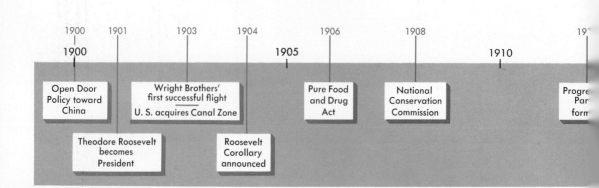

1900
1900
Open Door
Policy toward
China

1901
Theodore Roosevelt
becomes
President

1903
Wright Brothers'
first successful flight
U. S. acquires Canal Zone

1904
Roosevelt
Corollary
announced

1905

1906
Pure Food
and Drug
Act

1908
National
Conservation
Commission

1910

19
Progre
Par
form

As the twentieth century opened, the time seemed ripe to many Americans to attack some of the injustices in American society. The leaders in this Progressive Movement were intent upon establishing honest, responsive government and using it to protect the interests of all Americans. This was largely an urban reform movement, whereas the Populists had represented mainly a rural movement. Nevertheless, the Progressive Movement drew freely from the Populist demand that the federal government broaden its activities and use its powers to further the general welfare.

The success of the Progressive Movement depended in part on the work of journalists who exposed the inequalities in American society. It was greatly helped by President Theodore Roosevelt, who convinced the public that reform was necessary. During Roosevelt's administration the government began to break up the large trusts, regulate the railroads, and protect the rights of striking workers. Roosevelt's successor, William Howard Taft, broadened the movement. But Taft lacked Roosevelt's skill in dealing with conservative Republicans who opposed most progressive reforms. Thus, in 1912 the Republicans split into two factions, each running its own candidate in the presidential election.

This split enabled the Democratic candidate, Woodrow Wilson, to win an easy victory. He too was a progressive, and the reform movement reached its high point during his first administration. Wilson managed to lower the tariff, revise the banking system, and strengthen the regulation of trusts.

Meanwhile, the influence of the United States in world affairs continued to expand. The policies of Presidents Roosevelt and Taft resulted in the construction of the Panama Canal and an extension of the United States' influence among the Latin American republics. President Wilson conducted a spirited defense of American neutral rights after World War I broke out in Europe in 1914. But Germany's decision early in 1917 to use submarines in attacking and sinking neutral ships finally drew this country into the conflict. For President Wilson, submarine warfare was not only a violation of neutral rights but a threat to the security of all representative governments. In Wilson's words, therefore, America entered World War I to "make the world safe for democracy."

CHAPTER 26

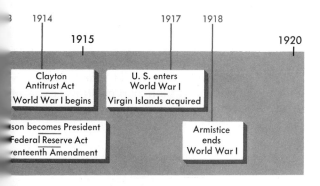

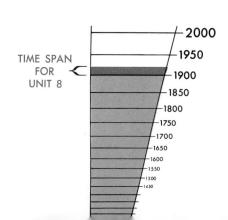

Theodore Roosevelt speaking

1900–1912

The Progressive
Movement
Sweeps the Country

[The] basic liberal strain in Roosevelt's personality did much for the success of the progressive movement. His very coming to the White House imparted to the whole government a vitality and a will to action which it had not known for years. . . . He aroused the entire nation to the need for action. And while he did little himself to solve the numerous questions he broached, he did create a national demand that these questions be met and answered. Roosevelt was the best publicity man progressivism ever had.

GEORGE E. MOWRY, "THEODORE ROOSEVELT AND THE PROGRESSIVE MOVEMENT"

It was obvious to many Americans at the beginning of the twentieth century that the growth of industry and cities had created pressing new problems. Among these, they realized, were corruption in politics and too much influence by big business in government. What came to be called the *Progressive Movement* was an effort to meet these challenges.

Though the Progressive Movement was related to the Populist revolt of the 1890's, it differed in certain respects. Instead of drawing its strength from discontented farmers, it attracted support chiefly from middle-class city dwellers. The Progressive Movement was basically an attempt to restore political control to the voters. By regulating big business and improving the machinery of government, the supporters of reform hoped to create better opportunities for ordinary citizens.

From 1900 until the United States became involved in World War I, progressive reformers in both parties strove to secure honest and efficient government and to put an end to special privilege. The progress sives' earliest successes came at the local and state level. But while Theodore Roosevelt was in the White House, he urged the adoption of reforms at the national level. He wanted the antitrust law enforced and the railroads regulated by the federal government. He also campaigned for the conservation of natural resources. Roosevelt's hand-picked successor, William Howard Taft, supported many reform measures. But Taft disappointed the progressives in the Republican Party and paved the way for a party split in 1912. This chapter will explain the origins of the Progressive Movement and follow its course through the Roosevelt and Taft administrations.

1 Progressives Demand Reforms

What were the sources of the Progressive Movement?   The Progressive Movement had its roots in earlier political ideas and movements. The late 1800's, as we have seen, had witnessed a number of protests against political corruption, the growth of business monopolies, and the exploitation of farmers, workingmen, and immigrants. The Liberal Republicans of 1872, for example, were followed by the Mugwumps in the election of 1884. Unrest on the farms sparked the Granger movement and finally led to the founding of the Populist Party.

Populist leaders had tried, without much success, to draw workingmen and middle-class city dwellers into their party. Many planks in the Populists' Omaha Platform had, in fact, appealed to urban voters. But city people had little or no interest in free silver, and some of the more outspoken western Populists made them uneasy. Hence Populist votes came largely from discontented farmers and people living in the silver-mining states. Nevertheless, the political revolt which began on the farms in the 1890's played an important part in progressive thinking. For the Progressive Movement, like Populism, was firmly rooted in the belief that the federal government must concern itself with the well-being of all citizens.

The progressives drew on newer sources of discontent as well as older ones. During the late 1800's, reformers had tried to improve government and physical conditions in the expanding urban centers. In 1894 they formed the National Municipal League, a coalition of local reform organizations, whose members played a leading role in launching the Progressive Movement.

Still other forces influenced the Progressive Movement. From Thomas Jefferson, progressives adopted the belief that every individual should have an opportunity to make the most of his talents. Moreover, they echoed Jefferson's conviction that political power could safely be vested in all of the people. The progressives drew from Alexander Hamilton's beliefs as well. They staunchly supported free enterprise and economic competition but felt that these had been undermined by the growth of monopolies. The progressives did not want to stifle industrial growth. Rather, they sought ways of adjusting American life to the changing conditions of the industrial age. Finally, it should be pointed out that the progressives firmly believed in a democratic system of government. The political reforms which they proposed were aimed at giving people more power at the polls and thus a greater voice in government.

Progressives object to continued growth of monopolies.   As we have seen, the Sherman Antitrust Act (page 500) had proved to be of little use in controlling the trusts. Few cases were prosecuted under this law; and when they were, the courts usually ruled in favor of the corporations. The Sherman Act failed either to regulate the behavior of the large trusts or to discourage the formation of new business combinations. Indeed, the trend toward large business organizations became more marked as a result of (1) the return of prosperity in the late 1890's, (2) the favorable attitude of the McKinley administration, and (3) the opening up of overseas markets. When a book entitled *The Truth about the Trusts* appeared in 1904, many Americans were startled to learn that three fourths of the 318 trusts in the country had been created since 1898.

This trend toward monopoly disturbed the progressives. They recognized the fact that the growth of industry had raised standards of living and created thousands of jobs. But they also realized that the formation of trusts ruined many small businessmen, reduced competition, and led to higher prices. Prices rose so rapidly between 1897 and 1913 that the cost of living shot up by 35 per cent. The progressives also accused some of the trusts of using their great power to destroy labor unions and keep wages low.

According to the progressives, the solution to the problem of the trusts was effective government regulation. Enforcement of the Sherman Antitrust Act, they argued, would break up the undesirable monopolies and create new economic opportunities. In this belief, the progressives had the strong support of many middle-income Americans. Caught in the pinch of rising prices, small businessmen, professional people, salesmen, clerks, and factory workers looked to the federal government for protection. They voted with enthusiasm for progressive candidates who promised to "curb the money power" or "bust the trusts."

Progressives are disturbed by inequalities in American life. Just as alarming to progressives as the growth of monopolies was the concentration of wealth in the hands of a few powerful families. The Census Bureau estimated in 1893 that 9 per cent of the population owned approximately 71 per cent of the country's wealth. A decade later 1 per cent of the population held nearly 87 per cent of the wealth. Poverty, on the other hand, was the lot of all too many Americans. In 1900 the average factory worker's pay was less than ten dollars a week. A woman working in a factory or as a servant was lucky to get six dollars a week, and children working at dangerous jobs in mines and mills received even less. Lacking adequate food, clothing, and shelter, the children of the poor had little chance to get an education and so had little hope for the future.

The wide range in personal income at the turn of the century was reflected by great differences in standards of living. In sharp contrast to the luxurious mansions of the rich were the squalid tenement houses in the cities, the weather-beaten dwellings of debt-ridden prairie farmers, and the rough cabins of Negro sharecroppers in the South. To lessen inequalities in American life, the progressives proposed the adoption of an income tax, but they felt a "living wage" for workers and a ban on child labor would be even more effective.

Journalists arouse public opinion. A number of writers and magazines helped awaken the American public to the need for reform. One of the first of these writers was Henry Demarest Lloyd. In *Wealth Against Commonwealth*, published in 1894, he surveyed the growth of the trusts and showed how they operated against the public interest.

Within the next few years, a group of new, moderate-priced magazines began to expose abuses in American business and politics. The magazine publisher S. S. McClure set the pattern by hiring able reporters and providing them with the time and money to write authoritative articles. The earliest of these was Ida M. Tarbell's "History of the Standard Oil Company," which started in *McClure's* in 1903. Miss Tarbell had spent six years finding the facts to document her charge that Standard Oil dealt ruthlessly with competitors, the government, and the public interest. Another sensational series of articles in *McClure's* was Lincoln Steffens' study of municipal corruption. He traveled to many cities to gather evidence of graft involving businessmen and local politicians. "The Shame of the Cities" shocked many readers and led to demands for reform.

These articles boosted circulation to such a degree that other magazines soon followed the lead of *McClure's*. In *Everybody's*, Thomas Lawson exposed the dishonest workings of the stock market in a series of articles entitled "Frenzied Finance." *Cosmopolitan* printed "The Treason of the Senate" by David Graham Phillips, showing how senators favored the railroads and large corporations.

This literature of exposure and protest was christened "muckraking" by President Theodore Roosevelt in 1906. Speaking of some of the more sensational journalists, he said they reminded him of the man in Bunyan's *Pilgrim's Progress* "who was offered the celestial crown for his muck-rake . . . but continued to rake the filth on the floor." The reporters ignored such criticism, however, and continued to investigate corruption. The historian George Mowry has said of the muckrakers: "If at times they bordered on the sensational, they at least exposed a picture of American politics and social conditions that had never before been revealed."

Other writers expose evil conditions. In addition to magazine articles, a number of muckraking books both informed and alarmed Americans. As we have seen, Jacob Riis' volumes about the slums made many readers aware of a pressing problem in the cities (page 472). Likewise, John Spargo's *The Bitter Cry of the Children* revealed shocking details of child labor. Burton J. Hendrick exposed fraudulent practices in *The Story of Life Insurance*.

Novelists also contributed to the literature of protest. Frank Norris described a bitter struggle between California wheat growers and the railroads in *The Octopus*. This book dramatized the power and influence of the railroads over the communities which they served. Another effective book was Winston Churchill's[1] *Coniston*, a study of the corrupt relationship between businessmen and urban political machines. The most eye-opening of these books, however, was Upton Sinclair's *The Jungle* (1906). This novel described the revolting conditions in Chicago's meat-packing plants.

Radicals take advantage of widespread discontent. The muckrakers and progressives maintained that they were criticizing American life because they wished to reform it. But some people took advantage of the widespread discontent of this period to seek revolutionary changes. Thus a belligerent union called the Industrial Workers of the World (IWW) called for the overthrow of the government and demanded that all industries and resources be owned by the workers. Members of the IWW, who included lumberjacks, miners, migrant farm laborers, and dock workers, felt they were not getting "a fair break" under existing economic conditions.

The Socialists call for government ownership. Although the Socialists took

One fourth of the workers in southern cotton mills at the turn of the century were children. They worked as much as thirteen hours a day, often operating dangerous machinery.

---

[1] This Winston Churchill was an American novelist, not the British statesman.

a less extreme position than the IWW, they advocated more far-reaching changes than the progressives. They believed that the government, representing the people as a whole, should own the means of production. This would eliminate fierce economic competition and would improve the condition of the working classes.

Eugene Debs had become a Socialist while he was serving his jail term after the Pullman strike (page 481). In 1900 Debs ran for the presidency on a Socialist platform calling for government ownership of the railroads, public utilities, and mines as well as a number of social and political reforms. Debs received fewer than 90,000 votes in this election; nevertheless, he helped to form the Socialist Party the next year. American Socialists differed somewhat from moderate Socialists in Europe and bore virtually no resemblance to the radical Socialists who seized power in Russia in 1917 (page 637). Instead they reflected Debs' hope of introducing modest reforms by winning elections.

▶ CHECK-UP

1. What ideas did the Progressive Movement draw from the Populists? From Jefferson? From Hamilton? What were the progressives' chief goals?

2. Why were the progressives concerned about the growth of monopolies? About inequalities in American life? How did the "muckrakers" influence public opinion?

3. How did the IWW and the Socialist Party seek to capitalize on the widespread discontent? What solutions did each propose?

- -

2 *Reforms Begin at the City and State Levels*

Among Americans who recognized the need for reform in the early 1900's, the Progressive Movement gained far more

supporters than either the Socialists or the IWW. In this section we shall see what the progressives accomplished in the cities and states. Later in the chapter we shall consider the progressive reforms undertaken by the federal government.

Aroused citizens act to end municipal corruption. Progressive reforms were first carried out in the cities. In the 1890's, New Yorkers again rebelled against Tammany Hall politicians (page 401) and elected honest officials who tried to stop the misuse of public funds. In Cleveland an influential businessman named Tom Johnson was won over to the reform cause. Johnson was elected mayor of Cleveland in 1901 and spent the next nine years fighting corruption. In nearby Toledo, Ohio, Samuel Jones used his power as mayor to apply the golden rule to city life. He lost some battles, but "Golden Rule" Jones endeared himself to the people and had the satisfaction of seeing his reforms continued by an able successor. In Milwaukee, a Socialist mayor named Emil Seidel headed the best administration the city had experienced in many years.

New forms of city government are introduced. The reformers sometimes found their efforts hampered by outdated city charters which state legislatures had granted decades before. As a result, reform groups sought, and in some states won, "home rule" for the cities — that is, the right of the voters to determine their own form of municipal government.

Some cities used their new freedom to try new types of government. One experiment came in the wake of a great disaster. When Galveston, Texas, was virtually destroyed by a tidal wave in 1900, the mayor and council were unable to cope with the crisis. In desperation the city set up a five-man commission, which was authorized to run the city government. The system worked so well that many other cities adopted a commission form of government. Dayton, Ohio, pioneered in setting up a city-manager government after it suffered a flood in 1913. Within a decade, some 300 cities hired city managers, who were responsible either to a commission or to a

*The civic spirit of the Progressive
years led cities to build more parks.
Chicago began to reclaim land from
Lake Michigan for park areas (above).
Wooded parks (left, in Kansas City)
offered a change of environment to
urban dwellers. Playgrounds in
densely populated cities (above, left,
in New York) provide children with
safe outlets for energy.*

city council. For greater efficiency in municipal government, a number of cities adopted better auditing and bookkeeping procedures, established civil service systems, and started training programs for firemen and policemen.

City governments took on some new responsibilities during the progressive era. Housing laws were passed requiring landlords to keep their property in good condition. Building codes which set minimum safety standards for new buildings were adopted. Many cities established juvenile courts to handle young offenders. Park and playground facilities were expanded, and the "city beautiful" movement gathered interest. This was an effort to set aside lake fronts, river banks, ravines, and wooded areas for public use in the cities. Among the most successful of these ventures were San Antonio's riverfront improvements, Kansas City's network of boulevard-parks, and Chicago's development of Lake Michigan beaches and forest preserves.

Reformers tackle the state governments. Strengthened by its successes in the cities, the reform movement soon spread to state governments. New York elected a vigorous reform governor named Charles Evans Hughes in 1906. Armed with evidence turned up by the muckrakers, Hughes succeeded in establishing state regulation of public utility companies and insurance firms. In California, Hiram Johnson used his power as governor to regulate the railroads.

Perhaps the most successful of the state reformers was Robert M. La Follette. Descendant of a French Huguenot settler, La Follette worked his way through the University of Wisconsin and practiced law until he was elected to Congress in 1884. La Follette worked with the Republican leaders and helped draft the McKinley tariff in 1890, but was defeated for re-election that year.

During the 1890's La Follette parted company with conservative Republicans and charted a program of reform for Wisconsin's state government. Elected governor in 1900, he found that lumber and railroad interests dominated the state legislature. La Follette waged a long and bitter fight against corrupt businessmen and their political allies before he secured the legislation he wanted. During 1903–1905, however, he won approval for his "Wisconsin idea" — a program of election reforms, changes in the tax system, and regulation of the railroads. Eloquently defending his proposals before the people of Wisconsin as well as nation-wide Chautauqua audiences, La Follette won a devoted following. He was a leading figure in the Progressive Movement as a reform governor and then as a United States senator (1906–1925).

State governments undergo many changes. Reformers believed that the best cure for political corruption at the state level was to give the voters a greater voice in the government. To prevent the party bosses from selecting candidates for office, the reformers devised the *direct primary*. This enabled the people to choose in a primary election the party can-

Voting booths, by enabling voters to mark their ballots in private, helped weaken the power of political bosses. Here a voting booth is hauled to a precinct in Cleveland in 1891.

didates who would run in a general election. Wisconsin enacted a direct primary law in 1903; ten years later almost every state in the country had a similar law.

Two other proposals that appealed to the progressives were the *initiative* and *referendum*. Both of these gave voters an opportunity to express their will on desired legislation. By signing a petition that proposed a law, a small percentage of voters could initiate legislation. If the state legislature failed to pass the voter-proposed law, the voters could again petition to have a referendum, or vote of the people, to see if the law had public support. If the bill was approved in the referendum, it became a law. The referendum also could be used to give voters an opportunity to reject laws already passed by the legislature. Starting in South Dakota in 1898, the initiative and referendum spread until half the states, mostly in the Midwest and the West, had adopted this method of legislation in one form or another.

Some states amended their constitutions to provide for *recall*. This device enabled the voters to remove an elected state official before his term expired. A few states applied the recall to judicial as well as executive officers.

The most significant of the progressive reforms at the state level was the direct election of United States senators. The Seventeenth Amendment, passed by Congress in 1912 and ratified the next year, gave the voters, rather than the state legislatures, the right to elect senators.

The reformers were sometimes disappointed because these reforms did not accomplish all that they expected. In some states, for example, party bosses were able to dominate primary elections. Nevertheless, the direct primary gave the voters an opportunity, if they made use of it, to influence the choice of candidates.

State legislatures pass social-welfare laws. As more and more people became interested in the reform movement, they began to look to the state legislatures for laws to protect the underprivileged. There were four basic types of laws:

(1) A drive against child labor resulted

Juvenile courts were established during the Progressive Era to deal with the special problems of children who got into trouble. Judge Benjamin Lindsay, shown here, pioneered in demonstrating the value of juvenile courts.

in state laws that established a minimum age (usually fourteen) for factory work and prohibited the employment of children for night work or on dangerous jobs.

(2) Legislation was also passed to limit the working hours of adults. More than half the states limited the work week for women to 60 hours and regulated the working hours of miners and others in hazardous occupations.

(3) In addition, state laws guaranteed compensation to workers for injuries received on the job. By 1917, four fifths of the states had some form of workmen's compensation law.

(4) The fourth type of social-welfare law established a minimum wage. Massachusetts passed the first minimum-wage law for women in 1912, and fifteen states had similar laws by 1923.

Employers who opposed these laws proceeded to test their constitutionality in the courts. In many cases the courts ruled that minimum-wage laws violated the right of the individual and his employer to make their own agreement. An Oregon law limiting the working day for women to ten hours was appealed all the way to the Supreme Court. Defending the state law was Louis Brandeis, a brilliant lawyer. Brandeis pointed out that long working hours for women resulted in disadvantages to families and therefore also to communities. Brandeis' argument was so convincing

that the Court decided the case of *Muller v. Oregon* in favor of the state law (1908). This decision was an important landmark, but it did not follow that all social-welfare laws were thereafter upheld by the courts. In 1923 the Supreme Court declared unconstitutional an act of Congress regulating the wages of women working in the District of Columbia. In this case (*Adkins v. Children's Hospital*) the Court returned to the *laissez-faire* concept that government regulation of wages violated the employee's freedom of contract.

Women work for reforms. American women played an important role in the Progressive Movement. They supported such political reforms as the direct election of senators, the direct primary, initiative, referendum, and recall. Women who had been active in social programs sponsored by settlement houses and churches persuaded their state legislatures to pass social-welfare laws. Many women's organizations worked tirelessly for measures to promote public health and safety and to improve the lot of wage earners.

▶ CHECK-UP

1. Why did reformers demand "home rule" for cities? What new systems of city government were introduced? What new responsibilities were accepted by city governments?

2. What political reforms were introduced at the state level? Explain each.

3. What social-welfare laws were passed? What role did women take in the reform movement?

. . . .

3   *Theodore Roosevelt Attacks Monopolies*

Theodore Roosevelt becomes President. Early in September, 1901, President McKinley journeyed to Buffalo, New York, to attend a Pan-American Exposition. At a public reception he was shot by an anarchist. Messengers were immediately dispatched to the Adirondacks to find the Vice-President, who was on a camping trip. When McKinley died eight days later, Theodore Roosevelt took the oath of office as President of the United States. Roosevelt's advance to the presidency alarmed such Republican bosses as Mark Hanna, who remembered the political independence Roosevelt had displayed as Governor of New York. The Republican leaders were only partly reassured by the new President's promise "to continue, absolutely unbroken, the policy of President McKinley, for the peace, prosperity, and honor of our beloved country."

Roosevelt launches progressive reform in the national government. No doubt Roosevelt was sincere about intending to continue McKinley's policies. When he entered the White House, Roosevelt had few ties with reformers. In fact, he had been extremely critical of the Populists and throughout the 1890's had supported the Republican stand on gold, tariff protection, and expansion. "I cannot say," Roosevelt later admitted, "that I entered the presidency with any deliberately planned and far-reaching scheme of social betterment."

Yet one of the elements of Roosevelt's greatness as chief executive was that he responded to the challenge of the times. Like other Americans, he was disturbed by the powerful position of the trusts and the plight of many working men and their families. Though he gave the "muckrakers" their nickname, he was strongly influenced by what they wrote. Roosevelt's years in the White House marked the beginning of progressive reforms at the national level. He called for a "square deal" for ordinary citizens and also promised to take action against the "malefactors of great wealth."

Both Roosevelt's contemporaries and later historians have argued about his motives. To some, he seemed to be a sincere convert to the Progressive Movement, who hoped to use his influence as President to secure needed reforms. William Allen White called him the "chief muckraker," and S. S. McClure said that "President Roosevelt was the most influential force in getting good things done that the country ever had." Others, however, were convinced that Roosevelt's actions had political motives. According to this view, his main ambition was to be elected President in 1904 and his sponsorship of reforms was intended to help him achieve that goal. Roosevelt never tackled the controversial problem of tariff reduction, however, and this prompted some critics to say that he was at heart only a lukewarm progressive.

Roosevelt was an energetic executive. Regardless of his motives, there was general agreement that Roosevelt was an effective publicity agent for the Progressive Movement. Energetic and resourceful, he used his tremendous personal popularity to arouse the interest of the American people in reform. His speeches always had a powerful impact upon the whole nation.

Roosevelt was a strong President in the tradition of Jackson and Lincoln, effectively using his office to influence politicians as well as voters. He believed a President should exercise all powers not expressly denied him by law or by the Constitution. It was not in his nature to sit back and let Congress, or the Supreme Court, or party bosses determine the course of events. Roosevelt had a hand in every major decision that was made during his administration, and he molded foreign pol-

(*Continued on page 558*)

Theodore Roosevelt

[1858–1919]

Theodore Roosevelt's parents were well-to-do New Yorkers who could trace their ancestry back to seventeenth-century New Amsterdam. As a student at Harvard College, young Roosevelt was interested in history and the study of plants and animals. But he decided not to become a college teacher and, after a brief stint of reading law, rejected that as a career too. Instead he amazed his wealthy friends by announcing his intention to go into politics. In his autobiography Roosevelt later recalled their warnings that only saloon-keepers and horse-car conductors got mixed up in politics. "I answered that if this were so, it merely meant that the people I knew did not belong to the governing class, and that the other people did — and that I intended to be one of the governing class."

Roosevelt joined a Republican organization and attended its meetings in a hall over a bar-room. He served for a time in the New York State legislature and then joined the Mugwumps in a vain effort to block Blaine's nomination in 1884. Roosevelt spent the summer of that year on his ranch in the Dakotas — riding, reading, and writing books on American history. In the fall he and his friend Henry Cabot Lodge broke with the Mugwumps and supported Blaine in the campaign. Two years later Roosevelt ran for mayor of New York City and lost. Shortly afterwards he married Edith Carow. Sagamore Hill, their home in Oyster Bay, Long Island, became the headquarters for a large and active family.

During the early 1890's Roosevelt was a member of the Civil Service Commission in Washington. But he soon returned to New York City as president of the Board of Police Commissioners. There he was constantly in the limelight, roving about the city to check on law enforcement and prowling the slums with Jacob Riis. President McKinley appointed Roosevelt Assistant Secretary of the Navy, a post he was happy to accept since he was already an ardent expansionist and disciple of Alfred Thayer Mahan. A war against Spain, said Roosevelt, would remind Americans of the "most valuable of all qualities, the soldierly virtues," and give them "something to think of which isn't material gain." He recounted his experiences in the Spanish-American War in *The Rough Riders*, a book published in 1898, the same year he was elected governor of New York. When he accepted the vice-presidential nomination in 1900, Roosevelt feared it was a dead-end job. But the Republican victory returned him to Washington, and the assassination of McKinley made him President.

For the next eight years the White House reverberated with the shouts of young children — boxing, wrestling, riding ponies on the lawn, roller-skating, and bicycling. The American public doted on news of the Roosevelt family and were amazed by the President's wide range of interests and his "strenuous life." An Englishman described the chief executive as "an interesting combination of St. Vitus and St. Paul."

Roosevelt found it difficult to retire from politics after 1909. Drawn into the bitter fight between Republican conservatives and progressives, his candidacy in 1912 helped the Democrats win. His last years were unhappy because he was denied an active role in World War I.

icy to a greater extent than any previous President.[2] Historians generally agree with Roosevelt's own analysis of his use of presidential authority: "I did not usurp power, but I did greatly broaden the use of executive power."

Roosevelt tackles the trusts. In his first message to Congress in December, 1901, the new President declared: "The biggest corporation, like the humblest citizen, should be held to strict compliance with . . . the fundamental law." He praised the captains of industry for their achievements, but he also warned: "There is a widespread conviction in the minds of the American people that . . . trusts are in certain of their features and tendencies hurtful to the general welfare." The President urged that the trusts be "supervised and within reasonable limits controlled." In other words, Roosevelt wanted to regulate the trusts, not drive them out of existence.

Within a few months of this message, Roosevelt instructed his Attorney General to bring suit against the Northern Securities Company (page 445) as an illegal monopoly in violation of the Sherman Antitrust Act. The public was surprised and businessmen were shocked by this action, since such powerful railroad figures as James J. Hill and Edward H. Harriman and the financier J. P. Morgan all were involved in the Northern Securities holding company. Nevertheless, in 1904 the Supreme Court ruled that the company must be broken up.

In 1903 Congress created a Bureau of Corporations as part of the newly established Department of Commerce and Labor. Roosevelt used evidence collected by this Bureau to bring cases against the meat-packing companies, Standard Oil, and the American Tobacco Company. The results of these and some 40 other antitrust cases were less decisive. But the President's victory over the Northern Securities Company had firmly established his reputation as a "trust-buster."

Roosevelt settles a coal strike. Besides regulating the trusts, the President

also wanted to see labor get a "square deal." "While I am President," he said, "I wish the laboring man to feel that he has the same right of access to me that the capitalist has; that the doors swing open as easily to the wage-worker as to the head of a big corporation — and no easier." His sympathy for the laboring man was tested in 1902 by a strike in the anthracite coal mines.

Led by John Mitchell of the United Mine Workers, the Pennsylvania coal miners walked off their jobs in May. They demanded a pay increase, a shorter working day, and recognition of their union. The mine-owners refused to meet any of these demands. Although Mitchell was willing to submit the union demands to arbitration, the mine-owners rejected that proposal too. George F. Baer, a leading mine operator, declared: "The rights and interests of the laboring man will be protected and cared for, not by the labor agitators, but by the Christian men to whom God, in His infinite wisdom, has given control of the property interests of the country."

When the deadlock continued until fall, Roosevelt called the company and union leaders to Washington and asked them to accept arbitration. The United Mine Workers agreed, but the mine operators refused. When the President threatened to send federal troops to run the mines, the operators finally agreed to accept the decision of a government commission. The miners then went back to work, and six months later the commission awarded them a wage increase and a nine-hour day.

Labor unions hailed the outcome of the anthracite coal strike as a victory. This was the first labor dispute in which the government had threatened to intervene on behalf of the strikers. Though President Roosevelt possessed no specific constitutional authority for such an action, he claimed that he had acted to protect the "public interest."

Roosevelt wins the election of 1904. The President's "trust-busting" activities, his action in the coal strike, and his vigorous foreign policy had won him great popularity. To be sure, the captains of indus-

---

[2] For foreign affairs during Theodore Roosevelt's presidency, see Chapter 28.

THEODORE ROOSEVELT'S REFORMS

THEODORE ROOSEVELT (1901-1908)	OBJECTIVES	ACTIONS TAKEN
established precedents for future government reforms in many fields.		
TRUSTS	Supervision and control of trusts "within reasonable limits."	1. 1902 suit against Northern Securities Company provided a pattern for later anti-monopoly action by the government. 2. Established Bureau of Corporations in 1903—forerunner of Federal Trade Commission.
LABOR	A "square deal" for the working man.	1. Arbitration commission appointed by Roosevelt in 1902 coal strike achieved wage settlement favorable to workers. The commission was a precedent for future government intervention on behalf of labor. 2. Proposed laws to improve conditions of labor.
RAILROADS	Regulation of freight rates to insure fair treatment of farmers. Implementation of ICC authority.	1. Elkins Act (1903) barred shippers from accepting rebates from railroads. 2. Hepburn Act (1906) permitted the Interstate Commerce Commission to establish rates based on its review of railroad's assets.
FOOD AND DRUGS	Protection for consumers from impure and harmful food and drug products.	1. Meat Inspection Act (1906) provided for government inspection and grading of meat; helped eradicate animal diseases. 2. Pure Food and Drug Act (1906) prohibited misbranding (improper labeling) and sale of adulterated foods and drugs across state lines.
CONSERVATION	Prevention of wasting of natural resources and the replenishment of existing supplies.	1. Roosevelt used executive authority to protect vast areas of forest land. 2. Newlands Reclamation Act (1902) established fund to finance irrigation projects. 3. Roosevelt fostered the setting up of wildlife preserves.

try and the "Old Guard" in the Republican Party were less than enthusiastic about Roosevelt. But the vast majority of delegates to the Republican convention in 1904 supported Roosevelt, and they nominated the President without a formal vote.

The Democrats, on the other hand, had more difficulty finding a suitable candidate. Roosevelt was sympathetic to many of the reforms they had supported in 1896 and 1900. It seemed pointless to run Bryan for a third time against an opponent far stronger than William McKinley. Furthermore, the Democratic convention was dominated by conservative delegates who denounced Roosevelt's administration as "spasmodic, erratic, sensational, spectacular, and arbitrary." They succeeded in nominating Judge Alton B. Parker, a conservative New Yorker, former law partner of Grover Cleveland, and supporter of the gold standard.

The contest proved a one-sided affair. Theodore Roosevelt swept the country, receiving two and a half million more votes than Parker. A third candidate in the 1904 election, Socialist Eugene Debs, polled more than four times as many votes as he had won in 1900. This vote reflected the feeling of some Americans that Roosevelt was not moving fast enough along the road of reform. The Socialist vote, however, was only 3 per cent of the total. Roosevelt won every state outside the Solid South and even carried the usually Democratic state of Missouri. Pleased with his sweeping victory, he made an announcement on the night of his election which was to plague him in later years: "Under no circumstances will I be a candidate for or accept another nomination."

New regulations are imposed on the railroads. Roosevelt interpreted the election returns as a demand from the voters for further action against big business. The regulation of railroads now received his attention. One piece of railroad legislation, the Elkins Act, had already been passed during Roosevelt's first administration (1903). The Elkins Act made it illegal for a shipper to accept a rebate (or discount), just as the Interstate Commerce Act had made it illegal for a railroad to grant one.

From the point of view of farmers and small businessmen, the major problem was the regulation of railroad rates. They wanted Congress to give the Interstate Commerce Commission power to examine the assets of a railroad company and then set reasonable rates. The Hepburn Act, passed in 1906, was a step in this direction. It permitted the ICC to set "just and reasonable rates." If railroad operators disputed a Commission ruling, the railroad rather than the Commission would have to take the case to court. The Hepburn Act also gave the Commission power to regulate express and sleeping-car companies, pipe lines, and railroad terminals. Roosevelt's backing was an important factor in the passage of the Hepburn Act.

The government regulates the production of food and drugs. Other federal legislation was aimed at protecting the public from harmful products. For some years government chemists in the Department of Agriculture had been aware that dangerous preservatives were used in canned goods. Muckraking journalists made this fact public and exposed still other undesirable procedures in the preparation of foods and drugs. No action was taken, however, until Upton Sinclair's novel *The Jungle* alerted the public to unsanitary practices in the meat-packing industry. Then, in 1906, Congress passed two important measures.

(1) The Meat Inspection Act authorized federal authorities to see that meat shipped in interstate commerce came from healthy animals and was packed under sanitary conditions. This federal law was paralleled by the passage of state laws. Though enforcement of the new legislation was not always effective, the laws helped put an end to the worst practices.

(2) The second law was directed against the sale of "medicines" advertised as cures for everything from coughs to cancer. The Pure Food and Drugs Act prohibited the "manufacture, sale or transportation of adulterated or misbranded or poisonous . . . foods, drugs, medicines, and liquors." Medicines had to carry a label accurately describing the contents, and manufacturers of foods and drugs were prohibited from using any harmful substance. Enforcement of this law was up to Dr. Harvey W. Wiley, a distinguished government chemist. Wiley established laboratories to test products and sent inspectors to check on methods of preparing food and drugs throughout the country.

Roosevelt calls attention to the need for conservation. Still another area in which Theodore Roosevelt saw an urgent need for reform was conservation. As early as the 1870's, the American Association for the Advancement of Science had warned that Americans were destroying their forests and wasting their natural resources. Forests were cut down without replanting, and little was done to prevent forest fires. Oil and natural gas were allowed to gush out of the ground unused, and only the choice veins of coal, the least expensive to mine, were worked. In spite of the rising volume of protests, Congress took no action until 1891, when it authorized the President to withdraw timber lands from public sale. Benjamin Harrison then set aside thirteen million acres as national forest reserves. Cleveland and McKinley more than doubled this area during their administrations. But the national reserves were only a small part of the total forest land, and other conservation problems continued to be ignored.

Theodore Roosevelt's love of the outdoors and his genius for making himself heard led him to dramatize the urgent need for conservation. In a special message to Congress, he warned:

> . . . There must be the look ahead. . . . The mineral wealth of the country, the coal, iron, oil, gas, and the like, does not reproduce itself, and . . . wastefulness in dealing with it today means that our descendants will feel the exhaustion a generation or two before they otherwise would.

To give added emphasis to the problem, Roosevelt called a Conservation Conference which met at the White House in 1908. Those attending included governors, congressmen, Cabinet members, scientists, businessmen, and conservation experts. They discussed control of forest fires, waste in mining, and use of water resources for irrigation, power, and inland navigation. They urged the establishment of a National Conservation Commission as well as state commissions. Later, Roosevelt sponsored a second conference, which included representatives from Canada, Newfoundland, and Mexico, to discuss the conservation problems of all North America.

Roosevelt takes action to conserve natural resources. Despite growing public interest in conservation, Congress paid little attention to the President's request for effective laws. Congress even refused to appropriate 25,000 dollars for the expenses of the National Conservation Com-

Serious efforts at conservation began under President Theodore Roosevelt, shown above with the naturalist and explorer John Muir, who helped establish Yosemite National Park. Conservation includes the protection of wild animals and birds (above right, a migratory waterfowl refuge) and fire prevention (right, a bulldozer builds a fire line in a national forest).

mission. Roosevelt, however, took advantage of the Forest Reserve Act of 1891 to withdraw millions of acres of timber land. In 1907 Congress attached an amendment to an appropriation bill which prohibited the President from withdrawing any more land. Roosevelt acted in characteristic fashion. He withdrew all the remaining forests in the public domain and then signed the appropriation bill! By the end of his second term Roosevelt had added about 150 million acres to the national forests. In addition, he withdrew from public sale 80 million acres of coal lands, nearly 5 million acres of phosphate lands, and over a million acres bordering on water-power sites.

When the President urged the appropriation of funds for irrigation projects, he found greater support in Congress. In large areas of the Southwest, potentially fertile land was not being used because of insufficient rainfall. Western politicians, led by Representative Francis Newlands of Nevada, wanted the government to finance the irrigation of this land. Roosevelt backed these efforts and in 1902 signed the Newlands Reclamation Act. This measure provided that money from the sale of public lands in sixteen western states be put into a "reclamation fund" for financing irrigation projects. Money received from the sale of water to settlers on the irrigated lands would be put into the fund for the reclamation of still more land. During the next four years, 28 projects were started for the irrigation of three million acres.

An economic panic occurs at the end of Roosevelt's administration. Despite Roosevelt's many achievements, his presidency ended on a discouraging note. A sudden break in the stock market in 1907 was followed by the failure of a dozen New York banks and several railroads. A number of small businesses also went into bankruptcy, and thousands of workers suffered wage cuts or layoffs. The panic was caused, in part, by the inability of banks to extend credit when needed. Another cause was the large amount of overpriced stock issued by corporations and holding companies. Industrialists and bankers, however, were quick to blame the panic

on the administration's "trust-busting" activities. Workers and many progressives in turn charged that the panic resulted from mismanagement by the trusts and from deals made by powerful financiers.

Roosevelt was inclined to agree that "malefactors of great wealth" were responsible for the panic. He appointed a commission to investigate the banks and their credit facilities but took no decisive action. Because the panic was not followed by a long depression as several earlier panics had been, Roosevelt's popularity remained high with most people.

▶ CHECK-UP

1. What was Theodore Roosevelt's conception of the presidency? What was his attitude toward trusts? Toward the coal strike?

2. What reforms were brought about by the Elkins Act? The Hepburn Act? The Meat Inspection Act? The Pure Food and Drugs Act?

3. Why was Roosevelt especially interested in conservation? What steps did he take to conserve timber, coal, and phosphate? To encourage irrigation?

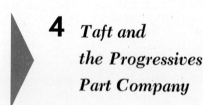

4 Taft and the Progressives Part Company

Roosevelt chooses his successor. As the election of 1908 approached, President Roosevelt felt that his two terms had been enough; and, in any case, he felt bound by his pledge not to accept another presidential nomination. He began to consider whom he should recommend to the Republican Party as a successor. Governor Charles Evans Hughes of New York had an outstanding record, but Secretary of State Elihu Root and Secretary of War William Howard Taft were much closer to Roosevelt. Though Root was able, his career as a corporation lawyer did not endear him to the reform wing of the party.

The President finally settled on William Howard Taft as his heir. Member of a prominent Cincinnati family, Taft had practiced law and had served as a prosecuting attorney and judge before distinguishing himself as the first governor of the Philippine Islands. In 1904 he had joined Roosevelt's Cabinet. Since Taft had had no part in domestic struggles, he was acceptable to both the reform and "Old Guard" factions of the Republican Party.

Roosevelt made sure of sufficient delegates at the 1908 convention to nominate Taft on the first ballot. The President also dictated the party platform, which praised his domestic and foreign policies and promised to continue them. Although Roosevelt was reluctant to spell out future reforms, the platform included several promises to attract the support of progressives. These included (1) currency reform, (2) further regulation of trusts and railroads, and (3) downward "revision of the tariff by a special session of Congress immediately following the inauguration of the next President."

Taft defeats Bryan. The Democrats, having suffered a resounding defeat in 1904 with a conservative candidate, turned again to William Jennings Bryan. The convention delegates nominated Bryan on the first ballot and then adopted a platform which promised far more than Roosevelt's Square Deal. The Democrats called for stronger antitrust laws and stricter enforcement, an income tax, the prohibition of injunctions in labor disputes, and drastic cuts in tariff rates.

In the election Taft received over a million votes more than his opponent and won a decisive margin in the electoral vote. Bryan carried the South, his home state of Nebraska, and also Nevada and Colorado.

Taft lacks Roosevelt's political skill. To be Roosevelt's successor was no easy task, and it was not entirely Taft's fault that he ran into difficulties. Roosevelt had whetted the appetite of the reformers without giving them all they wanted. Taft's unwillingness or inability to deliver everything the progressives desired soon led to a split between them and the conservative Republicans.

The new President's lack of political skill also widened the breach between these two factions. Unlike Roosevelt, he was incapable of dramatizing himself and his program. Taft was friendly, affable, and democratic, but he lived quietly and shunned the spotlight of publicity. Moreover, his judicial training and experience made him overly cautious, and he was reluctant to exercise powers not specifically granted the President by the Constitution or by legislation. Thus, Taft seemed indecisive and slow-moving by comparison with Roosevelt. Though an able administrator, he failed as a political leader to unify the factions within the Republican Party.

The Payne-Aldrich Tariff angers the progressives. As promised in the party's platform, President Taft called a special session of Congress to lower the tariff. The House quickly adopted a bill which reduced many rates and allowed some raw materials to come in duty-free. The Payne Bill then went to the Senate Finance Committee, whose chairman was Nelson W. Aldrich, a staunch conservative. This committee added nearly 850 amendments, most of which represented increases. Thus, instead of providing for a general reduction from the levels of the Dingley Act (page 526), the resulting bill actually increased rates.

President Taft was tactless in his handling of the tariff bill. At first he criticized the Senate's changes in the Payne Bill and encouraged the progressives to fight them. The progressive senators waged a stiff battle against every rate increase. These efforts naturally slowed up passage of the tariff measure in the Senate. When Taft, disturbed by this delay, began calling the progressives "demagogues," they understandably were outraged.

As finally passed in 1909, the Payne-Aldrich Tariff kept most of the Aldrich increases and provided an average rate slightly higher than the Dingley Act. Instead of letting the bill become law without his signature, Taft signed it. Then, speaking before an audience in Minnesota, the President said the Payne-Aldrich Tariff was "the best tariff bill that the Republican

William Howard Taft, shown here campaigning, was known for his good nature and large size. He was the only President also to serve as Chief Justice.

Party has ever passed, and therefore the best that has been passed at all."

The progressives challenge Taft's conservation policies. Controversy over the tariff had no sooner died down than Taft tangled with the progressives on conservation policy. Taft's Secretary of the Interior, Richard A. Ballinger, refused to withdraw from sale certain public lands valuable for their water power. When Ballinger claimed that the President's authority extended only to timber lands, Taft seemed to agree. Gifford Pinchot, who had been appointed Chief Forester by Roosevelt, thought that Ballinger and Taft were reversing Roosevelt's whole conservation effort. Moreover, he accused Ballinger of permitting valuable coal lands in Alaska to fall into private hands. After investigating the case, Taft fired Pinchot and thus widened the split between progressive and Old Guard Republicans.

Actually Taft was a firm believer in conservation. Because he questioned whether Roosevelt had possessed legal authority to withdraw from sale anything but timber lands, he persuaded Congress to give the President greater authority. By the end of Taft's administration nearly 59 million additional· acres of coal lands had been withdrawn from sale. In addition, Taft signed legislation permitting the government to buy over a million acres of land in the White Mountains and the southern Appalachians.

The Speaker of the House is deprived of power. The differences between progressive and conservative Republicans continued to grow sharper. This seemed particularly true in the House of Representatives, where the Speaker had almost dictatorial powers. The Speaker appointed all committees. He was himself chairman of the powerful Rules Committee, which determined procedure in the House and also decided its order of business. As the presiding officer of the House during debate, moreover, the Speaker could muzzle opposition by refusing to recognize members seeking the floor. At this time the Speaker was Joseph G. Cannon of Illinois, a member of the conservative faction of the Republican Party. The progressives accused Cannon of using his tremendous power as Speaker to keep them off committees, prevent them from speaking, and bury their measures in the Rules Committee.

In 1910, Representative George W. Norris of Nebraska proposed an amendment to the House rules. It provided that members of the Rules Committee be elected by the entire House. Speaker Cannon ruled the motion out of order, but after an all-night debate the progressive Republicans, joined by Democrats, overruled his decision and passed the amendment. In the following year all House committees were made elective. The Speaker was thus stripped of his control over House committees, including the powerful Rules Committee. During this bitter contest in the House, Taft once again failed to take a clear-cut stand. Although actually he felt that the Speaker was using his power unwisely, the President gave the impression of siding with Cannon. Thus Taft further infuriated the progressives.

Progressives make gains in the 1910 elections. When Theodore Roosevelt left the White House in March, 1909, he had traveled to Africa to hunt big game. It was not long before the progressives were writing to him about Taft's "treachery." Pinchot actually crossed the ocean to tell his former chief about the conservation quarrel. Even President Taft sent a pathetic note to Roosevelt, saying: "I have had a hard time. I have been conscientiously trying to carry out your policies, but my method of doing so has not worked smoothly."

At first Roosevelt refrained from giving advice to his successor or siding with the progressives. In the 1910 congressional elections, however, he made a number of speeches supporting progressive candidates and outlining a reform program that went far beyond anything Taft had proposed. Progressive candidates in both parties did well in the 1910 elections, while many of the Old Guard Republicans went down to defeat. So many Democrats were elected that they won control of the House of Representatives for the first time since 1892. Because President Taft had given strong support to conservative candidates, the election climaxed the misunderstanding between himself and the progressives. It also marked the beginning of a breach between Taft and Roosevelt.

Taft continues "trust-busting." Though Taft was losing the confidence of the progressives, he continued to support a program of reform. He was firmly convinced, for example, that the government should regulate giant industrial combinations and prosecute those violating the Sherman Act. Taft's Attorney General started nearly twice as many antitrust suits in four years as had been begun during Roosevelt's seven and a half years. In addition, Taft pushed to conclusion the cases which Roosevelt had started against the Standard Oil Company and the American Tobacco Company. In 1911 the Supreme Court ruled that both combinations violated the Sherman Act and had to be dissolved.

The "rule of reason" distinguishes between legal and illegal combinations. In the decisions affecting Standard Oil and American Tobacco, the Court laid down an important principle — the "rule of reason."

During Taft's presidency the government added the delivery of parcels to its postal service. Above, a Washington, D.C., mail truck was photographed on the first day of parcel post service in 1913. The number of packages handled by the Post Office has increased tremendously. Right, postal employees now use automated equipment to sort the flood of parcels.

The Court said this rule should be applied in judging business combinations. By the rule of reason, only those combinations were illegal which were "unreasonable" and "which would constitute an interference that is an undue restraint" of trade. Nine years later the Supreme Court went even further. It refused to dissolve the United States Steel Corporation, declaring that this company had not used unfair methods of competition and that *size alone* was no reason for dissolving a corporation.

Taft secures the enactment of progressive measures. In addition to the attack on big business, a number of progressive measures were enacted during Taft's administration. For one thing, the Interstate Commerce Commission's authority was extended to include telephone, telegraph, and cable companies. The Commission was empowered to examine the books of all companies under its authority and to set rates based on the true value of the company. Furthermore, the government provided postal savings banks at every post office, something the Populists had suggested in the 1890's. Over the protests of the private express companies, the government also established a parcel post service. The Sixteenth Amendment, authorizing the government to tax incomes, went into effect in 1913.

In addition, Taft permitted the federal government to take a more direct part in efforts to improve social conditions. He created a separate Department of Labor and established a Bureau of Mines to promote the health and welfare of miners. Creation of the federal Children's Bureau was hailed by persons seeking to ban child labor. Taft also signed a law limiting to eight hours the working day of all employees of the national government.

Other reforms during the Taft administration fulfilled Populist and progressive demands for honesty in government and increased power in the hands of voters. Civil-service laws were revised to cover many more employees. Another measure required publication of the names of persons who contributed to campaign funds in federal elections.

As Taft's administration drew to a close,

progressives were at odds with conservatives in both parties. Yet, in the years since McKinley's assassination, the Progressive Movement had won enthusiastic support from the American people. It had produced far-reaching reforms in city, state, and federal government. And it had convinced large numbers of both Democrats and Republicans that the government must protect the interests of citizens.

▶ CHECK-UP

1. Why did the Republicans nominate Taft in 1908? What future reforms did the Party's platform call for? How did Taft's views, personality, and lack of political skill create problems for the Republicans? (Consider the tariff and conservation issues.) How was the Speaker of the House stripped of his great power?

2. How did the "rule of reason" provide a basis for determining whether or not business combinations were illegal?

3. What important progressive legislation was enacted during Taft's administration?

• • • • • • • • • • • • • • • • • • • •

Clinching the Main Ideas in Chapter 26

The Progressive Movement borrowed freely from the reform movements of the post-Civil War years, particularly the Populist revolt of the 1890's. Unlike the Populist crusade, however, the Progressive Movement found its main support among urban middle-class Americans. Since the reform spirit spread into both major political parties, progressivism was a bipartisan movement.

The goals of the progressives were improvement of social conditions and more efficient democratic government. In the cities they introduced new forms of government and broadened the responsibilities of city administration. To make state government more responsive to the voters, the progressives introduced the initiative, referendum, and recall; direct primaries for selecting candidates; and the direct election of senators. Moreover, they prodded the state legislatures to pass laws establishing maximum hours and minimum wages and prohibiting child labor.

Progressive reform at the national level was launched by Theodore Roosevelt. The progressives hailed his attack on the trusts, regulation of the railroads, settling of the coal strike, and concern with conservation.

His successor, William Howard Taft, generally continued these policies. But Taft lost the progressives' support when he failed to take a clear-cut position on their side. Consequently, as Taft's term drew to a close, the progressives prepared for a showdown fight with the Republican Old Guard in the 1912 national convention.

Chapter Review

Terms to Understand

1. "rule of reason"
2. IWW
3. initiative
4. referendum
5. recall
6. Square Deal
7. muckraking
8. city manager
9. direct primary
10. Hepburn Act
11. Pure Food and Drugs Act
12. House Rules Committee
13. Old Guard Republican
14. Newlands Reclamation Act
15. Progressive Movement
16. commission government
17. social-welfare laws
18. Payne-Aldrich Tariff
19. Meat Inspection Act

What Do You Think?

1. Why did the growth of trusts become a major issue around 1900?

2. Why were Americans little concerned about conservation problems during the first century after independence?

3. "One of the elements of Roosevelt's greatness as chief executive was that he responded to the challenge of the times." Do you agree? Explain and illustrate.

4. Eugene V. Debs hoped to introduce socialism through the enactment of reform legislation in Congress and the state legislatures. Contrast his views and methods with those used by the Russian Bolshevik leader Lenin.

5. Why is it important that citizens vote in primary elections?

Using Your Knowledge of History

1. Read the text under the heading "Roosevelt settles a coal strike" (page 558). Have a committee report on these points: (a) What did the miners demand? (b) What was the reaction of the mine-owners? (c) What was the reaction of the general public? (d) Evaluate Baer's statement. (e) Evaluate the steps taken by the President.

2. Prepare a report on "The Roots of the Progressive Movement." Bring out the ideas the Progressives derived from each "root."

3. Does your state have a direct primary? Initiative? Referendum? Recall? Try to find out the extent to which these have been used in your state and how citizens generally feel about them.

Extending Your Knowledge of History

Richard Hofstadter provides an interesting interpretation in *The Age of Reform.* George Mowry writes about the Roosevelt and Taft administrations in *Theodore Roosevelt and the Progressive Movement.* H. F. Pringle's biography, *Theodore Roosevelt,* is more objective than Roosevelt's lively *Autobiography.* Louis Filler in *Crusaders for American Liberalism* provides biographical sketches of some progressives. *William Allen White's America,* edited by Walter Johnson, provides a broad view of this period. In *American Heritage* see "Jones vs. Jones," based on a book by William G. McLaughlin (April, 1961), on the Toledo reform mayor; "Bryan" (December, 1961) and "La Follette: The Promise Unfulfilled" (April, 1962), both by John A. Garraty; "The Coal Kings Come to Judgment" by Robert L. Reynolds (April, 1960) on the anthracite coal strike; and "A Lion in the Streets" by John A. Garraty (June, 1957) on J. P. Morgan and the panic of 1907.

CHAPTER 27

Federal Reserve Building,
Washington, D.C.

Wilson's First Administration Climaxes Domestic Reform

America stands for opportunity, America stands for a free field and no favor, America stands for a government responsible to the interests of all.

WOODROW WILSON, 1912

1912–1917

The Progressive Movement, having made gains under two Republican Presidents, continued after 1912 under the leadership of a Democrat. The rift between the two wings of the Republican Party had grown sharper as the presidential election of 1912 drew near. When the Republican convention, controlled by Taft and the conservative Republicans, ignored the demands of the reform group, the progressive Republican delegates organized a new party and nominated Theodore Roosevelt for President. Thus the contest became a three-cornered fight, involving Taft, Roosevelt, and a progressive Democratic candidate, Woodrow Wilson. The outcome was a victory for reform. Wilson won the presidency, and the Democrats received substantial majorities in Congress.

Woodrow Wilson's first term marked the climax of the progressive reform movement. Under his leadership, tariff, banking, and currency reforms were enacted; and effective antitrust laws were adopted. Congress also passed a host of other measures to "promote the general welfare." By 1916, most of the progressive demands had been fulfilled. Though not all reformers were completely satisfied, most of them believed that the Progressive Movement had helped to create "a government responsible to the interests of all."

1 *The Democrats Win in 1912*

The reform Republicans organize. Progressive Republicans, as we learned in the previous chapter, had considerable success in the congressional elections of 1910. Encouraged by these gains, they were determined to have the Republican Party nominate a progressive candidate in the next presidential contest. Early in 1911, therefore, they organized the National Progressive Republican League. Its purpose was to promote more reform legislation and to boost Robert M. La Follette as a candidate for President. Members of the League hoped to convince other Republicans that La Follette's "experience, his character, his courage, his record in constructive legislation, [and] his administrative ability meet the requirements of leadership."

Following his return from Africa, Theodore Roosevelt said nothing about running for a third term. Many observers suspected that he wanted to return to the White House, but any move in this direction would have violated his "no third term" pledge. Further, it would have been regarded as an insult to President Taft and would have dealt a serious blow to La Follette's hopes. Throughout 1911, Roosevelt maintained his silence. La Follette claimed he had an agreement with Roosevelt — though Roosevelt later denied it — that the former President would not be a candidate in 1912. On the basis of this assurance, La Follette began his campaign for the Republican nomination late in

1911. Strongly supported by the National Progressive Republican League, La Follette delivered a series of speeches in which he called for tariff reduction, stronger antitrust laws, and a federal commission to regulate business.

Theodore Roosevelt becomes a candidate. Early in 1912, Theodore Roosevelt changed his mind. His admirers had long pressed him to declare himself a candidate, and many progressives who respected La Follette nevertheless felt that Roosevelt would be a far stronger candidate. They supported La Follette until early February when, tired and ill, he delivered a rambling and ineffective speech. Many progressives took this occasion to switch their allegiance from the Wisconsin senator to the former President.

At Roosevelt's request, seven Republican governors sent him public letters asking him to declare his candidacy. Before Roosevelt answered, Taft slightingly referred to the progressive leaders as "political emotionalists." The Rough Rider's fighting spirit was aroused, and on February 24 he announced, "My hat is in the ring." La Follette's support melted away, and most of the Republican progressives closed ranks behind their former leader.

The Republican convention renominates President Taft. A struggle for delegates to the Republican convention started immediately. In the states which had direct presidential primaries, voters generally elected delegates who favored Roosevelt. In other states, the delegates were selected by the Republican Party organization, which was controlled by President Taft.

When the convention met at Chicago in June, the seats of about 250 delegates were contested. Taft's friends controlled the convention, and in settling the contests they seated only nineteen progressive delegates. When the Roosevelt delegates found themselves clearly in the minority, they refused to take any further part in the convention. The remaining delegates nominated Taft on the first ballot and drew up a party platform praising his administration for its constructive legislation. Nevertheless, the conservative Republicans were

. . . .

CHAPTER FOCUS

1. The Democrats win in 1912.

2. Wilson secures tariff, banking, and antitrust reforms.

3. The Progressive Era draws to a close.

A 1912 cartoon, titled "Trouble Ahead," showed President Taft and his Vice-President about to collide with the "Bull Moose" candidates, Theodore Roosevelt and Hiram Johnson. The election result was defeat for both sets of candidates.

in a gloomy mood. They realized that a split in the Republican Party would give the Democrats an excellent chance to elect the next President. One conservative grumbled, "The only question now is which corpse gets the most flowers."

The Progressive Party nominates Roosevelt. Outside the convention hall Roosevelt had assured his delegates that he was willing to run on an independent ticket and suggested the formation of a Progressive Party. The progressive delegates enthusiastically plunged into the work of organizing another convention, also to meet in Chicago.

The progressives assembled in an atmosphere of frenzied excitement. Most of the delegates were middle-class urban reformers or progressive politicians, with a sprinkling of wealthy businessmen. Missing from the convention were La Follette and his small band of followers. But the delegates were all enthusiastic Roosevelt fans and paid little attention to La Follette's absence. They roared their approval when Roosevelt told them: "We battle for the Lord." The convention responded to his speech with a rousing version of "Onward, Christian Soldiers."

The delegates nominated Roosevelt for the presidency and Hiram Johnson of Cali-

fornia for the vice-presidency. In its platform, the Progressive Party endorsed Roosevelt's Square Deal and called for still other reform measures. The platform supported changes which would give voters greater control of the government — direct primaries, the initiative, referendum, and recall, woman suffrage, and a swifter method of amending the Constitution. It also promised lower tariff rates, regulation of business combinations, conservation of natural resources, and such measures as minimum-wage laws, prohibition of child labor, social insurance, and an eight-hour work day.

The Democratic convention chooses Woodrow Wilson. The Democrats held their convention in Baltimore during the interval between the Republican and Progressive Party conventions. Democratic leaders realized that the Republican split improved the chances of a Democratic victory. A number of candidates, therefore, wanted the presidential nomination. William Jennings Bryan was not a candidate, but he controlled a number of western delegates and wanted to see a reform Democrat head the ticket. Governor Woodrow Wilson of New Jersey was the strongest progressive candidate, while most conservative Democrats favored "Champ"

Clark of Missouri, Speaker of the House of Representatives. Clark led in the early balloting but failed to win the necessary two thirds of the delegates. When Bryan threw his support to Wilson, other delegates jumped on the band wagon, and the New Jersey Governor was finally nominated on the forty-sixth ballot. The Democratic platform, though less detailed than that of the Progressive Party, was similar in tone. It called for a reduction in tariff rates, stricter antitrust legislation, banking and currency reform, publicity for campaign contributions, and conservation.

The campaign is dramatic. The 1912 election aroused more than usual interest. The quarrel between Roosevelt and Taft fascinated the voters, who eagerly awaited each exchange of insults. But Taft acted like a defeated candidate even before the campaign was well under way. The long-time Roosevelt supporters, on the other hand, were fired to even greater enthusiasm by the Progressive crusade. To the Republican elephant and the Democratic donkey was added the Bull Moose, symbol of the Progressives.[1] Roosevelt campaigned with his usual zest. He even insisted on delivering a speech in Milwaukee after he had been shot, but not seriously wounded, by a fanatic in the crowd. The real contest lay between Roosevelt and Woodrow Wilson. Wilson's eloquence surprised the voters. They found him well-informed, convincing, and self-confident.

While Wilson and Roosevelt differed sharply in personality, their party platforms were similar, each calling for progressive reforms. The greatest difference between them lay in their attitude toward the trusts. Roosevelt favored stricter regulation of the trusts; but nothing would be gained, he warned, "by breaking up a huge industrial organization *which has not offended otherwise than by its size.*" Wilson's campaign program, called the "New Freedom," emphasized "trust-busting" more than trust regulation. Wilson believed that the large trusts were a threat to democracy and a menace to small businessmen. He thought stricter antitrust laws should be passed to allow the courts to break up all large combinations. "If America is not to have free enterprise," said Wilson, "then she can have freedom of no sort whatever."

Wilson wins the election. Because of the split in the Republican Party, Wilson won a clear-cut victory. Taft gathered 8 electoral votes from two states, and Roosevelt won 88 electoral votes from six states. Wilson carried all the remaining states, with a total of 435 electoral votes. The Socialist Eugene Debs polled almost a million votes but won no electoral votes.

Though Wilson received less than half of the popular vote, he ran well in all sections of the country and had a united party behind him. The Democrats kept control of the House and won a majority of the seats in the Senate. Moreover, Wilson would be able to count on progressive Republicans in Congress to help enact the New Freedom program into law.

▶ CHECK-UP

1. Why did Roosevelt come to seek nomination for President in 1912? How was his nomination blocked in the Republican convention? What reforms were demanded in the Progressive Party's platform?

2. How did Wilson win the Democratic nomination? What reforms were called for in the Democratic platform? What was the outcome of the election?

. . . .

2 *Wilson Secures Tariff, Banking, and Antitrust Reforms*

---

[1] As early as 1900, Roosevelt had said in a letter to Mark Hanna, "I am as strong as a bull moose"; and he continued to use the term to describe a vigorous person.

Wilson exercises strong leadership. Woodrow Wilson entered the White House with clear ideas about the presidency. Although he believed in the constitutional principle of separation of powers among the three branches of government, Wilson intended to exert presidential leadership over Congress. He considered it his obligation to carry out the New Freedom program which the voters had approved in the election. Thus, in his messages to Congress he gave detailed recommendations for the passage of laws and then made skillful use of his power and influence as President to insure congressional action. Within months after the inauguration, observers noted with amazement that the new President was leading Congress "like a schoolmaster."

Wilson also established complete control over his Cabinet. When he named Bryan Secretary of State, many people expected the former party leader to dominate the Cabinet. But the President kept tight control over foreign policy, and when he and Bryan eventually disagreed, a new Secretary was appointed. Many patronage matters were left to Albert Burleson, Postmaster General, though Wilson kept an eye on this aspect of the administration, too. The President's closest adviser was Colonel Edward House, who declined a Cabinet position but worked efficiently behind the scenes.

Wilson asks for tariff revision. The first step in Wilson's program was to seek a reduction in tariff rates. By 1913 many Republicans as well as Democrats were convinced that excessively high tariffs were partly responsible for the increased cost of living. A month after he became President, Wilson went before a special session of Congress to read his tariff message in person. He was the first President to do this since Jefferson had established the custom of sending messages to Congress.

Representative Oscar Underwood introduced a bill to carry out the President's recommendations. The House quickly approved this bill's moderate cuts as well as a provision for an income tax. When the measure reached the Senate, however, the lobbyists for special interests prepared to amend it into another high-tariff act. Fearing that the bill would meet the same fate as most other tariff bills since the Civil War, President Wilson took an unusual step. He publicly denounced the "industrious and insidious" lobbyists at work in Washington and warned that they were trying "to overcome the interests of the public for their private profit." A Senate investigation then showed that many senators favoring high tariffs on steel, sugar, wool, and copper were large stockholders in industries dealing with these materials.

The Underwood Tariff is passed. Debate on the tariff continued throughout the summer, but by October, 1913, the Underwood Tariff Act had been approved by Congress and signed by the President. The free list was enlarged to include sugar, wool, iron ore, meats, agricultural implements, and other items. Altogether there were nearly 1000 cuts in tariff rates and fewer than 90 increases.

Lobbies

"Lobbies," or special interest groups, take their name from the lobbies or waiting rooms of Congress and the state legislatures. Here may be found pressure groups — lobbyists — who represent such special interests as industrial and business groups, farmers, workers, or veterans. The lobbyists put pressure on the lawmakers to act favorably in behalf of the special interests. Before the Seventeenth Amendment provided for the direct election of senators, many lawmakers were themselves active lobbyists for special interests.

The different lobbies use various tactics of persuasion, ranging from honest appeals for help to, in some cases, bribery or fraud. Lobbying in itself is not evil. In a democratic society, citizens have every right to express their needs and wishes to the government. It is true that most interest groups ask for concessions at the expense of others. But a wise legislature weighs the claims of conflicting groups in a situation of this kind and comes up with a compromise solution that is consistent with the general public interest.

(Continued on page 574)

Woodrow Wilson

[1856–1924]

A native of Virginia, Woodrow Wilson was educated at Princeton and the University of Virginia law school. He practiced law for a short time in Atlanta, Georgia, before enrolling in Johns Hopkins University where he earned a Ph.D. in political science. In 1890 he returned to Princeton as Professor of Jurisprudence and Politics. A stimulating teacher, Wilson became President of the university in 1902. Wilson's ability, sincerity, and high ideals enabled him to introduce drastic changes in the university's pattern of education. He raised academic standards, brought first-rate teachers to the campus, and established the tutorial system of instruction. But he ran into opposition in seeking to effect other changes. Refusing to compromise, Wilson resigned to run for the governorship of New Jersey.

George Harvey, the influential editor of *Harper's Weekly*, had urged Democratic politicians to run a candidate of Wilson's caliber if they wanted to win the governorship. They reluctantly agreed, and Wilson was elected in 1910. As governor, he surprised many observers by moving away from an earlier political conservatism to back progressive reforms. He persuaded the state legislature to pass a primary law, establish workmen's compensation, regulate public utilities companies, and permit cities to establish the commission form of government.

These spectacular successes brought Wilson to the attention of national Democratic leaders and helped him win the presidential nomination and election in 1912.

Wilson's eight years in the White House curiously paralleled his eight years as president of Princeton. In his first administration he scored one success after another—tariff reduction, banking reform, and regulation of the trusts. But during the second term, his refusal to compromise on the Treaty of Versailles led to bitter conflict with senators opposed to the Treaty. Wilson's valiant attempt to carry his case to the people in 1919 ended in a physical breakdown.

To many people Woodrow Wilson seemed aloof and withdrawn. Only the President's family and a few of his close associates knew the warmly responsive side of his complex personality. Yet Wilson's idealism and eloquence inspired millions of people all over the world who shared his hopes for a just and lasting peace. Every Armistice Day a crowd gathered outside his home in Washington to hear the ailing former President restate his belief that someday the United States would join the League of Nations. Thus, Woodrow Wilson can be considered the spiritual father of the United Nations, in addition to his roles as a successful initiator of domestic reforms and leader of the nation in World War I.

To make up for the loss in revenue, the Underwood Tariff increased rates on luxury items. But the most important source of new revenue was a personal income tax, which had been legalized by the Sixteenth Amendment (page 566). This tax was to be graduated so that persons with higher incomes paid at a higher rate. It began at 1 per cent on incomes of 3000 dollars and rose to 6 per cent on incomes over 500,000 dollars.

The effects of this first real tariff revision since the Civil War were never adequately tested. Soon after the new rates went into effect, World War I broke out in Europe, thus upsetting normal conditions of international trade. Nevertheless, the Underwood Act was an important victory for the President, who had shrewdly made use of public opinion to secure the enactment of this essential part of the New Freedom. Moreover, the act marked the beginning of the modern income tax, which eventually became a far more important source of revenue for the federal government than the tariff.

Banking and currency reform is needed. Another important part of Wilson's program had to do with banking and currency. The financial panic of 1907 (page 562) had made clear the need for a more flexible system of credit and transfer of currency. A number of sound banks had failed simply because they could not quickly change their assets into currency to meet the heavy demands of depositors wanting to draw out funds.[2] Besides, there was no way to transfer currency from a bank with adequate resources to one which needed temporary relief during a "run" by its depositors. The national banks could offer little help. The volume of notes or paper money which they could issue depended on the number of government bonds they owned (page 368). During times of prosperity and industrial growth,

when more currency was needed, the high price of bonds kept the banks from purchasing more bonds.

To enable banks to cope with sudden demands for currency, Congress in 1908 had passed the Aldrich-Vreeland Act. This measure allowed national banks, in time of need, to issue a limited amount of bank notes based on certain other securities than United States bonds. But the need for a thorough reform of the banking and currency system remained.

Two different approaches are suggested. In 1912 a report was submitted by the commission which President Roosevelt had appointed to study banking and credit facilities (page 562). It recommended the establishment of a central reserve bank with branches in the major cities. The bankers would control the entire system, and the government would have nothing to do with its operation. This practically amounted to restoring Hamilton's Bank of the United States (page 166), with control vested in the hands of private bankers. Most Democrats and Progressives, however, favored a decentralized system of reserve banks, to be supervised in some fashion by the federal government. They feared that control of the reserve banks by the bankers themselves would increase the power of the "money trust." Hence they argued for government representation on the board that would control the reserve banks.

The Federal Reserve Act is passed. Under the guidance of Representative Carter Glass of Virginia, a bill was proposed which would create reserve banks but leave control of them to private bankers. The progressives in Congress threatened to vote against this measure unless it were drastically amended; and, after careful study, Wilson decided that the Glass bill had to be changed. Going before Congress, he told its members: "The control of the system of banking . . . must be public, not private, must be vested in the Government itself, so that the banks may be the instruments, not the masters, of business and of individual enterprise and initiative." The progressive Republicans and Democrats had a stiff fight against the Repub-

---

[2] Banks make profits by lending money deposited with them. The notes received for these loans, and other property which the banks own, are known as assets. No bank has on hand, at any given moment, sufficient funds to pay back all of its depositors. A "run" on a bank develops when a large number of depositors become panicky and demand their money immediately.

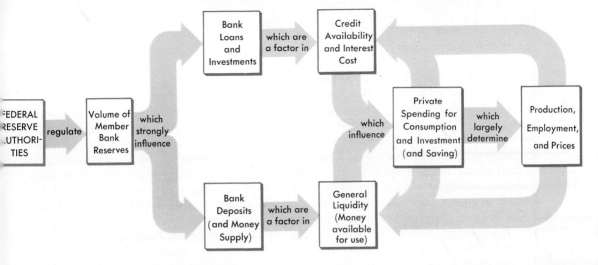

HOW THE FEDERAL RESERVE WORKS

This chart shows, in a simplified way, how actions taken by the Federal Reserve authorities influence total spending and thereby also affect employment, production, and prices.

lican Old Guard, but finally a bill providing for government control of reserve banks was passed in December, 1913.

By the terms of the Federal Reserve Act, the country was divided into twelve districts, each with a Federal Reserve Bank. The Federal Reserve Banks were bankers' banks, serving only member banks in their particular districts. Every national bank was required to join the system, and state banks were urged to do so. Each of the twelve Federal Reserve Banks had its own board of directors. The whole system was directed by a central Federal Reserve Board, composed of the Secretary of the Treasury, the Comptroller of the Currency, and six others appointed by the President.[3] The new law also provided for a new kind of currency, Federal Reserve notes.

The Federal Reserve System works well. When the Federal Reserve Act was passed in 1913, many private bankers and conservative Republicans were disturbed. They called the new system a dangerous "political bank" and a "communistic idea." Within a few years, however, even the bitterest foes of the Federal Reserve System had to admit that it was working well. The country's currency was much more

[3] The Secretary of the Treasury and the Comptroller were removed from the Board by the Banking Act of 1935.

flexible; that is, it could be expanded or contracted to meet changing conditions. During the financial strains of World War I, the reserve proved its ability to provide a flexible currency and greater stability for the banking structure of the country.

The Federal Reserve System controls credit. Under the new Federal Reserve System, ways of regulating credit were worked out to prevent rapid inflation or deflation, that is, a sharp decline or rise in the purchasing power of the dollar.

Each member bank was required to maintain a reserve account in its Federal Reserve Bank. The amount of this reserve, figured as a percentage of the member bank's deposits, was determined by the Federal Reserve System. The higher the reserve requirement, the less credit money the member banks would have available to lend customers. Thus, the reserve requirement could be used as a brake on lending in the event of dangerous inflation. When a member bank exhausted its supply of credit money, it could turn to the Federal Reserve Bank and ask for a loan. As security the member bank could offer *promissory notes* (promises of repayment with interest) signed by customers who had borrowed money from it, or it could give its own note. When the Federal Reserve Bank *rediscounts* (lends money on) the paper offered as security by the member bank, it charges interest on the loan. By raising or lowering the interest charged member banks on loans of this kind, the Federal Reserve System discourages or encourages business expansion. If a member bank cannot make money by re-discounting its paper and paying interest to the Federal Reserve Bank, it will either lend less money or charge higher interest (which in turn discourages borrowing).

The Federal Reserve Board can also re-quire its regional banks to rediscount notes for each other. As a result, funds that are not immediately needed in one section of the country can be transferred to another where there are pressing demands for credit.

Wilson considers new weapons to control trusts. Stricter control of the trusts was another important goal of Wilson's New Freedom. During the campaign of 1912 he had urged the adoption of anti-trust laws that would clearly define what business could and could not do. Theodore Roosevelt, on the other hand, had favored the establishment of a commission to police and advise the trusts; he had felt that additional laws were unnecessary. By 1914 it was clear to Wilson and his ad-visers, and to much of the general public, that not all big business was bad. Some combinations resulted in lower costs of production or in more efficient transportation and communication, which in turn

benefited all Americans. The real question, therefore, was how to eliminate unfair monopolies.

Finally, President Wilson decided that two steps were necessary. The first was to enact a new antitrust law which would clarify the Sherman Act by defining unfair practices. The second was to create a new regulatory commission to supervise corporations. These two steps embodied both Wilson's and Roosevelt's ideas on the control of trusts.

The Clayton Antitrust Act defines unfair business practices. The Clayton Antitrust Act (1914) was essentially an amendment to the Sherman Act. It plugged the loopholes in the earlier law and clearly defined illegal practices. The following were the most important provisions of the act:

(1) Price discrimination which would "lessen competition or tend to create a monopoly" was declared unlawful.

(2) A corporation was not allowed to acquire the stock of another company for the purpose of creating a monopoly.

(3) Interlocking directorates[4] were made illegal for the larger banks and for industrial corporations capitalized at a million dollars or over, which were or had been competitors.

The Federal Trade Commission is established. To carry out the second step

[4] In interlocking directorates the same men act as directors of different business organizations.

A continuing problem in recent American history is represented by this cartoon. To what extent should government interfere with banks and other business; to what extent should banks and other business interfere in government?

of Wilson's plan, Congress created the Federal Trade Commission in 1914. This commission was authorized to advise and regulate corporations carrying on interstate or foreign commerce. Composed of five members appointed by the President, it replaced Roosevelt's Bureau of Corporations (page 558). The Federal Trade Commission could order a corporation to stop unfair methods of competition. If the order was not obeyed, the Commission could apply to a court for aid in enforcing the ruling.

The Federal Trade Commission was supposed to bring the knowledge and advice of economic experts to the aid of both corporations and the courts. Businessmen were urged to consult the Commission if they had doubts about the legality of certain practices. And if Commission members found evidence that a trust was violating the law, they first consulted with the trust officers. If the violation continued, however, the Commission issued "cease and desist" orders. Only when a trust ignored the Commission's order was the case referred to the Attorney General for prosecution in federal courts. During Wilson's administration nearly 400 "cease and desist" orders were issued and most of them were obeyed. As a result, the number of antitrust cases that came into the courts was reduced.

Labor benefits from the Clayton Act. The Clayton Act not only laid down rules for corporations but also contained clauses favorable to organized labor. Ever since the Debs case (page 481), the courts had held that the Sherman Act applied to labor unions. An example was the Danbury Hatters Case. In 1902 the United Hatters of North America had called a strike against a hatmaker in Danbury, Connecticut, and declared a nation-wide boycott of his articles. The company promptly sued the union for damages under the Sherman Act, and in 1908 the Supreme Court upheld the claim. The boycott was declared a "conspiracy in restraint of trade."

Many progressives agreed with labor leaders that a union was not the same as a corporation and should not be prosecuted under the Sherman Act. The Clayton Act endorsed this belief by exempting labor unions from antitrust laws on the ground that "the labor of a human being is not a commodity or article of commerce." The act also permitted peaceful strikes and boycotts and prohibited the granting of an injunction in any industrial dispute "unless necessary to prevent irreparable injury to property."

Samuel Gompers and the American Federation of Labor hailed the Clayton Act as "labor's Magna Carta." Later, however, it proved a disappointment to labor. During the 1920's, courts interpreted the act in such a way that injunctions continued to be used to break up strikes.

▶ CHECK-UP

1. How was Wilson able to get Congress to enact the reforms of the New Freedom program? What changes were made in the tariff? Why was an income tax law passed?

2. Explain why the banks needed a more flexible system of credit and transfer of currency. How does the Federal Reserve System meet this need?

3. What were the important provisions of the Clayton Antitrust Act? Why was the Federal Trade Commission established? How does it operate? What provisions in the Clayton Act were intended to help labor?

. . . .

3 *The Progressive Era Draws to a Close*

The progressives call for still more legislation. After signing the Underwood Tariff Act, the Federal Reserve Act, the Federal Trade Commission Act, and the Clayton Antitrust Act, Wilson felt he had fulfilled his commitment to the voters. Toward the end of 1914 he stated that the New Freedom was "complete" and intimated to business leaders that there would be no more regulatory legislation. Moreover, national rivalries had plunged Europe into World War I, and the President was

The county agents of the Department of Agriculture play an important role in the nation's farm areas. For over 50 years these agents have advised farmers about crops (top left, in 1919) and helped them plan the best use of land (above, in a recent year). County agents also work with 4-H Clubs. Left, an agent explains to 4-H boys what "points" to look for in good stock.

finding it necessary to give more and more attention to foreign affairs.

The progressives, however, had little interest in the distant war, nor did they share the President's satisfaction with conditions at home. While they approved of the legislation that had been enacted, some wanted still stricter provisions in the Clayton Act. Most progressives also thought the federal government should regulate child labor and set minimum wages and maximum hours for workers. Moreover, they were not happy about the President's appointments to the Federal Reserve Board and the Federal Trade Commission. The progressives complained that members of these regulatory bodies were former bankers and businessmen having ties with the very organizations they were supposed to be policing.

As the next presidential election drew near, Wilson changed his attitude about additional progressive measures. One reason was that the Democrats had suffered some losses in the congressional elections of 1914. To win re-election in 1916, Wilson knew he would need not only to hold the Democratic vote but also to gain the support of many Progressive Republicans. As a result, during 1915 and 1916, Wilson backed a wide variety of reform legislation that satisfied the progressives in both parties.

Farm legislation is passed. During the fight over the Federal Reserve Act, Wilson had promised western progressives a bill that would make it easier for farmers to borrow money. The Federal Farm Loan Act (1916) fulfilled this promise. It established twelve federal land banks to finance loans for farmers through co-operative loan associations. Farmers could borrow up to 50 per cent of the value of their land and 20 per cent of the value of permanent improvements at an interest rate no higher than 6 per cent. This plan enabled farmers to borrow money at a much lower rate than they could from private bankers. The fact that loans could be repaid over a period of 33 years was another advantage.

Two other laws extended the educational activities of the Department of Agriculture. During Theodore Roosevelt's administration the department had sent agents into southern states to help farmers fight the boll weevil, which was destroying cotton plants. This *extension service* proved so successful that in 1914 Congress established it on a permanent basis by passing the Smith-Lever Act. This measure provided that an agent of the extension service should be placed in each rural county to help and advise farmers. These agents, whose salaries were paid by federal, state, and county funds, kept farmers informed about the latest agricultural research. The Smith-Hughes Act (1917) paid part of the salaries of teachers of agriculture, home economics, and other vocational subjects in public high schools.

The government fails to ban child labor. Wilson also supported a campaign for federal legislation against child labor. In 1916 (and again in 1919) Congress used its authority under the interstate commerce clause of the Constitution to pass laws forbidding child labor. But the Supreme Court declared these laws unconstitutional. Meanwhile, Congress approved an amendment to the Constitution banning child labor, but it failed to secure ratification in three fourths of the states. Not until the 1930's was the federal government able to deal with the child-labor problem (page 704).

Other laws favor organized labor. Throughout his administration President Wilson maintained cordial relations with organized labor. He named the first Secretary of Labor in 1913, selecting for this position a union man sponsored by the American Federation of Labor. The new Department of Labor made studies of wages, living costs, employment and unemployment, and strikes. Its experts were called on to help draft such measures as the Clayton Antitrust Act. Wilson also signed the Seamen's Act (1915), which raised the safety requirements on American ships and made it easier for merchant seamen to bargain with employers over contract terms.

In 1916 railroad workers threatened to stage a nation-wide strike unless they were granted an eight-hour day and paid time and a half for overtime. Wilson tried without success to avert the strike by mediation. But when the strike threatened to interfere with shipments of important war materials, Wilson gave in to the union demands. He asked Congress for an emergency law granting the railroad workers their demands. When the President signed this law (the Adamson Act), he was criticized by employers for "surrendering" to labor. But organized labor praised him for helping them achieve the eight-hour day, an objective they had first sought in the 1880's.

Wilson makes a controversial appointment to the Supreme Court. An action that especially pleased the progressives was Wilson's naming of Louis D. Brandeis (page 555) to the Supreme Court in 1916. Brandeis had advised Wilson during the 1912 campaign and helped formulate the Federal Reserve Act. His appointment provoked a storm of criticism in conserva-

This bronze bust of Louis Brandeis, by the sculptress Eleanor Platt, stands in the Supreme Court Library as a memorial to the justice known for his support of social and economic reforms.

The NAACP and the National Urban League, both founded in the early 1900's, continue today to seek improved opportunities for American Negroes. Shown here are Roy Wilkins (left), NAACP executive secretary, and Whitney Young, Jr., Urban League director.

tive circles, where Brandeis had long been mistrusted because of his support of liberal causes. Wilson stuck to his appointment, however, and eventually the Senate confirmed Brandeis, making him the first Jew to serve on the Supreme Court.

The Progressive Movement offers little hope to Negroes. Though the Progressive Movement touched most areas of American life, it did little for the country's ten million Negroes. Four fifths of them lived in the South, though Washington, Philadelphia, and New York had sizable Negro communities. Hard times in farming during the 1880's and early '90's had forced many southern Negroes off the land and into towns and cities. There they lived in crowded, ramshackle buildings and worked at unskilled jobs.

Southern state laws had already effectively segregated the Negro. He was forced to ride in separate railroad cars, eat in separate restaurants, attend separate theaters, and send his children to separate schools (page 397). The so-called "Jim Crow" laws had also prevented the southern Negro from voting. The movement of Negroes into the southern cities caused considerable tension. Although housing ordinances carefully defined the areas of the cities where the newcomers could live, there were frequent clashes between Negroes and whites, and serious riots sometimes broke out.

Articles in *McClure's* described the living conditions of the southern Negro, the

violence in the cities, and the lynchings of Negroes in rural areas. But most white people, in both South and North, still felt that Booker T. Washington's formula of time, patience, and education was the best solution (page 398).

Prejudice exists in the North. During these same years racial antagonisms also existed in many parts of the North. In fact, it was violence in Springfield, Illinois, which finally prompted Negro leaders to take action. In the summer of 1908 an unruly mob destroyed Negro homes and businesses, lynched two Negroes, and wounded scores of others before the Illinois militia could restore order. This shocking event prompted William Lloyd Garrison's grandson, Oswald Garrison Villard, to call a conference on Lincoln's birthday in 1909. Many prominent people, both white and Negro, attended. Foremost among the Negro leaders was William E. B. Du Bois. Born in Massachusetts, Du Bois had been educated at Fisk University, received several degrees from Harvard, and taught for a time at Atlanta University. There he became an outspoken critic of Booker T. Washington. Du Bois demanded that Negroes receive professional education and full economic, social, and political rights.[5]

Two Negro organizations are formed. Those attending the 1909 conference

[5] In old age, Du Bois became a Communist, renounced his American citizenship, and emigrated to Ghana. There he died in 1963.

agreed to establish a permanent organization, the National Association for the Advancement of Colored People (NAACP). Its officers, with the exception of Du Bois, were white. As director of publicity and research, Du Bois gathered statistics about violations of Negro rights and published a magazine, *The Crisis*. Other members of the NAACP worked for better police protection for Negroes and recognition of their political rights. The NAACP's legal committee carried the battle for Negro rights into the federal courts.

Other Negro leaders were disturbed about the limited job opportunities for colored people in the cities. In 1911 they formed the National Urban League for the purpose of improving social and economic conditions among Negroes living in cities. Among the supporters of this organization was Booker T. Washington.

The government gives Negroes little help. The national government offered Negroes little encouragement at this time. Presidents McKinley, Roosevelt, and Taft gave little attention to Negro problems, though they all highly regarded Booker Washington, who was a national figure at the turn of the century. In fact, Theodore Roosevelt invited Washington to dine at the White House, a tradition-shattering event which aroused much comment. At the meeting the two men discussed appointments of Negroes to government jobs. Later Roosevelt named a few Negro post-office workers, but the effect of these appointments was more than offset by his hasty action following a riot in Brownsville, Texas, in 1906. On the basis of inadequate evidence, and without a full trial, Roosevelt ordered a battalion of Negro soldiers discharged for allegedly participating in a riot. President Wilson had little interest in the problems of American Negroes, and in this respect he shared the general apathy of most white Americans.

The Progressive Movement brings important changes in America. Though the Progressive Movement generally ignored Negro problems, it did bring about tremendous changes in many other areas of American life. Perhaps the most important was the swing away from the *laissez-faire*

concept of government toward the belief that government must concern itself with the welfare of all citizens. Of course not everyone accepted this new point of view. Many Americans in both parties opposed the expansion of government responsibility, and for many years so did the courts. But most people favored, or generally accepted, this trend. In his *Autobiography*, the Kansas journalist William Allen White summed up the progressive spirit:

> Reform was in the air. In forging new weapons of democracy in the state legislatures and in the Congress, the people were setting out on a crusade. . . . A sudden new interest in the under dog was manifest in the land. He was not exalted, but universally the people began to understand what slums were, what sweatshops were, what exploited labor was, what absentee landlordism had become in our urban life, what railroad rates were doing to the farmer and to the consumer. . . . Some way, into the hearts of the dominant middle class of this country, had come a sense that their civilization needed recasting, that their government had fallen into the hands of self-seekers, that a new relation should be established between the haves and the have-nots. . . .

▶ CHECK-UP

1. Why did Wilson seek additional reform legislation in 1915–1916? How were farmers helped by the Federal Farm Loan Act? The extension service? The Smith-Hughes Act?

2. How were workers helped by the Department of Labor? What was the Adamson Act? Why was the appointment of Brandeis to the Supreme Court controversial?

3. How were Negroes disadvantaged in the South? In the North? What were the goals of the NAACP? Of the Urban League?

4. What was the basic change brought about by the Progressive Movement?

. . . .

Clinching the Main Ideas in Chapter 27

By 1912 the progressive reformers had made important gains in city, state, and federal governments. The presidential election held that year showed general endorsement of the Progressive Movement. Though President Taft ran for re-election, the main contest was between Theodore Roosevelt and Woodrow Wilson, both of whom believed in progressive reform. The personalities of the two men differed greatly, but they agreed on the need for downward revision of the tariff, an income tax, conservation, banking reform, and stricter control of the trusts. Wilson's victory in the election was regarded as a mandate from the voters for continuation of the reform movement.

Thanks to his powers of leadership and large progressive majorities in Congress, President Wilson was able to bring the Progressive Movement to an impressive climax. During the first two years of his administration the tariff was reduced, the Federal Reserve System was created, and two new antitrust measures were enacted. Unfair methods of competition were more clearly defined in the Clayton Act, while the Federal Trade Commission kept close scrutiny on the activities of corporations. Additional measures in 1915 and 1916 rounded out the reform program.

The progressive era had seen the acceptance of the idea that the central government had an obligation to protect the welfare of all citizens. The passage of progressive legislation and the creation of new federal agencies to carry out these laws were evidence of the great change that had taken place in American thinking during this period.

Chapter Review

Terms to Understand

1. New Freedom
2. Underwood Tariff
3. rediscount
4. NAACP
5. Smith-Hughes Act
6. promissory note
7. Adamson Act
8. extension service
9. Sixteenth Amendment
10. Clayton Antitrust Act
11. Bull Moose Party
12. Federal Reserve Act
13. Federal Trade Commission
14. Danbury Hatters Case
15. Federal Farm Loan Act
16. National Urban League

What Do You Think?

1. Compare the Republican victory in 1860 with the Democratic victory in 1912.

2. Why did the Republicans nominate Taft rather than Roosevelt in 1912?

3. Why was the Underwood Tariff quite different from the Payne-Aldrich Tariff?

4. What loopholes in the Sherman Antitrust Act were filled by the Clayton Antitrust Act?

5. Why did some Negro leaders in the early 1900's put greater stress on political equality than on economic opportunity, the goal stressed by Booker T. Washington?

Using Your Knowledge of History

1. Debate: *Resolved*, That more constructive legislation was enacted during Wilson's first term in office than during any other four-year period in our history.

2. Write an editorial such as might have appeared in a Progressive Wisconsin newspaper commenting on Roosevelt's nomination by the Progressive Party.

3. Write a 300-word essay on how the Federal Reserve System would cope with conditions like those that led to the Panic of 1907.

4. Write a letter giving the reaction of a Dakota wheat farmer to the Federal Farm Loan Act of 1916.

Extending Your Knowledge of History

A fine study of Wilson's administration is Arthur S. Link's *Woodrow Wilson and the Progressive Era, 1910–1917*. Harold U. Faulkner has written two books analyzing the social and economic changes of the early twentieth century: *The Quest for Social Justice, 1898–1914*, and *The Decline of Laissez Faire, 1897–1917*. A good one-volume biography of Woodrow Wilson has been written by John A. Garraty. See also Walter Lord's *The Good Years*, dealing with the period 1900–1914.

CHAPTER 28

The United States Becomes a World Power

A ship of the American fleet in 1909

In foreign affairs we must make up our minds that, whether we wish it or not, we are a great people and must play a great part in the world. It is not open to us to choose whether we will play that great part or not. We have to play it. All we can decide is whether we shall play it well or ill.

THEODORE ROOSEVELT

1900–1918

In the same years that the Progressive Movement was introducing reforms at home, our country's relations with the outside world were also undergoing change. As we saw in Chapter 25, the Spanish-American War brought an end to a century of relative isolation. Following this war, we held possession of the Philippine Islands and Puerto Rico and also felt responsible for the welfare of a free Cuba. Moreover, the United States had annexed the Hawaiian Islands. With these responsibilities, it was indeed not so much a question of whether we would "play a great part in the world" but whether we should "play it well or ill."

Under President Theodore Roosevelt, the United States began to take an active interest in the Far East. By preserving China's territorial integrity and restraining Japanese expansion, the United States hoped to protect American trade interests in the Far East and discourage other countries from threatening Hawaii or the Philippines. Presidents Taft and Wilson followed essentially the same policy in the Far East.

In the Caribbean, American policy called for preventing the intervention of European powers in the affairs of the Latin American republics and for constructing an interocean canal. What came to be known as "big stick diplomacy" and "dollar diplomacy" were used to further American interests both in the Far East and in the Caribbean.

1 *The United States Aids Cuba and Governs Island Possessions*

New territories offer challenging problems. The United States had entered the Spanish-American War to free Cuba. Not only did it achieve this goal but it also ended up with the responsibility of protecting and governing Puerto Rico and the Philippines. Americans had not expected to take on such a burden, and few in our government were prepared to carry out this new responsibility. To govern these islands as colonies seemed to conflict with the American tradition of self-government and independence. Yet the new possessions needed some kind of government as well as economic assistance. The fact that the former Spanish subjects lacked education and experience in self-government made the problem even more complex. Although Cuba had become an independent state, this island too needed help before it could stand on its own feet.

American aid helps Cuba. When the war ended in 1898, Cuba, though technically independent, was occupied by American troops under the command of General Leonard Wood. General Wood served as military governor of Cuba until 1902. During these years the Americans worked hard to rebuild the war-torn island. Food, medicine, and shelter were provided

. . . .

CHAPTER FOCUS

1. The United States aids Cuba and governs island possessions.
2. The United States favors an "Open Door" in the Far East.
3. Roosevelt wields a "Big Stick" in the Caribbean.
4. Wilson makes few changes in Latin American policy.

for the Cuban people. Ravaged cities were rebuilt, and American engineers supervised the construction of sanitary water supplies and sewage facilities. Roads, railroads, bridges, and hospitals were repaired. Schools were built, and the University of Havana was reopened. The Americans also helped put public finances in order and introduced changes in local government.

An even more startling achievement was the conquest of yellow fever in Cuba. For many years people had thought that unsanitary living conditions caused this dreaded disease. But Walter Reed, William C. Gorgas, and other American army doctors believed that the disease was spread by mosquitoes. To prove this theory, two of the doctors allowed themselves to be bitten by infected mosquitoes. Both contracted yellow fever and died of its effects, but their sacrifice served a great cause. Armed with knowledge of how the disease was spread, the army proceeded to clean up areas where the mosquitoes bred. By the time the American army withdrew from Cuba, it had rid the island of yellow fever.

A Cuban government is organized. In 1900 General Wood decided that the Cubans were ready to organize a government. He called for the election of delegates to a constitutional convention. Meeting in Havana, this convention drew up a constitution modeled on that of the United States. The constitution said nothing, however, about Cuba's relationship with its northern neighbor. While the American government was ready to approve Cuban independence, it expected to exercise some control over the new republic. In 1901, therefore, the United States Congress added the so-called Platt Amendment to an army appropriation bill. The Platt Amendment provided that the United States would give up its control of the island only when Cubans agreed to include in their constitution these guarantees:

(1) That the government of Cuba would neither make any treaty by which Cuba would give up its independence nor would it allow any foreign power to obtain control over any of its territory.

(2) That Cuba would contract no debt which could not be paid out of the ordinary revenues of the island.

(3) That Cuba would consent to the right of the United States "to intervene for the preservation of Cuban independence, the maintenance of a government adequate for the protection of life, property, and individual liberty, and for discharging the obligations with respect to Cuba imposed by the Treaty of Paris on the United States. . . ."

(4) That Cuba would sell or lease certain coaling or naval stations to the United States.

(5) That these provisions would be written into a permanent treaty with the United States.

The third section proved to be the heart of the Platt Amendment. Cubans objected to the idea of intervention in their affairs by the United States, but there was little they could do about it. The provisions of the Platt Amendment were included in the new Cuban constitution and were later embodied in a treaty with the United States. In 1902, the first Cuban president was installed, and American troops were

withdrawn. In the following year the United States, under the provisions of the Platt Amendment, leased from Cuba the land around Guantánamo Bay. The Americans developed, and still hold, an important naval base at this site.

American influence over Cuba remains strong. The Platt Amendment remained in effect until 1934. During that time the United States on several occasions took a hand in Cuban affairs. Presidents Theodore Roosevelt, Taft, and Wilson all sent troops at one time or another to maintain order in the island. In 1906, for example, the Americans suppressed a rebellion and stayed on for three years, until a new Cuban president was inaugurated.

American economic influence over Cuba continued to grow. A trade treaty assured Cuba of a 20 per cent cut in American tariff rates on exports to the United States. American products imported into Cuba, on the other hand, were favored by a 20-to-40 per cent cut in rates. This trade agreement increased American sales to Cuba and also

The fight against tropical diseases continues today. At left, above, a scientist holds fresh-water snails of a kind that spreads several diseases prevalent in tropical areas. These snails harbor certain flatworms that, when transmitted to man, severely damage vital organs and tissues. Walter Reed Army Hospital (above, right) is named for the medical officer who proved that mosquitos carry yellow fever and helped eliminate that disease from Cuba.

encouraged Americans to invest in the island's economy. The largest sums went into Cuban sugar plantations and refineries, but sizable investments were also made in government securities, railroads, public utilities, tobacco plantations, and mines. By the end of the 1920's American investors controlled an estimated two fifths of the total wealth of the island. More than four fifths of Cuba's exports went to the United States, and three quarters of her imports came from there.[1]

Puerto Rico gains some self-government. Because Puerto Rico became an American possession after the Spanish-American War, its story took a different course from that of Cuba. American military forces remained in Puerto Rico until 1900. In that year the Foraker Act established a civil government for the island. Its inhabitants were declared citizens of Puerto Rico (but not American citizens), entitled to the protection of the United States. A governor, with broad executive powers and the right to veto legislation, was to be appointed by the President of

[1] For later events in Cuba, see Chapters 34 and 38.

The Guantánamo naval station in Cuba provides the United States with a strategic base in the Caribbean. This picture shows the residential area and the naval station in the background.

the United States. The President was also to appoint an executive council of eleven men, five of them to be native Puerto Ricans. A legislative assembly would be elected by the Puerto Rican people.

In 1917, the Jones Act gave a larger degree of self-government to Puerto Rico. This act made Puerto Ricans citizens of the United States. It replaced the executive council with an elected senate, which became the upper house of the legislature. This change did not mean complete self-government, however, for the governor was still appointed by the President of the United States. Furthermore, acts of the Puerto Rican legislature could be set aside by the governor, the President, or the United States Congress.

Economic changes are made in Puerto Rico. Under American supervision, sanitary facilities were improved in Puerto Rico, and free compulsory schools were established. Roads were built, and public finances were reorganized. Americans made large investments in the Puerto Rican sugar plantations, and the United States imported most of the island's products — sugar, tobacco, coffee, and fruits. The establishment of complete free trade between Puerto Rico and the United States in 1901 helped expand the island's commerce. Yet the Puerto Rican economy remained sluggish. The rapid increase of population outstripped economic progress, and unemployment continued to be a serious problem.

Rebellion complicates the Philippine problem. Although the steps taken in Puerto Rico carried the United States along unfamiliar paths, even greater departures from American traditions proved necessary in the Philippines. Several factors complicated the situation there: (1) The Philippines consisted of more than 7000 islands, separated by some 7000 miles of ocean from our Pacific coast. (2) The seven million people represented all stages of civilization, from an advanced culture to barbarism. (3) Racial rivalries and religious tensions existed among the people, especially between the Moslem Moros and the Spanish-speaking Catholics.

Planning a suitable government under

Fort San Geronimo, a reminder of Puerto Rico's long period under Spanish rule, contrasts with the modern tourist hotels in San Juan, the capital city (left). The oil refinery above is another view representative of Puerto Rico's modern development.

these conditions would have been difficult enough. But the problem was still further complicated by the opposition of many Americans to the annexation of the Philippines. Moreover, a native rebellion soon broke out against United States rule.

When American troops captured Manila in 1898, they were aided by Filipinos already in revolt against Spain. These people believed the Americans were helping them win independence from Spain. The peace treaty, however, awarded the Philippine Islands to the United States. To the Filipinos, this decision (which had been reached without consulting their leaders) seemed merely an exchange of one master for another. As a result, a rebellion led by Emilio Aguinaldo broke out against the American occupation forces in 1899, and stubborn fighting continued for three years. Both sides resorted to guerrilla warfare — including the burning of villages and torture of prisoners. Americans who opposed the annexation of the islands were quick to point out that these were the very same tactics that Spain had used against the Cubans.

Civil government is organized in the Philippines. During the presidential campaign of 1900, President McKinley and his running mate, Theodore Roosevelt, defended American policy in the Philippines. An investigating commission had reported to the President that because of political inexperience and lack of education, the islanders were not ready for self-government. Largely as a result of this report, McKinley sent a second commission under William Howard Taft to establish civil government in the islands. Acts of Congress in 1901 and 1902 gave the President power to govern the islands and declared the inhabitants to be citizens of the Philippine Islands "entitled to the protection of the United States."

In 1901 Taft was named governor of the islands. A seven-man commission, of whom three members were Filipinos, organized local and provincial governments throughout the Christian parts of the islands. Governor Taft and his successors built schools, roads, and bridges, set up a public health program, and reorganized the financial and administrative systems. A separation between Church and state was effected. Land purchased from the Catholic orders was sold on easy terms to Filipino farmers.

The Filipinos demand more self-government. While most Filipinos favored these changes, they also wanted more self-government. In 1907 they were permitted to elect a legislative assembly, which shared some powers with the commission. Further gains were made after the Democratic Party, which had opposed acquisition of the Philippines, returned to power in the United States. The Jones Act of 1916 (not to be confused with the Jones Act of 1917 dealing with Puerto Rico) abolished the commission. It authorized

---

Puerto Rico on the Move

Many changes have taken place in Puerto Rico and the Philippines since the early 1900's. In recent years, for example, Puerto Rico has made important strides toward self-government and economic development. (See page 770 for the recent history of the Philippines.) Puerto Rico became a self-governing Commonwealth under American protection in 1952. Its citizens are also United States citizens and can move to the mainland without immigration restrictions.

For many years, poverty was widespread in Puerto Rico. In the 1940's, the Puerto Rican government, with American help, began "Operation Bootstrap" to improve conditions. Big plantations were broken up and land redistributed among poor farmers. Modern housing developments were built. The Puerto Rican government helped businessmen find factory locations, construct plants, and train people to work in them. Meanwhile, the Commonwealth has not neglected education and culture. Compulsory schooling has almost wiped out illiteracy, and colleges and universities are on the upswing. A project called "Operation Serenity" aims at preserving Puerto Rican traditions and encouraging arts and crafts.

---

the Filipinos to elect a senate as well as the assembly and extended suffrage to all adult males who could read and write. The governor-general, however, continued to be appointed by the President of the United States, and he retained his veto power over legislation. The Jones Act promised independence "as soon as a stable government can be established."

During President Wilson's closing days in office, he recommended that complete independence be granted to the Philippines, but the Republican Congress turned down his suggestion. Despite repeated requests for independence by the Filipinos, commissions sent to the Philippines during the 1920's reported that the time had not yet come for separation.

The constitutional status of the dependencies is fixed. Acquisition of Puerto Rico and the Philippines raised a knotty question about the constitutional rights of the inhabitants. Should the Constitution follow the American flag into the island possessions? Should the inhabitants enjoy the privileges conferred by the Constitution on American citizens? The treaty ending the Spanish-American War had declared that "the civil and political status of the native inhabitants hereby ceded to the United States shall be determined by Congress." But could Congress, in spite of the Constitution, limit freedom of speech or religion or the right to a jury trial in the new territories?

A provision of the Foraker Act of 1900, reducing the tariff rates on Puerto Rican products, prepared the way for a test in the Supreme Court. In this case, one of the so-called *Insular* ("island") *Cases*, the Supreme Court upheld the action of Congress by a five-to-four vote. It ruled that the clause of the Constitution requiring tariff duties to be uniform throughout the United States did not have to be applied to the newly acquired possessions. In other Insular Cases the Court ruled that civil rights, particularly trial by jury, were not guaranteed to inhabitants of territories which came under the jurisdiction of the United States. Thus, the Insular Cases determined that the Constitution did not "follow the flag." In other words, the peoples of the territories did not automatically acquire the rights of United States citizens.

Even after the Puerto Ricans received American citizenship, the Supreme Court ruled that their island was not by that act incorporated into the United States. The inhabitants of the island, therefore, were not necessarily entitled to the rights guaranteed by the Constitution. In effect, then, Congress was left to determine what civil rights *were* to be enjoyed by the inhabitants of the territories. It would also decide how much self-government they would exercise.

The country's armed forces are made more efficient. The acquisition of possessions caused the United States to take a greater interest in strengthening its armed forces. The Spanish-American War had revealed many shortcomings in the United States Army. When Theodore Roosevelt became President, he decided to shake up the army command and also to build up the navy. Thus, the regular army was enlarged and a number of service schools for officers were established. An act of Congress created a General Staff, whose presiding officer would serve as a military adviser to the Secretary of War.

Roosevelt had long been interested in strengthening the navy. Now he argued that the United States should have a navy second only to that of Great Britain. Since Germany was working toward the same goal, the United States would have to match Germany's large naval appropriations. Both Germany and Great Britain were beginning to build powerful battleships known as *dreadnoughts,* and the United States soon joined in this naval arms race. Roosevelt and his successors in the White House approved large expenditures for the navy because they regarded a strong fleet as essential for the protection of American interests and possessions in the Pacific and Caribbean.

▶ CHECK-UP

1. How did this country help newly independent Cuba? What was the Platt Amendment, and how did Cuba react to it? How did

trade agreements link the economies of Cuba and the United States?

2. Describe the government established for Puerto Rico under the Foraker Act. What rights were granted Puerto Rico in 1917? How did the United States help Puerto Rico? What problem remained unsolved?

3. What conditions made it difficult to establish a stable government in the Philippines? What efforts were made to help the Filipinos? How were they governed in the early 1900's? What further rights did the Filipinos obtain in 1907 and in 1916?

4. How was the status of dependencies and their peoples clarified in the Insular Cases?

. . . .

2 *The United States Favors an "Open Door" in the Far East*

The annexation of Pacific islands naturally increased American interest in the Far East. Acquisition of the Philippines also brought the United States into closer contact with Japan. Just beginning to establish itself as a world power, Japan viewed the western Pacific as its own sphere of influence.

Japan and European powers stake out claims in China. American ships had carried on trade with China since the early days of the republic. When the United States acquired the Philippines, it was hoped that this trade would increase. But conditions in China at the turn of the century were in a state of confusion. Defeated in a war with Japan in 1895, China had been compelled to surrender its claim to Korea and to cede the island of Formosa to Japan. Recognizing China's weakness, European powers began a scramble to force the Chinese to lease them important ports. Japan as well as France, Germany,

貴女裁縫之圖

The painting below is a Japanese portrait of Commodore Matthew C. Perry who opened up American trade with Japan in the 1850's (page 305).

American trade with the Orient resulted in an exchange of goods and ideas. For many years tea was the leading commodity in the China trade. Americans also valued fine Chinese porcelain like the tea set at left. Japan imported American machinery, including sewing machines (above). Some Japanese women even adopted western dress styles.

Britain, and Russia acquired "spheres of influence" in China. Thus they gained control over large areas of that country and enriched themselves by exploiting its natural resources.

Hay proposes an "open door." To maintain equal trading opportunities in China, the United States sought to stop the partitioning of that unhappy country. As President McKinley expressed it: "Asking only the open door for ourselves, we are ready to accord the open door to others." In the fall of 1899, Secretary of State John Hay tried to persuade the European nations and Japan to accept this Open Door Policy. He sent identical notes asking each nation to promise (1) to respect within its sphere of influence the trading privileges and vested interests of other nations; (2) to allow the Chinese tariff to continue in force and to be col-

lected by Chinese officials within all spheres of influence; and (3) to make no discrimination in charging port dues and railroad rates.

Most of the replies were cautious. The nations agreed in principle to Hay's proposal. But they were reluctant to commit themselves until they knew what the others would do. Hay realized it would be difficult, if not impossible, to secure firm agreement from each nation. In 1900, therefore, he simply announced that all the powers had approved the Open Door Policy.

The Chinese rebel against foreign interference. Meanwhile, a tide of resentment against European greed was rising within China. A patriotic society called the "Boxers" began to stir up hatred against the "foreign devils." This movement soon developed into organized rebellion. In 1900 bands of Boxers, joined by Chinese government forces, attacked and murdered missionaries and other foreign residents. They gained control of the area around the capital city, Peking, and cut off communication with the outside world. Foreigners in Peking took refuge in the British legation. The leading nations, including the United States, combined their forces to relieve the city. This international expedition entered Peking just in time to save the besieged diplomats and missionaries.

The angry European powers wanted to punish China by taking over still more of its territory. But Secretary Hay dispatched another round of notes urging that China be required only to pay for damages. United States policy, Hay declared, was to seek a solution that would "preserve Chinese territorial and administrative entity . . . and safeguard for the world the principle of equal and impartial trade with all parts of the Chinese Empire."

In the end, Hay's proposal was accepted by the European powers. China suffered no further loss of territory but was compelled to pay 333 million dollars to the various nations. Of this sum the United States was to receive some 24 million dollars. Only half this amount was needed to meet the claims of American citizens for losses suffered in the Boxer Rebellion. At a later time, therefore, the United States canceled the rest of the debt. The Chinese government set aside this amount to provide scholarships for Chinese students in the United States and also to help finance educational projects in China.

Roosevelt helps settle the Russo-Japanese War. China's problems did not end with the settlement of the Boxer Rebellion. Its obvious weakness encouraged both Japan and Russia to extend their influence in Korea and in Manchuria, a border province in northeastern China (map, page 592). Alarmed by Russian ambitions in the Far East, Japan had entered a defensive alliance with Great Britain in 1902. Japan then tried to persuade Russia to withdraw from Manchuria, which Russian troops had occupied following the Boxer Rebellion. Unable to reach an understanding, Japan launched a surprise attack on Russia in

1904. The modern, efficient Japanese army and navy won a series of surprising victories over the Russian forces. Nevertheless, the war seriously strained Japan's financial resources, and its diplomats secretly asked President Theodore Roosevelt to help settle the conflict.

Roosevelt was interested in the Russo-Japanese War for two reasons: (1) He wanted both Russia and Japan to uphold the Open Door Policy in the Far East. (2) He also feared that Japan, by seizing strategic territory from Russia or China, might become much more powerful. Such a situation, as Roosevelt saw it, might "possibly mean a struggle between them [Japan] and us in the future." For these reasons he agreed to serve as mediator.

Roosevelt invited both Russian and Japanese delegates to meet with him at Portsmouth, New Hampshire, in August, 1905. The victorious Japanese expected to receive not only Russian-held territory but a large payment of money as well. Roosevelt persuaded them to drop the claim for damages and also to reduce their demands for Russian territory. The peace treaty did,

The Russo-Japanese War was brought to an end by a treaty arranged at the peace conference sponsored by President Theodore Roosevelt.

SPHERES OF INFLUENCE IN THE FAR EAST

China was powerless to defend its territory against the encroachments of foreign nations. By 1900 several European powers had staked out spheres of influence in Chinese territory. Note that Japan also had begun to extend its influence beyond the home islands. See the map on page 725 for later Japanese expansion.

however, transfer Russian special interests in Manchuria to Japan, although the province was restored to China. The treaty also recognized Japan's special interest in Korea and ceded the southern half of the Russian island of Sakhalin to Japan. For his efforts to end the Russo-Japanese War, Roosevelt was awarded the Nobel Peace Prize. But his role in the negotiations angered many Japanese. They felt that Roosevelt had blocked their effort to obtain a badly needed sum of money.

Relations between Japan and the United States are troubled. Japanese resentment against the United States was further inflamed by the treatment of Oriental immigrants on our West Coast. As we saw in Chapter 22, prejudice against Asians had resulted in the exclusion of Chinese immigrants during the late 1800's.

Now politicians and labor leaders were demanding a ban on Japanese immigration, and western state legislatures were passing laws discriminating against Japanese already in the United States.

The situation came to a head in 1906, when the San Francisco school board ordered all Japanese children to attend a separate school. Newspapers in Japan called this a national insult and demanded action from Roosevelt. The President had no authority over San Francisco's schools, but he did exert pressure on the school board to reverse its decision. The segregation order was finally revoked when Roosevelt promised to do something about Japanese immigration. During 1907–1908 the two countries reached an understanding, which came to be called the Gentlemen's Agreement. In return for the lifting of the school segregation order, the Japanese government agreed not to issue passports to Japanese laborers wanting to enter the United States.[2]

The Gentlemen's Agreement effectively curbed Japanese immigration, but it did not put an end to state laws discriminating against Orientals. This situation was greatly resented in Japan, where the people assumed that all Americans regarded them as inferior. But few Japanese understood that the states had powers with which the federal government could not interfere.

Roosevelt sends the fleet around the world. To demonstrate American naval power, and thus make it easier to settle disagreements with Japan, President Roosevelt decided to send an American fleet on a cruise around the world. Although Congress at first refused to make an appropriation for this purpose, sufficient money was available to send the fleet to San Francisco. When the President declared it would stay there until Congress voted more funds, Congress gave way. The ships stopped at South American ports,

Hawaii, New Zealand, Australia, the Philippines, China, and Japan. In Yokohama the Japanese people welcomed the American sailors with enthusiasm. After a trip through the Suez Canal and across the Atlantic, the fleet returned to the United States. It arrived on February 22, 1909 — just in time to celebrate Washington's birthday. President Roosevelt proudly announced that sending the fleet around the world was "the most important service that I rendered to peace."

The Root-Takahira Agreement is signed. While the fleet was on its way, Japan and the United States signed the Root-Takahira Agreement (1908). In an exchange of notes, the two countries stated their desire to "encourage the free and peaceful development of their commerce" and agreed to maintain the existing situation in the Pacific area. This implied Japanese recognition of American sovereignty in the Philippines and American acknowledgment of Japanese influence in Manchuria and control of Korea. The agreement also provided that the two powers would respect the independence of China and support the Open Door. Finally, they agreed to consult with each other in the event of any threat to existing conditions in the areas concerned.

Taft promotes "dollar diplomacy." Theodore Roosevelt's successor, President Taft, applied another policy in the Far East. His Secretary of State, Philander C. Knox, had been a corporation lawyer having close ties with business interests. Knox and Taft favored an American foreign policy which would encourage American trade and investments in the Far East and Latin America. Such economic developments, they believed, would promote political and economic stability in these areas. The use of diplomatic influence to protect and advance American financial and commercial interests abroad became known as *dollar diplomacy.* President Taft defended it as a "most useful" policy which would "benefit . . . [all] countries concerned."

In the Far East, Secretary Knox justified "dollar diplomacy" on the grounds that the investment of American money in China

---

[2] An immigration act in 1907 denied admission to all Japanese who did not possess proper passports. This law was interpreted to exclude Japanese who came from island possessions of the United States or from any country other than Japan.

would help to keep the door open for American trade. He knew that British, German, and French bankers were planning to finance the construction of a railroad in central and southern China. After long negotiations, Knox secured the right for American bankers to participate in this project. Only a small amount of American capital, however, had been invested in China when President Taft and Secretary Knox left office.

Wilson is less enthusiastic about "dollar diplomacy." President Wilson held a very different view of "dollar diplomacy." He feared that large American loans and extensive commercial operations actually might threaten the independence of a country like China. The investments in China, said Wilson, "might conceivably [lead to] . . . forcible interference in the financial and even the political affairs of that great Oriental state." Hence in 1913 he withdrew government approval of the arrangement under which Americans helped to finance railroad construction in China. Four years later, however, the United States government gave its approval to American investments in China.

World War I strengthens Japan. Japanese territorial ambitions again became a problem during Wilson's administration. When World War I broke out in 1914, Japan seized the opportunity to strengthen its position in the Far East. Before the end of that year, Japan occupied a number of Germany's Far Eastern possessions. These included not only Kiaochow (*kyow'-chow'*), which China had leased to Germany, but also the entire Shantung peninsula (map, page 592) as well as islands in the Pacific. Assuming that the United States might protest but would take no action, Japan also decided to move directly against China. In 1915 the Japanese government presented China with the so-called Twenty-one Demands. Japan requested special economic privileges which, if granted, would close the Open Door and in effect establish Japanese control over China.

Secretary of State Bryan sent a sharp protest. He warned Japan that the United States would not recognize any treaty or action which impaired "the political or territorial integrity of the Republic of China, or the international policy relative to China commonly known as the open door policy." The American protest, in addition to pressure from the British government, led Japan to reduce its insulting demands on China.

Two years later, the United States and Japan attempted to reach an understanding over their aims in China. In signing the Lansing-Ishii Agreement, the two countries declared their support of the Open Door Policy and agreed to oppose any infringement of China's independence and territorial integrity. But the United States conceded that territorial nearness created "special relations between countries" and recognized that Japan had "special interests in China." This was a reference to Korea and Manchuria. There the matter rested until after the end of World War I (page 641).

▶ CHECK-UP

1. Why did the European powers seek "spheres of influence" in China during the late 1800's? What position did the United States take concerning this trend? What was the Boxer Rebellion? How was it suppressed? What terms were imposed on China?

2. What were the underlying causes of the Russo-Japanese War? Why did Roosevelt act as mediator to end the conflict? What were the terms of the peace? Why was Japan dissatisfied? What other factor increased tension between the United States and Japan?

3. What was the Gentlemen's Agreement? The Root-Takahira Agreement? What was the significance of each? What territorial gains were made by Japan in World War I? What were the Twenty-one Demands? How did the United States and Britain react to Japan's action? What concession was made in the Lansing-Ishii Agreement?

4. What is "dollar diplomacy"? What advantage was claimed for this policy by Secretary of State Knox? What fear was expressed by President Wilson?

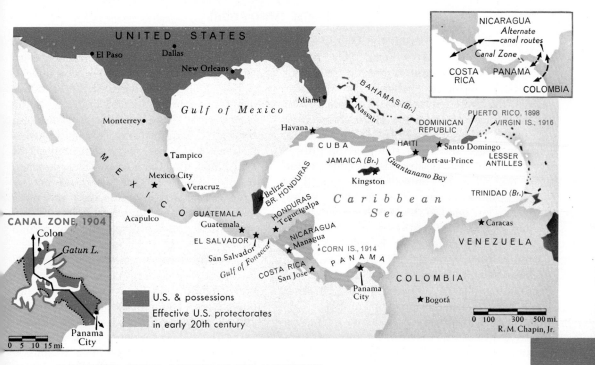

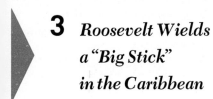

CANAL ZONE, 1904
Colon
Gatun L.
Panama City
0 5 10 15 mi.

CANAL ZONE, 1904 inset / main map labels:

UNITED STATES

El Paso • Dallas •
New Orleans •
Miami
Gulf of Mexico
Monterrey •
BAHAMAS (Br.)
Nassau
Havana ★
DOMINICAN REPUBLIC
PUERTO RICO, 1898
VIRGIN IS., 1916
• Tampico
CUBA
HAITI
Santo Domingo
JAMAICA (Br.)
Port-au-Prince
LESSER ANTILLES
Mexico City ★
Veracruz •
Guantanamo Bay
Kingston
M E X I C O
Belize
BR. HONDURAS
HONDURAS
C a r i b b e a n S e a
TRINIDAD (Br.)
Acapulco •
GUATEMALA
Guatemala ★
Tegucigalpa
EL SALVADOR
NICARAGUA
Managua
★ Caracas
San Salvador ★
Gulf of Fonseca
CORN IS., 1914
PANAMA
VENEZUELA
COSTA RICA
San José ★
Panama City
COLOMBIA
★ Bogotá

NICARAGUA
Alternate canal routes
Canal Zone
COSTA RICA   PANAMA
COLOMBIA

U.S. & possessions
Effective U.S. protectorates in early 20th century

0 100   300   500 mi.
R. M. Chapin, Jr.

THE UNITED STATES DOMINATES THE CARIBBEAN

The "big stick" and "dollar diplomacy" policies of the early 1900's made the Caribbean an "American lake." Note which areas became protectorates and which were actual possessions. The United States is planning construction of a second interoceanic canal (upper right).

3 Roosevelt Wields a "Big Stick" in the Caribbean

President Theodore Roosevelt's policy of showing American strength applied to Latin America as well as the Far East. He sometimes quoted an old proverb — "Speak softly and carry a big stick, and you will go far." In pursuing his goals in the Caribbean, Roosevelt did not always speak softly but he did frequently wield a "big stick." Roosevelt's Latin American goals were (1) to construct a canal across the Isthmus of Panama and (2) to keep European powers from interfering in the domestic affairs of Latin American countries.

Interest in a canal is revived. Americans had first considered the possibility

of a canal across Central America when the United States acquired California from Mexico. Two years later, in 1850, Great Britain and the United States signed the Clayton-Bulwer Treaty. This agreement provided that the two countries would jointly supervise the construction of an interocean canal. But American interest in such a project then declined because of the quarrel over slavery, the outbreak of the Civil War, and the building of transcontinental railroads.

When the United States entered the Spanish-American War, the need for a canal between the Caribbean and Pacific became apparent. A spectacular 14,000-mile cruise by the battleship *Oregon* around South America to Cuba drew attention to the need for a shorter water route. Military experts insisted that unless the United States built a canal, it would have to maintain powerful fleets in both the Atlantic and Pacific Oceans. Secretary of State Hay, therefore, asked the British to consider a treaty that would permit the United States to build and fortify a canal. The British were at first reluctant to give up their right to joint control. But when Hay made clear that the United States would go ahead with the project anyway, the British agreed to sign the Hay-Pauncefote Treaty (1901). This treaty set aside the Clayton-Bulwer agreement and permitted the construction of a canal to be controlled and policed by the United States. The canal, however, was to be "open to the vessels of commerce and of war of all nations" on equal terms.

The Panama route is selected. Two routes for the canal had been discussed — one through Panama (then a province of the Republic of Colombia) and the other through Nicaragua (map, page 595). One attempt had already been made to build a canal across the narrow Isthmus of Panama. As early as 1878, a French company had obtained from Colombia the right to build a canal there. Because of financial mismanagement and tropical disease, work on the project had ceased. After the Hay-Pauncefote Treaty was signed, the French company offered to sell its rights and equipment to the United States for 109 million dollars.

Meanwhile, United States engineers had made a report favoring a right-of-way through Nicaragua, and that country indicated strong interest in the project. Fear-ful that the United States might build the canal through Nicaragua, the French company reduced its price to 40 million dollars. In 1902, Congress authorized the President to purchase the rights and property of the French canal company. He was also authorized to acquire from Colombia perpetual control of a narrow strip of land across the isthmus and there to construct a canal. In case these arrangements could not be made "within a reasonable time and upon reasonable terms," the President was empowered to go ahead with the Nicaraguan route.

Colombia refuses our terms. Secretary of State Hay entered into negotiations with Colombia. A treaty was worked out under which Colombia would lease to the United States a strip of land six miles wide across the isthmus. The United States, in return, agreed to pay Colombia 10 million dollars in cash and 250,000 dollars annually. But Colombia had hoped for much better terms. After all, the French company's rights to the canal, for which the United States was willing to pay 40 million dollars, would revert to Colombia in less than one year. Although the United States Senate promptly ratified the treaty, the Colombian government rejected it.

Colombia's action angered President Roosevelt, who called the members of its government "blackmailers" and "bandits."

The excavation of the Panama Canal was one of the biggest engineering operations undertaken up to that time.

The impatient President vowed that Colombia would not be allowed "permanently to bar one of the future highways of civilization."

Panama revolts from Colombia. During the fall of 1903 the people of Panama grew restless. They feared that the United States might go ahead with plans to build the canal in Nicaragua, thus depriving them of an important artery of trade. Their fears were well-known to President Roosevelt, Secretary Hay, and the officials of the French canal company. In this tense situation an agent of the French company, Philippe Bunau-Varilla (boo-*noh'* vah-ree-*yah'*), took it upon himself to help the Panamanians organize a revolt against Colombia. He knew that the United States was bound by an 1846 treaty with New Granada (an earlier name for Colombia) to preserve freedom of transit across the isthmus. He guessed, moreover, that the American government would take action under this treaty in case of an uprising in Panama.

Realizing the likelihood of a revolution, the government at Washington did indeed send a warship, the U.S.S. *Nashville*, to Panama. Its mission was to make sure that, if a revolution broke out, there would be no interference with freedom of transit. The *Nashville* arrived on November 2. On the following day, Panamanian leaders staged a revolt against Colombia. The uprising quickly succeeded because the *Nashville* prevented Colombian military forces from reaching Panama.

A treaty is arranged with Panama. Three days later, the United States recognized the new government in Panama. Almost immediately Bunau-Varilla set out for Washington as the Republic of Panama's minister to the United States. Within a few days he and Secretary Hay negotiated a treaty that was satisfactory to both countries. By the terms of the Hay-Bunau-Varilla Treaty the United States (1) guaranteed the independence of the new republic; (2) paid Panama ten million dollars outright; and (3) promised to pay 250,000 dollars annually, beginning nine years after the ratification of the treaty. In return, Panama granted to the United States "in perpetuity," or forever, a zone ten miles wide across the entire country for the construction of a canal. Panama also granted permission to the United States to fortify the Canal Zone.[3]

Roosevelt's actions are criticized. Although the Senate ratified the treaty, Roosevelt was sharply criticized for his role in the Panama affair. Neither the President nor Secretary Hay had plotted the rebellion, but both had been aware of Bunau-Varilla's plans. Furthermore, the presence of the *Nashville* had virtually assured the success of the revolt. Many Americans felt that our government had violated Colombia's sovereign rights by aiding the rebels and that Roosevelt had been too hasty in recognizing the new government. The New York *American* said it would "rather forego forever the advantage of an inter-ocean waterway than gain one by such means as this."

Roosevelt was quick to defend his role in the Panamanian revolution. In a speech before Congress in December, 1903, he said: "I confidently maintain that the recognition of the Republic of Panama was an act justified by the interests of collective civilization. If ever a Government could be said to have received a mandate from civilization . . . the United States holds that position with regard to the interoceanic canal." Even after he left the White House, Roosevelt continued to defend his action. In a speech delivered in 1911 he explained:

> If I had followed traditional conservative methods, I would have submitted a dignified state paper of probably 200 pages to Congress and the debates on it would have been going on yet; but I took the Canal Zone and let Congress debate; and while the debate goes on the canal does also.

The Panama episode disturbs Latin American relations. Panama's revolt and our acquisition of the Canal Zone seriously disturbed relations between the United

---

[3] This treaty was amended several times (page 713).

States and Colombia. It also caused indignation and alarm among other Latin American states, who feared that Roosevelt might use his "big stick" against them. Colombia refused to recognize Panama's independence and demanded that the question of Colombian rights to the isthmus and interests in the canal be decided by arbitration. During Wilson's administration a treaty was drawn up with Colombia in which the United States apologized for its part in the Panamanian revolution and agreed to pay Colombia 25 million dollars. Roosevelt's friends in the Senate blocked this treaty. But in 1921, after Roosevelt's death, the United States paid Colombia this amount as an indemnity.

Construction of the canal is completed. The Hay-Bunau-Varilla Treaty had no sooner been signed than Roosevelt wanted to "make the dirt fly" in Panama. The project soon got under way. The President sent William Howard Taft to Panama as a special troubleshooter. Taft co-operated with the surgeon-general of the army, William C. Gorgas, in wiping out the threat of yellow fever. Meanwhile, the decision was made to let army engineers rather than private contractors build the canal. A canal with a series of locks was approved as being cheaper and easier to build than a sea-level canal. Colonel George W. Goethals directed construction, and in the summer of 1914 the first ocean steamer passed through the Panama Canal.

From both the commercial and military point of view, the Panama Canal had great importance. It shortened the water route from New York to San Francisco by 8000 miles. The saving in time and in the cost of operating a ship was worth many times the amount paid by a ship in tolls for the privilege of passing through the canal. The canal also made possible a quick shift of naval strength from one ocean to another.

The canal affects American foreign policy. In addition, the Panama Canal had important implications for the United States' foreign policy. Construction of the canal made the Caribbean one of the world's great highways of commerce. It was in this country's interest, therefore, to see that orderly governments were maintained in the Caribbean and that European powers did not interfere in the affairs of Latin American countries. The United States also needed to establish nearby naval bases for the defense of the Canal Zone, as well as for the protection of Puerto Rico and Cuba.

The United States forces a settlement of the Venezuelan debt. Even before plans for the canal had been completed, an event took place which demonstrated the United States' determination to uphold the Monroe Doctrine. In 1902 a crisis arose over Venezuela's inability to pay its debts to European creditors. To compel payment, Germany, Great Britain, and Italy established a blockade of Venezuelan ports; and German vessels even bombarded a Venezuelan fort and village. Furthermore, Germany refused to submit the quarrel to arbitration. President Roosevelt warned that the United States fleet would be sent to Venezuela if Germany tried to occupy that country's territory. Finally, Germany gave in, and a court of arbitration, to which the claims were referred, reduced the debts to one fifth of the original amount.

President Roosevelt enlarges the Monroe Doctrine. Close on the heels of the Venezuelan crisis came a similar problem in the Caribbean. The Dominican Republic owed large debts to European countries, who were threatening to use force to collect the money owed them. President Roosevelt believed that such interference posed a threat to American interests in the Caribbean. In his annual message to Congress in 1904, the President took a bold stand:

Chronic wrongdoing . . . may in America, as elsewhere, ultimately require intervention by some civilized nation, and in the Western Hemisphere the adherence of the United States to the Monroe Doctrine may force the United States, however reluctantly, in flagrant cases of such wrongdoing or impotence, to the exercise of an international police power.

Thus, the President warned that if any nation had to interfere in the affairs of a Latin American state which was not paying its foreign debts or whose stability was in question, it would be the United States.

In other words, Roosevelt interpreted the Monroe Doctrine as more than a warning to Europe to keep out of the Western Hemisphere. He regarded it as a positive doctrine, which authorized the United States to exercise leadership in the Western Hemisphere and put pressure on the Latin American republics to meet their international obligations. This interpretation of the Monroe Doctrine became known as the Roosevelt Corollary.

The Roosevelt Corollary is applied to the Dominican Republic. Faced with the necessity of accepting United States protection under the Roosevelt Corollary or risking European intervention, the Dominican Republic chose American protection. It entered into an agreement with President Roosevelt, by which the United States guaranteed the territorial integrity of the republic. In return, the United States was to supervise Dominican customs, take charge of the government's finances, and arrange for the payment of both its foreign and domestic debts. Although the United States Senate failed to ratify this agreement, Roosevelt appointed an American customs collector and assured him of the protection of American marines. In 1907 the Senate gave its approval to a slightly revised treaty, and the Dominican Republic became a protectorate of the United States. Under the American collector, customs receipts doubled and the finances of the republic were placed on a sound basis.

To critics of the Roosevelt Corollary, the President replied that he was actually protecting the independence of Latin American countries, not threatening it. When he was accused of using the Dominican crisis as a stepping stone toward annexation, he replied: "I want to do nothing but what a policeman has to do in Santo Domingo. As for annexing the island, I have about the same desire to annex it as a gorged boa constrictor might have to swallow a porcupine wrong end to."

Taft extends "dollar diplomacy" into the Caribbean. President Taft went even further than Roosevelt in "protecting" Latin American countries. He and Secretary of State Knox applied their policy of "dollar diplomacy" to this area as well as to the Far East. They believed that Americans should invest in the Latin American republics in order to head off European financiers. If the American investments were endangered by mismanagement or political disturbances, then the United States would intervene.

President Taft applied "dollar diplomacy" to several Caribbean countries. In 1912, for example, financial disorder and the threat of a revolution led him to intervene in Nicaragua. United States marines were sent to restore order and protect American lives and property. Nicaraguan finances were placed under American control, and the marines stayed on until the 1920's.

▶ CHECK-UP

1. What were the two goals of Theodore Roosevelt's Latin American policy? Why did American interest in an interoceanic canal decline after 1850? Why did it revive following the Spanish-American War? What agreement was reached with Britain? Why was the Panama route selected?

2. Why did Panama revolt? Why was this revolt successful? Why was Roosevelt's action criticized? What problems were overcome in building the canal? How did the canal affect American foreign policy?

3. What was the Roosevelt Corollary? How was it applied in the Dominican Republic? What were the consequences of "dollar diplomacy" in the Caribbean?

• •

 4 *Wilson Makes Few Changes in Latin American Policy*

Most Latin American states resented this country's use of the "big stick" and "dollar diplomacy," though there was little the small republics could do about these policies. When Woodrow Wilson became President, however, Latin Americans hoped that the new, Democratic administration might discontinue the policies of Roosevelt and Taft.

Wilson at first denounces "dollar diplomacy." The early actions of President Wilson and his Secretary of State, William Jennings Bryan, seemed to confirm this possibility. Soon after his inauguration, President Wilson denounced "dollar diplomacy" and said that his administration would not support any "special group of interests" — such as American investors in Latin America. He promised, moreover, that "the United States [would] never again seek one additional foot of territory by conquest."

Wilson continues the old policy. Despite their intentions, Wilson and Bryan found it desirable at times to use the "big stick" and "dollar diplomacy."

(1) In Nicaragua, for example, the marines remained and the United States continued to supervise the government's finances. The Bryan-Chamorro Treaty (1914) gave the United States important territorial rights in Nicaragua. According to the terms of this treaty, the United States acquired (for three million dollars) a right-of-way for an interoceanic canal through Nicaragua. We also leased a naval base on the Gulf of Fonseca in the Pacific and acquired long-term leases on Great Corn and Little Corn Islands in the Caribbean (map, page 595).

(2) Wilson also intervened in the troubled affairs of the republic of Haiti. By 1915, France, Great Britain, and Germany were threatening to seize control of the Haitian customs to insure payment of debts owed to them. Wilson sent marines to Haiti to restore order. He established American control of the Haitian customs, took over supervision of government finances, and arranged for an orderly repayment of the republic's foreign debts. A treaty ratified in 1916 legalized the American protectorate. American control brought some benefits to Haiti. Roads were built and sanitary conditions were improved.

(3) Meanwhile, Wilson expanded the United States' protectorate over the Dominican Republic. In 1916 American marines were landed in that country to put down political disturbances. For the next six years an American military government ruled the Dominican Republic. There, as in Haiti, American occupation led to the construction of roads, bridges, and wharves. Schools were built and sanitary conditions were improved. But to the people of Haiti and the Dominican Republic, these benefits did not compensate for their loss of independence.

(4) In 1916 American influence in the Caribbean was further extended by purchase of the Danish West Indies (now called the Virgin Islands) for 25 million dollars. These islands, located at the entrance to the Caribbean, were considered vital to the defense of the Panama Canal. The Virgin Islands were administered by a governor appointed by the President. Ten years later the inhabitants were made citizens of the United States, but they did not secure a legislative assembly until 1936.

Mexico attracts United States investments. Relations with Mexico proved the most troublesome of Latin American affairs during Wilson's administration. Under the dictatorial rule of Porfirio Diaz (*dee'* ahs), Mexico had the outward appearance of a well-knit federal state. Beneath the surface, however, lay ignorance and superstition, racial and class hatred, and economic discontent. Most of Mexico's land was owned by the members of a small privileged upper class, while nine out of ten Mexicans were landless peons who lived almost like serfs. Since Diaz had turned the rich natural resources of the country over to foreign capitalists for development, they, of course, supported his administration. Americans in particular took an active part in building railroads, developing rubber plantations, raising cattle, and exploiting the rich silver, lead, copper, and oil resources. By 1910 some 50,000 Americans lived in Mexico, and American investments had reached a total of a billion dollars.

The Mexican government is overthrown. In 1911 a political upheaval threatened American interests in Mexico. In that year the aged Diaz was toppled from power by Francisco Madero, who promised to introduce social, economic, and political reforms. Before Madero could carry out his program, however, he was challenged by other rebel leaders. They arrested Madero early in 1913 and executed him. Victoriano Huerta (*wehr'* tah), who had been Madero's commander-in-chief and was believed to have been responsible for his death, became president of Mexico.

Wilson adopts a policy of "watchful waiting." Huerta's violent seizure of power shocked President Wilson, who was inaugurated a month after Madero's death. Though European countries were quick to recognize Huerta's regime, President Wilson refused to do so. The United States, he said, "can have no sympathy with those who seek to seize the power of government to advance their own personal interests or ambitions." Wilson adopted a policy of "watchful waiting" — that is, of waiting until the dictator Huerta was overthrown just as Diaz had been. This was a departure from the usual American policy of recognizing new governments once they had established control of a country. Wilson, in effect, was declaring that the United States would recognize only those governments whose methods of attaining power met with American approval.

Wilson also took steps to encourage Huerta's opponents inside Mexico. He allowed arms and ammunition to be shipped to Venustiano Carranza and Pancho Villa (*vee'* yah), who were leading the opposition. Furthermore, Wilson persuaded Great Britain to withdraw its support from Huerta by promising concessions in the matter of Panama Canal tolls. Before the opening of the Canal, Congress had passed legislation exempting American coastwise shipping from paying tolls. Great Britain protested that this law violated the Hay-Pauncefote Treaty and gave an unfair advantage to American shippers. When Wilson persuaded Congress to repeal the Tolls Exemption Act, Great Britain agreed to go along with the President's policy of "watchful waiting" in Mexico.

American forces occupy Veracruz. In the spring of 1914, Wilson was forced to modify his Mexican policy. A squadron of American war vessels had been stationed near Tampico, Mexico, to protect American lives and property. When a supply party from the U.S.S. *Dolphin* landed at Tampico, the sailors were arrested and paraded through the streets to jail. Though they were soon allowed to return to their ship, Admiral Mayo demanded a formal apology and a 21-gun salute to the American flag. Huerta was willing to make the apology but refused to order the salute. President Wilson then asked Congress for authorization to use military force to obtain "the fullest recognition of the rights and dignity of the United States."

Further complicating the situation was the arrival at the Mexican port of Veracruz of a German merchant ship bringing machine guns and munitions to Huerta's forces. Wilson decided that drastic action was necessary. Without waiting for authority from Congress, he ordered armed intervention to prevent landing of the munitions. When American forces occupied Veracruz, Huerta promptly broke off relations with the United States.

This picturesque steeple on St. Croix, one of the American Virgin Islands, has been preserved from the time when the islands belonged to Denmark.

A new Mexican government is recognized. "Watchful waiting" had now developed into the threat of war with Mexico, the last thing that Wilson wanted. Alarmed by this turn of affairs, Argentina, Brazil, and Chile offered to mediate the quarrel. President Wilson accepted the offer of the so-called "ABC powers," and Huerta had no choice but to do the same. In a conference held at Niagara Falls, the mediators proposed a new constitutional government for Mexico. This proposal Huerta rejected. But finding himself in a hopeless position, the Mexican dictator resigned and fled to Europe. Mexico then came under the control of Carranza, and the American forces were withdrawn from Veracruz. When Carranza guaranteed that the lives and property of foreigners would be respected, the United States recognized him as head of the Mexican government (1915).

An expedition is launched against Villa. Wilson's Mexican troubles were not yet over. No sooner had Carranza succeeded to power than his former ally, Villa, turned against him. In revenge for aid given Carranza by the United States, Villa seized and executed eighteen Americans in northern Mexico. Two months later, he crossed the border, raided a town in New Mexico, and killed seventeen more Americans. A wave of anger swept the United States, and President Wilson announced that an expedition would be sent into Mexico to "get Villa dead or alive." Carranza reluctantly gave his consent, and General John J. Pershing led a military expedition into northern Mexico.

For almost a year Pershing's expedition searched northern Mexico for Villa. The Mexican people were openly hostile to the American troops. Finally, in February, 1917, shortly before the United States became involved in World War I, Wilson ordered Pershing and his troops to withdraw from Mexico. As we shall see later, relations with Mexico again became strained in the 1920's (page 643).

▶ CHECK-UP

1. What examples of using the "big stick" and of "dollar diplomacy" can be cited from Wilson's administration?

2. Why had Americans made investments in Mexico? Why did the Mexicans oust Diaz? Why was the United States unwilling to recognize Huerta? What events led Wilson to order American troops into Veracruz? What was the outcome of the dispute with Mexico?

. . . .

Clinching the Main Ideas in Chapter 28

By the early twentieth century the United States had won recognition as a world power. But Americans also realized that victory in the Spanish-American War had brought them new responsibilities. For three years they occupied Cuba, during which time yellow fever was conquered. Puerto Rico and the Philippines were given a limited degree of self-government; and, as in Cuba, Americans helped build roads, bridges, schools, hospitals, and sanitary facilities. At the same time American financial investments and increased trade tied Cuba, Puerto Rico, and the Philippines closely to the United States.

Acquisition of overseas territories affected the country's foreign policy. In the Far East, the United States sought to preserve the independence and territorial integrity of China and to uphold the principle of equal opportunity for trade. These considerations led Secretary of State Hay to propose the Open Door Policy and caused Presidents Roosevelt, Taft, and Wilson to oppose Japanese efforts to dominate the Far East.

In the Caribbean, the determining factor in American foreign policy came to be the security of the Panama Canal. Once Theodore Roosevelt had obtained the right to build the canal, American policy sought to insure the stability and independence of Latin American republics. Under the Roosevelt Corollary to the Monroe Doctrine, the United States claimed the right to intervene in a Latin American country if necessary to forestall intervention by a European power. At one time or another Roosevelt, Taft, and Wilson sent American armed forces into Nicaragua, the Dominican Republic, Haiti, Panama, and Mexico.

In addition, Presidents Roosevelt and Taft encouraged American businessmen and bankers to make investments in Latin American countries. Wielding the "big stick" and practicing "dollar diplomacy" furthered American foreign-policy goals in the Caribbean, but won this country few friends south of the border.

Chapter Review

Terms to Understand

1. "big stick"
2. Boxers
3. protectorate
4. ABC powers
5. Foraker Act
6. dollar diplomacy
7. Platt Amendment
8. Open Door Policy
9. Insular Cases
10. dreadnought
11. Hay-Pauncefote Treaty
12. Hay-Bunau-Varilla Treaty
13. Root-Takahira Agreement
14. Lansing-Ishii Agreement
15. "watchful waiting"
16. Jones Acts (1916 and 1917)
17. Twenty-one Demands
18. Gentlemen's Agreement
19. sphere of influence
20. Roosevelt Corollary

What Do You Think?

1. Compare the Monroe Doctrine and the Open Door Policy.

2. Read the third section of the Platt Amendment (page 585). Are these worthy goals? Explain. Why did Cubans object to the Amendment?

3. What were the causes of growing friction between this country and Japan during the early 1900's? Explain.

4. Why did Japan present the Twenty-one Demands to China? How did the United States and Britain react? How did the relations of these three countries gradually change?

5. How did the Latin American policies of Roosevelt and Taft differ from those of Wilson (a) in theory and (b) in practice?

Using Your Knowledge of History

1. Debate: *Resolved,* That the Constitution should follow the flag.

2. Members of the class might report on the events leading to the acquisition of the Canal Zone from the point of view of (a) the president of Colombia, (b) a leader in Panama's revolution, or (c) President Roosevelt.

3. Write an editorial evaluating the Roosevelt Corollary. Assume that this editorial would be published in a leading Latin American newspaper.

4. Look up the provisions of Britain's 1902 defensive alliance with Japan. Then write a brief essay explaining these provisions and why the alliance at the time was to the advantage of both powers.

Extending Your Knowledge of History

Two excellent studies of this country's role in world affairs are F. R. Dulles's *America's Rise to World Power, 1898–1954,* and Howard Beale's *Theodore Roosevelt and the Rise of America to World Power.* How the United States administered its new possessions is the subject of J. W. Pratt's *America's Colonial Experiment.* Our Caribbean policy is discussed by Dexter Perkins in two interesting books: *The United States and the Caribbean* and *History of the Monroe Doctrine.* In *American Heritage* see "Ambassadors to the Court of Theodore Roosevelt" by Nelson M. Blake (February, 1956), and "Black Jack's Mexican Goose Chase" by Leon Wolff (June, 1962).

CHAPTER 29

The United States Becomes Involved in the First World War

Infantrymen in World War I

1914–1918

The world must be made safe for democracy. Its peace must be planted upon the tested foundations of political liberty. We have no selfish ends to serve. We desire no conquest, no dominion. We seek no indemnities for ourselves, no material compensation for the sacrifices we shall freely make. . . . America is privileged to spend her blood and her might for the principles that gave her birth and happiness and the peace which she has treasured. God helping her, she can do no other.

WOODROW WILSON'S WAR MESSAGE
TO CONGRESS, APRIL, 1917

During the early years of the twentieth century American attention was focused on progressive reform at home and on the nation's enlarged responsibilities in the Caribbean and the Far East. Few Americans were well-informed about trends that had been developing in Europe — the growth of national pride, the race to build up armaments, the formation of military alliances, and rivalry for colonial empires. Many Americans assumed that future international conflicts could be resolved without the use of force. But this illusion was shattered in the summer of 1914 when the assassination of an Austrian archduke set in motion events which led to war.

At first President Wilson, like most Americans, saw no reason why the United States should become involved in this tragic conflict. He issued a proclamation of neutrality and asked the country to remain "impartial in thought as well as in action." As the war dragged on, however, Americans found it more and more difficult to remain neutral. By April, 1917, Germany's violation of neutral rights on the high seas and the threat which a German victory would pose prompted Wilson to ask Congress for a declaration of war.

The American entrance into World War I came at a critical point in the conflict and helped turn the tide in favor of the Allies. Before the fighting ended, President Wilson announced to the world his famous Fourteen Points. He hoped that these would help to establish and preserve world peace "upon the tested foundations of political liberty."

1 World War I Engulfs Europe

For centuries the countries of Europe had been concerned about maintaining the balance of power. When any one nation became too powerful, the others would combine against it. Thus Napoleon, who sought to build a European empire, found himself fighting Great Britain, Russia, Austria, Prussia, and many smaller states. After Napoleon's final defeat in 1815, the victorious powers arranged a peace settlement to prevent further French aggression. They also developed a plan under which the great powers could hold conferences to deal with issues which might provoke war. For a hundred years there was no general war in Europe.

International tension grows. Toward the end of the 1800's, however, certain conditions led to increased tension both in Europe and in other parts of the world.

(1) The rise of Germany as a great military power alarmed both France and Russia. (2) The development of German industry and trade disturbed Great Britain, especially after Germany began to build a powerful navy. (3) A growing spirit of nationalism made countries proud and warlike. (4) The Industrial Revolution caused countries to seek new sources of raw materials and new markets. In the scramble for colonies, conflicting claims led to international crises. (5) Increased rivalry and growing tension led European powers to begin an armaments race and to form rival alliances.

Rival alliances add to the danger of war. The European powers tried to protect themselves during this period of rapid change by making alliances and agreements with each other. Germany entered into a formal alliance with Austria-Hungary and later with Italy, thus forming the Triple Alliance. On the other hand, France, Great Britain, and Russia reached broad agreements and drew together in the Triple Entente. Great Britain also formed a defensive alliance with Japan.

In this tense atmosphere, conflicts between any two European powers threatened to involve the other members of the Triple Entente and the Triple Alliance. Thus, minor disputes could quickly become international crises. Quarrels between Austria-Hungary and Russia over territory in the Balkans and between France and Germany in Morocco brought Europe to the brink of war on several occasions before 1914. The danger of an international explosion was heightened by a naval arms race between Britain and Germany and by the build-up of military forces in all the major countries.

International peace conferences accomplish little. Two international peace conferences failed to reduce tension in Europe. The first of these conferences met in 1899 at The Hague in the Netherlands. Called at the suggestion of the Czar of Russia, it was attended by 26 nations, including the United States. The delegates could reach no agreement about disarmament, but they did establish a Permanent Court of Arbitration at The Hague. Countries involved in a dispute could submit

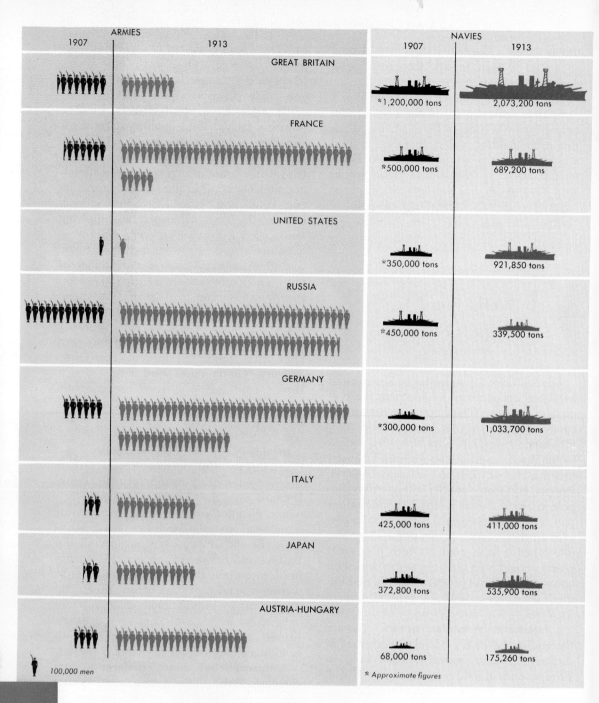

ARMIES			NAVIES	
1907	1913		1907	1913

GREAT BRITAIN

*1,200,000 tons / 2,073,200 tons

FRANCE

*500,000 tons / 689,200 tons

UNITED STATES

*350,000 tons / 921,850 tons

RUSSIA

*450,000 tons / 339,500 tons

GERMANY

*300,000 tons / 1,033,700 tons

ITALY

425,000 tons / 411,000 tons

JAPAN

372,800 tons / 535,900 tons

AUSTRIA-HUNGARY

68,000 tons / 175,260 tons

100,000 men

* Approximate figures

CHART STUDY

THE ARMAMENT RACE

This chart shows the increase in the size of the armies and navies of the major world powers from 1907 to 1913.

their quarrel to this tribunal; or they could appeal to a neutral nation or a commission of inquiry to settle their differences. Andrew Carnegie, a member of the American delegation to the conference, was so enthusias-tic about the Court of Arbitration that he donated money to build a "Peace Palace" at The Hague.

In 1907 President Theodore Roosevelt joined with the Russian Czar in calling a second peace conference at The Hague. Delegates representing 44 nations approved new rules concerning the conduct of war, but they failed to find any method of preventing war. The conference approved the Drago Doctrine, a principle which stemmed from Roosevelt's intervention in the financial affairs of Latin American countries. According to the Drago Doctrine,[1] debts should not be collected by force "unless the debtor country refused arbitration, or having accepted arbitration, failed to submit to the award."

Americans are interested in the peace movement. American interest in the peace movement was not limited to the Hague conferences alone. Church groups and women's clubs supported the movement, and many "peace" societies enlisted prominent businessmen as officers and directors. Andrew Carnegie, for instance, served as president of the New York Peace Society, and both President Wilson and Secretary of State Bryan were members of the American Peace Society. In 1910 a wealthy Boston publisher, Edwin Ginn, established the World Peace Foundation to publish studies in international law and international relations. That same year Carnegie granted an even larger sum to the Carnegie Endowment for International Peace. Many Americans read with approval *The Great Illusion*, written by an Englishman, Norman Angell. In this book Angell claimed that any future war would cause such widespread destruction that no country could win it.

The United States signs arbitration treaties. Further evidence of American interest in world peace was the signing of a number of arbitration treaties with other nations. Theodore Roosevelt, you will recall, had served as mediator to end the Russo-Japanese War. While he was President, the United States signed 25 treaties under which the treaty signers agreed to submit their disputes to the Hague Court. Presidents Taft and Wilson also supported arbitration. Secretary of State Bryan negotiated some thirty "cooling-off" treaties. These treaties provided that disputes which

Europe was still at peace in 1910 when royalty gathered in London for the funeral of Edward VII. Here are the German Kaiser (on the white horse) and (ahead of him) the new British king, George V.

could not be settled by the Hague Court would be referred to an international commission. To be sure, not all arbitration treaties received Senate approval, nor were all nations interested in entering into such agreements. Nevertheless, most Americans felt that no civilized country would launch a full-scale war.

World War I begins in the Balkans. The illusion that no great war could break out was shattered in the summer of 1914. An assassination in an Austrian province started a chain of events which plunged the major European powers into war. On June 28, 1914, the Austrian Archduke Francis Ferdinand and his wife were fatally shot by a young Serb in Sarajevo (sah-*rah*'yeh-voh), a town in what is now Yugoslavia.[2] By killing the heir to the Austrian throne, the assassin thought he was striking a blow for liberty. Austria, however, viewed the

---

[2] Sarajevo was the capital of the province of Bosnia. This province, populated largely by Serbs, had been part of the Turkish Empire until annexed by Austria-Hungary in 1908 over the protests of Serbia and Russia. The Serbs in Bosnia remained bitterly opposed to Austrian rule.

---

[1] It was proposed by Luis Drago, the Argentine foreign minister.

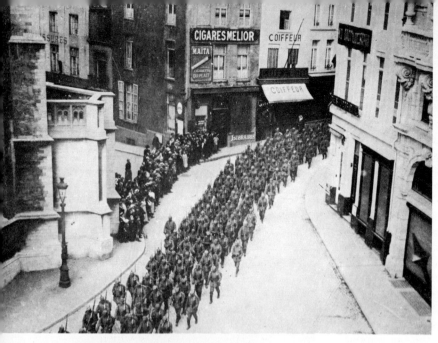

Belgians look on as a column of German troops marches through the streets of Brussels, in August, 1914.

attack as a challenge to its control over Bosnia. It assumed that the Serbian government had inspired the assassination and decided to punish Serbia.

Austria immediately sent a harsh ultimatum making extreme demands on Serbia. Though the Serbian government accepted practically all of these demands, Austria claimed that its reply was unsatisfactory. The Austrian government then began to mobilize its armed forces. For a tense month European diplomats worked to prevent a conflict between the two countries or at least to confine to the Balkan peninsula any war that broke out. But Britain's efforts to persuade Austria and Serbia to settle their differences by negotiation were thwarted because Austria had been assured of support from Germany. Serbia, on the other hand, was encouraged to hold firm by the Russians, who had long resented the extension of Austrian control in the Balkan peninsula. On July 28, Austria-Hungary declared war on Serbia.

Europe mobilizes. The system of alliances now began to drag other countries into the conflict. On the day after Austria's declaration, Russia started to mobilize its military forces. Alarmed by Russian preparations, the German Kaiser urged the Czar to withdraw the order for mobilization. When this was not done, Germany declared war against Russia on August 1. Meanwhile, France, allied with Russia, began to mobilize. When the French failed to declare their neutrality, Germany declared war on France and invaded Belgium.

Long before this crisis, German military leaders had planned their strategy in the event of war with Russia and France. Their plan called for a swift strike at France before the slow-moving Russian army could be mobilized for an invasion of Germany. To avoid a direct attack against the strongly fortified French border, the German armies were to cross neutral Belgium and tiny Luxemburg (map, page 619).

For 75 years Belgian neutrality had been guaranteed by an international agreement signed by Britain and other European powers. Germany's violation of Belgian neutrality both angered and alarmed the British. On August 4 the British government notified Germany that a state of war would exist if Belgian neutrality were not respected. When Germany ignored this demand, Britain declared war. Thus, within a week five great powers had stumbled into a general war which none of them wanted.

In time, the Allied nations included Britain, France, Russia, Serbia, Belgium, Romania, Japan, Portugal, Montenegro, Greece, and Italy. Italy, though a member of the Triple Alliance, at first declared her neutrality but in 1915 became one of the Allies by declaring war on Austria. The Central Powers included Germany, Austria-Hungary, Turkey, and Bulgaria.

The United States declares its neutrality. America's first response to the chain reaction which produced World War I was one of shock. Most Americans believed, however, that their country could stay out of the war. According to one magazine editorial, "Our isolated position and freedom from entangling alliances" offered the "cheering assurance that we are in no peril of being drawn into the European quarrel."

Americans were also reassured by their government's prompt declaration of neutrality. President Wilson appealed to the people to be "neutral in fact as well as in name" and "impartial in thought as well as in action." It was hoped that strict neutrality would enable the United States to steer clear of the storm that was sweeping over Europe.

▶ CHECK-UP

1. What is "balance of power"? How had European countries tried to maintain the "balance"? Why did international tensions increase in the late 1800's? What alliances were formed? Where did crises develop?

2. What was the purpose of the international conferences held in 1899 and in 1907? What was achieved at each? What was the purpose of arbitration treaties?

3. How did Austria-Hungary and Russia react to the assassination of Francis Ferdinand? How did the allies of each come into the war? What stand did the United States take?

. . . .

2 Wilson Strives to Keep the United States Neutral

Most Americans sympathize with the Allied nations. To be neutral "in thought as well as in action" proved difficult for most Americans. From the outset, a large majority of the people favored the Allied cause. Although they cared little about the fate of czarist Russia, they felt kinship with the democratic governments of France and Great Britain. Since Revolutionary War days, when Lafayette and the French had aided the Patriots, there had been friendly ties between France and the United States. As far as Britain was concerned, the ill feeling of the American Revolution and the War of 1812 had largely disappeared as the British government had become more democratic. Moreover, cultural ties and their common language had helped bind the Americans and British together. Of equal importance was the fact that Britain and the United States came to agree on a variety of questions over the years.

Allied propaganda also played an effective role in making Americans sympathize with the Allied cause. Great Britain controlled the transoceanic cables which carried most of the news published in America about the war. Thus, Americans read war news which favored the Allied cause. In their dispatches the British emphasized the devastation inflicted by the German march through Belgium and the inhumanity of Germany's submarine warfare.

Some Americans feel otherwise. Some people in the United States, however, favored the other side. Loyalty to the fatherland led some German and Austrian immigrants to voice support for the Central Powers. In addition, many Americans of Irish background hoped that involvement of British forces on the Continent would enable Ireland to win independence. And Jewish refugees who had fled persecution in Russia hoped for that country's defeat.

Americans lend money to the Allies. The early victories of the Central Powers aroused concern lest Germany become supreme in Europe. Many Americans not only favored the Allies but were willing to give them financial support. Determined to maintain strict neutrality, Secretary of State Bryan blocked a loan that private American investors wished to make to the French government. But in mid-1915, Bryan resigned as Secretary of State (page 612), and the government withdrew its objection to loans. Soon after, American bankers arranged a 500-million-dollar loan to the British and French governments. By the time the United States entered the war in April, 1917, American investors had pur-

On May 1, the day that the Lusitania *sailed from New York, the warning notice at left appeared in that city's newspapers. Six days later a German submarine torpedoed the liner, and many lives were lost. Above, passengers on a Spanish steamer watch and wonder as their ship, though neutral, is halted by a German submarine.*

chased Allied bonds to a total value of over two billion dollars. The 27 million dollars loaned to Germany seemed insignificant in comparison.

American trade with the Allies is important. Legally, American citizens were free to sell munitions and supplies to both the Central Powers and the Allies. But from the outset the volume of trade with the Allies was much larger. Great Britain's control of the sea lanes enabled her to block the shipment of supplies to the Central Powers. Thus American exports to Britain, France, Italy, and Russia exceeded three *billion* dollars in 1916, while exports to Germany and Austria-Hungary in the same year were valued at only one *million* dollars. Food, arms, and ammunition purchased from the United States were of vital importance in the Allied war effort.

The huge volume of trade with the Allies was also of great importance to the American economy. The high prices that American farmers received for their products enabled them to buy machinery for their farms and thus to increase their output. Even more startling were the earnings of American iron and steel companies and munitions manufacturers. Not only did some businessmen make fortunes out of the wartime trade with the Allies, but factory workers, whose wages kept rising, also shared in the general prosperity. During the two and a half years of American neutrality, trade with the Allies quadrupled and the American economy moved into high gear.

Britain restricts neutral trade with Germany. The nations that were waging war had the legal right to try to prevent the goods of neutral countries from reaching their enemies. Because of its superior naval power, Great Britain controlled the sea lanes leading to German ports, thus cutting off direct shipments to that country.

In addition, British ships stopped and searched neutral vessels destined for Germany and seized contraband goods. Under international law, contraband goods were usually understood to be military supplies such as arms and munitions. But Great Britain extended the contraband list to include foodstuffs and other articles which Germany had to import. Britain even insisted on searching neutral vessels destined for neutral ports, arguing that their cargoes might eventually reach the Central Powers.

During the early years of the war the American government repeatedly protested against Britain's interference with trade. The United States objected to Britain's definition of contraband and its high-handed manner of enforcing the blockade of German ports. Our government insisted, moreover, that British ships had no right to interfere with trade between neutral countries. Exasperated at Britain's continued violation of neutral rights on the high seas, Wilson asked on one occasion, "Can we any longer endure their intolerable course?" Yet the United States took no action except to send notes of protest. Although British practices cost American shippers time and money and violated international law, they involved no loss of life. More important, despite his intention of remaining neutral, the President believed that Britain was "fighting our fight," and he had no desire "to hinder or embarrass them [the British] in the prosecution of the war."

Germany begins submarine warfare. German violation of neutral rights proved far more serious. Though the German battle fleet was kept in harbor by the British blockade, German submarines were not. The submarine was a new weapon of war. Relatively light and frail, a submarine when surfaced could be destroyed by armed merchant ships. The submarine's effectiveness depended on surprise attack and quick retreat. Submarine commanders argued, therefore, that they could not follow the established practice of halting an enemy or neutral ship, searching its cargo for contraband, and removing passengers and crew before sinking the vessel.

During 1914 German submarines played only a minor role. But gradually the German government recognized that supplies were flowing freely to the Allies from neutral countries, whereas the British blockade was strangling trade with the Central Powers. Moreover, the fighting in western Europe seemed to have reached a deadlock, and it became clear that Germany's hopes depended on a quick victory. Under these circumstances the German government felt that it had to make full use of its submarines.

Early in February, 1915, Germany gave two weeks' notice that enemy merchant ships found in a war zone around Great Britain and Ireland would be sunk without warning. Neutral vessels entering this area would do so at their own risk. The American State Department promptly and vigorously protested. It solemnly warned Germany that she would be held to a "strict accountability" for the loss of American lives and property. The warning further stated that the United States would take action "to secure to American citizens the full enjoyment of their acknowledged rights on the high seas."

Despite the American protest, the German government would not retreat from its position. In fact, Germany insisted that submarine warfare was no more inhumane than the British blockade, which was keeping food from German civilians as well as troops. But this line of argument impressed neither the United States government nor the majority of its citizens. In 1915 it could hardly be said that the blockade was causing starvation on the Continent, whereas submarines were responsible for a heavy loss of life. Furthermore, claims for property losses caused by British restrictions on neutral trade could be settled later. But, as Wilson said, "the loss of life is irreparable."

The "Lusitania" is sunk. The full significance of submarine warfare was brought home to Americans by the sinking of the *Lusitania*. On the day that the British passenger liner sailed from New York, the German government placed a notice in the New York papers warning Americans that they traveled on Allied ships at their own risk. On May 7, 1915, off the coast of Ireland, the *Lusitania* was torpedoed. The liner sank within a few minutes, taking the

Though Wilson hoped to stay out of the war, he urged that the nation be ready to defend itself. Here, New York citizens march in a "Preparedness Parade" in support of the President's policy.

lives of nearly 1200 men, women, and children. Among them were 128 Americans.

The "Lusitania" crisis almost causes war. The sinking of the *Lusitania* nearly led to a break in relations between the United States and Germany. Some Americans, among them Theodore Roosevelt, urged an immediate declaration of war. Others, including Secretary of State Bryan, believed that the United States should take no action that might lead to war. This group argued that Americans should stay off the ships of warring nations.

President Wilson took a stand midway between these two extremes. He opposed a declaration of war, but he did warn the German government that American citizens had the right to travel as passengers on belligerent ships. He paid little attention to Germany's charge that the *Lusitania* was carrying munitions and other contraband.

Altogether the United States sent three notes to Germany, protesting the sinking of the *Lusitania* and seeking assurance that such an outrage would not be repeated. The second note was so strongly worded that Secretary of State Bryan resigned rather than sign it. The sharp protests of the new Secretary of State, Robert Lansing, finally brought results. In the fall of 1915, the German ambassador informed the United States that "liners will not be sunk by our submarines without warning and without safety of the lives of noncombatants, provided that the liners do not try to escape or offer resistance."

German agents engage in sabotage. Despite assurances that Germany would curb her submarines, the attacks continued and American lives were lost when an Italian liner was sunk in the Mediterranean. Meanwhile, German agents in the United States resorted to *sabotage* (the malicious destruction of property) to stop the flow of arms and supplies to the Allies. Bombs were placed on ships bound for Britain to destroy the vessels in midocean. Strikes were stirred up among workers in munitions plants, and explosions and fires destroyed factories producing war materials. This campaign of sabotage angered Americans and made them even more resentful of Germany's submarine warfare.

Germany makes the "Sussex" pledge. The submarine issue flared up again in March, 1916, when an unarmed French passenger ship, the *Sussex*, was attacked without warning. Several lives were lost, and many people were injured, including some Americans. This attack clearly violated Germany's promise. Wilson warned therefore that unless Germany abandoned its "relentless and indiscriminate" submarine warfare, the United States would "have no choice but to sever diplomatic relations."

Realizing that the United States was on the verge of declaring war, the German government yielded. In May, Germany renewed the pledge that merchant vessels would not be sunk "without warning and without saving human lives, unless these ships attempt to escape or offer resistance." The German government offered this *Sussex* pledge on condition that the United States force Great Britain to modify its illegal blockade. Wilson ignored this provision, but for the next few months German-American relations were less strained.

President Wilson urges preparedness. No one knew better than the President that the United States, as the leading neutral nation, was in a dangerous position. Both the *Lusitania* and the *Sussex* sinkings had brought the nation close to war, and Wilson had no way of knowing how long Germany would honor its latest pledge. He felt the United States should be prepared in case war did come. Theodore Roosevelt, Henry Cabot Lodge, and others had long been urging the President to take such steps. But many people in the Middle West, especially those of German origin, were less enthusiastic about readying the country for war. A number of progressives also opposed preparedness on the grounds that it would increase the likelihood of war and draw attention away from needed reforms at home.

In spite of opposition, Wilson pushed ahead with defense plans. As early as December, 1915, he had warned Congress of the need for such steps. A month later he told a midwestern audience: "I assure you that there is not a day to be lost. There may be at any moment a time when I cannot preserve both the honor and peace of the United States." After much prodding, Congress passed a National Defense Act in June, 1916. It increased the size of the regular army and provided for a national guard of 450,000 men, subject to the call of the President. In other legislation, Congress authorized the expenditure of more than 500 million dollars for the construction of battleships, submarines, and destroyers. A few months later, Congress approved the creation of a Council of National Defense to co-ordinate American industries and resources in the interests of national security.

Political parties prepare for the 1916 election. Wilson's popularity was high as the election of 1916 approached. His triple program of domestic reform, preparedness, and peace appealed to most Democrats and to many Republicans as well. The Democratic convention nominated him for re-election with great enthusiasm.

Theodore Roosevelt hoped to receive the Republican nomination. But conservative Republicans still resented his decision to bolt the party in 1912, and many of them opposed his warlike stand on foreign policy. The Republican convention instead nominated Charles Evans Hughes. Hughes had an outstanding record as a progressive governor of New York and at this time was serving as an associate justice on the Supreme Court. Roosevelt and most of the Progressives agreed to back Hughes.

Wilson wins re-election. During the campaign, Hughes toured the country and spoke to many gatherings. He was critical of Wilson's Mexican policy, of the Underwood Tariff (page 572), and of the Adamson Act (page 579); but in order to hold Progressive Republican votes, he endorsed most of Wilson's domestic program. With respect to the war in Europe, Hughes believed that Wilson had moved fast enough on preparedness and that he was successfully defending America's neutral rights on the high seas. Roosevelt's warlike campaign speeches embarrassed Hughes by giving the impression that the Republican

Wilson campaigners stressed prosperity, peace, and preparedness in the election of 1916.

Party favored war. The fact that Hughes failed to confer with the Progressive leader Hiram Johnson during a visit to California may have alienated some voters.

Wilson's efforts during the campaign were limited to speeches from the front porch of his summer home in New Jersey. But throughout the country Democrats campaigned actively, pointing with pride to the President's record. Especially effective was their campaign slogan: "He kept us out of war." They also charged that Hughes offered no real alternative to Wilson's program, and they dubbed the Republican candidate Charles "Evasive" Hughes.

The election of 1916 turned out to be one of the closest in history. Early returns from the East gave Hughes a commanding lead, and President Wilson went to bed on election night thinking he had lost. Then, as western ballots were counted, the Democrats gained and Wilson pulled ahead. Not until three days after the election, when the returns had come in from California, was Wilson's victory certain. Out of a total of over eighteen million votes cast, Wilson received 600,000 more popular votes than Hughes, while in the electoral college, the vote was 277 to 254. The President's re-election was a personal triumph. Even though registered Republicans had outnumbered registered Democrats, Wilson received three million more votes than in 1912. The Democrats also kept a narrow majority in the House and the Senate.

▶ CHECK-UP

1. Why did most Americans sympathize with the Allies? What steps were taken by Britain to cut off German trade? What was the United States' reaction?

2. How were submarines used by Germany to cut off trade between the United States and the Allies? What was this country's reaction? What other methods were used by Germany to keep the United States from helping the Allies?

3. What was the "Sussex" Pledge? What steps were taken by Wilson to prepare this country for war? Why? How was Wilson re-elected in 1916?

3 *The United States Enters the War*

Wilson favors "peace without victory." President Wilson interpreted the outcome of the election as a demand for peace, and he redoubled his efforts to find a way of ending the war. Sending notes to all the warring nations, he asked them to state the terms under which they would end the conflict. Because the replies he received were so far apart, Wilson prepared an outline of his own views on the kind of peace he thought the world needed. In January, 1917, Wilson presented these views in an address to the Senate.

"It must be a peace without victory," he said, for "victory would mean peace forced upon the loser, a victor's terms imposed upon the vanquished. . . . Only a peace between equals can last." Such a peace, declared the President, could be achieved only if the nations of the world recognized certain principles. Among these were government by the consent of the governed, equal rights for all nations, freedom of the seas, and the limitation of armaments on land and at sea. Wilson also included in this speech a proposal for a world peace organization. Though the President's ideas received much attention, his suggestion of "peace without victory" was unacceptable to both the Central Powers and the Allies.

Germany resumes unrestricted submarine warfare. The outlook for continued American neutrality faded when, on January 31, 1917, Germany announced its decision to resume unrestricted submarine warfare. The announcement stated that a war zone would be set up around the British Isles, along the French coast, and in the Mediterranean. Within this zone German submarines would attack all Allied or neutral ships. Once each week, one American passenger ship, plainly marked and carrying no contraband, might cross the Atlantic to England and one might return, if they followed a certain route.

Germany's decision to resume submarine attacks on American and other neutral ships was a calculated gamble. German military experts reasoned that "unrestricted" submarine warfare would break the blockade of German ports and cut off supplies from Great Britain. They realized that it would almost certainly bring the United States into the war on the side of the Allies. But they expected to crush the war-weary Allied armies before any sizable number of American reinforcements arrived in Europe.

The United States moves closer to war. Wilson answered the German declaration by breaking off diplomatic relations and dismissing the German ambassador in Washington. The President also asked Congress for authority to arm merchant ships. Action on this bill was delayed by a filibuster conducted by progressive senators. The President angrily denounced them as a "little group of willful men." When Wilson discovered that a statute passed in 1797 authorized the President to arm vessels without congressional approval, he acted at once to arm the merchant ships.

Meanwhile, British intelligence agents had notified the President that they had intercepted a message sent from German Foreign Secretary Zimmermann to the German minister in Mexico. The Zimmermann note proposed that if war broke out between Germany and the United States, Mexico should enter an alliance with Germany. Germany, in return, would help the Mexicans recover their "lost territory in New Mexico, Texas, and Arizona." When President Wilson released the text of the message, the American people were infuriated, and demands for action against Germany increased.

For several weeks Wilson played for time, hoping that a settlement might still be reached. Submarine warfare continued, however, and five American ships were sunk during the month of March alone. Until this time one reason for American reluctance to enter the war on the side of the Allies was that it would have meant aiding the Russian Czar. But in March, 1917, a revolution toppled the Czar from power and established a provisional (or temporary) government in Russia. This democratic government lasted for only half a year, but at the time Americans hoped that it meant an end to oppressive rule in Russia.

War is declared. On April 2, President Wilson went before a special session of Congress to deliver his war message. He reviewed Germany's violations of neutral rights and attacked the ruthless actions of the German government. He urged Congress to take the steps necessary to defend the United States and to help the Allies bring the war to a successful conclusion. "The world must be made safe for democracy," he said.

> It is a fearful thing to lead this great peaceful people into war. . . . But the right is more precious than peace, and we shall fight for the things which we have always carried nearest our hearts — for democracy, for the right of those who submit to authority to have a voice in their own Governments, for the rights and liberties of small nations, for a universal dominion of right by such a concert of free peoples as shall bring peace and safety to all nations and make the world itself at last free.

Four days later Congress declared war. The vote on the war resolution was 373 to 50 in the House and 82 to 6 in the Senate. The congressmen who opposed American entry into the war included a few pacifists and anti-war Socialists and some progressives. Many of them were convinced that the United States was going to war to protect her investments in the Allied cause. They believed Wilson's decision had been influenced by bankers and manufacturers of war materials, who might expect to profit from American entrance into the war and from an Allied victory. In the 1920's and '30's some historians repeated these same charges. But there is no evidence that Wilson was pressured by businessmen or that his decision stemmed from concern for the safety of American investments. The President, a majority of congressmen, and most Americans were prepared to fight to insure their country's security and to protect American rights.

The seriousness of the Allied situation becomes clear. The United States' entry into the war came at a critical time for the Allies. On the western front the British and French armies were barely holding their own. Morale suffered because of rumors that Russia would drop out of the war. Such an action would release hundreds of thousands of German soldiers for service on the western front. An Allied offensive in the Balkans was being pushed back by German, Austrian, and Bulgarian troops. Moreover, the Austrians appeared able to contain the Italian offensive. Indeed, with German aid Austria might launch a massive attack of its own.

The most serious problem for the Allies was the success of German submarine warfare. One out of every four ships that tried to reach Britain was being sunk. When the United States entered the war in April, Britain had enough grain to feed its population for only six or eight weeks. A high British official told the Wilson administration that the Germans would win "unless we can stop these losses — and stop them soon." But the number of German submarines was increasing.

The American navy goes into action. Less than a month after the declaration of war, American destroyers steamed into Queenstown on the southern coast of Ireland. They were soon followed by a number of cruisers and battleships. The American fleet co-operated with Allied warships in laying mines across the North Sea from the Orkney Islands to Norway. This mine field, as well as one across the Straits of Dover, proved effective in checking the coming and going of German submarines. During the course of the war American ships helped to maintain the blockade of Germany, "swept" German mines, and attacked German submarines.

Perhaps the American navy's most important contribution to winning the war was the development of the *convoy system*. The Allies had discussed the possibility of protecting merchant ships with escorts of destroyers and cruisers, but the idea had not yet been tried. When put into effect, the convoy system immediately proved successful. Allied shipping losses fell from 881,000 tons in April, 1917, to less than 300,000 tons by November. Not one of the ships carrying American troops to Europe was lost to German submarines. Thanks to the convoys, not only American "dough-

boys" but huge quantities of food and materials were safely transported to Europe.

An army is raised. Although the navy was ready for immediate action, it took time to raise, equip, train, and transport an American army to Europe. In May, 1917, Congress passed the Selective Service Act. It provided for the expansion of the regular army and national guard by enlistment and for the raising of a national army by a selective draft. All men between the ages of 21 and 30 (later 18 and 45) were required to register with local draft boards. Of the 24 million men who registered under the Selective Service Act, nearly 3 million were drafted. A lottery system in Washington determined the order in which these men were called up.

Camps were quickly established for the training of the soldiers. Each camp was a small city with complete facilities for housing and training thousands of men at a time. By the end of 1917 nearly two million recruits were being trained in 32 of these huge camps. Officers were trained in other camps and in Students' Army Training Corps, which were organized on college and university campuses.

Steps are taken to finance the war. After entering the war, the United States not only had to continue its loans to the Allies but also had to pay for its own war effort. During the remaining year and a half of World War I, the United States made loans of about seven billion dollars to the Allies. Most of this money was spent in this country for supplies. Meanwhile, the federal government's annual budget jumped from less than one billion dollars before the war to over twelve billion dollars in 1918. The Wilson administration met a third of the war's cost through taxation and sold long-term bonds to raise the rest of the money.

A series of revenue acts (1) increased income-tax rates, (2) provided that profits should be taxed if they were larger than during the prewar years 1911–1913, and (3) levied excise taxes on railroad tickets, telegraph and telephone messages, and such luxuries as tobacco, liquor, jewelry, automobiles, and theater tickets. Altogether

(*Continued on page 618*)

THE HOME FRONT IN WORLD WAR I

While American men served overseas during the First World War, their families contributed to the war effort at home. As never before in this country, the civilian population was affected by wartime conditions.

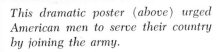

This dramatic poster (above) urged American men to serve their country by joining the army.

Farmers also increased their output, but Americans observed wheatless and meatless days to make food available for shipment overseas. Above, Herbert Hoover supervised the sending of food to Europe.

Industrial output rose to record heights as labor and management worked to produce the goods needed by the military services. Above, garment workers turn out army uniforms.

Children collected peach seeds (above), which were used in making gas masks. All Americans were urged to buy Liberty Bonds to help finance the war. Entertainers like Douglas Fairbanks helped sell the bonds (left).

these taxes paid about eleven billion dollars of the war costs.

Instead of issuing long-term bonds only in large denominations for sale to banks, the government sold bonds with face values as low as 50 dollars directly to the public. Actors and actresses, sports stars, government officials, and civic leaders helped to sell these Liberty Bonds. Posters urged every American — businessman, laborer, clerk, farmer, and school child — to buy bonds "until it hurts." Thrift stamps and war saving certificates reached even the smallest investor. In all, four Liberty Loans and a Victory Loan netted the United States government over 21 billion dollars.

Industry is mobilized for war. Equally important to the success of the war effort was the mobilization of American industry. It was essential to maintain the flow of supplies to the Allies. At the same time food, munitions, and equipment had to be provided for the American armed forces. Congress responded to this challenge by giving the President virtually unlimited powers over the economy for the duration of the war. (1) The President was authorized by law to obtain supplies for the army at prices which he would determine. (2) He was empowered to take possession of mines, factories, packing houses, railways, steamships, and all means of communication. (3) He could license the importation, manufacture, storage, and distribution of all necessities. President Wilson exercised these sweeping powers through a number of agencies, each responsible for a specific part of the war effort.

The most powerful of these agencies was the War Industries Board, whose chairman, Bernard Baruch, became the "czar" of the American economy. The War Industries Board fixed the prices of important war materials, determined what materials manufacturers could use, and to whom deliveries would be made.

The pressing need for ships to transport men and supplies overseas was met by the Shipping Board. It operated German ships caught in American ports at the beginning of the war and supervised the Emergency Fleet Corporation, which built some 700 merchant ships.

The Railroad Administration took over the railroads, the Pullman and express companies, and the inland waterways. Secretary of the Treasury William McAdoo ran the railroads as a single system, with common ticket offices, terminals, and equipment. Supply and troop trains moved on schedule, and reasonable profits were assured to the carriers. Both passenger and freight rates were increased during the war years, and so were the wages of railroad workers. While government management of the railroads met the war needs, it cost nearly one billion dollars.

Fuel and food are regulated. The government also set up agencies to insure the most efficient use of fuel and food. The Fuel Administration maintained adequate supplies of coal along the eastern seaboard for the fueling of ships bound for Europe. It also allocated coal to meet the needs of war-related industry. To conserve fuel for the war effort, the public was asked to observe "heatless" Mondays during the winter of 1917–1918 and to accept daylight saving time during the summer months. At one point in the war the Fuel Administration ordered all eastern manufacturing plants not engaged in war work to close down for five days.

The Food Administration was headed by Herbert Hoover, already well-known for efficient relief work in war-torn Belgium. Hoover was given sweeping powers over farmers, food processors and packers, and retailers, who sold products at prices set by the Food Administration. Farmers increased grain production almost 50 per cent in two years. The public co-operated with Hoover's plea to conserve food by observing wheatless and meatless days. Thousands of people turned flower gardens and vacant lots into vegetable gardens. "Food will win the war" became a national slogan.

Labor is mobilized. President Wilson realized the importance of enlisting the wholehearted support of American workers in the war effort. Defense plants, steel mills, shipyards, packing plants, railroads, and scores of other industries had to operate at full capacity, even though many workers were being drafted into the armed forces. Costly strikes which might have crippled

(*Continued on page 620*)

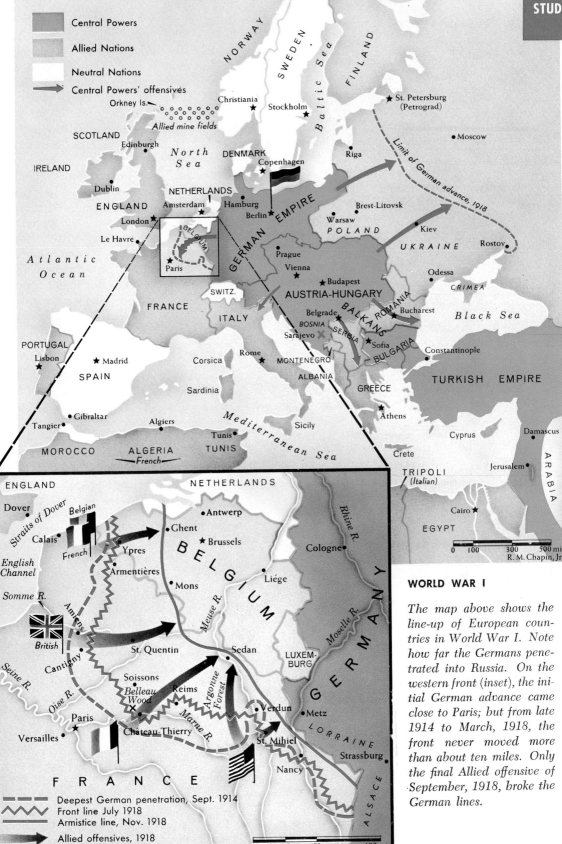

Central Powers

Allied Nations

Neutral Nations

Central Powers' offensives

NORWAY

SWEDEN

Baltic Sea

FINLAND

Orkney Is.

Christiania ★ Stockholm ●

Allied mine fields

● St. Petersburg (Petrograd)

● Moscow

SCOTLAND

Edinburgh ●

North Sea

DENMARK

Copenhagen ★

Riga ●

Limit of German advance, 1918

IRELAND

Dublin ●

NETHERLANDS

Amsterdam ★

Hamburg ●

Warsaw ●

Brest-Litovsk ●

Kiev ●

POLAND

UKRAINE

Rostov ●

ENGLAND

London ●

Berlin ●

GERMAN EMPIRE

BELGIUM

Le Havre ●

Paris ★

Prague ●

Vienna ●

Odessa ●

CRIMEA

Atlantic Ocean

SWITZ.

FRANCE

ITALY

★ Budapest

AUSTRIA-HUNGARY

Belgrade ●

BALKANS

ROMANIA

Bucharest ●

Black Sea

BOSNIA

Sarajevo ●

SERBIA

Sofia ●

BULGARIA

Constantinople ●

PORTUGAL

Lisbon ●

★ Madrid

SPAIN

Corsica

Rome ●

MONTENEGRO

ALBANIA

GREECE

TURKISH EMPIRE

Sardinia

Athens ●

Cyprus

Damascus ●

Tangier ●

● Gibraltar

Algiers ●

Mediterranean Sea

Sicily

Crete

Jerusalem ●

ARABIA

MOROCCO

ALGERIA
—French—

TUNIS

Tunis ●

TRIPOLI
(Italian)

Cairo ★

EGYPT

0   100   300   500 mi.
R. M. Chapin, Jr.

ENGLAND

NETHERLANDS

Dover ●

Straits of Dover

Belgian

● Antwerp

Rhine R.

Calais ●

French

Ghent ●

★ Brussels

Cologne ●

English Channel

Ypres ●

BELGIUM

Armentières ●

Liége ●

Somme R.

● Mons

Meuse R.

Amiens ●

British

St. Quentin ●

Sedan ●

LUXEM-
BURG

Moselle R.

GERMANY

Cantigny ●

Seine R.

Oise R.

Soissons ●

Reims ●

Belleau
Wood ✕

Argonne Forest

Verdun ●

Metz ●

Paris ★

Marne R.

Chateau-Thierry ●

St. Mihiel ●

LORRAINE

Versailles ●

Strassburg ●

F R A N C E

Nancy ●

ALSACE

‌‌‌‌ Deepest German penetration, Sept. 1914

Front line July 1918

Armistice line, Nov. 1918

Allied offensives, 1918

0   25   50   100 mi.

WORLD WAR I

The map above shows the line-up of European countries in World War I. Note how far the Germans penetrated into Russia. On the western front (inset), the initial German advance came close to Paris; but from late 1914 to March, 1918, the front never moved more than about ten miles. Only the final Allied offensive of September, 1918, broke the German lines.

the war effort had to be avoided even though workers had already begun to feel the pinch of rising prices. Wages had risen since 1914, but the economic boom had also raised the cost of living, and wartime shortages and restrictions were likely to cause continued inflation. Union members were understandably seeking further wage increases.

In dealing with these problems President Wilson consulted Samuel Gompers, president of the AFL and an advisory member of the Council of National Defense. Gompers assured the President that workingmen would support the government's war effort if their rights to organize unions and bargain for a "living wage" were protected. In return for a "no-strike" pledge, President Wilson promised to protect the rights of wage earners. He established a National War Labor Board and authorized it to settle all disputes between employers and employees. Many businessmen criticized Wilson's policy of co-operation with organized labor, but it proved essential to the success of the war effort.

Public opinion is mobilized. To ensure the support of the people, President Wilson appointed a Committee on Public Information. Its director, George Creel, enlisted teachers, ministers, business and professional men, artists, and civic leaders to write patriotic pamphlets and deliver four-minute speeches in theaters, concert halls, club rooms, and other gathering places. The purpose was to explain the causes and objectives of the war.

The Committee's publicity blamed Germany for starting the war and also accused the Germans of inhuman practices. This propaganda proved extremely effective, and Americans became aroused against anything German. Anyone who did not support the war effort — pacifists, anti-war Socialists, and German sympathizers — was harshly treated whether or not they actually aided the enemy. Schools dropped German-language courses, libraries removed German books from their shelves, and German music was banned at public concerts. Sauerkraut was even renamed "liberty cabbage."

The Espionage and Sedition Acts are passed. Congress passed strict laws to deal with those who opposed the war effort. The Espionage Act (1917) provided severe penalties for anyone who interfered with the draft or encouraged disloyalty. The Sedition Act (1918) extended these penalties to anyone who interfered with the sales of Liberty Bonds, tried to curtail production, or used "any disloyal, profane, scurrilous, or abusive language" about the American government or the armed forces. Under these laws, members of the IWW (page 551) were arrested and sentenced to jail. So too were many Socialists, including Eugene Debs. When cases arising from violation of the Espionage and Sedition Acts were appealed to the Supreme Court, both laws were upheld. But many Americans thought that these laws were needlessly harsh and out of place in a country that was waging a war for democracy.

▶ CHECK-UP

1. What were Wilson's views about a just peace? Why did Germany resume unrestricted submarine warfare? What developments brought the United States closer to war? What was the outlook for the Allies when this country entered the war?

2. How did the navy help the Allied cause? How was an American army raised? What steps were taken to finance the war? To mobilize industry? To conserve food and fuel? To mobilize public opinion?

- - - - - - - - - - - - - - -

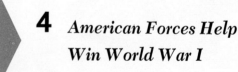

4 *American Forces Help Win World War I*

The American Expeditionary Force reaches France. Though the war-weary Allies were cheered by American preparations to take an active part in the war, they desperately needed immediate help. General John J. Pershing, commander of the American Expeditionary Force (AEF), reached Paris with his staff in June, 1917. The first regular army units arrived soon afterward. But these troops needed inten-

The United States' first fighter pilots saw action in World War I. Eddie Ricken-backer (above left), the leading American ace, shot down 26 enemy airplanes. But infantrymen made up the great majority of the armed forces (above right, landing in France). The men fought from trenches (below) until a direct attack on enemy positions called for "going over the top." Gas masks gave some protection against poison gas, which was used by both sides.

sive training in trench warfare before they were ready for battle. Though American soldiers first saw action in October, 1917, not until the next spring did they begin to arrive in large numbers. At the close of the struggle about two million American soldiers had served on European soil, and three quarters of them had seen combat.

The French and British wanted to use American troops to bring Allied units up to strength. But General Pershing, backed by President Wilson, felt that the Americans would be more effective in divisions commanded by their own officers. Although some Americans were used to reinforce Allied units, most of them served at the front under the direct command of General Pershing. After April, 1918, Pershing himself was subordinate to the Allies' supreme commander, the French Marshal Foch (*fohsh*).

Germany launches an offensive. The war had gone well for the Central Powers during the winter of 1917–1918. The Italians had suffered a crushing defeat at the hands of Germany and Austria in October, 1917. About the same time, the provisional Russian government was overthrown by the Communists (or Bolshevists), who were determined to withdraw from the war at any price.[3] In March, 1918, they accepted a humiliating peace with Germany at Brest-Litovsk (*brest′lih-tofsk′*). The Central Powers were then free to move their troops

[3] For a fuller account of the Bolshevist revolution, see pages 637–638.

from the eastern front to fight in the trenches of the western front.

In early 1918, Germany had about 300,000 more soldiers on the western front than did the Allies. Since the arrival of American troops would soon change this situation, the German strategists decided they must break through before that could happen. The German general staff, dominated by General Ludendorff, made plans for a final "victory drive" to begin in March.

The first blows were struck at the British and resulted in two important victories for the Germans. Next, the French were pushed back to the Marne River. But when Ludendorff launched an all-out offensive in mid-July, the Allied forces under Foch withstood the fury of the German attack. In fact, after three days they began a drive of their own. This counterattack was so successful that in two weeks the Germans were reeling back and never again assumed the offensive. Let us note briefly the part played by American troops in these last crucial months of the war.

American troops help stop the German drive. The timely arrival of large numbers of American troops helped to check the all-out German thrust. Late in May, 1918, American troops won their first victory by storming the fortified position of Cantigny (kahn-tee-*nyee'*). When the Germans reached the Marne River, only 50 miles from Paris, Pershing sent two American divisions to support the French. During June the Americans helped to check the German advance on Chateau-Thierry (shah-*toh'*-tyeh-*ree'*) and counterattacked there and at Belleau (beh-*loh'*) Wood. When the Germans made their last great effort to reach Paris in mid-July, some 85,000 American troops played an important role in checking the attack.

The Allied counteroffensive wins the war. With hundreds of thousands of American reinforcements coming into the line, Foch ordered an advance along the entire front. In the first stages of this counter-offensive Americans and French fought together in advancing across the Marne. In September the American army carried out its first major offensive at St. Mihiel

(*san'*mee-*yell'*), where the German line extended to the southeast of Verdun. Over a half million American soldiers fought in this battle. Wrote General Pershing: "An American army was an accomplished fact, and the enemy had felt its power. No form of propaganda could overcome the depressing effect on the morale of the enemy."

In the final weeks of the war, the American army moved down the Meuse River and through the Argonne Forest toward Sedan. Over a million Americans took part in the Meuse-Argonne operation. German military experts had regarded the Argonne Forest, heavily fortified with concrete entrenchments, barbed-wire entanglements, and sheltered machine-gun pits, as impenetrable. Every foot of the American advance over a 23-mile front was stubbornly resisted. More ammunition was fired in the Argonne than was used by the Union forces during the entire Civil War; and more than 100,000 American soldiers were killed or wounded. After advancing slowly but steadily for a month and a half, the Americans reached the outskirts of Sedan and cut the enemy's main line of communications. The advance of the American army was stopped only by the signing of an armistice on November 11.[4]

President Wilson presents the Fourteen Points. Throughout the last year and a half of World War I, President Wilson never lost sight of the goals for which he believed this country was fighting. In numerous speeches Wilson made it clear that our quarrel was with Germany's government and not with the German people. Moreover, he stressed the need to preserve international peace and order after the war was over. In January, 1918, in a speech before Congress, he outlined the *Fourteen Points* which he considered to be the "only possible program for world peace." They included the following principles:

(1) "Open covenants of peace, openly arrived at."

[4] Total American losses during World War I, at home and overseas, were approximately 115,000 dead and 200,000 wounded. By comparison, Russia lost 1,700,000 men killed in battle; Germany 1,800,000; France, 1,400,000; Britain, 900,000; and Austria-Hungary, 1,200,000.

(2) Freedom of the seas, in peace and war.

(3) The removal of all economic barriers and the establishment of equal opportunities for trade among all nations.

(4) The reduction of national armaments "to the lowest point consistent with domestic safety."

(5) An impartial adjustment of all colonial claims, in which "the interests of the populations concerned must have equal weight with the equitable claims of the government whose title is to be determined."

These were followed by specific points dealing with the future of Russia, Belgium, Alsace-Lorraine, Italy, the Balkan countries, Turkey, and Poland. Wilson's fourteenth point proposed a "general association of nations . . . for the purpose of affording mutual guarantees of political independence and territorial integrity to great and small states alike."

The Germans ask for an armistice. Wilson's Fourteen Points had a tremendous effect on the people of all the warring nations. Wilson gave voice to their hopes for an international order that would guarantee self-government and bar future wars. Members of the Allied governments, however, had reservations about the Fourteen Points. But while the outcome of the war was in doubt, they were still dependent on American man power and supplies. So they said little at this time about their objections to the principles outlined by Wilson.

At first, German leaders had scorned Wilson's Fourteen Points, for they had high hopes that their "victory drive" would win the war. But the failure of Germany's offensive in 1918 plus heavy losses and defeats demoralized the nation. Wilson's idealistic peace plans further undermined the confidence of the German people in their government. By September, German military and political leaders could read the handwriting on the wall. Their armies were on the verge of collapse; and their wartime partners were eager to make a separate peace. Bulgaria signed an armistice that month, and soon Austria-Hungary asked the Allies for terms of peace. Early

In New York, as in other cities, Americans thronged the streets to celebrate the end of the war in 1918.

in October the German government itself requested an armistice based on Wilson's Fourteen Points.

An armistice is signed. On November 8, Marshal Foch handed the armistice terms to the German representatives and gave them 72 hours in which to accept. Although the Allied demands were harsh, Germany was in no position to reject them. In several cities people were rising in rebellion against the Kaiser's government; mutiny had broken out in the German navy. The Kaiser himself fled to the Netherlands. The German representatives signed the armistice a few hours before the time limit ran out. At eleven o'clock on the morning of November 11, 1918, peace descended upon the battle-scarred fields of France.

Under the terms of the armistice, German troops had to pull out of Alsace-Lorraine and Luxemburg. Allied troops were to occupy German territory west of the Rhine, and a neutral zone was established on both banks of the river. Germany had to surrender arms and ammunition and its navy, including all submarines. Germany also had to renounce the treaty of Brest-Litovsk.

The armistice provided only for a cessation of hostilities on terms that made it impossible for Germany to renew the war. But the very fact that an armistice had been signed and the guns silenced was enough to set off wild celebrations on both sides of the Atlantic. To the American people President Wilson proclaimed: "Everything for which America fought has been accomplished. It will now be our fortunate duty to assist by example, by sober counsel, and by material aid in the establishment of just democracy throughout the world."

▶ CHECK-UP

1. What difference of opinion arose over the best way to use American troops? How successful were the Germans on the Russian front? The western front? What part did American troops play in the Allied drive that finally ended the war?

2. What were the Fourteen Points? What were the terms of the armistice?

. . . .

Clinching the Main Ideas in Chapter 29

The outbreak of World War I took Americans by surprise, for the international peace movement had led many of them to believe that no civilized nation would resort to war. President Wilson promptly declared the United States to be neutral, and most Americans seemed to believe that their country would be able to stay out of the conflict. Nevertheless, widespread sympathy for Britain and France caused Americans to lend money and sell supplies to the Allies. Germany ordered its submarines to attack both Allied and neutral vessels in an effort to cut off American supplies to the Allies. Wilson's protests after the sinking of the *Lusitania* and again after the sinking of the *Sussex* brought temporary relief from submarine attacks. But Wilson also prodded Congress to make preparations for war in case Germany revoked its *Sussex* pledge and again resorted to unrestricted submarine warfare. The President's handling of the European crisis, his record of progressive legislation, and his measures to insure preparedness helped him win a narrow victory in the election of 1916.

Early in 1917, Germany's resumption of unrestricted submarine warfare brought the United States into the war. Increased aid to the Allies and the immediate co-operation of the American navy helped the British and French hold the western front during 1917. By the spring of 1918, hundreds of thousands of American "doughboys" were ready to help check Germany's last great offensive and then to play a major role in the Allied counteroffensive which ended the war. The amazing mobilization of American industry and resources helped win the war. In formulating the Fourteen Points, President Wilson hoped to provide the basis for a just and lasting peace. Thus, having possessed little or no influence in European affairs in 1914, by the end of the war the United States had moved with swiftness into a position where it could determine the future of much of Europe.

Chapter Review

Terms to Understand

1. *Sussex* pledge
2. convoy system
3. Central Powers
4. Zimmermann note
5. mobilization
6. Triple Alliance
7. Triple Entente
8. Drago Doctrine
9. Court of Arbitration
10. the Allies
11. armistice
12. sabotage
13. Bolshevists
14. balance of power
15. Fourteen Points
16. National War Labor Board
17. Treaty of Brest-Litovsk
18. Meuse-Argonne operation

What Do You Think?

1. This chapter contains the statement "Rival alliances add to the danger of war" (page 605). Yet after World War II this country helped to organize a number of alliances (OAS, NATO, SEATO) to keep the peace. Explain.

2. Why did it prove impossible for Americans to be neutral "in thought as well as in action" in World War I?

3. Early in 1917 President Wilson expressed the view that the war must be ended by a "peace without victory." What did he mean? Why was this idea rejected by both sides?

4. The elimination of the eastern front was of great importance to Germany. Why? Yet about a year later the German war effort collapsed. Why?

5. Although the Allied governments had serious reservations about the Fourteen Points, they gave great publicity to them. Why? How did the Fourteen Points help to undermine the morale of the German people?

Using Your Knowledge of History

1. The German government contended that the sinking of the *Lusitania* was justified. Write a brief essay evaluating this argument.

2. Debate: *Resolved,* That the United States should have remained neutral in World War I.

3. In a two-column chart, list ways in which this country's rights as a neutral were violated by (a) Britain and (b) Germany. Why did the United States go to war with Germany and not Britain?

4. List what you consider the five most important contributions this country made to the victory of the Allies in World War I. Be ready to defend your list.

Extending Your Knowledge of History

Sympathetic accounts of Wilson's diplomacy are found in *American Neutrality, 1914–1917,* by Charles Seymour and *The World War and American Isolation 1914–1917,* by Ernest R. May. The isolationist point of view is presented by C. C. Tansill in *America Goes to War.* The fate of those who opposed the nation's war effort is discussed in *Opponents of War, 1917– 1918,* by H. C. Peterson and G. C. Fite. On the course of the war, see Hanson Baldwin's excellent short volume, *World War I: An Outline History.* Highly recommended are *The American Heritage History of World War I* and the companion record, "World War I Historic Music and Voices."

Analyzing Unit Eight

1. William Allen White called the Progressive Movement the period when America "turned the corner from conservatism." Under the *laissez faire* concept of government, what was the proper role of the federal government? How did the progressives modify this concept? What new powers did the government acquire during the Progressive Era?

2. The Progressive Movement was bipartisan in the sense that its supporters included both Democrats and Republicans. How does this fact help to account for the solid commitment of the American people to these sweeping reforms? What effect did the movement have on the two parties?

3. Do you agree that "American entry into World War I was precipitated by German submarine warfare, and that without this we probably would not have fought"? What part did the submarine play in drawing us into the war? Would our economic ties with the Allies, or the fact that our sympathies lay with the Allies, have drawn us into the war even without the submarine menace?

Unit 9 | The 1920's Bring Prosperity and Peril (1919-1932)

Fifth Avenue, New York City, in the 1920's

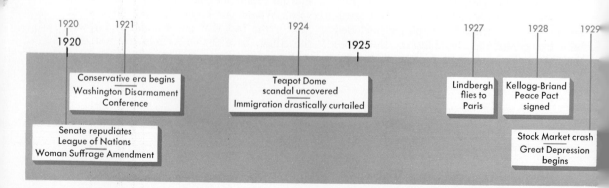

1920

1920

1921

1924

1925

1927

1928

1929

Conservative era begins
Washington Disarmament
Conference

Teapot Dome
scandal uncovered

Immigration drastically curtailed

Lindbergh
flies to
Paris

Kellogg-Briand
Peace Pact
signed

Senate repudiates
League of Nations

Woman Suffrage Amendment

Stock Market crash

Great Depression
begins

The crusading spirit that existed during the first two decades of the twentieth century came to a halt after World War I. Americans had confidently expected the peace settlement to carry out certain principles that President Wilson considered to be "the only possible program for world peace." At the Versailles Peace Conference, however, our allies weakened these principles with exceptions. And when the treaty, which included the plan for a League of Nations, reached the United States Senate, the President's political foes managed to defeat it. Meanwhile, Wilson's attempts to save the League had been cut short by his serious illness.

The Republicans won a sweeping victory in 1920. Sensing that the country's crusading spirit was evaporating, the Republicans called for a return to "normalcy." American disillusionment with world affairs was heightened by the collapse of several democratic European governments and the failure of our former allies to repay debts and loans. Nevertheless, the United States signed disarmament agreements and peace treaties in the 1920's and drew closer to its Latin American neighbors.

The zeal for reform likewise declined in domestic affairs. Businessmen found the Republican administrations of the 1920's responsive to their pleas for tariff protection, tax cuts, and lenient enforcement of federal laws by government agencies. Then the "golden twenties" came to a jarring end with the stock-market crash in 1929. There were basic economic causes for the collapse of the economy, but the American people blamed the Great Depression on the administration of President Herbert Hoover.

Until the depression struck, many Americans had paid little attention to affairs of state. They had been enjoying a wide variety of new products — from washing machines and vacuum sweepers to radios, movies, automobiles, and airplanes. By 1930 more people lived in cities than in the country, and American morals and manners were undergoing rapid changes. It is little wonder that many were willing to "let Europe stew in its own juice" and that most Americans were startled by the stock-market crash in 1929.

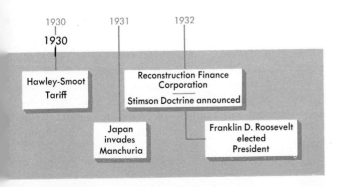

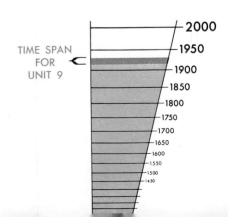

TIME SPAN FOR UNIT 9

CHAPTER 30

Wilson speaking for the League

The United States Rejects World Leadership

We must be now and forever for Americanism and Nationalism, and against Internationalism. There is no safety for us . . . if we do otherwise.

SENATOR HENRY CABOT LODGE, 1920

1919–1930

When World War I ended in November, 1918, many Americans and millions of other people throughout the world expected the peace treaty to follow the general outlines of President Wilson's Fourteen Points. They also looked forward to the establishment of an international organization to preserve the peace. So concerned was Wilson with the importance of writing the treaty that he himself headed the American delegation to the peace conference which met at Versailles. In the diplomatic bargaining, Wilson had to make many concessions to the Allies. Yet most of his Fourteen Points were visible in the final treaty, including the creation of the League of Nations. Wilson expected the United States Senate to give prompt ratification to the

Versailles Treaty. But his hopes were dashed by a small band of senators who opposed the treaty and American membership in the League of Nations.

Since the Republicans won the presidential elections of 1920, 1924, and 1928, they had the responsibility of conducting the country's foreign relations in the postwar years. They generally supported Senator Lodge's pledge "for Americanism and Nationalism, and against Internationalism." Yet it proved impossible for the United States to isolate itself from developments elsewhere in the world. Two problems in particular — disarmament and the failure of the Allies to repay wartime loans — kept this country in frequent contact with the major European nations. In addition, defense of the Panama Canal and American investments in Latin America required the United States to keep close watch on hemispheric affairs. In the Far East, meanwhile, fear and suspicion of Japan's intentions helped to shape American diplomacy during the 1920's.

1 President Wilson Helps Write the Versailles Treaty

Postwar Europe poses serious problems. For most Americans the adjustments that had to be made in the postwar years were difficult. Yet their problems seemed insignificant when compared to those faced by Europeans. About 60 million European men had served in World War I, and some 8 million of them had lost their lives. Billions of dollars in wealth had been wiped out. Large areas had been made unfit for cultivation, and hundreds of towns and villages were in ruins.

But physical destruction was only part of the story. Europe was also in a state of political upheaval. The ruling families of Russia, Germany, and Austria-Hungary had been toppled from power. Though supposedly the war had been fought and won to make the world "safe for democracy," there was strong opposition to democratic government in these three countries. The

When President Wilson visited the British and French capitals before the peace conference assembled, the people greeted him with great enthusiasm.

Russian Bolshevists were declaring their intention of spreading communism through the world by revolutionary means. In addition, small national groups throughout Europe were demanding self-government, or *self-determination,* thus complicating the task of redrawing the boundaries of the defeated countries. The peace conference that was to deal with this problem would also have to dispose of Germany's Asian and African colonies. Finally, the peace conference would have to consider the secret treaties and understandings which the delegates of various countries were determined to uphold.

President Wilson decides to go to Paris. Although no American President had ever traveled as far as Europe during his term of office, Wilson decided to head the American delegation to the peace conference. He justified this decision with the statement to Congress that "the peace settlements which are now to be agreed upon are of transcendent importance both to us and to the rest of the world, and I know of no business or interest which should take precedence of them." The President believed that his presence at the conference would help secure treaty terms based on the Fourteen Points. Moreover, he felt that no other American delegates would have as much personal prestige. In other words, he himself had to be present at the conference to fight for the kind of peace treaty he wanted.

Critics of President Wilson said it was unnecessary for him to go to Europe and even hinted that he sought personal glory. Some historians have argued that Wilson could have given firm instructions to American delegates and might have preserved more of the spirit of the Fourteen Points by staying at home. Looking back, it appears that Wilson's principal mistake was his failure to seek the co-operation of his political opponents in the United States Senate.

The Democrats lose control of Congress. During his first term in office Wilson had shown extraordinary political skill in working with Republican progressives and the various factions of his own party (Chapter 27). The result was a remarkable harvest of reform legislation. Then, during the war, party politics had been put aside as Republicans gave full support to the war effort.

By the time of the congressional elections of 1918, however, many people had become dissatisfied. Higher taxes, rising prices, economic controls, and the enactment of a wartime prohibition law caused many voters who had supported the Democrats in 1916 to change their minds. If the President had followed the usual custom of staying out of congressional elections, Democratic losses might have been less and the peace settlement might not have become a major political issue. But Wilson was angered by Republican attacks on the Fourteen Points and concerned about European reactions to possible Republican gains in Congress. Thus, at the last minute he appealed to the voters to return a Democratic majority to Congress. A Republican victory, he said, would be "interpreted on the other side of the water as a repudiation of my leadership."

Much to Wilson's dismay, the Republicans won control of the Senate by 49 seats to 47 and the House by 240 to 190. On the eve of the President's departure for Paris, Theodore Roosevelt declared: "Mr. Wilson has no authority whatever to speak for the American people at this time. His leadership has just been emphatically repudiated by them."

Wilson ignores the Republicans. The Republican margin in the Senate, though slim, gave that party the right to name the chairman and the majority of the members of all Senate committees. Chosen to head the Foreign Relations Committee, which would consider any treaty Wilson brought back, was Senator Henry Cabot Lodge, admittedly an opponent of the President. But Wilson refused to make any concessions to the Republican majority in the Senate or to regard the election results as disapproval of his policies. Said the President: "I have an implicit faith in Divine Providence and I am sure that by one means or another the great thing we have to do will work itself out."

Within the Republican Party there was considerable support for an international peace organization. Such prominent Republicans as William Howard Taft, Charles Evans Hughes, and Elihu Root agreed on the need for an international organization. Yet Wilson failed to include any of these men in the American delegation to the peace conference. Nor did he ask any member of the Senate, from either party, to accompany him to Paris as a delegate. Indeed, the only Republican delegate was a career diplomat who had not been active in party affairs for many years.

The "Big Four" dominate the peace conference. The peace conference met from January to June, 1919, at Versailles, just outside Paris. All the Allied nations sent delegates, but no representatives of the Central Powers took part in the negotiations. Nor was Communist Russia invited to the conference. The major decisions were made by the "Big Four" — Great Britain, France, Italy, and the United States. Representing Britain was Prime Minister David Lloyd George, who had just won an election in which he promised that severe penalties would be imposed on the Ger-

Representatives from the Allied nations met at the palace at Versailles (above) to arrange the peace treaty. At left are the "Big Four" leaders: Lloyd George of Great Britain, Orlando of Italy, Clemenceau of France, and Wilson.

mans. France was represented by Premier Georges Clemenceau, whose main concern at the conference was to guarantee his country's security. The Italian spokesman was Prime Minister Vittorio Orlando. He was determined to win for Italy all the territory that had been promised in secret treaties Italy had signed with the other Allies.

Secret agreements make the peace settlement difficult. Early in the conference the Allies called attention to secret agreements they had drawn up during the war. These had provided for dividing the spoils of war in case the Central Powers were defeated. France desired revenge against Germany, Italy claimed land from Austria, and all the Allies agreed that the Central Powers should pay war damages. They justified their demands on the grounds that Germany had forced even harsher terms of surrender on Russia in the treaty of Brest-Litovsk (page 621). Not surprisingly, these secret treaties ran counter to Wilson's Fourteen Points. In particular, they ignored the principle of self-determination. Thus the major difficulties at the peace conference stemmed from the conflict between the Allies' desire for a "hard" peace and Wilson's program for a "peace of justice."

The Covenant of the League of Nations is made a part of the treaty. Wilson was convinced that the best way to guarantee a lasting peace was through the organization of a league of nations. Such a body might later be able to correct any injustices included in the peace settlement. Wilson's proposal for the creation of an international body received prompt attention. Both the President and his close friend and adviser Colonel House were appointed to the commission to draw up a *covenant* (terms of agreement) for the league. When the Covenant was reported to the conference, it was immediately adopted.

After making certain that the League of Nations would be included in the peace treaty, Wilson returned to the United States to deal with pressing domestic problems. He soon found that a number of senators opposed American membership in any international organization. But the President said: "When the treaty comes back, gentlemen on this side will find the Covenant not only in it, but so many threads of the treaty

631

NEW NATIONS

— Boundaries of new nations created at Versailles

Territorial losses by:
Germany

Austria-Hungary

Bulgaria

Russia

1914 boundaries

To France
SYRIA AND LEBANON

PALESTINE TRANS- IRAQ
JORDAN
To Great Britain

To France

TOGOLAND CAMEROONS
To Belgium
RUANDA-URUNDI
To Great Britain
TANGANYIKA

S.W. AFRICA
To South Africa

Lost by:
Turkey
Germany

LEAGUE MANDATES

To Japan
NORTH PACIFIC ISLANDS
PHILIPPINE IS. Mariana Is.
Guam Marshall Is.
Palau Is.
Caroline Is.

NEW GUINEA
To Australia
SAMOA
To New Zealand

SWEDEN
NORWAY
Murmansk
Archangel
Baltic Sea
FINLAND
North Sea
ESTONIA U.
LATVIA S.
DENMARK Memel S.
Danzig LITHUANIA R.
GREAT BRITAIN
Polish "Corridor" EAST PRUSSIA
NETHERLANDS GERMANY POLAND
BELGIUM Occupied
LUXEMBURG Rhineland
Alsace- Saar CZECHOSLOVAKIA
Lorraine Basin
SWITZ. AUSTRIA HUNGARY
FRANCE ROMANIA
Corsica YUGOSLAVIA
ITALY BULGARIA Black Sea
Sardinia ALBANIA TURKEY
GREECE
Sicily
Crete Cyprus
Mediterranean Sea

R. M. Chapin, Jr.

THE TREATY OF VERSAILLES

For Germany, Austria-Hungary, and Russia, World War I meant sizable losses of territory as well as the overturn of their governments. In Africa and the Far East, possessions of the Central Powers were distributed among Allied nations.

tied to the Covenant, that you cannot dissect the Covenant from the treaty without destroying the whole vital structure." He did, however, listen to some Republicans who suggested amendments that would make the Covenant more attractive to the Senate. When Wilson returned to Paris, he succeeded in adding to the Covenant a provision that the Monroe Doctrine and American domestic affairs were not to come under the League's authority. Also, any nation was to have the right to withdraw after two years' notice.

The Treaty of Versailles is completed. On his return to the peace conference, Wilson had to contend with several difficult problems. These included (1) Clemenceau's demand that an independent buffer state be created from German territory west of the Rhine; (2) Italy's insistence on annexation of Austrian territory in which there was a small minority of Italian people; and (3) Japanese demands for Germany's holdings in China and the Pacific (page 594). Though exhausted and ill with influenza, Wilson put up a bitter fight against these and other extreme demands. The final terms of the Versailles Treaty did not incorporate all the principles Wilson had laid down in the Fourteen Points.

The principle of self-determination was embodied not only in the Versailles Treaty but in additional treaties signed with the Central Powers. As a result, the states of Czechoslovakia, Poland, Finland, Estonia, Latvia, and Lithuania were created; and Austria and Hungary became separate states. Moreover, the boundaries of Serbia (which became Yugoslavia after the war), Belgium, Italy, Greece, and Romania were enlarged. And Alsace-Lorraine was returned to France. (See map on page 632.) The treaty permitted Japan to retain her economic interests in the Shantung peninsula. She also received Germany's Pacific islands — the Carolines, Marshalls, and Marianas — but only as mandates,[1] not as permanent possessions.

In return for the inclusion of the League of Nations in the Versailles Treaty, Wilson agreed to harsh peace terms for Germany. The treaty stripped Germany of all its colonies. It allowed France to exploit the rich coal mines of the Saar Basin for fifteen years, and called for the Rhineland to be occupied by Allied troops for fifteen years. In addition, Germany was to pay five billion dollars in immediate reparations

(damages) and had to agree to pay an undetermined amount in the future. Germany was also forced to admit that it was responsible for the war. When the German delegates were called in to accept the Versailles Treaty, they protested. Powerless to do anything else, however, they signed on June 28, 1919.

The Covenant of the League of Nations establishes a world organization. Wilson pinned his hopes for the success of the treaty and the preservation of peace on the League of Nations. The Covenant provided for an Assembly, a Council, and a permanent Secretariat (official staff). The Assembly, which possessed final authority, consisted of delegates from the member states, each having one vote. It was to meet at stated intervals in Geneva, Switzerland. The Council consisted of representatives of nine powers — France, Great Britain, Italy, Japan, the United States, and four nonpermanent members to be chosen by the Assembly. Settlement of most major issues required unanimous votes in the Council and usually also in the Assembly. The Covenant also provided for a Permanent Court of International Justice, which came to be known as the World Court.

The purpose of the League of Nations was "to achieve international peace and security by the acceptance of obligations not to resort to war." Article X was regarded by Wilson and many others as the heart of the Covenant. It provided that "the members of the League undertake to respect and preserve as against external aggression the territorial integrity and existing political independence of all members of the League." Article XIII pledged the members (1) to submit to arbitration any disputes that might arise among them, (2) to carry out faithfully any awards or decisions made, and (3) to refrain from waging war on a nation which was carrying out such awards or decisions. Article XVI called for economic sanctions (penalties) as well as military measures against any members which waged war or broke promises to submit disputes to arbitration. Plans were also made for an international labor office.

To many, the dream of a world parliament seemed about to come true. To

---

[1] Nations that received territories as mandates administered these territories but were not supposed to fortify them. The governing nations were responsible to the League of Nations for their actions in the mandated territories.

Woodrow Wilson the League of Nations was "a definite guarantee of peace . . . a definite guarantee against the things which have just come near bringing the whole structure of civilization into ruin."

▶ CHECK-UP

1. What problems complicated the negotiations of a peace treaty after World War I? Why did President Wilson go to the peace conference? What problems stemmed from the Republican victory in the 1918 elections? How did Wilson make a mistake in failing to appoint any Republicans to the peace delegation?

2. What problems made the negotiations of a just peace difficult? What were the results of stressing the principle of self-determination? What concessions did Wilson make?

3. Describe the organization of the League of Nations. How was the League to preserve peace?

. . . .

2 *The Senate Rejects the Treaty and the League of Nations*

The Senate is divided over the League of Nations. When President Wilson submitted the Treaty of Versailles to the Senate (July, 1919), debate on the subject had already started. In their attitude toward the League, senators fell into three main groups. (1) There were a dozen or so "irreconcilables," ably led by William E. Borah, Hiram Johnson, and Robert M. La Follette. These men, many of them progressives, were determined to defeat the treaty and the League at any cost. (2) Another group of about 40 Democrats and a few Republicans were in favor of ratifying the treaty with little or no change. (3) The third group, mostly Republicans, favored modifying the treaty before ratification. They wanted to write in certain reservations and interpretations which would define more clearly the obligations of the United States under the League Covenant. Some senators in the third group favored substantial or even drastic reservations; others were "mild" reservationists.

All told, more than 80 senators — well over the necessary two-thirds majority — favored ratification in one form or another.

Lodge leads the fight to revise the League Covenant. The leader of those who favored reservations or limitations was Senator Henry Cabot Lodge. Before 1919, Lodge had spoken out in favor of an international organization to preserve the peace. But he found many things to criticize in the Covenant of the League of Nations. He especially objected to Article X, which, he argued, might involve the United States in a war to protect the territory of some foreign nation. Perhaps a more important reason for Lodge's objection to the League was his hostility toward Woodrow Wilson. These two strong-minded men had clashed before, and Lodge was now determined to use his power as Chairman of the Senate Foreign Relations Committee to amend or defeat Wilson's treaty.

The make-up of Lodge's Committee boded ill for the approval of the treaty and the League. A majority of its members were "irreconcilables." They were prepared to kill the treaty or, at the least, to amend it to the point where Wilson would be compelled either to accept a Lodge treaty or reject it. Wilson, on the other hand, made it very clear that he would not accept amendments or reservations. Such modifications would have to be submitted for approval to the other signers of the treaty, including Germany. This would leave the way open, Wilson felt, for other nations to submit their own amendments or reservations. Thus, the effectiveness of the League of Nations could be completely undermined.

The League receives popular support. When the treaty was submitted to the Senate, even Senator Lodge agreed that the great majority of the people were for it. Influential groups, such as the American Federation of Labor, the American Bar

Association, the American Bankers' Association, and the Federal Council of Churches, favored ratifying the treaty and entering the League. It is likely that with a few minor changes the treaty could have been ratified by the Senate in July, 1919.

Lodge delays Senate action on the League. Lodge knew that he needed time to rally support in the Senate for drastic revision and to persuade the public that membership in the League would weaken the United States. He spent two weeks reading aloud every word of the 300-page treaty to the Foreign Relations Committee. Several weeks of public hearings followed, during which the Committee listened to scores of people who objected to various provisions of the treaty or the Covenant. Meanwhile, the opponents of ratification spread anti-League propaganda across the country.

Wilson refuses to consider revision. During the summer of 1919 the Foreign Relations Committee worked on amendments to the treaty. The French ambassador assured Wilson that the Allies would gladly accept the amendments if it meant American participation in the League of Nations. But Wilson refused to accept any amendments. To the ambassador, he said: "I shall consent to nothing. The Senate must take its medicine." Wilson gave two reasons for his refusal to compromise. (1) He believed that changes in the Covenant ought to be made *after* the treaty went into effect. (2) He was still convinced that the vast majority of the American people wanted the treaty ratified without change.

Wilson appeals to the people. Wilson decided to appeal directly to the people for their support. Against his doctor's advice, he set out in early September on a long speaking tour. During the war years and at the peace conference the President had worked long hours under great pressure. Moreover, he had never fully recovered from his illness in Paris. Nevertheless, in three weeks he covered 9000 miles, delivering 37 major addresses and also speaking at countless stops from the rear platform of his train. The public response was generally enthusiastic, but the impact of Wil-

Henry Cabot Lodge of Massachusetts, who led the opposition to the League of Nations, was an author as well as a political figure. He served in the Senate for 30 years.

son's appeal was blunted by Senators Johnson and Borah, who for a time followed the President to attack the League. Then, in late September, 1919, after a speech at Pueblo, Colorado, Wilson became so ill that he canceled the remainder of the trip and returned to Washington. There, on October 2, the President suffered a stroke which left him partially paralyzed.

For weeks the President was a desperately sick man, though no one outside the White House knew the extent of his illness. His wife and his secretary shielded the President from all but the most important business. No information that "would twist the sword in his wound" was permitted to reach him. Though the President's speaking tour had won public sympathy for the League, it had no direct effect upon the senators who were considering the treaty.

The Foreign Relations Committee revises the treaty. On September 10, after Wilson had begun his tour, the Foreign Relations Committee reported the treaty to the Senate with 45 amendments and 4 reservations. But Democrats and moderate Republicans in the Senate voted down these amendments. Early in November, after Wilson's breakdown, the Committee reported 14 reservations, the so-called "Lodge reservations." Most important of these was a reservation which virtually nullified Article X of the Covenant. Under this reservation the United States assumed no obligation under Article X unless Congress by law or joint resolution so provided.

The treaty is defeated. Wilson's position on the League of Nations remained unchanged. The disabled President asked in a letter to "all true friends of the treaty" that they vote against the Lodge reservations. Apparently he still hoped that the treaty without reservations could command a two-thirds majority vote in the Senate. On November 19, 1919, the Senate ended its bitter debate and acted on the Lodge reservations. The treaty *with* these reservations was rejected by a combination of irreconcilables and loyal Democrats. Then the Senate voted on the treaty *without* reservations. This time the Wilson Democrats voted for the treaty, but the irreconcilables and the Lodge reservationists voted against it. The vote for the treaty fell far short of the necessary two-thirds majority.

During the winter of 1919–1920 considerable pressure was put on the Senate to reconsider the treaty. Church groups, lawyers, organized labor, and civic organizations urged American membership in the League. In March, 1920, the Senate again voted on the treaty with reservations. The ailing President again instructed Democrats to vote against the reservations, but some Democrats ignored his request and voted for the revised treaty. Though this time the treaty with reservations commanded a majority of the votes, it fell seven votes short of the necessary two thirds. After the treaty failed for a second time, Congress passed a joint resolution declaring the war at an end. Wilson vetoed this resolution, calling it "an ineffaceable stain upon the gallantry and honor of the United States."

Wilson hopes for a "solemn referendum" in 1920. President Wilson harbored hopes that the 1920 presidential election would be a "great and solemn referendum" on the treaty and the League. Victory for the Democrats, he felt, might enable the new President to secure ratification of the Versailles Treaty in the Senate.

James M. Cox, the Democratic candidate for President in 1920, did indeed favor ratification of the treaty and American membership in the League of Nations. The Republican Party was divided between opponents of the League and a pro-League faction led by Elihu Root, William Howard Taft, and Herbert Hoover. Neither the Republican presidential candidate, Warren G. Harding, nor the party platform took a definite stand on the League. During the campaign some Republicans interpreted the platform to mean support of the League with the Lodge reservations; others said it meant opposition to the League.

Harding rejects the League. A combination of many factors determined the outcome of the 1920 election (page 651). During the campaign, the League was discussed but in no sense was the election a "great and solemn referendum" on the issue. The Republicans won decisively, and the new President soon made his position on the League quite clear. In his inaugural address Harding said the United States sought no part "in directing the destinies of the Old World." In a later message to Congress, he said that if the League "is serving the Old World helpfully, more power to it. But it is not for us. The Senate has so declared, the executive has so declared, the people have so declared. Nothing could be more decisively stamped with finality." In July, 1921, Congress declared the war at an end and President Harding approved the resolution.

▶ CHECK-UP

1. What points of view about the League were held in the Senate? Why did Wilson refuse to consider compromise? Why did he appeal to the people to support the League?

2. What happened to the Versailles Treaty in the Foreign Relations Committee? In the Senate? What part did the League issue play in the 1920 election?

. . . .

3 *Americans Become Disillusioned with Events in Europe*

In the years after World War I many Americans were disappointed by developments across the Atlantic. They had expected that the Allied victory would strengthen the growth of democracy in Europe. Americans found it difficult to understand why democratic governments failed to root in Russia, Germany, and Italy, or in the new countries of eastern Europe. Nor could they understand why Great Britain and France were so slow in repaying the billions of dollars borrowed from the United States during the war. The American attitude toward Europe became one of disappointment, disillusion, and finally disgust. Many people expressed the opinion that the United States ought to withdraw from world affairs and let Europe "stew in its own juice."

Bolshevists establish a Communist state in Russia. A major disappointment stemmed from the Communist take-over in Russia. The first Russian Revolution in March, 1917, had overthrown the Czar, but the leaders of the new, republican government were in turn overthrown by the Bolshevists in November. Then, the Bolshevist government signed a peace treaty with Germany and withdrew from the war (page 621).

The provisional government set up in Russia after the Czar's overthrow was headed by Alexander Kerensky (top left, standing in a car). In November, 1917, Bolshevist troops stormed the headquarters of this government at the Winter Palace in Leningrad (above right, in a mural painting). The Bolshevists arrested many government officials, but Kerensky escaped and eventually went to live in the United States. The Bolshevist leader Nikolai Lenin (right) assumed power and immediately set about establishing a Communist dictatorship.

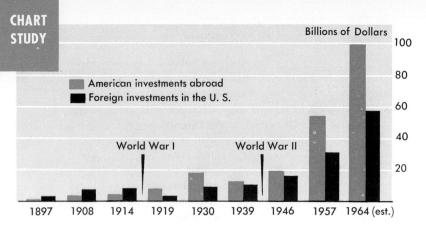

Billions of Dollars

■ American investments abroad
■ Foreign investments in the U. S.

World War I

World War II

100
80
60
40
20

1897   1908   1914   1919   1930   1939   1946   1957   1964 (est.)

THE UNITED STATES BECOMES A CREDITOR NATION

World War I changed the United States from a debtor to a creditor nation. Note, however, the substantial increase in foreign investments in this country since 1919.

The Bolshevist group, led by Nikolai Lenin, was an offshoot of the Russian Socialist movement. Like other Socialists, the Bolshevists opposed capitalism and believed that the state should own the means of production. But unlike many other Socialists, Lenin insisted that the provisional government would have to be overthrown before his brand of socialism could be established in Russia. Lenin and the Bolshevists formed a tightly disciplined band of revolutionaries. It was this Bolshevist "revolutionary vanguard" which seized power in Russia late in 1917.

Once in power, Lenin and the Bolshevists established a totalitarian state. This separated them from the Socialist parties in Russia and other countries. While Socialists believed the state should own the means of production, they also supported such democratic institutions as political parties, free elections, and civil liberties. The democratic Socialists believed that informed citizens would vote for a Socialist government. But under communism (as bolshevism came to be called), the Russian state was run by a small group of disciplined party leaders. There were no opposition parties, no free elections, and no freedom of the press, speech, or religion. Land, industry, and business were nationalized by the government. In theory, this property was owned in common by the people. Actually, however, the government was a dictatorship run by the leaders of the Communist Party. Lenin used force to crush a civil war and revolts by factory workers, farmers, and others who objected to the new government. With the help of the secret police, he eliminated effective opposition and created the first Communist state.

Russian communism frightens the West. The western democracies strongly opposed the police state which the Bolshevists established in the Soviet Union.[2] At the same time they were alarmed by Lenin's threat to spread communism throughout the world. In 1919 Lenin founded the Communist International to guide the work of Communist "revolutionary vanguards" in other countries. A number of Communist Parties were formed outside the Soviet Union, including one in the United States. Moreover, Communist uprisings broke out in Germany, Hungary, and Poland. Party members in these countries claimed that communism was the only answer to the political chaos, economic disorder, and hunger that troubled postwar Europe. The rise of communism led delegates to the Paris peace conference to share Herbert Hoover's fear that "the wolf is at the door of the world."

The Allies take limited action against the Bolshevists. During 1918–1921 fierce fighting went on between the "Red" Army of the Communists and the White Russians, who opposed the Communists. The Allies sent troops and supplies to help the White Russians. British, French, and American troops tried to undermine the Bolshevists by seizing the northern ports of Murmansk and Archangel (map, page 632). At the same time American and Japanese soldiers, using Vladivostok as a base, conducted a campaign against the Communists in eastern Siberia. But the Red Army won Russia's civil war, and the Allies discontinued their

[2] The Communists created the Union of Soviet Socialist Republics, which included Russia and other states such as the Ukraine. It is called the Soviet Union or the USSR for short.

limited operations. By early 1920, all American troops had been withdrawn from Russian soil, though Japanese forces held on until 1922.

Democratic regimes are unsuccessful in Germany and Italy. Also disturbing to most Americans was the failure of representative government in Germany and Italy. At the end of the war a republic was established in Germany, but many Germans associated the new government with the humiliating terms of the Treaty of Versailles. The "war guilt" clause of the treaty rankled in German minds. German hostility to France was kept alive by the French take-over in the Saar and by the Allied occupation of the Rhineland. Moreover, economic conditions were extremely shaky, and the question of reparations remained unsettled. As we shall see in Chapter 34, these conditions contributed to the rise of a German "strong man," Adolf Hitler.

Even before Hitler rose to power in Germany, Italy turned to a "strong man" named Benito Mussolini. The Italians had been disappointed in their gains at the peace table, and unemployment and a severe depression plagued their country during the postwar years. Communist organizers took advantage of discontent in Italy to build up an Italian Communist Party. But Mussolini, a former Socialist editor and war veteran, formed an organization of ex-soldiers called Fascists to fight the spread of communism. Claiming that he was saving the country from communism, Mussolini and the Fascists seized control of the Italian government in 1922. Although he allowed the king to remain, Mussolini set about making himself an absolute dictator. He glorified war, built up the army and navy, and talked about restoring to Italy the position of power it had held during the Roman Empire.

World War I makes the United States a creditor nation. American disappointment in the postwar years was not limited to political developments in Russia, Germany, and Italy. It stemmed also from troubles with wartime allies who owed the United States large sums of money. This was a new experience for this country, which before 1914 had been a debtor nation. After 1865, industrial expansion, railroad construction, and development of natural resources in the United States had attracted European investment capital. Indeed, by 1914 between five and six billion dollars of European capital had been invested in American stocks and bonds. Each year the owners of these securities received hundreds of millions of dollars in dividends and interest. Furthermore, American goods were shipped in foreign vessels, and much of our insurance was handled by foreign companies. To pay for these services, American gold was not actually shipped abroad; rather, the payments were made by shipping goods to Europe. Since we sold more than we bought (resulting in a surplus of exports over imports), part of the surplus was used to meet our obligations to European creditors.

World War I changed the United States from a debtor to a creditor country. During the early stages of World War I, greatly increased exports enabled the United States to pay off its European debts. Thereafter the Allies paid cash for American goods, and soon they were borrowing money to pay for the supplies needed to continue the war. From April, 1917, to the end of the war, the Allies borrowed nearly seven billion dollars in the United States. After the armistice was signed, they borrowed more than three billion dollars for war relief and rehabilitation. In a few short years, therefore, the United States had paid off more than five billion dollars owed to European creditors and made foreign loans of twice that amount.

The United States and the Allies disagree on payment of war debts. The British and French, who owed the United States the largest sums of money, expected to pay their obligations out of war reparations to be collected from Germany. The total amount of reparations levied upon Germany was 33 billion dollars. If this money actually had been paid to Britain and France, they in turn could have repaid the United States. But the Germans soon fell behind in their payments.

The United States refused to admit that there was any connection between German reparations and Allied war debts. Presidents Harding and Coolidge insisted that the Allies should meet their obligations no matter what the Germans did about making their reparations payments. As President Coolidge put it, "They hired the money, didn't they?"

For several reasons the British and French thought this attitude unreasonable. (1) They pointed out that high American tariff rates during the 1920's made it almost impossible for them to pay off the debts by trade. (2) Nor could they pay in gold because most of the world's gold supply was already in the United States. (3) In addition, they said, almost all of the money lent to them had been spent in the United States, thereby stimulating American industry and agriculture. (4) Moreover, because the war had been fought on European soil, the United States had escaped the destruction that hampered Europe's economic recovery. (5) Finally, they pointed out that British and French losses in man power had been far greater than American losses. In short, they argued that the United States ought to be willing to reduce or perhaps write off these financial obligations as its contribution to the united war effort.

The war debts remain unpaid. This dispute between the wartime allies continued throughout the 1920's. It helps to explain the American feeling of disillusion and the willingness to let Europe "stew in its own juice." But the United States government did attempt to improve economic conditions in Germany and to reduce reparations payments to a more realistic level. The Dawes Plan (1924) cut German reparations and provided for an American loan to Germany. In 1929 German reparations were reduced still further, and the period for making payments was extended to 1988. But these arrangements were soon upset by the severe depression which hit Europe and the United States. Though the American government in 1931 suspended all war-debt payments for a year, at the end of this period the debtor nations still were unable to resume payments. All told, Germany paid about four and a half billion dollars in reparations. The Allies in turn paid about two and a half billion dollars in war debts to the United States.

▶ CHECK-UP

1. How did the Communists come to power in Russia? What kind of government did they establish? Why were the western democracies opposed to communism? Why did democratic governments fail in Italy and Germany?

2. How did World War I make the United States a creditor nation? What problem arose when Germany failed to meet its reparations payments? Why did the Allies feel that the United States should reduce or cancel their war debts?

· · · · · · · · · · · · · ·

4 *The United States Plays a Limited Role in World Affairs*

Though the United States never joined the League of Nations, the world organization eventually came to include 60 countries. In the 1920's the League had some success in settling international disputes. Moreover, the League worked for disarmament; sought to control disease, the slave trade, and the drug trade; and tried to improve labor conditions throughout the world.

The United States takes part in League of Nations activities. At first, League communications to the United States government were ignored, for President Harding instructed the State Department not to answer them. But when it became evident that the League was discussing issues of vital interest to the United States, Secretary of State Hughes began to deal directly with the League staff. Unofficial American observers were sent to Geneva to sit with League committees dealing with nonpolitical matters. Beginning in 1924, delegates were sent to represent the United States formally at League conferences. By 1930 the United States had five permanent officials in Geneva to look after American interests. Although it played a small part in League activities, this country had no vote because it refused to join.[3] As Clemenceau wryly observed, the United States was represented "by an ear but not by a mouth."

The World Court is established. The Covenant of the League of Nations, as we have seen, provided for a Permanent Court of International Justice. Set up in 1920, the World Court was to consider all international disputes submitted to it by nations which became members of the Court. It could also give advisory opinions[4] on questions brought before it by the League's Council or Assembly. Membership in the Court was not limited to the countries in the League. In the United States there was considerable interest in the World Court because an American statesman, Elihu Root, had helped to outline its organization and functions. In addition, the United States had long favored the settlement of international disputes by arbitration.

The Senate rejects membership in the World Court. In spite of this interest, the suggestion that the United States join the World Court led to a long and bitter dispute. As early as 1923, President Harding asked the Senate to approve American membership but without success. President Coolidge also favored American membership, and in 1926 the Senate voted to join the World Court but included a number of reservations. These reservations were unacceptable to the other signers of the World Court treaty. Later, Elihu Root helped revise the constitution of the Court. Although the "Root Formula" was acceptable to the League, the State Department, and the members of the Court, the Senate withheld its approval.

The Paris Pact is adopted. Though some Americans were reluctant to submit their international disputes to the World Court, they were generally enthusiastic about a treaty to ban future wars. In 1927, Aristide Briand (bree-*ahn'*), the French Minister of Foreign Affairs, proposed such a treaty with the United States. Under this treaty both nations would agree never to use war "as an instrument of national policy" in their dealings with one another. Secretary of State Frank B. Kellogg said he thought other nations should be invited to join in such a declaration. As a result, the representatives of fifteen powers met at Paris in 1928 and signed the Paris Peace Pact, known also as the Kellogg-Briand Pact. Within a few years, more than 60 nations had agreed to "condemn recourse to war for the solution of international controversies, and renounce it as an instrument of national policy."

The United States Senate promptly ratified this treaty with only a single opposing vote. But the Paris Peace Pact depended solely on the good will of the countries that signed it, for there was no way of enforcing the terms of the treaty. It was, therefore, "a grandiose but essentially empty gesture," as one historian has pointed out.

The Washington Conference tackles the problem of disarmament. Americans were as enthusiastic about disarmament in the 1920's as they were about the peace pact. They realized that the arms race before World War I had helped to build up international tension. They were also concerned about Japan's postwar military build-up and the important positions that army and navy officers occupied in the Japanese government. Moreover, Japan had illegally begun to fortify the islands held as mandates from the League of Nations (page 633). Partly because of the situation in the Pacific, President Harding called for a disarmament conference to meet in Washington in the fall of 1921. Invitations were sent to all the major powers, except Russia, that were directly interested in the Far East.

Secretary of State Hughes startled the delegates to the conference by proposing that the naval powers set limits on the number of battleships in their navies. If necessary to keep within the accepted limit, a nation would scrap ships already built or

---

[3] President Harding reassured the anti-League forces by announcing that the United States "does not propose to enter now by the side door, or the back door or the cellar door."

[4] Opinions given in advance of actual cases heard by the Court.

Some of the leading participants in the Washington Conference of 1921 are shown here. Sixth from the right is Charles Evans Hughes, the American representative.

under construction. Even though the United States could outbuild other powers, Secretary Hughes offered to scrap the largest tonnage. The other nations at the conference immediately accepted this proposal. A treaty was drawn up which called for a ten-year "holiday" in the construction of capital ships (the class which included the largest warships). It also fixed the total tonnage in capital ships of the leading naval powers. Great Britain and the United States would have 525,000 tons each; Japan, 315,000 tons; and France and Italy, 175,000 tons each. Thus the strength of these five nations in capital ships would be in a ratio of 5-5-3-1⅔-1⅔. Though the delegates also discussed limitations on cruisers, destroyers, submarines, and land forces, no further agreements resulted.

The Washington Conference tries to preserve the "status quo" in the Far East. At the urging of Great Britain and the United States, delegates to the Washington Conference also adopted two treaties that were intended to restrain Japanese ambitions. The Four-Power Treaty, signed by the United States, Great Britain, Japan, and France, guaranteed the island possessions of each of these countries in the Pacific. It also called for the peaceful settlement of any disputes among the four countries. The Nine-Power Treaty was signed by these four countries as well as Belgium, China, Italy, the Netherlands, and Portugal.

It pledged support of the Open Door Policy in China.

The United States Senate gave its approval to the three treaties worked out by the Washington Conference during 1921–1922. It was widely believed at the time that an encouraging start had been made on the problem of disarmament and that the threat of Japanese imperialism in the Far East had been contained.

Later disarmament conferences accomplish little. The Washington Conference was followed by other disarmament conferences which were less successful. At a naval conference held at London in 1930, Great Britain, the United States, and Japan extended the "holiday" in the construction of capital ships to 1936. But an "escalator clause" permitted the signers to increase their armaments if other nations threatened their security. A year before the treaty was due to expire, Japan demanded naval equality with the United States and Britain as its price for continuing the agreement. When this demand was refused, Japan withdrew from the treaty.

Relations with Latin America improve. Although the United States continued its financial and military control in some Latin American countries during the 1920's, there were signs that the Roosevelt Corollary (page 599) was being modified. Secretary of State Hughes assured our southern neighbors that the United States did not want to "assert an overlordship" or "make our power the test of right in this hemisphere." He ended the military occupation of the Dominican Republic in 1924 and in the following year pulled American troops out of Nicaragua. But when civil war broke out in Nicaragua, United States marines again were sent to restore order. In 1927 President Coolidge's special representative, Henry L. Stimson, was able to arrange a truce and prepare the way for national elections in Nicaragua. Six years later the last American troops were withdrawn.

Meanwhile, at the Havana Inter-American Conference in 1928 the Latin American countries had protested against American military intervention. Recognizing the significance of this criticism, the United States State Department drew up a memorandum in effect renouncing the Roosevelt Corollary. It said that the Monroe Doctrine was "not an instrument of violence and oppression" but rather a guarantee of the "freedom, independence and territorial integrity [of the Latin American countries] against the imperialistic designs of Europe." This memorandum, which was made public in 1930, paved the way for a new trend in inter-American relations (page 712).

A misunderstanding with Mexico is peacefully settled. President Wilson had withdrawn American troops from Mexico early in 1917 (page 602), but friction between the two countries continued. The Mexican constitution adopted in 1917 struck a severe blow at American interests south of the Rio Grande. It declared that only Mexican citizens and Mexican companies might acquire land or receive the right to develop "mines, waters, or mineral fuels in the Republic of Mexico." Tension between the two countries was increased by the enactment in 1925 of a law stating that all petroleum deposits were owned by the Mexican nation. Although the United States State Department protested, the Mexican government proceeded to carry out this policy.

Some Americans called for intervention, but President Coolidge sent Dwight W. Morrow to Mexico in 1927 with instructions "to keep us out of war." Morrow proved to be an excellent ambassador. Genuinely in-

terested in the Mexican people, he soon won their respect and admiration. He further enhanced his position by helping to settle a dispute between the Mexican Catholic Church and the Mexican government. So far as American interests in Mexico were concerned, the Mexican government agreed to leave untouched those American oil rights that had been obtained before 1917. Although the dispute about American holdings in Mexico came up again in the 1930's, relations between the two countries remained relatively cordial.

▶ CHECK-UP

1. What was this country's relationship to League activities? What was the Paris Pact?

2. What agreements were reached at the Washington Disarmament Conference regarding naval strength? Concerning land holdings in the Far East? Why did Japan in time withdraw from the naval treaty?

3. Why did relations with Latin American countries improve in the late 1920's? What dispute arose from provisions in the 1917 Mexican constitution? How was it settled?

. . . .

Clinching the Main Ideas in Chapter 30

The great crusade to make the world "safe for democracy" ended in disillusion. A number of factors were responsible. Henry Cabot Lodge and the isolationists fought relentlessly to prevent American membership in the League of Nations. But President Wilson shared the blame for the League's defeat. His refusal to seek Republican co-operation and his stubborn rejection of any modifications in the Treaty of Versailles ruined its chances for ratification. Still other factors helped to shape the American postwar attitude. Among these were the spread of Russian communism and the problems of representative government in Germany and Italy. Moreover, many Americans were unable to understand why Great Britain and France did not pay their war debts.

But the United States was not completely isolated from world affairs in the decade after World War I. To a limited extent, it participated in League activities. The United States also worked with Great Britain, France, and other countries to find a formula for disarmament. But the initial success of the Washington Conference was never repeated.

In Latin American affairs, the United States gradually abandoned its policy of intervention. The re-interpretation of the Monroe Doctrine and Dwight Morrow's successful negotiations in Mexico pointed the way to improved relationships with the Latin American countries.

Chapter Review

Terms to Understand

1. World Court
2. Saar basin
3. Article X
4. communism
5. fascism
6. socialism
7. Covenant
8. reparations
9. Rhineland
10. mandate
11. Treaty of Versailles
12. League of Nations
13. self-determination
14. territorial integrity
15. economic sanctions
16. totalitarian state
17. Kellogg-Briand Pact
18. "escalator clause"
19. Four-Power Treaty
20. Washington Conference (1921)

What Do You Think?

1. Why did President Wilson feel that the inclusion of the Covenant in the Treaty of Versailles was more important than the specific terms dealing with territorial settlements?

2. Were Senate reactions to the League and the World Court more conservative than those of the American people? Explain.

3. How does one make the world "safe for democracy"?

4. During a war, statesmen may coin a phrase that helps to bring the conflict to an end but creates problems afterwards. For example, "The peoples of Austria-Hungary should be afforded opportunity for autonomous development." How did "self-determination" create more problems than it solved?

Using Your Knowledge of History

1. President Wilson added to the Covenant a provision that the Monroe Doctrine and American domestic affairs were not to come under the League's authority. Have a class discussion to consider (a) why this step was taken and (b) its significance.

2. The Treaty of Versailles stipulated that Germany was responsible for the war. Write a brief essay to bring out (a) why this was done and (b) whether it was true.

3. In a message to Congress, President Harding stated: ". . . it [the League] is not for us. The Senate has so declared, the executive has so declared, the people have so declared." Write an editorial indicating whether you agree with his statement and why.

4. How would you have explained to President Coolidge why Great Britain and France were slow in repaying the billions of dollars they had borrowed from the United States in World War I?

Extending Your Knowledge of History

Paul Birdsall's analysis in *Versailles Twenty Years After* is generally favorable to Woodrow Wilson. Quite critical, however, are Thomas A. Bailey's *Woodrow Wilson and the Lost Peace* and *Woodrow Wilson and the Great Betrayal*. Henry Cabot Lodge's role is explained by J. A. Garraty in *Henry Cabot Lodge*. President Wilson's appeal to the American people is described in *America in Crisis; Fourteen Crucial Episodes in American History*, edited by Daniel Aaron. Preston W. Slosson has an interesting analysis in *The Great Crusade and After, 1914–1928*. In *American Heritage*, see "Woodrow Wilson Wouldn't Yield" by Thomas A. Bailey (June, 1957); and "The Ordeal of Woodrow Wilson" by Herbert Hoover (June, 1958).

CHAPTER 31

The 1920's Are Marked by Political Conservatism and Social Change

"Jazz Age" cartoon

America's present need is not heroics but healing; not nostrums but normalcy, not revolution but restoration . . . not surgery but serenity.

WARREN G. HARDING, 1920

1919–1928

Ever since Theodore Roosevelt's years in the White House, the American people had been experiencing far-reaching changes in their way of life. Progressive reforms, which reached a climax in Wilson's first administration, had altered political, economic, and social patterns of living in the United States. When entrance into the First World War put a halt to such reforms, the nation was challenged to fight for the lofty goals of world peace and democracy. By the time the war was over, most Americans had had their fill of reforms and crusades. "Normalcy" was President Harding's prescription for the emotional letdown that Americans felt after World War I.

Actually the voters had already turned against the "crusaders" in the congressional elections of 1918. In the next three presidential elections, they went on to elect Republican candidates who promised to leave matters as they were. The administrations of the 1920's generally were friendly to businessmen, did little to aid the farmers, and ignored the problems of organized labor and immigrants. Although the Republicans ran into some opposition, their policies seemed to satisfy the majority of voters.

The 1920's were also a decade of social change. Such developments as the automobile, the airplane, motion pictures, and radio strikingly altered American life. New standards of behavior, new fashions of dress, and new forms of entertainment developed during the so-called "jazz age." But the growing emphasis on material things drew criticism from a number of writers and artists.

1 *Economic and Political Unrest Mark the Postwar Years*

An economic slump follows the war. During and after World War I, as we have seen, the United States had lent billions of dollars to its European allies. These countries had used the loans to purchase arms, food, and machinery in the United States. But during 1919–1920 the government cut back on foreign loans, ended defense contracts with manufacturers, and reduced aid to shipbuilders. The economic boom of the war years then turned into a "bust." Many business firms went bankrupt, and farm prices declined to almost half their wartime levels. The postwar depression continued for several years; and in shipping and farming, hard times lasted throughout the 1920's.

Unemployment was a serious problem. Many women who had taken jobs in defense plants during the war suddenly found themselves without a regular income. Thousands of men released from the armed forces began looking for jobs. Between 1918 and 1921 the number of unemployed jumped from half a million to over five

million. Negroes, who had been "the last to be hired," were "the first to be fired."

Congress subsidizes certain industries. When the war ended, the Railroad Administration was running the country's railroads (page 618). Spokesmen for organized labor wanted the government to continue operating the lines, while railroad owners insisted that control be restored to them. In the Esch-Cummins Transportation Act (1920), Congress adopted a compromise plan. The Interstate Commerce Commission was authorized to set rates that would yield a "fair return" to railroad stockholders. A Railway Labor Board was established to settle disputes between management and employees. Finally, the Esch-Cummins Act permitted railroads to merge in order to make their operations more efficient. In reversing its earlier antitrust policy toward the railroads, the government recognized the fact that the carriers faced increasing competition from waterways and the new trucking companies.

The shipping industry likewise received substantial government aid but with little supervision. The huge shipbuilding program of the war years had produced far more ships than were needed for peacetime foreign trade. In the Merchant Marine Act (1920), Congress agreed to sell government-owned ships to private companies for a fraction of their actual construction cost. To encourage American shipping, lower tariff rates were charged on goods carried to this country in American vessels. The act also granted generous mail subsidies to shippers.

In 1928 the government not only increased mail subsidies but also agreed to lend money to shippers interested in acquiring modern ships. This policy was intended to help the nation's idle shipyards. During the 1920's, the government also granted large subsidies to airlines which carried mail. Government aid to the railroads, shipping industry, and airlines helped them to survive the drastic economic changes which followed the war.

Growing unrest afflicts the labor movement. With the slowdown of industrial production after the war, many workers had

. . . .

CHAPTER FOCUS

1. Economic and political unrest mark the postwar years.

2. Republicans provide conservative government in the 1920's.

3. The 1920's witness important social and cultural changes.

their wages cut. At the same time, the removal of price controls allowed prices to rise. The labor unions, whose membership had increased during the war, made clear that they intended to hold onto their wartime gains. During 1919, almost 4000 strikes were called, involving more than four million workers. In three important strikes that year, labor suffered serious defeats.

(1) The first of these strikes involved the steel industry. Steelworkers wanted recognition of their union, better working conditions, and an eight-hour day. When the United States Steel Corporation refused to discuss any of these issues with union leaders, the steelworkers walked off their jobs. The steel companies brought in strikebreakers and hired private guards to end the strike. When violence broke out, both state and federal troops were called in to maintain order. The steel companies turned public opinion against the workers by publicizing the fact that the union leader, William Z. Foster, was a radical socialist. Although the strike ended in failure, a few years later the steel companies reduced the work day from twelve hours to eight. The steelworkers' union was not recognized, however, until the 1930's.

(2) The soft-coal miners also called a strike in 1919. They demanded higher wages and a 30-hour week, with employment spread over the entire year. Since the country was still technically at war, Attorney General A. Mitchell Palmer used his wartime powers to secure an injunction ordering the miners back to work. But the strikers were reluctant to return to the mines, even though their union leader, John L. Lewis, admitted defeat. With the country facing a coal shortage as winter approached, an arbitration board granted the miners a wage increase. The injunction, however, had blunted the effect of their strike.

(3) The third, and perhaps most dramatic, strike involved the Boston police force. These men went on strike when the police commissioner refused to recognize their right to join the American Federation of Labor. Many Boston veterans donned their army uniforms and volunteered to patrol the streets, but the mayor was able to maintain order with the help of state militia stationed in Boston. Governor Calvin Coolidge backed the police commissioner's decision not to rehire any of the strikers and sent in more state troops. When Samuel Gompers protested, Coolidge wired him: "There is no right to strike against the public safety by anybody, any time, anywhere." This terse communication made Governor Coolidge a national figure overnight.

Organized labor loses ground in the 1920's. Throughout the 1920's both government and public opinion were unsympathetic to organized labor. Membership in the AFL dropped from four million in 1920 to less than three million by 1923 and remained at that level for the rest of the decade. Manufacturers campaigned for adoption of the so-called "American plan." Under this plan, a factory would be an *open shop*, employing both union and non-union labor, rather than a *closed shop*, where only union members could work (page 478).

Workers make some gains. Despite such setbacks, labor had a share in the prosperity that followed the postwar depression in the early 1920's. Wages rose, and more workers were able to buy such new consumer products as radios, refrigerators, vacuum cleaners, washing machines, and even automobiles. Moreover, many companies improved working conditions. Modern plants were equipped with the latest safety devices. Attractive cafeterias, organized social activities, and dental and medical clinics were provided for employees. Some companies gave their workers annual bonuses or allowed them to buy company stock. *Company unions*, composed of employees of a single firm, were actively encouraged; employers were willing to discuss grievances with spokesmen for these organizations. It has been estimated that by 1929 about one and a half million workers belonged to company unions.

An American Communist Party is established. Communist organizers tried to take advantage of the discontent that existed among workingmen in the 1920's. The

Smoke still hung over Wall Street when this photograph was taken shortly after a bomb exploded in the busy area in 1920. The mystery of the explosion was never solved, but many people blamed it on "Reds."

leaders of the Communist movement that had developed in Russia during the war (page 637) hoped to find recruits among wage earners in capitalist countries. But in the United States and other industrialized countries, such as Britain, Germany, and Japan, the Communists were disappointed. American workers, though often at odds with their employers, had little interest in socialism and were openly hostile to American Communists.

The American Communists, like Russian Communists, were an offshoot of a socialist party. But their goal of political dictatorship and their disregard for civil liberties clearly distinguished them from Socialists. Thus, many American Socialists, including Eugene Debs, turned a deaf ear to the call from Moscow to endorse communism. But a few radical socialists formed the American Communist Party in 1920. Among the leaders of the new party were John Reed and William Z. Foster.

The "Red scare" is a reaction against radicalism. The Communist victory in Russia, the spread of communism in Europe, and the creation of a Communist Party in the United States alarmed many Americans. The threat of Communist growth, it should be remembered, came at the same time as other disturbing developments. These included the postwar economic adjustment, friction with wartime allies, the defeat of the Versailles Treaty in the Senate, and President Wilson's illness. As a result, the

United States went through a two-year period of fear and unrest over the rise of radicalism and its apparent threat to the American way of life.

Although neither the Industrial Workers of the World (page 551) nor the Communist Party had many members, they were blamed for many outbursts of disorder and violence in 1919–1920. Communist organizers were charged with instigating a general strike in Seattle. An alert clerk in the New York Post Office discovered bombs addressed to government officials. An explosion on Wall Street in front of the Morgan Company offices killed 38 persons and injured scores of others.

During the "Red scare," state legislatures passed strict laws against radicalism, and state officials arrested many agitators. Radical or left-wing publications were banned, and in New York State five legally elected Socialists were denied their seats in the legislature. Attorney General Palmer used the Espionage and Sedition Acts to arrest IWW members, Communists, and Socialists. About 550 aliens believed to be radicals were deported during 1919–1920.

Recovery from the "Red scare" is slow. The violation of constitutional rights in some of these cases did not go unchallenged. Charles Evans Hughes and the New York Bar Association protested when the five Socialists were barred from the state legislature. In a Supreme Court decision in 1919, Justice Oliver Wendell Holmes warned against unjustified violation of the right of free speech.[1] "The question in every case," he said, "is whether the words used . . . are of such a nature as to create a clear and present danger." The failure of the Attorney General to find as many dangerous radicals as he had claimed there were, also helped to quiet the fears of the public.

Nevertheless, throughout the 1920's there were lingering traces of postwar unrest. At one time or another, labor leaders, immigrants, political liberals, Negroes, and Jews were falsely accused of radicalism. The case of Sacco and Vanzetti helped to keep the issue alive. Nicola Sacco and Bartolomeo Vanzetti, both of them immigrants and anarchists, were arrested in 1920 and charged with committing a robbery and murder in Massachusetts. Tried in 1921, the two men were found guilty and condemned to death. Before the sentence was carried out, several prominent Americans charged that Sacco and Vanzetti had been condemned because of their political beliefs and not because of evidence linking them to the crime. Motions for appeal and investigations into the case delayed the execution of the two men until 1927. Even after their death, interest in the case continued. Many people remained convinced that Sacco and Vanzetti were victims of the intolerance bred by the "Red scare."

▶ CHECK-UP

1. Why did this country experience an economic slump immediately after World War I? What groups suffered most? Why? How did the government's policy toward the railroads change? Why? What industries were subsidized by the government? Why?

2. What important strikes were called in 1919? What was the outcome of each? Why did organized labor lose strength in the 1920's? What gains did workers make? Why was an American Communist Party organized?

3. What was the "Red scare"? What protests were made against violations of civil rights?

. . . .

[1] The case was *Schenck v. the United States,* in which the Court, by a unanimous decision, upheld the constitutionality of the Espionage Act.

2 *Republicans Provide Conservative Government in the 1920's*

Wilson's term ends in confusion. Political conflict marked the last two years of Woodrow Wilson's term in office. This situation grew out of the elections of 1918 (page 630), which had given the Republicans control of Congress. The President's illness made the situation worse. A semi-invalid, Wilson was unable to exercise leadership in either the Cabinet or Congress. During this time the Senate rejected the League of Nations, Congress canceled wartime contracts and removed wartime economic controls, and the Attorney General fanned the flames of the "Red scare."

Two constitutional amendments are adopted. Before the end of Wilson's term, two important amendments were added to the Constitution. By 1917 leaders in the prohibition movement had persuaded legislatures in well over half the states to outlaw the sale of alcoholic beverages. After the United States entered World War I, Congress prohibited the manufacture of liquor for the duration of the emergency. Meanwhile, the supporters of prohibition kept up their efforts to secure a constitutional amendment that would permanently outlaw the use of liquor throughout the country. In 1917 Congress approved the Eighteenth Amendment, which prohibited "the manufacture, sale or transportation of intoxicating liquors." It was ratified by the states in January, 1919, and went into effect one year later.

Another amendment gave women the right to vote. Under the leadership of Anna Howard Shaw and Carrie Chapman Catt, the women's rights movement had made significant progress in the years before World War I. By 1914 eleven states had granted the vote to women. The war efforts of American women proved the deciding factor in the campaign for suffrage. Their work

The ratification of the Nineteenth Amendment crowned the efforts of several generations of "suffragettes" (left). In 1920 women voted in a national election for the first time (right). Within a few years the country had its first woman governor, Nellie Tayloe Ross (lower left), who succeeded her husband as governor of Wyoming after his death in 1925. The 1920's also saw an increasing number of women enter the labor force, many of them as secretaries (lower right).

in defense plants and as nurses in the armed forces made it difficult for politicians to deny them the right to vote. By a narrow margin, Congress passed the Nineteenth Amendment in 1919. It was ratified in time for women to vote in the presidential election of 1920.

The parties nominate candidates. The Republican convention met in Chicago in 1920. When a deadlock developed among the leading contenders, the party bosses turned to a relatively unknown senator from Ohio, Warren G. Harding. Harding had few political enemies and no ties with the Progressives. Governor Calvin Coolidge of Massachusetts was nominated for the vice-presidency. As we saw in Chapter 30, the Republican platform was vague concerning the League of Nations and the Versailles Treaty. It did, however, recommend lower income taxes, repeal of the excess-profits tax, and higher tariff rates.

The Democrats, gloomy about their chances of retaining the presidency, met in San Francisco. Wilson's son-in-law, former Secretary of the Treasury McAdoo, wanted the nomination, and so too did Attorney General Palmer. But the delegates preferred the popular governor of Ohio, James M. Cox. As his running mate they chose the young Assistant Secretary of the Navy, Franklin D. Roosevelt. The Democratic platform praised the achievements of the Wilson administration and pledged "immediate ratification of the Treaty without reservations which would impair its essential integrity."

Harding is elected President. Cox and Roosevelt waged a vigorous campaign. Harding, on the other hand, stayed at home in Marion, Ohio, speaking occasionally from his front porch to visiting delegations. The Democrats tried to arouse interest in the League of Nations, while the Republicans played down international issues and called for a return to "normalcy."

The election results suggested that the American people were weary of crusades at home and abroad. Cox received only nine million votes compared to sixteen million for Harding. The Republicans carried the northern and western states, and even Tennessee, for a total of 404 electoral votes. The Republicans also won large majorities in the House and Senate. Nearly a million votes were cast for Eugene Debs, the Socialist candidate, who at the time was serving a jail sentence for violating the Sedition Act (page 620). The election of 1920 is best interpreted as a vote against Wilson's idealism and for the Republican promise to return the United States to "normalcy."

Harding appoints his Cabinet. The new President had edited the Marion (Ohio) *Daily Star* before his election to the United States Senate in 1914. He and his wife prided themselves on being "just folks." Handsome and friendly, Warren G. Harding was a popular President during his brief term in the White House. But he was essentially a man of limited intelligence and modest ambitions. Sensing that serious affairs of state were beyond his grasp, he named able men to the most important Cabinet posts. Charles Evans Hughes became Secretary of State, and Herbert Hoover accepted the job of Secretary of Commerce. To head the Treasury Department, Harding chose a wealthy Pittsburgh banker and industrialist, Andrew W. Mellon. On the other hand, Harding's friends Harry Daugherty, who became Attorney General, and Albert B. Fall, who became Secretary of the Interior, were incompetent. Lesser positions were given to Harding's long-time cronies, the so-called "Ohio gang."

The burdens of office prove too much for Harding. Within a few months of his inauguration, Harding told a friend, "I knew this job would be too much for me." He disliked making decisions, and he had neither the desire nor the ability to exercise strong leadership. Unscrupulous politicians had helped him win the nomination, and Harding's loyalty to his friends paved the way for large-scale graft and corruption.

Rumors of the illegal activities of the "Ohio gang" began to circulate early in 1923, and soon reached the ears of the President.

Exhausted by the responsibilities of his office and deeply disturbed by his friends' shady dealings, Harding's health began to decline. Yet in the summer of 1923 he undertook a speaking tour in the West and made a trip to Alaska. After returning to California, he collapsed. His illness was complicated by pneumonia and perhaps a stroke, and on August 2, 1923, President Harding died. The nation, which as yet knew little about the scandals, mourned the death of the handsome man who apparently had been a martyr to the burdens of the presidency. Years later, Herbert Hoover said of the unfortunate Harding, "We saw him gradually weaken not only from physical exhaustion but from mental anxiety." He knew that "he had been betrayed by a few of the men whom he had trusted."

The public learns of the scandals. Shortly after Harding's death, the extent of the graft and corruption in his administration was revealed to the American public. The director of the Veterans' Bureau, Charles R. Forbes, was found guilty of "almost unparalleled waste, recklessness, and misconduct" in handling construction contracts and in purchasing supplies for veterans' hospitals. Jesse Smith, a political friend of Harding's and the man behind many of the illegal deals of the "Ohio gang," committed suicide. A Senate investigating committee found Attorney General Daugherty guilty of misconduct for selling liquor permits as well as pardons and paroles to criminals.

The Teapot Dome scandal involves Secretary Fall. The most serious scandal involved the Department of the Interior. Shortly after his inauguration, President Harding transferred the control of certain naval oil reserves in Wyoming and California from the Navy to the Interior Department. Secretary of the Interior Albert Fall took advantage of the opportunity to lease these rich deposits to his friends in the oil industry and to make some money for himself. Without asking for competitive bids, Fall secretly leased the Teapot Dome Reserve in Wyoming to Harry Sinclair's

President Harding's original Cabinet included some notable figures. Harding is fourth from the left in front. Andrew Mellon and Charles Evans Hughes are sitting second and third from the left, and Vice-President Calvin Coolidge is on Harding's other side. Another future President, Herbert Hoover, is second from the right in the back. Involved in the scandals of Harding's administration were Albert B. Fall and Harry Daugherty (standing first and third from the left).

Mammoth Oil Company. In the same manner, he leased the Elk Hills Reserve in California to an oil company controlled by Edward Doheny. In return for these leases, Fall received several hundred thousand dollars. Fall's sudden wealth, some of which was spent on his ranch, attracted the attention of western senators.

After a long Senate investigation into Fall's illegal dealings, he was convicted in 1929 of accepting a bribe. Fall was fined 100,000 dollars and sentenced to a year in prison. Doheny and Sinclair, both of whom had bribed Fall, were acquitted, though Sinclair later went to jail for tampering with the jury at his trial. The Supreme Court canceled the oil leases on the grounds that they were tainted with "conspiracy, corruption, and fraud."

Coolidge becomes a popular President. At the time of Harding's death, Vice-President Calvin Coolidge was vacationing in Vermont. The oath of office was administered to him by his father, a justice of the peace, in a Vermont farmhouse lighted by kerosene lamps. The American people were touched by this transfer of great power in a setting of rural simplicity. They credited

Coolidge with wisdom and strength of character, partly because he was a man of few words. In the 1920's the people seemed to want a chief executive who was a symbol and a ceremonial figure, rather than an energetic leader like Theodore Roosevelt or Woodrow Wilson. Calvin Coolidge fulfilled their expectations.

The scandals of the Harding era did not rub off on Coolidge, who had had nothing to do with any of the culprits. As President, Coolidge forced Attorney General Daugherty to resign and prosecuted the men who were deep in graft and corruption. Most voters soon forgot about the scandals. Another reason for Coolidge's popularity was the return of prosperity. The postwar depression had lifted, and a period of rapid economic growth coincided with Coolidge's administration. For a few industries and most farmers, conditions did not improve much. But the majority of Americans basked in the sunshine of "Coolidge prosperity."

Coolidge wins the election of 1924. The Republican convention in 1924 almost unanimously chose Coolidge as its candidate for the presidency. Charles G. Dawes was named as his running mate. At the Democratic convention, there was a long and bitter contest between the supporters of William G. McAdoo and those who preferred Governor Alfred E. Smith of New York. McAdoo, a Protestant, was the choice of southern and western delegates who strongly supported Prohibition. Smith, on the other hand, was an urban candidate. He was a Catholic, opposed Prohibition, and favored continued immigration.

For more than a hundred ballots the convention was deadlocked over Smith and McAdoo. Finally, both withdrew in order to let the delegates nominate John W. Davis of West Virginia. Governor Charles Bryan of Nebraska, brother of the famous William Jennings Bryan, was named as the vice-presidential candidate.

During the campaign Davis and Coolidge spent most of their time belaboring a third-party candidate — Senator Robert M. La Follette. La Follette had been nominated by the Conference for Progressive Political Action — a combination of farmers, labor leaders, intellectuals, old-time progressives, and a few Socialists. Their platform promised government ownership of the railroads, an end to the use of injunctions in labor disputes, and relief for the farmers.

President Coolidge won the election with well over half the popular votes. Democratic strength was confined to the South, and La Follette carried only his own state of Wisconsin. The Republicans also kept control of Congress. In his inaugural address, Coolidge said he would continue the policies of the past four years.

Republican administrations aid business. Ever since the 1860's, businessmen had been influential in the Republican Party. During the administrations of Harrison and McKinley they had dominated party councils, but Theodore Roosevelt had pushed them into the background. For the Republican Party, the election of 1912 had been a showdown between the conservative faction headed by William Howard Taft and the Progressive faction headed by Roosevelt. Though neither won the election that year, the Old Guard had secured control of the party. Thereafter the Progressives had little say in party councils, and the Republicans spoke for the businessmen. Said Harding in 1920: "What we want in America is less government in business and more business in government." President Coolidge put it another way: "The business of the United States is business."

Almost all of the legislation passed by the Republicans in the 1920's met with the approval of businessmen. The government

Senator La Follette and his family listen to election returns. In 1920 one station had broadcast the outcome of the election, but in 1924 large numbers of Americans heard election results over the radio for the first time.

aided business in other ways as well. Throughout the decade, the government brought very few antitrust cases against corporations. As a result, thousands of new business mergers took place. In addition, Presidents Harding and Coolidge appointed businessmen to such regulatory commissions as the Federal Trade Commission (page 577) and the Interstate Commerce Commission (page 496).

The champion of business co-operation in the 1920's was Herbert Hoover, Secretary of Commerce under both Harding and Coolidge. Hoover helped businessmen form voluntary *trade associations.* Through these organizations, businessmen discussed common problems of production and marketing, factory efficiency, prices, and arbitration of industrial disputes. This sharing of information resulted in less competition and greater standardization of prices. Nevertheless, the Supreme Court ruled in 1925 that the trade associations did not violate the antitrust laws.

Taxes are lowered. Another way in which the Republican administrations aided business was by passing favorable tax laws. Though the country had a debt of 24 billion dollars in 1921, Secretary of the Treasury Mellon urged that taxes be reduced, especially on large personal incomes and on corporation income. Mellon believed that the money saved in taxes would be put back into business, thus creating new job opportunities for working people.

The Revenue Act of 1921 repealed the excess-profits tax which had been passed during World War I. It also lowered rates on high incomes. Further cuts were approved in the next few years. In spite of the lower tax rates, Mellon was able to reduce the national debt to 16 billion dollars by the end of the decade. Widespread prosperity and high tariffs brought the necessary revenue into the treasury.

Tariff rates are raised. During Harding's administration, the Republicans fulfilled their campaign promise to raise tariff rates. In 1921 Congress passed an Emergency Tariff Act, intended to help the farmers by raising rates on several agricultural imports. The next year Congress approved the Fordney-McCumber Act, which reduced the free list and established rates at the general level of the Payne-Aldrich Tariff (page 563). The Fordney-McCumber Act also authorized the President to raise or lower the rates whenever existing duties did not equalize costs of production at home and abroad. In actual practice this provision resulted in 32 increases during the Harding and Coolidge administrations. There were only five cuts in rates, and they applied to such unlikely imports as paintbrush handles and bobwhite quail.

The sharp increase in American tariff rates alarmed the countries of western Europe. For most of them it meant reduced trade with the United States, thus making it difficult for them to repay wartime loans through an exchange of goods. Many European countries struck back by raising tariff barriers on imports from the United States. As a result, international trade lagged in the 1920's. This situation hurt the American merchant marine and strained relations with our former allies.

Congress responds to the demands of veterans. During these same years important legislation was enacted to satisfy certain special-interest groups. The American Legion, founded in 1919, was active in politics much as the Grand Army of the Republic had been after the Civil War. The Legion demanded "adjusted compensation" for all veterans of World War I. That is, they sought bonuses which would equalize the difference between the low pay of soldiers and the high wages received by wartime industrial workers.

In 1922 Congress passed a bonus bill to provide "adjusted compensation." Although President Harding favored the measure, he vetoed it because Congress had made no provision for raising the necessary funds. Two years later Congress passed the bill again, and President Coolidge vetoed it on the same grounds. This time, however, veterans' organizations like the American Legion persuaded Congress to pass the measure over Coolidge's veto. The law provided for a bonus to be paid after twenty years. The amount was to depend on the veteran's length of service and the proportion of this

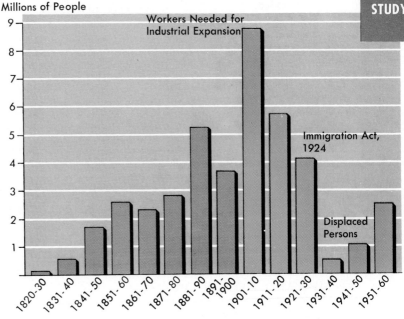

Millions of People

Workers Needed for
Industrial Expansion

Immigration Act,
1924

Displaced
Persons

War, restrictive legislation, and depression caused a decline in immigration after 1910. Fewer immigrants entered the United States in the years 1931–1940 than in any ten-year period since 1830.

time spent overseas. Earlier Congress had also established a Veterans' Bureau to care for hospitalized veterans.

Opponents of unrestricted immigration speak out. Another group that exerted pressure consisted of persons wanting to restrict immigration. Throughout the early 1900's opponents of unlimited immigration had charged that the foreign-born lowered American standards of living and swelled the ranks of paupers and criminals. During and immediately after the war, the immigrants were also accused of bringing in dangerous political ideas. Some were charged with being Communists.

As a result of such agitation, Congress in 1917 passed a literacy test bill, requiring immigrants to prove that they could read and write a language. Though President Wilson vetoed it, Congress passed the measure over his veto. Three years later the law was amended to exclude immigrants who were "members of the anarchistic and similar classes." Despite these restrictions, 805,000 immigrants entered the United States during 1921.

Congress establishes immigration quotas. To check the flow of Europeans to this country, Congress passed the Emergency Quota Act in 1921. This law limited the number of immigrants from each European country to 3 per cent of the number of

people of that nationality residing in the United States in 1910. But those who wanted to restrict immigration still were not satisfied. They felt it was important that the American population be predominantly white, "Anglo-Saxon," and Protestant. President Coolidge gave them his support by announcing that "new arrivals should be limited to our capacity to absorb them into the ranks of good citizenship. America must be kept American."

In 1924, therefore, Congress passed an immigration act which reduced the quota for each country to 2 per cent of the number of that nationality living in the United States in 1890. This measure not only reduced the number of immigrants admitted to about 160,000 a year but favored those who came from northern and western Europe. Furthermore, immigrants from Asia were specifically barred. This provision angered the Japanese, who had scrupulously lived up to the Gentlemen's Agreement (page 593). Citizens of Canada and the Latin American republics were not subject to quota restrictions.

The Immigration Act of 1924 further provided that, beginning in 1927, the total number of immigrants would be limited to 150,000 people per year. Each European country would be given a quota based upon the percentage of people of that national

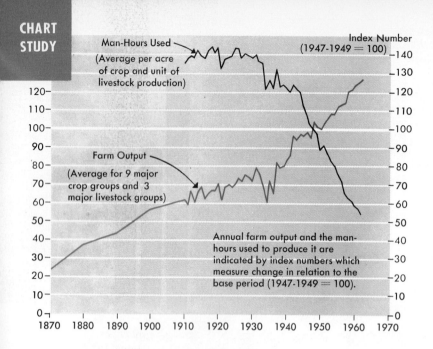

Man-Hours Used
(Average per acre
of crop and unit of
livestock production)

Index Number
(1947-1949 = 100)

Farm Output
(Average for 9 major
crop groups and 3
major livestock groups)

Annual farm output and the man-
hours used to produce it are
indicated by index numbers which
measure change in relation to the
base period (1947-1949 = 100).

**FARM PRODUCTION
IN THE UNITED STATES**

*Contrast the tremendous
growth in farm output with
the sharp decrease in man-
hours used in farming.*

origin in the United States population in
1920. Because the "national origins" of the
American population were difficult to determine, this last provision did not actually
go into effect until 1929. Then, the Great
Depression and, later, World War II completely changed the situation. In almost
every year from 1932 to 1945, less than one
third of the quota was filled. During the
depths of the depression in the 1930's there
were more people leaving the country than
there were immigrants arriving.

Farmers suffer hard times. "Coolidge
prosperity," as we have noted, did little for
the farmer. Land values and farm prices
had been high during the war years. But in
the 1920's they fell back to prewar levels.
One reason for lower prices was that the
use of new farm machinery and scientific
farming increased farm output by 30 per
cent between 1910 and 1925. During the
war years, the increased volume of farm
production had been easily absorbed, but
surpluses mounted in the 1920's — and surpluses meant lower prices. Also, American
farmers faced greater competition in the
world market. This competition came (1)
from the farmers of European countries that
had recovered from the ravages of the war
and (2) from the increased farm output of
Canada, Australia, Argentina, and Soviet
Russia. Still another factor was that nations
like China which could have used our

agricultural surpluses were unable to pay
for them. Finally, southern cotton growers
faced competition from new textiles, such
as rayon, as well as from cotton growers
in Russia, India, and Egypt. From 1919 to
1929 farm income dropped from fourteen
and a half billion dollars to a little over
eleven billion dollars.

**The "farm bloc" tries to improve the
situation.** Representatives from the agricultural states, both Democrats and Republicans, formed a "farm bloc" in Congress. The
farm bloc encouraged the formation of
farmers' co-operatives and in 1922 sponsored a law exempting such organizations
from antitrust acts. In the following year
Congress provided low-interest loans to
agricultural co-operatives as well as to individual farmers.

These measures failed, however, to improve the farmer's lot significantly. Farm
leaders then proposed a solution to the
problem of surpluses. Under this plan,
surpluses would be purchased by a government agency at prices based on prewar
averages. The government might hold surpluses until a poor crop year created a demand for them; or the surpluses might be
sold in the world market at prevailing
prices. Losses resulting from the sale of
surpluses at world market prices would be
met by collecting an "equalization fee"
from producers.

Throughout this country's history, immigrants have contributed to its growth and culture. Besides the immigrants mentioned elsewhere in this book, the three foreign-born Americans pictured here have made notable contributions. Enrico Fermi (left) came to this country from Italy in 1939 and helped develop the atomic bomb. Felix Frankfurter (center), born in Austria, served for many years as a justice of the Supreme Court. Dimitri Mitropoulos (right), born in Greece, became a leading conductor of symphonic and operatic orchestras.

The McNary-Haugen bill, embodying this plan, was passed by Congress in 1927 and again in 1928. Both times, however, President Coolidge vetoed it. He declared that the bill involved "unsound" government price-fixing, was unconstitutional, and would be of no real help to farmers. "Farmers have never made much money," said the President, who had once tried cultivating the rocky hillsides of Vermont. "I don't believe we can do much about it."

▶ CHECK-UP

1. How did the Eighteenth Amendment come to be passed? The Nineteenth Amendment? What points were stressed by Republicans and Democrats in the 1920 election? What interpretation can be made of the outcome?

2. What scandals marred Harding's administration? Why was Coolidge a popular President? What issues were raised in the 1924 election by the candidacies of Al Smith and Robert La Follette?

3. How did Republican administrations help business? Veterans? What restrictions were placed on immigration? Why? How did the immigration picture change after 1929?

4. Why did farmers experience hard times after World War I? What help was provided by Congress? What were the provisions of the McNary-Haugen bill?

. . . .

3 *The 1920's Witness Important Social and Cultural Changes*

Cities grow at the expense of the countryside. During the 1920's the number of farm workers in the American labor force decreased by about one million. Because of increased efficiency in production and low prices for farm products, farm people continued to migrate to the towns and cities. Many southern Negroes moved to northern industrial cities. Within the South, meanwhile, thousands of whites left tenant farming for city factory jobs. Most of the immigrants admitted during these years also settled in urban centers.

The growth of towns and cities at the expense of rural areas is reflected in census reports. In 1920, for the first time in American history, the census showed more than half the population living in towns and cities of 2500 people or more. During the 1920's, differences in outlook between city dwellers and rural people were highlighted by a number of controversies.

The Prohibition experiment has mixed results. One area of disagreement between rural and urban Americans was Prohibition. In January, 1920, the Prohibition Amendment went into effect. To enforce the Amendment, the Volstead Act had been passed in October, 1919. This law declared that the manufacture, sale, or transportation

of beverages containing more than one half of one per cent of alcohol was illegal.

The job of enforcement was turned over to a Prohibition commissioner and 1500 agents. These men were supposed to check on the production of industrial and medicinal alcohol (these were legal), to guard the country's borders against smuggling, and to make sure that no citizen brewed his own alcoholic beverages. When it became clear that more agents were needed, Congress doubled the number. Even so, the Prohibition agents were unable to catch many of the "rum-runners" who brought foreign liquor into sheltered harbors or transported it across the Canadian and Mexican borders. Nor could they catch the thousands of people who made alcoholic beverages in country stills or in their own basements. The Prohibition Amendment may have reduced the volume of liquor consumed in the United States. But it caused many people to violate a law which they regarded as a denial of their personal rights.

CHART STUDY

GROWTH OF POPULATION, 1910–1965

The concentration of population in urban areas increased rapidly in the twentieth century. By 1965 seven out of ten Americans were urban dwellers.

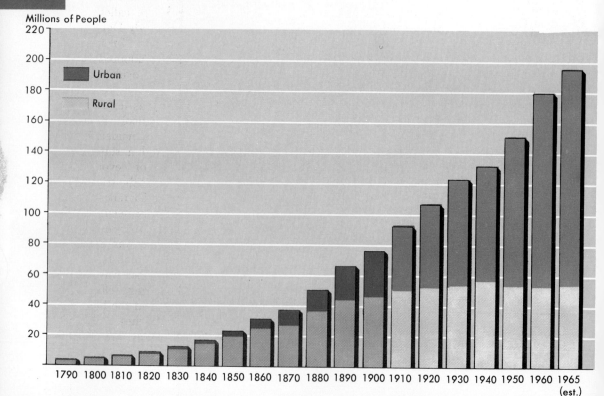

Millions of People

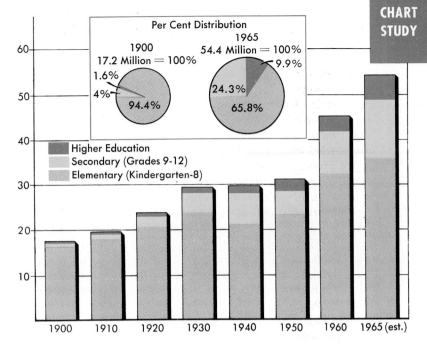

SCHOOL ENROLLMENT, 1900–1965

This graph shows the striking increase in the number of students enrolled in secondary schools and colleges. Compare enrollment above the elementary level in 1900 and in 1965.

Per Cent Distribution

1900
17.2 Million = 100%
1.6%
4%
94.4%

1965
54.4 Million = 100%
9.9%
24.3%
65.8%

■ Higher Education
■ Secondary (Grades 9-12)
■ Elementary (Kindergarten-8)

1900 1910 1920 1930 1940 1950 1960 1965 (est.)

Prohibition also had the unhappy result of encouraging bribery, corruption, and organized crime. The profits from selling illegal beer and liquor were immense, and "bootleggers" soon learned that some Prohibition agents could be bribed to overlook illegal activities. Organized gangs of "bootleggers" were even able to buy police protection in some cities. In Chicago, Al Capone built a criminal empire on the sale of beer and liquor and then branched into large-scale racketeering.

The strongest support for the Prohibition Amendment had come from rural America. In the cities many immigrants, accustomed to drinking beer and wine with their meals, regarded Prohibition as an infringement of their personal liberty. By the end of the 1920's many urban Americans — even non-drinkers — favored repeal of the Prohibition Amendment as one way of fighting organized crime. Though the Amendment had been passed with bipartisan support, Prohibition became a political issue by the end of the decade. The Republicans, though disappointed with enforcement of the law, generally wanted to continue the experiment; most Democrats favored repeal.

Some rural areas object to teaching about evolution. By the 1920's most urban churches had reconciled their religious beliefs with the scientific evidence supporting Darwin's theory of evolution (page 410). Moreover, they accepted new historical evidence about how and when various parts of the Bible had been written. In rural areas, however, many Protestants still held the view that the Bible was to be interpreted literally. Since they felt that Darwin's theory of evolution was in conflict with the biblical account of Creation, the *fundamentalists*, as they were called, did not want their children to study Darwinist ideas in their science courses. In several rural states, the legislatures adopted laws prohibiting the teaching of evolution in public schools.

In 1925 this kind of law was tested in a dramatic trial. A high-school biology teacher in Dayton, Tennessee, named John Scopes, intentionally violated a state law forbidding the teaching of evolution. Among the defense lawyers at the trial was the famous Chicago lawyer Clarence Darrow. Aiding the state in its prosecution of Scopes was William Jennings Bryan. The outcome of this unusual case was a technical victory for the fundamentalists, since the law was upheld and Scopes was fined 100 dollars. But the long-range effect of the Scopes trial was to weaken the hold of fundamentalism on rural churches.

New ideas in education are tried. Meanwhile, some educators were seeking ways of helping students adjust to the problems of urban, industrial life. To meet the growing demand for job training, the larger cities established vocational high schools. Junior high schools were founded to help students make the change from elementary to secondary school. The number of students attending colleges and universities jumped from about 600,000 in 1920 to over a million ten years later. This increased enrollment required a vast expansion of college and university campuses. New classrooms, laboratories, libraries, and dormitories were needed. To meet the demand for specialized training, many universities established graduate programs in medicine, dentistry, law, education, business administration, and journalism.

In the postwar decades, American schoolmen debated a theory about the nature of education put forward by John Dewey. Dewey taught at the University of Chicago and later at Columbia University. Taking issue with the long-accepted view of education, he insisted that book learning was not enough to prepare students for life in a rapidly changing world. Dewey argued that education should prepare young people to cope with real-life problems. They must discover relationships between what they study and the community in which they live. Their educational experience should prepare them to play an active role in their communities. Many educators staunchly resisted this so-called "progressive" theory of education. But it was applied in some private and public schools and influenced American education for years to come.

Racial tension increases. An unfortunate feature of American life from time to time has been the sudden outbreak of violence stemming from intolerance and prejudice. During the 1920's attacks were directed at such minority groups as Negroes, Jews, Catholics, and immigrants. Negroes in particular were the target for this kind of hostility.

Negroes faced prejudice in both the South and the North. Such organizations as the NAACP and Urban League (page 581) encountered opposition but kept up their demands for protection of their civil rights and better job opportunities for Negroes. During World War I, some 400,-000 Negroes served in the army,[2] about half of them in Europe where they experienced little or no discrimination. Naturally it was hard for these Negroes to return to the old system of segregation. But some southern whites were determined to maintain racial barriers, particularly against Negroes who had served in the army and returned to the South. During 1919 alone, more than 70 Negroes were lynched. Ten of these victims were servicemen.

In cities, hostility often stemmed from the fact that Negroes and whites were competing — in large numbers for the first time — for jobs and housing. During the war, the reduced flow of immigrants and the increased demand for workers had attracted several hundred thousand Negroes to industrial cities in the North. Their pay was low and their housing often cramped and inadequate. Yet they found somewhat greater freedom of movement in cities such as New York, Chicago, Detroit, Cleveland, and Pittsburgh than in the South. After the war these Negroes showed no intention of leaving the North. Moreover, many Negro servicemen chose to stay in the North at the end of the war.

During 1919, when defense plants closed down and white veterans came home to claim jobs, racial conflict sometimes broke out. More than 25 towns and cities had race riots that year. The most serious outbreak came in Chicago, where the Negro population had doubled within five years. A fight on a beach between Negroes and whites spread to other parts of the city, and for almost two weeks the police and state militia were unable to restore order. A total of 23 Negroes and 15 whites were killed and more than 500 people were injured. Nearly a thousand Negro families were left homeless as a result of pillaging and fires.

The Ku Klux Klan is revived. Fear and hatred of minority groups was inflamed by

---

[2] Negroes were barred from the Marine Corps, however, and discouraged from enlisting in the navy. In the army, they were allowed to serve in all branches except the air corps, where they were barred as pilots.

the activities of the revived Ku Klux Klan. The Klan of post-Civil War days had died out by the 1880's, but a new Klan was organized in Georgia in 1915. Its purpose was to restrict the rights and opportunities of Negroes, Catholics, Jews, and immigrants. Following the war, the Klan grew rapidly, and by 1924 it probably had four and a half million members. Though its chief strength was concentrated in the rural areas and small towns of the South and Middle West, active Klansmen could be found in cities as well as in the country. Using the violent methods of the earlier Klan, the hooded Klansmen terrorized their Negro and white victims.

At the height of its power in the 1920's, the Klan influenced elections in several states. But the tide began to turn when a Klan leader in Indiana was sent to prison for kidnapping a girl who later committed suicide. The exposure of the Klan's sordid activities came as a shock to many Americans, and membership in the organization dwindled.

Standards and values change. The 1920's witnessed a revolution in American manners and values. Young people especially ignored tradition. Girls, for example, shortened their skirts, rolled their stockings below their knees, and used cosmetics. The automobile freed young people from the watchful eye of chaperons.

Many adults also changed their ways. Women shortened their skirts — eventually to knee-length. They discarded cumbersome underskirts, thereby reducing the amount of material it took to dress a woman from 20 yards in 1914 to a mere 7 yards in 1928. Silk stockings replaced heavier cotton stockings, and new synthetic dress fabrics like rayon became popular. Women also followed the lead of young girls in bobbing their hair, wearing rouge and lipstick, and smoking.

American women "emancipate" themselves. Changing fashions in clothes were symbolic of a fundamental change in the role of women in American society. New labor-saving machines, such as the vacuum cleaner, refrigerator, and washing machine, had reduced the burden of household chores. At the same time more women were buying baked goods and using canned fruits and vegetables, thus reducing the time they had to spend in the kitchen. Moreover, newer houses were smaller in size and many families lived in apartments. Such changes meant that women had more free time.

As a result, the number of women with jobs sharply increased during the 1920's. Some who had taken defense jobs in 1917 continued to work after the war. Others were drawn into the labor market by the interesting range of office jobs that had become available to them and by the greater acceptance of women with professional training. The number of women holding full-time jobs rose from five million in 1900 to about eleven million by 1930. The increased economic independence of American women enabled some of them to terminate unhappy marriages. Thus, the divorce rate rose from 13 per 100 marriages in 1920 to almost 17 per 100 by the end of the decade.

The automobile comes of age. While people were adjusting to postwar social changes, a number of new mechanical developments were transforming American life. Though invented before the 1920's, the automobile, airplane, radio, and motion picture all came of age in that decade. It was the automobile that brought about the most important changes.

Throughout the nineteenth century, European and American inventors had tried to produce a "horseless carriage." In 1895 Charles B. Selden of Rochester, New York, secured a patent on a vehicle powered by a gasoline engine. By that time other Americans, including Henry Ford, were working on both gas and electric models. At the turn of the century there were about 8000 automobiles in the United States, most of them owned by wealthy families. A decade later, more than fifty companies were producing automobiles, among them Olds, Buick, Cadillac, Ford, Studebaker, and Packard.

The automobile brings about many changes. The economic and social changes brought about by the automobile were stag-

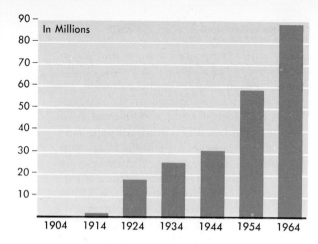

MOTOR VEHICLE REGISTRATIONS

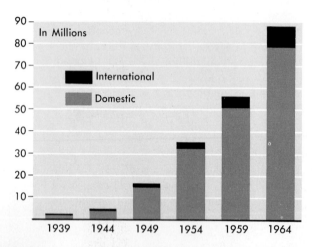

AIRLINE PASSENGERS

These charts show how the use of automobiles and airplanes zoomed. By 1964 more than 86 million motor vehicles were registered in the United States, and 88 million passengers were carried by scheduled airlines.

gering. From 1920 to 1930 the number of registered automobiles increased from 8 million to 23 million. By the end of the decade automobile production had become one of the country's largest industries, employing millions of workers. It encouraged the growth of related industries, and it made necessary the construction of adequate roads, financed by federal, state, and local governments. Garages, filling stations, and roadside stands all came into being as a result of the automobile.

This new means of transportation stimu-

lated the continuing growth of suburbs outward from the core of the cities. The expanding suburbs in turn attracted new stores and sometimes branch offices and factories. City buses began to replace other methods of local transportation, and buses also cut into railroad traffic. At the same time, the advantage of door-to-door pick-up and delivery enabled trucks to take over some of the freight previously shipped by rail. Families with automobiles began to vacation in distant states and national parks. The car also changed American dating patterns, and, some critics charged, lowered the moral standards of young people. In addition, it changed methods of crime, enabling gangsters to make quick "get-aways."

The airplane comes of age. The development of the airplane soon followed that of the automobile. The lightweight, high-powered gasoline engine made possible man's conquest of the air. After many trials, Orville and Wilbur Wright made a successful flight at Kittyhawk, North Carolina, in 1903. Airplanes were used in World War I, at first for scouting and later for combat. During the 1920's aircraft were improved in design and construction, airports were built, and regular service for passengers and mail got under way. The federal government speeded this development by giving profitable mail contracts to private air-transport companies.

Charles A. Lindbergh's spectacular solo flight across the Atlantic did much to arouse public interest in aviation. In May, 1927, Lindbergh took off from Roosevelt Field, New York, in *The Spirit of St. Louis,* a plane which he had helped design. Thirty-three and a half hours later, he landed at an airfield outside Paris. Overnight, "Lucky Lindy" became an international hero, a role which the shy young flier disliked. Other achievements in the field of aviation soon claimed the attention of the American public — Commander Richard Byrd's dramatic flight over the South Pole (1929) and Wiley Post's feat in circling the globe in less than eight days (1933).

The radio moves into American homes. The exciting news of Lindbergh's flight reached many Americans over their new radio sets. The radio resulted from prewar experimentation and invention by the Italian scientist Guglielmo Marconi and the Americans R. A. Fessenden and Lee de Forest. Though radio communication was used experimentally in World War I, the general public still regarded it as a toy for amateur scientists. Then, in November, 1920, the country's first broadcasting station, KDKA in Pittsburgh, carried the election returns. Still the public paid little attention to "wireless telephony" until President Harding installed a set in the White House. After that, the new industry grew rapidly. Other stations began broadcasting, and the major networks took shape. By the end of the 1920's there were ten million sets in use, bringing radio communication into half the homes in the United States.

Americans flock to the movies. The movies were also tremendously popular in the 1920's. As early as 1891 Thomas Edison had developed a motion-picture camera. Other inventors devised a machine to project the animated pictures onto a screen. The first film to tell a complete story, *The Great Train Robbery*, was produced in 1903.

Early films were shown in vacant stores to people willing to pay five cents for a ten-minute show. Soon longer films were made,

Although the number of automobiles increased tremendously during the 1920's, horses could still be useful, as the picture at left suggests. As good roads were built, fewer cars had to be hauled out of the mud.

Henry Ford's Model T (right) became one of the most popular of the early cars. Ford manufactured the Model T from 1908 to 1927.

Among the uses made of the new forms of transportation was the carrying of mail. The first air mail was flown between New York, Philadelphia, and Washington in 1918. The mail pilots flew their open-cockpit airplanes (left) even in bad weather, and many of them crashed.

their quality improved, and the actors began attracting loyal fans. By the end of World War I, most cities had large motion-picture theaters, and such stars as Charlie Chaplin, Lillian and Dorothy Gish, and Mary Pickford had become national idols. The most famous of the early directors was David W. Griffith, who released *The Birth of a Nation* in 1915. This film's portrayal of reconstruction has been criticized for its southern bias. But *The Birth of a Nation* was a technical landmark, for it demonstrated the dramatic possibilities of close-ups, fade-outs, switchbacks, mob scenes, and exciting pursuits.

Early in the 1920's movie producers made Hollywood, California, their headquarters. There they could shoot pictures outdoors all year round. The problem of co-ordinating a sound track with film was soon solved. The first big "talkie" was *The Jazz Singer,* starring Al Jolson (1927). Almost immediately sound movies replaced the silent pictures, and soon color was also added. By 1930 even the smallest towns had at least one movie house.

More Americans watch and participate in sports. General prosperity and a reduction in the work week gave Americans time not only to attend the movies but to attend sporting events also. Baseball and football games, boxing matches, and horse races were popular. College football games drew huge crowds, and broadcasts of games reached millions of listeners. Baseball continued to be America's favorite spectator sport. The game's greatest hero was Babe Ruth, who for many years held the record for most home runs (60) hit in a season. Jack Dempsey and Gene Tunney were among the best-known boxers. Large numbers of fans paid high prices for admission to their fights. Horse racing made money for promoters, attracted millions each year to the race tracks, and made "stars" of some thoroughbreds.

Sand-lot baseball and football were the favorite sports of many American youngsters of this decade. They and their elders also played tennis on public courts, and some Americans took up golf. In the 1920's many cities established municipal golf courses. The automobile carried thousands of people to lake and ocean beaches. New swimming resorts were established, public pools were built, and bathing beauty contests were introduced. Atlantic City held the first of its beauty pageants in 1921.

Jazz captures America's fancy. Jazz music, which was influenced by ragtime and the blues (page 510), gained wide popularity during the 1920's. Originated by Negro musicians in New Orleans, jazz had a distinct rhythm and structure of its own. By the first World War, jazz bands were playing in dance halls and night clubs in New Orleans, and a Dixieland Jazz Band was holding forth in Chicago. This band was the first to record jazz music.

Among the best-known early jazz musicians were Joseph "King" Oliver and Ferdinand "Jelly Roll" Morton. One member of Oliver's band was Louis Armstrong, a Negro born in New Orleans in 1900. In the 1920's Armstrong formed his own band and established a reputation in Chicago and New York as one of the country's leading jazz musicians. Later he toured Europe, introducing jazz music to enthusiastic audiences. Edward "Duke" Ellington arranged jazz compositions for a much larger band. He also toured Europe with great success in the 1930's. In the words of one historian: "Jazz was another American shot heard round the world! It has beaten its insidious rhythms into every corner of the globe."

Jazz also influenced American composers of other kinds of music. George Gershwin, a popular song writer of the 1920's, showed the jazz influence in his scores for such popular musicals as *Lady, Be Good* and *Strike Up the Band.* But Gershwin believed that jazz also could be used as "the basis of serious symphonic works of lasting value." During the 1920's the talented Gershwin wrote three symphonic masterpieces incorporating the elements of jazz — *Rhapsody in Blue,* the *Concerto in F,* and *An American in Paris.*

New magazines cater to special groups of readers. A wide variety of new magazines was launched in the 1920's, some of which are still thriving today. The *Reader's Digest* printed condensations of articles that

Since the 1920's, Duke Ellington (top left) and Louis Armstrong (above) have been leading figures in the jazz world. Ellington has composed many enduring songs (like "Mood Indigo") and is known for the sophisticated sound of his orchestra. Both he and Louis Armstrong, who learned to play the trumpet in a New Orleans orphanage, have become international favorites. Jazz influenced George Gershwin (left) in his scores for musical comedies and in such orchestral compositions as "Rhapsody in Blue" and "An American in Paris."

had appeared in other magazines. *Time,* one of the first weekly news magazines, made its appearance in 1923. Two years later the *New Yorker,* offering sophisticated cartoons, articles, and stories, was first published. A favorite magazine of college students was the *American Mercury,* founded and edited by Henry L. Mencken. He delighted — or infuriated — readers by his free-swinging attacks on those who believed in old-fashioned American virtues.

Gifted writers do some of their best work in the 1920's. It was the *American Mercury* which introduced readers to the work of F. Scott Fitzgerald, whose own life in many ways was typical of the "jazz age." *This Side of Paradise* was based on Fitzgerald's experiences at Princeton University. *The Great Gatsby* showed the transforma-

tion of an idealistic farm boy into a rich, disillusioned racketeer. Ernest Hemingway was one of many American writers and artists who lived in Paris during the 1920's. Hemingway depicted the life of Americans in Paris in *The Sun Also Rises.* In another novel, *A Farewell to Arms,* he portrayed an American soldier's disillusionment with war. Echoing Mencken's attack on middle-class life in America was Sinclair Lewis, the author of the novels *Main Street* and *Babbitt.*

A small magazine entitled *Poetry,* launched in Chicago in 1912, encouraged some of America's leading poets. One was Carl Sandburg, the son of Swedish immigrants, who held a variety of jobs before he turned to journalism in Chicago. Sandburg's *Chicago Poems* used common speech and even slang phrases to capture the spirit of the midwestern city. Vachel Lindsay and Edger Lee Masters were other Illinois poets who wrote about the Middle West. Masters' *Spoon River Anthology* painted word portraits of the citizens of an imaginary small town. Also making their appearance in *Poetry* magazine were Edna St. Vincent Millay and T. S. Eliot. Eliot's *The Waste Land,* which was critical of American civilization, became one of the most controversial and influential poems of the 1920's. One of the most widely read of American poets was Robert Frost. Many of Frost's poems dealt with New England rural life and yet had universal significance.

The first important American dramatist appears. In the 1920's many artists, authors, and musicians settled in Greenwich Village, the area around Washington Square in New York City. Their free and unconventional life startled other people, but the creativity of some of them greatly enriched American culture. Among the Greenwich Village group that summered in Provincetown, Massachusetts, was a young man named Eugene O'Neill. He helped to organize the Provincetown Players in 1916, and when they established a theater in New York, O'Neill began writing plays for them. *Bound East for Cardiff* drew on his own experience as a seaman and beachcomber. His later plays searched into the quirks of human nature, exploring the triumphs and shortcomings of man. For *The Emperor Jones, Desire Under the Elms, Strange Interlude, Mourning Becomes Electra,* and other plays, O'Neill won three Pulitzer Prizes in the 1920's and the Nobel Prize in 1936.

American artists are influenced by European painters. Adding to the excitement of life in Greenwich Village during World War I and the 1920's were the members of the "Ashcan School" of painting (page 486). Though often attacked by the critics, these artists continued to paint realistic canvases of the seamy side of urban life.

Yet even these painters were startled by the new European art displayed at the New York Armory in 1913. This show gave many Americans their first chance to see the work of European painters of the impressionist and abstract schools. The colorful impressionistic pictures were startling enough, but some of the more abstract paintings were dismissed by viewers and critics alike as "hideous," "crude," or the work of "a lunatic asylum." Nevertheless, the Armory Show had a tremendous influence on the subsequent development of American painting. A later generation of Americans acknowledged their debt to the European masters of modern art by arranging a second exhibition of the original Armory Show in New York in 1963.

▶ **CHECK-UP**

1. Why did towns and cities during the 1920's grow at the expense of rural areas? Why was it difficult to enforce prohibition? Why did lawlessness increase during the prohibition era? What hostility did minority groups face? Why?

2. What was the basic idea underlying "progressive" education? How did the role of women change in the 1920's?

3. What economic and social changes were brought about by the automobile? The airplane? The radio? Sports?

4. What were the important developments in such fields as literature, drama, art, popular music, and the movies?

. . . .

Clinching the Main Ideas in Chapter 31

American political leadership in the postwar years was uninspired. The Wilson administration, handicapped by the President's illness, did little to ease the change-over to peacetime conditions. Unemployment and prices shot up, strikes and racial conflict plagued the industrial centers, and the fear of political radicalism touched off the Red scare.

In 1920 the voters gave control of the federal government to the Republicans, only to learn within a few years that President Harding and the country had been victimized by corrupt officials. Harding's successor, Calvin Coolidge, continued the policy of "return to normalcy." Tax and tariff legislation passed during the 1920's was generally favorable to business. Attempts to help the farmers were, at best, feeble. In response to pressure groups, Congress adopted the quota system for immigration, thus greatly reducing the number of new-comers admitted each year.

During the 1920's, important changes took place in the country's economic, social, and cultural life. Big business continued to grow bigger. Workers, sharing in the prosperity of the times, were able to buy household appliances, radios, and even auto-mobiles. American youth rebelled against established social patterns, and adults soon followed their example. Women cut their hair, raised their hemlines, and left their kitchens to take jobs. People danced to jazz tunes, attended the new motion-picture theaters, or went for a drive in the "Model T." Yet somehow there was dissatisfaction with life in the "golden twenties," especially among the intellectuals. Their discontent was expressed in different styles by such writers as Lewis, Fitzgerald, Hemingway, and Eliot.

Chapter Review

Terms to Understand

1. Esch-Cummins Act
2. Eighteenth Amendment
3. Nineteenth Amendment
4. trade association
5. "national origins"
6. Volstead Act
7. Teapot Dome
8. company union
9. Red scare
10. Fordney-McCumber Act
11. "adjusted compensation"
12. Immigration Act (1924)
13. McNary-Haugen Bill
14. equalization fee
15. farm bloc
16. open shop
17. closed shop

What Do You Think?

1. Why did the economic boom of the war years turn into a "bust" right after the war?

2. Why did the nation prefer "normalcy" in the 1920's? What did this term imply? What was the alternative?

3. Why was there a "Red scare" after World War I?

4. In 1920 President Harding said: "What we want . . . is less government in business and more business in government." Explain. Do you agree? Why?

5. Why did race problems increase after World War I?

Using Your Knowledge of History

1. Debate: *Resolved,* That the automobile has made a greater change in American life than the radio.

2. Write a brief essay contrasting the conception of the presidency held by one of these pairs of Presidents: (a) Theodore Roosevelt and Calvin Coolidge; (b) Woodrow Wilson and Warren Harding.

3. Have a panel discussion on the Immigration Act of 1924. Evaluate the purpose of this law and the provision intended to carry out that purpose.

4. In a two-column chart, list (a) the arguments a prohibitionist might have advanced in favor of Prohibition and (b) the arguments an anti-prohibitionist might have advanced in favor of repeal.

Extending Your Knowledge of History

W. E. Leuchtenburg has written an excellent brief study of the 1920's, *The Perils of Prosperity.* For the political history of the decade, see Karl Schriftgiesser's *This Was Normalcy* and John D. Hicks' *Republican Ascendancy. Only Yesterday* by Frederick Lewis Allen is lively social history, and another good study is Lloyd Morris' *Postscript to Yesterday.* Herbert Asbury writes about Prohibition in *The Great Illusion.* William Allen White's biography of Coolidge is entitled *A Puritan in Babylon.* On the Scopes trial, see Ray Ginger's *Six Days or Forever?* For the Sacco-Vanzetti trial, see Francis Russell's "Sacco Guilty, Vanzetti Innocent?" in *American Heritage,* June, 1962. Highly recommended is the August, 1965, issue of *American Heritage,* entirely devoted to the 1920's.

CHAPTER 32

Stockbroker's office in the '20's

The Old Order
Faces a Crisis

In America today we are nearer a final triumph over poverty than in any land. The poorhouse has vanished from among us; . . . given a chance to go forward, we shall, with the help of God, be in sight of the day when poverty will be banished from this nation.

HERBERT HOOVER, 1928

1928–1932

When Herbert Hoover accepted the Republican nomination for the presidency in 1928, he expressed the hope that the day was in sight when poverty would be "banished from this nation." It is likely that many Americans — Republicans and Democrats alike — agreed with this happy prophecy. The voters apparently believed that another Republican administration could and would continue "Coolidge prosperity." Hoover's term of office had scarcely got under way, however, when the stock market began to waver and then plunged downward. After the "great crash" in the fall of 1929, the nation's economy fell off sharply. Factories and mines closed, trade dwindled, farm prices sagged, and banks failed. When Hoover left office four years later, one out of four American workers were jobless, and thousands were homeless and hungry.

It was President Hoover's misfortune to be blamed for this catastrophe. During the 1920's the Republicans had claimed credit for "Coolidge prosperity," and it was only natural that they were also held responsible for what was called the "Hoover depression." Yet the President showed more understanding in meeting the crisis than did many other Republicans. He tried to stabilize farm prices, and he was willing to use government funds to bolster banks, railroads, and major industries. Hoover drew the line, however, at appropriating federal funds for the relief of jobless people. Long before the end of Hoover's term, the voters had lost confidence in the Republican administration. In the election of 1932, they turned to the Democrats and elected Franklin D. Roosevelt to the presidency, hoping that he could solve the economic crisis.

1 Herbert Hoover Becomes President

The Republican convention nominates Hoover. In 1927, President Coolidge surprised everyone by announcing, "I do not choose to run for President in 1928." Possibly Coolidge hoped to be drafted by the convention, but most Republicans took his terse communication at face value. Influential politicians quickly switched their support to the Secretary of Commerce, Herbert Hoover.

Born on an Iowa farm, Hoover had been orphaned at an early age. But the industrious Quaker youth worked his way through Leland Stanford University in California and received an engineering degree. He soon rose to prominence as a mining engineer in the international oil industry. During the early years of World War I, he administered Belgian relief funds, but returned to the United States to head the Food Administration when this country entered the war. Hoover was so successful in these assignments that his name was mentioned for the presidency in 1920. Instead, however, he served Presidents Harding and Coolidge in the important post of Secretary of Commerce. Both professional politicians

. . . .

CHAPTER FOCUS

1. Herbert Hoover becomes President.
2. Prosperity comes to an end.
3. Hoover tries to stem the depression.
4. The Democrats win the 1932 election.

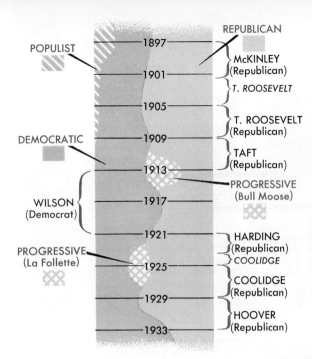

POLITICAL PARTIES, 1897–1933

In spite of the challenge of the Progressives, the Democratic and Republican Parties continued to win the support of most voters.

CHART STUDY

and businessmen favored Hoover in 1928. To many Americans who admired him, Herbert Hoover was the poor farm boy who had made his mark in business and international affairs.

The delegates to the Republican convention nominated Hoover on the first ballot. For the vice-presidency they selected Senator Charles Curtis of Kansas. This was the first time that a major party had given both nominations to men from states west of the Mississippi River.

The Democrats nominate Al Smith. The Democratic candidate in 1928 was the first presidential nominee of either major party to come from an urban, immigrant background. Born in the slums of New York, Alfred E. Smith attended Catholic schools until he went to work at the age of fifteen. He held a variety of jobs before joining Tammany Hall and winning election to the New York legislature in 1903. In the state capital he backed a number of reform measures and gained recognition as one of the best-informed members of the legislature. First elected governor of New York in 1918,

Al Smith waves to a campaign crowd in New York just a few days before the election in 1928. The New Yorkers loved him but the rest of the country was less enthusiastic.

Smith won re-election three times. Although he championed the interests of the cities and backed social legislation, "Al" Smith retained the confidence and support of conservative financial spokesmen. At the Democratic convention in 1928, Smith won the nomination on the first ballot, and the delegates chose Senator Joseph Robinson of Arkansas as his running mate.

The campaign reflects urban-rural differences. There was not much difference between the Republican and Democratic platforms in 1928. The Republicans claimed credit for "Coolidge prosperity" and hinted at tariff increases. Their campaign slogan was "a chicken in every pot and a car in every garage." The Democrats took a "me too" position in favor of prosperity and the tariff but, unlike the Republicans, endorsed the farm bloc's McNary-Haugen bill (page 657).

During the course of the campaign each of the candidates took a definite stand on Prohibition. Hoover called it "a great social and economic experiment, noble in motive and far-reaching in purpose," and he expressed a determination to continue it. Smith pointed out the difficulties of en-

forcement and the unfortunate side effects of Prohibition. He favored eventual repeal of the Eighteenth Amendment. The state governments, said Smith, should control the sale of liquor and the licensing of places that served it.

Of chief interest to most voters were the origin, experience, and connections of the two candidates. The fact that Smith was an Irish Catholic and came from "the sidewalks of New York" endeared him to many voters who came from immigrant stock, lived in cities, and were themselves Catholics. On the other hand, an active whispering campaign speculated on what would happen if a Catholic occupied the White House. Some anti-Catholics predicted that the Pope would run the country — perhaps from the Vatican, perhaps from the White House itself! Such appeals to prejudice lost Smith some votes, but they also solidified support for him in some areas of the country. Smith's stand on Prohibition also won him support.

As for Hoover, millions of Americans rallied to his cause because, as one of them said, "he is sprung from American soil and stock." Hoover's rapid rise as a mining engineer recalled the heroes of Horatio Alger's books, and his accomplishments as the "Great Humanitarian" in charge of international relief projects were well known. Americans who shared a rural background with the Republican candidate, who were Protestants, or who were active in the business community voted for Hoover. His support of Prohibition was an added virtue in their eyes.

The Republicans win the election. The election resulted in a substantial victory for the Republicans. Hoover won more than 21 million popular votes, while Smith received only 15 million. The Democratic electoral vote was a mere 87, compared to 444 for Hoover. The Republicans also won large majorities in both houses of Congress. Working for the Republican Party in this election was the issue of prosperity. As one historian has pointed out: "Given the temper of the 1920's and the success of the Republican Party in identifying itself with prosperity . . . , Smith's setback in 1928 was only to be expected. If Smith had been Protestant, dry, and born in a log cabin of good yeoman stock, he still would have been defeated on the Democratic ticket."

The election had two interesting features. For the first time since reconstruction, the Republicans ran well in the Solid South, carrying seven states in that section. At the same time, the Democrats made important gains in the large cities. For thirty years the Republicans had won substantial majorities in the cities. But in 1928 Smith broke this pattern by carrying some of the largest metropolitan centers.

Herbert Hoover takes office. There were few indications of the trouble that lay ahead when Hoover took office in March, 1929. His inaugural address was as optimistic as his campaign had been. Businessmen approved the President's decision to retain Andrew Mellon as Secretary of the Treasury. Henry L. Stimson, an authority on foreign policy and a recent Governor of the Philippines, was appointed Secretary of State. Leading figures in both parties expected good times to continue throughout the Hoover administration. Mellon solemnly proclaimed: "The high tide of prosperity will continue."

▶ CHECK-UP

1. Why did Republican politicians and businessmen favor the nomination of Hoover in 1928? What was the background of Al Smith?

2. What types of issues influenced voters in this campaign? What was the result?

· · · · · · · · · · · · · · · · · ·

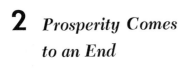

2 *Prosperity Comes to an End*

Prosperity seemed to be following a steady curve upward during the 1920's. To a large extent, this was an era of industrial expansion. Following the brief post-war depression, the output of American factories had risen sharply, partly because of more efficient management and the use of new machinery. The value of manufactured goods produced in the United States in 1929 had multiplied six times since 1900. The fact that many more Americans could purchase the new manufactured goods also stimulated productivity. Personal income rose to a point where American workers enjoyed the highest standard of living in the world. Yet reduction of income tax rates during the 1920's meant that the wealth of the country still was unevenly distributed. In 1928, 5 per cent of the population received 27 per cent of the country's basic income.

Mass production speeds industrial progress. Industrial progress owed much to *mass production,* the technique in which the new industry of automobile manufacturing pioneered. One of the first companies to bring together money, men, and machines in the combination called mass production was the Ford Motor Company. Ford installed expensive machinery to make the hundreds of parts that go into an automobile. These parts were stationed at the proper places alongside an *assembly line.* A bare automobile frame started at one end of the line, and as it moved along, each of many workers performed a single, specialized operation. Thus, at the end of the line, a completed automobile rolled off, ready to take to the road. Under this system the Ford factories in the early 1920's were able to turn out 8000 motor cars each day. "By 1926," writes one commentator, "it was a matter of thirty-three hours from the time iron ore left the bottom of a Great Lakes freighter until a new Ford honked for clearance on the open road." Mass-production methods spread throughout American industry (page 501).

The manufacture of automobiles accounted for nearly 13 per cent of the country's industrial production in 1929. It also gave a great boost to other industries, especially steel. In addition, it stimulated the demand for rubber, plate glass, nickel, lead, and petroleum products. New methods of refining made it possible to extract large

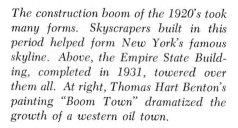

The construction boom of the 1920's took many forms. Skyscrapers built in this period helped form New York's famous skyline. Above, the Empire State Building, completed in 1931, towered over them all. At right, Thomas Hart Benton's painting "Boom Town" dramatized the growth of a western oil town.

quantities of gasoline from crude petroleum. By 1929 gasoline accounted for close to half the output of American oil refineries.

Factories and homes use electricity. Electricity likewise played an important role in the industrial expansion of the 1920's. In 1914 only 30 per cent of American factories had been run by electricity; nearly 70 per cent were operated by electricity in 1929. The amount of electricity produced in the 1920's more than doubled, and its uses were multiplied many times over. It operated such consumer items as radios, phonographs, lamps, toasters, telephones, washing machines, vacuum cleaners, and refrigerators. Electricity also ran machines and assembly lines in factories. Moreover, since manufacturers no longer depended on coal, they had more freedom in deciding where to build new plants.

The construction industry booms. Another industry which underwent vast expansion in the 1920's was building construction. New homes, shops, and factories provided steady work for the building trades in the early 1920's, and the demand for new construction remained high during "Coolidge prosperity." Almost every large city boasted of at least one skyscraper built in the 1920's, and New York's skyline changed dramatically. Twenty-story buildings had been commonplace in New York before 1914, but now skyscrapers like the 77-story Chrysler Building and the 102-story Empire State Building (1931), were erected. This latter structure was the tallest in the world. In the meantime, home construction in the suburbs boomed. New Yorkers spilled over into Queens; people in Cleveland built homes in Shaker Heights; Detroiters moved to Grosse Pointe. Suburbs also surrounded Chicago, St. Louis, San Francisco, and Los Angeles. A fantastic real-estate boom took place in Florida, where resort hotels and vacation homes went up at a startling rate. Construction in turn created major markets for glass, steel, brick, cement, lumber, and electrical and plumbing supplies.

The chemical and metal industries expand. Important new developments took place in the chemical and metallurgical industries. Lightweight metals like aluminum and magnesium were developed. Before World War I, the country's supplies of potash, nitrates, and dyes had come from abroad. But during and after the war, American industry filled these needs. A government-owned plant at Muscle Shoals in the Tennessee Valley produced essential nitrates during the war. New chemical companies grew up in the postwar years, and older ones vastly increased their production.

The 1920's also saw the appearance of many synthetic products. Though celluloid had been created as early as 1869, there was little market for synthetic plastics and fibers until after World War I. Bakelite, cellophane, lacquers, and synthetic fabrics then came into wide use. Rayon production, for example, multiplied nearly 70 times between 1914 and 1929. Both the chemical companies and the producers of synthetics maintained research laboratories and employed an increasing number of chemists. One of the most ingenious was George Washington Carver, a Negro chemist who had worked his way through high school and college. In his laboratory at Tuskegee Institute, Carver found ways of making shaving lotion and axle grease from peanuts, and library paste and tapioca from sweet potatoes.

Prosperity is unevenly spread. While industrial expansion brought prosperity to many Americans, pockets of depression existed throughout the 1920's. This situation resulted from several factors which we have already mentioned. Since prices on farm products remained low, the farmers' share of the national income steadily declined. The railroads were also in trouble, primarily because of growing competition from automobiles, trucks, buses, and airplanes. Another soft spot in the economy was coal mining. The sale of coal fell off as more and more industries switched to electricity, and as gas and oil-burning furnaces replaced coal units in homes and apartment buildings. Unemployment in the mining regions also resulted from the increased use of labor-saving machinery in the more profitable mines. Still another depressed industry in the 1920's was cotton textiles. Rayon and other synthetics cut into the sale of silk and wool, but the main victim was cotton. Moreover, the change in women's fashions reduced the total amount of fabric needed in their clothing.

Manufacturers produce more than can be consumed. The unemployed and low-income families could not afford the many products turned out by American industry. By the middle of the 1920's factories were turning out more automobiles and appliances than Americans could pay for in cash. The situation would have been helped if the surplus of manufactured goods on the mar-

Born of slave parents, George Washington Carver became an eminent chemist. Here he is shown conducting a chemistry class at Tuskegee Institute.

ket had forced prices down to a level where purchasers could have afforded them. But trade associations fixed the prices of many goods, and throughout the decade prices remained high. Another way to increase the number of buyers would have been for industries to pay higher wages and take less in corporate profits. But organized labor lacked the bargaining power to achieve this goal. Thus, wages did not rise fast enough to enable workers to purchase the vast amount of goods they were producing.

Americans buy on credit. For a number of years installment buying concealed the unhealthy gap between the amount of goods produced and the amount consumers could afford to buy. Americans were encouraged to purchase automobiles, household appliances, furniture, and other items on the installment plan. The buyer paid a fraction of the total cost of the item in cash at the time of the purchase. The balance was to be paid over a given number of months. Large sums of money were spent on advertising to persuade Americans that they needed certain items to "keep up with the Joneses." As a result, thousands of American families began to make purchases on credit. It has been estimated that by the late 1920's three out of every four radios and about 60 per cent of the automobiles and furniture were financed on the installment plan. Without consumer credit, many families might never have been able to obtain such useful items as refrigerators and washing machines. But it was all too easy for purchasers to ignore the fact that installment buying was really a form of indebtedness.

Buying on credit was encouraged in the stock market as well. Individuals could buy stock by putting only a fraction of the purchase price in the hands of a broker. This was known as buying stock *on margin.* As a result, large speculators could deal in thousands of shares without expending much capital, while people of modest incomes were encouraged to try their luck with a few shares of stock. Since most stocks rose in value during the 1920's, this appeared to be an easy way to make money. The fact that stocks could be purchased on

credit was a major reason for the mounting volume of stock market transactions.

Among those urging Americans to invest in stock was John Raskob, Chairman of the Democratic National Committee. In an article for *Ladies' Home Journal* entitled "Everybody Ought to be Rich," Raskob told his readers that if they invested fifteen dollars a week

in good common stocks, and allow the dividends and rights to accumulate, at the end of twenty years you will have at least $80,000 and an income from investments of around $400 a month. . . . And because income can do that, I am firm in my belief that anyone not only can be rich, but ought to be rich.

Warning signs are ignored. Toward the end of the 1920's there were indications that the bubble of prosperity might burst. Building construction fell off during 1928, sales of automobiles were down, and the number of unemployed rose. Nevertheless, installment buying increased, and in the spring of 1928, stock market prices suddenly shot up. The price of radio stock, for instance, doubled during the month of March. By the end of the summer industrial stocks had increased in value by almost 25 per cent. Dazzled by the hope of easy riches, thousands of Americans invested in stocks. When Hoover's election touched off another price increase, still more people poured their life savings into the stock market. Few of them realized that it was the flood of stock purchases that was forcing prices upward. Nor did they understand that the inflated stock prices bore little relation to the volume of production or sales of the companies whose securities they were buying.

The stock market crashes. The end came in October, 1929. Prices had wavered in September, but brokers encouraged Americans to go on buying. "Don't sell America short," was their slogan. Stock prices dipped on October 19 and again five days later. Despite the frantic efforts of bankers and stockbrokers to stem the decline in prices, a sharp drop occurred on October 29. On that day more than sixteen million shares of stock changed hands. By

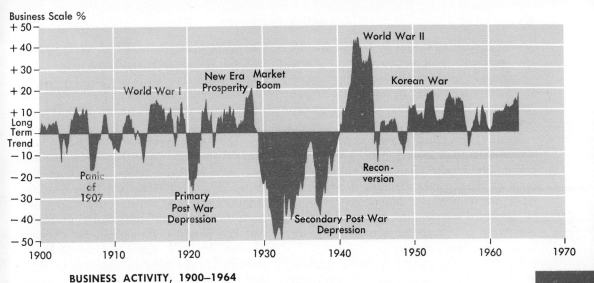

Business Scale %

BUSINESS ACTIVITY, 1900–1964

Note the contrast between the "Great Depression," which began in 1929, and the business boom which accompanied World War II. From 1945 to 1965, the ups and downs of the economy were less extreme and prosperity generally prevailed.

CHART STUDY

mid-November the value of the fifty leading stocks had been cut in half. The value of other securities had dropped by as much as 80 per cent. Thousands of Americans who had purchased stock "on margin" saw their savings wiped out in a matter of days. Securities which they actually owned were worth only a fraction of what they had paid for them. Since most investors were caught in the same dilemma, few wanted to buy. To sell, therefore, meant accepting the low market price.

The country's business and financial leaders tried to be optimistic. *The Wall Street Journal* insisted that "the wiping out of paper profits" would not "reduce the country's real purchasing power." President Hoover declared that "any lack of confidence in the economic future or the basic strength of the business of the United States is foolish." Yet people began to cut down on their purchases; manufacturers, uncertain of what lay ahead, reduced production and laid off workers. By the spring of 1930 it was clear that the stock market crash had touched off a major depression. A year after the crash, six million men were jobless. "There was hardly a man or woman in the country," wrote one historian, "whose attitude toward life had not been affected . . . by the sudden and brutal shattering of hope."

▶ CHECK-UP

1. Explain the relationship of the following items to the industrial boom of the 1920's: mass production, increased use of electricity, developments in the chemical industry, installment buying.

2. What "soft spots" were there in the economy? Why was industry producing more than consumers could buy? What possible danger did the increase of installment plan buying involve? What part did buying on margin play in the stock market?

3. What were the results of the stock market crash?

· · · · · · · · · · · · · · · · · ·

3 *Hoover Tries to Stem the Depression*

Hoover's appeal for voluntary action is ineffective. Like everyone else in the country, President Hoover was baffled by the economic collapse. He was convinced that the capitalist system remained sound. Said the President: "The fundamental busi-

675

ness of the country, that is, the production and distribution of commodities, is on a sound and prosperous basis." He thought the country was suffering only from "frozen confidence," and he talked about prosperity being "just around the corner."

To meet the crisis, Hoover urged voluntary rather than government action. He called upon businessmen not to cut employment or slash wages. He asked organized labor not to press for higher wages. And he appealed to the Red Cross and other charitable organizations to raise funds for the relief of needy families.

But decreasing sales and profits made it impossible for businessmen to maintain regular employment and wages. They began to fire workers and reduce wages. As the number of unemployed steadily mounted, private welfare organizations found themselves swamped with pleas for help. At the very time that these organizations needed more money to expand their relief work, fewer Americans were able to contribute money to charities.

The depression spreads. The "Great Depression," as it was called, had effects beyond our borders. After the stock market crash in 1929, American funds were withdrawn from Europe, thus creating a serious strain on the economy of European countries. Early in 1931 an important Austrian bank closed its doors, thus setting off financial panics in other countries. President Hoover felt that Europe's economic troubles aggravated the depression in the United States. In June, 1931, he proposed, and Congress accepted, the idea of a one-year *moratorium* (or suspension) on war-debt payments (page 640). But this move failed to improve the situation either in Europe or in the United States.

Meanwhile, employers in this country resorted to wholesale firings and wage cuts in order to stave off bankruptcy. The volume of manufacturing was cut in half between 1929 and 1932. As the purchasing power of families declined, shopkeepers, grocers, and retail stores saw their business melt away. Banks were compelled to foreclose on loans and mortgages. In the first three years of the depression, about 5100 banks failed.

Unemployment climbed to twelve million in 1932. In an industrial city like Cleveland, half of the men were out of work by that year. Between 1929 and 1932 the total spending power of all Americans fell from 83 billion dollars to 48 billion dollars.

The Agricultural Marketing Act fails to help the farmers. As we have seen, farmers had suffered hard times throughout the 1920's. Even before the depression began, Hoover had called a special session of Congress to deal with agricultural problems that had persisted throughout the decade. Though he had opposed the McNary-Haugen bill during the campaign, he realized that the government had to try in some way to stabilize farm prices and strengthen farm credit. Congress responded to Hoover's request by passing the Agricultural Marketing Act in 1929. This measure set up a Federal Farm Board with a special fund of 500 million dollars. From it, farm cooperatives could borrow money to pay for the costs of storing produce until prices were higher. The Farm Board itself tried to raise prices by buying up farm surpluses. It created a Grain Stabilization Corporation which purchased surplus wheat. For a while these operations kept the price of wheat in the United States slightly above the world figure. But when the Grain Stabilization Corporation ran out of money and stopped buying, the price dropped below the 1929 level. A Cotton Stabilization Corporation had a similar experience.

It was clear by 1931 that the Agricultural Marketing Act had failed to achieve its objectives. The price of wheat had fallen from a dollar a bushel in 1929 to 38 cents in 1932. Over the same period, cotton prices dropped from 16 cents a pound to 6 cents. Moreover, the government found itself with unmarketable surpluses of wheat and cotton, which further depressed the market. Yet the Agricultural Marketing Act marked the first time that federal funds had been used to regulate farm prices. Other schemes would be tried in the 1930's.

Congress raises tariff rates. President Hoover also asked the special session of Congress to make a "limited revision" downward of certain import duties. Before any

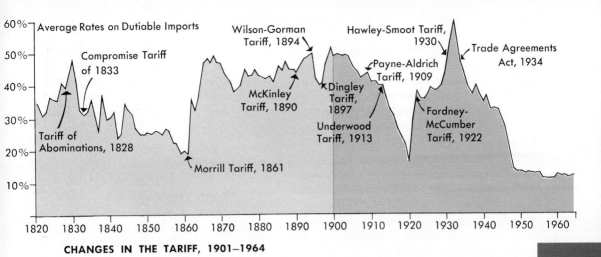

CHANGES IN THE TARIFF, 1901–1964

Notice that tariff rates reached the highest point in American history under the Hawley-Smoot Tariff. The Trade Agreements Act contributed to the sharp decline in duties after 1932.

bill was passed, however, the financial crash took place. Congress then decided to *raise* tariff rates in order to give still greater protection to American agriculture and industry. While the Hawley-Smoot Tariff Act was being written, a number of groups protested against Congress' plan to raise rates. Many farmers were convinced that higher tariffs would hurt them. Bankers and importers vigorously objected to a general rise in rates. Manufacturers who sold goods abroad feared that foreign countries would retaliate by raising barriers against American imports. A thousand members of the American Economic Association signed a petition urging President Hoover to veto the Hawley-Smoot Tariff.

Nevertheless, the President signed the bill into law in 1930. Within two years some 40 countries had adopted measures to cut down their imports of American goods. From 1929 to 1932 the foreign trade of the United States (exports plus imports) declined from ten billion dollars to three billion dollars. To be sure, the depression in the United States and Europe was responsible for much of this decline, but the Hawley-Smoot Tariff was also a factor.

Hoover supports a public-works program. As we have seen, President Hoover at first called for voluntary action to meet the economic crisis. He soon realized, however, that the government would also have to take action. Unlike many Republicans, President Hoover did not oppose the use of government funds to create jobs for the unemployed. Early in 1930 he approved an act of Congress which appropriated funds for the construction of public buildings and roads and for the improvement of rivers and harbors. The President felt that these steps would not only create badly needed jobs but would also stimulate business. Before he left office, he approved additional appropriations amounting to more than two billion dollars for public construction.

Hoover approves the Reconstruction Finance Corporation. Hoover was also willing to use government funds to bolster large businesses. During 1931 the number of bank failures increased sharply. Many utility companies, insurance firms, and mortgage companies also faced bankruptcy. To stave off further disaster, Hoover asked Congress to set up an agency for lending federal funds to business concerns. Early in 1932 Congress established the Reconstruction Finance Corporation (RFC) and authorized it to make loans to banks, railroads, insurance companies, mortgage companies, and other corporations. Within a year more than 5000 companies secured loans from the RFC. During the next administration, the scope of the RFC was vastly expanded, and loans were given to small businesses too.

Hoover rejects the Muscle Shoals power project. Though President Hoover was willing to lend government money to large companies, he steadfastly refused to let the government compete with any private business. This position led to a heated dispute over the Muscle Shoals project. At the end of the war the government found itself with a large dam and a nitrate plant at Muscle Shoals (page 673) on the Tennessee River. Progressives, among them Senator George Norris, urged the government to keep control of the dam, generate electric power, and sell it at reasonable prices to the people of the Tennessee River Valley. Conservatives, however, wanted the government to lease the dam to private enterprise.

In 1931 progressives in Congress succeeded in passing a bill authorizing the government to develop Muscle Shoals. But Hoover strongly opposed the measure. In his veto message, the President said:

There are many localities where the Federal Government is justified in the construction of great dams and reservoirs, . . . where they are beyond the capacity or purpose of private or local government capital to construct. In these cases power is often a by-product and should be disposed of by contract or lease. But for the Federal Government deliberately . . . to build up and expand . . . a power and manufacturing business is to break down the initiative and enterprise of the American people; it is destruction of equality of opportunity of our people; it is the negation of the ideals upon which our civilization has been based.

Supporters of the bill were unable to pass it over Hoover's veto, but government development of the Tennessee Valley became an issue in the next presidential campaign.

Hoover opposes direct relief. The President also firmly opposed the use of government funds for *direct* relief of the unemployed. He believed that this should be the responsibility of private organizations or of state and local governments. A number of cities and some state governments did administer relief programs. These varied from soup kitchens, bread lines, and the distribution of coal, flour, and lard to the payment of small weekly sums to the heads of families. The funds available for these relief programs were totally inadequate, however, and state and local leaders saw no way of raising additional money. After the Democrats won control of the House of Representatives in the 1930 elections, they presented Hoover with several bills requiring the federal government to sponsor a relief program for the unemployed. Hoover vetoed these measures on the grounds that direct government aid would be "impractical," "dangerous," and

Jobless people with nowhere else to go lived in crowded shacks on the outskirts of many cities. This picture shows Seattle's "Hooverville."

These veterans left St. Louis early in July, 1932, to march to Washington, even though Congress had already turned down the bonus bill.

"damaging to our whole conception of governmental relations."

This bitter struggle over who was to aid the unemployed seriously damaged Hoover's reputation as the "Great Humanitarian." Democrats asked the President why he had been willing to feed the starving Belgians during World War I but not American citizens in the depths of depression. Desperate men and women living in miserable wooden shanties on the edges of industrial cities called their communities "Hoovervilles." Throughout the United States the phrase "Hoover depression" replaced the favorite phrase of the 1920's, "Coolidge prosperity."

The army disperses the bonus marchers. As the depression grew worse, World War I veterans asked Congress to pay in full the bonus voted in 1924 (page 654). The veterans argued that this would help the nation's economy by placing money in circulation. In 1932, while Congress was considering such a bill, bands of jobless veterans marched on Washington to demonstrate in favor of the bonus bill. Some camped at the edge of the city in shacks and tents; others moved into unused government buildings near the Capitol. When the Senate defeated the bill, most of the bonus marchers went home.

The others, many of them both jobless and homeless, refused to leave Washington. Fearing violence, President Hoover finally ordered the United States Army to disperse

the veterans. Under the direction of Chief of Staff Douglas MacArthur, army troops ousted the bonus marchers and burned their shacks to the ground. Many Americans were shocked by this action. Said the Washington *News:* "What a pitiful spectacle is that of the great American Government, mightiest in the world, chasing unarmed men, women, and children with Army tanks."

The "lame duck" session is abolished. One of the closing events of the Hoover administration was the addition of an amendment to the Constitution. Senator Norris had long advocated an amendment that would abolish the short session of Congress.[1] A century before, when transportation was difficult, a long interval between the election of congressmen and the beginning of their new terms made sense. But in the twentieth century it was unnecessary, and the short session meant that so-called "lame duck" congressmen and a "lame duck" President might run the country for four months after failing to win re-election. Early in 1932, therefore, both houses of Congress approved an amendment to abolish the short session. Ratified by February, 1933, the Twentieth Amendment provided that congressmen take office on January 3 and that the President and Vice-President be inaugurated on January 20.

---

[1] From December following a presidential election to March 4, when new Presidents were inaugurated.

▶ CHECK-UP

1. Why did the depression continue to worsen? What was the Agricultural Marketing Act? The Hawley-Smoot Tariff? The Reconstruction Finance Corporation? How effective was each of these?

2. What was Hoover's attitude toward a public-works program? Muscle Shoals? Direct relief? Explain in each case.

3. What was the bonus march? What happened to the marchers?

4. What did the Twentieth Amendment provide for?

4 *The Democrats Win the 1932 Election*

The Republicans renominate President Hoover. In 1932 both parties held their conventions in Chicago — the Democrats in good spirits, the Republicans in very low spirits. The Republicans had lost control of Congress in 1930, and the economic situation had grown worse since then. Without much enthusiasm the Republican delegates renominated President Hoover on the first ballot. Their platform praised the administration's efforts to cope with the depression. Since many Republicans by this time doubted the wisdom of continuing Prohibition, their platform called for a national referendum on the matter.

The Democrats choose Governor Roosevelt. The strongest contender for the Democratic nomination was Franklin D. Roosevelt. He had served as Assistant Secretary of the Navy under Wilson, and had been the Democratic vice-presidential candidate in 1920. His political career had apparently been cut short in 1921 when an attack of polio left his legs crippled. But throughout the 1920's Roosevelt kept up his political contacts, and in 1928 he accepted the Democratic nomination for the governorship of New York. Much to everyone's surprise, Roosevelt was elected governor while Al Smith failed to carry the state as the party's presidential candidate. Roosevelt was an exceptionally able governor, but his independent decisions and appointments irritated Smith and destroyed their close friendship.

On the early ballots at the 1932 convention, Roosevelt had a majority but lacked the necessary two thirds. Smith and John Nance Garner of Texas controlled enough delegates to keep the convention deadlocked. On the fourth ballot the California delegation switched their votes from Garner to Roosevelt. The Texans followed Cali-

Franklin D. Roosevelt shattered tradition by flying to the Democratic convention. His plane had to land three times between Albany and Chicago — twice for gas and once for a storm. Here a crowd greets Roosevelt as he arrives in Chicago.

fornia's example and the convention stampeded to Roosevelt. Garner was then nominated for the vice-presidency.

The Democratic platform was brief but specific. It called for a reduction in government spending, a sound currency, reciprocal tariff agreements, state unemployment and old-age insurance, aid to agriculture, strict enforcement of the antitrust laws, participation in the World Court, independence for the Philippines, and outright repeal of the Prohibition Amendment. Governor Roosevelt started a new custom by coming to the convention to accept the nomination in person. His rousing speech to the delegates ended with these words: "I pledge you, I pledge myself, to a new deal for the American people." Roosevelt's program for action immediately became known as the "New Deal."

Roosevelt conducts a vigorous campaign. Roosevelt visited every section of the country during the campaign. He was smiling, confident, and optimistic, but his speeches were less specific than the Democratic platform. He would take an interest in "the forgotten man at the bottom of the economic pyramid," provide relief for the farmers, and revive the railroads. Roosevelt's promises to regulate the utility companies and develop public power won him the support of progressive Republicans like Hiram Johnson and George Norris. Many businessmen were reassured by Roosevelt's promise to cut government spending, balance the budget, and maintain a sound currency. Helping Roosevelt during the campaign were several university professors, who soon became known as the "brain trust." Roosevelt cheerfully acknowledged that he "trusted in brains," and he used the suggestions of Raymond Moley, Adolf Berle, and others in his speeches. Throughout the Democratic campaign, stress was put on the need for "bold, persistent experimentation" to cure the depression. Roosevelt said:

It is common sense to take a method and try it. If it fails, admit it frankly, and try another. But above all, try something. The millions who are in want will not stand by silently forever while the things to satisfy their needs are within easy reach.

President Hoover did not do much campaigning until October. His speeches were defensive and burdened with dull detail, and he appeared tired and gloomy. New Deal policies, he warned, would "endanger or destroy our system."

The Democrats win the election. The outcome of the election was no surprise. Roosevelt received 57 per cent of the popular vote compared to 40 per cent for Hoover. The Democrats carried every state in the country except Pennsylvania, Connecticut, Delaware, Maine, New Hampshire, and Vermont. The electoral vote was 472 for Roosevelt and 59 for Hoover. Republican senators and congressmen with long records of service were defeated by virtually unknown Democratic candidates. Many normally Republican states elected Democratic legislatures and governors.

The Socialists had expected an unusually large vote as a result of the widespread discontent, but their presidential candidate, Norman Thomas, polled fewer than 900,000 votes. The Communist presidential candidate, William Z. Foster, received 103,000 votes. Americans clearly preferred to give the opposition major party a chance to cure the nation's ills rather than turn to the Socialists or Communists.

Prohibition is repealed. Responding to the outcome of the election, Congress in February, 1933, approved a constitutional amendment providing for the repeal of Prohibition. The Twenty-first Amendment was submitted to the states and ratified late that year. Thus, a controversial experiment came to an end.

Roosevelt takes office in a time of crisis. The interval between Roosevelt's election and inauguration was an awkward period. Hoover and the President-elect conferred, but their views were too far apart for them to agree on a course of action. During the winter of 1932–1933, the depression grew worse. By March unemployment had climbed above thirteen million. A rash of bank failures convinced many Americans that it was best to keep their meager funds in a tin canister or tucked in a mattress. Angry farmers were taking the law into their own hands to prevent foreclosures on their homes and fields. Jobless, desperate men roamed from one city to another. And in almost every city men, women, and children could be found rummaging in garbage cans for scraps of food.

Inauguration Day, March 4, was cold, cloudy, and windy in Washington, D.C. But the new President instilled a measure of hope in the American people:

> This great nation will endure as it has endured, will revive and will prosper. So . . . let me assert my firm belief that the only thing we have to fear is fear itself — nameless, unreasoning, unjustified terror which paralyzes needed efforts to convert retreat into advance. . . . The people of the United States have not failed. In their need they have registered a mandate that they want direct, vigorous action. They have asked for discipline and direction under leadership. They have made me the present instrument of their wishes. In the spirit of the gift I take it.

▶ CHECK-UP

1. What were the planks in the 1932 Democratic platform? Why did the Democrats win the election?

2. Why was the Twenty-first Amendment adopted?

3. What developments had produced a crisis situation by early 1933?

. . . .

Clinching the Main Ideas in Chapter 32

Americans gave a vote of confidence to the Republicans in 1928 when they elected Herbert Hoover to the presidency. But within a few years they had turned against Hoover, blaming him for the economic disaster which overtook the country. Behind the stock market crash of 1929 were many causes — overproduction and underconsumption of manufactured goods, depression on the farms, and speculation in the stock market. It was the sudden, sharp drop in stock prices that touched off the "Great Depression," the worst the country had ever experienced.

At first, President Hoover hoped that voluntary action would cure the economic crisis. But as manufacturers cut back production, farm prices fell, and the number of unemployed mounted, Hoover proposed various remedial measures to Congress. The Agricultural Marketing Act failed to stabilize farm prices, and the Hawley-Smoot Tariff doubtless hurt rather than helped American industry. But Hoover's public-works projects and the Reconstruction Finance Corporation were approaches which the next administration would expand. The President's unwillingness to approve a federal relief program aroused much criticism. His opposition to direct relief and his drastic action against the bonus marchers seriously hurt his chances for re-election in 1932.

The Democrats waged a confident campaign that year. Their presidential candidate, Franklin D. Roosevelt, called for a "new deal" that would lift the country out of the depression and aid "the forgotten man at the bottom of the economic pyramid." Though Roosevelt's program was not spelled out in detail, his willingness to act appealed to distressed Americans. As a result, they gave the Democratic candidate an overwhelming vote in 1932.

Chapter Review

Terms to Understand

1. mass production
2. assembly line
3. RFC

4. purchasing power
5. bonus marchers
6. moratorium

7. synthetics
8. "brain trust"
9. public works

10. buying stock on margin
11. direct relief

Terms to Understand (Cont.)

12. Hawley-Smoot Tariff
13. "lame duck" session
14. metallurgical industries
15. Great Depression
16. Agricultural Marketing Act

What Do You Think?

1. The terms "overproduction" and "underconsumption" are both used to describe a condition which contributed to the Great Depression. Compare different ways of coping with such a situation.

2. The purchase of farm surpluses by the government is a plan that has been used to raise prices of farm commodities. How does it work? Why is it done?

3. During the 1920's many people bought stock "on margin." How did they expect to make money? How were they affected by the stock market crash?

4. President Hoover approved some plans for fighting the depression and opposed others. What standards seemed to guide his decisions? Do you agree with him? Why?

5. The 1932 Democratic platform called for reduced federal spending and a balanced budget. Was this a sound plank? Why?

Using Your Knowledge of History

1. Have each student list presidential races in which economic conditions during the preceding four years were of major importance in determining the outcome of the election. See if the class can reach agreement on a final list.

2. Prepare a two-column chart listing the advantages and disadvantages of making purchases on the installment plan.

3. Write an editorial for a Democratic newspaper, commenting on the methods used by the government to disperse the bonus marchers in 1932.

4. In accepting the nomination for the presidency in 1928, Herbert Hoover expressed the hope that the day was in sight when poverty would be "banished from this nation." Write a brief essay giving your reaction to this statement.

Extending Your Knowledge of History

Oscar Handlin has written a sympathetic book about an able Democratic leader, *Al Smith and His America*. A good study of the stock market crash is John Kenneth Galbraith's *The Great Crash, 1929*. See also Galbraith's "The Days of Boom and Bust" in *American Heritage* (August, 1958). On the early years of the depression, see Gilbert Seldes's *The Years of the Locust*. Richard Hofstadter has an interesting essay on Herbert Hoover in *The American Political Tradition and the Men Who Made It*. Walter Johnson discusses the Hoover administration in the opening chapters of *1600 Pennsylvania Avenue: Presidents and the People Since 1929*. In *American Heritage* see "Bonus March" by John D. Weaver (June, 1963).

Analyzing Unit Nine

1. How might President Wilson have avoided defeat of the Versailles Treaty in the United States Senate? Do you think that our participation in the League of Nations would have made any difference in the course of events during the 1920's?

2. Politicians often talked the language of isolation in the 1920's, but our foreign policy was usually at odds with these public statements. In what sense were our national interests affected by developments in the Far East? In Latin America? In Europe? How did the government seek to protect these interests?

3. How did the Republican administrations undermine the intent of many progressive reforms? What laws did they repeal or revise? In what sense could it be said that the United States had a "single-interest" government in the 1920's? Did this fact contribute to the stock-market crash in 1929?

Unit 10

Franklin D. Roosevelt Leads the Nation Through Depression and War (1933-1945)

President Roosevelt asks Congress for declaration of war

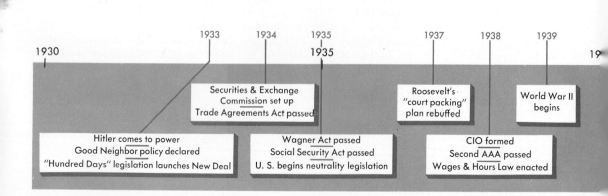

1930   1933   1934   1935   1937   1938   1939   19

1935

Securities & Exchange
Commission set up
Trade Agreements Act passed

Roosevelt's
"court packing"
plan rebuffed

World War II
begins

Hitler comes to power
Good Neighbor policy declared
"Hundred Days" legislation launches New Deal

Wagner Act passed
Social Security Act passed
U. S. begins neutrality legislation

CIO formed
Second AAA passed
Wages & Hours Law enacted

The voters in 1932 elected Franklin D. Roosevelt President, not so much for his previous political record as for his promise to act immediately to end the depression. Action was soon forthcoming. The New Deal bolstered and regulated the banks, regulated the stock market, raised farm prices, and provided jobs and relief for the unemployed. It also launched an ambitious program to stimulate and regulate the business community. The voters expressed overwhelming approval of the New Deal when they re-elected President Roosevelt in 1936 by an enormous margin.

During Roosevelt's second term, additional New Deal laws introduced permanent reforms in American life. Legislation provided for restrictions on crop production and subsidies to farmers who joined the program. This formula remains the basis of farm legislation today. The Social Security Act of 1935 set up systems of unemployment insurance and retirement pensions, which have since been vastly expanded by both Democratic and Republican administrations. And laws protecting the rights of workers to organize and bargain collectively with their employers, as well as establishing minimum wages and maximum hours, are still central to the working of our economic system.

The New Deal was in part a crisis program to save our faltering economy and our political system. While it did not solve all the problems of the depression decade, it accomplished enough to restore the faith of Americans in themselves and their form of government.

On the world front, the 1930's were marked by the spread of aggression — particularly by Nazi Germany under Hitler and by the war lords of Japan. For two years after World War II began in 1939, the United States was neutral, though supplying Britain with the materials needed to withstand the Nazi attack. German attacks on American ships in the North Atlantic brought us to the verge of war, but the final push was provided by the Japanese attack on Pearl Harbor. From the time the United States entered the war in December, 1941, until Roosevelt's death in April, 1945, the President and the British leader, Winston Churchill, masterminded the Allied war effort. Maintaining close contact with Russia, China, and other allies, Churchill and Roosevelt directed a powerful coalition that finally won total victory. Though he did not live to see the end of the war or the establishment of the United Nations, Franklin D. Roosevelt made significant contributions, both as a wartime leader and as an architect of peace.

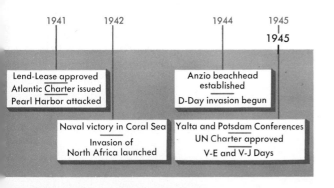

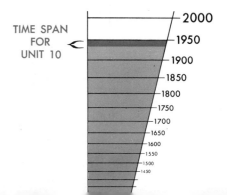

CHAPTER 33

CCC boys planting trees

1933–1940

Franklin D. Roosevelt
Introduces a
New Deal

. . . viewing the history of the New Deal as a whole, what seems outstanding about it is the drastic new departure that it marks in the history of American reformism. The New Deal was different from anything that had yet happened in the United States: different because its central problem was unlike the problems of Progressivism; different in its ideas and its spirit and its techniques.

RICHARD HOFSTADTER, "THE AGE OF REFORM," 1955

President Franklin D. Roosevelt took office at a time of crisis in American history — one of the most serious crises the country had yet faced. Steps taken during Hoover's administration had failed to halt the deepening depression, and by inauguration day in 1933, public confidence was at a low ebb. Out of economic and social chaos the new administration was pledged to bring order. President Roosevelt promised bolder experimentation, and action was soon forthcoming as the administration embarked on new programs in its determination to end the depression.

Much of the New Deal legislation had roots in the nation's past. The Democrats drew on (1) the ideas of the progressive era; (2) the expansion of government regulation during World War I; and (3) Hoover's experiments with trade associations, government loans to business, and government-sponsored public works projects. Yet the New Deal was a new departure. It was dealing with a sick economy, not a prosperous economy as had been the case in the progressive era. It greatly expanded the federal government's regulatory powers beyond anything previously undertaken. It also raised government spending to an unprecedented level in its efforts to

lift the country out of the depression. Many
of the New Deal reforms were considered
innovations at the time but are now generally accepted.

In pursuing these policies, the New Deal
stirred up much angry opposition. Nevertheless, its measures were overwhelmingly
endorsed by the voters. Perhaps the greatest
contributions of the New Deal were restoring public confidence in the American system and proving that a democracy could
cope with such a severe crisis.

1 *Franklin D. Roosevelt Takes Office*

**The New Deal is influenced by the
past.** Many historians have observed that
the "Roosevelt Revolution" of the 1930's
was really a new deal of the old cards. The
President and most of his political associates
were deeply influenced by the progressives
of the early 1900's. Franklin Roosevelt was
a strong admirer, for example, of his distant
relative, Theodore Roosevelt. The new
President had also been affected by the reform spirit of the Wilson administration, in
which he had served as Assistant Secretary
of the Navy. Moreover, Franklin Roosevelt
had shared the amazement of many Americans at the miracles performed by industry
during the First World War. During the
next decade, Roosevelt was a close observer

CHAPTER FOCUS

1. Franklin D. Roosevelt takes office.

2. The New Deal takes shape.

3. The New Deal consolidates its gains.

4. The final New Deal reforms are passed.

5. American culture flourishes during the
   New Deal years.

as his friend Al Smith introduced important
social legislation in New York State. Later,
as governor of New York himself (1929–
1933), Roosevelt promoted social reforms
and initiated a state relief program.

**Roosevelt is advised by the "brain
trust."** Roosevelt's "brain trust" advisers
continued to work with the President after
his election. Raymond Moley, Adolf Berle,
Rexford Tugwell, and later Felix Frankfurter proposed a wide variety of ideas,
helped draft bills for Congress, and sometimes helped administer new programs. The
President was willing to go far in trying out
different ideas. Like a quarterback in a
football game, the President called the
signals, but he frankly admitted that "future
plays will depend upon how the next one
works." The New Deal had no long-range
blueprint. The reformers played by ear,
and the result was, as one historian has said,
sometimes "harum-scarum."

**Many different groups support the
New Deal.** Roosevelt won the support of
a wide range of groups in 1932, and in the
years that followed, he showed great skill
in holding this coalition together. As the results of the 1932 election indicated, the
Democrats could count on the support of
the Solid South. Also, most midwestern
farmers believed that the Democrats would
use the power of the federal government to
bolster farm prices and provide easier credit.
City bosses in the industrial centers, who
had backed Smith in 1928, worked for
Roosevelt in the 1932 election. The President's willingness to let machine politicians
share in patronage contributed to his popularity in the cities.

Still other groups gave their support to
the New Deal. Organized labor became an
important part of the New Deal coalition.
Roosevelt's support of labor's right to organize and bargain collectively and his
efforts to limit hours and raise wages won
the enthusiastic backing of union members.
Immigrants also voted for the Democrats
because that party had opposed the immigration restrictions of the 1920's. Moreover,
a growing number of Negro voters abandoned their traditional ties with the Republican Party. Since the election of 1928,

Republicans, hoping to attract southern whites, had turned against longtime Negro Republican leaders in many southern states. For this reason, and because many Negroes, like many other Americans, blamed Hoover for the depression, Negroes were ready to switch their party allegiance. The New Deal programs of relief and public works helped millions of Negroes who had suffered great hardships during the early years of the depression. President Roosevelt gave them a feeling that the government was sincerely interested in improving their lot. Social workers and old-line progressives also backed Roosevelt, as he set out to introduce many programs which they had worked for without success in the Republican era.

Roosevelt's appointments reflect his diverse coalition. The President tried to give representation to most of these groups in the Cabinet or in other high government posts. As Postmaster General, he named James A. Farley, a New York politician who had managed his campaign for both the nomination and election. For Secretary of State, Roosevelt chose Cordell Hull of Tennessee, a dignified politician who had long fought for lower tariffs. Henry Morgenthau, Jr., a personal friend of the President and a Wall Street financier, became Secretary of the Treasury. For the post of Secretary of Agriculture, Roosevelt decided on Henry A. Wallace of Iowa. Heading the Department of the Interior and in charge of conservation projects was Harold L. Ickes, a former progressive. Frances Perkins, who had been Industrial Commissioner of New York in the late 1920's, accepted the post of Secretary of Labor. She thus became the first woman ever to serve in a presidential Cabinet. Harry Hopkins, a former social worker, administered relief programs in the early years of the New Deal and later became a close adviser of the President.

The country is anxious when Roosevelt takes office. "We are at the end of our string," said President Hoover in early March, 1933, as he prepared to turn the reins of government over to Roosevelt. In addition to unemployment in the cities, there were serious disorders in agricultural areas. Mobs of farmers prevented mortgage foreclosures, and some desperate farmers used violence against judges, bankers, and agents of insurance companies. According to one New York newspaper, "actual revolution already exists in the farm belt."

Moreover, the country's banks were on the verge of collapse. In early 1933 a growing number of bank failures created panic. So many people rushed to withdraw their savings that even soundly managed banks faced disaster. By the time of Roosevelt's inauguration, half the states had ordered banks to close in the hope that a banking "holiday" would stem the panic.

Roosevelt swings into action. "Only a foolish optimist can deny the dark realities of the moment," the new President said in his inaugural address. "This nation asks for action, and action now." On the day after his inauguration, President Roosevelt ordered all the banks in the country closed for four days. Then, he called a special session of Congress to begin on March 9. The President sent to Congress bills on a variety of subjects as fast as his advisers could write them. On the very first day of the special session, an Emergency Banking Act was introduced in Congress, passed, and signed by the President!

The government regulates the banks. The Emergency Banking Act approved the President's closing of the banks and forbade the hoarding or export of gold. The measure authorized government inspectors to investigate all banks. Sound banks were issued licenses and allowed to reopen; the unsound ones were denied licenses and thus put out of business. Both the Federal Reserve and the Reconstruction Finance Corporation were empowered to make loans to the sound banks which would help them meet depositors' demands. On March 12 the President addressed the American people by radio in the first of his many "fireside chats." He explained the government inspection system and told the people that the sound banks which reopened "would take care of all needs. . . . I can assure you that it is safer to keep your money in a reopened bank than under the mattress."

During the next two months more than 12,000 banks reopened, while fewer than 2000 banks were denied licenses. Both conservatives and liberals praised the Presi-

(Continued on page 690)

Franklin D. Roosevelt

[1882–1945]

Franklin Delano Roosevelt was born in Hyde Park, New York, the child of a wealthy family. After graduating from Harvard College, he studied law at Columbia University and then practiced law in New York City. In 1905 he married Eleanor Roosevelt, an intelligent and lively young lady who was his distant cousin and a favorite niece of President Theodore Roosevelt. Since Franklin Roosevelt showed some interest in Democratic politics, he was asked in 1910 to run for state senator from Dutchess County, where Hyde Park is located. Though this county had elected only one Democrat since 1856, Roosevelt won. He later quipped that he must have been mistaken for the former President.

As a state legislator, Franklin Roosevelt opposed Tammany Hall and the party bosses. Said one unhappy Democratic boss: "If we've caught a Roosevelt, we'd better . . . drop him off the dock. The Roosevelts run true to form, and this kid is likely to do for us what the Colonel is doing to the Republican Party, splitting it wide open." The young state senator supported such progressive measures as civil service laws, conservation proposals, direct primaries, woman suffrage, and welfare legislation. Re-elected in 1912, he helped Woodrow Wilson carry New York State. As a result, Franklin Roosevelt was appointed Assistant Secretary of the Navy. Roosevelt was deeply influenced by Wilson's progressivism, and he learned from the President's political successes as well as his failure with the League of Nations. Although defeated as Democratic vice-presidential candidate in 1920, Roosevelt favorably impressed both voters and party leaders. His future looked bright.

In the summer of 1921, while vacationing with his wife and five children on Campobello Island, Roosevelt was stricken with polio. Although both legs were paralyzed, his wife encouraged his resolve to lead as active a life as possible. By 1924 Roosevelt was able to appear before the Democratic national convention to nominate for the presidency his friend Governor Al Smith of New York. Four years later, when it was clear that Smith would win the presidential nomination, the Governor asked Roosevelt to run for the top post in New York State. Roosevelt agreed and was elected governor, even though Smith lost the state to Hoover. In 1932 Franklin Roosevelt won the Democratic nomination and was elected President.

During the twelve years that President and Mrs. Roosevelt occupied the White House, they made a deep impression on people all over the world. Mrs. Roosevelt shared the President's idealism and often made fact-finding trips for him. Millions of people were heartened by Franklin Roosevelt's charm, wit, courage, and optimism during the difficult years of depression and world war. Politicians admired FDR's ability to work with diverse groups and his skill in compromising on lesser matters in order to win on major issues. Frances Perkins said of him: "He made an indelible impression on his own country and on the world. . . . He grew to greatness by a full utilization of all of his talent and personality; he began where he was and used what he had. He ignored his handicaps . . . and let nothing hinder him from doing the work he had to do in the world. He was not born great but he became great."

dent's handling of the bank crisis. The journalist Walter Lippmann, who had been unenthusiastic about Roosevelt during the campaign, wrote: "In one week the nation, which had lost confidence in everything and everybody, has regained confidence in the government and in itself."

▶ CHECK-UP

1. On what sources did the New Deal draw for its policies? What was the "brain trust"? What groups supported the New Deal?

2. What was the nation's mood in March, 1933? How did President Roosevelt restore confidence in the banks?

. . . .

2 *The New Deal Takes Shape*

The special session of Congress, which met from March 9 through June 16, passed laws dealing with a wide variety of problems. The crisis atmosphere of this session, later known as the "Hundred Days," obviously could not last. But this period witnessed the launching of some of the New Deal's most important programs.

Congress increases banking security. Congress' first act of the special session had ended the banking panic. A few weeks later, in another banking measure (the Glass-Steagall Act), Congress provided for permanent government regulation of banks and credit. More banks were admitted to the Federal Reserve System, and the Reserve Board's authority over them was increased. Commercial banks were forbidden to use depositors' money to speculate in stocks and bonds. The act also created the Federal Deposit Insurance Corporation (FDIC), which insured every deposit up to 5,000 dollars in member banks.[1] (Later this limit was raised to 10,000 dollars.) A spokesman for the American Bankers Association assailed the new law as "unsound,

unscientific, unjust, and dangerous." Nevertheless, most American people again put their trust in those banks that the government approved and was willing to insure.

The SEC regulates the sale of stocks and bonds. Vivid memories of the 1929 crash caused most people also to recognize the need for government regulation of the stock exchanges. Two measures — the Federal Securities Act (1933) and the Securities and Exchange Act (1934)— empowered Congress to regulate sales of stocks and bonds. All securities offered for public sale had to be registered with a newly created Securities and Exchange Commission (SEC), which issued licenses to the stock exchanges. The SEC also required that firms make public certain information about securities they offered for sale. Moreover, the Federal Reserve Board was given authority to determine what percentage of the purchase price of stock had to be paid in cash.

The powers of the Securities and Exchange Commission were broadened during the following years. In 1935 the commission was authorized to regulate the financial practices of public-utility holding companies. Such companies had to prove their usefulness or else be broken up into smaller, competing units. At the end of the decade the SEC was also given control over investment trusts (companies that handled investments for their clients).

The United States goes off the gold standard. Another problem demanding attention in the early months of the New Deal was the dismally low price level. The advice that poured into the White House was contradictory. Some economists argued that the gold standard (the government's pledge to redeem all paper money with gold) should be maintained. Others insisted that the President should reduce the gold value of the dollar, or issue greenbacks (currency unbacked by gold or silver), or coin unlimited amounts of silver. In May, 1933, Congress gave the President vast powers to regulate the country's currency. He was

[1] All banks belonging to the Federal Reserve System automatically became members of the FDIC. Others were eligible if they met requirements. Most banks soon became members.

authorized to use any of the following means to bring about a rise in prices: (1) reduce the dollar's value in gold by as much as 50 per cent; (2) provide for the unlimited coinage of silver at any ratio of silver to gold, or (3) issue up to three billion dollars in greenbacks. Armed with these broad powers — which exceeded the demands of the most ardent Populists! — President Roosevelt proceeded with caution.

The congressional act forbidding the hoarding or export of gold (page 688) meant in effect that the United States had abandoned the gold standard. In June, 1933, Congress also passed a resolution canceling all obligations, public or private, to pay existing debts in gold. This act was immediately challenged in the courts and was eventually appealed to the Supreme Court. The Court ruled that abandonment of the gold standard was constitutional. Neither the government nor private debtors had to pay their obligations in gold.

Meanwhile, Congress was urging the President to devalue the gold dollar and to issue silver coins. In January, 1934, the President fixed the value of the dollar at about 59 cents in terms of its former value in gold. In other words, 35 of the new dollars would be needed, instead of about 21 of the old, to buy one ounce of gold. A few months later Congress passed a Silver Purchase Act. This measure obliged the government to maintain a reserve of silver

PRINCIPAL GOVERNMENT ANTI-DEPRESSION MEASURES OF THE 1930'S

This chart summarizes the policies and programs put into operation to meet the economic emergencies which faced the nation. Some measures contributed to more than one aspect of the attack on the depression.

CHART STUDY

EMERGENCY	RESULTING GOVERNMENT MEASURE
Stock market collapse, 1929	Federal Securities Act, 1933 Securities and Exchange Act, 1934
Bank failures and failure of the banking system	Emergency Banking Act, 1933 Glass-Steagall Act, 1933
Heavy unemployment	Federal Emergency Relief Administration, 1933 Public Works Administration, 1933 National Industrial Recovery Act, 1933 (to raise labor standards) Declared unconstitutional, 1935 Civilian Conservation Corps, 1935 (to provide employment) Social Security Act, 1935 (to aid the unemployed and the aged) Works Progress Administration, 1935
Low price level	President given power to regulate currency, 1933 United States abandoned gold standard, 1934 Silver Purchase Act, 1934

Business stagnation	Reconstruction Finance Corporation, 1932 (provisions
	    extended under New Deal)
	National Industrial Recovery Act, 1933 (to stimulate industry)
	    Declared unconstitutional, 1935
	Trade Agreements Act, 1934

Decline in farm income	Agricultural Adjustment Act, 1933 (to reduce farm surpluses
	    and raise prices paid the farmer)
	    Declared unconstitutional, 1936
	Agricultural Adjustment Act, 1938 (to restore farm
	    purchasing power to parity)

Depletion of natural resources	Tennessee Valley Authority, 1933 Civilian Conservation Corps, 1935 (to promote program of conservation)

and gold to back paper currency. One fourth of the value of the reserve would come from silver bullion; the rest from gold.

Considering the strong demand for action, and the vast powers given to the President by Congress, Roosevelt's experiments with the currency were modest. He avoided the danger of run-away inflation that would have resulted from reckless issuing of greenbacks. Instead he used silver and gold to back the devalued paper dollar. This helped to maintain the stability of the dollar, even though a dollar bill could no longer be exchanged for gold. Although Roosevelt's monetary policy put more money into circulation, it had little effect on prices. These remained much lower than the President had hoped.

The New Deal provides relief for the unemployed. The most urgent problem facing the President after the banking crisis was the desperate situation of millions of unemployed Americans. The outcome of the 1932 election had endorsed the principle that the federal government should come to their aid. But Roosevelt's advisers disagreed on whether the aid should be provided through direct relief payments or through an expanded public-works program. Since the unemployment problem needed immediate action, the President urged Congress to adopt several different measures.

To assist the states in their relief programs, Congress established the Federal Emergency Relief Administration (FERA). It was authorized to grant (not lend) 500 million dollars for direct emergency relief to state and local programs. FERA was administered by Harry Hopkins, who had headed New York State's relief program. Though direct relief was necessary in the early months of the New Deal, Hopkins believed that work relief was preferable to direct payments. A job, he said, "preserves a man's morale. It saves his skill. It gives him a chance to do something socially useful." Hence FERA sponsored work relief projects whenever possible.

The Civilian Conservation Corps (CCC) combined work relief for young men with badly needed conservation projects. Unemployed men between the ages of 18 to 25 could join the CCC. Assigned to work camps, they planted trees and worked on projects for preventing floods, soil erosion, and forest fires. They also built roads and dams and worked in the national parks. The government provided members of the corps with food, clothing, and shelter, and paid them 30 dollars a month, most of which was sent to their families. The CCC continued until 1941. By that time nearly three million young men had participated in this highly successful program.

The government finances public-works projects. In still another relief program of the "Hundred Days," Congress appropriated more than three billion dollars for public works. The program was intended not only to provide jobs but also to promote industrial recovery by stimulating the sale of building materials such as steel, cement, brick, lumber, and machinery. To put this program into operation, a Public Works Administration (PWA) was established, with Secretary of the Interior Ickes at its head. "Honest Harold" exercised such close supervision over PWA projects that it sometimes took many months to get the plans and contracts approved. But in time the PWA built schools, civic auditoriums, dams, bridges, roads, hospitals, sewage and water systems, and military airports, as well as two aircraft carriers.

The New Deal tries to help the farmers. The desperate situation of the nation's farmers was not overlooked during the New Deal's "Hundred Days." The President's advisers, Secretary of Agriculture Wallace, and spokesmen for farm organizations all agreed that agricultural surpluses were responsible for low farm prices. During the campaign there had been talk of a *voluntary allotment plan*, under which farmers would agree to limit their output of certain crops in order to cut down surpluses. In May, 1933, this plan was enacted into law as part of the Agricultural Adjustment Act. This act established the Agricultural Adjustment Administration (AAA), which was to secure promises from farmers to reduce the production of such staple crops as wheat, corn, rice, and tobacco. In return, the farmers would receive cash payments from the government. The program would be financed by a tax on such processors of farm products as meat packers, millers, and cotton ginners. The processing taxes would be passed on to consumers in higher prices. Secretary Wallace argued that "the slight contribution the consumer will make through retail prices will be more than compensated for by the revived power of farmers to buy the goods and services the city has to sell."

Many farmers had already done their spring planting by the time the act was passed. To participate in the AAA program, therefore, some of them had to plow up fields of cotton and wheat and slaughter young pigs to prevent a surplus of pork. This deliberate destruction of food at a time when thousands were hungry caused loud protests, though the government distributed the meat to relief programs. The dust storms which swept the Middle West during the 1930's helped cut production on many farms. This natural disaster plus the government controls resulted in higher farm prices. Between 1932 and 1936, yearly net farm income rose from less than two billion dollars to more than five billion dollars.

Congress passes the National Industrial Recovery Act. Like the farm program, the New Deal's plan for industrial recovery provided for government regulation of production. The situation in 1933 was so critical that even big business welcomed efforts by the government to start the wheels rolling again. Industrialists hoped that President Roosevelt would approve the trade associations formed in the 1920's (page 654) and allow them to establish fixed prices. Roosevelt agreed at this time that recovery was more likely to result from co-operation than from efforts to revive competition. But his price for approving a trade-association program was a promise from businessmen that they would grant concessions to their employees. These basic agreements were written into the National Industrial Recovery Act, passed by Congress in June, 1933.

Businessmen were called to Washington to draw up codes that would regulate each industry. They could set prices and production quotas for an entire industry, and the

Poverty-stricken by depression and by catastrophes of nature, many farmers of the Midwest migrated to the Pacific coast in the 1930's.

government promised not to prosecute them under the antitrust laws. But the National Recovery Administration (NRA) approved the codes only if they contained the following provisions for employees: (1) elimination of child labor; (2) a minimum wage of 30 to 40 cents an hour; (3) maximum working hours of 35 to 40 per week; and (4) the right of workers to form a union and bargain collectively with the employer.

The NRA was launched with high hopes and much publicity. Labor leaders compared the act to Lincoln's Emancipation Proclamation, and the President called it "the most important and far-reaching legislation ever enacted by the American Congress." Nearly 800 codes were approved, and manufacturers and retailers proudly displayed the NRA's Blue Eagle emblem bearing the legend "We Do Our Part."

The NRA loses favor. The initial enthusiasm, however, soon gave way to bickering and dissension. Small businessmen charged that they were being pushed to the wall by the larger companies. Labor leaders were aroused because some employers violated the provisions of the act. When small businessmen and labor leaders took their

The New Deal encompassed a variety of programs. The "Blue Eagle" (top left) symbolized the NRA experiment. President Roosevelt's interest in conservation led to the building of dams like Grand Coulee (above left) on the Columbia River in Washington. WPA activities, ranging from construction of the Hollywood Bowl (top right) to sewing projects (above right), created jobs for many workers.

complaints to the NRA, which was supposed to enforce the codes, they got little satisfaction. Soon they were calling the agency the "National Run Around." Big businessmen, encouraged by signs of economic recovery during 1934 and 1935, wanted to drop the codes and put an end to government regulation. Then, in 1935, the Supreme Court declared the National Industrial Recovery Act unconstitutional (page 697). By that time, however, the New Deal was ready to try other ways of protecting the rights of labor and of regulating business.

The Trade Agreements Act stimulates foreign trade. Another New Deal reform that concerned businessmen was a new tariff act. In his campaign, Roosevelt had suggested the revival of foreign trade as one way of lifting the country out of the depression. But he knew that a sharp cut in tariff rates would be difficult to get through Congress; and, if enacted, it could work hardship on manufacturers already in economic trouble. Thus, he and Secretary of State Cordell Hull urged the adoption of reciprocity treaties. The principle of reciprocity had first been introduced into tariff legislation in 1890 (page 506). Congress passed the Trade Agreements Act in 1934. It authorized the President to negotiate reciprocal trade agreements without submitting such "treaties" to the Senate for approval. By 1940 the United States had reciprocal trade agreements with 26 countries and was exporting twice as much to "treaty" nations as to all others.

Congress establishes the Tennessee Valley Authority. The New Deal project most persistently criticized by businesmen was the Tennessee Valley Authority (TVA), established by Congress in May, 1933. This program was an outgrowth of the Muscle Shoals project (page 678), which the Democrats had promised to expand. During the "Hundred Days," however, President Roosevelt suggested a more sweeping program to Congress. He proposed that the government undertake the development of the entire Tennessee River Valley, an area which had been plagued for years by floods and erosion. On the President's recommendation, Congress established the Tennessee Valley Authority. This agency was authorized not only to develop and operate power plants but also to restore forests, halt erosion, and build dams for flood control and improvement of navigation. Further, it was to advance the "economic and social well-being of the people" living in the Tennessee Valley.

TVA was given all the powers of a private corporation, together with the right of eminent domain.[2] It started a broad pro-

[2] This is the power to take private property for public use, provided that owners receive reasonable compensation.

gram to help the people living in an area of some 40,000 square miles in seven states (map, page 696). TVA improved five existing dams, built a number of new ones, constructed power plants, and sold electricity at low rates as a "yardstick" for private utility companies in the area. It also taught farmers how to check soil erosion, encouraged co-operatives and small industries, promoted public health, built low-cost housing, and provided recreation facilities.

Critics assail TVA. Businessmen protested TVA's direct competition with private power companies. One of the most outspoken opponents of TVA was Wendell L. Willkie, president of a private utility company in the Tennessee Valley. TVA's low charges for electricity could be explained, businessmen said, by the fact that part of its operating expenses were charged to flood control and improvement of navigation. TVA officials denied the charge, declaring that private power companies would still be able to make money even if they lowered rates. In fact, the TVA "yardstick" had the effect of lowering electric rates almost everywhere in the country. As a result, the use of electricity sharply increased. Two lawsuits against TVA were appealed to the Supreme Court, but in both cases the Court upheld its constitutionality.

The New Deal proposes other conservation measures. TVA was the New Deal's

An Oklahoma farmer and his sons struggle against the wind and flying dust in this photograph of the 1930's. Drought and wind made much of the Great Plains a "dust bowl" during the depression years.

Paducah · *Ohio R.* · KY. · Tennessee watershed boundary · VA.

Mississippi R. · TENN. · ★ Nashville · Oak Ridge · N.C. · Knoxville · Asheville

Memphis · *Tennessee R.* · Chattanooga

MISS. · *Muscle Shoals* · G A. · Major dam ▮

ALA. · Area serviced by TVA electrical power

TENNESSEE RIVER PROFILE

Chickamauga · Watts Bar · Fort Loudoun
Guntersville · Hales Bar
Wheeler
Wilson
Kentucky · Pickwick
815 ft.
←*Ohio R.*
Miles →
up stream 23 · 207 259 275 · 349 · 431 471 · 530 602
R. M. Chapin, Jr.

THE TENNESSEE VALLEY AUTHORITY

The development of TVA brought significant changes to a region long plagued by floods and unemployment. The taming of the Tennessee River has resulted in improved navigation and flood control and has provided cheap electric power for an area reaching into several states. Note that the "profile" identifies the Tennessee River dams shown on the map.

most spectacular conservation program, but many others were also undertaken. Franklin D. Roosevelt, like Theodore Roosevelt, had a deep interest in conservation. In 1934 he appointed a National Resources Board, with Harold Ickes as chairman, to prepare an inventory of the nation's resources. In its report, this board warned that two thirds of the country's land had been damaged by erosion and that some 35 million acres of farm land had been "essentially destroyed." Forests that were still privately owned were inadequately protected against fire. The report also pointed out that erosion and forest loss destroyed natural safeguards against floods and droughts.

Even before the board began its study, many Americans had become painfully familiar with the problem of drought. Throughout the 1930's dust storms swept through the Great Plains. People spoke of this part of the country as the "dust bowl." The situation was so serious in Oklahoma and Arkansas that thousands of families abandoned their farms and migrated to other states.

New Deal legislation included a number of conservation programs. As we have seen,

the CCC boys worked on conservation projects. The NRA lumber codes sought to protect timber resources. Many of the public-works projects — dams, flood-control programs, parks, and wild-life refuges — were vital parts of the conservation program. In addition, Ickes proposed planting clusters of trees in a strip one hundred miles wide and more than a thousand miles long, from Canada to Mexico, through the middle of the "dust bowl." By 1942, over 100 million trees had been planted in the Great Plains. As the trees grew, they helped break the dust storms and preserve the moisture in midwestern farmland. The government also helped to relocate farm families whose land had become hopelessly arid, and it taught farmers how to prevent erosion of their fields.

▶ CHECK-UP

1. What steps were taken to insure the security of bank deposits? To regulate holding companies and the sale of stocks and bonds? Why was the gold content of the dollar reduced? Why did the government establish a reserve of gold and silver to back paper currency?

2. What steps were taken to help the unemployed? The farmers? Industry? Labor? How effective were these in each case? How was foreign trade stimulated?

3. What were the goals of TVA? On what grounds was it criticized? What did TVA achieve? In what other ways did the New Deal further conservation?

. . . .

3 *The New Deal Consolidates Its Gains*

The New Deal measures described so far are often called the "first New Deal." They were overwhelmingly endorsed by the voters in 1934 and again in 1936. Because of certain adverse Supreme Court decisions, however, New Dealers enacted additional laws to protect the rights of wage earners and to raise farm income. To these fundamental reforms, Congress added a broad program of unemployment compensation and retirement pensions. The next sections of this chapter deal with this important legislation — often called the "second New Deal."

The Democrats make gains in the 1934 elections. As Congress enacted the New Deal measures into law, voices were raised in opposition. Some bankers, stockbrokers, and manufacturers protested against the restrictions of the SEC and NRA. Some farmers opposed the compulsory quotas enforced by the AAA, while spokesmen for utility companies objected to the TVA "yardstick." These critics generally shared former President Hoover's fear that the New Deal was undermining American initiative, individualism, and liberty. Opponents of the New Deal also charged that the expanding powers of the federal government threatened to destroy the rights of the states and the tradition of local government. Nevertheless, in the congressional elections of 1934, the Democrats increased their large majorities in both houses of Congress. Only once before in the twentieth century had the party in power done so in the off-year elections.[3]

The Supreme Court rejects the NRA. Although the voters endorsed the New Deal in the 1934 elections, the administration suffered a defeat early the next year when the Supreme Court ruled the NRA codes unconstitutional. Roosevelt's advisers had argued that the NRA was a proper use of the congressional power to regulate interstate commerce. In a test case, however, the Supreme Court ruled unanimously that Congress had unconstitutionally delegated power to the President to draft the codes. Roosevelt charged that the conservative judges were still living in the "horse-and-buggy" era, but privately he admitted that administration of the codes was becoming "an awful headache."

The Wagner Act is passed. After the NRA was declared unconstitutional, Congress rescued some of that program's labor reforms by passing a new law. In July, 1935, the President signed the National Labor Relations Act, commonly called the Wagner Act. It gave organized labor the same right to bargain collectively that had been guaranteed by the NRA. In addition, it placed restrictions on employers who tried to force employees into company unions or who sought to prevent them from joining labor unions. The act was to be enforced by a National Labor Relations Board (NLRB).

Organized labor makes great gains under the NLRB. The protection given to organized labor by the NRA had brought about some increase in union membership. The American Federation of Labor claimed a million new members between 1933 and 1935. But after the passage of the Wagner Act, organized labor made even greater gains. The NLRB was empowered to hold elections in plants to determine which union would represent workers in collective bargaining. If workers were penalized by their employers for union activity, they could appeal to the Board and the Board could

[3] That was in 1902 under Theodore Roosevelt.

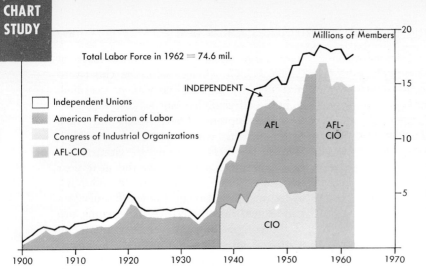

Total Labor Force in 1962 = 74.6 mil.

Millions of Members

INDEPENDENT

☐ Independent Unions
▧ American Federation of Labor
▨ Congress of Industrial Organizations
▨ AFL-CIO

AFL

AFL-CIO

CIO

1900   1910   1920   1930   1940   1950   1960   1970

**GROWTH OF ORGANIZED
LABOR**

*Notice the tremendous in-
crease in union membership
since 1933. Nevertheless,
under a fourth of the na-
tion's workers were orga-
nized in 1962.*

take the employers into court. Thus, the
Wagner Act gave new incentive to union
organizers.

The CIO is formed. At the same time,
however, the Wagner Act encouraged dissension within the ranks of the AFL. For
many years some labor leaders, including
John L. Lewis of the United Mine Workers,
had wanted to organize employees in the
mass-production industries. They felt that
industrial unions, embracing all workers in
a particular industry, would be much
stronger than the AFL's craft unions. After
a clash between labor leaders at the 1935
AFL convention, Lewis and his followers
formed the Committee for Industrial Organization (CIO). They began organizing
workers in the automotive, steel, rubber,
textile, electrical, and radio industries, and
soon claimed nearly as many members as
the AFL. Those industrial unions which
joined the CIO were expelled from the
AFL. In 1938, the CIO adopted its own
constitution and changed its name to the
Congress of Industrial Organizations. John
L. Lewis became the first CIO president.

During its drive to organize industrial
workers, the CIO made use of a new
weapon — the *sit-down strike.* Instead of
leaving a plant and setting up picket lines,
striking workers stayed at their posts and
refused to leave. Thus they prevented employers from using strikebreakers to continue production. General Motors and the
Chrysler Corporation gave in to sit-down
strikers and recognized CIO unions in their

plants. In 1937 the giant United States Steel
Corporation surprised everyone by recognizing the CIO steelworkers' union without
a strike. The smaller Republic Steel Corporation resisted the union organizers, however, and violence flared up in Chicago,
Youngstown (Ohio), and Cleveland. Not
until 1941 did the CIO gain recognition
from the "Little Steel" companies. By that
time the AFL and CIO each had more than
four million members.

Work relief programs are continued.
Persistent unemployment throughout the
1930's kept the government in the business
of work relief. The early direct-relief programs had already given way to work
relief under the PWA (page 692). In
1935 a new agency, the Works Progress
Administration (WPA), was established
with Harry Hopkins at its head. This agency
administered all relief work projects except
for the CCC and PWA, which were continued separately. By 1943 the WPA had
completed more than 250,000 public-works
projects and had given work to more than
eight million people.

Relief programs are criticized. Critics
of the relief programs pointed out that in
spite of the spending of billions of dollars,
unemployment never fell below 14 per cent
of the labor force during the 1930's. They
accused reliefers of loafing on the job. They
also charged that the WPA and PWA were
aimed at securing votes for the Democrats.
New Deal supporters replied that government spending helped revive the economy

by stimulating the sale of building supplies and by putting money into the hands of workers who could then buy consumer goods. Moreover, the public-works projects benefited communities. Almost every town and city in the nation acquired at least one school, park, road, bridge, hospital, library, or auditorium. Most important, they argued, the New Deal relief programs gave meaningful jobs to men who would otherwise have been idle, discouraged, and destitute.

The Social Security Act is passed. One of the most far-reaching New Deal reforms was the adoption of a federal program to free people from the insecurity of old age and the hazards of unemployment. This idea had first been suggested during the progressive era. By the 1930's a number of states had adopted programs providing for old-age pensions and unemployment compensation financed by employers, employees, and the state governments. The depression revived demands for a federal program of the same kind. Roosevelt's ad-

visers drafted such a measure, and in August, 1935, Congress passed the Social Security Act by a large margin.

There were three parts to this important measure:

(1) *Old-age insurance.* The law set up a compulsory old-age insurance system with benefits for workers who retired at 65 and who had participated in the plan. The old-age insurance plan was to be administered by the federal government and financed by a compulsory pay-roll tax on both employers and employees.

(2) *Unemployment insurance.* The federal government set minimum standards for an unemployment insurance program, but the exact terms of the program and its administration were left to the states. Funds were raised by a compulsory pay-roll tax on employers. Benefits to unemployed workers ranged from five to fifteen dollars a week and lasted in most states for no longer than fifteen weeks.

(3) *Aid to dependent people.* The federal government agreed to match funds

© *Karsh, Ottawa*

Two former coal miners led the AFL and the CIO in the 1930's. William Green (above) had succeeded Samuel Gompers as president of the AFL in 1924. John L. Lewis (top left), a leader in the CIO's withdrawal from the AFL, served as the new union's first president. In 1952, George Meany (left) succeeded Green as the AFL's top officer and three years later became president of the AFL-CIO when the two organizations merged (page 793).

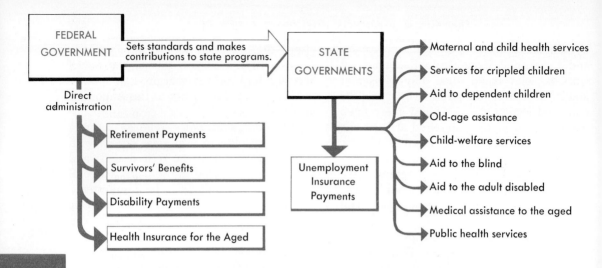

FEDERAL GOVERNMENT

Sets standards and makes contributions to state programs.

STATE GOVERNMENTS

Direct administration

Retirement Payments

Survivors' Benefits

Disability Payments

Health Insurance for the Aged

Unemployment Insurance Payments

Maternal and child health services

Services for crippled children

Aid to dependent children

Old-age assistance

Child-welfare services

Aid to the blind

Aid to the adult disabled

Medical assistance to the aged

Public health services

CHART STUDY

HOW THE SOCIAL SECURITY SYSTEM WORKS

This chart shows how Social Security is administered. Note the relationship between the federal program and the programs of the individual states.

raised by the states for aid to several categories of dependent people. Destitute men and women over 65 could draw old-age pensions (they were too old to participate in the old-age insurance program). Aid was given to the blind and the crippled, and pensions were paid to dependent mothers with small children.

By 1940, 50 million workers were participating in Social Security, and both major parties had accepted Social Security as a permanent reform. As originally enacted, the program did not cover certain categories of workers — such as employees of nonprofit institutions, government workers, merchant seamen, itinerant laborers, domestic workers, self-employed professional people, and farmers. But later laws extended coverage to some of these people and also increased the size of benefits.

The New Deal is attacked for doing too little. Most critics of the New Deal attacked it for introducing too many changes. But other critics of President Roosevelt tried to build up a following by saying that the New Deal had not accomplished enough. One of these was Dr. Francis E. Townsend, an elderly physician in California, who urged the government to pay a 200-dollar monthly pension to every person over 60 years old. Townsend Clubs sprang up in every part of the United States. Another

was Father Charles E. Coughlin, a priest whose weekly radio broadcasts reached a large audience. He assailed President Roosevelt for failing to nationalize banks, public utilities, and natural resources.

Huey P. Long of Louisiana was the most persuasive of those who offered radical solutions to end the depression. First as governor and then as senator, Long had built up a powerful political machine in his home state. He then gained a national following by proposing that the wealthy be heavily taxed and that every family be guaranteed a 2500-dollar annual income. The "Kingfish," as he was called, addressed thousands of audiences who supported his "Share the Wealth" program. Huey Long was eyeing the presidency for 1936, and some New Dealers thought he could win between three and four million votes. Motivated in part by the desire to cut down the size of Long's following, the New Dealers proposed higher taxes on large incomes. The Revenue Act of 1935 placed a 75 per cent tax on incomes above five million dollars and levied new taxes on corporations. Before the presidential campaign began, Huey Long was assassinated.

Several candidates enter the 1936 campaign. In 1936, Townsend, Coughlin, and some of Huey Long's followers combined forces to organize the Union Party.

They offered as a presidential candidate William Lemke, a Republican congressman from North Dakota. Other candidates of minor parties in 1936 were Norman Thomas, nominated by the Socialists, and Earl Browder, the Communist candidate.

The Republican Party nominated Governor Alfred M. Landon of Kansas for the presidency. He was one of the few Republican governors elected in 1932 and 1934, and he had the additional recommendation of having balanced his state's budget. Frank Knox, a Chicago newspaper publisher, was nominated for the vice-presidency. The Republican platform proclaimed: "America is in peril." It criticized the Democrats for increasing the national debt, invading the rights of the states, harassing businessmen and farmers with government regulations, and destroying the morale of people on relief. The Republicans invited "all Americans, irrespective of party, to join us in defense of American institutions."

The Democratic convention renominated Roosevelt and Garner without a formal ballot, and the platform naturally lavished praise on the New Deal. Roosevelt, addressing the cheering delegates, had this reply for his Republican critics: "These economic royalists complain that we seek to overthrow the institutions of America. What they really complain of is that we seek to overthrow their power."

The Democrats sweep the country. During the campaign "Alf" Landon repeated the Republican charges against the New Deal. President Roosevelt — smiling, confident, and determined — toured the country in October. He reminded the people that since 1932, unemployment had fallen from twelve million to nine million while national income had risen from 42 billion dollars to 65 billion dollars. Most of the country's newspapers opposed the President's re-election. They had little influence, however, on the millions of Americans who listened to Roosevelt's "fireside chats" on their radios and who had benefited from New Deal measures.

The outcome of the election was a landslide for Roosevelt. He won almost 28 million popular votes to Landon's 16 and a half million. The Democrats carried every state in the Union except Maine and Vermont and also kept their large majorities in both houses of Congress. Votes won by the Socialist, Communist, and Union candidates totaled only a little over a million.

▶ CHECK-UP

1. Why did the New Deal sponsor the Wagner Act? How did it help organized labor? Why was the CIO formed?

2. What programs were provided in the Social Security Act?

3. What was the WPA? What criticisms were made of New Deal relief programs? What individuals accused the New Deal of doing too little?

4. What candidates sought the presidency in 1936? What was the outcome?

. . . .

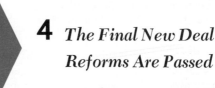

4 *The Final New Deal Reforms Are Passed*

The President seeks to "pack" the Supreme Court. Roosevelt's sweeping victory in 1936 was followed by an unexpected setback — the defeat of his plan to enlarge the Supreme Court. Not only had the Supreme Court found the NRA unconstitutional (page 697), but in nine cases involving New Deal measures, the administration's legislation had been upheld only twice. Doubtless Roosevelt's overwhelming victory in the 1936 election encouraged him to propose a plan that would ensure more favorable decisions from the Court. The President wished to appoint (up to a total of fifteen) a new Supreme Court justice for each one who did not retire on reaching the age of 70. At the time, six of the nine Supreme Court justices were 70 or older. Therefore, the President's plan would have permitted him to appoint six justices; and this would have been enough to counter-

THAT COMPASS DOESN'T POINT THE WAY I WANT TO GO. CHANGE IT. NOW!

Roosevelt's court-packing plan alarmed many people, even some who had been New Deal supporters. One cartoonist compared Roosevelt to an admiral trying to change a basic law of nature.

balance those justices who were anti-New Deal. The President's proposal, made early in 1937, came as a surprise to Congress and the American people.

The "court-packing" plan, as it was soon called, started a heated discussion. New Deal supporters argued that it was necessary to reform the Supreme Court to make it more responsive to the wishes of Congress. They also pointed out that Congress had the unquestioned constitutional authority to determine the number of justices on the Supreme Court. But Roosevelt's critics insisted that his real intention was to limit the powers of the Court. Charging that the President was trying to "pack" the Supreme Court with New Dealers, they opposed any change that would upset the balance of power among the three branches of the government.

"A switch in time saves nine." While the debate was still raging, the Supreme Court handed down several decisions favorable to the New Deal. In opinions handed down during the spring of 1937, the Su-

preme Court upheld both the Wagner Act and the Social Security Act. The Court's approval of these important New Deal programs gave rise to the quip — "a switch in time saves nine." After weeks of bitter debate, the Senate finally voted against the "court-packing" proposal.

New Dealers were soon saying, however, that the President had lost a battle but won the war against the Supreme Court. One justice retired in 1937, and Roosevelt appointed a liberal senator from Alabama, Hugo L. Black. Six more retirements in the next four years gave Roosevelt the opportunity to change substantially the membership of the country's highest court. After 1937 the Supreme Court took a more liberal attitude toward New Deal legislation.

The Court issue loses support for the New Deal. The Court fight resulted in a political setback for the Democrats. It seemed to confirm the warnings of the Republicans that Roosevelt was taking constitutional shortcuts and undermining American democracy. Many persons who had voted for Roosevelt in 1936 were disturbed by his attempt to change the Supreme Court. Some progressives, including Senator Burton K. Wheeler of Montana, parted company with the President over the Court issue. Increasing opposition also came from many Southerners, who feared that a New Deal Court would declare racial segregation unconstitutional. After 1937, southern conservatives voted more and more with the Republicans. It was this coalition of Republicans and southern Democrats that finally brought an end to New Deal reform legislation.

A recession in 1937 leads to further controversy. An economic recession[4] in 1937 gave Roosevelt's opponents additional ammunition. From 1933 until mid-1937 there had been a slow but steady rise in prices, an increase in national income, and a decline in unemployment. But this trend was reversed in the summer of 1937. Prices of agricultural products fell, and unemployment jumped to ten million in 1938.

[4] A *recession* is an economic decline less severe than a depression.

Supporters of the New Deal said that the recession had been caused by large farm surpluses and by the reduction in government spending on relief programs. They called for larger appropriations for the WPA, liberal RFC loans, and new farm legislation. Roosevelt's supporters also wanted his administration to take a tougher attitude toward business and to pass new laws protecting the rights of wage earners.

Critics of the New Deal replied that the "Roosevelt recession" had resulted from unwise taxes levied on business and from excessive federal spending. They rejected the view that government spending was necessary for "pump-priming" purposes, that is, to stimulate industry and to increase consumer spending. These critics stressed the fact that the President had not only failed to keep his promise to balance the budget but had also permitted the national debt nearly to double in size. Many Republicans and conservative Democrats sincerely believed that the recession could be brought to an end and financial stability restored only if the federal budget were balanced. Nevertheless, New Deal opponents in Congress were not strong enough to block the passage in 1938 of two major New Deal laws — the second AAA and the Wages and Hours Law.

New farm legislation is passed. Early in 1936, before the "court-packing" controversy, the Supreme Court had ruled that the Agricultural Adjustment Act (page 692) was unconstitutional. According to the Court, the AAA interfered with states' rights by putting limits on production, and the processing tax was an improper use of Congress' power to levy taxes. Early in 1938 Congress again tackled the problem of farm surpluses and passed a second Agricultural Adjustment Act. This second AAA made *marketing* of basic crops, rather than production, the point of control. Its chief provisions were these:

(1) The Secretary of Agriculture would decide how much cotton, corn, wheat, tobacco, and rice could be marketed in any year. If two thirds of the producers of these five staple crops voted to accept marketing quotas, the AAA would assign each pro-

ducer a certain acreage allotment. Farmers who exceeded their allotments had to pay a tax on their excess sales.

(2) Farmers who agreed to limit their crops would receive benefit payments from the government. These were called *parity payments* because they were intended to restore farm purchasing power to parity (equality) with the purchasing power of the years before World War I.

(3) Farmers could also receive *commodity loans* on surpluses. The surpluses were to be stored and marketed when prices were higher, at which time the farmers would have to repay the loans.

(4) Farmers who planted soil-building crops and improved the fertility of their lands would receive benefit payments. Those farmers who refused to co-operate with the AAA program were to be denied parity and conservation payments and commodity loans.

The farm situation improves. In 1939 the Supreme Court upheld the provisions of the second Agricultural Adjustment Act. The measure seemed to have some effect in reducing surpluses and raising farm prices. But critics of the act pointed out that most of the payments and financial benefits went to large farmers, not to small operators or tenant farmers. Then, following the outbreak of World War II in 1939, foreign demand for American farm products increased. After the United States entered the war in 1941, this country and its allies consumed the total production of American farms. Thus the troublesome problem of farm surpluses was solved, not by the AAA but by the advent of war. In the postwar years the familiar problems of farm surpluses returned to plague the nation's farmers and the government.

Congress regulates wages and hours. The second major act of 1938 benefited labor. The Supreme Court ruling against the NRA had meant an end to the minimum-wage and maximum-hour provisions of the codes. As a result, there were demands for new federal legislation to regulate wages, hours, and child labor. Not until 1938, however, did President Roosevelt give his support to such a bill. Congress then passed the Fair Labor Standards Act (or Wages and Hours Law) over the strong opposition of Republicans and southern Democrats. This law applied to companies engaged in interstate commerce. It provided that the hours of industrial workers had to be limited to 44 per week, and this was to be lowered to 40 per week within three years. The minimum wage of these employees was set at 25 cents an hour in 1938, and had to be increased to 40 cents an hour within eight years. The act also required workers to be at least sixteen years old and restricted the employment of people under eighteen to non-hazardous occupations.

A unanimous decision of the Supreme Court in 1941 upheld every provision of the Wages and Hours Law. Thus, the long fight for a federal law to ban child labor and to put a "ceiling" on hours and a "floor" under wages finally succeeded. The law did not apply to certain categories of workers, including farm laborers, domestic workers, clerks in stores, and seamen. But since 1938, this basic measure has been amended many times to cover more workers and to raise the minimum wage. Like Social Security, the Fair Labor Standards Act has become a permanent part of American domestic policy.

New Deal legislation strengthened the government's authority to regulate drug manufacture. Here, a government scientist examines a counterfeit tablet to determine its content and origin.

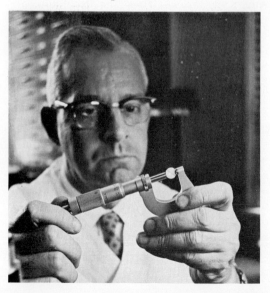

Additional New Deal measures are passed. Among the many other problems dealt with by the New Deal was housing. Government agencies made loans to homeowners to prevent foreclosures on mortgages. Moreover, the Federal Housing Administration (FHA) loaned money to middle-income families for repairs and improvements or for the construction of new houses. Congress also created the United States Housing Authority to help state and local agencies clear slums and provide new housing facilities. By 1941 homes for more than 200,000 families had been built.

In 1938 Congress also strengthened the Pure Food and Drugs Act of 1906 (page 560). In the Food, Drug, and Cosmetics Act the government imposed stricter regulation and higher standards in the manufacture of food, drugs, and cosmetics. Moreover, the act provided heavy penalties for the misbranding of products and for false or misleading advertising claims.

Finally, in 1938 the administration adopted a tougher attitude toward the trusts. The government launched a trust-busting program which recalled Theodore Roosevelt's attack on big business. The New Deal's drive was especially aimed at the practice of setting prices by agreement with competitors. By 1941 a number of companies had agreed to abandon price-fixing agreements.

The conservative coalition brings the New Deal to a close. As the congressional elections of 1938 approached, the lines were clearly drawn between the liberal, New Deal Democrats and the conservative Democrats who were allied with the Republicans. The New Deal Democrats wanted to (1) increase the regulatory powers of the federal government; (2) continue government spending; (3) aid the underprivileged; and (4) pursue the drive against the trusts. The conservatives wanted to (1) check the power of the federal government and preserve states' rights; (2) reduce federal spending; (3) abandon expensive relief programs; (4) curb the strength of organized labor; and (5) halt the antitrust drive.

Roosevelt knew that he would need more liberal Democrats in Congress if he wanted to continue the New Deal. Thus, he asked the voters in 1938 to support liberal rather than conservative candidates. But his efforts were unsuccessful. Conservative Democratic and Republican candidates attracted more votes than New Deal Democrats, and the Republicans won additional seats in both the House and Senate. Although the Democrats kept their majorities in both houses of Congress, the conservative coalition could outvote the New Dealers after this election. The President admitted as much when he told the new Congress in January, 1939, that henceforth his objective would be "to preserve our reforms."

Congress approves administrative changes. The new Congress did pass legislation providing for some changes in government administration. Ever since the days of Theodore Roosevelt, there had been talk of overhauling the federal administrative service. The creation of the New Deal's "alphabet agencies" had intensified the problem of overlapping authority and duplication of effort. Although a presidential fact-finding committee recommended far-reaching changes, Congress merely authorized the President to regroup or abolish certain government agencies.

Opponents of the New Deal proposed an administrative reform of their own. They had long suspected that people on relief were pressured to vote Democratic. So in 1939 and 1940 Congress passed two measures to "prevent pernicious political activities." These laws (the Hatch Acts) made it illegal for anyone to pressure voters who happened to be on the relief rolls. They also forbade federal administrative officials from taking part in federal elections or contributing to candidates running in those elections.

How do historians evaluate the New Deal? During the turbulent decade of the 1930's charges and countercharges were hurled by ardent New Dealers and angry conservatives. Former President Hoover thought that the New Deal amounted to "national regimentation . . . its very spirit is government direction, management, and dictation of social and economic life."

Today few historians would say the

"*It's All Part of a Great Big Plan*" was the title of this cartoon making fun of the professors in Roosevelt's brain trust.

New Deal destroyed American liberties. In fact, one historian has stated that "the shortcomings of the New Deal vanish in the general perspective of its . . . restoration of democracy as a workable way of life." It cannot be denied, however, that Franklin Roosevelt increased the authority of the federal government at the expense of the states. Roosevelt's critics point out that his massive aid programs increased the national debt during his first two terms from 19 billion dollars to 43 billion dollars without really solving unemployment or farm surpluses. They also claim that he upset the balance of power between employer and employee by regulating business at the same time that he extended government protection to organized labor.

On the other hand, most historians believe that the New Deal — or something equally daring and experimental — was necessary to save American democracy in the depression years. While not all of Roosevelt's programs were wise or workable, most of them have had lasting significance. Few Americans today would abandon the Social Security system, minimum-wage and maximum-hour laws, or

Eleanor Roosevelt, shown here with Mary McLeod Bethune, became an important national figure in her own right. Among her many interests was the securing of equal rights and opportunities for minority groups. Mrs. Bethune founded Bethune-Cookman College in Florida and served as its president for many years.

government regulation of banks and stock exchanges. In fact, the Republican Party platform endorsed all of these measures as early as 1940. This bipartisan support of the major New Deal reforms remained unchallenged for many years.

Minority groups make gains in the 1930's. One hundred years from now historians may well say that one of the significant achievements of the New Deal was the opening up of opportunities for minority groups within American society. Even during the progressive era the government had paid little attention to the problems of Negroes, for example. Unfortunately discrimination was present in New Deal relief programs when these were administered by state agencies or individuals prejudiced against the Negro. Despite this limitation, such New Deal measures as the Farm Security Administration, the various housing authorities, and the CCC provided opportunities for Negroes that had not existed earlier.

Moreover, members of minority groups were appointed to major government posts. Robert C. Weaver and William H. Hastie, both Negroes, held responsible positions in the Interior Department, and Mary McLeod Bethune, a Negro educator, served as an official in the National Youth Adminis-

tration.[5] President Roosevelt also appointed a larger number of Jews and Catholics to federal judgeships than had any previous President. Leaders of organized labor had a voice in formulating government policies, and Roosevelt was the first President to appoint a woman to the Cabinet. In the long run, this movement toward a more democratic society will stand out as one of the major contributions of the New Deal.

▶ CHECK-UP

1. Why did Roosevelt try to "pack" the Supreme Court? Why did his suggestion lead to controversy? What was the outcome?

2. What views were expressed about causes of the 1937 recession? What new farm legislation was passed? What was the result? What legislation was enacted to regulate wages and hours? To improve housing? To strengthen the Pure Food and Drug Act?

3. How did New Deal Democrats and the conservatives differ on goals? What happened to the reform program after 1938? Why?

4. How do historians evaluate the New Deal? What gains were made by minority groups under the New Deal?

. . . .

[5] The NYA was a work-relief program for persons between the ages of 16 and 25.

5 *American Culture Flourishes During the New Deal Years*

The New Deal encourages the arts. In the 1930's, for the first time in American history, the federal government undertook the responsibility of aiding the creative arts. Roosevelt believed that artists, musicians, actors, and writers were entitled to government aid during the depression, just as much as farmers and other workers were. Several WPA projects were designed to encourage the fine arts. The Federal Arts Project subsidized painters and sculptors who produced works of art for post offices, other public buildings, and parks. WPA orchestras gave free school concerts as well as public performances. WPA funds also supported theatrical groups, which staged dramatic performances in parts of the country that otherwise could not have seen live theater. The Federal Writers Project employed teachers and writers to collect documents, write local histories, and prepare guidebooks and surveys.

Writers explore American problems. Many readers found escape from the realities of the depression in Margaret Mitchell's *Gone With the Wind*. A romantic story of southern life during the Civil War and after, this was one of the best-selling novels of the 1930's. But the depression awakened in many fiction writers a new sense of social responsibility. In their novels they sought to describe the sufferings of underprivileged people and thus stir the consciences of those who were better off. In the 1930's John Dos Passos completed his trilogy *U.S.A.* (a novel in three parts). In it he portrays the unhappiness and frustrations of rich and poor, immigrants and native-born, the educated and the illiterate. The tragedy of the "Okies" who trekked westward from the dust bowl to California was captured by John Steinbeck in *The Grapes of Wrath*.

Of the writers of the 1920's whom we read about in Chapter 31, Ernest Hemingway was probably the most creative in the following decade. One of his best novels, published in 1940, was *For Whom the Bell Tolls*. This study of life and death in the Spanish Civil War (page 719) helped make Americans conscious of the struggle going on in Europe.

A young writer from North Carolina, Thomas Wolfe, displayed his literary talents in four autobiographical novels. In the first of these, *Look Homeward, Angel*, he described his boyhood. Wolfe's great promise

A "New Deal" for the Indians

Franklin Roosevelt's advisers realized that the Indian policy laid down in the Dawes Act of 1887 (page 429) had not worked very well. This plan of "turning Indians into red-skinned whites" had made many Indian tribes wards of the federal government. Schools on the reservations ignored Indian arts and crafts and discouraged tribal customs but did little to prepare the Indians for absorption into American patterns of living. Moreover, though the Indians owned separate parcels of land, the soil was often too poor to support them. In the twentieth century, oil was found on some Indian lands, but most of the tribes barely managed to eke out an existence.

John Collier, Roosevelt's Commissioner of Indian Affairs, worked out a "New Deal for the American Indians." The Wheeler-Howard Act of 1934 tried to revive community life on the reservations. It provided for more self-government and for the holding of land by the tribe rather than by individuals. Indians were instructed in soil conservation and methods of raising livestock, and there was a strong revival of interest in Indian culture, including arts and crafts. Under this program the number of Indians, which had fallen to 240,000 in 1920, began to increase. By 1960 there were more than 520,000 Indians in the United States.

as a writer was cut short with his death at
the age of 38. Among the most powerful of
the new voices in the 1930's, though not
recognized as such at the time, was that of
William Faulkner. Negroes, poor whites,
planters, merchants, politicians, and Indians
appeared in his epic novels of life in
Yoknapatawpha County, an imaginary section of the deep South which bore a close
resemblance to Faulkner's native Mississippi. Richard Wright, a gifted young Negro
writer, described his early life in *Black Boy*.

Artists respond to the depression. Some
painters met the economic and social upheavals of the 1930's by reaffirming their
faith in the American past. Artists like
Grant Wood, John Steuart Curry, and
Thomas Hart Benton had little interest in
depicting urban slums or experimenting
with abstract styles. Their manner of painting was realistic and direct, and their favorite themes were rural or historical. Grant
Wood specialized in Iowa farm scenes and
studies of the men and women who tilled
the soil. His famous painting "American

Gothic" was the most popular picture displayed at the Chicago Exposition in 1933.
Thomas Hart Benton, grandnephew of Missouri's first senator, painted scenes of the
Missouri countryside. Some of his murals
were commissioned by the federal government. Curry, a native of Kansas and a professor of art at the University of Wisconsin,
found his inspiration in the midwestern
countryside.

Other painters of the depression years
depicted the misery of the urban poor.
Reginald Marsh sketched and painted many
facets of New York City life — the subways,
beaches, store windows, street signs, and
tugboats. Marsh made no attempt to
glamorize his subjects, thus prompting John
Steuart Curry to ask why he always had to
take "a worm's-eye view." Ben Shahn and
Jack Levine were talented young painters
who worked on WPA projects in the 1930's.
Their work combined social criticism with
biting realism.

**Entertainers help dispel the depression
gloom.** Though the 1930's were grim years,

THE AMERICAN SCENE

AMERICANS OF THE 1930'S

as seen by BEN SHAHN

In his poster for the Resettlement Administration (below, left), Shahn caught the despair of
a midwestern farmer whose land had been
ravaged by the dust storms of the 1930's. The
picture below (part of a mural now in the Department of Health, Education, and Welfare
Building) reflects a more hopeful scene — carpenters at work as the country began to make
its way out of the depression.

Americans did not lose the ability to laugh. The best-known humorist of the 1920's and '30's was Will Rogers, "the Cowboy Philosopher." Born in Oklahoma, he was part Cherokee and quipped that he "had just enough white in me to make my honesty questionable." At the time of Roosevelt's inauguration, he delighted troubled Americans by saying: "The whole country is with him, just so he does something. If he burned down the capitol we would cheer and say, 'Well, we at least got a fire started anyhow.'" The whole country mourned when Will Rogers died in an airplane crash in Alaska in 1935.

Other favorite entertainers of the 1930's were radio comedians and motion-picture stars. Only a few of the earlier actors and actresses were able to make the transition to the "talkies," and such new stars as Cary Grant, Greta Garbo, and Shirley Temple claimed the limelight in the 1930's.

Americans of the depression years also enjoyed the work of several talented composers. Cole Porter, Irving Berlin, and George Gershwin (page 664) were among America's favorite songwriters. Gershwin's spoof of a presidential election, *Of Thee I Sing,* won the first Pulitzer Prize ever awarded to a musical play. In 1935, two years before his death, Gershwin completed the opera *Porgy and Bess* about Negro life on the Charleston water front. Large dance bands gradually replaced the small jazz groups in the 1930's, and band leaders developed written arrangements known as "swing." Benny Goodman became the "King of Swing," while other big-name bands were those of Tommy Dorsey, Glenn Miller, and Gene Krupa.

Finally, it should be noted that although Americans usually found their entertainment close to home in the 1930's, enough of them journeyed to Chicago in 1933 and New York in 1939 to make financial successes of the world's fairs held by those cities. Chicago's Century of Progress Exposition commemorated the hundredth anniversary of the city's founding. The New York fair celebrated international ties and the advance of civilization; yet before its gates were closed, Europe had plunged into the Second World War.

▶ CHECK-UP

1. How did the New Deal encourage the arts?

2. What writers and artists found their themes in depression conditions?

3. What types of entertainment were characteristic of the depression years?

. . . .

Clinching the Main Ideas in Chapter 33

The American people were desperate and confused when Franklin Roosevelt took office in 1933. Though the new President had no well-planned blueprint for lifting the country out of the depression, he and his advisers immediately swung into action. They used whatever techniques had worked in the progressive era and the 1920's and also devised new approaches as they went along.

The key pieces of New Deal legislation extended the power of the federal government into areas of American life that had been hardest hit by the economic collapse. Government regulation of banks, stock exchanges, and public-utility companies was welcomed by most Americans. Likewise, many people approved of New Deal relief measures since private industry was unable to provide jobs and neither state or local governments could shoulder the cost of assisting unemployed families. Because of the crisis atmosphere, Congress was willing to use its authority to impose farm quotas and business codes and to authorize the President to inflate the currency.

Heavy government spending, or "pump-priming," in the early years of the New Deal undoubtedly helped revive both industry and agriculture. As the country began to make a slow recovery from the depression, more and more people objected to government regulations. Opponents of the New Deal made little headway in the 1936 election, but Roosevelt's "court-packing plan" played into their hands. It destroyed Roosevelt's political coalition and helped conservative southern Democrats and Republicans make substantial gains in the congressional elections of 1938.

Although New Deal legislation came to a

halt after 1938, such programs as TVA, AAA, Social Security, the Wagner Act, and the Fair Labor Standards Act marked important changes in America's social and economic life. Moreover, the revival of po-

litical opposition to New Deal Democrats and the reverses which Roosevelt suffered in 1937 and 1938 showed that the President had not undermined individual rights or freedom of expression.

Chapter Review

Terms to Understand

1. FDIC
2. SEC
3. FERA
4. CCC
5. PWA
6. WPA
7. AAA
8. NRA
9. NLRB
10. CIO
11. FHA
12. recession
13. dust bowl
14. banking "holiday"
15. TVA "yardstick"
16. "pump-priming"
17. parity payments
18. industrial union
19. sit-down strike
20. Social Security Act
21. minority groups
22. Fair Labor Standards Act

What Do You Think?

1. During President Roosevelt's first two terms, New Deal spending added 24 billion dollars to the national debt without solving the problems of unemployment or farm surpluses. Evaluate this statement.

2. Opponents of the New Deal made little headway until President Roosevelt's "court-packing" plan played into their hands. How did this happen and why?

3. Critics of President Roosevelt claim that he upset the balance of power between employer and employee by regulating business at the same time that he extended government protection to organized labor. Explain and give examples. What do you conclude?

4. Which of the New Deal programs have had lasting significance? Explain why in each case.

5. Early in 1934 the value of the new dollar was fixed at about 59 per cent of its former value in gold. What effect on prices was expected? Did this happen? Why?

Using Your Knowledge of History

1. Debate: *Resolved,* That "no person shall be elected to the office of the President more than twice. . . ."

2. Briefly explain how the position of New Deal Democrats was likely to differ from that of conservative Democrats and Republicans on each of these issues: (a) the federal government's regulatory powers; (b) states' rights; (c) federal spending; (d) relief programs; (e) organized labor; (f) the antitrust drive.

3. Write an editorial advocating or opposing a river valley development program, similar to TVA, in the region where you live.

4. Historians have observed that the "Roosevelt Revolution" was really a new deal of the old cards. Do you agree? Briefly explain why each New Deal step or program was either an "old" or a "new" card.

Extending Your Knowledge of History

Two good brief accounts of Roosevelt's administration are Dexter Perkins's *The New Age of Franklin Roosevelt* and D. W. Brogan's *The Era of Franklin D. Roosevelt.* For economic history of the 1930's, see Broadus Mitchell's *Depression Decade; From New Era to New Deal.* Dixon Wecter's *Age of the Great Depression, 1929–1941,* deals with the social history of those years. An excellent one-volume biography is *Roosevelt: The Lion and the Fox* by James MacGregor Burns. Interesting chapters on Roosevelt can be found in Hofstadter's *American Political Tradition* and Walter Johnson's *1600 Pennsylvania Avenue.* The tragedy of the depression era is vividly captured by James David Horan in *The Desperate Years: A Pictorial History of the Thirties.*

CHAPTER 34

The United States Moves from Isolation to Involvement in World War II

German bomber over London

War is a contagion, whether it be declared or undeclared. It can engulf states and peoples remote from the original scene of hostilities. We are determined to keep out of war, yet we cannot insure ourselves against the disastrous effects of war and the dangers of involvement . . . we cannot have complete protection in a world of disorder in which confidence and security have broken down.

FRANKLIN D. ROOSEVELT, OCTOBER 5, 1937

1933–1941

In the early 1930's, recovery from the Great Depression was the primary concern of most Americans. They were troubled by the rise of fascism in Italy, nazism in Germany, and a militaristic government in Japan, but they felt unable — and unwilling — to do anything about these developments. The inability of the League of Nations to halt aggressor nations further strengthened American isolationists — those who opposed participation by the United States in international affairs. As a result, isolationist congressmen succeeded in pass-

ing neutrality acts intended to keep the United States out of another war. At the same time, President Roosevelt's Good Neighbor Policy improved our relations with Latin American countries.

Toward the end of the 1930's, the American attitude toward aggressor nations began to change. Developments in Europe and the Far East had become alarming. Germany, Italy, and Japan were carrying out ever more reckless acts of aggression, confident that the democracies and the League of Nations would not interfere.

Against this somber background, President Roosevelt warned the American people that their neutrality laws could not guarantee the security of the United States "in a world of disorder."

After Europe was plunged into war in 1939, a bitter debate raged in Congress and throughout the country over whether or not the United States should aid the western democracies. Nazi Germany's brutal assaults in Europe finally convinced Americans that Hitler had to be stopped. By 1941 the United States was giving Great Britain all aid short of war. Japan's attack on Pearl Harbor finally pushed this country into World War II.

1 Relations with Latin America Improve

Hoover inaugurates a new policy toward Latin America. When Herbert Hoover was elected President in 1928, our relations with the countries of Latin America were strained by years of "big stick" and "dollar diplomacy." For this reason the President-elect made a good-will tour of Latin America to assure our neighbors that their fears of American intervention were "unfounded." Hoover backed up his words with actions. He withdrew American troops from Nicaragua and recognized newly elected governments in eight Latin American nations. Moreover, Hoover refused to

· ·

CHAPTER FOCUS

1. Relations with Latin America improve.

2. The United States seeks to safeguard its neutrality.

3. The outbreak of war affects American policy.

4. The United States is drawn into World War II.

intervene in El Salvador when that country failed to meet its financial obligations to United States bankers.

Roosevelt formulates the Good Neighbor Policy. This new approach to Latin American relations was carried further by Franklin D. Roosevelt. In his inaugural address in 1933, President Roosevelt said that the United States would follow "the policy of the good neighbor — the neighbor who resolutely respects himself and, because he does so, respects the rights of others — the neighbor who respects his obligations and respects the sanctity of his agreements in and with a world of neighbors."

During the next eight years Roosevelt and Secretary of State Cordell Hull worked hard to put this Good Neighbor Policy into effect. As we shall see in this section, the United States refrained from intervention in Latin American affairs and encouraged the settlement of disputes through arbitration. The United States also negotiated reciprocal trade treaties and promoted cultural exchanges between the peoples of North and South America. And, as the world situation grew more threatening, our government took part in planning for the collective security of this hemisphere.

The United States renounces intervention. At Pan American conferences during the 1930's, American delegates spelled out the intent of the Good Neighbor Policy. Thus, at the Montevideo Conference in 1933, Secretary Hull approved a pact declaring that "no state has the right to intervene in the internal or external affairs of another." At the Buenos Aires Conference three years later, the United States reaffirmed this policy. These inter-American agreements were a direct reversal of the position taken by Theodore Roosevelt some thirty years earlier.

This new policy toward Latin America was soon put to the test. In 1933 the government of Cuba was overthrown. Though the United States at first withheld recognition of the new government, it did not send troops. The next year, in a new treaty between the two countries, the United States gave up its right to intervene in Cuba as provided under the Platt Amendment

The changed attitude of the United States toward the Latin American countries was reflected in the meetings shown here. Above, Nicaraguan officials greeted President-elect Herbert Hoover during his good-will tour of Latin America in 1928. This policy was continued in the 1930's. At right, Secretary of State Cordell Hull talks with a Latin American representative at the 1938 Pan-American Conference.

(page 585). The United States also withdrew troops from Haiti, thus ending its protectorate, though it retained financial control over that country. A treaty signed with Panama in 1936 (though not ratified until 1939) increased our annual payment for canal rights from 250,000 dollars to 430,000 dollars.[1]

The United States renounces dollar diplomacy. In line with the Good Neighbor Policy, the United States also abandoned "dollar diplomacy" (page 599). That is, our government no longer maintained that it had a right to intervene in Latin American affairs to protect private American investments. This new policy was demonstrated in 1938 when the Mexican government seized American and British oil properties in Mexico. The Roosevelt administration admitted the right of Mexico to take over the foreign oil holdings but demanded adequate payment to the former American owners. The Mexican government was willing to pay for the surface property rights, though not for the underground oil and minerals. In spite of pressure from American businessmen, Roosevelt and Secretary Hull insisted that a solution to this issue be sought through diplomatic channels. After several years of negotiations, the dispute was finally settled when the oil companies accepted an award of some 24 million dollars in full payment. The diplomatic handling of the problem had helped to preserve friendly relations between the United States and Mexico.

Reciprocal trade treaties help improve relations. The Trade Agreements Act of 1934 (page 694) also contributed to better relations among the countries of the Western Hemisphere. This act paved the way for greatly increased trade between the United States and the Latin American nations and with Canada as well. Moreover, the United States made loans of over three

[1] In 1955 another treaty raised the annual payment to 1,930,000 dollars.

billion dollars to Latin American governments for the construction of roads, bridges, hospitals, schools, and water and sewage systems. Unlike earlier American investments in private industrial ventures, the government loans were made not for profit but to help raise the standard of living in the Latin American countries.

Cultural exchange programs are established. As a part of its Good Neighbor Policy, the United States promoted "cultural exchange" with its southern neighbors. Artists, writers, actors, dancers, and musicians participated in this successful program, thus making people in this country increasingly aware of Latin American viewpoints and cultures. Though interrupted by World War II, the cultural exchange program was resumed in the 1950's.

The Western Hemisphere moves toward collective security. As aggressor nations grew bolder in other parts of the world, President Roosevelt expressed his concern about protecting the Western Hemisphere against attack. In 1936 he journeyed to Buenos Aires to open the Inter-American Conference for the Maintenance of Peace. This conference declared that a threat of foreign attack against any nation in the Western Hemisphere would be considered a threat to all American republics. Even more significant was the action taken at a Pan American Conference held at Lima, Peru, in 1938. Under the leadership of Secretary Hull, this conference adopted the Declaration of Lima. In this collective-security pact, the American nations agreed to defend themselves and each other against any outside threat.

Though Canada was not a party to the Declaration of Lima, President Roosevelt made clear that plans for the collective security of the hemisphere included our northern neighbor as well. In 1938 the President traveled to Canada and delivered an important speech at Kingston, Ontario: "I give to you assurance that the people of the United States will not stand idly by if the domination of Canadian soil is threatened by any other empire." Thus, even before World War II broke out in Europe, the United States had strengthened its relations with Latin America and Canada. Equally important, it had taken steps to provide for the collective security of the New World.

▶ CHECK-UP

1. What steps did the Hoover and Roosevelt administrations take to improve relations with Latin America?

2. What steps were taken by Western Hemisphere nations to insure collective security?

. . . .

2 *The United States Seeks to Safeguard Its Neutrality*

In the years between the two World Wars (1918–1939), the United States and other democratic nations watched with alarm the rise of totalitarian governments in Russia, Italy, Germany, and Japan. The first of these four countries to use force in expanding at the expense of its neighbors was Japan.

Japan takes advantage of civil war in China. During the 1920's Japanese military officers gained the upper hand in their country's government (page 641). Eager to make Japan the dominant country in East Asia, the Japanese militarists blamed the United States for having thwarted Japanese expansion into China. Many people in Japan agreed with the army and navy commanders that their country had good reasons for closing the Open Door, by force if necessary.

Civil war in China played into the hands of the Japanese militarists. The Manchu ruler of China had been overthrown in 1911 and a republic established. But many provincial warlords ignored the central government. In the 1920's a Nationalist government under Chiang Kai-shek (chee-*ahng' kye'shek'*) tried to achieve unity and to introduce urgently needed reforms. Progress was disappointingly slow because the government became involved in a struggle for power with Chinese Communists. The resulting chaos led the Japanese militarists to believe that the time had come to take over Manchuria and to extend Japanese influence in China. The fact that the Western powers, struggling with the depression, would be reluctant to intervene in behalf of China also prompted Japan to act.

Manchuria becomes a puppet state. In 1931 the Japanese war lords launched a full-scale invasion of Manchuria and soon conquered all of that region. Manchuria was proclaimed the sovereign state of Manchukuo (man-choo-*kwoh'*). Actually, it became a Japanese puppet state.

Japan quits the League. The Japanese invasion violated several treaties and was a direct challenge to the League of Nations. China had appealed to the League when Japanese troops moved into Manchuria, but nothing was done to halt the invasion. The League did appoint a commission to investigate this act of aggression. Its report condemned the Japanese for invading Manchuria and for establishing the puppet state of Manchukuo. It also recommended that Manchuria be established as a self-governing state within the republic of China. When the League Assembly adopted the report of the commission, Japan walked out of the Assembly and soon afterward resigned from the League. Japan insisted that it had the right and the obligation to keep order in the Far East.

The United States protests the Manchurian conquest. Japan's conquest of Manchuria came at an awkward time for the United States. The year 1932 witnessed the end of Hoover's term, a presidential election, and the low point of the depression. Most Americans had little interest in far-off Manchuria. Secretary of State Stimson discussed with President Hoover the possibility of imposing economic sanctions (penalties) against Japan, but the President felt that such action might lead to war. Instead, therefore, the Secretary of State formulated the so-called Stimson Doctrine, warning the Japanese that the United States did not intend to "recognize any situation, treaty, or agreement" which might be brought about by the use of force. The Japanese militarists deeply resented the Stimson Doctrine. But they moved ahead with plans for exploiting the rich resources of the "independent" state of Manchukuo.

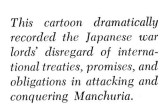

This cartoon dramatically recorded the Japanese war lords' disregard of international treaties, promises, and obligations in attacking and conquering Manchuria.

President Franklin Roosevelt, concerned with the problems of the depression, took no effective action against Japan. He and Secretary of State Cordell Hull insisted that American treaty rights be recognized in the Far East. But they did not want to provoke Japan at a time when no one in the United States wanted war. Moreover, 25 per cent of this country's foreign trade was with Japan as against 2 per cent with China. There the matter rested until Japan began a full-scale attack on China in 1937 (page 720).

Hitler rises to power in Germany. Meanwhile, the republic established in Germany after World War I had encountered serious difficulties (page 639). Many Germans held it responsible for the humiliating terms of the Treaty of Versailles. Others blamed their government for the economic ills that plagued Germany after World War I. The country's political and economic troubles worsened during the depression of the 1930's. These conditions help to explain how Adolf Hitler was able to take over the German government.

Hitler was an Austrian of humble parentage whose early life had been marked by failure and unhappiness. During World War I, Hitler served in the German army. After the war he plotted with other discontented Germans against the republican government. While serving a prison term, he wrote *Mein Kampf* ("My Struggle"), a vehement book outlining his reckless plans for Germany. By holding out glittering promises to all who were discontented, Hitler and his Nazi Party[2] attracted many followers. In 1933, Hitler was named to the high office of chancellor. Voted unlimited powers for four years by the German legislature, Hitler made Germany a Nazi dictatorship. *Der Fuehrer* ("the leader") suppressed opposition parties and gained control of all branches of the government.

Hitler establishes a totalitarian state. Under Hitler's dictatorship, every phase of German life was controlled by the Nazi Party, and every individual had to bow to the will of the state. Freedom of speech disappeared, newspapers were censored, schools taught Nazi propaganda, and freedom of religion was restricted. The state closely regulated both labor and industry, and Nazi planners mobilized the country's resources to expand the arms industry and make Germany self-sufficient. Though anyone who spoke out against the government was punished, German Jews suffered most at the hands of the Nazis. Hitler and his top advisers declared their intention of establishing a "master race" in Germany. Since the Jews did not fit into Hitler's idea of a "pure" German race, they were ruth-

[2] The full name of his party was National Socialist German Workers' Party. *Nazi* was a shortened form of its German name.

Nazi Persecutions

To unite the German people, Adolf Hitler used a trick that is as old as history. The Nazi dictator played on people's emotions by inciting them to hate minority groups, especially Jews. Hitler claimed that the Germans were a "pure race" and charged that the Jews were radicals who had gained control of Germany. Other minorities — foreigners, liberal thinkers, and clergymen — were also accused of disloyalty to Germany.

The action taken against the scapegoat minorities followed a set pattern. First came denunciations of the victims by the Nazis. Incited to fear and hatred by these charges, other Germans resorted to mob violence against the accused. Next for the victims came loss of jobs, citizenship, and other common rights and privileges. Finally these people were arrested without cause, imprisoned and tortured in concentration camps, and then put to death in a gas chamber or in other ways.

The millions of Jews killed by the Nazis were victims of "genocide," or the systematic destruction of a religious, national, or racial group. The world's horror over the Nazi atrocities has since been expressed in war crimes trials of Nazi leaders and in a United Nations resolution outlawing genocide.

lessly persecuted. Many Jews sought refuge in other countries. Before World War II ended, the Nazis murdered six million Jews in Germany and German-occupied lands.

Hitler prepares for aggression. By the mid-1930's it was evident that Hitler's ambitions extended far beyond the boundaries of Germany. Soon after *Der Fuehrer's* takeover in 1933, Germany quit the League of Nations. In his speeches, Hitler denounced as unfair Germany's treatment under the Treaty of Versailles and asserted his country's right to expand. At first in secret, but later openly, he set about making Germany a powerful military state. In 1935 Hitler proclaimed that Germany would no longer respect the disarmament provision of the Versailles Treaty. Compulsory military service was restored, and the German air and naval forces were built up. In the following year German troops moved into the Rhineland (page 633), which had been demilitarized (stripped of fortifications) under the Versailles agreement.

Stalin seeks to strengthen the Soviet Union. Some years before Hitler's rise to power in Germany, a Communist totalitarian government had become well-established in Russia. Within four years after the death of Lenin (page 638) in 1924, Joseph Stalin had eliminated rival leaders and seized power in the Soviet Union. In order to build up industrial production, Stalin launched the first of a series of five-year plans in 1928. Efforts were made to increase the available supply of power and to introduce modern machinery both in factories and on the large "collective" farms. Although Russia's industrial output rose, the people's standard of living remained far below that of western Europe.

The dictators use similar methods. Stalin's totalitarian state was similar in many respects to Nazi Germany and Fascist Italy. In all three countries a single political party ruled the state; the party leaders stamped out civil liberties and used force to maintain order. Schools and the press came under strict government control. Industrialists, labor leaders, professional people, and artists all had to bow to the commands of the ruling party. Each of the three dictators used secret police to uncover opponents of the state. In Russia, anti-Communists or Communists who opposed Stalin's iron rule were sentenced to slave labor in Siberia or executed.

The Communist state differed from the other dictatorships in its attitude toward the private ownership of property. Fascism and nazism permitted private ownership of land, business, and industry, though the Italian and German governments kept tight controls over both management and labor. In the Soviet Union, on the other hand, the state owned all factories of any size. The state also eliminated private ownership of land and held tight control over all farmers.

The United States recognizes the Soviet Union. Though other countries had recognized the Communist government in Russia soon after its establishment, the United States had not. In the 1920's, the American government withheld recognition on the grounds that the Soviets refused to pay debts incurred while Russia was ruled by the czars. Another reason was resentment of Soviet direction and supervision of the American Communist Party's activities. Nevertheless, American trade with Russia increased, and the Soviet government hired American companies and engineers to build industries in Russia.

When Franklin Roosevelt became President, there was growing sentiment in favor of recognizing Soviet Russia. The main reason was the hope of increased trade. One isolationist senator said, "There are billions of dollars' worth of future orders in Russia for American workers to fill." Late in 1933, President Roosevelt announced that diplomatic recognition had been granted to the Soviet Union. In return, the Russians agreed to refrain from encouraging Communist activity in the United States and to negotiate a settlement of American claims against the Soviet government. But the Soviet Union failed to live up to its end of the bargain. No agreement was reached on a settlement of American claims, and Communist activity continued in the United States. Nor did American trade with Russia increase significantly.

Isolationists gain strength in the United States. The rise to power of totalitarian governments and the aggressive ambitions

Mussolini (top left) was the first of the European dictators to undertake aggression. The Ethiopians resisted the Italian attack, but their camel corps (above) were ineffective against modern weapons. Meanwhile, Hitler (top right) built up his military forces. Germany and Italy also aided Franco in the Spanish Civil War. At right, Spanish Loyalists scale a stone wall to attack Fascist snipers.

of Japan soured many Americans on any form of international co-operation. Even many who had once favored membership in the League of Nations lost their enthusiasm for that organization in the early 1930's. Indeed, after Japan's take-over in Manchuria, few Americans believed that the League could either stop aggressors or bring about disarmament. There was a growing feeling that the United States should avoid foreign entanglements and concentrate on the problems of the depression. Some old-time progressives, like Senators William Borah and Hiram Johnson, feared that the New Deal reforms would be endangered if the United States took action against aggressor nations.

Italy attacks Ethiopia. The failure of the League of Nations to halt the Japanese conquest of Manchuria had not gone unnoticed by the European dictators. Mussolini had long talked about building a new empire to revive Italy's past glory. In 1935 he launched an attack against the African kingdom of Ethiopia. The poorly armed Ethiopians could offer little resistance to Italian tanks and airplanes, and their country was soon reduced to the position of a conquered Italian province.

The League of Nations branded Italy an

aggressor, and its members voted to apply economic sanctions. This action caused Mussolini to take Italy out of the League. But neither Great Britain nor France would support an embargo on Italian imports of gasoline, which were vital to Mussolini's war effort. Nor was the Suez Canal closed to Italian troops and supplies. Britain and France feared that such moves might drive Italy into an alliance with Germany. But Hitler gave his blessing to the Italian venture anyway, and about the same time ordered his troops into the Rhineland. In October, 1936, Hitler and Mussolini joined hands in the "Rome-Berlin Axis," thus forming the partnership also known as the Axis powers.

The United States adopts a Neutrality Act. Italy's attack on Ethiopia prompted American isolationists to seek the passage of neutrality legislation. The Neutrality Act of 1935 declared that the President (1) should prohibit for six months the shipment of arms to warring powers and (2) should forbid American citizens to travel, except at their own risk, on the ships of nations at war. Roosevelt and Secretary of State Hull would have preferred an embargo on arms shipments to aggressor nations while permitting the sale of arms to nations defending themselves. But the isolationists felt that if the United States was to keep out of foreign quarrels, it could not afford to distinguish between aggressors and the victims of aggression. In February, 1936, Congress extended the Neutrality Act for fifteen months and prohibited loans or credits to nations at war.

The Spanish Civil War poses a dilemma to Americans. The isolationists had not taken into account the dangers which a European *civil* war might present to the United States. Such a conflict erupted in Spain in 1936. General Francisco Franco and his followers, including many Spanish Fascists, rebelled against the Spanish republican government. Germany and Italy aided Franco, while Soviet Russia helped the Loyalists (those who supported the government). For the next three years civil war raged in Spain. By 1939 the outcome was clear. Spain fell under the control of Franco, who established a totalitarian state.

The brutal fighting of the Spanish Civil War and the involvement of Germany, Italy, and Russia made it difficult for Americans to ignore the conflict. Some American Catholics sided with Franco, for most of the Spanish clergy supported him. Other Americans sympathized with Franco because they felt a Loyalist victory would lead to a Communist government in Spain. On the other hand, many people in this country viewed the conflict as a testing ground between representative government and Fascist totalitarianism. They thought the United States should aid the Loyalists. Also voicing support for the Loyalists were members of the American Communist Party and Communist-sympathizers. But American isolationists were unmoved by the issues involved in the Spanish Civil War. They were determined at all costs to prevent the United States from aiding either Franco or the Loyalists.

Congress passes a second neutrality law. In May, 1937, Congress passed a second Neutrality Act. It retained the restrictions of the earlier legislation and made it illegal for Americans to travel on ships of warring nations. A new "cash-and-carry" provision was added to this Neutrality Act. Belligerent nations were allowed to buy non-military goods from the United States if they paid cash and transported the goods in their own ships. Most Americans continued to hope that these laws could keep the country from becoming involved in Europe's seemingly endless troubles.

▶ CHECK-UP

1. How was Japan able to establish a puppet state in Manchuria? What protests did the League of Nations and the United States make? With what effect?

2. How did Hitler come to power in Germany? How did he establish a totalitarian state? Prepare for aggression? How did Stalin make the USSR more powerful? In what respects were the methods used by the dictators similar?

3. Why did this country decide to recognize the USSR? Why did isolationist views gain strength? What did the League and the democratic powers do to deter Italian aggression in Ethiopia?

4. Why did the United States adopt a Neutrality Act? What were its provisions? What changes were made in the second Neutrality Act?

5. How did the Spanish Civil War pose a dilemma for this country?

• • • • • • • • • • • • • • • • • •

3 *The Outbreak of War Affects American Policy*

Japan wages war on China. Japan's success in Manchuria had whetted that country's desire for conquest. When fighting broke out between Japanese and Chinese troops near Peiping (Peking) in 1937, Japan had an excuse to start a full-scale invasion of China's northern provinces. Although the Japanese never officially declared war on China, their attack was another step in a carefully prepared plan to gain control of East Asia.

Toward the end of 1937, Japanese airplanes bombed and sank the United States gunboat *Panay* on the Yangtze River and also destroyed three American tankers. Japan apologized for the insult to the American flag and paid damages. Nevertheless, Japan's undeclared war on China compelled the United States to reconsider its neutral position. Speaking in Chicago a few months after the fighting began in China, President Roosevelt called for a "quarantine" of aggressor nations. He used this opportunity to warn the American people that no nation could "completely . . . isolate itself from economic and political upheaval in the rest of the world."[3] The President's "quarantine" speech indicated that he was beginning to consider ways of insuring collective security for the law-abiding nations of the world. But it provoked much criticism from persons who thought the United

States should not become involved in the troubles of other countries.

Germany becomes an aggressor. Meanwhile, Hitler had built up a powerful military force and was ready to begin carrying out his own plan of expansion. In early 1938, Hitler's army occupied Austria without firing a shot. Next, he demanded that Czechoslovakia give up the Sudetenland, an area with a large German-speaking population. The Czechs were willing to fight if France and Britain supported them. But these two countries were not ready to risk war. Instead, they arranged a conference with Hitler. At Munich in September, 1938, Hitler and Mussolini met with Prime Ministers Chamberlain of Britain and Daladier of France. Adopting a policy of appeasement ("peace at any price"), France and Great Britain signed a pact with Hitler agreeing to separation of the Sudetenland from Czechoslovakia. Hitler solemnly promised: "This is the last territorial claim I have to make in Europe." On his return to England from Munich, Chamberlain announced that the statesmen of Europe had secured "peace with honor . . . peace in our time."

Aggression continues. Unfortunately, neither Hitler's promise nor Chamberlain's prediction held true. Once Hitler occupied the Sudetenland, Czechoslovakia was helpless. In March, 1939, German troops occupied the remainder of that unfortunate country. Soon the Nazis also took the Baltic port of Memel from Lithuania. Moreover, in April, Mussolini's troops occupied Albania. (The map on page 725 shows the extent of Axis aggression in Europe.)

Britain and France reconsider appeasement. The summer days of 1939 were the lull before the storm. Having lost all faith in Hitler's promises, leaders in Great Britain and France reconsidered the wisdom of appeasement. The British and French governments pledged themselves to give assistance and even military aid to countries like Poland and Turkey, which were in danger of attack from Germany. Great Britain and France also hastened the build-up of their army, naval, and air forces.

[3] The quotation on page 711 is also from this speech.

The British cartoonist David Low summed up the double-dealing of the Nazi and Soviet dictators in this drawing. Though they had previously called each other "scum of the earth" and "bloody assassin," they willingly signed a non-aggression pact when it was to their mutual advantage.

Hitler and Stalin sign a non-aggression pact. Hitler was not impressed by these gestures. With his attention now fixed on Poland, he demanded the free city of Danzig and control of a strip of land across the Polish Corridor. Tension mounted throughout August. Then Hitler dismayed all Europe by announcing that he had signed a non-aggression pact with Soviet Russia. The Nazis and Communists had long been bitter enemies. But the signing of this pact dashed all hopes that Russia would help to defend Poland against a German attack. In fact, to the Soviet Union the pact was a device that made possible the take-over of eastern Poland plus additional territory in Estonia, Latvia, Lithuania, Finland, and Romania.

Hitler invades Poland. Events now moved swiftly toward war. President Roosevelt's last-minute appeals to Hitler had no effect, and Germany renewed its demands on Poland. But Britain and France repeated the promise of support for the latest victim of Nazi bullying, and the Poles refused to surrender any territory. On September 1, 1939, *Der Fuehrer* sent his armies into Poland, and German planes began bombing Polish cities. Two days later, Britain and France declared war on Germany. Soon afterward, Russian forces moved into Poland from the east.

The United States proclaims its neutrality. President Roosevelt invoked the Neutrality Act against the belligerents and issued a declaration of American neutrality. In a radio broadcast, the President stated:

"This nation will remain a neutral nation, but I cannot ask that every American remain neutral in thought as well." The President added: "Even a neutral has a right to take account of facts. Even a neutral cannot be asked to close his mind or his conscience." Public-opinion polls showed that although most Americans wanted to stay out of the war, a sizable majority hoped Britain and France would win.[4]

Congress revises the neutrality law. Before the outbreak of World War II, Roosevelt had voiced his objections to the Neutrality Acts. Such legislation "played right into the hands of the aggressor nations," he pointed out, by assuring them that their victims could not get military supplies from the United States. Thus "the aggressor nations . . . were actually encouraged by our laws to make war upon their neighbors." When war broke out in Europe, the President was even more convinced of the need to change the neutrality laws. He called Congress into special session and requested authority to sell arms and other supplies to Britain and France. He also asked for renewal of the cash-and-carry provision (page 719), which had expired in May. Roosevelt thus hoped to keep American merchant ships from carrying military cargoes into combat zones where they might be attacked by Hitler's submarines.

In the late fall of 1939, after long and

---

[4] A poll in October, 1939, showed that 84 per cent favored Britain and France, only 2 per cent sided with Germany and Italy, and 14 per cent had no opinion.

heated debate, Congress passed a third Neutrality Act. It gave the President essentially what he wanted. (1) The embargo on the sale of arms, munitions, and implements of war was repealed. (2) All commerce with the belligerents was to be on a cash-and-carry basis. (3) The granting of loans to belligerents was prohibited. (4) Americans, except in special cases, were not to travel on belligerent ships. (5) American vessels were forbidden to enter the war zone. (6) American merchant vessels were not permitted to arm.

This neutrality law was something of a compromise. Those who wanted to aid Britain and France approved of the lifting of the arms embargo. But the isolationists were pleased with the cash-and-carry provision, the ban on loans, and the restrictions on American travelers and vessels. In effect, the Neutrality Act of 1939 sacrificed the principle of freedom of the seas for which the United States had fought in two earlier wars, and drove our merchant marine from the North Atlantic.

A "phony war" strengthens the isolationists. Although Britain and France had promised assistance to Poland, they were in no position to give effective military support. While the German divisions rolled into Poland from the west, Russian troops moved in from the east. In less than a month, Polish resistance was crushed. After the conquest of Poland, there was little fighting for seven months. The expression "phony war" was coined to describe the quiet winter of 1939–1940. In western Europe, both the German and French armies retired behind strongly fortified positions, leading some people to expect a long siege of trench warfare as in World War I. Some felt that Germany would be content with the conquest of Poland. Others found comfort in rumors of peace offers.

American isolationists were encouraged by the lack of military activity during the winter of 1939–1940. Those who wanted the United States to stay out of the European war had various motives. Some German-Americans and Italian-Americans supported the isolationists because they did not want war between the United States

and their homelands. There were a few Nazis and Fascists who hoped to see a totalitarian system established in this country. Communists and Communist-sympathizers were active isolationists so long as the German-Russian non-aggression pact was in force. Some Irish-Americans, who felt bitter toward Great Britain because of its past treatment of Ireland, favored isolation. Still other Americans took this position in order to continue their political fight against President Roosevelt. And some New Dealers feared that foreign entanglement would turn attention from needed reforms at home.

One group of isolationists formed an "America First Committee." They hoped to win support for a hands-off foreign policy and to prevent Congress from extending aid to Britain and France. Perhaps the most prominent member of the America First Committee was Charles A. Lindbergh. The famous aviator argued that the German air force was invincible and that the United States should let Hitler have his way in Europe.[5] The isolationists felt certain that Hitler had no designs on the Western Hemisphere.

A Nazi blitzkrieg ends the "phony war." The "phony war" ended in April, 1940, when Hitler sent his armed forces into neutral Denmark and Norway. Though British and French forces tried to help Norway, the Nazis established control over most of that country within a few weeks. In May the Nazi *blitzkrieg* ("lightning war") was unleashed against the neutral Low Countries — the Netherlands, Luxemburg, and Belgium — and France. The German air force bombed airports, transportation centers, and cities. Motorized army divisions swept across Belgium and northern France to the sea, ruthlessly killing civilians who got in the way. The British expeditionary force was pushed back to Dunkirk on the English Channel and was evacuated to England by June 4.

Early in June the German forces slashed southward into France. The French army crumpled before the Nazi onslaught, and the roads were crowded with retreating

[5] When the United States entered the war, Lindbergh fully supported the American war effort.

soldiers and panic-stricken civilians. Realizing that France was doomed, Mussolini declared war on June 10. President Roosevelt observed: "The hand that held the dagger has struck it into the back of its neighbor." Before the end of the month, France signed an armistice, turning over half the country to Hitler's occupation forces. The rest of France came under the rule of a French government with headquarters at Vichy. But the Vichy government had to obey Hitler's orders. Thus, in less than three months the Germans had overrun Denmark, Norway, the Netherlands, Belgium, Luxemburg, and France. Great Britain now stood alone against Germany and Italy.

Support for intervention grows in America. The alarming events in Europe strengthened the hand of those Americans who wanted to aid Great Britain. The brutal Nazi conquests proved that Hitler was deadly serious in his goal of establishing German supremacy in Europe. The war was clearly a contest between representative governments respecting individual freedom, on the one hand, and ruthless totalitarianism, on the other. Moreover, the Nazi victories threatened to bring the war closer to the United States. Both France and the Netherlands had colonies in the Western Hemisphere that the Nazis might wish to use as bases. The activities of Ger-

Mechanized warfare characterized World War II. At top left, German tanks cross the Czech border in 1939. Airplanes carried out many different kinds of missions, including the dropping of parachute invasion troops (left, Germans landing in Crete in 1941). Bombers left heavy destruction behind them. The aerial view above shows American flying fortresses bombing a Nazi-held air field in France in 1943.

man and Italian agents in South America indicated that the Axis powers did have plans to extend their influence into the Western Hemisphere.

President Roosevelt stressed the need to strengthen American defenses and give all possible aid to Great Britain. A growing number of Americans approved this policy. To counteract the influence of the America First Committee, people who favored aid to Britain organized the "Committee to Defend America by Aiding the Allies."

The British fight on. When France fell, Winston Churchill, the new British Prime Minister, warned his country: "The Battle of Britain is about to begin. Upon this battle depends the survival of Christian civilization." Throughout the summer and fall of 1940, Hitler's planes bombed British cities, inflicting great damage in an attempt to "soften" the island for an invasion. But the valiant Royal Air Force fought the Nazi attackers with courage and skill. By fall it was clear that the British could not be bombed into defeat. If the Nazis tried to invade, said Churchill, "We shall defend our Island, whatever the cost may be. We shall fight on the beaches, we shall fight on the landing grounds, we shall fight in the fields and in the streets, we shall fight in the hills; we shall never surrender."

The United States aids Britain. Americans were deeply stirred by British courage. A public-opinion poll in September, 1940, showed that 60 per cent of those questioned felt it was more important to help Britain than to stay out of the war. In that same month President Roosevelt arranged a "destroyers for bases" deal with Great Britain. Britain urgently needed destroyers to fight off German submarines and keep shipping lanes open to the United States. So the American government exchanged 50 over-age destroyers for 99-year leases on air and naval bases in Bermuda, Newfoundland, Jamaica, and other British possessions in the Western Hemisphere.

Roosevelt made the arrangement by executive agreement, rather than treaty, in order to avoid a long delay by isolationists in the Senate. His critics called the destroyers-bases deal a "dictatorial" act, but Congress

ultimately indicated its approval by appropriating funds to recondition the ships. Churchill later wrote that this agreement "brought the United States definitely nearer to us and to the war, and it was the first of a long succession of increasingly unneutral acts in the Atlantic which were of the utmost service to us. It marked the passage of the United States from being neutral to being non-belligerent."

The United States strengthens its defenses. For months following the outbreak of war in Europe, Congress had voted only modest increases in appropriations for the armed forces. But the Nazi blitzkrieg underlined the growing danger. In May, 1940, therefore, Congress voted large sums to increase the size of the army, build a two-ocean navy, and meet the President's request for "at least 50,000 planes a year." Then, in September, while the Battle of Britain raged, a Selective Service Act established compulsory peacetime military service for the first time in American history. It provided for the registration of all men between the ages of 21 and 35. By November the first draftees had been called for military training.

The American nations plan for hemispheric defense. Meanwhile, the nations of the Western Hemisphere had agreed to strengthen their solidarity. In 1939, a Pan American Conference at Panama adopted a declaration of general neutrality. It also drew a "safety belt" in the oceans around the Americas south of Canada, and warned nations at war not to commit hostile acts within this zone. At the next Pan American conference, held in Havana in July, 1940, delegates took steps to prevent the growth of Nazi influence in Latin America. The conference also decided that if a European power lost its independence, its American possessions should be placed under a Pan American trusteeship.

The Panama and Havana agreements did not apply to Canada, since it did not attend the Pan American conferences. But President Roosevelt consulted with the Canadian Prime Minister about North American defenses, and the two countries established a joint-defense board.

THE AXIS AT ITS ZENITH

The expansion of the Rome-Berlin-Tokyo Axis brought the Allied cause to low ebb by late 1942. In Europe, Hitler and Mussolini held territory reaching from the Arctic to Africa, from Vichy France to the gates of Stalingrad. In Asia, Tokyo held large areas of China and controlled the Pacific from Burma to the Aleutians (dashed color line).

MAP STUDY

R. M. Chapin, Jr.

0   500   1,000   2,000 mi.

The Axis

Territory controlled by the Axis in late 1942

Vichy French controlled

Allied controlled

Neutral

NEW ZEALAND

AUSTRALIA

U. S. S. R.

OUTER MONGOLIA

CHINA

MANCHUKUO
1931

Tokyo

Aleutian Is.
1942

Midway
Is.

Wake Is.
1941

Gilbert Is.
1941

Truk Is.

Guam, 1941

NEW GUINEA
1942

PHILIPPINE IS.
1942

BORNEO
1941

DUTCH EAST INDIES
1942

MALAYA
1941

BURMA
1942

1941

SWEDEN

NORWAY
1940

FINLAND

ESTONIA

LATVIA
1940

LITHUANIA

U. S. S. R.

Moscow

1941

Kiev
1939

Stalingrad

DENMARK, 1940

GREAT BRITAIN

IRELAND

BENELUX
1940

Berlin

POLAND, 1939

Sudetenland, 1938

CZECHOSLOVAKIA, 1939

1938

AUSTRIA

HUNGARY

ROMANIA

YUGOSLAVIA
1941

BULGARIA

Rome

FRANCE
1940

SPAIN

PORTUGAL

ALBANIA
1939

GREECE
1940

TURKEY

SYRIA

LEBANON

FRENCH NORTH AFRICA

LIBYA (It.)

EGYPT

El Alamein

ETHIOPIA (It.)
1935

FRENCH WEST AFRICA

▶ CHECK-UP

1. Why did Japan invade China? How did Germany take over Austria and the Sudetenland? How was Germany able to take over the rest of Czechoslovakia? Why did Hitler and Stalin sign a non-aggression pact? What was the result?

2. How did Britain and France begin to change their policy toward Hitler? What changes were made in American neutrality laws? Why did many Americans favor isolation?

3. How did the Nazis take over Denmark, Norway, the Low Countries, and much °of France?

4. What was the effect of the Nazi victories on opinion in this country? How did the United States help Britain? How did we strengthen our defenses? What plans were made for hemispheric defense?

. . . .

4 *The United States Is Drawn into World War II*

Willkie challenges Roosevelt in 1940. A week after the fall of France, the Republican convention met in Philadelphia to select a presidential candidate for the election of 1940. It was clear that American foreign policy would be a leading issue in the campaign. Delegates who favored aid to Britain, as well as many rank-and-file Republicans throughout the country, favored Wendell Willkie. A personable lawyer and businessman, Willkie had once been a Democrat but had joined the Republican Party because he opposed such New Deal programs as TVA (page 695). In international affairs, however, Willkie backed Roosevelt's preparedness measures and favored giving Britain all aid short of war. His nomination was a defeat for the isolationist wing of the Republican Party.

President Roosevelt said nothing about his political plans until the Democratic convention met in July. Then he sent a message to the delegates saying that he had no desire to run for a third term. But apparently few of the delegates, or of Democrats throughout the country, regarded the two-term tradition as sacred. Using the slogan "Don't swap horses in mid-stream," Democratic leaders argued that the foreign situation was too perilous for the party to consider any candidate other than Franklin Roosevelt. The convention enthusiastically nominated the President for a third term and approved his choice of Secretary of Agriculture Wallace as the vice-presidential candidate.

During the campaign the Republican candidate hit hard on the third-term issue and called for greater defense efforts. Willkie undertook a whirlwind campaign tour during which he covered some 30,000 miles in 34 states. Though warmly received wherever he spoke, he could not break up the coalition of urban, southern, and western voters that had elected Roosevelt twice before. The President did no active campaigning until late in the fall.

Roosevelt wins a third term. On election day, Roosevelt received over 27 million votes, while more than 22 million were cast for Willkie. The President won 449 electoral votes to 82 for the Republican candidate. Willkie, however, had won respect with his high-level campaign and had strengthened those within his party who favored aiding Britain. During Roosevelt's third term, Willkie carried out a number of foreign assignments for the President.

Roosevelt clarifies American policy. The President interpreted his re-election as approval by the American people of all-out aid to Britain short of war. His annual message to Congress in January, 1941, was an important statement on foreign policy. He declared that the United States was committed to a program of national defense and to the support of countries that were resisting aggression. The President also stated: "We look forward to a world founded upon four essential human freedoms." These were defined as (1) "freedom of speech and expression"; (2) "freedom of every person to worship God in his own way"; (3) "freedom from want"; and (4) "freedom from fear." This fourth point, said the President, would require "a world-wide reduction of armaments to such a point . . . that no nation will be in a position to commit an act of physical aggression against any neighbor."

To carry out the promise of support to nations resisting aggression, the President asked Congress to approve the delivery of armaments to "those nations which are now in actual war with aggressor nations. Our most useful and immediate role is to act as an arsenal for them as well as for ourselves. They do not need man power. They do need billions of dollars worth of the weapons of defense."

The Lend-Lease Act is passed. Roosevelt had discussed the possibility of making the United States an "arsenal of democracy" during consultations with the British government in 1940. Churchill had informed the President that the British desperately needed munitions and supplies but were running out of cash to purchase them. The United States, however, could not lend money to Britain, since the neutrality acts prohibited loans to belligerents. President Roosevelt hit upon the idea of lending Britain goods rather than money.

In January, 1941, a Lend-Lease bill was introduced in Congress. It would authorize the President to sell, lease, or lend war materials to any nation whose defense he considered vital to America's safety. In return the United States would accept "payment in kind," that is, return of the goods after the war, or "any other direct or indirect benefit which the President deems satisfactory." In a "fireside chat" to the American people, Roosevelt said the Lend-Lease bill was like lending a garden hose to a neighbor whose house was on fire. Isolationists in Congress insisted that the measure would drag us into war. Nevertheless, public opinion favored the measure, and Congress passed it in March. An initial appropriation of seven billion dollars launched the Lend-Lease program.

The United States moves closer to war. It was one thing to manufacture war materials and lend them to Britain; it was an-

Wendell Willkie attracted a big crowd when campaigning in Chicago in 1940. Of the four Republicans who faced Franklin Roosevelt in a presidential election, Willkie won the largest total of popular votes.

other to get them there. As the flow of American goods increased, the Germans stepped up their submarine warfare in the North Atlantic. To help the British navy meet this threat, the United States took steps to protect merchant ships carrying supplies across the Atlantic. American air and naval bases were established in Greenland and Iceland, and navy patrols were authorized to help protect convoys bound for England.

Meanwhile, the United States had seized all ships of Axis and Axis-dominated countries in our ports. German and Italian assets in the United States were frozen (could not be used), and German and Italian consulates were closed on the grounds that they promoted subversive activity. By July, 1941, all German and Italian diplomats had left the United States.

Churchill and Roosevelt announce the Atlantic Charter. Suddenly, in June, 1941,

In July, 1941, American forces replaced British troops in Iceland to defend that strategic island from German attack. American marines lived in these prefabricated huts.

Hitler changed the nature of the war by invading Soviet Russia despite the non-aggression pact signed by the two dictators. Hitler doubtless hoped that a blitzkrieg attack would knock the Russians out of the conflict, thus giving Germany access to the wheat of the Ukraine, the oil of the Caucasus, and the output of Soviet factories. Germany would then be master of the European continent.

By this turn of events, Communist Russia became an ally of Great Britain (and, in effect, of the United States). Both Churchill and Roosevelt were outspoken foes of communism. But under the circumstances they could not ignore the advantage of having a powerful ally on the eastern flank of the Axis powers. With the nature of the war thus changed, Churchill and Roosevelt felt it desirable to make clear their countries' aims.

The two Western leaders met on shipboard off the coast of Newfoundland in August, 1941. After conferring for several days, they issued a document known as the Atlantic Charter. The Charter listed "common principles in the national policies of their respective countries on which they base their hopes for a better future for the world." It endorsed the following principles, several of which were similar to those contained in Wilson's Fourteen Points:

(1) No territorial aggrandizement.

(2) No territorial changes without the approval of the people concerned.

(3) Self-government for all peoples.

(4) Free access for all countries to trade and raw materials.

(5) Economic co-operation of all nations.

(6) Freedom from fear and want.

(7) Freedom of the seas.

(8) World disarmament and the abandonment of the use of force.

American ships are attacked in the North Atlantic. The increasing flow of Lend-Lease supplies to Great Britain and Russia heightened the danger of armed conflict in the North Atlantic. Hitler had made clear that ships carrying supplies to Britain or Russia would be torpedoed. By the late summer of 1941, the United States Navy was escorting merchant ships as far as Iceland, where British warships then took over. Before long, German submarines attacked an American destroyer and sank two merchant ships. Roosevelt, therefore, asked Congress to repeal the section of the Neutrality Act of 1939 which prohibited the arming of merchant ships. While the isolationists sought to block this change, two more American destroyers were attacked by German submarines. Congress responded by passing an act which not only allowed the arming of merchant ships but also permitted them to enter combat zones and deliver Lend-Lease goods directly to British ports. Thus, by November, 1941, the United States was in effect an ally of Great Britain, though technically not at war with Nazi Germany.

American relations with Japan worsen. While aid to Britain brought the United

States closer to war, developments in the Far East also affected American neutrality. Despite the loss of China's northern provinces and some coastal territory, Chiang Kai-shek doggedly kept up the fight against the Japanese invaders (page 720). The United States made loans to China to enable Chiang to buy war supplies in this country. At the same time, however, American firms were selling war materials to Japan, which had the cash to buy whatever it needed. During 1938, for instance, the United States actually supplied Japan with nine tenths of its scrap metal and copper and two thirds of its oil. But in July, 1939, our government announced that its long-standing trade treaty with Japan would be canceled at the end of six months. When extreme militarists took over the Japanese government in the following summer, Roosevelt banned the sale of aviation gasoline to Japan and sharply restricted the export of oil and scrap metal.

The Japanese answer to these changes in American policy was to join the Axis. Japan signed a mutual-assistance pact with Germany and Italy, thus forming the Rome-Berlin-Tokyo Axis. After Hitler unleashed his attack on the Soviet Union, Japanese military commanders felt free to carry out their plans for a "new order in Greater East Asia." In 1941, they compelled the French Vichy government to permit Japanese occupation of northern Indo-China. The United States then froze Japanese assets in this country. Japan struck back by freezing American assets. President Roosevelt then warned the Japanese that if they seized any further territory, the United States would take "any and all steps" necessary to safeguard its interests.

Negotiations fail. The Japanese imperialists were ready for war. Nevertheless, in November, 1941, the Japanese government sent a special envoy to the United States to talk with Secretary Hull. Japan demanded that the United States (1) stop aid to China, (2) approve Japanese conquests in China and Indo-China, (3) restore normal trade relations, and (4) "supply Japan a required quantity of oil."

Hull presented stiff American counter-

Flame and smoke billow into the air after the Japanese attack on the Naval Air Station at Pearl Harbor on December 7, 1941. The attack destroyed many ships and airplanes and caused heavy loss of life.

proposals. Japan must (1) recognize the Chinese Nationalist government of Chiang Kai-shek, (2) withdraw its troops from China and Indo-China, and (3) sign a non-aggression pact with other nations in the Far East before the United States would resume trade relations. On December 1 the Japanese rejected Hull's demands but asked that negotiations be continued.

The talks went on, even though Hull had no hope of reaching a settlement. On November 26 he told Secretary of War Stimson: "I have washed my hands of it, and it is now in the hands of you and Knox [the Secretary of the Navy], the Army and Navy." American intelligence agents had deciphered Japanese coded messages indicating that Japan would take action if the talks failed. Warnings were sent therefore to American forces in the Pacific. Most experts assumed that the Japanese would attack Thailand, Malaya, the Dutch East Indies, or possibly the Philippines. But in late November, a Japanese task force left the Kurile islands bound for Hawaii.

War comes at Pearl Harbor. Early on the morning of Sunday, December 7, carrier-based Japanese airplanes bombed air strips and the naval base at Pearl Harbor in Hawaii. Taken by surprise, the Americans suffered staggering losses. About 150 airplanes were destroyed on the ground, and 19 ships were sunk or badly damaged. Several thousand soldiers, sailors, officers, and civilians were killed or wounded.

On the next day President Roosevelt addressed a joint session of Congress. Calling December 7, 1941, "a date which will live in infamy," he asked for a declaration of war against Japan. With only one dissenting vote, Congress complied. On December 11, Germany and Italy declared war on the United States, and Congress unanimously declared war against these two countries.

▶ CHECK-UP

1. What was the significance of Wendell Willkie's views on foreign policy? How did Roosevelt clarify this country's policy?

2. What was the Lend-Lease Act? The Atlantic Charter? How did this country move closer to war with Germany?

3. Why did relations with Japan become increasingly less friendly? What demands did the United States make on Japan, and vice versa? What action brought us into World War II?

. . . .

Clinching the Main Ideas in Chapter 34

During the early and mid-1930's most Americans continued to be disillusioned with affairs in Europe. Totalitarian governments had taken root in Germany, Italy, and Russia, and it soon became clear that these governments were bent on aggression against weaker countries. Meanwhile, in the Far East, Japan too had set out on a course of conquest at the expense of China. Many Americans believed their country's best interests would be served by staying out of the conflicts in Europe and Asia. Thus Congress passed a series of Neutrality Acts intended to prevent American involvement in foreign wars. Meanwhile, as the Good Neighbor Policy led to improved relations with Latin America, the nations of this hemisphere began to consult on measures for common defense.

After 1937, as Europe moved toward war, many Americans heeded President Roosevelt's warning that neutrality legislation could not guarantee the country's safety. Once World War II had broken out in Europe, Congress changed these laws to permit the sale of war supplies to Britain and France. The false peace of the "phony war," however, strengthened the hand of American isolationists. Not until the Nazis had conquered Denmark, Norway, the Low Countries, and France did Congress appropriate large sums for American defense. The German threat to Great Britain led to increased American aid in the form of the destroyers-bases deal and the Lend-Lease Act. Convoying war supplies across the North Atlantic to Britain brought the United States still closer to war with Germany. But it was the Japanese attack on Pearl Harbor which actually plunged the United States into World War II.

Chapter Review

Terms to Understand

1. isolationists
2. appeasement
3. four freedoms
4. Nationalist China
5. puppet state
6. "master race"
7. Stimson Doctrine
8. collective farm
9. Polish Corridor
10. "cash and carry"
11. Lend-Lease Act
12. Rome-Berlin Axis
13. non-aggression pact
14. Vichy government
15. Atlantic Charter
16. Good Neighbor Policy
17. collective-security pact
18. America First 'Committee
19. "destroyers for bases" deal

What Do You Think?

1. Why did the Mexican government in 1938 seize American oil properties in Mexico? What was significant about the way a settlement was reached? Discuss these related issues: reasons for national ownership, the importance of efficient development, the need to attract foreign capital.

2. What factors have to be considered in determining the value of a collective-security pact to member states?

3. The League of Nations could neither stop aggressors nor bring about disarmament. Why?

4. What was this country's stand with respect to the rights of a neutral nation in World War II? World War I? The Napoleonic wars? How do you account for any differences?

5. Since World War II, this country has cooperated fully with the United Nations and has accepted heavy world-wide responsibilities. How, then, do you account for the country's isolationist policies after World War I?

Using Your Knowledge of History

1. Make two lists, one for Europe and one for Asia, of events which brought the United States into World War II. In a class discussion try to reconcile any differences.

2. Compare the major points included in the Atlantic Charter and the Fourteen Points. Which ideas are included in both?

3. Write a letter to a newspaper giving your reactions to the Neutrality Act of 1939. Assume that you are either an isolationist or in favor of aiding Britain and France.

4. Write an essay pointing out characteristics that totalitarian states have in common.

Extending Your Knowledge of History

A brief summary of American foreign policy in the 1930's is Allan Nevins's *The New Deal and World Affairs*. E. O. Guerrant has written *Roosevelt's Good Neighbor Policy*. A good study of the background to World War II is Hajo Holborn's *The Political Collapse of Europe*. Selig Adler in *The Isolationist Impulse: Its Twentieth Century Reaction* traces this country's reaction to developments in Europe. Walter Johnson writes about those Americans who disagreed with the isolationists in *The Battle Against Isolation*. On American policy in the Pacific, see *The Road to Pearl Harbor* by Herbert Feis and *Pearl Harbor: Warning and Decision* by Roberta Wohlstetter. An informative presentation of the 1940 election can be found in M. E. Dillon's *Wendell Willkie*. Frederick Lewis Allen gives a lively account of the social changes of the 1930's in *Since Yesterday*.

CHAPTER 35

Atomic mushroom cloud

The United States Plays a Crucial Role in World War II

Victory in this war is the first and greatest goal before us. Victory in the peace is the next. That means striving toward the enlargement of the security of man here and throughout the world.

FRANKLIN D. ROOSEVELT, 1943

1941–1945

The surprise attack on Pearl Harbor gave the American people a strong sense of unity. The bitter argument about whether the United States should aid the Allies now seemed pointless. Even the staunchest isolationist agreed that there was no other course than to fight and win a war against the Axis powers. The President said in his war message: "I believe I interpret the will of the Congress and of the people when I assert that we will not only defend ourselves to the uttermost but will make very certain that this form of treachery shall never endanger us again."

The American and British war efforts were closely co-ordinated by Roosevelt and Churchill, who met frequently to discuss strategy. The defeat of Hitler and Mussolini and the freeing of the conquered peoples became their immediate goal. The war against Japan was left chiefly to the United States, and did not end until two atomic bombs had been dropped on Japanese cities.

The Allies banded together not only to defeat the Axis powers but also to win the peace. Planning for another world organization began as early as 1943. American delegates played an important part in preliminary conferences and in the creation of the United Nations Organization at San Francisco in 1945. In sharp contrast to the bitter debate over ratification of the League of

Nations, the Senate approved American membership in the United Nations by an overwhelming vote.

Said President Roosevelt in 1945: "We have learned that we must live as men, and not as ostriches, nor as dogs in the manger. We have learned to be citizens of the world, members of the human community." The major contribution of this country to the Allied victory and our support of the United Nations showed that the United States had realized its world responsibilities.

1 *The Allies Stem the Axis Advance*

The Allies agree to fight together. Within a month after Pearl Harbor, delegates from 26 nations that were fighting the Axis powers met in Washington. They signed a declaration endorsing the principles of the Atlantic Charter, pledging their full resources to the war effort, and promising not to make a separate peace. The Allies — or the "United Nations," as President Roosevelt referred to them — agreed to "defend life, liberty, independence, and religious freedom, and to preserve human rights and justice in their own lands as well as in other lands." The Soviet Union joined in the Allied Declaration; but, as later events proved, the Communists had no intention of granting liberty to the Russian people or independence to any lands they occupied during the war. Nevertheless, the declaration stated the broad purposes of

. . . .

CHAPTER FOCUS

1. The Allies stem the Axis advance.
2. The United States mobilizes its resources for the war effort.
3. The Allies achieve victory.
4. The United Nations is established.

the countries allied together in the life-and-death struggle against the Axis powers.

Latin America supports the United States. As we learned in Chapter 34, the United States was concerned about the possibility of an Axis attack on Latin America. In January, 1942, an Inter-American Conference of Foreign Ministers assembled at Rio de Janeiro. The foreign ministers agreed to recommend to their governments that they break diplomatic relations with Japan, Germany, and Italy. All the Latin American nations eventually followed the recommendation of the conference, though Argentina did not take this step until 1944. About half of the Latin American nations, including Brazil and most of Central America, went further and declared war on the Axis. The Latin American states co-ordinated their shipping with ours, supplied us with raw materials, and suppressed the activities of Nazi agents. Brazil gave vital assistance in making the South Atlantic safe for shipping, and also sent an expeditionary force to Italy. The co-operation of the Latin American countries during World War II greatly aided the United States.

American-British war efforts are closely co-ordinated. The Allied nations worked together more efficiently than did Germany, Italy, and Japan. War production, transportation, use of troops, and overall strategy were planned in a series of major conferences held from time to time. The United States and Great Britain had a particularly close relationship. As soon as the United States entered the war, the American and British Chiefs of Staff were combined. Thus, the two countries pooled their forces.

This joint military effort was strengthened by the close personal relationship of President Roosevelt and Prime Minister Churchill. They met often and became warm friends. Churchill once cabled the President, "It is fun to be in the same decade with you." On many occasions, of course, the two leaders or their military advisers failed to agree. But General George Marshall later described the British-American co-operation as "the most complete unification of military effort ever achieved by two allied nations."

Roosevelt and Churchill met a number of times during World War II to decide Allied policy. Here they are shown at the Atlantic Charter meeting aboard a British battleship in August, 1941.

The liberation of Europe receives priority. One of the first decisions of the Anglo-American military planners was to strike hardest at Hitler. Some Americans demanded immediate action against the Japanese to avenge the attack on Pearl Harbor. But most American military and government leaders agreed that the Allied effort should be directed first against enemies in Europe. Germany and Italy were menacing the North Atlantic and Mediterranean shipping lanes and were threatening to close the vitally important Suez Canal. The Axis powers already controlled most of the European continent, and it was essential to prevent their conquest of Russia and Britain. Finally, the Germans had many agents at work in Latin America and presented a greater threat to the Western Hemisphere than did Japan.

Japan wins impressive victories. The decision to strike at Hitler before Japan meant that the United States could do little in the Pacific area until sufficient ships, planes, and troops became available. Thus, the "Hitler-first" strategy plus the losses at Pearl Harbor gave the Japanese a golden opportunity, and they made the most of it. Japanese jungle fighters overran the Malay Peninsula and captured the great British naval base of Singapore in February, 1942. The Japanese then pressed on through Burma to the very gateway of India and cut off supplies to China over the Burma Road. After a bitter struggle, the Dutch East Indies fell to the Japanese, leaving Australia as the only Allied stronghold in the South Pacific.

Meanwhile, Japanese forces had attacked American outposts in the Pacific. Guam and Wake Island were captured in December, 1941. To the north, Attu and Kiska in the western Aleutian Islands were also lost. (See the map on the next page for the war in the Pacific.)

The Philippines fall. While the Japanese were picking off isolated American islands and overrunning the East Indies, a fierce battle raged in the Philippines. American and Filipino troops, under General Douglas MacArthur, offered stubborn resistance to the invaders. Nevertheless, early in January, 1942, Manila surrendered, and the American forces retired to the Bataan peninsula and the island of Corregidor in Manila Bay. Despite heroic fighting against overwhelming odds, Bataan surrendered in April, Corregidor in May. General MacArthur escaped to Australia, where he became Supreme Allied Commander in the Southwest Pacific. Before leaving the Philippines, MacArthur made a dramatic promise to return and free the islands.

Two naval victories encourage the United States. American morale was bolstered in April, 1942, by the first air raid on the Japanese homeland. Led by Major General James Doolittle, a squadron of American planes took off from a carrier and bombed Tokyo and other cities in Japan. But more important militarily were two naval victories which helped stem the Japanese advance in the Pacific. A Japanese task force had attacked New Guinea, a vital link in communications between the United States and Australia. In May, American and Australian naval forces met the Japanese in the Coral Sea, and after a fierce battle between carrier-based airplanes, the Japanese withdrew. A month later, the enemy tried to capture Midway Island, but American forces led by Admiral

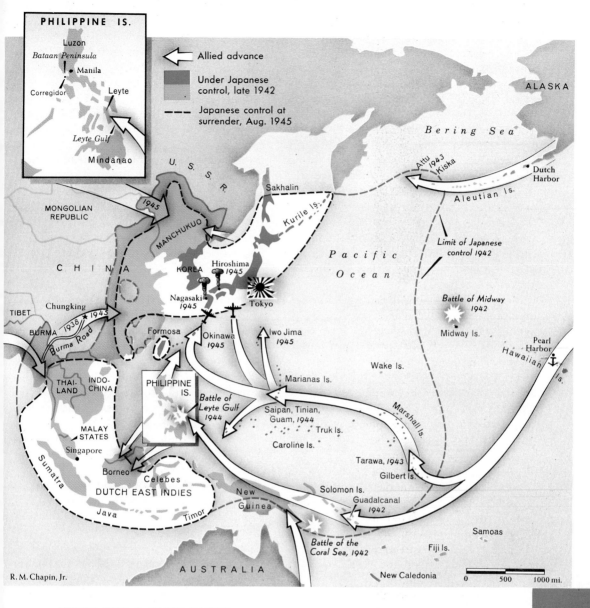

PHILIPPINE IS.

Luzon
Bataan Peninsula
Manila
Corregidor
Leyte
Leyte Gulf
Mindanao

← Allied advance

Under Japanese control, late 1942

--- Japanese control at surrender, Aug. 1945

ALASKA

Bering Sea

Attu 1943 Kiska

Dutch Harbor

Aleutian Is.

U. S. S. R.

Sakhalin

Kurile Is.

MONGOLIAN REPUBLIC

1945

MANCHUKUO

Limit of Japanese control 1942

Pacific Ocean

C H I N A

KOREA

Hiroshima 1945

Battle of Midway 1942

Chungking

Nagasaki 1945

Tokyo

Midway Is.

TIBET

BURMA 1938 1943

Burma Road

Formosa

Okinawa 1945

Iwo Jima 1945

Wake Is.

Pearl Harbor

Hawaiian Is.

THAI-LAND

INDO-CHINA

PHILIPPINE IS.

Battle of Leyte Gulf 1944

Marianas Is.

Saipan, Tinian, Guam, 1944

Truk Is.

Marshall Is.

MALAY STATES

Singapore

Caroline Is.

Tarawa, 1943

Gilbert Is.

Sumatra

Borneo

Celebes

DUTCH EAST INDIES

Java

Timor

New Guinea

Solomon Is.

Guadalcanal 1942

Samoas

Battle of the Coral Sea, 1942

Fiji Is.

R. M. Chapin, Jr.

AUSTRALIA

New Caledonia

0   500   1000 mi.

WORLD WAR II IN THE PACIFIC

The Allies used sea, air, and land operations to defeat Japan. Occupation of key islands provided air fields which brought still other islands, and eventually the Japanese homeland, under heavy bomber attack. When the atomic bombs were dropped, territory controlled by Japan had shrunk to the areas within black dashed lines.

MAP STUDY

Chester Nimitz inflicted heavy losses on the Japanese fleet. The Americans kept control of Midway and eliminated the threat of a Japanese invasion of Hawaii.

The Japanese advance is stopped at Guadalcanal. The Japanese offensive was finally halted at Guadalcanal in the Solomon Islands. American marines captured Henderson Field on Guadalcanal in Au-

gust, 1942, and began to extend their control throughout the island. Japanese forces counterattacked, and the fierce fighting reached a climax in November. A three-day naval battle was costly for both sides, but the Japanese finally withdrew from the Solomon Islands. The American victory at Guadalcanal marked a turning point in the fight against Japan. But the enemy was still strongly entrenched in the Gilbert, Caroline, and Marshall Islands, as well as in the Philippines and in southeast Asia. Victory in the Pacific had to await the turning of the tide in the European theater of war.

German forces threaten North Africa. Despite the victories in the Coral Sea, off Midway, and on Guadalcanal, the spring and summer of 1942 brought dark days for the Allies. German and Italian forces occupied all of North Africa from Tunisia to the Egyptian border. A German tank corps under General Rommel was threatening to smash into Egypt and seize the Suez Canal. (See the map on page 743 for the war in Europe and Africa.)

Meanwhile, Stalin was urging Churchill and Roosevelt to make a direct attack against Germany and thereby draw Nazi forces away from the Russian front. Churchill, however, wanted American forces to enter the North African campaign. He argued that it was essential to liberate North Africa, protect the Suez Canal, and reopen the Mediterranean to Allied shipping. By the summer of 1942 President

Erwin Rommel, commander of the German forces in North Africa, was one of the most brilliant of Hitler's generals. Later involved in a plot to kill the dictator, Rommel took poison in 1944.

Roosevelt had been won over to the British point of view. He realized that the Allies still lacked sufficient resources for a direct assault on Germany. Moreover, control of North Africa and the Suez Canal was vital to the defense of other parts of the British Empire.

American forces help liberate Africa. The German General Rommel, called the "Desert Fox," pushed back the British forces defending Egypt to El Alamein, not far from the Nile. But the British began a counteroffensive in October and within a few weeks drove the Nazis out of Egypt. Then, in early November, British and American forces made surprise landings in Morocco and Algeria. The French government in North Africa, supposedly loyal to the Vichy government (page 723), made only a show of resistance. In fact, a Vichy official, Admiral Darlan, surrendered to the Allied commander, General Dwight D. Eisenhower, and prepared the way for the rapid Allied advance across French North Africa. While General Eisenhower pushed into Tunisia from the west, British forces continued attacking the German army retreating westward across Libya. By May, 1943, the remnants of Rommel's forces in Tunisia had surrendered to the Allies.

The Russians turn back the German forces. Meanwhile, the prospect of an Axis victory in Russia had evaporated. When the Germans launched their attack on the Soviet Union in June, 1941, they advanced on a front from the Baltic to the Black Sea. Within four months the Germans had pushed the Russian armies close to Moscow, and a million Soviet troops had been captured. Hitler was confident that the military power of the Communists was destroyed. But the Russian retreat had overextended German lines of communication. Moreover, the Soviet "scorched-earth" policy (destroying all the resources of the country as they retreated) denied Germany the fruits of victory. Holding firm before Leningrad, Moscow, and Sevastopol, the Russians not only checked the German advance but during the winter and following spring regained nearly one fourth of the territory lost.

In the summer of 1942, German motorized units rolled southward, seeking the oil of the Caucasus. Although the invaders gained victories, their advance ground to a halt before Stalingrad, the port on the Volga through which much of this oil was shipped. When winter came, the Russians once more resumed the offensive. Thereafter they never lost the initiative.

Submarine warfare is checked. During 1942 Germany made a determined effort to increase the effectiveness of its submarine warfare. The Nazi command sent almost all its submarines to the Atlantic to attack oil tankers, cargo ships, and vessels transporting American troops to Europe. German submarines sank large numbers of Allied ships, causing heavy loss of life among American and British seamen. By the summer of 1943, however, the picture began to change. The United States Navy developed effective methods for hunting down the submarine "wolf packs." Air patrols and new detection devices helped antisubmarine vessels find their targets. More than 90 German U-boats were destroyed in the summer of 1943, and at the same time the construction of American ships moved into high gear. During the rest of the war American troops and supplies moved across the Atlantic in greater safety.

The Allies take the initiative in the air. The Royal Air Force had won supremacy in the air over England in 1940 (page 724). But the British were unable to strike directly at Germany until their aircraft production had increased. It was in 1941 that they began to attack German factories and transportation centers. After the United States entered the war, American planes joined in these air attacks. From air bases in North Africa, Allied planes also bombed industrial targets in Italy. In 1943, radar bombing was introduced. Radar made possible "precision" bombing under cover of darkness and bad weather. The Allied bombing raids weakened civilian morale in Germany and Italy.

▶ CHECK-UP

1. What pledges did the Allies make to each other? How did Latin American countries contribute to the war effort? How did the United States and Britain work together? Why was priority given to the liberation of Europe?

2. What gains were made by Japan following the attack on Pearl Harbor? What was the significance of Allied victories in the Coral Sea, off Midway, and at Guadalcanal?

3. How did the German advance in North Africa threaten the Allies? How did the British and Americans defeat the enemy in Africa? How did the Allies cope with German submarine warfare? Why did air strikes become an increasingly important factor in the war?

4. How were the Russians able to check and then turn back the German invasion?

• •

2 *The United States Mobilizes Its Resources for the War Effort*

With the coming of war, the United States suddenly faced problems very different from those of the depression years. As never before, winning a war depended on efficient use of man power and production.

Twelve million Americans serve in World War II. Thanks to the Selective Service Act passed in 1940 (page 724), the United States had a well-trained army of one and a half million men when Pearl Harbor was attacked. But once the United States entered the war, the army, navy, and air force were rapidly expanded. Training camps, ammunition depots, naval and submarine bases, and air fields were built here and abroad. A new Selective Service law required all men between the ages of 18 and 64 to register. Those between 18 and 45 became liable for military service. Men who were not drafted were assigned by the War Manpower Commission to vital war industries where trained workers were badly needed. For the first time in American history, large numbers of women were recruited by the armed forces. By the end of the war more than 250,000 women had joined the army (WACS), the navy (WAVES), the coast guard (SPARS), and the marines. Many other women served as military nurses. America's total armed forces numbered twelve million by 1945.

American production is vastly increased. Soon after Pearl Harbor, the President established the War Production Board to mobilize the country's resources and industry. The WPB placed government contracts for war supplies and determined which manufacturers would receive raw materials and man power. Despite some administrative tangles and occasional shortages of oil and rubber, production increased spectacularly.

The automobile industry gave up the manufacture of passenger cars to produce airplanes and tanks, as well as trucks and other vehicles needed by a modern army. Other peacetime industries also converted to war production. Shipyards speeded up production until in the summer of 1943 five ships a day were being launched. A new synthetic rubber industry had to be created during the war years because Japanese conquests had cut off the supply of crude rubber from Southeast Asia. As factories producing essential materials worked around the clock, the average work week jumped from 38 to 44 hours, and average factory wages doubled between 1939 and 1945. Many women took jobs in defense factories. Corporate profits also doubled. Moreover, though the farm population decreased during the war years, agricultural output increased and farm income more than doubled. War production thus helped solve the problem of unemployment and boosted the national income from 73 billion dollars in 1939 to 181 billion dollars in 1945.

The cost of the war is enormous. The cost of World War II to the United States was more than 300 billion dollars, about thirteen times the amount spent in World War I. Approximately 40 per cent of the total cost of the Second World War was met by increased taxation; the remainder was added to the national debt. As a result, the national debt skyrocketed from 40 billion dollars in 1939 to 258 billion in 1945.

Sale of war bonds and savings stamps brought the government over 100 billion dollars. Income taxes and luxury taxes were raised to unprecedented levels. The number of income-tax payers rose from 4 million in 1939 to more than 42 million in 1945. Rates as high as 94 per cent were imposed on the largest incomes. In addition, the practice of *withholding* income taxes was introduced. Under this system employers withheld federal income taxes from their employees' pay checks and turned the money over to the government.

Many wartime restrictions are imposed on the home front. By and large, Americans accepted heavy taxes and other wartime burdens without grumbling. But shortages of important items and the threat of inflation made necessary a system of price control and rationing. The Office of Price Administration (OPA) was set up to prevent inflation. It imposed price ceilings (limits) on a wide variety of consumer goods, and the War Labor Board tried to limit increases in wages and salaries. When shortages developed, the OPA began to ration certain consumer items. This meant that civilians could only buy specified quantities of sugar, meat, fats, coffee, canned goods, shoes, gasoline, fuel oil, and tires. The OPA also controlled rents. Prices did inch up, despite OPA controls and rationing, but such measures prevented serious inflation.

There were other inconveniences, but civilians accepted them as necessary to the war effort. Shortages of gasoline and tires limited automobile transportation, and the space available for civilian travel on airplanes and trains was reduced. The possibility of air and submarine attack caused cities to hold practice air raids and blackouts and to order the dimming of lights in coastal areas. People served on draft boards or as air raid wardens, auxiliary policemen and firemen, and hospital and Red Cross aides. Women wore straight skirts rather than pleated ones to save material; cuffs were abandoned on men's trousers for the same reason. Women factory workers began to wear trousers — a fashion change which survived the end of the war.

Scientists make a vital contribution to the war effort. Aware of the importance of

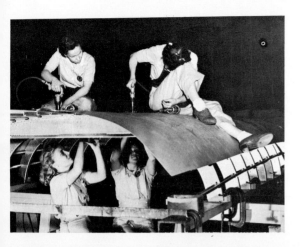

American industry produced enormous quantities of material and vehicles needed by the armed forces during World War II. The two photos at left above show how women filled vital jobs in defense factories, replacing the men who had gone to war. Shipyards performed miracles. Scenes like this christening at San Francisco (above right) were frequent as the yards swiftly turned out new vessels.

scientific research in the war effort, the government gave support and encouragement to scientists. The Office of Scientific Research and Development, headed by Vannevar Bush, welcomed refugee scientists from Italy and Germany and co-ordinated their work with British and American scientists. The results were impressive. British research on radar prior to 1940 enabled their planes to intercept German bombers in the Battle of Britain. Working together, Allied scientists then developed methods of detecting submarines with the form of radar called *sonar*. They also developed short-range rockets. Medical researchers produced the powerful pesticide DDT and

the antibiotic penicillin. They found new ways of fighting tropical diseases, introduced more effective methods of treating burns, and devised new surgical techniques.

Allied scientists produce atomic energy. The most significant scientific advance of the war years was the harnessing of atomic energy. In 1939 Albert Einstein and other scientists told President Roosevelt that the Nazis were experimenting with atomic fission and might produce a nuclear bomb. They urged that this country begin work on such a weapon. Thus, Roosevelt authorized the secret Manhattan District Project to develop an atomic bomb. Under the direction of Italian-born Enrico Fermi, the

The renowned scientist Albert Einstein (above) left Germany in 1932 to come to this country. Charles Drew, a Negro surgeon (right), helped save many lives during World War II by his work on the preservation and storage of blood.

first man-made nuclear chain reaction took place in a laboratory at the University of Chicago in 1942. This successful experiment ushered in the atomic era. But it required many more months of work to translate this knowledge into a nuclear weapon. A team of physicists built the first atomic bomb at Los Alamos, New Mexico, and successfully exploded it on July 16, 1945.

Most minority groups fare better in World War II. There was relatively little agitation against German-Americans and Italian-Americans during World War II, partly because the government did not seek to "mobilize patriotism" as it had in World War I. Furthermore, there were fewer foreign-born citizens, and not many of them sympathized with the regimes of Hitler or Mussolini.

The unusual conditions of the war years enabled Negro Americans to win new opportunities. Negro leaders called attention to the contradiction in fighting totalitarianism abroad while continuing the system of segregation in this country.[1] Their first goal was to increase employment opportunities for Negroes in defense plants. In 1941,

A. Philip Randolph, president of the Brotherhood of Sleeping Car Porters, threatened to lead a Negro march on Washington unless the President took action. As a result, Roosevelt issued an executive order forbidding defense industries to discriminate against Negroes in hiring workers. A Fair Employment Practices Committee was established to carry out this order. The work of the FEPC, as well as the man power shortage, opened new employment opportunities to Negroes. Some segregation practices were also abandoned in the armed services. And in 1944, NAACP lawyers won an important victory in the fight for civil rights. The Supreme Court ruled that state laws excluding Negroes from primary elections violated the Fifteenth Amendment.

The drive for Negro rights increased racial tension during the war years. Some employers and southern whites opposed the FEPC, and the 1944 Court decision was unpopular in some southern states. But the most serious demonstration of anti-Negro feeling occurred in Detroit, a city to which many southern Negroes and whites had come to work in defense plants. Egged on by agitators, Negroes and whites clashed on a hot Sunday afternoon in June, 1943. Federal troops finally put down the riot, but not until 34 lives had been lost.

[1] More than a million Negroes served in the American armed forces during World War II; half a million of them went overseas.

One group of people who suffered a great injustice during the war were the Japanese-Americans. The government, fearing sabotage in the event of a Japanese invasion, moved those on the West Coast to inland relocation centers. The American Civil Liberties Union denounced this action as "the worst single wholesale violation of civil rights of American citizens in our history." Despite this discrimination, many Americans of Japanese ancestry served with honor and courage in the United States armed forces. After the war, the government in effect recognized its error and appropriated funds to compensate these Japanese-Americans.

Roosevelt wins a fourth term. During the war years, the United States held its congressional and presidential elections as usual, proving the strength of a democracy even in times of national emergency. The Republicans made gains in the congressional elections of 1942 and had high hopes for victory in the next presidential election. At their convention in 1944, the Republicans nominated Governor Thomas E. Dewey of New York for President and Governor John W. Bricker of Ohio for Vice-President.

At the Democratic convention President Roosevelt was quickly renominated. But there was disagreement over the choice of a running mate. Vice-President Wallace had the support of many New Dealers, while the choice of the southern conservative delegates was James Byrnes of South Carolina. Finally the convention settled on Senator Harry S. Truman of Missouri, an able politician and a popular member of the upper house.

In the campaign, Dewey found no fault with the President's conduct of the war, endorsed plans for an international organization, and approved the broad outlines of the New Deal. All he could promise the voters was better administration. The President, stung by the charge that he was "a tired old man," waged a vigorous campaign, climaxed by a day-long drive in an open car through a heavy rain in New York City. The election proved to be Roosevelt's closest victory. He and Truman received less than 25 million votes to 22 million for Dewey and Bricker. The electoral vote was 432 to 99.

The Democrats kept their majority in the Senate and increased their strength in the House.

▶ CHECK-UP

1. What contributions to the war effort were made by the United States in terms of armed forces? Industrial production? Agricultural production? How did the country finance its war costs? Check inflation? Cope with shortages of important products?

2. How did scientists help to win the war?

3. What efforts were made during the war to secure equal treatment for Negroes? Why were Japanese-Americans living on the West Coast "re-located"? Why was this unjust?

• • • • • • • • • • • • • • • • • • • •

3 *The Allies Achieve Victory*

Section 1 of this chapter told how the Allies brought the Axis advance to a halt and began to take the offensive. In this section we shall see how Allied military forces closed in on the Axis powers and won complete victory.

Roosevelt and Churchill meet at Casablanca. In January, 1943, President Roosevelt and Prime Minister Churchill met at Casablanca, Morocco, with their chiefs of staff. The Allied leaders reached a number of important decisions at this conference. Top American military advisers favored the early creation of a "second front." They felt that the time was ripe for an invasion of France and a direct assault on Germany. But Churchill again argued against such a strike. He believed that the conquest of North Africa should be followed by an attack on the "soft underbelly" of the Axis. By this he meant Sicily and the Italian mainland and perhaps the Balkans. Such a campaign, he pointed out, would tie up many German and Italian troops and thus indirectly relieve pressure on the Russians. Churchill's argument carried, and it was agreed to invade Sicily and Italy as soon as the North African fighting was brought to an end.

Churchill and Roosevelt also discussed the war in the Pacific. They agreed that enough war materials, ships, planes, and men should be sent to the Pacific to permit General MacArthur and Admiral Nimitz to launch an offensive against the Japanese. Finally, it was decided at Casablanca that the war should end only with the "unconditional surrender" of the Axis powers.

The Allies invade Italy. As soon as enough landing craft had been assembled in North Africa, the Allies were ready to invade Italy. Under the command of General Eisenhower, a combined British and American force landed on Sicily in July, 1943, and took over that island in little more than a month. Meanwhile, discouraged by defeats in a war for which they had little enthusiasm, the Italians overthrew Mussolini. The new Italian government speedily

The drawings of cartoonist Bill Mauldin showed Americans at home how the battle-weary "GI's" managed to keep a sense of humor.

"Spring is here."

concluded a truce with the British and the Americans. But the German reaction to this turn of events was to occupy most of Italy and to treat the Italians as a conquered people. In September the Allied forces landed on the Italian mainland and began their advance northward.

The Allied troops had to fight a long and costly campaign to clear Italy of the well-entrenched German troops. In early 1944, Allied troops landing at Anzio, 30 miles south of Rome, suffered heavy casualties. Not until four months later did the Allies take Rome. Their progress northward continued to be slow and hard-fought. In April, 1945, anti-Fascist Italians captured and executed Mussolini.

Allied leaders meet at Moscow, Cairo, and Teheran. While British and American forces were fighting their way northward in Italy, the Russians were continuing their drive against the German invaders. During the summer and fall of 1943, they pushed the Germans back to the Dnieper River. With Moscow freed from the threat of German attack, the foreign ministers of Great Britain, the United States, and Russia met there in October. The Anglo-American spokesmen promised to invade Nazi-held Europe in 1944, and the Russians agreed to declare war against Japan after Hitler was defeated.

In the following month Churchill and Roosevelt met with Chiang Kai-shek in Cairo to talk about the war in the Pacific. Hampered by Communist opposition within China, Chiang Kai-shek was making little headway against the Japanese. Churchill and Roosevelt agreed to increase the flow of supplies to the Chinese. Out of the Cairo conference came the promise that both Manchuria and Formosa would be returned to China after the war and that Korea would be granted independence.

Churchill and Roosevelt then traveled on to Teheran, the capital of Iran, where they met with Stalin. This was the first Allied conference in which Stalin took part and the first time that Roosevelt and Stalin met. Churchill and Roosevelt reported definite plans to invade western Europe in May or June of 1944, and Stalin re-affirmed the promise to declare war on Japan as soon as

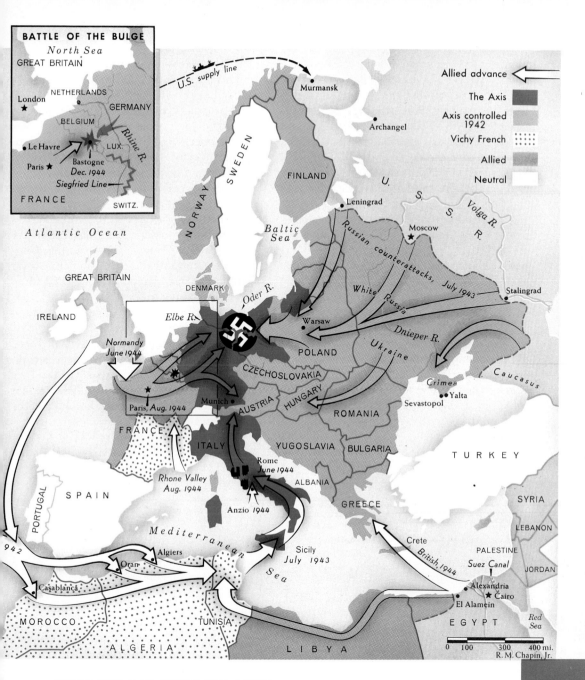

BATTLE OF THE BULGE

North Sea

GREAT BRITAIN

NETHERLANDS

London ★

GERMANY

BELGIUM

Le Havre •

LUX.

Rhine R.

Paris ★

Bastogne
Dec. 1944

Siegfried Line

FRANCE

SWITZ.

Atlantic Ocean

U.S. supply line

Murmansk •

Allied advance

The Axis

Axis controlled
1942

Vichy French

Allied

Neutral

• Archangel

SWEDEN

NORWAY

FINLAND

U.

S.

S.

Volga R.

• Leningrad

Moscow
★

Russian counterattacks, July 1943

• Stalingrad

Baltic Sea

GREAT BRITAIN

DENMARK

Oder R.

Elbe R.

IRELAND

Normandy
June 1944

• Warsaw

White Russia

Dnieper R.

POLAND

CZECHOSLOVAKIA

Ukraine

Crimea

Caucasus

•• Yalta

Sevastopol

Paris, Aug. 1944

Munich •

AUSTRIA

HUNGARY

ROMANIA

FRANCE

ITALY

YUGOSLAVIA

BULGARIA

TURKEY

Rome
June 1944

Rhone Valley
Aug. 1944

ALBANIA

SYRIA

PORTUGAL

SPAIN

Anzio 1944

GREECE

LEBANON

Mediterranean

Crete

PALESTINE

Suez Canal

JORDAN

942

Algiers •

Sicily
July 1943

British 1944

• Alexandria

★ Cairo

Oran •

Sea

• El Alamein

Casablanca •

MOROCCO

TUNISIA

EGYPT

Red
Sea

ALGERIA

LIBYA

0   100   300   400 mi.

R. M. Chapin, Jr.

WORLD WAR II IN EUROPE AND AFRICA

To crush the Axis, the western Allies counterattacked in North Africa and then invaded Italy and France. Driving eastward from France and westward from Russia, the Allies swept across Germany, thus destroying the Nazi state.

Germany surrendered. The future of Poland was also discussed. The three leaders agreed that Russia would retain part of eastern Poland, while the Poles, in return, would receive territory from Germany.

The Allies land in Normandy. The long-awaited invasion of western Europe began on June 6, 1944 — D-Day. Allied military leaders had carefully planned the operation. Heavy bombing of the French coast had disrupted German transport and communication. But heavy German fire met the 120,000 troops who landed on the Normandy beaches the first day of the invasion. The enemy fought the invaders from concrete pillboxes, protected by barbed wire, mines, tank traps, and formidable artillery. Nevertheless, two months later more than one million British and American soldiers were fighting in northern France under the command of General Eisenhower. Meanwhile, another Allied army had landed in southern France and was fighting its way up the Rhone valley. The French underground harassed Nazi communications, thus aiding the Allied advance. By October, 1944, all of France was liberated. The retreating Germans lost 500,000 men, many planes and tanks, and huge quantities of munitions and supplies.

The cross-Channel invasion was paralleled by a great Russian offensive on the eastern front. Russian armies had occupied Bulgaria and Romania and were driving into Hungary and Yugoslavia. Farther north, the Red° Army invaded Finland, which in 1941 had joined in the German attack on Russia. By the time France had been freed, Russian troops were fighting their way into Poland and Czechoslovakia.

The Allies invade Germany from east and west. With British, French, and American forces advancing toward German soil and Russian troops marching through Poland, many people thought the war was almost over. But they failed to take into account the insane determination of Hitler. The German leader ordered that the Allied advance be resisted to the bitter end and demanded that German officers adopt a "scorched-earth" policy as they retreated.

By mid-September, 1944, American forces had entered Germany. In November, General Eisenhower launched an attack on Germany's heavily defended Siegfried Line. But in December a desperate German counterattack drove twenty miles into Allied lines before it was halted at Bastogne. This Battle of the Bulge took the lives of thousands of Allied soldiers, but it exhausted the German troops and proved to be their last offensive. Meanwhile, the Russian troops were driving toward the Oder River in eastern Germany.

The United States advances in the Pacific. In the Pacific theater of war (page

Part of the great fleet of Allied warships that landed in Normandy on D-Day is shown above. At right, Dwight Eisenhower, commander-in-chief of the operation, confers with Field Marshal Bernard Montgomery, who commanded Allied ground forces in the invasion.

The "Big Three" leaders — Churchill, Roosevelt, and Stalin — met at Yalta early in 1945. Some two months later, President Roosevelt was dead.

735), the Allied strategy called for "island-hopping" advances against the Japanese. Instead of clearing the enemy off every island, American forces attacked only the most important Japanese holdings in the Pacific. In February, 1944, an American naval force took the Marshall Islands. By mid-summer, Admiral Nimitz had captured Guam and Saipan, less than 1500 miles from Japan. From these bases American bombers began attacking the enemy homeland.

In October, 1944, General MacArthur returned to the Philippines with an invasion force, thus carrying out the promise he had made in the dark days of 1942. A few days after the invasion, the greatest naval battle in history was fought in the Gulf of Leyte. The Japanese suffered a staggering defeat, losing most of the striking power of their fleet. During the following winter, MacArthur's troops pressed on toward Manila, while Nimitz's forces continued their leap-frogging approach to Japan.

The Big Three meet at Yalta. In February, 1945, Churchill, Roosevelt, and Stalin met at Yalta in the Crimea for the most important of their wartime conferences. They discussed both military strategy and the postwar settlement. The Big Three agreed to disarm Germany after its defeat, and to divide the country into four occupation zones to be administered by Britain, the United States, Russia, and France. Another basic decision at Yalta concerned the political future of nations in eastern Europe

— Poland, Czechoslovakia, Hungary, Bulgaria, Romania, and Yugoslavia. The Soviet Union, whose troops had occupied most of eastern Europe, promised to hold free elections in these countries.

The Big Three also discussed the situation in the Far East. American military advisers wanted Soviet assistance in the war against Japan. They had warned the President that an invasion of Japan might cost the lives of a million American soldiers, and that victory would not be achieved before 1946. After some prodding by Roosevelt and Churchill, Stalin agreed to declare war on Japan within three months after the surrender of Germany. In exchange Stalin was promised the restoration of the Kurile Islands and southern Sakhalin. Despite the earlier pledge to Chiang Kai-shek (page 742), Russia was promised special privileges in Manchuria at the close of the war. Stalin, however, promised Roosevelt to sign a "pact of friendship and alliance" with the Chiang Kai-shek government.

Roosevelt's critics later charged that he and Churchill paid too high a price for Soviet participation in the war against Japan. But no one at that time could have foreseen that the atomic bomb would so quickly end the war with Japan. Indeed, in February, 1945, the scientists at Los Alamos could not even be sure that their experiment would succeed.

Roosevelt's critics also accused him of "giving away" eastern Europe to the Communists at Yalta. Prior to this conference, Churchill had shown some awareness of the danger of a Communist take-over, particularly in the Balkans. But both leaders hoped that Stalin would live up to his promises concerning free elections in the eastern European countries. Even if they had mistrusted Stalin's intentions, there was no way short of war to *force* the Communists to hold free elections in eastern Europe. Both Churchill and Roosevelt believed that the establishment of a world organization of nations provided the only real assurance of peace. And they had Stalin's promise that Russia would co-operate in a peacetime United Nations. In such an organization problems that had not been solved during the war could be given consideration.

Soviet actions inspire distrust. Early in 1945, with Russian, American, and British troops pushing into Germany, Stalin took steps to advance Soviet interests without regard for the views of Roosevelt and Churchill. Even before the Yalta meetings, the Soviet Union had recognized a Communist-led regime in Poland, despite British and American protests. When the Soviets soon after the Yalta conference also installed a Communist government in Romania, they openly violated the pledge of free elections. Moreover, Stalin charged Roosevelt and Churchill with attempting to negotiate a separate peace with Germany.

Roosevelt and Churchill watched these Soviet maneuvers with concern. The President dismissed the Russian charges about a separate peace effort as "vile misrepresentations." Roosevelt also sent Stalin a sharply worded message concerning "the lack of progress made in carrying out. . . . the political decisions which we reached at Yalta, particularly those relating to the Polish question." In a message to Churchill regarding dealings with the Russians, Roosevelt said, "We must be firm."

Roosevelt dies before the end of the war. Worn out by the heavy burdens of his office, the President went to Warm Springs, Georgia, to rest. There, on April 12, 1945, President Roosevelt died of a cerebral hemorrhage. He was, said one historian, "as truly a casualty of war as any man who died in battle." Roosevelt's death denied

him the privilege of seeing the total defeat of the Axis powers. It also meant that he was spared the tragedy of seeing the wartime co-operation with the Soviet Union turn into a "cold war" between communism and democracy.

Germany surrenders. By February, 1945, the Allies had regained the territory lost in the Battle of the Bulge and were ready to launch their final drive into Germany. They crossed the Rhine River in March, while the Russians crossed the Oder River and raced westward toward Berlin. Concerned about Stalin's violation of the Yalta agreements, Churchill believed that Allied troops should try to reach Berlin before the Russians. For military reasons, however, General Eisenhower felt that the Allies should concentrate on destroying the German armies. Both Roosevelt and his successor, President Truman, sided with Eisenhower. As a result, it was the Russians who took Berlin at the end of April.

The fall of Berlin spelled the end of Nazi Germany. Hitler committed suicide in his underground fortification as the Russians entered the city. American and Russian troops met on the Elbe River late in April, and the remaining German forces began to surrender. The fighting in northern Italy ended on May 2. Five days later a German field marshal signed an unconditional surrender at Allied headquarters in Rheims. On May 8 (V-E Day), the war in Europe officially came to an end.

American forces drive closer to Japan. While the European conflict was grinding to a close, General MacArthur's forces were defeating the Japanese in the Philippines. The Americans recaptured Manila in February, 1945, and after months of hard fighting drove the enemy from the island of Luzon.

As Admiral Nimitz's forces drew nearer the Japanese homeland, they found the enemy determined to fight to the last man. In February, American marines landed on Iwo Jima, a tiny island 750 miles from Tokyo. It took one month and 20,000 American casualties to capture this island. But the air base on Iwo Jima allowed the Americans to step up their bombings of Japanese cities. American naval and land forces then

An aerial view of the Allied attack on Iwo Jima (above) showed the white trails of invading ships and Mount Suribachi in the background but gave no hint of the savage fighting necessary to capture the island. Marines in the South Pacific often had to fight in jungle terrain. Only guns and ammunition stay dry as marines in the picture at right struggle through jungle swamps on an island near New Guinea.

invaded the large island of Okinawa, still closer to Japan. Japanese suicide pilots flew their planes into American warships in a vain effort to drive off the attacking fleet. Nearly 200 American ships were damaged or destroyed by these tactics, and the total American casualties in the Okinawa campaign reached 45,000. But the conquest of Okinawa late in June gave the United States an important base less than 400 miles from Japan.

Atomic bombs force Japan to surrender. In July the heads of the Allied nations met at Potsdam, Germany. It was there that President Truman received word of the successful atomic explosion at Los Alamos (page 740). The Allied leaders then issued an ultimatum to Japan: "The alternative to surrender is prompt and utter destruction." The Potsdam ultimatum did not spell out the nature of the destruction, and the Japanese government chose to ignore it. One official dismissed it as "unworthy of public notice."

President Truman was convinced that the Japanese war lords would never surrender until American troops had invaded and conquered the home islands. The cost in American lives, judging from the Iwo Jima and Okinawa campaigns, would be enormous. Consequently, the President made the fateful decision to use the atomic bomb. At the time the first atomic bomb was dropped, President Truman told the world that he realized "the tragic significance" of his decision. We had beaten Nazi scientists in "the race of discovery," he said, and "having found the bomb we have used it. . . . We have used it in order to shorten the agony of war, in order to save the lives of thousands and thousands of young Americans."

On August 6 the awesome new weapon was dropped on the Japanese city of Hiroshima. Equal to the explosive power of 20,000 tons of TNT, the atomic bomb did as much damage as would a thousand airplanes dropping conventional bombs. Two days later, the Soviet Union declared war on Japan and invaded Manchuria. Still the

Japanese would not surrender. On August 9, a second atomic bomb was dropped on the city of Nagasaki, with even more devastating results. The Japanese government then agreed to unconditional surrender, asking only that the emperor be allowed to remain as head of state. On September 2 (V-J Day), the official surrender terms were signed aboard the American battleship *Missouri* in Tokyo Bay.

▶ CHECK-UP

1. What agreements were reached by Allied leaders at conferences in Casablanca? Moscow? Cairo? Teheran? Why did the Allies invade Italy? What were the results?

2. How did the Allies strike at Germany from the east and the west? What agreements were reached at Yalta? What tensions developed in relations with the USSR? How did the war in Europe come to an end?

3. Why was "island-hopping" used in the war with Japan? Why were atomic bombs used to bring the conflict to a close?

· · · · · · · · · · · · · · · · · ·

4 *The United Nations Is Established*

Americans favor international co-operation. Long before the end of the war, American leaders were giving thought to the postwar settlement. Public opinion in the United States definitely favored a worldwide organization of nations to prevent future aggression and to avoid another world war. In September, 1943, the House of Representatives passed a resolution introduced by Representative J. William Fulbright of Arkansas. The resolution called for American participation in an international organization with enough power to establish and maintain world peace.

The first official approval of a postwar successor to the League of Nations came at the Moscow conference of foreign ministers in 1943. The Moscow Pact called for the establishment of an "international organization, based on the principle of the sovereign equality of all peace-loving states, and open to membership by all such states . . . for the maintenance of international peace and security." This document was signed by representatives of the United States, Britain, the Soviet Union, and China. The United States Senate endorsed the proposal of American participation in such an organization by a vote of 85 to 5.

Concrete plans are made for international co-operation. During 1943 and 1944 several important steps were taken to further the goal of international co-operation. One was the creation of the United Nations Relief and Rehabilitation Administration (UNRRA). Its function was to assist the people in the countries liberated from the Nazis. Another was the meeting in July, 1944, of financial experts from 44 countries at Bretton Woods, New Hampshire, to

General Douglas MacArthur (left) and other high-ranking Allied officers look on as the Japanese sign surrender papers on the battleship Missouri *in 1945.*

plan for postwar economic co-operation. They set up an International Bank for Reconstruction and Development and also proposed an International Monetary Fund to stabilize currencies threatened by inflation.

A month after the Bretton Woods Conference, delegates of the United States, Britain, Russia, and later China met at Dumbarton Oaks, a mansion in Washington, D.C. They gathered for the purpose of drafting a charter for the proposed world organization, by this time referred to as the United Nations Organization. The general recommendations of this conference provided the basis for the plan later adopted at San Francisco.

Plans are made at Yalta for the San Francisco Convention. The Russians had raised a number of questions about the proposed UN organization worked out at Dumbarton Oaks. Roosevelt and Churchill hoped to settle these issues when they met with Stalin at Yalta early in 1945. The Dumbarton Oaks draft called for a General Assembly, with representatives from all member nations, and a smaller Security Council, which would include the Big Three as permament members. Stalin proposed that the permanent members of the Security Council have veto power over all major decisions. He also insisted that each of the sixteen republics of the Soviet Union have a vote in the General Assembly. Churchill and Roosevelt agreed to the veto power in the Security Council, but they objected to Stalin's demand for sixteen votes in the General Assembly. When Roosevelt implied that the United States might be entitled to 48 votes, Stalin gave way and agreed to three votes — one for the Soviet Union, one for the Ukraine, and one for White Russia. Finally, the Big Three issued a call for the United Nations to meet in San Francisco in April, 1945, to approve a charter.

The United Nations prepare a charter. In planning for the San Francisco Conference, President Roosevelt tried to avoid Woodrow Wilson's errors. The Charter of the United Nations was kept entirely separate from any peace treaty. Moreover, to attend the San Francisco meeting, the Presi-

One of Harry Truman's first important acts as President was to welcome the Allied nations at the San Francisco Conference only a few days after Franklin Roosevelt's death.

dent appointed a bipartisan delegation, which included a Republican and a Democrat from each house of Congress. It was Franklin Roosevelt's successor, President Harry Truman, however, who welcomed the delegates from 50 nations. "If we do not want to die together in war," said President Truman, "we must learn to live together in peace."

The Charter adopted by the San Francisco Conference included the following provisions:

(1) A General Assembly of all member nations might discuss any question or any matter within the scope of the United Nations Charter.

(2) A Security Council was to consist of the United States, Great Britain, the Soviet Union, France, and China as permanent members plus six non-permanent members chosen by the Assembly. It was authorized to investigate international disputes, foster their peaceful settlement, and take diplomatic, economic, and military action against aggressors. The Security Council could make decisions on important matters by the affirmative vote of seven members, includ-

ing the five permanent members. Thus, each of the "Big Five" nations had a veto power over the actions of the Council. In settling international disputes, however, the nations involved in a particular dispute had no vote.

(3) An Economic and Social Council, responsible to the General Assembly and including numerous commissions and agencies, was to seek solutions to social and economic problems. None of the commissions or agencies was to be hampered by the veto.

(4) An International Court of Justice was to pass judgment on the legal aspects of international disputes submitted to it.

(5) A Trusteeship Council was to investigate conditions in territories that were held in trust by the United Nations and to advise the Assembly on the supervision of such territories.

(6) Provision was also made for a Permanent Secretariat, headed by a Secretary-General, to co-ordinate the work of the United Nations.

The United Nations Charter is ratified. The Charter was to become effective when it was ratified by the "Big Five" powers and by a majority of the 45 other nations that had signed the Charter. In the United States Senate, action was prompt and decisive. Twenty-five years before, that body had rejected the League of Nations. But in July, 1945, the Senate debated the United Nations Charter for only six days and then approved it by an overwhelming vote. By October, enough other nations had ratified the Charter to make the new world organization a reality.

▶ CHECK-UP

1. How were plans for an international organization furthered by the Moscow Pact? By UNRRA? By the Bretton Woods, Dumbarton Oaks, and Yalta conferences?

2. What bodies were provided for in the United Nations Charter? What was to be the function of each?

3. What sentiment existed in the United States concerning membership in the United Nations organization?

* * * * * * * * * * * * * * * * * * * *

Clinching the Main Ideas in Chapter 35

The United States played a crucial role in winning the Second World War. This war, to an even greater extent than the First World War, affected the lives of almost all Americans. Over twelve million men and women served in the various branches of the nation's armed forces, while civilians on the home front gave all possible support to the war effort.

Dark days followed the attack at Pearl Harbor, as Japanese forces made conquests in Southeast Asia and threatened to rule the Pacific. But American naval and air power soon halted the Japanese advance and began the recapture of strategic islands in the Pacific. Meanwhile, Allied landings in Africa, Italy, and France and the Russian counterattack on the eastern front turned the tide in Europe. A few months after the collapse of Nazi Germany, the dropping of atomic bombs on two Japanese cities forced Japan to surrender.

The Allied coalition was an uneasy one in many respects. Roosevelt and Churchill and their staffs worked together well. But the Western powers never achieved the same degree of understanding or co-operation with the Soviet Union. After the Teheran Conference, Roosevelt, Churchill, and Stalin issued a statement saying they were "friends in fact, in spirit, and in purpose." This hopeful atmosphere generally still prevailed at Yalta where the Big Three reached important decisions bearing on the postwar settlement. Within a few weeks after this conference, however, Stalin's violation of the Yalta promises disturbed Roosevelt and angered Churchill.

Because of Roosevelt's untimely death in April, 1945, his successor, Harry Truman, presided over the San Francisco conference that established the United Nations. The United States Senate quickly approved this country's membership in the UN. It was, however, Franklin Roosevelt and Winston Churchill who had been the architects of the military victory which ended World War II in 1945, and of the new world organization which was established by the Allied nations in that same year.

Chapter Review

Terms to Understand

1. radar
2. sonar
3. V-E Day
4. V-J Day
5. UNRRA
6. Moscow Pact
7. Burma Road
8. FEPC
9. WPB
10. OPA
11. cold war
12. Manhattan District Project
13. United Nations
14. Security Council
15. Yalta Conference
16. Trusteeship Council
17. Economic and Social Council
18. Bretton Woods Conference
19. Dumbarton Oaks Conference
20. San Francisco Conference
21. French underground
22. Battle of the Bulge

What Do You Think?

1. Contrast the strategies advocated by Churchill and by Stalin in 1942 and 1943. Why did each advocate the course of action he did?

2. What are the implications of the fact that between 1939 and 1945 national income in this country increased from 73 billion to 181 billion dollars, while the number of persons paying federal income tax increased from 4 million to 42 million?

3. On what grounds have the agreements approved by Roosevelt at Yalta been criticized? Evaluate these criticisms.

4. Since 1941 the United States has "realized its world responsibilities." What policies that have been adopted can be cited to support this point of view?

Using Your Knowledge of History

1. Debate: *Resolved,* That President Truman was justified in using the atomic bomb to end the war with Japan.

2. In a two-column chart, contrast procedures followed by Wilson and by Roosevelt and Truman in seeking to insure participation by this country in a world peace organization.

3. Write a letter to a newspaper defending or criticizing the "relocation" of the West Coast Japanese-Americans.

4. Write a brief essay expressing your views concerning the Allied policy of unconditional surrender in World War II.

Extending Your Knowledge of History

A brief survey of the war is *War for the World* by Fletcher Pratt. In *Strategy and Compromise,* Samuel E. Morison analyzes wartime strategy. Hanson W. Baldwin's *Great Mistakes of the War* is more critical of Allied decisions. Dwight D. Eisenhower recounts his wartime experiences in *Crusade in Europe.* For a description of the home front, see *While You Were Gone,* edited by Jack Goodman. The soldier's view is recorded by Ernie Pyle's *Brave Men* and Bill Mauldin's *Up Front.*

Analyzing Unit Ten

1. The historian Samuel Eliot Morison wrote that the New Deal was as "American as a bale of hay." What earlier reforms and political experiments influenced the New Deal? What was *new* in Roosevelt's legislative program?

2. The New Deal was both an emergency program to meet the challenge of the depression and a reform movement to remedy injustices. What steps were taken by President Roosevelt to cure the depression? What long-range reforms did he sponsor? To what extent did these stem from the reaction to Republican "rule" in the 1920's?

3. During the 1930's, American isolationists felt that they were realists in taking into account lessons learned during World War I. What conclusions did they draw from this country's participation in World War I? How did their conclusions influence the formulation of American foreign policy during the 1930's? Why did many Americans support the isolationists during the mid-1930's but break away from them toward the end of the decade?

Unit 11 | The United States Exercises World Leadership (1945-Today)

President Kennedy and Indian Prime Minister Nehru in 1961

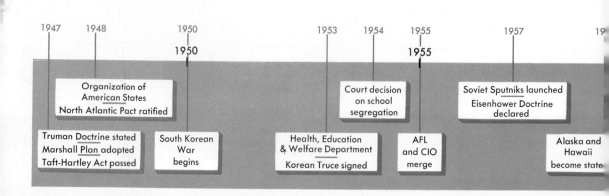

1947 1948   1950   1953   1954   1955   1957   19

1950   1955

Organization of
American States
North Atlantic Pact ratified

Court decision
on school
segregation

Soviet Sputniks launched
Eisenhower Doctrine
declared

Truman Doctrine stated
Marshall Plan adopted
Taft-Hartley Act passed

South Korean
War
begins

Health, Education
& Welfare Department

Korean Truce signed

AFL
and CIO
merge

Alaska and
Hawaii
become state

fter World War II, there was no breathing spell during which Americans did not have to be concerned about the rest of the world. Even before the fighting ended, it was apparent that the Russians were determined to impose Communist rule on countries they had liberated from the Nazis. In fact, the avowed purpose of Soviet leaders was to spread communism throughout the world. President Truman responded to this challenge with firmness, particularly when Communist pressures threatened Greece, Turkey, and Berlin. American aid administered through the Marshall Plan helped restore the shattered economies of west European nations; and American leadership helped organize the North Atlantic Treaty Organization for mutual defense against Communist aggression.

The cold war was not restricted to Europe. The United States and other United Nations countries beat back a Communist invasion of South Korea. In the 1950's President Eisenhower had to cope with Communist threats in Southeast Asia, the Middle East, and elsewhere. During his brief presidency, John F. Kennedy won a decisive showdown when the Russians established missile bases in Cuba. More recently President Johnson has sought to save South Vietnam from Communist domination.

Hanging like a dark cloud over these cold-war conflicts has been the threat of nuclear warfare. A limited test ban between the United States and Russia in 1963 was a step in the right direction but fell far short of an effective disarmament program. The ever-present threat of atomic destruction increases the danger of every local conflict, as does the fact that more nations are developing nuclear weapons.

During the period since World War II, Americans have been grappling with important economic and social problems. President Truman had urged Congress, without success, to approve a national health insurance and an effective guarantee of Negro civil rights. During the Eisenhower years Negroes began a broad-based movement to obtain equal civil rights. Before his tragic assassination President Kennedy called for sweeping legislation in this area. Then President Johnson pushed a civil rights program through Congress after he entered the White House. Because of his skill in working with Congress, and with the help of heavy Democratic majorities, Johnson also secured passage of a far-reaching program of social welfare measures.

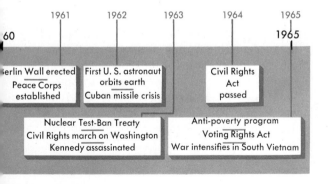

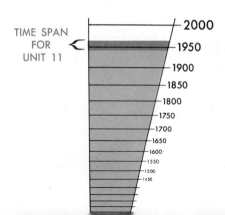

CHAPTER 36

The Cold War
Presents New
Challenges

We have got to understand that all our lives the danger, the uncertainty, the need for alertness, for effort, for discipline will be upon us.

DEAN ACHESON, 1946

American and Soviet representatives meet at tenth UN session

1945–1960

After every other war in their history, Americans had enjoyed a period of relaxation — a breather, so to speak. But no such interlude followed the Second World War. The hope of many Americans that the Western powers and the Soviet Union would continue their wartime co-operation was soon dashed. Instead, the Soviet Union made clear its intention of extending communism throughout the world and showed no desire to co-operate with the Western powers within the United Nations. Less than a year after the end of the war, Winston Churchill spoke of the "iron curtain" that sealed off Com-munist-held territory in eastern Europe. Americans soon realized that the democracies were engaged in a "cold war" with Communist totalitarianism and that the danger and the uncertainty of the war years were by no means over.

Thrust into the presidency by Roosevelt's death, President Truman met the challenge with courage and imagination both in Europe and in Asia. From 1945 until the Korean War, his bold proposals in foreign policy were endorsed by both Democrats and Republicans in Congress. The Marshall Plan hastened the economic recovery of Europe, and the North Atlantic

Treaty Organization provided for a common defense against Soviet Russia.

President Eisenhower, who took office in 1953, also had bipartisan support in foreign affairs. His persistent, though unsuccessful, search for a disarmament formula that the Russians would accept and his willingness to "go to the summit" to lessen cold-war tensions were applauded by the American people. Meanwhile, the number of trouble spots involved in the cold war multiplied as crises inflamed such far-flung areas as Southeast Asia, the Middle East, and Latin America.

1 *Postwar Friction Develops Between Russia and the West*

When Harry Truman heard that President Roosevelt was dead, he felt, he said, as if "the stars and all the planets fell on me." He asked reporters to pray for him, for "I've got the most terribly responsible job any man ever had." Truman did indeed inherit enormous responsibilities. The long war in Europe was drawing to a close, and the question of what to do with conquered Germany demanded attention. Moreover, it was impossible to predict when the struggle with Japan would end. And, as Harry Truman took the oath of office, the United Nations conference was about to convene in San Francisco (page 749).

. . . .

CHAPTER FOCUS

1. Postwar friction develops between Russia and the West.

2. Communist aggression is checked in Germany and Korea.

3. The cold war continues under President Eisenhower.

The Allied powers consider the fate of Germany. Shortly after Germany surrendered, President Truman, Prime Minister Clement Attlee of Great Britain, and Soviet Premier Stalin met in Potsdam (page 747) to lay plans for the future of Germany. They agreed to divide Germany into four military zones of occupation, to be supervised by an Allied Control Council of American, British, French, and Soviet generals. Germany was to be disarmed and to pay reparations, and the Nazi leaders were to stand trial as war criminals.

During 1945 and 1946 an international military court at Nuremberg, Germany, heard the sickening story of Nazi brutality. Of the top Nazi officials, ten were hanged, eight sentenced to prison and one committed suicide. Less important Nazis were turned over to special courts, the "denazification" courts, for trial. In the American zone over 500,000 Germans were found guilty of war crimes and other offenses.

The Western powers revise their German policy. The war trials were one point on which the four powers could agree with respect to Germany. But in other matters there was continued conflict. In the eastern zone the Soviets dismantled German factories and shipped machinery and anything else they thought they could use to the Soviet Union. Moreover, the Soviets proceeded to set up a Communist government in their zone. Repeated protests by American, British, and French officials in the Allied Control Council had no effect. After 1946, therefore, the Western powers gradually changed their German policy. Instead of repressing the Germans, they began to encourage economic recovery. They also took steps to unite the British, French, and American occupation zones in preparation for restoring independence to West Germany.

Two German states are formed. In May, 1949, the three western zones became the German Federal Republic. The Soviet Union responded by establishing a so-called German Democratic Republic in the eastern zone. The cold war, therefore, produced two Germanies: one democratic and bound to the Western powers by economic and political ties; the other a satellite of the Soviet Union.

Peace treaties are signed with eastern European states. At the Potsdam Conference it had been agreed that a Council of Foreign Ministers was to draw up peace treaties with the enemy countries. Serving on the Council were the foreign ministers of the major Allied powers. For about a year the Council worked on the details of peace treaties with Italy, Finland, Bulgaria, Hungary, and Romania. The meetings were marked by constant wrangling between the Soviet representative and the spokesmen for the Western powers. It became clear that the Soviet Union would not permit the holding of free elections in Bulgaria, Hungary, and Romania, all of which were occupied by Soviet troops. But in order to secure Soviet approval of peace treaties with Italy and Finland, the Western powers accepted Russia's terms for the other three countries. No progress was made at that time in working out peace treaties for Austria and Germany.

American occupation forces govern Japan. Because of Russian opposition in Europe, President Truman resolved that American troops would carry out the occupation of Japan. A Far Eastern Commission in Washington and an Allied Council in Tokyo represented the countries which had fought against Japan, but their duties were merely advisory. Actual power lay in the hands of General Douglas MacArthur, who gave orders to the Japanese emperor and government. The emperor was stripped of his political power and his claims to divinity. He was permitted, however, to retain his title and his position as head of state. As in Germany, the wartime leaders of Japan were tried for their war crimes. Premier Tojo and six others were executed, and 4000 lesser officials were sentenced to prison terms.

Under General MacArthur's direction, political, social, and economic life in Japan underwent tremendous changes. Large land holdings and huge industrial organizations were broken up, thereby greatly reducing the power of the former ruling classes. A new constitution provided for an elected legislature and guaranteed the civil rights of all Japanese citizens. Women were given the right to vote, a democratic school system was established, and workers were encouraged to form trade unions.

In 1951 the Allies (not including the USSR) signed a peace treaty with Japan. The treaty ended the American occupation and permitted Japan to establish a small defense force. At the same time, the United States and Japan signed a treaty allowing the United States to maintain military bases in Japan.

The United States tries to help Chiang Kai-shek's government. China, the United States' wartime ally, presented more of a problem in the postwar era than did Japan. Throughout World War II, President Roosevelt had at times tried to deal with Chiang Kai-shek as an ally equal in stature to Churchill and Stalin. It was the President's hope that Chiang would eventually be able to put his own house in order and help defeat Japan. President Truman continued this policy. The Chinese were included in the Council of Foreign Ministers and given a permanent seat in the UN Security Council.

Chiang Kai-shek's government had contributed less than hoped for to the winning of World War II. Although Europe had top priority, the United States provided Chiang with arms, munitions, and medicines. But even President Roosevelt was discouraged by the ineffective Nationalist campaign against the Japanese. Moreover, corruption and dictatorial rule weakened the Nationalist government. By the war's end, millions of Chinese had made common cause with the Chinese Communists, headed by Mao Tse-tung (*mah'* oh *dzoo' doong'*).

In an effort to prevent civil war, President Truman sent General George C. Marshall to China late in 1945. Marshall brought the Nationalists and Communists together for talks that might lead to a coalition government. After months of negotiations, however, General Marshall concluded that neither side was willing to co-operate with the other. He placed the blame equally on the fanatic Communists and the "irreconcilable groups" supporting

Tokyo, the world's biggest metropolitan area, is a city of sharp contrasts. Behind the peaceful grounds of the imperial palace (above left) rises a background of office and factory buildings. Modern and traditional dress can both be seen on downtown streets (left). Though traffic within Tokyo is as congested as in any other modern city, a speedy monorail and superhighways (above) provide fast transportation outside the city.

Chiang who were "interested in the preservation of their own feudal control of China."

In 1947 General Albert Wedemeyer was sent to China in an effort to break the deadlock. Although his report gave evidence of the corruption and inefficiency of the Nationalist government, he concluded that extensive aid to Chiang Kai-shek was the only way to defeat the Communists. Between 1945 and 1949 Congress granted more than three billion dollars in aid to the Chinese Nationalists. But frequent American requests that Chiang Kai-shek undertake political, economic, and social reforms brought no results.

The Communist conquest of China disturbs Americans. Chiang's inability to cope with his country's long-standing problems caused the Chinese army and people to lose confidence in his government. Communist forces drove Nationalist troops out of Manchuria and continued to make further gains. Near the end of 1949 Chiang Kai-shek, a small band of loyal followers, and the remnant of his army retreated to the island of Formosa. The Communists established control over the mainland.

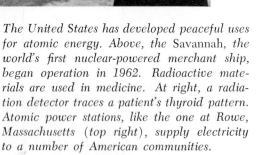

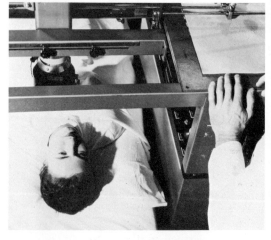

The United States has developed peaceful uses for atomic energy. Above, the Savannah, *the world's first nuclear-powered merchant ship, began operation in 1962. Radioactive materials are used in medicine. At right, a radiation detector traces a patient's thyroid pattern. Atomic power stations, like the one at Rowe, Massachusetts (top right), supply electricity to a number of American communities.*

The fall of China to the Communists touched off a bitter debate in the United States. Administration supporters blamed Chiang for his failure to rally the Chinese people. General Wedemeyer said the Nationalist defeat was due to "lack of spirit. It was not the lack of equipment. In my judgment they could have defended the Yangtze [River] with broomsticks if they had the will to do it." But President Truman's critics charged that too much attention had been paid to Communist threats in Europe and not enough to Communist aggression in China. China could have been saved, they claimed, if the State Department had not allowed prejudice against Chiang to stand in the way of giving the Nationalists all-out support.

Two things were clear in the "Chinese tangle." At no time during the postwar years had either the Republicans or the Democrats been willing to send American troops into China and thus risk a third world war. Moreover, neither party was willing to have the United States recognize the new Communist government of China. Britain and many other countries extended diplomatic recognition to Communist China. But the United States and the United Nations continued to treat Chiang's government on Formosa as the legitimate government of China. Furthermore, the American government saw to it that Nationalist China kept its seat in the UN Security Council and that the Communist "People's Republic" of China was denied admission to the UN.

No agreement is reached on atomic control. The United States' use of atomic bombs against Japan had created a problem that concerned all nations — how to control this fearsome new weapon. Until 1949 the United States was the only country in the world with atomic weapons. President Truman had made it clear that we would not endanger world peace by giving atomic secrets to other countries. It was known, however, that Russian scientists were working on atomic weapons. Hence, it was urgent that some type of international control be established.

In 1946 the United States proposed that the UN establish an International Atomic Development Authority, which would regulate the use of atomic energy throughout the world. The UN agency would have the right to inspect all atomic plants and to punish countries which violated its rules. This plan was approved by most UN members. But the Soviet Union refused to agree to inspection by an outside agency of atomic plants within its territory. The Russians offered a counter-proposal which called for (1) the destruction of the United States' stockpile of atomic bombs and (2) an agreement by all nations not to make atomic weapons. The Soviet plan would have permitted each country to enforce the agreement within its own borders.

The United States was willing to destroy its bombs but not until a system of international inspection had been established. Truman declared that the United States would surrender its atomic monopoly whenever the Soviet Union accepted UN inspection. The Soviets refused, and discussions stalled. Meanwhile, the United States created an Atomic Energy Commission to pursue peaceful uses of atomic power.

The Soviet Union establishes satellites in eastern Europe. The Soviet Union's obstinacy in the UN and in the Council of Foreign Ministers deepened the rift between the Communists and the Western powers. Fear and suspicion increased as Russia put Communists in control of the governments of Poland, Romania, Bulgaria, Czechoslovakia, Albania, and Hungary.[1]

[1] Three other east European states — Estonia, Lithuania, and Latvia — had been annexed by the Soviet Union at the beginning of World War II. In Yugoslavia a national Communist government rose to power without Soviet aid.

Thus, these nations became Soviet satellites. Though independent in name, they were in fact dominated by the Soviet Union.

As soon as the Communists came to power in the satellite nations, they eliminated freedom of speech and of the press. Then they imprisoned their political opponents or executed them. Such tactics disturbed Russia's former allies. Though some Americans still hoped for postwar co-operation with the Soviet Union, most became disillusioned and angry. Some even talked about using the bomb on the Russians while the United States still had a monopoly.

The United States adopts a policy of containment. In 1947, President Truman and his advisers reluctantly decided on a "get tough" policy toward the Russians. This attitude was shared by the British. In a speech delivered at Fulton, Missouri, in 1946, Winston Churchill stressed the need for a policy of strength:

> From Stettin in the Baltic to Trieste in the Adriatic, an iron curtain has descended across the Continent. . . . I do not believe that Soviet Russia desires war. What they desire is the fruits of war and the indefinite expansion of their power and doctrines. . . . I am convinced that there is nothing they admire so much as strength, and there is nothing for which they have less respect than weakness, especially military weakness.

A strong defense was also advocated by George F. Kennan, an American foreign policy expert. He wrote that the American attitude "toward the Soviet Union must be that of a long-term, patient but firm and vigilant containment of Russian expansive tendencies." In other words, the United States must wage the cold war by *containing* communism within the iron-curtain countries.

The Truman Doctrine checks the spread of communism. The containment policy was put to the test in 1947. Since the war, British troops had been helping the Greek government in its fight to put down a Communist-directed rebellion. Facing a financial crisis at home, the British informed President Truman that they would have to withdraw their troops from Greece. This withdrawal would almost certainly have meant the triumph of communism in Greece and probably in Turkey as well.

President Truman met this challenge with a bold proposal. He asked Congress to appropriate 400 million dollars for aid to Greece and Turkey. The President's explanation of the need to block Communist expansion has come to be known as the Truman Doctrine. Said Truman:

> I believe that it must be the policy of the United States to support free peoples who are resisting attempted subjugation by armed minorities or by outside pressures. . . . The free peoples of the world look to us for support in maintaining their freedoms. If we falter in our leadership, we may endanger the peace of the world — and we shall surely endanger the welfare of this nation.

Members of both parties supported aid for Greece and Turkey. This bipartisan support was due in part to Senator Arthur Vandenberg, the Republican chairman of the Senate Foreign Relations Committee, who had formerly been an isolationist. It also reflected the respect that both Democrats and Republicans had for George Marshall, who in 1947 became Secretary of State. By 1950 the United States had granted about 650 million dollars in aid to Greece and Turkey and had helped both countries fight off the threat of Communist expansion.

The Marshall Plan aids European recovery. The financial crisis that had forced Britain to pull out of Greece was typical of postwar troubles in other western European nations. In addition to a shortage of capital, crops were poor, UNRRA aid (page 748) was coming to an end, and in France and Italy Communist Parties were making gains. "The patient is sinking," said Secretary of State Marshall, "while the doctors deliberate." In June, 1947, Marshall announced that European economic recovery was a major goal of American foreign policy:

> Our policy is directed not against any country or doctrine but against hunger, poverty, desperation, and chaos. . . . Any government that is willing to assist in the task of recovery will find full co-operation, I am sure, on the part of the United States government.

Representatives of Britain, France, Italy, and other European countries, including the Soviet Union and its satellites, met in Paris to discuss "the Marshall plan." The Communist nations soon withdrew, but the countries of western Europe plus Turkey and Greece were enthusiastic about the American offer of aid. By mid-September sixteen countries had drawn up a four-year European Recovery Program. Its aims were to increase production, control inflation, and promote European economic co-operation by lowering trade barriers.

While Congress debated the European Recovery Program in early 1948, the Communists boldly seized control of Czechoslovakia. Spurred on by this development, Congress approved the program and established the Economic Co-operation Administration to carry it out. When the European Recovery Program came to an end in 1951, it had revitalized the economies of the sixteen participating countries. Moreover, it helped to undermine the appeal of the Communist Parties in western Europe.

The Organization of American States is established. The cold war not only strengthened the United States' ties with western Europe but also led to closer ties within the Western Hemisphere. In 1947 a special conference of American republics was held at Rio de Janeiro, Brazil. Its purpose was to work out a regional plan of defense within the framework of the United Nations. The Rio Pact pledged the United States and the other American republics to "regard an armed attack on any American state as an attack on all the American states." This historic treaty, quickly ratified by the United States Senate, was the first regional pact approved by the United Nations.

Another inter-American conference met at Bogotá, Colombia, in 1948. Latin American delegates hoped that the United States would propose a "little Marshall Plan" to stimulate their sagging economies. But the United States was more interested in ending Communist agitation in Latin America. Communist-inspired riots in Bogotá at the time of the conference emphasized the need for action. The delegates adopted a strong anti-Communist resolution and

UNRRA fed many refugees during and after World War II. Here children of several nationalities have a nourishing meal at a displaced persons camp in Austria in 1946.

agreed to resist Communist activities in the hemisphere. They also formed an Organization of American States (OAS) to enforce the Rio Pact. An Inter-American Defense Council was created for consultation on mutual defense.

The United States supports the UN. In contrast to its isolationist attitude after World War I, the United States gave strong support to the infant United Nations during the postwar years. The world organization held its first meetings in London but soon moved to New York City, where land had been contributed for the construction of a permanent headquarters. American delegates to the United Nations actively assisted in the formation of several UN agencies. Among them were the International Refugee Organization, the World Health Organization, the Food and Agriculture Organization, the International Labor Organization, and the United Nations Educational, Scientific, and Cultural Organization (UNESCO).

As time went on, the UN General Assembly came to wield almost as much power as the Security Council. This development resulted from the Soviet Union's frequent use of the veto to block Security Council action. During the UN's first ten years, the Soviet Union exercised its veto more than 60 times, while the United States did not use its veto at all.

The UN secures a truce in Palestine. One of the UN's first major endeavors was to seek a solution to the difficult Palestine problem. Since the end of the First World War, Great Britain had held Palestine as a League of Nations mandate. During and after World War II, many European Jewish refugees sought to enter Palestine, but British officials turned them away in order to keep peace with the Arabs.

In 1947, Britain turned over the Palestine problem to the United Nations, and the General Assembly voted to partition the troubled land between Arabs and Jews. When the British mandate ended in May, 1948, the Palestine Jews proclaimed the new state of Israel, and President Truman immediately extended diplomatic recognition. There followed a bitter war between Israelis and Arabs, but the United Nations managed to arrange an armistice in 1949. The American Negro statesman Ralph J. Bunche played an important part in this settlement as the UN mediator. Jews in the United States contributed large sums of money to the new state. But American volunteers also helped the International Refugee Organization care for thousands of impoverished Arabs expelled from Israel.

▶ CHECK-UP

1. How did the Western powers and the Soviet Union disagree concerning Germany? What was the result? What peace treaties were concluded with east European countries?

2. What changes were brought about by the American occupation of Japan? What efforts

THE UNITED NATIONS AND RELATED AGENCIES

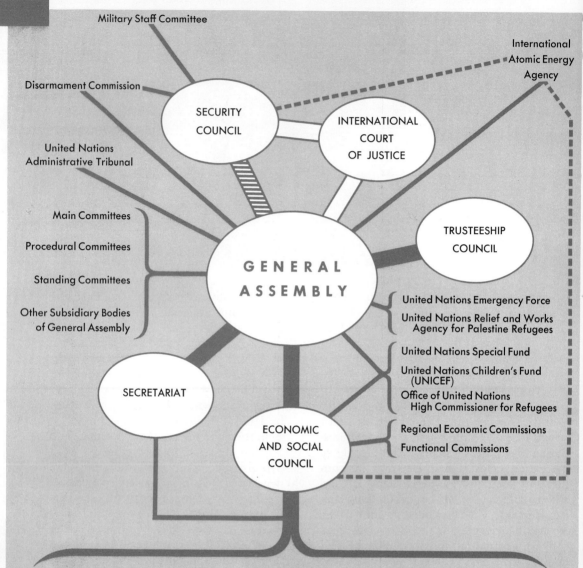

Military Staff Committee

International
Atomic Energy
Agency

Disarmament Commission

SECURITY
COUNCIL

INTERNATIONAL
COURT
OF JUSTICE

United Nations
Administrative Tribunal

Main Committees

Procedural Committees

Standing Committees

Other Subsidiary Bodies
of General Assembly

GENERAL
ASSEMBLY

TRUSTEESHIP
COUNCIL

United Nations Emergency Force

United Nations Relief and Works
Agency for Palestine Refugees

United Nations Special Fund

United Nations Children's Fund
(UNICEF)

Office of United Nations
High Commissioner for Refugees

SECRETARIAT

Regional Economic Commissions

Functional Commissions

ECONOMIC
AND SOCIAL
COUNCIL

THE SPECIALIZED AGENCIES

- International Labor Organization

- Food and Agriculture Organization
  of the United Nations

- United Nations Educational, Scientific
  and Cultural Organization

- World Health Organization

- International Development Association

- International Bank for Reconstruction
  and Development

- International Finance Corporation

- International Monetary Fund

- International Civil Aviation Organization

- Universal Postal Union

- International Telecommunication Union

- World Meteorological Organization

- Inter-Governmental Maritime
  Consultative Organization

- International Trade Organization
  (General Agreement on Tariffs and Trade)

were made to bolster Chiang Kai-shek's government? Why were the Communists able to take over in China? What was the American attitude?

3. Why did this country and the Soviet Union fail to reach agreement on the control of atomic power? How did the Russians establish satellite states in eastern Europe? How did the Truman Doctrine and the Marshall Plan help to contain communism?

4. Why was the OAS established? In what ways did the United States co-operate with the UN after the war? How did the UN help to end the fighting in Palestine?

. . . .

2 *Communist Aggression Is Checked in Germany and Korea*

Truman proposes aid to underdeveloped countries. In the fall of 1948, Harry Truman won election to the presidency in his own right (page 786). In his inaugural speech in January, 1949, the President proposed "a bold new program" to aid the "underdeveloped areas" of the world. He said that the United States could help stop the spread of communism in four ways. These included (1) continued support of the United Nations, (2) financial aid to promote world-wide economic stability, and (3) aid to the free nations, such as we were giving through the Marshall Plan. (4) The fourth way — or *Point Four*, as it came to be called — was to make American scientific and industrial knowledge available to the underdeveloped countries. Such a program would provide technical assistance to countries that wanted help in developing their own resources.

The Point Four Program was launched in 1950 with an appropriation of 35 million dollars. By the time Truman left office, more than 300 million dollars had been spent on Point Four projects in Asia, Africa, and Latin America. America's "technical missionaries" were then at work in 33 countries improving agriculture; raising health standards; planning dams and power and irrigation projects; and teaching people to read and write.

The cold war intensifies. Meanwhile, the rift between Communist Russia and the Western powers deepened. The dispute over the city of Berlin was a case in point. Agreement had been reached at Potsdam that Berlin, though located well within the Soviet zone of Germany, would be divided into four sectors. Each of these was to be administered by one of the four occupying powers — France, Britain, the United States, and the Soviet Union. As we have seen, the Western powers had not been able to reach any understanding with the Soviet Union about peace terms for Germany or plans for the reunification of that divided country. Convinced that the Soviet Union wanted to take over all of Germany, the Western powers decided to unify their zones in western Germany and build a bulwark against communism. In June, 1948, they introduced a new cur-

Ralph Bunche (left), shown here with Trygve Lie, UN Secretary-General in 1948, received the 1950 Nobel peace prize for his role in negotiating the armistice between Arabs and Jews in Palestine (page 761).

Berliners watch an American transport plane coming in for a landing soon after the airlift started in 1948. Such flights kept the people of West Berlin supplied with food and fuel during the Russian blockade of land routes.

rency for their area and extended its use to West Berlin.

An airlift breaks the Berlin blockade. The Communists countered with a blockade of all highway, river, and rail traffic into Berlin. Frustrated by the success of the Marshall Plan in western Europe, the Communists hoped to save face by forcing the Allies out of Berlin. The Western powers realized that if they submitted to the blockade, they would be starved out of Berlin within a short time. If they used force to break the blockade, they would risk starting a third world war. A third possibility was suggested by General Lucius Clay, the American commander in Germany. He proposed using American and British planes to airlift supplies into Berlin. Truman accepted the idea, and the airlift began immediately.

By the fall of 1948, more than 5000 tons of supplies were being flown into Berlin each day. The spectacular airlift continued through the winter. When the Russians saw that the airlift was increasing the prestige of the Western powers, they had second thoughts. In May, 1949, the Russians called off the blockade.

The North Atlantic Pact is signed. Communist policy in Berlin and elsewhere convinced the Western powers that a military alliance was necessary to insure the security of western Europe. Already Britain, France, Belgium, the Netherlands, and Luxemburg had signed the Brussels Pact, providing for military and economic cooperation. President Truman felt that a broader military pact, including Canada and the United States, would be an added defense against Communist aggression in Europe. As a result, the North Atlantic Pact was signed in 1949 by the United States, Canada, Great Britain, France, Italy, Belgium, the Netherlands, Denmark, Norway, Portugal, Luxemburg, and Iceland.[2]

These twelve nations established the North Atlantic Treaty Organization (NATO) to guard the security of western Europe and the North Atlantic. They agreed to consult whenever "the territorial integrity, political independence or security of any of the parties is threatened." They also agreed that "an armed attack against one or more of them . . . shall be considered an attack against them all" and would be met by armed force. Like the Organization of American States, the North Atlantic Treaty Organization was a re-

[2] Greece and Turkey joined NATO in 1952 and West Germany two years later.

gional agreement approved by the United Nations. The United States Senate ratified the North Atlantic Pact and also sanctioned the use of American forces in a NATO army. General Eisenhower resigned the presidency of Columbia University to become the first commander of the NATO forces in 1951.

Russia explodes an atomic bomb. The troublesome problem of nuclear control became more acute in September, 1949, when Soviet scientists startled the world by exploding an atomic bomb. Since the United States no longer held a monopoly on nuclear weapons, both its defense plans and its cold-war strategy had to take into account this new development. President Truman was determined to avoid war, for now the Soviet Union might be able to strike back by dropping atomic bombs on American cities. At the same time, the President's scientific advisers debated the morality of making an even more powerful nuclear weapon — the hydrogen bomb. President Truman ended the debate in January, 1950, by ordering work to proceed on the deadly H-bomb.

The fact that the Soviet Union had nuclear weapons did not greatly change our European policy. But it did strengthen American determination to aid countries resisting Communist activity within their borders. When the European Recovery Program came to an end in 1951, it was replaced by the Mutual Security Agency. Within two years this agency administered more than thirteen billion dollars in foreign aid. The NATO defense area was extended eastward to include Greece and Turkey, and six American divisions were stationed in Europe. Congress appropriated more than six billion dollars to supply military aid to our European allies between 1949 and 1953.

The Communists take over North Korea. Meanwhile, in the Far East the Communist powers were ready to make their next move. It had been decided at the Cairo conference (page 742) that after the war Korea would be restored as an independent nation. At the war's end the Soviet Union had occupied the northern part of Korea, and the United States the southern half.[3] Although both countries had agreed to help form a unified Korean government, the growing suspicion between the Soviet Union and the United States made this impossible. Consequently, two separate governments were established — a Communist state in North Korea and the democratic Republic of South Korea, which was recognized by the UN. The Soviet armies withdrew in 1948, leaving the Communist government well-armed. The American forces, in turn, withdrew from Korea the following year.

War breaks out in Korea. Near the end of June, 1950, North Korean troops crossed the thirty-eighth parallel to invade South Korea. To permit the Republic of South Korea to fall under Communist control would have damaged the prestige of the United Nations. Yet to defend South Korea might have brought Communist China and even the Soviet Union into the contest and touched off another world war. Fully aware of the risks involved, the President asked Secretary of State Dean Acheson to bring the matter before the UN Security Council. President Truman later described his decision with respect to Korea as the toughest one he had to make.

At this time the Soviet delegate was temporarily boycotting the Security Council because it had refused to recognize Red China. Unhampered by the Soviet veto, the Council demanded the immediate withdrawal of the invading North Korean troops. It also called upon UN members to come to the aid of South Korea. President Truman promptly ordered American air and ground forces, under the command of General MacArthur, into Korea. Before long, sixteen nations were fighting side by side in what was called a UN "police action." At first, American troops accounted for most of the United Nations force, but the South Koreans eventually put more men into the battle lines than all the other UN troops combined.

Despite superior naval and air power, the UN forces were soon driven back to a

---

[3] The two zones were divided by the thirty-eighth parallel of latitude.

narrow beachhead in the southeast corner of the peninsula. In September, 1950, General MacArthur executed a brilliant counterattack, landing UN forces at Inchon far behind the enemy lines. By October he had driven the Communists from almost all South Korean territory.

The objectives of the Korean War change. The United Nations then had to decide whether to stop at the thirty-eighth parallel or to carry the fight into North Korea. The General Assembly concluded that "the establishment of a unified, independent, and democratic Korea" required the defeat of the Communists. It therefore authorized the UN forces to move into North Korea. General MacArthur pressed on toward the Yalu River, the boundary between Korea and China. Reports that the Chinese might intervene were forwarded to the UN command, but MacArthur discounted this information. Nevertheless, late in November, large numbers of Chinese forces crossed the Yalu River and soon drove the UN army well below the thirty-eighth parallel. Said General MacArthur, "We face an entirely new war." By March, 1951, however, UN forces had regained most of the territory south of the thirty-eighth parallel.

MacArthur and Truman disagree on Korean policy. Meanwhile, attention within

UN forces, composed of men from sixteen nations, fought in rugged hills (above) to repel the Communist invasion of South Korea. Truce talks between UN and Communist officials (right) continued for two years before an agreement was reached. Many American soldiers befriended Korean war orphans. At top right, a GI helps a Korean boy pull on a pair of American cowboy boots.

the United States focused on a dispute between President Truman and General MacArthur. The General blamed the reverses in Korea on the administration's policy. He called for a more aggressive policy, including the bombing of Chinese bases in Manchuria, a blockade of the Chinese coast, and use of Chinese Nationalist forces. Some members of Congress and many other Americans agreed with MacArthur that such tactics were necessary to knock the Chinese Communist "volunteers" out of the war.

President Truman and most UN members, on the other hand, believed that the "police action" in Korea should remain a limited war. Bombing Manchuria would almost certainly have brought China into the war as a full-scale participant. This, in turn, might have drawn the Soviet Union into the conflict and thus led to another world war. General Omar Bradley, Chairman of the Joint Chiefs of Staff, warned that war with China would be "the wrong war in the wrong place, at the wrong time, and with the wrong enemy." Waging a limited war in Korea was frustrating; but most members of Congress and most of the American people preferred the "police action" in Korea to all-out war against China.

Truman dismisses MacArthur. General MacArthur's defiance of the President seemed to threaten the American tradition of civilian control over the military forces. Therefore, Truman relieved MacArthur of his command in Korea and his control of the occupation forces in Japan. The President said: "MacArthur left me no choice — I could no longer tolerate his insubordination." The General's supporters were furious over the President's brusque dismissal. They gave MacArthur a hero's welcome when he returned to the United States and arranged for him to address Congress. A Senate investigation into the General's dismissal clearly brought out the differences in points of view on Far Eastern policy.

Truce talks begin in Korea. Both sides had suffered heavy losses in Korea. In June, 1951, the Soviet delegate at the United Nations suggested peace talks. Armistice negotiations soon began but

dragged on for two full years. It seemed impossible to reach any agreement on a cease-fire line or on means of enforcing an armistice. A particularly difficult question was what to do with captured Chinese and North Koreans who did not want to return to their Communist homelands. While the negotiations were stalled, occasional fighting and air activity continued. Americans, who were paying a large part of the costs of the war, became increasingly disturbed as the talks failed to end the war. Nevertheless, Communist aggression against South Korea had been turned back.

▶ CHECK-UP

1. How did Truman seek to help underdeveloped countries? How did Britain and the United States cope with Communist efforts to take over West Berlin and western Germany? Why was NATO organized? What was this country's reaction to the explosion of an atomic bomb by Russia?

2. How did war break out in Korea? What action was taken by the UN? By the United States? What differences developed between MacArthur and Truman concerning Korean policy? Why did it prove difficult to end the fighting in Korea?

. . . .

3 *The Cold War Continues Under President Eisenhower*

The frustrations of the Korean War and the Communist conquest of China played a major role in the election of 1952 (page 790). The American people elected the first Republican President in 20 years. But the change of power in Washington brought no letup in the tensions of the cold war. President Eisenhower and his Secretary of State, John Foster Dulles, met head-on the challenges of continued Communist aggression, as crises developed in the Far and Middle East, Europe, and Latin America. Meanwhile, new developments in nuclear warfare and the beginning of the "space race" also heightened world tension.

A truce is signed in Korea. During the campaign in 1952, General Eisenhower had pledged that, if elected, he would go to Korea. He fulfilled this campaign promise a month after the election, but his trip to Korea bore no immediate results. Truce negotiations dragged on, and fighting continued to flare up from time to time. A turning point finally came in the spring of 1953. Stalin's death gave the new Soviet leaders an opportunity to change their position, and in July, 1953, an armistice was finally signed. It provided for a political conference to settle the fate of prisoners of war who did not want to return to their homelands. The next year the United States signed a mutual-defense treaty with South Korea, and since then has given considerable financial aid to the South Korean government. But the signing of the Korean truce did not mean an end to cold-war problems in Asia. China and French Indo-China were especially troublesome areas.

A mutual-security pact is signed with Chiang Kai-shek. During the 1952 election campaign John Foster Dulles had criticized the "containment" policy of the Truman administration. He talked about replacing it with a more "dynamic" policy of "liberation" for the people of Communist countries. Chiang Kai-shek, encouraged to hope for American support in an invasion of the Chinese mainland, moved Nationalist troops to Quemoy and Matsu. These islands lay just a few miles off the Chinese coast (see map on next page).

In 1954 Dulles negotiated a mutual-security pact with Chiang Kai-shek. By this pact, the United States promised to defend Formosa and the Pescadores Islands, but not Quemoy and Matsu unless an attack on them was part of an attack on Formosa. Chiang agreed not to launch an invasion of the mainland unless the United States gave its consent. The Senate ratified this pact, but the situation in the Formosa Straits remained unsettled. Though the Chinese Communists periodically bombarded Quemoy and Matsu, they did not risk an invasion of the offshore islands.

The French lose Indo-China. Meanwhile, attention was focused on Southeast Asia, where Communist forces were about to win a significant victory. French dominance in Indo-China had been broken by Japan during World War II. Although French rule was re-established after the war, Communist forces had been trying to drive the French out of Indo-China. By 1954 the French position had become precarious. The war was unpopular in France, and the people of Indo-China had no enthusiasm for French rule. Moreover, Red China was aiding the Communist rebels in Indo-China. Though the United States had sent military supplies to the French, President Eisenhower refused an appeal for American troops. Following the collapse of French resistance in May, 1954, an international conference was held at Geneva. Negotiations led to a political settlement under which the independence of Cambodia and Laos was guaranteed. Vietnam was temporarily divided at the seventeenth parallel, and Communist guerrilla fighters were to withdraw to North Vietnam.[4] Elections in 1956 were supposed to reunite North and South Vietnam. Though the United States participated in the Geneva conference, it refused to sign the agreements because it felt that too many concessions had been made to the Communists.

The United States signs a Southeast Asia defense pact. Secretary Dulles hoped that a defense pact with other concerned countries would prevent further Communist aggression in Southeast Asia. Consequently, in September, 1954, the United States joined with the Philippines, Thailand, Pakistan, Britain, France, Australia, and New Zealand in the Southeast Asia Treaty Organization (SEATO). The eight nations agreed to respond to attacks by aggressors, but they did not establish a

---

[4] Cambodia, Laos, and Vietnam had been provinces in the French protectorate of Indo-China.

WORLD TROUBLE SPOTS

During the cold war years, certain areas of the world have emerged as special trouble spots. Note that in several areas, trouble has broken out more than once. Some of these crises have brought the world to the brink of war. Outbreaks of violence in any of these trouble spots may threaten world peace and security.

R. M. Chapin, Jr.

Communist world

RED CHINA

Cease fire line, 1953
Occupied by Red China since 1962
JAMMU & KASHMIR
War 1965
U.S.S.R.
Rawalpindi
WEST PAKISTAN
INDIA
Delhi

War 1950-53
N. KOREA
S. KOREA
JAPAN
Yalu R.
Peking
Cease fire line
RED CHINA
U.S. 7th Fleet
Formosa Strait
Taipei
NATIONALIST CHINA
Matsu I.
Quemoy
Pescadores Is.

RED CHINA
U.S. 7th Fleet
War since 1960
Gulf of Tonkin
Hanoi
N. VIET NAM
LAOS
Cease fire line, 1954
1965 U.S. Escalation
S. VIET NAM
Saigon
THAILAND
CAMBODIA
Civil War 1960-62

TURKEY
SYRIA
LEBANON
CYPRUS
Civil War 1964
U.S. Marines 1958
ISRAEL
Jerusalem
TRANS-JORDAN
SAUDI ARABIA
A R A B
EGYPT
Cairo
Suez Canal
Red Sea
War 1956
U.S. 6th Fleet
N A T I O N S

EAST GERMANY
Berlin Wall, 1961
West Berlin
WEST GERMANY
Hamburg
Helmstedt
Berlin Autobahn
Frankfurt
Berlin Airlift 1948-49

FAR EAST
SOUTH EAST ASIA
U.S.S.R.
RED CHINA
KASHMIR
MIDDLE EAST
GERMANY
AFRICA
CARIBBEAN
U.S.A.

UGANDA
RWANDA
BURUNDI
TANZANIA
REPUBLIC OF THE CONGO
CONGO REP.
Leopoldville
Congo R.
Civil War 1960
KATANGA
Elizabethville
ANGOLA
ZAMBIA
Lusaka
Kariba Dam
Salisbury
RHODESIA

Fla.
U.S. Missile Blockade 1962
C U B A
DOMINICAN REPUBLIC
HAITI
JAMAICA
U.S. Intervention 1965
Bay of Pigs 1961
Canal Zone, 1964
PANAMA

769

MAP STUDY

separate military force. SEATO extended its protection to South Vietnam, Laos, and Cambodia — all possible targets of Communist expansion. Some countries in Southeast Asia — India, Burma, and Indonesia — preferred to steer a neutral course between the United States and the Soviet Union.

The Western European Union is created. Communist aggression in Southeast Asia alarmed the countries of western Europe. Having recovered from the economic setbacks of World War II, these nations began to build up their own defenses against communism. In 1954, Great Britain, France, Italy, Belgium, the Netherlands, Luxemburg, and West Germany formed the Western European Union. The seven countries agreed to maintain their own national armies; West Germany was allowed to raise up to twelve divisions, and these were to be under NATO command. The sovereignty of West Germany also was recognized with two exceptions: (1) She could not manufacture atomic, biological, or chemical weapons; (2) the Western powers had the right to station troops in

West Berlin until East and West Germany were unified.

International tension lessens. After Stalin's death in 1953, the leaders of the Soviet Union engaged in a fierce struggle for power. Eventually Nikita Khrushchev (kroosh-*choff'*) emerged as the most powerful figure in the USSR. The new Soviet leader surprised the Western world by talking about "peaceful co-existence" with capitalist nations. Moreover, the Soviet Union agreed to a peace treaty with Austria and withdrew its troops from that country. Winston Churchill had been urging a meeting of world leaders at the "summit" — a high-level conference that might reduce the tensions of the cold war. By 1955 the feeling was growing that such a meeting might have fruitful results.

Many people hoped that a summit conference might revive discussion of the problem of arms control. The Soviet Union had exploded a hydrogen bomb in 1953, and both the Soviet Union and the United States were testing ever more powerful weapons. As nuclear tests increased the amount of radioactive material in the atmosphere, scientists warned that "fallout" of this material might endanger human health for generations to come.

The "Big Four" leaders meet in Geneva. In July, 1955, the heads of government of the United States, Great Britain, France, and the Soviet Union met in Geneva, Switzerland. The atmosphere was friendly, and President Eisenhower proposed that the United States and the Soviet Union each allow the other to carry out aerial inspection of their territory. But the only agreement reached at the summit meeting was that the "Big Four" foreign ministers meet to discuss German reunification and Eisenhower's "open-skies" proposal. These meetings, held a few months later, ended in deadlock, and the relaxed "spirit of Geneva" soon dissolved.

A crisis develops in the Middle East. Increasing Arab nationalism in the Middle East presented both a threat and a challenge to the United States and the Soviet Union. Just as the Communists hoped to win new satellites in this trouble area, so

---

Freedom for the Philippines

One member of the SEATO pact was the Republic of the Philippines. In 1946, just eight years before, this new nation had been born. As you read in Chapter 28, the Filipinos had repeatedly asked for independence from the United States. In 1934 Congress passed legislation promising the Philippines freedom after a period of trial self-government, with final independence scheduled for 1946. But World War II threatened this timetable. In 1941 the Japanese made war on the United States and overran the Philippines. More than two years passed before American forces returned to the islands and, together with their Filipino comrades, freed the Philippines from Japanese rule. Then, in 1946, independence became a fact. In April of that year, the Filipinos elected Manuel Roxas to be their president, and on July 4 — our own nation's birthday — the Republic of the Philippines came into existence.

Egyptians cheered President Nasser as he drove through Cairo (above) soon after his nationalization of the Suez Canal in 1956. A UN Emergency Force supervised the cease-fire that followed Israel's invasion of Egypt. Above, right, UNEF soldiers from India manned a post on the armistice line. When a pro-Nasser revolution threatened in Lebanon, the United States sent troops to help the Lebanese government. Right, American marines began to withdraw when the danger had passed.

the Western powers hoped to win the confidence of Arab leaders. The situation was complicated, however, by Arab hostility to Israel. The Arabs also resented the fact that Britain and France still held territory in Africa. Gamal Abdel Nasser, who came to power in Egypt in 1954, vowed to drive the Israelis "into the sea" and to end British control over the Suez Canal. The Canal had long been operated by a corporation in which the chief stockholders were the British government and French investors.

Secretary Dulles tried to head off a conflict by persuading the British to withdraw their troops from the Suez Canal Zone. The United States and Britain also offered to help Nasser build the Aswan High Dam on the upper Nile River. Not to be outdone, the Soviet Union approached Egypt

about a loan for the Aswan Dam. It also signed a trade agreement to buy Egyptian cotton in exchange for arms. Egyptian troops used these weapons to carry out raids across the Israeli border.

Nasser's dealings with the Soviet Union and his recognition of Communist China caused a shift in United States policy. Dulles abruptly announced in July, 1956, that the United States was withdrawing its offer to help build the dam. Nasser struck back by nationalizing the Suez Canal and forbidding Israeli ships to use it.

Fighting flares up in Egypt. Britain and France insisted that Nasser's seizure of the Suez Canal threatened western Europe, which depended on that waterway for much of its oil from the Middle East. The British government hoped that the United

States would support Britain and France in taking action against Nasser. But Dulles urged the British and French to agree to international management of the Canal.

The tense situation was heightened late in October, 1956, when Israel launched an attack on Egypt. Two days later Britain and France, without informing the United States, joined the attack. The American government exerted pressure on Israel, Britain, and France to end the fighting. The UN Assembly also called for an immediate cease-fire, and the Soviet Union threatened to send "volunteers" to Egypt unless the attack was halted. On November 6, Britain and France accepted a cease-fire, and a United Nations Emergency Force moved into Egypt to supervise the withdrawal of troops.

The Suez crisis had serious consequences. For one thing, it strained relations between the United States and its allies Great Britain and France. Also, it left Nasser in control of the Suez Canal and increased his dependence on the Soviet Union for military and financial aid. Moreover, it encouraged Nasser to hope that he could dominate other Arab countries.

The United States sends troops to Lebanon. Unsettled conditions in the Middle East caused the Eisenhower administration to declare its intention of defending countries in that part of the world against Communist aggression. The President asked Congress for emergency military and economic aid "to secure and protect the territorial independence" of Middle Eastern countries "against overt armed aggression from any nation controlled by international communism."

This Eisenhower Doctrine was put to the test in 1958. When a pro-Nasser movement threatened the security of Lebanon, that country appealed to the United States for assistance. American marines were rushed to Lebanon. At the same time British forces responded to a call for help from the King of Jordan. The Soviet Union vigorously objected to the American and British action but did not intervene. A few months later, when the safety of the pro-Western governments of Lebanon and Jordan seemed assured, American and British troops were withdrawn.

New crises occur in Europe. Meanwhile, cold-war crises concerning Europe underlined the tense situation that continued to exist there. Those who had hoped for a fundamental change in Soviet policy toward its satellites following Stalin's death were disappointed. The Communist states, though termed "people's democracies," remained dictatorships. When the courageous Hungarian people rose up

The head of a Joseph Stalin monument lies in a Budapest street after being pulled down by Hungarian patriots during the ill-fated revolution of 1956. This photograph is from a film smuggled out by Hungarian refugees.

against their Communist government in October, 1956, Russian tanks and troops moved in and soon crushed the rebellion. As fleeing Hungarians tried to reach the Austrian and Yugoslavian borders, many Americans urged intervention by the United States or the UN. Though the UN Assembly adopted a resolution calling for the withdrawal of Soviet troops, no action was taken, in part because the Suez crisis had developed in the meantime.

Two years later, another crisis threatened when Khrushchev revived the Berlin issue. Without prior warning, he announced that the time had come to "give up the remnants of the occupation regime in Berlin." Khrushchev proposed that all of Berlin, including the western zone, be made a "free city"; all troops would be withdrawn and access to the city would be controlled by the Communist East German government. Unless the Western powers agreed to this solution within six months, Khrushchev warned, the Soviet Union would sign a separate peace treaty with East Germany. This would make permanent the division of Germany; and the announcement clearly implied that if such a treaty were signed, East Germany might impose another blockade on West Berlin.

Secretary Dulles made clear that the United States had no intention of abandoning the two million people of West Berlin. Meeting in Paris, the Western foreign ministers restated their determination "to maintain their position and rights in Berlin, including the right of free access." They offered, however, to consider Berlin's future in a discussion focused on the problems of Germany and European security.

Another summit conference is proposed. Khrushchev relieved the tension early in 1959 by indicating his willingness to extend the Berlin deadline if the Western leaders would agree to a summit conference. Secretary of State Christian Herter (who had replaced Dulles[5]) represented the United States at a foreign ministers' conference intended to prepare the ground-

[5] Illness had forced Secretary Dulles to resign. He died during the foreign ministers' conference.

Khrushchev's presence at UN meetings in the fall of 1960 resulted in a stormy session. The Soviet leader demanded the resignation of UN Secretary-General Dag Hammarskjold.

work for a summit meeting. Though no agreement was reached, the pressure to hold a high-level conference continued. Vice-President Richard Nixon toured Russia and Poland in the summer of 1959, and in the fall Khrushchev visited the United States.

The summit conference breaks up. Finally it was agreed to hold the muchheralded summit conference at Paris in May, 1960. Just as world leaders gathered in Paris, however, an unfortunate combination of circumstances broke up the conference. An enraged Khrushchev announced that an American airplane had been discovered flying over the Soviet Union and had been shot down. The United States government admitted that for several years high-flying U-2 airplanes had been photographing Soviet territory. It argued that such flights were necessary to protect the free world against surprise attack by the Soviet Union. When Khrushchev demanded that the President apologize for the flights, Eisenhower accepted full responsibility but refused to apologize. The Western allies rallied to the President's support. But the summit meeting collapsed before it even began.

The arms race continues. The tensions of the U-2 episode contributed to the failure of an international disarmament conference to reach any agreement. Through the 1950's the deadly arms race had continued as the United States and Russia stockpiled atomic and hydrogen bombs, resulting in a nuclear "balance of terror." Both countries had also begun to develop guided missiles armed with nuclear warheads. By 1957 the United States had successfully tested intermediate-range missiles that could travel 1500 to 3000 miles. But in that same year the Soviet Union announced that it had perfected an intercontinental missile. If true, it would mean that the Russians had rockets far more powerful than any developed by this country. The United States hastened its development of long-range rockets.

The space race begins. The Soviet announcement was confirmed in October, 1957, when powerful booster rockets launched Sputnik, the world's first space satellite, into orbit around the earth. Sputnik was followed the next month by the even larger Sputnik II, weighing more than a thousand pounds. It reached an altitude of more than a thousand miles. Two years later Soviet scientists scored another victory when they crash-landed a Lunik rocket on the surface of the moon.

Americans were alarmed by this evidence that Russia had taken the lead in rocket development. Spurred on by the Soviet achievements, Congress adopted several measures to step up national defense. Appropriations were increased, the Defense Department was reorganized, and a National Aeronautics and Space Administration (NASA) was created to plan for the exploration of outer space. Early in 1958 the United States launched its first satellite, Explorer I, weighing about 31 pounds. In time, larger Explorer, Vanguard, and Discoverer satellites were launched. Late in 1958, the United States successfully testfired an intercontinental Atlas missile and launched another Atlas missile into orbit.

Unrest pervades Latin America. Latin America did not escape the unrest and tension that prevailed throughout most of the world during the 1950's. While the United States was preoccupied with cold-war crises elsewhere in the world, its relations with its neighbors in this hemisphere worsened. Following World War II, political and social unrest had swept Latin American countries as the people demanded greater political freedom and economic reforms. Taking advantage of this discontent, Communist agents began to make their way into labor unions, student organizations, and the armed forces and to establish left-wing political parties. Ambitious military officers also made use of unsettled conditions to seize control of governments; by 1954 thirteen Latin American presidents were military men. Some leaders met the rising tide of criticism by imposing dictatorial rule.

What the Latin Americans wanted most from the United States was economic aid. The Latin American nations hoped for increased trade with the United States and hinted that Latin America needed a "little Marshall Plan" (page 760). The United States did not respond to either of these requests, but it did give the Latin American countries half a billion dollars in Point Four assistance and military aid. In the eyes of most Latin Americans, these programs were entirely inadequate to meet their countries' needs. Moreover, military aid usually found its way into the hands of army officers who supported the dictatorships. And the American government alienated many people in Latin America by failing to denounce some of the dictators. Popular uprisings overturned dictatorial regimes in Peru, Venezuela, and Argentina; yet resentment against the United States remained strong. When Vice-President Nixon and his wife visited South America in 1958, angry mobs stoned their limousine in Lima, Peru, and Caracas, Venezuela. Such expressions of anti-American feeling led the United States to re-examine its Latin American policy.

Castro comes to power in Cuba. Meanwhile, the people of Cuba sought to free themselves from the harsh rule of a dictator named Batista. A guerrilla uprising against the Cuban dictator won sympathy throughout the hemisphere, and in 1959, Batista fled the country. The leader of the successful rebellion, Fidel Castro, formed a new government and promised to carry out political, economic, and social reforms. But enthusiasm for Castro faded in the United States when Communists gained influence over the movement and Castro began to restrict political liberties, refused to hold a promised free election, and nationalized American-owned property. The Cuban leader became increasingly hostile toward the United States, and signed a trade treaty with the Soviet Union in 1960. The American government responded by suspending purchases of Cuban sugar (the mainstay of the Cuban economy) and cutting off all exports to Cuba except food and medicine. In January, 1961, Castro ordered a sharp reduction in the American embassy staff in Havana. Among the last actions of the Eisenhower administration was the breaking of diplomatic relations with Cuba.

▶ CHECK-UP

1. How was a truce arranged in Korea? What were the terms of the mutual security pact with Chiang Kai-shek? What was the result of the French defeat in Indo-China? What was the purpose of SEATO?

2. Why was the Western European Union organized? What agreements were reached with West Germany? Why did European tensions ease somewhat after 1953? What was the outcome of the Geneva conference?

3. What factors contributed to the Suez crisis? How was the crisis resolved? Why was the Eisenhower Doctrine formulated? How was it tested in Lebanon?

4. What was the Soviet response to the Hungarian revolt? How did the United States respond to Khrushchev's proposals regarding Berlin? What happened to the 1960 summit conference? What advances were made by Russia in the nuclear arms race and exploration of space? By the United States?

5. Why did unrest increase in Latin America? Why did anti-United States feeling increase? How did Castro come to power in Cuba? Why did this country's relations with Castro become increasingly unfriendly?

Fidel Castro led a successful rebellion against a hated dictator but failed to introduce the democratic reforms he had promised to the Cuban people.

Clinching the Main Ideas in Chapter 36

Suddenly elevated to the presidency in 1945, Harry Truman faced the enormous challenge of formulating a postwar settlement in Europe. Moreover, as leader of the free world, he also had to prevent the spread of communism. For two years he tried to co-operate with the Soviet Union. Then, convinced that the Soviet Union would not co-operate with the Western powers, Truman moved decisively to contain the Communists. The Truman Doctrine, the Marshall Plan, the Berlin airlift, and NATO all helped to stop Communist expansion in Europe. The Organization of American States and Point Four aid helped to check Communist subversion in Latin America. And in the Far East, the Communists were halted in Korea. The United States was unable, however, to do anything to stop their take-over of China without resorting to all-out war. This the country was unwilling to risk.

During President Eisenhower's administration there was no lasting reduction of cold-war tension. Soviet and Chinese Communists probed for weaknesses in Southeast Asia, the Middle East, Berlin, and Latin America. The United States answered these challenges by extending the system of regional pacts and giving aid to nations threatened by Communist aggression. The launching of Sputnik demonstrated the Soviet Union's lead in rocket development, and Communist propaganda made the most of Soviet achievements in space. Meanwhile, the rise to power of a pro-Communist government in Cuba brought the cold war still closer to America.

Chapter Review

Terms to Understand

1. iron curtain
2. Korean War
3. Formosa
4. Rio Pact
5. space race
6. satellite
7. Point Four
8. NATO
9. AEC
10. OAS
11. WHO
12. NASA
13. SEATO
14. Marshall Plan
15. Berlin airlift
16. Brussels Pact
17. Potsdam Conference
18. Truman Doctrine
19. Nuremberg trials
20. German Federal Republic
21. People's Republic of China
22. Western European Union
23. Eisenhower Doctrine
24. "people's democracies"
25. summit conference

What Do You Think?

1. Contrast American and Soviet views on control of the atomic bomb.
2. Why did the United States put pressure on Britain, France, and Israel to end their attack on Egypt during the Suez crisis?
3. Why did the Soviet Union cease to cooperate with the Western powers when Germany was defeated?
4. Would a "little Marshall Plan" for Latin America have been inconsistent with this country's goal of ending Communist agitation in that region? Explain.
5. How did General MacArthur differ from President Truman in his views on policy in the Korean War? Why did each advocate the views he did?

Using Your Knowledge of History

1. Make a chart pointing out similarities and differences in the provisions of the Covenant of the League of Nations and of the Charter of the United Nations.
2. Write a brief essay explaining why the Communists were able to take over mainland China after World War II.
3. Arrange a panel discussion to bring out reasons why SEATO has been unable to prevent Communist aggression in Southeast Asia.
4. Prepare a two-column chart to show the differences in Allied policy in occupied Germany and Japan.

Extending Your Knowledge of History

Two brief and readable summaries of the postwar decades are Eric Goldman's *The Crucial Decade — and After* and Herbert Agar's *The Price of Power: America Since 1945.* A good biography of Truman is Jonathan Daniels's *The Man of Independence.* Interesting studies of Truman as President can be found in *The Truman Administration: Principles and Practices,* edited by Louis Koenig. General Lucius Clay writes about the Berlin crisis in *Decision in Germany.* On the Truman-MacArthur conflict, see Richard Rovere and Arthur M. Schlesinger, Jr., *The General and the President, and the Future of American Foreign Policy.* H. A. Kissinger analyzes the new weapons in *Nuclear Weapons and Foreign Policy. The Wine Is Bitter: The United States and Latin America* by Milton Eisenhower describes relations with those countries in the 1950's.

BUILDING FOR THE TWENTIETH CENTURY

Architects of our day create buildings to meet the needs and satisfy the tastes of twentieth-century Americans. Glass, steel, and concrete are the basic materials from which most of these buildings are constructed. Modern architecture, as shown by the buildings pictured on pages 777–780, is an expression of our times.

Howard Sochurek

Present-day builders use new equipment and techniques. Above, giant cranes erected the huge Gateway Arch that towers over St. Louis. This stainless steel arch was designed by Eero Saarinen. Right, steel girders form the skeleton of a skyscraper under construction in New York.

Concrete cast around a steel skeleton provides extra strength, as in the hotel below, part of Century City in California.

Many cities are rebuilding their business centers. A glass building of unusual shape dominates downtown Hartford, Connecticut (below).

Howard Sochurek

Louis Sullivan said a skyscraper should be "every inch a proud and soaring thing." He relieved utilitarian designs with rich ornamentation, as in the Wainwright Building, below (St. Louis, 1891).

Imaginative use of materials gives beauty to modern structures. Right, Mies van der Rohe designed the gleaming, bronze-sheathed Seagram Building (New York). Eero Saarinen's design for the General Motors Research Center (below, near Detroit) has influenced the planning of other industrial buildings. Glazed tile adds color to some of the walls.

The function of a building influences architectural design. Sweeping lines characterize this terminal building, designed by Eero Saarinen, at Dulles International Airport near Washington, D.C. (above).

The Solomon R. Guggenheim Museum, New York

Pictures are hung along a spiral ramp in New York's Guggenheim Museum (above), designed by Frank Lloyd Wright. Good acoustical engineering is essential in an auditorium like Philharmonic Hall in New York's Lincoln Center (right).

© Ezra Stoller

Some designs are adaptable to different kinds of buildings. The geodesic dome (right) is a framework of equilateral triangles. Invented by Buckminster Fuller, the dome can cover large areas without internal supports. This building is a bank in Oklahoma.

Good design is as important in homes as in public buildings. Frank Lloyd Wright's "Falling Waters" (above) near Bear Run, Pennsylvania, seems to grow out of its natural setting. The interior (above, right) is designed for informal living.

West Coast architects have continued Wright's emphasis on natural materials and natural settings. Redwood sheathing is used in this house (left), designed by H. H. Harris, on a Berkeley hillside near San Francisco.

The growing concentration of people in and around cities has led architects to design new residential complexes. Reston, Virginia, near Washington, D.C., is the first "instant city." This self-contained community includes attractive houses and apartments, schools, stores and business buildings, and recreation facilities; but woodland areas are within walking distance. At right, Lake Anne Village (shown here under construction) is the first of seven villages to be built within Reston.

CHAPTER 37

Truman and Eisenhower Deal With Difficult Problems at Home

Suburban community

Every segment of our population and every individual has a right to expect from our government a fair deal.

HARRY S. TRUMAN, 1949

We demand that the federal government give needed assistance cheerfully, but in ways that will protect the traditional relationship between federal and local government.

DWIGHT D. EISENHOWER, 1960

1945–1960

In their handling of foreign affairs Presidents Truman and Eisenhower generally could count on the support of leaders of both political parties. But this was not true of domestic policies in the postwar years. President Truman called for a program of sweeping reforms, only to have a conservative coalition in Congress reject most of his proposals. Though he won a stunning victory at the polls in 1948, Republicans and southern Democrats managed to defeat his Fair Deal reforms in the House and the Senate.

In 1952 the voters ended twenty years of Democratic rule by electing to the presidency a popular World War II general, Dwight D. Eisenhower. Describing himself as a "modern Republican," Eisenhower believed in international co-operation, firm opposition to Communist aggression, and acceptance of the major reforms of the New Deal era. But he felt that further reforms, such as Truman's Fair Deal program, were unnecessary. The conservative coalition in Congress agreed with Eisenhower. Moreover, it shared the President's view that the federal budget should be balanced and that some of the burdens of government should be shifted from Washington to the states.

Meanwhile, American society underwent significant changes in the 1950's. Economic prosperity was widespread, and most families were able to improve their standard of living. But the continued growth of cities and suburbs placed new burdens on the schools, crowded existing housing facilities, and created problems for urban governments. One of the most significant developments of the 1950's was the rapid stride of Negro Americans toward equal rights and opportunities. Though some critics charged that American society tended to conform to standards set by mass advertising and television, public interest in the arts had seldom been greater.

1 *Truman Calls for Fair Deal Reforms*

Truman succeeds to the presidency. Harry Truman's brief experience as Vice-President had not provided much training for the presidency. Born in Lamar, Missouri, Truman had served in World War I and tried his hand at farming and merchandising before turning to politics. He was elected to judgeships in Missouri with the help of the Kansas City Democratic machine, and then went to the United States Senate in 1934. Re-elected six years later, he distinguished himself as chairman of a Senate committee investigating defense contracts. This, in addition to his midwestern origin, helped put him on the Democratic ticket in 1944. Then, as we have seen, Franklin Roosevelt's death put

· ·

CHAPTER FOCUS

1. Truman calls for Fair Deal reforms.
2. Eisenhower follows a more conservative policy.
3. A prosperous society undergoes many changes.

Harry Truman in the White House. Truman's humility on becoming President soon gave way to self-assurance. As he got the feel of the office, he began to replace members of Roosevelt's Cabinet with appointees of his own.

Demobilization is hurried. One of the first problems to face the new President after Germany's surrender was the general demand to "bring the boys home." Although sizable military forces would be required to occupy Japan and Germany, Congress exerted strong pressure on President Truman to demobilize the armed forces. Truman was swayed by these demands, and within a year after the end of the war, the number of men under arms had been reduced from twelve million to three million. At the same time, defense contracts were abruptly terminated and Lend-Lease aid to the Allies was halted.

A "GI Bill of Rights," passed by Congress in 1944, provided many benefits for the discharged servicemen. This measure entitled veterans to mustering-out pay as well as hospitalization and unemployment insurance for one year. Moreover, it enabled them to secure government loans for building or purchasing homes and acquiring farms or businesses. Equally important, the bill provided financial assistance to veterans who wished to enroll in colleges or vocational schools. The GI Bill of Rights helped to ease the nation's transition to peacetime conditions. It enabled veterans to continue their education before seeking employment, and the spending of their government benefits helped to stimulate the economy.

Price controls are ended. During the war both farmers and businessmen had complained about price controls (page 738). It was a foregone conclusion that these groups would call for an end to such controls as soon as the war was over. The fact that a wave of strikes in 1946 led to substantial wage increases further angered producers, who were still bound by price ceilings. President Truman, however, recognized that the removal of controls would lead to higher prices, since the wartime backlog of demand for consumer items

Homeward bound troops in late 1945 march up the gangplank of an American ship in a French port (left). The end of the war meant many changes in the American economy, as defense factories converted to peacetime production. In the picture at lower left, for example, men assemble kitchen stoves in a workroom still cluttered with airplane parts. The military jeep proved adaptable to such peacetime uses as hauling a trailer load of hay (below).

would far outstrip production. Because wage earners would be hardest hit by inflation, labor leaders urged the President to continue price controls.

Congress and the President could reach no understanding on a bill to extend price ceilings. When controls lapsed in June, 1946, prices immediately shot up. In a single month, food prices rose nearly 14 per cent. Alarmed by this inflation, Congress passed a control measure, but it proved impossible to roll back the price increases. Then, at the end of the year, Congress lifted all controls except those on rents, sugar, and rice. As a result, prices

increased nearly 25 per cent during 1946–1947. This was more than the total price increase during the entire period of World War II.

The Republicans win control of Congress. The quarrel between President Truman and Congress over price controls was shot through with politics; 1946 was an election year, and each party blamed the other for inflation. In addition, there was great concern about the wave of strikes. The Republicans campaigned with the slogan "Had enough?" Apparently the voters had, for the Republicans won majorities in both houses of Congress for the first time since 1930. They also captured 25 governorships. Republican Party leaders confidently forecast a presidential victory in 1948.

Truman proposes new reforms. The election of a Republican Congress failed to discourage President Truman. In 1945 he had already outlined to Congress his proposals for extending the New Deal. These included construction of public housing, health insurance, a permanent Fair Employment Practices Committee (page 740), broader Social Security coverage, and a higher minimum wage. Now he asked the newly elected Congress to enact these measures into law. President Truman also asked Congress to consider the recommendations of his Committee on Civil Rights, which was composed of leading Negro and white citizens. In its report, the Committee recommended the creation of a permanent FEPC, anti-lynching and anti-poll-tax laws, stricter civil-

Senator Robert A. Taft, the son of President William Howard Taft, won the title "Mr. Republican" because of his outstanding party leadership. A conservative, Taft opposed most Democratic legislation but supported government aid for housing and education.

rights statutes, and the effective enforcement of such laws. But Congress took no action on these recommendations.

An important measure which Congress and President Truman did agree on was the National Security Act, passed in 1947. It united the army, navy, and air force under a single Secretary of Defense. It also created the National Security Council, the National Security Resources Board, and the Central Intelligence Agency to help the government wage the cold war against communism.

Congress passes the Taft-Hartley Act. Many Americans were alarmed by the wave of strikes in 1946, by organized labor's demand for wage increases, and by the rising cost of living. Their anger was aimed at such labor leaders as John L. Lewis of the United Mine Workers. A coal strike was settled after the government took over the mines, but within a few months Lewis decided he had had enough of government operation and abruptly canceled the union contract. The government secured a court injunction against Lewis and, when he ignored it, imposed a heavy fine on the union. Lewis then called the men back to work.

Senator Robert Taft of Ohio and other congressmen felt that the Wagner Act (page 697) gave organized labor far too much power. They urged new legislation to protect the rights of employers and to prevent strikes from interfering with the delivery of essential goods and services. Under Taft's leadership — and against the protests of liberal Democrats, President Truman, and labor leaders — Congress passed a new labor law in 1947. This was the Taft-Hartley Act or Labor-Management Relations Act. Although President Truman vetoed the bill, its supporters were able to enact it into law over his veto. The new law affirmed labor's right to organize and bargain collectively, and it retained the National Labor Relations Board. But it changed labor policy in several important respects:

(1) It required a 60-day notice (a "cooling off" period) before a contract could be ended by either employer or union. If the national health or safety should be en-

dangered, the Attorney General could secure an injunction postponing a threatened strike or lockout for 80 days.

(2) It outlawed the closed shop (page 647), but permitted the *union shop* (in which non-union workers may be hired on condition that they join the union at once) if the majority of employees voted for it.

(3) Unions were forbidden to establish secondary boycotts (page 478), to call jurisdictional strikes,[1] to refuse to bargain collectively with an employer, to put pressure on non-union workers, or to charge unusually high initiation and membership fees.

(4) Both employers and unions might sue for damages for breach of contract.

(5) Unions were forbidden to contribute to political campaign funds.

(6) Unions were ordered to file copies of their constitutions and by-laws, schedules of fees, lists of officers, and other information with the Secretary of Labor.

(7) Officers of unions seeking NLRB recognition were required to swear that they were not Communists and did not support any organization advocating the overthrow of the United States government.

The Republican Congress passes other measures. Another bill passed over President Truman's veto provided for a tax cut of nearly five billion dollars. The Republican Congress also expressed its disapproval of President Franklin Roosevelt's long tenure of office by passing the Twenty-second Amendment, which limited any future President to two terms. This Amendment was ratified and went into effect in 1951. In addition, Congress changed the order of presidential succession in favor of men elected to office. An act adopted in 1947 provided that in the absence of both a President and a Vice-President, the Speaker of the House and then the Senate President *pro tempore*[2] would succeed to the presidency ahead of Cabinet members.

[1] A jurisdictional strike is one growing out of a dispute between two unions over which of them will do a certain job or organize a certain group of workers.

[2] The member of the Senate elected to preside in the absence of the Vice-President.

Quarrels erupt in the Democratic Party. Stunned by their defeat at the polls in 1946, the Democrats felt pessimistic about the outcome of the next presidential election. Many New Deal Democrats felt that President Truman was too close to party "bosses" and that he lacked the idealism of President Roosevelt. Some labor leaders were angry with Truman for his part in the coal strike and blamed him for not blocking passage of the Taft-Hartley Act. Southern Democrats, upset by Truman's civil-rights program, charged that he was playing politics to win Negro votes in the North.

Another serious rift developed over foreign policy. Henry Wallace, who had become Secretary of Commerce in 1945, argued that the administration's foreign policy was too tough on the Russians and caused them to mistrust the West. After Wallace delivered a major address condemning the Truman policy, the President removed him from the Cabinet. Nevertheless, Wallace continued his criticism, hammering away on the theme that the Marshall Plan was really a "Martial Plan" that might lead to war with the Soviet Union.

The parties name their candidates. Their victories in the congressional elections in 1946 and the quarrels within the Democratic Party convinced the Republicans that they would win the presidency in 1948. The outstanding man in the Republican Party was Senator Robert A. Taft of Ohio. But Taft's views on foreign policy and domestic affairs were not shared by many Republicans who supported the bipartisan foreign policy and approved of major New Deal reforms. The Republican convention, therefore, nominated Governor Dewey of New York, the 1944 candidate, and chose Governor Earl Warren of California to be his running mate. The Republican platform approved Truman's stand against Soviet aggression but called for a more conservative domestic policy.

At the Democratic convention, the delegates renominated President Truman and chose Senator Alben Barkley of Kentucky as their vice-presidential candidate. The Democratic platform praised the President's

A jubilant President Truman displays an early edition of the Chicago Tribune, *which mistakenly announced a Dewey victory.*

foreign policy and endorsed his proposals for domestic reform. Over the opposition of southern delegates, the convention approved a strong civil-rights plank, calling for a permanent FEPC and the enactment of anti-lynching and anti-poll-tax laws.

Other presidential candidates were offered by two factions of dissatisfied Democrats. (1) Even before the regular party convention met, Henry Wallace had organized left-wing Democrats into a new Progressive Party. It nominated Wallace for the presidency on a platform calling for sweeping social reforms and co-operation with the Soviet Union. (2) Dissatisfied southern Democrats formed the States' Rights Democratic Party, commonly called the Dixiecrat Party. They nominated Governor J. Strom Thurmond of South Carolina as their candidate for the presidency. The Dixiecrats hoped that they could prevent any presidential candidate from getting a majority of the electoral votes and thus throw the election into the House of Representatives.

Truman's chances look slim. Few people except Truman himself thought he could win against such overwhelming odds. After the political conventions had been held, the President called a special session of Congress and challenged the Republicans to carry out the promises of domestic reform included in their platform. Because

nothing came of this session, Truman waged his campaign on the theme of the "do-nothing" Congress. While public-opinion polls and newspapers confidently predicted a Truman defeat, the scrappy President conducted a "one-man crusade" throughout the country. In contrast, Governor Dewey waged an overconfident campaign, speaking in general terms and saying nothing to endanger the expected Republican victory. Some disgruntled Republicans called it a "me-too" campaign.

Truman wins an upset victory. On election night the Chicago *Tribune* put out a special edition announcing in banner headlines "Dewey Defeats Truman." But much to the surprise of everyone, the Democrats won a stunning victory. Truman polled 24 million votes and Governor Dewey nearly 22 million. The President received 303 electoral votes to the Republican candidate's 189. Wallace and Thurmond each won about a million votes, and the latter candidate succeeded in carrying four southern states.

President Truman's supporters were jubilant. They predicted that the Democratic majorities elected to both houses of Congress would now enable the President to put through his program. But their prophecy was soon proved wrong. The same coalition of Republicans and southern Democrats that had blocked reform legislation in the late 1930's and in the postwar years continued to block Truman's recommendations during his second term.

Truman again requests domestic reforms. When he addressed Congress early in 1949, President Truman gave his domestic program a name — the Fair Deal — and described it as "an extension of the New Deal." He called for civil-rights legislation, broader Social Security coverage, a higher minimum wage, more public housing, health insurance, and application of the TVA idea (page 695) to other rivers. He also proposed that agricultural benefits be increased and that the Taft-Hartley Act be repealed.

None of these proposals was new; the President had suggested all of them earlier. But the Congress elected in 1948, like the previous Congress, showed a definite lack of interest. A majority of its members felt that the government should not undertake expensive new welfare programs. They were more concerned with protecting states' rights, reducing taxes and the government debt, regulating organized labor, and freeing business from excessive government regulation. Some congressmen were strongly opposed to Truman's civil rights program.

Congress goes its own way. Congress did accept a few of the President's proposals. It raised the minimum wage from 40 cents an hour to 75 cents. Social Security payments were increased, and coverage was extended to ten million additional workers. A new housing act provided money for slum clearance and the construction of new housing for low-income families. Congress continued the system of parity payments for farmers but turned down an administration plan intended to reduce agricultural surpluses. Congress also rejected a plan for national health insurance, and took no action on civil-rights legislation. A few minor revisions were made in the Taft-Hartley Act.

A new immigration act is passed. Since the end of the war, President Truman had been asking Congress to liberalize the immigration laws. He thought that the quota system (page 655) should be changed and that "displaced persons," who had been made homeless by the war, should be admitted. By 1950, Congress had admitted some 600,000 displaced persons. Two years later Congress passed a new immigration law but ignored the President's recommendations. The McCarran-Walter Act kept the quota system, though it lifted the long-time ban on Oriental immigration by establishing small quotas for Asian peoples. Other provisions of the bill denied admission to immigrants with past Communist associations, and provided for the deportation of aliens with Communist or "subversive" backgrounds. Truman vetoed the McCarran Act, but Congress passed the measure a second time with the necessary two-thirds majority.

The United States investigates Communist sympathizers. When President Truman began his "tough" policy against the Russians (page 759), he established a commission to investigate government employees and dismiss those who sympathized with communism. Later he created a Loyalty Review Board to pass judgment on government workers accused by the FBI of being Communist agents or "security risks." During the rest of Truman's term in office some 500 persons held to be security risks were removed from the government payroll, while more than three million were cleared.

Meanwhile, the House Un-American Activities Committee startled the nation with the perplexing case of Alger Hiss. Hiss had served in the State Department from 1936 to 1947. In 1948 a self-confessed former spy, Whittaker Chambers, testified before the House Committee that Hiss had been a Communist spy in the 1930's. Hiss denied the charge and sued Chambers for slander. Since more than seven years had elapsed, the statute of limitations[3] protected Hiss from being prosecuted for espionage. He was, however, tried for perjury, but the jury was unable to agree on a verdict. At a second trial, Hiss was convicted and sentenced to five years in prison. Some liberals maintained that Hiss

---

[3] This law provides that a person may not be prosecuted for a crime that took place more than seven years earlier.

was the victim of an overzealous Un-American Activities Committee, while conservatives believed that the courts had vindicated the House Committee. Soon after the Soviet Union exploded its first atomic bomb (page 765), a naturalized British scientist admitted having given top-secret information to the Russians. Americans began to wonder how many Communist agents were posing as upright, loyal citizens.

Communists are convicted under the Smith Act. The government had already taken steps to restrict Communist activities in the United States. The Smith Act, passed in 1940, had made it illegal for anyone to teach or advocate the overthrow of the government or to belong to any group which sought that goal. In 1949 eleven top leaders of the American Communist Party were convicted of violating the Smith Act. They appealed to the Supreme Court, which upheld the convictions. The Court ruled that the Smith Act was constitutional, for a conspiracy to overthrow the government constituted what Justice Oliver Wendell Holmes had described in 1919 as a "clear and present danger" (page 649). A minority of the justices, however, believed that the Smith Act violated the rights guaranteed to all Americans in the First Amendment.

The McCarran Internal Security Act is passed. Because Congress felt that the Smith Act did not provide a sufficient safeguard against Communist activities, it passed the McCarran Internal Security Act in 1950. This act not only outlawed Communist organizations but required them to publish their records. All members of the Communist Party and of Communist-front organizations had to register with the Attorney General. Communists were barred from employment in defense plants and were denied passports. Immigrants who had once been members of totalitarian organizations were prohibited from entering the United States. As it turned out, this provision made it difficult for people escaping from iron-curtain countries to find refuge in the United States.

President Truman vetoed the McCarran Act on the grounds that it punished people for their ideas, not their deeds. "In a free country," he said, "we punish men for the crimes they commit but never for the opinions they have." But Congress passed the measure over the President's veto.

McCarthy publicizes the Communist issue. Early in 1950, Senator Joseph McCarthy of Wisconsin made a sensational charge. McCarthy claimed that he had the names of 205 (later he said 57) Communists "still working and making policy" in the State Department. The Senate promptly appointed a subcommittee to look into McCarthy's charges. Since not one of the charges could be proved, the committee branded the Republican senator's speech a "fraud and a hoax." Undaunted, McCarthy broadened his attack and accused the "whole group of twisted-thinking New Dealers" of being Communists.

The Communist issue became a formidable political weapon. Scores of public officials climbed on the bandwagon by charging that others were "soft on communism." McCarthy went after bigger game. He accused former Secretary of State George C. Marshall of disloyalty and questioned the loyalty of Secretary of State Dean Acheson and President Truman. Across the country, professors, teachers, authors, librarians, and labor leaders who advocated social reform or criticized the nation's foreign policy were accused of being Communist sympathizers or active Communist agents. The spread of "McCarthyism" reminded many Americans of the "Red scare" hysteria that followed World War I.

Dissatisfaction with the Truman administration increases. Fear of Communist infiltration was only one reason for growing unrest in the United States during the early 1950's. The conflict in Korea (page 767) was especially discouraging. People began to wonder why American lives were being sacrificed in that far-off land. Moreover, the economic strain of the Korean War caused a rise in the cost of living. The government again imposed wage and price controls, and these restrictions further irritated many people.

Strikes in steel, coal, oil, and other industries during 1952 also inconvenienced

A general and a governor faced each other in the 1952 election. In the first picture, General and Mrs. Eisenhower are being greeted by Thomas E. Dewey, the Republican presidential candidate in the two previous elections. The Democratic candidate, Governor Adlai Stevenson of Illinois, and his running mate, Senator John Sparkman of Alabama, appear in the picture at right.

the public. Truman tried to settle the steel strike by arbitration. When that failed, he ordered government seizure of the steel plants. The President felt he had the authority to do this because of the emergency created by the Korean War. But the steel companies appealed to the Supreme Court, which found no authority in the Constitution or in law for the President's action.

The Republicans, already looking with confidence to the 1952 elections, were pleased to discover evidence of corruption in Washington. Officials in the Reconstruction Finance Corporation had accepted freezers and mink coats for their wives in return for granting RFC loans. Moreover, a few agents in the Bureau of Internal Revenue and the tax division of the Department of Justice had accepted "pay-offs" to settle tax cases. Though the President cleaned house in these departments, he moved too slowly to satisfy his critics.

Meanwhile, a Senate subcommittee, headed by Estes Kefauver, a Democrat from Tennessee, was investigating organized crime. Its televised hearings attracted a nation-wide audience, which saw notorious gang leaders talk about their ties with big-

city politicians — most of them Democrats. The Republicans argued that such ties provided one more reason for ending twenty years of Democratic rule.

▶ CHECK-UP

1. What benefits were provided veterans after World War II? Why did an inflationary period follow the war? What reforms did Truman advocate? With what success?

2. Why did Congress pass the Taft-Hartley Act? What were its provisions? Why did Congress pass the Twenty-second Amendment? How was presidential succession changed?

3. Why did rifts develop in the Democratic Party? What candidates ran for President in 1948? What was the outcome?

4. What reforms were included in Truman's Fair Deal? Why were many of them turned down by Congress? Which were passed? What was the McCarran-Walter Act?

5. How did communism in government become an issue? What were the provisions of the Smith Act? The McCarran Internal Security Act? What charges were made by Senator McCarthy? Why did dissatisfaction with the Truman administration increase?

. . . .

CHAPTER THIRTY-SEVEN

2 Eisenhower Follows a More Conservative Policy

Candidates are nominated for the election of 1952. Since the Republicans had high hopes of winning the presidency in 1952, there was a spirited contest within the party for control of the convention delegates. Conservative Republicans, particularly in the Midwest, supported Senator Taft of Ohio, but moderate Republicans preferred General Dwight Eisenhower. Well-known to all Americans for his wartime service, the General had the advantage of having no previous political associations. When the Republican convention met, Taft had more delegates than Eisenhower, but the General's supporters prevented contested Taft delegates from being seated. As a result, Eisenhower was nominated on the first ballot. The delegates chose Senator Richard M. Nixon of California as Eisenhower's running mate. The Republican platform was sufficiently vague to satisfy both conservative and moderate Republicans. The conservatives gave support to Eisenhower in the campaign, though there was lingering bitterness about the party's rejection of Taft.

Under the Twenty-second Amendment (page 156), President Truman was eligible to run for another term, but he announced in March that he would not be a candidate. He indicated his preference for Governor Adlai E. Stevenson of Illinois as the Democratic nominee. Though Stevenson was reluctant to run for President, the Democratic convention nominated him on the third ballot. For the vice-presidency the Democrats chose Senator John Sparkman of Alabama. Their platform reaffirmed the Fair Deal and promised action on civil rights.

The Republicans win the election. The Republicans based their campaign on "Korea, communism, and corruption." As we saw in Chapter 36, Eisenhower won much support by his promise to "go to Korea and try to end the war." The General also lashed out at corruption in Washington and called for lower taxes and less government regulation of business. Nixon developed the theme of Communist infiltration into the government, charging "that Mr. Truman, Dean Acheson and other administration officials for political reasons covered up this Communist conspiracy and attempted to halt its exposure."

In his campaign, Governor Stevenson promised to "talk sense to the American people." He spoke of the "long, patient, costly struggle which alone can assure triumph" in the cold war. His strong support of Fair Deal objectives won him the backing of liberals and organized labor. Stevenson's eloquent, witty speeches appealed to intellectuals. But his promise to advance civil rights alarmed many southern whites.

On election day, Eisenhower won nearly 34 million popular votes, while Stevenson received over 27 million. The Republicans carried 39 states (including four southern ones) to win 442 electoral votes; the Democrats had only 89 electoral votes from nine states. Yet the victory was a personal one for Eisenhower and far from a clean sweep for Republican candidates for other offices. The Republicans gained control of Congress by a very narrow margin — 48 to 47 in the Senate (with one independent) and 221 to 213 in the House of Representatives. Until his untimely death in 1953, Senator Taft was the dominant force in the Senate.

Eisenhower takes over as President. At the age of 62, General Eisenhower became the country's thirty-fourth President. Unlike many of his predecessors, he did not believe in trying to force his views on Congress. In fact, he talked about "restoring the constitutional balance" and letting congressmen "vote their own consciences." One historian has observed that the President "proved to be the very antithesis [opposite] of the stereotype of the professional soldier. Instead of issuing commands, he made requests. Instead of attacking his opponents, he sought to conciliate them." There was one carry-over from Eisenhower's army career, however; this was the reorganization of the White House staff along the lines of a military staff system. The chief of the executive staff was former Governor Sherman Adams of New Hampshire. All information (except in the field of foreign affairs) passed through his office, and he made the final decision about what to place on the President's desk.

The President's closest adviser in the Cabinet was Secretary of State John Foster Dulles. A wealthy lawyer, Dulles had wide experience in foreign affairs and had helped negotiate the Japanese peace treaty. In formulating domestic policy, the most influential member of the Cabinet was Secretary of the Treasury George M. Humphrey, a successful businessman from Ohio. To the new Cabinet post of Secretary of Health, Education, and Welfare, Eisenhower named a woman, Oveta Culp Hobby of Texas.

The Senate censures McCarthy. McCarthyism was as troublesome a problem for Eisenhower as it had been for Truman. The Wisconsin senator continued to make charges concerning Communist influence in the federal government, despite the fact that his own party was now in control. Nor was McCarthy impressed by the fact that Eisenhower abolished the Loyalty Review Board and established special security boards in each department and agency. Senator McCarthy insisted that Communists were being sheltered in the Central Intelligence Agency, in the State Department, and elsewhere in the government.

Early in 1954 McCarthy launched an investigation of the Army Signal Corps installations in New Jersey. The army struck back with charges that McCarthy was trying to secure special privileges for one of his former staff members. A special Senate committee investigated McCarthy's activities, and recommended public censure of the Wisconsin senator. In December, 1954, the Senate voted to condemn McCarthy for conduct "unbecoming a member of the United States Senate." After the vote of censure, McCarthy's influence declined.

Republicans try to reduce the federal government's operations. President Eisenhower pleased Taft supporters when he promised to make the federal government "smaller rather than bigger" and to find "things it can stop doing instead of seeking new things to do." Wage and price controls imposed during the Korean War were lifted; rent controls were retained only in areas of severe housing shortages. Moreover, the Reconstruction Finance Corporation was abolished, the federal budget was reduced, and the number of government employees was cut back. The Eisenhower administration also sought to transfer certain governmental functions to the states. Thus, offshore oil deposits were turned over to the states, making possible private (rather than federal government) development of these resources.

The Eisenhower administration likewise encouraged private rather than public development of hydroelectric power and atomic energy. When the Atomic Energy Commission asked for additional electric power from TVA, Congress decided to let private power companies supply the needed electricity. Without competitive bidding, it awarded the so-called Dixon-Yates contract to private companies, thereby touching off a furious political quarrel. In 1955 this controversial contract was canceled, though

Secretary of State Dulles (left) and Vice-President Nixon (center) greeted Chancellor Konrad Adenauer when the German leader arrived in Washington for conferences with President Eisenhower.

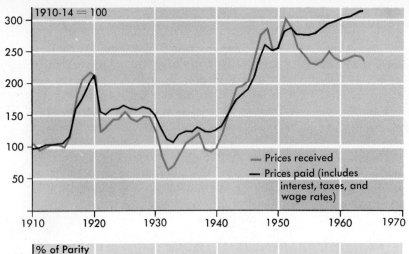

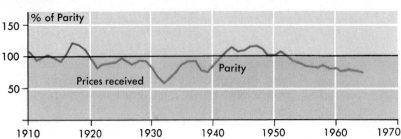

THE FARM PROBLEM

This chart shows that since 1951 prices paid by the farmer have exceeded those he has received. The parity ratio, therefore, has been below 100.

private power companies were encouraged to build their own dams. Moreover, the Atomic Energy Act of 1954 permitted private industry to develop atomic power.

Congress approves new expenditures. Throughout the 1950's Congress favored a moderate domestic policy which right-wing Republicans called too "socialistic" and which liberal Democrats considered too conservative. But it satisfied the coalition of moderate Republicans and southern Democrats, and President Eisenhower accepted most of its legislation.

Among the expenditures which Congress authorized during Eisenhower's first term was the St. Lawrence Seaway project. Three former Presidents had urged the construction of a channel around the rapids in the St. Lawrence River and other improvements to open the Great Lakes to ocean shipping. When Canada announced that it would undertake this project on its own, the Senate finally ratified a treaty providing for joint Canadian-American construction (1954). Opened to traffic in 1959, the waterway enabled ocean-going ships to reach Great Lakes ports.

Congress also extended Social Security coverage to ten million more people in

1954 and declared an additional four million people eligible for unemployment compensation. A public housing program provided for some 80,000 housing units. In 1956 Congress allocated 33 billion dollars for a thirteen-year highway-building program. The Trade Agreements Act (page 694), which for a time had been renewed only from year to year, was extended for a three-year period in 1955 (and in 1958 for four years). In addition, Congress approved the expenditure of more than 22 billion dollars for foreign aid between 1953 and 1960.

The administration tackles financial problems. After the Korean War ended in 1953 (page 768), cuts in defense appropriations reduced government expenditures by several billion dollars. This reduction in government spending was partly responsible for a temporary slow-down in the nation's economy. But the recession soon lifted and the economy moved ahead to a new high level of production. A tax cut in 1954, more liberal credit policies, and a swelling demand for consumer goods helped nourish the economic boom.

Meanwhile, prices and the cost of living climbed upward. Economists differed as to the cause of this inflation. Some blamed it on organized labor's demand for higher wages. Others blamed it on employers who met these wage demands by increasing prices. Still others argued that government spending was a major factor in the rising cost of living.

The Eisenhower administration made a determined effort to balance the federal budget and succeeded in doing so in 1956 and 1957. But the President found that continued heavy spending for national defense, plus expenditures for foreign aid and essential programs at home, made it impossible to balance the budget every year or to reduce the national debt.

President Eisenhower is re-elected. The Democrats looked forward to the 1956 presidential election with growing confidence. Two years before, in the congressional elections, they had regained a narrow margin over the Republicans in both the House and Senate. Moreover, though Eisenhower had lost none of his popularity, his health had become a political issue. In September, 1955, he suffered a heart attack, and less than a year later he was hospitalized for an emergency abdominal operation. But the President made speedy recoveries from both illnesses.

In 1956, the Democratic convention again nominated Adlai Stevenson and this time chose Senator Estes Kefauver for the vice-presidency. A week later the Republicans unanimously selected Eisenhower and Nixon to head their ticket. The Republicans based their campaign on the three "P's" — popularity, prosperity, and peace. The President was at the height of his popularity with the American people, and there was little the Democrats could do about it. Eisenhower won the election by an overwhelming majority — 35½ million to 26 million in the popular vote, and 457 to 74 in the electoral vote. But the President's popularity did not carry over to other Republican candidates. For the first time in more than a century a winning President failed to carry either house of Congress. Leadership in Congress fell to two moderate Democrats, both from Texas — Speaker of the House Sam Rayburn and

Lyndon B. Johnson, Majority Leader of the Senate.

Farm problems continue. Throughout the 1950's the country continued to face the problem of how to enable the farm population to share in the general prosperity. The Republicans had criticized President Truman's farm program as costly and unsuccessful. Eisenhower's Secretary of Agriculture, Ezra Taft Benson, proposed a new policy of flexible rather than fixed government price supports for farm products. Congress agreed to change price supports from 90 per cent of parity to a flexible scale, ranging from 82.5 to 90 per cent. It was hoped that this program would sustain farm income and still reduce crop surpluses. In addition, a "soil bank" plan provided payments to farmers who withdrew acres from production.

This farm program had no more success, however, than the programs of other administrations. Farm surpluses remained a problem. During the 1950's, output per man-hour on the farms continued to rise because of improved machinery, new agricultural techniques, advances in scientific plant breeding, and the introduction of new crops. Thus, farm production increased, despite the fact that five million people left the countryside for the cities. Although the government's price-support program cost five times as much in 1960 as it had in 1952, the income of farm families actually declined over this period. Small farmers who did not participate in the price-support program were especially hard-hit.

Organized labor faces new problems. Union members, like farmers, had to adjust to changing conditions in the 1950's. In 1955, the rival AFL and CIO formed a unified labor federation, representing some fifteen million American workers. President George Meany of the AFL became president of the new AFL-CIO, and Walter Reuther, the CIO president, became vice-president and head of the Industrial Union Department. Differences between industrial unions and craft unions, however, continued to cause friction in the new organization.

One problem that faced organized labor

in the 1950's was getting its share of the growing industrial income made possible by increased productivity. Congress raised the minimum wage to one dollar per hour for a 40-hour week in interstate industries. And fringe benefits (including pensions, medical care, and paid vacations) were at a new high level. But wage increases and fringe benefits were often offset by the rising cost of living.

The most serious problem for organized labor was *automation* — the use of electronic controls to operate machines. Automation greatly reduced the number of workers needed in many plants and thus threatened workers' security. How to make use of the new electronic devices to increase the efficiency of production and also to avoid unemployment was a major challenge to both employers and employees.

New labor legislation is passed. Still another labor problem was the growing evidence that a small number of unions were mismanaging pension and welfare funds and were involved in unsavory deals with racketeers and gangsters. Senator John McClel-

---

Two More Stars Added to the Flag

The parade of new states into the Union, which had halted in 1912 with the admission of New Mexico and Arizona, was resumed in 1959. In that year Alaska and Hawaii received statehood, becoming the forty-ninth and fiftieth states respectively.

The new states set a notable precedent in that they were noncontiguous (did not adjoin their sister states). Alaska, the largest state in area, is separated from the 48 continental states by a strip of Canada. Hawaii, of course, is an island group in the Pacific Ocean about 2400 miles southwest of California.

Surprisingly, Hawaii is not the smallest state in the Union in area but ranks ahead of Connecticut, Delaware, and Rhode Island. In 1965 its estimated population was 711,000, while Alaska's was 253,000. The location of both Hawaii and Alaska gives them strategic importance as military bases.

---

lan of Arkansas began an investigation of racketeering in labor unions. The president of the Teamsters Brotherhood, Dave Beck, was charged with misappropriating union funds, and he eventually went to jail. The Teamsters then elected James Hoffa to head their union. Since damaging evidence against Hoffa had been brought to light by the McClellan committee, the AFL-CIO evicted the Teamsters union from the labor federation.

As a result of the investigation, Congress passed a law giving the government greater control over organized labor. The Landrum-Griffin Act (1959) was designed to enforce democratic procedures and financial honesty in labor unions. It provided a "Bill of Rights" for union members and required the use of secret ballots in union elections. The law prohibited convicts and members of the Communist Party from serving as union officers and business agents. Unions were required to submit detailed reports to the Secretary of Labor concerning pension and welfare funds.

Court rulings declare segregation illegal. During President Eisenhower's administration, Negro Americans increased their demands for first-class citizenship. Since Congress had not acted on President Truman's requests for civil-rights legislation, Negro leaders continued to seek justice in the courts. Lawyers of the National Association for the Advancement of Colored People carried cases to the Supreme Court and won a number of victories. In 1948 the Court ruled that restrictive real-estate covenants[4] could not be legally enforced. Another Court decision ruled that a state college or university had to admit Negroes unless the state provided equivalent programs in an institution open to them. Separate facilities for Negroes and whites on interstate trains and buses were also prohibited. And the Court ruled that segregated public parks, playgrounds, beaches, and golf courses were illegal.

The Supreme Court rules against school segregation. The most important

[4] Agreements not to sell houses in specified areas to certain types of people.

Some states which had required public school segregation firmly resisted the Court ruling; others began to integrate schools. Above left, students at a desegregated school in Louisville, Kentucky, move through the corridors. Thurgood Marshall (above right) argued the case for integrated schools before the Supreme Court. Marshall later was appointed United States Solicitor General.

decision came in May, 1954 (*Brown v. Board of Education of Topeka*). In this historic ruling the Supreme Court set aside the 1896 decision (page 397) that had upheld "separate but equal" school facilities for Negro children. The Court declared unanimously that "in the field of public education, the doctrine of 'separate but equal' has no place. Separate educational facilities are inherently unequal." The decision affected seventeen states and the District of Columbia, all of which had laws requiring segregation in public schools. Aware of the difficulty of changing a long-established pattern, the Court handed down another decision a year later, calling for segregated school systems to make "a prompt and reasonable start" on plans for integration.

Reaction to the Court's decision is mixed. Many Northerners and a small minority of southern whites joined with Negroes in approving the Supreme Court's decision. In the border states, many whites disapproved of the ruling, but were prepared to obey it as the law of the land. In the states of the Deep South, opponents of the decision declared they would prevent integration as long as possible.

Progress toward school integration, therefore, followed an uneven course. In the District of Columbia and in most border states, schools proceeded to integrate without any serious trouble. But disturbances broke out over the admission of Negro students to a white school in Clinton, Tennessee, and the enrollment of a Negro girl in the University of Alabama. The most serious trouble came in Little Rock, Arkansas, in 1957. The local school board had agreed to admit nine Negro students to Central High School, but Governor Orval Faubus intervened and used the Arkansas national guard to bar their entrance. When President Eisenhower persuaded the Governor to remove the na-

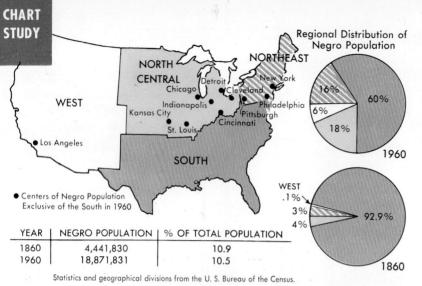

Regional Distribution of
Negro Population

DISTRIBUTION OF NEGRO POPULATION, 1860 AND 1960

Notice the shift in regional distribution of the Negro population since 1860. Large numbers of Negroes have migrated to urban centers outside the South.

● Centers of Negro Population
Exclusive of the South in 1960

YEAR	NEGRO POPULATION	% OF TOTAL POPULATION
1860	4,441,830	10.9
1960	18,871,831	10.5

Statistics and geographical divisions from the U. S. Bureau of the Census.

---

tional guard, unruly mobs threatened the safety of the Negro students. Finally, the President sent federal troops to Little Rock and ordered the Arkansas national guard into federal service. When order was restored, the Negro students entered the school and the troops were withdrawn.

In Virginia the state legislature passed laws aimed at closing schools faced by court orders to admit Negroes. The legislature also adopted a plan to use public funds to pay the tuition of students in schools of their choice. In 1959 a start was made at desegregating schools in Norfolk and Arlington, Virginia. Prince Edward County, however, closed its public schools. White children in that county attended private schools supported in part by public funds, but Negroes, choosing to continue the fight for desegregation, had no official schools until the Supreme Court in 1964 ordered desegregated public schools to be reopened.

The civil-rights movement makes gains. Meanwhile, other developments furthered the drive for equal rights and opportunities. The Eisenhower administration completed the job, started by Truman, of ending segregation in the armed services. More Negroes were hired for government jobs. And Congress passed the first civil-rights acts since reconstruction.

The Civil Rights Act of 1957 was designed to give federal protection to Negroes wanting to vote. It created a Civil Rights Commission to investigate cases in which state or local officials interfered with Negro registration or voting. Federal judges could order election officials to register qualified voters. Another Civil Rights Act, passed in 1960, made it a federal offense to threaten voters with violence.

Negro leaders were quick to follow up the court decisions and civil-rights laws. Bolstered by the 1954 Supreme Court ruling, they won many lower court decisions outlawing segregation practices. In Montgomery, Alabama, a young minister, Dr. Martin Luther King, Jr., helped direct a Negro boycott aimed at ending segregation in buses. This economic pressure, plus court decisions, led to the desegregation of the Montgomery bus system. A believer in non-violence, King urged his followers to meet physical assaults with passive resistance. Well-disciplined groups of Negro demonstrators prayed, sang, or marched with placards to achieve their goals.

Early in 1960 four Negro college students sat down at a white lunch counter in Greensboro, North Carolina. Soon the "sit-in" movement swept the South. Hundreds of Negro students, often accompanied by whites, staged "sit-ins" at lunch counters, department stores, libraries, and movie theaters. When the students were arrested for violating local segregation laws, they chose to go to jail and appeal their cases rather than pay fines. As a result of the "sit-in" movement, many southern cities desegregated lunch counters, stores, and theaters.

Dissatisfaction with the administration grows. By 1958, though President Eisenhower's personal popularity remained high, there was increasing discontent with the Republican administration. Reasons for this dissatisfaction included a recession in 1958, farm discontent, and criticism of the actions of several high government officials.

Toward the end of 1957 the economy had skidded into a serious slump. By the next spring, industrial production was down 14 per cent and unemployment had risen to more than five million. Unemployment insurance payments kept many families from serious want; and the government eased credit restrictions and speeded up defense spending and the highway construction program. Though these measures helped to stimulate the economy, the Democrats were able to use the "Eisenhower recession" as a campaign issue.

Another source of discontent was the government's farm policy. As we have seen, farm surpluses continued to be a problem throughout the 1950's. By 1958 farmers had apparently concluded that Secretary of Agriculture Benson's policies were not going to relieve their situation.

The opposition also took advantage of the fact that the Republicans, who had promised to "clean up the mess" in Washington, had some embarrassing scandals of their own. Sherman Adams, the Assistant to the President, had accepted gifts from a businessman seeking government favors. Democrats and even some Republicans who resented Adams' influence called for his dismissal. President Eisenhower resisted, saying "I need him," but Adams finally resigned.

Democrats widen their lead in Congress. In November, 1958, the Democrats won an impressive victory at the polls. They increased their majority in the Senate, 62 to 34, and in the House, 282 to 153. This was the largest margin either party had held in Congress since Roosevelt's sweeping victory in 1936. The Republicans took consolation in the upset election of Nelson Rockefeller as Governor of New York, and they hoped to mend their fences before the next presidential contest.

▶ CHECK-UP

1. What issues did the Republicans stress in the 1952 campaign? What were Eisenhower's views about the role of the President? About the scope of the federal government's operations?

2. What new expenditures were voted by Congress? On what issues did the Republicans base their campaign in 1956? With what result?

3. How did the Republican administration deal with farm problems? What problems confronted labor? What were the provisions of the Landrum-Griffin Act?

4. What Court rulings extended and protected the civil rights of Negroes? What different reactions were provoked by the Court's school decision? How did the Civil Rights Acts of 1957 and 1960 seek to safeguard Negroes' right to vote? What use was made of peaceful demonstrations in the civil rights movement?

5. Why did dissatisfaction with the Republican administration increase after 1957? How was this reflected in the 1958 elections?

* * * * * * * * * * * * * * * * * * * *

3 *A Prosperous Society Undergoes Many Changes*

Despite the tensions of the cold war and disagreements on domestic policy, the American economy made sharp advances in the 1950's and early 1960's. This unprecedented prosperity allowed many people to raise their standard of living and broaden the variety of their leisure-time activities.

Most Americans share in the economic prosperity. The vastly increased production of American industry during the 1950's brought material rewards for most American families. Economists have estimated that the average American worker received

Vacationing Americans may fly to foreign countries, drive to camping grounds, or go to local beaches (left, New York City's Coney Island). As the population grows and industrial and urban development continues, wilderness areas grow smaller. To preserve areas of natural beauty and interest, the government maintains national parks. The campground above is part of Zion National Park in Utah.

roughly 50 per cent more income at the end of the 1950's than he had just before World War II. Of equal significance was the fact that national income was more evenly distributed than at any time in the American past. In 1929, for example, more than two thirds of all American families had received yearly incomes of 4000 dollars or under. By 1963, less than a third were in this bracket, while half of all American families received from 4000 to 10,000 dollars a year.

The income of city families increased by a larger proportion than did that of farm families. Though declining farm prosperity was the chief reason, another was that cities provided greater opportunities for women to find jobs. By the 1950's one out of every three women was holding down a full-time job (chart, page 485). Urban Negroes also enjoyed a rise in earning power; better education, a wider variety of available jobs, and minimum wage laws were responsible. More Negroes found employment in clerical and sales jobs, in skilled factory jobs, and in the professions.

Americans enjoy a high standard of living. The larger incomes of most American families went into material goods and services rather than savings. Many families moved to the suburbs, buying a small plot of land with a one-story or split-level ranch house. New household appliances took their place beside the familiar vacuum sweeper, washing machine, and refrigerator. Increasing numbers of Americans hastened to equip their homes with dishwashers, freezers, clothes dryers and hair dryers, electric coffee pots and skillets, food blenders and mixers, television, high-fidelity phonographs, air-conditioners, power lawn-mowers, and extension telephones.

Many families had two cars in their garages, and a growing number owned summer cottages and boats. Still another sign of prosperity was the increasing amount of pleasure travel. Eight million Americans traveled abroad during the decade of the 1950's, and a much larger number took long vacation trips within the United States. Because most Americans preferred to travel in their own cars or by airplane, the passenger income of railroads and bus companies suffered. In many large cities commuter rail lines closed down because former passengers chose to drive their automobiles to and from work.

"Pockets" of poverty still exist. While most Americans shared in the economic prosperity of the postwar years, some did not. In *The Affluent Society,* John Kenneth Galbraith observed that poverty was no longer "a massive affliction" as in the 1930's. But for some people, poverty was a very real thing. Almost every city still had large slum areas, where people with little or no education and few job skills were crowded into substandard housing. Many of them existed on relief payments.

In a few areas of the country, poverty resulted from the depressed state of certain industries. Coal-mining, for instance, was hurt by the increased use of oil, gas, and electricity. A growing number of mines were forced to close down. Those that stayed open introduced labor-saving machinery to make their operations profitable. Thus, thousands of coal miners, especially in Pennsylvania and West Virginia, lost their jobs. Other Americans whose incomes remained low were small farmers who did not participate in the parity program.

Still another group of people who lived in poverty were the migrant farm workers. These people moved from one area of the country to another, wherever unskilled farm labor was needed. Often of Negro, Mexican, or Puerto Rican background, these families traveled north with the harvest season, seldom earning more than a thousand dollars a year. Their children had little chance to get an education.

The population increases rapidly. Another significant development of the postwar era was a sharp rise in population. The total number of Americans jumped from 140 million in 1945 to 180 million by 1960.[5] More than three million immigrants were admitted during this period, but the major reasons for the population increase were a high birth rate and a longer life span. A trend toward earlier marriage and larger families produced a bumper crop of babies in the 1950's. At the same time, the use of antibiotics and new surgical techniques helped reduce the death rate. By 1960 the average life span was 70 years.

The West grew faster than any other part of the country. California especially attracted people from other states. In the 1960's it passed New York as the most populous state in the Union. While urban communities continued to grow in the 1950's, the most startling rate of growth was in the suburbs. By 1960 nearly 55 million Americans were suburbanites. Some 70 per cent of the population lived in urban or suburban communities. A new term — *megalopolis* — was coined to refer to an extensive area covering several major centers of population. Social scientists applied this term, for example, to the densely settled coastal area reaching from Boston to Washington, D.C. (map, page 816).

Critics worry about American conformity. Some observers claimed that television, increased travel, and the rapid growth of the suburbs (especially those with almost identical houses) reflected a growing "sameness" in American life. More and more people were holding so-

[5] By 1966 the population was estimated to be 200 million.

called "white-collar" jobs; they worked as salesmen and office personnel or held professional, managerial, and executive positions. Their incomes, clothes, houses, entertainment, and recreation all tended to be similar. Said one historian, "More people than ever before had white-collar jobs, white-collar incomes, white-collar educations, and white-collar values." Some Americans regarded this development as a natural consequence of the continued expansion of the American middle class. But critics charged that the trend toward conformity led Americans to avoid independent thought and controversy and to seek personal security rather than individual achievement.

American schools are subjected to criticism. This re-examination of goals in American life carried over into the field of education. The country's public schools came under close scrutiny, especially after the launching of Sputnik in 1957. Many Americans concluded that the Russians were beating us in space because the Soviet educational program required more of students. Critics of the American high-school curriculum demanded the elimination of "frills" and asked for greater emphasis on science and mathematics. It was also proposed that schools make advanced courses available to gifted students. Both the government and private foundations provided funds to develop better programs in science, mathematics, foreign languages, and other subject areas. As a result, advanced-placement programs have enabled bright high-school students in many schools to take college-level courses. The colleges, in turn, have revised freshman and sophomore courses to meet the needs of well-prepared high-school graduates.

POPULATION TRENDS

MAP STUDY

The ten states with the largest number of people are indicated in color in the map below. Note that California has captured first place in population rank. As the arrow at top right shows, the country's center of population has moved steadily westward. The pyramid of age groups (lower right) compares population in 1965 and in 1980 as projected by demographic experts.

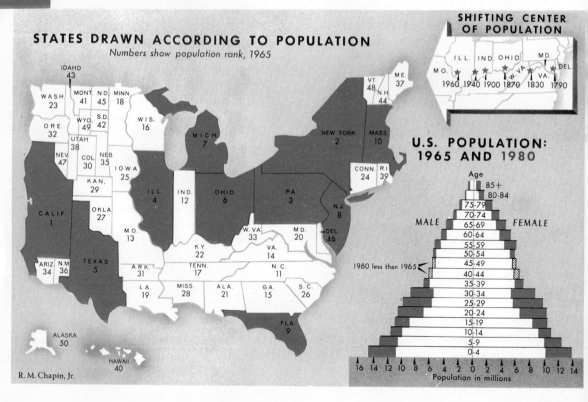

SHIFTING CENTER OF POPULATION

STATES DRAWN ACCORDING TO POPULATION
Numbers show population rank, 1965

U.S. POPULATION: 1965 AND 1980

R. M. Chapin, Jr.

Another problem which faced both schools and colleges in the 1950's was the sharp increase in enrollments. Population growth was chiefly responsible, but another factor was the desire of a greater percentage of young people to go to college.

Television entertains America. The charge of conformity in the 1950's was most often aimed at television. While radio and the movies had captured the hearts of Americans in the 1920's, the great love affair of the post-World War II generation was with television. Though experiments with television had begun in the 1930's, sets were not generally available until the late 1940's. But within ten years nearly 85 per cent of American homes acquired television sets, and some had two or three. Many families depended on the "TV" for their news, weather reports, and entertainment.

Television's tremendous popularity brought varied reactions. Many critics claimed that advertisers had too much influence on the scheduling of television programs. It was also charged that both advertisers and television executives underrated viewers' intelligence. As a result, said the critics, television channels were clogged with westerns, crime dramas, and low-grade comedy shows. Others, however, pointed out that television also broadcast many stimulating programs. They cited original television dramas, productions of well-known plays and operas, symphonic concerts, documentaries, interviews with public figures, and coverage of political campaigns and other special news events.

The movie theaters felt the competition of television. From 1945 to 1960 attendance fell from 90 million a week to 40 million. The motion-picture industry tried to meet the competition in several ways. Drive-in theaters sought to lure patrons from the highways. Some producers hired foreign stars, made their films in exotic parts of the world, or spent millions in producing "epics." American movies still had their stars, but Hollywood had lost much of its glamour.

Americans show a lively interest in the arts. One answer to the charge of conformity was the steadily growing interest of Americans in literature, drama, music, art, and architecture. Critics were amazed at the huge numbers of paperbound books and long-playing records bought by middle-income Americans. More people also acquired original prints, paintings, and pieces of sculpture for their homes. In addition, large numbers visited local museums, attended concerts and ballets, and supported drama groups. Across the country, theaters and concert halls were built to accommodate the "cultural explosion."

The attention given to "best-seller" lists and the growing membership of book clubs indicated the public's interest in new books. This was sparked in part by the work of young writers inspired by experiences in World War II. Other novelists and playwrights explored psychological problems or criticized the social scene.

Americans buy paperbound books. One of the best indications of the growing interest in literature during the 1950's and 1960's was the phenomenal sale of paperbound books. Some paperbound editions had been published before and during World War II. But a few years after the war, publishers began offering a much wider variety of these inexpensive books — nonfiction, classics, and serious modern novels as well as detective stories and other "light" reading. By 1960 paperbacks were accounting for three fourths of all books sold in the United States.

American music wins acclaim. The long-playing record, introduced in 1948, had the same success in the field of music that the paperback had in publishing. Interest in music reached a new high as Americans bought millions of "LP's" of symphonic music, operas, jazz, and popular and folk songs.

A leading figure in American music since the 1930's has been Aaron Copland, composer of symphonies, ballets, operas, and film scores. Copland had an ambition "to write a work that would immediately be recognized as American in character." He did this in his ballet scores *Billy the Kid* and *Appalachian Spring*. Both of these works drew on folk songs and American legends.

Oklahoma! *by Richard Rodgers and Oscar Hammerstein II delighted audiences with its vivacious songs and dancing (left).*

The American composer Aaron Copland wrote the score for Rodeo *(right) and other ballets with American themes. Like* Oklahoma!, *Copland's* Rodeo *had a western background and cowboy characters.*

The conductor Leonard Bernstein (left) is noted for his musical comedy scores as well as his symphonic compositions. Bernstein's television broadcasts have contributed to young people's appreciation of music.

Jazz had been the first American music to make an impression on other countries. By the mid-1900's American composers of symphonies, ballets, and musicals had also won world-wide recognition. American orchestras and performers toured foreign countries playing to enthusiastic audiences. Both at home and abroad, people enjoyed the blending of song, drama, and dance in American musical comedies. Perhaps the most successful of the postwar musical-comedy composers was Richard Rodgers, who collaborated with Oscar Hammerstein II in such memorable productions as *Oklahoma!* and *South Pacific.* By far the most popular musical of the 1950's was *My Fair Lady* by Alan Jay Lerner and Frederick

Loewe. An especially versatile musician of the postwar period was Leonard Bernstein, composer of the musical *West Side Story.* Bernstein has also written symphonic music and serves as conductor of the New York Philharmonic Orchestra.

American art and architecture flourish. By the postwar years American artists had developed a style of painting that commanded attention in Europe in much the same way the Armory Show (page 666) had awakened painters in the United States. Artists working in the new style, called *abstract expressionism,* did not try to show recognizable objects or themes. Jackson Pollock, for example, painted enormous canvases with multi-colored, interwoven lines. Other artists continued to work in the realistic tradition. Probably the best-known of these painters in the postwar years were Andrew Wyeth and Edward Hopper.

American architecture at mid-century was strongly influenced by Frank Lloyd Wright. His plans for private homes, his industrial building for the Johnson Wax Company, and his unusual Guggenheim Museum in New York were all daring designs which set standards for other architects. More recent outstanding architects have developed their own individual styles. (See the picture story on pages 777–780.)

▶ CHECK-UP

1. What evidence is there that most Americans shared in the prosperity of the 1950's? Why did some areas and some groups remain poor? What population trends developed?

2. What criticism was made concerning "sameness" in American life? (Consider television in this connection.) What changes were introduced in education?

3. What evidence is there of growing American interest in the arts? What trends have developed in American music? In art and architecture?

. . . .

Clinching the Main Ideas in Chapter 37

While President Truman's foreign policy usually enjoyed bipartisan support, his domestic policy met with opposition. Congress enacted little of his Fair Deal program. Moreover, such measures as the Taft-Hartley Act and the McCarran Internal Security Act were passed over Truman's veto. President Truman reached the peak of his popularity in 1948 with his upset victory in the election that year. Thereafter, the Korean War, fear of Communist infiltration into the government, and the exposure of corruption in Washington caused voters to turn away from the Democratic Party.

President Eisenhower took office in 1953, thus ending twenty years of Democratic control of the presidency. During the Eisenhower administration, Congress followed a middle-of-the-road course. While extending some of the New Deal programs, such as Social Security and minimum-wage legislation, it balked at undertaking further reform. The most far-reaching change in American life in the 1950's came as a result of the Supreme Court decision against segregation in the public schools. Encouraged by this ruling, Negro Americans stepped up their efforts to achieve full civil rights.

During the postwar years the United States enjoyed a period of unprecedented prosperity. It provided many Americans with the leisure time and the extra money to buy books and records, visit museums, and attend concerts and plays. But pockets of poverty continued to exist. This fact plus the Russian lead in space technology and the desire of many people to broaden the drive for equal opportunity set the stage for a lively presidential contest in 1960.

Chapter Review

Terms to Understand

1. Fair Deal	5. Smith Act	9. soil bank	13. Dixon-Yates
2. AFL-CIO	6. security risks	10. pockets of poverty	contract
3. CIA	7. automation	11. cultural explosion	14. Landrum-Griffin
4. FBI	8. megalopolis	12. GI Bill of Rights	Act

Terms to Understand (Cont.)

15. National Security
    Act
16. Taft-Hartley Act
17. "white collar
    values"
18. Un-American
    Activities
    Committee
19. McCarran
    Internal
    Security Act
20. *Brown v. Board
    of Education*
21. Civil Rights Acts
    of 1957 and 1960

What Do You Think?

1. Since the labor force and production for civilian use were both greater after the war, why did prices rise sharply during the period 1946–1947?

2. Despite the fact that most Americans have shared in the prosperity of the postwar years, "pockets of poverty" have persisted. Why?

3. Why did these Republican campaign slogans have wide appeal: "Korea, communism, and corruption" in 1952; "popularity, prosperity, and peace" in 1956?

4. Compare the Red "scares" after World Wars I and II. What was the underlying cause in each case?

5. What values and policies has Martin Luther King stressed in the civil-rights movement? Why?

Using Your Knowledge of History

1. Prepare a two-column chart listing major gains in the civil-rights movement since World War II. Use these headings: "Court Decisions" and "New Legislation."

2. One result of the cold war has been the greater stress on seeking excellence in American education. Plan a panel discussion to bring out possible advantages and disadvantages of this emphasis.

3. Write a letter to a newspaper giving your reaction to the idea of the growing "sameness" in American life.

4. Debate: *Resolved,* That a re-grouping of liberals and conservatives in the two major political parties to form a Liberal Party and a Conservative Party would be in the public interest.

Extending Your Knowledge of History

Two readable biographies which reflect different points of view are M. J. Pusey's *Eisenhower the President* and Marquis Childs' *Eisenhower: Captive Hero.* For developments during Eisenhower's first administration, see R. J. Donovan's *Eisenhower, the Inside Story* or Richard Rovere's *Affairs of State: The Eisenhower Years.* Alistair Cooke, a reporter at the Hiss trial, writes about the case in *A Generation on Trial.* Samuel Lubell analyzes the political balance of power during the postwar years in *The Future of American Politics.* The contrast between American life in the early 1900's and in the post-World War II years is the theme of Frederick Lewis Allen's *The Big Change: America Transforms Itself.* For more about American life during the 1950's, see John Kenneth Galbraith's *The Affluent Society* and *The 1950's: America's "Placid" Decade,* edited by Joseph Satin. On civil rights, see A. M. Rose's *The Negro in Postwar America* and Louis Lomax's *The Negro Revolt.*

CHAPTER 38

Presidents Kennedy
and Johnson
Introduce Changes

We stand today on the edge of a New Frontier — the frontier of the 1960's — a frontier of unknown opportunities and perils — a frontier of unfulfilled hopes and threats.

Woodrow Wilson's New Freedom promised our nation a new political and economic framework. Franklin Roosevelt's New Deal promised security and succor to those in need. But the New Frontier of which I speak is not a set of promises — it is a set of challenges. It sums up, not what I intend to offer the American people, but what I intend to ask of them.

JOHN F. KENNEDY, JULY 15, 1960

Satellite in space (artist's drawing)

1960–Today

In his speech accepting the Democratic presidential nomination, John F. Kennedy outlined the challenges of a New Frontier for Americans in the 1960's. He went on to win the presidency and occupied the White House for less than three years before his tragic assassination. But in that brief time he posed a number of challenges to the American people. He placed the support of the executive branch behind the civil rights movement. To grant equal rights to *all* citizens, he said, was to fulfill the democratic principles on which

this government rested. Keenly interested in the exploration of space, he launched a program designed to land an American on the moon by 1970. Kennedy tried to thwart Communist aggression in several new trouble spots around the globe. But at the same time he realized that the Communist bloc was undergoing changes and that agreement might be reached with the Russians in some areas.

In November, 1963, Lyndon B. Johnson took over the duties of the presidency and soon proved himself an able leader. He

completed many of Kennedy's programs
and proposed new ones of his own. Conservatives, alarmed by the nature and pace
of these domestic changes, rallied around
Senator Barry Goldwater in the election of
1964. But Johnson's huge vote indicated that
most Americans seemed ready and willing
to meet the challenges of the 1960's.

1 *President Kennedy Points to a New Frontier*

The parties select their candidates.
After their victories in the 1958 congressional elections, the Democrats were optimistic about their chances in the 1960
presidential campaign. Among those who
sought the Democratic nomination were
Senators John F. Kennedy of Massachusetts, Hubert Humphrey of Minnesota, and
Lyndon B. Johnson of Texas. Kennedy was
only 43 years old and a Roman Catholic.
He had done well in several presidential
primaries, especially in West Virginia, a
predominantly Protestant state. This convinced many delegates to the Democratic
convention that his youth and his religion
would not be serious handicaps. As a result, Kennedy was nominated on the first
ballot. Lyndon B. Johnson was named as
his running mate. The Democratic platform promised to regain America's "position of pre-eminence" in defense and world
affairs. Moreover, it promised a number of
domestic reforms — federal aid to public
schools, medical care for the elderly under
Social Security, full employment, and an
end to racial discrimination.

. . . .

CHAPTER FOCUS

1. President Kennedy points to a New
   Frontier.

2. President Johnson plans for a Great
   Society.

3. The cold war takes dangerous turns.

Vice-President Richard Nixon was the
favorite for the Republican nomination.
But moderate Republicans preferred Governor Nelson Rockefeller of New York and
called for a platform that would include a
strong civil rights plank, domestic reforms,
and an expanded defense program. On the
eve of the Republican convention, Nixon
met secretly with Rockefeller in New York
City and agreed to most of the Governor's
terms. Nixon was nominated on the first
ballot, and the Republican platform called
for strong action on civil rights and an
overhaul of the nation's military program.
UN Ambassador Henry Cabot Lodge was
named as the vice-presidential candidate.
Conservative Republicans, disgruntled over
liberal control of the party ever since Willkie's nomination in 1940, were determined
to name their own candidate in 1964.

The campaign is spirited. Since the
platforms of the two parties were similar,
the voters concentrated on the candidates
and their views. Kennedy emphasized the
need to "get America moving again." The
Democratic candidate met the question of
his religion head on. Before a gathering
of Protestant ministers in Houston, he said:
"I believe in an America where the separation of Church and State is absolute."

When the campaign began, Vice-President Nixon was far better known than his
opponent. But four nationally televised debates between the candidates showed Senator Kennedy to be a well-informed, effective speaker. Watched by more than half
the people in the country, the debates were
the turning point of the campaign. Alarmed
by the rising popularity of the Democratic
candidate, Nixon asked President Eisenhower to come to his aid. In the closing
days of the campaign, the President drew
large and enthusiastic crowds in Pennsylvania, Ohio, and New York.

Kennedy wins by a narrow margin.
On election night early returns from the
South and East indicated a substantial lead
for Kennedy. But results from the Middle
West and Pacific states made the outcome
uncertain. Not until the following day was
it clear that Kennedy had won with an
electoral vote of 303 to Nixon's 219. In the

In popular vote, the 1960 election was one of the closest of this century. At top left, John F. Kennedy addresses a crowd at Hyde Park, New York, during the campaign. Above, Richard Nixon and his running mate, Henry Cabot Lodge, respond to an ovation at the Republican convention. The television networks covered the campaign in detail and used computers to forecast the outcome. Left, cameras in a television studio focus on state returns during the election night broadcast.

popular vote Kennedy received a margin of only one tenth of one per cent of the ballots cast.

Kennedy ran best in the heavily populated, industrial states. He won a substantial majority of the Negro and Catholic votes, did well with organized labor, carried the large cities, and cut into some suburban areas. Nixon carried several southern states, three New England states, and most of the Middle and Far West. One historian summed up the 1960 election by observing that there were only two safe conclusions: "The Republican party was in no danger of becoming a hopeless minority without Eisenhower" and "a Roman Catholic was no longer automatically barred from winning the nation's highest office."

The spirit of the New Frontier catches hold. The youth and personality of John F. Kennedy evoked a warm response from many Americans. Of Irish background, he was educated at Harvard, served with distinction in the navy during World War II, and won election to the House of Representatives in 1946. Six years later he was elected to the Senate. While recuperating from surgery on his back, he wrote *Profiles in Courage,* which won a Pulitzer Prize. In 1956 Kennedy narrowly missed the Democratic vice-presidential nomination. His presidential victory in 1960 at the age of 43 made him the youngest man ever elected to the White House.

Kennedy's moving inaugural address reflected the idealism of the younger generation as well as an understanding of the

country's heritage. The principles of 1776
— liberty and freedom — are "still at issue
around the globe," he said.

> Let the word go forth from this time and
> place, to friend and foe alike, that the torch
> has been passed to a new generation of
> Americans — born in this century, tempered
> by war, disciplined by a hard and bitter
> peace, proud of our ancient heritage — and
> unwilling to witness or permit the slow un-
> doing of those human rights . . . to which
> we are committed today at home and
> around the world.

The new President chose Dean Rusk,
head of the Rockefeller Foundation, as his
Secretary of State. A Republican, Robert
McNamara of the Ford Motor Company,
became Secretary of Defense. Adlai Stevenson was named Ambassador to the United
Nations, and the President's brother, Robert
F. Kennedy, was appointed Attorney General. The President drew heavily on college faculties for advisers and consultants,
staff members, and diplomats. But the
most important person on the New Frontier
was the President himself. Dedicated, energetic, and witty, Kennedy soon won the
admiration and respect of most Americans.
Elsewhere in the world, millions of people
were convinced that the torch had indeed
"passed to a new generation of Americans."

**The conservative coalition in Congress
remains strong.** The men in the executive
branch of the government were eager to
get America "moving again," but Congress
had other ideas. Though the Democrats
held a majority in both houses, the familiar
coalition of Republicans and southern
Democrats was able to control congressional action. Thus, Kennedy's proposal
for federal aid to public schools was
blocked, and his request for a Department
of Urban Affairs was turned down. A
Medicare bill, to provide health insurance
for the aged under Social Security, died in
the Senate. And Congress substantially
pared down the President's requests for
foreign aid.

Some legislation is passed. Yet a number of important measures were approved.
At the President's request, Congress established the Peace Corps. Members of this
organization received brief intensive training and then were sent to underdeveloped
countries to serve as teachers, engineers,
agricultural experts, nurses, and technicians. By 1966 the Peace Corps had 15,000
volunteers serving in 46 countries. Its success led several western European nations
to launch similar programs.

Congress also gave the President broad
powers over tariff rates in order to meet
the competition of the European Common
Market. When Belgium, the Netherlands,
Luxemburg, France, West Germany, and
Italy formed the Common Market in 1957,
they planned to lower tariff barriers among
themselves and adopt a common tariff policy toward other countries. As a result,
American economists recommended that
this country's rates on Common Market
goods be reduced, to increase the sale of
American goods to Common Market countries. The Trade Expansion Act of 1962
permitted the President to lower tariffs by
as much as 50 per cent over a five-year
period and to eliminate others entirely.
The act provided for "adjustment assistance" to those American industries which
would face the stiffest competition from
European imports.

**Kennedy is concerned about poverty
and unemployment.** In spite of the general prosperity of the country when President Kennedy took office, there were pockets of poverty in certain areas, and the
unemployment rate stood at about 6 per
cent. The spread of automation (page 794)
had the effect of eliminating many jobs.
Computers replaced bookkeepers and
clerks; photographic equipment replaced
typists; machines performed the work of
men on assembly lines and in industrial
control rooms. The new machines created
jobs as well, but only skilled workers could
qualify for these positions. As a result,
there was a sharp decline in the demand
for manual laborers. The rate of unemployment among unskilled workers shot
up to 13 per cent.

President Kennedy secured from Congress a number of measures designed to
help the country's poor. Federal aid was

granted to cities and communities for urban renewal programs. The Housing Act of 1961 provided nearly five billion dollars to replace slum dwellings with public housing. An Area Redevelopment Act made additional funds available for "distressed areas" which had an unusually high rate of unemployment. Federal loans and grants would help to retrain workers and attract new industries to these areas. Congress also raised the minimum wage rate to a dollar and a quarter per hour and extended minimum-wage protection to nearly four million additional workers.

To encourage economic growth and thus create new jobs, President Kennedy pro-posed a thirteen-billion-dollar cut in income taxes. He hoped that a tax cut would give workers more take-home pay and thus enable them to purchase more goods. Cuts in business taxes, moreover, would permit companies to expand their operations. But Congress failed to take any action on the tax bill during Kennedy's administration.

Kennedy takes a stand on civil rights. Though President Kennedy had promised vigorous action on civil rights, he relied on executive action rather than new legislation during his first two years in office. He created a Committee on Equal Employment Opportunity, which sought to persuade firms holding government contracts

President Kennedy's advisers on foreign affairs and national defense included (from left to right in picture at top left) General Maxwell Taylor, Secretary of State Dean Rusk, and Secretary of Defense Robert McNamara. Among the New Frontier programs were job retraining (above, a young man learns how to operate a bulldozer) and the Peace Corps. At left, a Peace Corps worker in Colombia gives some eager children their first taste of raw turnip.

Leaders of the 1963 March on Washington, including Martin Luther King (second from left), met with President Kennedy at the White House. The group included religious, labor, and civil rights leaders.

to provide equal job opportunities for Negroes. The Justice Department had some success in enforcing the Civil Rights Acts of 1957 and 1960 (page 796). Moreover, the Interstate Commerce Commission banned discrimination in terminals or on buses, trains, or airlines involved in interstate transportation. And in 1962 the President signed an executive order prohibiting racial or religious discrimination in housing financed with federal funds.

Meanwhile, Congress took action on civil rights by approving the Twenty-fourth Amendment. This Amendment prohibited any state from requiring a citizen to pay a poll tax in order to vote in federal elections. After ratification by the states, the Amendment became law in 1964.

Integration in the Deep South meets resistance. By the fall of 1962, Mississippi, South Carolina, and Alabama were the only states which operated completely segregated school systems. Their resistance to integration was challenged by a Supreme Court order directing the University of Mississippi to admit James H. Meredith, a Negro resident of that state. University trustees and officials agreed to obey the Court order, but Governor Ross Barnett refused to let Meredith register.

President Kennedy and the Attorney General acted decisively to uphold the Supreme Court order. Federal marshals accompanied Meredith to the campus; federal troops were stationed nearby; and the Mississippi National Guard was federalized to remove it from the Governor's command. The President made a special television appeal to the people of Mississippi to comply with the law. But rioting broke out on the university campus, leaving two people dead and many injured. Nevertheless, Meredith was registered and eventually became the first known Negro to graduate from the University of Mississippi. In 1963, Alabama and South Carolina also admitted Negro students to their universities, thus bringing at least token integration to public universities of all the southern states.

Negroes demonstrate against discrimination. The slow pace of integration left many civil rights leaders less than satisfied. One hundred years after the Emancipation Proclamation, Negroes still suffered discrimination in all parts of the country. Nine years after the Supreme Court decision declaring school segregation unconstitutional, only 1 per cent of the Negro children in the South were attending integrated schools. Moreover, the recent establishment of many independent states in Africa heightened the awareness of American Negroes that they were "second-class" citizens in their own country.

During 1963, civil rights demonstrators in the North as well as the South protested discrimination in housing, schools, jobs, hotels and motels, restaurants, and amusement parks. In Birmingham, Alabama, thousands of Negroes, including school children, staged mass demonstrations to protest against that city's rigid system of segregation. City officials used fire hoses, police dogs, and electric prod sticks to break up the demonstrations. Officials from the Justice Department finally brought together representatives from both sides to discuss differences. But this uneasy truce was endangered when a Negro church in Birmingham was bombed, killing four children in a Sunday school class.

The largest civil rights demonstration was an orderly mass rally held in Washington, D.C., in August. Some 200,000 white and Negro citizens gathered at the Washington Monument and walked to the Lincoln Memorial. There they heard Martin Luther King and other civil rights leaders speak. President Kennedy endorsed this "March on Washington" and invited the leaders to meet with him at the White House.

A new civil rights act is proposed. President Kennedy approved the civil rights demonstrations, saying they were in the American tradition. But increased outbreaks of violence convinced him that new legislation was necessary to secure for Negroes those rights which many whites refused to grant them. He therefore proposed to Congress a sweeping civil rights bill. This legislation would (1) guarantee equal access for Negroes to all public facilities such as hotels, restaurants, places of amusement, and stores; (2) speed up school integration; (3) launch a broad attack on job discrimination; and (4) provide training programs for unskilled Negro workers.

In defense of his civil rights bill, the President made a powerful appeal to the American people. Over national television he told them:

We are confronted primarily with a moral issue. It is as old as the Scriptures and is as clear as the American Constitution. The heart of the question is whether all Americans are to be afforded equal rights and

equal opportunities. . . . And this nation, for all its hopes and all its boasts, will not be fully free until all its citizens are free. . . . It is time to act in the Congress, in your state and local legislative body, and, above all, in all of our daily lives.

Whether widespread public support for the bill would be translated into congressional action remained unanswered during President Kennedy's administration. But Kennedy's definition of the civil rights movement as a challenge to American democracy was one of his most important contributions as President.

The assassination of President Kennedy shocks the world. In November, 1963, President Kennedy flew to Texas for a three-day speaking tour of the state. Accompanied by Vice-President Johnson and Texas Governor John Connally, Jr., and their wives, the Kennedys arrived at the Dallas airport on November 22. As the presidential motorcade drove through downtown Dallas, three shots rang out from a building along the route. One bullet injured Governor Connally; the other

An hour and a half after President Kennedy's death, Lyndon B. Johnson was sworn in as President of the United States. At his side in the presidential airplane were Mrs. Johnson and Mrs. Kennedy, the late President's widow.

two struck the President, wounding him fatally.[1]

Under heavy security guard, Vice-President Johnson was escorted back to the presidential airplane. There, less than two hours after the assassination, he took the oath of office as President of the United States. The plane, bearing the former President's body, Mrs. Kennedy, President and Mrs. Johnson, and presidential aides, took off for Washington. For the next three days a grief-stricken nation and millions of overseas viewers watched the solemn pageantry of a state funeral unfold on their television screens. Following a funeral mass attended by an unprecedented gathering of foreign heads of state and diplomats, John F. Kennedy was buried in Arlington Cemetery on a hillside overlooking the Potomac River.

The entire world mourned the loss of President Kennedy. As its memorial the British government deeded to the United States an acre of land at Runnymede. It was in the meadow at Runnymede that English barons had forced King John to accept the Magna Carta, a first step on the road that eventually led to representative government in Great Britain and the United States. The Runnymede site was dedicated in 1965, the 750th anniversary of that historic event. In this country a flame burning at the grave in Arlington Cemetery became a symbol of the memories and hopes of the thousand days of John F. Kennedy's presidency.

▶ CHECK-UP

1. What factors contributed to Kennedy's victory in the election of 1960? What important legislation did he sponsor? What was his stand on civil rights?

---

[1] The President's assassin was Lee Harvey Oswald, an emotionally disturbed former marine who had once defected to the Soviet Union. Two days after the assassination, as Oswald was being transferred from the city jail to the county jail in Dallas, he was shot by a Dallas night-club operator. President Johnson appointed a commission, headed by Chief Justice Earl Warren, to investigate the circumstances surrounding the assassination. The commission's report confirmed that Oswald alone had planned and carried out the murder of President Kennedy.

2. Which of Kennedy's legislative proposals were passed by Congress? Which were blocked?

. . . .

2 *President Johnson Plans for a Great Society*

The new President assumes leadership. The only consolation for many Americans in November, 1963, was the smooth transfer of power to the new administration. President Kennedy's Cabinet members and staff stayed at their posts to serve President Johnson. The new chief executive assured our allies of his determination to honor the nation's foreign commitments. Furthermore, he reminded Congress that action on the late President's legislative program would be a fitting memorial.

Johnson assumed his great responsibilities with broader training than any previous Vice-President elevated to the highest office. Born and raised in Texas, Johnson had been elected to the House of Representatives in 1938. He served in the navy during World War II and then won election to the Senate in 1948. His political skill as Democratic floor leader of the Senate in the 1950's attracted the attention of many people, including John F. Kennedy, then a Massachusetts senator. Moreover, Johnson had surprised his southern friends by strongly supporting the Civil Rights Acts of 1957 and 1960.

Nine years older than Kennedy, Lyndon Johnson had reached maturity in the 1930's and was strongly influenced by Franklin D. Roosevelt's political style and New Deal goals. Johnson did not have Kennedy's ease with words or his knowledge of foreign affairs. But the new President was a seasoned politician who knew how to cajole Congress into action and how to seek broad public support for his policies.

(*Continued on page 817*)

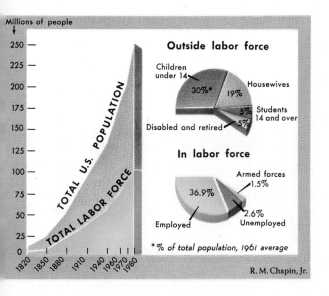

Millions of people

Outside labor force

Children under 14 — 30%*
Housewives 19%
Students 14 and over 5%
Disabled and retired 5%

In labor force

Armed forces 1.5%
Employed 36.9%
Unemployed 2.6%

* % of total population, 1961 average

R. M. Chapin, Jr.

AMERICA AT WORK

Workers play a vital role in a highly industrialized society. This fact is reflected in the charts on this page, which present significant statistics about the number of American workers and the types of work they do. Pages 814–815 show the country's major areas of economic activity, while page 816 describes "megalopolis," the world's most highly developed industrial area.

The graph above shows the size of the labor force from 1820 to 1960 with projected figures for 1970 and 1980. Population growth and a greater proportion of women workers have enlarged the labor force. While the United States was an agricultural nation, unemployment was less of a problem. But as industry expanded, more and more workers were exposed to the risk of unemployment. The graph at right indicates the number of jobless people at intervals since 1900 and the percentage of the total civilian labor force which the unemployed represent.

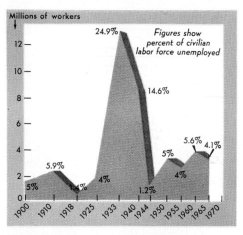

Millions of workers

Figures show percent of civilian labor force unemployed

24.9%
14.6%
5.9%
5.6% 4.1%
5% 5%
4% 4%
1.4% 4%
1.2%

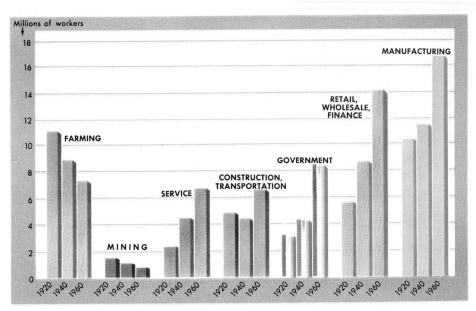

Millions of workers

FARMING
MINING
SERVICE
CONSTRUCTION, TRANSPORTATION
GOVERNMENT
RETAIL, WHOLESALE, FINANCE
MANUFACTURING

The shifts in major occupational groups between 1920 and 1960 are shown in the chart above. The decreasing number of workers in farming and mining does not mean reduced production but reflects the use of machines and new processes. Note that the number of local, state, and federal government employees has tripled. The map on the next two pages shows where important fields of economic activity are concentrated throughout the United States.

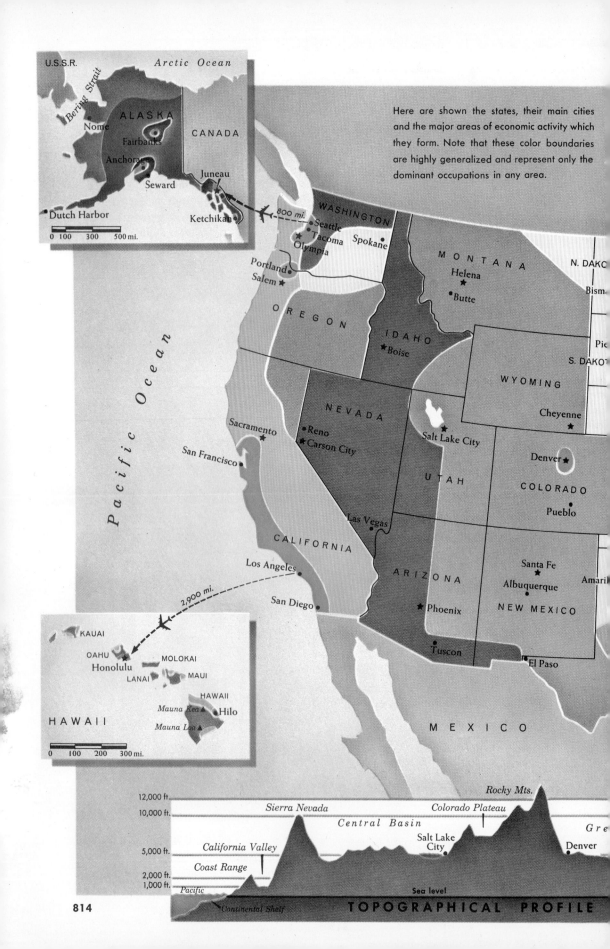

U.S.S.R.
Arctic Ocean

Bering Strait
ALASKA
CANADA
Nome
Fairbanks
Anchorage
Seward
Juneau
Dutch Harbor
Ketchikan

0   100   300   500 mi.

800 mi.

Here are shown the states, their main cities
and the major areas of economic activity which
they form. Note that these color boundaries
are highly generalized and represent only the
dominant occupations in any area.

WASHINGTON
Seattle
Tacoma
Spokane
Olympia

Portland
Salem

O R E G O N

MONTANA
Helena
Butte

N. DAKO

Bism

IDAHO
Boise

Pie

S. DAKO

WYOMING

Cheyenne

Pacific Ocean

Sacramento

San Francisco

NEVADA
Reno
Carson City

Salt Lake City

UTAH

Denver

COLORADO
Pueblo

Las Vegas

CALIFORNIA

Los Angeles

2,900 mi.

San Diego

ARIZONA

Phoenix

Santa Fe
Albuquerque

NEW MEXICO

Amaril

Tuscon

El Paso

KAUAI
OAHU
Honolulu
MOLOKAI
LANAI
MAUI
HAWAII
Mauna Kea ▲
Mauna Loa ▲
Hilo

HAWAII

0   100   200   300 mi.

MEXICO

12,000 ft.
Rocky Mts.

10,000 ft.
Sierra Nevada
Colorado Plateau

Central Basin
Gre

Salt Lake
City
Denver

5,000 ft.
California Valley

2,000 ft.
Coast Range

1,000 ft.
Pacific
Sea level

Continental Shelf
TOPOGRAPHICAL PROFILE

814

Industrial concentrations
Dairying
Mining
Fruits and truck farming
Range livestock
Grains and farm livestock
Fibres, tobacco, general agriculture
Timber and pulpwood

CANADA

Quebec

L. Superior

MINNESOTA
Duluth

Montreal

Ottawa

MAINE
Augusta

MICHIGAN

L. Huron

Montpelier
VT. N.H.
Portland
Concord

NEW
YORK

Minneapolis
St. Paul
WISCONSIN
Madison

L. Michigan

Lansing

Toronto

L. Ontario

Buffalo

Albany

MASS.
Boston

Hartford
CONN.
Providence
R.I.

IOWA
Des Moines

Milwaukee

Detroit

L. Erie

PA.

Trenton

New York
N.J.

Chicago
Gary

Cleveland

Pittsburgh
Harrisburg

Philadelphia
Dover DEL.

EBRASKA
Lincoln

ILLINOIS
INDIANA

OHIO
Columbus

MD.

Springfield

Indianapolis

Cincinnati

Washington, D.C.
W. VA.
Charleston
VA.

Annapolis

Kansas City

St. Louis

Louisville

Norfolk

Topeka

Jefferson City

Frankfort

Richmond

KANSAS

MISSOURI

KENTUCKY

Raleigh

Tulsa

Nashville

N. CAROLINA
Charlotte

OKLAHOMA
klahoma City

ARKANSAS

TENNESSEE
Memphis
Chattanooga

S. CAROLINA
Columbia

Ft. Worth

Little Rock

Birmingham
Atlanta

GEORGIA

Dallas

Shreveport
LOUISIANA

MISSISSIPPI
Jackson

ALABAMA
Montgomery

Savannah

TEXAS

Natchez

Mobile

Jacksonville

Austin

Baton Rouge

Tallahassee

Houston
an Antonio
Galveston

New Orleans

FLORIDA

Tampa

Gulf of Mexico

Miami

Atlantic Ocean

0   100   300   500 mi.
R. M. Chapin, Jr.

ains

Central   Lowlands

Appalachians

5,000 ft.

Missouri R.   Mississippi R.

Pittsburgh

Coastal Plain

2,000 ft.

New York

1,000 ft.

Atlantic

OF THE UNITED STATES

Continental Shelf

815

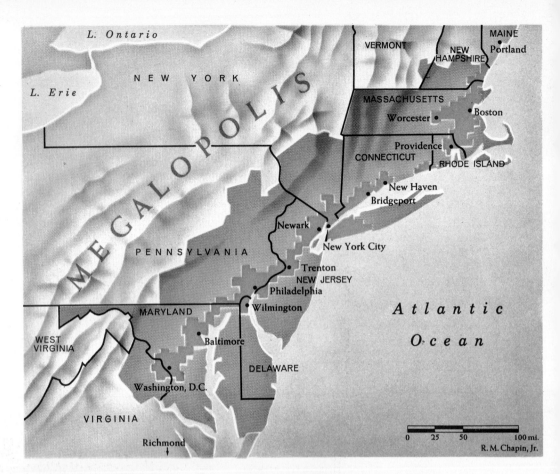

L. Ontario

L. Erie

NEW YORK

VERMONT

MAINE
Portland

NEW
HAMPSHIRE

MASSACHUSETTS
Worcester • Boston •

Providence •
CONNECTICUT
RHODE ISLAND

New Haven •
Bridgeport •

MEGALOPOLIS

PENNSYLVANIA

Newark •

New York City •

Trenton •
NEW JERSEY

Philadelphia •

Wilmington •

MARYLAND

WEST
VIRGINIA

Baltimore •

DELAWARE

Washington, D.C. •

VIRGINIA

Richmond •

Atlantic

Ocean

0   25   50   100 mi.

R. M. Chapin, Jr.

Megalopolis was once the name of a flourishing community in ancient Greece. Although the city was destroyed long ago, its name — meaning "great city" — has lived on. The term "megalopolis" has recently been applied to the densely populated northern half of our Atlantic seaboard.

The roots of this modern megalopolis were planted long before the twentieth century. As we have seen (map, page 465), New England and Middle Atlantic ports dominated the nation's commerce as early as 1790. Good harbors as well as locations at the mouths of important rivers contributed to the growth of these early American cities. As industry rapidly expanded, urban centers enlarged. Farm areas and small towns near the seaboard cities filled with commuting urban workers. Thus, suburbs gradually surrounded the core cities. By 1960, metropolitan areas formed an almost continuous belt from southern New Hampshire to northern Virginia. This area is what we call megalopolis. (On the above map, the red tone indicates the entire extent of megalopolis; blue shows the core cities.) Within this coastal strip, comprising only one and a half per cent of the nation's land, lived 37 million people

in 1960. This was almost 20 per cent of the total American population. Megalopolis included 30 per cent of the nation's manufacturing operations.

This northeastern "super-city," despite its wealth and productive power, suffers to a severe degree the problems of individual metropolitan areas (page 823). Among its headaches are air and water pollution, urban blight, and massive traffic congestion. In the next few years, as the population within megalopolis multiplies, existing modes of transportation will become even less adequate than they are today. But plans are already under way (backed by the federal government) to develop high-speed ground transportation between Boston and Washington, D.C.

Megalopolis is the leading example of a national trend. Population experts have identified at least twenty other "urban clusters" in the making. Among them are the midwestern area reaching from South Bend through Chicago to Green Bay, and the Pacific coast area between Los Angeles and San Francisco. The problems of all these emerging super-cities must be met, not by the individual metropolitan areas within them, but by each megalopolis as a whole.

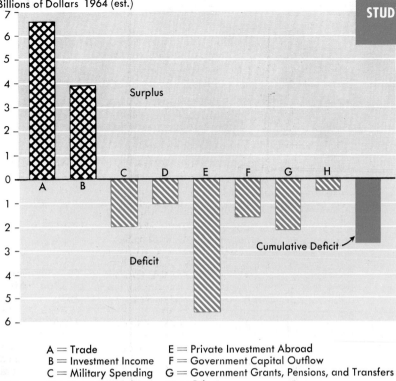

Billions of Dollars 1964 (est.)

BALANCE OF PAYMENTS, 1964

This chart shows a balance of payments gap in 1964 of approximately 2.8 billion dollars. Note the areas in which dollars leaving the country exceeded the dollars we received.

A = Trade
B = Investment Income
C = Military Spending
D = Tourist Spending
E = Private Investment Abroad
F = Government Capital Outflow
G = Government Grants, Pensions, and Transfers
H = Others

The government tackles the balance of payments gap. President Johnson faced several economic problems which had also troubled the two previous administrations. One of these problems was the "balance of payments gap." Since World War I the United States had been a creditor nation, exporting more than it imported and therefore earning money on its foreign trade and investments abroad. The overall situation changed in the 1950's. By that time western Europe and Japan had recovered from the damage of World War II. They were producing surpluses of manufactured goods for sale in foreign countries, including the United States. More important, American corporations were spending hundreds of millions of dollars to buy outright or to acquire part ownership of plants and industries in foreign lands. Furthermore, the United States was spending billions of dollars on foreign aid and on the support of its armed forces stationed overseas. Still another factor was the sharp increase in the number of Americans traveling abroad during the 1950's.

By the close of the decade, our annual expenditures overseas exceeded by three billion dollars the money coming into the United States from foreign trade and investments. This gap in the balance of payments was met by withdrawing gold from the federal reserve. Unless the balance could be restored, the stability of the dollar might eventually be endangered. The government, therefore, took a number of steps to reduce the "dollar gap." Our allies were asked to share part of the cost of maintaining American troops stationed in their countries; and the families of servicemen were asked to remain in the United States. Businessmen were given tax credits as an incentive to modernize their plants. This would enable them to compete more efficiently with foreign producers. In addition, each American tourist was permitted to bring back from abroad only 100 dollars' worth of duty-free goods instead of 500 dollars' worth. Moreover, President Johnson asked people to spend their vacation funds in American territory rather than in foreign countries.

The administration guards against inflation. The prosperity of the 1950's and

817

the continued economic expansion of the 1960's posed the threat of inflation. If the cost of living were to increase sharply, the gains of the nation's economic growth would be wiped out. To guard against too much money flowing into the economy, the Federal Reserve Board kept an eye on the loan policies of Federal Reserve Banks. In late 1965 the Board raised the interest rate to reduce the threat of inflation.

Because of the possibility of inflation, both Kennedy and Johnson took an interest in the signing of new contracts between labor unions and management. Both Presidents insisted that increased benefits for workers should come out of the profits from increased productivity. If employers were to raise retail prices to absorb wage increases, the cost of living would edge upward for all consumers. In 1962 the major steel companies and the United Steelworkers signed a noninflationary contract. President Kennedy praised both sides for their "industrial statesmanship." When the steel companies then tried to increase prices, Kennedy denounced this action, and the price increases were canceled. In 1965 the Johnson administration persuaded the aluminum and copper industries to cancel price increases.

Labor leaders are concerned about job security. During the mid-1960's, job security continued to be a problem. Automation remained a threat to the jobs of unskilled and semiskilled workers. Employers were eager to introduce labor-saving devices, and in many industries it was essential to do so in order to compete with foreign producers. But at the same time union spokesmen sought to maintain job security for their members. Thus, longshoremen struck when mechanized packaging and loading devices threatened their jobs. To prevent the elimination of firemen from diesel locomotives and the adoption of new work rules, the railroad unions carried their protest all the way to the Supreme Court. The Court ruled in favor of the railroads. In 1964 a nation-wide rail strike was narrowly averted by last-minute negotiations carried on at the White House. President Johnson insisted that the two

sides settle the dispute by collective bargaining to avoid a crippling strike or government intervention.

A new approach to the problem of job security was included in a contract which went into effect in 1963 between the Kaiser Steel Corporation and the United Steelworkers. Employees were assured that they would get nearly one third of all savings that resulted from increased productivity. Economists hoped that this formula — the use of savings from automation to retrain workers and provide job security — would help other industries adjust to new conditions.

Congress passes the Civil Rights Act of 1964. After the death of President Kennedy, some conservatives hoped that Johnson would modify the New Frontier program. They soon found, however, that Johnson was genuinely interested in domestic reforms. For example, he called for prompt action from Congress on the civil rights bill. Approval was won in the House by a large majority, but the struggle in the Senate was long and bitter. Finally, to bring the bill to a vote, it was necessary to impose cloture.[2] This was the first time that such a procedure had been used to break a civil rights filibuster. The Senate then passed the bill by a vote of 73 to 27. In July the President signed the Civil Rights Act of 1964 into law.

This act was one of the most far-reaching laws ever passed by Congress. (1) It required standardized voting requirements for Negroes and whites in all states and provided that cases of alleged voting discrimination should go to special courts with direct appeal to the Supreme Court for speedy action. (2) It prohibited discrimination in almost all public accommodations — hotels, motels, restaurants, theaters, sports arenas, gas stations, and stores. (3) To speed up school desegregation, it empowered the Attorney General to initi-

[2] The cloture rule must be approved by a two-thirds majority of those voting in the Senate. It restricts each member to one hour of debate on the bill under consideration. The Senate seldom uses the cloture rule because of its cherished tradition of unlimited debate.

ate or intervene in cases where Negroes could not afford to fight a court case or were threatened with losing their jobs if they started legal action. (4) The act also offered financial aid to school districts that needed help in beginning a program of desegregation. And it instructed government agencies to withhold federal funds from school districts which continued to maintain segregated schools. (5) Finally, the measure prohibited discrimination on the basis of race or sex by employers, labor unions, and employment agencies engaged in interstate commerce. Federal funds would be cut off from any project, private or state, which practiced discrimination in hiring.

The Civil Rights Act goes into effect. The voting rights provisions and the public accommodations sections of the new law went into effect immediately. Civil rights groups were ready to test the public accommodations provision; but, to the surprise of many, compliance with the law was prompt and widespread. A restaurant owner in Atlanta appealed his case to the Supreme Court to test the constitutionality of the measure. But the Court rendered a unanimous decision upholding the Civil Rights Act. A North Carolina newspaper expressed the views of many Southerners when it said: "Nobody has to like the law. But the time of resistance is clearly past. The time for as painless adjustment to it as possible has arrived. . . . The law is here."

Under the section of the Civil Rights Act concerning schools, the Commissioner of Education announced that federal funds would be cut off from school districts which did not effectively integrate Negro and white students. This threat produced some results. By the fall of 1965, about 6 per cent of the Negro public school children in eleven southern states were attending classes with white children.

The employment provisions of the act went into effect in 1965. But cases involving discrimination in unions and in hiring

The 1965 Voting Rights Act (page 820) authorized federal examiners to register voters in states and areas where Negroes had been discouraged from voting. Below, a federal examiner goes over registration forms with two would-be voters in Alabama.

The drugstore counter in New Orleans shown above was integrated without disturbance in 1962. The 1964 Civil Rights Act outlawed segregation at lunch counters or restaurants that still refused to serve Negroes.

and promotion are harder to decide than those concerning service in a restaurant or motel. It will take some time to determine the effectiveness of this provision of the Civil Rights Act.

The Voting Rights Act of 1965 is passed. In many areas of the South the voting rights provisions of the Civil Rights Act were tested and found inadequate. During the summer of 1964 northern civil rights workers went to Mississippi to establish "Freedom Schools" for Negroes and to impress on them the importance of registering and voting. Many white Mississippians resented these efforts, and a few resorted to violence. Three civil rights workers were murdered, and others were assaulted or had their headquarters damaged by bombs or fire.

Early in 1965 a voter registration drive led by Martin Luther King in Selma, Alabama, met heavy resistance. Of 15,000 Negro residents of voting age in the county, only 335 were registered when King started his campaign. Local white officials used minor regulations to thwart the registration drive, and Negro impatience swelled. Television coverage of these injustices moved scores of white people across the country to join the demonstrations in Selma. Local opposition resulted in the murders of a Negro boy, a Boston minister, and a Detroit housewife, crimes for which no convictions were secured.

The use of violence by some southern whites prompted President Johnson to call for still another federal law to guarantee the constitutional rights of Negroes. Passed by Congress in 1965, the Voting Rights Act abolished literacy tests and other voting restrictions in those states and counties where less than 50 per cent of the voting-age population had participated in the 1964 election. Federal examiners were to be appointed to register voters in those areas which refused to obey the new law. By 1966, compliance with the Voting Rights Act had added thousands of Negroes to the lists of registered voters. Federal registrars were sent to a number of southern counties which chose to ignore the law.

Civil rights legislation alone does not solve the problem. By 1966 the country had a basic framework of laws guaranteeing the civil rights of all citizens. But adherence to the *spirit* of these laws would require many adjustments on the part of white citizens throughout the country. Segregated patterns of housing had resulted in *de facto*[3] school segregation in many cities, especially in the North. Moreover, discrimination in employment and job advancement often worked hardships on Negroes and other minority groups. Many Americans hoped that these injustices could be remedied by state laws, city ordinances, and voluntary action. It would not then be necessary for the federal government to intervene. In a commencement address at Howard University, President Johnson made it clear that he shared this hope. Referring to the barriers of prejudice which still existed, he said they "must be overcome if we are ever to reach the time when the only difference between Negroes and whites is the color of their skins."

Violence stresses the need for action. In spite of the new civil rights laws, some Negroes felt that the doors of opportunity were not opening fast enough. As a result, riots broke out in Negro sections of New York City, Los Angeles, and Rochester, New York. Recurring instances of white violence against Negroes and civil rights workers in the South and of Negro violence against city administrations elsewhere in the country were tragic reminders of the urgent need to resolve the civil rights problem.

Johnson launches a war on poverty. Just as President Johnson enlarged on Kennedy's civil rights program, so he broadened the attack on poverty and unemployment. Soon after he took office, the President persuaded Congress to pass the tax cut which Kennedy had proposed (page 809). The next year, at the President's request, Congress eliminated or reduced many of the excise taxes which had been in effect since World War II. The adminis-

---

[3] This Latin phrase (literally "from the fact") is applied to segregation that results not from intentional separation but from other factors.

tration hoped that the money made available for consumer spending by these tax cuts would stimulate the economy. But it also recognized that this stimulus to the economy was not enough to win an "unconditional war on poverty." There were nearly nine million families in the United States with incomes below 3000 dollars a year, and it was Johnson's desire to help these people.

In 1964 Congress created an Office of Economic Opportunity to supervise a variety of antipoverty programs. (1) A Job Corps would provide vocational training and remedial education for unemployed young men and women, most of them school drop-outs. (2) A domestic version of the Peace Corps, called Volunteers in Service to America (VISTA), would offer training and education to people in migrant labor camps, Indian reservations, city slums, and poverty-stricken rural areas. (3) Under the Community Action Program, federal grants would be used by cities, communities, and states to run antipoverty programs of their own design. (4) Part-time jobs for needy high school and college students and small loans to individual businessmen and farmers constituted another way of aiding low-income families.

Some Americans oppose domestic reforms. In an era of rapid change it was understandable that some people would feel the country was moving too fast or in the wrong direction. The civil rights crusade, for example, aroused opposition from both white and Negro extremists. In many areas of the South, White Citizens Councils and the revived Ku Klux Klan resisted the drive for Negro rights. A few Negroes were drawn to the Black Muslims, an organization which favored separation from white society and demanded an all-Negro state within this country. A split within the ranks of the Black Muslims, and the assassination of Malcolm X, a former leader in the organization, dealt a blow to this movement.

More important numerically were the "ultra-conservatives," also called the "far right," who opposed most of the changes which had taken place in American society since the 1920's. They called the New

Northern civil rights demonstrations were often aimed at de facto segregation. Here, demonstrators led by a Negro clergyman protest racial imbalance in Boston's public schools.

Deal, the Fair Deal, and the Democratic reforms of the 1960's "socialistic"; and they criticized President Eisenhower for failing to stop the trend while he was in office. The "ultra-conservatives" also claimed that the Supreme Court was undermining the Constitution with many of its decisions. They objected, for example, to its rulings on civil rights cases and to a 1962 decision that required election districts for state legislatures to have substantially equal populations. Two years after this ruling, the Court applied the same "one man, one vote" rule to congressional districts. Since this principle would increase the representation of the cities and suburbs, conservatives feared that rural areas would lose power and influence in the state legislatures and in Congress. Finally, supporters of the "far right" were disturbed by American foreign policy. They particularly objected to foreign aid and co-operation with the United Nations.

Conservatives capture the Republican Party. The most popular conservative political leader in the early 1960's was Senator Barry Goldwater of Arizona. The conservatives hoped to capture control of the Republican Party and nominate Goldwater for the presidency in 1964.

Other possibilities for the Republican candidacy were Henry Cabot Lodge (the Ambassador to South Vietnam), Governor Rockefeller, Governor George Romney of Michigan, and former Vice-President Nixon. All of these men were moderate Republicans, and most observers expected one of them to win the nomination. Thus, the country paid close attention to the primaries but generally ignored those states which chose their convention delegates by other methods. By the time Goldwater narrowly won the California primary, however, he was sure of enough delegates to be within easy striking distance of the nomination. In the last few weeks before the convention, Governor William Scranton of Pennsylvania made a desperate effort to win enough delegates to prevent the right-wing capture of the Republican nomination. But the convention selected Goldwater as its candidate and endorsed a conservative platform.

Barry Goldwater gave up his Senate seat to run for President. He voiced the views of conservative Republicans and also won the vote of many southern Democrats.

The campaign issues are sharply defined. President Johnson's nomination by the Democrats was assured, but his choice of a running mate was left up in the air until their convention had assembled. He chose Senator Humphrey of Minnesota, and the delegates ratified this choice. The convention adopted a platform endorsing the Kennedy-Johnson policies.

During the campaign Johnson sought to broaden the support he already had. Businessmen were told that the best guarantee of economic prosperity was a Democratic administration which could balance the demands of labor and capital. Civil rights advocates needed no convincing that their movement would fare better under Johnson than under Goldwater. Liberals approved the President's emphasis on creation of a "Great Society," while professional politicians admired Johnson's control over Congress. The President, in short, held the Democratic coalition together and made deep inroads into traditionally Republican support.

Goldwater pitched his campaign to attract those Americans who opposed the developments of the past thirty years. He claimed that the federal government had unjustifiably invaded the rights of the states. He was critical of New Deal measures which the majority of Americans had long since taken for granted. He opposed the antipoverty program and federal action on civil rights. In foreign affairs he called for a more aggressive policy against communism.

Johnson wins by a landslide. The outcome of the election was no surprise. Johnson received 61 per cent of the popular vote, and the Democrats won large majorities in both houses of Congress. Goldwater carried only six states — Arizona, Alabama, Georgia, Louisiana, Mississippi and South Carolina. "I want the mandate of this election to be written strong and clear," said President Johnson, "so that none will mistake the meaning." His decisive victory did indeed constitute a mandate for further reform and a defeat for Goldwater's conservative position. Moderate Republicans faced a difficult task regaining control of their party. Meanwhile, Democratic majorities in Congress pushed ahead with Johnson's plans for building a "Great Society."

Congress approves sweeping reforms. During 1965 Congress doubled appropriations for the poverty program and authorized an economic development program for depressed areas in the eleven-state Appalachian Mountain region. Two education bills involved sharp departures from tradition. One measure provided more than a billion dollars for the country's elementary schools, most of it to be distributed by the states to their neediest school districts. But the remainder of the money was earmarked for textbooks, laboratories, and supplementary programs to be shared by public and parochial schools. The second measure provided more than two billion dollars for colleges and universities in the form of construction grants, support for new programs, loans to needy students, and the country's first federally financed college scholarships.

The long-discussed Medicare bill was enacted into law during 1965. It provided medical insurance under Social Security for people over 65. To meet the costs of this program, Social Security taxes were increased. Immigration policy was drastically revised when Congress eliminated the national origins quotas (page 655). The new law set a limit of 170,000 immigrants each year from countries outside the Western Hemisphere. People with relatives in the United States or with special skills are to be given priority; no more than 20,000 immigrants from any single country can enter in a given year. Immigration from countries of the Western Hemisphere, previously unrestricted, will be limited to 120,000 annually after 1968.

One measure which met defeat was a bill calling for repeal of Section 14b of the Taft-Hartley Act. This section authorizes states to pass "right to work" laws. Such laws forbid compulsory union membership as a requirement for holding a job.

Another action taken by Congress was to approve a Twenty-fifth Amendment to the Constitution and send it to the states

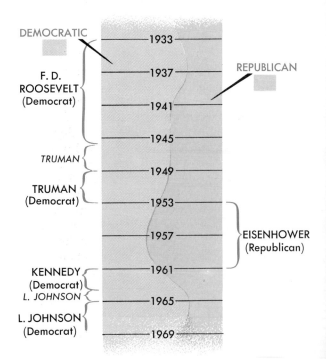

POLITICAL PARTIES, 1933 TO THE PRESENT

Compare the party ties of Presidents from 1897 to 1933 with those of Presidents from 1933 to the present. (See chart, page 669.)

CHART STUDY

for ratification. This Amendment would authorize the President to name a Vice-President if that office should become vacant. It would also enable a Vice-President to assume the duties of the presidency in case the President were seriously disabled. In addition, as we have seen, Congress passed the Voting Rights Act.

The importance of urban problems is recognized. By 1965 approximately 70 per cent of the American people were living in urban areas. Nearly all cities faced complex problems of mass transportation, urban renewal, shortages of parks and recreation areas, air and water pollution, unemployment among unskilled workers, and *de facto* school segregation. For many years the federal and state governments had paid little attention to these urgent problems. The Supreme Court decisions calling for "one man, one vote" in state legislatures and the House of Representatives (page 821) would in time give city dwellers and suburbanites a larger voice in government. But even before the full effects of these rulings were felt, Congress acted on some urban problems.

Over seven billion dollars was appropriated in 1965 for a four-year program of urban renewal and public-housing construction. Laws were passed allowing the federal government to take action on air and water pollution if the states failed to tackle these problems. Congress approved a highway "beautification" program and took steps to add to the nation's parks and recreation areas. In addition, the Civil Rights Act of 1964, the Voting Rights Act, and the new education measures were certain to increase federal involvement in urban problems. As a start toward the orderly administration of some of these programs, Congress created a Department of Housing and Urban Development. As Secretary of the new Department, Johnson appointed Robert C. Weaver, the first Negro to serve in a presidential Cabinet.

The scope and volume of the legislation passed in 1965 provided a sharp contrast with the amount of action taken when the conservative coalition had controlled Congress. President Johnson said of the new legislation, the next task is to "make sure it works properly."

▶ CHECK-UP

1. What stand did Johnson take on foreign and domestic affairs on becoming President?

2. What are the causes of the "balance of payments gap"? How did the administration try to cope with it? With inflation? How has job security become a problem?

3. What stand did President Johnson take on civil rights? What were the provisions of the Civil Rights Act of 1964? Of the Voting Rights Act of 1965? What efforts were made to eliminate poverty?

4. What were the issues of the 1964 election? What were the implications of the outcome?

5. What additional legislation did Johnson request? With what success?

. . . .

Two pressing challenges facing American cities today are traffic congestion (left) and air and water pollution. Right, a blanket of industrial smoke spreads over Los Angeles. The Department of Housing and Urban Development, headed by Robert C. Weaver (right, below) aims at helping cities solve their problems.

New rapid-transit systems may help some cities ease their transportation problem. Streamlined trains like the one at left will carry commuters on an extensive rapid-transit system now being built in the San Francisco area.

3 *The Cold War Takes Dangerous Turns*

The cold war between the Western world and the Communist nations remained the chief concern in foreign affairs during the 1960's. The United States continued to oppose Communist aggression whether it was inspired by Soviet Russia or Red China. But there were signs that the capacity of the Communist bloc for united action was weakened by (1) Chinese-Russian rivalry and (2) the desire of east European Communist states to make more decisions for themselves.

Kennedy and Khrushchev meet in Vienna. Shortly after President Kennedy took office in 1961, he met with Premier Khrushchev in Vienna for a private exchange of views. The Soviet leader presented stiff demands for "immediate" peace treaties with the two Germanies and the withdrawal of all foreign troops. He threatened to sign his own treaty with East Germany if he did not get his way. Also, Khrushchev rejected a ban on the testing of atomic weapons.

The reasons for Khrushchev's stand on international control of atomic testing were soon apparent. In the fall of 1961, the world was shocked by the Soviet Union's announcement that it was about to end an unofficial three-year moratorium on nuclear tests in the atmosphere. There followed some 40 or 50 Soviet tests, including the explosion of a bomb equal to more than 50 million tons of TNT. When the Soviet Union still refused to accept a test-ban treaty, President Kennedy reluctantly announced that the United States would also resume testing, at first underground and then in the atmosphere. World-wide concern about the danger of radioactive fallout kept the test-ban talks going. But the negotiators could find no basis for agreement on the problem of inspection.

Berlin remains a danger spot. Khrushchev's German demands also strained East-West relations. The Western allies were

An escaping East Berlin woman dangles from a building on the Berlin frontier as Communist police try to pull her back. West Berliners on the ground finally managed to rescue her.

determined not to give up their rights in Berlin. President Kennedy said: "We cannot and will not permit the Communists to drive us out of Berlin, either gradually or by force." Kennedy's preparations to defend West Berlin convinced Khrushchev that the Western allies would not give way. He therefore relaxed his deadline for an "immediate" German treaty. But the deadlock continued over the larger question of German reunification and a German treaty.

Meanwhile, East Germany had closed the boundary between East and West Berlin in order to stem the flow of refugees from the Communist world. In August, 1961, the Communists sealed off their sector of the city with a wall of concrete blocks and barbed wire. A few brave Germans managed to tunnel under the wall, climb over it, or crash vehicles through it. Other refugees, less fortunate, were killed or captured by East German guards. To the rest of the world the Berlin Wall was an admission of failure by the East German Communist government.

The cold war spreads to the Congo. Wherever former colonies were struggling to establish independent governments, Communist agents were ready to stir up trouble. This happened in Africa when the Republic of the Congo received its independence from Belgium in 1960. Desperately short of trained leaders, the country soon dissolved into warring factions, with Communist agitators adding to the confusion. When the Congo President asked the United Nations for help, UN security forces were sent in to try to restore order. The United States gave strong moral and financial support to the UN mission. Soviet Russia, however, objected to the Congo operation and refused to pay the dues assessed UN members for its maintenance. No solution was found for the UN financial dilemma, but the Congo was saved from Communist domination. Katanga Province, a rich mining area which had tried to secede from the Congo, was finally brought under the control of the central government. In 1964, the UN force was withdrawn.

The UN dues dispute leads to inaction. The Soviet failure to pay its assessments led to a deadlock in the UN General Assembly. The UN Charter provided that if a member fails to pay its dues for more than two years, it loses its vote in the Assembly. To avoid any showdown between the United States and the Soviet Union over this provision, the General Assembly avoided taking any vote during its 1964–1965 session. Thus, the Assembly could take no action, even on urgent matters. To end this paralysis, the United States in the late summer of 1965 dropped its demand that the Soviet Union pay its assessments or lose its voting rights in the Assembly.

The Alliance for Progress is launched. While events in far parts of the world demanded attention, the United States could not ignore serious problems in this hemisphere. Continuing poverty and unrest encouraged Communist agitators to seek a foothold in Latin America. To meet this threat, President Kennedy wanted to improve our relations with the Latin American countries, help stabilize governments that were democratic, raise standards of living, and thwart Communist propaganda. To achieve these goals, he proposed a new emphasis on social and economic reform.

Early in 1961 President Kennedy outlined a program known as the Alliance for Progress. It promised 20 billion dollars in aid over a ten-year period, half the money to come from the United States government, the rest from private American investors. In return, the Latin American countries were to promote democratic government, agricultural reform, and a higher standard of living for wage earners. At an Inter-American Conference in Uruguay, all the countries of Latin America — with the exception of Cuba — joined the Alliance.

A number of these countries used the aid to good advantage. But there were difficulties. Throughout Latin America the large landowners were reluctant to accept land-redistribution programs, and wealthy Latin Americans resisted new laws designed to make them pay their fair share of taxes. Despite the Alliance's emphasis on democratically supported governments, during the early 1960's the governments of Guatemala, Ecuador, Honduras, and the Dominican Republic were overturned by military leaders.

An attempt to unseat Castro fails. Meanwhile, in Cuba, Fidel Castro was establishing close ties with the Communists (page 775). Thousands of Cubans fled to the United States. They were eager to secure American military aid for an invasion of their homeland. On taking office, Kennedy learned that Eisenhower had already agreed to train and equip Cuban refugees for such a venture. A few members of Kennedy's staff advised the new President to drop the idea. But other advisers believed that an invasion would trigger a large-scale rebellion in Cuba and result in the overthrow of Castro. President Kennedy acted on their advice.

In April, 1961, an invasion force of 1500 Cuban exiles landed at the Bay of Pigs on the southern coast of the island. The operation had been planned with American aid. But the invaders lacked adequate air cover or naval artillery support and were soon taken prisoner by Castro's forces. No contact was made with the Cuban underground and no uprising took place.

This discouraging failure had widespread results. Some Latin American countries called the invasion a new form of American "imperialism." Khrushchev threatened to send Soviet troops to defend Cuba against American aggression. The failure of the invasion strengthened Castro's hold on the Cuban people, and he soon established even closer ties with the Communists. In response to a torrent of criticism, Kennedy took full responsibility for the disaster. But thereafter he kept a tighter rein on foreign policy and increasingly depended on his own judgment rather than his advisers'.

Kennedy quarantines Cuba. Cuba was now a Soviet satellite and Castro was exporting Communist agents to other Latin American countries. The Organization of American States voted to exclude Cuba from membership, and the United States tightened its trade embargo against the Castro regime. The Soviet Union responded by increasing its trade with Cuba and sending arms and military technicians.

In October, 1962, American airplanes carrying out a surveillance of Cuba established the fact that long-range missile sites were being prepared. In a television address, President Kennedy informed the nation that these missile sites were capable of sending nuclear weapons a distance of 2000 miles. The President announced that the United States navy and air force would establish a blockade around Cuba to prevent delivery of "offensive military equipment." In addition, the American government asked the UN Security Council to back its demand that all missile bases in Cuba be dismantled immediately. Kennedy said: "It shall be the policy of this nation to regard any nuclear missile launched from Cuba against any nation in the Western Hemisphere as an attack by the Soviet Union on the United States requiring a full retaliatory response on the Soviet Union."

For a few days the United States and Soviet Union stood at the brink of nuclear war. But Soviet ships carrying jet aircraft and military supplies to Cuba changed course rather than risk an encounter with American ships or planes enforcing the blockade. When America's allies and the OAS gave strong support to President Kennedy's stand, Soviet Premier Khrushchev agreed to remove the offensive weapons under UN supervision. In return, he asked that the United States lift its blockade and agree not to invade Cuba. Castro, however, refused to permit on-site inspection. Nevertheless, the Soviet Union promptly began removing the missiles, and the United States carried out its own inspection by aerial surveillance. The blockade was then lifted.

The outcome of the crisis was a clear-cut victory for the United States and the free world. It convinced Khrushchev that President Kennedy was prepared to use force if necessary to block Soviet domination of any country in Latin America. The Soviet leader had therefore decided not to risk touching off a nuclear holocaust by pushing his plans in Cuba.

A nuclear test-ban treaty is signed. Throughout the difficulties in Berlin, the Congo, and Cuba, Kennedy had kept the door open for negotiations with the Russians. He especially wanted to reach an understanding on the question of testing nuclear weapons in the atmosphere. In June, 1963, President Kennedy repeated his willingness to talk about this matter, and Khrushchev soon announced that he would agree to discuss the banning of atmospheric tests.

Negotiators for the United States, Britain, and the Soviet Union signed a treaty in August which prohibited all but underground nuclear tests (these produce little or no fall-out). President Kennedy hailed the treaty as "a shaft of light cut into the darkness. According to the ancient Chinese proverb, a journey of a thousand miles must begin with a single step. . . . Let us take that first step." The United States Senate ratified the test-ban treaty in September by a vote of 80 to 19. More than a hundred other countries also agreed to the

Under Communist leadership, China has struggled to build up heavy industry like steelmaking (left). But Red China's agricultural output still cannot feed its huge population, recently estimated at 750 million. Above, Chinese boys and girls train for militia duty with fixed bayonets.

treaty, though France, Communist China, and Cuba refused to sign.

Strains appear behind the iron curtain. The fact that the Soviet Union signed the test-ban treaty while Communist China did not reflected the growing differences between the two countries. For more than a decade China had been dependent on the Soviet Union for military and industrial goods and had generally followed the Russian lead in Communist policy. But during Khrushchev's years in power, the Soviet Union underwent many changes. The Russian people demanded and got more consumer goods. The harsh police state of Stalin's day gave way to a less harsh, though still totalitarian, government. The Soviet Union's aggressive foreign policy softened as a result of repeated reverses and heavy expenses.

Meanwhile, China under Mao Tse-tung and Premier Chou En-lai was making strenuous efforts to catch up with the twentieth century. The government imposed rigidly planned programs on the Chinese people to increase agricultural and industrial output. Although the Soviet Union refused to share nuclear information with the Chinese, Communist China was able to explode its first atomic bomb in 1964. The most important difference between the two countries, however, concerned interpretation of Communist methods and goals. Chinese leaders believed in a more aggressive policy and even claimed they were not afraid of nuclear war. They aided guerrilla fighters in Southeast Asia, harassed their Indian neighbors, and sent agitators into Africa and Latin America.

The missile crisis in Cuba and the test-ban treaty widened the rift in the Communist bloc. China accused the Soviet Union of selling out to the capitalist countries. Khrushchev retorted that the Chinese leaders were brutal Stalinists. Both nations sought the support of other Communist countries. When Khrushchev was suddenly removed from power in 1964, Western leaders feared that the new Soviet rulers might revert to earlier policies and heal the breach with China. But the new Soviet government seemed to continue Khrushchev's policy of a more relaxed rule at home and a less adventurous foreign policy abroad. Most of the Communist countries in Europe remained under Russian influence. But the belligerent Chinese Communists made headway in those areas of the world where underdeveloped countries were looking for a short cut to higher standards of living.

Strains also appear in the Western alliance. The free-world alliance was also experiencing difficulties in the 1960's. France's failure to sign the test-ban treaty was symbolic of the disagreement within the Western alliance. General Charles de Gaulle had come to power in France in 1958 with a chip on his shoulder against the "Anglo-Saxons," as he called the British and Americans. He resented their domination of the NATO alliance. He frequently disagreed with policies which Britain and the United States supported in the United Nations, such as the peace-keeping operation in the Congo. Also, while Britain and the United States wanted to prevent the spread of nuclear capability, de Gaulle was determined to make France a full-fledged nuclear power. In 1960 France exploded its first nuclear bomb in the Sahara Desert. De Gaulle also established diplomatic relations with Communist China.

At the heart of de Gaulle's ambition was a desire to re-establish France as the dominant country in western Europe. For this reason he vetoed Britain's application to join the Common Market (page 808). And he sought to convince other countries that in case of a showdown with the Soviet Union, the United States would not risk nuclear war to defend its NATO allies. De Gaulle wanted western Europe to chart its own course independent of the United States. None of the countries of western Europe was ready to abandon NATO or to accept French domination of the Common Market. But de Gaulle touched a sensitive nerve when he said that Europe had outgrown the need for American leadership.

Laos and South Vietnam are endangered. Meanwhile, a major threat to world peace was developing in Southeast Asia, where Communist guerrilla fighters threat-

American military forces first went to South Vietnam as advisers. Below, United States Special Forces men teach Vietnamese how to use modern weapons to protect their villages against Vietcong attacks.

The American forces in Vietnam gradually took on a combat role. Helicopters (above) have proved especially useful to men fighting in the Vietnamese jungles and rice paddies.

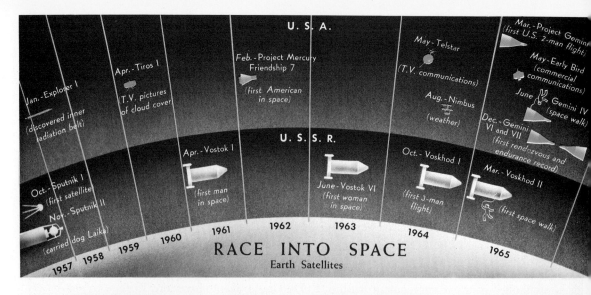

RACE INTO SPACE
Earth Satellites

U.S.A.

Jan.- Explorer I
(discovered inner radiation belt)

Apr.- Tiros I
T.V. pictures of cloud cover

Feb.- Project Mercury Friendship 7
(first American in space)

May- Telstar
(T.V. communications)

Aug.- Nimbus
(weather)

Mar.- Project Gemini
(first U.S. 2-man flight)

May- Early Bird
(commercial communications)

June - Gemini IV
(space walk)

Dec.- Gemini VI and VII
(first rendezvous and endurance record)

U.S.S.R.

Oct.- Sputnik I
(first satellite)

Nov.- Sputnik II
(carried dog Laika)

Apr.- Vostok I
(first man in space)

June - Vostok VI
(first woman in space)

Oct.- Voskhod I
(first 3-man flight)

Mar.- Voskhod II
(first space walk)

1957   1958   1959   1960   1961   1962   1963   1964   1965

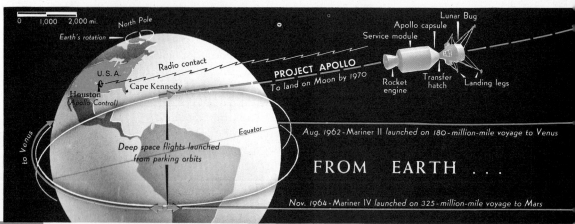

FROM EARTH . . .

0   1,000   2,000 mi.
North Pole
Earth's rotation
Radio contact
U.S.A.
Cape Kennedy
Houston (Apollo Control)
Deep space flights launched from parking orbits
Equator
to Venus

PROJECT APOLLO
To land on Moon by 1970

Service module
Apollo capsule
Lunar Bug
Rocket engine
Transfer hatch
Landing legs

Aug. 1962 - Mariner II launched on 180-million-mile voyage to Venus

Nov. 1964 - Mariner IV launched on 325-million-mile voyage to Mars

MAP STUDY

THE EXPLORATION OF SPACE

Man has made tremendous progress in knowledge of space. The upper panel surveys important "firsts" in the American and Soviet satellite programs. The United States hopes to send men to the moon in the Apollo spacecraft (lower panel).

ened the independence of the countries carved out of French Indo-China (page 768). In Laos, three groups were vying for power — one was pro-Western, one was pro-Communist, and the third wanted Laos to remain neutral. Secretary of State Dulles had firmly opposed neutralist control of Laos, but President Kennedy was willing to explore the possibilities of such a settlement. Negotiators met at Geneva in 1961, and in the following year the Laotian civil war ended. A system of government was set up under three ruling princes — one neutral, one pro-Western, and one pro-Communist. Furthermore, a pact guaran-

teeing the neutrality of Laos was signed by fourteen nations.

Ever since 1954 North Vietnam had been aiding Communist guerrillas (the Viet Cong) in their struggle to overthrow the government of South Vietnam. During the Kennedy administration the United States sent over 10,000 servicemen as advisers, instructors, pilots, and supporting units to help the South Vietnamese government crush the Viet Cong. In President Kennedy's opinion, preserving the independence of South Vietnam was of "vital interest" to the United States.

After President Johnson took office, he

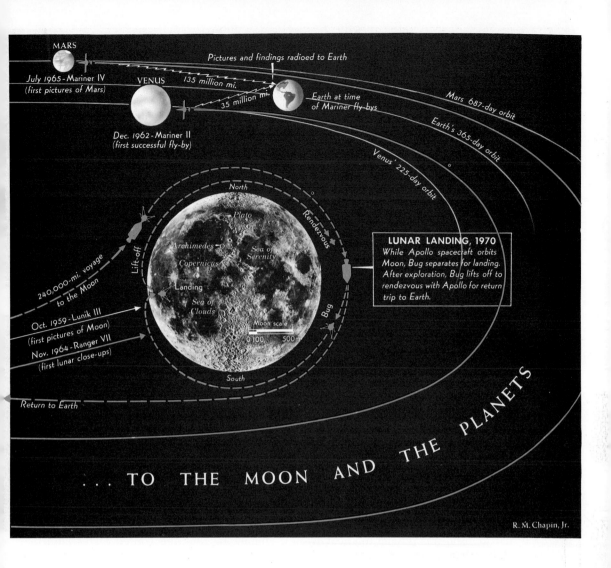

MARS
July 1965-Mariner IV
(first pictures of Mars)

Pictures and findings radioed to Earth

VENUS
135 million mi.

Dec. 1962-Mariner II
(first successful fly-by)

35 million mi.

Earth at time
of Mariner fly-bys

Mars 687-day orbit

Earth's 365-day orbit

Venus' 225-day orbit

North

Plato

Rendezvous

Archimedes
Sea of
Serenity

Copernicus

LUNAR LANDING, 1970
*While Apollo spacecraft orbits
Moon, Bug separates for landing.
After exploration, Bug lifts off to
rendezvous with Apollo for return
trip to Earth.*

Lift-off

Landing

Sea of
Clouds

240,000-mi. voyage
to the Moon

Oct. 1959-Lunik III
(first pictures of Moon)
Nov. 1964-Ranger VII
(first lunar close-ups)

Bug

Moon scale

0 100   500m

South

Return to Earth

... TO THE MOON AND THE PLANETS

R. M. Chapin, Jr.

*The Lunar "Bug" will separate from the Apollo spacecraft to land on the moon.
Information gathered from the Mariner probes will help space scientists plan for
exploration of Mars and Venus and perhaps the other planets.*

continued to follow the Kennedy policy of limited support for the South Vietnamese government. Then, in the summer of 1964, North Vietnamese torpedo boats attacked two American destroyers in the Gulf of Tonkin. In response, Johnson ordered an air strike against North Vietnamese coastal bases. But during the presidential campaign that fall he made it clear that he did not want to broaden the war by turning it into an attack on North Vietnam.

The Vietnamese war escalates. Shortly after the election, President Johnson was forced to alter his policy concerning Vietnam. Communist gains prompted Johnson

to increase the American military commitment to 190,000 men by the early months of 1966. American planes bombed North Vietnamese supply routes, bridges, and other military targets. Johnson announced that if the Viet Cong would end the war, the United States would give generous financial support to a UN-sponsored plan for development of Southeast Asia. The President hoped to make the North Vietnamese less dependent on Communist China by including them in the economic development program. But North Vietnam did not accept this proposal.

Although a large majority of Americans

Two Gemini spacecraft were only a few feet apart in this photograph taken by one of the orbiting Astronauts during the historic rendezvous mission of December, 1965.

munist take-over in the rebel movement, Johnson sent some 20,000 American troops to the Dominican Republic.

The United States' action in sending troops to the Dominican Republic violated the OAS charter and reminded Latin Americans of "big stick" diplomacy (page 595). On the other hand, the Organization of American States did not want Castro Communists establishing a beachhead in another country. At the urging of the United States, therefore, the OAS sent an inter-American force to replace the American troops and enforce a cease-fire in the Dominican Republic. After negotiating with leaders of different factions, OAS mediators established a provisional government. But continuing outbursts of violence threatened the stability of this government.

The space race continues. During the unrelenting tensions of the cold war, Americans were somewhat cheered by their country's accomplishments in the exploration of space. The Soviet space program was also moving ahead, but American scientists seemed to be slowly closing the gap.

This country put its first astronaut into orbit early in 1962 when John Glenn circled the earth three times. The following year an American completed a twenty-two orbit flight. In 1964 the United States launched Saturn I, a rocket weighing 38,000 pounds, almost three times heavier than any the Russians had put up. This was an important step in our long-range program to put a man on the moon. Then, in 1965, a series of Gemini flights proved man's ability to remain in space for days at a time without suffering ill effects.

Efforts in space were not restricted to manned flights and rocket thrust. In 1962 Mariner II probed to within 21,000 miles of the planet Venus, sending back valuable scientific information. Telstar and other communications satellites relayed live television programs between the continents. American space probes sent back photographs of the moon's surface and of the planet Mars. In early 1966 a Soviet unmanned spacecraft made a "soft" landing on the moon and radioed back to earth close-up photographs.

supported Johnson's policies, there were critics at home and abroad. Some people felt that Johnson was relying too heavily on a military solution rather than a negotiated settlement. Others said the danger of getting into a land war with China far outweighed any gains that might result from the air attacks on North Vietnam. In early 1966, President Johnson halted the bombing of North Vietnam for 37 days while intensive efforts were made to move the Vietnamese conflict to the conference table. When bombing resumed, the President asked the United Nations Security Council to help in the continuing "pursuit of peace."

The United States intervenes in the Dominican Republic. In the midst of the Vietnam dilemma, Johnson found himself caught in another trouble spot. In April, 1965, a rebellion broke out in the Dominican Republic. The President dispatched 400 marines to Santo Domingo to protect American lives. Then, when officials reported that there was danger of a Com-

To land on the moon will require more than knowledge of the lunar surface. The space crew will need to leave their spaceships and survive in an airless environment. The Russians took the first step in this direction in 1965 when one of their Cosmonauts left his space vehicle and floated in space, attached to his ship by a thin cord. The United States soon duplicated this achievement when an Astronaut left his Gemini capsule and remained in space for twenty minutes. The American space program scored a first when Astronauts succeeded in maneuvering two Gemini spacecraft within a foot of each other while in orbit. This "rendezvous" maneuver is an essential stage in the Apollo moon program.

▶ CHECK-UP

1. What was the outcome of the Vienna meeting of Kennedy and Khrushchev? Why was the Berlin Wall built? How did the cold war spread to Africa? Why was the Alliance for Progress launched?

2. How did Kennedy deal with the Cuban missile crisis? What was the significance of the test-ban treaty?

3. What issues have tended to divide the Communist countries? The Western alliance?

4. How did the cold war spread to Southeast Asia? How has the war in Vietnam "escalated"? Why did the United States intervene in the Dominican Republic? What were the results?

5. What are recent developments in the space race?

. . . .

Clinching the Main Ideas in Chapter 38

The events recorded in Chapter 38 may well be viewed in the light of earlier developments during the twentieth century. The Progressive Movement of the early 1900's and the New Deal reforms of the 1930's had expanded the regulatory powers of the federal government in response to the needs of farmers, wage earners, and consumers.

Much that took place under Presidents Kennedy and Johnson was a further development of these trends. The federal government extended its activities into new fields such as education and the increasingly complex problems of America's great cities. The decision of the Kennedy and Johnson administrations to place the full force of the federal government behind the drive for equal rights and equal opportunities for all citizens, especially Negroes and the urban and rural poor, was a logical outgrowth of earlier reforms. This decision seems likely to influence the course of events for years to come.

The country's role in foreign affairs can be viewed in a similar light. Theodore Roosevelt was the first President to announce that as a world power we had to become involved in international events whether we wanted to or not. This involvement was demonstrated in World Wars I and II. In each of these wars, the United States reluctantly entered to preserve its own security. Abraham Lincoln once said that the Declaration of Independence promised "not alone to the people of this country but also to the world . . . that in due time the weights should be lifted from the shoulders of all men." Presidents Kennedy and Johnson, as well as Truman and Eisenhower, sought to fulfill the broader meaning which Lincoln found in the Declaration. They did so by their strong support of the United Nations, their quest for control of atomic weapons, their opposition to Communist aggression, and their assistance to independent governments in all parts of the world.

A prominent Frenchman, André Malraux, has captured in a few words the essence of the American contribution to world affairs in the twentieth century. During a visit to the United States in 1962, Malraux offered a toast "to the only nation that has waged war but not worshipped it, that has won the greatest power in the world but not sought it, that has wrought the greatest weapon of death but not wished to wield it; and may it [the United States] inspire men with dreams worthy of its action."

Chapter Review

Terms to Understand

1. New Frontier
2. Medicare
3. Peace Corps
4. Viet Cong
5. Berlin Wall
6. "far right"
7. Great Society
8. Alliance for Progress
9. VISTA
10. Trade Expansion Act
11. Civil Rights Act of 1964
12. Voting Rights Act
13. balance of payments gap
14. Area Redevelopment Act
15. Housing Act of 1961
16. Common Market
17. Freedom Schools
18. *de facto* segregation
19. March on Washington

What Do You Think?

1. In accepting the Democratic nomination for President, John F. Kennedy said: ". . . the New Frontier . . . is not a set of promises — it is a set of challenges." What did he mean?

2. Why might it be desirable to retain high federal taxes during periods of full employment and to cut taxes when the economy slumps? Explain.

3. Although the dollar value of American exports exceeds that of imports, the balance of payments gap persists. Why?

4. Some hold that civil rights legislation infringes on the reserved powers of the state.

Do you agree? What is the constitutional basis for this legislation?

5. What are the major causes of unrest in Latin America? How can these be remedied?

Using Your Knowledge of History

1. Debate: *Resolved,* That the best interests of the Republican Party will be served if it reflects conservative views.

2. Write a letter to a newspaper giving your reaction to the principle of "one man, one vote."

3. Plan a panel discussion on the subject of this country's policy in Southeast Asia.

4. Prepare a two-column chart to bring out the advantages and problems of automation.

Extending Your Knowledge of History

John Kennedy: A Political Profile is a good biography by James MacGregor Burns. Two books on the New Frontier are *Kennedy* by Theodore Sorensen and *A Thousand Days* by Arthur M. Schlesinger, Jr. On recent presidential campaigns, see T. H. White's *The Making of the President, 1960* and *The Making of the President, 1964.* William S. White is the author of *The Professional: Lyndon B. Johnson.* For relations with Europe, see Drew Middleton's *The Atlantic Community: A Study in Unity and Disunity.*

Analyzing Unit Eleven

1. American foreign policy during the cold war has differed markedly from the policies pursued during the 1920's and 1930's. What has the post-World War II generation learned from the mistakes of earlier generations? How has this knowledge influenced the decision of Americans to play an active role in world affairs?

2. The federal government in the 1920's was dominated by businessmen who talked the language of *laissez faire.* Today the federal government is responsive to the demands of businessmen, farmers, consumers, organized labor, and Negroes. How and why has this

change come about? How has it affected the position of each of the groups that now have a voice in the federal government?

3. President Kennedy considered his civil rights bill a measure to enforce the Fourteenth and Fifteenth Amendments. "Now the time has come," he said, "for this nation to fulfill its promise." What rights were guaranteed to the Negroes by the Fourteenth Amendment? By the Fifteenth Amendment? By the Civil Rights Act of 1875? Why were these rights denied them for so many years? Why was the time ripe for action on civil rights in the early 1960's? What has been accomplished so far?

REFERENCE SECTION

For Further Reading

General References

Johnson, A., and Malone, D., eds., *Dictionary of American Biography* (22 vols.)

Lord, C. L. and E. H., *Historical Atlas of the United States*

Morris, Richard B., *Encyclopedia of American History*

Paullin, C. O., *Atlas of the Historical Geography of the United States*

Sources

Bailey, T. A., ed., *The American Spirit*

Commager, H. S., ed., *America in Perspective*

Commager, H. S., ed., *Documents of American History*

Commager, H. S., and Nevins, Allan, eds., *The Heritage of America*

Handlin, Oscar, ed., *This Was America*

Hofstadter, Richard B., ed., *Great Issues in American History*

General Accounts

Bailey, T. A., *The American Pageant: A History of the Republic*

Handlin, Oscar, *The Americans*

Hicks, John, Mowry, George E., and Burke, Robert E., *The Federal Union* and *The American Nation*

Hofstadter, R., Miller, W., and Aaron, D., *The American Republic*

Miller, William, *A New History of the United States*

Morison, S. E., and Commager, H. S., *The Growth of the American Republic*

Morison, S. E., *The Oxford History of the American People*

Multi-volume Series

Boorstin, D. J., ed., *The Chicago History of American Civilization*

Commager, H. S., and Morris, R. B., eds., *The New American Nation Series*

David, H., and others, eds., *The Economic History of the United States*

Fine, S., and Brown, G. S., *The American Past*

Johnson, A., ed., *Chronicles of America*

Stephenson, W. H., and Coulter, E. M., eds., *A History of the South*

Taylor, G. R., ed., *Problems in American Civilization*

Special Accounts

The American Heritage Book of Indians

The American Heritage Book of the Pioneer Spirit

The American Heritage History of the Great West

Bailey, T. A., *A Diplomatic History of the American People*

Billington, R. A., *Westward Expansion*

Burchard, J., and Bush-Brown, A., *The Architecture of America*

Chase, Gilbert, *America's Music*

Dulles, F. R., *Labor in America*

Eliot, Alexander, *Three Hundred Years of American Painting*

Fite, Gilbert C., and Reese, Jim E., *An Economic History of the United States*

Franklin, John Hope, *From Slavery to Freedom: A History of American Negroes*

Gabriel, R. H., *The Course of American Democratic Thought*

Handlin, Oscar, *The Uprooted*

Kelly, A. H., and Harbison, W. A., *The American Constitution*

Logan, Rayford W., *The Negro in the United States: A Brief History*

Pratt, J. W., *A History of United States Foreign Policy*

Shannon, F. A., *America's Economic Growth*

Taubman, Howard, *The Making of the American Theatre*

Wade, Richard C., *The Negro in American Life*

Pictorial and Illustrated Histories

Athearn, Robert G., *The American Heritage New Illustrated History of the United States* (16 vols.)

Butterfield, Roger, *The American Past*

Life History of the United States (12 vols.)

The number of books available in paperbound editions is constantly growing. To see which of the books in these lists are available in paper, consult Paperbound Books in Print, *published by* R. R. Bowker Co., 1180 Avenue of the Americas, New York, N.Y., 10036.

ADDITIONAL UNIT READING SUGGESTIONS

UNIT 1

Two volumes in *The Life History of the United States* deal with this period: Volume 1, *The New World: Prehistory to 1774*, and the first half of Volume 2, *The Making of a Nation, 1775–1789*.

For more information on the European background of American colonization, see Louis B. Wright's *The Atlantic Frontier* and A. L. Rowse's *The Expansion of Elizabethan England*. Ernle Bradford is the author of a brisk biography of Sir Francis Drake, *The Wind Commands Me*. A study of the African cultural roots of the Negro slaves is *A Glorious Age in Africa: The Story of Three Great African Empires* by Daniel Chu and Elliott Skinner. For more material on the background of the American Indians, consult *The Indian in America's Past* by Jack D. Forbes and *The American Heritage Book of Indians*.

An interesting analysis of Franklin's influence can be found in V. W. Crane's *Benjamin Franklin and a Rising People*. Stewart Holbrook writes about the Boston Post Road in *The Old Post Road*. Ola E. Winslow has written two fine biographies which reveal many facets of colonial life: *Samuel Sewall of Boston* and *Jonathan Edwards, 1703–1758*. M. L. Starkey is the author of *The Devil in Massachusetts, A Modern Inquiry into the Salem Witch Trials*. For an unusual but fascinating view of the colonial period, see Daniel Boorstin's *The Americans: The Colonial Experience*.

A brief but well-balanced account of events leading up to the Revolution and the course of the war itself is *The Birth of the Republic, 1763–1789*, by Edmund S. Morgan. Two good surveys of the causes of the war are John C. Miller's *Origins of the American Revolution* and L. H. Gipson's *The Coming of the Revolution, 1763–1775*. *Background to Glory* by John Bakeless is an interesting biography of George Rogers Clark. Willard Wallace writes with understanding in *Traitorous Hero: The Life and Fortunes of Benedict Arnold*. Naval aspects of the war are brilliantly treated by Samuel Eliot Morison in *John Paul Jones: A Sailor's Biography*. For military history, see Richard M. Ketchum's *The Battle for Bunker Hill;* Bernhard Knollenberg's *Washington and the Revolution;* John C. Miller's *Triumph of Freedom;* or J. R. Alden's *The American Revolution, 1775–1783*.

For developments on the frontier, see two books by Dale Van Every — *Forth to the Wilderness: The First American Frontier, 1754–1774*, and *A Company of Heroes: The American Frontier, 1775–1783*.

A number of fine historical novels are based on events in North America during the 1600's and 1700's. Willa Cather's *Shadows on the Rock* is set in Quebec during the period of French rule. Colonial life in Massachusetts comes to life in Anya Seton's *The Winthrop Woman* and Esther Forbes's *Johnny Tremain*. General Burgoyne and the American campaign against him are featured in Walter D. Edmonds's *Drums Along the Mohawk* and Kenneth Roberts's *Rabble in Arms*. Benedict Arnold's assault on Quebec inspired Kenneth Roberts to write *Arundel*, and the same author deals with the Revolution from the Loyalist viewpoint in *Oliver Wiswell*.

UNIT 2

Events in this unit are covered in the last half of Volume 2 and the first half of Volume 3 in *The Life History of the United States* — *The Making of a Nation, 1775–1789* and *The Growing Years, 1789–1829*. See also the first five chapters in *The American Heritage History of the Great West*.

Allan Nevins discusses the social, economic, and political changes that took place after 1776 in *The American States During and After the Revolution*. The role of Congress in the 1780's is treated in *The Reluctant Rebels: The Story of the Continental Congress, 1774–1789*, by Lynn Montrose. For information about the delegates to the Philadelphia convention, see Nathan Schachner's *Founding Fathers* and Richard Hofstadter's first chapter in *The American Political Tradition*.

Richard B. Morris has edited a paperbound collection of Hamilton's writings, *The Basic Ideas of Alexander Hamilton*. The conflict in political principles between Federalists and Republicans is the theme of *Jeffersonian Principles and Hamiltonian Principles*, edited by James T. Adams. Leland Baldwin is the author of *Whiskey Rebels; The Story of a Frontier Uprising*. For additional information on the last Federalist President, see Gilbert Chinard's *Honest John Adams*.

Richard Hofstadter presents a stimulating interpretation of Thomas Jefferson in the second chapter of *The American Political Tradition.* Allen Johnson has written *Jefferson and His Colleagues,* while Adrienne Koch has dealt with the close relationship between the third and fourth Presidents in *Jefferson and Madison: The Great Collaboration.* For naval developments in this period, see Donald Barr Chidsey's *The American Privateers* and Glenn Tucker's *Dawn Like Thunder: The Barbary Wars and the Birth of the United States Navy.* The American policy of economic coercion is handled by L. M. Sears in *Jefferson and the Embargo.* Dale Van Every provides a lively description of Jefferson's frontier supporters in *Men of the Western Waters.* On the War Hawks, see Charles M. Wiltse's *John C. Calhoun* and Bernard Mayo's *Henry Clay: Spokesman of the New West.* Also of interest is Julius W. Pratt's *Expansionists of 1812.*

The economic and social developments of this period are covered by John Krout and Dixon R. Fox in *The Completion of Independence, 1790–1830.* The role of cities in the development of the West is explained by Richard Wade in *The Urban Frontier: The Rise of Western Cities, 1790–1830.* On the introduction of the steamboat see Thomas Boyd's *Poor John Fitch* and James Thomas Flexner's *Steamboats Come True.* The American effort to establish cultural independence is the main theme of Russel Blaine Nye's *The Cultural Life of the New Nation, 1776–1830.*

Thomas Jefferson stars in Elizabeth Page's historical novel, *Tree of Liberty,* while Alexander Hamilton is featured in Gertrude Atherton's *The Conqueror.* A famous story set in the 1790's is *The Man Without a Country* by Edward Everett Hale. Hildegarde Hawthorne writes about the Lewis and Clark expedition in *Westward the Course.* Dale Van Every's fiction is as good as his history; see *Westward the River* and *Our Country Then: Tales of Our First Frontier.* Odell Shepard writes about Tecumseh and the pirate Jean Lafitte in *Holdfast Gaines.* *Horseshoe Bend* by Bruce Palmer and John C. Giles is a lively story of Jackson and the Creek Indians. C. S. Forester's *Captain from Connecticut* deals with naval aspects of the War of 1812. So do two books by J. E. Jennings, *Tall Ships* and *Salem Frigate,* and two by Kenneth Roberts, *The Lively Lady* and *Captain Caution.*

UNIT 3

Highly recommended are Volumes 3 and 4 of *The Life History of the United States* — *The Growing Years, 1789–1829,* and *The Sweep Westward, 1829–1849* — and Chapters 6–10 of *The American Heritage History of the Great West.*

An outstanding historian who dealt with sectionalism in American history is Frederick Jackson Turner. His essays on this subject were edited by Max Farrand and Avery Craven under the title *The Significance of Sections in American History.* Other studies include Everett Dick's *The Dixie Frontier* and R. C. Buley's two-volume *The Old Northwest: Pioneer Period, 1815–1840.* *The Paths of Inland Commerce* by A. B. Hulbert deals with transportation in this period.

There are a number of fine biographical studies of political figures. William N. Chambers's *Old Bullion Benton, Senator from the New West* paints a sympathetic picture of Thomas Hart Benton. Van Buren's political skills are depicted by Holmes Alexander in *The American Talleyrand.* Clement Eaton wrote *Henry Clay and the Art of American Politics,* and Richard N. Current is the author of *Daniel Webster and the Rise of National Conservatism.*

Alexis de Tocqueville, a French traveler, was a perceptive observer of American life in the Jacksonian Era. His valuable *Democracy in America* is available in several editions. For special aspects of the reform movement, see John Krout's *The Origins of Prohibition,* and Helen Marshall's *Dorothea Dix: Forgotten Samaritan.* Educational reform is the subject of S. L. Jackson's *America's Struggle for Free Schools* and Louise Hall Tharp's *Until Victory: Horace Mann and Mary Peabody.* Carl Bode examines the demand for adult education in *The American Lyceum, Town Meeting of the Mind.* On the origins and growth of Mormonism, see Fawn Brodie's *No Man Knows My History: The Life of Joseph Smith;* M. R. Werner's *Brigham Young;* and R. B. West's *Kingdom of the Saints.* For biographies of some of the outstanding authors of this period, see R. L. Rusk's *The Life of Ralph Waldo Emerson,* Howard Doughty's *Francis Parkman,* and Van Wyck Brooks's *The World of Washington Irving.*

Leaders of the westward movement come to life in Allan Nevins's *Frémont, Pathmaker of the West,* Marquis James's *The Raven: A Biography of Sam Houston,* and J. A. Shackford's *David Crockett: The Man and the Legend.* A well-written history of the Mexican War is *Rehearsal for Conflict* by A. H. Bill. The relation between the westward movement and the political crisis can be studied in greater detail in C. B. Going's *David Wilmot, Free Soiler* and W. E. Dodd's *Expansion and Con-*

flict. An interesting study of the politics of compromise is *America's Silver Age: The State-craft of Clay, Webster, and Calhoun* by Gerald Johnson.

Samuel Hopkins Adams wrote an entertaining historical novel about the canal era called *Canal Town.* Irving Stone features Rachel Jackson in *The President's Lady* and Jessie Benton Frémont in *Immortal Wife.* Paul I. Wellman based his novel *Magnificent Destiny* on the friendship between Andrew Jackson and Sam Houston. A. B. Guthrie's *The Way West* is a fine novel about the journey from Missouri to Oregon. Don Berry's *Moontrap* is a story of two men in Oregon in 1850. *Doctor in Buckskin* by T. D. Allen deals with the Whitmans in Oregon. Vardis Fisher used the Mormon epic in *Children of God,* while the forty-niners figure in S. E. White's *Gold* and Robert Lewis Taylor's *The Travels of Jaimie McPheeters.*

UNIT 4

The fifth volume of *The Life History of the United States* provides a survey of this period — *The Union Sundered, 1849–1865.* See also Chapters 10–12 of *The American Heritage History of the Great West.* For a strikingly different view of American life in the prewar decades, see Daniel Boorstin's *The Americans: The National Experience.*

For further information on the impact of science and technology, see J. A. Kouwen-hoven's *Made in America,* and Roger Bur-lingame's *March of the Iron Men.* An outstanding historian of immigration, Marcus Lee Hansen, wrote *The Atlantic Migration, 1607–1860,* and *The Immigrant in American History.* The reaction of some native-born Americans to the immigrants is the subject of Ray Billington's *The Protestant Crusade, 1800–1860.* Useful biographies include Russel B. Nye's *William Lloyd Garrison and the Humanitarian Reformers;* James D. Horan's *Mathew Brady: Historian With a Camera;* and John Tasker Howard's *Stephen Foster: America's Troubadour.*

Clement Eaton's *Freedom of Thought in the Old South* is a study of southern intellectual life. W. E. Dodd's *The Cotton Kingdom* is still useful, but it should be supplemented with the new material in D. L. Cohn's *The Life and Times of King Cotton.* The northern view of slavery and slaveholders is analyzed in H. R. Floan's *The South in Northern Eyes, 1831 to 1861.* Two biographical studies of fire-eaters are *George Fitzhugh: Propagandist of the Old*

South by Harvey Wish and *Edmund Ruffin, Southerner* by Avery Craven.

The political effects of the Kansas-Nebraska Act are analyzed by Roy Nichols in *Bleeding Kansas* and *The Disruption of American Democracy.* Lincoln's handling of the secession crisis is the subject of Kenneth Stampp's *And the War Came.* David Donald's *Charles Sumner and the Coming of the Civil War* is an interesting book.

David Donald has also written a provocative book of essays entitled *Why the North Won the Civil War.* Paul Angle and Earl S. Miers edited eyewitness accounts of the war in *The Tragic Years, 1860–1865.* Bell Wiley has described the soldiers' life in *The Life of Johnny Reb* and *The Life of Billy Yank.* The atmosphere of the northern capital is reconstructed by Margaret Leech in *Reveille in Washington, 1860–1865.* James Bishop is the author of *The Day Lincoln Was Shot.* Among the many biographies of Civil War figures are J. W. Thomason's *Jeb Stuart,* Hudson Strode's *Jefferson Davis,* and Lloyd Lewis's *Sherman, Fighting Prophet.*

Two historical novels make use of the drama of the underground railroad — *Fire Bell in the Night* by C. N. Robertson and *The Glass Dove* by Sally Carrighar. Kansas in the 1850's is the setting for Margaret Lynn's *Land of Promise.* Among the best of the Civil War historical novels are Ben Ames Williams's *A House Divided;* Stark Young's *So Red the Rose;* Ellen Glasgow's *The Battleground;* Clifford Dowdey's *Where My Love Sleeps;* Harold Frederic's *The Copperhead;* Stephen Crane's *The Red Badge of Courage;* and Margaret Mitchell's *Gone With the Wind.* Stephen Vincent Benét wrote an epic poem about the war, *John Brown's Body.* Books by three distinguished authors who lived through the Civil War are *Ambrose Bierce's Civil War,* Herman Melville's *Battle-Pieces,* and Walt Whitman's *Drum-Taps.*

UNIT 5

Highly recommended is Volume 6 of *The Life History of the United States* — *The Union Restored, 1861–1876.* A vivid description of the South immediately after the war was written by J. T. Trowbridge in *The Desolate South.* For more information about the Ku Klux Klan, see S. F. Horn's *The Invisible Empire.* *Old Thad Stevens* by Richard N. Current explores the motives and the maneuvers of the Radical Republicans. Of great interest is the chapter on Senator Edmund G.

Ross in John F. Kennedy's *Profiles in Courage*. Claude G. Bowers's *The Tragic Era, the Revolution after Lincoln* and George F. Milton's *The Age of Hate: Andrew Johnson and the Radicals* should be weighed against a more recent study, *Andrew Johnson and Reconstruction* by E. L. McKitrick. An understanding of southern white attitudes can be found in R. B. Nixon's biography, *Henry W. Grady, Spokesman of the New South*.

Useful for studying the Gilded Age is Roy Nichols's *The Stakes of Power, 1845–1877*. See also *The Dreadful Decade, 1869–1879* by D. C. Seitz. For biographies of men who drifted with the currents of the 1870's and 1880's, see W. B. Hesseltine's *Ulysses S. Grant, Politician* and W. A. Swanberg's *Jim Fisk: The Career of an Improbable Rascal*. Other historians have studied individuals who fought the prevailing currents of the Gilded Age. See, for example, C. M. Fuess's *Carl Schurz, Reformer;* G. G. Van Deusen's *Horace Greeley: Nineteenth Century Crusader;* and Harry Barnard's *Rutherford B. Hayes and His America*.

UNIT 6

Vigilante organizations are the subject of Wayne Gard's *Frontier Justice*. Stanley Vestal has written *Mountain Men* and a book on Indian warfare, *Warpath and Council Fire*. An excellent study of the Indians is John C. Collier's *Indians of the Americas*. Arthur Chapman has written *The Pony Express,* and J. B. Frantz and J. E. Choate, Jr., examine life on the range in *The American Cowboy*. A colorful phase of the farmers' westward march is the subject of *The Sod-House Frontier* by Everett Dick. Solon J. Buck examines the farmers' reaction to hardships in *The Granger Movement* and *The Agrarian Crusade*.

For the growth of industrialism and its impact, see the seventh volume in *The Life History of The United States — The Age of Steel and Steam, 1877–1890*. More specialized studies include J. R. Smith's *The Story of Iron and Steel;* Lewis Corey's *The House of Morgan;* and Warren Tute's *Atlantic Conquest: The Men and Ships of the Glorious Age of Steam*. For more material about inventors, see Richard N. Current's *The Typewriter and the Men Who Made It;* Orlando Stevenson's *Alexander Graham Bell;* and H. G. Garbedian's *Thomas Alva Edison*. Biographical studies of businessmen include Allan Nevins's *Study in Power: John D. Rockefeller;* Burton J. Hendrick's *The Life of Andrew Carnegie;* and H. G. Prout's *A Life of George Westinghouse*.

Dixon Wecter provides a colorful description of high society in *The Saga of American Society*. Wayne Andrews includes an excellent discussion of the architectural standards of the period in *Architecture, Ambitions, and Americans*. Aline Saarinen writes about the businessmen's art collections in *The Proud Possessors*. One of the most interesting collectors comes to life in *Mrs. Jack: A Biography of Isabella Stewart Gardner* by Louise Hall Tharp. *John Sloan: A Painter's Life* by Van Wyck Brooks and *John Singer Sargent* by Charles Mount offer interesting contrasts.

John Higham describes the immigrants' reception in *Strangers in the Land*. The plight of the urban poor and efforts to help them are described in *From the Depths: The Discovery of Poverty in the United States* by Robert Bremner. For Jacob Riis's ties with the urban reformers, see his interesting autobiography, *The Making of an American*. For more information on labor disputes, see J. W. Coleman's *The Molly Maguire Riots* and Henry David's *The History of the Haymarket Affair*. Samuel Gompers's autobiography, *Seventy Years of Life and Labor*, is useful. Also see Bernard Mandel's *Samuel Gompers: A Biography*.

Students might want to read some of the novels and stories mentioned in the text — those by Rölvaag, Mark Twain, Harte, Garland, and Cather on the Middle and Far West; and those by Howells, Wharton, James, Alger, Crane, and O. Henry on life in the cities. In addition, Joseph Kirkland's *Zury* and E. W. Howe's *The Story of a Country Town* deal with problems of Midwesterners. Edna Ferber wrote about Oklahoma pioneers in *Cimarron*, while Owen Wister set his novel *The Virginian* in Wyoming cattle country. Wallace Stegner has written two fine books about the West — *Beyond the Hundredth Meridian* and *Wolf Willow*. Political corruption is dealt with in A. C. Train's *Tassels on Her Boots* and Winston Churchill's *Coniston*.

UNIT 7

Volume eight of *The Life History of the United States* covers much of the material included in this unit — *Reaching for Empire, 1890–1901*. So too does Harold U. Faulkner's *Politics, Reform and Expansion, 1890–1900*.

James Bryce's comments about the United States in the 1880's are interesting. His *American Commonwealth* is available in many editions. Biographical studies of the leading Republicans include A. Sievers's *Benjamin*

Harrison; W. A. Robinson's *Thomas B. Reed;* and D. S. Muzzey's *James G. Blaine.* Ida Tarbell described the struggles over tariff legislation in *The Tariff in Our Times.* Irving Wallace has written a biography of P. T. Barnum, *The Fabulous Showman,* and John Krout is the author of an entertaining book about sports, *The Annals of American Sport.*

Stanley L. Jones has written *The Presidential Election of 1896,* and D. L. McMurry has studied *Coxey's Army.* For biographies of the reform leaders, see *Tom Watson: Agrarian Rebel* by C. Vann Woodward; *Pitchfork Ben Tillman* by F. B. Simkins; *Ignatius Donnelly* by Martin Ridge; *James B. Weaver* by F. E. Haynes; and *Eagle Forgotten: The Life of John Peter Altgeld* by Harry Barnard.

On the background of the Spanish-American War, see W. D. Puleston's *Mahan;* Walter Millis's *The Martial Spirit;* and A. K. Weinberg's *Manifest Destiny. Admirals of American Empire* by R. S. West has interesting material on Dewey. For the annexation of Hawaii, see S. K. Stevens's *American Expansion in Hawaii, 1842–1898.* H. Wayne Morgan covers all these developments in *America's Road to Empire: The War with Spain and Overseas Expansion.*

UNIT 8

For treatment of material in this unit, see two volumes of *The Life History of The United States* — Volume 9, *The Progressive Era, 1901–1917,* and the first part of Volume 10, *War, Boom and Bust, 1917–1932.*

To get a better understanding of the Progressive Movement, sample the autobiographies of some of its leading figures. See the autobiographies of Robert M. La Follette and William Allen White; Gifford Pinchot's *Breaking New Ground;* Tom Johnson's *My Story;* and Brand Whitlock's *Forty Years of It.* An interesting study of the crusading journalists is C. C. Regier's *The Era of the Muckrakers.* Hermann Hagedorn's story of the Roosevelts is delightful — *The Roosevelt Family of Sagamore Hill.* The observations of the country's leading humorist during these years, Finley Peter Dunne, are presented in *Mr. Dooley on Ivrything and Ivrybody.*

H. C. F. Bell analyzes Wilson's appeal to the public in *Woodrow Wilson and the People.* Alpheus T. Mason has written a biography of Wilson's friend and adviser in *Brandeis.* For the role of political radicals before and during World War I, see Ray Ginger's biography of Debs, *The Bending Cross,* and *Wobbly* by

Ralph Chaplin. On race relations, see Ray Stannard Baker's *Following the Color Line,* the relevant chapters in John Hope Franklin's *From Slavery to Freedom,* and Rayford Logan's *The Betrayal of the Negro.*

Gerstle Mack writes about the Panama Canal in *The Land Divided,* and Roosevelt's Far Eastern policy is the subject of T. A. Bailey's *Theodore Roosevelt and the Japanese-American Crises.* Bernard Baruch describes the amazing economic mobilization of 1917–1918 in *American Industry in the War.* Just as valuable is Margaret Coit's biography, *Mr. Baruch.* The contributions of the army and navy are discussed in Laurence Stallings's *The Doughboys* and E. E. Morison's *Admiral Sims and the Modern American Navy.*

Novels by muckrakers and reformers include Upton Sinclair's *The Jungle;* Brand Whitlock's *The 13th District* and *The Turn of the Balance;* and Frank Norris's *The Pit.* Joseph Hergesheimer used the iron and steel industry as the background for *The Three Black Pennys.* Robert Cantwell writes about labor troubles in a western lumber mill in *The Land of Plenty,* while Ernest Poole chose New York longshoremen for his novel *The Harbor.* Farm families play the leading role in S. L. Winther's *Take All to Nebraska,* Willa Cather's *One of Ours,* and Russell Laman's *Manifest Destiny. Falcons of France* by C. B. Nordhoff and J. N. Hall concerns the pilots of World War I. French warfare is unforgettably described by E. M. Remarque in *All Quiet on the Western Front.* The opening month of the war is the setting for Barbara Tuchman's exciting *The Guns of August.* A popular play of the World War I period, later made into a movie, was *What Price Glory?* by M. Anderson and L. Stallings.

UNIT 9

Volume 10 of *The Life History of the United States* — *War, Boom, and Bust, 1917–1932* — is excellent.

For additional information on President Wilson's last years, see Herbert Hoover's *The Ordeal of Woodrow Wilson* and Gene Smith's *When the Cheering Stopped.* See Robert Murray's *Red Scare: A Study in National Hysteria* for that aspect of the years 1919–1921. S. H. Adams writes about the Harding scandals in *Incredible Era.* On the economic developments of the 1920's, consult George Soule's *Prosperity Decade,* and J. W. Prothro's *Dollar Decade. Ford: The Times, The Man, The Company* is an interesting biography by Allan

Nevins and F. E. Hill. Other biographical studies that give a feeling for the decade are William Manchester's *Disturber of the Peace: The Life of H. L. Mencken;* Donald Day's *Will Rogers: A Biography;* and Arthur Mizener's *The Far Side of Paradise: A Biography of F. Scott Fitzgerald.* On the 1928 presidential campaign, see Edmund A. Moore's *A Catholic Runs for President.* George Norris's autobiography, *Fighting Liberal,* is an interesting account of his lonely battle in the Senate.

For more information on the development of the airplane, see *The American Heritage History of Flight.* Marshall W. Stearns has written an interesting volume entitled *The Story of Jazz.* On the revolutionary changes in painting, see Milton W. Brown's *American Painting from the Armory Show to the Depression.* O'Neill and other dramatists are discussed by Lloyd Morris in *Curtain Time: The Story of the American Theater.* Reading any of the novels, poems, or plays mentioned in Chapter 31 would be rewarding.

UNIT 10

Volume 11 of *The Life History of the United States — New Deal and Global War, 1933–1945 —* is highly recommended.

Many of the leading figures in the 1930's have written about their experiences. David Lilienthal is the author of *TVA: Democracy on the March,* while Harold L. Ickes gives a lively account of the decade in *The Autobiography of a Curmudgeon.* Raymond Moley is critical of many New Deal policies in his book *After Seven Years.* Eleanor Roosevelt's volume, *This I Remember,* is interesting. On the President as viewed by his associates, see *Jim Farley's Story* and Frances Perkins's *The Roosevelt I Knew.* For the New Deal's social welfare policies, see Grace Abbott's *From Relief to Social Security.* Selig Perlman has written an informative book entitled *Labor in the New Deal Decade.* E. S. Corwin evaluates the Court controversy and its outcome in *Constitutional Revolution.* John Gunther's biography, *Roosevelt in Retrospect,* is good; and Eric F. Goldman's *Rendezvous with Destiny* is a lively account of the decade.

Charles A. Beard is critical of Roosevelt's conduct of foreign policy in *President Roosevelt and the Coming of the War.* Beard's charges are refuted by Basil Rauch in *Roosevelt: From Munich to Pearl Harbor.* *Life's Picture History of World War II* is good, and Winston Churchill's superb account of the war is available in a condensed one-volume edition.

Sumner Welles, who served in the State Department, has written *Seven Decisions That Shaped History.* Donald M. Nelson describes his wartime experiences in *Arsenal of Democracy,* the story of America's war production. E. R. Stettinius has written *Lend-Lease* and discusses the Yalta Conference in *Roosevelt and the Russians.* The co-ordination of scientific research during the war is the subject of J. P. Baxter's *Scientists Against Time.*

American life in the depression decade is portrayed in an anthology edited by Louis Filler, *The Anxious Years: America in the Nineteen Thirties.* The struggles of New York Jews during the 1930's is dealt with in Michael Gold's *Jews Without Money* and Clifford Odets's play *Awake and Sing.* Another novel with a depression background is Nathaniel West's *Miss Lonelyhearts.*

Ernest Hemingway's *For Whom the Bell Tolls* describes the role of an American volunteer in the Spanish Civil War. John Hersey's *A Bell for Adano* is set in wartime Italy. William L. White writes about the war in the Philippines in *They Were Expendable.* The impact of the war on American families is the subject of MacKinlay Kantor's *Happy Land.* Marion Hargrove tells of a soldier's experiences in his amusing *See Here, Private Hargrove.* Pearl Buck explores the moral implications of the use of the atomic bomb in *Command the Morning.*

UNIT 11

The last volume in *The Life History of the United States — The Great Age of Change, From 1945 —* is useful. Many of the leading figures of the last twenty years have written of their experiences. Harry Truman's *Memoirs* should be compared with James F. Byrnes's *Speaking Frankly* and Robert A. Taft's *A Foreign Policy for Americans.* Dwight Eisenhower is the author of two books about his administration, *Mandate for Change* and *Waging Peace,* under the series title *The White House Years.* Other accounts of the Eisenhower period are Richard M. Nixon's *Six Crises;* Sherman Adams's *First-hand Report;* Ezra Taft Benson's *Cross Fire: The Eight Years with Eisenhower;* and Emmet John Hughes's *The Ordeal of Power.* President Kennedy's speeches have been published under the title *The Burden and the Glory.* Adlai E. Stevenson wrote about his UN experiences in *Looking Outward: Years of Crisis at the United Nations.* For Barry Goldwater's views, see *Conscience of a Conservative.*

For the contrast between American life in the early twentieth century and in the postwar years, see Frederick Lewis Allen's *The Big Change*. *The Taft Story* is a biography of the Ohio senator by William S. White. Studies of American society in the postwar years include William H. Whyte's *The Organization Man;* C. W. Mills's *White Collar* and *The Power Elite;* David Riesman's *The Lonely Crowd;* and Daniel Boorstin's *The Image: Or What Happened to the American Dream*. For more information on the importance of urban problems, see *The Exploding Metropolis* by the editors of *Fortune* and *The Squeeze: Cities Without Space* by Edward Higbee. Bernard Rosenberg and D. M. White take a dim view of cultural standards in *Mass Culture*. Alvin Toffler sharply disagrees with them in *The Culture Consumers: A Study of Art and Affluence in America*.

James MacGregor Burns has written *The Deadlock of Democracy: Four-Party Politics in America*, a study of the divisions within each party. It is interesting to compare this book with Richard E. Neustadt's *Presidential Power*. Oscar Handlin explores the forms of discrimination, both northern and southern, in *Fire-Bell in the Night*. *Dark Ghetto* by Kenneth Clark is a penetrating analysis of the problems of urban Negroes. Also see Martin Luther King's *Why We Can't Wait*. George Sullivan tells *The Story of the Peace Corps* through 1964. On Kennedy's assassination, see *Four Days* by the editors of *American Heritage* and the authoritative *Warren Report*.

W. W. Rostow's *The United States in the World Arena* is a stimulating essay on foreign policies. For evaluations of Secretary of State Dulles, see *Duel at the Brink* by Roscoe Drummond and Gaston Coblentz, and Richard Goold-Adams's *John Foster Dulles: A Reappraisal*. Two useful studies of our relations with Europe are *Alliance Born of Danger* by Charles Cerami and *The End of Alliance: America and the Future of Europe* by Ronald Steele. C. L. Sulzberger analyzes our relations with the uncommitted nations in *Unfinished Revolution: America and the Third World*.

Important Dates

c. 1000 Leif Ericson reaches North America.
1487 Dias reaches Cape of Good Hope.
1492 Columbus lands at San Salvador.
1493 Pope draws first Line of Demarcation.
1497 Cabot explores North American coast.
1498 Da Gama reaches India.
1513 Balboa discovers Pacific. De Leon discovers Florida.
1519 Magellan begins voyage around world.
Cortés starts conquest of Mexico.
1532 Pizarro begins conquest of Peru.
1534 Cartier explores St. Lawrence River.
1541 De Soto discovers Mississippi River.
1565 St. Augustine, Florida, founded.
1588 Spanish Armada defeated.
1603 Champlain begins explorations of St. Lawrence River.
1607 Jamestown founded.
1609 Henry Hudson explores Hudson River.
1619 Virginia House of Burgesses first meets.
First Negroes brought to Virginia as bound servants.
1620 Mayflower Compact. Pilgrims land at Plymouth.
1624 James I makes Virginia a royal colony.
1630 Puritans establish Massachusetts Bay Colony.
1634 Maryland founded.
1636 Roger Williams founds Providence, R.I.
Connecticut founded.
Harvard College founded.
1643 New England Confederation formed.
1647 School Law adopted by Massachusetts.
1649 Toleration Act passed in Maryland.
1660 Navigation Act passed by Parliament.
1661 Slavery legalized in Virginia.
1664 English take New Netherland.

1673 Charles Town (Charleston), S.C., founded.
Marquette and Joliet explore Mississippi River.
1680 New Hampshire separated from Massachusetts.
1682 Philadelphia is founded.
La Salle reaches mouth of Mississippi River.
1686 Dominion of New England formed.
1688 "Glorious Revolution" in England.
1689 War begins between England and France.
1691 Massachusetts Bay and Plymouth colonies are merged.
1693 College of William and Mary founded.
1699 Woolens Act restricts colonial industry.
1704 Delaware founded.
1733 Georgia founded.
Molasses Act.
1738 New Jersey becomes separate royal colony.
1750 Iron Act.
1754 Albany Congress meets.
French and Indian War begins.
1759 English capture Quebec.
1760 George III becomes king.
1763 Treaty of Paris signed.
Proclamation line bars colonists from Indian territory.
1764 Sugar and Currency Acts.
1765 Stamp Act.
1766 Stamp Act repealed.
1767 Townshend Acts.
1770 Boston Massacre.
1772 Committees of Correspondence formed.
1773 Boston Tea Party.
1774 Coercive ("Intolerable") Acts.
Quebec Act.
First Continental Congress meets.
1775 Battles of Concord and Lexington.
Second Continental Congress assembles.
Battle of Bunker Hill.
1776 Paine's *Common Sense* published.
Declaration of Independence.
Washington takes Trenton.
1777 Burgoyne surrenders at Saratoga.

1779 George Rogers Clark wins Northwest.
1781 Articles of Confederation go into effect.
Cornwallis surrenders at Yorktown.
1783 Treaty of Paris signed.
1785 Land Ordinance of 1785.
1787 Northwest Ordinance.
Constitution drafted.
1789 **Washington becomes President.**
First Congress under the Constitution meets.
French Revolution begins.
1791 Bill of Rights ratified.
First Bank of the United States chartered.
Hamilton issues *Report on Manufactures.*
1793 Cotton gin invented.
Washington issues Proclamation of Neutrality.
1794 Whiskey Rebellion.
Battle of Fallen Timbers.
1795 Jay and Pinckney Treaties ratified.
1797 **John Adams becomes President.**
1798 Alien and Sedition Acts.
Kentucky and Virginia Resolutions.
1800 Washington, D.C., becomes capital.
1801 **Thomas Jefferson becomes President.**
Naval expedition against Barbary pirates.
1803 *Marbury v. Madison.*
Louisiana is purchased.
1804 Lewis and Clark embark on expedition.
1807 Embargo Act.
Fulton's steamboat is successful.
1809 **James Madison becomes President.**
Non-Intercourse Act replaces Embargo Act.
1811 National Road started.
Indians defeated at Tippecanoe.
1812 War declared against Great Britain.
Detroit falls to British.
1814 Hartford Convention.
Treaty of Ghent.
1815 Battle of New Orleans.
1816 Protective tariff adopted.
Second Bank of the United States chartered.
1817 **James Monroe becomes President.**

Era of Good Feelings begins.

Rush-Bagot Agreement signed.

1819 Panic of 1819.

Spain cedes Florida.

McCulloch v. Madison.

1820 Missouri Compromise.

1821 First public high school.

1822 U.S. recognizes independence of Latin American states.

1823 Monroe Doctrine.

1825 **John Quincy Adams becomes President.**

Erie Canal completed.

1828 Tariff of Abominations passed.

South Carolina *Exposition and Protest.*

1829 **Andrew Jackson becomes President.**

1830 Webster-Hayne debate.

First successful run of a steam locomotive on Baltimore and Ohio Railroad.

1831 First nominating convention held.

The Liberator appears.

McCormick invents reaper.

Nat Turner leads slave revolt in Virginia.

1832 Jackson vetoes Bank Bill.

South Carolina nullifies tariffs.

1833 Congress adopts Compromise Tariff.

New York *Sun* brings out penny daily.

American Antislavery Society formed.

1836 Texas declares independence from Mexico.

House adopts Gag Rule.

Specie Circular issued.

1837 **Martin Van Buren becomes President.**

Panic of 1837.

Horace Mann begins educational reforms.

1840 Independent Treasury system established.

Whig victory ends Jacksonian Era.

1841 **William Henry Harrison becomes President; succeeded by John Tyler.**

1842 Webster-Ashburton Treaty.

Ether first used in surgery.

1844 Telegraph put into use.

1845 Texas annexed.

James K. Polk becomes President.

Famine drives Irish to America.

1846 Mexican War begins.

Oregon boundary fixed.

1847 Wilmot Proviso defeated.

1848 Mexican Cession.

Women's Rights Convention at Seneca Falls, N.Y.

Free Soil Party organized.

1849 **Zachary Taylor becomes President.**

California gold rush.

Know-Nothing Party formed.

1850 **Millard Fillmore succeeds to presidency.**

Compromise of 1850 adopted.

1852 *Uncle Tom's Cabin* appears.

1853 **Franklin Pierce becomes President.**

Gadsden Purchase.

1854 Perry opens Japan to American commerce.

Republican Party formed.

Kansas-Nebraska Act.

1856 Violence erupts in "Bleeding Kansas."

1857 **James Buchanan becomes President.**

Dred Scott decision.

Panic of 1857.

1858 Lincoln-Douglas debates.

1859 John Brown raids Harpers Ferry.

First oil well drilled.

1860 **Lincoln elected President.**

South Carolina secedes.

Pony Express established.

1861 Confederacy formed.

Morrill Tariff adopted.

Abraham Lincoln becomes President.

Firing on Fort Sumter begins Civil War.

1862 *Monitor* and *Merrimac* clash.

Homestead Act.

"Greenbacks" issued.

Morrill Act sets up land-grant colleges.

Mississippi River opened to Vicksburg.

1863 Emancipation Proclamation becomes effective.

National Banking System adopted.

Battle of Gettysburg.

Surrender of Vicksburg.

1864 Grant opens drive to Richmond.

Sherman takes Atlanta and Savannah.

1865 Lee surrenders at Appomattox.

Lincoln assassinated; **Andrew Johnson succeeds to presidency.**

Thirteenth Amendment ratified.

1866 Atlantic cable successful.

National Labor Union organized.

Texas ranchers organize first "long drive."

1867 Reconstruction Act.

Beginning of Granger movement.

Alaska purchased.

1868 Andrew Johnson impeached.

Fourteenth Amendment adopted.

1869 **Ulysses S. Grant becomes President.**

First transcontinental railroad completed.

Knights of Labor founded.

1870 Fifteenth Amendment ratified.

National Woman Suffrage Association formed.

1871 Ku Klux Act.

Treaty of Washington settles *Alabama* claims.

Tweed Ring exposed.

1872 Amnesty Act.

Credit Mobilier scandal.

1873 Panic of 1873.

1874 Chautauqua movement started.

Women's Christian Temperance Union formed.

1875 Civil Rights Act passed.

1876 Sioux uprising wipes out Custer's force.

Bell invents telephone.

Election returns disputed.

1877 **Rutherford B. Hayes becomes President.**

Last federal troops removed from South.

Railroad strike.

1878 Greenback Party organized.

Bland-Allison Act.

Edison invents phonograph.

1879 Edison invents incandescent light bulb.

1881 **James A. Garfield becomes President.**

Booker T. Washington founds Tuskegee Institute.

Garfield assassinated; **Chester Arthur succeeds to presidency.**

1882 Standard Oil trust organized.

Chinese immigration restricted.

1883 Pendleton Act sets up Civil Service Commission.

1885 Importation of contract labor barred.

Grover Cleveland becomes President.

1886 Presidential Succession Act.

Haymarket Riot.

Granger laws ruled unconstitutional.

End of organized Indian resistance.

American Federation of Labor formed.

1887 Dawes Act assigns land to Indians.

Interstate Commerce Act.

Hatch Act promotes agricultural research.

1889 **Benjamin Harrison becomes President.**

First Pan-American Conference.

Hull House founded by Jane Addams.

1890 Sherman Antitrust Act.

Sherman Silver Purchase Act passed.

McKinley Tariff adopted.

End of frontier line announced.

1892 Populist Party organized.

Homestead Strike.

1893 **Grover Cleveland becomes President.**

Panic of 1893.

Sherman Silver Act repealed.

Columbian Exposition at Chicago.

1894 Pullman Strike.

Wilson-Gorman Tariff.

1895 Insurrection in Cuba against Spanish rule.

Venezuelan boundary dispute.

Plessy v. Ferguson upholds "separate-but-equal" education.

1896 Bryan defeated in free-silver campaign.

1897 **William McKinley becomes President.**

Dingley Tariff raises rates to new high.

Klondike gold rush.

1898 War declared against Spain.

Hawaii annexed.

Puerto Rico, Guam, and Philippines acquired.

1899 Peace of Paris ratified.

First Hague Peace Conference.

1900 Gold Standard Act.

Open Door Policy for China proclaimed.

Boxer Rebellion in China.

1901 Platt Amendment authorizes intervention in Cuba.

U.S. Steel Corporation organized by J. P. Morgan.

McKinley assassinated; **Theodore Roosevelt succeeds to presidency.**

Hay-Pauncefote Treaty.

1902 Federal suit against Northern Securities Company opened.

Newlands Reclamation Act.

1903 Elkins Act strengthens ICC.

Direct primary adopted in Wisconsin.

Alaska boundary settled.

1904 Roosevelt Corollary.

1905 IWW founded.

Treaty of Portsmouth ends Russo-Japanese War.

1906 Hepburn Act regulates railroad rates.

Pure Food and Drugs Act.

Meat Inspection Act.

1907 Panic of 1907.

"Gentlemen's Agreement" reached with Japan.

Second Hague Peace Conference adopts Drago Doctrine.

1908 National Conservation Commission established.

U.S. fleet circles globe.

Root-Takahira Agreement.

1909 **William H. Taft becomes President.**

"Dollar diplomacy" espoused.

Payne-Aldrich Tariff.

NAACP founded.

1911 National Urban League founded.

1912 Marines land in Nicaragua.

Progressive Party nominates Theodore Roosevelt.

1913 Sixteenth Amendment authorizes income tax.

Woodrow Wilson becomes President.

Seventeenth Amendment provides for popular election of senators.

Underwood Tariff lowers rates.

Federal Reserve Act.

1914 Smith-Lever Act.

World War I begins in Europe; U.S. neutrality proclaimed.

Panama Canal opened.

Federal Trade Commission and Clayton Antitrust Acts.

1915 *Lusitania* sunk by German submarine.

Marines land in Haiti.

U.S. intervenes in Dominican Republic.

1916 Border campaign against Villa.

Germany makes *Sussex* pledge.

National Defense Act expands regular army.

1917 Virgin Islands purchased.

Germany resumes unrestricted submarine warfare.

Smith-Hughes Act provides federal aid to education in agriculture and trades.

U.S. declares war on Germany.

Selective Service Act.

American Expeditionary Force lands in France.

Revolution in Russia.

1918 Wilson states Fourteen Points.

Bolsheviks negotiate separate peace with Germany.

Battles of Château-Thierry and Belleau Wood.

St. Mihiel and Argonne offensives.

Armistice ends war.

1919 Prohibition Amendment adopted.

Strike wave.

"Red Scare" begins.

Treaty of Versailles.

1920 League of Nations repudiated by Senate.

Woman suffrage Amendment adopted.

Radio station KDKA begins broadcasting.

1921 **Warren Harding becomes President.**

Washington Naval Disarmament Conference.

1922 Fordney-McCumber Act.

Mussolini comes to power in Italy.

1923 **Calvin Coolidge succeeds to presidency.**

Dawes Plan for Germany adopted.

1924 Teapot Dome scandal.
Immigration drastically curtailed.
1927 McNary-Haugen Bill vetoed.
Lindbergh flies to Paris.
1928 Kellogg-Briand Pact.
1929 **Herbert Hoover becomes President.**
Stock market crash; Great Depression begins.
1930 Hawley-Smoot Tariff.
1931 Japan invades Manchuria.
1932 RFC established.
Stimson Doctrine announced.
1933 **Franklin D. Roosevelt becomes President.**
Prohibition repealed.
Hitler becomes German chancellor.
Good Neighbor Policy declared.
Bank holiday.
Emergency Banking Act.
CCC, AAA, and NRA established.
Federal Securities Act.
Federal Emergency Relief Act.
TVA created.
Soviet Union recognized.
1934 Gold Reserve Act.
Securities and Exchange Commission established.
Trade Agreements Act.
1935 WPA established.
Wagner Act.
Social Security Act.
First Neutrality Act.
1937 Second Neutrality Act.
President's "court-packing" plan rebuffed.
Japan invades China.
1938 Second AAA passed.
CIO organized.
Wages and Hours Law.
Munich Conference.
Declaration of Lima.
1939 Hatch Act.
Germany invades Poland; World War II begins in Europe.
Declaration of Panama.
Neutrality policy modified.
1940 Nazi blitzkrieg begins.
Havana Conference.
Selective Service Act.
1941 Lend-Lease approved.
Atlantic Charter issued.
Pearl Harbor attacked; U.S. enters Second World War.

1942 Rio Conference.
Bataan and Corregidor surrender.
Battle of the Coral Sea; Guadalcanal offensive launched.
Allies land in North Africa.
1943 Sicily invaded.
Moscow, Cairo, and Teheran Conferences.
1944 Anzio beachhead established.
Rome liberated.
D-Day; Allies land in France.
Paris liberated.
Battle of the Bulge.
1945 Yalta Conference.
Roosevelt dies; **Harry Truman succeeds to presidency.**
United Nations Charter approved.
Germany surrenders (V-E Day).
Potsdam Conference.
Atomic bombs dropped on Japan.
Japan surrenders (V-J Day).
1946 Price controls lifted.
Philippines become independent.
1947 Truman Doctrine.
Marshall Plan adopted.
Taft-Hartley Act.
National Security Act.
1948 Organization of American States (OAS) established.
Berlin airlift.
1949 Point Four Program announced.
North Atlantic Treaty signed (NATO).
Russia explodes atomic bomb.
Mainland China controlled by Communists.
1950 UN intervention in Korea.
1951 Twenty-Second Amendment limits presidency to two terms.
1953 **Dwight Eisenhower becomes President.**
Department of Health, Education, and Welfare created.
Korean truce signed.
1954 Supreme Court rules against public school segregation.
SEATO formed.

1955 Geneva summit conference.
AFL and CIO merger.
Montgomery bus boycott.
1956 Suez Canal crisis.
Hungarian uprising.
1957 Soviet Sputniks launched.
Eisenhower Doctrine.
Civil Rights Act.
1958 First American satellite launched.
1959 Landrum-Griffin Act.
Castro comes to power in Cuba.
Alaska and Hawaii become states.
1960 U-2 incident upsets Paris summit meeting.
Civil Rights Act.
Congo crisis develops.
1961 **John F. Kennedy becomes President.**
Kennedy-Khrushchev talks in Vienna.
Berlin wall erected.
Alliance for Progress started.
Peace Corps established.
1962 First U.S. Astronaut orbits earth.
Trade Expansion Act.
Poll tax Amendment adopted.
Cuban missile crisis.
1963 Nuclear test-ban treaty.
Civil rights "March on Washington."
Kennedy assassinated; **Lyndon Johnson succeeds to presidency.**
1964 Federal tax cuts.
Civil Rights Act.
"War on Poverty" program outlined.
Communist China explodes atomic bomb.
1965 Anti-poverty legislation enacted.
Voting Rights Act.
U.S. commitment to South Vietnam increased.
U.S. troops intervene in Dominican Republic.
Immigration policy liberalized.
Department of Housing and Urban Development created.
1966 Senate holds hearings on Vietnam conflict.
New GI Bill of Rights adopted.

THE STATES OF THE UNITED STATES OF AMERICA

NO.	STATE NAME	DATE OF ADMISSION	POPULATION (1960 CENSUS)	NUMBER OF REPRESENTATIVES (1960 APPORTIONMENT)	AREA IN SQUARE MILES	CAPITAL
1	Delaware	1787	446,292	1	2,057	Dover
2	Pennsylvania	1787	11,319,366	27	45,333	Harrisburg
3	New Jersey	1787	6,066,782	15	7,836	Trenton
4	Georgia	1788	3,943,116	10	58,876	Atlanta
5	Connecticut	1788	2,535,234	6	5,009	Hartford
6	Massachusetts	1788	5,148,578	12	8,257	Boston
7	Maryland	1788	3,100,689	8	10,577	Annapolis
8	South Carolina	1788	2,382,594	6	31,055	Columbia
9	New Hampshire	1788	606,921	2	9,304	Concord
10	Virginia	1788	3,966,949	10	40,815	Richmond
11	New York	1788	16,782,304	41	49,576	Albany
12	North Carolina	1789	4,556,155	11	52,712	Raleigh
13	Rhode Island	1790	859,488	2	1,214	Providence
14	Vermont	1791	389,881	1	9,609	Montpelier
15	Kentucky	1792	3,038,156	7	40,395	Frankfort
16	Tennessee	1796	3,567,089	9	42,244	Nashville
17	Ohio	1803	9,706,397	24	41,222	Columbus
18	Louisiana	1812	3,257,022	8	48,523	Baton Rouge
19	Indiana	1816	4,662,498	11	36,291	Indianapolis
20	Mississippi	1817	2,178,141	5	47,716	Jackson
21	Illinois	1818	10,081,158	24	56,400	Springfield
22	Alabama	1819	3,266,740	8	51,609	Montgomery
23	Maine	1820	969,265	2	33,215	Augusta
24	Missouri	1821	4,319,813	10	69,686	Jefferson City
25	Arkansas	1836	1,786,272	4	53,104	Little Rock
26	Michigan	1837	7,823,194	19	58,216	Lansing
27	Florida	1845	4,951,560	12	58,560	Tallahassee
28	Texas	1845	9,579,677	23	267,339	Austin
29	Iowa	1846	2,757,537	7	56,290	Des Moines
30	Wisconsin	1848	3,951,777	10	56,154	Madison
31	California	1850	15,717,204	38	158,693	Sacramento
32	Minnesota	1858	3,413,864	8	84,068	St. Paul
33	Oregon	1859	1,786,687	4	96,981	Salem
34	Kansas	1861	2,178,611	5	82,264	Topeka
35	West Virginia	1863	1,860,421	5	24,181	Charleston
36	Nevada	1864	285,278	1	110,540	Carson City
37	Nebraska	1867	1,411,330	3	77,227	Lincoln
38	Colorado	1876	1,753,947	4	104,247	Denver
39	North Dakota	1889	632,446	2	70,665	Bismarck
40	South Dakota	1889	680,514	2	77,047	Pierre
41	Montana	1889	674,767	2	147,138	Helena
42	Washington	1889	2,853,214	7	68,192	Olympia
43	Idaho	1890	667,191	2	83,557	Boise
44	Wyoming	1890	330,066	1	97,914	Cheyenne
45	Utah	1896	890,627	2	84,916	Salt Lake City
46	Oklahoma	1907	2,328,284	6	69,919	Oklahoma City
47	New Mexico	1912	951,023	2	121,666	Santa Fe
48	Arizona	1912	1,302,161	3	113,909	Phoenix
49	Alaska	1959	226,167	1	586,400	Juneau
50	Hawaii	1959	632,772	2	6,424	Honolulu
	District of Columbia		763,956		69	
			179,323,175	435	3,615,211	

PRINCIPAL DEPENDENCIES OF THE UNITED STATES

DEPENDENCY	DATE OF ACQUISITION	POPULATION (1960 CENSUS)	AREA IN SQUARE MILES	CAPITAL, OR PRINCIPAL CITY
Puerto Rico	1899	2,349,544	3,435	San Juan
Guam	1899	67,044	212	Agana
American Samoa	1900	20,051	76	Pago Pago
Panama Canal Zone	1904	42,122	553	Balboa
Virgin Islands	1917	32,099	133	Charlotte Amalie
Total		2,510,860	4,409	

PRESIDENTS AND VICE-PRESIDENTS OF THE UNITED STATES

PRESIDENT	BORN	DIED	DATE OF INAUGURATION	PARTY ELECTING PRESIDENT	STATE*	VICE-PRESIDENT	STATE*
George Washington	1732	1799	1789	None	Virginia	John Adams	Massachusetts
George Washington	1732	1799	1793	None	Virginia	John Adams	Massachusetts
John Adams	1735	1826	1797	Federalist	Massachusetts	Thomas Jefferson	Virginia
Thomas Jefferson	1743	1826	1801	Dem.–Republican	Virginia	Aaron Burr	New York
Thomas Jefferson	1743	1826	1805	Dem.–Republican	Virginia	George Clinton	New York
James Madison	1751	1836	1809	Dem.–Republican	Virginia	George Clinton	New York
James Madison	1751	1836	1813	Dem.–Republican	Virginia	Elbridge Gerry	Massachusetts
James Monroe	1758	1831	1817	Dem.–Republican	Virginia	Daniel D. Tompkins	New York
James Monroe	1758	1831	1821	Dem.–Republican	Virginia	Daniel D. Tompkins	New York
John Quincy Adams	1767	1848	1825	Nat.–Republican	Massachusetts	John C. Calhoun	South Carolina
Andrew Jackson	1767	1845	1829	Democratic	Tennessee	John C. Calhoun	South Carolina
Andrew Jackson	1767	1845	1833	Democratic	Tennessee	Martin Van Buren	New York
Martin Van Buren	1782	1862	1837	Democratic	New York	Richard M. Johnson	Kentucky
William H. Harrison	1773	1841	1841	Whig	Ohio	John Tyler	Virginia
John Tyler	1790	1862	(1841, April)	Whig	Virginia		
James K. Polk	1795	1849	1845	Democratic	Tennessee	George M. Dallas	Pennsylvania
Zachary Taylor	1784	1850	1849	Whig	Louisiana	Millard Fillmore	New York
Millard Fillmore	1800	1874	(1850, July)	Whig	New York		
Franklin Pierce	1804	1869	1853	Democratic	New Hampshire	William R. King	Alabama
James Buchanan	1791	1868	1857	Democratic	Pennsylvania	John C. Breckinridge	Kentucky
Abraham Lincoln	1809	1865	1861	Republican	Illinois	Hannibal Hamlin	Maine
Abraham Lincoln	1809	1865	1865	Republican	Illinois	Andrew Johnson	Tennessee
Andrew Johnson	1808	1875	(1865, April)	Republican	Tennessee		
Ulysses S. Grant	1822	1885	1869	Republican	Illinois	Schuyler Colfax	Indiana
Ulysses S. Grant	1822	1885	1873	Republican	Illinois	Henry Wilson	Massachusetts
Rutherford B. Hayes	1822	1893	1877	Republican	Ohio	William A. Wheeler	New York
James A. Garfield	1831	1881	1881	Republican	Ohio	Chester A. Arthur	New York

President	Born	Died	Term	Party	Residence*	Vice President	Residence*
Chester A. Arthur	1830	1886	(1881, Sept.)	Republican	New York		
Grover Cleveland	1837	1908	1885	Democratic	New York	Thomas A. Hendricks	Indiana
Benjamin Harrison	1833	1901	1889	Republican	Indiana	Levi P. Morton	New York
Grover Cleveland	1837	1908	1893	Democratic	New York	Adlai E. Stevenson	Illinois
William McKinley	1843	1901	1897	Republican	Ohio	Garret A. Hobart	New Jersey
William McKinley	1843	1901	1901	Republican	Ohio	Theodore Roosevelt	New York
Theodore Roosevelt	1858	1919	(1901, Sept.)	Republican	New York		
Theodore Roosevelt	1858	1919	1905	Republican	New York	Charles W. Fairbanks	Indiana
William H. Taft	1857	1930	1909	Republican	Ohio	James S. Sherman	New York
Woodrow Wilson	1856	1924	1913	Democratic	New Jersey	Thomas R. Marshall	Indiana
Woodrow Wilson	1856	1924	1917	Democratic	New Jersey	Thomas R. Marshall	Indiana
Warren G. Harding	1865	1923	1921	Republican	Ohio	Calvin Coolidge	Massachusetts
Calvin Coolidge	1872	1933	(1923, August)	Republican	Massachusetts		
Calvin Coolidge	1872	1933	1925	Republican	Massachusetts	Charles G. Dawes	Illinois
Herbert Hoover	1874	1964	1929	Republican	California	Charles Curtis	Kansas
Franklin D. Roosevelt	1882	1945	1933	Democratic	New York	John N. Garner	Texas
Franklin D. Roosevelt	1882	1945	1937	Democratic	New York	John N. Garner	Texas
Franklin D. Roosevelt	1882	1945	1941	Democratic	New York	Henry A. Wallace	Iowa
Franklin D. Roosevelt	1882	1945	1945	Democratic	New York	Harry S. Truman	Missouri
Harry S. Truman	1884		(1945, April)	Democratic	Missouri		
Harry S. Truman,	1884		1949	Democratic	Missouri	Alben W. Barkley	Kentucky
Dwight D. Eisenhower	1890		1953	Republican	New York	Richard M. Nixon	California
Dwight D. Eisenhower	1890		1957	Republican	Pennsylvania	Richard M. Nixon	California
John F. Kennedy	1917	1963	1961	Democratic	Massachusetts	Lyndon B. Johnson	Texas
Lyndon B. Johnson	1908		(1963, Nov.)	Democratic	Texas		
Lyndon B. Johnson	1908		1965	Democratic	Texas	Hubert H. Humphrey	Minnesota

* Residence at time of election.

Acknowledgments and Credits

The authors and publisher wish to express their appreciation to the following individuals and organizations who gave permission to quote copyright material: Brandt & Brandt, for permission to quote from *A Book of Americans* by Rosemary and Stephen Vincent Benét, published by Holt, Rinehart and Winston, Inc. Copyright, 1933 by Rosemary and Stephen Vincent Benét. Copyright renewed, 1961, by Rosemary Carr Benét. Hastings House, Publishers, Inc., for permission to quote from *Old Jules*, copyright 1935 by Mari Sandoz, reproduced by permission of Hastings House, Publishers, Inc. The Macmillan Company, for permission to quote from *A Son of the Middle Border* by Hamlin Garland, copyright 1917, and from *The Autobiography of William Allen White* by William Allen White, copyright 1946. The University of Wisconsin Press, for permission to quote from *Theodore Roosevelt and the Progressive Movement* by George E. Mowry, copyright 1946 by the Regents of the University of Wisconsin. William L. White, for permission to quote from *Masks in a Pageant* by William Allen White, copyright 1928.

Statistical sources for most of the charts in this book were *Historical Statistics of the United States, Statistical Abstract of the United States*, and other publications of the United States government. Exceptions were as follows: page 197, National Industrial Conference Board; page 237, Porter, *History of Suffrage in the United States;* pages 250, 521, and 675, Cleveland Trust Company, Cleveland, Ohio; page 300, Whelpton, "Occupational Groups in the United States, 1820–1920," *Journal of the American Statistical Association*, September, 1926; page 575, Board of Governors of the Federal Reserve System; page 606, *Statesman's Yearbook;* page 762, United Nations Organization.

Thanks are also extended to the persons and organizations listed below for their courtesy in making pictures available for reproduction. The following abbreviations have been used for a few sources from which many illustrations have been obtained: Bettmann — The Bettmann Archive; Brown — Brown Brothers; Culver — Culver Pictures, Inc.; LC — Library of Congress; NYHS — Courtesy of the New-York Historical Society, New York City; NYPL — New York Public Library; UPI — United Press International; WW — Wide World Photos, Inc.

xvi Painting by Johannes Oertel, NYHS.
2 Courtesy of the American Museum of Natural History.
5 Historical Pictures Service.
6 Helge Ingstad.
14 (top left) Western Ways; (top right) Courtesy of Museum of the American Indian, Heye Foundation; (bottom left) Thomas Gilcrease Institute, Tulsa, Okla.; (bottom right) Courtesy History Division, Los Angeles County Museum.
27 Trustees of the British Museum.
36 (top left) Detail from engraving by William Burgis; NYHS; (middle left) National Gallery of Art, Index of American Design; (bottom left) Bureau of New Orleans News; (right) Department of Conservation and Development, Raleigh, North Carolina.
49 (top left) A. Devaney; (right) David Lawlor.
50 (top right) Courtesy of the Abby Aldrich Rockefeller Folk Art Collection, Williamsburg, Virginia; (middle left) David Lawlor; (bottom right) Colonial Williamsburg, Williamsburg, Virginia.
51 (top left) A. Devaney; (center) Richard Merrill Photo; (middle right) Thomas L. Williams; (bottom left) Old Sturbridge Village Photo.
52 (top left) Painting by John Wollaston, National Portrait Gallery, London; (top right) H. Armstrong Roberts.
60 Chase Manhattan Bank, Money Museum.
61 Brown.
63 (top left) Historical Society of Pennsylvania; (top right and center) The Franklin Institute Science Museum; (bottom right) University of Pennsylvania.
70 Historical Pictures Service.
80 (top left) Emmett Collection, NYPL; (top center) LC; (top right) Bettmann; (bottom) Stokes Collection, NYPL.
81 (top left) Culver; (top right) The Metropolitan Museum of Art, Gift of Mrs. Russell Sage, 1910; (middle right) The Metropolitan Museum of Art, Arthur H. Hearn Fund, 1950, Copyright Associated American Artists, New York; (bottom) Bancroft Collection, NYPL.
85 (top left and right) Fort Ticonderoga; (bottom) From the collections of the Historical Society of Pennsylvania.
88 (top) The Metropolitan Museum of Art, Bequest of William Nelson, 1905; (middle) Thomas Jefferson Memorial Foundation; (bottom) University of Virginia.
93 Detail from mural in Virginia State Capitol, Dementi Studio.
95 LC.
111 (left) Seidman; (right) General Dynamics.
113 (left) Shelburne Museum, Inc.; (center) Historical Pictures Service; (right) Trustees of the British Museum.
116 National Gallery of Art, Garbisch Collection.
118 Detail of mural by Albert Herter, State Historical Society of Wisconsin.
123 Ewing Galloway.
125 Historical Society of Pennsylvania.
127 (left) Culver; (right) National Park Service.
161 Detail from engraving by Amos Doolittle, Stokes Collection, NYPL.
167 Portrait by John Trumbull, National Archives.
173 Burton Historical Collection of the Detroit Public Library.
177 (left and right) Massachusetts Historical Society; (center) The Metropolitan Museum of Art, Gift of I. N. Phelps Stokes, Edward S. Hawes, Alice Mary Hawes, Marion Augusta Hawes, 1937.
180 LC.
181 Harvard College Library.
183 Portrait by Rembrandt Peale, Culver.
192 Historical Society of Pennsylvania.
195 Detail of wash drawing by Thomas Birch, NYHS.
200 Smithsonian Institution, Bureau of American Ethnology.
205 (top and bottom left) Smithsonian Institution.
208 (top) Smithsonian Institution.
212 Josiah Gregg, *Commerce of the Prairies*, 1850.
214 Detail of engraving by Krimmel, National Park Service.
217 Portrait by Chester Harding.
222 Bettmann.
225 (left) Stokes Collection, NYPL; (top right) Maryland Historical Society; (bottom right) William Clements Library.

226 National Audubon Society.

235 Print by Robert Cruickshank, White House Collection.

239 Portrait by Asher B. Durand, NYHS.

242 (top left) Bettmann; (top right) Brown; (bottom) Painting by George Peter Alexander in Faneuil Hall, Boston.

245 American Antiquarian Society.

251 NYHS.

252 Indiana Historical Society Library.

255 Detail of "The Country Election," 1851–1852, by George Caleb Bingham, 1811–1879, The City Art Museum of St. Louis.

257 Association of American Railroads.

262 (top left) Collection of Edward W. C. Arnold, Museum of the City of New York; (top right) Bettmann; (center) Culver.

266 (right) Through the courtesy of Boatmen's National Bank, St. Louis.

267 (top left) LC; (top right) National Park Service; (bottom right) Sleepy Hollow Restorations.

269 (left) Utah State Historical Society; (right) Salt Lake City Chamber of Commerce.

274 Josiah Gregg, *Commerce of the Prairies*, 1850.

276 Culver.

281 (top and bottom left) Paintings by George A. Catlin, Courtesy of The American Museum of Natural History; (top right) Courtesy of Western Americana Collection, Yale University Library; (bottom right) Museum of the American Indian, Heye Foundation.

282 (top left) Painting by Alfred Miller, Northern Natural Gas Company Collection, Joslyn Art Museum, Omaha, Nebraska; (top right) Library, State Historical Society of Colorado; (bottom left) Painting by Alfred Miller, Courtesy of Western Americana Collection, Yale University Library; (bottom right) Culver.

283 (middle right) Painting by A. D. O. Browere, Knoedler Galleries, courtesy TIME-LIFE Books; (bottom) NYHS.

284 (top) Nooning on the Platte, Albert Bierstadt, American, 1830–1902, City Art Museum of St. Louis; (middle right) Painting by Karl Bodmer, Courtesy of Western Americana Collection, Yale University Library; (bottom left and right) Sketches by J. Goldsborough Bruff, The Huntington Library, San Marino, California.

296 LC.

298 NYHS.

301 (top left) The Singer Company; (top right) The Goodyear Tire and Rubber Company; (bottom left) State Historical Society of Wisconsin; (bottom right) Historical Pictures Service.

309 Brown.

310 (left) Bettmann.

311 (top left and center) Brown; (bottom) Culver; (right) Bettmann.

314 *American Magazine of Useful and Entertaining Knowledge*, 1839.

317 (top right) From the original in the Louisiana State Museum, New Orleans, La., courtesy American Heritage Publishing Co., Inc.; (middle left) Smithsonian Institution; (bottom) Collection of Mr. and Mrs. Screven Lorillard, Far Hills, N.J., photo by Cullen.

318 (top right) Painting by W. P. Chappel, The Edward W. C. Arnold Collection, lent by the Metropolitan Museum of Art, photograph courtesy Museum of The City of New York; (middle) Lithograph by N. Currier, The J. Clarence Davies Collection, Museum of the City of New York; (bottom) NYPL, photo by Francis G. Mayer.

319 (top left and right) Watercolors by Nicolino Calyo, Museum of The City of New York; (middle right) The Historical Society of Pennsylvania; (bottom left) Watercolor by John Searle, NYHS.

320 (top left) Missouri Historical Society; (bottom left) *Godey's Magazine and Lady's Book*, Feb. 1844.

321 Bettmann.

323 Benson J. Lossing, *Pictorial Field Book of the Civil War*, 1868.

325 (left) Historical Pictures Service; (right) Brown.

326 (top left) National Park Service; (bottom left) Southern Highlands Handicraft Guild, Ed Dupuy photo; (right) Asheville Chamber of Commerce.

331 (top) Lithograph by Currier and Ives, Culver; (left) Smithsonian Institution; (bottom right) Unpublished sketchbook of T. K. Wharton, NYPL.

334 LC.

336 Painting by Eastman Johnson, The Brooklyn Museum.

340 (top left) Brown; (bottom right) Culver.

345 (top left) Missouri Historical Society, St. Louis; (top right)

American Museum of Photography; (bottom left) The Chamber of Commerce of Metropolitan St. Louis; (bottom right) Western Reserve Historical Society.

350 (left) Brown; (right) LC.

354 Detail from drawing "General McClellan's Sixth Pennsylvania Cavalry Regiment Ready to Embark at Alexandria for Old Point Comfort," The Cooper Union Museum, New York.

356 *Harper's Weekly*, May 4, 1861.

357 LC.

362 LC.

363 (top left and right) LC; (bottom) U.S. Signal Corps Photo from Brady Collection, National Archives.

366 Currier and Ives print, LC.

369 (top left) Bettmann; (top right) LC; (middle right) Chase Manhattan Bank, Money Museum; (bottom left) U.S. Signal Corps Photo from Brady Collection, National Archives.

377 Culver.

380 Culver.

382 LC.

386 (left) Culver; (right) Bettmann.

392 Penn Community Services, Inc.

393 Lithograph by Currier and Ives.

396 (top left) Culver; (bottom right) Jackson Insurance Agency, Birmingham, Alabama.

398 Bettmann.

400 *Frank Leslie's Illustrated Newspaper*, May 20, 1876.

402 (middle left) *Harper's Weekly*, Nov. 7, 1871, Culver; (bottom left) *Harper's Weekly*, Jan. 15, 1870; (top and bottom right) Culver.

406 (top) The Cooper Union Museum, New York; (bottom) Owned by Mrs. Edwin S. Webster.

409 *Frank Leslie's Illustrated Newspaper*, Sept. 11, 1875.

412 (left) Bettmann.

418 LC.

422 (top left) LC; (middle left) Denver Public Library Western Collection; (top right) National Archives; (bottom) LC, photo by C. H. Grabill.

424 (left) *Historic Sketches of the Cattle Trade of the West and Southwest*; (right) Charles Russell, from the original oil painting in Woolaroc Museum, Bartlesville, Oklahoma.

430 (top left) West Point Museum Collection; (bottom left) Smithsonian Institution, Bureau of American Ethnology;

663 (top left) Culver; (top right) Ford Motor Company Archives; (bottom left) Brown.
665 (top left and right) Brown; (bottom left) Bettmann.
668 Courtesy McDonnell and Company, New York City.
670 Culver.
672 (top left) Culver; (bottom right) From the collection of The Memorial Art Gallery of the University of Rochester.
673 Culver.
678 WW.
679 Brown.
680 WW.
684 WW.
686 WW.
689 Brown.
693 LC.
694 (top left) Brown; (top right) Works Projects Administration, National Archives; (bottom left) U.S. Department of Agriculture; (bottom right) State Historical Society of Wisconsin.
695 LC.
699 (top right) Culver; (bottom left) UPI.
702 From HALF CENTURY by J. N. Darling, by permission of Duell, Sloan & Pearce, Inc., copyright, 1962, by Meredith Publishing Co.
704 FDA Photo.
705 Hutton, The Philadelphia *Inquirer.*
706 UPI.
708 (left) LC; (right) Department of Health, Education, and Welfare.
711 UPI.
713 UPI.
715 Jerry Doyle, The Philadelphia *Daily News.*
718 (top left) WW; (bottom left, top and bottom right) UPI.
721 © 1941 Simon & Schuster, by permission of author's estate.

723 (top left) WW. (bottom left and right) UPI.
727 UPI.
728 WW.
729 WW.
732 U.S. Air Force Photo.
734 UPI.
736 UPI.
739 (top left) National Archives; (bottom left) WW; (right) Bethlehem Steel Corp.
740 (left) UPI; (right) American Red Cross.
742 From BILL MAULDIN'S ARMY, by Bill Mauldin, Copyright 1944, 1945 by United Feature Syndicate, Inc., permission of William Sloane Associates, Inc.
744 UPI.
745 UPI.
747 (left) WW; (right) UPI.
748 UPI.
749 United Nations.
752 UPI.
754 WW.
757 WW.
758 (left) U.S. Atomic Energy Commission; (top right) Yankee Atomic Energy Company; (bottom right) Oak Ridge Operations Office.
761 UNRRA Photograph from United Nations.
763 WW.
764 UPI.
766 (top left and bottom right) U.S. Army; (top right) UPI.
771 (top left) WW; (top right) United Nations; (bottom right) UPI.
772 UPI.
773 WW.
775 WW.
777 (middle right) Photography for Industry.
778 (top left) Courtesy, The Museum of Modern Art, New York, New York.

779 (top) Federal Aviation Agency.
780 (middle left) Julius Shulman, Inc.; (bottom right) Executive Office, Reston, Virginia
781 Ewing Galloway.
783 WW.
784 Culver.
785 UPI.
789 WW.
791 WW.
795 (left) WW; (right) UPI.
798 (top left) Pan American World Airways; (top right) National Park Service; (bottom left) Ewing Galloway.
802 (top left) Courtesy of the Vandamm Collection, the Theatre Collection, the New York Public Library, Astor, Lenox and Tilden Foundations; (bottom left) Leonard Bernstein photographed during recording session for Columbia Records, from the Penguin Collection.
805 National Aeronautics and Space Administration.
807 (top left) UPI; (top right) WW.
809 (top left and right) UPI; (bottom left) Peace Corps Photo by Paul Conklin.
810 WW.
811 UPI.
819 WW.
821 Jonathan Thomas, *The Christian Science Monitor.*
822 UPI.
824 (top left and top right) WW; (bottom left) San Francisco Bay Area Rapid Transit District; (middle right) UPI.
825 UPI.
828 (left) Fernand Gigon-PIX; (right) Goskin Sipahoiglu, Black Star.
829 (left) Claude Jacoby-PIX; (right) WW.
832 WW.

Index

This index includes references not only to the text but to maps, charts, and pictures as well. These may be identified as follows: *m* refers to a map; *c* refers to a chart; *p* refers to a picture.

A

ABC powers, 602
Abilene, Kansas, 424, *m* 425
Abolitionists, in Jacksonian Era, 270–271; oppose annexation of Texas, 277; oppose Mexican War, 287; in mid-1800's, 309–312, *p* 310–311
Acadia, in New France, *m* 18, 19; in French and Indian Wars, 41, 42, *m* 42. *See also* Nova Scotia
Acheson, Dean, 765, 788
Adams, Andy, 425
Adams, Charles Francis, *p* 177; minister to Britain, 355, 372; and election of 1872, 405
Adams, Henry, quoted, 400
Adams, John, *p* 87; quoted, 65, 82, 83, 170; defends British soldiers, 79; in Second Continental Congress, 94, 96; seeks Dutch aid, 102; negotiates with British, 105; and Treaty of 1783, 112, 113; as minister to Britain, 124, 127; as Vice-President, 162, 171; as President, 175–178
Adams, John Quincy, *p* 177; and Treaty of Ghent, 206; as Secretary of State, 215, 219, 220, 222; as minister to Britain, 218; quoted, 230; elected President, 230–231; as President, 231–233; opposes Gag Rule, 309–310
Adams, Samuel, *p* 87; quoted on taxation of colonies, 78; organizes Committees of Correspondence, 82; and Coercive Acts, 84; in first Continental Congress, 84; and Battle of Concord, 89, 90; not at Constitutional Convention, 127
Adams, Sherman, 791, 797
Adamson Act, 579
Adams-Onís Treaty, 219–220, 221
Addams, Jane, 483, *p* 483
Adirondack Mountains, 55
Adkins v. Children's Hospital, 555
Administration of Justice Act, 83
Adult education, 264, 509
Adventists, 268
Adventures of Huckleberry Finn, 433
Adventures of Tom Sawyer, 433
Affluent Society, 799
AFL. *See* American Federation of Labor
AFL-CIO, merger, 793; evicts Teamsters, 794
Africa, and Portuguese exploration, 8–10, *m* 9; Negroes brought to America from, 47, 48; in World War II, *m* 743; today, *m* 769
Age of Innocence, 461
Age of the Moguls, 457
Agricultural Adjustment Acts, first, 692, 693; second, 703
Agricultural Marketing Act, 676

Agriculture, of Indians, 13; in New France, 19; in English colonies, 53, 54, 55, 56, 57; and western transportation, 224; after 1815, 228, 260; use of machinery in, 256, 300, 434–435; in prewar South, 322, 327; in postwar South, 384, 394–395, 435; on Great Plains, 431, 435–439; in Middle West, 435; problems of, in late 1800's, 435–439; crop acreage west of the Mississippi, *c* 435; Cleveland vetoes aid bill, 494–495; farmers in politics of 1890's, 516; legislation passed under Wilson, 578–579; government aid, sought in 1920's, 656–657; output, *c* 656; government policy under Hoover, 676; and New Deal, 692–693, 696, 703; during World War II, 738; in 1950's, 787, 793, 797; farm prices since 1951, *c* 792; migrant, workers, 799; number of workers, 1920–1960, *c* 813
Agriculture, Department of, 435, 560, 579
Aguinaldo, Emilio, 587
Air brake, 445
Air force, in World War II, 734, 737, 745
Airplanes, 646, 662; number of passengers, *c* 662
Alabama, territory, 198; admitted, 224; secedes, 349, *m* 359; population rank, *m* 800; today, *m* 815
Alabama, 372; claims, 413–414
Alabama River, 323, *m* 360
Alamo, 276, *p* 276
Alaska, Russian claims in, *m* 40, 221, 222, 223; population and resources, *m* 414; purchased, 415; gold discovered, 526; boundary dispute, 532; becomes state, 794; population rank, *m* 800; today, *m* 814
Albania, 720, *m* 725, 759
Albany, N.Y., founded, 37, *m* 37; in Revolution, *m* 106, 107; and Erie Canal, 224–225, 260, *m* 302; and railroads, 301, *m* 303, 304
Albany Plan of Union, 42–43, 72
Aldrich, Nelson W., 563
Aldrich-Vreeland Act, 574
Aleutian Islands, *m* 414; seal dispute, 531; in World War II, 734, *m* 735
Alger, Horatio, 461
Algeria, 736, *m* 743
Algiers, pirates of, 190, 191, *m* 202
Algonquin Indians, *m* 42
Alien and Sedition Acts, 176–177, 182
Allegheny Mountains, 55, *m* 74, *m* 109
Allen, Ethan, 95
Alliance for Progress, 826
Alliances, Farmers', 439, 516
Allied Control Council, 755
Allies, in World War I, 608, 609; in World War II, 733
Allison, William, 411
Alsace-Lorraine, *m* 619, 623, *m* 632, 633
Altgeld, John Peter, 474, *p* 475, 476, 481
Amazon River, *m* 221
Ambrister, Robert, 219
Amendment of Constitution, provided for, 134. *See also under number of each Amendment*
America, origin of name, 11

America First Committee, 722, 724
American Antislavery Society, 271, 312
American Association for the Advancement of Science, 560
American Bankers' Association, 635
American Bar Association, 634–635
American Civil Liberties Union, 741
American Colonization Society, 270
American Crisis, 105
American Economic Association, 677
American Expeditionary Force, 620–622
American Federation of Labor, formed, 477–478; refuses to support Debs, 481; favors League, 634; membership in 1920's, 647; membership in 1930's, 697; and CIO, 698, 793
American in Paris, 664
American Legion, 654
American Medical Association, 263
American Mercury, 665
American Party (Know-Nothing), 307–342
American Peace Society, 607
American Philosophical Society, 62
American plan, in labor, 647
American Railway Union, 480, 481, 505
American Red Cross, 368
American Samoa, 534, *m* 540
American Society for the Promotion of Temperance, 269
American Sugar Refining Company, 456, 500
American System, 226–227
American Telephone and Telegraph Company, 448
American Tobacco Company, 558, 565
Ames, Oakes, 404–405
Amherst, Jeffrey, 43, 44, 72
Amnesty Act, 394
Amusements, in mid-1800's, 315; in late 1800's, 511; in 1920's, 663–664; in 1930's, 708–709; television, 801
Anchorage, Alaska, *m* 414
Anderson, Robert, 356
Andes, *m* 15
Andover Academy, 121
André, John, 112
Andros, Sir Edmund, 33–34
Anesthetics, 263
Angell, Norman, 607
Anglican Church, created, 23; in southern colonies, 29, 61, 68; Columbia Univ. founded by, 62; in Virginia, 119
Angola, *m* 9, 10, *m* 769
Annapolis, Md., 34, *m* 35, 127
Anthony, Susan B., 485
Antietam, Md., *m* 360, 365, 373
Antifederalists, 132, 134, 165
Anti-Imperialist League, 543
Anti-Masons, 237, 249
Antin, Mary, 463
Anti-Saloon League, 484
Antislavery movement. *See* Abolitionists
Antitrust legislation, Sherman Act, 500, 505; Clayton Act, 576
Antwerp, 4, *m* 4
Anzio, 742, *m* 743
Apache Indians, 427, *m* 428, 429
Appalachian Mountains, 42, 55, *m* 74, 823
Appalachian Spring, 801
Appeal of the Independent Democrats in Congress, 339
Appomattox, *m* 374, 376